# THE PRINCETON REVIEW

# K&W GUIDE TO
# COLLEGES
## FOR THE LEARNING
## DISABLED

### 1998 EDITION

## ERRATA

Dear Customer,

Due to an error in compiling the data for this book, some of the SAT II requirements for certain colleges are incorrect. A complete and correct list of SAT II requirements is available free of charge by calling Random House customer services at 1-800-726-0600 during the hours of 8:30 to 5:00 EST. Please accept our apologies. We have corrected this error for future printings.

The Princeton Review

W9-CYA-999

"Filling a glaring need for reliable information about programs for students with learning differences, the *K&W Guide to Colleges for the Learning Disabled* is a comprehensive, accurate, and valuable addition to any college counselor's professional library."

**Andrew Roth, Dean of Enrollment Services,**
**Mercyhurst College (PA)**

"The *K&W Guide* has been most helpful and is very thorough... Until now, I've not found so much useful material available in such concentrated format. So happy to have discovered your book!"

**A parent of three sons with learning disabilities,**
**Cardiff by the Sea, California**

"I knew something had to exist. My tenth grade son will thrive in a correct college setting... I saw it mentioned in *USA Today*."

**Parent of a student with learning disabilities,**
**Santa Fe, New Mexico**

"The *K&W Guide* is distinctive in its design. The Landmark students who have used it have found that it sets the standard for clear presentation of pertinent material."

**Director of Admissions,**
**Landmark College**

"Many colleges have programs and services for students with learning disabilities. A very informative guidebook you might want to consult is The *K&W Guide to Colleges for the Learning Disabled*."

**Jeffrey Zaslow,**
**Chicago Sun Times**

"[The *K&W Guide*] is outstanding in content, scope, coverage, and authority. . . the authors have developed a major new reference source in a field that is crying for reference material."

**Jack Hicks, Administrative Librarian at the Deerfield Public Library,**
**Deerfield, Illinois**

THE PRINCETON REVIEW

# K&W GUIDE TO
# COLLEGES
## FOR THE LEARNING DISABLED

**1998 EDITION**

## BY MARYBETH KRAVETS
## AND IMY WAX

*Random House, Inc.*
*New York  1997*

*http://www.randomhouse.com*

Princeton Review Publishing, L.L.C.
2315 Broadway
New York, NY   10024
E-mail: info@review.com

Copyright © 1997 by Princeton Review Publishing, L.L.C.

All rights reserved under International and Pan-American Copyright Conventions. Published in the United States by Random House, Inc., New York, and simultaneously in Canada by Random House of Canada Limited, Toronto.

ISBN: 0-375-75043-6
ISSN: 1094-9356

Manufactured in the United States of America on partially recycled paper.

9  8  7  6  5  4  3  2  1

Editor: Amy Zavatto
Production editor: Amy Bryant
Production manager: Greta Englert

# CONTENTS

# ACKNOWLEDGMENTS

To the families of Marybeth Kravets and Imy F. Wax for their patience and support in this endeavor: Alan, Wendy, Steve, Allison, Connor, Mark, Sara, David, Cathy, Dan, Howard, Lisa, Gary, Debrah, and Greg.

To Deerfield High School and High School District 113 for their ongoing support of learning disability programs and services and their belief in promoting the development of independence for all students—and guiding them to make good decisions for life after high school.

To all of the colleges who responded to the questionnaire requesting information and who provide services and programs to promote the educational endeavors and dreams of students with learning disabilities.

To Dr. Pamela Adelman, Adele Anger, Michael Barron, Debrah, Emily, Diane Gibson, Stephanie Gordon, Darlene Huntley, Jeanne Kincaid, Esq., Adam Lava, Lynne Luskin, KM, and Valerie O'Connor for sharing their thoughts and experiences with learning disabilities.

To Stephanie Gordon, learning disability specialist, Deerfield High School, Deerfield, Illinois, for her professional assistance.

To Dr. Lynne Schaeffer, professor of English, for her professional assistance with editing and proofing.

To Dennis Fraser, LaserType, Inc. in Deerfield, Illinois, for his endless patience and assistance.

To Karen Rodgers Photography for the authors' pictures.

# DEDICATION

This book is a labor of love written to help individuals throughout the world who have been identified as having learning disabilities or attention deficit disorders. And just as importantly, for those who have never been officially identified. And of course, for all of the families, professionals, and friends who know someone who has a learning disability.

# FOREWORD

It is my pleasure to introduce this fourth edition of *The Princeton Review K & W Guide to Colleges for the Learning Disabled*. As Chairman of the National Center for Learning Disabilities, I congratulate The Princeton Review on this excellent resource. There is an enormous need for information sharing of this kind. So many helping organizations, programs, schools, and materials exist that benefit individuals with learning disabilities—people just need to have access to them. This book achieves this goal in a very effective way.

My heart goes out to all children and adults with learning disabilities, as well as to their families. Given my experiences with my daughter, I can certainly empathize with the constant struggles so many young people face throughout their school years and after they transition to the work world. Accurate diagnosis, proper interventions, and informed and caring support of parents, teachers, and professionals can make a difference in assuring that these children and adults enjoy productive and satisfying lives. An important first step is to have access to accurate and useful resources and information.

When I first found out my daughter had learning disabilites, my instinct was to do everything humanly possible to help her. Much to my shock and dismay, I learned there was little help available. I felt alone and helpless. At that time, I wondered if other families and professionals were going through the same frustrations and disappointments. I now realize they were . . . and still are! If only this type of resource had been around twenty years ago!

As one of the nation's leading not-for-profit organizations committed to helping individuals with learning disabilities, the National Center for Learning Disabilities considers the sharing of accurate information and referrals to services as one of our highest priorities. In fact, our efforts in this area began in the early 1980s, when we published the Guide for Parents of Children with Learning Disabilities. This effort later evolved into NCLD's National Information and Referral Service, which today provides free information and referrals to local, state, and national resources, including diagnostic clinics, camps, and specialized schools.

We applaud The Princeton Review K&W Guide to Colleges for the Learning Disabled. This book captures so many types of helpful resources for parents, teachers, counselors, physicians, and advocates. It is sure to be a valuable addition to your library.

Anne Ford
Chairman, National Center for Learning Disabilities
New York, NY

# INTRODUCTION

The *K&W Guide to Colleges for the Learning Disabled* was conceived independently by the authors over twenty years ago, but it took until 1987 for the paths of the authors to cross.

Imy Wax is a licensed psychotherapist and educational consultant. She is also the mother of two—one with a learning disability and the other with a learning disability and Attention Deficit Hyperactivity Disorder (ADHD). The truth is that this book is really a dedication to Imy's daughter, who at the age of two was identified with multiple learning disabilities, a large delay in her language skills, and a dismal prognosis for her future. All of those professionals proclaimed doom and gloom and indicated that a traditional public elementary and high school experience would not be possible; college was never even mentioned.

However, Imy always saw the glass as half full rather than half empty, and she absolutely refused to accept such a diagnosis. She set goals, became a visionary, and exerted significant influence for her daughter to compensate for the limitations. She became an advocate for her daughter: She researched; she read every book and every article she could find; and she gave herself hope to believe in her child and in herself. Imy made it her goal to understand the learning disability and the strategies that would best contribute to her daughter's well being.

Imy's daughter ultimately attended both public school and a special private school for students with learning disabilities. When her daughter was in the eighth grade in private school, Imy volunteered in the College Resource Center at Deerfield High School so that she could get a better grasp on what might be in store for her daughter if she were to enroll in her local public high school. This was in 1987, and the paths of the two authors crossed for the first time.

Marybeth Kravets is the College Consultant at Deerfield High School, where Imy volunteered. Deerfield High School is a public high school that has comprehensive programs and services for students with learning disabilities (LD) and Attention Deficit Hyperactivity Disorder (ADHD). Deerfield High School is also a school from which 98 percent matriculate to college, including those students identified as LD or ADHD. Imy discovered that her daughter could be accommodated in the high school, and that the professionals there had hopes of mainstreaming her into regular college preparatory courses with appropriate accommodations and modifications.

Hidden under Imy's "coat of hope," however, lived the growing anxiety she experienced every time she listened to a college representative visiting with students at the high school. It seemed to her that all colleges were after the same student: At least a 3.0 GPA, an ACT score of 24 or SAT score of 1000, a ranking in the top 50 percent of the class, and a four-year curriculum consisting of every subject at Deerfield High School. Imy's daughter had begun ninth grade in all special education courses, which were individualized to meet her special needs. By junior year, she had mainstreamed into college preparatory courses in English, science, fine arts, and social studies, but was still enrolled in special education classes in math. She was not even close to learning about algebra (the typical freshman curriculum), and she had never taken a foreign language.

One day, Imy asked to meet with Marybeth to talk about her concern that there was not enough information about colleges that were prepared to accommodate students with learning disabilities. As the two began to explore the available resources for information, they realized that most guidebooks only offer computer-generated information, which says almost the same thing about every college regarding special services and special admissions. Thus began their search for more pertinent information to help Imy in her quest for a possible match for her daughter, and to help Marybeth provide better college counseling for the students at her high school.

The two developed a series of questions geared to soliciting very precise, comprehensive, and succinct information that gleaned not only facts, but insight. They were interested in special programs and basic services as well as the college's sensitivity to the learning disabled population. The first questionnaire resulted in responses from over 1,000 colleges and universities. This information was invaluable not only as the authors worked on plans for Imyís daughter, but for other students, parents, and professionals who were dealing with the same scenario all over the country. The *K&W Guide to Colleges for the Learning Disabled* was then created.

The first edition of the book included extensive information about 150 colleges. The next two editions grew in size and information. Marybeth and Imy have now embarked on the all-new fourth edition of the guide, with information detailing over 300 colleges and universities. They have also formed a new and exciting partnership with The Princeton Review and Random House as their publishers.

This edition of the *K&W Guide* has been expanded to include more information, more tips and strategies, and more colleges and universities. With detailed information about what specific colleges do and do not provide, students can determine if the services or programs offered match their individual needs. This guide should be used as a reference and resource to explore and identify appropriate colleges and universities. In this edition, you'll find:

- Special programs and services for students with multiple learning disabilities or for those needing limited accommodations.

- What professionals need to know in order to help advise and counsel students and parents in this search process.

- Detailed information about general and special admission procedures, the application process, services, programs, accommodations, remedial or developmental courses, and opportunities for basic skills classes.

- Policies and procedures regarding course waivers or substitutions.

- General profiles of the colleges and universities.

The main focus of the *K&W Guide* is to provide comprehensive information about the services or programs availableat colleges and universities for students with learning disabilities. However, all of the institutions detailed in this guide also offer accommodations to students with documented Attention Deficit Hyperactivity Disorder. Many colleges and universities will include students with LD or ADHD in their structured programs or special services. Although ADHD is not a learning disability, students could be diagnosed with both ADHD and LD. In most high schools, students identified as only ADHD are categorized under "other health related disabilities" and protected by Section 504 of the Rehabilitation Act of 1973. These students can request and receive accommodations in high school and

college, as long as they present current and appropriate documentation from a certified professional.

Colleges that provide descriptions of the level of support and accommodations available on their campuses, whether they are basic services complying to the mandates of Section 504 or enhanced services that go beyond the mandates, provide this population of students with the best opportunity for good decision-making. The end result is that students will make college choices where the services match their needs.

Students and their parents are encouraged to read the college catalogs, talk to the admission staff and the directors of the special support services, and visit the campuses. Before planning a trip, however, begin with a thorough reading of this Guide. Any student needs to have her priorities in order to determine the criteria for selecting a college that is appropriate. The most important criterion for students with learning disabilities is the availability of the necessary level of services.

The student with unique learning needs should approach the college search with the goal of identifying colleges that will fill all of his needs—educationally, culturally, and socially. There is not just one right college for any student, non-learning disabled or learning disabled. Students need to explore options and select several colleges that will provide a successful environment.

Although no single source can provide all of the information needed to make an educated decision about an appropriate college choice, the availability of other resource books with extensive information is very limited. The ultimate goal of the *K&W Guide* is to give descriptive and honest information so that all students, even in the most remote sections of the country, have equal access to this knowledge. This guide is the first place to look for, and differentiate between, colleges providing:

- **Structured Programs:** Schools that have specific programs for LD with much more than the mandated services: special admission procedures, specialized and trained professionals, compensatory strategies, one-on-one tutoring, additional fees, compulsory participation, and monitoring.

- **Coordinated Services:** Schools that have some involvement with admission decisions, voluntary and not compulsory participation, more than just mandated services, small or no fees, and less structure.

- **Basic Services:** Schools that comply to Section 504 mandates, rarely have specialized LD staff, do not have monitoring, and are totally dependent on student advocacy.

The authors gratefully acknowledge the time and effort of all of the service providers at the colleges and universities who responded to our request for current information about their services and programs. It is these colleges and others like them who are willing to work closely with these students, believe in empowering students to articulate their needs, and help students to become independent and successful learners as they seek to pursue a college education.

It is essential that college services and accommodations for individuals with learning disabilities be visible, honored, funded, maintained, and expanded to meet the needs of identified students. This population is being identified in school earlier; this means that they are being provided with individualized educational plans to meet their needs, becoming self-advocates, learning compensatory skills, and transitioning in greater numbers from high school to college.

This must be a joint effort. The colleges and universities need to support the efforts of the ongoing learning process of these individuals. Those who believe should reach out to those who do not understand. Those who do not understand should open their minds to the fact that this is a neurological disability that is lifelong; it does not go away. The authors of this Guide applaud these students. No children elect to be born with a learning disability. However, if they hold fast to their dreams and aspirations and look beyond the imperfections and hidden handicaps, they can make things happen.

# THOUGHTS FROM . . .

## A High School Learning Disability Specialist

As a high school teacher of students with learning disabilities, I have seen many students go through the process of selecting a post-secondary setting to meet their individual needs. The success of this search is dependent upon a number of variables; however, certain of these variables appear to be high on the list of importance. First, you must be able to understand and articulate the nature of your learning disability. This means stating your strengths and weaknesses as well as understanding what kinds of accommodations are (and will be) helpful/necessary. You must be realistic in your college search. That is, you must assess how well a post-secondary setting is equipped to meet your needs, as well as how equipped you are to meet the demands of the institution. Learning as much as you can about a variety of colleges and universities will allow you to make an informed decision. The *K & W Guide* is an important tool for acquiring that knowledge.

Students, you must use your high school time to learn to advocate for yourself. This skill will not only help you in high school and college but in many future aspects of your life. Use the resources available to you in your high school to learn this important aspect of communication. Finally, prioritize the different aspects of your college search. With success as your goal, plan for what will enhance your chances. Learn all you can from resources available at your high school as well as resources like the *K & W Guide*. With an understanding of your own specific needs as well as an understanding of what a college/university can provide for you, you will be able to find the best match you can. Good luck in your search.

Stephanie Gordon, M.A.
Learning Disabilities Specialist

# A College Learning Disability Specialist

After more than fifteen years of offering programs and services for college students with learning disabilities, we know that there are certain factors that enhance the student's ability to achieve academic success. What are these factors, and how can we help students take advantage of them?

First, these factors involve acquiring knowledge and skills that will prepare them for college and seeking out supportive services necessary for their success once they are in college. Specifically, these factors include:

a. participating in college-bound high school curricula, particularly English classes, which require students to do more rigorous reading and writing assignments;

b. learning strategies that enable students to compensate for their learning disabilities;

c. developing advocacy skills, so students are prepared to explain their learning disabilities to advisors and professors and request the appropriate reasonable accommodations;

d. receiving academic advice from someone who understands the student's learning disability and its impact on college-level work; and

e. taking advantage of the supportive services, including assistance from LD specialists, subject-matter tutors, and personal and career counselors.

Second, supportive parents, understanding teachers, services from qualified learning disabilities specialists, and knowledgeable counselors and physicians can help students acquire sufficient understanding and acceptance of their learning disabilities. Such an understanding is important in order for students to develop a positive attitude toward the teaching/learning environment. Students with positive attitudes have proven far more likely to have the motivation to acquire the necessary knowledge and skills in spite of their learning disabilities, as well as being more likely to take advantage of support services available to them.

Today, many colleges and universities have excellent services available for college students with learning disabilities. The *K&W Guide* is designed to help students find these schools and identify the right match for each student. Once the match is made, a strong partnership in which both the student and the institution honors their commitment can certainly lead to a high degree of academic success.

Dr. Pamela Adelman
Director of the Learning Opportunities Program
Barat College, Lake Forest, Illinois

# A College Learning Disability Specialist

Students, parents, and school personnel all have as their goal the appropriate placement of students with learning disabilities in an environment intended to give them the best chance to succeed in college. The *K&W Guide To Colleges For The Learning Disabled* provides an excellent starting point for those interested in matching students with the colleges and the LD programs and/or services most suited to their needs.

Theoretically, students select a college because it has the majors they are interested in pursuing. Realistically, many students with learning disabilities, as well as students with no learning disabilities, are searching to find their niche and may not know what major they want when they begin their search during their junior year in high school. Therefore, selecting a college with the appropriate support often becomes the primary focus. The major will come later.

What can students do to improve their chances of being admitted by the college and LD program of their choice? How will they know the right program when they see it?

The answers involve course selection in high school and early exploration of college LD options. Learning disabled college programs and support services have increased dramatically in the past ten years, but not at the rate of demand. Candidates for the limited spots in the existing programs must demonstrate the ability to handle college coursework if they want to be considered for these openings. While in high school, students must work with their parents and school personnel to balance the demands of college preparatory coursework with their mental health. If students are not enrolled in almost all college preparatory courses by their junior year, they may need to consider alternatives to a four-year college. Community college, a post grad year in high school, or a specialized college for students with learning disabilities may be the best starting place for these students.

Grades are important, but a C grade in a college prep course is viewed more favorably than a higher grade in a non-college prep course. Some students must work closely with LD teachers, regular classroom teachers, and tutors to successfully meet these resources. Motivation and perseverance are important personal qualities for college-bound students with learning disabilities, but they don't make up for solid preparation.

Let's assume a student with learning disabilities has taken a rigorous course load. What's the next step in improving this student's chances of being selected? The answer is to begin the college selection process early. During sophomore year, write to colleges requesting information about LD programs or services, as well as more general information. The *K&W Guide* is an excellent resource to use in determining colleges to explore as possible options. Examine the college catalogue, which lists the general requirements to graduate. Colleges vary widely on these requirements, so it may be possible to avoid or minimize the impact of a deficit area.

Begin preparing your own materials according to the timeline set by the college. If current documentation of your learning disability is required, arrange for the appropriate testing, preferably in the junior year. In my experience, delays in receiving the documentation have been responsible for students being eliminated from consideration. For example, Loras College requires prospective students to send a transcript and current testing to the college for an evaluation before a visit is scheduled. Some students are advised to pursue other options at this point if the program at Loras College does not meet the needs of the students.

Once visits to the college have been arranged, prepare questions for the LD personnel and other college representatives you'll be meeting. Marybeth Kravets and Imy Wax, the authors of the *K&W Guide*, provide sample questions and offer other suggestions in this guide regarding the campus visit. Ask to talk with students with learning disabilities who receive support services or participate in the LD program. Meet with professors in your areas of interest. Note class size, campus layout, living quarters, and recreational facilities while on tour. Stay overnight in a residence hall. All of these arrangements can be made through the admissions office.

The services and programs provided vary from college to college, but, in general, support services include tutors, notetakers, special equipment, taped textbooks, and advice and assistance in arranging special testing accommodations. Full programs, such as the program I direct at Loras College, have the support services I've listed, but also provide direct contact with program personnel on a regular basis in classes and weekly meetings. I would advise selecting those colleges that have full programs. Reducing services is easier than increasing services where they don't exist. Full structured programs provide more options and flexibility than do support services.

By senior year in high school you should complete your visits and should call or write the LD personnel at the campuses you want to attend. Let them know that you want to be seriously considered at their college. Most students and their parents have strong feelings about the colleges they've visited. Trust your feelings. You know what you need. Arrange for letters of recommendation, complete the application, request to have official ACT/SAT results sent to the colleges, and write a personal statement about your learning disability. All that remains is waiting for the acceptance letter. I hope you receive an acceptance to the college of your choice. If it doesn't come, remember that "success doesn't follow one path; look for other routes or accept a temporary detour but don't stop learning."

Diane Gibson, M.A.
Director, Learning Disabilities Program
Loras College, Dubuque, Iowa

# A High School Student with Learning Disabilities

*A letter from a high school student to the director of admissions*

Dear Director:

My name is Emily and I am a senior in high school. I am applying to your university for the fall. My college counselor suggested I write to you about my learning disability and my ACT score.

I was first diagnosed with my learning disability in sixth grade. At that time, I received special assistance on a daily basis, which continued until sophomore year in high school. Since that time I have been on consultation, which simply means I have the opportunity to check in with a learning specialist if needed. My learning disability involves long-term retrieval and auditory comprehension. I am very comfortable with my disability as I know what my strengths and weaknesses are and how to compensate. One of my strengths involves visual processing. I know that I learn better when I take notes, record my lectures, talk to the teachers about what we discussed in class, and make note cards. In high school, I have been involved in a learning resource program. I understand my learning profile, know how to seek assistance, and have developed strong self-advocacy skills. I feel the way to my success is patience, being able to confront my peers, teachers, and tutors about any academic problems or concerns, and, most of all, to work hard at everything that I do.

I believe that my ACT score of 20 does not present an accurate picture of what I can accomplish. Because of my long-term retrieval difficulties, my math score was much lower on my ACT, while my present grade in trigonometry and related topics is an A. This shows that I am able to do well in classes with help and perseverance.

I know that I could work successfully in your college environment. I am confident that I would receive the support services that I need to apply the skills I have acquired in order to be a good student. Please review my application by assessing my growth, the challenge of the courses I have taken, and the fact that I do meet your grade point average requirement for admission and merely fall short in the ACT by a small margin. Feel free to contact me should you need more information.

Sincerely,

Emily

# A Prospective Graduate Student with a Learning Disability

I can't believe that I am actually studying for the GRE Exam and have submitted applications for graduate school. At the age of two I was diagnosed with multiple learning disabilities, and my family was given a negative prognosis about my future ability to be educated in a traditional school setting. I have had to overcome many obstacles and learn multiple compensatory skills in order to accomplish academic and social success.

I applied to a number of colleges and picked the one that offered me a maximum amount of support, and where the faculty are understanding and accepting of my need for accommodations. I was given the option of a pass/fail grade in a few courses where my learning disability was most severe. I majored in communications with a concentration in film. I spent my summers during college involved in various internships that provided me with the opportunity to graduate with experience in my field. The combination of my high GPA (I was on the Dean's List several semesters), and my summer work experience has opened doors for me to attend graduate school.

I know my learning disability will never go away, but that does not mean I will let it get in my way. I have struggled throughout my academic life, but I have never felt that I had no future potential. I don't believe that parents should give up on their child when they hear the word LD. I also don't think students should feel sorry for themselves. It's not a bad thing to have a learning disability; it just means a lot of extra work. I can understand why parents may worry, but giving up is not the answer. After all, the child feels bad already because there's often a feeling of not being worth anything. If parents have a positive attitude toward their children then the children will develop good feelings about themselves.

There was a time when I hated everything and everyone, because I thought I was the most terrible person in the world because of my learning problems. My disabilities were so complex. However, my parents had a positive attitude—and that helped me to begin to feel better about myself. In school I was often treated differently and the other kids made fun of me because I had trouble following directions or doing math. However, I learned a lot of skills to compensate for these problem areas, and I also learned to avoid those people who were not capable of being understanding.

I know that I will never outgrow my learning disabilities. In graduate school and in work I will continue to have to develop skills and techniques to get around my weaknesses, but my desire to achieve will keep me actively pursing my life's dream. My positive attitude, good work ethics, willingness to always keep trying, and acceptance of my disabilities have helped me to develop positive feelings about myself. Now I have positive feelings about the future too.

Debrah

# A Parent

When this fourth edition of the *K&W Guide* is published, my daughter will have just graduated from college. I don't consider this an extraordinary feat. But others who never knew her personally and who saw her through the eyes of test results are surprised. For those who have not read this section in the previous editions of the *K&W Guide*, you may not be familiar with the history and the dynamics involved in achieving this important milestone.

Throughout both my clinical and educational consulting practices I have focused on the dreams that both parents and their children share for the future. My schooling prepared me to challenge, ask questions, and develop sensitivity to those who I would see, but it was my experience as the mother to two children with special needs that taught me how to reach beyond the obvious and navigate the unknown.

My daughter and I developed a bond that began with her depending on me and ended with my respecting her independence, ability, and sensitivity to others. When she was young it was my job to develop as much knowledge and understanding about her learning style, cognitive processing, and socialization ability as possible, so that I could provide what was necessary. To do this I needed to hold on to my dreams for her future. When she was four years old I started looking for colleges that would accommodate her needs. This was my goal for her. By challenging the professionals who gave me a negative prognosis, and by keeping my eye on the objective, a very stimulating environment was created for her.

My daughter has challenged those who could not believe and, more importantly, proved to herself that she could achieve her dream. She is graduating college and is deciding on a graduate program. She has developed a career for herself and is focused on reaching her goals. There is little doubt now from anyone that she will be successful.

My son has his own unique learning style. He is now going off to college. His vision for himself is different from that of his sister, but nevertheless attainable. He, too, has had to learn how to be a successful student in spite of his academic challenges. While his history has not had all the ups and downs of his sister, they are no less important.

I have learned how to value the small steps that children take as they grow. I have great pleasure when I can empower parents to believe that their investments in their child will yield great rewards in the future. It is really the dream that we have when our children are born that needs to stay kindled long after the diagnosis is given.

Imy F. Wax
Mother of Debrah and Greg
Co-author of the *K&W Guide*

# A Parent

Life as a single-mother of six children, ranging in age from eleven to twenty-five, has been like a "magical mystery tour." Life as the mother of an eighteen-year-old son, who is both "gifted and LD and ADHD" has been like being on a roller coaster, Ferris wheel, and merry-go-round all at the same time. My son is now a senior in high school, and we have been "trail blazers" since he entered school. We have successfully gone through both a due process hearing for technology accommodations (requesting a laptop computer for my son who has severe dysgraphia but is a gifted writer), and a major U. S. Department of Education—Office of Civil Rights complaint filed against the town's schools on behalf of all students with learning disabilities.

My son has never taken a foreign language and has been advised not to take one because the "foreign language department has found that students with LD don't do well in foreign languages." In its place, my son has taken technical education, which he loves. My dilemma as his mother was whether he should continue with technical education or take a foreign language. My gut feeling was to let him continue the technical education, but I was afraid and nervous that this guidance would close doors of opportunity for him. It was so hard to know what to do because he had not decided exactly where he wanted to go to college and what he would like to study. I tried to stay in the background, except when I was needed. I tried to guide, not decide, but at the same time: How can we make a knowledgeable, good decision if we don't know what colleges want or how they will interpret a decision like not taking a foreign language because of the learning disability's impact on his ability to learn this subject? According to your guide, it is apparently all decided on a "case by case" basis, which makes it so difficult to know what to do. The *K & W Guide* has been so helpful in providing us with comprehensive information. Especially because we have had to rely on their own resources to seek out and identify options for post-secondary education. Thank you so much for writing this book and for your personal introductions.

KM
Mother in Rhode Island

# A Parent

Refusing to buy into the negative prognosis by his guidance counselor and others that my son, Brian, wouldn't be accepted into any college, I set out to provide Brian with the opportunity for a college education.

My husband is a professor at a large public university. His colleagues in the Learning Disability Services Program there readily admitted that they were not in a position to deal with disabilities of the sort Brian suffers. But they were more than helpful by providing me with several reference books on colleges with LD programs. By far, the most helpful of these was the *K&W Guide*. It provided the most appropriate and succinct resources of any of the texts I reviewed for evaluating and applying to colleges.

When it became necessary that I return the *K&W Guide* to the university, I nearly panicked! Where was I to get another? No one locally seemed to know. Taking the bull by the horns, I wrote Marybeth Kravets to order a new guide directly from her.

In due course I received the volume, and using it, applied to a number of colleges that had programs that seemed appropriate to Brian's needs. He was accepted to fifteen of them! One of them even offered him an academic scholarship. Without the *K&W Guide*, I would not have known about these opportunities.

The *K&W Guide* is, in my opinion, the definitive source of guidance for students, parents, and professionals in applying to the right school (a school with the right programs and resources for a student with a learning disability). The insights and knowledge gained from reading and using this guide gives direction to what would otherwise be a maze of information about thousands of colleges. It provides a means of controlling what could otherwise be an uncontrollable situation.

Once the selection of a college has been made, the *K&W Guide* still has enormous value. These days, students change majors and colleges often. If Brian decides to change his career path, the *K&W Guide* will help him to decide on his next choice.

Brian has decided to enter an old, traditional New England college this fall. The school has a well-established and comprehensive LD support program, and, very importantly to Brian, an active lacrosse program. The athletic department understands and supports Brian's needs.

A year ago, Brian was a frustrated, almost hopeless young man. He saw no future for himself except as a relatively uneducated, low-paid worker. Now he knows that he has more opportunities than many of his non-LD friends. None of this would have happened without the *K&W Guide*.

Valerie O'Connor

# A Parent

As the parent of a son with learning disabilities, the authors asked me to give my perspective on the college search process. When we started our "homework" for the right school, there were very few resources available, [which were] often vague and misleading. None gave the depth and wisdom that the *K&W Guide* provides. In this book, readers will find detailed information about learning disability programs as well as admissions criteria for general admission and learning disability admission, if different. Readers will also find answers to important questions many may not have thought to ask. The questions and guidelines provided can be used to research and make decisions about college selections.

Our children are learning disabled, and the first step in selecting the right school is to acknowledge and accept this fact. While learning disabled can be a broad-based term, it signifies that our children do learn differently. I was so very proud of my son Adam when I heard him discuss his learning disability clearly and intelligently with administrators, teachers, and fellow students as we visited campuses. Your child should be able to say what the disability is (decoding, processing, reversal, etc.), how it manifests itself in the learning process, and what services are required to help compensate. Whether your child needs untimed tests, taped text books, or frequent tutoring, the goal is to match the student with the college that offers services that will allow for success at the college level. This guidebook, along with a realistic understanding of your child's needs, is almost all you will need to select appropriate schools.

From a parent's point of view, I have some inside tips that might help. When you and your child visit selected campuses, do schedule an interview with the learning disability services director and ask to meet learning disabled students participating in the program. Ask students how they arrange for the help they need and what kind of academic advisors they have. These students can be an invaluable source of information about campus life, dorms, and activities.

Another suggestion is to prepare your student to be assertive in college. For example, Adam knew that he needed to sit in the front of the classroom to concentrate better and avoid distractions. He learned that he had to introduce himself as a student with learning disabilities to his professors and make his requests known. In another situation, Adam had to ask his economics professor to rephrase a question so he could understand it. The point I'm trying to make is that our children have to know what kind of learning works best and have the confidence to seek help, use the services offered, and speak up as the need arises. We need our students to learn to compensate and live comfortably with their learning disability. It may be hidden, but it is always there.

I am the parent of a son with learning disabilities. If you are a parent reading this, I have been where you are. Adam did not talk until he was four, and he could not truly read until he was ten. Today, Adam has graduated from college with, believe it or not, a degree in communications and a minor in history. Not bad for a child who couldn't talk or read. His goal has been reached through determination and commitment to himself, with support from his family, teachers, and friends.

Fortunately, the help parents and students need in selecting the right college begins with this guide. So good reading, and most of all good luck, as you open up a new and very exciting chapter of your life.

Lynne Luskin
Highland Park, Illinois

## A College Director of Admission

Twenty-eight years ago, when I first became an admission officer at a medium-sized public university in Texas, my mentors and colleagues suggested to me that I would encounter applicants who had not performed very well in high school. I was told to expect that some of those students would "claim" to have a reading problem and others would actually use the term dyslexia. It seems that many of my admission colleagues were somewhat dubious about the true extent of such a disability (although the term dyslexia was not in widespread use at the time). It is with horror that I look back on those times when many of us simply discounted such students as just being lazy, dumb, or under-prepared.

We are blessed today by greater knowledge about these conditions and, more importantly, by compassionate understanding of those individuals who cope with one or more of the growing list of what we now call learning disabilities. Often these students exhibit superior intellectual capacity but lack the facility to mark the appropriate bubble or write an answer on paper in the prescribed time period. They are a resource that cannot be overlooked or swept aside by our application of some of the more odious and inappropriate labels used in the past.

We must take risks along with these students in order to help them develop their potential. We have learned that there are many disorders that impact an individualís ability to learn but do not impair their intellectual capacity. I am pleased to say that now there are many more of my colleagues who understand these needs and, working carefully with disabilities specialists and faculty, are developing ways to provide these students with the opportunity for a higher education.

At Iowa, the office of admissions has a special relationship with the office of services for disabled students, and have operated a very successful program of alternative admission consideration for such students. We strive to enroll students with excellent academic records who also have displayed personal achievement outside of the classroom. Students with learning disabilities who have used the resources available to them to their fullest potential are the ones we seek.

A diverse student body with a variety of talents, interests, and backgrounds is necessary to truly deserve a label of university. Iowa welcomes applications from students with documented learning disabilities and/or attention deficit disorder. The staff in the office of services for disabled students, as well as those in the office of admissions, carefully evaluates the overall academic performance of these students for evidence that they will be able to successfully pursue a demanding and rigorous collegiate program. We keep in mind that we are looking for students with the ability to do college work reflected in the strength of the courses that they have taken, as well as the compensatory strategies that they have employed during their high school years.

Some students fulfill all of our regular admission requirements despite documented learning disabilities. This does not mean that they no longer need compensatory strategies or a special office to assist them in advising faculty of their special needs. They do. We have had excellent success at Iowa with our special admission process for students with learning disabilities who do not meet our regular admission requirements, and recent data suggest that with proper attention as many as eight out of ten such students succeed at the university. Faculty are recruited to be partners in this process, although we are not always perfect in our efforts and as successful as we might want to be.

We recognize that the decision for students to self-identify as learning-disabled is a personal choice. A student's decision not to self-identify is respected. However, it has been our experience that students with learning disabilities who do acknowledge the existence of a disability and seek assistance early are more likely to achieve academic success than those who wait for problems to develop. It was not too long ago that such students probably would never graduate from high school. Even if they did, they could not look forward to a future with very many options for employment.

Thankfully we are making breakthroughs for many of these students—and now are at the plateau of providing access and opportunities for higher education. While there are programs like Iowa's that are beginning to achieve success, we have by no means provided a paradigm that is consistently accepted and used throughout the country. That will come only through our making public the successes and failures of those of us who have met the challenge and taken the risk. This book, the *K&W Guide to Colleges for the Learning Disabled*, is certainly one of those resources I hope will be widely used in that effort.

While we are working to educate our colleagues, to modify our systems to accommodate these students, and to provide them with the opportunity to obtain the education that they desire, we also must begin to work as partners with industry. It will not be enough to provide an environment where an individual can complete a university degree and yet fail miserably in the world of work because of its lack of understanding and inappropriate job placement procedures. Our experience at Iowa is that these students desperately want to succeed, and they want to stand on the merits of their own achievements. To deny them the opportunity to be an asset at the highest level of their ability is to squander a valuable human resource, creating an unnecessary and unwanted liability for society. I urge students with learning disabilities and their families to demand the services they need and to be patient with those of us in the education establishment, as we seek to understand. I also encourage educators at all levels to be sensitive to and aware of these individuals as a resource not to be wasted, and to work diligently to provide educational opportunity to all.

Michael Barron
Director of Admissions
University of Iowa

## An Adult with a Learning Disability

Whenever I am asked how my learning disability has affected my life I say, "Only for the better." This is because I don't know how my life would be without my learning disability. Since I was diagnosed at the age of six I have been, and always will be, dealing with my disability, which is dyslexia.

After years of counseling, tutors, and special academic programs, I have learned the skills to compensate for my weaknesses and promote my strengths. With four years of college under my belt and almost four years in the work place, I have realized the hidden benefit of my learning disability. You might inquire: What could be a possible benefit from not being able to spell without looking words up in a dictionary or reversing numbers and letters in simple daily work?

Well, I'll tell you. It is the ability to completely concentrate and focus on the task I am doing. Concentration is the key. The study tips and the note-taking techniques helped in school, but in the "real world" it's not enough. This skill of total concentration did not come overnight, and it is harder than it sounds. I have learned to block out all distractions, focus on what I am doing, and carefully review my work, concentrating on not making the common mistakes that I am prone to make because of my disability.

I did not learn this from tutors or special programs, but instead over the course of my life. I capitalize on my strengths to do what I am naturally good at, like personnel communication and comprehension. These offset my weaknesses in reading and math.

To explain what I mean by all of this, let me tell you about my job. I am a salesman. I work with people and try to build a relationship with them. This part of my job emphasizes my strength, as I am very comfortable speaking to people. However, in my job I must also know all of the products. This translates into a great deal of reading—and I am an extremely slow reader. Thus the strategies I have learned about focus and concentration help to keep me on track. I take my time when I am learning new information and when I am finished I know it backwards and forwards. This feeds into my comfort level when interacting with clients. Skimming over something is pointless. I either need to take extra time and learn it my way or not even bother.

The hardest part of my job is doing the mathematical calculations. I never thought I would have to tackle mathematics again. Who would have thought I would need to know how to figure out a conversion formula for changing linear yardage to square feet, or how to figure the cost of a plastic bag when all I have to work with is the price of the raw plastic? Yet these are some of the things I do on a daily basis. It might not sound difficult to most people, but as a dyslexic, I hit the 6 button on my calculator by mistake because my eyes tell me it is the 9 button. It is in these circumstances that my disability is a hindrance and a savior. I call upon my skills of concentration and block out everything but the task at hand. It is not easy to do this. I tend to get frustrated and tired of everything being an ordeal. Nothing is ever routine or simple. When I treat work in a cursory manner I start to make mistakes, and when mistakes come they start to grow like weeds.

I learned early in school from my mother that it was going to take longer for me to do my homework, write my papers, and learn new information. However, it must not stop me from doing any of these things. It is not a wise move to think that you can cover up your weaknesses and not try to improve on them. This is a sure way for failure. It became clear to me that if I did not give my work 100 percent of my attention all of the time, I was only cheating myself.

I had to struggle to overcome my learning disability in college. I recall that during my senior year, I opted to challenge myself and take a Russian literature course. I had to read books like *War and Peace*. Why would someone who needs to spend five minutes on a page take a course that deals with complicated issues in a 1,000-page book?

Well, I'll tell you. I needed to test myself to see if I could take the time and read all those pages. My college days were numbered, and the "real world" was only months away. I needed to prove to myself that if I concentrated I could learn the material. I did not take the course to prove that I was smart enough, I already knew that I was intelligent enough to understand the material. Instead I needed to see if I had the determination, the dedication, and the self-sacrifice to take the time and do the work. Most of all, I needed to see if I could block out all of the distractions that are present in your last semester of college, and take the hours upon hours I knew it would require to read all those pages. There would be no skimming over dull spots. I was going to have to read every word in the book. I knew that going in.

Trust me—there are much easier ways to sharpen the mind then Tolstoy. After I finished that class I realized that I had the ability to do anything I wanted as long as I took my time, did a thorough job, and concentrated on my work just like my mother always told me. By the way, I received an A in that class.

Adam Lava
Sales Manager, A. Lava & Sons

## An Adult with a Learning Disability

Learning disabilities. So many emotions and thoughts accompany such a simple phrase. I remember being diagnosed in sixth grade and thinking, "I'm different." Well, I've been different for years now and it's not such a bad thing—if you learn to accept it and understand it.

I have now completed college and graduate school. I used to laugh when my family and friends said, "If you put your mind to it, anything is possible." Now instead of laughing I smile, because I know that it's true and that I'm working toward accomplishing a major goal.

I would like to highlight some hints on how to be a successful learning disabled student in college:

- Have a goal; know what you want to be or do and always keep that goal in mind when classes become difficult. Don't give up!

- Know your learning disability. You are the one going to college and attending classes. You're going to need to be able to express your needs and ask for extra resources, if needed.

- Be your own self-advocate. If you need help, get it! If you have a question, ask! No one will ask if you need help or have questions. Take it upon yourself. It is your responsibility.

- Most importantly, find a college that fits your needs both academically and personally. Make sure you feel comfortable there in all aspects.

I won't lead you down the primrose path. College is Difficult (with a capital "D"). Most of the time you will be studying twice as hard to get the same grades as the students who don't even open a book. But if college is what you want, and you are willing to work harder and longer for what you want, it is well worth it.

I feel I have accomplished major goals in my life. I have completed college, graduate school, married a wonderful husband, and secured a job in my field as the teacher for a classroom of pre-school toddlers. I know my learning disabilities are life long, and each day I utilize the compensatory skills I have learned. Remember, being different isn't bad—in fact, it is what makes the world go round, and so interesting to live in.

Darlene Huntley, B.S., M.A.
National—Louis University, Evanston, Illinois
Teacher at Greentree-Rivertree North

## An Attorney on Disability Law

The *K&W Guide to Colleges for the Learning Disabled* offers potential students and their families the opportunity to make an educated decision when selecting the proper college or university designed to meet the student's needs, in light of her learning disability. Although nearly every college in the country is subject to Section 504 of the Rehabilitation Act and many also fall within the coverage of the Americans with Disabilities Act (ADA) (both of which prohibit discrimination on the basis of disability), the range of accommodations and services offered by each institution varies considerably.

The following information is designed to assist the student and family in helping to understand what the law minimally requires, determining if the student requires more, and what other services might be available. I begin with a brief outline of how the laws differ for students from kindergarten through twelfth grade from those individuals in a higher-education institution. This will provide a framework for my further comments.

| K-12 | Higher Education |
|------|------------------|
| Guaranteed an education | Have no right to an education |
| Districts must screen and identify | Students responsible for identification |
| Free evaluation | Student pays for evaluations |
| District must develope a plan | Students responsible for plan |
| IEP | No IEP |
| District ensures plan implemented | Students responsible for plan |
| Right to fundamental services | No fundamental rights |
| Right to due process hearing | No right to due process |
| Parents are legal advocates | Students act as own advocate |

**Admissions:** Generally, institutions of higher education may not inquire about one's disability prior to acceptance, unless the inquiry is made for affirmative action purposes. However, students and families should consider contacting the college's Section 504/ ADA Coordinator, or the Disabled Student Services Office (DSS), to determine what services the student is likely to receive if accepted by the college. The DSS office may also be helpful in advising the student whether to disclose her disability in the application. Additionally, should the student choose to enroll at the college, the DSS office can advise the student as to what documentation he may need, in order to ensure that he receives timely and effective services.

**Documentation:** Documentation serves two important purposes: 1) It establishes that the student has a disability as defined by Section 504 and the ADA; and 2) guides the college in providing appropriate accommodations for the adult learner. Many colleges require that documentation be conducted within the past three years. Moreover, as federal law does not obligate a college to conduct assessments, a student should consider requesting that her high school update the assessment, consistent with any requirements of the college in which the student seeks enrollment. For example, some colleges have established guidelines for the type of documentation they require. Checking with the DSS office in advance, however, may yield information about what assessments the college may provide the student free of charge.

**Accommodations:** At a minimum, a student with a learning disability should be able to expect the following accommodations, if the nature of the disability requires such adjustments and is supported by the documentation: A reduced course load, extended time to complete tests and assignments, extended time to complete degree requirements, a note-taker, course substitution of nonessential courses, a quiet testing room, books on tape, the right to tape-record classes, and in some cases, an alternate format for taking tests. The law does not obligate an institution of higher education to provide all recommended accommodations, but rather effective accommodations. A student should therefore not presume that what he received in high school will necessarily be honored at the post-secondary level.

With respect to courseload, often students with disabilities benefit greatly from taking less than the average number of courses, particularly during the first year, as the student transitions to the rigors of higher education. Nonetheless, as many students with learning disabilities may take five or more years to complete an undergraduate degree, it is important to consider the impact a reduced course load may have upon financial aid. Although most loans and scholarships should be pre-rated, rather than lost entirely, colleges handle this issue in a variety of ways. Again, the DSS office should be able to apprise the student of the college's policy.

A critical consideration for college selection is determining the college's general education requirement imposed on all students in order to obtain a degree as well as requirements for graduating with a particular major. Many colleges/universities require one or more courses in foreign language and mathematics. For some students with learning disabilities, no amount of accommodation will result in their successful completion of such requirements. It cannot be emphasized enough how vital it is to review such requirements before selecting your college, as such requirements typically need not be waived based upon disability.

**Services:** Beyond the accommodations mentioned above, colleges often provide a vast array of additional services. Although a college may not charge for legally mandated accommodations, it may impose a fee for services that go beyond the minimal legal requirements. For example, as discussed throughout this guide, some colleges provide tutoring by personnel specifically trained in working with students with learning disabilities. As tutoring is considered to be a personal service, and not an accommodation, a college may generally charge for such services, to the extent they go beyond the minimum legal standard. Other such services may include: Assessments, study-skills training, priority registration, counseling, and case management services.

**Securing Accommodations:** Each campus has its own unique system for providing students with disability-related accommodations. Many give the student a letter detailing recommended accommodations, with instructions to the student to approach the professors in each course so that classroom accommodations are provided in a timely fashion. Some DSS offices send the letter directly to the student's professors. However, the former approach is the trend, as it promotes self-advocacy, a necessary skill for the student's long-term success, both as a student and in the future, as an employee. Although many professors have received training on the ADA and Section 504, many have not. Therefore, should a professor fail to agree to the recommendations or neglect to carry them out, it is imperative that the student promptly notify the DSS office, which should intervene on the student's behalf. Unlike public high school, civil rights laws in institutions of higher education do not require that the institution monitor the student's progress or shadow the student to ensure that the accommodations are provided and effective. Again, it is up to the student to take affirmative steps when problems arise. Remember, no one is likely to ever know if a notetaker fails to consistently show for a class unless the student notifies the DSS office.

**As a Final Cautionary Note:** Students with hidden disabilities, such as learning disabilities, often wish to attempt college without accommodation. Many students have been "labeled" their entire educational lives and are committed to attempting college on their own terms, without special assistance. Although some succeed without accommodation, court and agency rulings have consistently ruled that a student who fails to take advantage of available disability-related accommodations does so at his peril. Although the ADA is based on promoting success, it also gives individuals with disabilities the right to fail. Before making a decision to forego accommodations, I strongly encourage the student to consult with the DSS office.

> Jeanne M. Kincaid, Esq., a noted legal authority on disability law and education, graduated from the University of Oregon School of Law. She writes and lectures widely in the area of disability law and education, and serves as a due process special education hearing officer for the state of New Hampshire. Ms. Kincaid is also an adjunct faculty member of the University of New Hampshire's Graduate School of Education and the Franklin Pierce Law Center. Ms. Kincaid is co-author of *Section 504, the ADA and the Schools,* and is a contributing author to the publication *Disability Compliance for Higher Education.*

# GETTING READY

The purpose of the *K&W Guide* is to help students with learning disabilities acquire the basic knowledge necessary to begin the college exploration process and get ready to make appropriate college selections.

## To get ready students need to:

- Understand their strengths and weaknesses.
- Be able to articulate the nature of their learning disabilities.
- Understand the compensatory skills developed to accommodate the learning differences.
- Describe the services received in high school.
- Identify short-term and long-term goals.
- Select appropriate college choices to match individual needs.

## Guidelines for the search and selection process

### Self Assessment:

- What is the student's learning disability?
- When was the disability diagnosed?
- What is the student's level of performance in high school?
- Is the student enrolled in college-prep courses, modified courses, or individualized, special-education courses?
- What are the student's individual strengths and weaknesses?
- Is it easier for the student to learn from a lecture, from reading the material, or having the material read to her?
- Does the student perform better on written assignments or oral presentations?
- Which subjects are easier, and which are more difficult?
- What are the student's most favorite and least favorite courses and why?
- What are the student's short-term and long-term goals?
- Are these goals realistic?

- Is the student striving to improve in academic areas?

- What accommodations are being provided?

- Is the student actively utilizing resource assistance and learning compensatory strategies?

- What does the student plan to study in college?

- What skills and competencies are required for the career goals being pursued?

- When were the last diagnostic tests given?

- What level of services/accommodations are needed in college? Structured programs, comprehensive services, or basic services?

## Articulation:

- Does the student understand the disability?

- Can the student describe the learning disability?

- Does the student comprehend how the disability impacts on learning?

- Can the student explain the nature of the disability?

- Can the student explain the accommodations being utilized as well as any curriculum modifications received?

- Can the student explain necessary accommodations to teachers?

## Academic Assessment:

- Does the student have difficulty with written language?
    - —using appropriate words
    - —organizing thoughts
    - —writing lengthy compositions
    - —using correct punctuation and sentence structure
    - —expressing thoughts clearly

- Does the student have trouble with verbal expression?
    - —retrieving appropriate words
    - —understanding what others are saying
    - —using words in the correct context
    - —carrying on conversations

- Does the student have a problem with hand-eye coordination?
    - —finding certain information on a page
    - —performing tasks that require fine motor coordination

- Does the student get frustrated reading?
  - —decoding unfamiliar words
  - —understanding reading assignments
  - —completing reading assignments within a time frame
- Does the student often misspell words?
  - —mix up the sequence of letters
  - —become confused when spelling irregular words
- Does the student experience difficulty performing mathematics?
  - —multiplication table and fractions
  - —sequencing of steps of various mathematical questions
- What are the student's study habits?
  - —attentive in class for an extended period of time
  - —easily distracted
  - —needs extra time to respond to questions
  - —note-taking skills
  - —memory
  - —time management
  - —time orientation
  - —organization
- How is the student's handwriting ability?
  - —assignments are difficult to read
  - —appropriate capitalization used
  - —stays within the lines when writing
  - —leaves enough space between words

### Exploration and Timelines:
- Sophomore year
  - —explore options
  - —meet with counselor and case manager
  - —review testing and documentation
  - —write for information
  - —contact the service providers on the college campus

- Junior year
  - —review achievement level
  - —review the level of services in high school
  - —identify the level of services needed in college
  - —visit colleges
  - —register for the ACT/SAT: standardized or non-standardized?*
- Senior year
  - —submit general applications
  - —submit special applications (if required)
  - —schedule interviews
  - —write essays (if required)
  - —disclose learning disability to college
  - —release current psychoeducational testing*
  - —release documentation of other health related disabilities*
- Students under the age of eighteen must have their parents' signature to release information to each of the colleges.

---

*Not all students with learning disabilities are eligible for a non-standardized administration of the ACT/SAT. The American College Testing Center (ACT) and Educational Testing Services (SAT) ultimately have the authority to approve special testing accommodations. To be eligible to take a test non-standardized the student must:

- have a diagnosed disability requiring test modifications
- have supporting documentation: #IEP, 504 Plan, or professional evaluation
- be receiving these test accommodations in the high school

To request a non-standardized ACT/SAT, you must submit to ACT/ETS:

- a special application
- a description of the diagnosed disability
- psychcoeducational evaluation
- a list of all tests or assessments used to identify the disability
- the results of all tests and a description of the identified limitations
- the credentials of the evaluator
- a description of the requested accommodations
- a statement describing why the disability qualifies the student for the requested accommodations

## Campus Visits:

- The student should call to make an arrangement for a visit.
- Visit while classes are in session.
- Meet with admissions and special support service providers.
- Take a guided tour.
- Attend a class.
- Eat a meal on campus.
- Drive around the boundaries of the campus.
- Take pictures, take notes, and talk to students on campus.
- Take parents or family members along (but not in the interview).
- Pick up college catalogue, view book, video, and support service brochures.
- Write thank-you notes.

## Interview:

- Prepare for interviews
  - —know strengths and weaknesses
  - —know the accommodations needed
  - —know how to describe learning disability
- If an interview is required prior to an admission decision
  - —view the interview as an opportunity
  - —prepare a list of questions
  - —know that interviews, if required, are either required of all applicants or required for a special program or special admission practice
- Questions the Director of Support Services may ask:
  - —When was the learning disability first diagnosed?
  - —What type of assistance has the student been receiving in high school?
  - —What kind of accommodations will the student need in college?
  - —Can the student describe the learning difficulties?
  - —Can the student articulate strengths and weaknesses?
  - —How has the disability affected the student's learning?
  - —What high school courses were easy (or more difficult)?
  - —Is the student comfortable with the learning disability?
  - —Can the student self-advocate?

—What does the student plan to choose as a major?

—Is the student motivated?

- Questions students and/or parents may ask:

—What are the admission requirements?

—Is there any flexibility in admission policy? Course substitutions? GPA?

—What is the application procedure?

—Is a special application required?

—What auxiliary testing is required?

—Are there extra charges or fees for the special programs or services?

—Are there remedial or developmental courses?

—What is the procedure for requesting waivers or substitutions?

—Who is the contact person for learning disabilities?

—What are the academic qualifications of the individual who provides services to students with learning disabilities?

—What services and accommodations are available: Testing accommodations? Note takers? Books on tape? Skills classes? Support groups? Priority registration? Professional tutors? Peer tutors? Advising? Computer-aided technology? Scribes? Proctors? Oral tests? Use of computers and spell-checker in class? Use of calculators in class? Distraction-free environment for tests? Learning disability specialists? Advocacy with professors? Faculty in services?

—How long has the program been in existence?

—How many students are receiving services?

—How long can students access services?

—What is the success rate of students receiving services?

- For a successful interview:

—Develop a list of questions.

—Know the accommodations needed .

—Provide new information .

—Practice interviewing .

—Be able to describe strengths and weaknesses.

—Talk about extracurricular activities.

—Take notes.

—Get the business card of the interviewer.

—Try to relax.

—Have fun!

## Recommendations:

- Descriptive letters from counselors, teachers, and case managers.

- Have recommenders address learning style, degree of motivation, level of achievement, abilities, attitudes, self-discipline, determination, creativity, mastery of subject matter, academic risks, and growth.

- Have a teacher describe the challenge in a difficult course.

- Advise recommenders when letters are due.

We have just highlighted some of the areas of importance. Now it is time to begin to use the information in this guide that describes the various programs and services in the colleges and universities in the United States.

# How To Use This Guide

The *K & W Guide to Colleges for the Learning Disabled* includes information on colleges and universities that offer services to students with learning disabilities. No two colleges are identical in the programs or services they provide, but there are some similarities. For the purpose of this guide, the services and programs at the various colleges have been grouped into three categories.

## Structured Programs (SP)

Colleges with Structured Programs offer the most comprehensive services for students with learning disabilities. The director and/or staff are certified in learning disabilities or related areas. The director is actively involved in the admission decision and often, the criteria for admission may be more flexible than general admission requirements. Services are highly structured and students are involved in developing plans to meet their particular learning styles and needs. Often students in Structured Programs sign a contract agreeing to actively participate in the program. There is usually an additional fee for the enhanced services. Students who have participated in a Structured Program or Structured Services in high school such as Learning Disabilities Resource Program, individualized or modified coursework, tutorial assistance, academic monitoring, notetakers, test accommodations, or skill classes might benefit from exploring colleges with Structured Programs or Coordinated Services.

## Coordinated Services (CS)

Coordinated Services differ from Structured Programs in that the services are not as comprehensive. These services are provided by at least one certified learning disability specialist. The staff is knowledgeable and trained to provide assistance to students to develop strategies for their individual needs. The director of the program or services may be involved in the admission decision, or be in a position to offer recommendations to the admission's office on the potential success of the applicant, or to assist the students with an appeal if denied admission to the college. To receive these services generally requires specific documentation of the learning disability—students are encouraged to self-identify prior to entry. Students voluntarily request accommodations or services in the Coordinated Services category, and there may be specific skills courses or remedial classes available or required for students with learning disabilities who are admitted probationally or conditionally. High school students who may have enrolled in some modified or remedial courses, utilized test accommodations, required tutorial assistance, but who typically requested services only as needed, might benefit from exploring colleges with Coordinated Services or Services.

# Services (S)

Services is the least comprehensive of the three categories. Colleges offering Services generally are complying with the federal mandate requiring reasonable accommodations to all students. These colleges routinely require documentation of the disability in order for the students with learning disabilities to receive accommodations. Staff and faculty actively support the students with learning disabilities by providing basic services to meet the needs of the students. Services are requested on a voluntarily basis, and there may be some limitations as to the degree of services available. Sometimes, just the small size of the student body allows for the necessary personal attention to help students with learning disabilities succeed in college. High school students requiring minimum accommodations, but who would find comfort in knowing that services are available, knowing who the contact person is, and knowing that this person is sensitive to students with learning disabilities, might benefit from exploring colleges providing Services or Coordinated Services.

# Categories Used to Describe the Programs and Services at Colleges and Universities

The following categories will describe the topics of information used in this guide. Each college in the book is covered on two pages, beginning with pertinent information describing the learning disability program or services. This is followed by special admission procedures, specific information about services offered, and concluding with general college information. Some categories are answered with N/A (not applicable), NR (not reported), or N/I (not indicated), as not all colleges were able to answer or fit into every category included in this guide. When the authors were unable to locate the information, you'll see and N/I. When The Princeton Review was unable to locate the information, you'll see an NR.

The authors have made a conscientious effort to provide the most current information possible. However, names, costs, dates, policies and other information are always subject to change and colleges of particular interest or importance to the reader should be contacted directly for verification of the data.

1. **School Name**

   address, phone, fax, email, and website

2. **State Abbreviation**

3. **Support:**

   SP—Structured Program
   CS—Coordinated Services
   S—Services

4. **Institution:**

   Type of institution (two-year or four-year; public or private)

5. **Comments:**

   A brief description of the program and services—may include philosophy, goals, and objectives

6. **Program Name:**

   Name of special program or services

7. **Program Director:**

   Designated person in charge of program or services and his or her telephone number

8. **Contact Person:**

   Person to write to or call with questions and his or her phone number (if different from program director)

9. **Admissions:**

   Description of any special admission procedure or requirements and/or special applications

10. **College Entrance Exams Required:**

    Standardized tests taken prior to admission

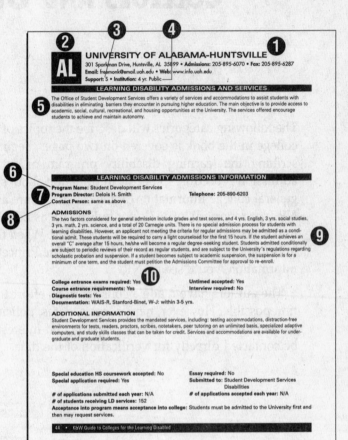

## 11. Untimed Accepted:

If untimed entrance exams are admissible

## 12. Course Entrance Requirements:

Specific high school courses and other requirements for admission

## 13. Interview:

A required or recommended meeting between the student and the director of the program or admissions

## 14. Diagnostic Tests:

Psychoeducational evaluation (WISC-R WAIS-R; Woodcock-Johnson; WPAT; PIAT; SDAT)

## 15. Documentation:

A summary of the interpretation and description of standardized tests and IEP (Individualized Educational Plan)

## 16. Additional Information:

Detailed information about services and accommodations

## 17. Special Education

Coursework accepted: College-prep special-ed classes

## 18. Essay Required:

Student's personal statement or answer to specific questions or description of disability

## 19. Special Application Required:

Separate application for special program or services

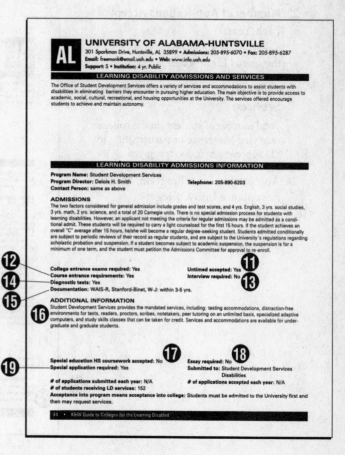

## 20. Submitted to:

Application should be submitted to program director and/or to the office of admissions

## 21. Number of Applications Submitted Each Year:

Number of students who apply yearly for the special LD program

## 22. Number of Applications Accepted Each Year:

Number of applicants admitted into the special LD program

## 23. Number of Students Receiving Services:

Total number of students at the college receiving assistance or participating in LD support services or program

## 24. Acceptance into Program Means Acceptance into College:

Whether the student needs acceptance from the university or college to gain acceptance in to the LD program.

**UNIVERSITY OF ALABAMA-HUNTSVILLE**
301 Sparkman Drive, Huntsville, AL 35899 • Admissions: 205-895-6070 • Fax: 205-895-6287
Email: freemonk@email.uah.edu • Web: www.info.uah.edu
Support: S • Institution: 4 yr. Public

### LEARNING DISABILITY ADMISSIONS AND SERVICES

The Office of Student Development Services offers a variety of services and accommodations to assist students with disabilities in eliminating barriers they encounter in pursuing higher education. The main objective is to provide access to academic, social, cultural, recreational, and housing opportunities at the University. The services offered encourage students to achieve and maintain autonomy.

### LEARNING DISABILITY ADMISSIONS INFORMATION

**Program Name:** Student Development Services
**Program Director:** Delois H. Smith          **Telephone:** 205-890-6203
**Contact Person:** same as above

**ADMISSIONS**
The two factors considered for general admission include grades and test scores, and 4 yrs. English, 3 yrs. social studies, 3 yrs. math, 2 yrs. science, and a total of 20 Carnegie units. There is no special admission process for students with learning disabilities. However, an applicant not meeting the criteria for regular admissions may be admitted as a conditional admit. These students will be required to carry a light courseload for the first 15 hours. If the student achieves an overall "C" average after 15 hours, he/she will become a regular degree-seeking student. Students admitted conditionally are subject to periodic reviews of their record as regular students, and are subject to the University's regulations regarding scholastic probation and suspension. If a student becomes subject to academic suspension, the suspension is for a minimum of one term, and the student must petition the Admissions Committee for approval to re-enroll.

**College entrance exams required:** Yes          **Untimed accepted:** Yes
**Course entrance requirements:** Yes          **Interview required:** No
**Diagnostic tests:** Yes
**Documentation:** WAIS-R, Stanford-Binet, W-J: within 3-5 yrs.

**ADDITIONAL INFORMATION**
Student Development Services provides the mandated services, including: testing accommodations, distraction-free environments for tests, readers, proctors, scribes, notetakers, peer tutoring on an unlimited basis, specialized adaptive computers, and study skills classes that can be taken for credit. Services and accommodations are available for undergraduate and graduate students.

**Special education HS coursework accepted:** No          **Essay required:** No
**Special application required:** Yes          **Submitted to:** Student Development Services
                                                                                                    Disabilities
# of applications submitted each year: N/A          # of applications accepted each year: N/A
# of students receiving LD services: 152
**Acceptance into program means acceptance into college:** Students must be admitted to the University first and then may request services.

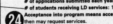

### 25. Learning Center:

Room or center used for delivery of services

### 26. Notetaker:

Someone who volunteers or is paid to takes notes in class/lecture

### 27. Professional Tutors:

Number of professional tutors

### 28. Kurzuweil Personal Reader:

Reading machines

### 29. Scribes:

Someone assigned to write for students

### 30. Peer Tutors:

Number of tutors who are college students with the necessary skills to provide content tutoring in a specific subject

### 31. LD Specialists:

Number of LD Specialist on staff

### 32. Proctors:

Someone assigned to oversee students during exams

### 33. Maximum Number of Hours Per Week for Services:

The number of hours of services/tutoring given to each student each week and for each course

### 34. Allowed in Exams:

Whether professors allow the use of a calculator, dictionary, computer or spell-checker in class during exams

### 35. Oral Exams:

Exams read to the student

### 36. Extended Test Time:

Additional time allowed for tests

### 37. Priority Registration:

Students are permitted to register for classes prior to other students

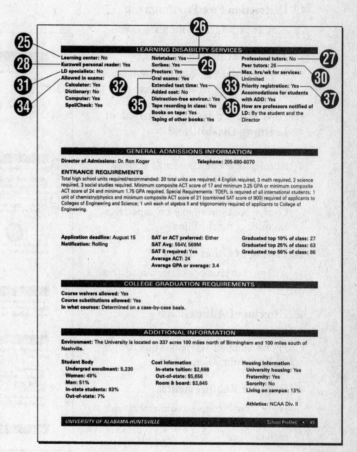

**LEARNING DISABILITY SERVICES**

Learning center: No
Kurzweil personal reader: Yes
LD specialists: No
Allowed in exams:
 Calculator: Yes
 Dictionary: No
 Computer: Yes
 SpellCheck: Yes
Notetaker: Yes
Scribes: Yes
Proctors: Yes
Oral exams: Yes
Extended test time: Yes
Added cost: No
Distraction-free environ.: Yes
Tape recording in class: Yes
Books on tape: Yes
Taping of other books: Yes
Professional tutors: No
Peer tutors: 26
Max. hrs/wk for services: Unlimited
Priority registration: Yes
Accomodations for students with ADD: Yes
How are professors notified of LD: By the student and the Director

**GENERAL ADMISSIONS INFORMATION**

Director of Admissions: Dr. Ron Koger          Telephone: 205-890-6070

ENTRANCE REQUIREMENTS
Total high school units required/recommended: 20 total units are required; 4 English required, 3 math required, 2 science required, 3 social studies required. Minimum composite ACT score of 17 and minimum 3.25 GPA or minimum composite ACT score of 24 and minimum 1.75 GPA required. Special Requirements: TOEFL is required of all international students; 1 unit of chemistry/physics and minimum composite ACT score of 21 (combined SAT score of 900) required of applicants to Colleges of Engineering and Science; 1 unit each of algebra II and trigonometry required of applicants to College of Engineering.

Application deadline: August 15
Notification: Rolling

SAT or ACT preferred: Either
SAT Avg: 554V, 569M
SAT II required: Yes
Average ACT: 24
Average GPA or average: 3.4

Graduated top 10% of class: 27
Graduated top 25% of class: 63
Graduated top 50% of class: 86

**COLLEGE GRADUATION REQUIREMENTS**

Course waivers allowed: Yes
Course substitutions allowed: Yes
In what courses: Determined on a case-by-case basis.

**ADDITIONAL INFORMATION**

Environment: The University is located on 337 acres 100 miles north of Birmingham and 100 miles south of Nashville.

Student Body
 Undergrad enrollment: 5,230
 Women: 49%
 Men: 51%
 In-state students: 93%
 Out-of-state: 7%

Cost Information
 In-state tuition: $2,698
 Out-of-state: $5,856
 Room & board: $3,645

Housing Information
 University housing: Yes
 Fraternity: Yes
 Sorority: No
 Living on campus: 13%

 Athletics: NCAA Div. II

UNIVERSITY OF ALABAMA-HUNTSVILLE                    School Profiles • 45

## 38. Added Cost:

Yearly additional fee for services and/or program

## 39. Accomodations for Students with Attention Deficit Disorder:

Services or accommodations are provided for students with ADD

## 40. Distraction Free Environment:

A quiet private room for tests/exams

## 41. Tape Recording in Class:

The professor may allow a student to use a tape recorder during class

## 42. How Are Professors Notified of Learning Disabilities?

The person(s) responsible for notifying a professor about a student's disability

## 43. Books on Tape from RFB:

Course books available on tape from Recordings for the Blind

## 44. Taping of Other Books

A service to tape books not already on tape

## 45. Director of Admissions:

Person in charge of general admissions Phone Number: Telephone number for Office of Admissions

## 46. Entrance Requirements:

High school course requirements for admission and other additional information

## 47. Application Deadline:

Date the application is due to admissions office

## 48. SAT ACT Preferred:

Which admissions test the college/university prefers

## 49. Graduated:

How many students graduated in the top 10, 25, and 50 percent of their class

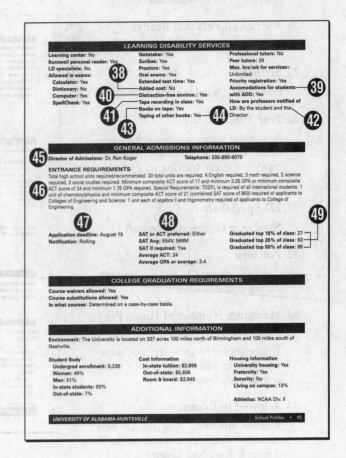

### LEARNING DISABILITY SERVICES

Learning center: No
Kurzweil personal reader: Yes
LD specialists: No
Allowed in exams:
Calculator: Yes
Dictionary: No
Computer: Yes
SpellCheck: Yes
Notetaker: Yes
Scribes: Yes
Proctors: Yes
Oral exams: Yes
Extended test time: Yes
Added cost: No
Distraction-free environ.: Yes
Tape recording in class: Yes
Books on tape: Yes
Taping of other books: Yes
Professional tutors: No
Peer tutors: 26
Max. hrs/wk for services:
Unlimited
Priority registration: Yes
Accomodations for students
with ADD: Yes
How are professors notified of
LD: By the student and the
Director

### GENERAL ADMISSIONS INFORMATION

Director of Admissions: Dr. Ron Koger          Telephone: 205-890-6070

ENTRANCE REQUIREMENTS
Total high school units required/recommended: 20 total units are required; 4 English required, 3 math required, 2 science required, 3 social studies required. Minimum composite ACT score of 17 and minimum 3.25 GPA or minimum composite ACT score of 24 and minimum 1.75 GPA required. Special Requirements: TOEFL is required of all international students; 1 unit of chemistry/physics and minimum composite ACT score of 21 (combined SAT score of 900) required of applicants to Colleges of Engineering and Science; 1 unit each of algebra II and trigonometry required of applicants to College of Engineering.

Application deadline: August 15
Notification: Rolling
SAT or ACT preferred: Either
SAT Avg: 554V, 569M
SAT II required: Yes
Average ACT: 24
Average GPA or average: 3.4
Graduated top 10% of class: 27
Graduated top 25% of class: 63
Graduated top 50% of class: 86

### COLLEGE GRADUATION REQUIREMENTS

Course waivers allowed: Yes
Course substitutions allowed: Yes
In what courses: Determined on a case-by-case basis.

### ADDITIONAL INFORMATION

Environment: The University is located on 337 acres 100 miles north of Birmingham and 100 miles south of Nashville.

Student Body
Undergrad enrollment: 5,230
Women: 49%
Men: 51%
In-state students: 93%
Out-of-state: 7%
Cost Information
In-state tuition: $2,698
Out-of-state: $5,656
Room & board: $3,645
Housing Information
University housing: Yes
Fraternity: Yes
Sorority: No
Living on campus: 13%

Athletics: NCAA Div. II

*UNIVERSITY OF ALABAMA-HUNTSVILLE*                                      School Profiles • 45

## 50. SAT Average

A suggested score or range of scores on the Scholastic Assessment Test

## 51. SAT II:

Content-oriented tests required by some colleges for admission (entry will only appear if SAT II is required)

## 52. Average ACT:

A suggested score or range of scores on the American College Test

## 53. Average GPA:

Grade Point Average (for freshmen applicants)

## 54. Waivers:

Students may be excused from taking specific courses required for graduation

## 55. Course Substitutions:

Students may take alternative classes to fulfill requirements for graduation

## 56. In What Courses?

The subjects for which students request waivers or substitutions

## 57. Environment:

Geographical area of the college

## 58. Student Body

The undergraduate enrollment, as well as the percent of women, men, in and out of state students

## 59. Cost Information:

In-satate tuition, out-of-state tuition, and room and board costs

## 60. Housing Information

Whether on campus, fraternity, or sorority housing available, and percent of students living on campus

## 61. Athletics:

Inter-Collegiate Athletic Association

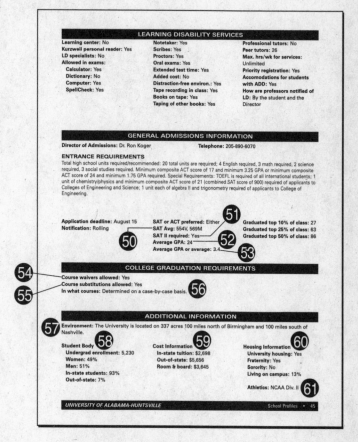

# SCHOOL PROFILES

# UNIVERSITY OF ALABAMA

Box 870132, Tuscaloosa, AL 35487 • **Admissions:** 205-348-5666 • **Fax:** 205-348-9046
**Email:** uaadmit@ua1vm.ua.edu • **Web:** www.ua.edu
**Support:** CS • **Institution:** 4 yr. Public

## LEARNING DISABILITY ADMISSIONS AND SERVICES

Any student enrolled with a documented LD is eligible for services and accommodations. The Assistant Director for Disability Services coordinates services through the Center for Teaching and Learning. Students must provide documentation including a written report of an LD evaluation; a summary of areas of testing; actual test scores; overall summary and diagnosis; and recommendations and suggested strategies for student, professors, and academic advisors. The assessment battery must be comprehensive and include: WAIS-R; achievement test in written language, reading, and math; appropriate cognitive processing evaluations in language, visual-spatial, memory, and executive functioning; social-emotional development; and others as determined by psychologist. Disability Services may request further testing.

## LEARNING DISABILITY ADMISSIONS INFORMATION

**Program Name:** Disability Services
**Program Director:** Pat Friend-NeSmith          **Telephone:** 205-348-4285
**Contact Person:** Melonie Bearden

### ADMISSIONS

All students must meet regular entrance requirements. Students with learning disabilities must be admitted to the university prior to seeking accommodations for their disability. An interview is recommended with Learning Disability Services. Applicants with a GPA under 2.0 or ACT under 19 may be invited to interview. Examples of a 'Restricted' Fall admission are: GPA 1.80-1.99 and ACT 23 or SAT 960; GPA 2.80-2.99 and ACT 18 or SAT 740; GPA 3.0-3.19 and ACT 17 or SAT 690. Students with acceptable GPA but not tests or vice-versa may be considered for Summer Trial Admissions.

**College entrance exams required:** Yes          **Untimed accepted:** Yes
**Course entrance requirements:** Yes          **Interview required:** Recommended
**Diagnostic tests:** Yes
**Documentation:** WAIS-R;W-J; Cognitive processing evaluations: within 3 yrs.

### ADDITIONAL INFORMATION

Accommodations are tailored to individual needs according to diagnostic testing. Accommodations include: early registration; testing modifications; academic aids such as taping lectures, use of calculators, dictionaries, spell checkers, study cards for mathematics tests involving application of lengthy formulas, and note takers; taped materials and reading assistance. Services include: Special courses and instruction such as Academic Skills Development, Academic Potential, reading courses and career exploration courses; tutoring; study skills; writing and spelling; counseling; technology lab; and an Independent study lab. UA also sponsors a summer camp called "College Camp" designed for students with LD/ADD who want to prepare for the rigor of the academic challenges of freshman year in college. The focus is on communication; advocacy; academic skills; learning strategies; note-taking skills; study skills; reading; writing; and math skills, and self-presentation skills. LD and ADD attend different two week sessions, and the cost is $400.

**Special Ed HS coursework accepted:** Yes, if teacher is certified in the area
**Essay required:** No
**Special application required:** No          **Submitted to:** N/A
**# of applications submitted each year:** 50          **# of applications accepted each year:** N/I
**# of students receiving LD services:** 226
**Acceptance into program means acceptance into college:** Students must be admitted to the university first and then may request services.

## LEARNING DISABILITY SERVICES

Learning center: Yes
Kurzweil personal reader: Yes
LD specialists: 2
Allowed in exams:
  Calculator: Yes
  Dictionary: Yes
  Computer: Y/N
  SpellCheck: Y/N

Notetaker: Yes
Scribes: Yes
Proctors: Yes
Oral exams: Yes
Extended test time: Yes
Added cost: None
Distraction-free environ.: Yes
Tape recording in class: Yes
Books on tape: Yes
Taping of other books: Yes

Professional tutors: Yes
Peer tutors: Yes
Max. hrs/wk for services: 2
Priority registration: Yes
Accomodations for students
with ADD: Yes
How are professors notified of
LD: By the student with verification from Disability Services

## GENERAL ADMISSIONS INFORMATION

Director of Admissions: Dr. Randall Dahl          Telephone: 800-933-BAMA

### ENTRANCE REQUIREMENTS

Total high school units required/recommended: 20 total units are required; 4 English required, 3 math required, 3 science required, 1 foreign language required, 3 social studies required, 1 history required. Minimum composite ACT score of 22 (combined SAT I score of 1030) and minimum 2.0 GPA in core academic courses required. Special requirements: A portfolio is required for art program applicants; an audition is required for music program applicants; TOEFL is required of all international students.

Application deadline: April 15
Notification: Rolling

SAT or ACT preferred: Either
Average ACT: 24
Average GPA: 3.2

Graduated top 10% of class: 21
Graduated top 25% of class: 61
Graduated top 50% of class: 92

## COLLEGE GRADUATION REQUIREMENTS

Course waivers allowed: No
Course substitutions allowed: Yes
In what courses: Core curriculum has built-in substitutions: computer language for foreign language; logic for math.

## ADDITIONAL INFORMATION

Environment: The university is located 55 miles from the city of Birmingham.

Student Body
  Undergrad enrollment: 14,195
  Women: 51%
  Men: 49%
  In-state students: 68%
  Out-of-state: 32%

Cost Information
  In-state tuition: $2,470
  Out-of-state: $6,268
  Room & board: $3,680

Housing Information
  University housing: Yes
  Fraternity: Yes
  Sorority: Yes
  Living on campus: 27%

  Athletics: NR

# UNIVERSITY OF ALABAMA-HUNTSVILLE

301 Sparkman Drive, Huntsville, AL 35899 • **Admissions:** 205-895-6070 • **Fax:** 205-895-6287
**Email:** freemonk@email.uah.edu • **Web:** www.info.uah.edu
**Support:** S • **Institution:** 4 yr. Public

## LEARNING DISABILITY ADMISSIONS AND SERVICES

The Office of Student Development Services offers a variety of services and accommodations to assist students with disabilities in eliminating barriers they encounter in pursuing higher education. The main objective is to provide access to academic, social, cultural, recreational, and housing opportunities at the university. The services offered encourage students to achieve and maintain autonomy.

## LEARNING DISABILITY ADMISSIONS INFORMATION

**Program Name:** Student Development Services
**Program Director:** Delois H. Smith                    **Telephone:** 205-890-6203
**Contact Person:** Same as above

### ADMISSIONS

The two factors considered for general admission are grades and test scores, and 4 yrs. English, 3 yrs. social studies, 3 yrs. math, 2 yrs. science, and a total of 20 Carnegie units. There is no special admission process for students with learning disabilities. However, an applicant not meeting the criteria for regular admissions may be admitted as a conditional admit. These students will be required to carry a light courseload for the first 15 hours. If the student achieves an overall "C" average after 15 hours, he/she will become a regular degree-seeking student. Students admitted conditionally are subject to periodic reviews of their record as regular students, and are subject to the university's regulations regarding scholastic probation and suspension. If a student becomes subject to academic suspension, the suspension is for a minimum of one term, and the student must petition the Admissions Committee for approval to re-enroll.

**College entrance exams required:** Yes           **Untimed accepted:** Yes
**Course entrance requirements:** Yes              **Interview required:** No
**Diagnostic tests:** Yes
**Documentation:** WAIS-R, Stanford-Binet, W-J: within 3-5 yrs.

### ADDITIONAL INFORMATION

Student Development Services provides the mandated services, including: testing accommodations, distraction-free environments for tests, readers, proctors, scribes, notetakers, peer tutoring on an unlimited basis, specialized adaptive computers, and study skills classes that can be taken for credit. Services and accommodations are available for undergraduate and graduate students.

**Special education HS coursework accepted:** No      **Essay required:** No
**Special application required:** Yes                **Submitted to:** Student Development Services Disabilities

**# of applications submitted each year:** N/A        **# of applications accepted each year:** N/A
**# of students receiving LD services:** 152
**Acceptance into program means acceptance into college:** Students must be admitted to the university first and then may request services.

## LEARNING DISABILITY SERVICES

**Learning center:** No
**Kurzweil personal reader:** Yes
**LD specialists:** No
**Allowed in exams:**
  **Calculator:** Yes
  **Dictionary:** No
  **Computer:** Yes
  **SpellCheck:** Yes

**Notetaker:** Yes
**Scribes:** Yes
**Proctors:** Yes
**Oral exams:** Yes
**Extended test time:** Yes
**Added cost:** No
**Distraction-free environ.:** Yes
**Tape recording in class:** Yes
**Books on tape:** Yes
**Taping of other books:** Yes

**Professional tutors:** No
**Peer tutors:** 26
**Max. hrs/wk for services:** Unlimited
**Priority registration:** Yes
**Accomodations for students with ADD:** Yes
**How are professors notified of LD:** By the student and the Director

## GENERAL ADMISSIONS INFORMATION

**Director of Admissions:** Dr. Ron Koger

**Telephone:** 205-890-6070

### ENTRANCE REQUIREMENTS

Total high school units required/recommended: 20 total units are required; 4 English required, 3 math required, 2 science required, 3 social studies required. Minimum composite ACT score of 17 and minimum 3.25 GPA or minimum composite ACT score of 24 and minimum 1.75 GPA required. Special requirements: TOEFL is required of all international students; 1 unit of chemistry/physics and minimum composite ACT score of 21 (combined SAT score of 900) required of applicants to Colleges of Engineering and Science; 1 unit each of algebra II and trigonometry required of applicants to College of Engineering.

**Application deadline:** August 15
**Notification:** Rolling

**SAT or ACT preferred:** Either
**SAT Avg:** 554V, 569M
**Average ACT:** 24
**Average GPA:** 3.4

**Graduated top 10% of class:** 27
**Graduated top 25% of class:** 63
**Graduated top 50% of class:** 86

## COLLEGE GRADUATION REQUIREMENTS

**Course waivers allowed:** Yes
**Course substitutions allowed:** Yes
**In what courses:** Determined on a case-by-case basis.

## ADDITIONAL INFORMATION

**Environment:** The university is located on 337 acres 100 miles north of Birmingham and 100 miles south of Nashville.

**Student Body**
  **Undergrad enrollment:** 5,230
  **Women:** 49%
  **Men:** 51%
  **In-state students:** 93%
  **Out-of-state:** 7%

**Cost Information**
  **In-state tuition:** $2,698
  **Out-of-state:** $5,656
  **Room & board:** $3,645

**Housing Information**
  **University housing:** Yes
  **Fraternity:** Yes
  **Sorority:** No
  **Living on campus:** 13%

  **Athletics:** NCAA Div. II

# UNIVERSITY OF ALASKA-ANCHORAGE

3211 Providence Drive, Anchorage, AK 99508 • **Admissions:** 907-786-1480
**Email:** ayenrol@alaska.edu • **Web:** www.uaa.alaska.edu
**Support:** S • **Institution:** 2 yr. & 4 yr. Public

## LEARNING DISABILITY ADMISSIONS AND SERVICES

The University of Alaska-Anchorage provides equal opportunities for students who experience disabilities. Academic support services are available to students with learning disabilities. Staff trained to work with students with disabilities provide specialized assistance. To allow time for planning and scheduling assistance, students are encouraged to contact the Disability Support Services Office several weeks before registration each semester. Ongoing communication with the staff throughout the semester is encouraged.

## LEARNING DISABILITY ADMISSIONS INFORMATION

**Program Name:** Disability Support Services
**Program Director:** Lyn Stoller
**Contact Person:** Same as above

**Telephone:** 907-786-4530

### ADMISSIONS

While formal admission is encouraged, the university has an open enrollment policy that allows students to register for courses in which they have adequate background. Open enrollment does not guarantee subsequent formal admission to certificate or degree programs. Individuals with learning disabilities are admitted via the standard admissions procedures that apply to all students submitting applications for formal admission. Students with documentation of a learning disability are eligible to receive support services once they are enrolled in the university.

**College entrance exams required:** Not for open enrollment   **Untimed accepted:** Yes
**Course entrance requirements:** Not for open enrollment   **Interview required:** No
**Diagnostic tests:** Yes
**Documentation:** WJ; WRAT; WAIS-R; or other appropriate tests: prefer within 3 years

### ADDITIONAL INFORMATION

Slingerland Language Arts classes are available for all students in the areas of vocabulary building and study skills. There is no separate tutoring for students with learning disabilities. Tutorial help is available in the Reading and Writing Labs and the Learning Resource Center for all students. Services and accommodations are available for undergraduate and graduate students.

**Special education HS coursework accepted:** Yes, if regular level classes
**Essay required:** No
**Special application required:** No                              **Submitted to:** N/A
**# of applications submitted each year:** N/A                   **# of applications accepted each year:** All who request
**# of students receiving LD services:** 90
**Acceptance into program means acceptance into college:** UAA has open enrollment; students are accepted to the university and then may request services.

## LEARNING DISABILITY SERVICES

**Learning center:** No
**Kurzweil personal reader:** Yes
**LD specialists:** No
**Allowed in exams:**
  **Calculator:** No
  **Dictionary:** Yes
  **Computer:** Yes
  **SpellCheck:** Yes

**Notetaker:** Yes
**Scribes:** Yes
**Proctors:** Yes
**Oral exams:** Yes
**Extended test time:** Yes
**Added cost:** None if in tutoring lab; Private tutoring cost is variable
**Distraction-free environ.:** Yes
**Tape recording in class:** Yes
**Books on tape:** Yes
**Taping of other books:** Yes

**Professional tutors:** Yes
**Peer tutors:** Yes
**Max. hrs/wk for services:** No; referred to same tutors as all other students
**Priority registration:** Yes
**Accomodations for students with ADD:** Yes
**How are professors notified of LD:** By the student or Program Director

## GENERAL ADMISSIONS INFORMATION

**Director of Admissions:** Linda Berg-Smith

**Telephone:** 907-786-1480

### ENTRANCE REQUIREMENTS
Total high school units required/recommended: 13 total units are recommended; 4 English recommended, 3 math recommended, 2 science recommended, 22 social studies recommended. Minimum 2.5 GPA required. Special requirements: A portfolio is required for art program applicants. An RN is required for nursing program applicants. TOEFL is required of all international students. At least 45 college credits and minimum score of 176 on Pre-Professional Skills Test (PPST) required of B.Ed. program applicants.

**Application deadline:** Rolling
**Notification:** Rolling

**SAT or ACT preferred:** Either
**SAT Avg:** 422V, 459M
**Average ACT:** 20

## COLLEGE GRADUATION REQUIREMENTS

**Course waivers allowed:** No
**Course substitutions allowed:** Yes
**In what courses:** Decided on an individual, case-by-case basis

## ADDITIONAL INFORMATION

**Environment:** The University of Alaska is an urban campus on 350 acres 7 miles from downtown Anchorage.

**Student Body**
  **Undergrad enrollment:** 16,746
  **Women:** 56%
  **Men:** 44%
  **In-state students:** 96%
  **Out-of-state:** 4%

**Cost Information**
  **In-state tuition:** $1,035
  **Out-of-state:** $3,105
  **Room & board:** $6,310

**Housing Information**
  **University housing:** Yes
  **Fraternity:** No
  **Sorority:** No
  **Living on campus:** 7%

  **Athletics:** NCAA Div. II

# UNIVERSITY OF ALASKA-FAIRBANKS

Suite 102 Signers Hall, Fairbanks, AK 99775 • **Admissions:** 907-474-7521 • **Fax:** 907-474-5379
**Email:** fnaws@aurora.alaska.edu • **Web:** www.uaf.edu
**Support:** S • **Institution:** 4 yr. Public

## LEARNING DISABILITY ADMISSIONS AND SERVICES

The University of Alaska is committed to providing equal opportunity to students with disabilities. Services for Students with Disabilities (SSD) at UAF provides assistance to students with permanent or temporary disabilities. The purpose of SSD is to enable students who have disabilities to be successful in college. Campus Services include the Academic Advising Center, which is responsible for advising incoming freshmen and students with undeclared majors. It provides explanations of programs and requirements, assists students with choosing a major, selecting electives, and choosing classes consistent with their academic and career goals. Student Support Services provides academic and personal support including developmental classes and tutoring for students who are economically disadvantaged, do not have a parent who graduated from college, or have a documented disability. DisAbled Students of UAF provides peer support groups for UAF students experiencing disabilities. The Student Development and Learning Center provides tutoring, individual instruction in basic skills and counseling, career planing services, and assessment testing. Services for Students with Disabilities welcomes inquiries and seeks to make the college experience a success for students with disabilities.

## LEARNING DISABILITY ADMISSIONS INFORMATION

**Program Name:** Services for Students with Disabilities
**Program Director:** Diane Preston, Coordinator        **Telephone:** 907-474-5655
**Contact Person:** Same as above

### ADMISSIONS

There is no special admissions process for students with LD. The university has a liberal admissions policy. To qualify for admission freshman students must meet one of the following: Associate Degree program requires a high school diploma or GED, and a "C" average with 14 credits to enter a baccalaureate degree program; Baccalaureate Degree requires a high school diploma with a 2.0 GPA, and admission to specific programs requires different combinations of GPA and high school courses. Students must also complete, with a minimum GPA of 2.5, a core curriculum including 4 yrs. English, 3 yrs. math, 3 yrs. social sciences, and 3 yrs. natural or physical sciences. Foreign language is recommended. Students can be provisionally accepted if they make up course deficiencies with a "C" or better in each of the developmental or university courses, and complete 9 credits of general degree requirements with a "C" or better. Being accepted to the university does not depend on minimum test scores; however these test scores are used to determine placement in English, math, and other freshman-level courses.

| | |
|---|---|
| **College entrance exams required:** No | **Untimed accepted:** N/A |
| **Course entrance requirements:** Yes | **Interview required:** No |
| **Diagnostic tests:** Yes | |
| **Documentation:** WAIS-R | |

### ADDITIONAL INFORMATION

Services include: Individual counseling to determine necessary accommodations; arrangements for special services such as readers, scribes, and notetakers; advocacy with faculty and staff; assistance to faculty and staff in determining appropriate accommodations; help in determining specific needs for students with learning disabilities; and referral to campus and community agencies for additional services. Basic study skill classes are offered for all students and may be taken for credit. There is a special summer program for precollege freshmen with learning disabilities. Services and accommodations are provided for undergraduate and graduate students.

| | |
|---|---|
| **Special education HS coursework accepted:** Yes | **Essay required:** No |
| **Special application required:** No | **Submitted to:** N/A |
| **# of applications submitted each year:** N/A | **# of applications accepted each year:** N/A |
| **# of students receiving LD services:** Approximately 60-70 | |

**Acceptance into program means acceptance into college:** Students must be admitted to the university and then request services.

## LEARNING DISABILITY SERVICES

**Learning center:** No
**Kurzweil personal reader:** Yes
**LD specialists:** No
**Allowed in exams:**
 **Calculator:** Yes
 **Dictionary:** Yes
 **Computer:** Yes
 **SpellCheck:** Yes

**Notetaker:** Yes
**Scribes:** Yes
**Proctors:** Yes
**Oral exams:** Yes
**Extended test time:** Yes
**Added cost:** N/I
**Distraction-free environ.:** Yes
**Tape recording in class:** Yes
**Books on tape:** Yes
**Taping of other books:** Yes

**Professional tutors:** No
**Peer tutors:** N/I
**Max. hrs/wk for services:** N/I
**Priority registration:** N/I
**Accomodations for students with ADD:** N/I
**How are professors notified of LD:** By the student and the Director of Support Services

## GENERAL ADMISSIONS INFORMATION

**Director of Admissions:** Ann Tremarello       **Telephone:** 907-474-7500

### ENTRANCE REQUIREMENTS

Total high school units required/recommended: Sixteen total units are required; 2 total units are recommended; 4 English required, 3 math required, 3 science required, 2 foreign language recommended, 3 social studies required. Minimum 2.0 cumulative GPA required; 2.5 GPA in 16-unit program of study. Special requirements: TOEFL is required of all international students; 3.5 units of math required of engineering program applicants; 4 units of math required of computer science, math, and statistics program applicants.

**Application deadline:** August 1
**Notification:** Rolling

**SAT or ACT preferred:** Either

**Graduated top 10% of class:** 16
**Graduated top 25% of class:** 34
**Graduated top 50% of class:** 61

## COLLEGE GRADUATION REQUIREMENTS

**Course waivers allowed:** No
**Course substitutions allowed:** Yes
**In what courses:** Depends on documentation

## ADDITIONAL INFORMATION

**Environment:** NR

**Student Body**
 **Undergrad enrollment:** 7,393
 **Women:** 59%
 **Men:** 41%
 **In-state students:** 90%
 **Out-of-state:** 10%

**Cost Information**
 **In-state tuition:** $2,160
 **Out-of-state:** $6,480
 **Room & board:** $3,690

**Housing Information**
 **University housing:** Yes
 **Fraternity:** Yes
 **Sorority:** Yes
 **Living on campus:** 22%

 **Athletics:** NCAA Div. II

# SHELDON JACKSON COLLEGE

801 Lincoln Street, Sitka, AK 99835 • **Admissions:** 907-747-5221 • **Fax:** 907-747-5212
**Email:** trnopic@acad1.alaska.edu
**Support:** CS • **Institution:** 4 yr. Private

## LEARNING DISABILITY ADMISSIONS AND SERVICES

People vary and are "differently abled." The College seeks to help students find their forté, best learning modes, and best modes of expression; and seeks to help students prepare to find the greatest possible joy in vocation and service to others. The college seeks guidance from the students in its effort to guide them toward the aids and resources that will be the most helpful and meaningful. The Sheldon Jackson College Achievement Program provides individualized attention, a structured academic program, and special support services during the students' first semester. This program is designed to provide a structured support system that will allow students to succeed in college. Students sign a Participation Agreement. This program also addresses the out-of-classroom experiences. Additional attention and support services are provided by the Office of Residence Life, including giving appropriate information to trained Residence Advisors. Residence Advisors provide encouragement on the peer level.

## LEARNING DISABILITY ADMISSIONS INFORMATION

**Program Name:** Learning Assistance Program
**Program Director:** Alice Zellhuber          **Telephone:** 907-747-5235
**Contact Person:** Same as above

### ADMISSIONS

Students not meeting the general admission requirements who have apparent learning difficulties will be given the opportunity to enter Sheldon Jackson College through the Achievement Program. Generally these students have a GPA below a 2.0, but have average to above average intelligence, are motivated to attend classes, can meet deadlines in completing assignments, and are willing to seek help when needed. The Office of Admissions sends a letter, including a Participation Agreement, to any applicant who meets the criteria for the Program. If the student attains a minimum 2.0 GPA at the end of the first semester, the student will no longer be accountable to the Achievement Program conditions and requirements, but will have the option of continuing to utilize the Program's services. ACT/SAT are not used for admission, but are used for comparative purposes after sophomore year.

**College entrance exams required:** Yes            **Untimed accepted:** N/A
**Course entrance requirements:** N/I              **Interview required:** No
**Diagnostic tests:** No
**Documentation:** Varies; often the WAIS-R; W-J-R: within 3 years

### ADDITIONAL INFORMATION

The Academic Programs Committee coordinates the Achievement Program. The committee evaluates each participant based on semester GPA, a recommendation of the assigned advisor, etc. The Learning Resource Center provides the academic resources for the Program. The LRC Coordinator serves as an advisor. Additional faculty and administrative advisors are assigned when needed. Advisors instruct the Academic Success Skills classes; determine orientation activities; advise during registration; monitor academic progress; liaison with faculty; and instruct students to write narratives describing their classes and demonstrate responsibility for behavior relating to academic progress. Participants agree to enroll in Academic Success Skills Class; participate in New Student Orientation; attend all classes regularly; attend all scheduled meetings with advisor; review all course syllabi with advisor; attend study hall, tutoring sessions and resource labs; and communicate academic difficulties.

**Special education HS coursework accepted:** Individually evaluated
**Essay required:** No
**Special application required:** Yes            **Submitted to:** Admissions Office if GPA is below 2.0
**# of applications submitted each year:** 3-6    **# of applications accepted each year:** Virtually all
                                                  who request services.
**# of students receiving LD services:** 3-8
**Acceptance into program means acceptance into college:** Students must request services after admission.

## LEARNING DISABILITY SERVICES

**Learning center:** Yes
**Kurzweil personal reader:** Yes
**LD specialists:** 1
**Allowed in exams:**
  **Calculator:** Y/N
  **Dictionary:** Y/N
  **Computer:** Y/N
  **SpellCheck:** Y/N

**Notetaker:** Yes
**Scribes:** Yes
**Proctors:** Yes
**Oral exams:** Yes
**Extended test time:** Yes
**Added cost:** No
**Distraction-free environ.:** Yes
**Tape recording in class:** Yes
**Books on tape:** Yes
**Taping of other books:** Yes

**Professional tutors:** 1-2
**Peer tutors:** 2-5
**Max. hrs/wk for services:** 30
**Priority registration:** No
**Accomodations for students with ADD:** No
**How are professors notified of LD:** By the student and the Program Director

## GENERAL ADMISSIONS INFORMATION

**Director of Admissions:** Lance Williamson

**Telephone:** 907-747-5221

### ENTRANCE REQUIREMENTS
High school diploma or GED equivalent

**Application deadline:** Rolling
**Notification:** NR

**SAT or ACT preferred:** NR

## COLLEGE GRADUATION REQUIREMENTS

**Course waivers allowed:** Yes
**Course substitutions allowed:** Yes
**In what courses:** Students petition the Academic Programs Committee

## ADDITIONAL INFORMATION

**Environment:** The College is located on 345 acres in a small town 800 miles north of Seattle.

**Student Body**
  **Undergrad enrollment:** NR
  **Women:** NR
  **Men:** NR
  **In-state students:** 46%
  **Out-of-state:** 54%

**Cost Information**
  **In-state tuition:** $9,000
  **Out-of-state:** $9,000
  **Room & board:** $4,800

**Housing Information**
  **University housing:** Yes
  **Fraternity:** No
  **Sorority:** No
  **Living on campus:** 80%

  **Athletics:** NAIA

# AZ ARIZONA STATE UNIVERSITY

P.O. Box 870112, Tempe, AZ 85287-0112 • **Admissions:** 602-965-7788 • **Fax:** 602-965-3610
**Email:** ugradadm@asuvm.inre.asu.edu • **Web:** www.asu.edu
**Support:** CS • **Institution:** 4 yr. Public

## LEARNING DISABILITY ADMISSIONS AND SERVICES

ASU's Disabled Student Resources (DSR) program strives to facilitate resources, services, and auxiliary aids to allow each qualified student with disabilities to equitably access educational, social, and career opportunities. Students utilizing the services through the DSR Program are mainstreamed in all courses. Support is available but students need to be assertive and have a desire to succeed. The services are geared to the needs of the particular student and are individually based. Each student is encouraged to seek out methods for attaining the highest possible goals. All services and accommodations are provided upon request on an individual basis as appropriate for qualified/eligible individuals with learning disabilities.The goal of DSR is to assist the student in becoming academically and socially independent.

## LEARNING DISABILITY ADMISSIONS INFORMATION

**Program Name:** Disabled Student Resources  (DSR)
**Program Director:** Deb Taska                **Telephone:** 602-965-6484
**Contact Person:** Gale Johnson               **Telephone:** 602-965-1235

### ADMISSIONS

Students with LD submit the regular ASU application. Students should self-disclose their LD and submit documentation. Courses required: 4 yrs. English, 4 yrs. math , 3 yrs. science, 2 yrs. social science, and 1 yr. fine arts. Arizona residents must rank in the top quarter or have a 22 ACT/930 SAT or a 3.0 GPA. Non-residents must rank in the top quarter or have a 24 ACT/1010 SAT or a 3.0 GPA. Non-residents who have a strong high school background and who rank in the top 50% or have a GPA of 2.5-2.9 will be considered individually. To appeal a denial applicant should: write a letter stating reasons for wanting to attend ASU and describing ability for success; send 3 recommendations showing motivation and perseverance; and send a transcript showing gradual upward trend in courses and grades. If applicant is ultimately denied after an appeal or 6 hours of credit or less is desired per semester, a non-degree seeking application is available. Transcripts are not required. Students can earn up to 15 non-degree hours to be applied toward a degree program. Non-degree candidates may live in residential housing at ASU.

**College entrance exams required:** Yes                **Untimed accepted:** Yes
**Course entrance requirements:** Yes                **Interview required:** Recommended
**Diagnostic tests:** Yes
**Documentation:** WAIS-R; W-J; WRAT-R and other appropriate tests: within 3 years

### ADDITIONAL INFORMATION

Academic support accommodations include: consultation; individualized program recommendations; registration information and advisement referrals; academic tutoring; Computer Technology Center; learning strategies instruction; library research assistance; supplemental readers in coordination with RFB; mastery of Alternative Learning Techniques lab; in-class notetaking; testing accommodations; and diagnostic testing referrals. DSR provides in-service training for faculty/staff. Services and accommodations are available for undergraduate and graduate students.

**Special education HS coursework accepted:** Yes, but must be approved
**Essay required:** No
**Special application required:** No                **Submitted to:** N/A
**# of applications submitted each year:** 100          **# of applications accepted each year:** 50+
**# of students receiving LD services:** 400+ are currently receiving services
**Acceptance into program means acceptance into college:** Students must be admitted to the university first and them may request services.

## LEARNING DISABILITY SERVICES

**Learning center:** Yes
**Kurzweil personal reader:** Yes
**LD specialists:** 3
**Allowed in exams:**
  **Calculator:** Yes
  **Dictionary:** Yes
  **Computer:** Yes
  **SpellCheck:** Yes

**Notetaker:** Yes
**Scribes:** Yes
**Proctors:** Yes
**Oral exams:** Yes
**Extended test time:** Yes
**Added cost:** None
**Distraction-free environ.:** Yes
**Tape recording in class:** Yes
**Books on tape:** Yes
**Taping of other books:** Yes

**Professional tutors:** 0
**Peer tutors:** 8
**Max. hrs/wk for services:** As needed; limited to Trio Grant participants
**Priority registration:** Yes
**Accomodations for students with ADD:** Yes
**How are professors notified of LD:** By the student

## GENERAL ADMISSIONS INFORMATION

**Director of Admissions:** Dolan Evanovich          **Telephone:** 602-965-2604

### ENTRANCE REQUIREMENTS

Total high school units required/recommended: 16 total units are required; 4 English required, 4 math required, 3 science required, 2 foreign language required, 1 social studies required, 1 history required. Minimum combined SAT I score of 1040 (composite ACT score of 22), rank in top quarter of secondary school class, or minimum 3.0 GPA recommended of in-state applicants; minimum combined SAT I score of 1110 (composite ACT score of 24), rank in top quarter of secondary school class, or minimum 3.0 GPA recommended of out-of-state applicants. Special requirements: An audition is required for music program applicants; TOEFL is required of all international students.

**Application deadline:** Rolling
**Notification:** Rolling

**SAT or ACT preferred:** Either
**SAT Avg:** 540V, 544M
**Average ACT:** 23
**Average GPA:** 3.2

**Graduated top 10% of class:** 24
**Graduated top 25% of class:** 49
**Graduated top 50% of class:** 82

## COLLEGE GRADUATION REQUIREMENTS

**Course waivers allowed:** No
**Course substitutions allowed:** Yes
**In what courses:** Math and foreign language substitutions are granted by college standards committees as appropriate to documentation of related disability and a history of attempts.

## ADDITIONAL INFORMATION

**Environment:** Arizona State University is a city school about 5 miles from Phoenix.

**Student Body**
  **Undergrad enrollment:** 31,859
  **Women:** 50%
  **Men:** 50%
  **In-state students:** 72%
  **Out-of-state:** 28%

**Cost Information**
  **In-state tuition:** $2,009
  **Out-of-state:** $8,377
  **Room & board:** $4,287

**Housing Information**
  **University housing:** Yes
  **Fraternity:** Yes
  **Sorority:** Yes
  **Living on campus:** 17%

  **Athletics:** NCAA Div. I

# UNIVERSITY OF ARIZONA

Tucson, AZ 85721 • **Admissions:** 520-621-3237 • **Fax:** 520-621-9799
**Email:** kwood@arizona.edu • **Web:** www.arizona.edu
**Support:** SP • **Institution:** 4 yr. Public

## LEARNING DISABILITY ADMISSIONS AND SERVICES

SALT empowers students with LD to succeed in their pursuit of higher education. Supporting the ideal of education for life, SALT encourages and provides experiences and opportunities to build confidence beyond the classroom. SALT encourages growth and independence-training individuals to improve learning, expression, and decision making. A major philosophy is to provide intensive service for the first year with the goal of increasing independence as the student learns the coping strategies to succeed in college. The following guidelines clarify the process of documenting a LD at UA: assessment and testing must be comprehensive and include a diagnostic interview and results of a neuropsychological or psychoeducational evaluation; results must include a specific diagnosis and actual test scores; evaluation by a qualified professional; testing must be current; recommended accommodations should include a rationale that correlates the accommodations to specific test results and clinical observations. Students providing documentation express a desire to qualify for consideration as an individual with a disability. Being identified as LD/ADD does not afford any individual automatic access to university accommodations or for privileges as an individual with disabilities. The university has established guidelines to meet diverse needs while maintaining the integrity of academic and nonacademic programming.

## LEARNING DISABILITY ADMISSIONS INFORMATION

**Program Name:** Strategic Alternative Learning Techniques (SALT)
**Program Director:** Diane Perreira                    **Telephone:** 520-621-1427
**Contact Person:** Shirley Ramsey                      **Telephone:** 520-621-3652

### ADMISSIONS

The majority of students with disabilities seeking admission to UA meet the general admission requirements. Candidates with disabilities, desiring special consideration, are expected to provide all documentation they feel necessary to represent the specific circumstances. If the candidate has a learning disability or attention deficit disorder, is requesting special consideration, and is seeking admission to the SALT Center, the student should submit all documentation of disability directly to UA admissions. Students may apply to SALT at any time beginning in August preceding their senior year of high school. A student may submit documentation with the SALT application as well, but one copy MUST accompany the UA application for admission to receive special consideration. Whenever possible, the SALT Center will announce its decision regarding a student's application for admission to SALT concurrent with the university's notification of acceptance. Incomplete records at SALT could delay a decision. Students denied admission to UA will not be considered for SALT.

**College entrance exams required:** Yes                    **Untimed accepted:** Yes
**Course entrance requirements:** Yes                      **Interview required:** No
**Diagnostic tests:** Yes
**Documentation:** WAIS-R; W-J: within 3 years

### ADDITIONAL INFORMATION

Basic services include advocacy, auxiliary aids for classroom accommodations, and special testing; there is no charge for these services. Enhanced services provide a full service program with academic monitoring, registration assistance, staff contact and trained learning specialists, tutoring, a writing enhancement program, a specially equipped computer learning laboratory, and personalized tutorial services. Each student works with a trained specialist to identify learning preferences, learning strategies, and appropriate compensatory, productive learning techniques. There is a fee for enhanced services. Support services include both academic programs and counseling components. Students receive assistance with academic planning and registration followed by regularly scheduled staff contact to monitor progress. A Drop-In-Center is available for study, tutoring, and student/staff interaction. The SALT Program is staffed by persons trained and experienced in working with students with LD.

**Special education HS coursework accepted:** No             **Essay required:** Yes
**Special application required:** Yes                         **Submitted to:** SALT Coordinator
**# of applications submitted each year:** 500+              **# of applications accepted each year:** 200
**# of students receiving LD services:** 475
**Acceptance into program means acceptance into college:** No, students are admitted to the university and then to SALT.

# LEARNING DISABILITY SERVICES

**Learning center:** Yes
**Kurzweil personal reader:** No
**LD specialists:** Yes
**Allowed in exams:**
  **Calculator:** Yes
  **Dictionary:** Yes
  **Computer:** Yes
  **SpellCheck:** Yes

**Notetaker:** Yes
**Scribes:** Yes
**Proctors:** Yes
**Oral exams:** Yes
**Extended test time:** Yes
**Added cost:** $1,500 freshman year per semester
**Distraction-free environ.:** Yes
**Tape recording in class:** Yes
**Books on tape:** Yes
**Taping of other books:** No

**Professional tutors:** Yes
**Peer tutors:** 100+
**Max. hrs/wk for services:** Varies
**Priority registration:** Yes
**Accomodations for students with ADD:** Yes
**How are professors notified of LD:** By the student

# GENERAL ADMISSIONS INFORMATION

**Director of Admissions:** Lori Goldman (interim)　　　**Telephone:** 520-621-3237

## ENTRANCE REQUIREMENTS

Total high school units required/recommended: 11 total units are required; 4 English required, 3 math required, 4 math recommended, 2 science required, 2 social studies required, 1 history required. Eighteen units recommended. Minimum combined SAT I score of 1040 (composite ACT score of 22), rank in top half of secondary school class, or minimum 2.5 GPA required of in-state applicants; minimum combined SAT I score of 1110 (composite ACT score of 24), rank in top quarter of secondary school class, or minimum 3.0 GPA required of out-of-state applicants. Special requirements: Additional requirements for architecture, education, engineering, music, theatre, and pharmacy program applicants.

**Application deadline:** April 1
**Notification:** Rolling

**SAT or ACT preferred:** Either
**SAT Avg:** 463V, 532M
**Average ACT:** 23

**Graduated top 10% of class:** 30
**Graduated top 25% of class:** 58
**Graduated top 50% of class:** 88

# COLLEGE GRADUATION REQUIREMENTS

**Course waivers allowed:** Yes
**Course substitutions allowed:** Yes
**In what courses:** Math and Foreign Language

# ADDITIONAL INFORMATION

**Environment:** Situated in downtown Tucson on 325 acres, the university is surrounded by the Santa Catalina Mountain range in the Sonora Desert.

**Student Body**
  **Undergrad enrollment:** 26,468
  **Women:** 51%
  **Men:** 49%
  **In-state students:** 71%
  **Out-of-state:** 29%

**Cost Information**
  **In-state tuition:** $1,940
  **Out-of-state:** $8,308
  **Room & board:** $4,190

**Housing Information**
  **University housing:** Yes
  **Fraternity:** Yes
  **Sorority:** Yes
  **Living on campus:** 70%

  **Athletics:** NCAA Div. I

# NORTHERN ARIZONA UNIVERSITY

P.O. Box 4132, Flagstaff, AZ 86011 • **Admissions:** 520-523-5511 • **Fax:** 520-523-6023
**Email:** undergraduateadmissions@nau.edu • **Web:** www.nau.edu
**Support:** SP • **Institution:** 4 yr. Public

## LEARNING DISABILITY ADMISSIONS AND SERVICES

The goal of the Learning Disabilities Center is to assist students in achieving their academic goals while at the same time creating an environment conducive to learning and building self-esteem. The belief is that in providing supportive assistance the student will become an independent learner and self-advocate. The Learning Disabilities Center is a part of Disability Support Services.

## LEARNING DISABILITY ADMISSIONS INFORMATION

**Program Name:** Disability Support Services
**Program Director:** Marsha Fields, Ed.D
**Contact Person:** Karen Wise

**Telephone:** 520-523-2261
**Telephone:** 520-523-7252

### ADMISSIONS

There is no special admissions for students with learning disabilities. General admission requirements for unconditional admission include: 4 yrs. English, 4 yrs. math, 2 yrs. social science with 1 yr. being American history, 3 yrs. lab science in biology, chemistry, physics or earth science, and 1 yr. fine arts; 3.0 GPA or the upper 25% of the graduating class or SAT of 930 for resident students or 1010 for non-residents or an ACT of 22 for residents or 24 for non-residents. Conditional admissions is possible with a 2.5-2.99 GPA or top 50% of graduating class and ACT/ SAT scores. Exceptional admission may be offered to 10% of the new freshmen applicants or transfer applicants.

**College entrance exams required:** Yes
**Course entrance requirements:** Yes
**Diagnostic tests:** Yes
**Documentation:** 1 aptitude and 1 achievement test; within 3 years

**Untimed accepted:** Yes
**Interview required:** No

### ADDITIONAL INFORMATION

Skills classes are available in notetaking, study techniques, reading, memory and learning, overcoming math anxiety, speed reading, time management, test taking strategies, "How To Make Math Easy," "How To Get Started Writing," "How To Edit Writing," and "How To Prepare For Final Exams." There is a special summer program for precollege freshmen with learning disabilities, and all services continue through the summer. All services and accommodations are available for undergraduate and graduate students.

**Special education HS coursework accepted:** Y/N with approval from Admissions     **Essay required:** No
**Special application required:** No                         **Submitted to:** N/A
**# of applications submitted each year:** 200 applicants self-disclose yearly     **# of applications accepted each year:** N/I
**# of students receiving LD services:** 140
**Acceptance into program means acceptance into college:** Students must be admitted to the university first and then may request services.

# LEARNING DISABILITY SERVICES

**Learning center:** Yes
**Kurzweil personal reader:** No
**LD specialists:** 1
**Allowed in exams:**
 **Calculator:** Yes
 **Dictionary:** Yes
 **Computer:** Yes
 **SpellCheck:** Yes

**Notetaker:** Yes
**Scribes:** Yes
**Proctors:** Yes
**Oral exams:** Yes
**Extended test time:** Yes
**Added cost:** None
**Distraction-free environ.:** Yes
**Tape recording in class:** Yes
**Books on tape:** Yes
**Taping of other books:** Yes

**Professional tutors:** No
**Peer tutors:** Yes
**Max. hrs/wk for services:** Tutoring is 2 hrs. per week,per subject; other services are unlimited
**Priority registration:** Yes
**Accomodations for students with ADD:** Yes
**How are professors notified of LD:** By the student

# GENERAL ADMISSIONS INFORMATION

**Director of Admissions:** Molly Carter          **Telephone:** 520-523-6002

## ENTRANCE REQUIREMENTS

Total high school units required/recommended: 16 total units are required; 4 English required, 3 math required, 2 science required, 2 social studies required. Rank in top half of secondary school class, minimum 2.5 GPA, or minimum composite ACT score of 22 (combined SAT I score of 1040) required of in-state applicants; rank in top half of secondary school class, minimum 2.5 GPA, or minimum composite ACT score of 24 (combined SAT I score of 1110) required of out-of-state applicants. Special requirements: Additional requirements for business, dental hygiene, education, engineering, forestry, nursing, and speech pathology/audiology program applicants.

**Application deadline:** April 1
**Notification:** Rolling

**SAT or ACT preferred:** ACT
**SAT Avg:** 500V, 520M
**Average ACT:** 22
**Average GPA:** 3.22

**Graduated top 10% of class:** 20
**Graduated top 25% of class:** 40
**Graduated top 50% of class:** 80

# COLLEGE GRADUATION REQUIREMENTS

**Course waivers allowed:** Yes
**Course substitutions allowed:** Yes
**In what courses:** There is a math substitution program for individuals with a math learning disability. It only applies to lower level liberal arts math.

# ADDITIONAL INFORMATION

**Environment:** The university is located on 320 acres in an urban area.

**Student Body**
 **Undergrad enrollment:** 14,250
 **Women:** 54%
 **Men:** 46%
 **In-state students:** 80%
 **Out-of-state:** 20%

**Cost Information**
 **In-state tuition:** $2,060
 **Out-of-state:** $7,826
 **Room & board:** $3,400

**Housing Information**
 **University housing:** Yes
 **Fraternity:** Yes
 **Sorority:** Yes
 **Living on campus:** 52%

 **Athletics:** NCAA Div. I

# AR

# HARDING UNIVERSITY

900 East Center, Searcy, AR 72149 • **Admissions:** 501-279-4407 • **Fax:** 501-279-4865
**Email:** admissions@harding.edu • **Web:** www.harding.edu
**Support:** CS • **Institution:** 4 yr. Private

## LEARNING DISABILITY ADMISSIONS AND SERVICES

The philosophy and goals of Student Support Services are to foster an institutional climate supportive of the success of high-risk (first-generation, low-income, or disabled) students at Harding University. SSS strives to deliver a program of services that will result in increasing the college retention and graduation rates of these students. Each student in the program receives a high level of personal attention to and support for his/her needs throughout the school year. Students meet with an academic counselor concerning their specific needs. Students are given the opportunity to discuss their needs and goals with someone to help them better understand what they are. There are many workshops offered to provided students with hands-on learning. Additionally there is a Ropes Course, which consists of three levels of activities on a special outdoor obstacle course. These are: Readiness Level Activities consisting of games and problem-solving activities; Low Elements using various apparatus to pose problems for the group to overcome; and High Elements, where mountain climbing techniques and safety procedures are used to allow the individual to reach goals with the support of the group. The Ropes Course teaches a variety of skills ranging from communication to trust and faith to working as a team. "People can learn to overcome many fears by overcoming just one."

## LEARNING DISABILITY ADMISSIONS INFORMATION

**Program Name:** Student Support Services (SSS)
**Program Director:** Dr. Linda Thompson          **Telephone:** 501-279-4416
**Contact Person:** Jennifer Hurd                 **Telephone:** 501-279-4101

### ADMISSIONS

Admission criteria for students with learning disabilities are the same as for students in general, except that scores made on special administrations of college entrance exams ( ACT/SAT) are accepted. These scores, however, must meet the accepted admissions criteria. Students who score 18 or below on the ACT ( or equivalent SAT) are admitted into the Developmental Studies Program called Advance. Transfer students with low GPA are accepted on probation.  Course requirements include 4 yrs. English, 3 yrs. math, 3 yrs. social studies, and 2 yrs. science; 2 yrs. of foreign language are recommended. The minimum GPA is a 2.0.  The Director of SSS makes admission decisions for the Program and the Director of Admission determines admissibility into the university.

**College entrance exams required:** Yes          **Untimed accepted:** Yes
**Course entrance requirements:** Yes             **Interview required:** No
**Diagnostic tests:** Yes
**Documentation:** Any recognized test battery: No limitation on how recent

### ADDITIONAL INFORMATION

Testing accommodations are provided with documented evidence of a disability. These accommodations include: extended time on exams, readers, taking the test in parts with breaks; use of computer with spellcheck; and providing a distraction-free environment. Classroom accommodations may include: computer with spellcheck; extra time for proof-reading and editing of written assignments; notetaker; books on tape; and taping outside reading assignments.  Professors do not receive documentation or explanation unless the student signs a release form that would permit the release of such sensitive information. Each semester the student is asked to sign a permission form designating which professors should receive letters. Skills classes for college credit are offered in Beginning Algebra, Basic English, College Reading, and Study Skills. The CAPS-coaches and players mentoring program targets primarily students with ADD/ADHD.

**Special education HS coursework accepted:** No          **Essay required:** No
**Special application required:** No                       **Submitted to:** N/A
**# of applications submitted each year:** 48              **# of applications accepted each year:** 48
**# of students receiving LD services:** 36
**Acceptance into program means acceptance into college:** Students must be admitted to the university first and then may request services.

## LEARNING DISABILITY SERVICES

**Learning center:** Yes
**Kurzweil personal reader:** No
**LD specialists:** 1
**Allowed in exams:**
  **Calculator:** Yes
  **Dictionary:** Yes
  **Computer:** Yes
  **SpellCheck:** Yes

**Notetaker:** Yes
**Scribes:** Yes
**Proctors:** Yes
**Oral exams:** Yes
**Extended test time:** Yes
**Added cost:** No
**Distraction-free environ.:** Yes
**Tape recording in class:** Yes
**Books on tape:** Yes
**Taping of other books:** Yes

**Professional tutors:** Yes
**Peer tutors:** 15
**Max. hrs/wk for services:**
Unlimited
**Priority registration:** Yes
**Accomodations for students
with ADD:** Yes
**How are professors notified of
LD:** By the Director and student

## GENERAL ADMISSIONS INFORMATION

**Director of Admissions:** Mike Williams          **Telephone:** 501-279-4407

### ENTRANCE REQUIREMENTS
Total high school units required/recommended: 4 English required, 4 math required, 3 science required, 2 foreign language required, 3 social studies required. Minimum composite ACT score of 19, rank in top half of secondary school class, and minimum 2.5 GPA required. Special requirements: A portfolio is required for art program applicants; an audition is required for music program applicants.

**Application deadline:** June 1
**Notification:** Rolling

**SAT or ACT preferred:** Either
**SAT Range:** 420–550V, 450–610M
**Average ACT:** 24
**Average GPA:** 3.2

**Graduated top 10% of class:** 38
**Graduated top 25% of class:** 68
**Graduated top 50% of class:** 89

## COLLEGE GRADUATION REQUIREMENTS

**Course waivers allowed:** No
**Course substitutions allowed:** No
**In what courses:** N/A

## ADDITIONAL INFORMATION

**Environment:** The university is located on 200 acres in a small town 50 miles northeast of Little Rock.

**Student Body**
  **Undergrad enrollment:** 3,464
  **Women:** 53%
  **Men:** 47%
  **In-state students:** 25%
  **Out-of-state:** 75%

**Cost Information**
  **In-state tuition:** $5,775
  **Out-of-state:** $5,775
  **Room & board:** $3,802

**Housing Information**
  **University housing:** Yes
  **Fraternity:** No
  **Sorority:** No
  **Living on campus:** 75%

  **Athletics:** NAIA

# HENDERSON STATE UNIVERSITY

1100 Henderson Street, Arkadelphia, AR 71999 • **Admissions:** 870-230-5028 • **Fax:** 870-230-5066
**Email:** hardwrv@oaks.hsu.edu • **Web:** www.hsu.edu
**Support:** S • **Institution:** 4 yr. Public

## LEARNING DISABILITY ADMISSIONS AND SERVICES

The university does not offer a specialized curriculum, but shares the responsibility with students for modifying procedures to meet individual needs. The aim of the Student Support Services Program, to those students who qualify, is to provide needed support that the student can use to have a positive experience at the university. This Program, which is federally funded, monitors academic progress and provides individuals with information and assistance in educational, personal, and career concerns. The Office of Disability Services, which provides 504 accommodations, requires students to provide: documentation of the disability from a licensed professional; a professional recommendation for specific accommodations; and a detailed explanation of why the accommodations are needed. The university reserves the right to request additional information to clarify need for services and to verify the professional's credentials and expertise relevant to the recommendations. The university also reserves the right to retain an independent expert to evaluate the student's documentation. Note: If a course requirement is essential to a program and a student with a disability cannot fulfill that requirement, the student is not "qualified" for the program within the definition of the Americans with Disabilities Act.

## LEARNING DISABILITY ADMISSIONS INFORMATION

**Program Name:** Student Support Services (SSS)
**Program Director:** Kathy Muse
**Contact Person:** Vickie Faust, Coordinator

**Telephone:** 501-230-5251

### ADMISSIONS

Admissions decisions are made by the Office of Admission. Unconditional admission requires 19 ACT or equivalent SAT and 2.0 GPA. Conditional admission must have a GPA of 1.25 after 12 college semester hours and may be required to participate in a program through the Office of Retention. First-time freshmen applicants with a 15 ACT must apply by 7/15 and submit supplemental materials (including LD documentation) for review by admissions. Once an individual has been admitted to HSU, he/she may apply to the Student Support Services program to request special services and accommodations. Documentation verifying the learning disability is necessary to determine eligibility and need for services. A personal interview is required.

**College entrance exams required:** Yes
**Course entrance requirements:** Yes
**Diagnostic tests:** Yes
**Documentation:** Will accept a variety of tests: WAIS-R; HTP/DAP; WRAT-R; B-G

**Untimed accepted:** Yes
**Interview required:** Yes

### ADDITIONAL INFORMATION

Program modifications could include: extended time to complete degree requirements, substitutions of specific courses, and/or adaptations of specific courses. Policy information for course substitution is available through Disability Services. Services include: academic survival and study skills in time management, notetaking, test preparation, and goal setting and attainment; academic assistance in class scheduling, working cooperatively with faculty and staff, and academic accommodations; tutorial assistance through one-on-one assistance with peer tutors, notetakers, scribes, test proctors, lab partners; and career awareness, counseling and human development through career exploration, contact with outside agencies, activities for cultural development, personal and academic counseling, and advisement to assist students in coping with situations that may affect a successful academic program. The university offers development coursework in reading, English, and intermediate algebra for credit, but not towards graduation.

**Special education HS coursework accepted:** No
**Special application required:** Yes
**# of applications submitted each year:** N/I
**# of students receiving LD services:** 18

**Essay required:** No
**Submitted to:** SSS (contact person)
**# of applications accepted each year:** N/I

**Acceptance into program means acceptance into college:** Students must be admitted to the university first and then may request services (there is an appeal process).

# LEARNING DISABILITY SERVICES

Learning center: No
Kurzweil personal reader: Yes
LD specialists: No
Allowed in exams:
  Calculator: Yes
  Dictionary: Yes
  Computer: Yes
  SpellCheck: Yes

Notetaker: Yes
Scribes: Yes
Proctors: Yes
Oral exams: Yes
Extended test time: Yes
Added cost: None
Distraction-free environ.: Yes
Tape recording in class: Yes
Books on tape: Yes
Taping of other books: No

Professional tutors: No
Peer tutors: 15
Max. hrs/wk for services: As needed
Priority registration: Yes
Accomodations for students with ADD: Yes
How are professors notified of LD: By the student and Program Coordinator

# GENERAL ADMISSIONS INFORMATION

Director of Admissions: Tom Gattin

Telephone: 501-230-5135

## ENTRANCE REQUIREMENTS

Total high school units required/recommended: 20 total units are required; 4 English required, 4 English recommended, 2 math required, 4 math recommended, 2 science required, 3 science recommended, 2 social studies required, 1 history required, 2 history recommended. Minimum composite ACT score of 16 and minimum 2.5 GPA required. Special requirements: TOEFL is required of all international students.

Application deadline: Rolling
Notification: Rolling

SAT or ACT preferred: ACT
SAT Avg: 490V, 540M
Average ACT: 21
Average GPA: 3.1

Graduated top 10% of class: 12
Graduated top 25% of class: 50
Graduated top 50% of class: 70

# COLLEGE GRADUATION REQUIREMENTS

Course waivers allowed: Y/N
Course substitutions allowed: Y/N
In what courses: There is an appeal process available, although waivers or substitutions are rarely approved.

# ADDITIONAL INFORMATION

Environment: The university is located on 132 acres in a small town 60 miles southwest of Little Rock.

Student Body
  Undergrad enrollment: 3,252
  Women: 55%
  Men: 45%
  In-state students: 93%
  Out-of-state: 7%

Cost Information
  In-state tuition: $1,980
  Out-of-state: $3,960
  Room & board: $2,856

Housing Information
  University housing: Yes
  Fraternity: No
  Sorority: Yes
  Living on campus: 35%

  Athletics: NR

# UNIVERSITY OF THE OZARKS

**AR**

415 College Avenue, Clarksville, AR 72830 • **Admissions:** 501-979-1227 • **Fax:** 501-979-1355
**Web:** www.dobson.ozarks.edu
**Support:** SP • **Institution:** 4 yr. Private

## LEARNING DISABILITY ADMISSIONS AND SERVICES

The Jones Learning Center believes that students with specific learning disabilities are entitled to services that allow them to compete with other students. The Learning Center Program emphasizes a total learning environment. Instruction is individualized and personalized. Enhanced services include individualized programming; a technology unit; centralized accessibility; and a supportive atmosphere with low student to staff ratio, which provides students even greater opportunity to realize their true academic potential. Ideas, instructional materials, and activities are presented on a variety of different levels commensurate with the educational needs of the individual student. This program is very comprehensive in every area. At the beginning of each semester the course load and needs of the student are assessed to determine what services will be needed.

## LEARNING DISABILITY ADMISSIONS INFORMATION

**Program Name:** Jones Learning Center
**Program Director:** Julia Frost
**Contact Person:** Debby Mooney

**Telephone:** 501-979-1403
**Telephone:** 501-979-1422

### ADMISSIONS

Students complete a special application and a regular admissions application. Applicants must be 18 or older; complete high school or obtain a GED; demonstrate average or above average IQ; have a learning disability as a primary disability; provide diagnostic information from previous evaluations; complete the admissions packet; visit campus; and participate in a 2-day psychoeducational evaluation that includes interviews. Applicants with some areas of concern for the admissions committee may be admitted on a 1-year trial basis. This Conditional Admission is only available to students applying to the Jones Learning Center. There are no specific high school courses and no minimum ACT/SAT scores required for admission. Admission decisions are made by the Admissions Committee. Most students admitted have a learning disability as their primary disability. Motivation is a key factor in the admission decision. March 15 is the deadline for applications although some extensions may be allowed.

**College entrance exams required:** Yes
**Course entrance requirements:** No
**Diagnostic tests:** Yes
**Documentation:** MMPI; WAIS-R; W-J: within 1 year

**Untimed accepted:** Yes
**Interview required:** Yes

### ADDITIONAL INFORMATION

Students are assigned to a program coordinator who is responsible for the individualized planning of the students' program of study, acts as an advocate, and monitors the students' progress. Services are offered in Phases, with Phase I offering the maximum services. The Phases are adjusted as needed based upon academic performance, cooperation with the Learning Center, and anticipated needs for the following semester. Students receive help understanding learning styles, utilizing strengths, circumventing deficits, building skills, and becoming independent learners and self-advocates. Skills classes are offered in study skills, fundamentals of communication (for credit), reading and math, and English/writing. Students sign a contract of participation each semester. Students with ADD and LD may receive services from the Learning Center. Students with only ADD may request accommodations from the Section 504 Coordinator.

**Special education HS coursework accepted:** Yes
**Special application required:** Yes
**# of applications submitted each year:** N/I
**# of students receiving LD services:** 65
**Acceptance into program means acceptance into college:** Students admitted to the Learning Center are automatically accepted to the university.

**Essay required:** Yes
**Submitted to:** Program Director
**# of applications accepted each year:** 20-30

## LEARNING DISABILITY SERVICES

**Learning center:** Yes
**Kurzweil personal reader:** Yes
**LD specialists:** 16
**Allowed in exams:**
  **Calculator:** Y/N
  **Dictionary:** Yes
  **Computer:** Yes
  **SpellCheck:** Yes

**Notetaker:** Yes
**Scribes:** Yes
**Proctors:** Yes
**Oral exams:** Yes
**Extended test time:** Yes
**Added cost:** $9,500 per year depending on the phase of service.
**Distraction-free environ.:** Yes
**Tape recording in class:** Yes
**Books on tape:** Yes
**Taping of other books:** Yes

**Professional tutors:** 16
**Peer tutors:** 90
**Max. hrs/wk for services:** 44
**Priority registration:** No
**Accomodations for students with ADD:** Yes
**How are professors notified of LD:** By the student and Program Director

## GENERAL ADMISSIONS INFORMATION

**Director of Admissions:** Michael Heater

**Telephone:** 501-979-1227

### ENTRANCE REQUIREMENTS

Total high school units required/recommended: 15 total units are required; 4 English required, 2 math required, 2 science required, 2 foreign language required, 2 social studies required, 2 history required. Minimum composite ACT score of 18 (combined SAT I score of 800) and minimum 2.0 GPA required. Special requirements: TOEFL is required of all international students.

**Application deadline:** Rolling
**Notification:** Rolling

**SAT or ACT preferred:** ACT
**Average ACT:** 21
**Average GPA:** 3.3

**Graduated top 10% of class:** 21
**Graduated top 25% of class:** 44
**Graduated top 50% of class:** 87

## COLLEGE GRADUATION REQUIREMENTS

**Course waivers allowed:** No
**Course substitutions allowed:** Yes
**In what courses:** A policy is being written for substitutions for college algebra and foreign language.

## ADDITIONAL INFORMATION

**Environment:** The university is located on 56 acres, 100 miles northwest of Little Rock. Clarksville is a town of 5,000 residents in the Arkansas River Valley.

**Student Body**
  **Undergrad enrollment:** 573
  **Women:** 55%
  **Men:** 45%
  **In-state students:** 69%
  **Out-of-state:** 31%

**Cost Information**
  **In-state tuition:** $7,000
  **Out-of-state:** $7,000
  **Room & board:** $3,400

**Housing Information**
  **University housing:** Yes
  **Fraternity:** No
  **Sorority:** No
  **Living on campus:** 60%

  **Athletics:** NAIA

# BAKERSFIELD COLLEGE

Bakersfield, CA 93305 • **Admissions:** 805-395-4301

**Support:** CS • **Institution:** 2 yr. Public

## LEARNING DISABILITY ADMISSIONS AND SERVICES

The goals of the Bakersfield College Learning Disabilities Program are to foster academic success, encourage life-long learning, and ensure that students with disabilities have an equitable opportunity for success in an educational setting. The LD Program at BC provides services for students with learning disabilities and assist with transferring to 4-year colleges, gaining AA degrees, completing certificates in specialized fields, and developing as an individual. There are no special classes, and students attend regular classes and are expected to compete on that level. Services include counseling, tutoring, test accommodations, readers, study skills classes, and individualized instructional materials. Bakersfield offers a variety of services designed to maximize success for students in their college courses.

## LEARNING DISABILITY ADMISSIONS INFORMATION

**Program Name:** Supportive Services Program
**Program Director:** Dr. Don Johnson
**Contact Person:** Joyce Kirst (LD Director)

**Telephone:** 805-395-4334
**Telephone:** 805-395-4520

### ADMISSIONS

There is no special application for admission. The College has an 'open-door' policy. Students must meet the California Community College LD Eligibility Model, which includes an IQ of 80+, a processing deficit, and a discrepancy between aptitude and achievement. Students with recent testing from high school may submit this evaluation. The LD program will give students the Woodcock-Johnson assessment to determine the existence of a learning disability, if they enter College without a diagnosis of a learning disability. These students will be allowed to access services while waiting to be tested. All students take a College-designed test called 'Asset' that is similar to an ACT and helps the College obtain curricular information used in placement. This test is given timed and untimed.

**College entrance exams required:** No
**Course entrance requirements:** No
**Diagnostic tests:** Yes
**Documentation:** WAIS-R; W-J I & II: within 1 year (testing available on campus)

**Untimed accepted:** N/A
**Interview Required:** No

### ADDITIONAL INFORMATION

All courses have reading level requirements and some have prerequisites that must be met before entrance. It is recommended that students be able to read at least at a 6th grade level in order to be successful in the College courses. Often students reading below 6th grade level are unable to find courses that are appropriate. Skills courses are offered in Reading, math, writing, and study strategies. Students with Attention Deficit Disorder will receive Section 504 accommodations from Disabled Student Services.

**Special education HS coursework accepted:** Yes
**Special application required:** No
**# of applications submitted each year:** 100
**# of students receiving LD services:** 300+

**Essay required:** No
**Submitted to:** N/A
**# of applications accepted each year:** All who apply

**Acceptance into program means acceptance into college:** Student must be admitted to the College first and then may request services.

## LEARNING DISABILITY SERVICES

**Learning center:** Yes
**Kurzweil personal reader:** Yes
**LD specialists:** 3
**Allowed in exams:**
  **Calculator:** Yes
  **Dictionary:** Yes
  **Computer:** Yes
  **SpellCheck:** Yes

**Notetaker:** Yes
**Scribes:** Yes
**Proctors:** Yes
**Oral exams:** Yes
**Extended test time:** Yes
**Added cost:** None
**Distraction-free environ.:** Yes
**Tape recording in class:** Yes
**Books on tape:** Yes
**Taping of other books:** yes

**Professional tutors:** 5
**Peer tutors:** 50
**Max. hrs/wk for services:** 2
hours tutoring for each class
**Priority registration:** Yes
**Accomodations for students
with ADD:** Yes
**How are professors notified of
LD:** By the student

## GENERAL ADMISSIONS INFORMATION

**Director of Admissions:** N/I

**Telephone:** 805-395-4301

**ENTRANCE REQUIREMENTS**
Open admissions.

**Application deadline:** Rolling
**Notification:** NR

**SAT or ACT preferred:** NR

## COLLEGE GRADUATION REQUIREMENTS

**Course waivers allowed:** No
**Course substitutions allowed:** Yes
**In what courses:** The decision to grant a substitution is made on an individual basis and course substitutions vary.

## ADDITIONAL INFORMATION

**Environment:** The College is located on a 175-acre campus 100 miles north of Los Angeles.

**Student Body**
  **Undergrad enrollment:** 12,267
  **Women:** 56%
  **Men:** 44%
  **In-state students:** 99%
  **Out-of-state:** 1%

**Cost Information**
  **In-state tuition:** $140
  **Out-of-state:** $3,500

**Housing Information**
  **University housing:** Yes
  **Fraternity:** No
  **Sorority:** No
  **Living on campus:** 1%

  **Athletics:** Intercollegiate sports

# CALIFORNIA POLYTECHNIC STATE UNIVERSITY-SAN LUIS OBISPO

San Luis Obispo, CA 93407 • **Admissions:** 805-756-2311 • **Fax:** 805-756-5400
**Email:** dp141@calpoly.edu • **Web:** www.calpoly.edu
**Support:** CS • **Institution:** 4 yr. Public

## LEARNING DISABILITY ADMISSIONS AND SERVICES

The goal of the Program is to help students with learning disabilities use their learning strengths. Disabled Student Services (DSS) assists students with disabilities in achieving access to higher education, promotes personal and educational success, and increases the awareness and responsiveness of the campus community. DSS is actively involved with students and faculty and provides a newsletter and open house to keep the college population aware of who it is and what it does. Incoming students are encouraged to meet with DSS staff to receive assistance in the planning of class schedules. This allows for the selection of appropriate classes to fit particular needs and personal goals.

## LEARNING DISABILITY ADMISSIONS INFORMATION

**Program Name:** Disabled Student Services (DSS)
**Program Director:** William Bailey                    **Telephone:** 805-756-1395
**Contact Person:** Ann Fryer

### ADMISSIONS

Students with LD must meet the same admission criteria as all applicants, and should submit a general admission application to the Admissions Office. General requirements include: 4 yrs. English, 3 yrs. math, 1 yr. U.S. history or government, 1 yr. lab science, 2 yrs. foreign language, 1 yr. fine arts, and 3 yrs. electives. On a case-by-case basis, foreign language substitutions may be allowed. The general application does have an optional question (#21) that the student can mark that states, "If you have a ... learning disability, enter a Y in the box. Special services may be available to accommodate your disability." Students who self-disclose will receive information. Students may be considered for special admission on an individual basis. The special admission process requires: an autobiographical statement regarding how the specific disability has adversely impacted the student's academic progress; a reference statement verifying the student's motivation and potential to succeed; official high school and/or college transcript; and documentation of disability. Decisions are made by the admissions office.

**College entrance exams required:** Yes          **Untimed accepted:** Yes
**Course entrance requirements:** Yes          **Interview required:** No
**Diagnostic tests:** Yes
**Documentation:** WAIS-R; WISC-R; W-J; Achievement tests: within 3-5 years

### ADDITIONAL INFORMATION

Incoming students are strongly urged to schedule an appointment with DSS to receive assistance in the planning of classes. DSS may recommend the services of the Academic Skills Center of Student Academic Services, and enrollment in English and math classes offering additional support. There is also a Peer Mentoring program, a Partners for Success program, and a career mentoring program available to all students. Students requesting accommodations, which include using a calculator, computer, dictionary, or spellcheck during an exam, will need the professor's permission. Services and accommodations are available to undergraduate and graduate students.

**Special education HS coursework accepted:** Depends on the articulation agreement
**Essay required:** No
**Special application required:** No                    **Submitted to:** N/A
**# of applications submitted each year:** 150          **# of applications accepted each year:** N/I
**# of students receiving LD services:** 382
**Acceptance into program means acceptance into college:** Students must be admitted to the university first and then may request services.

## LEARNING DISABILITY SERVICES

**Learning center:** No
**Kurzweil personal reader:** Yes
**LD specialists:** 2
**Allowed in exams:**
  **Calculator:** Yes
  **Dictionary:** Yes
  **Computer:** Yes
  **SpellCheck:** Yes

**Notetaker:** Yes
**Scribes:** Yes
**Proctors:** Yes
**Oral exams:** Yes
**Extended test time:** Yes
**Added cost:** None
**Distraction-free environ.:** Yes
**Tape recording in class:** Yes
**Books on tape:** Yes
**Taping of other books:** RFB

**Professional tutors:** 3
**Peer tutors:** 28
**Max. hrs/wk for services:**
Depends on the service
**Priority registration:** Yes
**Accomodations for students with ADD:** Yes
**How are professors notified of LD:** By the student

## GENERAL ADMISSIONS INFORMATION

**Director of Admissions:** James Maraviglia          **Telephone:** 805-756-2913

### ENTRANCE REQUIREMENTS

Total high school units required/recommended: 15 total units are required; 4 English required, 3 math required, 1 science required, 2 foreign language required, 1 history required. Electives should include 1 unit of visual/performing arts. Special requirements: A portfolio is required for art program applicants; an audition is required for music program applicants.

**Application deadline:** Nov. 30
**Notification:** Rolling

**SAT or ACT preferred:** Either
**SAT Avg:** 532V, 569M
**Average ACT:** 23
**Average GPA:** 3.5

**Graduated top 10% of class:** 40
**Graduated top 25% of class:** 68
**Graduated top 50% of class:** 91

## COLLEGE GRADUATION REQUIREMENTS

**Course waivers allowed:** No
**Course substitutions allowed:** Yes
**In what courses:** On a case-by-case basis, individuals may be granted course substitutions in quantitative reasoning (in very limited non-math related majors) and foreign language with department approval.

## ADDITIONAL INFORMATION

**Environment:** The campus is located 100 miles north of Santa Barbara.

**Student Body**
  **Undergrad enrollment:** 15,947
  **Women:** 43%
  **Men:** 57%
  **In-state students:** 96%
  **Out-of-state:** 4%

**Cost Information**
  **In-state tuition:** $2,075
  **Out-of-state:** $5,904
  **Room & board:** $5,553

**Housing Information**
  **University housing:** Yes
  **Fraternity:** Yes
  **Sorority:** Yes
  **Living on campus:** 16%

  **Athletics:** NCAA Div. II

# CALIFORNIA STATE POLYTECHNIC UNIVERSITY-POMONA

3801 West Temple Avenue, Pomona, CA 91768 • **Admissions:** 909-869-2000 • **Fax:** 909-869-4529
**Email:** cppadmit@csupomona.edu • **Web:** www.csupomona.edu
**Support:** S • **Institution:** 4 yr. Public

## LEARNING DISABILITY ADMISSIONS AND SERVICES

The mission of the Office of Disabled Student Services is to help students with disabilities compete on an equal basis with their non-disabled peers by providing reasonable accommodations that will allow them access to any academic program or to facilitate participation in any university activity that is offered to fellow students. The major purposes of DSS are: To determine reasonable accommodations based on disability as assessed by knowledgeable professionals; to emphasize self-advocacy; to maximize learning experience and to continuously assess students' needs; to actively recruit and increase retention and graduation rates of students with disabilities and provide greater educational equity; to facilitate the university in meeting requirements of the Americans with Disabilities Act; and to prepare students with disabilities for life, leadership, and careers in a changing world.

## LEARNING DISABILITY ADMISSIONS INFORMATION

**Program Name:** Disabled Student Services (DSS)
**Program Director:** John Hanna
**Contact Person:** Jane Mathis-Lowe

**Telephone:** 909-869-4611
**Telephone:** 909-869-3270

### ADMISSIONS

Students must meet the university's regular entrance requirements, including: "C" or better in the subject requirements of 4 yrs. English, 3 yrs. math, 1 yr. U.S. history, 1 yr. lab science, 2 yrs. foreign language, 1 yr. visual or performing arts, and 3 yrs. electives; and a qualifiable eligibility index based on high school GPA and scores on either ACT or SAT. Applicants with LD are encouraged to complete college prep courses. However, if students are unable to fulfill a specific course requirement because of a learning disability, alternative college prep courses may be substituted. Substitutions may be granted in foreign language, lab science, and math. Substitutions may be authorized on an individual basis after review and recommendation by applicant's guidance counselor in consultation with the director of DSS. Course substitutions could limit access to some majors. Students who self-disclose are reviewed by DSS, which provides a recommendation to admissions.

**College entrance exams required:** Yes
**Course entrance requirements:** Yes
**Diagnostic tests:** Yes
**Documentation:** Psychoeducational evaluations; within 3 years

**Untimed accepted:** Yes
**Interview required:** No

### ADDITIONAL INFORMATION

Support services include counseling, advocacy services, registration, notetakers, readers, tutors, testing accommodations, and specialized equipment. Skills classes are not offered through DSS, but are available in other departments in the areas of reading skills, test preparation, test-taking strategies, and study skills. Services and accommodations are available to undergraduate and graduate students. Cal Poly offers a summer program for any high school student.

**Special education HS coursework accepted:** N/I
**Special application required:** No
**# of applications submitted each year:** 60+
**# of students receiving LD services:** 200+

**Essay required:** No
**Submitted to:** N/A
**# of applications accepted each year:** 55+

**Acceptance into program means acceptance into college:** No, must be accepted to the university first and then may request services.

# LEARNING DISABILITY SERVICES

**Learning center:** Yes
**Kurzweil personal reader:** Yes
**LD specialists:** Yes
**Allowed in exams:**
  **Calculator:** Yes
  **Dictionary:** Yes
  **Computer:** Yes
  **SpellCheck:** Yes

**Notetaker:** Yes
**Scribes:** Yes
**Proctors:** Yes
**Oral exams:** Yes
**Extended test time:** Yes
**Added cost:** None
**Distraction-free environ.:** Yes
**Tape recording in class:** Yes
**Books on tape:** Yes
**Taping of other books:** Yes

**Professional tutors:** No
**Peer tutors:** 50+
**Max. hrs/wk for services:** Limited
**Priority registration:** Yes
**Accomodations for students with ADD:** Yes
**How are professors notified of LD:** By the student and the Program Director

# GENERAL ADMISSIONS INFORMATION

**Director of Admissions:** Dena Bennett, Supervisor        **Telephone:** 909-869-2991

## ENTRANCE REQUIREMENTS

Total high school units required/recommended: 15 total units are required; 4 English required, 3 math required, 1 science required, 2 foreign language required, 1 history required. Electives should include 1 unit of visual/performing arts. Minimum grade of C, index of 2800 for SAT I (694 for ACT) required of in-state applicants; minimum eligibility index of 3402 for SAT I (842 for ACT) required of out-of-state applicants. In-state applicants with minimum 3.0 GPA and out-of-state applicants with minimum 3.6 GPA are eligible regardless of test scores. Special requirements: Higher GPA required of architecture program applicants; out-of-state applicants not admitted to this program.

**Application deadline:** Rolling
**Notification:** Rolling

**SAT or ACT preferred:** Either
**SAT Avg:** 463V, 511M
**SAT II required:** Yes
**Average ACT:** 19

# COLLEGE GRADUATION REQUIREMENTS

**Course waivers allowed:** No
**Course substitutions allowed:** Yes
**In what courses:** It depends on the nature of the disability. Foreign language and math are the most common.

# ADDITIONAL INFORMATION

**Environment:** The university is located on 1,437 acres in a suburban area 30 miles east of Los Angeles.

**Student Body**
  **Undergrad enrollment:** 14,874
  **Women:** 42%
  **Men:** 58%
  **In-state students:** 97%
  **Out-of-state:** 3%

**Cost Information**
  **In-state tuition:** $1,893
  **Out-of-state:** $7,797
  **Room & board:** $5,850

**Housing Information**
  **University housing:** Yes
  **Fraternity:** No
  **Sorority:** No
  **Living on campus:** 7%

  **Athletics:** NCAA Div. II

# CALIFORNIA STATE UNIVERSITY-NORTHRIDGE

18111 Nordhoff Street, Northridge, CA 91330 • **Admissions:** 818-677-3700 • **Fax:** 818-177-3766
**Email:** admissions@csun.edu
**Support:** CS • **Institution:** 4 yr. Public

## LEARNING DISABILITY ADMISSIONS AND SERVICES

The Office of Disabled Student Services recognizes that students with learning disabilities can be quite successful in a university setting if appropriate educational support services are offered to them. In an effort to assist students with learning disabilities in reaching their full potential, the Program offers a comprehensive and well coordinated system of educational support services that allow students to be judged on the basis of their ability rather than disability. The professional staff includes LD Specialists trained in the diagnosis of learning disabilities and the provision of educational support services. Additionally, the Program employs graduate students (Educational Support Specialists) who work under the direction of the professional staff and assist students with study skills, time management procedures, test-taking techniques, and other individualized programs.

## LEARNING DISABILITY ADMISSIONS INFORMATION

**Program Name:** Office of Disabled Student Services
**Program Director:** Steve Loving, Coordinator          **Telephone:** 818-885-2684
**Contact Person:** Lee Axelrod/ Jennifer Zvi

### ADMISSIONS

There is no special admission process. However, the Special Admission Committee of Disabled Student Services makes recommendations to the Admissions Office. Students must get a "C" or better in: 4 yrs. English, 3 yrs. math, 1 yr. U.S. history.,1 yr. science, 2 yrs. foreign language, 1 yr. visual/performing arts, and 3 yrs. electives. Students with LD may request course substitutions. An eligibility index combining GPA and ACT or SAT is used, and grades used are from 10th-12th grade (bonus points for honor courses). Index is calculated by multiplying GPA by 800 and adding SAT, or multiply GPA by 200 and add 10 times the ACT. California residents need an index of 2800 using SAT or 694 using ACT. Non-residents must have a minimum index of 3402 (SAT) or 842 (ACT). No test scores needed if GPA is a 3.0+ for residents or 3.61 for non-residents.

| | |
|---|---|
| **College entrance exams required:** Yes | **Untimed accepted:** Yes |
| **Course entrance requirements:** Yes | **Interview required:** Suggested but not required |
| **Diagnostic tests:** Yes | |
| **Documentation:** Standard diagnostic tests; within 3 years | |

### ADDITIONAL INFORMATION

Testing accommodations may be arranged through the Program without the 'integrity' of the test being sacrificed. The Computer Access Lab provides computers along with professional assistance. The Program and the CSUN Career Center work cooperatively to assist students with LD in planning and attaining their career goals. Diagnostic testing is available for students who suspect they may have a learning disability. Counselors are available to assist students in meeting their social/emotional needs as well as their academic requirements. Assistance in developing appropriate learning strategies is provided on an individual basis. Additionally, a support group for students with learning disabilities meets regularly. There are also workshops, a reader service, and notetakers. Services and accommodations are available for undergraduate and graduate students.

| | |
|---|---|
| **Special education HS coursework accepted:** Yes | **Essay required:** No |
| **Special application required:** No | **Submitted to:** N/A |
| **# of applications submitted each year:** N/I | **# of applications accepted each year:** N/I |
| **# of students receiving LD services:** 351 | |

**Acceptance into program means acceptance into college:** Students must be accepted to the university first and then may request services.

## LEARNING DISABILITY SERVICES

**Learning center:** Yes
**Kurzweil personal reader:** Yes
**LD specialists:** 2
**Allowed in exams:**
  **Calculator:** Y/N
  **Dictionary:** Y/N
  **Computer:** Y/N
  **SpellCheck:** Y/N

**Notetaker:** Yes
**Scribes:** Yes
**Proctors:** Yes
**Oral exams:** Yes
**Extended test time:** Yes
**Added cost:** None
**Distraction-free environ.:** Yes
**Tape recording in class:** Yes
**Books on tape:** Yes
**Taping of other books:** Yes

**Professional tutors:** No
**Peer tutors:** Yes
**Max. hrs/wk for services:** 1 hr./ each credit unit per week
**Priority registration:** Yes
**Accomodations for students with ADD:** Yes
**How are professors notified of LD:** By the student

## GENERAL ADMISSIONS INFORMATION

**Director of Admissions:** Lorraine Newlon          **Telephone:** 818-885-3773

### ENTRANCE REQUIREMENTS

Total high school units required/recommended: 15 total units are required; 4 English required, 3 math required, 1 science required, 2 foreign language required, 1 history required. Electives should include 1 unit of visual/performing arts. Minimum grade of "C," index of 2800 for SAT I (694 for ACT) required of in-state applicants; minimum eligibility index of 3402 for SAT I (842 for ACT) required of out-of-state applicants. In-state applicants with minimum 3.0 GPA and out-of-state applicants with minimum 3.6 GPA are eligible regardless of test scores. Special requirements: Additional requirements for business, computer science, engineering, and physical therapy program applicants.

**Application deadline:** Nov. 30          **SAT or ACT preferred:** Either          **Graduated top 25% of class:** 33
**Notification:** Rolling          **Graduated top 50% of class:** 33

## COLLEGE GRADUATION REQUIREMENTS

**Course waivers allowed:** Yes
**Course substitutions allowed:** Yes
**In what courses:** Math

## ADDITIONAL INFORMATION

**Environment:** A large suburban campus in the San Fernando Valley northwest of Los Angeles

**Student Body**
  **Undergrad enrollment:** 21,720
  **Women:** 55%
  **Men:** 45%
  **In-state students:** 95%
  **Out-of-state:** 5%

**Cost Information**
  **In-state tuition:** $1,970
  **Out-of-state:** $7,820
  **Room & board:** $5,071

**Housing Information**
  **University housing:** Yes
  **Fraternity:** Yes
  **Sorority:** Yes
  **Living on campus:** 8%

  **Athletics:** NCAA Div. II

# CALIFORNIA STATE UNIVERSITY-SAN BERNARDINO

5500 University Parkway, San Bernardino, CA 92407 • **Admissions:** 909-880-5200
**Support:** CS • **Institution:** 4 yr. Public

## LEARNING DISABILITY ADMISSIONS AND SERVICES

The Learning Disability Program is dedicated to assuring each student an opportunity to experience equity in education. Each student must complete an assessment and then the staff helps to develop compensatory methods for handling assignments and classroom projects. Careful attention is paid to helping the student acquire learning skills and formulating and implementing specific strategies for notetaking and management of written materials. An Individual Educational Plan is designed for each student as a result of the psychometric assessment, personal interview, and academic requirements. The emphasis of the Plan is to assist the students with a learning disability in finding techniques to deal with the disabilities in college and in the job market.

## LEARNING DISABILITY ADMISSIONS INFORMATION

**Program Name:** Learning Disability Program
**Program Director:** Barbara Sovereign
**Contact Person:** Same as above

**Telephone:** 909-880-5239

### ADMISSIONS

Applicants with learning disabilities must follow the same application procedure as all students. Special admission may be requested through the Learning Disability Program if the student has a deficiency in course entrance requirements. The Director of the LD Program provides recommendations on the admissibility of those students who do not meet regular admissions requirements. Occasionally the special admit will consider students who are below the required GPA or test scores. These requirements can be substituted and the student can make up the deficiency on campus once enrolled.

**College entrance exams required:** Yes
**Course entrance requirements:** Yes
**Diagnostic tests:** Yes
**Documentation:** WAIS-R; WRAT-R: within 3 years

**Untimed accepted:** Yes
**Interview required:** No

### ADDITIONAL INFORMATION

Specific services include: assessment counseling, tutoring arrangements, proofreading, and paper writing assistance. There is a peer support group for students with learning disabilities. Students on academic probation have two quarters to raise their GPA to a 2.0. The LD Program provides continual academic support.The Director of the LD Program provides social skills training and career and job counseling, including interviewing techniques. In addition, the Office for Disability Services helps students with pre-employment job preparation.

**Special education HS coursework accepted:** Y/N
**Special application required:** No
**# of applications submitted each year:** N/I
**# of students receiving LD services:** 139
**Acceptance into program means acceptance into college:** No, must be admitted to the university first and then may request services.

**Essay required:** No
**Submitted to:** N/A
**# of applications accepted each year:** N/I

# LEARNING DISABILITY SERVICES

**Learning center:** Yes
**Kurzweil personal reader:** Yes
**LD specialists:** 2
**Allowed in exams:**
  **Calculator:** Yes
  **Dictionary:** Yes
  **Computer:** Yes
  **SpellCheck:** Yes

**Notetaker:** Yes
**Scribes:** Yes
**Proctors:** Yes
**Oral exams:** Yes
**Extended test time:** Yes
**Added cost:** None
**Distraction-free environ.:** Yes
**Tape recording in class:** Yes
**Books on tape:** Yes
**Taping of other books:** Yes

**Professional tutors:** Yes
**Peer tutors:** No
**Max. hrs/wk for services:** As needed, as available
**Priority registration:** Yes
**Accomodations for students with ADD:** Yes
**How are professors notified of LD:** By the student

# GENERAL ADMISSIONS INFORMATION

**Director of Admissions:** Cheryl Smith          **Telephone:** 909-880-5190

## ENTRANCE REQUIREMENTS

Total high school units required/recommended: 13 total units are required; 3 English required, 2 math required, 1 science required, 2 foreign language required, 1 social studies required, 1 history required. Minimum grade of C, eligibility index of 3072 for SAT I (741 for ACT) required of in-state applicants; minimum eligibility index of 3402 for SAT I (822 for ACT) required of out-of-state applicants. In-state applicants with minimum 3.1 GPA and out-of-state applicants with minimum 3.6 GPA are eligible regardless of test scores. Special requirements: TOEFL is required of all international students.

**Application deadline:** Sept. 15          **SAT or ACT preferred:** Either
**Notification:** Rolling

# COLLEGE GRADUATION REQUIREMENTS

**Course waivers allowed:** No
**Course substitutions allowed:** Yes
**In what courses:** Math, if the criteria of 'Developmental Arithmetic Disorder' is met.

# ADDITIONAL INFORMATION

**Environment:** The university is located on 375 acres in a rural area 5 miles west of Bakersfield.

**Student Body**
  **Undergrad enrollment:** 11,007
  **Women:** 59%
  **Men:** 41%
  **In-state students:** 97%
  **Out-of-state:** 3%

**Cost Information**
  **In-state t:uition** $1,869
  **Out-of-state:** $7,773
  **Room & board:** $4,380

**Housing Information**
  **University housing:** Yes
  **Fraternity:** Yes
  **Sorority:** Yes
  **Living on campus:** 4%

  **Athletics:** NCAA Div. III

# UNIVERSITY OF CALIFORNIA-BERKELEY

Office of Undergraduate Admission and Relations with Schools, 110 Sproul Hall #5800, Berkeley, CA 94720-5800 • **Admissions:** 510-642-3175 • **Email:** ouars@uclink.berkeley.edu
**Web:** www.berkeley.edu
**Support:** CS • **Institution:** 4 yr. Public

## LEARNING DISABILITY ADMISSIONS AND SERVICES

DSP seeks to ensure that students with disabilities have equal access to educational opportunities and student life at UC Berkeley. DSP works to sustain a supportive environment that provides appropriate and necessary disability-related accommodations, enables students to demonstrate their knowledge and skills, facilitates students' success in academic pursuits, and promotes independence. DSP's services assist students as they develop their skills and the qualities needed to meet their educational, personal, and professional goals. DSP also works to support the efforts of the campus community to ensure full participation of students with disabilities in every aspect of university life. DSP is a recipient of a TRIO Student Support Services Grant. Funds are used to provide a variety of services for students, helping them to complete graduation requirements and plan successful post-graduation educations or careers. For services, DSP must have verification of the disability on file. Students with LD must submit a psychoeducational evaluation done by a qualified professional. Students with ADD must submit a letter from a qualified professional who has an expertise in diagnosing ADD in adults. Additional testing may be requested if it is deemed necessary for the planning and provision of appropriate accommodations and services.

## LEARNING DISABILITY ADMISSIONS INFORMATION

**Program Name:** Disabled Student's Program (DSP)
**Program Director:** N/A **Telephone:** 510-642-0518
**Contact Person:** Connie Chiba **Telephone:** 510-642-0518

### ADMISSIONS

An LD specialist and Admission specialist are available to meet with students with LD interested in applying to UC Berkeley. These specialists will review the applicant's high school or college transcript and give advice on how to proceed with the application. DSP works closely with the Office of Admissions and Records. There are two tiers for admission: Tier I is an automatic admission; Tier II applicants may need other criteria to be admitted. The impact of a disability could be a factor in an admission for a Tier II applicant. When an applicant indicates on the application that there is a disability, DSP contacts the applicant to request information, documentation of the disability, and a statement from the applicant about the impact of the disability on his/her life and academic achievement. DSP uses this information to answer questions about the applicant from Admissions. UC Berkeley seeks to identify students with disabilities who have a high potential for success if provided with appropriate accommodation and support services.

**College entrance exams required:** Yes **Untimed accepted:** Yes
**Course entrance requirements:** Yes **Interview required:** No
**Diagnostic tests:** Yes
**Documentation:** WAIS-R; W-J: WRAT: within 3 years

### ADDITIONAL INFORMATION

DSP staff provide the following services: recommending and ensuring the provision of academic accommodations; consulting with instructors about accommodations; authorizing auxiliary services; teaching academic strategies and study skills; promoting on-campus awareness; academic advising; adaptive technology; support groups; a special section of the course "Facilitating Success" for students with LD and ADD that centers on understanding learning differences, maximizing strengths, academic planning, research, writing, exam preparation, and using university resources; priority registration; specialist to help in developing problem-solving strategies and solutions to difficult problems; and a series of informational workshops on topics like understanding disabilities and individual learning styles, improving reading, writing, and research efficiency, memory strategies, self-advocacy, computer applications that facilitate learning, and career or graduate school planning. Specialists may recommend a reduced course load.

**Special education HS coursework accepted:** No **Essay required:** Yes
**Special application required:** No **Submitted to:** N/A
**# of applications submitted each year:** N/A **# of applications accepted each year:** N/A
**# of students receiving LD services:** 500
**Acceptance into program means acceptance into college:** Must be admitted to the university first and then may request services.

**Learning center:** Yes
**Kurzweil personal reader:** Yes
**LD specialists:** 4
**Allowed in exams:**
  **Calculator:** Y/N
  **Dictionary:** Y/N
  **Computer:** Yes
  **SpellCheck:** Yes

**Notetaker:** Yes
**Scribes:** Yes
**Proctors:** Yes
**Oral exams:** Yes
**Extended test time:** Yes
**Added cost:** $8-$15 per hour
**Distraction-free environ.:** Yes
**Tape recording in class:** Yes
**Books on tape:** Yes
**Taping of other books:** Yes

**Professional tutors:** 4
**Peer tutors:** Yes
**Max. hrs/wk for services:** Tutors used are 'vendors' and not DSP staff
**Priority registration:** Yes
**Accomodations for students with ADD:** Yes
**How are professors notified of LD:** By the student and Program Director

# GENERAL ADMISSIONS INFORMATION

**Director of Admissions:** Bob Laird          **Telephone:** 510-642-0200

## ENTRANCE REQUIREMENTS

Total high school units required/recommended: 15 total units are required; 4 English required, 3 math required, 4 math recommended, 2 science required, 3 science recommended, 2 foreign language required. Minimum 3.4 GPA required of out-of-state applicants. In-state applicants with minimum 3.3 GPA are eligible regardless of test scores. Applicants with minimum combined SAT I score of 1400 (composite ACT score of 31) and minimum combined SAT II scores of 1730 (in-state) or 1850 (out-of-state), with no score below 530 on any one test, are eligible on the basis of test scores alone. Special requirements: An audition is required for music program applicants. TOEFL is required of all international students.

**Application deadline:** Nov. 30
**Notification:** March 31

**SAT or ACT preferred:** Either
**SAT Avg:** 664V, 632M
**Average GPA:** 3.84

**Graduated top 10% of class:** 95
**Graduated top 25% of class:** 100
**Graduated top 50% of class:** 100

# COLLEGE GRADUATION REQUIREMENTS

**Course waivers allowed:** Yes
**Course substitutions allowed:** Yes
**In what courses:** Foreign language requirement can be substituted with cultural courses on a case-by-case basis. Math waivers are considered on a case-by-case basis.

# ADDITIONAL INFORMATION

**Environment:** The 1,232-acre campus is in an urban area, 10 miles east of San Francisco.

**Student Body**
  **Undergrad enrollment:** 21,358
  **Women:** 49%
  **Men:** 51%
  **In-state students:** 90%
  **Out-of-state:** 10%

**Cost Information**
  **In-state tuition:** $4,354
  **Out-of-state:** $12,748
  **Room & board:** $7,226

**Housing Information**
  **University housing:** Yes
  **Fraternity:** Yes
  **Sorority:** Yes
  **Living on campus:** 25%

  **Athletics:** NCAA Div. I

# UNIVERSITY OF CALIFORNIA-LOS ANGELES

405 Hilgard Avenue, Los Angeles, CA  90024 • **Admissions:** 310-825-3101 • **Fax:** 310-206-1206
**Email:** ugadm@saonnet.ucla.edu • **Web:** www.ucla.edu
**Support:** CS • **Institution:** 4 yr. Public

## LEARNING DISABILITY ADMISSIONS AND SERVICES

UCLA complies with State, Federal and university guidelines that mandate full access for students with disabilities, including learning disabilities. UCLA complies with the requirement to provide reasonable accommodations for documented students to allow them to participate in their academic program to the greatest extent possible. Students with other documented types of learning disabilities, including Attention Deficit (Hyperactive) Disorder, and Traumatic Brain Injury are also served by the Learning Disabilities Program. The UCLA Learning Disabilities Program is coordinated by a full-time learning disabilities specialist, and offers a full range of accommodations and services. Services are individually designed, and include counseling, special test arrangements, notetaker services, readers, priority enrollment, adaptive technology, and individual tutoring. An active support group provides opportunities for students to discuss mutual concerns and enhance learning strategies. Workshops and speakers address skill development and topics of interest. In the Peer-Mentor Program continuing students with learning disabilities serve as resources to entering students.

## LEARNING DISABILITY ADMISSIONS INFORMATION

**Program Name:** UCLA Learning Disabilities Program
**Program Director:** Arline Halper, Ed.D.          **Telephone:** 310-825-1501
**Contact Person:** Same as above

### ADMISSIONS

There are no special admissions criteria for students with learning disabilities. All applicants are required to submit scores from the SAT I  or ACT and SAT II ( including the Writing Test, Mathematics-Level 1 or 2,  and either English Literature, Foreign Language, Science, or Social Studies). To be competitive students usually score in the high 20's on the ACT or high 1100's on the SAT I and between 500-600 on each of the SAT II Subject Tests. High school courses required are: 4 yrs. English, 2 yrs. history/social science, 3 yrs. math, 2 yrs. foreign language (3 yrs. recommended), 2 yrs. lab science ( 3 yrs. recommended), and 2 yrs. electives. Additional criteria are based on an eligibility index using test scores and class rank. Selected students are admitted for winter and offered the opportunity to take fall extension classes (based on space availability). The LD specialists provide disability-related information to admissions staff. Applicants are encouraged to send copies of LD documentation, and a personal statement to the Coordinator of LD Program.

**College entrance exams required:** Yes          **Untimed accepted:** Yes
**Course entrance requirements:** Yes          **Interview required:** No
**Diagnostic tests:** Yes
**Documentation:** At least the W-J; WAIS-R;  within 3 years

### ADDITIONAL INFORMATION

LD Program includes: tutors for individual classes; Peer Mentors; support group meetings; learning skills workshops; advocacy; referrals to campus resources; priority enrollment; orientation program; LD screening; and disability management counseling by LD specialist including disability awareness, learning and time management strategies, self-advocacy skills, and interpretation of evaluation reports. Compensations could include alternatives in (1) printed materials: taped textbooks, computerized voice synthesizer, RFB; (2) test-taking procedures: extended time, proctor to assist with reading and writing, distraction-free test area, computer for essay exams, alternative test formats including essay-type rather than multiple choice-type or taped exams rather than written exams, use of calculator or spellchecker; (3) notetaking: notetakers, taped lecture; (4) writing essays and papers: word processors with voice synthesizers, composition tutors; (5) reduced courseload; and (6) extended time to complete a program

**Special education HS coursework accepted:** No          **Essay required:** Yes
**Special application required:** No          **Submitted to:** N/A
**# of applications submitted each year:** 350          **# of applications accepted each year:** N/I
**# of students receiving LD services:** 201
**Acceptance into program means acceptance into college:** Students must be admitted to the university first and then may request services.

# LEARNING DISABILITY SERVICES

**Learning center:** No
**Kurzweil personal reader:** Yes
**LD specialists:** 2
**Allowed in exams:**
 **Calculator:** Yes
 **Dictionary:** Yes
 **Computer:** Yes
 **SpellCheck:** Yes

**Notetaker:** Yes
**Scribes:** Yes
**Proctors:** Yes
**Oral exams:** Yes
**Extended test time:** Yes
**Added cost:** None
**Distraction-free environ.:** Yes
**Tape recording in class:** Yes
**Books on tape:** Yes
**Taping of other books:** Yes

**Professional tutors:** No
**Peer tutors:** Yes
**Max. hrs/wk for services:**
Unlimited
**Priority registration:** Yes
**Accomodations for students
with ADD:** Yes
**How are professors notified of
LD:** By the student

# GENERAL ADMISSIONS INFORMATION

**Director of Admissions:** Rae Lee Siporin

**Telephone:** 310-825-3101

## ENTRANCE REQUIREMENTS

Total high school units required/recommended: 15 total units are required; 4 English required, 3 math required, 4 math recommended, 2 science required, 3 science recommended, 2 foreign language required. Minimum 2.82 GPA required of in-state applicants; minimum 3.4 GPA required of out-of-state applicants. In-state applicants with minimum 3.3 GPA are eligible regardless of test scores; in-state applicants with minimum combined SAT I score of 1400 (composite ACT score of 31) and minimum combined SAT II score of 1650 (with minimum score of 500 on any one test) are eligible on the basis of test scores alone. Special requirements: A portfolio is required for art program applicants. An audition is required for music program applicants. Additional requirements for applicants to School of the Arts and School of Theatre, Film, and Television.

**Application deadline:** Nov. 30
**Notification:** March 15

**SAT or ACT preferred:** Either
**SAT Avg:** 603V, 633M
**SAT II Required:** Yes
**Average ACT:** 25
**Average GPA:** 4

**Graduated top 10% of class:** 87
**Graduated top 25% of class:** 100
**Graduated top 50% of class:** 100

# COLLEGE GRADUATION REQUIREMENTS

**Course waivers allowed:** No
**Course substitutions allowed:** Yes
**In what courses:** Foreign language and math

# ADDITIONAL INFORMATION

**Environment:** The university is located on 419 acres in an urban area of Los Angeles.

**Student Body**
 **Undergrad enrollment:** 23,914
 **Women:** 52%
 **Men:** 48%
 **In-state students:** 95%
 **Out-of-state:** 5%

**Cost Information**
 **In-state tuition:** $4,050
 **Out-of-state:** $13,034
 **Room & board:** $6,490

**Housing Information**
 **University housing:** Yes
 **Fraternity:** Yes
 **Sorority:** Yes
 **Living on campus:** 24%

 **Athletics:** NCAA Div. I

# UNIVERSITY OF CALIFORNIA-SAN DIEGO

9500 Gilman Drive, 0337, La Jolla, CA 92093-0337 • **Admissions:** 619-534-4831
**Email:** admissionsinfo@ucsd.edu • **Web:** www.admissions.ucsd.edu
**Support:** CS • **Institution:** 4 yr. Public

## LEARNING DISABILITY ADMISSIONS AND SERVICES

The Office for Students with Disabilities' (OSD) primary objective is to integrate mainstream students with learning disabilities into campus programs, services, and activities. Academic accommodations are designed to meet a student's disability-related needs without fundamentally altering the nature of the instructional program or altering any directly related licensing requirement. This program is not intended to provide remediation. OSD's Peer Mentoring program is designed to bridge the gap by matching new students who have disabilities (Mentees) with continuing students (Mentors) who have the same major, interests, and/or disabilities. A Peer Mentor is a trusted guide, friend, and peer counselor who assists the new student with areas of adjustment and transition into university life. Through active listening and sharing of personal experience, the Mentor guides and advises the Mentee so that a smooth transition can transpire. Mentors and Mentees meet as a group once a week, and provides for informal meetings and serve as a place to receive emotional support from several students who understand and have something in common. The group also gives students a place where they can feel comfortable to discuss issues. Topics covered in the past include: problem-solving techniques, study strategies, test-taking problems, and social issues.

## LEARNING DISABILITY ADMISSIONS INFORMATION

**Program Name:** Office for Students with Disabilities (OSD)
**Program Director:** Roberta J. Gimblett          **Telephone:** 619-534-4382
**Contact Person:** Moshe "Micky" Witztum          **Telephone:** 619-534-4382

## ADMISSIONS

There is no special admissions process for students with Learning Disabilities. All applicants must meet the same admission criteria. Students need to check the box in Item 43 of the application if they wish to receive information about university resources and services available. They may also check Item 44 to identify their learning disability. This information will have no bearing on eligibility for admission and will be treated confidentially. Course requirements include: 2 yrs. social science (including U.S. history and 1/2 yr. government), 4 yrs. English, 3 yrs. math, 2 yrs. lab science, 2 yrs. foreign language (courses taken in 7th or 8th grade may be used to fulfill part of this requirement), 2 yrs. electives. There is an Eligibility Index based on ACT/SAT and GPA such as 2.82 GPA and 36 ACT/1590-1600 SAT up to 3.29 GPA and 12 ACT/490-570 SAT. Meeting the Eligibility Index requirements does not guarantee admission. There is a Summer Bridge Program for conditional admits that is available to a specific group of students.

**College entrance exams required:** Yes          **Untimed accepted:** Yes
**Course entrance requirements:** Yes          **Interview required:** No
**Diagnostic tests:** Yes
**Documentation:** WAIS-R and/or W-J-R: within 3 yrs.

## ADDITIONAL INFORMATION

Student seeking accommodations must provide a comprehensive written evaluation that meets the following requirements: Assessment must be comprehensive and include: Aptitude (WAIS-R with subtest scores and/or W-J-R ); Achievement (W-J-R; Information Processing (WAIS-R subtests or W-J-R-cognitive portions); within 3 years; diagnostic report with written summary of educational, medical, and family histories and behavioral observation; test scores, testing procedures followed, interpretation, dates, evaluator; specified intracognitive and/or cognitive-achievement discrepancies; statement of how the LD substantially interferes with the student's educational progress; and recommendations for academic accommodations. Academic accommodations are designed to meet disability-related needs without fundamentally altering the program; are not remedial; and may include part-time enrollment, exception to minimum academic progress requirements, substitution of course work required for graduation, and alternative test formats.

**Special education HS coursework accepted:** Y/N- Admissions by individual college
**Essay required:** Yes
**Special application required:** No          **Submitted to:** OSD for Peer Mentoring
**# of applications submitted each year:** 40-50          **# of applications accepted each year:** 30
**# of students receiving LD services:** 86
**Acceptance into program means acceptance into college:** Students are admitted to the college and then reviewed for LD services.

## LEARNING DISABILITY SERVICES

**Learning center:** Yes
**Kurzweil personal reader:** Yes
**LD specialists:** 1
**Allowed in exams:**
  **Calculator:** Yes
  **Dictionary:** N/I
  **Computer:** Yes
  **SpellCheck:** Yes

**Notetaker:** Yes
**Scribes:** Yes
**Proctors:** Yes
**Oral exams:** Yes
**Extended test time:** Yes
**Added cost:** None
**Distraction-free environ.:** Yes
**Tape recording in class:** Yes
**Books on tape:** No
**Taping of other books:** RFB

**Professional tutors:** N/I
**Peer tutors:** N/I
**Max. hrs/wk for services:** Unlimited hours depends on the number of students requesting
**Priority registration:** Yes
**Accomodations for students with ADD:** Yes
**How are professors notified of LD:** By the student and the Program Director

## GENERAL ADMISSIONS INFORMATION

**Director of Admissions:** Dr. Richard Backer

**Telephone:** 619-534-3160

### ENTRANCE REQUIREMENTS

Total high school units required/recommended: 15 total units are required; 4 English required, 3 math required, 4 math recommended, 2 science required, 2 foreign language required, 3 foreign language recommended, 2 history required. Minimum 3.4 GPA required of out-of-state applicants. In-state applicants with minimum 3.3 GPA are eligible regardless of test scores. Applicants with minimum combined SAT I score of 1100 (composite ACT score of 27) and minimum combined SAT II scores of 1650 (in-state) or 1730 (out-of-state), with no score below 500 on any one test, are eligible on the basis of test scores alone. Special requirements: TOEFL is required of all international students.

**Application deadline:** November 30
**Notification:** March 15

**SAT or ACT preferred:** Either
**SAT Avg:** 593V, 632M
**SAT II required:** Yes
**Average ACT:** 25
**Average GPA:** 3.96

**Graduated top 10% of class:** 95
**Graduated top 25% of class:** 100
**Graduated top 50% of class:** 100

## COLLEGE GRADUATION REQUIREMENTS

**Course waivers allowed:** Yes
**Course substitutions allowed:** Yes
**In what courses:** Foreign language

## ADDITIONAL INFORMATION

**Environment:** NR

**Student Body**
  **Undergrad enrollment:** 14,623
  **Women:** 50%
  **Men:** 50%
  **In-state students:** 98%
  **Out-of-state:** 2%

**Cost Information**
  **In-state tuition:** $4,198
  **Out-of-state:** $8,984
  **Room & board:** $6,836

**Housing Information**
  **University housing:** Yes
  **Fraternity:** No
  **Sorority:** No
  **Living on campus:** 29%

  **Athletics:** NCAA Div. III

# UNIVERSITY OF CALIFORNIA-SANTA BARBARA

**CA**

Santa Barbara, CA 93106 • **Admissions:** 805-893-2485 • **Fax:** 805-893-8779
**Email:** appinfo@ucsb.edu • **Web:** www.ucsb.edu
**Support:** CS • **Institution:** 4 yr. Public

## LEARNING DISABILITY ADMISSIONS AND SERVICES

The Disabled Student Program (DSP) is a department within the Division of Student Affairs that works to increase the retention and graduation ratio of students with temporary and permanent disabilities, assure equal access to all educational and academic programs, and foster student independence. The university is strongly committed to maintaining an environment that guarantees students with disabilities full access to educational programs and activities. The DSP office serves as campus liaison regarding issues and regulations related to students with disabilities. DSP provides reasonable accommodations to students with learning disabilities; specific accommodations are determined on an individual basis. Admitted students should send LD documentation to DSP and schedule an appointment with the LD specialist. Accommodations and academically related services are not designed to provide remediation, but to accommodate a perceptual disorder that impairs the student's ability to acquire, process, or communicate information. Each accommodation will be made available to the extent that it does not compromise the academic integrity of the student's program. In all cases, it is the student's responsibility to communicate special needs to the professor and/or DSP.

## LEARNING DISABILITY ADMISSIONS INFORMATION

**Program Name:** Disabled Student Program (DSP)
**Program Director:** Diane Glenn        **Telephone:** 805-893-2182
**Contact Person:** Same as above

### ADMISSIONS

There is no special application for students with learning disabilities. All students must meet the same admission criteria. However, students are encouraged to self-disclose the existence of a learning disability. Students should use their autobiographical statement to address their disability and how they have coped with it in high school. All documentation is submitted to the Office of Admissions, including tests and letters that could be helpful in determining the student's ability to succeed in college. Special circumstances qualifying students for "special action" admissions is viewed on a case-by-case basis, such as waiving foreign language, math, and science. General admission requirements include 4 yrs. English, 3 yrs. math, 1 yr. world history, 1 yr. U.S. history, 2 yrs. lab science, 2 yrs. foreign language, 2 yrs. electives. The ACT or SAT is required and 3 SAT II in English Composition, Math, and one other additional subject. DSP does not admit students but may consult with Admissions. Admission decisions are made by admission officers and consultation from an LD specialist regarding documentation submitted.

**College entrance exams required:** Yes        **Untimed accepted:** Yes
**Course entrance requirements:** Yes        **Interview required:** No
**Diagnostic tests:** Yes
**Documentation:** WAIS-R; WRAT; Nelson-Denny; Achievements; W-J: within 3 years

### ADDITIONAL INFORMATION

Academic accommodations may include substitution of courses required for graduation, non-remedial individualized tutoring, and instruction in reading and writing strategies and in compensatory study skills. Academic support services include priority registration, aids with reading, writing, notetakers, test taking, proofreading, and liaison with faculty. Skills classes and tutoring are provided through CLASS, the Campus Learning Assistance Program. These classes are available for all students on campus. DSP Office does not have the space to provide areas for testing accommodations, but individual professors assist by securing space. Services and accommodations are available for undergraduate and graduate students.

**Special education HS coursework accepted:** Yes        **Essay required:** Yes
**Special application required:** No        **Submitted to:** N/A
**# of applications submitted each year:** 500        **# of applications accepted each year:** N/I
**# of students receiving LD services:** 220
**Acceptance into program means acceptance into college:** Students must be accepted to the university first and then may request services.

# LEARNING DISABILITY SERVICES

**Learning center:** No
**Kurzweil personal reader:** Yes
**LD specialists:** 1
**Allowed in exams:**
  **Calculator:** Yes
  **Dictionary:** No
  **Computer:** Yes
  **SpellCheck:** Yes

**Notetaker:** Yes
**Scribes:** Yes
**Proctors:** Yes
**Oral exams:** Yes
**Extended test time:** Yes
**Added cost:** None
**Distraction-free environ.:** Yes
**Tape recording in class:** Yes
**Books on tape:** Yes
**Taping of other books:** Yes

**Professional tutors:** Yes
**Peer tutors:** Yes
**Max. hrs/wk for services:** 1 hour per week individually and 3 hours per week for group work
**Priority registration:** Yes
**Accomodations for students with ADD:** Yes
**How are professors notified of LD:** By the student via a letter from DSP

# GENERAL ADMISSIONS INFORMATION

**Director of Admissions:** William Villa          **Telephone:** 805-893-3246

## ENTRANCE REQUIREMENTS

Total high school units required/recommended: 15 total units are required; 4 English required, 3 math required, 2 science required, 2 foreign language required, 1 social studies required, 1 history required. Electives should include 1 unit of visual/performing arts. Minimum 2.82 GPA required of in-state applicants; those with minimum combined SAT I score of 1300 (composite ACT score of 31) and combined SAT II score of 1650 (with minimum score of 500 on any one SAT II) are eligible on the basis of test score alone. Minimum 3.4 GPA required of out-of-state applicants; those with combined SAT I score of 1300 (composite ACT score of 31) and combined SAT II score of 1730 (with minimum score of 500 on any one SAT II) are eligible on the basis of test score alone. Special requirements: A portfolio is required for art program applicants; an audition is required for music program applicants; TOEFL is required of all international students; audition required of performing arts program applicants.

**Application deadline:** Nov. 30
**Notification:** March 15

**SAT or ACT preferred:** Either
**SAT Avg:** 549V, 569M
**SAT II Required:** Yes
**Average GPA:** 3.5

**Graduated top 10% of class:** 93
**Graduated top 25% of class:** 100
**Graduated top 50% of class:** 100

# COLLEGE GRADUATION REQUIREMENTS

**Course waivers allowed:** No
**Course substitutions allowed:** Yes
**In what courses:** Substitutions depend on documentation and an attempt by the student to take the course. Typically the requests for substitutions are in math and foreign language. Requests for substitutions of course work are reviewed by a committee. Substitutions are designed to meet student needs, but not alter major requirements.

# ADDITIONAL INFORMATION

**Environment:** The university is located on 813 acres in a small city 10 miles west of Santa Barbara.

**Student Body**
  **Undergrad enrollment:** 16,281
  **Women:** 53%
  **Men:** 47%
  **In-state students:** 95%
  **Out-of-state:** 5%

**Cost Information**
  **In-state tuition:** $4,098
  **Out-of-state:** $12,492
  **Room & board:** $6,131

**Housing Information**
  **University housing:** Yes
  **Fraternity:** Yes
  **Sorority:** Yes
  **Living on campus:** 19%

  **Athletics:** NCAA Div. I

# UNIVERSITY OF CALIFORNIA-SANTA CRUZ

**CA**

1156 High Street, Cook House, Santa Cruz, CA 95064 • **Admissions:** 408-459-0111 • **Fax:** 408-459-4452
**Email:** admissions@cats.ucsc.edu • **Web:** www.ucsc.edu
**Support:** CS • **Institution:** 4 yr. Public

## LEARNING DISABILITY ADMISSIONS AND SERVICES

The Disability Resource Center is committed to making all programs, services, and activities accessible to students with disabilities. Services are free of charge, entirely voluntary, and provided at the request of the student. Recent documentation that verifies the disability must state the nature of the disability and what accommodations are required. Service coordinators are available to speak to the student to discuss the disability, goals and solutions, as well as strategies for a successful academic year.

## LEARNING DISABILITY ADMISSIONS INFORMATION

**Program Name:** Disability Resource Center
**Program Director:** Margaret Keith
**Contact Person:** Sharyn Martin

**Telephone:** 408-459-2089

### ADMISSIONS

Students with LD should self-disclose and submit documentation to DRC. Students not admissible may request special consideration through DRC. This option is limited to a small percentage of applicants. DRC evaluates documentation; reviews economic background, age, talents, life experiences, community contributions, and essay; and makes a recommendation to Admissions. Three recommendations are required. Regular admissions requires 15 academic credits: 4 yrs. English; 3 yrs. math; 2 yrs. history; 2 yrs. laboratory science (3 recommended); 2 yrs. foreign language (3 recommended); 2 electives. Students may be admitted with 3.31 (3.4 out-of state) GPA alone, or by exams alone. An SAT I of 1300 or ACT of 31 and 3 SAT II Tests with total scores of 1650 (1730 out-of-state) with no individual SAT II score below 500 will result in admission.

**College entrance exams required:** Yes
**Course entrance requirements:** Yes
**Diagnostic tests:** Yes
**Documentation:** WAIS-R; W-J-R preferred, not required: within 3 years

**Untimed accepted:** Yes
**Interview required:** No

### ADDITIONAL INFORMATION

The Disability Resource Center offers learning and study skills programs. Students can receive assistance in developing and improving reading, writing, listening, notetaking, and problem-solving abilities. There are mini courses to improve skills in math, science, and preparing for graduate school entrance tests. With permission the DRC staff will advise instructors of the nature of the disability, as well as help students plan for a student-faculty meeting. Proofreading services are available for help in correcting spelling and punctuation errors, footnoting, and formatting. Notetaking services are intended to supplement class attendance and not replace it. Notetakers are not obligated to take notes for classes the student misses. Students are encouraged to contact DRC as early as possible to request services. There is a pilot 'Bridge Program' for select incoming freshmen.

**Special education HS coursework accepted:** N/I
**Special application required:** No
**# of applications submitted each year:** 195
**# of students receiving LD services:** 210-250

**Essay required:** Yes
**Submitted to:** N/A
**# of applications accepted each year:** 122

**Acceptance into program means acceptance into college:** Students must be admitted to the university first (can appeal a denial) and then may request services.

# LEARNING DISABILITY SERVICES

**Learning center:** No
**Kurzweil personal reader:** No
**LD specialists:** 1.5
**Allowed in exams:**
  **Calculator:** Y/N
  **Dictionary:** Y/N
  **Computer:** Y/N
  **SpellCheck:** Y/N

**Notetaker:** Yes
**Scribes:** Yes
**Proctors:** Yes
**Oral exams:** Yes
**Extended test time:** Yes
**Added cost:** None
**Distraction-free environ.:** Yes
**Tape recording in class:** Yes
**Books on tape:** Yes
**Taping of other books:** Yes

**Professional tutors:** No
**Peer tutors:** Varies
**Max. hrs/wk for services:** For tutoring: 2 hrs.
**Priority registration:** Yes
**Accomodations for students with ADD:** Yes
**How are professors notified of LD:** By the student and Program Coordinator

# GENERAL ADMISSIONS INFORMATION

**Director of Admissions:** J. Michael Thompson    **Telephone:** 408-459-5453

## ENTRANCE REQUIREMENTS

Total high school units required/recommended: 15 total units are required; 4 English required, 3 math required, 4 math recommended, 2 science required, 3 science recommended, 2 foreign language required, 3 foreign language recommended, 1 social studies required, 1 history required. SAT II Subject Tests in Writing, Mathematics, and a third test are required. Minimum 3.4 GPA required of out-of-state applicants. In-state applicants with minimum 3.3 GPA are eligible regardless of test scores. Applicants with minimum combined SAT I score of 1400 (composite ACT score of 31) and minimum combined SAT II scores of 1760 (in-state) or 1850 (out-of-state), with no score below 530 on any one test, are eligible on the basis of test scores alone. Special requirements: An audition is required for music program applicants; TOEFL is required of all international students.

**Application deadline:** Nov. 30
**Notification:** March 15

**SAT or ACT preferred:** Either
**SAT Avg:** 570V, 565M
**SAT II required:** Yes
**Average ACT:** 23
**Average GPA:** 3.5

**Graduated top 10% of class:** 94
**Graduated top 25% of class:** 100
**Graduated top 50% of class:** 100

# COLLEGE GRADUATION REQUIREMENTS

**Course waivers allowed:** No
**Course substitutions allowed:** Yes
**In what courses:** Made on a case-by-case basis, but rarely given

# ADDITIONAL INFORMATION

**Environment:** The university is located above Monterey Bay and the Pacific Ocean on 2,000 acres of redwood forest.

**Student Body**
  **Undergrad enrollment:** 8,629
  **Women:** 60%
  **Men:** 40%
  **In-state students:** 93%
  **Out-of-state:** 7%

**Cost Information**
  **In-state tuition:** $4,136
  **Out-of-state:** $12,530
  **Room & board:** $6,429

**Housing Information**
  **University housing:** Yes
  **Fraternity:** No
  **Sorority:** No
  **Living on campus:** 45%

  **Athletics:** NCAA Div. III

# KINGS RIVER COMMUNITY COLLEGE

**CA**

Reedley, CA 93654-2099 • **Admissions:** 209-638-3641

**Support:** CS • **Institution:** 2 yr. Public

## LEARNING DISABILITY ADMISSIONS AND SERVICES

The mission of Disabled Student Service is to provide resources to encourage and support independent academic, social, and personal skill development. The College aims to provide reasonable accommodations and to teach learning strategies to students with Learning Disabilities so that they may be successful in a college setting. This involves workshops, classes, services, and accommodations to equalize learning potential for students with veritable Learning Disabilities.

## LEARNING DISABILITY ADMISSIONS INFORMATION

**Program Name:** Disabled Student Service
**Program Director:** Lynn Mancini
**Contact Person:** Debbie Norman

**Telephone:** 209-638-0332

### ADMISSIONS

Admissions is 'open door' to any student with a high school diploma or equivalent. Students must meet the eligibility model set by the California Community College Chancellor's Office to receive services for Learning Disabilities. This model includes information from: (1) intake screening; (2) measured achievement; (3) measured ability; (4) processing deficit; (5) aptitude-achievement discrepancy; and (6) survey of academic attributes-self-reporting measure of adaptive behavior. Students with learning disabilities, requesting LD accommodations, must present with a history of special education and current records within three years of evaluation. If the student has a GPA below a 2.0 there must be evidence of the ability to benefit from a college education, and a placement test is given.

**College entrance exams required:** No
**Course entrance requirements:** No
**Diagnostic tests:** Yes
**Documentation:** Cognitive- Common WAIS; W-J-R Cog; SPM; SB: within 3 years

**Untimed accepted:** N/A
No

### ADDITIONAL INFORMATION

Remedial courses are available in math and English. Tutoring is offered to all students for no additional fee. Guidance class work is offered and recommended to all students with learning disabilities. This course provides strategies and techniques on 'How to be successful college students'. There are modules in study strategies, test taking skills, organizational skills, time management, and utilizing the resources at the College. Skills classes for credit are offered in math, reading, sentence writing, and written language. LD specialists on the staff of Disabled Student Services provide services to students with learning disabilities. Scribes are not common, and they encourage the use of computers. The area provided for a distraction-free environment is better than a classroom, but not completely quiet. Tape recorders are allowed by most professors. Students requesting the use of a computer, dictionary, spellchecker, or calculator in an exam will need the professor's permission.

**Special education HS coursework accepted:** Yes
**Special application required:** No
**# of applications submitted each year:** 100
**# of students receiving LD services:** 137

**Essay required:** No
**Submitted to:** N/A
**# of applications accepted each year:** 83%

**Acceptance into program means acceptance into college:** Students must be admitted to the College first and then may request services.

# LEARNING DISABILITY SERVICES

**Learning center:** Yes
**Kurzweil personal reader:** Yes
**LD specialists:** Yes
**Allowed in exams:**
  **Calculator:** Yes
  **Dictionary:** Y/N
  **Computer:** Yes
  **SpellCheck:** Yes

**Notetaker:** Yes
**Scribes:** Y/N
**Proctors:** Yes
**Oral exams:** Yes
**Extended test time:** Yes
**Added cost:** None
**Distraction-free environ.:** Y/N
**Tape recording in class:** Y/N
**Books on tape:** Yes
**Taping of other books:** No

**Professional tutors:** Yes
**Peer tutors:** N/A
**Max. hrs/wk for services:** Unlimited
**Priority registration:** Yes
**Accomodations for students with ADD:** Yes
**How are professors notified of LD:** By the student and the Program Director

# GENERAL ADMISSIONS INFORMATION

**Director of Admissions:** Moire Charters

**Telephone:** 209-638-3611

## ENTRANCE REQUIREMENTS
High school diploma or GED equivalent

**Application deadline:** NR
**Notification:** NR

**SAT or ACT preferred:** NR

# COLLEGE GRADUATION REQUIREMENTS

**Course waivers allowed:** No
**Course substitutions allowed:** No
**In what courses:** They have been successful in obtaining two waivers in math, but it is difficult to get and needs clear documentation with extraordinary affects.

# ADDITIONAL INFORMATION

**Environment:** The college is located on 350 ares in a rural area.

**Student Body**
  **Undergrad enrollment:** 6,722
  **Women:** 63%
  **Men:** 37%
  **In-state students:** 98%
  **Out-of-state:** 2%

**Cost Information**
  **In-state tuition:** $300
  **Out-of-state:** $3,390

**Housing Information**
  **University housing:** Yes
  **Fraternity:** No
  **Sorority:** No
  **% Living on campus:** 88%

  **Athletics:** Intramural

# UNIVERSITY OF THE PACIFIC

3601 Pacific Avenue, Stockton, CA 95211 • **Admissions:** 209-946-2211 • **Fax:** 209-946-2413
**Email:** admission@uop.edu • **Web:** www.uop.edu
**Support:** CS • **Institution:** 4 yr. Private

## LEARNING DISABILITY ADMISSIONS AND SERVICES

There is no special program for students with learning disabilities, but the university does have a Learning Disabilities Support program. This Program offers assistance through tutoring, study skills classes, support groups, and testing accommodations. Students register for services after admission by contacting the Educational Resource Center. Student confidentiality is protected. The ultimate goal is for the student to earn a degree that is 'unmodified and unflagged.' Faculty and staff are dedicated to providing students with learning disabilities all reasonable accommodations so that they may enjoy academic success. The LD Support Program helps keep UOP in compliance with the Americans with Disabilities Act and Section 504 of the Rehabilitation Act. Compliance is accomplished without compromising UOP standards, placing undue financial or administrative burden on the university, fundamentally altering the nature of programs, or extending unreasonable accommodations.

## LEARNING DISABILITY ADMISSIONS INFORMATION

**Program Name:** Learning Disabilities Support
**Program Director:** Howard Houck, Coordinator           **Telephone:** 209-946-3219
**Contact Person:** Same as above

### ADMISSIONS

UOP welcomes students with learning disabilities. Although there is no special admission procedure, students are given special consideration. No minimum ACT/SAT requirement. There are two alternative methods for admissions: (1) Probationary Admissions for the marginal student: "C/D" average with no special requirements, but the university advisor is notified of status, no required test score, and no quota regarding the number of students admitted; and (2) Special Admissions: students who begin college courses in the summer prior to freshman year and receive at least a "C" average in 2 courses and 1 study skills class (can take those courses at any local community college).

**College entrance exams required:** Yes          **Untimed accepted:** Yes
**Course entrance requirements:** Yes          **Interview required:** No
**Diagnostic tests:** Yes
**Documentation:** WAIS-R; W-J: within 3 years

### ADDITIONAL INFORMATION

All admitted students are eligible for LD services with the appropriate assessment documentation. The Educational Resource Center is open to all students on campus. Skills courses for credit are available in reading, study skills, writing, and math. Services and accommodations are available for undergraduate and graduate students. The university offers a special summer program for pre-college freshmen students with learning disabilities.

**Special education HS coursework accepted:** Yes          **Essay required:** Yes
**Special application required:** No          **Submitted to:** N/A
**# of applications submitted each year:** N/I          **# of applications accepted each year:** N/I
**# of students receiving LD services:** 150
**Acceptance into program means acceptance into college:** Students must be accepted to the university first and then may request services.

**Learning center:** Yes
**Kurzweil personal reader:** Yes
**LD specialists:** 4
**Allowed in exams:**
  **Calculator:** Yes
  **Dictionary:** Yes
  **Computer:** Yes
  **SpellCheck:** Yes

**Notetaker:** Yes
**Scribes:** Yes
**Proctors:** Yes
**Oral exams:** Yes
**Extended test time:** Yes
**Added cost:** None
**Distraction-free environ.:** Yes
**Tape recording in class:** Yes
**Books on tape:** Yes
**Taping of other books:** Yes

**Professional tutors:** 10
**Peer tutors:** 40
**Max. hrs/wk for services:** Unlimited
**Priority registration:** Yes
**Accomodations for students with ADD:** Yes
**How are professors notified of LD:** By the Program Coordinator

# GENERAL ADMISSIONS INFORMATION

**Director of Admissions:** Edward Schoenberg          **Telephone:** 209-946-2211

## ENTRANCE REQUIREMENTS

Total high school units required/recommended: 16 total units are recommended; 4 English recommended, 3 math recommended, 2 science recommended, 2 foreign language recommended, 1 history recommended. Special require-ments: An audition is required for music program applicants; TOEFL is required of all international students; 4 units of math and 3 units of lab science recommended of science and technical program applicants.

**Application deadline:** March 1
**Notification:** Rolling

**SAT or ACT preferred:** Either
**SAT Avg:** 547V, 573M
**Average ACT:** 19
**Average GPA:** 3.4

**Graduated top 10% of class:** 38
**Graduated top 25% of class:** 74
**Graduated top 50% of class:** 90

# COLLEGE GRADUATION REQUIREMENTS

**Course waivers allowed:** Yes
**Course substitutions allowed:** Yes
**In what courses:** N/I

# ADDITIONAL INFORMATION

**Environment:** The university is located on 150 acres 90 miles east of San Francisco.

**Student Body**
  **Undergrad enrollment:** 2,758
  **Women:** 56%
  **Men:** 44%
  **In-state students:** 80%
  **Out-of-state:** 20%

**Cost Information**
  **In-state tuition:** $18,260
  **Out-of-state:** $18,260
  **Room & board:** $5,526

**Housing Information**
  **University housing:** Yes
  **Fraternity:** Yes
  **Sorority:** Yes
  **Living on campus:** 50

  **Athletics:** NCAA Div. I

# UNIVERSITY OF REDLANDS

P.O. Box 3080, 1200 East Colton Avenue, Redlands, CA 92373-0999 • **Admissions:** 800-455-5069
**Fax:** 909-335-4089
**Email:** admit@uor.edu • **Web:** www.uor.edu
**Support:** S • **Institution:** 4 yr. Private

## LEARNING DISABILITY ADMISSIONS AND SERVICES

Students identified as learning disabled are eligible for tutoring and individual assistance from Academic Support Services. While the university does not have a formal program for students with learning disabilities, the goal is to help students succeed in college once they are enrolled. Although the services and accommodations offered are minimal, they do comply to the mandates of Section 504 of the Rehabilitation Act of 1973. Academic Support Services is sensitive to the needs of students with disabilities, and strives to provide the services and accommodations that are identified in the professional documentation.

## LEARNING DISABILITY ADMISSIONS INFORMATION

**Program Name:** Academic Support Service
**Program Director:** Judy Strack Bowman
**Contact Person:** Same as above

**Telephone:** 909-335-4079

### ADMISSIONS

Students with learning disabilities are required to submit the general application form and meet the same admission standards as all applicants. 'Faculty admits' are for those students whose GPA's or SAT/ACT scores do not meet admissions standards, but who show promise of success in college. The Director of Academic Support Services is involved in the admission decision for students with learning disabilities.

**College entrance exams required:** Yes
**Course entrance requirements:** Yes
**Diagnostic tests:** No
**Documentation:** Helpful after admission

**Untimed accepted:** Yes
**Interview required:** Recommended

### ADDITIONAL INFORMATION

Study skills courses are available as well as basic skills classes in math, writing, and learning strategies. Students have access to tutoring on a one-to-one basis. The Director of Academic Support Services will work with students to assist them in identifying their needs and securing appropriate accommodations. However, it is the students' responsibility to seek out help and request assistance.

**Special education HS coursework accepted:** Yes
**Special application required:** No
**# of applications submitted each year:** Unknown
**# of students receiving LD services:** 40-50
**Acceptance into program means acceptance into college:** Students must be admitted to the university first and then may request services.

**Essay required:** Yes
**Submitted to:** N/A
**# of applications accepted each year:** N/I

**Learning center:** No
**Kurzweil personal reader:** No
**LD specialists:** No
**Allowed in exams:**
  **Calculator:** Yes
  **Dictionary:** Yes
  **Computer:** Yes
  **SpellCheck:** Yes

**Notetaker:** Yes
**Scribes:** Yes
**Proctors:** Yes
**Oral exams:** No
**Extended test time:** Yes
**Added cost:** None
**Distraction-free environ.:** Yes
**Tape recording in class:** Yes
**Books on tape:** Yes
**Taping of other books:** No

**Professional tutors:** No
**Peer tutors:** Yes
**Max. hrs/wk for services:** As needed
**Priority registration:** No
**Accomodations for students with ADD:** Yes
**How are professors notified of LD:** By the student and Program Director

## GENERAL ADMISSIONS INFORMATION

**Director of Admissions:** Paul Driscoll          **Telephone:** 909-335-4074

### ENTRANCE REQUIREMENTS

Total high school units required/recommended: 4 English recommended, 3 math recommended, 2 science recommended, 1 social studies recommended, 2 history recommended, 2 foreign language recommended. Minimum combined SAT I score of 950 and minimum 2.85 GPA recommended. Special requirements: An audition is required for music program applicants; interview required of applicants to Johnston Center for Individualized Learning.

**Application deadline:** March 1
**Notification:** Rolling

**SAT or ACT preferred:** Either
**SAT Avg:** 546V, 544M
**Average ACT:** 23
**Average GPA:** 3.4

**Graduated top 10% of class:** 33
**Graduated top 25% of class:** 64
**Graduated top 50% of class:** 90

## COLLEGE GRADUATION REQUIREMENTS

**Course waivers allowed:** Yes
**Course substitutions allowed:** Yes
**In what courses:** N/I

## ADDITIONAL INFORMATION

**Environment:** The university is located on 130 acres in a small town 60 miles east of Los Angeles.

**Student Body**
  **Undergrad enrollment:** 1,318
  **Women:** 55%
  **Men:** 45%
  **In-state students:** 72%
  **Out-of-state:** 28%

**Cost Information**
  **In-state tuition:** $18,300
  **Out-of-state:** $18,300
  **Room & board:** $7,096

**Housing Information**
  **University housing:** Yes
  **Fraternity:** Yes
  **Sorority:** Yes
  **Living on campus:** 78

  **Athletics:** NCAA Div. III

# SAN DIEGO STATE UNIVERSITY

San Diego, CA 92182 • **Admissions:** 619-594-6871
**Email:** admissions@sdsu.edu • **Web:** www.sdsu.edu
**Support:** CS • **Institution:** 4 yr. Public

## LEARNING DISABILITY ADMISSIONS AND SERVICES

The Learning Disability Program at San Diego State is under the umbrella of Disabled Student Services. The LD Program is designed to provide assessment, accommodations, and advocacy. Students must provide documentation prior to receiving services. Students with learning disabilities may be assessed using nationally standardized batteries. The university believes that students with learning disabilities can be successful at San Diego State and will try to provide the appropriate services to foster their success.

## LEARNING DISABILITY ADMISSIONS INFORMATION

**Program Name:** Disabled Student Services
**Program Director:** Dr. Frank Siehien, Coordinator        **Telephone:** 619-594-6473
**Contact Person:** Same as above

### ADMISSIONS

Students with learning disabilities who are not admissible by the general admission criteria or who are denied admission, may request a review through special admission. Students need to write a letter to the Director of the LD Program, explaining why they feel they should be admitted. Three recommendations are required for special admit. No student will be admitted with a GPA below 2.0. Students must provide documentation verifying the disability and meeting the California State definition of a learning disability. The Director of Disabled Student Services reviews documentation and makes a recommendation to the Admissions Office.

**College entrance exams required:** No          **Untimed accepted:** Yes
**Course entrance requirements:** Yes          **Interview required:** Recommended
**Diagnostic tests:** Yes
**Documentation:** W-J: WAIS-R with WRAT-R; within 3 years

### ADDITIONAL INFORMATION

Students are encouraged to get volunteer notetakers from among other students enrolled in the class. Students with learning disabilities may request permission to tape a lecture. Students will also need permission from the professor to use a calculator, dictionary, computer, or spellchecker in exams. Tutoring services are provided at no charge. High Tech Center is a learning center available for all students with disabilities. Services and accommodations are available for undergraduates and graduated students.

**Special education HS coursework accepted:** No          **Essay required:** Yes
**Special application required:** No          **Submitted to:** N/A
**# of applications submitted each year:** N/A          **# of applications accepted each year:** N/A
**# of students receiving LD services:** 750
**Acceptance into program means acceptance into college:** Students must be admitted to the university first and then may request services.

# LEARNING DISABILITY SERVICES

**Learning center:** Yes
**Kurzweil personal reader:** Yes
**LD specialists:** 2.5
**Allowed in exams:**
  **Calculator:** Y/N
  **Dictionary:** Y/N
  **Computer:** Y/N
  **SpellCheck:** Y/N

**Notetaker:** Yes
**Scribes:** No
**Proctors:** Yes
**Oral exams:** No
**Extended test time:** Yes
**Added cost:** None
**Distraction-free environ.:** Yes
**Tape recording in class:** Yes
**Books on tape:** Yes
**Taping of other books:** Yes

**Professional tutors:** No
**Peer tutors:** Yes
**Max. hrs/wk for services:**
Depends on needs
**Priority registration:** Yes
**Accomodations for students
with ADD:** Yes
**How are professors notified of
LD:** By the student

# GENERAL ADMISSIONS INFORMATION

**Director of Admissions:** Dr. Nancy C. Sprotte      **Telephone:** 619-594-6871

## ENTRANCE REQUIREMENTS
Total high school units required/recommended: 15 total units are required; 4 English required, 3 math required, 1 science required, 2 foreign language required, 1 history required. Electives should include 1 unit of visual/performing arts. Minimum grade of C, eligibility index of 2800 for SAT I (674 for ACT) required of in-state applicants; minimum eligibility index of 3402 for SAT I (822 for ACT) required of out-of-state applicants. In-state applicants with minimum 3.0 GPA and out-of-state applicants with minimum 3.6 GPA are eligible regardless of test scores. Special requirements: Specific GPA required of nursing, radio/TV, engineering, and business program applicants.

**Application deadline:** November 30
**Notification:** Rolling

**SAT or ACT preferred:** Either
**SAT Avg:** 476V, 486M
**Average ACT:** 20
**Average GPA:** 3.1

**Graduated top 10% of class:** 12
**Graduated top 25% of class:** 42
**Graduated top 50% of class:** 86

# COLLEGE GRADUATION REQUIREMENTS

**Course waivers allowed:** No
**Course substitutions allowed:** Yes
**In what courses:** Substitutions based on attempts and disability-related issues

# ADDITIONAL INFORMATION

**Environment:** San Diego State is located on 300 acres 12 miles from the ocean.

**Student Body**
  **Undergrad enrollment:** 29,331
  **Women:** 55%
  **Men:** 45%
  **In-state students:** 97%
  **Out-of-state:** 3%

**Cost Information**
  **In-state tuition:**
  **Out-of-state:** $5,904
  **Room & board:** $4,700

**Housing Information**
  **University housing:** Yes
  **Fraternity:** Yes
  **Sorority:** Yes
  **Living on campus:** 10

  **Athletics:** NCAA Div. I

# SAN FRANCISCO STATE UNIVERSITY

1600 Holloway, San Francisco, CA 94132 • **Admissions:** 415-338-2411
**Email:** admissions@sfsu.edu • **Web:** www.sfsu.edu
**Support:** CS • **Institution:** 4 yr. Public

## LEARNING DISABILITY ADMISSIONS AND SERVICES

The Disability Resource Center (DRC) is available to promote and provide equal access to the classroom and to campus-related activities. A full range of support services is provided in order that students may define and achieve personal autonomy at SFSU. The staff is sensitive to the diversity of disabilities, including those only recently recognized as disabilities requiring reasonable accommodations. Confidential support services are available for all students with a verified temporary or permanent disability who are enrolled at the university. All students registered with DRC are eligible for disability management advising. This consists of helping students access services from DRC, manage DRC services and school in general, problem solve conflicts/concerns that are disability related with individuals, programs, and services on campus, and understand "reasonable accommodation" under the law. The DRC seizes every opportunity to educate the campus community about reasonable accommodations for students with disabilities. Generally the campus community is sensitive, but if an oversight occurs, students do have protection under Section 504 and ADA. Students are encouraged to contact DRC for guidance in pursuing a grievance. Resolution of a violation can often be achieved informally without completing the formal grievance procedure.

## LEARNING DISABILITY ADMISSIONS INFORMATION

**Program Name:** Disability Resource Center (DRC)
**Program Director:** Kimberly Bartlett, Ph.D.                    **Telephone:** 415-338-2472
**Contact Person:** Deidre Defreese                               **Telephone:** 415-338-6356

### ADMISSIONS

Students with LD apply to the university using the regular application process. If the student is not eligible for regular admission for a disability-related reason, DRC can provide special admissions assistance. To obtain special admissions assistance, students need to register with the DRC office, provide verification of the disability, and notify the Admissions Office that the DRC has the appropriate verification. When these steps have been taken, the Admissions Office will consult with DRC before denying admission. The Admission contact person can request substitutions of high school courses in math, foreign language, and science. Students with LD who are judged unable to fulfill specific requirements may take courses substitutions. Substitutions are authorized on an individual basis after review and recommendation by the high school counselor. Students taking substitutions must have 15 units of college prep study. High school case-managers may write summaries and provide a clinical judgment. DRC wants information about achievement deficits and may require the student to attend an admissions interview.

**College entrance exams required:** Yes                  **Untimed accepted:** Yes
**Course entrance requirements:** Yes                     **Interview required:** Yes
**Diagnostic tests:** Yes
**Documentation:** Full LD diagnostic testing; ach. in reading, written language, & math: within 3 years

### ADDITIONAL INFORMATION

The Disability Resource Center offers a drop-in-center with available tutorial services. The Disability Resource Center can also arrange for test accommodations and notetakers and will advocate for the student. The staff is very involved and offers comprehensive services through a team approach. There are no developmental courses offered at the university. However, there are skills classes. Students with documented learning disabilities may request assistance in locating tutors. Other services may include registration assistance, campus orientation, notetakers, readers, test-taking assistance, assessment of the learning disability, tutoring, disability-related counseling, and referral information.

**Special education HS coursework accepted:** N/I        **Essay required:** No
**Special application required:** Yes                    **Submitted to:** DRC
**# of applications submitted each year:** N/A           **# of applications accepted each year:** N/I
**# of students receiving LD services:** 400
**Acceptance into program means acceptance into college:** Students must be admitted to the university first and then may request services.

## LEARNING DISABILITY SERVICES

**Learning center:** No
**Kurzweil personal reader:** Yes
**LD specialists:** 3
**Allowed in exams:**
  **Calculator:** Yes
  **Dictionary:** Yes
  **Computer:** Yes
  **SpellCheck:** Yes

**Notetaker:** Yes
**Scribes:** Yes
**Proctors:** Yes
**Oral exams:** Yes
**Extended test time:** Yes
**Added cost:** None
**Distraction-free environ.:** Yes
**Tape recording in class:** Yes
**Books on tape:** Yes
**Taping of other books:** No

**Professional tutors:** Yes
**Peer tutors:** Yes
**Max. hrs/wk for services:** Limited
**Priority registration:** Yes
**Accomodations for students with ADD:** Yes
**How are professors notified of LD:** By the student with letter of documentation from DRC

## GENERAL ADMISSIONS INFORMATION

**Director of Admissions:** Patricia Wade          **Telephone:** 415-338-2017

### ENTRANCE REQUIREMENTS

Total high school units required/recommended: 15 total units are required; 4 English required, 3 math required, 2 science required, 2 foreign language required, 1 history required. Minimum grade of C, minimum eligibility index of 2800 for SAT I (694 for ACT) required of in-state applicants; minimum eligibility index of 3402 for SAT I (842 for ACT) required of out-of-state applicants. In-state applicants with minimum 3.0 GPA and out-of-state applicants with minimum 3.6 GPA are eligible regardless of test scores. Special requirements: A portfolio is required for art program applicants; an audition is required for music program applicants.

**Application deadline:** November 30
**Notification:** Rolling

**SAT or ACT preferred:** Either
**SAT Avg:** 372V, 444M
**Average ACT:** 19

## COLLEGE GRADUATION REQUIREMENTS

**Course waivers allowed:** Yes
**Course substitutions allowed:** Yes
**In what courses:** Decisions are made on a case-by-case basis.

## ADDITIONAL INFORMATION

**Environment:** The school is located in downtown San Francisco on a 130-acre campus.

**Student Body**
  **Undergrad enrollment:** 19,102
  **Women:** 57%
  **Men:** 43%
  **In-state students:** 99%
  **Out-of-state:** 1%

**Cost Information**
  **In-state tuition:** $1,982
  **Out-of-state:** $9,362
  **Room & board:** $5,225

**Housing Information**
  **University housing:** Yes
  **Fraternity:** No
  **Sorority:** No
  **Living on campus:** 6

  **Athletics:** NCAA Div. II

SAN FRANCISCO STATE UNIVERSITY

# CA

# UNIVERSITY OF SAN FRANCISCO

2130 Fulton Street, San Francisco, CA 94117 • **Admissions:** 415-422-6563 • **Fax:** 415-422-2217
**Web:** www.usfca.edu
**Support:** CS • **Institution:** 4 yr. Private

## LEARNING DISABILITY ADMISSIONS AND SERVICES

The University of San Francisco believes that students with learning disabilities are capable of succeeding and becoming contributing members of the university community and society. To this end, USF provides educational support and assistance to those students whose goals are successful completion of college and who take an active participatory role in their own education. Services provided enable students to achieve grades that accurately reflect their ability, promote healthy self-images, remediate deficit areas, and promote USF's LD program by conducting in-services for faculty, admissions and other staff, providing brochures, advertising services, and working closely with faculty to provide accommodations to students with learning disabilities.

## LEARNING DISABILITY ADMISSIONS INFORMATION

**Program Name:** Services to Student with Learning Disabilities
**Program Director:** Cally Salzman                    **Telephone:** 415-422-6876
**Contact Person:** or Tom Merrell

### ADMISSIONS

If a student who is a borderline admit self-discloses on the regular application form, the Director of USF Services reviews the documentation and gives an evaluation before an admission decision is made. The final decision is made jointly between the Director of the Program and the Office of Admissions. Students who are accepted to the university under "conditional" status are encouraged to participate in the Summer Forward program. This voluntary program focuses on the academic needs of the students and prepares them for the demands of college life.

**College entrance exams required:** Yes                    **Untimed accepted:** Yes
**Course entrance requirements:** Yes                    **Interview required:** Recommended
**Diagnostic tests:** Yes
**Documentation:** WAIS-R: W-J: within 3 years

### ADDITIONAL INFORMATION

Services include: trained tutors, instruction in study skills and coping strategies, academic advising, maintaining regular contact with the LD coordinator, diagnostic testing, individual or small group instruction for educational skills building, and helping students improve their understanding of their learning disability. Services and accommodations are available for undergraduate and graduate students. Students with Attention Deficit Disorder request services through Disability Related Services.

**Special education HS coursework accepted:** Yes if meet admission requirements    **Essay required:** Yes
**Special application required:** No                    **Submitted to:** N/A
**# of applications submitted each year:** N/A                    **# of applications accepted each year:** 10
**# of students receiving LD services:** 155
**Acceptance into program means acceptance into college:** Students must be admitted to the university first and then may request services.

## LEARNING DISABILITY SERVICES

**Learning center:** Yes
**Kurzweil personal reader:** No
**LD specialists:** 2
**Allowed in exams:**
  **Calculator:** Y/N
  **Dictionary:** Y/N
  **Computer:** Yes
  **SpellCheck:** Yes

**Notetaker:** No
**Scribes:** Yes
**Proctors:** Yes
**Oral exams:** Yes
**Extended test time:** Yes
**Added cost:** None
**Distraction-free environ.:** Yes
**Tape recording in class:** Yes
**Books on tape:** Yes
**Taping of other books:** Yes

**Professional tutors:** No
**Peer tutors:** Yes
**Max. hrs/wk for services:** 5-8 hours
**Priority registration:** No
**Accomodations for students with ADD:** Yes
**How are professors notified of LD:** By the student and Program Director

## GENERAL ADMISSIONS INFORMATION

**Director of Admissions:** William A. Henley          **Telephone:** 415-422-6886

### ENTRANCE REQUIREMENTS

Total high school units required/recommended: 20 total units are recommended; 4 English recommended, 3 math recommended, 2 science recommended, 2 foreign language recommended, 3 social studies recommended. Rank in top quarter of secondary school class and minimum 3.0 GPA recommended. Special requirements: TOEFL is required of all international students.

**Application deadline:** February 15
**Notification:** Rolling

**SAT or ACT preferred:** SAT
**SAT Range:** 480–600 Verbal, 480–600 Math
**ACT Range:** 21–26
**Average GPA:** 3.3

**Graduated top 10% of class:** 25
**Graduated top 25% of class:** 55
**Graduated top 50% of class:** 88

## COLLEGE GRADUATION REQUIREMENTS

**Course waivers allowed:** No
**Course substitutions allowed:** Yes
**In what courses:** Decision is made on an individual basis depending on the diagnosis.

## ADDITIONAL INFORMATION

**Environment:** The University of San Francisco is located on 52 acres in the heart of the city.

**Student Body**
  **Undergrad enrollment:** 4,570
  **Women:** 62%
  **Men:** 38%
  **In-state students:** 78%
  **Out-of-state:** 22%

**Cost Information**
  **In-state tuition:** $14,920
  **Out-of-state:** $14,920
  **Room & board:** $6,934

**Housing Information**
  **University housing:** Yes
  **Fraternity:** Yes
  **Sorority:** No
  **Living on campus:** 32

  **Athletics:** NCAA Div. I

# SAN JOSE STATE UNIVERSITY

**CA**

1 Washington Square, San Jose, CA 95192 • **Admissions:** 408-283-7500 • **Fax:** 408-924-2050
**Email:** contact@anret.sjsu.edu • **Web:** www.sjsu.edu
**Support:** CS • **Institution:** 4 yr. Public

## LEARNING DISABILITY ADMISSIONS AND SERVICES

The goal of the Disabled Student Services is to provide appropriate academic adjustments and support services to students with disabilities while training them to become self-advocates and to develop maximum independence. The Disability Resource Center provides services to students and consultation to faculty to empower every department so that they can mainstream individuals with disabilities.

## LEARNING DISABILITY ADMISSIONS INFORMATION

**Program Name:** Disabled Student Services
**Program Director:** Martin Schulter
**Contact Person:** Joan Kilbourne

**Telephone:** 408-924-6000

### ADMISSIONS

There is no special admissions for students with learning disabilities. Students must have at least a 2.0 GPA, and a sliding scale is used combining GPA and test scores. Only courses from grades 10–12 are used to compute GPA. High school courses required are: 4 yrs. English, 3 yrs. math, 1 yr. lab science, 1 yr. U.S. history, 2 yrs. foreign language, 1 yr. visual and performing arts, and 3 yrs. electives. Foreign language admission requirements are waived for students with learning disabilities. Those students not meeting general entrance criteria can petition the Exceptional Admissions Committee of the Admissions Office. These students must submit a personal statement and 2 letters of recommendations, plus disclosure of their learning disability, to be eligible for special consideration. The Admissions Committee has a representative from Disabled Student Services.

**College entrance exams required:** Yes
**Course entrance requirements:** Yes
**Diagnostic tests:** Yes
**Documentation:** W-J; and/or WAIS-R; and other skills tests: within 3 years

**Untimed accepted:** Yes
**Interview required:** No

### ADDITIONAL INFORMATION

No skills courses are offered. All services and accommodations available are provided to undergraduate and graduate students. Professional tutoring is not provided by the staff of Disabled Student Services. Tutoring is accessed through other departments on campus. Books on tape are provided through RFB. Students who request the use of a calculator in an exam will need to secure permission from the professor, as well as have appropriate documentation identifying this is a necessary accommodation to compensate for the disability. Students who are transferring to San Jose State University from another campus in California do not need to provide new documentation of the learning disability.

**Special education HS coursework accepted:** Yes
**Special application required:** No
**# of applications submitted each year:** N/I
**# of students receiving LD services:** 500+

**Essay required:** No
**Submitted to:** N/A
**# of applications accepted each year:** N/I

**Acceptance into program means acceptance into college:** Students must be admitted to the university first and then may request services.

## LEARNING DISABILITY SERVICES

**Learning center:** No
**Kurzweil personal reader:** Yes
**LD specialists:** 1
**Allowed in exams:**
  **Calculator:** Y/N
  **Dictionary:** Y/N
  **Computer:** Yes
  **SpellCheck:** Yes

**Notetaker:** Yes
**Scribes:** Yes
**Proctors:** Yes
**Oral exams:** Yes
**Extended test time:** Yes
**Added cost:** None
**Distraction-free environ.:** Yes
**Tape recording in class:** Yes
**Books on tape:** Yes
**Taping of other books:** Yes

**Professional tutors:** No
**Peer tutors:** No
**Max. hrs/wk for services:**
Limited, case-by-case
**Priority registration:** Yes
**Accomodations for students with ADD:** Yes
**How are professors notified of LD:** By the student

## GENERAL ADMISSIONS INFORMATION

**Director of Admissions:** Marilyn Radisch          **Telephone:** 408-924-2012

### ENTRANCE REQUIREMENTS

Total high school units required/recommended: 15 total units are required; 4 English required, 3 math required, 1 science required, 2 foreign language required, 1 history required. Electives should include 1 unit of visual/performing arts. Minimum grade of C, eligibility index of 2800 for SAT I (694 for ACT) required of in-state applicants; minimum eligibility index of 3402 for SAT I (842 for ACT) required of out-of-state applicants. In-state applicants with minimum 3.0 GPA and out-of-state applicants with minimum 3.6 GPA are eligible regardless of test scores. Special requirements: TOEFL is required of all international students; portfolio required of graphic and interior design program applicants; interview recommended of nursing, occupational therapy, and graphic/interior design program applicants; engineering program limited to state residents.

**Application deadline:** Rolling          **SAT or ACT preferred:** Either
**Notification:** Rolling          **SAT Avg:** 372V, 466M
                                          **Average ACT:** 19

## COLLEGE GRADUATION REQUIREMENTS

**Course waivers allowed:** Yes
**Course substitutions allowed:** Yes
**In what courses:** General education quantitative reasoning substitution on case-by-case bases.

## ADDITIONAL INFORMATION

**Environment:** The university is located on 117 acres in an urban area in the center of San Jose.

**Student Body**
  **Undergrad enrollment:** 20,993
  **Women:** 51%
  **Men:** 49%
  **In-state students:** 99%
  **Out-of-state:** 1%

**Cost Information**
  **In-state tuition:** $2,017
  **Out-of-state:** $7,921
  **Room & board:** $5,786

**Housing Information**
  **University housing:** Yes
  **Fraternity:** Yes
  **Sorority:** Yes
  **Living on campus:** 5%

  **Athletics:** NCAA Div. I

# SANTA CLARA UNIVERSITY

**CA**

500 El Camino Real, Santa Clara, CA 95053 • **Admissions:** 408-554-4700 • **Fax:** 408-554-5255
**Email:** ugadmissions@scu.edu • **Web:** www.scu.edu
**Support:** S • **Institution:** 4 yr. Private

## LEARNING DISABILITY ADMISSIONS AND SERVICES

The primary mission of the Student Resource Center is to enhance academic progress, promote social involvement, and build bridges connecting the various services of the university for all students. This goal is met by providing: academic intervention programs; opportunities to increase students' personal understanding of their disability; role models; and community outreach. Disabled Student Resources is a resource area within the SRC that helps to ensure equal access to all academic and programmatic activities for students with disabilities. This goal is met through the provision of Academic Support Services, contact with other university offices, educational programming on disability issues for the university, and, most importantly, assistance in teaching students effective self-advocacy skills under the student development model.

## LEARNING DISABILITY ADMISSIONS INFORMATION

**Program Name:** Disabled Student Resources (DSR)
**Program Director:** Ramon A. Chacon, Assistant Director     **Telephone:** 408-554-4109
**Contact Person:** Same as above

### ADMISSIONS

All students submit the same general application. Santa Clara takes pride in the personal nature of its admission process. All applicants are carefully reviewed. Freshman applicants are offered admission based upon (1) high school record; (2) ACT/SAT; (3) recommendations; and (4) personal factors. Applicants submitting a non-standardized ACT/SAT are encouraged to write a personal statement to assist the admission committee in evaluating the application.

**College entrance exams required:** Yes                     **Untimed accepted:** Yes
**Course entrance requirements:** Yes                       **Interview required:** No
**Diagnostic tests:** Yes
**Documentation:** Psycho-educational evaluations administered by qualified professional

### ADDITIONAL INFORMATION

The Student Resource Center staff meets individually with student. Some of the academic accommodations provided by DSR include notetaking, library assistance, proofreading, and test accommodations. Other support services include priority registration; tutoring or academic counseling: and workshops on legal issues and self-advocacy. The SRC is in the process of purchasing computer-aided technology to assist the students. LD assessments are available on campus for a fee of $600. Graduate students with learning disabilities are offered the same services and accommodations as those provided for undergraduate students. Students can be better served if the professional documentation they submit specifically identifies the accommodations needed for the student to be successful in college. This should include the student's strengths and weaknesses and any required modifications.

**Special education HS coursework accepted:** No          **Essay required:** Yes
**Special application required:** No                        **Submitted to:** N/A
**# of applications submitted each year:** N/I             **# of applications accepted each year:** N/I
**# of students receiving LD services:** 100
**Acceptance into program means acceptance into college:** Students must be accepted to university first and then may request services.

# LEARNING DISABILITY SERVICES

**Learning center:** No
**Kurzweil personal reader:** No
**LD specialists:** No
**Allowed in exams:**
  **Calculator:** Yes
  **Dictionary:** Yes
  **Computer:** Yes
  **SpellCheck:** Yes

**Notetaker:** Yes
**Scribes:** Yes
**Proctors:** Yes
**Oral exams:** Yes
**Extended test time:** Yes
**Added cost:** None
**Distraction-free environ.:** Yes
**Tape recording in class:** Yes
**Books on tape:** Yes
**Taping of other books:** Yes

**Professional tutors:** No
**Peer tutors:** Yes
**Max. hrs/wk for services:** 1 hour per course or more if necessary
**Priority registration:** Yes
**Accomodations for students with ADD:** Yes
**How are professors notified of LD:** By the student and DSR Director

# GENERAL ADMISSIONS INFORMATION

**Director of Admissions:** Charlene Aguilar          **Telephone:** 408-554-4700

## ENTRANCE REQUIREMENTS

Sixteen total units are recommended; 4 English recommended, 3 math recommended, 1 science recommended, 3 foreign language recommended, 1 history recommended. Electives should be chosen from advanced courses in foreign language, math, lab science, or history. Special requirements: An audition is required for music program applicants; TOEFL is required of all international students.

**Application deadline:** January 15
**Notification:** Rolling

**SAT or ACT preferred:** SAT
**SAT Range:** 530–620V, 540–640M
**SAT II required:** Yes
**Average GPA:** 3.5

**Graduated top 10% of class:** 38
**Graduated top 25% of class:** 70
**Graduated top 50% of class:** 92

# COLLEGE GRADUATION REQUIREMENTS

**Course waivers allowed:** No
**Course substitutions allowed:** Yes
**In what courses:** Foreign language, math, science—all done on an individual basis

# ADDITIONAL INFORMATION

**Environment:** Located 1 hour south of San Francisco in "Silicon Valley," 3 miles from San Jose airport and 4 hours from Lake Tahoe.

**Student Body**
  **Undergrad enrollment:** 4,230
  **Women:** 53%
  **Men:** 47%
  **In-state students:** 67%
  **Out-of-state:** 33%

**Cost Information**
  **In-state tuition:** $16,455
  **Out-of-state:** $16,455
  **Room & board:** $7,026

**Housing Information**
  **University housing:** Yes
  **Fraternity:** Yes
  **Sorority:** Yes
  **Living on campus:** 43%

  **Athletics:** NCAA Div. I

# SANTA ROSA JUNIOR COLLEGE

Santa Rosa, CA 95401 • **Admissions:** 707-527-4011

**Support:** CS • **Institution:** 2 yr. Public

## LEARNING DISABILITY ADMISSIONS AND SERVICES

The Disability Resources Department provides students with disabilities equal access to a community college education through specialized instruction, disability-related support services, and advocacy activities. Santa Rosa Junior College is a state-supported school that accepts all students with learning disabilities who apply and meet the mandatory state eligibility requirements that verify their learning disability. If a student is eligible for the Program, an Individualized Educational Plan is developed and implemented. Students may participate in a combination of special and mainstream college classes with appropriate support services as needed.

## LEARNING DISABILITY ADMISSIONS INFORMATION

**Program Name:** Disability Resources
**Program Director:** Pattie Wegman
**Contact Person:** Betty Smiley

**Telephone:** 707-527-4906
**Telephone:** 707-527-4278

### ADMISSIONS

Admission to Santa Rosa is open to students with a high school diploma or a GED. There are no specific requirements for admission. Students with learning disabilities must meet state eligibility requirements verifying a learning disability to qualify to receive services. Students must demonstrate: average to above average intellectual ability, adequate measured achievement in at least one academic area or employment setting, a severe processing deficit in one or more areas, a severe discrepancy between aptitude and achievement in one or more academic areas, and adaptive behavior appropriate to a college setting. Students may also qualify on the basis of a communicative disorder and head injuries. All students must demonstrate appropriate behavior and an ability to benefit from the instructional program.

**College entrance exams required:** No
**Course entrance requirements:** No
**Diagnostic tests:** Yes
**Documentation:** W-J parts 1 & 2; WAIS-R

**Untimed accepted:** No
**Interview required:** Yes

### ADDITIONAL INFORMATION

The Learning Skills Program offers small specialized classes in the following areas for non-transferable credit: basic academic skills, guidance/independent living, sensory-motor integration, and speech and language. Support services include assessment for learning disabilities, counseling, tutoring, speech/language skills development, and liaison. Skills classes are offered in spelling, writing, math, study strategies, computers, and art process. All of these courses may be taken for college credit.

**Special education HS coursework accepted:** Y/N
**Special application required:** No
**# of applications submitted each year:** 100

**Essay required:** No
**Submitted to:** N/A
**# of applications accepted each year:** All who qualify

**# of students receiving LD services:** 350
**Acceptance into program means acceptance into college:** Students must be admitted to the college first and then may request services.

## LEARNING DISABILITY SERVICES

**Learning center:** Yes
**Kurzweil personal reader:** Yes
**LD specialists:** 3
**Allowed in exams:**
  **Calculator:** Yes
  **Dictionary:** Yes
  **Computer:** Yes
  **SpellCheck:** Yes

**Notetaker:** Yes
**Scribes:** Yes
**Proctors:** Yes
**Oral exams:** No
**Extended test time:** Yes
**Added cost:** None
**Distraction-free environ.:** Yes
**Tape recording in class:** Yes
**Books on tape:** Yes
**Taping of other books:** No

**Professional tutors:** 10
**Peer tutors:** No
**Max. hrs/wk for services:**
Decided on an individual basis
**Priority registration:** Yes
**Accomodations for students with ADD:** Yes
**How are professors notified of LD:** By the student and the LD Specialist

## GENERAL ADMISSIONS INFORMATION

**Director of Admissions:** Ricardo Navarrette          **Telephone:** 707-527-4685

### ENTRANCE REQUIREMENTS
High school diploma or GED equivalent.

**Application deadline:** None
**Notification:** NR

**SAT or ACT preferred:** Not required

## COLLEGE GRADUATION REQUIREMENTS

**Course waivers allowed:** Yes
**Course substitutions allowed:** Yes
**In what courses:** Decided on a case-by-case basis

## ADDITIONAL INFORMATION

**Environment:** The college is located on 93 acres with easy access to San Francisco.

**Student Body**
  **Undergrad enrollment:** 28,223
  **Women:** 59%
  **Men:** 41%
  **In-state students:** 98%
  **Out-of-state:** 2%

**Cost Information**
  **In-state tuition:** $315
  **Out-of-state:** $3,630

**Housing Information**
  **University housing:** Yes
  **Fraternity:** No
  **Sorority:** No
  **Living on campus:** 21.5%

  **Athletics:** Intercollegiate

# SIERRA COLLEGE

Rocklin, CA 95677 • **Admissions:** 916-624-3333

**Support:** CS • **Institution:** 2 yr. Public

## LEARNING DISABILITY ADMISSIONS AND SERVICES

The goals of the program are: to assist students with learning disabilities in reaching their academic/vocational goals, and to help the students strengthen and develop their perceptual skills; and to provide the support needed to maximize student success. Sierra College subscribes to the psychometric-evaluation model established by the California Community College System. This six-step process includes: (1) intake screening; (2) measured achievement; (3) ability level; (4) processing deficit; (5) aptitude-achievement discrepancy; and (6) eligibility recommendation. Students are evaluated individually through the Learning Disabilities Orientation course. This is a mainstreamed program with no special classes, but it does provide support and accommodations for students with learning disabilities.

## LEARNING DISABILITY ADMISSIONS INFORMATION

**Program Name:** Learning Opportunities Center
**Program Director:** Dr. James Hirschinger     **Telephone:** 916-781-0599
**Contact Person:** Denise Stone                **Telephone:** 916-789-2697

### ADMISSIONS

Sierra College has an open admissions policy for those students who meet the regular entrance requirements and who have completed testing and evaluation by a Learning Disabilities Specialist. ACT/SAT are not required, and there are no cut-offs for GPA, class rank, or test scores. Additionally, no specific courses are required for admission. Any student who holds a high school diploma or GED is admitted. Services are provided to all enrolled students with appropriate documentation.

**College entrance exams required:** No          **Untimed accepted:** N/A
**Course entrance requirements:** No            **Interview required:** No
**Diagnostic tests:** Yes
**Documentation:** WISC-R:WAIS-R: W-J: within 3 years

### ADDITIONAL INFORMATION

In order to receive services and accommodations, students must meet the eligibility requirements set forth by the state of California for students with learning disabilities. Skills courses are available in reading, math, writing, study strategies, English as a Second Language, and spelling. These skills classes are offered for college credit. In addition, students can get assistance in test-taking techniques, priority registration, and peer tutoring. Other services include: assessment and evaluation of learning disabilities; individual education plans; identification of students' learning styles and modalities; perceptual training programs; test-taking facilitation; compensatory learning strategies/techniques; computer-assisted instruction; and classroom accommodations.

**Special education HS coursework accepted:** Yes     **Essay required:** No
**Special application required:** No                  **Submitted to:** N/A
**# of applications submitted each year:** 200        **# of applications accepted each year:** N/I
**# of students receiving LD services:** 400+
**Acceptance into program means acceptance into college:** Students must be admitted to the college first and then may request services.

## LEARNING DISABILITY SERVICES

**Learning center:** Yes
**Kurzweil personal reader:** No
**LD specialists:** 3
**Allowed in exams:**
  **Calculator:** Yes
  **Dictionary:** Yes
  **Computer:** Yes
  **SpellCheck:** Yes

**Notetaker:** Yes
**Scribes:** No
**Proctors:** Yes
**Oral exams:** Yes
**Extended test time:** Yes
**Added cost:** None
**Distraction-free environ.:** Yes
**Tape recording in class:** Yes
**Books on tape:** Yes
**Taping of other books:** Yes

**Professional tutors:** No
**Peer tutors:** 100
**Max. hrs/wk for services:**
Unlimited
**Priority registration:** Yes
**Accomodations for students
with ADD:** Yes
**How are professors notified of
LD:** By the student and Program
Director

## GENERAL ADMISSIONS INFORMATION

**Director of Admissions:** Mandy Davies

**Telephone:** 916-781-0525

### ENTRANCE REQUIREMENTS
High school diploma or GED equivalent

**Application deadline:** NR
**Notification:** NR

**SAT or ACT preferred:** NR

## COLLEGE GRADUATION REQUIREMENTS

**Course waivers allowed:** Yes
**Course substitutions allowed:** Yes
**In what courses:** Waivers or substitutions are provided on an individual basis

## ADDITIONAL INFORMATION

**Environment:** The school is located on a 327-acre campus in a rural setting with easy access to Sacramento.

**Student Body**
  **Undergrad enrollment:** 15,057
  **Women:** 56%
  **Men:** 44%
  **In-state students:** 99%
  **Out-of-state:** 1%

**Cost Information**
  **In-state tuition:** $0
  **Out-of-state:** $3,120

**Housing Information**
  **University housing:** Yes
  **Fraternity:** No
  **Sorority:** No
  **Living on campus:** 1%

  **Athletics:** Intercollegiate

# SONOMA STATE UNIVERSITY

1801 East Cotati Avenue, Rohnert Park, CA 94928 • **Admissions:** 707-664-2778 • **Fax:** 707-664-4060
**Email:** admitme@sonoma.edu • **Web:** www.sonoma.edu
**Support:** CS • **Institution:** 4 yr. Public

## LEARNING DISABILITY ADMISSIONS AND SERVICES

The goal of the program is to provide accommodations and equal access to students with learning disabilities and to help them become self-advocates. Services at Sonoma State University are provided primarily through two offices on campus. The Disability Resource Center offers support services such as support groups and advocacy, and the Learning Skills Services provides diagnostic testing as well as academic support and skill development. Both offer one-to-one sessions and workshops given by specialists in various subject areas. In addition, a campus Tutorial Program offers individual peer tutoring.

## LEARNING DISABILITY ADMISSIONS INFORMATION

**Program Name:** Disability Resource Center (DRC)
**Program Director:** Anthony Tusler  **Telephone:** 707-664-2166
**Contact Person:** Bill Clopton  **Telephone:** 707-664-2677

### ADMISSIONS

Admission is based on a combination of high school GPA, test scores, and college preparatory classes. SAT/ACT score requirements depend on the GPA. However, a 2.0 GPA is the absolute minimum. Students with learning disabilities submit a general application. If a limited number of required courses are missing, students can be granted a Conditional Admission and these courses must be made up in college. Students not meeting either Regular or Conditional Admissions may initiate a request for Special Admissions by writing a letter to the DRC Director providing information about strengths and weaknesses, and why special admission is needed. LD diagnostic evaluation and 2 letters of recommendations are also required for Conditional Admission. All special admission applicants are interviewed in person or by phone. Special admission is only available to designated groups of students. The staff of DRC makes recommendations, but the final decision is made by the Office of Admission.

**College entrance exams required:** Yes  **Untimed accepted:** Yes
**Course entrance requirements:** Yes  **Interview required:** No
**Diagnostic tests:** Yes
**Documentation:** W-J and other tests: within 5 years

### ADDITIONAL INFORMATION

DRC does not offer skills classes or tutoring. Reading, writing, and math are offered through the Learning Skills Services. Tutorial assistance is available in the Tutorial Center. Services and accommodations are offered to undergraduate and graduate students.

**Special education HS coursework accepted:** Yes  **Essay required:** No
**Special application required:** Y/N  **Submitted to:** DRC for special admit
**# of applications submitted each year:** 50  **# of applications accepted each year:** 35
**# of students receiving LD services:** 250
**Acceptance into program means acceptance into college:** Students must be admitted to the university first and then may request services.

## LEARNING DISABILITY SERVICES

**Learning center:** No
**Kurzweil personal reader:** No
**LD specialists:** 1
**Allowed in exams:**
  **Calculator:** Yes
  **Dictionary:** Yes
  **Computer:** Yes
  **SpellCheck:** Yes

**Notetaker:** Yes
**Scribes:** Yes
**Proctors:** Yes
**Oral exams:** Yes
**Extended test time:** Yes
**Added cost:** None
**Distraction-free environ.:** Yes
**Tape recording in class:** Yes
**Books on tape:** Yes
**Taping of other books:** Yes

**Professional tutors:** No
**Peer tutors:** No
**Max. hrs/wk for services:** Varies
**Priority registration:** Yes
**Accomodations for students with ADD:** Yes
**How are professors notified of LD:** By the student with written verification from DRC

## GENERAL ADMISSIONS INFORMATION

**Director of Admissions:** Frank Tansy          **Telephone:** 707-664-2778

### ENTRANCE REQUIREMENTS

Total high school units required/recommended: 15 total units are required; 4 English required, 3 math required, 1 science required, 2 foreign language required, 1 history required. Electives should include 1 unit of visual/performing arts. Minimum grade of C, eligibility index of 2800 for SAT I (694 for ACT) required of in-state applicants; minimum eligibility index of 3402 for SAT I (842 for ACT) required of out-of-state applicants. Special requirements: A portfolio is required for art program applicants; an audition is required for music program applicants; an RN is required for nursing program applicants; TOEFL is required of all international students.

**Application deadline:** Nov. 30
**Notification:** January 30

**SAT or ACT preferred:** Either
**SAT Avg:** 505V, 505M
**Average GPA:** 3.3

**Graduated top 10% of class:** 24
**Graduated top 25% of class:** 53
**Graduated top 50% of class:** 89

## COLLEGE GRADUATION REQUIREMENTS

**Course waivers allowed:** No
**Course substitutions allowed:** Yes
**In what courses:** Allowed sometimes in math by petition; the university offers an alternative math class to fulfill the General Education requirements.

## ADDITIONAL INFORMATION

**Environment:** The school is located on 220 acres with easy access to San Francisco.

**Student Body**
  **Undergrad enrollment:** 5,868
  **Women:** 60%
  **Men:** 40%
  **In-state students:** 99%
  **Out-of-state:** 1%

**Cost Information**
  **In-state tuition:** $2,130
  **Out-of-state:** $8,034
  **Room & board:** $5,455

**Housing Information**
  **University housing:** Yes
  **Fraternity:** Yes
  **Sorority:** Yes
  **Living on campus:** 12%

  **Athletics:** NCAA Div. II

# UNIVERSITY OF SOUTHERN CALIFORNIA

University Park, Los Angeles, CA 90089 • **Admissions:** 213-740-1111 • **Fax:** 213-740-6208
**Web:** www.usc.edu
**Support:** CS • **Institution:** 4 yr. Private

## LEARNING DISABILITY ADMISSIONS AND SERVICES

Disability Services and Programs is responsible for delivery of service to students with learning disabilities. They offer a comprehensive support program in the areas of educational therapy, content area tutoring, study skills instruction, special exam administration, liaison with textbook taping services, advocacy, and network referral system. The learning specialists, graduate assistants, and learning assistants are available to students for academic therapy. A computer lab is available for computer-assisted learning and for word processing when working with a staff person. After admission, students with LD are counseled by advisors who dialogue with the learning specialist, and who are sensitive to special needs. Educational counseling is done by the learning specialist. Off-campus referrals are made to students desiring comprehensive diagnostic testing. The support structure for students with documented learning disabilities is one that is totally individualized. There is no 'special program' per se. Support is given at the request of the student. The Learning Disabilities Specialist and/or grad assistants at USC are prepared to act as advocates when appropriate for any student experiencing academic problems, that are related to the learning disability. USC aims to assure close, personal attention to its students even though it is a large campus.

## LEARNING DISABILITY ADMISSIONS INFORMATION

**Program Name:** Disability Services and Programs
**Program Director:** Janet Eddy, Ph.D.                    **Telephone:** 213-740-0776
**Contact Person:** Same as above

## ADMISSIONS

There are no special admissions for students with learning disabilities. Course requirements include 4 yrs. English, 3 yrs. math, 2 yrs. natural science, 2 yrs. social studies, and 4 year-long electives. Students must petition to have waivers or substitutions in any of the entrance requirements. It is helpful for comparison purposes to have both timed and untimed SAT or ACT test results. Students with LD documentation and a 3.0 GPA could have a base SAT of 830. Transfer students are admitted on the basis of their college course work. However, in some cases high school records and test scores may be requested. It is the student's responsibility to provide recent educational evaluations for documentation as part of the admissions application process. Testing must be current within 3 years, or 5 years for transfer or returning students.

**College entrance exams required:** Yes          **Untimed accepted:** Yes
**Course entrance requirements:** Yes             **Interview required:** No
**Diagnostic tests:** Yes
**Documentation:** WAIS-R; W-J; Achievement tests: within 3 years

## ADDITIONAL INFORMATION

The services provided are modifications that are determined to be appropriate for students with learning disabilities. During the first 3 weeks of each semester, students are seen on a walk-in basis by the staff in the Learning Disabilities Support Services. After that time, an appointment is necessary. Students requesting assistance must have a planning appointment with an LD specialist or grad assistant; provide a copy of the current class schedule; and be sure that eligibility has been determined by documentation of specific learning disabilities. Learning Assistance most often involves one-to-one attention for academic planning, scheduling, organization, and methods of compensation. Students may have standing appointments with learning assistants and subject tutors. After one "no-show" or 3 canceled appointments, standing appointments will be canceled. Course accommodations could include taping of lectures; notetaking; extended time for tests; use of word processor; proofreader; limiting scheduling of consecutive exams; and advocacy.

**Special education HS coursework accepted:** Yes       **Essay required:** Yes
**Special application required:** No                     **Submitted to:** N/A
**# of applications submitted each year:** N/A          **# of applications accepted each year:** N/A
**# of students receiving LD services:** 224
**Acceptance into program means acceptance into college:** No, must be accepted to the university first and then may request services.

**Learning center:** Yes
**Kurzweil personal reader:** Yes
**LD specialists:** 1
**Allowed in exams:**
  **Calculator:** Y/N
  **Dictionary:** Y/N
  **Computer:** Yes
  **SpellCheck:** Yes

**Notetaker:** Yes
**Scribes:** Yes
**Proctors:** Yes
**Oral exams:** Yes
**Extended test time:** Yes
**Added cost:** None
**Distraction-free environ.:** Yes
**Tape recording in class:** Yes
**Books on tape:** Yes
**Taping of other books:** Yes

**Professional tutors:** Yes
**Peer tutors:** 28
**Max. hrs/wk for services:** 2 hrs per class, may be extended
**Priority registration:** No
**Accomodations for students with ADD:** Yes
**How are professors notified of LD:** By the student and a letter from the Director

## GENERAL ADMISSIONS INFORMATION

**Director of Admissions:** Duncan Murdoch          **Telephone:** 213-740-8775

### ENTRANCE REQUIREMENTS

Total high school units required/recommended: 16 total units are required; 4 English required, 3 math required, 2 science required, 2 foreign language required, 2 social studies required. Special requirements: A portfolio is required for art program applicants; an audition is required for music program applicants; supplemental application required of cinema/television program applicants.

**Application deadline:** January 31
**Notification:** April 1

**SAT or ACT preferred:** Either
**SAT Avg:** 579V, 608M
**SAT II required:** Yes
**NACT Required:** No
**Average ACT:** 25
**Average GPA:** 3.6

**Graduated top 10% of class:** 43
**Graduated top 25% of class:** 72
**Graduated top 50% of class:** 93

## COLLEGE GRADUATION REQUIREMENTS

**Course waivers allowed:** Yes
**Course substitutions allowed:** Yes
**In what courses:** May petition for substitution for foreign language. LD specialist decides if appeal is valid, and writes a letter recommending course substitutions. Courses valid for substitutions include literature in translation, linguistics, classics, logic, and computer languages.

## ADDITIONAL INFORMATION

**Environment:** The university is located on 150 acres in an urban area, 2 miles south of downtown Los Angeles.

**Student Body**
  **Undergrad enrollment:** 13,716
  **Women:** 48%
  **Men:** 52%
  **In-state students:** 68%
  **Out-of-state:** 32%

**Cost Information**
  **In-state tuition:** $19,516
  **Out-of-state:** $19,516
  **Room & board:** $6,714

**Housing Information**
  **University housing:** Yes
  **Fraternity:** Yes
  **Sorority:** Yes
  **Living on campus:** 80%

  **Athletics:** NCAA Div. I

# STANFORD UNIVERSITY

Stanford, CA 94305 • **Admissions:** 415-723-2091 • **Fax:** 415-725-2846
**Email:** admissions@stanford.edu • **Web:** www.stanford.edu
**Support:** CS • **Institution:** 4 yr. Private

## LEARNING DISABILITY ADMISSIONS AND SERVICES

Since its creation in 1983, the Disability Resource Center has provided direct academic services for students with learning disabilities. It also serves as an advocacy group to assist students who encounter accessibility problems, and facilitate special arrangements for housing and campus activities. In addition to its function as a service organization, the Center is also a community center, a place where students with disabilities may come to meet, work, and socialize with one another.

## LEARNING DISABILITY ADMISSIONS INFORMATION

**Program Name:** Disability Resource Center
**Program Director:** Joan Bisagno, Ph.D.          **Telephone:** 415-723-1066
**Contact Person:** Same as above

### ADMISSIONS

Stanford seeks to enroll students with excellent academic records, who show evidence of personal achievement outside the classroom, and who have used the resources available to them to their fullest potential. The policy on the admissions of students with learning disabilities makes clear there is no separate academic program. Students should take a strong college preparatory curriculum, including honors and Advanced Placement courses. The university will look at ACT/SAT test scores in context of the learning disability. Typically, applicants to Stanford rank in the top 10% from a public high school or the top 20-30% in a private high school.

**College entrance exams required:** Yes          **Untimed accepted:** Yes
**Course entrance requirements:** Yes          **Interview required:** No
**Diagnostic tests:** Yes
**Documentation:** Psychoeducational evaluation: within 3 years

### ADDITIONAL INFORMATION

Students seeking services or accommodations for specific learning disabilities or attention deficit disorders must submit psychoeducational evaluations that are recent enough to reflect current levels of functioning. There are no skill courses offered. Tutoring is available on campus through the Center for Teaching and Learning. A peer support group is available. Services and accommodations are offered to undergraduate and graduate students.

**Special education HS coursework accepted:** No          **Essay required:** Yes
**Special application required:** No          **Submitted to:** N/A
**# of applications submitted each year:** 60          **# of applications accepted each year:** N/I
**# of students receiving LD services:** 100
**Acceptance into program means acceptance into college:** Students must be accepted to the university first and then may request services.

**Learning center:** Yes
**Kurzweil personal reader:** Yes
**LD specialists:** Yes
**Allowed in exams:**
  **Calculator:** Y/N
  **Dictionary:** Y/N
  **Computer:** Y/N
  **SpellCheck:** Yes

**Notetaker:** Yes
**Scribes:** Yes
**Proctors:** Yes
**Oral exams:** Yes
**Extended test time:** Yes
**Added cost:** None
**Distraction-free environ.:** Yes
**Tape recording in class:** Yes
**Books on tape:** Yes
**Taping of other books:** Yes

**Professional tutors:** No
**Peer tutors:** Yes
**Max. hrs/wk for services:** Limited amount of tutoring hours per week
**Priority registration:** No
**Accomodations for students with ADD:** Yes
**How are professors notified of LD:** By the student and the Program Director

## GENERAL ADMISSIONS INFORMATION

**Director of Admissions:** Dean Jim Montoya       **Telephone:** 415-723-2091

### ENTRANCE REQUIREMENTS

Solid secondary school program recommended of applicants, including strongest possible background in English, math, science, one foreign language, and social studies. Special requirements: TOEFL is required of all international students.

**Application deadline:** December 15
**Notification:** April 1

**SAT or ACT preferred:** Either
**SAT Avg:** 703V, 709M
**SAT II required:** Yes
**Average ACT:** 32

**Graduated top 10% of class:** 89
**Graduated top 25% of class:** 96

## COLLEGE GRADUATION REQUIREMENTS

**Course waivers allowed:** No
**Course substitutions allowed:** Yes
**In what courses:** Course substitutions for foreign language.

## ADDITIONAL INFORMATION

**Environment:** Stanford University is located about 30 minutes south of San Francisco.

**Student Body**
  **Undergrad enrollment:** 6,550
  **Women:** 50%
  **Men:** 50%
  **In-state students:** 51%
  **Out-of-state:** 49%

**Cost Information**
  **In-state tuition:** $20,490
  **Out-of-state:** $20,490
  **Room & board:** $7,340

**Housing Information**
  **University housing:** Yes
  **Fraternity:** Yes
  **Sorority:** No
  **Living on campus:** 93%

  **Athletics:** NCAA Div. I

# WHITTIER COLLEGE

13406 Philadelphia, Whittier, CA 90608 • **Admissions:** 562-907-4238 • **Fax:** 562-907-4870
**Email:** admission@whittier.edu • **Web:** www.whittier.edu
**Support:** S • **Institution:** 4 yr. Private

## LEARNING DISABILITY ADMISSIONS AND SERVICES

Learning Support Services is designed to assist at-risk students, including students with learning disabilities. The Director of Learning Support Services provides assistance to students with documented disabilities. Accommodation requests are made through the Director's office. Students with disabilities must make their needs known to the Director of LSS in order to receive accommodations. To arrange for services students must self-disclose the learning disability, and make an individual appointment to discuss their accommodation requests with the Director. The Learning Support Services offers peer tutoring, workshops on study skills, and basic English and math skills assistance. These services are provided at no cost.

## LEARNING DISABILITY ADMISSIONS INFORMATION

**Program Name:** Learning Support Services
**Program Director:** Gail Harris                                    **Telephone:** 310-907-4840
**Contact Person:** Same as above

### ADMISSIONS

There is no special admissions process for students with learning disabilities. All applicants are expected to meet the same admission criteria. Students must submit the ACT or SAT I and have a minimum of a 2.0 GPA; the recommended courses include 4 yrs. English, 3-4 yrs. math, 2-3 yrs. foreign language, 2-3 yrs. social studies, and 2-3 yrs. lab science. Waivers are considered on a case-by-case basis.

**College entrance exams required:** Yes                **Untimed accepted:** Yes
**Course entrance requirements:** Yes                    **Interview required:** No
**Diagnostic tests:** Yes
**Documentation:** WAIS-R, W-J-R: within 3 years

### ADDITIONAL INFORMATION

Skills courses are offered for credit in time management, test-taking strategies, text reading, and note taking. The use of calculators, dictionary, computer, or spellchecker in exams would be considered on a case-by-case basis depending on appropriate documentation and student needs. The availability of tutors is posted regularly on the Tutoring Board; if no tutor is posted in the subject needed, Learning Support Services will find a tutor for the student within one day to one week from the request date; all the tutors are professor recommended. Workshops are given on a regular basis; students may meet with a Basic Skills tutor for additional help; a Basic Skills computer lab is available to students to enhance basic English and math skills. Students with appropriate documentation will have access to notetakers, readers, extended exam time, and alternative exam locations.

**Special education HS coursework accepted:** Yes        **Essay required:** Yes
**Special application required:** Yes                    **Submitted to:** Program Director
**# of applications submitted each year:** 10-15        **# of applications accepted each year:** N/A
**# of students receiving LD services:** Approximately 30
**Acceptance into program means acceptance into college:** Students must be admitted to the college and then reviewed for LD services.

## LEARNING DISABILITY SERVICES

**Learning center:** Yes
**Kurzweil personal reader:** No
**LD specialists:** No
**Allowed in exams:**
  **Calculator:** Y/N
  **Dictionary:** Yes
  **Computer:** Yes
  **SpellCheck:** Yes

**Notetaker:** Yes
**Scribes:** Yes
**Proctors:** Yes
**Oral exams:** Yes
**Extended test time:** Yes
**Added cost:** None
**Distraction-free environ.:** Yes
**Tape recording in class:** Yes
**Books on tape:** Yes
**Taping of other books:** Yes

**Professional tutors:** No
**Peer tutors:** 40+
**Max. hrs/wk for services:** Unlimited
**Priority registration:** Y/N
**Accomodations for students with ADD:** Yes
**How are professors notified of LD:** By the student and the Program Director

## GENERAL ADMISSIONS INFORMATION

**Director of Admissions:** Douglas Locker          **Telephone:** 310-907-4238

### ENTRANCE REQUIREMENTS

Total high school units required/recommended: 17 total units are recommended; 4 English recommended, 3 math recommended, 3 science recommended, 2 foreign language recommended, 2 social studies recommended, 3 history recommended. Special requirements: TOEFL is required of all international students.

**Application deadline:** Rolling
**Notification:** Rolling

**SAT or ACT preferred:** SAT
**SAT Avg:** 536V, 528M
**SAT II required:** Yes
**Average ACT:** 22
**Average GPA:** 3

**Graduated top 10% of class:** 27
**Graduated top 25% of class:** 52
**Graduated top 50% of class:** 81

## COLLEGE GRADUATION REQUIREMENTS

**Course waivers allowed:** No
**Course substitutions allowed:** No
**In what courses:** There are no waivers or substitutions for math or foreign language.

## ADDITIONAL INFORMATION

**Environment:** NR

**Student Body**
  **Undergrad enrollment:** 1,301
  **Women:** 55%
  **Men:** 45%
  **In-state students:** 77%
  **Out-of-state:** 23%

**Cost Information**
  **In-state tuition:** $18,624
  **Out-of-state:** $18,624
  **Room & board:** $6,230

**Housing Information**
  **University housing:** Yes
  **Fraternity:** No
  **Sorority:** No
  **Living on campus:** 57%

  **Athletics:** NCAA Div. III

# UNIVERSITY OF COLORADO-BOULDER

Campus Box 30, Boulder, CO 80309 • **Admissions:** 303-492-6301
**Email:** apply@colorado.edu • **Web:** www.colorado.edu
**Support:** CS • **Institution:** 4 yr. Public

## LEARNING DISABILITY ADMISSIONS AND SERVICES

The philosophy of the Learning Disabilities Program (LDP) is one of empowering students to become independent learners. The Program centers around an interactive diagnostic-prescriptive model that utilizes "self-acknowledgment" of the learning disability as a means to assist academic and personal growth.  With this foundation, the student develops compensatory strategies and builds a network of resources. A profile of individual strengths and weaknesses is developed between the student and the diagnostician. This information enables the student to understand how learning occurs and how strategies may be developed. The students are encouraged to access other resources offered by the university community. The goal of the program is to help students be successful within this academic community and provide them with skills and tools to be productive members of society. Students are encouraged to build a network of resources including the utilization of the LD program services.

## LEARNING DISABILITY ADMISSIONS INFORMATION

**Program Name:** Learning Disabilities Program (LDP)
**Program Director:** Terri Bodhaine                     **Telephone:** 303-492-5613
**Contact Person:** Same as above

### ADMISSIONS

Initially there is no separate admissions process or criteria for students with LD. All applicants are considered under the competitive entrance requirements for the college to which they apply.  For the College of Arts and Sciences the requirements include: 4 yrs. English, 3 yrs. math, 3 yrs. natural science (must include chemistry or physics, and include 2 yrs. of lab science), 3 yrs. social science, and 3 yrs. foreign language. There are no waivers on course requirements, and all students are expected to meet the same entrance and exit requirements.  If not admissible under these criteria, applicants will then be wait-listed. After the competitive deadline of 2/15 all wait-listed applicants will be reviewed. At this time, the LD Program reviews applications from students with learning disabilities, factoring in the diagnostic information provided. The review process examines the "match" between the student's profile, entrance-exit requirements, and the program support services.

**College entrance exams required:** Yes          **Untimed accepted:** Yes
**Course entrance requirements:** Yes             **Interview required:** No
**Diagnostic tests:** Yes
**Documentation:** WAIS-R; WISC-R; WJ-R; other standardized tests: within 3 years

### ADDITIONAL INFORMATION

Services are provided through Disability Services, of which the LD Program is a component. The LDP provides limited tutorial support to eligible students. Unlimited tutorial support is available privately. Other services include advocacy and support; evening writing lab; cooperative learning seminar associated with an academic course; and individual sessions with LD specialists. Students requesting the use of a computer, spellchecker, dictionary or calculator in exams will need the permission of the professor. Lectures may be taped with the professor's permission. Priority registration is provided only if it directly responds to the disability. Support services and accommodations are available to undergraduate and graduate students. Students may seek an assessment to determine the possibility of the existence of a learning disability by paying $250. The LD Program will respond to all students with appropriate documentation who request services.

**Special education HS coursework accepted:** Yes          **Essay required:** Yes
**Special application required:** No                        **Submitted to:** N/A
**# of applications submitted each year:** N/A             **# of applications accepted each year:** N/A
**# of students receiving LD services:** 250
**Acceptance into program means acceptance into college:** Students must be admitted to the university first and then may request services.

## LEARNING DISABILITY SERVICES

**Learning center:** No
**Kurzweil personal reader:** No
**LD specialists:** 4
**Allowed in exams:**
  **Calculator:** Y/N
  **Dictionary:** Y/N
  **Computer:** Yes
  **SpellCheck:** Yes

**Notetaker:** No
**Scribes:** No
**Proctors:** Yes
**Oral exams:** No
**Extended test time:** Yes
**Added cost:** For private tutoring
**Distraction-free environ.:** Yes
**Tape recording in class:** Y/N
**Books on tape:** No
**Taping of other books:** No

**Professional tutors:** N/A
**Peer tutors:** N/A
**Max. hrs/wk for services:** Unlimited
**Priority registration:** Yes
**Accomodations for students with ADD:** Yes
**How are professors notified of LD:** By the student

## GENERAL ADMISSIONS INFORMATION

**Director of Admissions:** Gary Kelsey

**Telephone:** 303-492-6301

### ENTRANCE REQUIREMENTS

Total high school units required/recommended: 18 total units are required; 4 English required, 4 math required, 3 science required, 3 foreign language required, 3 social studies required. Special requirements: An audition is required for music program applicants; TOEFL is required of all international students; 4 units of math required of business/administration and engineering/applied science program applicants; chemistry and physics required of engineering/applied science program applicants; 3 units of foreign language and 3 units of social studies required of arts/sciences and business/administration program applicants.

**Application deadline:** February 15
**Notification:** Rolling

**SAT or ACT preferred:** Either
**SAT Range:** 450–560V, 530–650M
**ACT Range:** 22–28

**Graduated top 10% of class:** 28
**Graduated top 25% of class:** 65
**Graduated top 50% of class:** 93

## COLLEGE GRADUATION REQUIREMENTS

**Course waivers allowed:** No
**Course substitutions allowed:** No
**In what courses:** Decisions on academic requirements are within the domain of the academic deans. Decisions are made on an individualized basis. There are no waivers/substitutions for entrance to College of Arts & Science.

## ADDITIONAL INFORMATION

**Environment:** The school is located at the base of the Rocky Mountains 45 minutes from Denver.

**Student Body**
  **Undergrad enrollment:** 20,006
  **Women:** 47%
  **Men:** 53%
  **In-state students:** 65%
  **Out-of-state:** 35%

**Cost Information**
  **In-state tuition:** $2,790
  **Out-of-state:** $14,463
  **Room & board:** $4,370

**Housing Information**
  **University housing:** Yes
  **Fraternity:** Yes
  **Sorority:** Yes
  **Living on campus:** 25%

  **Athletics:** NCAA Div. I

# UNIVERSITY OF COLORADO-COLORADO SPRINGS

P.O. Box 7150, 1420 Austin Bluffs Parkway, Colorado Springs, CO 80933 • **Admissions:** 719-262-3000 •
**Fax:** 719-262-3116
**Email:** admrec@mail.uccs.edu • **Web:** www.uccs.edu
**Support:** CS • **Institution:** 4 yr. Public

## LEARNING DISABILITY ADMISSIONS AND SERVICES

University of Colorado-Colorado Springs is committed to providing equal educational opportunity for all students who meet the academic admission requirements. The purpose of Supplemental Services is to provide comprehensive support to meet the individual needs of students with disabilities.

## LEARNING DISABILITY ADMISSIONS INFORMATION

**Program Name:** Supplemental Services
**Program Director:** JoAnne Hill                    **Telephone:** 719-593-3265
**Contact Person:** Same as above

### ADMISSIONS

An applicant's learning disability is not considered in an admission decision. All applicants are required to meet the Minimum Academic Preparation Standards (MAPS), including: 4 yrs. English, 3 yrs. math (4 yrs. for engineering and business), 3 yrs. natural science, 2 yrs. social science, 2 yrs. foreign language, and 1 yr. elective; fine and performing arts are encouraged. Courses taken before 9th grade are accepted as long as the documentation provided shows that the courses were completed. Successfully completing 2 years of foreign language will satisfy the foreign language requirement regardless of whether the courses were taken before the 9th grade. Students with deficiencies may be admitted to the university provided they meet the other admission standards of test scores, rank in class, and GPA (minimum of 2.8), and provided they make up any deficiencies in the MAPS prior to graduation.

**College entrance exams required:** Yes          **Untimed accepted:** Yes
**Course entrance requirements:** Yes             **Interview required:** No
**Diagnostic tests:** Yes
**Documentation:** WAIS; W-J-R; within 3-5 yrs. depending on age of student

### ADDITIONAL INFORMATION

Students with learning disabilities receive information in their acceptance letter about contacting Supplemental Services if they wish to request accommodations or services. Courses are offered in study skills, reading, test performance, stress reduction, time management, math, science, and writing skills. Notetakers are rarely available, but supplemental services offers the use of volunteers who use carbonless paper provided by the support services. Services and accommodations are available for undergraduate and graduate students with learning disabilities.

**Special education HS coursework accepted:** No      **Essay required:** No
**Special application required:** No                 **Submitted to:** N/A
**# of applications submitted each year:** Unknown    **# of applications accepted each year:** N/A
**# of students receiving LD services:** 39
**Acceptance into program means acceptance into college:** Students must be accepted and enrolled in the university prior to requesting services.

# LEARNING DISABILITY SERVICES

**Learning center:** No
**Kurzweil personal reader:** Yes
**LD specialists:** 1
**Allowed in exams:**
  **Calculator:** Yes
  **Dictionary:** Yes
  **Computer:** Yes
  **SpellCheck:** Yes

**Notetaker:** Yes
**Scribes:** Yes
**Proctors:** Yes
**Oral exams:** Yes
**Extended test time:** Yes
**Added cost:** None
**Distraction-free environ.:** Yes
**Tape recording in class:** Yes
**Books on tape:** Yes
**Taping of other books:** Yes

**Professional tutors:** No
**Peer tutors:** 9
**Max. hrs/wk for services:** 3 hrs. per week with individual exceptions
**Priority registration:** Yes
**Accomodations for students with ADD:** Yes
**How are professors notified of LD:** By the student and the Director of support services

# GENERAL ADMISSIONS INFORMATION

**Director of Admissions:** Randall E. Kouba          **Telephone:** 719-593-3265

## ENTRANCE REQUIREMENTS
Total high school units required/recommended: 16 total units are required; 4 English required, 3 math required, 3 science required, 2 foreign language required, 2 social studies required. Minimum composite ACT score of 24 recommended. Special requirements: TOEFL is required of all international students; requirements are higher for business and engineering program applicants.

**Application deadline:** July 1
**Notification:** Rolling

**SAT or ACT preferred:** Either
**SAT Range:** 470–585V, 470–640M
**ACT Range:** 20–26
**Average GPA:** 3.3

**Graduated top 10% of class:** 15
**Graduated top 25% of class:** 40
**Graduated top 50% of class:** 79

# COLLEGE GRADUATION REQUIREMENTS

**Course waivers allowed:** No
**Course substitutions allowed:** Yes
**In what courses:** Dependent on documentation and the course of student. No waivers are provided, only substitutions.

# ADDITIONAL INFORMATION

**Environment:** NR

**Student Body**
  **Undergrad enrollment:** 4,159
  **Women:** 57%
  **Men:** 43%
  **In-state students:** 87%
  **Out-of-state:** 13%

**Cost Information**
  **In-state tuition:** $2,118
  **Out-of-state:** $8,438
  **Room & board:** $5,400

**Housing Information**
  **University housing:** Yes
  **Fraternity:** No
  **Sorority:** No
  **Living on campus:** 1%

  **Athletics:** NCAA Div. II

# UNIVERSITY OF DENVER

University Hall, Room 155, 2199 South University Boulevard, Denver, CO 80208
**Admissions:** 800-525-9495 • **Fax:** 303-871-3301
**Email:** admission@du.edu • **Web:** www.du.edu
**Support:** CS • **Institution:** 4 yr. Private

## LEARNING DISABILITY ADMISSIONS AND SERVICES

Learning Effectiveness Program (LEP) is a comprehensive program structured to provide students with individualized support. Through educational therapy and the use of academic counselors, LEP works with students one-to-one to determine their learning styles and to develop skills that will make them successful university students. Students are encouraged in three crucial areas of skill development: self-advocacy, articulation of strengths and weaknesses, and independent learning strategies. Cognitive strategy development is a basic part of individual sessions with a learning specialist. Students in LEP do not take special classes, and are expected to participate in regular course work. One important aspect of LEP involves reducing anxiety about learning in a college environment. Cognitive strategy development is a basic part of individualized sessions with the learning specialist and focuses on higher-level thought processes and planning to strengthen or compensate for lower-level processing deficits. Non-traditional study skills designed to increase reading, writing, and memory skills are taught to each student. Students are treated as responsible adults and are expected to participate willingly.

## LEARNING DISABILITY ADMISSIONS INFORMATION

**Program Name:** Learning Effectiveness Program  (LEP)
**Program Director:** Ted F. May                          **Telephone:** 303-871-4293
**Contact Person:** Moris Price                           **Telephone:** 800-525-9495

### ADMISSIONS

Admissions to the university and LEP is a process carried out by Admissions and LEP. Potential candidates with LD must submit a general admissions application, essay, recommendations, activity sheet, high school transcript, and ACT/SAT scores. Students must also provide: documentation of LD/ADHD; recent diagnostic tests; the completed LEP Intake Form provided upon disclosure of an LD; and a letter from a counselor, teacher, or LD specialist.  The recommendation from an LD specialist is critical and should describe the students' learning style and the support services necessary for success. Strengths, weaknesses, maturity level, ability to handle frustration, and feelings about limitations should also be included. Students must have at least a C+ average. A foreign language is not required, however, a successful background in college prep classes is desirable. LEP works closely with the Admissions Office to thoroughly evaluate the application. A campus visit and interview is recommended after submission of all documentation and testing. Interviews should be scheduled as far in advance as possible.

**College entrance exams required:** Yes              **Untimed accepted:** Yes
**Course entrance requirements:** Yes                **Interview required:** Recommended
**Diagnostic tests:** Yes
**Documentation:** WAIS-R ; W-J: ADHD Battery: within 3 years

### ADDITIONAL INFORMATION

LEP services are only available to students who are participating in the Program. It is highly recommended that students participate in the comprehensive Program during their first two years at DU.  However, students who feel that they need only basic accommodations and do not wish to participate in the comprehensive program should contact Disabled Person's Resources at 303-871-2278 to make those arrangements. The use of a calculator, dictionary, computer, or spellchecker require the professor's permission. Services and accommodations are, indirectly, available for undergraduate and graduate students. The University of Denver has a special summer program for high school students with learning disabilities. Learning disability assessments are available on campus for $650.

**Special education HS coursework accepted:** No        **Essay required:** Yes
**Special application required:** Yes                    **Submitted to:** assistant to the Director of LEP
**# of applications submitted each year:** 250          **# of applications accepted each year:** 50-60
**# of students receiving LD services:** 130
**Acceptance into program means acceptance into college:** Joint decision by LEP and Admissions

# LEARNING DISABILITY SERVICES

**Learning center:** Yes
**Kurzweil personal reader:** Yes
**LD specialists:** 4
**Allowed in exams:**
  **Calculator:** Y/N
  **Dictionary:** Y/N
  **Computer:** Y/N
  **SpellCheck:** Y/N

**Notetaker:** No
**Scribes:** Yes
**Proctors:** Yes
**Oral exams:** Yes
**Extended test time:** Yes
**Added cost:** $2,550 per year
**Distraction-free environ.:** Yes
**Tape recording in class:** Yes
**Books on tape:** Yes
**Taping of other books:** Yes

**Professional tutors:** 10
**Peer tutors:** Yes
**Max. hrs/wk for services:** No limit with academic counselor/ 1 hr. per wk per class for content tutoring
**Priority registration:** Yes
**Accomodations for students with ADD:** Yes
**How are professors notified of LD:** By the student

# GENERAL ADMISSIONS INFORMATION

**Director of Admissions:** Roger Campbell

**Telephone:** 303-871-2036

## ENTRANCE REQUIREMENTS

Total high school units required/recommended: 4 English recommended, 3 math recommended, 3 science recommended, 2 foreign language recommended. Minimum combined SAT I score of 850 (composite ACT score of 18), rank in top quarter of secondary school class, and minimum 2.8 GPA recommended. Special requirements: An audition is required for music program applicants. Essay required of all applicants. Portfolio recommended of art program applicants.

**Application deadline:** February 15
**Notification:** after January 1

**SAT or ACT preferred:** Either
**SAT Avg:** 544V, 554M
**Average ACT:** 24
**Average GPA:** 3.40

**Graduated top 10% of class:** 28
**Graduated top 25% of class:** 57
**Graduated top 50% of class:** 83

# COLLEGE GRADUATION REQUIREMENTS

**Course waivers allowed:** No
**Course substitutions allowed:** Yes
**In what courses:** In the area of foreign language

# ADDITIONAL INFORMATION

**Environment:** The university has a 230-acre campus 7 miles southeast of Denver.

**Student Body**
  **Undergrad enrollment:** 2,951
  **Women:** 52%
  **Men:** 48%
  **In-state students:** 41%
  **Out-of-state:** 59%

**Cost Information**
  **In-state tuition:** $17,532
  **Out-of-state:** $17,532
  **Room & board:** $5,538

**Housing Information**
  **University housing:** Yes
  **Fraternity:** Yes
  **Sorority:** Yes
  **Living on campus:** 54%

  **Athletics:** NCAA Div. II

# UNIVERSITY OF NORTHERN COLORADO

Greeley, CO 80639 • **Admissions:** 970-351-2881 • **Fax:** 970-351-1837
**Email:** qqullick@mail.unionnorthco.edu • **Web:** www.univnorthco.edu
**Support:** S • **Institution:** 4 yr. Public

## LEARNING DISABILITY ADMISSIONS AND SERVICES

Although the university does not offer a formal learning disability program, individual assistance is provided whenever possible. The office of Disability Access Center (DAC) provides access, accommodations, and advocacy for UNC students who have documented disabilities. Academic needs are determined by the documentation and a student interview. DAC provides test accommodations, adaptive hardware and software, learning strategies, organizational skills, and a reader program. Students requesting accommodations at UNC must provide test instruments that measure general intellect, aptitude, and more specific information processing tests; academic and vocational measures of achievement; and a clinical interview, which is the primary measure of previous educational and psychological functioning.

## LEARNING DISABILITY ADMISSIONS INFORMATION

**Program Name:** Disability Access Center (DAC)
**Program Director:** Nancy Kauffman
**Contact Person:** Same as above

**Telephone:** 970-351-2289

### ADMISSIONS

There is no special admission process for students with learning disabilities. All students are expected to meet the general admission requirements. These requirements include 4 yrs. English, 3 yrs. math, 2 yrs. science, 2 yrs. social sciences, and 4 yrs. electives. The Disability Access Program provides a special "window" for admitting students who do not meet UNC's freshman admission requirements but want to earn full admission into a degree program. Students wishing to participate in this program need to complete the special form and return it to the Admissions Office. Each applicant is judged on an individual basis.

**College entrance exams required:** Yes
**Course entrance requirements:** Yes
**Diagnostic tests:** Yes
**Documentation:** Diagnostic Battery administered by a certified professional: within 3 years

**Untimed accepted:** Yes
**Interview required:** Recommended

### ADDITIONAL INFORMATION

Students do not need to be learning disabled to apply for this DAC program. Students enrolled in the Directed Admission Program must take 12 hours of college credit and earn a GPA of 2.0 after one or two semesters in order to remain at UNC. Workshops are offered in student skills, organizational skills, study strategies, and time management. These workshops are electives and are not for credit. Services and accommodations are available for undergraduate and graduate students.

**Special education HS coursework accepted:** Yes
**Special application required:** No
**# of applications submitted each year:** N/A
**# of students receiving LD services:** 80-100

**Essay required:** No
**Submitted to:** N/A
**# of applications accepted each year:** N/A

**Acceptance into program means acceptance into college:** Students must be admitted to the university first and then may request services.

## LEARNING DISABILITY SERVICES

**Learning center:** Yes
**Kurzweil personal reader:** Yes
**LD specialists:** No
**Allowed in exams:**
  **Calculator:** Yes
  **Dictionary:** Yes
  **Computer:** Yes
  **SpellCheck:** Yes

**Notetaker:** Yes
**Scribes:** Yes
**Proctors:** Yes
**Oral exams:** Yes
**Extended test time:** Yes
**Added cost:** None
**Distraction-free environ.:** Yes
**Tape recording in class:** Yes
**Books on tape:** Yes
**Taping of other books:** Y/N

**Professional tutors:** No
**Peer tutors:** 20
**Max. hrs/wk for services:** Varies
**Priority registration:** Yes
**Accomodations for students with ADD:** Yes
**How are professors notified of LD:** Preferably by the student and Program Director

## GENERAL ADMISSIONS INFORMATION

**Director of Admissions:** Gary Gullickson

**Telephone:** 970-351-2881

### ENTRANCE REQUIREMENTS

Total high school units required/recommended: 15 total units are required; 4 English recommended, 3 math recommended, 2 science recommended, 2 social studies recommended. Composite ACT score of 22 (combined SAT I score of 1000R), rank in top 2/5 of secondary school class, and 2.8 GPA recommended. Special requirements: An audition is required for music program applicants; TOEFL is required of all international students.

**Application deadline:** August 15
**Notification:** Rolling

**SAT or ACT preferred:** Either
**SAT Avg:** 510V, 507M
**Average ACT:** 22
**Average GPA:** 3.2

**Graduated top 10% of class:** 11
**Graduated top 25% of class:** 34
**Graduated top 50% of class:** 74

## COLLEGE GRADUATION REQUIREMENTS

**Course waivers allowed:** No
**Course substitutions allowed:** No
**In what courses:** N/A

## ADDITIONAL INFORMATION

**Environment:** The university is located on 240 acres in a small town 50 miles north of Denver.

**Student Body**
  **Undergrad enrollment:** 8,594
  **Women:** 59%
  **Men:** 41%
  **In-state students:** 88%
  **Out-of-state:** 12%

**Cost Information**
  **In-state tuition:** $1,914
  **Out-of-state:** $8,416
  **Room & board:** $4,270

**Housing Information**
  **University housing:** Yes
  **Fraternity:** Yes
  **Sorority:** Yes
  **Living on campus:** 30%

  **Athletics:** NCAA Div. II

# REGIS UNIVERSITY

**CO**

3333 Regis Boulevard, Denver, CO 80221-1099 • **Admissions:** 303-458-4900 • **Fax:** 303-964-5534
**Email:** regisadm@regis.edu • **Web:** www.regis.edu
**Support:** SP • **Institution:** 4 yr. Private

## LEARNING DISABILITY ADMISSIONS AND SERVICES

The Freshman Commitment Program offers a specialized program for approximately 40 students who show sufficient evidence of motivation and ability to succeed in college, even though they may not have the required GPA or test scores. Recommendations from high school teachers and evidence of extracurricular activities, as well as all other information a student provides, are considered for selection of these students. The goals of the Commitment Program are to provide a means for underachieving students to enter college; to provide the support needed to be a successful learner; and to help students develop the analytical processes that lead to high achievement. Students remain in the Program for two semesters and if they are successful they are admitted into the university. To be successful, students must attend and pass all required Commitment courses with a "C" or better; cannot fall below a 1.8 GPA in non-Commitment courses; may not participate in varsity sports, forensics, or other activities that could interfere with class attendance; and must limit outside work, events, or other extracurricular activities that could impact their scholastic success.

## LEARNING DISABILITY ADMISSIONS INFORMATION

**Program Name:** Freshman Commitment Program
**Program Director:** Victoria McCabe, Ph.D.                    **Telephone:** 303-458-3572
**Contact Person:** same or Greg Miller                        **Telephone:** 303-458-4900

### ADMISSIONS

There is no special admission procedure for students with learning disabilities. Although an interview is not required, the college would prefer that the student visit the school and have a minimum GPA of C+, an SAT of 830, or ACT of 17. Students need to show sufficient evidence of motivation and ability to succeed in college, even though they may not have the required GPA or test scores. Recommendations from counselors and evidence of extracurricular activities will be used in their decision-making process. The Director of the Program is part of the admission decision for students applying to the Freshman Commitment Program.

**College entrance exams required:** Yes                 **Untimed accepted:** Yes
**Course entrance requirements:** Yes                    **Interview required:** Recommended
**Diagnostic tests:** No
**Documentation:** No preference; will accept a wide range

### ADDITIONAL INFORMATION

Students remain in the Program for the year and, with successful completion, are officially admitted to the college. They must pass all required Commitment courses with a "C" or better; not fall below a 2.0 GPA in non-Commitment coursework; and agree not to participate in varsity sports or other activities that may interfere with class attendance while involved in the Program. There are Learning Support Courses, study groups, and tutorials as needed. Two study rooms are staffed by tutors during the daytime and in the evening. All students must pass 3 hours of math, but there is a Math Learning Support Course or a Remedial Math class available for students to take prior to taking the regular college algebra class. The Program offers learning support classes in reading skills, writing skills, and study skills, which apply toward elective credit. Special advising; tutoring; diagnostic academic testing; and study and testing assistance are other services offered.

**Special education HS coursework accepted:** Yes        **Essay required:** Yes
**Special application required:** No                      **Submitted to:** N/A
**# of applications submitted each year:** 100-125       **# of applications accepted each year:** 90
**# of students receiving LD services:** 35

**Acceptance into program means acceptance into college:** Students are reviewed by Freshman Commitment and a recommendation is provided to the Admissions Committee for a final decision.

## LEARNING DISABILITY SERVICES

**Learning center:** Yes
**Kurzweil personal reader:** No
**LD specialists:** 1
**Allowed in exams:**
  **Calculator:** Y/N
  **Dictionary:** Yes
  **Computer:** Y/N
  **SpellCheck:** Yes

**Notetaker:** No
**Scribes:** No
**Proctors:** Yes
**Oral exams:** Y/N
**Extended test time:** Yes
**Added cost:** $1,350 one-time fee
**Distraction-free environ.:** Yes
**Tape recording in class:** Yes
**Books on tape:** No
**Taping of other books:** No

**Professional tutors:** 2
**Peer tutors:** 12
**Max. hrs/wk for services:**
Individual basis, as needed
**Priority registration:** Yes
**Accomodations for students with ADD:** Yes
**How are professors notified of LD:** By the student and the Program Director

## GENERAL ADMISSIONS INFORMATION

**Director of Admissions:** Penny St. John

**Telephone:** 800-388-2366 ext. 4900

### ENTRANCE REQUIREMENTS

Total high school units required/recommended: 16 total units are recommended; 4 English recommended, 2 math recommended, 2 science recommended, 2 foreign language recommended, 2 social studies recommended, 1 history recommended. Minimum 2.5 GPA recommended.

**Application deadline:** August 1
**Notification:** Rolling

**SAT or ACT preferred:** Either
**SAT Avg:** 530V, 521M
**SAT II required:** No
**Average ACT:** 22
**Average GPA:** 3.08

## COLLEGE GRADUATION REQUIREMENTS

**Course waivers allowed:** Yes/some
**Course substitutions allowed:** Yes/some
**In what courses:** All students must take 3 hours of math. Foreign culture courses are substituted for foreign language if the documentation verifies a disability.

## ADDITIONAL INFORMATION

**Environment:** The university is on a 90-acre campus in a suburban area of Denver.

**Student Body**
  **Undergrad enrollment:** 1,160
  **Women:** 56%
  **Men:** 44%
  **In-state students:** 53%
  **Out-of-state:** 47%

**Cost Information**
  **In-state tuition:** $14,900
  **Out-of-state:** $14,900
  **Room & board:** $6,100

**Housing Information**
  **University housing:** Yes
  **Fraternity:** No
  **Sorority:** No
  **Living on campus:** 48%

  **Athletics:** NCAA Div. II

CO

# UNIVERSITY OF SOUTHERN COLORADO

2200 Bonforte Boulevard, Pueblo, CO 81001 • **Admissions:** 719-549-2461 • **Fax:** 719-549-2419
**Email:** vasquez@uscolo.edu • **Web:** www.uscolo.edu
**Support:** S • **Institution:** 4 yr. Public

## LEARNING DISABILITY ADMISSIONS AND SERVICES

The Disabilities Services Office, an affiliate of the Learning Assistance Center, strives to provide optimal services to students who have disabilities to enhance learning and increase retention. Students with learning disabilities or attention deficit disorder are encouraged to submit additional documentation, as well as letters of recommendation from counselors, teachers, or special education specialists. Documentation must include a comprehensive psychological evaluation with diagnostic and description of manifestations of the disability to the learning environment with recommendations for specific accommodations.

## LEARNING DISABILITY ADMISSIONS INFORMATION

**Program Name:** Disabilities Services Office
**Program Director:** Rose M.E. Duran
**Contact Person:** Same as above

**Telephone:** 719-549-2292

### ADMISSIONS

All first-time freshmen must submit their high school transcripts with GPA and ACT/SAT scores along with the general application. There is no special admission procedure for students with disabilities, but all information submitted will be considered in making an admission decision. Twenty percent of the freshmen applicants are eligible for admission based on criteria in addition to GPA and test scores. Students who do not meet the general admission criteria should submit letters of recommendation with information describing their ability to be successful in the university curriculum. Since there are no course requirements for admission, only recommendations, waivers are not necessary.

**College entrance exams required:** Yes
**Course entrance requirements:** Recommended
**Diagnostic tests:** Yes
**Documentation:** Psychoeducational evaluations; within 3 years

**Untimed accepted:** Yes
**Interview required:** No

### ADDITIONAL INFORMATION

Skills classes are offered in notetaking strategies, study skills, and textbook reading strategies. The request for the use of a dictionary, computer, or spellchecker during exams will depend on the student's documented needs and permission from the professor. Students with specific needs are encouraged to provide documentation that specifically identifies the specific disability and the accommodations identified to compensate for the deficit. Services and accommodations are available for undergraduate and graduate students.

**Special education HS coursework accepted:** Yes
**Special application required:** No
**# of applications submitted each year:** N/A
**# of students receiving LD services:** 14
**Acceptance into program means acceptance into college:** Students must be admitted and enrolled and then may request services.

**Essay required:** No
**Submitted to:** N/A
**# of applications accepted each year:** N/A

## LEARNING DISABILITY SERVICES

**Learning center:** Yes
**Kurzweil personal reader:** Yes
**LD specialists:** No
**Allowed in exams:**
　**Calculator:** Y/N
　**Dictionary:** Y/N
　**Computer:** Y/N
　**SpellCheck:** Y/N

**Notetaker:** Yes
**Scribes:** Yes
**Proctors:** Yes
**Oral exams:** Yes
**Extended test time:** Yes
**Added cost:** No
**Distraction-free environ.:** Yes
**Tape recording in class:** Yes
**Books on tape:** Yes
**Taping of other books:** Yes

**Professional tutors:** 1
**Peer tutors:** 5
**Max. hrs/wk for services:** Unlimited
**Priority registration:** Yes
**Accomodations for students with ADD:** Yes
**How are professors notified of LD:** By the student and the Director of Support Services

## GENERAL ADMISSIONS INFORMATION

**Director of Admissions:** Christie Kangas

**Telephone:** 719-549-2292

### ENTRANCE REQUIREMENTS

Total high school units required/recommended: 15 total units are recommended; 4 English recommended, 3 math recommended, 3 science recommended, 2 foreign language recommended, 3 social studies recommended. Minimum composite ACT score of 19 (combined SAT I score of 825), rank in top half of secondary school class, and minimum 2.5 GPA recommended. Special requirements: Separate applications required of industrial engineering and nursing program applicants.

**Application deadline:** July 22
**Notification:** Rolling

**SAT or ACT preferred:** Either
**SAT Avg:** 460V, 476M
**Average ACT:** 20
**Average GPA:** 3

**Graduated top 10% of class:** 9
**Graduated top 25% of class:** 30
**Graduated top 50% of class:** 65

## COLLEGE GRADUATION REQUIREMENTS

**Course waivers allowed:** No
**Course substitutions allowed:** Yes
**In what courses:** Waivers are not allowed, but substitutions may be arranged, determined on an individual basis.

## ADDITIONAL INFORMATION

**Environment:** NR

**Student Body**
　**Undergrad enrollment:** 4,056
　**Women:** 53%
　**Men:** 47%
　**In-state students:** 89%
　**Out-of-state:** 11%

**Cost Information**
　**In-state tuition:** $2,171
　**Out-of-state:** $7,988
　**Room & board:** $4,508

**Housing Information**
　**University housing:** Yes
　**Fraternity:** Yes
　**Sorority:** No
　**Living on campus:** 10

　**Athletics:** NAIA

# BRIARWOOD COLLEGE

Southington, CT 06489 • Admissions: 860-628-4751

**Support:** S • **Institution:** 2 yr. Private

## LEARNING DISABILITY ADMISSIONS AND SERVICES

Briarwood College is a very small school and provides support as needed on a one-to-one basis between student and professor. There is no program for students with learning disabilities, rather there are services for all students with disabilities. Briarwood attempts to educate all students in the way in which they best learn, while building knowledge of and skill in handling their disabilities and while building advocacy skills. The faculty is involved in working with students to provide accommodations related to their learning disability. The Coordinator services and monitors the student's progress each semester. The Psychologist on staff interprets all documentation and provides each of the student's professors with a clear understanding of the disability and the accommodations necessary.

## LEARNING DISABILITY ADMISSIONS INFORMATION

**Program Name:** Services for Students with Disabilities
**Program Director:** N/I
**Contact Person:** Barbara Mackay, Registrar                **Telephone:** 860-628-4751 ext. 22

### ADMISSIONS

Briarwood is willing to admit any student with a learning disability and work with the student to offer support and accommodations. Admissions is 'open door,' and there are no cutoffs for GPA, class rank or test scores. If the student self-identifies as learning disabled, a meeting is arranged, prior to the start of classes, between the prospective student, Dean of Students, Academic Dean of intended major, and the Coordinator of Services (parents can attend). The purpose of this meeting is to determine if the student's program choice is wise or realistic in light of the student's learning disability.

**College entrance exams required:** No                **Untimed accepted:** Yes
**Course entrance requirements:** Yes                **Interview Required:** Recommended
**Diagnostic tests:** No, but helpful
**Documentation:** Any testing acceptable

### ADDITIONAL INFORMATION

Provisional Admittance requires students to take a 'College Survival' course and be monitored as to their academic progress. Conditional Admittance requires students to take a 'College Survival' course, be monitored, plus successfully complete an English or math course (or both) prior to admittance. Follow-up is done frequently by the Coordinator's office, and a personal record is kept on each student containing a brief description of the learning disability, positive points about the student, how they are being served at Briarwood, and how they progress each semester. In addition to accommodations made by instructors, there is a great deal of one-on-one in classes and in the Learning Resource Center, which is open to all students. Students need permission from the professor to use a calculator, computer, spellchecker, or a dictionary in an exam. There is a summer program for precollege freshmen with learning disabilities, and they may take remedial English, remedial math, and study skills.

**Special education HS coursework accepted:** Yes, if accepted for HS graduation
**Essay required:** No
**Special application required:** No                **Submitted to:** N/A
**# of applications submitted each year:** N/A      **# of applications accepted each year:** N/A
**# of students receiving LD services:** 30 approximately
**Acceptance into program means acceptance into college:** Students must be admitted to the college first and then may request services if documented.

# LEARNING DISABILITY SERVICES

**Learning center:** Yes
**Kurzweil personal reader:** No
**LD specialists:** No
**Allowed in exams:**
  **Calculator:** Yes
  **Dictionary:** Y/N
  **Computer:** Yes
  **SpellCheck:** Y/N

**Notetaker:** Yes
**Scribes:** Yes
**Proctors:** Yes
**Oral exams:** Yes
**Extended test time:** Yes
**Added cost:** None
**Distraction-free environ.:** Yes
**Tape recording in class:** Yes
**Books on tape:** Yes
**Taping of other books:** No

**Professional tutors:** Yes
**Peer tutors:** Yes
**Max. hrs/wk for services:**
Unlimited
**Priority registration:** Yes
**Accomodations for students
with ADD:** Yes
**How are professors notified of
LD:** By the student

# GENERAL ADMISSIONS INFORMATION

**Director of Admissions:** Debra LaRoche

**Telephone:** 860-628-4751

## ENTRANCE REQUIREMENTS
High school diploma or GED equivalent

**Application deadline:** NR
**Notification:** NR

**SAT or ACT preferred:** NR

# COLLEGE GRADUATION REQUIREMENTS

**Course waivers allowed:** Yes
**Course substitutions allowed:** Yes
**In what courses:** Individually assessed and determined by Program Director.

# ADDITIONAL INFORMATION

**Environment:** The college is located in a small town on 32 acres with easy access to Hartford.

**Student Body**
  **Undergrad enrollment:** 302
  **Women:** 75%
  **Men:** 25%
  **In-state students:** 95%
  **Out-of-state:** 5%

**Cost Information**
  **In-state tuition:** $8,847
  **Out-of-state:** $8,847

**Housing Information**
  **University housing:** Yes
  **Fraternity:** N/A
  **Sorority:** N/A
  **Living on campus:** 40%

  **Athletics:** Intercollegiate

# UNIVERSITY OF CONNECTICUT

Storrs, CT 06269 • **Admissions:** 860-486-3137 • **Fax:** 860-486-1476
**Email:** admiss8@uconn.edu • **Web:** www.uconn.edu
**Support:** CS • **Institution:** 4 yr. Public

## LEARNING DISABILITY ADMISSIONS AND SERVICES

The major goal of the University Program for College Students with LD (UPLD) is to assist qualified students with learning disabilities to become independent and successful learners within the regular university curriculum. The Program is designed to complement and support, but not to duplicate, the university's existing campus services and programs. Three types of program services are offered along a continuum leading to independence: (1) direct instruction in which students meet with learning specialists weekly to learn compensatory skills to strengthen learning strategies; (2) monitoring for students who need periodic contact; and (3) consultation for students wishing to consult with UPLD staff on a student-initiated basis. Most students find that it is beneficial to access services at the Direct Instruction Level, and to progress at an individual rate through the UPLD Continuum as they experience increasing confidence and competence. UPLD staff are available to help students access additional campus resources. Staff of UPLD are not qualified to serve as academic advisors. Students are fully integrated within every program at the university.

## LEARNING DISABILITY ADMISSIONS INFORMATION

**Program Name:** University Program for College Students with LD (UPLD)
**Program Director:** Joan M. McGuire, Ph.D.      **Telephone:** 860-486-0178
**Contact Person:** Same as above

### ADMISSIONS

Students are encouraged to self-identify on the general application form. This disclosure will result in a letter from the university outlining the recommended documentation that can voluntarily be submitted to UPLD. There must be clear and specific evidence and identification of a learning disability. Professionals conducting assessments and rendering diagnosis of specific learning disabilities must be qualified to do so. Reports must include names and titles of evaluators. All documentation should be received prior to the admission decision. For those students who voluntarily self-identify there is an LD admission committee to review those applications. No WRAT-R accepted. Typically the profile of the admitted student is: top third with college prep classes; or 2.5 as transfer student; 920 SAT or equivalent ACT; above average intellectual potential; and strong personal motivation for college study. If students do not meet the general criteria for admission, voluntarily submitted documentation is considered through a cooperative procedure between Admissions and UPLD.

**College entrance exams required:** Yes      **Untimed accepted:** Yes
**Course entrance requirements:** Yes      **Interview required:** No
**Diagnostic tests:** Yes
**Documentation:** WAIS-R;W-J Psychoeducational Battery-R; TOWL; TASK: current

### ADDITIONAL INFORMATION

Trained staff work with students on developing learning strategies. Individual structured sessions are planned weekly, biweekly, or monthly. Students are encouraged to plan their coursework to ensure success, which could include a reduced courseload and extending the time period for degree completion. Training in self-advocacy skills encourages students to consult directly with faculty regarding modifications and alternative testing procedures. Learning specialists assist students and identify and monitor their needs. This process culminates in the development of an individualized, comprehensive, educational plan that is cooperatively generated by the student, the Learning Specialist, and UPLD administrative staff. Other services offered include university counseling and career planning; math and writing centers; and mental health services. The Center for Students with Disabilities coordinates requests for proctors or scribes, as well as providing services to students with attention deficit disorder without a diagnosed learning disability.

**Special education HS coursework accepted:** No      **Essay required:** No
**Special application required:** No      **Submitted to:** N/A
**# of applications submitted each year:** 350+      **# of applications accepted each year:** 40-50
**# of students receiving LD services:** 160-170
**Acceptance into program means acceptance into college:** Student must be admitted to the university first and then may request services.

# LEARNING DISABILITY SERVICES

**Learning center:** Yes
**Kurzweil personal reader:** No
**LD specialists:** 5
**Allowed in exams:**
  **Calculator:** Y/N
  **Dictionary:** Y/N
  **Computer:** Y/N
  **SpellCheck:** Y/N

**Notetaker:** Yes
**Scribes:** No
**Proctors:** Yes
**Oral exams:** Yes
**Extended test time:** Yes
**Added cost:** None
**Distraction-free environ.:** Y/N
**Tape recording in class:** Yes
**Books on tape:** Yes
**Taping of other books:** Yes

**Professional tutors:** No
**Peer tutors:** No
**Max. hrs/wk for services:** 2-3 hours per week
**Priority registration:** Yes
**Accomodations for students with ADD:** Yes
**How are professors notified of LD:** By the student

# GENERAL ADMISSIONS INFORMATION

**Director of Admissions:** Dr. Ann Huckenbeck          **Telephone:** 860-486-3137

## ENTRANCE REQUIREMENTS

Total high school units required/recommended: 16 total units are required; 4 English required, 3 math required, 2 science required, 2 foreign language required, 2 social studies required. Minimum combined SAT I score of 1000 and rank in top third of secondary school class recommended of in-state applicants; minimum combined SAT I score of 1000 and rank in top quarter of secondary school class recommended of out-of-state applicants. Special requirements: TOEFL is required of all international students; audition required for music and drama program applicants.

**Application deadline:** March 1
**Notification:** Rolling

**SAT or ACT preferred:** SAT
**SAT Avg:** 553V, 559M

**Graduated top 10% of class:** 23
**Graduated top 25% of class:** 59
**Graduated top 50% of class:** 95

# COLLEGE GRADUATION REQUIREMENTS

**Course waivers allowed:** No
**Course substitutions allowed:** Yes
**In what courses:** To get substitutions in foreign language or math: Provide current documentation substantiating a severe language-based LD or dyscalculia and how it impacts on these subjects; submit case history and student statement; Committee reviews and sends recommendations to the Dean.

# ADDITIONAL INFORMATION

**Environment:** University of Connecticut is located 30 miles northeast of Hartford.

**Student Body**
  **Undergrad enrollment:** 11,336
  **Women:** 50%
  **Men:** 50%
  **In-state students:** 81%
  **Out-of-state:** 19%

**Cost Information**
  **In-state tuition:** $5,242
  **Out-of-state:** $13,760
  **Room & board:** $5,462

**Housing Information**
  **University housing:** Yes
  **Fraternity:** Yes
  **Sorority:** Yes
  **Living on campus:** 65%

  **Athletics:** NCAA Div. I

# FAIRFIELD UNIVERSITY

1073 North Benson Road, Fairfield, CT 06430 • **Admissions:** 203-254-4100 • **Fax:** 203-254-4007
**Email:** admis@fair1.fairfield.edu • **Web:** www.fairfield.edu
**Support:** CS • **Institution:** 4 yr. Private

## LEARNING DISABILITY ADMISSIONS AND SERVICES

Student Support Services offers appropriate academic accommodations to students with disabilities. Students with learning disabilities must provide documentation from an appropriate testing agent. Students are offered meetings with a professional who has a background in teaching students with disabilities. Letters are sent to professors upon students' request. Students are urged to be self-advocates.

## LEARNING DISABILITY ADMISSIONS INFORMATION

**Program Name:** Student Support Services
**Program Director:** Rev. W. Laurence O'Neil, S.J.
**Contact Person:** Linda Tribuzio

**Telephone:** 203-254-4000, ext. 2445

### ADMISSIONS

There is no special admissions process for students with learning disabilities. Admission criteria include: top 40% of graduating class or better; "B" average; 1100 SAT or 25 ACT; counselor recommendations; and college prep courses including 4 yrs. English, 3-4 yrs. math, 2-4 yrs. foreign language, 1-3 yrs. lab science, and 2-3 yrs. history. Once students have been admitted and have enrolled they may initiate a contact for services.

**College entrance exams required:** Yes
**Course entrance requirements:** Yes
**Diagnostic tests:** Yes
**Documentation:** W-J; Stanford; WAIS-R: within 3 years

**Untimed accepted:** Yes
**Interview required:** No

### ADDITIONAL INFORMATION

Skills courses are offered in study skills, notetaking strategies, time management skills, and strategies for success. These skills courses are not for credit. Services and accommodations are available for undergraduate and graduate students.

**Special education HS coursework accepted:** Yes
**Special application required:** No
**# of applications submitted each year:** N/A
**# of students receiving LD services:** 25

**Essay required:** No
**Submitted to:** N/A
**# of applications accepted each year:** N/A

**Acceptance into program means acceptance into college:** Students must be accepted to the university first and then may request services.

## LEARNING DISABILITY SERVICES

**Learning center:** No
**Kurzweil personal reader:** Yes
**LD specialists:** 1
**Allowed in exams:**
  **Calculator:** Yes
  **Dictionary:** Yes
  **Computer:** Yes
  **SpellCheck:** Yes

**Notetaker:** Yes
**Scribes:** Yes
**Proctors:** Yes
**Oral exams:** Yes
**Extended test time:** Yes
**Added cost:** None
**Distraction-free environ.:** Yes
**Tape recording in class:** Yes
**Books on tape:** Yes
**Taping of other books:** No

**Professional tutors:** No
**Peer tutors:** 80+
**Max. hrs/wk for services:** Unlimited
**Priority registration:** Yes
**Accomodations for students with ADD:** Yes
**How are professors notified of LD:** By the student and Program Director

## GENERAL ADMISSIONS INFORMATION

**Director of Admissions:** David Flynn          **Telephone:** 203-254-4100

### ENTRANCE REQUIREMENTS

Total high school units required/recommended: 17 total units are required; 3 English required, 4 English recommended, 3 math required, 2 science required, 2 foreign language required, 3 social studies required, 1 history required. Rank in top two-fifths of secondary school class recommended.

**Application deadline:** March 1
**Notification:** April 1

**SAT or ACT preferred:** SAT
**SAT Avg:** 552V, 555M
**Average ACT:** 25

**Graduated top 10% of class:** 17
**Graduated top 25% of class:** 52
**Graduated top 50% of class:** 87

## COLLEGE GRADUATION REQUIREMENTS

**Course waivers allowed:** No
**Course substitutions allowed:** Yes
**In what courses:** Typically in math or foreign language

## ADDITIONAL INFORMATION

**Environment:** The university is located on 200 acres in a suburban area 60 miles northeast of New York City.

**Student Body**
  **Undergrad enrollment:** 3,100
  **Women:** 52%
  **Men:** 48%
  **In-state students:** 30%
  **Out-of-state:** 70%

**Cost Information**
  **In-state tuition:** $17,900
  **Out-of-state:** $17,900
  **Room & board:** $7,024

**Housing Information**
  **University housing:** Yes
  **Fraternity:** No
  **Sorority:** No
  **Living on campus:** 80%

  **Athletics:** NCAA Div. I

# UNIVERSITY OF HARTFORD

200 Bloomfield Avenue, West Hartford, CT 06117 • **Admissions:** 860-768-4296 • **Fax:** 860-768-4961

**Email:** admission@uhavax.hartford.com • **Web:** www.hartford.edu

**Support:** CS • **Institution:** 2 yr. & 4 yr. Private

## LEARNING DISABILITY ADMISSIONS AND SERVICES

The Learning Plus program is a support service available to any University of Hartford student who has been diagnosed with a Learning Disability. Students who have sent their documentation to Learning Plus will be advised to contact the Director during the first week of classes. The Director will meet with each student to discuss his or her disability, appropriate services, and classroom accommodations. Students who choose to disclose their disability will meet with their professors to discuss the accommodations that will be most effective in the classroom. Students can also receive instruction at Learning Plus from masters-level professionals. Instruction is provided in time management, organization strategies, reading, writing, mathematics, and course-specific study techniques. Some students with learning disabilities choose not to avail themselves of Learning Plus Services. That is their privilege. The Director of Learning Plus maintains confidential files of all documentation, should students request services at any time during their college career.

## LEARNING DISABILITY ADMISSIONS INFORMATION

**Program Name:** Learning Plus
**Program Director:** Sharon Truex          **Telephone:** 860-768-4522
**Contact Person:** Same as above

### ADMISSIONS

Students with learning disabilities do not apply to the Learning Plus program, but do apply directly to one of the nine schools and colleges within the university. If admitted, students with learning disabilities may then elect to receive the support services offered. The Admissions Committee pays particular attention to the student's individual talents and aspirations, especially as they relate to programs available at the university. Some borderline applicants may be admitted as a summer admission. Course requirements include 4 yrs. English, 3-3.5 yrs. math, 2 yrs. science, 2 yrs. social studies, plus electives. Substitutions are allowed on rare occasions and depend on disability and major. Students may also apply to Hillyer College, which is a 2-year program with more flexible admission criteria.

**College entrance exams required:** Yes          **Untimed accepted:** Yes
**Course entrance requirements:** Yes          **Interview required:** No
**Diagnostic tests:** Yes
**Documentation:** WISC-R or WAIS-R; Achievement tests; IEP: within 3 years

### ADDITIONAL INFORMATION

Learning Plus is voluntary and students are required to seek assistance and to maintain contact. All modifications are determined on a case-by-case, course-by-course basis. The learning specialists are not content tutors. It is their goal to help students develop learning strategies and understand specific course material. Students are responsible for disclosing their LD to their professors. The university offers a 2-year program in the Hillyer College. This is a developmental program, with flexible admission standards, offering many services. Hillyer provides students with the opportunity to be in a college atmosphere and, if successful, transfer into the 4-year program. Hillyer is not necessarily for students with LD, although some students with LD are enrolled. Skills classes are offered in study skills and math, and all LD services and accommodations are available for undergraduate and graduate students.

**Special education HS coursework accepted:** Sometimes    **Essay required:** No
**Special application required:** No                        **Submitted to:** N/A
**# of applications submitted each year:** N/A              **# of applications accepted each year:** N/A
**# of students receiving LD services:** 200
**Acceptance into program means acceptance into college:** Students must be accepted to the university first and then may request services.

## LEARNING DISABILITY SERVICES

**Learning center:** Yes
**Kurzweil personal reader:** No
**LD specialists:** 1
**Allowed in exams:**
  **Calculator:** Yes
  **Dictionary:** Y/N
  **Computer:** Y/N
  **SpellCheck:** Y/N

**Notetaker:** Yes
**Scribes:** Yes
**Proctors:** Yes
**Oral exams:** Y/N
**Extended test time:** Yes
**Added cost:** None
**Distraction-free environ.:** Yes
**Tape recording in class:** Yes
**Books on tape:** No
**Taping of other books:** Yes

**Professional tutors:** 6
**Peer tutors:** No
**Max. hrs/wk for services:** 1 time per week; more with math or writing tutors as needed
**Priority registration:** No
**Accomodations for students with ADD:** Yes
**How are professors notified of LD:** By the student

## GENERAL ADMISSIONS INFORMATION

**Director of Admissions:** Richard A. Zeiser      **Telephone:** 860-768-4296

### ENTRANCE REQUIREMENTS

Total high school units required/recommended: 16 total units are recommended; 4 English recommended, 2 math recommended, 2 science recommended, 2 social studies recommended. Special requirements: A portfolio is required for art program applicants; audition is required for music program applicants; RN is required for nursing program applicants.

**Application deadline:** Rolling
**Notification:** Rolling

**SAT or ACT preferred:** SAT
**SAT Avg:** 528V, 524M
**SAT II required:** Yes
**Average ACT:** 21

**Graduated top 10% of class:** 11
**Graduated top 25% of class:** 35
**Graduated top 50% of class:** 69

## COLLEGE GRADUATION REQUIREMENTS

**Course waivers allowed:** No
**Course substitutions allowed:** Yes
**In what courses:** On rare occasions; depends on disabilities and major.

## ADDITIONAL INFORMATION

**Environment:** The university is located on a 320-acre campus in a residential section of West Hartford 90 minutes from Boston.

**Student Body**
  **Undergrad enrollment:** 5,354
  **Women:** 48%
  **Men:** 52%
  **In-state students:** 37%
  **Out-of-state:** 63%

**Cost Information**
  **In-state tuition:** $16,380
  **Out-of-state:** $16,380
  **Room & board:** $6,890

**Housing Information**
  **University housing:** Yes
  **Fraternity:** No
  **Sorority:** No
  **Living on campus:** 73%

  **Athletics:** NCAA Div. I

# MITCHELL COLLEGE

New London, CT 06320 • **Adimissions:** 800-443-2811

**CT**

**Support:** SP • **Institution:** 2 yr. Private

## LEARNING DISABILITY ADMISSIONS AND SERVICES

The Learning Resource Center offers intensive academic support for college students with learning disabilities who are accepted into the program. The primary goal of the program is to stimulate the development of learning skills and strategies that are necessary for successful and independent functioning on the college level. The program is designed for students with at least average intelligence and adequate basic skills who have taken high school classes designed for college preparation and who are adequately motivated.

## LEARNING DISABILITY ADMISSIONS INFORMATION

**Program Name:** Learning Resource Center (LRC)
**Program Director:** Joseph Madaus, Ph.D.
**Contact Person:** Same as above

**Telephone:** 860-701-5142

### ADMISSIONS

Students with identified specific learning disabilities may apply for admission through the LRC program. Students must complete an application process that includes submitting high school transcript; background information form; WAIS-R with subtest scores; LD teacher report with current achievement testing results for reading, writing, and math; and an informal writing sample sent directly to the LRC office. An interview with the LRC staff may be requested following a review of the completed application. Academic curriculum should be mainstreamed in high school. An upward trend in grades is helpful. The Director of the Learning Resource Center reviews the documentation and records and makes a recommendation to the Admissions Office. There is a required summer session for those on a probationary admission in order to demonstrate ability and motivation.

**College entrance exams required:** Yes
**Course entrance requirements:** Yes
**Diagnostic tests:** Yes
**Documentation:** WAIS-R with sub scores, achievement tests, informal writing sample: within 3 years

**Untimed accepted:** Yes
**Interview required:** Yes

### ADDITIONAL INFORMATION

During the first year students are expected to be in the LRC 4 hours weekly, 2 of these hours are with an English tutor, and 2 hours with a Learning Specialist exploring personal ways of learning. In the second year students can elect to participate full-time, part-time, or not at all. Other features of the Program include individualized learning strategies and instruction and drop-in Content Review sessions. If a student needs more than 5 hours per week of tutoring, additional hours may be accessed at the Professional Tutoring Center on campus. LRC students are expected to fulfill all degree requirements for their chosen major, and follow all requirements and procedures in the student catalog. There is a special summer program for high school students with learning disabilities.

**Special education HS coursework accepted:** Yes
**Special application required:** Yes
**# of applications submitted each year:** 300
**# of students receiving LD services:** 120

**Essay required:** Yes
**Submitted to:** Admissions
**# of applications accepted each year:** 200

**Acceptance into program means acceptance into college:** Students are reviewed by both the Program and Admissions, but the final decision is with Admissions. Once admitted students may request services.

## LEARNING DISABILITY SERVICES

**Learning center:** Yes
**Kurzweil personal reader:** No
**LD specialists:** 10
**Allowed in exams:**
  **Calculator:** No
  **Dictionary:** Yes
  **Computer:** Yes
  **SpellCheck:** Yes

**Notetaker:** Yes
**Scribes:** Yes
**Proctors:** Yes
**Oral exams:** Yes
**Extended test time:** Yes
**Added cost:** $3,952 per year
**Distraction-free environ.:** Yes
**Tape recording in class:** Yes
**Books on tape:** Yes
**Taping of other books:** No

**Professional tutors:** 8
**Peer tutors:** No
**Max. hrs/wk for services:** 5 hours per week; additional hours available at Professional Tutoring Center
**Priority registration:** Yes
**Accomodations for students with ADD:** Yes
**How are professors notified of LD:** By the student and the Program Director

## GENERAL ADMISSIONS INFORMATION

**Director of Admissions:** Arthur Forst

**Telephone:** 860-701-5037

**ENTRANCE REQUIREMENTS**
A minimum of a "C" average is required.

**Application deadline:** 3/31
**Notification:** NR

**SAT or ACT preferred:** NR

## COLLEGE GRADUATION REQUIREMENTS

**Course waivers allowed:** No
**Course substitutions allowed:** Yes
**In what courses:** There is no foreign language requirement. Substitution is allowed for math but students need to initiate request and attempt one course with accommodations. There must be documentation to substantiate the request.

## ADDITIONAL INFORMATION

**Environment:** The school is located on the banks of the Thames River approximately 1 hour from Hartford, and 1 hour from Providence, Rhode Island.

**Student Body**
  **Undergrad enrollment:** 525
  **Women:** 48%
  **Men:** 52%
  **In-state students:** 48%
  **Out-of-state:** 52%

**Cost Information**
  **In-state tuition:** $11,935
  **Out-of-state:** $11,935

**Housing Information**
  **University housing:** Yes
  **Fraternity:** No
  **Sorority:** No
  **Living on campus:** 93%

  **Athletics:** NJCAA

# SOUTHERN CONNECTICUT STATE UNIVERSITY

501 Crescent Street, New Haven, CT 06515 • **Admissions:** 203-392-5644 • **Fax:** 203-392-5727
**Email:** adminfo@scsu.ctstateu • **Web:** scwww.ctstateu.edu
**Support:** CS • **Institution:** 4 yr. Public

## LEARNING DISABILITY ADMISSIONS AND SERVICES

The purpose of the Disability Resource Office is to ensure educational equity for students with disabilities. The Office works to provide access to full participation in all aspects of campus life. The Office assists students in arranging for individualized accommodations and support services. The Office is a resource to students, faculty, and the university at large. Use of the Disability Resource Office services is voluntary and confidential. The Disability Resource Office provides academic, career, and personal support for all university students with disabilities, including students with specific learning disabilities and attention-deficit disorders. The Disability Resource Office is a component of Student Supportive Services.

## LEARNING DISABILITY ADMISSIONS INFORMATION

**Program Name:** Disability Resource Office (DRO)
**Program Director:** Suzanne Tucker
**Contact Person:** Above and Debbie Fairchild

**Telephone:** 203-392-6828

### ADMISSIONS

There is no special admissions process for students with learning disabilities. All applicants must meet the same criteria. Conditional Admission is considered and based on the following: WAIS scores and subscores, achievement tests, SAT/ACT scores, and transcript. Applicants who wish DRO to be involved in the admission decision, should note "disability" on the application, which goes to Admissions. They should also submit current psychoeducational testing information to DRO.

**College entrance exams required:** Yes
**Course entrance requirements:** Yes
**Diagnostic tests:** Yes
**Documentation:** Psychoeducational testing given by professional; within 3 years

**Untimed accepted:** Yes
**Interview required:** No

### ADDITIONAL INFORMATION

The DRO assists students in arranging for individualized accommodations and support services. Services are available to both prospective and current students as follows: prospective students should attend one of the several workshops offered each fall for prospective students and their parents seeking information regarding the program and should obtain an application to the university. Current students should make an appointment with the office and bring educational documentation including achievement testing and psychoeducational evaluation or medical documentation. Services include course selection and registration; course and testing accommodations; support from Learning Specialists in developing time management and study skills, in identifying strengths and weaknesses, and in acquiring compensatory strategies; liaison with faculty and university departments; and advocacy and self-advocacy information and training. Services and accommodations are available for undergraduate and graduate students.

**Special education HS coursework accepted:** N/I
**Special application required:** No
**# of applications submitted each year:** N/A
**# of students receiving LD services:** 400

**Essay required:** Yes
**Submitted to:** N/A
**# of applications accepted each year:** N/A

**Acceptance into program means acceptance into college:** Student must be admitted to the university first and then may request services.

## LEARNING DISABILITY SERVICES

**Learning center:** Yes
**Kurzweil personal reader:** Yes
**LD specialists:** 3
**Allowed in exams:**
  **Calculator:** Yes
  **Dictionary:** Yes
  **Computer:** Yes
  **SpellCheck:** Yes

**Notetaker:** Yes
**Scribes:** Yes
**Proctors:** Yes
**Oral exams:** Yes
**Extended test time:** Yes
**Added cost:** None
**Distraction-free environ.:** Yes
**Tape recording in class:** Yes
**Books on tape:** Yes
**Taping of other books:** Yes

**Professional tutors:** No
**Peer tutors:** Yes
**Max. hrs/wk for services:**
Usually 1/2 hr. per week
**Priority registration:** Y/N
**Accomodations for students
with ADD:** Yes
**How are professors notified of
LD:** By the student

## GENERAL ADMISSIONS INFORMATION

**Director of Admissions:** Sharon Brennan          **Telephone:** 203-392-6161

### ENTRANCE REQUIREMENTS

Total high school units required/recommended: 17 total units are required; 4 English required, 3 math required, 2 science required, 2 foreign language required, 2 social studies required, 1 history required. Minimum combined SAT I score of 800 required; 900 recommended. Special requirements: TOEFL is required of all international students.

**Application deadline:** Rolling
**Notification:** Rolling after
December 1

**SAT or ACT preferred:** Either
**SAT Avg:** 466V, 451M

**Graduated top 10% of class:** 3
**Graduated top 25% of class:** 19
**Graduated top 50% of class:** 53

## COLLEGE GRADUATION REQUIREMENTS

**Course waivers allowed:** Yes
**Course substitutions allowed:** Yes
**In what courses:** Foreign language

## ADDITIONAL INFORMATION

**Environment:** The university is located on 168 acres in an urban area 35 miles south of Hartford, and 90 miles from New York City.

**Student Body**
  **Undergrad enrollment:** 7,568
  **Women:** 55%
  **Men:** 45%
  **In-state students:** 93%
  **Out-of-state:** 7%

**Cost Information**
  **In-state tuition:** $2,062
  **Out-of-state:** $6,674
  **Room & board:** $5,566

**Housing Information**
  **University housing:** Yes
  **Fraternity:** Yes
  **Sorority:** Yes
  **Living on campus:** 32%

  **Athletics:** NCAA Div. II

# WESTERN CONNECTICUT STATE UNIVERSITY

181 White Street, Danbury, CT 06810 • **Admissions:** 203-837-9000
**Email:** qubon@wcsu.ctstateu.edu • **Web:** wcsu.ctstateu.edu/homepage.html
**Support:** CS • **Institution:** 4 yr. Public

## LEARNING DISABILITY ADMISSIONS AND SERVICES

Two primary purposes of Disabled Student Services are to provide the educational development of disabled students, and to improve understanding and support in the campus environment. Students with learning disabilities will be assisted in receiving the services necessary to achieve their goals.

## LEARNING DISABILITY ADMISSIONS INFORMATION

**Program Name:** Students with Disabilities Services
**Program Director:** Helen Kreuger                    **Telephone:** 203-837-9252
**Contact Person:** Same as above

### ADMISSIONS

Students with learning disabilities submit the general application form. No alternative admission policies are offered. Students should have a 2.5 GPA (C+ or better) and the average SAT is 894. (ACT may be substituted). Students are encouraged to self-disclose their disability on the application, and submit documentation to be used after admission to determine services and accommodations.

**College entrance exams required:** Yes                    **Untimed accepted:** Yes
**Course entrance requirements:** Yes                      **Interview required:** Recommended
**Diagnostic tests:** Yes
**Documentation:** Psychoeducational evaluation; within 3 years

### ADDITIONAL INFORMATION

Services include priority registration, tutoring, testing accommodations, and advocacy and counseling. The university does not offers any skills classes. The university offers a special summer program for precollege freshmen with learning disabilities. Services and accommodations are available for undergraduate and graduate students.

**Special education HS coursework accepted:** Yes          **Essay required:** No
**Special application required:** No                       **Submitted to:** N/A
**# of applications submitted each year:** N/A             **# of applications accepted each year:** N/A
**# of students receiving LD services:** 70
**Acceptance into program means acceptance into college:** Student must be admitted to the university first and then may request services.

# LEARNING DISABILITY SERVICES

**Learning center:** No
**Kurzweil personal reader:** No
**LD specialists:** 1
**Allowed in exams:**
  **Calculator:** Yes
  **Dictionary:** No
  **Computer:** Y/N
  **SpellCheck:** Y/N

**Notetaker:** Yes
**Scribes:** Yes
**Proctors:** Yes
**Oral exams:** Yes
**Extended test time:** Yes
**Added cost:** $2 per hr. for peer tutor
**Distraction-free environ.:** Yes
**Tape recording in class:** Yes
**Books on tape:** Yes
**Taping of other books:** Yes

**Professional tutors:** 1
**Peer tutors:** Varies
**Max. hrs/wk for services:** As needed
**Priority registration:** Y/N
**Accomodations for students with ADD:** Yes
**How are professors notified of LD:** By the student and the Disability Specialist

# GENERAL ADMISSIONS INFORMATION

**Director of Admissions:** Delmore Kinney

**Telephone:** 203-837-9000

## ENTRANCE REQUIREMENTS

Total high school units required/recommended: 16 total units are required; 4 English required, 3 math required, 4 math recommended, 2 science required, 2 foreign language required, 2 social studies required, 1 history required. Minimum combined SAT I score of 900, rank in top half of secondary school class, and minimum 2.5 GPA required. Special requirements: An audition is required for music program applicants.

**Application deadline:** April 1
**Notification:** Rolling

**SAT or ACT preferred:** SAT

**Graduated top 10% of class:** 7
**Graduated top 25% of class:** 23
**Graduated top 50% of class:** 65

# COLLEGE GRADUATION REQUIREMENTS

**Course waivers allowed:** Yes
**Course substitutions allowed:** Yes
**In what courses:** As required by the student's disability

# ADDITIONAL INFORMATION

**Environment:** The university is located on 315 acres, 60 miles from New York City.

**Student Body**
  **Undergrad enrollment:** 4,679
  **Women:** 51%
  **Men:** 49%
  **In-state students:** 87%
  **Out-of-state:** 13%

**Cost Information**
  **In-state tuition:** $2,012
  **Out-of-state:** $6,510
  **Room & board:** $4,496

**Housing Information**
  **University housing:** Yes
  **Fraternity:** No
  **Sorority:** No
  **Living on campus:** 31%

  **Athletics:** NCAA Div. III

# UNIVERSITY OF DELAWARE

U.S.P.S. 077580, Newark, DE 19716 • **Admissions:** 302-831-8123 • **Fax:** 302-831-6905
**Email:** admissions@.udel.edu • **Web:** www.udel.edu
**Support:** CS • **Institution:** 4 yr. Public

## LEARNING DISABILITY ADMISSIONS AND SERVICES

The University of Delaware is committed to providing reasonable and timely academic accommodations for students with disabilities. The Academic Services Center focuses primarily on serving students with learning disabilities. ASC is not a program but rather a Center that provides services and accommodations to help students. The Center works jointly with other units. The staff has been trained to understand learning disabilities and is available to assist faculty, one-on-one, in providing accommodations for students. Students with learning disabilities who are independent and able to self-advocate will be the most successful on campus. Students who are concerned about learning problems or who are seeking academic accommodations must first complete an educational consultation. The purpose of the consultation is to decide if additional educational testing is necessary or to verify a previously diagnosed learning disability. Once identified students are eligible for services and ample assistance is available.

## LEARNING DISABILITY ADMISSIONS INFORMATION

**Program Name:** Academic Services Center
**Program Director:** David Johns
**Contact Person:** Ruth Smith

**Telephone:** 302-831-8167
**Telephone:** 302-831-1639

### ADMISSIONS

Students must be 'otherwise qualified' for university admissions, which means they must meet university and college admissions criteria with untimed SAT scores counted as the equivalent of regular or standard administered SAT scores. Students are encouraged to self-disclose and occasionally IQ test scores can offset a lower ACT/SAT score. A good place to disclose is on the essay portion of the application. Delaware residents not meeting standard admission requirement may request an alternative admit through 'summer qualifier.'

**College entrance exams required:** Yes
**Course entrance requirements:** Yes
**Diagnostic tests:** Yes
**Documentation:** WAIS-R; WRAT-R; W-J-R: within 3 years

**Untimed accepted:** Yes
**Interview required:** Recommended

### ADDITIONAL INFORMATION

Skills courses are offered in Academic Self-Management and Study Skills and Critical Thinking. ASC offers a remedial course in reading, writing, and spelling, which also serves as a support group for students with LD. The Math Center offers a remedial Math course and the English Department offers a writing course. There is also a writing center where students can receive feedback on their essays. Students have access to pre-admission information; individualized needs assessment; priority registration; consultation and advocacy; and referrals for other services. Students with ADD are provided joint counseling between ASC and the counseling center.

**Special education HS coursework accepted:** Y/N
**Special application required:** No
**# of applications submitted each year:** N/A
**# of students receiving LD services:** 450

**Essay required:** No
**Submitted to:** N/A
**# of applications accepted each year:** N/A

**Acceptance into program means acceptance into college:** Students must be admitted to the university first and then may request LD services.

# LEARNING DISABILITY SERVICES

**Learning center:** No
**Kurzweil personal reader:** No
**LD specialists:** Yes
**Allowed in exams:**
  **Calculator:** Yes
  **Dictionary:** Yes
  **Computer:** N/I
  **SpellCheck:** Yes

**Notetaker:** Yes
**Scribes:** Yes
**Proctors:** Yes
**Oral exams:** Y/N
**Extended test time:** Yes
**Added cost:** Based on individual financial need
**Distraction-free environ.:** Yes
**Tape recording in class:** Yes
**Books on tape:** Yes
**Taping of other books:** No

**Professional tutors:** No
**Peer tutors:** 40
**Max. hrs/wk for services:** Varies: students make appointments
**Priority registration:** Yes
**Accomodations for students with ADD:** Yes
**How are professors notified of LD:** By the student and Program Director

# GENERAL ADMISSIONS INFORMATION

**Director of Admissions:** N. Bruce Walker          **Telephone:** 302-831-1209

## ENTRANCE REQUIREMENTS

Total high school units required/recommended: Sixteen total units are required; 24 total units are recommended; 4 English required, 4 English recommended, 2 math required, 4 math recommended, 2 science required, 4 science recommended, 2 foreign language required, 4 foreign language recommended, 1 social studies required, 3 social studies recommended, 2 history required, 2 history recommended. Special requirements: TOEFL is required of all international students.

**Application deadline:** March 1
**Notification:** Rolling

**SAT or ACT preferred:** SAT
**SAT Range:** 530–620V, 540–630M
**Average GPA:** 3.2

**Graduated top 10% of class:** 22
**Graduated top 25% of class:** 55
**Graduated top 50% of class:** 91

# COLLEGE GRADUATION REQUIREMENTS

**Course waivers allowed:** No
**Course substitutions allowed:** Yes
**In what courses:** Foreign language; The Educational Affairs Committee of the College of Arts and Sciences makes decisions on a case-by-case basis. Students are asked to attempt the class and work closely with a tutor before submitting a petition for a substitution.

# ADDITIONAL INFORMATION

**Environment:** The 1,100-acre campus is in a small town 12 miles southwest of Wilmington and mid-way between Philadelphia and Baltimore.

**Student Body**
  **Undergrad enrollment:** 14,829
  **Women:** 58%
  **Men:** 42%
  **In-state students:** 42%
  **Out-of-state:** 58%

**Cost Information**
  **In-state tuition:** $3,990
  **Out-of-state:** $11,250
  **Room & board:** $4,590

**Housing Information**
  **University housing:** Yes
  **Fraternity:** Yes
  **Sorority:** Yes
  **Living on campus:** 53%

  **Athletics:** NCAA Div. I

# AMERICAN UNIVERSITY

4400 Massachusetts Avenue, NW, Washington, DC 20016 • **Admissions:** 202-885-1000
**Fax:** 202-885-6014
**Email:** mheer@american.edu • **Web:** www.american.edu
**Support:** CS • **Institution:** 4 yr. Private

## LEARNING DISABILITY ADMISSIONS AND SERVICES

Respect for individual differences is the cornerstone of services for students with learning disabilities. The goal of American University's Support Service is to facilitate the expression of students' strengths by providing the support needed for students to achieve. The support services are coordinated by the Center for Psychological and Learning Services. This is a one-year program for freshmen, and after the first year, a staff person is available for providing basic skills tutorial sessions. Enrollment in the Learning Services Program will not guarantee success, but it will give students the support and help to gain confidence. The Center (CPLS) offers an array of support services that facilitate students' academic and personal achievements.

## LEARNING DISABILITY ADMISSIONS INFORMATION

**Program Name:** Learning Services Program
**Program Director:** Helen Steinberg          **Telephone:** 202-885-3360
**Contact Person:** Same as above

### ADMISSIONS

Students with LD must be admitted to the university and then to the Learning Services Program. Students who wish to have program staff consult with Admissions about their LD during the admissions process must submit a Supplemental Application to the Learning Services Program that requires documentation of the LD. Students using a 'Common Application' should indicate interest in the Program on their application. Special education courses taken in high school may be accepted if they meet the criteria for the Carnegie Units. The academic credentials of successful applicants with LD fall within the range of regular admissions criteria; the mean GPA is 2.9 for LD admits and 3.2 for regularly admitted students; ACT ranges from 24-28 or SAT 1100-1270. The admission decision is made by a special admissions committee and is based on the high school record, recommendations, and all pertinent diagnostic reports. For selected students, admission to the university will be contingent upon enrollment in the Program; for others, the Learning Services Program will be optional though strongly recommended.

**College entrance exams required:** Yes          **Untimed accepted:** Yes
**Course entrance requirements:** Yes          **Interview required:** Recommended
**Diagnostic tests:** Yes
**Documentation:** Psychoeducational evaluation; WAIS-R; WISC-R: within 3 years

### ADDITIONAL INFORMATION

Students have an academic advisor experienced in advising students with LD. All entering freshmen have the same requirements including College Writing (a section is reserved for students in the Program) and College Reading. Students meet weekly with a learning specialist for individual tutorial sessions that help them further develop college-level reading, writing, and study strategies. Peer tutors assist with course content tutoring. Individual and group counseling is offered through Psychological Services. The staff of the Program will speak with professors with students' written permission. All modifications are based upon diagnostic testing and educational recommendations and students are held to the same academic standards but may meet these standards through non-traditional means. As sophomores, basic skills tutorial sessions are offered on an 'as needed' basis.

**Special education HS coursework accepted:** Yes, if it meets college prep standards
**Essay required:** Yes
**Special application required:** Yes          **Submitted to:** Learning Services Program
**# of applications submitted each year:** 170          **# of applications accepted each year:** 50
**# of students receiving LD services:** N/I
**Acceptance into program means acceptance into college:** Students must be admitted to the university first and then may request services.

**Learning center:** Yes
**Kurzweil personal reader:** Yes
**LD specialists:** 5
**Allowed in exams:**
  **Calculator:** Y/N
  **Dictionary:** Y/N
  **Computer:** Y/N
  **SpellCheck:** Y/N

**Notetaker:** No
**Scribes:** Yes
**Proctors:** Yes
**Oral exams:** Y/N
**Extended test time:** Yes
**Added cost:** $1,000 per semester
**Distraction-free environ.:** Yes
**Tape recording in class:** Yes
**Books on tape:** No
**Taping of other books:** RFB

**Professional tutors:** Yes
**Peer tutors:** Yes
**Max. hrs/wk for services:** Varies
**Priority registration:** Yes
**Accomodations for students with ADD:** Yes
**How are professors notified of LD:** By the student and the Program Director

## GENERAL ADMISSIONS INFORMATION

**Director of Admissions:** Marcelle Heerschap

**Telephone:** 202-885-6000

### ENTRANCE REQUIREMENTS
Total high school units required/recommended: 15 total units are required; 4 English required, 3 math required, 3 science required, 2 foreign language required, 2 social studies recommended.

**Application deadline:** February 1
**Notification:** April 1

**SAT or ACT preferred:** SAT
**SAT Avg:** 604V, 579M
**SAT II required:** Yes
**Average ACT:** 26
**Average GPA:** 3.2

**Graduated top 10% of class:** 30
**Graduated top 25% of class:** 72
**Graduated top 50% of class:** 94

## COLLEGE GRADUATION REQUIREMENTS

**Course waivers allowed:** No
**Course substitutions allowed:** Yes
**In what courses:** Foreign language on a case-by-case basis; math department does not offer waivers/course substitutions. A special section of finite math is offered for students with learning disabilities. This section meets 3 rather than 2 days a week and has a professor and a math tutor who are familiar with learning disabilities.

## ADDITIONAL INFORMATION

**Environment:** The university is located on 77 acres close to the nation's Capital.

**Student Body**
  **Undergrad enrollment:** 5,433
  **Women:** 59%
  **Men:** 41%
  **In-state students:** 5%
  **Out-of-state:** 95%

**Cost Information**
  **In-state tuition:** $18,300
  **Out-of-state:** $18,300
  **Room & board:** $7,350

**Housing Information**
  **University housing:** Yes
  **Fraternity:** No
  **Sorority:** No
  **Living on campus:** 60%

  **Athletics:** NCAA Div. I

# THE CATHOLIC UNIVERSITY OF AMERICA

Cardinal Station, Washington, DC 20064 • **Admissions:** 202-319-5305 • **Fax:** 202-319-6533
**Email:** cua-admissions@cua.edu • **Web:** www.cua.edu
**Support:** CS • **Institution:** 4 yr. Private

## LEARNING DISABILITY ADMISSIONS AND SERVICES

The university has an Advisory Committee on Students with Learning Disabilities that is composed of faculty members and administrators with expertise in a variety of specialized areas. The committee assists students with any learning disability that might preclude their full participation in university academic activities. The Office of Multicultural and Special Services is not a program for students with learning disabilities. However, a specially designated 'Support Service' team, which includes an LD consultant, provides assistance and advocacy to students with learning disabilities based on individual needs and learning differences. The goals of the services are to facilitate academic success, support personal growth, and encourage self-advocacy. Students with LD are required to meet the same academic standards as other students at the university. If a documented disability will affect the way in which an otherwise academically qualified student completes course and/or degree requirements, the student is entitled to a reasonable procedural modification in the methods by which requirements must be met. The cognizant dean has the right to waive requirements that prevent students from successfully completing required coursework.

## LEARNING DISABILITY ADMISSIONS INFORMATION

**Program Name:** Multicultural and Special Services
**Program Director:** Lorraine I. Krusa            **Telephone:** 202-319-5618
**Contact Person:** Bonnie McClellan

### ADMISSIONS

Applicants will be notified through existing admissions material of optional procedures to be followed in identifying themselves as learning disabled. These optional procedures are intended to enhance the applicants's opportunity for admission to the university and will not be used to discriminate against the individual. If an otherwise intellectually qualified applicant feels that there are weaknesses in admissions material due to a pre-existing learning disability and voluntarily informs the Office of Admissions, the application will be referred to a Special Admissions Committee for review. The review process will be used to provide a fuller assessment of the total student than regular admissions material might provide. In addition to the regular university admission requirements, the following criteria will be utilized for consideration under special admissions: diagnostic reports certifying the LD and ability to do college work; 3 teacher evaluations from the most recent teachers of math, English and one other subject; a supervised writing sample on a topic of the applicant's choice; and an interview.

**College entrance exams required:** Yes          **Untimed accepted:** Yes
**Course entrance requirements:** Yes        **Interview required:** Yes
**Diagnostic tests:** Yes
**Documentation:** WAIS-R; ach. battery of reading comp., written language, math; within 3 years

### ADDITIONAL INFORMATION

Students with a learning disability that impairs the ability to acquire a foreign language may submit scores from the Modern Language Aptitude Test for possible waiver of the university's foreign language requirement. The decision to grant a waiver is based on an individual's learning history, documentation of a disability that impairs foreign language acquisition, and future educational goals. Services include advocacy, advising and referral to tutoring or study skills, faculty consultation and support, assistance in arranging notetakers and recorded texts, support and positive feedback, tape recording, extended time on tests, and reasonable extension of deadlines on written papers.

**Special education HS coursework accepted:** No      **Essay required:** Yes
**Special application required:** No               **Submitted to:** N/A
**# of applications submitted each year:** N/A     **# of applications accepted each year:** N/A
**# of students receiving LD services:** 125
**Acceptance into program means acceptance into college:** Students must be admitted to the university first and then may request services.

# LEARNING DISABILITY SERVICES

**Learning center:** Yes
**Kurzweil personal reader:** Yes
**LD specialists:** 1
**Allowed in exams:**
  **Calculator:** N/I
  **Dictionary:** N/I
  **Computer:** Yes
  **SpellCheck:** N/I

**Notetaker:** Yes
**Scribes:** Yes
**Proctors:** Yes
**Oral exams:** Yes
**Extended test time:** Yes
**Added cost:** None
**Distraction-free environ.:** Yes
**Tape recording in class:** Yes
**Books on tape:** Yes
**Taping of other books:** Yes

**Professional tutors:** No
**Peer tutors:** 40
**Max. hrs/wk for services:** As available
**Priority registration:** Yes
**Accomodations for students with ADD:** Yes
**How are professors notified of LD:** By the student and the Advisor

# GENERAL ADMISSIONS INFORMATION

**Director of Admissions:** Kate Lafrance          **Telephone:** 202-319-5615

## ENTRANCE REQUIREMENTS

Total high school units required/recommended: 17 total units are required; 21 total units are recommended; 4 English required, 3 math required, 4 math recommended, 3 science required, 4 science recommended, 2 foreign language required, 4 social studies required. Special requirements: An audition is required for music program applicants; biology, chemistry, language, math, and social science are required of nursing program applicants.

**Application deadline:** Rolling
**Notification:** Rolling

**SAT or ACT preferred:** Either
**SAT Range:** 550–660V, 520–640M
**ACT Range:** 24–28

**Graduated top 10% of class:** 40
**Graduated top 25% of class:** 63
**Graduated top 50% of class:** 90

# COLLEGE GRADUATION REQUIREMENTS

**Course waivers allowed:** No
**Course substitutions allowed:** Yes
**In what courses:** In foreign language

# ADDITIONAL INFORMATION

**Environment:** The university is situated in northeast DC within minutes of the Capitol.

**Student Body**
  **Undergrad enrollment:** 2,380
  **Women:** 53%
  **Men:** 47%
  **In-state students:** 3%
  **Out-of-state:** 97%

**Cost Information**
  **In-state tuition:** $16,500
  **Out-of-state:** $16,500
  **Room & board:** $7,036

**Housing Information**
  **University housing:** Yes
  **Fraternity:** No
  **Sorority:** No
  **Living on campus:** 55%

  **Athletics:** NCAA Div. III

# GEORGE WASHINGTON UNIVERSITY

2121 I Street, NW, Washington, DC 20052 • **Admissions:** 202-994-6040 • **Fax:** 202-994-0325
**Email:** gwadm@gwis2.circ.gwu.edu • **Web:** www.gwu.edu
**Support:** CS • **Institution:** 4 yr. Private

## LEARNING DISABILITY ADMISSIONS AND SERVICES

Disability Support Services (DSS) was established to provide support to disabled students so that they might participate fully in university life, derive the greatest benefit from their educational experiences, and achieve maximum personal success. Services are designed to eliminate competitive disadvantages in an academic environment while preserving academic integrity. The staff is committed to providing student-centered services that meet the individual needs of each student. The ultimate goal of DSS is to assist students with disabilities as they gain knowledge to recognize strengths, accommodate differences, and become strong self-advocates. Staff are available to discuss issues such as course load, learning strategies, academic accommodations, and petitions for course waivers or substitutions. DSS offers individual assistance in addressing needs not provided through routine services. Students with LD must provide documentation, including a comprehensive diagnostic interview, psychoeducational evaluation, and a treatment plan; the report should include test scores and an interpretation of overall intelligence, information processing, executive functioning, spatial ability, memory, motor ability, achievement skills, reading, writing, and math, and a specific diagnosis and description of the student's functional limitations in an educational setting.

## LEARNING DISABILITY ADMISSIONS INFORMATION

**Program Name:** Disability Support Services
**Program Director:** Christy Willis
**Contact Person:** Stefanie Coale

**Telephone:** 202-994-8250
**Telephone:** 202-994-6590

### ADMISSIONS

GW does not discriminate on the basis of handicap in the recruitment and admission of students. There are no separate admissions procedures or criteria for disabled students. The minimal course requirements include 2 yrs. math (prefer 4), 4 yrs. English, 2 yrs. foreign language (prefer 4), 2-3 yrs. social sciences (prefer 4), and 2-3 yrs. science (prefer 4). The score range for the ACT is 25-30 or SAT 1160-1320. The SAT II is optional. Since there is no automatic referral from Admissions or other campus offices, students are encouraged to contact DSS directly prior to or upon admission.

**College entrance exams required:** Yes
**Course entrance requirements:** Yes
**Diagnostic tests:** Recommended
**Documentation:** WAIS-R; neuropsychological or psychoeducational evaluation: within 3 years

**Untimed accepted:** Yes
**Interview required:** No

### ADDITIONAL INFORMATION

Students need to make a specific request for services or accommodations. Based upon the documentation, the Director of DSS authorizes the needed academic adjustments. DSS provides services without charge, including advocacy, readers, scribes, test proctors, LD advising, and assistance with registration and notetaking. Students may be referred for additional services, including diagnostic testing, tutors, and specialized non-credit courses that are available on a fee basis. There is a learning disabilities support group that meets twice monthly throughout the academic year. This group focuses on issues important to students with LD and/or ADD. In addition to providing an opportunity for peer support, the group discusses topics ranging from study strategies, notetaking, and the planning of papers, to social issues facing the GW student with LD/ADD. GW alumni offer a Mentorship Program to help GW students learn to overcome the obstacles presented by their disabilities and to succeed at the university and professionally.

**Special education HS coursework accepted:** Yes
**Special application required:** No
**# of applications submitted each year:** N/A
**# of students receiving LD services:** 220

**Essay required:** Yes
**Submitted to:** N/A
**# of applications accepted each year:** N/A

**Acceptance into program means acceptance into college:** Students must be accepted by the university first and then reviewed for services with Disability Support Services.

**Learning center:** No
**Kurzweil personal reader:** Yes
**LD specialists:** 1
**Allowed in exams:**
 **Calculator:** Yes
 **Dictionary:** Yes
 **Computer:** Yes
 **SpellCheck:** Yes

**Notetaker:** No
**Scribes:** Yes
**Proctors:** Yes
**Oral exams:** Y/N
**Extended test time:** Yes
**Added cost:** None
**Distraction-free environ.:** Yes
**Tape recording in class:** Yes
**Books on tape:** RFB
**Taping of other books:** No

**Professional tutors:** N/I
**Peer tutors:** Yes
**Max. hrs/wk for services:** Unlimited
**Priority registration:** Yes
**Accomodations for students with ADD:** Yes
**How are professors notified of LD:** By the student and the Program Director

# GENERAL ADMISSIONS INFORMATION

**Director of Admissions:** Frederic Siegal          **Telephone:** 1-800-447-3765

## ENTRANCE REQUIREMENTS
Total high school units required/recommended: 16 total units are required; 4 English required, 2 math required, 2 science required, 2 foreign language required, 1 social studies required, 1 history required. Special requirements: An audition is required for music program applicants; TOEFL is required of all international students; 4 units of math (2 algebra, 1 plane geometry, 1/2 plane trigonometry, 1/2 precalculus), 1 unit of physics, and 1 unit of chemistry required of engineering program applicants.

**Application deadline:** December 1
**Notification:** March 15

**SAT or ACT preferred:** Either
**SAT Range:** 560–660V, 550–650M
**SAT II required:** Yes
**ACT Range:** 24–29

**Graduated top 10% of class:** 41
**Graduated top 25% of class:** 78
**Graduated top 50% of class:** 97

# COLLEGE GRADUATION REQUIREMENTS

**Course waivers allowed:** Yes
**Course substitutions allowed:** Yes
**In what courses:** The decision to grant a waiver or substitution is up to the Dean of the particular college. DSS can only give recommendations, and all decisions are done on a case-by-case basis.

# ADDITIONAL INFORMATION

**Environment:** NR

**Student Body**
 **Undergrad enrollment:** 6,581
 **Women:** 55%
 **Men:** 45%
 **In-state students:** 9%
 **Out-of-state:** 91%

**Cost Information**
 **In-state tuition:** $19,065
 **Out-of-state:** $19,065
 **Room & board:** $6,910

**Housing Information**
 **University housing:** Yes
 **Fraternity:** Yes
 **Sorority:** No
 **Living on campus:** 54%

 **Athletics:** NCAA Div. I

# GEORGETOWN UNIVERSITY

37th and O Streets, NW, Washington, DC 20057 • **Admissions:** 202-687-3600 • **Fax:** 202-687-5084
**Email:** guadmiss@gunet.georgetown.edu • **Web:** www.georgetown.edu
**Support:** CS • **Institution:** 4 yr. Private

## LEARNING DISABILITY ADMISSIONS AND SERVICES

Georgetown University will not discriminate against or deny access to any otherwise qualified handicapped student. Learning Services requires that all students with learning disabilities provide documentation. Once the disability is on record the university will provide reasonable accommodations. Learning Services will advise students about their college course work. With student permission Learning Services will provide faculty members with an information sheet listing strengths and weaknesses that characterize the student's learning abilities and disabilities.

## LEARNING DISABILITY ADMISSIONS INFORMATION

**Program Name:** Learning Services
**Program Director:** Dr. Norma Jo Eitington      **Telephone:** 202-687-6985
**Contact Person:** Same as above

### ADMISSIONS

Students with learning disabilities are admitted under the same competitive standards used for all students. Students are encouraged to self-disclose their disability and send documentation to the Learning Center. Services are offered to enrolled students.

**College entrance exams required:** Yes          **Untimed accepted:** Yes
**Course entrance requirements:** Yes             **Interview required:** No
**Diagnostic tests:** Yes
**Documentation:** Psychoeducational evaluation: within 3 years

### ADDITIONAL INFORMATION

Students may take courses in effective reading, study skills, time management, notetaking, testing strategies, and stress management. Some of the services offered include diagnostic testing, quiet study rooms, study skills training, and support groups. All entering students take the Nelson Denny Reading Test to determine their ability in comprehension and vocabulary.

**Special education HS coursework accepted:** No      **Essay required:** Yes
**Special application required:** No                 **Submitted to:** N/A
**# of applications submitted each year:** N/A       **# of applications accepted each year:** N/A
**# of students receiving LD services:** 110
**Acceptance into program means acceptance into college:** Students must be admitted to the university first and then may request services.

**Learning center:** Yes
**Kurzweil personal reader:** Yes
**LD specialists:** 1
**Allowed in exams:**
  **Calculator:** Yes
  **Dictionary:** Y/N
  **Computer:** Yes
  **SpellCheck:** Yes

**Notetaker:** Yes
**Scribes:** N/I
**Proctors:** N/I
**Oral exams:** Yes
**Extended test time:** Yes
**Added cost:** No
**Distraction-free environ.:** Yes
**Tape recording in class:** Yes
**Books on tape:** Yes
**Taping of other books:** Yes

**Professional tutors:** No
**Peer tutors:** Yes
**Max. hrs/wk for services:**
Tutorial referrals
**Priority registration:** Yes
**Accomodations for students
with ADD:** Yes
**How are professors notified of
LD:** By the student and Program
Director

## GENERAL ADMISSIONS INFORMATION

**Director of Admissions:** Charles Deacon          **Telephone:** 202-687-3600

### ENTRANCE REQUIREMENTS

Total high school units required/recommended: 4 English recommended, 3 math recommended, 2 science recommended, 2 foreign language recommended, 2 social studies recommended. Special requirements: TOEFL is required of all international students; 4 units of math and 3 units of science required of math and science program applicants; chemistry, biology, and physics required of nursing program applicants; language background required of foreign service and language program applicants.

**Application deadline:** January 10
**Notification:** April 1

**SAT or ACT preferred:** Either
**SAT Range:** 620–720V, 610–710M
**SAT II required:** Yes
**ACT Range:** 26–31

**Graduated top 10% of class:** 79
**Graduated top 25% of class:** 92
**Graduated top 50% of class:** 99

## COLLEGE GRADUATION REQUIREMENTS

**Course waivers allowed:** No
**Course substitutions allowed:** Yes
**In what courses:** Foreign language can be substituted if not required for major

## ADDITIONAL INFORMATION

**Environment:** The college is located on 110 acres 1 1/2 miles north of downtown Washington, D.C.

**Student Body**
  **Undergrad enrollment:** 6,338
  **Women:** 52%
  **Men:** 48%
  **In-state students:** 2%
  **Out-of-state:** 98%

**Cost Information**
  **In-state tuition:** $21,216
  **Out-of-state:** $21,216
  **Room & board:** $8,091

**Housing Information**
  **University housing:** Yes
  **Fraternity:** No
  **Sorority:** No
  **Living on campus:** 80%

  **Athletics:** NCAA Div. I

# BEACON COLLEGE

Leesburg, FL 34748 • **Admissions:** 352-787-7660

**Support:** SP • **Institution:** 4 yr. Private

## LEARNING DISABILITY ADMISSIONS AND SERVICES

Beacon College offers students with LD a unique opportunity to achieve their goals and pursue a collegiate degree. The college offers academic programs supplemented by appropriate accommodations and tutorial support services that help students prepare for a meaningful role in society. The college believes that individuals learn at different rates and in different ways and that it is the college's responsibility to discover and use the educational techniques best suited to the student. The college provides AA and BA in Human Services and General Studies. The Human Services programs are designed to stimulate the students' interest in intellectual, philosophical, social, and public issues. The General Studies Program provides a well-rounded liberal arts education or the opportunity to pursue a concentration addressing student's interest or career goals. The program's strength lies in the small student-teacher ratios and its support services. Daily study labs concentrate on development of study and organization skills, as well as test-taking strategies. Support groups are provided to foster interpersonal growth, social problem solving, self-advocacy, and time management skills. Beacon students consider themselves non-traditional learners who can benefit from the flexible, student-centered teaching style that Beacon College offers throughout the curriculum.

## LEARNING DISABILITY ADMISSIONS INFORMATION

**Program Name:** Beacon College
**Program Director:** Deborah Brodbeck, Ph.D.          **Telephone:** 352-787-7660
**Contact Person:** Debora Townley

### ADMISSIONS

Applicants must submit current academic reports and test scores, recent psychoeducational evaluations documenting a learning disability, and records that may help clarify presenting learning problems. Students must also submit a high school transcript, personal statements, and 3 recommendations. All applicants must have a high school diploma or the GED. Each applicant must have an interview prior to an admission decision being made. Provisional acceptance is available to students requiring remedial work in reading and writing. There are no specific high school courses required for admission, and courses taken in a special education curriculum are accepted. The college does not require either the ACT or SAT. The admission decision is made by the Director of Admission and the Program Director.

**College entrance exams required:** No                 **Untimed accepted:** Yes
**Course entrance requirements:** No                   **Interview required:** Yes
**Diagnostic tests:** Yes
**Documentation:** Psychoeducational evaluations; WAIS-R; within 2 years

### ADDITIONAL INFORMATION

Class size averages 7 students so faculty can identify and address individual strengths and weaknesses. Tutorials concentrate on the process of learning, and students take a proactive role in their learning, and are mentored to be responsible and self-reliant. The tutorial staff use a learning-process oriented approach to facilitate skill development. Individual Sessions help with study and time management skills  and personal attention to increase self-esteem and academic success. Content-specific Small Group Sessions help develop collaborative learning; reinforce problem-solving strategies; and model effective study or notetaking skills. Open Lab Sessions allow for independent work on homework, papers, or special projects; and provide access to tutors for academic support. The Field Placement Program is used for practical application of course work; the Residential Life Program assists with social problem solving skills, self-advocacy, developing self-confidence, and improving time management and organizational abilities.

**Special education HS coursework accepted:** Yes      **Essay required:** Yes
**Special application required:** No                   **Submitted to:** N/A
**# of applications submitted each year:** N/A         **# of applications accepted each year:** N/A
**# of students receiving LD services:** All
**Acceptance into program means acceptance into college:** Students are admitted directly into the College and the Program simultaneously.

# LEARNING DISABILITY SERVICES

**Learning center:** Yes
**Kurzweil personal reader:** Yes
**LD specialists:** 4
**Allowed in exams:**
  **Calculator:** Yes
  **Dictionary:** Yes
  **Computer:** Yes
  **SpellCheck:** Yes

**Notetaker:** Yes
**Scribes:** Yes
**Proctors:** Yes
**Oral exams:** Yes
**Extended test time:** Yes
**Added cost:** Part of the total tuition
**Distraction-free environ.:** Yes
**Tape recording in class:** Yes
**Books on tape:** Yes
**Taping of other books:** N/I

**Professional tutors:** 6
**Peer tutors:** N/A
**Max. hrs/wk for services:** Unlimited
**Priority registration:** Yes
**Accomodations for students with ADD:** Yes
**How are professors notified of LD:** Training orientation

# GENERAL ADMISSIONS INFORMATION

**Director of Admissions:** Debora Townley          **Telephone:** 352-787-7660

## ENTRANCE REQUIREMENTS
High school diploma with general education requirements.

**Application deadline:** NR          **SAT or ACT preferred:** NR
**Notification:** NR

# COLLEGE GRADUATION REQUIREMENTS

**Course Waivers Allowed:** N/A
**Course Substitutions Allowed:** N/A
**In what courses:** The college meets the individual needs of all students

# ADDITIONAL INFORMATION

**Environment:** The college is located in the city of Leesburg 1 hour from Orlando.

**Student Body**
  **Undergrad enrollment:** 45
  **Women:** 50%
  **Men:** 50%
  **In-state students:** 9%
  **Out-of-state:** 91%

**Cost Information**
  **In-state tuition:** $18,000
  **Out-of-state:** $18,000

**Housing Information**
  **University housing:** Yes
  **Fraternity:** No
  **Sorority:** No
  **Living on campus:** 100%
  **Athletics:** NR

# FLORIDA A&M UNIVERSITY

Suite 112, Foote-Hilyer Administration Center, Tallahassee, FL 32307 • **Admissions:** 904-599-3796
**Fax:** 904-561-2428
**Email:** bcox@nsi.famu.edu • **Web:** www.famu.edu
**Support:** CS • **Institution:** 4 yr. Public

## LEARNING DISABILITY ADMISSIONS AND SERVICES

Florida A&M offers an education for students with LD and meets the challenge consistent with the objective indicated by the LDEC club name, "Excellence Through Caring." The goals of the LDEC are threefold: first, students with specific learning disabilities can successfully pursue college level studies with a reasonable level of expectation for degree success; second, preparation for college level studies for students with specific learning disabilities should begin early, and third, postsecondary students should actively engage in developmental learning. The need for life-long learning is evident in the ever-changing society and for the learning disabled person is mandatory for continued success. Tutoring for developmental learning is a major component. The Program does not offer 'blanket' accommodations, but services offered are very comprehensive, such as preparation classes for tests, adapted courses, opportunities for test retakes, alternative courses, and academic activities structured according to students' diagnostic evaluation. A reduced course load is considered a viable option to maintaining an acceptable GPA. The LDEC is a multifaceted program providing psychoeducational evaluation, personalized prescription, and comprehensive support services.

## LEARNING DISABILITY ADMISSIONS INFORMATION

**Program Name:** Learning Development and Evaluation Center (LDEC)
**Program Director:** Dr. Sharon M. Wooten          **Telephone:** 904-599-8474
**Contact Person:** Dr. William Hudson/Mrs. Gwen McGee          **Telephone:** 904-599-3180

### ADMISSIONS

Acceptance into the LDEC does not ensure admission to the university. If students with learning disabilities apply and are rejected, they may ask for 'special admission' consideration and send verifying information of a learning disability. The Office of Admissions gives all information to the LDEC Director for a recommendation for admission to the university based upon acceptance into the LDEC program. Applicants must have a high school diploma, take the ACT/SAT, have a recent psychoeducational evaluation, and if admitted, agree to attend a summer program. Most students who have learning disabilities and who seek admission through the LDEC enter Florida A&M through the special admission process. ACT scores should be 12 or higher. The required GPA is 1.7 or above.

**College entrance exams required:** Yes          **Untimed accepted:** Yes
**Course entrance requirements:** Yes          **Interview required:** Recommended
**Diagnostic tests:** Yes
**Documentation:** W-J: WRAT; TOWL: within 3 years

### ADDITIONAL INFORMATION

Specific course offerings in reading, study skills, English, and math with additional class meetings and assignments to meet the individual needs of the students are available. Students must register for reading and student life skills courses each semester until the student and program staff feel that optimal learning development skills have been reached. When appropriate, students may have a peer tutor attend classes and take notes (student and tutor will exchange notes in the LDEC) or the peer tutor may only need to help the student organize notes from a taped lecture. LDEC offers a two-week Summer Transition Program (required for incoming students with LD) to students entering 11th or 12th grade or recent graduates from high school. This Program provides students a chance to focus on certain skills such as memory, technology, or a particular academic area. Mastery of the College Study Skills Institute provides a firm foundation for students with learning disabilities to enhance success in college and their future employment.

**Special education HS coursework accepted:** Y/N          **Essay required:** Yes
**Special application required:** Yes          **Submitted to:** Director of Program
**# of applications submitted each year:** 40-60          **# of applications accepted each year:** 20-25
**# of students receiving LD services:** 123
**Acceptance into program means acceptance into college:** Students are admitted directly into LDEC and attend the summer LD program as part of special admissions to the university.

## LEARNING DISABILITY SERVICES

**Learning center:** Yes
**Kurzweil personal reader:** Yes
**LD specialists:** 3
**Allowed in exams:**
  **Calculator:** Yes
  **Dictionary:** Yes
  **Computer:** Yes
  **SpellCheck:** Yes

**Notetaker:** Yes
**Scribes:** Yes
**Proctors:** Yes
**Oral exams:** Yes
**Extended test time:** Yes
**Added cost:** None
**Distraction-free environ.:** No
**Tape recording in class:** Yes
**Books on tape:** Yes
**Taping of other books:** Yes

**Professional tutors:** Yes
**Peer tutors:** Yes
**Max. hrs/wk for services:** Varies
**Priority registration:** No
**Accomodations for students with ADD:** Yes
**How are professors notified of LD:** By the student and the Program Director

## GENERAL ADMISSIONS INFORMATION

**Director of Admissions:** Barbara Cox          **Telephone:** 904-599-3796

### ENTRANCE REQUIREMENTS

Total high school units required/recommended: 19 total units are required; 4 English required, 3 math required, 3 science required, 2 foreign language required, 3 social studies required. Minimum combined SAT I score of 1010 (composite ACT score of 21) and minimum 2.5 GPA required. Special requirements: TOEFL is required of all international students.

**Application deadline:** May 9
**Notification:** Rolling

**SAT or ACT preferred:** Either
**Average ACT:** 20
**Average GPA:** 3.15

**Graduated top 25% of class:** 40
**Graduated top 50% of class:** 40

## COLLEGE GRADUATION REQUIREMENTS

**Course waivers allowed:** Yes
**Course substitutions allowed:** Yes
**In what courses:** Varies; it depends on the major elective requirements and the disability of the individual

## ADDITIONAL INFORMATION

**Environment:** The university is located on 419 acres 169 miles west of Jackson.

**Student Body**
  **Undergrad enrollment:** 9,877
  **Women:** 58%
  **Men:** 42%
  **In-state students:** 77%
  **Out-of-state:** 23%

**Cost Information**
  **In-state tuition:** $1,981
  **Out-of-state:** $7,898
  **Room & board:** $3,281

**Housing Information**
  **University housing:** Yes
  **Fraternity:** No
  **Sorority:** No
  **Living on campus:** 30%

  **Athletics:** NCAA Div. I

# FLORIDA ATLANTIC UNIVERSITY

P.O. Box 3091, Boca Raton, FL 33431 • **Admissions:** 561-367-3040 • **Fax:** 561-367-2758
**Email:** admisweb@acc.fau.edu • **Web:** www.fau.edu
**Support:** CS • **Institution:** 4 yr. Public

## LEARNING DISABILITY ADMISSIONS AND SERVICES

The Disabled Student Services offers equal access to a quality education by providing reasonable accommodations to qualified students. Students who have a documented learning disability may receive strategy tutoring from the LD Specialist by appointment. Students are expected to be self-sufficient and strong self-advocates. There is a Counseling Center with professionally trained staff to help students with interpersonal conflicts and concerns, test anxiety, poor concentration, and guidance services.

## LEARNING DISABILITY ADMISSIONS INFORMATION

**Program Name:** Office for Students with Disabilities (OSD)
**Program Director:** Beverly Warde                      **Telephone:** 561-367-3880
**Contact Person:** Same as above

### ADMISSIONS

There is no special application process for students with learning disabilities. However, students with learning disabilities may be eligible to substitute for certain admission requirements. Students not meeting admission criteria may be admitted by a faculty admission committee, if they possess the potential to succeed in university studies or will enhance the university. Supporting documentation explaining circumstances that adversely affected the student's past academic performances will be required. An admissions counselor will assess each applicant in developing supporting materials to be presented to the committee by the Director of Admissions. Students are expected to have a minimum ACT of 20 or SAT of 860. A sliding scale is used with GPA and test scores. Students who self-disclose and are admitted are than reviewed for Services. In some cases these students are reviewed by the OSD, which provides a recommendation to admissions.

| | |
|---|---|
| **College entrance exams required:** Yes | **Untimed accepted:** Yes |
| **Course entrance requirements:** Yes | **Interview required:** No |
| **Diagnostic tests:** Yes | |

**Documentation:** WAIS-R; Academic achievements; processing tests: within 3 years

### ADDITIONAL INFORMATION

The WISC-R may not be substituted for the WAIS-R. Students requesting special consideration may be referred to the committee through faculty/staff recommendations to the Director of Admissions or through a written request to the Director from the applicant. The students should self-disclose and provide current documentation. These files are reviewed by the Director of LD services and a recommendation is given to the Office of Admissions. The final decision is made by the Admissions Office.

| | |
|---|---|
| **Special education HS coursework accepted:** No | **Essay required:** Yes |
| **Special application required:** No | **Submitted to:** N/A |
| **# of applications submitted each year:** N/A | **# of applications accepted each year:** N/A |
| **# of students receiving LD services:** 110 | |

**Acceptance into program means acceptance into college:** Students must be accepted to the university first (can appeal a denial) and then may request services.

## LEARNING DISABILITY SERVICES

**Learning center:** No
**Kurzweil personal reader:** Yes
**LD specialists:** 2
**Allowed in exams:**
  **Calculator:** Y/N
  **Dictionary:** Yes
  **Computer:** Yes
  **SpellCheck:** Yes

**Notetaker:** Yes
**Scribes:** Yes
**Proctors:** Yes
**Oral exams:** Y/N
**Extended test time:** Yes
**Added cost:** None
**Distraction-free environ.:** Yes
**Tape recording in class:** Yes
**Books on tape:**
**Taping of other books:** Y/N

**Professional tutors:** N/I
**Peer tutors:** N/I
**Max. hrs/wk for services:**
Determined at the first meeting
**Priority registration:** No
**Accomodations for students
with ADD:** Yes
**How are professors notified of
LD:** By the student and a letter
from OSD

## GENERAL ADMISSIONS INFORMATION

**Director of Admissions:** Richard Griffin          **Telephone:** 561-367-3040

### ENTRANCE REQUIREMENTS
Total high school units required/recommended: 19 total units are required; 4 English required, 3 math required, 3 science required, 2 foreign language required, 3 social studies required. Minimum combined SAT I score of 900 and minimum 2.5 GPA recommended. Special requirements: An audition is required for music program applicants; TOEFL is required of all international students.

**Application deadline:** July 1
**Notification:** Rolling

**SAT or ACT preferred:** Either
**SAT Avg:** 523V, 531M
**Average ACT:** 21
**Average GPA:** 3.46

## COLLEGE GRADUATION REQUIREMENTS

**Course waivers allowed:** No
**Course substitutions allowed:** Yes
**In what courses:** Individually determined

## ADDITIONAL INFORMATION

**Environment:** The university is located on 1,000 acres 1 1/2 miles from the ocean and in proximity to Miami and Ft. Lauderdale.

**Student Body**
  **Undergrad enrollment:** 15,995
  **Women:** 59%
  **Men:** 41%
  **In-state students:** 92%
  **Out-of-state:** 8%

**Cost Information**
  **In-state tuition:** $2,080
  **Out-of-state:** $7,850
  **Room & board:** $4,680

**Housing Information**
  **University housing:** Yes
  **Fraternity:** No
  **Sorority:** No
  **Living on campus:** 8%

  **Athletics:** NCAA Div. II

# UNIVERSITY OF FLORIDA

Undergraduate Admissions, 201 Criser Hall, Gainesville, FL 32611 • **Admissions:** 352-392-1365
**Email:** spritz@nw.mail.ufl.edu • **Web:** www.ufsa.ufl.edu/sfa/sfa.html
**Support:** S • **Institution:** 4 yr. Public

## LEARNING DISABILITY ADMISSIONS AND SERVICES

The University of Florida offers a full range of support services designed to assist students with learning disabilities. Support services are individually tailored to each student's needs and those supports may be modified to meet the specific demands and requirements of individual courses. Advisement and support services are available to students on an as-needed basis. Assistance can be provided regarding registration, learning strategies, classroom accommodations, and the University of Florida petition process.

## LEARNING DISABILITY ADMISSIONS INFORMATION

**Program Name:** Office for Students with Disabilities
**Program Director:** James Costello
**Contact Person:** Same as above

**Telephone:** 352-392-1260

### ADMISSIONS

The student with learning disabilities applies to the university under the same guidelines as all other students. However, students with learning disabilities may request a separate review. Students should check #27 on the general application to request information and submit a personal statement describing how their learning disabilities may have had an impact or an effect on their grade point average or standardized test scores if applicable. The required SAT or ACT varies according to the student's GPA. Students denied admission may petition for a review of their application. This review process petition should be directed to the Director of the Office of Student Services.

**College entrance exams required:** Yes
**Course entrance requirements:** Yes
**Diagnostic tests:** Yes
**Documentation:** WAIS-R; WISC-R; W-J-R; psychoeducational evaluation: within 3 years

**Untimed accepted:** Yes
**Interview required:** Recommended

### ADDITIONAL INFORMATION

Skills workshops are offered in reading, notetaking, memory, and time management. OSS sponsors 'Preview,' an early registration and orientation program. Assistance can be provided regarding learning strategies, classroom accommodations, and petitions. Services are available to focus on strategic learning strategies and success strategies.

**Special education HS coursework accepted:** Yes
**Special application required:** No
**# of applications submitted each year:** N/A
**# of students receiving LD services:** 101

**Essay required:** To explain learning disability
**Submitted to:** N/A
**# of applications accepted each year:** N/A

**Acceptance into program means acceptance into college:** Students must be admitted to the university first (can appeal a denial) and then may request services.

## LEARNING DISABILITY SERVICES

**Learning center:** No
**Kurzweil personal reader:** Yes
**LD specialists:** No
**Allowed in exams:**
  **Calculator:** Yes
  **Dictionary:** Yes
  **Computer:** Yes
  **SpellCheck:** Yes

**Notetaker:** Yes
**Scribes:** Yes
**Proctors:** Yes
**Oral exams:** Yes
**Extended test time:** Yes
**Added cost:** None
**Distraction-free environ.:** No
**Tape recording in class:** Yes
**Books on tape:** Yes
**Taping of other books:** Yes

**Professional tutors:** Yes
**Peer tutors:** Yes
**Max. hrs/wk for services:** NR
**Priority registration:** Yes
**Accomodations for students with ADD:** Yes
**How are professors notified of LD:** By the student and Program Director

## GENERAL ADMISSIONS INFORMATION

**Director of Admissions:** William Kolb

**Telephone:** 352-392-1365

### ENTRANCE REQUIREMENTS

Total high school units required/recommended: 15 total units are required; 4 English required, 3 math required, 3 science required, 2 foreign language required, 3 social studies required. Minimum combined SAT I score of 970 (composite ACT score of 20) and minimum 2.0 GPA required. Special requirements: A portfolio is required for art program applicants; an audition is required for theatre and music program applicants.

**Application deadline:** February 1
**Notification:** March 24

**SAT or ACT preferred:** SAT
**SAT Range:** 560–670V, 580–680M
**ACT Required:** No
**ACT Range:** 25–29
**Average GPA:** 3.85

**Graduated top 10% of class:** 54
**Graduated top 25% of class:** 85
**Graduated top 50% of class:** 97

## COLLEGE GRADUATION REQUIREMENTS

**Course waivers allowed:** Yes
**Course substitutions allowed:** Yes
**In what courses:** Foreign language and math; individually decided on a case-by-case basis

## ADDITIONAL INFORMATION

**Environment:** The university is located on 2,000 acres in a small city 115 miles north of Orlando, Florida, and 20 minutes from the Gainesville airport.

**Student Body**
  **Undergrad enrollment:** 30,008
  **Women:** 48%
  **Men:** 52%
  **In-state students:** 92%
  **Out-of-state:** 8%

**Cost Information**
  **In-state tuition:** $1,793
  **Out-of-state:** $7,038
  **Room & board:** $4,500

**Housing Information**
  **University housing:** Yes
  **Fraternity:** Yes
  **Sorority:** Yes
  **Living on campus:** 21%

  **Athletics:** NCAA Div. I

# LYNN UNIVERSITY

3601 North Military Trail, Boca Raton, FL 33431 • **Admissions:** 561-994-0770 • **Fax:** 561-241-3552
**Email:** admission@lynnuniversity.edu • **Web:** www.lynn.edu
**Support:** SP • **Institution:** 4 yr. Private

## LEARNING DISABILITY ADMISSIONS AND SERVICES

Academic support services provide assistance to help students remain in college. The Academic Resource Center (ARC) is available to all students. In The Advancement Program (TAP), students enroll in regular college courses and concurrently in elective credit courses designed for this program. One three-credit specialized course is offered in the first semester. This course, Language and Learning, is diagnostic and offers an opportunity for students to explore their strengths, learning styles, and college skills. A research based text, *Frames of Mind*, is required reading. Programs are scheduled for each individual with special consideration, usually resulting in a reduced academic course load. Tutorials, both individual and group, and study groups are facilitated by TAP personnel. Language and writing skills development support is provided by English and education professors.

## LEARNING DISABILITY ADMISSIONS INFORMATION

**Program Name:** The Advancement Program (TAP)
**Program Director:** Marsha Glines, Ph.D.          **Telephone:** 561-994-0770
**Contact Person:** Mary Ann Crosta

### ADMISSIONS

Students should submit the general application to Lynn University. Admissions criteria are dependent on the level of services required. Students needing the least restrictive Level I services should have taken college prep high school courses. Component III applicants may have been enrolled in more individualized high school courses, and may have lower IQ scores; admission is very flexible. Some students may be admitted provisionally after submitting official information. Other students may be admitted conditionally into the Frontiers Program. Typically these students have an ACT of 18 or lower or an SAT of 800 or lower. Students admitted conditionally take a reduced course load; no science for first semester; and 1 1/2 hours of scheduled tutoring. The Precollege Program, LEAP, is an eight-week program that may be required for some students or suggested for others prior to admission to the university. This Program is designed for students with learning disabilities and it is diagnostic in nature. Other students not admissible to the university may be offered the opportunity to attend the LEAP Program for an entire year.

**College entrance exams required:** Yes          **Untimed accepted:** Yes
**Course entrance requirements:** Yes          **Interview required:** Recommended
**Diagnostic tests:** Yes
**Documentation:** Psychoeducational testing: within 3 years

### ADDITIONAL INFORMATION

All tests are monitored by TAP personnel, and advocacy work with faculty is provided by the Director. TAP students may choose any major as they work toward degree completion in subsequent years. Students who continue to need support services after one year will continue in the program for specific tutoring, untimed tests and program guidance as needed. Skills classes are offered for credit in Language and Learning Development. There is also one-to-one tutoring with professional tutors. Students with LD have the opportunity to take an evening program in Physical Fitness. Students choose AA or BA degrees. Lynn University also offers a comprehensive and nurturing support service for students with different learning needs or abilities. The Lynn Educational Alternative Program (LEAP) in the Adirondack Mountains at Old Forge, New York, offers year-round transition programs in Hospitality/Food Service or Human Service. Lynn also offers a summer program for high school students with learning disabilities.

**Special education HS coursework accepted:** Yes          **Essay required:** Requested
**Special application required:** No          **Submitted to:** N/A
**# of applications submitted each year:** 300          **# of applications accepted each year:** 200
**# of students receiving LD services:** Approximately 110
**Acceptance into program means acceptance into college:** Students must be accepted into the university first and then offered services through TAP

# LEARNING DISABILITY SERVICES

**Learning center:** Yes
**Kurzweil personal reader:** No
**LD specialists:** 2
**Allowed in exams:**
  **Calculator:** Yes
  **Dictionary:** Yes
  **Computer:** Y/N
  **SpellCheck:** Yes

**Notetaker:** Yes
**Scribes:** Yes
**Proctors:** Yes
**Oral exams:** Yes
**Extended test time:** Yes
**Added cost:** $3,850 per year
**Distraction-free environ.:** No
**Tape recording in class:** Yes
**Books on tape:** No
**Taping of other books:** No

**Professional tutors:** 12
**Peer tutors:** No
**Max. hrs/wk for services:** Unlimited
**Priority registration:** Yes
**Accomodations for students with ADD:** Yes
**How are professors notified of LD:** By the student and the Program Director

# GENERAL ADMISSIONS INFORMATION

**Director of Admissions:** Jim Sullivan

**Telephone:** 561-994-0770

## ENTRANCE REQUIREMENTS

Total high school units required/recommended: 20 total units are recommended; 4 English recommended, 3 math recommended, 3 science recommended, 2 social studies recommended, 2 history recommended. Special requirements: A portfolio is required for art program applicants.

**Application deadline:** Rolling
**Notification:** Rolling

**SAT or ACT preferred:** Either
**SAT Avg:** 440V, 450M
**Average ACT:** 21

# COLLEGE GRADUATION REQUIREMENTS

**Course waivers allowed:** No
**Course substitutions allowed:** Yes
**In what courses:** Math and foreign language

# ADDITIONAL INFORMATION

**Environment:** The university is located on 123 acres in a suburban area on Florida's Gold Coast.

**Student Body**
  **Undergrad enrollment:** 1,450
  **Women:** 48%
  **Men:** 52%
  **In-state students:** 30%
  **Out-of-state:** 70%

**Cost Information**
  **In-state tuition:** $15,450
  **Out-of-state:** $15,450
  **Room & board:** $6,250

**Housing Information**
  **University housing:** Yes
  **Fraternity:** No
  **Sorority:** No
  **Living on campus:** 70%

  **Athletics:** NAIA

# BRENAU UNIVERSITY

1 Centennial Circle, Gainesville, GA 30501 • **Admissions:** 770-543-62990 • **Fax:** 770-534-6114
**Email:** upchurch@lib.brenau.edu • **Web:** www.brenau.edu
**Support:** CS • **Institution:** 4 yr. Private

## LEARNING DISABILITY ADMISSIONS AND SERVICES

The Brenau Learning Center is a program for students with a diagnosed learning disability or attention deficit disorder. Students must also have average to above average academic aptitude with an adequate high school preparation for college studies. The Program is designed to provide support services for students as they attend regular college courses. It also offers a more structured learning environment as well as the freedom associated with college living. Full-time students enroll in 4 or 5 courses per semester. Learning Center students receive academic advising from the college, as well as the Director of the Program. Students have the opportunity to register early, which allows them to take required courses at the appropriate time in their college career. Many students become inactive in the Program as they experience success and require less assistance. They may re-enter the Program at any time. Brenau University attempts to offer a more personalized caring approach to college education. Faculty are very supportive of students who request extra help. So, in addition to receiving special services from the Learning Center, staff, and tutors, the student is being educated in an environment conducive to learning.

## LEARNING DISABILITY ADMISSIONS INFORMATION

**Program Name:** Learning Center (LC)
**Program Director:** Vincent Yamilkoski, Ed.D.                    **Telephone:** 770-534-6134
**Contact Person:** J. Janet Payne                    **Telephone:** 770-534-6133

### ADMISSIONS

Regular admission criteria include an SAT of 900+ or ACT of 18+, and a GPA of 2.5+. Applicants with an LD not meeting regular admission criteria may be admitted through a 'Learning Center Admission' and must participate in the LD Program. These students should be "college-able," and motivated and have appropriate high school preparation. Students must have the intellectual potential and academic foundation to be successful. Applicants must provide documentation. Not all students with a diagnosed learning disability are eligible for the Program; the learning differences must not be the primary result of emotional problems. Both the Director of the LC and the Director of Admissions make a decision after reviewing SAT/ACT scores, academic performance and preparation, counselor's recommendation and other letters of reference, test results contained in the psychological evaluation, and a campus interview.

**College entrance exams required:** Yes                    **Untimed accepted:** Yes
**Course entrance requirements:** Yes                    **Interview required:** Yes
**Diagnostic tests:** Yes
**Documentation:** WAIS-R; Individual achievement scores in reading and math: within 3 years

### ADDITIONAL INFORMATION

Learning Center students can register early and receive regular academic advising from the Director of the Program. Study skills, including word processing, reading, and math skills classes are offered for credit. At all service levels students may take tests in an extended-time format where oral assistance is available. Learning Center students begin tutoring with professional tutors during the first week of the term and contract to regularly attend tutoring sessions throughout the semester. All LC students may receive one hour of educational support per week in addition to scheduled tutoring. Students may be tutored in one to four academic classes per semester. Skills classes in word processing, time management, study skills, and research may be taken for credit. LD services and accommodations are available for undergraduate and graduate students. Courses are offered in the summer and entering freshman are encouraged to attend. Summer school allows students to get ahead with courses and take a reduced course load the first year.

**Special education HS coursework accepted:** Yes                    **Essay required:** Yes
**Special application required:** No                    **Submitted to:** N/A
**# of applications submitted each year:** N/A                    **# of applications accepted each year:** N/A
**# of students receiving LD services:** 50
**Acceptance into program means acceptance into college:** Students can be reviewed by the LD Program Director, but must be admitted by the university and then may request services.

**Learning center:** Yes
**Kurzweil personal reader:** Yes
**LD specialists:** 2
**Allowed in exams:**
  **Calculator:** Yes
  **Dictionary:** Yes
  **Computer:** Yes
  **SpellCheck:** Yes

**Notetaker:** Yes
**Scribes:** Yes
**Proctors:** Yes
**Oral exams:** Yes
**Extended test time:** Yes
**Added cost:** $800 per course
**Distraction-free environ.:** Yes
**Tape recording in class:** Yes
**Books on tape:** Yes
**Taping of other books:** Yes

**Professional tutors:** 30
**Peer tutors:** No
**Max. hrs/wk for services:** 10
**Priority registration:** Yes
**Accomodations for students with ADD:** Yes
**How are professors notified of LD:** By the Program Director

## GENERAL ADMISSIONS INFORMATION

**Director of Admissions:** Dr. John Upchurch       **Telephone:** 770-534-6100

### ENTRANCE REQUIREMENTS

Total high school units required/recommended: 4 English recommended, 3 math recommended, 2 science recommended, 3 social studies recommended, 7-9 electives recommended.

**Application deadline:** Rolling
**Notification:** NR

**SAT or ACT preferred:** NR
**SAT Avg:** 527V, 512M

## COLLEGE GRADUATION REQUIREMENTS

**Course waivers allowed:** No
**Course substitutions allowed:** No
**In what courses:** N/A

## ADDITIONAL INFORMATION

**Environment:** Brenau University is in a small town setting 50 miles northeast of Atlanta in the foothills of the Blue Ridge Mountains.

**Student Body**
  **Undergrad enrollment:** NR
  **Women:** NR
  **Men:** NR
  **In-state students:** 81%
  **Out-of-state:** 19%

**Cost Information**
  **In-state tuition:** $10,350
  **Out-of-state:** $10,350
  **Room & board:** $6,330

**Housing Information**
  **University housing:** Yes
  **Fraternity:** No
  **Sorority:** Yes
  **Living on campus:** 25%

  **Athletics:** NAIA

# DEKALB COLLEGE
Clarkston, GA 300212 • **Admissions:** 404-229-4000

**Support:** CS • **Institution:** 2 yr. Public

## LEARNING DISABILITY ADMISSIONS AND SERVICES

The Center for Disability Services (CDS) was created to assure that all students who have disabilities have access to all aspects of the educational experience at DeKalb College. Appropriate support services are provided as required for each student's academic success. Any student entering DeKalb for the first time must learn to adjust to the new environment. For all students, including the students with disabilities, the adjustment is not always an easy one. They must learn to cope on a daily basis with obstacles that may impede their academic and social performance at college. The goal of the CDS is to supply students with disabilities those auxiliary aids that will allow them to compete and participate equally with the rest of the student body. Full participation means providing the students with an equal opportunity to succeed, as well as an opportunity to fail. Students who have a disability, are addressed with respect to their personal dignity, academic endeavors, and life goals on behalf of the staff of the Center for Disability Services.

## LEARNING DISABILITY ADMISSIONS INFORMATION

**Program Name:** Center for Disability Services
**Program Director:** Lisa Fowler                      **Telephone:** 404-299-4118
**Contact Person:** Louise Cebula                      **Telephone:** 404-299-4120

### ADMISSIONS
There is no special admission process for students with learning disabilities. All applicants must submit the general application; have a high school diploma or the GED; and have a GPA of 1.8 or a verbal SAT I of 330 or a math SAT I of 310 or ACT of 13 English and 14 Math. The minimum GPA is 1.8.  Course requirements include 4 yrs. English, 3 yrs. math, 3 yrs. science (physical science and 2 lab courses from biology, chemistry, physics or related), 3 yrs. social sciences (American and world history, economics and government), and 2 yrs. foreign language. Provisional admission is allowed for students to satisfy deficiencies. Students may request a substitution for the required foreign language courses, but permission is subject to approval by the Regents' Committee for Learning Disorders.

**College entrance exams required:** Yes               **Untimed accepted:** Yes
**Course entrance requirements:** Yes                 **Interview Required:** No
**Diagnostic tests:** Yes
**Documentation:** WAIS-R; WISC-R; WISC-III; Stanford Binet; within 3 years

### ADDITIONAL INFORMATION
Learning Disability Criteria acceptable by the Georgia Board of Regents include documentation within 3 years; average broad cognitive functioning demonstrated on an individually administered intelligence test; specific cognitive processing deficits documented with an assessment instrument plus an individually administered IQ test, in executive functions, memory, fine motor, and selective attention/perception; social-emotional assessment that doesn't suggest primary emotional basis for results;  oral language assessment; significant specific achievement deficits relative to potential, which must be documented in the areas of written language, reading, and math; utilization of assessment instruments with appropriate age norms; and all standardized measures must be represented by standard score or percentile ranks based on published norms. Skills courses for credit are offered in study strategies, test-taking strategies, and self-help workshops. The center also provides trained tutors, readers, and notetakers.

**Special education HS coursework accepted:** Yes, if they
meet course requirements                              **Essay required:** No
**Special application required:** No                  **Submitted to:** N/A
**# of applications submitted each year:** N/A        **# of applications accepted each year:** N/A
**# of students receiving LD services:** Approximately 150
**Acceptance into program means acceptance into college:** Students must be admitted to the college and then may request services.

# LEARNING DISABILITY SERVICES

**Learning center:** No
**Kurzweil personal reader:** Yes
**LD specialists:** 2
**Allowed in exams:**
  **Calculator:** Yes
  **Dictionary:** Yes
  **Computer:** Yes
  **SpellCheck:** Yes

**Notetaker:** Yes
**Scribes:** Yes
**Proctors:** Yes
**Oral exams:** Yes
**Extended test time:** Yes
**Added cost:** None
**Distraction-free environ.:** Yes
**Tape recording in class:** Yes
**Books on tape:** RFB
**Taping of other books:** Yes

**Professional tutors:** 3
**Peer tutors:** No
**Max. hrs/wk for services:** Varies
**Priority registration:** Yes
**Accomodations for students with ADD:** Yes
**How are professors notified of LD:** By the student and the counselor

# GENERAL ADMISSIONS INFORMATION

**Director of Admissions:** James Squires

**Telephone:** 404-299-4546

## ENTRANCE REQUIREMENTS

A high school diploma or the GED equivalent; a GPA or 1.8 or a Verbal SAT of 330, Math 310; or ACT of 13 in English, 14 Math. Course requirements include: 4 years English, 3 years math, 3 years science, 3 years social sciences, and 2 years foreign language.

**Application deadline:** NR
**Notification:** NR

**SAT or ACT preferred:** NR

# COLLEGE GRADUATION REQUIREMENTS

**Course waivers allowed:** Yes
**Course substitutions allowed:** Yes
**In what courses:** Foreign language—it must be approved by Department Chair as relevant to specific disability

# ADDITIONAL INFORMATION

**Environment:** NR

**Student Body**
  **Undergrad enrollment:** NR
  **Women:** NR
  **Men:** NR
  **In-state students:** NR
  **Out-of-state:** NR

**Cost Information**
  **In-state tuition:** NR
  **Out-of-state:** NR

**Housing Information**
  **University housing:** NR
  **Fraternity:** NR
  **Sorority:** NR
  **Living on campus:** NR

  **Athletics:** NR

# EMORY UNIVERSITY

**GA**

1380 South Oxford Road, NE, Atlanta, GA 30322 • **Admissions:** 404-727-6036 • **Fax:** 404-727-4303
**Email:** admiss@emory.edu • **Web:** www.emory.edu
**Support:** CS • **Institution:** 4 yr. Private

## LEARNING DISABILITY ADMISSIONS AND SERVICES

It is the policy of Emory University to ensure that all services and accommodations are accessible to students with disabilities in accordance with ADA, Section 504, and other pertinent federal, state, and local disabilities anti-discrimination laws. Reasonable accommodations will be made on an individualized basis. It is the responsibility of the students to seek available assistance and establish their needs. The Disabled Student Services Program has a number of goals for its students, including coordinating services to provide equal access to programs, services, and activities; reducing competitive disadvantage in academic work; providing individual counseling and referral; serving as an advocate for student needs; providing a variety of support services; and serving as a liaison between students and university officers or community agencies. Disabled Student Services will send a memorandum to professors to support accommodation requests from students. DSS acknowledges to the professor that they have received sufficient verification to support the request, and will provide the professor with the identified accommodations necessary.

## LEARNING DISABILITY ADMISSIONS INFORMATION

**Program Name:** Disabled Student Services
**Program Director:** Deborah H. Hyde Ph.D., Coordinator        **Telephone:** 404-727-1070
**Contact Person:** Same as above

### ADMISSIONS

Students with learning disabilities are required to submit everything requested by the Office of Admission for regular admissions. Untimed SAT/ACT may be submitted in lieu of the timed test. Teacher and/or counselor recommendations may be weighted more heavily in the admissions process. A professional diagnosis of the learning disability with recommended accommodations is helpful. Essentially, each student with a disability is evaluated individually, and admitted based on potential for success in the Emory environment, taking into consideration the necessary accommodations requested. Documentation is required for services, not admissions. Once admitted, the Admissions Office sends a Self-Identification Form in the acceptance packet to each student who discloses a learning disability.

**College entrance exams required:** Yes          **Untimed accepted:** Yes
**Course entrance requirements:** Yes          **Interview required:** No
**Diagnostic tests:** Yes
**Documentation:** WAIS-R; W-J; WRAT: Psychoeducational battery; Bender-Gestalt: within 1 year

### ADDITIONAL INFORMATION

The needs of students with learning disabilities are met through counseling and referral advocacy, and a variety of support services. Deans are notified by a report each semester of students who have self-identified as having a learning disability. Tutoring is offered on a one-to-one basis or in small groups in most subjects. Students also are eligible for priority registration. Skills classes are offered, and the coordinator can monitor and track students to follow their progress. The coordinator meets with students to assess needs and develop an Individualized Service Plan for each. The coordinator is also an advocate for students and provides information to faculty to help with their understanding of providing accommodations to students with learning disabilities. The Emory Students Enabling Association provides a support network for students with disabilities.

**Special education HS coursework accepted:** No          **Essay required:** Yes
**Special application required:** No          **Submitted to:** N/A
**# of applications submitted each year:** N/A          **# of applications accepted each year:** N/A
**# of students receiving LD services:** 54
**Acceptance into program means acceptance into college:** Students must be admitted to the university and then may request services.

## LEARNING DISABILITY SERVICES

**Learning center:** Yes
**Kurzweil personal reader:** No
**LD specialists:** 1
**Allowed in exams:**
  **Calculator:** Yes
  **Dictionary:** Yes
  **Computer:** Yes
  **SpellCheck:** Yes

**Notetaker:** Yes
**Scribes:** Yes
**Proctors:** Yes
**Oral exams:** Yes
**Extended test time:** Yes
**Added cost:** None
**Distraction-free environ.:** Yes
**Tape recording in class:** Yes
**Books on tape:** Yes
**Taping of other books:** Yes

**Professional tutors:** Yes
**Peer tutors:** Yes
**Max. hrs/wk for services:** 4 hours per course
**Priority registration:** Yes
**Accomodations for students with ADD:** Yes
**How are professors notified of LD:** By the student and Program Director

## GENERAL ADMISSIONS INFORMATION

**Director of Admissions:** Daniel C. Walls          **Telephone:** 404-727-6036

### ENTRANCE REQUIREMENTS

Total high school units required/recommended: 16 total units are required; 4 English required, 3 math required, 2 science required, 2 foreign language required, 2 social studies required. Minimum 3.0/3.5 GPA required. Special requirements: An audition is required for music program applicants.

**Application deadline:** January 15
**Notification:** April 1

**SAT or ACT preferred:** Either
**SAT Avg:** 570V, 650M
**Average ACT:** 28
**Average GPA:** 3.7

**Graduated top 10% of class:** 81
**Graduated top 25% of class:** 98
**Graduated top 50% of class:** 100

## COLLEGE GRADUATION REQUIREMENTS

**Course waivers allowed:** No
**Course substitutions allowed:** Yes
**In what courses:** Decision made on a case-by-case basis

## ADDITIONAL INFORMATION

**Environment:** The 631-acre campus is in a suburban section 5 miles northeast of Atlanta.

**Student Body**
  **Undergrad enrollment:** 5,736
  **Women:** 53%
  **Men:** 47%
  **In-state students:** 20%
  **Out-of-state:** 80%

**Cost Information**
  **In-state tuition:** $20,870
  **Out-of-state:** $20,870
  **Room & board:** $6,800

**Housing Information**
  **University housing:** Yes
  **Fraternity:** Yes
  **Sorority:** Yes
  **Living on campus:** 65%

  **Athletics:** NCAA Div. III

# GEORGIA SOUTHERN UNIVERSITY

Landrum Box 8033, Statesboro, GA 30460 • **Admissions:** 912-681-5531 • **Fax:** 912-681-5635

**Email:** adm37@svmsi.cc.gasou.edu • **Web:** www.gasou.edu

**Support:** CS • **Institution:** 4 yr. Public

## LEARNING DISABILITY ADMISSIONS AND SERVICES

Georgia Southern University wants all students to have a rewarding and pleasant college experience. The university offers a variety of services specifically tailored to afford students with learning disabilities an equal opportunity for success. These services are in addition to those provided to all students and to the access provided by campus facilities. Opportunities available through the Disabled Student Services program include Special Registration, which allows students to complete the course registration process without going through the standard procedure, and Academic/Personal Assistance for students who are having difficulty with passing a class and need help with time management, note-taking skills, study strategies, and self-confidence. The university has a support group designed to help students with disabilities deal with personal and academic problems related to their disability.

## LEARNING DISABILITY ADMISSIONS INFORMATION

**Program Name:** Disabled Student Services
**Program Director:** Wayne Akins
**Contact Person:** Same as above

**Telephone:** 912-871-1566

### ADMISSIONS

There is no special admissions procedure for students with learning disabilities. The university system feels that all applicants must meet the same minimum requirements. Courses required for admission include: 4 yrs. English, 3 yrs. math, 3 yrs. science, 2 yrs. foreign language, and 3 yrs. social studies. The minimum SAT I Verbal score is 480 and Math is 440. The minimum GPA is 2.0.

**College entrance exams required:** Yes
**Course entrance requirements:** Yes
**Diagnostic tests:** Yes
**Documentation:** WAIS-R, WRAT, KAIT: within 3 years

**Untimed accepted:** Yes
**Interview required:** No

### ADDITIONAL INFORMATION

To ensure the provision of services, the Disabled Student Services office requests that any student with Learning Disabilities who will need accommodations and/or assistance identify him/herself as a student with a disability as soon as possible by either returning the Voluntary Declaration of Disability form found in the admissions acceptance packet or by contacting the Disabled Student Services office directly.

**Special education HS coursework accepted:** Yes
**Special application required:** No
**# of applications submitted each year:** N/A
**# of students receiving LD services:** 200

**Essay required:** N/I
**Submitted to:** N/A
**# of applications accepted each year:** N/A

**Acceptance into program means acceptance into college:** Students must be admitted to the university first and then be reviewed for services.

# LEARNING DISABILITY SERVICES

**Learning center:** No
**Kurzweil personal reader:** No
**LD specialists:** Yes
**Allowed in exams:**
  **Calculator:** Yes
  **Dictionary:** Yes
  **Computer:** Yes
  **SpellCheck:** Yes

**Notetaker:** Yes
**Scribes:** Yes
**Proctors:** Yes
**Oral exams:** Yes
**Extended test time:** Yes
**Added cost:** None
**Distraction-free environ.:** Yes
**Tape recording in class:** Yes
**Books on tape:** Yes
**Taping of other books:** Yes

**Professional tutors:** No
**Peer tutors:** 25
**Max. hrs/wk for services:** Unlimited
**Priority registration:** Yes
**Accomodations for students with ADD:** Yes
**How are professors notified of LD:** By the student

# GENERAL ADMISSIONS INFORMATION

**Director of Admissions:** Dale Wasson

**Telephone:** 912-681-5391

## ENTRANCE REQUIREMENTS

Total high school units required/recommended: 15 total units are required; 17 total units are recommended; 4 English required, 3 math required, 3 science required, 2 foreign language required, 3 social studies required. Minimum SAT I scores of 480 Verbal and 440 Math and minimum 2.0 GPA required.

**Application deadline:** August 1
**Notification:** Rolling

**SAT or ACT preferred:** Either
**SAT Avg:** 438V, 487M

# COLLEGE GRADUATION REQUIREMENTS

**Course waivers allowed:** No
**Course substitutions allowed:** Yes
**In what courses:** Substitutions have only been granted in foreign language and a deficit area.

# ADDITIONAL INFORMATION

**Environment:** NR

**Student Body**
  **Undergrad enrollment:** 12,594
  **Women:** 45%
  **Men:** 55%
  **In-state students:** 86%
  **Out-of-state:** 14%

**Cost Information**
  **In-state tuition:** $2,055
  **Out-of-state:** $5,934
  **Room & board:** $3,696

**Housing Information**
  **University housing:** Yes
  **Fraternity:** Yes
  **Sorority:** Yes
  **Living on campus:** 21%

  **Athletics:** NCAA Div. I

# GEORGIA STATE UNIVERSITY

University Plaza, P.O. Box 4009, Atlanta, GA 30303 • **Admissions:** 404-651-2000 • **Fax:** 404-651-4811
**Email:** admits@langate.gsu.edu • **Web:** www.gsu.edu
**Support:** S • **Institution:** 4 yr. Public

## LEARNING DISABILITY ADMISSIONS AND SERVICES

Georgia State University is committed to helping each student, including those students with disabilities, realize his/her full potential. This commitment is fulfilled through the provision of reasonable accommodations to ensure equitable access to its programs and services for all qualified students with disabilities. In general, the university will provide accommodations for students with disabilities on an individualized and flexible basis. It is the student's responsibility to seek available assistance and to make his/her needs known. All students are encouraged to contact the Office of Disability Services and/or Student Support Services in the early stages of their college planning. The preadmission services include information regarding admission requirements and academic support services. Students should register with both services before classes begin. This will assure that appropriate services are in place prior to the first day of classes. As a rule, the university does not waive academic requirements because of any disability. Therefore, the student should carefully evaluate degree requirements early in his/her studies. The only exception to this policy is if there is a documented learning disability that would hinder the learning of a foreign language, in which case a student may petition for a substitution in the foreign language requirement.

## LEARNING DISABILITY ADMISSIONS INFORMATION

**Program Name:** Office of Disability Services
**Program Director:** Dr. Carole L. Pearson
**Contact Person:** Same as above

**Telephone:** 404-651-1487

### ADMISSIONS

Students with learning disabilities must meet the same admission criteria as all other applicants. The university uses a predicted GPA of 2.1 for admission to a degree program or a GPA of 1.8 for admission to Learning Support Systems. This is determined by the ACT/SAT I score and the high school GPA. The higher the GPA, the lower the ACT/SAT can be and vice versa. Course requirements include 4 yrs. English, 3 yrs. science, 3 yrs. math, 3 yrs. social science, and 2 yrs. foreign language. (Substitutions are allowed for foreign language if the student has documentation that supports the substitution.) Students may appeal an admission decision if they are denied, and could be offered a probationary admission. If a student contacts the Office of Disability Services and provides documentation of a learning disability, the office will write the Admissions Office and verify the existence of the learning disability.

**College entrance exams required:** Yes          **Untimed accepted:** Yes
**Course entrance requirements:** Yes            **Interview required:** No
**Diagnostic tests:** Yes
**Documentation:** WAIS-R;Stanford-Binet; KBIT;WJ-R;WRAT-R; within 3 years

### ADDITIONAL INFORMATION

To receive services for LD students must submit documentation that evaluates: intelligence; academic achievement in reading, math, and written language; auditory/phonological processing; language; visual-perceptual-spatial-constructural; attention; memory; executive function; motor; and social emotional. student support services provides individual and group counseling; tutoring; advocacy; taped texts; advising; readers; learning lab; computer training; and referral for diagnosis of LD. The University Counseling Center provides study skills training; test-taking strategies; note-taking skills; textbook reading skills; test anxiety and stress management; time management; organizational techniques; thesis and dissertation writing; and personal counseling. Passport is a special section of the Personal and Academic Development Seminar Class offered through Learning Support Program, and is specifically designed for students with LD. The Office of Disability Services offers Advisement; study lab; readers; and testing accommodations.

**Special education HS coursework accepted:** Yes       **Essay required:** No
**Special application required:** N/A                    **Submitted to:** N/A
**# of applications submitted each year:** N/A          **# of applications accepted each year:** N/A
**# of students receiving LD services:** 112
**Acceptance into program means acceptance into college:** Students must be admitted to the university first and then may request services or accommodations.

# LEARNING DISABILITY SERVICES

**Learning center:** No
**Kurzweil personal reader:** Yes
**LD specialists:** N/I
**Allowed in exams:**
  **Calculator:** Yes
  **Dictionary:** Yes
  **Computer:** Yes
  **SpellCheck:** Yes

**Notetaker:** Yes
**Scribes:** Yes
**Proctors:** Yes
**Oral exams:** Yes
**Extended test time:** Yes
**Added cost:** None
**Distraction-free environ.:** Yes
**Tape recording in class:** Yes
**Books on tape:** Yes
**Taping of other books:** Yes

**Professional tutors:** No
**Peer tutors:** 22
**Max. hrs/wk for services:** 4-5 hours per week; based on need and availability of space and staff
**Priority registration:** No
**Accomodations for students with ADD:** Yes
**How are professors notified of LD:** By the student and by letter from ODS if requested

# GENERAL ADMISSIONS INFORMATION

**Director of Admissions:** Dr. Rob Sheinkopf

**Telephone:** 404-651-2467

## ENTRANCE REQUIREMENTS

Total high school units required/recommended: 15 total units are required; 4 English required, 3 math required, 3 science required, 2 foreign language required, 1 social studies required, 2 history required. Minimum SAT I scores of 400 in both Verbal and Math (ACT scores of 21 English and 19 Math) and minimum 2.0 GPA required. Special requirements: An audition and theory placement test is required for music program applicants; TOEFL is required of all international students; additional requirements for applicants to the College of Health Science.

**Application deadline:** July 1
**Notification:** Rolling

**SAT or ACT preferred:** Either
**SAT Avg:** 427V, 476M
**SAT II required:** Yes
**Average ACT:** 20

# COLLEGE GRADUATION REQUIREMENTS

**Course waivers allowed:** No
**Course substitutions allowed:** Yes
**In what courses:** On a case-by-case basis with the recommendation of the student's major department

# ADDITIONAL INFORMATION

**Environment:** NR

**Student Body**
  **Undergrad enrollment:** 16,786
  **Women:** 59%
  **Men:** 41%
  **In-state students:** 92%
  **Out-of-state:** 8%

**Cost Information**
  **In-state tuition:** $2,385
  **Out-of-state:** $8,640
  **Room & board:** $3,600

**Housing Information**
  **University housing:**
  **Fraternity:** No
  **Sorority:** No
  **Living on campus:** NR

  **Athletics:** NCAA Div. I

# UNIVERSITY OF GEORGIA

Athens, GA 30602 • **Admissions:** 706-542-2112
**Email:** undergrad@admissions.uga.edu • **Web:** www.uga.edu
**Support:** CS • **Institution:** 4 yr. Public

## LEARNING DISABILITY ADMISSIONS AND SERVICES

The purpose of the LDC is to provide support and direct services to students who demonstrate a specific learning disability so that they may function as independently as possible while at the university. The objectives of the program are to: (1) identify the nature of the learning disability; (2) assist students in understanding their disability; (3) coordinate information about other support services; (4) offer informal group interaction; (5) recommend modifications for the Regents Exam (required to graduate) and program of study where appropriate; (6) consult with faculty and; (7) provide direct remediation and tutorial assistance. All UGA students whose learning disabilities have been confirmed by the Learning Disabilities Center are eligible for support services. Students must meet the Learning Disability Criteria acceptable by the Georgia Board of Regents, including documentation within 3 years; average broad cognitive functioning; specific cognitive processing deficits; social-emotional assessment that doesn't suggest primary emotional basis for results; oral language assessment; significant specific achievement deficits relative to potential documented in the areas of written language, reading, and math; utilization of assessment instruments with appropriate age norms; and all standardized measures must be represented by standard score or percentile ranks based on published norms.

## LEARNING DISABILITY ADMISSIONS INFORMATION

**Program Name:** Learning Disabilities Center (LDC)
**Program Directors:** Dr. Noel Gregg/ Dr. Rosemary Jackson    **Telephone:** 706-542-4589
**Contact Person:** Sebrena Mason                            **Telephone:** 706-542-4658

### ADMISSIONS

Students with learning disabilities are encouraged to self-disclose on the general application form. This disclosure sets the process in motion, and the Admissions Office notifies the LDC. LDC contacts the applicant and offers to discuss services available, and then refers the students' name back to Admissions (to the attention of Ann Ralph). LDC provides the Admissions Office with a diagnosis to assist with an admission decision. Students must submit documentation of their disability to be considered for special admissions. Admissions may be flexible with GPA and test scores, but students should take college prep courses in high school. GPA is the most important criterion and the subscore on the Verbal section of the ACT/SAT is more weighted than Math. Required SAT and GPA are adjusted in relation to general admission averages. The final decision is made by the Admissions Office.

| | |
|---|---|
| **College entrance exams required:** Yes | **Untimed accepted:** Yes |
| **Course entrance requirements:** Yes | **Interview required:** Yes |
| **Diagnostic tests:** Yes | |

**Documentation:** WAIS-R (or other IQ test); Achievement assessment: within 3 years

### ADDITIONAL INFORMATION

Individual tutoring is provided by LD specialists 2 hours per week. Specialists address individual strengths and weaknesses in the context of specific courses and help with learning strategies for all courses and course content for many courses. Students meet with LD specialists to register quarterly and design a schedule that considers their LD along with curriculum requirements. Students are assisted in communicating their disabilities and learning needs with their instructors. An ongoing group is led by the staff psychologist to help students accept their disabilities, recognize their strengths, and cope with the challenges of the college environment. Modifications for assignments and tests are designed to meet students' specific needs. Skills classes for college credit are offered to all students at UGA in study techniques, time management, problem-solving, research paper writing, and career selection. Students with ADD are serviced by Disability Services but receive very little individual attention.

| | |
|---|---|
| **Special education HS coursework accepted:** Yes | **Essay required:** No |
| **Special application required:** Yes | **Submitted to:** Contact LDC |
| **# of applications submitted each year:** 100 | **# of applications accepted each year:** N/A |
| **# of students receiving LD services:** 300 | |

**Acceptance into program means acceptance into college:** Students must be admitted to the university first and then may request services.

## LEARNING DISABILITY SERVICES

**Learning center:** Yes
**Kurzweil personal reader:** Yes
**LD specialists:** 5
**Allowed in exams:**
  **Calculator:** Yes
  **Dictionary:** Yes
  **Computer:** Yes
  **SpellCheck:** Yes

**Notetaker:** Yes
**Scribes:** Yes
**Proctors:** Yes
**Oral exams:** Yes
**Extended test time:** Yes
**Added cost:** None
**Distraction-free environ.:** Yes
**Tape recording in class:** Yes
**Books on tape:** Yes
**Taping of other books:** Yes

**Professional tutors:** 5
**Peer tutors:** No
**Max. hrs/wk for services:**
Special tutoring 2 hours per
week
**Priority registration:** Yes
**Accomodations for students
with ADD:** Yes
**How are professors notified of
LD:** By student and the Director
of the Program

## GENERAL ADMISSIONS INFORMATION

**Director of Admissions:** Dr. Nancy G. McDuff          **Telephone:** 706-542-2112

### ENTRANCE REQUIREMENTS

Total high school units required/recommended: 15 total units are required; 4 English required, 3 math required, 3 science required, 2 foreign language required, 3 social studies required. Minimum combined SAT I score of 900 (or equivalent ACT score) and minimum 3.0 GPA recommended. Special requirements: An audition is required for music program applicants; TOEFL is required of all international students; SAT II in foreign language required of applicants planning to continue study of that language; plane geometry, trigonometry, chemistry, and physics recommended for B.S. program applicants; combined SAT I score of 1000 recommended for business administration program applicants.

**Application deadline:** February 1
**Notification:** April 1

**SAT or ACT preferred:** SAT
**SAT Avg:** 599V, 590M
**Average GPA:** 3.6

**Graduated top 10% of class:** 43
**Graduated top 25% of class:** 79
**Graduated top 50% of class:** 98

## COLLEGE GRADUATION REQUIREMENTS

**Course waivers allowed:** No
**Course substitutions allowed:** Yes
**In what courses:** Varies by college

## ADDITIONAL INFORMATION

**Environment:** The university is located on a large campus 80 miles from Atlanta.

**Student Body**
  **Undergrad enrollment:** 22,301
  **Women:** 54%
  **Men:** 46%
  **In-state students:** 84%
  **Out-of-state:** 16%

**Cost Information**
  **In-state tuition:** $2,694
  **Out-of-state:** $7,875
  **Room & board:** $4,045

**Housing Information**
  **University housing:** Yes
  **Fraternity:** Yes
  **Sorority:** Yes
  **Living on campus:** 26%

  **Athletics:** NCAA Div. I

# GA

# REINHARDT COLLEGE

Waleska, GA 30183 • **Admissions:** 770-479-1454

**Support:** SP • **Institution:** 2 yr. Private

## LEARNING DISABILITY ADMISSIONS AND SERVICES

The Academic Support Office (ASO) provides assistance to students with specific learning abilities or attention deficit disorders. Students are enrolled in regular college courses. The Program focuses on compensatory skills and provides special services in academic advising and counseling, individual and group tutoring, assistance in writing assignments, notetaking, testing accommodations, and taped texts. The ASO was established in 1982 to provide assistance to students with learning disabilities who meet regular college entrance requirements, have a diagnosed LD, and may or may not have received any LD services in the past due to ineligibility for high school services, or a recent diagnosis.

## LEARNING DISABILITY ADMISSIONS INFORMATION

**Program Name:** Academic Support Office (ASO)
**Program Director:** Sylvia Robertson          **Telephone:** 770-720-5567
**Contact Person:** Same as above

### ADMISSIONS

Applicants with learning disabilities should request an ASO admission packet from admissions; complete the regular application;  check the ASO admission box; fill out the supplemental form from ASO;  provide I.E.P.'s from as many years of high school as possible, psychological evaluations documenting the disability, and 3 references addressing aptitude, motivation, ability to set realistic goals, interpersonal skills, and readiness for college; and submit SAT/ACT scores. Students applying to the ASO Program may be asked to interview with the ASO staff.

**College entrance exams required:** Yes          **Untimed accepted:** Yes
**Course entrance requirements:** Yes          **Interview Required:** Yes
**Diagnostic tests:** Yes
**Documentation:** WISC-R; WAIS-R; W-J or WRAT: within 3 years

### ADDITIONAL INFORMATION

The Academic Support Office is staffed by four full-time faculty members. Additional tuition is required for students enrolled in ASO tutorials.  A generous financial aid program is available to all qualified students. Skills classes are available through Student Development.

**Special education HS coursework accepted:** No          **Essay required:** Yes
**Special application required:** Yes          **Submitted to:** Admissions Office
**# of applications submitted each year:** 70          **# of applications accepted each year:** 30
**# of students receiving LD services:** 60
**Acceptance into program means acceptance into college:** Students are admitted jointly by the college and ASO.

# LEARNING DISABILITY SERVICES

**Learning center:** Yes
**Kurzweil personal reader:** Yes
**LD specialists:** 4
**Allowed in exams:**
  **Calculator:** Yes
  **Dictionary:** No
  **Computer:** Yes
  **SpellCheck:** Yes

**Notetaker:** Yes
**Scribes:** Yes
**Proctors:** Yes
**Oral exams:** Yes
**Extended test time:** Yes
**Added cost:** Fee for tutoring: $112 per credit hour
**Distraction-free environ.:** Yes
**Tape recording in class:** Yes
**Books on tape:** Yes
**Taping of other books:** No

**Professional tutors:** 4
**Peer tutors:** Yes
**Max. hrs/wk for services:** Unlimited
**Priority registration:** Yes
**Accomodations for students with ADD:** Yes
**How are professors notified of LD:** By the student and Program Director

# GENERAL ADMISSIONS INFORMATION

**Director of Admissions:** Tim Copeland

**Telephone:** 770-479-1454

## ENTRANCE REQUIREMENTS

3 years math, 3 years science.

**Application deadline:** NR
**Notification:** NR

**SAT or ACT preferred:** NR

# COLLEGE GRADUATION REQUIREMENTS

**Course waivers allowed:** No
**Course substitutions allowed:** No
**In what courses:** N/A

# ADDITIONAL INFORMATION

**Environment:** The college is located on a 600-acre campus in a small town 40 miles from Atlanta.

**Student Body**
  **Undergrad enrollment:** 650
  **Women:** 55%
  **Men:** 45%
  **In-state students:** 95%
  **Out-of-state:** 5%

**Cost Information**
  **In-state tuition:** $5,040
  **Out-of-state:** $5,040

**Housing Information**
  **University housing:** Yes
  **Fraternity:** N/R
  **Sorority:** N/R
  **Living on campus:** 66%

  **Athletics:** NJCAA

# UNIVERSITY OF IDAHO

**ID**

Moscow, ID 83844-4140 • **Admissions:** 208-885-6326 • **Fax:** 208-885-9061
**Email:** nss@uidaho.edu • **Web:** www.uidaho.edu
**Support:** S • **Institution:** 4 yr. Public

## LEARNING DISABILITY ADMISSIONS AND SERVICES

Student Support Services is an Educational Assistance Program that offers participating students academic and personal support services necessary to reach their educational goals. Designed to complement existing resources on campus, this federally funded program offers students opportunities to identify and pursue educational and career goals, establish and improve academic performance, and balance the challenges of university and personal life. SSS provides highly individualized assistance, which often makes the difference in a student's persistence with his/her educational plan. Tutoring is available from 1 to 3 hours per week, per class. One hour per week is with a professional counselor, the rest with peer tutors. A math specialist is available. Enrollment is limited to the first 200 students on a first come first served basis. To qualify for services a student must be a United States citizen; accepted for enrollment or currently enrolled; and be either financially limited or from a first generation family or physically or learning disabled; in addition, a student must show a need for and a potential to benefit from the Student Support Services Program.

## LEARNING DISABILITY ADMISSIONS INFORMATION

**Program Name:** Student Support Services (SSS)
**Program Director:** Meredith Goodwin
**Contact Person:** Same as above

**Telephone:** 208-885-6746

### ADMISSIONS

Students must meet the general admission requirements. However, special admission and probationary admission are available. A staff person from SSS is part of the special admissions committee for students with disabilities who do not meet regular admissions criteria. These students typically are denied admission but may reapply, submit additional information and documentation, and request a review of their application. Students admitted specially or on probation must successfully complete 14 credits in 4 core areas over 3 semesters.

**College entrance exams required:** Yes
**Course entrance requirements:** Yes
**Diagnostic tests:** Yes
**Documentation:** WAIS-R;  W-J: within 3 years

**Untimed accepted:** Yes
**Interview required:** No

### ADDITIONAL INFORMATION

Students with learning disabilities who participate in the Student Support Services Program will receive assistance with learning strategies, organization and time management, career advisory and employment readiness, advocacy, academic advisory, and instruction in unprepared areas in reading, writing, and math. An academic plan is mutually developed and students take an active role in their education. Students with learning disabilities enrolled at the University of Idaho, who exhibit a need for and the potential to benefit from the SSS program, will be eligible to participate. There are no LD specialists, but the Director of SSS has had extensive training. The office of Student Disability Services serves as a 'clearinghouse' to direct students with disabilities to various services on campus. The Computer Lab has software programs that are useful for students with learning disabilities.

**Special education HS coursework accepted:** On a
case-by-case basis
**Special application required:** Yes
**# of applications submitted each year:** 200
**# of students receiving LD services:** 90
**Acceptance into program means acceptance into college:** Students must be admitted to the university first and then may request LD services.

**Essay required:** No
**Submitted to:** Special Admission Committee
**# of applications accepted each year:** All

## LEARNING DISABILITY SERVICES

**Learning center:** No
**Kurzweil personal reader:** No
**LD specialists:** No
**Allowed in exams:**
  **Calculator:** Yes
  **Dictionary:** Yes
  **Computer:** Yes
  **SpellCheck:** Yes

**Notetaker:** Yes
**Scribes:** Yes
**Proctors:** Yes
**Oral exams:** Yes
**Extended test time:** Yes
**Added cost:** None
**Distraction-free environ.:** Yes
**Tape recording in class:** Yes
**Books on tape:** Yes
**Taping of other books:** Yes

**Professional tutors:** Yes
**Peer tutors:** Yes
**Max. hrs/wk for services:** Varies: 1-3 hrs. per week, per class
**Priority registration:** NR
**Accomodations for students with ADD:** Yes
**How are professors notified of LD:** By the student

## GENERAL ADMISSIONS INFORMATION

**Director of Admissions:** Peter Brown

**Telephone:** 208-885-6326

### ENTRANCE REQUIREMENTS

Total high school units required/recommended: 4 English required, 3 math required, 3 science required, 1 foreign language required, 3 social studies required. Applicants evaluated on a sliding scale based on secondary school GPA and ACT or SAT I scores.

**Application deadline:** August 1
**Notification:** Rolling

**SAT or ACT preferred:** Either
**SAT Avg:** 540V, 517M
**Average ACT:** 23
**Average GPA:** 3.5

**Graduated top 10% of class:** 20
**Graduated top 25% of class:** 49
**Graduated top 50% of class:** 80

## COLLEGE GRADUATION REQUIREMENTS

**Course waivers allowed:** No
**Course substitutions allowed:** Yes
**In what courses:** Math and foreign language. Students must request by petition.

## ADDITIONAL INFORMATION

**Environment:** The university is located on a 800-acre campus in a small town 90 miles south of Spokane, Washington.

**Student Body**
  **Undergrad enrollment:** 7,107
  **Women:** 43%
  **Men:** 57%
  **In-state students:** 67%
  **Out-of-state:** 33%

**Cost Information**
  **In-state tuition:** $1,942
  **Out-of-state:** $7,742
  **Room & board:** $3,680

**Housing Information**
  **University housing:** Yes
  **Fraternity:** Yes
  **Sorority:** Yes
  **Living on campus:** 60%

  **Athletics:** NCAA Div. I

# BARAT COLLEGE

700 East Westleigh Road, Lake Forest, IL 60045 • **Admissions:** 847-295-4260 • **Fax:** 847-604-6300

**Support:** SP • **Institution:** 4 yr. Private

## LEARNING DISABILITY ADMISSIONS AND SERVICES

The Learning Opportunities Program (LOP) is designed to meet the needs of college students with specific learning disabilities. The Program began in 1980 and is approximately 6% of the Barat population. The Program aims to help enrollees achieve success, prepare for a responsive and independent life, and to function effectively in the classroom, in their chosen profession, and in their personal lives. During the first year students focus, as needed, on oral and written communication, reading and math skills, and effective study habits. An LD specialist works one-on-one with each student to plan and implement an individually designed program. Students are involved in ongoing measurement and self-evaluation.

## LEARNING DISABILITY ADMISSIONS INFORMATION

**Program Name:** Learning Opportunities Program (LOP)
**Program Director:** Dr. Pamela Adelman
**Contact Person:** Same as above

**Telephone:** 847-234-3000, ext. 631

### ADMISSIONS

Barat will consider for admission those students who have a history or current diagnosis of a specific learning disability. These students should have average or above-average ability, a strong desire to succeed in college, and a willingness to work hard. Stage I for the students is to complete the application, send 2 recommendations, transcripts, SAT or ACT, case history, and LD tests. The teacher in high school or the case-manager should complete a special report. The LOP will notify the student about Stage II of the process, which includes past evaluation, reports, health information, and placement tests and interviews. The decision is made jointly by Admissions and LOP. High risk students who do not apply through the LOP are admitted on contract, which allows them to get additional assistance.

**College entrance exams required:** Yes
**Course entrance requirements:** Yes
**Diagnostic tests:** Yes
**Documentation:** WAIS-R or WISC-R or WISC-III: within 4 years

**Untimed accepted:** Yes
**Interview required:** Yes

### ADDITIONAL INFORMATION

No credit is given for participation in the LOP. Students receive credit for course work the same as other students. Additional instruction includes Barat's Writing Center, the Language Lab, the Math Center, the Typing Lab, the Library, and the Life/Career Planning Center. LOP students meet weekly for 2 hours with LD specialists and can have additional hours with tutors supervised by the specialist. LD specialists provide remediation as well as subject matter tutoring.

**Special education HS coursework accepted:** No
**Special application required:** Yes
**# of applications submitted each year:** 60-80
**# of students receiving LD services:** 40-50

**Essay required:** Yes
**Submitted to:** Admissions and the LOP
**# of applications accepted each year:** 15-20

**Acceptance into program means acceptance into college:** Students are admitted cooperatively by LOP and Admissions.

# LEARNING DISABILITY SERVICES

**Learning center:** No
**Kurzweil personal reader:** No
**LD specialists:** 4
**Allowed in exams:**
  **Calculator:** Yes
  **Dictionary:** Yes
  **Computer:** Yes
  **SpellCheck:** Yes

**Notetaker:** Yes
**Scribes:** Yes
**Proctors:** Yes
**Oral exams:** Yes
**Extended test time:** Yes
**Added cost:** $600-1,500 per semester
**Distraction-free environ.:** Yes
**Tape recording in class:** Yes
**Books on tape:** Yes
**Taping of other books:** Yes

**Professional tutors:** Yes
**Peer tutors:** Yes
**Max. hrs/wk for services:** Varies
**Priority registration:** N/A
**Accomodations for students with ADD:** Yes
**How are professors notified of LD:** By the student and Program Director

# GENERAL ADMISSIONS INFORMATION

**Director of Admissions:** Douglas Schacke          **Telephone:** 847-295-3000

## ENTRANCE REQUIREMENTS

Total high school units required/recommended: 16 total units are recommended; 4 English recommended, 2 math recommended, 2 science recommended, 2 foreign language recommended, 2 social studies recommended, 1 history recommended. Minimum composite ACT score of 20 (combined SAT I score of 900), rank in top half of secondary school class, and minimum 2.5 GPA recommended. Special requirements: An RN is required for nursing program applicants; audition required of dance program applicants.

**Application deadline:** Rolling
**Notification:** Rolling

**SAT or ACT preferred:** ACT
**Average ACT:** 22
**Average GPA:** 3.1

**Graduated top 10% of class:** 15
**Graduated top 25% of class:** 42
**Graduated top 50% of class:** 56

# COLLEGE GRADUATION REQUIREMENTS

**Course waivers allowed:** No
**Course substitutions allowed:** No
**In what courses:** Determined on an individual basis

# ADDITIONAL INFORMATION

**Environment:** The college is located on a 30-acre campus in the suburbs 25 miles north of Chicago.

**Student Body**
  **Undergrad enrollment:** 719
  **Women:** 68%
  **Men:** 32%
  **In-state students:** 72%
  **Out-of-state:** 28%

**Cost Information**
  **In-state tuition:** $12,570
  **Out-of-state:** $12,570
  **Room & board:** $4,966

**Housing Information**
  **University housing:** Yes
  **Fraternity:** No
  **Sorority:** No
  **Living on campus:** 57%

  **Athletics:** NR

# DEPAUL UNIVERSITY

1 East Jackson Boulevard, Chicago, IL 60604 • **Admissions:** 312-362-8300 • **Fax:** 312-362-5289
**Email:** admitdpu@wppost.depaul.edu • **Web:** www.depaul.edu
**Support:** CS • **Institution:** 4 yr. Private

## LEARNING DISABILITY ADMISSIONS AND SERVICES

PLuS is designed to service students with learning disabilities who can reason, think cognitively, and are motivated to succeed in college. The immediate goals are to remediate the students' existing skills and to teach coping strategies when remediation is not feasible. The ultimate goal is to impart academic and study skills that will enable the students to function independently in the academic environment and competitive job market. PLuS provides intensive help on a one-to-one or small group basis. It is designed to assist with regular college courses, to improve learning deficits, and to help the student learn compensatory skills. Students and learning disability specialists meet for 2 hours per week for at least the first year of college. The ultimate goal is to make sure that the strategies being taught will benefit students not only at the university but also in the competitive job market.

## LEARNING DISABILITY ADMISSIONS INFORMATION

**Program Name:** Productive Learning Strategies (PLuS)
**Program Director:** Karen Wold
**Contact Person:** Same as above

**Telephone:** 312-325-7000, ext.1706

### ADMISSIONS

There is no separate admission process for students with learning disabilities. Students with learning disabilities must be accepted to DePaul University before they can be accepted to PLuS. The diagnostic testing that is required, if done within the last 3 years, will be used in the evaluation. Admission criteria include a GPA of 2.5, top 40% of class, and ACT 21 or SAT 890. If the student does not have the required testing, the university will administer the appropriate assessments. Some students who are considered "high potential" but who have borderline admission criteria may qualify for admissions through the Bridge Program. This is an enhancement program for incoming freshmen. Bridge students may have an ACT of 18-20 or SAT of 860-890. (This program is not for students with learning disabilities although some students are learning disabled.) Bridge students must begin in a summer program prior to freshman year. Some students can be admitted on a probationary basis as Special Students. Adult students (over 24) can be admitted through the Adult Admissions Program.

**College entrance exams required:** Yes
**Course entrance requirements:** Yes
**Diagnostic tests:** Yes
**Documentation:** Complete diagnostic battery: within 3 years

**Untimed accepted:** Yes
**Interview required:** Yes, for PLuS

### ADDITIONAL INFORMATION

Skills courses in many areas are offered. PLuS is housed in the Reading and Learning Lab and the Program is only available to students with learning disabilities. Many of the services requested are offered through Disabled Student Services. Students who do the best at DePaul and the PLuS Program are students who are highly motivated and who have received LD resource support in grade school and high school. Services and accommodations are available for undergraduate and graduate students.

**Special education HS coursework accepted:** Yes, unless they are developmental
**Special application required:** Yes
**# of applications submitted each year:** 20-25
**# of students receiving LD services:** 42

**Essay required:** Yes
**Submitted to:** Director of Program
**# of applications accepted each year:** 15-20

**Acceptance into program means acceptance into college:** Students must be admitted to the university first and then may request services.

## LEARNING DISABILITY SERVICES

**Learning center:** Yes
**Kurzweil personal reader:** No
**LD specialists:** 7
**Allowed in exams:**
 **Calculator:** Yes
 **Dictionary:** No
 **Computer:** Yes
 **SpellCheck:** Yes

**Notetaker:** No
**Scribes:** Yes
**Proctors:** Yes
**Oral exams:** Yes
**Extended test time:** Yes
**Added cost:** $250 for 1 hr. per week; $400 for 2 hrs. per week with LD specialist
**Distraction-free environ.:** Yes
**Tape recording in class:** Yes
**Books on tape:** Yes
**Taping of other books:** Yes

**Professional tutors:** 7
**Peer tutors:** Yes
**Max. hrs/wk for services:** 2
**Priority registration:** Yes
**Accomodations for students with ADD:** Yes
**How are professors notified of LD:** By the student

## GENERAL ADMISSIONS INFORMATION

**Director of Admissions:** Ellen Cohen

**Telephone:** 312-362-8146

### ENTRANCE REQUIREMENTS

Total high school units required/recommended: 16 total units are required; 4 English required, 2 math required, 2 science required, 2 social studies required, 2 history required. Additional units of math and science are recommended. Special requirements: An audition is required for music and theater program applicants; RN is required for nursing program applicants.

**Application deadline:** August 15
**Notification:** Rolling

**SAT or ACT preferred:** Either
**SAT Avg:** 511V, 554M
**Average ACT:** 25

**Graduated top 10% of class:** 30
**Graduated top 25% of class:** 58
**Graduated top 50% of class:** 89

## COLLEGE GRADUATION REQUIREMENTS

**Course waivers allowed:** Yes
**Course substitutions allowed:** Yes
**In what courses:** This depends on the student's major course requirements. Courses that are not required for the major can be waived.

## ADDITIONAL INFORMATION

**Environment:** DePaul is an urban campus located in Chicago's Lincoln Park area on a 3-acre campus 3 miles north of the downtown area.

**Student Body**
 **Undergrad enrollment:** 9,788
 **Women:** 57%
 **Men:** 43%
 **In-state students:** 70%
 **Out-of-state:** 30%

**Cost Information**
 **In-state tuition:** $12,750
 **Out-of-state:** $12,750
 **Room & board:** $5,500

**Housing Information**
 **University housing:** Yes
 **Fraternity:** No
 **Sorority:** No
 **Living on campus:** 25%

 **Athletics:** NCAA Div. I

# EASTERN ILLINOIS UNIVERSITY

600 Lincoln Avenue, Charleston, IL 61920 • **Admissions:** 217-581-2223 • **Fax:** 217-581-7060
**Email:** admissns@www.eiu.edu • **Web:** www.eiu.edu
**Support:** S • **Institution:** 4 yr. Public

## LEARNING DISABILITY ADMISSIONS AND SERVICES

EIU will provide services as deemed effective and reasonable to assist students with learning disabilities to obtain access to the university programs. Students applying to the university who are requesting support services and/or accommodations from the Office of Disability Services are required to submit documentation to verify eligibility under Section 504. The assessment and diagnosis of specific learning disabilities must be conducted by a qualified professional. The written diagnostic evaluation report should include the following information: diagnostic report clearly stating the learning disability and the rationale for the diagnosis; the tests administered and the specific scores including grade level scores, standard scores, and percentile scores; descriptive written text beyond that which is provided on a typical IEP and including qualitative information about the student's abilities; recommendations for accommodations that include specific suggestions based on the diagnostic evaluation results and supported by the diagnosis; and identifying information about the evaluator/diagnostician. The diagnostic tests should be current within the last 3 years; should be comprehensive and include a battery of more than one test and/or subtest; should include at least one instrument to measure aptitude or cognitive ability; and should include at least one measurement in reading, written language, and math.

## LEARNING DISABILITY ADMISSIONS INFORMATION

**Program Name:** Office of Disability Services
**Program Director:** Martha Jacques     **Telephone:** 217-581-6583
**Contact Person:** Same as above

### ADMISSIONS

All applicants must meet the same admission criteria. There is no special admission process for students with learning disabilities. General admission requires students to (1) rank in the top half of the class and have a minimum ACT of 18 or SAT of 860 or (2) rank in the top three-quarters of the class and have a minimum ACT of 22 or SAT of 1020. Additionally, all students must have 3 yrs. of English, 3 yrs. math, 3 yrs. social science, 3 yrs. laboratory science, and 2 yrs. electives. Once admitted, students with learning disabilities or attention deficit disorder must provide appropriate documentation in order to access services and accommodations.

**College entrance exams required:** Yes     **Untimed accepted:** Yes
**Course entrance requirements:** Yes     **Interview required:** No
**Diagnostic tests:** Yes
**Documentation:** WAIS-R; WJ-R; Stanford Binet; within 3 years

### ADDITIONAL INFORMATION

Students should meet with the Office of Disability Services to discuss accommodations or make further arrangements as needed. Some services provided include priority registration; alternate format for classroom materials; notetakers; assistance locating tutors and liaison with tutors to develop effective study strategies; proctors; and liaison with instructors. Skills classes can be arranged in time management, notetaking, test taking, and study strategies.

**Special education HS coursework accepted:** Yes,     **Essay required:** No
if college preparatory
**Special application required:** No     **Submitted to:** N/A
**# of applications submitted each year:** N/A     **# of applications accepted each year:** N/A
**# of students receiving LD services:** 80-90
**Acceptance into program means acceptance into college:** Must be admitted and be enrolled and then request services.

## LEARNING DISABILITY SERVICES

**Learning center:** No
**Kurzweil personal reader:** Yes
**LD specialists:** No
**Allowed in exams:**
  **Calculator:** Yes
  **Dictionary:** Y/N
  **Computer:** Y/N
  **SpellCheck:** Yes

**Notetaker:** Yes
**Scribes:** Yes
**Proctors:** Yes
**Oral exams:** Yes
**Extended test time:** Yes
**Added cost:** $5 per hour with Honors Tutorial
**Distraction-free environ.:** Yes
**Tape recording in class:** Yes
**Books on tape:** Yes
**Taping of other books:** Yes

**Professional tutors:** No
**Peer tutors:** No
**Max. hrs/wk for services:** N/A
**Priority registration:** Yes
**Accomodations for students with ADD:** Yes
**How are professors notified of LD:** Both by student and Director

## GENERAL ADMISSIONS INFORMATION

**Director of Admissions:** Dale Wolf

**Telephone:** 217-581-2223

### ENTRANCE REQUIREMENTS

Total high school units required/recommended: 13 total units are required; 2 total units are recommended; 4 English required, 3 math required, 3 science required, 2 foreign language, and 3 social studies required. Minimum composite ACT score of 22 and rank in top 3/4 of secondary school class, or minimum composite ACT score of 18 and rank in top 1/2 of secondary school class required. Special requirements: An audition is required for music and theatre program applicants.

**Application deadline:** Rolling
**Notification:** Rolling

**SAT or ACT preferred:** ACT
**Average ACT:** 22

**Graduated top 10% of class:** 9
**Graduated top 25% of class:** 38
**Graduated top 50% of class:** 85

## COLLEGE GRADUATION REQUIREMENTS

**Course waivers allowed:** No
**Course substitutions allowed:** Yes
**In what courses:** Foreign language and math

## ADDITIONAL INFORMATION

**Environment:** NR

**Student Body**
  **Undergrad enrollment:** 10,106
  **Women:** 58%
  **Men:** 42%
  **In-state students:** 97%
  **Out-of-state:** 3%

**Cost Information**
  **In-state tuition:** $2,052
  **Out-of-state:** $6,156
  **Room & board:** $3,434

**Housing Information**
  **University housing:** Yes
  **Fraternity:** Yes
  **Sorority:** Yes
  **Living on campus:** 52%

  **Athletics:** NCAA Div. I

# ILLINOIS STATE UNIVERSITY

2200 Admissions, Normal, IL 61790 • **Admissions:** 309-438-2181 • **Fax:** 309-438-7234
**Email:** ppabell@ilstu.edu • **Web:** www.ilstu.edu
**Support:** CS • **Institution:** 4 yr. Public

## LEARNING DISABILITY ADMISSIONS AND SERVICES

The mission of the Disability Concerns Office is to ensure the full and equal participation for persons with disabilities in the university community through empowering individuals, promoting equal access, encouraging self-advocacy, reducing attitudinal and communication barriers, and providing appropriate accommodation. The Disability Concerns Program is designed to work with students who have learning disabilities on becoming academically and socially successful while attending Illinois State University. The success of Disability Concerns is due largely to the fact that the majority of services are provided by volunteers. After a review of the appropriate documentation by the Coordinator of the learning disability services and a consultation, accommodations can then be determined based on the needs of the individual. A psychoeducational evaluation completed when the individual was 17 or older is required. It should include test scores and the following: the diagnosis, including specific areas of the disability; the impact the disability has on the academic performance of the student; and the accommodations suggested in view of the impact on learning of the student's disability.

## LEARNING DISABILITY ADMISSIONS INFORMATION

**Program Name:** Disability Concerns
**Program Director:** Dr. Judith Smithson
**Contact Person:** Ann Caldwell

**Telephone:** 309-438-5853

### ADMISSIONS

Admissions criteria for students with learning disabilities are the same as for other students at this time. Applicants with questions should contact the Disability Concerns Office. In general, students are admissible if they are in the top three-fourths of their high school class and have an ACT of 20 or better. High school courses required include: 4 yrs. English, 3 yrs. math, 2 yrs. social science, 2 yrs. science. Students with learning disabilities who are borderline admits or who are denied admission, may self-disclose and ask to be reviewed by Disability Concerns. The Director will review the documentation and make a recommendation to admissions.

**College entrance exams required:** Yes
**Course entrance requirements:** Yes
**Diagnostic tests:** Yes

**Untimed accepted:** Yes
**Interview required:** No

**Documentation:** Psychological evaluation given by School or Clinical Psychologist: recent

### ADDITIONAL INFORMATION

The following are options for accommodations based on appropriate documentation and needs: notetakers; peer tutors; readers; scribes; peer mentors; taped textbooks; Arkenstone Reader; computers; testing accommodations; conference with LD specialist; and quiet studyrooms. LD support groups meet monthly. LMS (Learning Through Mini Sessions) are designed to help students make college academics and college life a little less stressful. Sessions could include stress management; self advocacy; test anxiety; communication skills; and organizational skills.

**Special education HS coursework accepted:** Yes
**Special application required:** No
**# of applications submitted each year:** N/A
**# of students receiving LD services:** 91

**Essay required:** No
**Submitted to:** N/A
**# of applications accepted each year:** N/A

**Acceptance into program means acceptance into college:** Students must be admitted to the university first and then may request services.

**Learning center:** Yes
**Kurzweil personal reader:** Yes
**LD specialists:** Yes
**Allowed in exams:**
  **Calculator:** Yes
  **Dictionary:** Yes
  **Computer:** Yes
  **SpellCheck:** Yes

**Notetaker:** Yes
**Scribes:** Yes
**Proctors:** Yes
**Oral exams:** Yes
**Extended test time:** Yes
**Added cost:** None
**Distraction-free environ.:** Yes
**Tape recording in class:** Yes
**Books on tape:** Yes
**Taping of other books:** Yes

**Professional tutors:** 2
**Peer tutors:** Yes
**Max. hrs/wk for services:** Unlimited
**Priority registration:** Yes
**Accomodations for students with ADD:** Yes
**How are professors notified of LD:** By the student and/or the Program Director

# GENERAL ADMISSIONS INFORMATION

**Director of Admissions:** Steve Adams

**Telephone:** 309-438-2262

## ENTRANCE REQUIREMENTS

Total high school units required/recommended: 15 total units are required; 4 English required, 3 math required, 2 science required, 2 social studies required. Minimum composite ACT score of 17 and rank in top half of secondary schoool class or minimum composite ACT score of 23 and rank in 3/4 of secondary school class required. Special requirements: An audition is required for music program applicants.

**Application deadline:** Rolling
**Notification:** Rolling

**SAT or ACT preferred:** ACT
**SAT II required:** Yes
**Average ACT:** 22

**Graduated top 10% of class:** 11
**Graduated top 25% of class:** 33
**Graduated top 50% of class:** 77

# COLLEGE GRADUATION REQUIREMENTS

**Course waivers allowed:** Yes
**Course substitutions allowed:** Yes
**In what courses:** Considered on a case-by-case basis

# ADDITIONAL INFORMATION

**Environment:** The university is located on 850 acres in a small town 125 miles south of Chicago, and 180 miles north of St. Louis.

**Student Body**
  **Undergrad enrollment:** 16,773
  **Women:** 57%
  **Men:** 43%
  **In-state students:** 99%
  **Out-of-state:** 1%

**Cost Information**
  **In-state tuition:** $2,952
  **Out-of-state:** $8,856
  **Room & board:** $3,840

**Housing Information**
  **University housing:** Yes
  **Fraternity:** Yes
  **Sorority:** Yes
  **Living on campus:** 35%

  **Athletics:** NCAA Div. I

# UNIVERSITY OF ILLINOIS-URBANA-CHAMPAIGN

506 South Wright Street, Urbana, IL 61801 • **Admissions:** 217-333-0302 • **Fax:** 217-244-7124
**Email:** admission@uiuc.edu • **Web:** www.uiuc.edu
**Support:** CS • **Institution:** 4 yr. Public

## LEARNING DISABILITY ADMISSIONS AND SERVICES

The Division of Rehabilitation Education Services (DRES) assists qualified students with disabilities in the pursuit of their higher education objectives. Additionally, DRES assists students with disabilities in gaining access to and benefiting from all the related experiences that are an integral part of a University of Illinois education. The design of the Urbana-Champaign campus in combination with the programming of DRES enhance access to campus academic and extracurricular programs. Professional staff are also available at DRES to assist university students in the following areas: planning and implementing academic accommodations, obtaining additional aids (e.g., interpreters, readers/writer), obtaining modified test accommodations, counseling, and priority registration/scheduling assistance.

## LEARNING DISABILITY ADMISSIONS INFORMATION

**Program Name:** Rehabilitation Education Services
**Program Director:** Interim Director
**Contact Person:** Brad Hedrick

**Telephone:** 217-333-4600
**Telephone:** 217-333-4602

### ADMISSIONS

Applicants with learning disabilities are expected to meet the same admission criteria as all other applicants. Any tests for undergraduate and graduate admissions taken with accommodations are considered as competitive. Students are encouraged to provide diagnostic evidence from a licensed clinical examiner of their learning disabilities and to use the "Background Statement" section on the application to provide additional information that could be useful in understanding the student's academic history. The university admits students to particular colleges on the basis of class rank and ACT/SAT scores. Prospective students should contact the appropriate college for complete course requirements.

**College entrance exams required:** Yes
**Course entrance requirements:** Yes
**Diagnostic tests:** Yes
**Documentation:** W-J Cognitive Battery; WAIS-R; within 3 years

**Untimed accepted:** Yes
**Interview required:** Yes

### ADDITIONAL INFORMATION

Accommodations are individually student centered. The student is expected to declare and document all concurrent disabilities for which services are expected. The design and implementation of accommodations depend on the student's perspective of his/her functional limitations relative to the academic requirements of each course. Timely communication to the learning disability specialist of any situations that are projected to need accommodations during the semester is essential. Individual inquiries and early contacts prior to campus residency strengthen the process of accommodation.

**Special education HS coursework accepted:** N/I
**Special application required:** No
**# of applications submitted each year:** N/A
**# of students receiving LD services:** 90
**Acceptance into program means acceptance into college:** Students must be admitted to the university first and then may request services.

**Essay required:** Y/N
**Submitted to:** N/A
**# of applications accepted each year:** N/A

# LEARNING DISABILITY SERVICES

**Learning center:** No
**Kurzweil personal reader:** Yes
**LD specialists:** 1
**Allowed in exams:**
  **Calculator:** Yes
  **Dictionary:** Yes
  **Computer:** Yes
  **SpellCheck:** Yes

**Notetaker:** Yes
**Scribes:** Yes
**Proctors:** Yes
**Oral exams:** Yes
**Extended test time:** Yes
**Added cost:** No
**Distraction-free environ.:** Yes
**Tape recording in class:** Yes
**Books on tape:** N/I
**Taping of other books:** Yes

**Professional tutors:** N/I
**Peer tutors:** N/I
**Max. hrs/wk for services:** Unlimited
**Priority registration:** Yes
**Accomodations for students with ADD:** Yes
**How are professors notified of LD:** By the student

# GENERAL ADMISSIONS INFORMATION

**Director of Admissions:** Martha Moore          **Telephone:** 217-333-0302

## ENTRANCE REQUIREMENTS

Total high school units required/recommended: 15 total units are required; 4 English required, 3 math required, 4 math recommended, 2 science required, 2 foreign language required, 2 social studies required. Special requirements: An audition is required for music program applicants; professional interest statement recommended for some programs.

**Application deadline:** January 1
**Notification:** Rolling

**SAT or ACT preferred:** Either
**SAT Avg:** 608V, 640M
**SAT II required:** Yes
**Average ACT:** 27
**Average GPA:** 3.5

**Graduated top 10% of class:** 51
**Graduated top 25% of class:** 86
**Graduated top 50% of class:** 99

# COLLEGE GRADUATION REQUIREMENTS

**Course waivers allowed:** No
**Course substitutions allowed:** Yes
**In what courses:** Substitutions are given on an individual basis

# ADDITIONAL INFORMATION

**Environment:** The university is on an urban campus 130 miles south of Chicago

**Student Body**
  **Undergrad enrollment:** 26738
  **Women:** 46%
  **Men:** 54%
  **In-state students:** 91%
  **Out-of-state:** 9%

**Cost Information**
  **In-state tuition:** $3,150
  **Out-of-state:** $8,580
  **Room & board:** $4,560

**Housing Information**
  **University housing:** Yes
  **Fraternity:** Yes
  **Sorority:** Yes
  **Living on campus:** 31%

  **Athletics:** NCAA Div. I

# LINCOLN COLLEGE

Lincoln, IL 62656 • **Admissions:** 800-569-0556

**Support:** S • **Institution:** 2 yr. Private

## LEARNING DISABILITY ADMISSIONS AND SERVICES

Lincoln College is committed to enhancing student achievement through supportive service community efforts in combination with parental involvement. The college offers personal attention and a number of supportive services to assist students. The Academic Enrichment Program meets every day to improve fundamental learning skills in writing, reading, mathematics, and oral communication. Study skills and study habits are also emphasized. Tutoring is assigned and each student's course schedule is strictly regulated. The Breakfast Club is for students who are failing two or more classes. These students meet with the college President and the Academic Dean to discuss ways to change direction and achieve academic success. Class attendance is monitored and faculty members inform the Dean weekly if a student has missed class. Advisors help students to change counter-productive behaviors regarding attendance. C.A.S.P. (Concerned about Student Progress) warnings are sent the 5th week of each semester to provide an early indicator of below average performance, and allow students time to recover and change behaviors. The Connection Program targets incoming freshmen who may benefit from an established peer group. These groups of 8-10 meet with professors and foster awareness and build relationships.

## LEARNING DISABILITY ADMISSIONS INFORMATION

**Program Name:** Supportive Educational Services
**Program Director:** Paula Knopp/Tina Smith          **Telephone:** 800-569-0556
**Contact Person:** Roderick S. Rumler, Director of Admissions

### ADMISSIONS

There is no special admissions process for students with learning disabilities. Students must submit the general application, a high school transcript, and counselor recommendation. Students with sub-17 ACT scores are required to attend the one-week Academic Development Seminar prior to the fall semester. Upon completing the Academic Development Seminar a student's probationary status is removed. Students may be admitted and placed into a split semester, which means the student will take two courses per nine weeks if this is recommended by the Academic Development Seminar.

| | |
|---|---|
| **College entrance exams required:** Yes | **Untimed accepted:** Yes |
| **Course entrance requirements:** Yes | **Interview Required:** Yes |
| **Diagnostic tests:** No | |
| **Documentation:** N/A | |

### ADDITIONAL INFORMATION

Lincoln College offers the Academic Development Seminar for students the week before fall semester starts. Students learn writing and speaking skills; effective library skills; and science lab orientation. They develop effective student techniques; lab and field orientation; methods to evaluate social science graphs, charts and maps; and concepts and values in the humanities. The Academic Writing Seminar is also offered one week in the summer to cover crucial college skills such as writing skill development; note-taking techniques; exam tips; writing and speaking skills; writing to define and classify; college expectations; analytical thinking and writing; and writing to understand and evaluate.

| | |
|---|---|
| **Special education HS coursework accepted:** No | **Essay required:** No |
| **Special application required:** No | **Submitted to:** N/A |
| **# of applications submitted each year:** N/A | **# of applications accepted each year:** N/A |
| **# of students receiving LD services:** N/A | |

**Acceptance into program means acceptance into college:** Admitted to the college and then reviewed for supportive services.

## LEARNING DISABILITY SERVICES

**Learning center:** No
**Kurzweil personal reader:** No
**LD specialists:** No
**Allowed in exams:**
  **Calculator:** Yes
  **Dictionary:** Yes
  **Computer:** Yes
  **SpellCheck:** Yes

**Notetaker:** No
**Scribes:** No
**Proctors:** No
**Oral exams:** No
**Extended test time:** Yes
**Added cost:** Tutoring is free
**Distraction-free environ.:** Yes
**Tape recording in class:** Yes
**Books on tape:** RFB
**Taping of other books:** RFB

**Professional tutors:** 7
**Peer tutors:** 20-30
**Max. hrs/wk for services:**
Unlimited
**Priority registration:** Yes
**Accomodations for students
with ADD:** Yes
**How are professors notified of
LD:** By the student

## GENERAL ADMISSIONS INFORMATION

**Director of Admissions:** Roderick S. Rumler

**Telephone:** 800-569-0556

### ENTRANCE REQUIREMENTS
NR

**Application deadline:** NR
**Notification:** NR

**SAT or ACT preferred:** NR

## COLLEGE GRADUATION REQUIREMENTS

**Course waivers allowed:** No
**Course substitutions allowed:** No
**In what courses:** N/A

## ADDITIONAL INFORMATION

**Environment:** NR

**Student Body**
  **Undergrad enrollment:** NR
  **Women:** NR
  **Men:** NR
  **In-state students:** NR
  **Out-of-state:** NR

**Cost Information**
  **In-state tuition:** NR
  **Out-of-state:** NR

**Housing Information**
  **University housing:** NR
  **Fraternity:** NR
  **Sorority:** NR
  **Living on campus:** NR

  **Athletics:** NR

# NATIONAL-LOUIS UNIVERSITY

2840 Sheridan Road, Evanston, IL 60201 • **Admissions:** 847-256-6771 • **Fax:** 847-465-0593
**Web:** www.nlu.nl.edu
**Support:** CS • **Institution:** 4 yr. Private

## LEARNING DISABILITY ADMISSIONS AND SERVICES

The Center for Academic Development is designed to assist students with learning disabilities to pursue and complete a college education. It is a supportive program for students admitted by the university and enrolled in regular and developmental college courses. While the total services furnished in this program are provided by the university to all students who might experience difficulty with a regular college curriculum, emphasis is placed on individual program planning, tutoring, monitoring, arranged counseling, and special testing for the learning disabled. The center provides peer tutoring, liaison with faculty, academic advising, and career/ emotional counseling for students who make reasonable progress toward a degree in one of the college programs.

## LEARNING DISABILITY ADMISSIONS INFORMATION

**Program Name:** Center for Academic Development
**Program Director:** Anna Hammond
**Contact Person:** Same as above

**Telephone:** 847-475-1100, ext. 2357

### ADMISSIONS

Students must meet regular admission requirements of a 2.0 GPA in non-remedial academic courses. Interested students should indicate on the supplemental application form the nature of their learning disability and return the form to the Admissions Office. An informal assessment session is held with the applicants by a learning specialist. Students forward all requested reports to Admissions with authorization for release of information. Students should submit a statement from a diagnostician that they can function at college level. Social service or psychiatric reports should also be submitted. The Learning Specialist evaluates reports and admits 10 students each fall and they must participate in the summer Bridge Program and LD counseling group. Alternative admission for all students is offered through Provisional Admission and/or Summer Admission.

**College entrance exams required:** Yes
**Course entrance requirements:** Yes
**Diagnostic tests:** Yes
**Documentation:** WISC; W-J: within 5 years

**Untimed accepted:** Yes
**Interview required:** Yes

### ADDITIONAL INFORMATION

The Center for Academic Development is staffed by specialists. Special services provided include Summer Bridge Program; developmental reading, writing, and math courses; special advising and orientation; assistance in registration; individualized tutoring and monitoring; organizational and student skill training; academic and career counseling; and an arrangement with faculty for modification of course presentation and examination. Support services and accommodations are offered to undergraduate and graduate students. The PACE Program is housed on this campus. This is a non-credit transition program for students with low IQ scores who want to experience residential living and develop life skills. These students have the opportunity to get work experience as Teacher Aides or in Human Resources. (Contact Dr. Robert Harth 847-256-5150.s)

**Special education HS coursework accepted:** No
**Special application required:** No
**# of applications submitted each year:** NR
**# of students receiving LD services:** 5

**Essay required:** Yes
**Submitted to:** N/A
**# of applications accepted each year:** NR

**Acceptance into program means acceptance into college:** Students must be accepted to the university first and then may request services.

**Learning center:** Yes
**Kurzweil personal reader:** No
**LD specialists:** 2
**Allowed in exams:**
  **Calculator:** Yes
  **Dictionary:** Yes
  **Computer:** Yes
  **SpellCheck:** Yes

**Notetaker:** Yes
**Scribes:** Yes
**Proctors:** Yes
**Oral exams:** Yes
**Extended test time:** Yes
**Added cost:** None
**Distraction-free environ.:** Yes
**Tape recording in class:** Yes
**Books on tape:** Yes
**Taping of other books:** No

**Professional tutors:** 2
**Peer tutors:** 5
**Max. hrs/wk for services:** 6 hours per week with professional tutor
**Priority registration:** Yes
**Accomodations for students with ADD:** Yes
**How are professors notified of LD:** By the student and the Program Director

## GENERAL ADMISSIONS INFORMATION

**Director of Admissions:** Randall Berd, Director of Enrollment        **Telephone:** 847-475-1100

### ENTRANCE REQUIREMENTS
4 yrs. English, 3 yrs. social studies, 2 yrs. math, 2 yrs. science; 2.0 GPA in regular academic courses, interviews are highly recommended.

**Application deadline:** Rolling
**Notification:** NR

**SAT or ACT preferred:** NR
**SAT II required:** Yes
**Average ACT:** 18

**Graduated top 10% of class:** 5
**Graduated top 25% of class:** 21
**Graduated top 50% of class:** 59

## COLLEGE GRADUATION REQUIREMENTS

**Course waivers allowed:** No
**Course substitutions allowed:** No
**In what courses:** All students must pass an English Competency Exam and a Math Competency Exam

## ADDITIONAL INFORMATION

**Environment:** Formerly known as National College of Education, the school is located in Evanston on 12 acres in a suburban neighborhood 12 miles north of Chicago.

**Student Body**
  **Undergrad enrollment:** NR
  **Women:** 72%
  **Men:** 28%
  **In-state students:** 95%
  **Out-of-state:** 5%

**Cost Information**
  **In-state tuition:** $12,150
  **Out-of-state:** $12,150
  **Room & board:** $5,256

**Housing Information**
  **University housing:** Yes
  **Fraternity:** No
  **Sorority:** No
  **Living on campus:** 5%

  **Athletics:** NAIA

# NORTHERN ILLINOIS UNIVERSITY

DeKalb, IL 60115 • **Admissions:** 815-753-0446
**Email:** admissions-info@niu.edu • **Web:** www.niu.edu
**Support:** CS • **Institution:** 4 yr. Public

## LEARNING DISABILITY ADMISSIONS AND SERVICES

The main goal of the Center for Access Ability Resources (CAAR) is to create and maintain a supportive atmosphere to assist students with learning disabilities develop self-esteem, self-advocacy skills, and effective strategies for college success. CAAR is staffed by personnel who are supportive and sensitive to students. CAAR provides a comprehensive range of support services that are integrated within the university resources. Assistance must be requested by the student. The LD Coordinator assists students in identifying appropriate accommodations, compensatory, and remediation strategies, and in the utilization of both on and off campus resources. The goal is to enhance student success through an individualized program of support services. To request and initiate services, students must submit to CAAR the necessary and appropriate official documentation verifying the disability. BOLD (Building On Learning Differences) provides academic and personal support to individuals with learning disABILITIES, to be a resource for people interested in acquiring knowledge about learning disABILITIES, and to create an environment promoting positive interaction for all people. The goal is to nurture an environment that will both foster advocacy for, and awareness of, persons with learning disABILITIES.

## LEARNING DISABILITY ADMISSIONS INFORMATION

**Program Name:** Center for Access-Ability Resources (CAAR)
**Program Director:** Nancy Kasinski                **Telephone:** 815-753-1303
**Contact Person:** Sharon Wyland, LD Coordinator

### ADMISSIONS

Regular admission requires: 50-99% class rank and 19 ACT or 34-49% class rank and 23 ACT; 3 yrs. math, 2 yrs. science, 2 yrs. social studies, and 1 yr. art, music, foreign language, or theater. Students with LD not meeting the minimum requirements may request special consideration (through CAAR for Illinois residents only) by submitting the regular application and a letter disclosing the LD and/or ADD; applications are forwarded to the LD Coordinator who contacts students regarding the special consideration and who requests: current documentation, three letters of recommendation, and a possible on-campus interview. Provisional admission requires no deficiencies in English or math and only one deficiency in any of the other areas of social science, lab science, or elective. This decision is made by Admissions and the LD Coordinator.

**College entrance exams required:** Yes          **Untimed accepted:** Yes
**Course entrance requirements:** Yes             **Interview required:** Yes for CAAR
**Diagnostic tests:** Yes
**Documentation:** I.Q.; Achievement tests; summary by a psychologist: within 3 years

### ADDITIONAL INFORMATION

Students admitted provisionally must earn a minimum of 15 semester hours during the first two semesters and achieve a cumulative GPA of at least 2.0. Academic resources include priority registration; exam accommodations; limited tutoring; individualized study skill learning strategy advisement and instruction by LD specialists; reading and study techniques course taught by LD specialist; foreign language course substitution with documentation; and taped texts. Advocacy services include orientation; self-advocacy training; liaison with faculty; information on LD/ADD-related events; support group (BOLD); and in-service training for faculty. Advisement Resources include academic advising; referrals to University Counseling; and support and consultation to staff. Diagnostic evaluation resources include cognitive and achievement testing for a fee; ADD evaluation and treatment; and referral to private diagnostician. Not all students are eligible for services.

**Special education HS coursework accepted:** Yes, by approval of Admissions  **Essay required:** Yes, for CAAR
**Special application required:** No                **Submitted to:** N/A
**# of applications submitted each year:** N/A       **# of applications accepted each year:** N/A
**# of students receiving LD services:** 250
**Acceptance into program means acceptance into college:** Students admitted may request services. Students denied admission may appeal decision and once admitted may request services.

## LEARNING DISABILITY SERVICES

**Learning center:** No
**Kurzweil personal reader:** Yes
**LD specialists:** 1
**Allowed in exams:**
  **Calculator:** Y/N
  **Dictionary:** Y/N
  **Computer:** Yes
  **SpellCheck:** Y/N

**Notetaker:** Yes
**Scribes:** Yes
**Proctors:** Yes
**Oral exams:** Yes
**Extended test time:** Yes
**Added cost:** No
**Distraction-free environ.:** Yes
**Tape recording in class:** Yes
**Books on tape:** Yes
**Taping of other books:** Yes

**Professional tutors:** No
**Peer tutors:** Yes
**Max. hrs/wk for services:**
Unlimited within reason
**Priority registration:** Yes
**Accomodations for students
with ADD:** Yes
**How are professors notified of
LD:** By the student or by student
request to Program Director

## GENERAL ADMISSIONS INFORMATION

**Director of Admissions:** Robert Burk

**Telephone:** 815-753-8300

### ENTRANCE REQUIREMENTS

Total high school units required/recommended: 13 total units are required; 4 English required, 3 math required, 3 science required, 2 social studies required. Minimum composite ACT score of 19 and rank in top half of secondary school class or minimum composite ACT score of 23 and rank in top 2/3 of secondary school class required. Special requirements: An audition is required for music program applicants.

**Application deadline:** August 1
**Notification:** Rolling

**SAT or ACT preferred:** ACT
**Average ACT:** 22

**Graduated top 10% of class:** 10
**Graduated top 25% of class:** 33
**Graduated top 50% of class:** 76

## COLLEGE GRADUATION REQUIREMENTS

**Course waivers allowed:** No
**Course substitutions allowed:** Yes
**In what courses:** Primarily foreign language and math, but each request for a substitution is reviewed on a case-by-case basis.

## ADDITIONAL INFORMATION

**Environment:** The school is located on 460 acres in a small town 65 miles from Chicago.

**Student Body**
  **Undergrad enrollment:** 16,423
  **Women:** 54%
  **Men:** 46%
  **In-state students:** 96%
  **Out-of-state:** 4%

**Cost Information**
  **In-state tuition:** $3,036
  **Out-of-state:** $9,106
  **Room & board:** $3,600

**Housing Information**
  **University housing:** Yes
  **Fraternity:** Yes
  **Sorority:** Yes
  **Living on campus:** 36%

  **Athletics:** NCAA Div. I

# ROOSEVELT UNIVERSITY

430 South Michigan Avenue, Chicago, IL 60605 • **Admissions:** 312-341-3515 • **Fax:** 312-341-3523
**Email:** dessimm@admrs6k.roosevelt.edu • **Web:** www.roosevelt.edu
**Support:** SP • **Institution:** 4 yr. Private

## LEARNING DISABILITY ADMISSIONS AND SERVICES

The goal of the Learning and Support Services Program (LSSP) is to provide a highly individualized support system that will help students discover their learning style. The staff works with each student individually on reading comprehension, writing skills, note-taking, study skills, time management skills and test-taking skills. Roosevelt's small classroom size provides an opportunity for students to get to know their professors, and the faculty has been very responsive to the needs of LSSP students. The program is for students who would otherwise experience difficulty with a regular college curriculum. Emphasis is placed on individual program planning, tutoring, arranged counseling, and modified test taking. The program helps students to define their strengths so that they can overcome their weaknesses and become independent, successful college students.

## LEARNING DISABILITY ADMISSIONS INFORMATION

**Program Name:** Learning and Support Services Program (LSSP)
**Program Director:** Nancy Litke
**Contact Person:** Same as above
**Telephone:** 312-341-3810

### ADMISSIONS

There is a special admissions process through LSSP. Students write a letter to the LSSP director to request services and state the purpose and reason for seeking help. After reviewing the letter an informal interview assessment is held with the student by LSSP staff. Applicants send reports to the LSSP with authorization for release of information. These reports should include the following: (1) most recent transcript and confidential records; (2) health and academic history; (3) test results and reports, including achievement, individual I.Q. or other measurements of academic performance; and (4) the latest IEP. The LSSP staff will evaluate the reports and an admission meeting will be held to determine eligibility and possible enrollment. Students may be admitted during the summer with probationary status.

**College entrance exams required:** Yes
**Course entrance requirements:** Yes
**Diagnostic tests:** Yes
**Documentation:** All psycho-educational testing: within 3 years
**Untimed accepted:** Yes
**Interview required:** Yes

### ADDITIONAL INFORMATION

The Learning and Support Services Program is only available to students with learning disabilities. Assistance is available in course selection, required course readings, assignments, and more. A major department advisor is assigned to each student. Depending on individual needs, tutoring assistance may include course-related training, reading, writing, and spelling. Help is offered in specific problem areas such as note taking, basic skills improvement, time management, and organization. Qualified counseling psychologists help students cope with personal concerns and advise them on career goals. Students are encouraged to use Roosevelt's Learning Resource Center and Writing Laboratory. Services and accommodations are available to undergraduate and graduate students. Students with learning disabilities are not required to take the Roosevelt University Assessment Test.

**Special education HS coursework accepted:** No
**Special application required:** Yes
**# of applications submitted each year:** Varies
**# of students receiving LD services:** 20
**Essay required:** Yes, for LSSP
**Submitted to:** Program Director
**# of applications accepted each year:** Varies
**Acceptance into program means acceptance into college:** Students are admitted directly into the university through LSSP.

## LEARNING DISABILITY SERVICES

**Learning center:** Yes
**Kurzweil personal reader:** No
**LD specialists:** 2
**Allowed in exams:**
  **Calculator:** Yes
  **Dictionary:** Y/N
  **Computer:** Y/N
  **SpellCheck:** Y/N

**Notetaker:** Yes
**Scribes:** Yes
**Proctors:** Yes
**Oral exams:** Yes
**Extended test time:** Yes
**Added cost:** $1,000 per semester
**Distraction-free environ.:** Yes
**Tape recording in class:** Yes
**Books on tape:** Yes
**Taping of other books:** No

**Professional tutors:** 2
**Peer tutors:** Yes
**Max. hrs/wk for services:** 2 hours per week plus unlimited time in writing lab
**Priority registration:** Yes
**Accomodations for students with ADD:** Yes
**How are professors notified of LD:** By the student and the Director of the Program

## GENERAL ADMISSIONS INFORMATION

**Director of Admissions:** Michael Dessimoz          **Telephone:** 312-341-2440

### ENTRANCE REQUIREMENTS

Total high school units required/recommended: 15 total units are recommended; 4 English recommended, 3 math recommended, 2 science recommended, 2 foreign language recommended, 2 social studies recommended, 1 history recommended. Minimum composite ACT score of 20, rank in top half of secondary school class, and minimum 2.5 GPA required. Special requirements: An audition is required for music and theatre program applicants.

**Application deadline:** July 31
**Notification:** Rolling

**SAT or ACT preferred:** Either
**Average ACT:** 19

**Graduated top 10% of class:** 15
**Graduated top 25% of class:** 35
**Graduated top 50% of class:** 65

## COLLEGE GRADUATION REQUIREMENTS

**Course waivers allowed:** Yes
**Course substitutions allowed:** Yes
**In what courses:** Depends on department

## ADDITIONAL INFORMATION

**Environment:** Roosevelt University is located in an urban area in downtown Chicago.

**Student Body**
  **Undergrad enrollment:** 4,279
  **Women:** 59%
  **Men:** 41%
  **In-state students:** 79%
  **Out-of-state:** 21%

**Cost Information**
  **In-state tuition:** $10,830
  **Out-of-state:** $10,830
  **Room & board:** $5,500

**Housing Information**
  **University housing:** Yes
  **Fraternity:** No
  **Sorority:** No
  **Living on campus:** 6%

  **Athletics:** NR

# SHIMER COLLEGE

Waukegan IL 60079-0500 • **Admissions:** 847-623-8400

**Support:** S • **Institution:** 4 yr. Private

## LEARNING DISABILITY ADMISSIONS AND SERVICES

Shimer has no specific program for students with learning disabilities. Some students with relatively mild learning disabilities who have been unsuccessful in other settings have been successful at Shimer because of the unusual approach to education. Shimer offers an integrated curriculum where students read original sources and not textbooks. Students gather to discuss the books in small groups. Shimer has been able to meet the needs of students with learning disabilities who are motivated to seek this kind of education. Students are responsible for seeking the supportive help they want. The class size varies from 8 to 12 students, and a great deal of individual attention is available to all students.

## LEARNING DISABILITY ADMISSIONS INFORMATION

**Program Name:** N/A
**Program Director:** N/A
**Contact Person:** David B. Buchanan

**Telephone:** N/A
**Telephone:** 847-249-7174

### ADMISSIONS

Admissions standards are the same for all students. Admissions is based on whether or not the college feels it can provide the services necessary for successful learning. Students are encouraged to have a personal interview, which can be conducted by telephone, write a personal essay, submit ACT/SAT scores, submit letters of recommendations, and have the psychoeducational reports sent to the admissions office. There are no minimum GPA or specific high school courses required. ACT/SAT scores are not used in the admission decision.

**College entrance exams required:** No
**Course entrance requirements:** Yes
**Diagnostic tests:** No
**Documentation:** Writing sample

**Untimed accepted:** N/A
**Interview Required:** Yes

### ADDITIONAL INFORMATION

Skills courses are offered to all students for credit in writing, reading, math, study strategies, and learning strategies. Classes are never larger than 12 students. All courses are conducted through discussion and all course reading is from original sources. Extraordinary support is available to all students by faculty, staff, and other students.

**Special education HS coursework accepted:** Yes
**Special application required:** No
**# of applications submitted each year:** N/A
**# of students receiving LD services:** N/I

**Essay required:** Yes
**Submitted to:** N/A
**# of applications accepted each year:** N/A

**Acceptance into program means acceptance into college:** Students are admitted to the college first and then may request services.

**Learning center:** No
**Kurzweil personal reader:** No
**LD specialists:** No
**Allowed in exams:**
  **Calculator:** Yes
  **Dictionary:** Yes
  **Computer:** Yes
  **SpellCheck:** Yes

**Notetaker:** No
**Scribes:** No
**Proctors:** No
**Oral exams:** Yes
**Extended test time:** Yes
**Added cost:** None
**Distraction-free environ.:** Yes
**Tape recording in class:** No
**Books on tape:** Yes
**Taping of other books:** Yes

**Professional tutors:** Yes
**Peer tutors:** Yes
**Max. hrs/wk for services:**
Unlimited
**Priority registration:** No
**Accomodations for students with ADD:** No
**How are professors notified of LD:** By the student

## GENERAL ADMISSIONS INFORMATION

**Director of Admissions:** David B. Buchanan          **Telephone:** 847-249-7174

### ENTRANCE REQUIREMENTS
High school transcript, 1 letter of recommendation.

**Application deadline:** NR          **SAT or ACT preferred:** NR
**Notification:** NR

## COLLEGE GRADUATION REQUIREMENTS

**Course waivers allowed:** No
**Course substitutions allowed:** No
**In what courses:** N/A

## ADDITIONAL INFORMATION

**Environment:** The school is located in a city setting 40 miles north of Chicago and 40 miles south of Milwaukee.

**Student Body**
  **Undergrad enrollment:** 119
  **Women:** 57%
  **Men:** 43%
  **In-state students:** 67%
  **Out-of-state:** 33%

**Cost Information**
  **In-state tuition:** $11,200
  **Out-of-state:** $11,200

**Housing Information**
  **University housing:** Yes
  **Fraternity:** No
  **Sorority:** No
  **Living on campus:** 40%

  **Athletics:** Intramural sports

# SOUTHERN ILLINOIS UNIVERSITY-CARBONDALE

Carbondale, IL 62901 • **Admissions:** 618-536-4405
**Email:** jcarl@saluki-mail.siu.edu • **Web:** www.siu.edu
**Support:** SP • **Institution:** 4 yr. Public

## LEARNING DISABILITY ADMISSIONS AND SERVICES

Achieve Program is an academic support program for students with learning disabilities. Students are accepted on a first come, first serve basis providing they qualify for the program. Students are enrolled in regular college courses and are never restricted from any course offerings. Freshman year students are enrolled as full-time students but are restricted to 12 semester hours. As students become more successful they may enroll in more semester hours. Students have access to individualized tutoring, taped texts, test accommodations, remedial classes, developmental writing course, test proctoring, and advocacy service.

## LEARNING DISABILITY ADMISSIONS INFORMATION

**Program Name:** Achieve Program
**Program Director:** Barbara Cordoni, Ed.D.          **Telephone:** 618-453-6120
**Contact Person:** Sally DeDecker/ Amy Shaw          **Telephone:** 618-453-6131

### ADMISSIONS

Application to the university and the Program are separate. University application requires a general application form, ACT scores and transcript. Applicants to Achieve Program are required to provide: Achieve application, $50 application fee, recent photo, and documentation of the LD. There is a fee of $1,000 for diagnostic testing (some fee waivers available) which is required before admissions. The Project Achieve application can be submitted any time during high school (the earlier the better). Students who self-disclose on their applications will have them reviewed by the Program, which provides a recommendation to Admissions. The required 20 ACT can be waived for Achieve Program applicants. For students not automatically admitted, Southern offers a selected admissions through the Center for Basic Skills. In addition there is a 2-year Associates Program that will consider admitting students not meeting minimum standards for regular admission.

**College entrance exams required:** Yes          **Untimed accepted:** Yes
**Course entrance requirements:** Yes          **Interview required:** Recommended
**Diagnostic tests:** Yes
**Documentation:** WAIS-R, Slingerland, WRAT-R, WIAT, etc.: within 3 years

### ADDITIONAL INFORMATION

Students take tests in 5 subject areas and are assigned specific classes within those course areas. Peer tutors are assigned to assist students with: understanding course material, studying and preparing for exams, homework assignments, projects, written work and time management. Notetakers are hired to go into classes and take notes for students who demonstrate difficulty with visual-motor, auditory-memory-to-motor and auditory comprehension tasks. Students must attend classes even if they are receiving notetaking support. Students may take exams and quizzes in Achieve office, and may receive extended time, as well as a reader or writer if needed. Students may have textbooks and other written material taped. Some students will benefit from remediation of reading, spelling, math and/or organizational deficits. Achieve students may take a developmental writing course before attempting the required English course. Graduate assistants work with students on a one-to-one basis so that the students my have individual attention.

**Special education HS coursework accepted:** Yes          **Essay required:** No
**Special application required:** Yes          **Submitted to:** Achieve Program
**# of applications submitted each year:** 175          **# of applications accepted each year:** 75
**# of students receiving LD services:** 175
**Acceptance into program means acceptance into college:** Students are admitted concurrently to the University and Achieve Program.

## LEARNING DISABILITY SERVICES

**Learning center:** Yes
**Kurzweil personal reader:** No
**LD specialists:** 13
**Allowed in exams:**
  **Calculator:** Y/N
  **Dictionary:** Yes
  **Computer:** Y/N
  **SpellCheck:** Yes

**Notetaker:** Yes
**Scribes:** Yes
**Proctors:** Yes
**Oral exams:** Yes
**Extended test time:** Yes
**Added cost:** $1,850 per semester; $925 half-time
**Distraction-free environ.:** Yes
**Tape recording in class:** Yes
**Books on tape:** Yes
**Taping of other books:** Yes

**Professional tutors:** Yes
**Peer tutors:** Yes
**Max. hrs/wk for services:** Unlimited
**Priority registration:** Yes
**Accomodations for students with ADD:** Yes
**How are professors notified of LD:** By the student and the Program Director

## GENERAL ADMISSIONS INFORMATION

**Director of Admissions:** Roland Keim
**Telephone:** 618-453-4381

### ENTRANCE REQUIREMENTS

Total high school units required/recommended: 15 total units are required; 4 English required, 3 math required, 3 science required, 3 social studies required. Minimum composite ACT score of 20 or rank in top half of secondary school class and composite ACT score of 18 required. Special requirements: TOEFL is required of all international students. Additional admissions requirements vary by department.

**Application deadline:** Rolling
**Notification:** Rolling

**SAT or ACT preferred:** ACT
**ACT required:** Yes
**Average ACT:** 22

**Graduated top 10% of class:** 11
**Graduated top 25% of class:** 31
**Graduated top 50% of class:** 66

## COLLEGE GRADUATION REQUIREMENTS

**Course waivers allowed:** No
**Course substitutions allowed:** Yes
**In what courses:** Foreign language and math

## ADDITIONAL INFORMATION

**Environment:** The campus lies at the edge of the Shawnee National Forest 6 hours south of Chicago.

**Student Body**
  **Undergrad enrollment:** 18,712
  **Women:** 41%
  **Men:** 59%
  **In-state students:** 87%
  **Out-of-state:** 13%

**Cost Information**
  **In-state tuition:** $2,550
  **Out-of-state:** $7,650
  **Room & board:** $3,489

**Housing Information**
  **University housing:** Yes
  **Fraternity:** Yes
  **Sorority:** Yes
  **Living on campus:** 22%

  **Athletics:** NCAA Div. I

# SOUTHERN ILLINOIS UNIVERSITY-EDWARDSVILLE

Edwardsville, IL 62026 • **Admissions:** 618-692-3705 • **Fax:** 618-292-2081
**Web:** www.siue.edu
**Support:** S • **Institution:** 4 yr. Public

## LEARNING DISABILITY ADMISSIONS AND SERVICES

SIUE's philosophy is to assist students in becoming as independent as possible, and every effort has been made to eliminate barriers to learning. SIUE offers a full range of resources to support students with disabilities and help them attain their educational goals. Reaching goals starts with pre-admission planning and an assessment of the student's abilities and interests. The Coordinator in the Office of Disability Support Services will develop an understanding of the student's individual needs through counseling and academic advising. Early planning and testing will insure that special needs are taken into consideration and that students can enjoy the full benefit of an educational experience at SIUE. Students are encouraged to contact the DSS as soon as they decide to enroll at the university in order to plan an individualized support program. SIUE does not have special classes for students with learning disabilities, however, the university does offer academic development classes for all students who need to develop their math, reading, and writing skills. New Horizons is an organization for students, faculty, and staff who are concerned with issues facing students with disabilities on campus. New Horizons' activities include advocacy, fund raising, guest speakers, and social activities.

## LEARNING DISABILITY ADMISSIONS INFORMATION

**Program Name:** Disabled Student Services (DSS)
**Program Director:** Jane Floyd-Hendley          **Telephone:** 618-692-3782
**Contact Person:** Same as above

### ADMISSIONS

Students with learning disabilities are required to submit the same general application form as all other students. Students should submit documentation of their learning disability in order to receive services once enrolled. This documentation should be sent to DSS. Regular admissions criteria include: 4 yrs. English, 3 yrs. math, 3 yrs. science, 3 yrs. social science, 2 yrs. foreign language (students with deficiencies need to check with the Office of Admission); a class rank in the top 2/3, and an ACT minimum of 17 (average is 21) or SAT of 640-680. Students denied admission may appeal the decision.

**College entrance exams required:** Yes          **Untimed accepted:** Yes
**Course entrance requirements:** Yes          **Interview required:** No
**Diagnostic tests:** Yes
**Documentation:** Psychoeducational evaluation: within 5 years

### ADDITIONAL INFORMATION

The advisers of DSS will assist students with learning disabilities with pre-admission planning, including an assessment of abilities and interests. Counseling and academic advisement provides assistance in developing an understanding of individual needs. Skills classes are available in math, writing, and reading. Current resources include testing accommodations, assistance in writing/reading exams, assistance with library research, tutoring, and volunteer notetakers. In addition, the Coordinator of DSS acts as a liaison with faculty and staff regarding learning disabilities and accommodations needed by students. Services and accommodations are available for undergraduate and graduate students.

**Special education HS coursework accepted:** Y/N          **Essay required:** No
**Special application required:** No          **Submitted to:** N/A
**# of applications submitted each year:** N/A          **# of applications accepted each year:** N/A
**# of students receiving LD services:** 50
**Acceptance into program means acceptance into college:** Students must be accepted to the university first and then may request LD services.

## LEARNING DISABILITY SERVICES

**Learning center:** No
**Kurzweil personal reader:** Yes
**LD specialists:** No
**Allowed in exams:**
  **Calculator:** Yes
  **Dictionary:** Yes
  **Computer:** Yes
  **SpellCheck:** Yes

**Notetaker:** Yes
**Scribes:** Yes
**Proctors:** Yes
**Oral exams:** Yes
**Extended test time:** Yes
**Added cost:** None
**Distraction-free environ.:** Yes
**Tape recording in class:** Yes
**Books on tape:** No
**Taping of other books:** No

**Professional tutors:** No
**Peer tutors:** Yes
**Max. hrs/wk for services:** Unlimited
**Priority registration:** Yes
**Accomodations for students with ADD:** Yes
**How are professors notified of LD:** By the student and Program Director

## GENERAL ADMISSIONS INFORMATION

**Director of Admissions:** Christa Oxford          **Telephone:** 618-692-2010

### ENTRANCE REQUIREMENTS

Total high school units required/recommended: 4 English required, 3 math required, 3 science required, 2 foreign language required, 3 social studies required, 2 history required. Special requirements: A portfolio is required for art program applicants. An audition is required for music program applicants. Additional admissions requirements vary by department.

**Application deadline:** August 4
**Notification:** Rolling

**SAT or ACT preferred:** ACT
**SAT II required:** Yes
**Average ACT:** 21

**Graduated top 10% of class:** 13
**Graduated top 25% of class:** 39
**Graduated top 50% of class:** 78

## COLLEGE GRADUATION REQUIREMENTS

**Course waivers allowed:** No
**Course substitutions allowed:** No
**In what courses:** N/A

## ADDITIONAL INFORMATION

**Environment:** The university is located on 2,664 acres 18 miles northeast of St. Louis.

**Student Body**
  **Undergrad enrollment:** 8,610
  **Women:** 57%
  **Men:** 43%
  **In-state students:** 87%
  **Out-of-state:** 13%

**Cost Information**
  **In-state tuition:** $1,928
  **Out-of-state:** $5,784
  **Room & board:** $3,238

**Housing Information**
  **University housing:** Yes
  **Fraternity:** No
  **Sorority:** No
  **Living on campus:** 15%

  **Athletics:** NCAA Div. II

# WESTERN ILLINOIS UNIVERSITY

1 University Circle, Macomb, IL 61455 • **Admissions:** 309-295-1414 • **Fax:** 309-298-3111
**Email:** karen_helmers@wiu.edu • **Web:** www.wiu.edu
**Support:** S • **Institution:** 4 yr. Public

## LEARNING DISABILITY ADMISSIONS AND SERVICES

Western Illinois University is committed to justice, equity, and diversity. Academically qualified students who have disabilities are an important part of our student body. Providing equal opportunities for students with disabilities is a campus-wide responsibility and commitment. Personnel with the university work with students to modify campus facilities and programs to meet individual needs. Disability Support Services is responsible for coordinating support services for Western Illinois University students who have disabilities. It is important to note that while services are available, there is no formal program for students with learning disabilities. WIU does not provide any remedial programs or offer any specialized curriculum. Students requesting accommodations must provide documentation verifying the specific learning disability. P.R.I.D.E. (Promoting the Rights of Individuals with Disabilities Everywhere) is an organization comprised of students with and without disabilities. Members work together to remove attitudinal barriers within the university community. The group sponsors awareness-raising activities and serves as a resource for faculty, staff, and students who are interested in disability issues.

## LEARNING DISABILITY ADMISSIONS INFORMATION

**Program Name:** Disability Support Services
**Program Director:** Joan Green          **Telephone:** 309-298-2512
**Contact Person:** Same as above

### ADMISSIONS

Students with learning disabilities must meet the same admission criteria as all applicants, which includes 4 yrs. English, 3 yrs. social studies, 3 yrs. math, 3 yrs. science, and 2 yrs. electives. Applicants must also have a 22 ACT/ SAT 1010 or have an ACT score of 18/SAT 850 and rank in the upper 50% of their class. Students not meeting these standards may be considered for alternative admission through The Academic Services Program, which provides an opportunity for admission to a limited number of students yearly who do not meet the regular WIU admissions. Students considered for alternative admissions must have an ACT of 15/SAT 600 and a C average. The application should be supported by a letter of recommendation from the counselor and a letter of appeal from the student. These students must have an interview. Students can be admitted if a review of their transcript and references indicate they are prepared for college-level work, and if they agree to participate in the Office of Academic Services Program. These students are on academic probation for the first semester.

**College entrance exams required:** Yes          **Untimed accepted:** Yes
**Course entrance requirements:** Yes          **Interview required:** Y/N
**Diagnostic tests:** Yes
**Documentation:** Psycho-educational assessment: within 3 years

### ADDITIONAL INFORMATION

Students admitted through the Academic Services Program enter the university on academic probation and must earn a minimum 1.75 GPA in order to continue the next semester. Students remain in this program until they have earned a minimum of 27 semester hours, have achieved a minimum grade point average of 2.00, and have declared a major. While in this program, students take the same classes as regularly admitted freshman and may participate in all university activities except fraternities and sororities. There are tutoring support services available to all WIU students through laboratories for writing and math which are staffed by the English and mathematics departments. Students can receive one-to-one help with study skills including time management, notetaking skills, and exam preparation. There is tutoring available in some subjects, but there is no guarantee for tutoring in all subjects. Some tutors charge between $4-$7 per hour, and some tutorials offered through the Office of Academic Services are free.

**Special education HS coursework accepted:** No          **Essay required:** No
**Special application required:** No          **Submitted to:** N/A
**# of applications submitted each year:** N/A          **# of applications accepted each year:** N/A
**# of students receiving LD services:** 107
**Acceptance into program means acceptance into college:** Students must be admitted to the university and then be reviewed for services.

## LEARNING DISABILITY SERVICES

**Learning center:** No
**Kurzweil personal reader:** No
**LD specialists:** No
**Allowed in exams:**
  **Calculator:** Yes
  **Dictionary:** Yes
  **Computer:** Yes
  **SpellCheck:** Yes

**Notetaker:** No
**Scribes:** No
**Proctors:** No
**Oral exams:** Yes
**Extended test time:** Yes
**Added cost:** None
**Distraction-free environ.:** Yes
**Tape recording in class:** Yes
**Books on tape:** Yes
**Taping of other books:** Yes

**Professional tutors:** No
**Peer tutors:** Yes
**Max. hrs/wk for services:** Unlimited
**Priority registration:** Yes
**Accomodations for students with ADD:** Yes
**How are professors notified of LD:** By the student and the Program Director

## GENERAL ADMISSIONS INFORMATION

**Director of Admissions:** Karen Helmers

**Telephone:** 309-298-3100

### ENTRANCE REQUIREMENTS

Total high school units required/recommended: 15 total units are recommended; 4 English recommended, 3 math recommended, 3 science recommended, 3 social studies recommended. Minimum combined SAT I score of 1010 (composite ACT score of 22) or minimum combined SAT I score of 850 (composite ACT score of 18) and rank in top half of secondary school class required. Special requirements: An audition is required for music program applicants. TOEFL is required of all international students.

**Application deadline:** NR
**Notification:** NR

**SAT or ACT preferred:** Either
**SAT II required:** Yes
**Average ACT:** 21

**Graduated top 10% of class:** 8
**Graduated top 25% of class:** 26
**Graduated top 50% of class:** 63

## COLLEGE GRADUATION REQUIREMENTS

**Course waivers allowed:** No
**Course substitutions allowed:** No
**In what courses:** N/A

## ADDITIONAL INFORMATION

**Environment:** NR

**Student Body**
  **Undergrad enrollment:** 9,644
  **Women:** 51%
  **Men:** 49%
  **In-state students:** 93%
  **Out-of-state:** 7%

**Cost Information**
  **In-state tuition:** $2,040
  **Out-of-state:** $6,120
  **Room & board:** $3,613

**Housing Information**
  **University housing:** Yes
  **Fraternity:** Yes
  **Sorority:** Yes
  **Living on campus:** 44%

  **Athletics:** NCAA Div. I

# ANDERSON UNIVERSITY

1100 East Fifth Street, Anderson, IN 46012 • **Admissions:** 765-641-2328 • **Fax:** 765-641-3851
**Email:** info@anderson.edu • **Web:** www.icusc.org/anderson/achome.htm
**Support:** CS • **Institution:** 4 yr. Private

## LEARNING DISABILITY ADMISSIONS AND SERVICES

It is the philosophy of Anderson University that those students who are qualified and have a sincere motivation to complete a college education should be given every opportunity to work towards that goal. Students with specific learning disabilities may be integrated into any of the many existing services at the Kissinger Learning Center or more individual programming may be designed. Students receive extensive personal contact through the program. The Director of the Program schedules time with each student to evaluate personal learning style in order to assist in planning for the most appropriate learning environment. One of the most successful programs is the individual or small group tutorial assistance. Social and emotional support are also provided. The college strives to provide the maximum amount of services necessary to assist students with learning disabilities in their academic endeavors, while being careful not to create an over-dependency.

## LEARNING DISABILITY ADMISSIONS INFORMATION

**Program Name:** Program for Learning Disabilities
**Program Director:** Rinda Vogelgesang
**Contact Person:** Same as above

**Telephone:** 317-641-4226

### ADMISSIONS

Students with learning disabilities who apply to Anderson do so through the regular admission channels. Documentation of a specific learning disability must be included with the application. Upon request for consideration for the program, prospective students are expected to make an on-campus visit, at which time a personal interview is arranged with the program director. All applicants are considered on an individual basis.

**College entrance exams required:** Yes

**Untimed accepted:** Yes

**Course entrance requirements:** Yes

**Interview required:** Yes

**Diagnostic tests:** Yes

**Documentation:** WAIS-R or WISC-R: within 3 years

### ADDITIONAL INFORMATION

Freshmen enrolled in the Program are typically limited to 12-13 credit hours of course work during the first semester, including a 2-hour study skills class. As students become more independent and demonstrate the ability to deal with increased hours, an additional course load may be considered. The Kissinger Learning Center offers a variety of services, including a Writing Assistance Program directed by a faculty member of the English Department. Individuals needing further assistance receive a diagnostic evaluation which enables staff to work more efficiently with school personnel in creating programs to fit the needs of students with learning disabilities. Students are fully integrated into the university and are expected to meet the same academic standards as all other students.

**Special education HS coursework accepted:** No

**Essay required:** No

**Special application required:** No

**Submitted to:** N/A

**# of applications submitted each year:** N/A

**# of applications accepted each year:** N/A

**# of students receiving LD services:** 60

**Acceptance into program means acceptance into college:** It is a joint decision between Admissions and the program.

## LEARNING DISABILITY SERVICES

**Learning center:** Yes
**Kurzweil personal reader:** Yes
**LD specialists:** 1.5
**Allowed in exams:**
  **Calculator:** Yes
  **Dictionary:** Yes
  **Computer:** Yes
  **SpellCheck:** Yes

**Notetaker:** No
**Scribes:** Yes
**Proctors:** Yes
**Oral exams:** Yes
**Extended test time:** Yes
**Added cost:** None
**Distraction-free environ.:** Yes
**Tape recording in class:** Yes
**Books on tape:** Yes
**Taping of other books:** No

**Professional tutors:** 3
**Peer tutors:** 30
**Max. hrs/wk for services:** Unlimited
**Priority registration:** No
**Accomodations for students with ADD:** Yes
**How are professors notified of LD:** By the student and/or LD Specialist

## GENERAL ADMISSIONS INFORMATION

**Director of Admissions:** Jim King

**Telephone:** 317-641-4080

### ENTRANCE REQUIREMENTS

High school units required/recommended: 4 English required, 2 math required, 3 math recommended, 2 science required, 1 social studies required, 1 history required. Minimum combined SAT I score of 700 and minimum 2.0 GPA required. Special requirements: An audition is required for music program applicants. TOEFL is required of all international students.

**Application deadline:** September 1
**Notification:** Rolling

**SAT or ACT preferred:** SAT
**SAT Avg.:** 533V, 549M
**Average ACT:** 25
**Average GPA:** 3.4

**Graduated top 10% of class:** 32
**Graduated top 25% of class:** 61
**Graduated top 50% of class:** 88

## COLLEGE GRADUATION REQUIREMENTS

**Course waivers allowed:** No
**Course substitutions allowed:** Yes
**In what courses:** Considered on an individual basis

## ADDITIONAL INFORMATION

**Environment:** Anderson University is located on 100 acres 40 miles northeast of Indianapolis.

**Student Body**
  **Undergrad enrollment:** 2,097
  **Women:** 55%
  **Men:** 45%
  **In-state students:** 61%
  **Out-of-state:** 39%

**Cost Information**
  **In-state tuition:** $11,840
  **Out-of-state:** $11,840
  **Room & board:** $3,980

**Housing Information**
  **University housing:** Yes
  **Fraternity:** No
  **Sorority:** No
  **Living on campus:** 64%

  **Athletics:** NAIA

# INDIANA UNIVERSITY

Bloomington, IN 47405 • **Admissions:** 812-855-0661 • **Fax:** 812-855-5102
**Email:** iuadmit@indiana.edu • **Web:** www.indiana.edu/iub
**Support:** CS • **Institution:** 4 yr. Public

## LEARNING DISABILITY ADMISSIONS AND SERVICES

There is no specific program at Indiana University for students with learning disabilities. The services provided are supportive services necessary to help students pursue their academic objectives. The Briscoe Academic Support Center offers free assistance to all IU students, night and day. During the day the Center is used for study groups, meetings, and advising. In the evenings it provides free tutoring, advising, and academic support to assist with course assignments and studying. No appointments are necessary.

## LEARNING DISABILITY ADMISSIONS INFORMATION

**Program Name:** Office of Disabled Student Services
**Program Director:** Steve Morris
**Contact Person:** Lynn Flinders

**Telephone:** 812-855-7578

### ADMISSIONS

There is no special admission process for students with learning disabilities. Each applicant is reviewed individually. IU is concerned with the strength of the college-prep program, including senior year; grade trends; and the student's class rank. Students falling below the minimum standards may receive serious consideration if their grades have been steadily improving in a challenging college-prep program. Conversely, declining grades and/or a program of less demanding courses are often reasons to deny. The minimum admission standards include: 4 yrs. English, 3 yrs. math, 1 yr. science, 2 yrs. social science, 6 yrs. (4 yrs. for in-state) foreign language or additional math, science, social science, or computer science. Students usually rank in the top 1/3 out-of-state and top 50% in-state. ACT/SAT are used primarily for advising.

**College entrance exams required:** Yes
**Course entrance requirements:** Yes
**Diagnostic tests:** Yes
**Documentation:** Intelligence Tests; Achievement Tests; within 3 years

**Untimed accepted:** Yes
**Interview Required:** No

### ADDITIONAL INFORMATION

The LD specialist at IU assists students with LD. Accommodations can be made to provide: test modifications, tutoring support for 3 hours per week per subject, Note Network sets up accounts for students for no fee, books on tape, adaptive technology, priority registration for students needing books on tape. There are no individual appointments with the LD specialist. Students must provide appropriate documentation. Students need to request that ODSS notify professors about the their LD. Two years of foreign language are required for a degree from the College of Arts and Science. Students with a disability that impacts their ability to learn a foreign language must attempt one semester and the Dean will monitor the student's sincere effort to succeed. If the student is unsuccessful there will be a discussion of alternatives. There is an alternative track in Spanish for students with LD. There are also special tracks of math courses and one is a remedial math course for credit. Services are available for undergrads and graduates.

**Special education HS coursework accepted:** No
**Special application required:** No
**# of applications submitted each year:** N/A
**# of students receiving LD services:** 193

**Essay required:** No
**Submitted to:** N/A
**# of applications accepted each year:** N/A

**Acceptance into program means acceptance into college:** Students must be admitted to the university first and then may request services.

## LEARNING DISABILITY SERVICES

**Learning center:** No
**Kurzweil personal reader:** Yes
**LD specialists:** 1
**Allowed in exams:**
  **Calculator:** Yes
  **Dictionary:** Yes
  **Computer:** Yes
  **SpellCheck:** Yes

**Notetaker:** Yes
**Scribes:** Yes
**Proctors:** Yes
**Oral exams:** N/I
**Extended test time:** Yes
**Added cost:** No
**Distraction-free environ.:** Yes
**Tape recording in class:** Yes
**Books on tape:** Yes
**Taping of other books:** Yes

**Professional tutors:** No
**Peer tutors:** Varies
**Max. hrs/wk for services:** Varies
**Priority registration:** Yes
**Accomodations for students with ADD:** Yes
**How are professors notified of LD:** By the student and the Director

## GENERAL ADMISSIONS INFORMATION

**Director of Admissions:** Robert Magee

**Telephone:** 812-855-0661

### ENTRANCE REQUIREMENTS

Total high school units required/recommended: 14 total units are required; 19 total units are recommended; 4 English required, 3 math required, 1 science required, 2 social studies required. Rank in top 1/3 of secondary school class and completion of nineteen year-long academic courses recommended. Students with modest class rank but rising grades in challenging academic programs are encouraged to apply. Special requirements: An audition is required for music program applicants. TOEFL is required of all international students.

**Application deadline:** February 15
**Notification:** Rolling

**SAT or ACT preferred:** Either
**SAT Avg.:** 466V, 530M
**Average ACT:** 24

**Graduated top 10% of class:** 25
**Graduated top 25% of class:** 72
**Graduated top 50% of class:** 96

## COLLEGE GRADUATION REQUIREMENTS

**Course waivers allowed:** No
**Course substitutions allowed:** Yes
**In what courses:** Foreign language, depending on the documentation and the individual situation. There is an alternative track in Spanish for students with LD. There are also special tracks of math courses and one is a remedial math course for credit.

## ADDITIONAL INFORMATION

**Environment:** NR

**Student Body**
  **Undergrad enrollment:** 27,480
  **Women:** 55%
  **Men:** 45%
  **In-state students:** 60%
  **Out-of-state:** 27%

**Cost Information**
  **In-state tuition:** $3,326
  **Out-of-state:** $10,890
  **Roam & board:** $4,220

**Housing Information**
  **University housing:** Yes
  **Fraternity:** Yes
  **Sorority:** Yes
  **Living on campus:** 49%

  **Athletics:** NR

# INDIANA WESLEYAN UNIVERSITY

4201 South Washington Street, Marion, IN 46953 • **Admissions:** 317-677-2138 • **Fax:** 317-677-2333
**Email:** mcnbc@indwes.edu • **Web:** www.indwes.edu
**Support:** S • **Institution:** 4 yr. Private

## LEARNING DISABILITY ADMISSIONS AND SERVICES

The services offered are designed to assist students who have documented learning disabilities, through advocacy and provision of appropriate accommodations. Student Support Services (SSS) provides tutoring, counseling, notetakers, and test accommodations. The Learning Center is available to all students who seek assistance with raising the quality of their academic work. Developmental educational courses are offered in reading improvement, fundamentals of communication and skills for academic success.

## LEARNING DISABILITY ADMISSIONS INFORMATION

**Program Name:** Student Support Services
**Program Director:** Dr. Neil McFarlane
**Contact Person:** Same as above

**Telephone:** 317-677-2257

### ADMISSIONS

The Office of Admissions seeks students with at least a 2.0 GPA, 840 SAT or 20-21 ACT. Students with a GPA under a 2.0 can be admitted provisionally and there are no cut-off scores for ACT or SAT. In addition, some students may be offered an admission which allows them to take 7-8 credit hours in Bible studies, learning skills, and speech. These students may live in the dorm and participate in campus activities. Successful completion of these 7-8 credits lead to regular admission. The admission decision is made jointly by the Office of Admissions and SSS.

**College entrance exams required:** Yes
**Course entrance requirements:** Yes
**Diagnostic tests:** Yes
**Documentation:** WAIS-R: WRAT; others as related to disability: within 3 years

**Untimed accepted:** Yes
**Interview required:** No

### ADDITIONAL INFORMATION

All admitted students are given the Nelson Denny Reading Test. If they score below 10.7 they are required to take developmental reading, writing and study skills classes. SAT Verbal score below 350 or ACT English below 14 will also be indicators that the student should take developmental reading and fundamentals of communication classes.

**Special education HS coursework accepted:** No
**Special application required:** Yes
**# of applications submitted each year:** N/I
**# of students receiving LD services:** 11

**Essay required:** No
**Submitted to:** Director of Student Services
**# of applications accepted each year:** N/I

**Acceptance into program means acceptance into college:** Students are admitted to the university and to the program simultaneously.

# LEARNING DISABILITY SERVICES

**Learning center:** Yes
**Kurzweil personal reader:** Yes
**LD specialists:** No
**Allowed in exams:**
  **Calculator:** Yes
  **Dictionary:** No
  **Computer:** No
  **SpellCheck:** No

**Notetaker:** Yes
**Scribes:** Yes
**Proctors:** Yes
**Oral exams:** Yes
**Extended test time:** Yes
**Added cost:** None
**Distraction-free environ.:** Yes
**Tape recording in class:** Yes
**Books on tape:** Yes
**Taping of other books:** Yes

**Professional tutors:** Yes
**Peer tutors:** 35+
**Max. hrs/wk for services:** 1/2 hour per student per course
**Priority registration:** N/I
**Accomodations for students with ADD:** Yes
**How are professors notified of LD:** By the student

# GENERAL ADMISSIONS INFORMATION

**Director of Admissions:** Herb Frye

**Telephone:** 317-674-6901

## ENTRANCE REQUIREMENTS

10 units of college-preparatory English, math, science, foreign language, social studies, and electives required. Minimum 2.0 GPA required. Special requirements: An audition is required for music program applicants.

**Application deadline:** August 15
**Notification:** Rolling

**SAT or ACT preferred:** Either

**Graduated top 10% of class:** 20
**Graduated top 25% of class:** 48
**Graduated top 50% of class:** 78

# COLLEGE GRADUATION REQUIREMENTS

**Course waivers allowed:** No
**Course substitutions allowed:** No
**In what courses:** N/A

# ADDITIONAL INFORMATION

**Environment:** The university is located on a 50-acre campus in a rural city 65 miles from Indianapolis and 50 miles south of Fort Wayne.

**Student Body**
  **Undergrad enrollment:** 1,947
  **Women:** 62%
  **Men:** 38%
  **In-state students:** 76%
  **Out-of-state:** 24%

**Cost Information**
  **In-state tuition:** $10,260
  **Out-of-state:** $10,260
  **Room & board:** $4,042

**Housing Information**
  **University housing:** Yes
  **Fraternity:** No
  **Sorority:** No
  **Living on campus:** 40%

  **Athletics:** NAIA

# UNIVERSITY OF INDIANAPOLIS

**IN**

1400 East Hanna Avenue, Indianapolis, IN 46227 • **Admissions:** 317-788-3368 • **Fax:** 317-788-3300
**Email:** admissions@gandfl.uindy.edu • **Web:** www.uindy.edu
**Support:** SP • **Institution:** 4 yr. Private

## LEARNING DISABILITY ADMISSIONS AND SERVICES

The University of Indianapolis offers a full support system for students with learning disabilities called B.U.I.L.D. (Baccalaureate for University of Indianapolis Learning Disabled). The goal of this program is to help students with learning disabilities reach their academic potential. Helen Keller expressed their goal: "Although the world is full of suffering, it is also full of the overcoming of it." Services are extensive and the staff is very supportive and knowledgeable about learning disabilities. The Program Directors feel that 3/4 of all learning disabilities are related to a coordination problem that goes back to crawling. Physical exercises are implemented as part of the program to improve coordination. These crawling exercises are behind the theory that 75% of all students with learning disabilities suffer from an immature symmetric tonic neck reflex because they didn't crawl long enough as a baby. They feel that the crawling problems continue later in life and make it uncomfortable for students to sit straight for long periods of time or to complete simple writing assignments. They find that the crawling exercises show results after a few months.

## LEARNING DISABILITY ADMISSIONS INFORMATION

**Program Name:** B.U.I.L.D.
**Program Directors:** Patricia A. Cook, Ph.D., and Nancy O'Dell, Ph.D.    **Telephone:** 317-788-3369
**Contact Person:** Patricia A. Cook, Ph.D., and Nancy O'Dell, Ph.D.

### ADMISSIONS

Students with documented learning disabilities must meet the university admissions requirements; however, flexibility is allowed to consider individual strengths. The student must submit the following: regular application for admission; B.U.I.L.D. application; high school transcript; current documentation regarding I.Q. scores, reading and math proficiency levels, primary learning style, and major learning difficulty; recommendations from an LD teacher discussing the applicant's main areas of strength and weakness, a mainstream teacher or guidance counselor, and an optional letter from an employer. After the Directors of B.U.I.L.D. review the information, interviews will be arranged for those applicants being considered for final selection. Students with LD denied admission who have not submitted an application for B.U.I.L.D. will automatically receive an application. Once this application is on file, the student will be reviewed by the B.U.I.L.D. Program Directors who will determine admissibility based on this new information. Acceptance into the B.U.I.L.D. Program is determined by the Program Directors.

**College entrance exams required:** Yes          **Untimed accepted:** Yes
**Course entrance requirements:** Yes          **Interview required:** Yes
**Diagnostic tests:** Yes
**Documentation:** I.Q. tests; reading and math tests: within 3 years

### ADDITIONAL INFORMATION

Tutorial supervisors assign tutors to each student in B.U.I.L.D. All students must have at least 2 hours per week of individualized tutoring. Notetaking, books on tape, test modifications, and group study are also provided. Course substitution is a possibility, but has not yet been necessary. B.U.I.L.D. offers 2 special courses to meet university requirements for English and math proficiency, and all other classes are regular classes. Students are limited to 12 hours each semester until they can demonstrate academic success indicating they can handle the demands of a heavier course load. Other services include: diagnostic testing as needed, remediation for specific motoric difficulties of writing, individualization of classroom assignments, test individualization, required supervised study tables, and study-skills courses. There is a "freshman orientation" session of 2 weeks for students who need "brush up" help.

**Special education HS coursework accepted:** Yes          **Essay required:** No
**Special application required:** Yes          **Submitted to:** B.U.I.L.D.
**# of applications submitted each year:** 50-60
**# of applications accepted each year:** 20-25
**# of students receiving LD services:** 40
**Acceptance into program means acceptance into college:** Students must be admitted by the University and then admitted to B.U.I.L.D. If not accepted by Admissions a committee confers.

# LEARNING DISABILITY SERVICES

**Learning center:** Yes
**Kurzweil personal reader:** No
**LD specialists:** 5
**Allowed in exams:**
  **Calculator:** Yes
  **Dictionary:** Y/N
  **Computer:** Y/N
  **SpellCheck:** Y/N

**Notetaker:** Yes
**Scribes:** Yes
**Proctors:** Yes
**Oral exams:** Yes
**Extended test time:** Yes
**Added cost:** $3,600/year
**Distraction-free environ.:** Yes
**Tape recording in class:** Yes
**Books on tape:** Yes
**Taping of other books:** Yes

**Professional tutors:** 5
**Peer tutors:** 6
**Max. hrs/wk for services:** Unlimited
**Priority registration:** Yes
**Accomodations for students with ADD:** Yes
**How are professors notified of LD:** By the student and the Program Director with student approval

# GENERAL ADMISSIONS INFORMATION

**Director of Admissions:** Mark T. Weigand       **Telephone:** 317-788-3350

## ENTRANCE REQUIREMENTS

Total high school units required/recommended: 12 total units are required; 4 English required, 2 math required, 2 science required, 2 foreign language required, 2 social studies required, 1 history required. Minimum combined SAT I score of 920 (composite ACT score of 20) and rank in top 1/2 of secondary school class required. Special requirements: TOEFL is required of all international students. Portfolio required of art scholarship applicants. Audition required of music scholarship applicants.

**Application deadline:** Rolling
**Notification:** Rolling

**SAT or ACT preferred:** Either
**SAT range:** 450–570 V, 450–580M
**SAT II required:** Yes
**ACT range:** 18–25

**Graduated top 10% of class:** 25
**Graduated top 25% of class:** 55
**Graduated top 50% of class:** 77

# COLLEGE GRADUATION REQUIREMENTS

**Course waivers allowed:** No
**Course substitutions allowed:** Yes
**In what courses:** Substitution will be considered for foreign language and math with documentation

# ADDITIONAL INFORMATION

**Environment:** The 60-acre campus in a suburban neighborhood is located 10 miles south of downtown Indianapolis.

**Student Body**
  **Undergrad enrollment:** 2,906
  **Women:** 60%
  **Men:** 40%
  **In-state students:** 83%
  **Out-of-state:** 17%

**Cost Information**
  **In-state tuition:** $12,350
  **Out-of-state:** $12,350
  **Room & board:** $4,330

**Housing Information**
  **University housing:** Yes
  **Fraternity:** No
  **Sorority:** No
  **Living on campus:** 60%

  **Athletics:** NCAA Div. II

# MANCHESTER COLLEGE

**IN**

604 College Avenue, North Manchester, IN 46962 • **Admissions:** 800-852-3648 • **Fax:** 219-982-5043
**Email:** admissioninfo@mc.edu • **Web:** www.manchester.edu
**Support:** CS • **Institution:** 4 yr. Private

## LEARNING DISABILITY ADMISSIONS AND SERVICES

Manchester College does not have a specific program for students with learning disabilities. The college is, however, very sensitive to all students. The key word at Manchester College is "Success" which means graduating in 4 years. The college wants all students to be able to complete their degree in 4 years. The college does provide support services to students identified as disabled to allow them to be successful. The goal is to assist students in their individual needs.

## LEARNING DISABILITY ADMISSIONS INFORMATION

**Program Name:** Services for Students with Disabilities
**Program Director:** Denise L.S. Howe
**Contact Person:** Same as above

**Telephone:** 219-982-5076

### ADMISSIONS

Students with learning disabilities submit the regular application form, and are required to meet the same admission criteria as all other applicants. Students are admitted to the college and use the support services as they choose. If special consideration for admission is requested, it is done individually, based on potential for graduation from the college. Manchester considers a wide range of information in making individual admission decisions. Students are encouraged to provide information beyond what is required on the application form if they believe it will strengthen their application or help the college to understand the students' performance or potential. Students who self-disclose the existence of a learning disability and are denied can ask to appeal the decision and have their application reviewed in a "different" way. The key question that will be asked is if the student can graduate in 4 years or at the most 5 years.

**College entrance exams required:** Yes
**Course entrance requirements:** Yes
**Diagnostic tests:** Yes
**Documentation:** Psycho-educational evaluation: within 3 years

**Untimed accepted:** Yes
**Interview required:** Yes

### ADDITIONAL INFORMATION

College Study Skills, for one credit, is offered. There is also a support group which meets biweekly. There are no developmental courses offered. There is a Learning Center which provides tutoring for all students at the college. The college is in the process of developing a handbook that will describe services for students with disabilities. Services and accommodations are offered to undergraduate and graduate students.

**Special education HS coursework accepted:** Y/N
**Special application required:** No
**# of applications submitted each year:** N/A
**# of students receiving LD services:** 35-40

**Essay required:** No
**Submitted to:** N/A
**# of applications accepted each year:** N/A

**Acceptance into program means acceptance into college:** Students must be accepted to college first and then may request services.

# LEARNING DISABILITY SERVICES

**Learning center:** Yes
**Kurzweil personal reader:** No
**LD specialists:** 1
**Allowed in exams:**
  **Calculator:** Y/N
  **Dictionary:** Y/N
  **Computer:** Y/N
  **SpellCheck:** Yes

**Notetaker:** Yes
**Scribes:** Yes
**Proctors:** Yes
**Oral exams:** Yes
**Extended test time:** Yes
**Added cost:** None
**Distraction-free environ.:** Yes
**Tape recording in class:** Yes
**Books on tape:** Yes
**Taping of other books:** No

**Professional tutors:** No
**Peer tutors:** 40+
**Max. hrs/wk for services:** Unlimited
**Priority registration:** No
**Accomodations for students with ADD:** Yes
**How are professors notified of LD:** By the student and Program Director

# GENERAL ADMISSIONS INFORMATION

**Director of Admissions:** David McFadden

**Telephone:** 219-982-5055

## ENTRANCE REQUIREMENTS
Total high school units required/recommended: 8 English recommended, 6 math recommended, 4 science recommended, 2 foreign language recommended, 2 social studies recommended, 2 history recommended. Minimum combined SAT I score of 900, rank in top half of secondary school class, and minimum 2.3 GPA in college preparatory courses recommended. Special requirements: An audition is required for music program applicants. TOEFL is required of all international students.

**Application deadline:** August 1
**Notification:** Rolling

**SAT or ACT preferred:** Either
**SAT Avg.:** 518V, 524M
**SAT II required:** Yes
**Average ACT:** 22
**Average GPA :** 3.0

**Graduated top 10% of class:** 24
**Graduated top 25% of class:** 55
**Graduated top 50% of class:** 78

# COLLEGE GRADUATION REQUIREMENTS

**Course waivers allowed:** No
**Course substitutions allowed:** No
**In what courses:** Waivers or substitutions have never been requested.

# ADDITIONAL INFORMATION

**Environment:** The college is located in North Manchester 35 miles west of Fort Wayne.

**Student Body**
  **Undergrad enrollment:** 1,030
  **Women:** 48%
  **Men:** 52%
  **In-state students:** 86%
  **Out-of-state:** 14%

**Cost Information**
  **In-state tuition:** $12,070
  **Out-of-state:** $12,070
  **Room & board:** $4,330

**Housing Information**
  **University housing:** Yes
  **Fraternity:** No
  **Sorority:** No
  **Living on campus:** 72%

  **Athletics:** NAIA

# UNIVERSITY OF NOTRE DAME

113 Main Building, Notre Dame, IN 46556 • **Admissions:** 219-631-7505 • **Fax:** 219-631-8865
**Email:** admissions.admissio.1@nd.edu • **Web:** www.nd.edu
**Support:** S • **Institution:** 4 yr. Private

## LEARNING DISABILITY ADMISSIONS AND SERVICES

At the University of Notre Dame, students with disabilities may use a variety of services intended to reduce the effects that a disability may have on their educational experience. Services do not lower course standards or alter essential degree requirements, but instead give students an equal opportunity to demonstrate their academic abilities. Students can initiate a request for services by registering with the Office for Students with Disabilities (OSD), and providing information that documents the disability. Individual assistance is provided in selecting the services that will provide access to the academic programs and facilities of the university.

## LEARNING DISABILITY ADMISSIONS INFORMATION

**Program Name:** Office for Students with Disabilities
**Program Director:** Scott Howland                     **Telephone:** 219-631-7141
**Contact Person:** Same as above

### ADMISSIONS

The university does not have a special admission process for students with learning disabilities. All students submit the same application and are expected to meet the same admission criteria. Admission to the university is highly competitive. The university seeks to enroll an exceptionally distinguished student body from among its broadly diverse and richly talented applicant pool. The admission office prides itself on reviewing each application individually and with care. Students are expected to have 4 yrs. English, 4 yrs. math, 4 yrs. science, 2 yrs. foreign language, 2 yrs. social studies, and 3 yrs. of additional courses from these previous areas.

**College entrance exams required:** Yes          **Untimed accepted:** Yes
**Course entrance requirements:** Yes            **Interview required:** No
**Diagnostic tests:** Yes
**Documentation:** WAIS-R, Woodcock-Johnson; within 3 years

### ADDITIONAL INFORMATION

Services for students with learning disabilities or attention deficit disorder include taped textbooks, notetakers, assistance with developing time management skills and learning strategies, and screening and referral for diagnostic testing.  All students with disabilities are given assistance in developing a positive working relationship with faculty, facilitation of classroom accommodations, liaison with Vocational Rehabilitation and other state and local agencies, informal academic, personal and vocational counseling, and referral to other university resources. Services and accommodations are available for undergraduate and graduate students.

**Special education HS coursework accepted:** N/I       **Essay required:** Yes
**Special application required:** N/A                   **Submitted to:** N/A
**# of applications submitted each year:** N/A          **# of applications accepted each year:** N/A
**# of students receiving LD services:** 20-30
**Acceptance into program means acceptance into college:** Students must be accepted by the university before they can access services.

## LEARNING DISABILITY SERVICES

**Learning center:** No
**Kurzweil personal reader:** Yes
**LD specialists:** No
**Allowed in exams:**
  **Calculator:** Yes
  **Dictionary:** Yes
  **Computer:** Yes
  **SpellCheck:** Yes

**Notetaker:** Yes
**Scribes:** Yes
**Proctors:** Yes
**Oral exams:** Yes
**Extended test time:** Yes
**Added cost:** No
**Distraction-free environ.:** Yes
**Tape recording in class:** Yes
**Books on tape:** Yes
**Taping of other books:** Yes

**Professional tutors:** No
**Peer tutors:** No
**Max. hrs/wk for services:** N/A
**Priority registration:** Yes
**Accomodations for students with ADD:** Yes
**How are professors notified of LD:** By the student and the Director

## GENERAL ADMISSIONS INFORMATION

**Director of Admissions:** Kevin Rooney          **Telephone:** 219-631-7505

### ENTRANCE REQUIREMENTS

Total high school units required/recommended: 16 total units are required; 20 total units are recommended; 4 English required, 4 English recommended, 3 math required, 4 math recommended, 2 science required, 4 science recommended, 2 foreign language required, 2 history required, 4 history recommended. Special requirements: A portfolio is required for art program applicants. An audition is required for music program applicants. TOEFL is required of all international students.

**Application deadline:** January 9
**Notification:** April 7

**SAT or ACT preferred:** Either
**SAT Avg.:** 641V, 662M
**SAT II required:** Yes
**Average ACT:** 29

**Graduated top 10% of class:** 80
**Graduated top 25% of class:** 96
**Graduated top 50% of class:** 99

## COLLEGE GRADUATION REQUIREMENTS

**Course waivers allowed:** N/I
**Course substitutions allowed:** N/I
**In what courses:** N/I

## ADDITIONAL INFORMATION

**Environment:** NR

**Student Body**
  **Undergrad enrollment:** 7,857
  **Women:** 45%
  **Men:** 55%
  **In-state students:** 9%
  **Out-of-state:** 91%

**Cost Information**
  **In-state tuition:** $20,000
  **Out-of-state:** $20,000
  **Room & board:** $4,850

**Housing Information**
  **University housing:** Yes
  **Fraternity:** No
  **Sorority:** No
  **Living on campus:** 84%

  **Athletics:** NCAA Div. I

# PURDUE UNIVERSITY

**IN**

West Lafayette, IN 47907 • **Admissions:** 765-494-4600 • 765-494-0544
Email: ADMISSIONS@adms.purdue.edu • **Web:** www.purdue.edu
**Support:** CS • **Institution:** 4 yr. Public

## LEARNING DISABILITY ADMISSIONS AND SERVICES

Purdue University offers support services to students with LD. There is an LD specialist available to provide ongoing counseling, communication with the professors, and referral to other services on campus. The Adaptive Program staff is prepared to assist students in gaining independence and achieving their potential at Purdue. For the program staff to determine appropriate academic adjustments, documentation that states the current functional limitations resulting from the student's LD is required. Functional limitations may be specific academic skill deficits (reading comprehension, spelling, math calculations, etc.) and/or learning (short-term auditory memory, visual perception, processing speed, etc.). Written verification includes: a psychoeducational evaluation signed by a certified or registered psychologist containing the diagnosis of a specific LD; a report of Annual Review that determines eligibility for LD services; or a signed letter from a certified or registered psychologist. Other useful information might include: recommendations regarding needed academic adjustments; descriptions of academic adjustments and/or classroom accommodations that the students has successfully utilized in the recent past; or previous evaluations, Annual Reviews, and Transition Evaluations, etc.

## LEARNING DISABILITY ADMISSIONS INFORMATION

**Program Name:** Adaptive Program (AP)
**Program Director:** Paula Micka
**Contact Person:** Same as above

**Telephone:** 765-494-1247

### ADMISSIONS

All students with learning disabilities must meet regular university admission requirements. Documentation and letters from an LD specialist will help in making the admission decision. Some majors are more competitive for admission than others. Admitted students are encouraged to contact Adaptive Program as early as possible to identify accommodations necessary for successful completion of college.

**College entrance exams required:** Yes
**Course entrance requirements:** Yes
**Diagnostic tests:** Yes
**Documentation:** Academic potential (IQ), Processing & Achievement: within 3 years

**Untimed accepted:** Yes
**Interview:** Recommended

### ADDITIONAL INFORMATION

Students should meet with AP Staff about needs as soon as possible. Academic support services include: advising, course selection and scheduling; computer center; personal counseling and ombudsman services; tutoring services including the Learning Center which provides free help in learning strategies for time management, lecture notetaking, and test taking skills, and a writing lab; adjustments in testing conditions such as extended time, distraction-free environment, and a Testing Center for students who need extra time which cannot be accommodated in the academic department; Alternative methods of testing including reader and/or scribe, oral exams, or alternative means of "marking" answers. The student should be in contact with his/her instructor within the first 3 weeks of class for regular semesters if any special access or classroom accommodations are required. "Academic Self-esteem Enhancement" is a 3-credit course offered to students with learning disabilities. Services are available for undergraduates and graduates.

**Special education HS coursework accepted:** Yes
**Special application required:** No
**# of applications submitted each year:** N/A
**# of students receiving LD services:** 343

**Essay required:** No
**Submitted to:** N/A
**# of applications accepted each year:** N/A

**Acceptance into program means acceptance into college:** Students must be accepted to university first and then may request services.

**Learning center:** No
**Kurzweil personal reader:** Yes
**LD specialists:** 3
**Allowed in exams:**
  **Calculator:** Yes
  **Dictionary:** Yes
  **Computer:** Y/N
  **SpellCheck:** Y/N

**Notetaker:** Yes
**Scribes:** Yes
**Proctors:** Yes
**Oral exams:** Yes
**Extended test time:** Yes
**Added cost:** None
**Distraction-free environ.:** Yes
**Tape recording in class:** Yes
**Books on tape:** Yes
**Taping of other books:** Yes

**Professional tutors:** Yes
**Peer tutors:** Yes
**Max. hrs/wk for services:** As needed
**Priority registration:** No
**Accomodations for students with ADD:** Yes
**How are professors notified of LD:** By the student and the Program Director

## GENERAL ADMISSIONS INFORMATION

**Director of Admissions:** Doug Christiansen          **Telephone:** 314-494-1776

### ENTRANCE REQUIREMENTS

Total high school units required/recommended: 4 English required, 2 math required, 1 science required, 1-2 history and social studies recommended.

**Application deadline:** NR
**Notification:** NR

**SAT or ACT preferred:** NR
**SAT Avg:** 528V, 490-630M
**Average ACT:** 24

**Graduated top 10% of class:** 26
**Graduated top 25% of class:** 57
**Graduated top 50% of class:** 89

## COLLEGE GRADUATION REQUIREMENTS

**Course waivers allowed:** Yes
**Course substitutions allowed:** Yes
**In what courses:** Math and foreign language if they are not considered an essential component for a degree.

## ADDITIONAL INFORMATION

**Environment:** Purdue University is located in West Lafayette on the Wabash River about 65 miles northwest of Indianapolis.

**Student Body**
  **Undergrad enrollment:** 26,401
  **Women:** 42%
  **Men:** 58%
  **In-state students:** 74%
  **Out-of-state:** 26%

**Cost Information**
  **In-state tuition:** $3,210
  **Out-of-state:** $10,640

**Housing Information**
  **University housing:** Yes
  **Fraternity:** Yes
  **Sorority:** Yes
  **Living on campus:** 47%

  **Athletics:** NCAA Div. I

# SAINT FRANCIS COLLEGE (IN)

2701 Spring Street, Fort Wayne, IN 46808 • **Admissions:** 219-434-3279 • **Fax:** 219-434-3183
**Web:** www.sfc.edu
**Support:** CS • **Institution:** 4 yr. Private

## LEARNING DISABILITY ADMISSIONS AND SERVICES

The Office of Academic Support Services (ASS) assists all students who wish to improve their basic skills in reading, writing, and math. The office also assists and acts as an advocate for students with learning disabilities. The Academic Support Services strives to provide students with learning disabilities with the special services and academic support needed to achieve success in the college environment.

## LEARNING DISABILITY ADMISSIONS INFORMATION

**Program Name:** Academic Support Services
**Program Director:** Sandra Pass
**Contact Person:** Same as above

**Telephone:** 219-434-3288

### ADMISSIONS

There is no special admission process for students with learning disabilities. Entrance is based on an overall evaluation of the student's high school transcript, recommendations and tests. The minimum ACT is 19 or SAT of 800. Automatic admission is given to students with a 920 SAT. College prep course requirements include: 4 yrs. English, 3 yrs. math, 2 yrs. lab science, 2 yrs. social studies, and 2 yrs. foreign language. The minimum GPA is 2.2. Some students may be asked to come to campus for an interview and/or to write a personal statement or essay. Students may be admitted "on warning," on a 13-hour limit or a part-time basis.

**College entrance exams required:** Yes
**Course entrance requirements:** Yes
**Diagnostic tests:** Yes
**Documentation:** Determined on an individual basis: within 5 years

**Untimed accepted:** Yes
**Interview required:** Y/N

### ADDITIONAL INFORMATION

Incoming freshmen may be asked to take placement exams in reading, writing, and math to determine appropriate beginning level courses. Curriculum consideration is given to applicants whose test scores show that a limited number of credit hours would be helpful. Skills classes are offered in reading, writing, and math. The Academic Support Services also serves as a student advocate and informs professors regarding the student's learning disability.

**Special education HS coursework accepted:** Yes
**Special application required:** No
**# of applications submitted each year:** N/A
**# of students receiving LD services:** 7
**Acceptance into program means acceptance into college:** Students must be admitted to the college first and then may request services.

**Essay required:** Y/N
**Submitted to:** N/A
**# of applications accepted each year:** No limit

## LEARNING DISABILITY SERVICES

**Learning center:** Yes
**Kurzweil personal reader:** No
**LD specialists:** 1
**Allowed in exams:**
  **Calculator:** Y/N
  **Dictionary:** Yes
  **Computer:** No
  **SpellCheck:** Yes

**Notetaker:** Yes
**Scribes:** No
**Proctors:** No
**Oral exams:** Yes
**Extended test time:** Yes
**Added cost:** None
**Distraction-free environ.:** Yes
**Tape recording in class:** Yes
**Books on tape:** Yes
**Taping of other books:** Y/N

**Professional tutors:** No
**Peer tutors:** Varies
**Max. hrs/wk for services:** Unlimited
**Priority registration:** No
**Accomodations for students with ADD:** No
**How are professors notified of LD:** By the student and the Program Director

## GENERAL ADMISSIONS INFORMATION

**Director of Admissions:** Scott Flanagan          **Telephone:** 219-434-3264

### ENTRANCE REQUIREMENTS

Total high school units required/recommended: 16 total units are recommended; 4 English recommended, 3 math recommended, 2 science recommended, 2 foreign language recommended, social studies recommended, 2 history recommended. Minimum combined SAT I score of 920 (composite ACT score of 19), rank in top 1/2 of secondary school class, and minimum 2.0 GPA required. Special requirements: 1 unit each of algebra, biology, and chemistry required of nursing program applicants.

**Application deadline:** Rolling
**Notification:** Rolling

**SAT or ACT preferred:** Either
**SAT Avg.:** 480V, 473M
**SAT II required:** Yes
**Average ACT:** 21
**Average GPA:** 2.97

**Graduated top 10% of class:** 13
**Graduated top 25% of class:** 38
**Graduated top 50% of class:** 77

## COLLEGE GRADUATION REQUIREMENTS

**Course waivers allowed:** No
**Course substitutions allowed:** No
**In what courses:** N/A

## ADDITIONAL INFORMATION

**Environment:** The 70-acre campus is located west of Fort Wayne.

**Student Body**
  **Undergrad enrollment:** 954
  **Women:** 73%
  **Men:** 27%
  **In-state students:** 84%
  **Out-of-state:** 16%

**Cost Information**
  **In-state tuition:** $10,710
  **Out-of-state:** $10,710
  **Room & board:** $4,270

**Housing Information**
  **University housing:** Yes
  **Fraternity:** No
  **Sorority:** No
  **Living on campus:** 20%

  **Athletics:** NAIA

# UNIVERSITY OF SOUTHERN INDIANA

8600 University Boulevard, Evansville, IN 47712 • **Admissions:** 812-464-1765 • **Fax:** 812-465-7154
**Email:** enroll.ucs@smtp.usi.edu • **Web:** www.usi.edu
**Support:** S • **Institution:** 4 yr. Public

## LEARNING DISABILITY ADMISSIONS AND SERVICES

The philosophy of the Counseling Center is to help students function more effectively in the educational environment by assisting in overall personal development. The goal of the Disability Support Services is to help students overcome/compensate for obstacles relating to a physical, emotional, or learning disability.

## LEARNING DISABILITY ADMISSIONS INFORMATION

**Program Name:** Counseling Center
**Program Director:** James Browning
**Contact Person:** Leslie Swanson

**Telephone:** 812-464-1867

### ADMISSIONS

Admissions criteria is the same for all students; however, the admissions office will always work with students on an individual basis if needed. In general, students with a 3.6 GPA or higher are admitted with honors. Students with a 2.0-3.5 GPA are admitted in good standing, and students with a GPA below a 2.0 are accepted conditionally. The conditional admissions procedure is for new freshmen who earned below a 2.0 in English, math, science and social studies. The following are required for those admitted conditionally: Freshman seminar; 2.0 GPA; register through the University Division rather than a specific major; take no more than 12 credit hours. ACT/SAT scores are used for placement purposes.

**College entrance exams required:** Yes
**Course entrance requirements:** Yes
**Diagnostic tests:** Yes
**Documentation:** Any which identify specific disability

**Untimed accepted:** Yes
**Interview required:** No

### ADDITIONAL INFORMATION

In order to receive support services, documentation of a learning disability must be provided by the student. Skills classes are offered in basic grammar, algebra review, reading and study skills. Credit is given for the hours, but the grades are Pass/No Pass. There are no notetakers, but special supplies are provided to allow the students to get other students to carbon their notes in class. Other services include counseling, advocacy, and career planning. Services and accommodations are available for undergraduate and graduate students.

**Special education HS coursework accepted:** Yes
**Special application required:** Yes
**# of applications submitted each year:** 25
**# of students receiving LD services:** 40
**Acceptance into program means acceptance into college:** Students must be admitted to the university first and then may request services.

**Essay required:** No
**Submitted to:** Contact person
**# of applications accepted each year:** N/A

## LEARNING DISABILITY SERVICES

**Learning center:** Yes
**Kurzweil personal reader:** No
**LD specialists:** No
**Allowed in exams:**
  **Calculator:** Yes
  **Dictionary:** Yes
  **Computer:** Yes
  **SpellCheck:** Yes

**Notetaker:** Y/N
**Scribes:** Yes
**Proctors:** Yes
**Oral exams:** Yes
**Extended test time:** Yes
**Added cost:** None
**Distraction-free environ.:** Yes
**Tape recording in class:** Yes
**Books on tape:** Yes
**Taping of other books:** Yes

**Professional tutors:** N/I
**Peer tutors:** Yes
**Max. hrs/wk for services:** Unlimited
**Priority registration:** Yes
**Accomodations for students with ADD:** Yes
**How are professors notified of LD:** By the student

## GENERAL ADMISSIONS INFORMATION

**Director of Admissions:** Timothy Buecher          **Telephone:** 812-464-1765

### ENTRANCE REQUIREMENTS

Total high school units required/recommended: 4 English recommended, 4 math recommended, 2 science recommended, 2 social studies recommended.

**Application deadline:** August 1
**Notification:** NR

**SAT or ACT preferred:** NR
**SAT Avg:** 478V, 477M
**Average ACT:** 18

**Graduated top 10% of class:** 9
**Graduated top 25% of class:** 26
**Graduated top 50% of class:** 55

## COLLEGE GRADUATION REQUIREMENTS

**Course waivers allowed:** Not recommended
**Course substitutions allowed:** Yes
**In what courses:** Physical education; others are at the discretion of the Department Chairperson. Substitutions are recommended over waivers. Foreign language is not required for graduation.

## ADDITIONAL INFORMATION

**Environment:** The university is located on 300 acres in a suburban area 150 miles south of Indianapolis.

**Student Body**
  **Undergrad enrollment:** 7,324
  **Women:** 57%
  **Men:** 43%
  **In-state students:** 94%
  **Out-of-state:** 6%

**Cost Information**
  **In-state tuition:** $2,400
  **Out-of-state:** $5,888
  **Room & board:** $1,920

**Housing Information**
  **University housing:** Yes
  **Fraternity:** Yes
  **Sorority:** Yes
  **Living on campus:** 24%

  **Athletics:** NCAA Div. II

# VINCENNES UNIVERSITY

**IN**

Vincennes, IN 47591 • **Admissions:** 800-742-9198

**Support:** CS • **Institution:** 2 yr. Public

## LEARNING DISABILITY ADMISSIONS AND SERVICES

Students Transition into Education Program (STEP) is an LD support program for students in the mainstream. Students' strengths rather than deficits are the emphasis; compensatory techniques rather than remediation are the thrust. STEP is designed to give students the opportunity to develop their own unique abilities, to achieve their highest academic potential, develop a sense of self-worth, and the skills needed to function and learn independently in college. STEP students must enroll 4 semesters in Coping in College I-IV: the course teaches requisite social, study, and self-awareness skills; serves as a support group; the curriculum is practical and emphasizes active thinking, independent learning, student accountability, and the acquisition of specific strategies proven to improve academic performance. Coping in College I addresses self advocacy, compensatory techniques, coping, adaptation, stress, and socialization; II emphasizes socialization and metacognitive skills; III further develops social skills and solidifies study skills; IV emphasizes career planning, job-search and social skills, and includes the STEP retreat. Cope Student Support Services is a program designed to help students with all aspects of the college experience. This is a Trio Program requiring that the student meet 1 of 3 requirements: first generation college student, low income, or disabled.

## LEARNING DISABILITY ADMISSIONS INFORMATION

**Program Name:** Students Transition into Education Program  (S.T.E.P.)
**Program Director:** Jane Kavanaugh **Telephone:** 812-888-4485
**Contact Person:** Susan Laue **Telephone:** 812-888-4212

### ADMISSIONS

Students with learning disabilities must submit the general application form to Vincennes University. Vincennes offers open-door admissions to any student with a high school diploma or the GED. Students with learning disabilities must apply separately to STEP: send the STEP application; psychological evaluation; and letters of recommendation from LD specialists, counselors or teachers; submit all requested information to STEP. Once accepted, students reserve a spot with a deposit of $105 to STEP. Admission to the Program is based on completion of the application process, determination of student eligibility, available funding, and space remaining. Space in the Program is limited. Early application is important. Students applying to Cope should apply separately to the university prior to applying to STEP Students are accepted on the basis of eligibility, potential and need assessment, and available space.

**College entrance exams required:** Yes **Untimed accepted:** Yes
**Course entrance requirements:** No **Interview Required:** Yes
**Diagnostic tests:** Placement tests
**Documentation:** Psycho-educational evaluation: within 3 years

### ADDITIONAL INFORMATION

STEP benefits include: LD specialist for individualized tutoring/remediation; professional/peer tutoring; specialized remedial and/or support classes; weekly academic monitoring; coordinated referral to Counseling/Career Center; special classes; carbonless paper for notetaking; reduced class load; audit class before taking test modifications; papers rather than tests; alternative ways to demonstrate competency. STEP does not exempt students from classes, exempt students from class requirements, or provide taped books and notetakers. Cope provides: individual counselor to assist with needs; tutoring; progress reports; academic advising; appropriate accommodations; academic support groups; workshops on study skills, test anxiety, self-esteem, and interview skills. The Study Skills Center is open to all students and offers: free tutoring; study skills classes in spelling, study skills, success strategies, and learning strategies; individualized materials to help improve performance in problem areas; assessment center; study skills lab.

**Special education HS coursework accepted:** Yes **Essay required:** No
**Special application required:** Yes **Submitted to:** STEP
**# of applications submitted each year:** 200 **# of applications accepted each year:** 60
**# of students receiving LD services:** 200
**Acceptance into program means acceptance into college:** Students must apply separately to the university and STEP or Cope. Students will be accepted to the university and then to STEP or Cope.

# LEARNING DISABILITY SERVICES

**Learning center:** Yes
**Kurzweil personal reader:** Yes
**LD specialists:** 12
**Allowed in exams:**
  **Calculator:** Y/N
  **Dictionary:** Y/N
  **Computer:** Y/N
  **SpellCheck:** Y/N

**Notetaker:** Y/N
**Scribes:** Y/N
**Proctors:** Yes
**Oral exams:** Y/N
**Extended test time:** Yes
**Added cost:** $300 per/semester for STEP; No fee for Cope
**Distraction-free environ.:** Yes
**Tape recording in class:** Yes
**Books on tape:** RFB
**Taping of other books:** No

**Professional tutors:** 20
**Peer tutors:** 60
**Max. hrs/wk for services:** Unlimited
**Priority registration:** Yes
**Accomodations for students with ADD:** Yes
**How are professors notified of LD:** By the student

# GENERAL ADMISSIONS INFORMATION

**Director of Admissions:** Stephen M. Simonds          **Telephone:** 812-888-4313

## ENTRANCE REQUIREMENTS
Open admissions.

**Application deadline:** NR
**Notification:** NR

**SAT or ACT preferred:** NR

# COLLEGE GRADUATION REQUIREMENTS

**Course waivers allowed:** Yes
**Course substitutions allowed:** Yes
**In what courses:** Handled individually

# ADDITIONAL INFORMATION

**Environment:** The school is located on 95 acres 45 minutes south of Terre Haute.

**Student Body**
  **Undergrad enrollment:** 7,211
  **Women:** 43%
  **Men:** 57%
  **In-state students:** 91%
  **Out-of-state:** 9%

**Cost Information**
  **In-state tuition:** $1,786
  **Out-of-state:** $3,120

**Housing Information**
  **University housing:** Yes
  **Fraternity:** Yes
  **Sorority:** Yes
  **Living on campus:** 48%

  **Athletics:** NJCAA

# CORNELL COLLEGE

600 First Street, Mount Vernon, IA 52314 • **Admissions:** 319-895-4477 • **Fax:** 319-895-4451
**Email:** admissions@cornell-iowa.edu • **Web:** www.cornell-iowa.edu
**Support:** S • **Institution:** 4 yr. Private

The services for students with learning disabilities are developed individually based upon identified needs. The process is only initiated after a student self-identifies on the application for admission. There is a support group during orientation week to facilitate adjustment to college, in general, and to Cornell's One Course At A Time. Cornell College is unusual in that it has what is called a 'block system' of study. The student takes 1 course at a time for a period of 3 1/2 weeks. Students usually take 8 blocks each year. The services at Cornell assist students to 'learn the system' and successfully compete in the mainstream with reasonable accommodations.

## LEARNING DISABILITY ADMISSIONS INFORMATION

**Program Name:** Student Support Services
**Program Director:** Connie Rosene                    **Telephone:** 319-895-4292
**Contact Person:** Same as above

### ADMISSIONS

The admission decision is made by the Office of Admissions. The Director of Student Support Services may be asked to confer with Admissions. Requests must be made for special review of admissions files for persons who want any part of the regular admission criteria waived. Students should submit as much information as possible regarding their learning disability to be used in making an admission decision. Cornell admits 25 high-risk students yearly on a conditional basis; not all of them have learning disabilities. These students, upon admission, would be in constant contact with the Director of the Student Services for a period covering 4-blocks and would have to maintain a 2.0 GPA to be fully admitted. Students may be admitted conditionally with or without support.

**College entrance exams required:** Yes                    **Untimed accepted:** Yes
**Course entrance requirements:** Yes                    **Interview required:** Recommended
**Diagnostic tests:** Yes
**Documentation:** Standardized intelligence and achievement tests: within 3 years

### ADDITIONAL INFORMATION

Students who are successful at focusing on one area at a time will probably benefit from the block system. There is an emphasis on reading and reading comprehension. If a student has a weakness in this area may find this type of learning environment very challenging. Skills courses are offered in writing and study skills. Tutoring is available in most subjects on a one-to-one basis.

**Special education HS coursework accepted:** No                    **Essay required:** Yes
**Special application required:** No                    **Submitted to:** N/A
**# of applications submitted each year:** N/A                    **# of applications accepted each year:** N/I
**# of students receiving LD services:** 10-12
**Acceptance into program means acceptance into college:** Students must be accepted to the college first and then may request LD services.

## LEARNING DISABILITY SERVICES

**Learning center:** No
**Kurzweil personal reader:** No
**LD specialists:** No
**Allowed in exams:**
  **Calculator:** Yes
  **Dictionary:** Yes
  **Computer:** Yes
  **SpellCheck:** Yes

**Notetaker:** Yes
**Scribes:** No
**Proctors:** No
**Oral exams:** Yes
**Extended test time:** Yes
**Added cost:** None
**Distraction-free environ.:** Yes
**Tape recording in class:** Yes
**Books on tape:** Yes
**Taping of other books:** Y/N

**Professional tutors:** No
**Peer tutors:** 12
**Max. hrs/wk for services:** Unlimited
**Priority registration:** No
**Accomodations for students with ADD:** Yes
**How are professors notified of LD:** By the student or the Program Director

## GENERAL ADMISSIONS INFORMATION

**Director of Admissions:** Kevin Crockett

**Telephone:** 319-895-4215

### ENTRANCE REQUIREMENTS

Total high school units required/recommended: 15 total units are recommended; 4 English recommended, 3 math recommended, 3 science recommended, 2 foreign language recommended, 4 social studies recommended. Minimum composite ACT score of 20 (minimum combined SAT I score of 820), rank in top half of secondary school class, and minimum 2.6 GPA recommended.

**Application deadline:** March 1
**Notification:** April 1

**SAT or ACT preferred:** Either
**SAT Avg:** 600V, 570M
**Average ACT:** 25
**Average GPA:** 3.27

**Graduated top 10% of class:** 26
**Graduated top 25% of class:** 56
**Graduated top 50% of class:** 86

## COLLEGE GRADUATION REQUIREMENTS

**Course waivers allowed:** No
**Course substitutions allowed:** Yes
**In what courses:** Usually in any course not considered critical to the major.

## ADDITIONAL INFORMATION

**Environment:** The school is located on 110 acres in a small town of 2,000 people 15 miles from Cedar Rapids and 20 miles from Iowa City.

**Student Body**
  **Undergrad enrollment:** 1,105
  **Women:** 60%
  **Men:** 40%
  **In-state students:** 26%
  **Out-of-state:** 74%

**Cost Information**
  **In-state tuition:** $17,080
  **Out-of-state:** $17,080
  **Room & board:** $4,670

**Housing Information**
  **University housing:** Yes
  **Fraternity:** No
  **Sorority:** No
  **Living on campus:** 88%

  **Athletics:** NCAA Div. III

# IA DRAKE UNIVERSITY

2507 University, Des Moines, IA 50311 • **Admissions:** 515-271-3181 • **Fax:** 515-271-2831
**Email:** admitinfo@acad.drake.edu • **Web:** www.drake.edu
**Support:** S • **Institution:** 4 yr. Private

## LEARNING DISABILITY ADMISSIONS AND SERVICES

The Disability Resource Center purpose is to facilitate and enhance the opportunity for students with any type of disability to successfully complete their post-secondary education.The DRC is committed to enriching the academic experience of Drake students with disabilities through individualized assessment of accommodations and resource needs. To initiate a request for services, students should contact the DRC. An appointment will be made with a staff member to begin the registration process. Students are encouraged to meet with a DRC counselor each semester to identify accommodations that are needed. It is the students' responsibility to self-identify that they have a learning disability; to provide professional documentation of their disability; and to request the accommodations that they need. Drake's Disability Resource Center supports a student organization. The association offers students the opportunity to meet with one another for support, networking, learning opportunities and socializing. The DRC office maintains a collection of information on disabilities, and there are many sources on the instruction and evaluation of students with disabilities. DRC encourages faculty, staff, and students to contact the office if they are interested in this type of information.

## LEARNING DISABILITY ADMISSIONS INFORMATION

**Program Name:** Disability Resource Center (DRC)
**Program Director:** Amy Desenberg-Wihes          **Telephone:** 515-271-3100
**Contact Person:** Roxanne Sciorrotta            **Telephone:** 515-271-1835

### ADMISSIONS

There is no special admission process for students with learning disabilities. All applicants are expected to meet the same admission criteria including: 16 academic college prep courses with a minimum of 4 yrs. English, 2 yrs. math, 2 yrs. science, 2 yrs. social studies, 1 yr. history, and 2 yrs. foreign language; 21 ACT or 970 SAT; and a minimum of a 2.0 GPA. Students must be admitted and enrolled in the university prior to seeking accommodations or services for a learning disability.

**College entrance exams required:** Yes          **Untimed accepted:** Yes
**Course entrance requirements:** Yes             **Interview required:** No
**Diagnostic tests:** Yes
**Documentation:** WAIS; Woodcock-Johnson: within 3 years

### ADDITIONAL INFORMATION

The DRC can offer students: appointments at the pre-admission and pre-enrollment stages; review of Drake's policies and procedures regarding students with disabilities; identification and coordination of classroom accommodations; assessment of service needs; notetakers, scribes and readers; referral to appropriate campus resources; advocacy and liaison with university community; and training on the use of assistive technology. Services provided by the DRC do not lower any course standards or change any requirements of a particular degree. The services are intended to allow equal access and provide an opportunity for students with disabilities to demonstrate their abilities.

**Special education HS coursework accepted:** Yes     **Essay required:** Recommended
**Special application required:** No                  **Submitted to:** N/A
**# of applications submitted each year:** N/A        **# of applications accepted each year:** N/A
**# of students receiving LD services:** 27
**Acceptance into program means acceptance into college:** Students must be admitted to the university first and then may request LD services.

**Learning center:** No
**Kurzweil personal reader:** No
**LD specialists:** No
**Allowed in exams:**
  **Calculator:** Y/N
  **Dictionary:** Yes
  **Computer:** Yes
  **SpellCheck:** Yes

**Notetaker:** Yes
**Scribes:** Yes
**Proctors:** Yes
**Oral exams:** Yes
**Extended test time:** Yes
**Added cost:** None
**Distraction-free environ.:** Yes
**Tape recording in class:** Yes
**Books on tape:** No
**Taping of other books:** No

**Professional tutors:** No
**Peer tutors:** N/A
**Max. hrs/wk for services:** unlimited
**Priority registration:** No
**Accomodations for students with ADD:** Yes
**How are professors notified of LD:** By the student and the Program Director

## GENERAL ADMISSIONS INFORMATION

**Director of Admissions:** Thomas Willoughby      **Telephone:** 515-271-3181

### ENTRANCE REQUIREMENTS

Total high school units required/recommended: 16 total units are required; 4 English recommended, 2 math recommended, 2 science recommended, 2 foreign language recommended, 2 social studies recommended, 2 history recommended. Minimum composite ACT score of 18, rank in top two-fifths of secondary school class, and minimum 2.5 GPA required. Special requirements: An audition is required for music program applicants. An RN is required for nursing program applicants.

**Application deadline:** March 1
**Notification:** Rolling

**SAT or ACT preferred:** Either
**SAT Avg:** 560V, 575M
**Average ACT:** 25
**Average GPA:** 3.5

**Graduated top 10% of class:** 37
**Graduated top 25% of class:** 67
**Graduated top 50% of class:** 89

## COLLEGE GRADUATION REQUIREMENTS

**Course waivers allowed:** No
**Course substitutions allowed:** No
**In what courses:** A special request can be made with appropriate documentation. Requests are evaluated individually.

## ADDITIONAL INFORMATION

**Environment:** The campus is located in the suburbs of Des Moines.

**Student Body**
  **Undergrad enrollment:** 3,630
  **Women:** 59%
  **Men:** 41%
  **In-state students:** 30%
  **Out-of-state:** 70%

**Cost Information**
  **In-state tuition:** $14,380
  **Out-of-state:** $14,380
  **Room & board:** $4,920

**Housing Information**
  **University housing:** Yes
  **Fraternity:** Yes
  **Sorority:** Yes
  **Living on campus:** 53%

  **Athletics:** NCAA Div. I

# IA GRINNELL COLLEGE

P.O. Box 805, Grinnell, IA 50112 • **Admissions:** 515-269-3600 • **Fax:** 515-269-4800
**Email:** askgrin@admin.grin.edu • **Web:** www.grin.edu
**Support:** S • **Institution:** 4 yr. Private

## LEARNING DISABILITY ADMISSIONS AND SERVICES

Grinnell College is dedicated to educating young people whose achievements show a high level of intellectual capacity, initiative, and maturity. Every year, this highly qualified group of students includes people with learning disabilities. Grinnell is committed to providing academic adjustments and reasonable accommodations for students with disabilities who are otherwise qualified for admission. Many of Grinnell's characteristics make it a positive educational environment for all students: an open curriculum, small classes, easy access to professors, and an openness to diversity. The Director of Academic Advising coordinates services for students with LD; arranges for academic accommodations; acts as a liaison to the faculty and offers personal, individual assistance. Once students are admitted and they accept the offer of admission, Grinnell likes to plan with them for any reasonable accommodation they will need in order to enjoy a successful experience. Students have the responsibility to make their needs known. The most important factors to college success are seeking help early and learning to be self-advocates. Students are encouraged to notify the Director of Academic Advising about their needs before they arrive for the first semester. For planning purposes, sooner is always better.

## LEARNING DISABILITY ADMISSIONS INFORMATION

**Program Name:** Academic Advising Office
**Program Director:** N/A
**Contact Person:** Jo Calhoun

**Telephone:** N/A
**Telephone:** 515-269-3702

### ADMISSIONS

Grinnell welcomes applications from students with learning disabilities. While they have the same admission standards for all students, they do accept untimed standardized test scores. They also advise students to document their needs in the application for admission and how the learning disabilities may have affected the secondary school performance. They are looking for a strong scholastic record from high school, recommendations, satisfactory results on the ACT/SAT, and specific units of high school course work including: 4 yrs. English, 3 yrs. math, 3 yrs. social studies, 3 yrs. science, 3 yrs. foreign language; the average ACT is 30 and the average SAT is 1308; over 85% of the admitted students are from the top 20% of the class; and students are encouraged to have an interview either on or off campus.

**College entrance exams required:** Yes
**Course entrance requirements:** Yes
**Diagnostic tests:** Yes
**Documentation:** Flexible: within 3 years

**Untimed accepted:** Yes
**Interview required:** No

### ADDITIONAL INFORMATION

Students need to meet with professors and the Director of Academic Advising in order to plan for their individual needs. The Office of Academic Advising coordinates services for students and arranges for academic accommodations. The ADA Task Force ensures compliance with the Americans with Disabilities Act. The Reading Lab helps students improve reading speed, vocabulary, and reading comprehension; the Director of Academic Advising assists students with LD in identifying effective academic strategies. The Science and Math Learning Center provides instruction in math and science courses for students who want to strengthen their background in these areas. Student tutoring will help students make arrangements for tutoring at no charge. Additional resources include: referral for LD testing, reduced course loads, untimed exams, personal counseling, and volunteers who are willing to read to students with learning disabilities. Skills classes for credit are offered in reading, writing and math.

**Special education HS coursework accepted:** Yes, if they are academic solids
**Essay required:** Yes
**Special application required:** N/A
**# of applications submitted each year:** N/A
**# of students receiving LD services:** 23

**Submitted to:** N/A
**# of applications accepted each year:** N/A

**Acceptance into program means acceptance into college:** Students must be admitted to the College first and then may request LD services.

## LEARNING DISABILITY SERVICES

**Learning center:** No
**Kurzweil personal reader:** No
**LD specialists:** No
**Allowed in exams:**
  **Calculator:** Yes
  **Dictionary:** Yes
  **Computer:** Yes
  **SpellCheck:** Yes

**Notetaker:** Yes
**Scribes:** No
**Proctors:** No
**Oral exams:** Yes
**Extended test time:** Yes
**Added cost:** None
**Distraction-free environ.:** Yes
**Tape recording in class:** Yes
**Books on tape:** RFB
**Taping of other books:** No

**Professional tutors:** 7
**Peer tutors:** 50
**Max. hrs/wk for services:**
Unlimited
**Priority registration:** No
**Accomodations for students
with ADD:** Yes
**How are professors notified of
LD:** By the Director of services

## GENERAL ADMISSIONS INFORMATION

**Director of Admissions:** Vince Cuseo

**Telephone:** 515-269-3600

### ENTRANCE REQUIREMENTS

Total high school units required/recommended: 16 total units are required; 4 English required, 3 math required, 3 science recommended, 3 foreign language recommended, 3 social studies recommended. Special requirements: TOEFL is required of all international students.

**Application deadline:** February 1
**Notification:** April 1

**SAT or ACT preferred:** Either
**SAT Avg:** 677V, 650M
**Average ACT:** 29

**Graduated top 10% of class:** 62
**Graduated top 25% of class:** 89
**Graduated top 50% of class:** 98

## COLLEGE GRADUATION REQUIREMENTS

**Course waivers allowed:** No
**Course substitutions allowed:** No
**In what courses:** Not applicable because Grinnell has no general education requirements.

## ADDITIONAL INFORMATION

**Environment:** The College is located on 95 acres in a small town 55 miles east of Des Moines.

**Student Body**
  **Undergrad enrollment:** 1,314
  **Women:** 55%
  **Men:** 45%
  **In-state students:** 15%
  **Out-of-state:** 85%

**Cost Information**
  **In-state tuition:** $17,142
  **Out-of-state:** $17,142
  **Room & board:** $5,152

**Housing Information**
  **University housing:** Yes
  **Fraternity:** No
  **Sorority:** No
  **Living on campus:** 85%

  **Athletics:** NCAA Div. III

# INDIAN HILLS COMMUNITY COLLEGE

**IA**

525 Grandview Ave., Ottumwa, IA 52501 • **Admissions:** 515-683-5111

**Support:** SP • **Institution:** 2 yr. Public

## LEARNING DISABILITY ADMISSIONS AND SERVICES

The Transition Program is a post-secondary educational program for students with special needs. The program is designed to meet the special educational and developmental needs of high school graduates who wish to increase their educational achievement and vocational potential, but who are unable or unprepared to cope with the demands of a traditional college program. It is designed to meet the individual needs of students. Special diagnostic and remedial techniques and approaches are used. Individualized instruction is provided to help students develop competency in basic skills.

## LEARNING DISABILITY ADMISSIONS INFORMATION

**Program Name:** Transition Program
**Program Director:** Judy Brickey
**Contact Person:** Same as above

**Telephone:** 515-683-5125

### ADMISSIONS

Students enroll with widely varying levels of achievement and differing goals, and some discover that they can move ahead more quickly. Applicants are required to submit a portfolio which is reviewed by a selection committee. Many eventually enter one or more of the Indian Hills credit courses. A decision to move into college credit courses is made by staff members, parents, and the student involved. This is a self-paced program. Students must be enrolled full time in the Transition Program. Applicants are required to submit a portfolio which is reviewed by a selection committee.

**College entrance exams required:** No: they use the Asset
**Course entrance requirements:** No
**Diagnostic tests:** Yes
**Documentation:** WAIS-R or WISC-R and W-J-R: within 3 years

**Untimed accepted:** Yes
**Interview required:** Yes

### ADDITIONAL INFORMATION

The 1 year Transition Program is an alternative college program for students with special needs. Upon completion students are awarded a certificate representing post-secondary preparation and training. The course of study in the Transition Program is based on individual needs and expectations. An average course load would consist of 5 classes in English, literature, math, study skills, and an elective.

**Special education HS coursework accepted:** No
**Special application required:** No
**# of applications submitted each year:** 25-30
**# of students receiving LD services:** 20, within program; 50-75 campus wide
**Acceptance into program means acceptance into college:** Students are admitted directly into the Transition Program except for the Health Occupations Programs.

**Essay required:** No
**Submitted to:** N/A
**# of applications accepted each year:** 20

## LEARNING DISABILITY SERVICES

**Learning center:** Yes
**Kurzweil personal reader:** No
**LD specialists:** 2
**Allowed in exams:**
  **Calculator:** Y/N
  **Dictionary:** Yes
  **Computer:** Yes
  **SpellCheck:** Yes

**Notetaker:** Yes
**Scribes:** Yes
**Proctors:** Yes
**Oral exams:** Yes
**Extended test time:** Yes
**Added cost:** Total cost $6000-$7000. Includes tuition, room and board.
**Distraction-free environ.:** Yes
**Tape recording in class:** Yes
**Books on tape:** RFB
**Taping of other books:** RFB

**Professional tutors:** Yes
**Peer tutors:** Yes
**Max. hrs/wk for services:** Based on need
**Priority registration:** No
**Accomodations for students with ADD:** Yes
**How are professors notified of LD:** Depends on the wishes of the student

## GENERAL ADMISSIONS INFORMATION

**Director of Admissions:** Jane Sapp

**Telephone:** 515-683-5155

### ENTRANCE REQUIREMENTS
Required for some: 3 math.

**Application deadline:** NR
**Notification:** NR

**SAT or ACT preferred:** ACT

## COLLEGE GRADUATION REQUIREMENTS

**Course waivers allowed:** No
**Course substitutions allowed:** No
**In what courses:** N/A

## ADDITIONAL INFORMATION

**Environment:** The College is located on 400 acres about 2 hours east of Iowa City or west of Des Moines.

**Student Body**
  **Undergrad enrollment:** 3,279
  **Women:** 50%
  **Men:** 50%
  **In-state students:** 93%
  **Out-of-state:** 7%

**Cost Information**
  **In-state tuition:** $1,375
  **Out-of-state:** $1,800

**Housing Information**
  **University housing:** Yes
  **Fraternity:** No
  **Sorority:** No
  **Living on campus:** 15%

  **Athletics:** NJCAA

# IOWA STATE UNIVERSITY

100 Alumni Hall, Office of Admissions, Ames, IA 50011 • **Admissions:** 515-294-5836
**Fax:** 515-294-6106
**Email:** admissions@iastate.edu • **Web:** www.iastate.edu
**Support:** CS • **Institution:** 4 yr. Public

## LEARNING DISABILITY ADMISSIONS AND SERVICES

ISU is committed to providing equal opportunities and to facilitating the personal growth and development of all students. Several departments and organizations cooperate to accomplish these goals. The LD Specialist assists students with issues relating to LD and helps them adjust to the university setting; provides a review of students' most current LD evaluation and documentation to determine the accommodations needed; offers assistance in articulating needs to faculty and staff and may serve as a liaison in student/staff negotiations. Documentation should include: demographic data about the student and examiner's qualifications; behavioral observation of the way students present themselves, manner of dress, verbal and nonverbal communication, interpersonal skills and behavior during testing; a narrative describing developmental and educational history; a description of the effect of the LD on academic learning; a report of the results of an assessment of intellectual functioning (including WAIS-R or WISC-R); a report of the results of academic testing including Woodcock-Johnson; testing for Foreign Language substitute; and specific recommendations concerning academic compensatory strategies and whether the student qualifies for specific academic accommodations.

## LEARNING DISABILITY ADMISSIONS INFORMATION

**Program Name:** Disability Resources
**Program Director:** Joyce Packwood
**Contact Person:** Gwen Woodward

**Telephone:** 515-294-1020

### ADMISSIONS

If a student is LD and does not meet minimum requirements, the student can request a review. However, this is not a program for students with extreme deficits. Iowa State is looking for students who can succeed, have good verbal skills and have an upward trend in grades. Students not meeting high school course requirements, but otherwise qualified, may be admitted after an individual review. They will look at the pattern on the ACT, not just the score. General admission requirements include: 4 yrs. English, 3 yrs. math, 3 yrs. science, 2 yrs. social studies (3 yrs. for liberal arts and sciences plus 2 yrs. foreign language); 3 yrs. of high school foreign language satisfies the requirement to graduate from Iowa State; ACT 19 (SAT is accepted); requirements for students from out-of-state may be more difficult; there is an admission index indicating student rank and ACT scores. There is also a Summer Trial Program for students not regularly admissible through test scores or class rank; students take 6 credits and get C or better; these students are often in the top 3/4 of their class but may have a 25 ACT.

**College entrance exams required:** Yes
**Course entrance requirements:** Yes
**Diagnostic tests:** Yes
**Documentation:** WAIS-R; or WISC-R (Part II) or WRAT-R: within 3 years

**Untimed accepted:** Yes
**Interview required:** No

### ADDITIONAL INFORMATION

The Academic Learning Lab is a "learning how-to-learn" center designed to help all students; counselors work one-to-one to evaluate and identify problem study habits and devise strategies to improve them. The Learning Lab, Tutoring and Student Support Services are in one area called The Academic Success Center. ASC coordinates services including counseling, teaching reading and study skills, and provides a list of tutors. The Writing Center, available for all students, helps students to write papers. The English Department has a list of approved proofreaders. The LD Specialist provides information about readers, notetakers, and scribes. SI is an academic assistance program attached to very difficult courses. Peer SI leaders, who have demonstrated competence in the course, attend classes and conduct bi-weekly sessions to help students learn and study the course material. Student Support Services is a federally funded program for LD and others qualified to receive academic support in the form of free tutoring and skill-building workshops.

**Special education HS coursework accepted:** Yes
**Special application required:** No
**# of applications submitted each year:** N/A
**# of students receiving LD services:** 210
**Acceptance into program means acceptance into college:** Students must be admitted to the university first and then may request LD services.

**Essay required:** No
**Submitted to:** N/A
**# of applications accepted each year:** N/A

# LEARNING DISABILITY SERVICES

**Learning center:** No
**Kurzweil personal reader:** Yes
**LD specialists:** 1
**Allowed in exams:**
  **Calculator:** Yes
  **Dictionary:** Yes
  **Computer:** Yes
  **SpellCheck:** Yes

**Notetaker:** Yes
**Scribes:** No
**Proctors:** No
**Oral exams:** Yes
**Extended test time:** Yes
**Added cost:** $6/hr. charge for notetaker
**Distraction-free environ.:** Yes
**Tape recording in class:** Yes
**Books on tape:** Yes
**Taping of other books:** No

**Professional tutors:** No
**Peer tutors:** Varies
**Max. hrs/wk for services:** Unlimited
**Priority registration:** No
**Accomodations for students with ADD:** Yes
**How are professors notified of LD:** By the student

# GENERAL ADMISSIONS INFORMATION

**Director of Admissions:** Phil Caffrey        **Telephone:** 515-294-0815

## ENTRANCE REQUIREMENTS

Total high school units required/recommended: 12 total units are required; 4 English required, 3 math required, 3 science required, 2 social studies required. Rank in top half of secondary school class required. Special requirements: TOEFL is required of all international students. 1 additional unit of social studies and 2 units of a single foreign language required of applicants to College of Liberal Arts and Sciences.

**Application deadline:** Rolling
**Notification:** Rolling

**SAT or ACT preferred:** ACT
**SAT Avg:** 542V, 573M
**SAT II required:** Yes
**Average ACT:** 24
**Average GPA:** 3.4

**Graduated top 10% of class:** 26
**Graduated top 25% of class:** 57
**Graduated top 50% of class:** 91

# COLLEGE GRADUATION REQUIREMENTS

**Course waivers allowed:** Yes
**Course substitutions allowed:** Yes
**In what courses:** Courses depend on a case-by-case evaluation. Substitutions are allowed.

# ADDITIONAL INFORMATION

**Environment:** Iowa State University is located on a 1,000 acre campus about 30 miles north of Des Moines.

**Student Body**
  **Undergrad enrollment:** 18,235
  **Women:** 43%
  **Men:** 57%
  **In-state students:** 83%
  **Out-of-state:** 17%

**Cost Information**
  **In-state tuition:** $2,470
  **Out-of-state:** $8,284
  **Room & board:** $3,508

**Housing Information**
  **University housing:** Yes
  **Fraternity:** Yes
  **Sorority:** Yes
  **Living on campus:** 35%

  **Athletics:** NCAA Div. I

# UNIVERSITY OF IOWA

107 Calvin Hall, Iowa City, IA 52242 • **Admissions:** 319-335-3847 • **Fax:** 319-333-1535
**Email:** admissions@uiowa.edu • **Web:** www.uiowa.edu
**Support:** CS • **Institution:** 4 yr. Public

## LEARNING DISABILITY ADMISSIONS AND SERVICES

The mission of SDS is to provide students with disabilities the opportunity to obtain a quality education and develop into well-integrated, self-reliant graduates. The purpose is to reduce or eliminate any disadvantages that may exist. Students with learning disabilities are provided with an individualized, cooperatively planned program of services. SDS staff members strike an important balance between working closely with individuals while still nurturing their independence and self-reliance. Advocacy for students is an important component of the office's services. To be eligible to receive support services students must provide documentation verifying the LD/ADD. This information is used in designing a program of support services that reflects individual needs and abilities. Students who self-identify and seek assistance early are more likely to achieve academic success. SDS offers information, advice, and referral services to students and parents. Individual meetings, campus visits, as well as telephone inquiries are welcome. The summer orientation program features information and activities designed to orient students with learning disabilities to the university.

## LEARNING DISABILITY ADMISSIONS INFORMATION

**Program Name:** Student Disability Services (SDS)
**Program Director:** Donna Chandler
**Contact Person:** Mary Richard, Coordinator

**Telephone:** 319-335-1462

### ADMISSIONS

There is a "special considerations" procedure for students not meeting general admission requirements and do not believe their academic record accurately reflects their ability to do college work. Students must submit: a general application, transcript and test scores; a letter disclosing the disability and requesting "special consideration," describing how the disability affected academic performance and what accommodations and compensation strategies are used to strengthen performance in deficit areas; a description of resources used and a statement explaining why the student may not have completed high school requirements, if applicable; letters from two people, not related, who can attest to the applicant's ability to be successful; a diagnostic report verifying the disability and providing information both about the process and findings of the diagnostic assessment. The report should contain specific recommendations concerning the eligible academic accommodations, including whether the students qualifies for foreign language or math substitutions, and be signed by a licensed professional with the license number.

**College entrance exams required:** Yes

**Course entrance requirements:** Yes

**Diagnostic tests:** Yes

**Untimed accepted:** Yes

**Interview required:** No

**Documentation:** WAIS-R; Academic Achievement; Cognitive processing deficits: within 3 yrs.

### ADDITIONAL INFORMATION

Students requesting services and resources from Student Disability Services must self disclose and provide appropriate evidence of the disability. Use of services is the student's choice and it is the responsibility of each individual to determine whether or not to utilize the available services. Services available through SDS include but are limited to: pre-admission counseling and information, new student orientation, advocacy and liaison with university community, priority registration, support groups, course modification, alternative exam arrangements; Learning Strategies Program including topics such as time management, reading comprehension, notetaking, test taking and writing, assistance in acquiring taped books, assistance in obtaining notetaking services; and tutoring through New Dimensions in Learning program, which offers group tutoring free of charge to eligible students. Tutors are trained and provide general study skills tutoring. The demands for service often out-number the available resources.

**Special education HS coursework accepted:** Yes, if they are fully weighted
**Essay required:** Yes
**Special application required:** Y/N
**# of applications submitted each year:** 100+
**# of students receiving LD services:** 450

**Submitted to:** Admissions
**# of applications accepted each year:** N/A

**Acceptance into program means acceptance into college:** They are the same, but if denied, students may appeal decision.

# LEARNING DISABILITY SERVICES

**Learning center:** No
**Kurzweil personal reader:** Yes
**LD specialists:** 1
**Allowed in exams:**
  **Calculator:** Yes
  **Dictionary:** Yes
  **Computer:** Yes
  **SpellCheck:** Yes

**Notetaker:** Yes
**Scribes:** Yes
**Proctors:** Yes
**Oral exams:** Yes
**Extended test time:** Yes
**Added cost:** None
**Distraction-free environ.:** Yes
**Tape recording in class:** Yes
**Books on tape:** No
**Taping of other books:** Yes

**Professional tutors:** No
**Peer tutors:** Yes
**Max. hrs/wk for services:** Only limited by availability of staff
**Priority registration:** Yes
**Accomodations for students with ADD:** Yes
**How are professors notified of LD:** By the student and the Program Director

# GENERAL ADMISSIONS INFORMATION

**Director of Admissions:** Michael Barron       **Telephone:** 319-335-3847

## ENTRANCE REQUIREMENTS

Total high school units required/recommended: 15 total units are required; 4 English required, 3 math required, 3 science required, 2 foreign language required, 3 social studies required. Rank in top half of secondary school class required of in-state applicants; rank in top 30% of secondary school class required of out-of-state applicants; admissions index based on class rank and ACT or SAT I scores used for all applicants who do not meet these requirements. Special requirements: A portfolio is required for art program applicants. An audition is required for music program applicants. TOEFL is required of all international students. Specific requirements vary by college.

**Application deadline:** May 15
**Notification:** Rolling

**SAT or ACT preferred:** Either
**SAT Range:** 510–630V, 520–640 M
**ACT Range:** 22–27
**Average GPA:** 3.37

**Graduated top 10% of class:** 22
**Graduated top 25% of class:** 51
**Graduated top 50% of class:** 90

# COLLEGE GRADUATION REQUIREMENTS

**Course waivers allowed:** No
**Course substitutions allowed:** Yes
**In what courses:** Foreign language and math.

# ADDITIONAL INFORMATION

**Environment:** The university is on a 1,900 acre campus in a small city 180 miles east of Des Moines.

**Student Body**
  **Undergrad enrollment:** 18,586
  **Women:** 54%
  **Men:** 46%
  **In-state students:** 69%
  **Out-of-state:** 31%

**Cost Information**
  **In-state tuition:** $2,566
  **Out-of-state:** $9,422
  **Room & board:** $3,825

**Housing Information**
  **University housing:** Yes
  **Fraternity:** Yes
  **Sorority:** Yes
  **Living on campus:** 30%

  **Athletics:** NCAA Div. I

# LORAS COLLEGE

1450 Alta Vista, Dubuque, IA 52004 • **Admissions:** 319-588-7100 • **Fax:** 319-588-7964
**Email:** adms@loras.edu •
**Support:** SP • **Institution:** 4 yr. Private

## LEARNING DISABILITY ADMISSIONS AND SERVICES

Loras College provides a supportive, comprehensive program for the motivated individual with a learning disability. The college believes that students can be successful in Loras's competitive college environment if they have had adequate preparation, and if they are willing to work with program staff and take responsibility for their own learning. The LD Program staff has two full-time specialists to serve as guides and advocates, encouraging and supporting students to become independent learners. Students with learning disabilities who are enrolled in college preparatory courses in high school are the most appropriate candidates for the Loras program. Often high school students who previously were in LD programs, but are not currently receiving services, are appropriate candidates for the program if they have taken college prep classes.

## LEARNING DISABILITY ADMISSIONS INFORMATION

**Program Name:** Learning Disabilities Program
**Program Director:** Dianne Gibson                    **Telephone:** 319-588-7134
**Contact Person:** Darlene Colbert

### ADMISSIONS

Suggested steps for admission to the program: students may contact the Program Director in junior year and request an early assessment of their chances for admission; the admission process will be explained and students will receive an application; arrange for an evaluation documenting the learning disability if the evaluation is more than 2 years old, to include the WAIS-R, as well as achievement/diagnostic tests of reading, written expression, and math; send the evaluation when completed; submit transcript with 4 yrs. English, 3 yrs. math, 3 yrs. social studies, 2-3 yrs. science; ACT/SAT; and 3 letters of recommendation should be submitted by Oct. 1 of the senior year.  Criteria for admission include: strong average intelligence, class rank close to or above 50%; 2.0 GPA (minimum), 16+ ACT or 750 SAT. Students must be able to present their needs, strengths and interests in a required interview with the LD Director that is scheduled for those who are invited to visit after all materials have been received.  An admission decision is made by the Director of the LD Program.

**College entrance exams required:** Yes          **Untimed accepted:** Yes
**Course entrance requirements:** Yes             **Interview required:** Yes
**Diagnostic tests:** Yes
**Documentation:** WAIS-R or WISC-R; WJ cognitive and Ach. batteries: within 2 years

### ADDITIONAL INFORMATION

First year students attend "Learning Strategies" class which includes instruction in college reading and writing skills, time management, and organizational skills. Priority registration is only available for the first semester. Students have weekly meetings with LD staff for planning and tutoring. There is a math requirement for graduation, and students may request daily assistance if needed. In addition to individual attention and support, the Loras Learning Disabilities Program provides many special services and facilities including: tutors; notetakers; typists; a reading machine; a study workroom; computers and software programs chosen particularly for students with learning disabilities. Additional resource labs are available on campus to assist all students with written expression, math or computer needs.

**Special education HS coursework accepted:** Yes          **Essay required:** Yes
**Special application required:** Yes                        **Submitted to:** Program Director
**# of applications submitted each year:** 65              **# of applications accepted each year:** 16-20
**# of students receiving LD services:** 65
**Acceptance into program means acceptance into college:** Students are admitted into the LD Program and the College simultaneously. The decision is made by the LD Director.

# LEARNING DISABILITY SERVICES

**Learning center:** Yes
**Kurzweil personal reader:** Yes
**LD specialists:** 1
**Allowed in exams:**
  **Calculator:** Y/N
  **Dictionary:** Y/N
  **Computer:** Y/N
  **SpellCheck:** Yes

**Notetaker:** Yes
**Scribes:** No
**Proctors:** Yes
**Oral exams:** Y/N
**Extended test time:** Yes
**Added cost:** Per semester: $1100 1st year; $900 other yrs.; $650 serv. only
**Distraction-free environ.:** Yes
**Tape recording in class:** Y/N
**Books on tape:** Yes
**Taping of other books:** Yes

**Professional tutors:** No
**Peer tutors:** 10-12
**Max. hrs/wk for services:** No maximum
**Priority registration:** Yes
**Accomodations for students with ADD:** Yes
**How are professors notified of LD:** By the student

# GENERAL ADMISSIONS INFORMATION

**Director of Admissions:** Teddi Joyce

**Telephone:** 319-588-7236

## ENTRANCE REQUIREMENTS

Total high school units required/recommended: 17 total units are recommended; 4 English recommended, 3 math recommended, 3 science recommended, 2 foreign language recommended, 3 social studies recommended, 2 history recommended. Minimum composite ACT score of 20 and rank in top half of secondary school class recommended.

**Application deadline:** August 15
**Notification:** Rolling

**SAT or ACT preferred:** Either
**SAT Avg:** 536V, 564M
**SAT II required:** Yes
**Average ACT:** 23
**Average GPA:** 3.5

**Graduated top 10% of class:** 21
**Graduated top 25% of class:** 42
**Graduated top 50% of class:** 87

# COLLEGE GRADUATION REQUIREMENTS

**Course waivers allowed:** No
**Course substitutions allowed:** No
**In what courses:** Waivers are considered on a case-by-case basis. Math waivers are possible, but students must attempt certain classes before waivers would be granted.

# ADDITIONAL INFORMATION

**Environment:** The College is located on 66 hilltop acres in NE Iowa overlooking the Mississippi River.

**Student Body**
  **Undergrad enrollment:** 1,736
  **Women:** 52%
  **Men:** 48%
  **In-state students:** 56%
  **Out-of-state:** 44%

**Cost Information**
  **In-state tuition:** $11,800
  **Out-of-state:** $11,800
  **Room & board:** $4,000

**Housing Information**
  **University housing:** Yes
  **Fraternity:** No
  **Sorority:** No
  **Living on campus:** 62%

  **Athletics:** NCAA Div. III

# UNIVERSITY OF NORTHERN IOWA

1222 West 27th Street, Cedar Falls, IA 50614 • **Admissions:** 319-273-2281
**Email:** admissions@uni.edu • **Web:** www.uni.edu
**Support:** S • **Institution:** 4 yr. Public

## LEARNING DISABILITY ADMISSIONS AND SERVICES

The Office of Disability Services is dedicated to serving the special needs of students at the University of Iowa. The Office of Disability Services works with students to ensure that all persons with disabilities have access to university activities, programs and services. Specialized services are provided to enhance the overall academic, career and personal development of each person with a physical, psychiatric or learning disability. Services are available to currently enrolled students who must apply for services, and provide appropriate documentation to substantiate the claimed disability. RUN (Restrict Us Not) is a recognized student organization, sponsored by the Office of Disability Services. RUN provides students with the opportunities for developing leadership and self-advocacy skills as well as providing social activities.

## LEARNING DISABILITY ADMISSIONS INFORMATION

**Program Name:** Disability Services
**Program Director:** Dr. Edward F. Morris
**Contact Person:** Jane Slykhuis, Coordinator

**Telephone:** 319-273-2676
**Telephone:** 319-273-2676

### ADMISSIONS

There is no special admission process for students with learning disabilities. Students with disabilities are considered for admission on the same basis as all other applicants, and must meet the same academic standards. Students must have 4 yrs. English, 3 yrs. math, 3 yrs. science, 3 yrs. social studies, 2 yrs. academic elective (can be foreign language). The university will accept college preparatory courses taken through the special education department of the high school. Students must rank in the top 50% of their class, and submit either the ACT or the SAT.

**College entrance exams required:** Yes
**Course entrance requirements:** Yes
**Diagnostic tests:** Yes
**Documentation:** Psycho-educational evaluation; within 3 years

**Untimed accepted:** Yes
**Interview required:** No

### ADDITIONAL INFORMATION

Services available include: individualized pre-enrollment interview and orientation to disability services; preferred registration; list of students interested in serving as academic aides; alternative testing arrangements; auxiliary aides. The Center for Academic Achievement services all students at UNI who wish to receive additional academic support outside of the classroom. The Center provides students with a variety of supportive services that will enhance academic achievement and success. Students may access help in Writing Assistance in any of their classes. Students may schedule a single appointment to work on a specific assignment or a regular appointment to work on a variety of assignments. Assistance with math skills is also available in the Math Lab. Services include one-to-one and small group instruction; individual instruction and practice through a variety of self-instructional modes and review lessons to support the development and practice of concepts/skills taught in math courses. Drop-in hours are available.

**Special education HS coursework accepted:** Yes, if they are college prep
**Essay required:** No
**Special application required:** No
**# of applications submitted each year:** N/A
**# of students receiving LD services:** N/A
**Acceptance into program means acceptance into college:** Students must be admitted to the university first and then may request services.

**Submitted to:** N/A
**# of applications accepted each year:** N/A

# LEARNING DISABILITY SERVICES

**Learning center:** No
**Kurzweil personal reader:** Yes
**LD specialists:** No
**Allowed in exams:**
  **Calculator:** Yes
  **Dictionary:** No
  **Computer:** No
  **SpellCheck:** Yes

**Notetaker:** Yes
**Scribes:** Yes
**Proctors:** Yes
**Oral exams:** Yes
**Extended test time:** Yes
**Added cost:** None
**Distraction-free environ.:** Yes
**Tape recording in class:** Yes
**Books on tape:** Yes
**Taping of other books:** Yes

**Professional tutors:** No
**Peer tutors:** 9
**Max. hrs/wk for services:** Based on availability
**Priority registration:** Yes
**Accomodations for students with ADD:** Yes
**How are professors notified of LD:** By the student and the Director

# GENERAL ADMISSIONS INFORMATION

**Director of Admissions:** Clark Elmer

**Telephone:** 319-273-2281

## ENTRANCE REQUIREMENTS

Total high school units required/recommended: 15 total units are required; 4 English required, 3 math required, 3 science required, 3 social studies required. English units should include 1 unit of composition; math units should include 1 unit of algebra. Electives must be selected from listed required subject areas or from foreign language or humanities. Rank in top half of secondary school class required. Special requirements: A portfolio is required for art program applicants. An audition is required for music program applicants. TOEFL is required of all international students.

**Application deadline:** August 15
**Notification:** Rolling

**SAT or ACT preferred:** ACT
**Average ACT:** 23

**Graduated top 10% of class:** 18
**Graduated top 25% of class:** 48
**Graduated top 50% of class:** 94

# COLLEGE GRADUATION REQUIREMENTS

**Course waivers allowed:** Yes
**Course substitutions allowed:** Yes
**In what courses:** The university is in the process of establishing guidelines for waiver/substitutions in math and foreign language.

# ADDITIONAL INFORMATION

**Environment:** NR

**Student Body**
  **Undergrad enrollment:** 11,405
  **Women:** 57%
  **Men:** 43%
  **In-state students:** 96%
  **Out-of-state:** 4%

**Cost Information**
  **In-state tuition:** $2,470
  **Out-of-state:** $6,688
  **Room & board:** $3,272

**Housing Information**
  **University housing:** Yes
  **Fraternity:** Yes
  **Sorority:** Yes
  **Living on campus:** 36%

  **Athletics:** NCAA Div. I

# SAINT AMBROSE UNIVERSITY

518 West Locust Street, Davenport, IA 52803 • **Admissions:** 319-383-8888 • **Fax:** 319-333-6297
**Email:** poconnor@saimck.sai.edu • **Web:** www.sau.edu
**Support:** CS • **Institution:** 4 yr. Private

## LEARNING DISABILITY ADMISSIONS AND SERVICES

St. Ambrose University's Services for Students with Disabilities is two dimensional. The first dimension is the education of the faculty to the specific needs of students. The second dimension is the development of services that allow programmatic access to students with disabilities. The key to both dimensions is the Coordinator of Services for Students with Disabilities. It is the responsibility of this individual to prepare seminars for the faculty and staff, to advise students, and to be the conscience of the St. Ambrose University Community in regards to students with disabilities. Students with learning disabilities are provided with an individual program of services. Services do not lower academic standards, but rather, just help level the "playing field" for individuals with disabilities. The Coordinator works with students to develop skills and select accommodations to compensate for their learning disabilities and become their own advocate.

## LEARNING DISABILITY ADMISSIONS INFORMATION

**Program Name:** Services for Students with Disabilities
**Program Director:** Andy Kaiser                    **Telephone:** 319-333-6275
**Contact Person:** Same as above

### ADMISSIONS

Students meeting minimum admission requirements are not required to send additional information for admission purposes, but it is helpful in providing effective services. The general admission criteria includes: ACT 20 and above or 950 SAT or above; 2.5 GPA; and no specific courses are required. Students not meeting minimum requirements for admission may request special consideration by submitting 1) a regular application accompanied by a letter directed to the Dean of Admissions including; a description of the LD, how the student has compensated for academic deficits, what resources were utilized in high school, and whether the student has independently requested accommodations. 2) Written assessment of learning problems (including all test scores) done by a certified professional, clearly stating that the student is LD and/or ADD. 3) Recommendations from teachers who have first-hand knowledge of the student's academic abilities and 4) scheduling a meeting with the Coordinator of Services. Students may also attend the Summer Transition Program to assess their ability for regular admission.

**College entrance exams required:** Yes               **Untimed accepted:** Yes
**Course entrance requirements:** Yes                  **Interview required:** No
**Diagnostic tests:** Yes
**Documentation:** WAIS-R; Woodcock-Johnson: within 3 years

### ADDITIONAL INFORMATION

A 4-week Summer Transition Program is available for college-bound students with learning disabilities; students take "Intro to Psychology," Tutoring and Study Skills Sessions where they receive instruction on study skills, notetaking, textbook reading, memorization strategies and test preparation; LD Seminar which is an informal discussion group on topics such as rights and responsibilities of LD, selecting accommodations, understanding LD, self advocacy; "Socializing in College" relates to making new friends, dealing with stress, communication skills. Tutors attend the Psych class and assist students in applying learning skills to their course work. Special courses are available during the school year in reading, learning strategies and college survival skills. Other services include academic advising; access to text-to-speech software; liaison with outside agencies; and one-to-one instruction to help students compensate for their learning disability. Services and accommodations are available to undergraduate and graduate students.

**Special education HS coursework accepted:** Yes        **Essay required:** No
**Special application required:** No                     **Submitted to:** N/A
**# of applications submitted each year:** N/A           **# of applications accepted each year:** N/A
**# of students receiving LD services:** 80
**Acceptance into program means acceptance into college:** Students must be admitted to the university first and then may request LD services.

# LEARNING DISABILITY SERVICES

**Learning center:** No
**Kurzweil personal reader:** No
**LD specialists:** 1
**Allowed in exams:**
 **Calculator:** Yes
 **Dictionary:** Yes
 **Computer:** Yes
 **SpellCheck:** Yes

**Notetaker:** Yes
**Scribes:** Yes
**Proctors:** Yes
**Oral exams:** Yes
**Extended test time:** Yes
**Added cost:** None
**Distraction-free environ.:** Yes
**Tape recording in class:** Yes
**Books on tape:** Yes
**Taping of other books:** Yes

**Professional tutors:** 2
**Peer tutors:** 25
**Max. hrs/wk for services:** 3-4
**Priority registration:** No
**Accomodations for students with ADD:** Yes
**How are professors notified of LD:** By the student

# GENERAL ADMISSIONS INFORMATION

**Director of Admissions:** Patrick O'Connor

**Telephone:** 319-333-6300

## ENTRANCE REQUIREMENTS

Total high school units required/recommended: 16 total units are required; 4 English required, 2 math required, 2 science required, 1 foreign language required, 2 social studies required, 1 history required. Minimum composite ACT score of 20 (combined SAT I score of 780), rank in top half of secondary school class, and minimum 2.5 GPA required.

**Application deadline:** Rolling
**Notification:** Rolling

**SAT or ACT preferred:** ACT
**Average ACT:** 22

**Graduated top 10% of class:** 12
**Graduated top 25% of class:** 48
**Graduated top 50% of class:** 91

# COLLEGE GRADUATION REQUIREMENTS

**Course waivers allowed:** No
**Course substitutions allowed:** No
**In what courses:** N/A

# ADDITIONAL INFORMATION

**Environment:** The campus is located in an urban area 180 miles west of Chicago.

**Student Body**
 **Undergrad enrollment:** 1,735
 **Women:** 55%
 **Men:** 45%
 **In-state students:** 68%
 **Out-of-state:** 32%

**Cost Information**
 **In-state tuition:** $11,740
 **Out-of-state:** $11,740
 **Room & board:** $4,420

**Housing Information**
 **University housing:** Yes
 **Fraternity:** No
 **Sorority:** No
 **Living on campus:** 47%

 **Athletics:** NAIA

# IA WALDORF COLLEGE

Forest City, IA 50436 • **Admissions:** 800-292-1903

**Support:** CS • **Institution:** 2 yr. Private

## LEARNING DISABILITY ADMISSIONS AND SERVICES

The Learning Disabilities Program fully integrates learning disabled students into mainstream courses. The program features a special orientation session, academic advising, tutoring, specialized services, and developmental courses. They take a holistic approach to address the social, emotional and academic needs of the person with a learning disability. The LDP is learning strategies based. Students are accepted as individuals with the potential to succeed in college. The students have the opportunity to participate fully in college life and to experience academic success. Students benefit from a 12 to 1 student to instructor ratio, and a 5 to 1 student to computer ratio. To be eligible for the Waldorf LDP, students must meet the following criteria: students must have psychological and achievement test results, preferably no more than two years old; students must have been involved with intervention on some level during high school; and students must exhibit a positive attitude and potential for good college success when appropriate learning strategies and coping skills are used.

## LEARNING DISABILITY ADMISSIONS INFORMATION

**Program Name:** Learning Disabilities Program
**Program Director:** Rebecca Hill
**Contact Person:** Same as above

**Telephone:** 515-582-8207

### ADMISSIONS

There is no special admissions process for students with learning disabilities. LDP students go through the regular admission procedures. General admission requirements include: 4 yrs. English, 2 yrs. math, and science; ACT 15+. There is a probationary admission for students not meeting the regular criteria. Students will be asked to participate in a special interview, either by phone or in person, in order to be considered for LDP. The number of spaces in LDP is limited. The stronger candidates are reviewed and admitted by the Office of Admission; the students with weaker records, who have a documented learning disability, are reviewed by the LDP Director and the Office of Admission and they make a joint decision on admission.

| | |
|---|---|
| **College entrance exams required:** Yes | **Untimed accepted:** Yes |
| **Course entrance requirements:** Yes | **Interview required:** Yes |
| **Diagnostic tests:** Yes | |
| **Documentation:** Psycho-educational evaluation: within 3 yrs. | |

### ADDITIONAL INFORMATION

Services in the LDP include the following: specialized academic advising regarding schedules and academic classes; priority time and scheduling with the Learning Specialist; counseling services available upon referral or request; special orientation for LDP students at the beginning of the academic year, prior to the arrival of the other students; tutor time above and beyond the regular services available to all students; specialized materials and/or technology for LD students; priority assignment for developmental and study skills classes; as needed academic and psychological testing with a learning style emphasis; instructor notification of learning disability; and academic progress monitoring which will be shared with the student, and parents if permission is given. There are skills classes for credit in study skills, math/pre-algebra, reading and writing. There is a two day LD orientation prior to the beginning of the regular freshman orientation in the fall.

| | |
|---|---|
| **Special education HS coursework accepted:** Yes | **Essay required:** No |
| **Special application required:** No | **Submitted to:** N/A |
| **# of applications submitted each year:** N/A | **# of applications accepted each year:** N/A |
| **# of students receiving LD services:** 30 | |

**Acceptance into program means acceptance into college:** Students are either admitted directly into the college and then request LDP or are reviewed by LDP and a joint decision is made.

# LEARNING DISABILITY SERVICES

**Learning center:** Yes
**Kurzweil personal reader:** No
**LD specialists:** 1
**Allowed in exams:**
  **Calculator:** Yes
  **Dictionary:** Yes
  **Computer:** Yes
  **SpellCheck:** Yes

**Notetaker:** Yes
**Scribes:** N/A
**Proctors:** Yes
**Oral exams:** Yes
**Extended test time:** Yes
**Added cost:** $400 per semester/
fresh year.; $300 per semester/
soph year.
**Distraction-free environ.:** Yes
**Tape recording in class:** Yes
**Books on tape:** Yes
**Taping of other books:** No

**Professional tutors:** 2
**Peer tutors:** 25
**Max. hrs/wk for services:**
Unlimited
**Priority registration:** Yes
**Accomodations for students
with ADD:** Yes
**How are professors notified of
LD:** By the Program Director

# GENERAL ADMISSIONS INFORMATION

**Director of Admissions:** Steve Lovick

**Telephone:** 515-582-8112

## ENTRANCE REQUIREMENTS
NR

**Application deadline:** NR
**Notification:** NR

**SAT or ACT preferred:** NR

# COLLEGE GRADUATION REQUIREMENTS

**Course waivers allowed:** No
**Course substitutions allowed:** No
**In what courses:** N/A

# ADDITIONAL INFORMATION

**Environment:** NR

**Student Body**
  **Undergrad enrollment:** NR
  **Women:** NR
  **Men:** NR
  **In-state students:** NR
  **Out-of-state:** NR

**Cost Information**
  **In-state tuition:** NR
  **Out-of-state:** NR

**Housing Information**
  **University housing:** Yes
  **Fraternity:** NR
  **Sorority:** NR
  **Living on campus:** NR

  **Athletics:** NR

# KS KANSAS STATE UNIVERSITY

Anderson Hall Room 1, Manhattan, KS 66506 • **Admissions:** 913-532-6250 • **Fax:** 913-532-6393
**Email:** kstate@ksu.edu • **Web:** www.ksu.edu
**Support:** CS • **Institution:** 4 yr. Public

## LEARNING DISABILITY ADMISSIONS AND SERVICES

Kansas State provides a broad range of support services to students with learning disabilities through Disabled Student Services, as well as through numerous other university departments. Under DSS the Services for Learning Disabled Students serves as a liaison between students and instructors. The goals of the program are to recommend and provide accommodations and assistance tailored to the students' needs. Faculty and staff are sensitive to the special needs of the students and will work with them in their pursuit of educational goals. DSS works with students to plan accommodations that best aid the students to overcome areas of difficulty. DSS does not modify or reduce the content of courses. Rather, DSS helps to set up ways for students to demonstrate academic knowledge without interference from the disability. To qualify for services students must provide DSS with documentation of a learning disability which includes: a complete record of all testing administered; a signed statement from professional documenting LD; information about strengths and weaknesses to help plan accommodations best suited to the student's needs. Many of the services provided take time to arrange. Consequently, students are encouraged to apply for services early in the process of planning for college.

## LEARNING DISABILITY ADMISSIONS INFORMATION

**Program Name:** Disabled Student Services(DSS)
**Program Director:** Gretchen Holden
**Contact Person:** Andrea Blair

**Telephone:** 913-532-6441

### ADMISSIONS

There is no special admissions process for students with learning disabilities. Kansas State has open admissions for state residents. Out-of-state students must meet some basic requirements for general admissions to the university including: academic courses recommended 4 yrs. English, 3 yrs. math, 3 yrs. science, 3 yrs. social studies, and 2 yrs. foreign language. Special consideration may be given when requested. To be eligible for support services the student must provide verification of a learning disability. Students should have their records of their learning disabilities sent to DSS. A signed statement documenting a learning disability will qualify students for services. More specific information about strengths and weaknesses will help DSS plan accommodations best suited to students' needs. Application for support services can be made by contacting Services for Learning Disabled Students. Many services provided take time to arrange so they encourage early applications.

**College entrance exams required:** Yes          **Untimed accepted:** Yes
**Course entrance requirements:** Yes          **Interview required:** No
**Diagnostic tests:** Yes
**Documentation:** WAIS; W-J: within 3 years

### ADDITIONAL INFORMATION

Students with learning disabilities are eligible for a broad range of supportive services such as: test-taking accommodations; readers; assistance in obtaining taped texts; notetakers; taped lectures; priority registration; and free tutoring. It is sometimes difficult to find tutors in more specialized classes, but the office works with Educational Supportive Services to arrange tutors for students with LD. If a tutor is not currently available, the office will contact the professor to attempt to find a qualified tutor. All students must attend an orientation meeting on an individual basis prior to registration freshman year. Special courses are offered in: Enhanced University Experience to learn notetaking, textbook reading, and test taking skills; math review for students experiencing difficulty with arithmetical computations; intermediate algebra; and college algebra. Services and accommodations are available for undergraduate and graduate students.

**Special education HS coursework accepted:** Yes          **Essay required:** No
**Special application required:** No          **Submitted to:** N/A
**# of applications submitted each year:** N/A          **# of applications accepted each year:** All admitted to University with documentation

**# of students receiving LD services:** 240
**Acceptance into program means acceptance into college:** Students must be admitted to the university first and then may request LD services.

## LEARNING DISABILITY SERVICES

Learning center: No
Kurzweil personal reader: Yes
LD specialists: 1
Allowed in exams:
  Calculator: Yes
  Dictionary: Y/N
  Computer: Y/N
  SpellCheck: Y/N

Notetaker: Yes
Scribes: Yes
Proctors: Yes
Oral exams: Yes
Extended test time: Yes
Added cost: None
Distraction-free environ.: Yes
Tape recording in class: Yes
Books on tape: Yes
Taping of other books: Yes

Professional tutors: No
Peer tutors: Yes
Max. hrs/wk for services: .
Unlimited
Priority registration: Yes
Accomodations for students
with ADD: Yes
How are professors notified of
LD: By the student

## GENERAL ADMISSIONS INFORMATION

Director of Admissions: Richard Elkins     Telephone: 913-532-6250

### ENTRANCE REQUIREMENTS
Total high school units required/recommended: 4 English recommended, 3 math recommended, 3 science recommended, 2 foreign language recommended, 3 social studies recommended. Strong ACT scores and secondary school class rank recommended. Special requirements: Selective criteria required of architecture program applicants.

Application deadline: Rolling
Notification: Rolling

SAT or ACT preferred: ACT
SAT II required: Yes
Average ACT: 23
Average GPA: 3.3

Graduated top 25% of class: 52

## COLLEGE GRADUATION REQUIREMENTS

Course waivers allowed: Yes
Course substitutions allowed: Yes
In what courses: Math and foreign language.

## ADDITIONAL INFORMATION

Environment: The university is located on 664 acres in a suburban area 125 miles west of Kansas City.

Student Body
  Undergrad enrollment: 16,935
  Women: 46%
  Men: 54%
  In-state students: 89%
  Out-of-state: 11%

Cost Information
  In-state tuition: $2,400
  Out-of-state: $8,400
  Room & board: $3,500

Housing Information
  University housing: Yes
  Fraternity: Yes
  Sorority: Yes
  Living on campus: 22%

  Athletics: NCAA Div. I

# UNIVERSITY OF KANSAS

Office Of Admissions, 126 Strong Hall, Lawrence, KS 66045 • **Admissions:** 785 864-3911
**Fax:** 785-864-5006
**Email:** be.a.jayhawk@st37.eds.ukans.edu • **Web:** www.ukans.edu
**Support:** S • **Institution:** 4 yr. Public

## LEARNING DISABILITY ADMISSIONS AND SERVICES

The university tries to accommodate the student with LD by understanding the student's ability and individualizing the services as much as possible. K.U.'s philosophy is one of mainstreaming students with disabilities, including LD. Thus, there are no special classes, resource room, tutoring services, or other services specifically for the student with a LD. Course requirements and academic standards are not reduced. Rather, once the LD is adequately documented, the student receives classroom accommodations to meet specific individual needs. The Center also serves as a referral agent to other resources at the university and in the Lawrence community. Integration and mainstreaming, decentralized services with appropriate accommodations centrally coordinated, and student involvement and responsibility are critical aspects of the university's philosophy. Documentation is necessary and should include a recent diagnostic report of LD, and LD programs and progress will need to be identified. Students are encouraged to begin planning early so that programs are in place at the beginning of the semester to facilitate studies. The goal of SAC is to facilitate independence in preparation for needs after graduation.

## LEARNING DISABILITY ADMISSIONS INFORMATION

**Program Name:** Student Assistance Center (SAC)
**Program Director:** Lorna Zimmer
**Contact Person:** Mike Shuttic, Coordinator
of Serv/ Assist. Dir.

**Telephone:** 913-864-4064
**Telephone:** 913-864-4064

### ADMISSIONS

All applicants are admitted using the same criteria. Students unable to meet admission criteria because of a LD should submit a personal statement providing additional information, such as no foreign language taken in high school because of the LD. Applicants should contact SAC for information and an early assessment of needs. It is important to include recent documentation or diagnosis, and samples of students' work and parent and student statements regarding educational history. Regular admission requires 1 "C" average in Board of Regent courses including 4 yrs. English; 3 yrs. of college prep math; 3 yrs. natural science; 3 yrs. social science; 2 yrs. foreign language or 2) an ACT of 24 and a 2.0 GPA or 3) a 3.0 GPA and no cut-off on the ACT. The university is very concerned that a student with LD be competitive in this academic environment. If admission criteria are not met because of a learning disability, the applicant should submit documentation and counselor recommendation, and the Director of SAC will review and make a recommendation to admissions to waive requirements.

**College entrance exams required:** Yes
**Course entrance requirements:** Yes
**Diagnostic tests:** Yes
**Documentation:** WAIS-R; W-J; Detroit Test of Learning; within 3 years

**Untimed accepted:** Yes
**Interview required:** Recommended

### ADDITIONAL INFORMATION

Skill workshops are available in study skills, time management, listening, notetaking, calculus, speed and reading comprehension, learning a foreign language, and preparing for exams. SAC also serves as an advocate or liaison for students. Tutoring services for students who meet qualifications are available through Supportive Educational Services at no cost. Private tutors can also be hired by the student for specific subjects. In neither instances are the tutors specifically trained regarding learning disabilities. SAC does not offer a reduced standard for academic performance, special classes, supplemental instruction, a learning center, special tutorial program, or exemption to graduation requirements. Services and accommodations are available for undergraduate and graduate students.

**Special education HS coursework accepted:** Yes, if they are really college preparatory
**Essay required:** No
**Special application required:** No
**# of applications submitted each year:** N/A
**# of students receiving LD services:** 149

**Submitted to:** N/A
**# of applications accepted each year:** N/A

**Acceptance into program means acceptance into college:** Students must be admitted to the university first (can appeal a denial) and then may request services.

**Learning center:** No
**Kurzweil personal reader:** Yes
**LD specialists:** No
**Allowed in exams:**
 **Calculator:** Yes
 **Dictionary:** Yes
 **Computer:** Yes
 **SpellCheck:** Yes

**Notetaker:** Yes
**Scribes:** Yes
**Proctors:** No
**Oral exams:** Yes
**Extended test time:** Yes
**Added cost:** None
**Distraction-free environ.:** Yes
**Tape recording in class:** Yes
**Books on tape:** Yes
**Taping of other books:** Yes

**Professional tutors:** Yes
**Peer tutors:** Yes
**Max. hrs/wk for services:**
Negotiated
**Priority registration:** No
**Accomodations for students
with ADD:** Yes
**How are professors notified of
LD:** By the student and the
Coordinator of Services

## GENERAL ADMISSIONS INFORMATION

**Director of Admissions:** Alan Cerveny

**Telephone:** 913-864-3911

### ENTRANCE REQUIREMENTS

Total high school units required/recommended: 15 total units are recommended; 4 English recommended, 3 math recommended, 3 science recommended, 2 foreign language recommended, 3 social studies recommended. Open admissions policy for in-state applicants who are graduates of accredited secondary schools. Composite ACT score of 24, minimum 3.0 GPA at the end of junior year of high school, or minimum 2.5 GPA required of out-of-state applicants. Special requirements: An audition is required for music program applicants. Portfolio may be requested of art or design program applicants.

**Application deadline:** April 1
**Notification:** Rolling

**SAT or ACT preferred:** Either
**Average ACT:** 24

**Graduated top 10% of class:** 25
**Graduated top 25% of class:** 30
**Graduated top 50% of class:** 84

## COLLEGE GRADUATION REQUIREMENTS

**Course waivers allowed:** No
**Course substitutions allowed:** Yes
**In what courses:** Generally in the area of math, English, or foreign language.

## ADDITIONAL INFORMATION

**Environment:** The 1,000 acre campus is located in a small city 40 miles west of Kansas City.

**Student Body**
 **Undergrad enrollment:** 16,659
 **Women:** 51%
 **Men:** 49%
 **In-state students:** 70%
 **Out-of-state:** 30%

**Cost Information**
 **In-state tuition:** $1,965
 **Out-of-state:** $8,269
 **Room & board:** $3,736

**Housing Information**
 **University housing:** Yes
 **Fraternity:** Yes
 **Sorority:** Yes
 **Living on campus:** 22%

 **Athletics:** NCAA Div. I

# EASTERN KENTUCKY UNIVERSITY

**KY**

Lancaster Avenue, Richmond, KY 40475 • **Admissions:** 606-622-2106 • **Fax:** 606-622-1020
**Web:** www.eku.edu
**Support:** CS • **Institution:** 4 yr. Public

## LEARNING DISABILITY ADMISSIONS AND SERVICES

The mission of Project SUCCESS is to respond effectively and efficiently to the individual educational needs of eligible university students with learning disabilities through a cost-effective, flexible program of peer tutors, workshops, group support and program referral. Upon admittance, Project SUCCESS develops an individualized program of services which serve to enhance the academic success of each student. The services a student utilizes will be determined in a conference between the student and the program coordinator. All services are offered free of charge to the student. EKU also offers a summer orientation for students with learning disabilities. The orientation is designed to smooth the transition between high school and college. To apply for participation in Project SUCCESS, students are encouraged to visit both the campus and the Office of Judicial Affairs and Services for Students with Disabilities. The student will be asked to fill out an application and provide appropriate, current documentation of the disability. The application for services through Project SUCCESS is in no way connected to admission to EKU. Students must first be admitted to EKU in order to work with the program.

## LEARNING DISABILITY ADMISSIONS INFORMATION

**Program Name:** Project SUCCESS
**Program Director:** Harry Moberly, Jr.          **Telephone:** 606-622-1500
**Contact Person:** Teresa Belluscio             **Telephone:** 606-622-6396

### ADMISSIONS

There is no special admissions criteria to the university for students with learning disabilities. All applicants must meet the general admission criteria. EKU is an open admission school for residents of the Commonwealth of Kentucky. Out-of-state applicants must have: 4 yrs. English, 3 yrs. math, 2 yrs. science, 1 yr. social studies, 1 yr. history, 9 units of electives; minimum ACT 21 or SAT I 870; rank in the top 50% of the class; and have a minimum 2.5 GPA. Students must be admitted and enrolled in the university in order to be eligible for entrance into Project SUCCESS. To participate in Project SUCCESS students must provide the most recent documentation, the testing should indicate both ability and achievement and contain a diagnosis of LD/ADHD; present with an IQ commensurate with college achievement; provide 2 letters of recommendation, one addressing the student's academic abilities and the other an area of interest outside of school; Project SUCCESS application; copy of transcript; copy of ACT/SAT; and have a personal interview with the program coordinator.

**College entrance exams required:** Yes          **Untimed accepted:** Yes
**Course entrance requirements:** Yes            **Interview required:** Yes
**Diagnostic tests:** Yes
**Documentation:** Achievement; Aptitude: within 3 years

### ADDITIONAL INFORMATION

Project SUCCESS services provided include: one-on-one tutoring; notetaking services; books on tape; test accommodations; advocacy; weekly seminars. Skills classes are offered in study skills, reading skills, weekly workshops in transition, time management, learning and study strategies, test taking skills, developmental math, and developmental reading and developmental writing. A special summer program for pre-college freshmen with learning disabilities is offered. All services and accommodations are available for undergraduate and graduate students.

**Special education HS coursework accepted:** Yes          **Essay required:** No
**Special application required:** Yes                      **Submitted to:** Program Coordinator
**# of applications submitted each year:** 60              **# of applications accepted each year:** 45
**# of students receiving LD services:** 125
**Acceptance into program means acceptance into college:** Students must be admitted to the university first and then may apply to Project SUCCESS.

**Learning center:** No
**Kurzweil personal reader:** Yes
**LD specialists:** 1
**Allowed in exams:**
  **Calculator:** Yes
  **Dictionary:** Yes
  **Computer:** Yes
  **SpellCheck:** Yes

**Notetaker:** Yes
**Scribes:** Yes
**Proctors:** Yes
**Oral exams:** Yes
**Extended test time:** Yes
**Added cost:** None
**Distraction-free environ.:** Yes
**Tape recording in class:** Yes
**Books on tape:** Yes
**Taping of other books:** Yes

**Professional tutors:** No
**Peer tutors:** 22
**Max. hrs/wk for services:** Unlimited
**Priority registration:** No
**Accomodations for students with ADD:** Yes
**How are professors notified of LD:** By the student and the Program Director

# GENERAL ADMISSIONS INFORMATION

**Director of Admissions:** James L. Grigsby        **Telephone:** 606-622-2106

## ENTRANCE REQUIREMENTS

Total high school units required/recommended: 20 total units are required; 4 English required, 3 math required, 2 science required, 1 social studies required, 1 history required. Minimum composite ACT score of 21 (combined SAT I score of 870), rank in top half of secondary school class, and minimum 2.5 GPA required of out-of-state applicants. Special requirements: TOEFL is required of all international students. Higher requirements for allied health, business, and nursing program applicants.

**Application deadline:** Rolling          **SAT or ACT preferred:** ACT
**Notification:** Rolling                 **ACT Required:** Yes

# COLLEGE GRADUATION REQUIREMENTS

**Course waivers allowed:** Yes
**Course substitutions allowed:** Yes
**In what courses:** Waivers and substitutions are determined on a case-by-case basis.

# ADDITIONAL INFORMATION

**Environment:** The university is located on 350 acres in a small town 20 miles south of Lexington.

**Student Body**
  **Undergrad enrollment:** 14,558
  **Women:** 56%
  **Men:** 44%
  **In-state students:** 92%
  **Out-of-state:** 8%

**Cost Information**
  **In-state tuition:** $1,970
  **Out-of-state:** $5,450
  **Room & board:** $3,396

**Housing Information**
  **University housing:** Yes
  **Fraternity:** Yes
  **Sorority:** Yes
  **Living on campus:** 58%

  **Athletics:** NCAA Div. I

# LEXINGTON COMMUNITY COLLEGE

Cooper Drive, Lexington, KY 40506-0235 • **Admissions:** 606-257-4872

**Support:** S • **Institution:** 2 yr. Public

## LEARNING DISABILITY ADMISSIONS AND SERVICES

Lexington Community College has made a firm commitment to providing high quality post-secondary education to persons with disabilities. The program goals are two-fold. First, the program seeks to ensure equal access and full participation for persons with disabilities in post-secondary education. Second, the program strives to empower students with disabilities to obtain the life skills necessary for a fulfilling productive lifestyle after leaving LCC. Students can request services by visiting DSS. Students with learning disabilities must provide psychological testing which has been completed within the last three years to receive services. Full participation in the DSS Program is encouraged from the initial admission contact throughout the student's academic career. Students are encouraged to assume full responsibility in securing the reasonable accommodations needed for a particular academic program. Positive peer contacts as well as guidance from the DSS Coordinator and other faculty and staff also play a major role in encouraging participation in the DSS program.

## LEARNING DISABILITY ADMISSIONS INFORMATION

**Program Name:** Disability Support Services
**Program Director:** Veronica Miller          **Telephone:** 606-257-3566
**Contact Person:** Same as above

### ADMISSIONS

LCC offers an "open door" admission to all applicants who meet the following requirements: proof of a high school diploma or the GED; ACT for placement not admission; 4 yrs. English, algebra I & II, biology, chemistry or physics, U.S. history, and geometry; any areas of deficiency can be made up at LCC before enrolling in college courses; there is no required GPA or class rank. Students may live in the residence halls at the University of Kentucky and attend classes at LCC which is located on the same campus as the university. There is an articulation agreement between LCC and the University of Kentucky.

**College entrance exams required:** Yes                    **Untimed accepted:** Yes
**Course entrance requirements:** Yes                       **Interview required:** No
**Diagnostic tests:** Yes
**Documentation:** Psycho-educational evaluation: within 3 years

### ADDITIONAL INFORMATION

DSS Program provides a full range of services including: academic advising; career counseling; supportive counseling; specialized computer software; recorded textbooks; notetaker; readers; writers/scribes; tutors; and testing accommodation. The DSS Coordinator serves as student liaison with college faculty, staff and administrators, vocational rehabilitational counselors, and various other social service agencies. The DSS office routinely works with community agencies on behalf of current and prospective students with disabilities. A case management approach is used to ensure continuity of services between agencies. LD assessments are available on campus for $175-200. Students must be admitted to the college and may voluntarily request support services. Study Strategies is offered for college credit. The Athena Club is a student organization created to assume an advocacy role on behalf of students with disabilities at LCC through education, recruiting, support groups, and social opportunities.

**Special education HS coursework accepted:** N/I          **Essay required:** No
**Special application required:** No                        **Submitted to:** N/A
**# of applications submitted each year:** N/A             **# of applications accepted each year:** N/A
**# of students receiving LD services:** 135+
**Acceptance into program means acceptance into college:** Students must be admitted to LCC and then may request services.

## LEARNING DISABILITY SERVICES

**Learning center:** No
**Kurzweil personal reader:** No
**LD specialists:** No
**Allowed in exams:**
  **Calculator:** Yes
  **Dictionary:** No
  **Computer:** Yes
  **SpellCheck:** Yes

**Notetaker:** Yes
**Scribes:** Yes
**Proctors:** Yes
**Oral exams:** Yes
**Extended test time:** Yes
**Added cost:** N/I
**Distraction-free environ.:** Yes
**Tape recording in class:** Yes
**Books on tape:** Yes
**Taping of other books:** Yes

**Professional tutors:** 15
**Peer tutors:** 15
**Max. hrs/wk for services:** N/I
**Priority registration:** No
**Accomodations for students with ADD:** Yes
**How are professors notified of LD:** By the student and the Program Director

## GENERAL ADMISSIONS INFORMATION

**Director of Admissions:** Shelbie Hugle          **Telephone:** 606-257-4872

### ENTRANCE REQUIREMENTS
NR

**Application deadline:** NR          **SAT or ACT preferred:** NR
**Notification:** NR

## COLLEGE GRADUATION REQUIREMENTS

**Course waivers allowed:** No
**Course substitutions allowed:** Yes
**In what courses:** Students may request substitutions for any course with appropriate documentation.

## ADDITIONAL INFORMATION

**Environment:** NR

**Student Body**
  **Undergrad enrollment:** NR
  **Women:** NR
  **Men:** NR
  **In-state students:** NR
  **Out-of-state:** NR

**Cost Information**
  **In-state tuition:** NR
  **Out-of-state:** NR

**Housing Information**
  **University housing:** Yes
  **Fraternity:** NR
  **Sorority:** NR
  **Living on campus:** NR

  **Athletics:** NR

# THOMAS MORE COLLEGE

Thomas More Parkway, Crestview Hills, KY 41017 • **Admissions:** 606-344-3332 • **Fax:** 606-344-3638
**Email:** cantralk@thomasmore.edu • **Web:** www.thomasmore.edu
**Support:** S • **Institution:** 4 yr. Private

## LEARNING DISABILITY ADMISSIONS AND SERVICES

Thomas More College's Student Support Services program is committed to the individual academic, personal, cultural/social and financial needs of the student. It is committed to promoting sensitivity and cultural awareness of the population served and to promoting varied on/off campus services and events that enhance the student's educational opportunities. A variety of support services are offered including developmental courses, peer tutoring, and individual counseling. Students with deficits in speech/language, study skills, written expression, ongoing additional skills, perceptual skills, reading, speaking, math, fine motor and ADD/ADHD with or without LD are admissible. Students may need 5 years to graduate. The college offers small classes, excellent faculty, and solid preparation for the future.

## LEARNING DISABILITY ADMISSIONS INFORMATION

**Program Name:** Student Support Services
**Program Director:** Barbara S. Davis
**Contact Person:** Same as above

**Telephone:** 606-344-3521

### ADMISSIONS

There is no separate application required for an applicant with learning disabilities. All students must submit the general application for admission. A Student Support Services staff person is part of the Admission's Committee. Students with learning disabilities may be conditionally admitted so that they can receive extra support. General admission criteria includes: a recommendation for 4 yrs. English, 2 yrs. math , 2 yrs. science, 2 yrs. social studies, 2 yrs. foreign language; foreign language requirements may be substituted for and possibly math as well;  ACT 19-23 and a few below 19 or 950 SAT; rank in top 50% of class; and a B– average. The college can waive ACT/SAT scores after considering the students' LD status. A WAIS-R is not required, but diagnostic testing is encouraged before enrolling, as it is required to be on file before student can access services.

**College entrance exams required:** Yes
**Course entrance requirements:** Yes
**Diagnostic tests:** Yes
**Documentation:** Tests given by school district: prefer within 3 years

**Untimed accepted:** Yes
**Interview required:** Recommended

### ADDITIONAL INFORMATION

Students with learning disabilities could be limited to 12-13 hours the first semester. Students' progress will be monitored. Some students may be required to take developmental courses based on the college's assessment of reading, writing, and math skills. Skills classes are paired with World History and there is college credit for skill classes in study skills, reading and math. Some students are admitted on a conditional status and are given additional support through Student Support Services.

**Special education HS coursework accepted:** Yes
**Special application required:** No
**# of applications submitted each year:** N/A
**# of students receiving LD services:** N/A

**Essay required:** No
**Submitted to:** N/A
**# of applications accepted each year:** N/A

**Acceptance into program means acceptance into college:** Students are admitted to the College and then reviewed for LD services.

**Learning center:** No
**Kurzweil personal reader:** No
**LD specialists:** No
**Allowed in exams:**
  **Calculator:** No
  **Dictionary:** Y/N
  **Computer:** No
  **SpellCheck:** No

**Notetaker:** Yes
**Scribes:** Yes
**Proctors:** Yes
**Oral exams:** Yes
**Extended test time:** Yes
**Added cost:** None
**Distraction-free environ.:** Yes
**Tape recording in class:** Yes
**Books on tape:** Yes
**Taping of other books:** Yes

**Professional tutors:** 3
**Peer tutors:** 20
**Max. hrs/wk for services:** 3-5 hours per week or as needed
**Priority registration:** Yes
**Accomodations for students with ADD:** Yes
**How are professors notified of LD:** By the student and the Program Director

## GENERAL ADMISSIONS INFORMATION

**Director of Admissions:** Katy Daugherty

**Telephone:** 606-344-3324

### ENTRANCE REQUIREMENTS

Total high school units required/recommended: 16 total units are required; 4 English recommended, 2 math recommended, 2 science recommended, 2 foreign language recommended, 2 social studies recommended. Minimum composite ACT score of 20 (combined SAT I score of 900), rank in top half of secondary school class, and minimum B average required.

**Application deadline:** August 15
**Notification:** Rolling

**SAT or ACT preferred:** Either
**SAT Avg:** 510V, 660M
**Average ACT:** 23
**Average GPA:** 3.11

**Graduated top 10% of class:** 18
**Graduated top 25% of class:** 42
**Graduated top 50% of class:** 67

## COLLEGE GRADUATION REQUIREMENTS

**Course waivers allowed:** Yes
**Course substitutions allowed:** Yes
**In what courses:** Foreign language and math.

## ADDITIONAL INFORMATION

**Environment:** The College is located on a 160 acre campus 8 miles from Cincinnati.

**Student Body**
  **Undergrad enrollment:** 1,237
  **Women:** 53%
  **Men:** 47%
  **In-state students:** 61%
  **Out-of-state:** 39%

**Cost Information**
  **In-state tuition:** $10,970
  **Out-of-state:** $10,970
  **Room & board:** $4,500

**Housing Information**
  **University housing:** Yes
  **Fraternity:** No
  **Sorority:** No
  **Living on campus:** 33%

  **Athletics:** NAIA

# WESTERN KENTUCKY UNIVERSITY

**KY**

1 Big Red Way, Bowling Green, KY 42101 • **Admissions:** 502-745-2551 • **Fax:** 502-745-6402
**Web:** www.wku.edu
**Support:** S • **Institution:** 4 yr. Public

## LEARNING DISABILITY ADMISSIONS AND SERVICES

The goal of the Office of Affirmative Action is to foster the full and self-directed participation of persons with disabilities attending the university. The service is established to facilitate the participation of students at Western Kentucky University by providing information on services, acting as liaison with faculty and staff for reasonable accommodation, and providing learning disability services. ODS coordinates support services so that students can be self-sufficient and can develop to their maximum academic potential. To be eligible for these services, documentation from a licensed professional must be provided. This documentation must be no more than three years old, state the nature of the disability, and clearly describe the kinds of accommodations recommended. Once accepted students should provide the documentation; discuss the disability and ways to accommodate special needs; arrange to take placement tests and register for classes early; contact instructors to learn what each instructor will require in terms of grading criteria, amount of weekly reading, number and types of homework assignments and tests; order books on tape; and request alternative testing conditions, notetakers; and readers. Students needing specialized help beyond that offered by the university may need to seek financial assistance.

## LEARNING DISABILITY ADMISSIONS INFORMATION

**Program Name:** Office of Affirmative Action
**Program Director:** Huda Melky
**Contact Person:** Same as above

**Telephone:** 502-745-5121

### ADMISSIONS

There is no special admissions process for students with learning disabilities. All applicants must meet the same admission criteria. High school courses required include: 4 yrs. English, 3 yrs. math, 2 yrs. social science, and 2 yrs. lab science (biology, physics and chemistry). In-state residents must have a minimum 2.3 GPA or 18 ACT; out-of-state students must have a minimum 2.3 GPA and 18 ACT or 990 SAT. Factors considered for admission are ACT/SAT; high school performance; any post-secondary record; recommendations; personal qualifications and conduct; interview; and complete and accurate information listed on the application for admission.Students can be admitted by exception through the Director of Admissions. Western Kentucky University's Community College will admit students who do not meet high school course requirements.

**College entrance exams required:** Yes
**Course entrance requirements:** Yes
**Diagnostic tests:** Yes
**Documentation:** Psycho-educational evaluation

**Untimed accepted:** Yes
**Interview required:** No

### ADDITIONAL INFORMATION

The Program for students with LD offers students: adapted test administrations; taped textbooks; short-term loan of special equipment; reading referral services; faculty liaison; peer tutoring; academic, personal and career counseling; and assisting with the Reading and Learning Labs. Academic advisors assist students in course selection. The university combines intensive academic advisement with special seminars to provide support during the freshman year. The University Counseling Services Center provides assistance in personal, social, emotional and intellectual development. Skills classes are offered in math, reading, vocabulary, study skills and English through the Community College. College credit is given for these classes. Services and accommodations are available for undergraduate and graduate students.

**Special education HS coursework accepted:** No
**Special application required:** Yes
**# of applications submitted each year:** 50
**# of students receiving LD services:** 250

**Essay required:** No
**Submitted to:** Program Director
**# of applications accepted each year:** 50

**Acceptance into program means acceptance into college:** Students must be admitted to the university first and then may request LD services.

## LEARNING DISABILITY SERVICES

**Learning center:** No
**Kurzweil personal reader:** No
**LD specialists:** No
**Allowed in exams:**
  **Calculator:** Yes
  **Dictionary:** Yes
  **Computer:** Yes
  **SpellCheck:** Yes

**Notetaker:** Yes
**Scribes:** Yes
**Proctors:** Yes
**Oral exams:** Yes
**Extended test time:** Yes
**Added cost:** None
**Distraction-free environ.:** Yes
**Tape recording in class:** Yes
**Books on tape:** Yes
**Taping of other books:** Yes

**Professional tutors:** 15
**Peer tutors:** 20
**Max. hrs/wk for services:** Unlimited
**Priority registration:** Yes
**Accomodations for students with ADD:** Yes
**How are professors notified of LD:** By the student and the Program Director

## GENERAL ADMISSIONS INFORMATION

**Director of Admissions:** Dr. Cheryl Chambless          **Telephone:** 502-745-5422

### ENTRANCE REQUIREMENTS

Total high school units required/recommended: 20 total units are required; 4 English required, 3 math required, 2 science required, 2 social studies required. Minimum composite ACT score of 17 and minimum 2.2 GPA required of in-state applicants; minimum composite ACT score of 19 and minimum 2.2 GPA required of out-of-state applicants. Special requirements: TOEFL is required of all international students. Admission to department (in addition to university) required of dental hygiene and nursing program applicants.

**Application deadline:** August 1
**Notification:** Rolling

**SAT or ACT preferred:** ACT
**Average ACT:** 21

## COLLEGE GRADUATION REQUIREMENTS

**Course waivers allowed:** No
**Course substitutions allowed:** Yes
**In what courses:** Courses can be substituted but are handled on a case-by-case basis.

## ADDITIONAL INFORMATION

**Environment:** The university is located on 200 acres in a suburban area 65 miles north of Nashville.

**Student Body**
  **Undergrad enrollment:** 12,618
  **Women:** 55%
  **Men:** 45%
  **In-state students:** 82%
  **Out-of-state:** 18%

**Cost Information**
  **In-state tuition:** $1,740
  **Out-of-state:** $5,220
  **Room & board:** $3,110

**Housing Information**
  **University housing:** Yes
  **Fraternity:** Yes
  **Sorority:** Yes
  **Living on campus:** 33%

  **Athletics:** NCAA Div. I

# LOUISIANA COLLEGE

P.O. Box 560, Pineville, LA 71359 • **Admissions:** 800-487-1906 • **Fax:** 318-487-7550
**Email:** admissions@andria.lacollege.edu • **Web:** www.lacollege.edu
**Support:** SP • **Institution:** 4 yr. Private

## LEARNING DISABILITY ADMISSIONS AND SERVICES

The goal of PASS is to facilitate the academic success of students with disabilities and to serve as an advocate for the students. This highly individualized, limited enrollment program provides support services and personal attention to students who need special counseling, tutoring, or classroom assistance. Three levels of services are provided. Level I students are required to attend weekly group and individual counseling and tutoring sessions; the emphasis at this level is to provide individualized help to ensure the student's successful transition to college and to overcome any identifiable disability. Level II students have, at a minimum, completed 24 hours of college credit at Louisiana College with at least a 2.3 grade point average; regularly scheduled individual counseling sessions continue to be provided; all other services continue to be available to the student as needed. Level III students have learned to overcome their disability and are independently achieving college success; these students will have their progress monitored by the staff. Any student not maintaining a 2.3 GPA must remain or return to Level I.

## LEARNING DISABILITY ADMISSIONS INFORMATION

**Program Name:** Program to Assist Student Success (PASS)
**Program Director:** Vickie Kelly                    **Telephone:** 318-487-7629
**Contact Person:** Same as above

### ADMISSIONS

All qualified applicants must submit the regular application, meet the general criteria for admission to Louisiana College and have a diagnosed learning disability (or physical handicap). Successful applicants must have the intellectual potential (average to superior), the appropriate academic foundation (class standing and/or ACT/SAT scores), and the personal desire and motivation to succeed. The PASS Director and staff make the final decision about admission to the program after reviewing the following: 20 or above on ACT or 930 or above on SAT; 4 yrs. English, 3 yrs. science, 3 yrs. social studies, and 3 yrs. math; 2.0 GPA; counselors recommendation and other letters of reference; psychological or medical reports; and a 750 word essay outlining why the student feels he/she can succeed in college. At least one personal interview with student and parent(s) is required. Students are encouraged to apply early and will be advised of admission on or after May 31. There is an application evaluation fee of $125. Students may appeal to the Appeal's Board if they are denied admission.

| | |
|---|---|
| **College entrance exams required:** Yes | **Untimed accepted:** Yes |
| **Course entrance requirements:** Yes | **Interview required:** Yes |
| **Diagnostic tests:** Yes | |

**Documentation:** WAIS-R or WISC-R, or other appropriate tests: within 1 year

### ADDITIONAL INFORMATION

Tutoring sessions are conducted in all subjects taken by Level I students. Additional tutorial help is available at the higher levels as needed. At all service levels, students may take untimed tests at the PASS Center. The PASS Staff will carefully work with individual professors and the student's academic advisor to coordinate and accommodate the student's learning needs. Students admitted to the PASS Program will remain in the program as long as they are at Louisiana College. Non-compliance with any component of the program may result in a student's dismissal from the Program and from the college. Skills classes are offered in study techniques, test taking strategies, time management through Orientation and private tutoring from a PASS staff member. Incoming freshmen are encouraged to attend one summer session (5 weeks) to become familiar with the campus and college life.

| | |
|---|---|
| **Special education HS coursework accepted:** No | **Essay required:** Yes |
| **Special application required:** Yes | **Submitted to:** Program Director |
| **# of applications submitted each year:** 10-20 | **# of applications accepted each year:** 7-12 |
| **# of students receiving LD services:** 25 | |

**Acceptance into program means acceptance into college:** Students must be admitted to the College first and then may request admission to PASS.

## LEARNING DISABILITY SERVICES

**Learning center:** Yes
**Kurzweil personal reader:** Yes
**LD specialists:** 1
**Allowed in exams:**
  **Calculator:** Y/N
  **Dictionary:** Y/N
  **Computer:** Yes
  **SpellCheck:** Yes

**Notetaker:** Yes
**Scribes:** Yes
**Proctors:** Yes
**Oral exams:** Yes
**Extended test time:** Yes
**Added cost:** Per semester: Level I/$850; Level II/ $435; Level III/ $200
**Distraction-free environ.:** Yes
**Tape recording in class:** Yes
**Books on tape:** Yes
**Taping of other books:** Yes

**Professional tutors:** 3
**Peer tutors:** 15
**Max. hrs/wk for services:** Unlimited
**Priority registration:** Yes
**Accomodations for students with ADD:** Yes
**How are professors notified of LD:** By the student and the Program Director

## GENERAL ADMISSIONS INFORMATION

**Director of Admissions:** Karen Gregoczyk

**Telephone:** 318-487-7629

### ENTRANCE REQUIREMENTS

Total high school units required/recommended: 17 total units are required; 4 English required, 3 math required, 3 science required, 3 social studies required. Minimum composite ACT score of 20 (or SAT I equivalent) or minimum composite ACT score of 14, rank in top half of secondary school class, and minimum 2.0 GPA required. Special requirements: An audition is required for music program applicants. TOEFL is required of all international students.

**Application deadline:** Rolling
**Notification:** August 15

**SAT or ACT preferred:** ACT
**Average ACT:** 23
**Average GPA:** 3.3

**Graduated top 10% of class:** 35
**Graduated top 25% of class:** 64
**Graduated top 50% of class:** 90

## COLLEGE GRADUATION REQUIREMENTS

**Course waivers allowed:** No
**Course substitutions allowed:** Yes
**In what courses:** Possibly will allow substitutions; appeal must be made to special committee. However, the Director of PASS rarely makes such a recommendation.

## ADDITIONAL INFORMATION

**Environment:** The College is located on 81 acres in a small town, 1 mile northeast of Alexandria.

**Student Body**
  **Undergrad enrollment:** 1,003
  **Women:** 59%
  **Men:** 41%
  **In-state students:** 95%
  **Out-of-state:** 5%

**Cost Information**
  **In-state tuition:** $4,488
  **Out-of-state:** $4,488
  **Room & board:** $1,529

**Housing Information**
  **University housing:** Yes
  **Fraternity:** Yes
  **Sorority:** Yes
  **Living on campus:** 45%

  **Athletics:** NAIA

# LOUISIANA STATE UNIVERSITY-BATON ROUGE

Baton Rouge, LA 70803 • **Admissions:** 504-388-1175 • **Fax:** 504-388-4433

**Email:** admit@unix1.sncc.lsu.edu • **Web:** www.lsu.edu

**Support:** CS • **Institution:** 4 yr. Public

## LEARNING DISABILITY ADMISSIONS AND SERVICES

The purpose of the Office of Services for Students with Disabilities is to assist any student who finds his or her disability to be a barrier to achieving educational and /or personal goals. The office provides support services to students with learning disabilities. The Office of Services for Students with Disabilities has a strong commitment to improving individual choices, personal control of essential resources, and integration into the university community. The consequences of a disability may include specialized requirements, therefore, the particular needs of each student are considered on an individual basis. SSD dedicates its efforts to meeting both the needs of students with disabilities and the interests of faculty, staff, and the university as a whole. It is the practice of SSD that issues concerning accommodations of students with disabilities in academic and other programs and activities be resolved between the student requesting the accommodation and the university employee representing the department within which the academic program or service is located. After intervention, if the student does not find the provision of an accommodation satisfactory, the student may file a formal grievance.

## LEARNING DISABILITY ADMISSIONS INFORMATION

**Program Name:** Office of Services for Students with Disabilities
**Program Director:** Traci Bryant                    **Telephone:** 504-388-5919
**Contact Person:** Laura Brackin

### ADMISSIONS

There is no special admissions process for students with learning disabilities. All applicants must meet the general admission requirements including: 4 yrs. English, 3 yrs. math (including algebra I and II and an advanced math), biology, chemistry and physics, American and world history or world geography or history of western civilization and one additional social studies, foreign language, 1/2 year of computers, and 2 academic electives; ACT 20 or above or SAT 910 or above but the exact scores are dependent on an individual student record; 2.3 GPA. If an applicant does not meet the general admission criteria but is borderline, the student can be admitted through the Access Program.

**College entrance exams required:** Yes           **Untimed accepted:** Yes
**Course entrance requirements:** Yes              **Interview required:** No
**Diagnostic tests:** Yes
**Documentation:** WAIS-R: W-J: within 3 years

### ADDITIONAL INFORMATION

Specialized support services are based on individual student's disability based needs. Services available include: disability management counseling; adaptive equipment loan; notetakers; referral for tutoring; assistance with enrollment and registration; liaison assistance and referral to on-campus and off-campus resources; services and agencies; supplemental orientation to the campus; and advocacy on behalf of students with campus faculty, staff, and students. Students with learning disabilities who are requesting services must provide current documentation. The decision to provide accommodations and services is made by the SSD after reviewing documentation. There is a Learning Assistance Center which is open to all students on campus. Services and accommodations are available to undergraduate and graduate students.

**Special education HS coursework accepted:** Yes       **Essay required:** Yes
**Special application required:** No                     **Submitted to:** N/A
**# of applications submitted each year:** N/A          **# of applications accepted each year:** N/A
**# of students receiving LD services:** Approximately 450
**Acceptance into program means acceptance into college:** Students must be accepted to the university first and then may request LD services.

# LEARNING DISABILITY SERVICES

**Learning center:** Yes
**Kurzweil personal reader:** No
**LD specialists:** 1
**Allowed in exams:**
  **Calculator:** Yes
  **Dictionary:** Yes
  **Computer:** N/I
  **SpellCheck:** Yes

**Notetaker:** Yes
**Scribes:** Yes
**Proctors:** Yes
**Oral exams:** Yes
**Extended test time:** Yes
**Added cost:** None
**Distraction-free environ.:** Yes
**Tape recording in class:** Yes
**Books on tape:** Yes
**Taping of other books:** Yes

**Professional tutors:** Yes
**Peer tutors:** Yes
**Max. hrs/wk for services:**
Unlimited
**Priority registration:** Yes
**Accomodations for students
with ADD:** Yes
**How are professors notified of
LD:** By the student and the
Program Director

# GENERAL ADMISSIONS INFORMATION

**Director of Admissions:** Lisa Harris          **Telephone:** 504-388-1175

## ENTRANCE REQUIREMENTS

Total high school units required/recommended: 17 total units are required; 4 English required, 3 math required, 3 science required, 2 foreign language required, 3 social studies required. Minimum 2.3 GPA required. Special requirements: A portfolio is required for art program applicants. An audition is required for music program applicants. TOEFL is required of all international students.

**Application deadline:** June 1
**Notification:** Rolling

**SAT or ACT preferred:** ACT
**Average ACT:** 23
**Average GPA:** 3.1

**Graduated top 10% of class:** 26
**Graduated top 25% of class:** 51
**Graduated top 50% of class:** 79

# COLLEGE GRADUATION REQUIREMENTS

**Course waivers allowed:** Yes
**Course substitutions allowed:** Yes
**In what courses:** Foreign language and math.

# ADDITIONAL INFORMATION

**Environment:** The campus is in an urban area in Baton Rouge.

**Student Body**
  **Undergrad enrollment:** 21,413
  **Women:** 50%
  **Men:** 50%
  **In-state students:** 90%
  **Out-of-state:** 10%

**Cost Information**
  **In-state tuition:** $2,687
  **Out-of-state:** $5,987
  **Room & board:** $3,570

**Housing Information**
  **University housing:** Yes
  **Fraternity:** Yes
  **Sorority:** Yes
  **Living on campus:** 24%

  **Athletics:** NCAA Div. I

# UNIVERSITY OF NEW ORLEANS

Lake Front, New Orleans, LA 70148 • **Admissions:** 504-280-6595 • **Fax:** 504-280-5522
**Email:** admissions@uno.edu • **Web:** www.uno.edu
**Support:** S • **Institution:** 4 yr. Public

## LEARNING DISABILITY ADMISSIONS AND SERVICES

The University of New Orleans is committed to providing all students with equal opportunities for academic and extra-curricular success. The Disabled Student Services Office coordinates all services and programs. In addition to serving its primary functions as a liaison between the student and the university, the Office provides a limited number of direct services to students with all kinds of permanent and temporary disabilities. Services begin when a student registered with the university contacts the DSS Office, provides documentation of the disability, and requests assistance. DSS encourages student independence, program accessibility, and a psychologically supportive environment, so students may achieve their educational objectives. DSS also seeks to educate the campus community about disability issues.

## LEARNING DISABILITY ADMISSIONS INFORMATION

**Program Name:** Disabled Student Services (DSS)
**Program Director:** Janice Lyn
**Contact Person:** Same as above

**Telephone:** 504-286-6222

### ADMISSIONS

University of New Orleans does not have any special admissions process for students with learning disabilities. Students with learning disabilities should submit the general application form and are expected to meet the same admission standards as all other applicants. Any student who is denied admission may apply to the College Life Program which is designed as an alternative admissions for 'high risk' students (not only students with learning disabilities). This program is for students who need assistance in one or more academic areas. The students remain with this program until they are able to remediate their deficits and then transfer into the appropriate college.

**College entrance exams required:** Yes
**Course entrance requirements:** Yes
**Diagnostic tests:** Yes
**Documentation:** Psycho-educational evaluation: within 3 years

**Untimed accepted:** Yes
**Interview required:** No

### ADDITIONAL INFORMATION

The DSS provides regular support services to all UNO students. Drop-in tutoring for Math and writing is available. Audio tapes are also available in math and English course. Tutors are available in the Learning Resource Center and Testing Centers in the Library for test taking, adaptive technology, and/or test administration.  Developmental courses are offered in Math and English and skills classes are available for assistance in study techniques. PREP START is a special summer outreach program for recent high school graduates to gain admission to the university.

**Special education HS coursework accepted:** N/I
**Special application required:** No
**# of applications submitted each year:** N/A
**# of students receiving LD services:** 100

**Essay required:** No
**Submitted to:** N/A
**# of applications accepted each year:** N/A

**Acceptance into program means acceptance into college:** Students must be admitted to the university first and then request services.

**Learning center:** Yes
**Kurzweil personal reader:** Yes
**LD specialists:** No
**Allowed in exams:**
  **Calculator:** Yes
  **Dictionary:** Yes
  **Computer:** Yes
  **SpellCheck:** Yes

**Notetaker:** Yes
**Scribes:** Yes
**Proctors:** Yes
**Oral exams:** Yes
**Extended test time:** Yes
**Added cost:** None
**Distraction-free environ.:** Yes
**Tape recording in class:** Yes
**Books on tape:** Yes
**Taping of other books:** Yes

**Professional tutors:** No
**Peer tutors:** No
**Max. hrs/wk for services:** N/A
Referred to the Learning Resource Center
**Priority registration:** No
**Accomodations for students with ADD:** Yes
**How are professors notified of LD:** By the student and the Program Director

# GENERAL ADMISSIONS INFORMATION

**Director of Admissions:** Roslyn Shelley          **Telephone:** 504-286-6595

## ENTRANCE REQUIREMENTS

Total high school units required/recommended: 18 total units are required; 4 English required, 3 math required, 3 science required, 2 foreign language required, 2 social studies required, 1 history required. Minimum composite ACT score of 20 (combined SAT I score of 950) or minimum 2.0 GPA required. Special requirements: A portfolio is required for art program applicants. An audition is required for music program applicants. TOEFL is required of all international students.

**Application deadline:** August 21
**Notification:** Rolling

**SAT or ACT preferred:** ACT
**SAT Avg:** 530V, 507M
**Average ACT:** 20
**Average GPA:** 2.83

**Graduated top 25% of class:** 39
**Graduated top 50% of class:** 76

# COLLEGE GRADUATION REQUIREMENTS

**Course waivers allowed:** No
**Course substitutions allowed:** Yes
**In what courses:** Foreign language and math with appropriate documentation.

# ADDITIONAL INFORMATION

**Environment:** The university is located on 345 acres in downtown New Orleans.

**Student Body**
  **Undergrad enrollment:** 11,689
  **Women:** 56%
  **Men:** 44%
  **In-state students:** 94%
  **Out-of-state:** 6%

**Cost Information**
  **In-state tuition:** $2,362
  **Out-of-state:** $5,154
  **Room & board:** $3,386

**Housing Information**
  **University housing:** Yes
  **Fraternity:** Yes
  **Sorority:** No
  **Living on campus:** 5%

  **Athletics:** NCAA Div. I

# NICHOLLS STATE UNIVERSITY

P.O.Box 2004 Univ. Station, Thibodaux, LA 70310 • **Admissions:** 504-448-4145 • **Fax:** 504-448-4929
**Web:** server.nich.edu
**Support:** S • **Institution:** 4 yr. Public

## LEARNING DISABILITY ADMISSIONS AND SERVICES

The Center for the Study of Dyslexia offers assistance to serious, capable, students with learning disabilities at Nicholls State University who seek to earn an undergraduate degree. They believe that everyone has the right and the obligation to pursue the fulfillment of their learning potential. The center's programs are data driven, goal oriented, and committed to change. They are committed to continually question and evaluate their own practices. They have their own research program and have close ties with leading scholars and researchers in dyslexia. The center is impressed with multisensory, linguistic, and direct instructional approaches, but to maintain their own integrity, they project an orientation that is objective, open-minded, and directed toward the future. The goals they have are focused on the need to increase the understanding of dyslexia and to upgrade and improve the accessibility and quality of the services that individuals with dyslexia depend upon to help them to become self-sufficient, well-adjusted, and contributing members of society.

## LEARNING DISABILITY ADMISSIONS INFORMATION

**Program Name:** Center for the Study of Dyslexia
**Program Director:** Dr. Carol S. Ronka
**Contact Person:** Randall Moore          **Telephone:** 504-448-4214

### ADMISSIONS

There is no special admissions process for students with learning disabilities. The college has an "open  admissions policy" for all graduates of high school or a GED. The college recommends that students have 4 yrs. English, 3 yrs. math, 3 yrs. science, 3 yrs. social studies, and 2 yrs. foreign language. ACT/SAT are not required for admission. The average high school GPA is 2.7 and the average ACT is 20. There are a limited number of openings in the Center and students should apply early to assure space. The Program seeks highly motivated students who have been diagnosed as having a learning disability and who have been successfully mainstreamed in college prep courses throughout the four years of high school. Admission decisions are made after careful review of all submitted documentation. Students may be selected for admission to the Center, or may be placed on a waiting list. The final decision is based upon selecting the option best suited to providing a successful experience at NSU for the student.

| | |
|---|---|
| **College entrance exams required:** Yes | **Untimed accepted:** Yes |
| **Course entrance requirements:** Yes | **Interview required:** Yes |
| **Diagnostic tests:** Yes | |
| **Documentation:** Any psycho-educational evaluation: within 3 years | |

### ADDITIONAL INFORMATION

The Dyslexia Center provides support system; equipment; remediation; academic planning; resources; and assistance. With the student's permission, letters requesting appropriate classroom and testing accommodations are written for professors. Typical accommodations may include but are not limited to: extended time; use of an electronic dictionary; oral reader; or use of a computer. Students meet weekly with an identified academic assistant and are enrolled in regular college classes. Other campus services for students with disabilities include the Office for Students with Disabilities; the Testing Center for special testing accommodations such as extended time or a quiet room; the Tutorial Learning Center for tutoring assistance; the University Counseling Center which provides counseling directed at self-encouragement, self-esteem, assertiveness, stress management, and test anxiety; and the Computer Lab for assistance with written assignments.

| | |
|---|---|
| **Special education HS coursework accepted:** Yes | **Essay required:** No |
| **Special application required:** Yes | **Submitted to:** Program Director |
| **# of applications submitted each year:** 25 | **# of applications accepted each year:** 20 |
| **# of students receiving LD services:** 20 | |

**Acceptance into program means acceptance into college:** Students are admitted to the university first and then request to be reviewed for LD services.

# LEARNING DISABILITY SERVICES

**Learning center:** Yes
**Kurzweil personal reader:** Yes
**LD specialists:** N/I
**Allowed in exams:**
  **Calculator:** Yes
  **Dictionary:** Yes
  **Computer:** Yes
  **SpellCheck:** Yes

**Notetaker:** No
**Scribes:** Yes
**Proctors:** Yes
**Oral exams:** Yes
**Extended test time:** Yes
**Added cost:** $300 per/semester
**Distraction-free environ.:** Yes
**Tape recording in class:** Yes
**Books on tape:** No
**Taping of other books:** No

**Professional tutors:** 1
**Peer tutors:** No
**Max. hrs/wk for services:** Unlimited
**Priority registration:** No
**Accomodations for students with ADD:** Yes
**How are professors notified of LD:** By the student

# GENERAL ADMISSIONS INFORMATION

**Director of Admissions:** Becky Durocher          **Telephone:** 504-448-4507

## ENTRANCE REQUIREMENTS

Total high school units required/recommended: 4 English recommended, 3 math recommended, 3 science recommended, 2 foreign language, 3 social studies recommended. Open admissions policy for graduates of approved secondary schools. Special requirements: TOEFL is required of all international students.

**Application deadline:** August 15          **SAT or ACT preferred:** ACT
**Notification:** Rolling          **SAT II required:** Yes

# COLLEGE GRADUATION REQUIREMENTS

**Course waivers allowed:** No
**Course substitutions allowed:** No
**In what courses:** N/A

# ADDITIONAL INFORMATION

**Environment:** NR

**Student Body**
  **Undergrad enrollment:** 6,355
  **Women:** 59%
  **Men:** 41%
  **In-state students:** 98%
  **Out-of-state:** 2%

**Cost Information**
  **In-state tuition:** $2,017
  **Out-of-state:** $2,592
  **Room & board:** $2,700

**Housing Information**
  **University housing:** Yes
  **Fraternity:** No
  **Sorority:** No
  **Living on campus:** 18%

  **Athletics:** NCAA Div. I

## ME   UNIVERSITY OF NEW ENGLAND

Hills Beach Road, Biddeford, ME 04005 • **Admissions:** 207-283-0171 ext. 2297 • **Fax:** 207-286-3678
**Email:** kberry@mailbox.une.edu • **Web:** www.une.edu
**Support:** SP • **Institution:** 4 yr. Private

## LEARNING DISABILITY ADMISSIONS AND SERVICES

The primary goal of the Individual Learning Program is to promote and enhance the learning process for students with learning disabilities. The ILP is a voluntary, comprehensive intervention program for students who have a documented LD. The program is developmental rather than remedial—a way to help students meet and overcome their learning disabilities in order to get the most out of their college education. Students receive individually planned, sequenced curricula with support services to meet their particular needs for 4 years if required. The ILP operates on levels of program intervention, which lets students make a gradual transition into assitance-free college study. The level is determined by the faculty at the time of admission to the program. After the first semester in the ILP and for each subsequent semester, students and the learning specialist decide if the student should remain in the program at the initial level of intervention, if the student is eligible to move to a different level or if the student should be released or dismissed from the program altogether. If released, students may reapply at any time and the fee is pro-rated. Dismissal indicates not meeting 70% of the Individualized College Plan objectives with 70% accuracy, and students must wait a year to reapply.

## LEARNING DISABILITY ADMISSIONS INFORMATION

**Program Name:** Individual Learning Program  (ILP)
**Program Director:** Pamela M. Leone, Ph.D.             **Telephone:** 207-283-0171 ext.532
**Contact Person:** Admissions Office                    **Telephone:** 207-283-0171 ext. 385

### ADMISSIONS

Admissions to UNE and the ILP is a process carried out jointly by the Office of Admissions and ILP. No single criterion is used, but factors considered are GPA, level of difficulty of high school courses, social/emotional maturity, and verbal ability. Students should submit the following; transcript, 2 recommendations, educational/psychological evaluations, and scores from assessments of academic functioning. A personal interview with faculty of the ILP is required.  The ACT/SAT are not used in the admission process. The Verbal sub-score on the WAIS-R is very important. Interested students may request a pre-screening. Application to the ILP constitutes an applicant's self-declaration of the presence of a learning disability. General admission criteria include: 4 yrs. English, 3 yrs. math, 3 yrs. science, 2 yrs. history, 2 yrs. social studies; recommendations; activities. Conditional acceptances are granted to students who have displayed a weakness in an academic area, but have proven themselves overall.  These students must maintain a particular GPA and take a limited course load. Admission decision is done by ILP and admissions.

**College entrance exams required:** No                 **Untimed accepted:** Yes
**Course entrance requirements:** Depends on applicant's  **Interview required:** Yes
intended major
**Diagnostic tests:** Yes
**Documentation:** WAIS-R; W-J; Tests of academic achievement : within 1 year

### ADDITIONAL INFORMATION

All students in the ILP meet regularly with a learning specialist. These sessions offer the opportunity for the students to understand their learning disability and develop an individual learning style, refine study strategies and learn study skills. Study Skill and Learning Strategy classes are offered for credit. Students discuss issues related to social adjustment and stress management. If a student has a learning disability but is not in need of ILP, there is an Office of Scholastic Support for Students with Disabilities (OSSSD) which will try to provide effective accommodations to the student. Services and accommodations are available for undergraduate and graduate students.

**Special education HS coursework accepted:** Yes       **Essay required:** Yes
**Special application required:** Yes                   **Submitted to:** Admissions; check box for ILP on
                                                        application
**# of applications submitted each year:** 25-35        **# of applications accepted each year:** 30%
**# of students receiving LD services:** 25
**Acceptance into program means acceptance into college:** Students who request ILP will be reviewed by ILP who make a recommendation to Admission, and students are admitted to both simultaneously.

**Learning center:** Yes
**Kurzweil personal reader:** No
**LD specialists:** 1.5
**Allowed in exams:**
  **Calculator:** Yes
  **Dictionary:** Yes
  **Computer:** Yes
  **SpellCheck:** Yes

**Notetaker:** No
**Scribes:** Yes
**Proctors:** Yes
**Oral exams:** Yes
**Extended test time:** Yes
**Added cost:** Level III: $3,500 per/yr; Level II: $2,600 per/yr; Level I: $1,500 per/yr.
**Distraction-free environ.:** Yes
**Tape recording in class:** Yes
**Books on tape:** Yes
**Taping of other books:** No

**Professional tutors:** 4-6
**Peer tutors:** 20-30
**Max. hrs/wk for services:** Individualized and unlimited
**Priority registration:** Yes
**Accomodations for students with ADD:** Yes
**How are professors notified of LD:** By the student and the Director

## GENERAL ADMISSIONS INFORMATION

**Director of Admissions:** Patricia T. Cribby

**Telephone:** 207-283-0171 ext. 297

### ENTRANCE REQUIREMENTS

Total high school units required/recommended: 18 total units are recommended; 4 English required, 3 math required, 2 science required, 3 science recommended, 2 social studies required, 3 social studies recommended, 2 history required, 3 history recommended. Special requirements: An RN is required for nursing program applicants. Interview required of nursing program applicants. Evidence of job shadowing required of occupational therapy and physical therapy program applicants.

**Application deadline:** Rolling
**Notification:** Rolling

**SAT or ACT preferred:** SAT
**SAT Avg:** 510V, 510M
**SAT II required:** Yes
**Average GPA:** 3.1

**Graduated top 10% of class:** 19
**Graduated top 25% of class:** 48
**Graduated top 50% of class:** 82

## COLLEGE GRADUATION REQUIREMENTS

**Course waivers allowed:** Yes
**Course substitutions allowed:** Yes
**In what courses:** On a case-by-case basis only after a reasonable attempt has been made to succeed in any given course.

## ADDITIONAL INFORMATION

**Environment:** The 121-acre campus is in a rural area 16 miles east of Portland.

**Student Body**
  **Undergrad enrollment:** 1,402
  **Women:** 69%
  **Men:** 31%
  **In-state students:** 53%
  **Out-of-state:** 47%

**Cost Information**
  **In-state tuition:** $13,575
  **Out-of-state:** $13,575
  **Room & board:** $5,595

**Housing Information**
  **University housing:** Yes
  **Fraternity:** No
  **Sorority:** No
  **Living on campus:** 50%

  **Athletics:** NAIA

# SOUTHERN MAINE TECHNICAL COLLEGE

**ME**

Fort Rd., South Portland, ME 04106 • **Admissions:** 207-767-9520

**Support:** CS • **Institution:** 2 yr. Public

## LEARNING DISABILITY ADMISSIONS AND SERVICES

The Learning Assistance Center Program is designed to offer academic support to students through various individualized services. The college acknowledges that all students have certain strengths and weaknesses. Students can get tutors in their most difficult courses; learn about their specific learning style; improve concentration and memory; study more efficiently for tests; learn how to manage their time better; learn the basic skills that are the foundation of their specific technology; and use a computer for typing perfect lab reports, term papers and resumes. The NoveNET Learning Lab at SMTC uses a specially designed set of lessons and offers an alternative to Adult Education or other classes to complete high school level math, science and English. The Learning Lab is a good place to become re-acquainted with oneself as a learner; students can start using it anytime during the school year and work at their own pace; they can study only the lessons that they need; they can work at home on their own personal computer; there is an instructor available during regular lab hours; the instruction meets SMTC's prerequisite admissions requirements; it has day and evening hours; it allows students to earn credit for work in certain courses in the lab by Credit-by-Examination.

## LEARNING DISABILITY ADMISSIONS INFORMATION

**Program Name:** Learning Assistance Center
**Program Director:** Gail Rowe                          **Telephone:** 207-767-9536
**Contact Person:** Same as above

### ADMISSIONS

All students must meet the same admission criteria. There is no special admissions process for students with learning disabilities.  All students have access to Learning Assistance Center including those with a diagnosed learning disability. Applicants must submit a high school transcript, essay, and recommendation. Interviews are required. Students must have 2 yrs. algebra, 1 yr. biology, physics or chemistry for most programs. SAT I is required for applicants to the Associate Degree Programs who have been out of high school two years or less. The ACT is not required. Students are expected to have a "C" average with at least a "C" in prerequisite courses. Assessment tests sometimes are required as well.

**College entrance exams required:** Yes (for some degrees)  **Untimed accepted:** Yes
**Course entrance requirements:** Yes                        **Interview required:** Recommended
**Diagnostic tests:** Recommended
**Documentation:** Psycho-educational report: within 3 years

### ADDITIONAL INFORMATION

Students with diagnosed LD, as well as any students with academic needs, are provided with: tutoring by faculty and students; access to NovaNET; access to resources in study skills, in the form of personal advising/counseling, skill inventories, and study guides; and for LD, access to academic accommodations such as untimed exams, testing in a quiet area, and notetakers or readers. Other services are: learning assessments; diagnosing of learning problems; diagnosing learning styles; faculty consulting; curriculum development; preparation of materials to assist students in all courses; study skills counseling; academic advising; counseling and support for students with learning disabilities; access to multimedia self-teaching materials including computer assisted instruction, videotapes, and audio cassettes; microcomputers, typewriters, and tape recorders. The college administers the MAPS test to any student who has not provided scores from the ACT or SAT.

**Special education HS coursework accepted:** Yes      **Essay required:** Yes
**Special application required:** No                            **Submitted to:** N/A
**# of applications submitted each year:** N/A          **# of applications accepted each year:** N/A
**# of students receiving LD services:** 60
**Acceptance into program means acceptance into college:** Students must be admitted to the College first and then may request to receive services.

# LEARNING DISABILITY SERVICES

Learning center: Yes
Kurzweil personal reader: No
LD specialists: 1
Allowed in exams:
 Calculator: Y/N
 Dictionary: Y/N
 Computer: Y/N
 SpellCheck: Y/N

Notetaker: Y/N
Scribes: Y/N
Proctors: Y/N
Oral exams: Yes
Extended test time: Yes
Added cost: None
Distraction-free environ.: Yes
Tape recording in class: Yes
Books on tape: Yes
Taping of other books: No

Professional tutors: Yes
Peer tutors: 4-6
Max. hrs/wk for services: As
needed
Priority registration: No
Accomodations for students
with ADD: Yes
How are professors notified of
LD: By the student and the
Program Director

# GENERAL ADMISSIONS INFORMATION

Director of Admissions: Robert A. Weimont          Telephone: 207-767-9520

## ENTRANCE REQUIREMENTS
Total high school units required/recommended: 2 math required, 1 science required.

Application deadline: Rolling
Notification: NR

SAT or ACT preferred: SAT
needed for AAS program.

# COLLEGE GRADUATION REQUIREMENTS

Course waivers allowed: No
Course substitutions allowed: Yes
In what courses: Limited

# ADDITIONAL INFORMATION

Environment: The College, part of the Maine Technical College System, is located on a 50-acre campus.

Student Body
 Undergrad enrollment: 2,410
 Women: NR
 Men: NR
 In-state students: NR
 Out-of-state: NR

Cost Information
 In-state tuition: NR
 Out-of-state: NR

Housing Information
 University housing: NR
 Fraternity: NR
 Sorority: NR
 Living on campus: NR

 Athletics: NR

# ME
# UNITY COLLEGE

HC78 Box 1, Unity, ME 04988 • **Admissions:** 207-948-3131 •
**Email:** admissions@unity.unity.edu •
**Support:** CS • **Institution:** 4 yr. Private

## LEARNING DISABILITY ADMISSIONS AND SERVICES

Unity College offers services for students with learning disabilities and encourages them to begin their studies in the summer prior to freshman year in the Summer Institute. The Institute provides an opportunity for students to become familiar with the college, and is an effective way to prepare for college coursework. The LRC provides a program for bright, highly motivated students. Once admitted, students with learning disabilities follow a carefully coordinated program that combines regular coursework, supportive services, and intensive individual work on academic skills development. The LD specialist meets regularly with students, monitoring progress and ensuring personal contact. The LRC's staff is composed of faculty members, a learning disabilities specialist, a counselor, and tutors. The staff is available to help students develop effective learning strategies, with special emphasis placed on individual student needs. Most importantly, the LRC gives necessary attention to each student's academic and personal growth. With the support of the LRC, students can gain confidence, knowledge and skills to complete a high quality college education.

## LEARNING DISABILITY ADMISSIONS INFORMATION

**Program Name:** Learning Resource Center (LRC)
**Program Director:** James Horan                          **Telephone:** 207-948-3131 ext. 241
**Contact Person:** Ann Dailey                             **Telephone:** 207-948-3131 ext. 236

### ADMISSIONS

To apply for admission students with learning disabilities should submit the general college application and the results of recent diagnostic testing including a WAIS. Students should submit other diagnostic materials which indicate their level of functioning. SAT and ACT scores are not required but should be submitted if available. Students also must send two letters of recommendation and their official high school transcript. The Office of Admissions may require an on-campus interview, on-campus testing, or submission of additional supporting materials. Students with learning disabilities may request an interview with the Director of Student Support Services. Other students may be admitted with the stipulation that they attend the Summer Institute and be successful prior to being admitted as a student for the fall semester. Other factors used in the admission decision include special talents, leadership, activities, alumni status, and personality. Students not regularly admissible are reviewed by the LD specialist who provides a recommendation to Admissions and a joint decision is made.

**College entrance exams required:** No              **Untimed accepted:** N/A
**Course entrance requirements:** No               **Interview required:** Yes
**Diagnostic tests:** Yes
**Documentation:** WAIS-R: within 2 years

### ADDITIONAL INFORMATION

The Summer Institute ($1,295), required of some incoming freshmen, is a 4 week pre-college program offering basic academic skills in writing, math, study strategies, computers, Unity College orientation, as well as the natural environment of Maine. The Institute includes credit and non-credit courses and individual tutorial assistance. Students meet with an academic advisor and pre-register for fall courses. Learning disability specialists are on staff and services during the school year include: specialized academic advising, support groups, taped texts, tutoring on a one-to-one basis or small group, skills remediation in reading, math, spelling, written language and learning techniques. Special courses, mostly for credit, are offered in composition, math, reading, college survival skills and study skills. This Program is curriculum based, designed to foster independence, and allow students to achieve maximum academic goals and maximum potential.

**Special education HS coursework accepted:** Yes       **Essay required:** Yes
**Special application required:** No                     **Submitted to:** N/A
**# of applications submitted each year:** N/A          **# of applications accepted each year:** N/A
**# of students receiving LD services:** 25-30
**Acceptance into program means acceptance into college:** Students must be admitted to the College prior to requesting services from the Learning Resource Center.

# LEARNING DISABILITY SERVICES

**Learning center:** Yes
**Kurzweil personal reader:** No
**LD specialists:** 1
**Allowed in exams:**
  **Calculator:** Yes
  **Dictionary:** Yes
  **Computer:** Yes
  **SpellCheck:** Yes

**Notetaker:** Yes
**Scribes:** Yes
**Proctors:** Yes
**Oral exams:** Y/N
**Extended test time:** Yes
**Added cost:** None
**Distraction-free environ.:** Y/N
**Tape recording in class:** Yes
**Books on tape:** Yes
**Taping of other books:** No

**Professional tutors:** 5 faculty
**Peer tutors:** 10-12
**Max. hrs/wk for services:** Unlimited
**Priority registration:** Yes
**Accomodations for students with ADD:** Yes
**How are professors notified of LD:** By the student and the Program Director

# GENERAL ADMISSIONS INFORMATION

**Director of Admissions:** John Craig, Ed.D.          **Telephone:** 207-948-3131 ext. 231

## ENTRANCE REQUIREMENTS
Total high school units required/recommended: 4 English recommended, 4 math recommended, 4 science recommended, 2 foreign language recommended, 4 social studies recommended.

**Application deadline:** August 15
**Notification:** NR

**SAT or ACT preferred:** SAT

**Graduated top 10% of class:** 3
**Graduated top 25% of class:** 15
**Graduated top 50% of class:** 75

# COLLEGE GRADUATION REQUIREMENTS

**Course waivers allowed:** Yes
**Course substitutions allowed:** Yes
**In what courses:** Waivers and substitutions are handled on an individual basis for each student.

# ADDITIONAL INFORMATION

**Environment:** The College is located on 185 acres in a rural community about 20 miles from Waterville.

**Student Body**
  **Undergrad enrollment:** 470
  **Women:** 26%
  **Men:** 74%
  **In-state students:** 33%
  **Out-of-state:** 67%

**Cost Information**
  **In-state tuition:** $10,330
  **Out-of-state:** $10,330
  **Room & board:** $5,050

**Housing Information**
  **University housing:** Yes
  **Fraternity:** No
  **Sorority:** No
  **Living on campus:** 60%

  **Athletics:** NAIA

# MD COLUMBIA UNION COLLEGE

7600 Flower Avenue, Takoma Park, MD 20912 • **Admissions:** 301-891-4080 • **Fax:** 301-891-4167
**Email:** admissions@cuc.edu • **Web:** www.cuc.edu
**Support:** CS • **Institution:** 4 yr. Private

## LEARNING DISABILITY ADMISSIONS AND SERVICES

The Columbia Union College Summer Start Program is designed for students who do not meet college entrance requirements. Summer Start is an intensive 6 week academic program that provides students with a strong review of basic math and English, as well as reading and study skills. The program also gives students an opportunity to learn employment-seeking skills such as resume writing and interviewing techniques. Summer Start is designed for students who are willing to invest the time and effort required to become successful college students.

## LEARNING DISABILITY ADMISSIONS INFORMATION

**Program Name:** Summer Start
**Program Director:** Betty Howard, Ph.D.
**Contact Person:** Same as above

**Telephone:** 301-891-4106

### ADMISSIONS

There is no special application or admissions procedure for students with learning disabilities. Students must submit the general application form for admission. Student should have taken the following courses in high school: 4 yrs. English, 2 yrs. math, 2 yrs. science, 2 yrs. history, and 4 electives. Interviews are required. The minimum SAT is a 450 on the Verbal and the Math sections or an ACT of 18. It is recommended that students have a GPA of 2.25 or higher. The college will consider non-academic criteria such as activities, alumni relationships, special talents and personal attributes.

**College entrance exams required:** Yes
**Course entrance requirements:** Yes
**Diagnostic tests:** No
**Documentation:** Evaluation done on site

**Untimed accepted:** Yes
**Interview required:** Yes

### ADDITIONAL INFORMATION

Summer Start and Learning Assistance Program offers admission to students not usually admitted due to academic or economic disadvantage.

**Special education HS coursework accepted:** Yes
**Special application required:** No
**# of applications submitted each year:** N/I
**# of students receiving LD services:** 6-8

**Essay required:** Yes, for English placement
**Submitted to:** N/A
**# of applications accepted each year:** N/I

**Acceptance into program means acceptance into college:** Students must be admitted to the College first (may appeal a denial) and then may request services.

**Learning center:** Yes
**Kurzweil personal reader:** No
**LD specialists:** Yes
**Allowed in exams:**
  **Calculator:** Yes
  **Dictionary:** Yes
  **Computer:** Yes
  **SpellCheck:** Yes

**Notetaker:** No
**Scribes:** N/I
**Proctors:** No
**Oral exams:** Yes
**Extended test time:** N/I
**Added cost:** $1,081 for Summer Start
**Distraction-free environ.:** N/I
**Tape recording in class:** Yes
**Books on tape:** Yes
**Taping of other books:** No

**Professional tutors:** Yes
**Peer tutors:** Yes
**Max. hrs/wk for services:** 4
**Priority registration:** No
**Accomodations for students with ADD:** Yes
**How are professors notified of LD:** By the student and Program Director

## GENERAL ADMISSIONS INFORMATION

**Director of Admissions:** Cindy Carrrend        **Telephone:** 301-891-4080

### ENTRANCE REQUIREMENTS

Total high school units required/recommended: 14 total units are recommended; 4 English recommended, 2 math recommended, 2 science recommended, 2 history recommended. Minimum SAT I scores of 450 in both Verbal and Math (composite ACT score of 18) and minimum 2.25 GPA recommended. Special requirements: TOEFL is required of all international students.

**Application deadline:** August 15
**Notification:** Rolling

**SAT or ACT preferred:** Either
**SAT Avg:** 490V, 468M
**Average ACT:** 21
**Average GPA:** 3.1

**Graduated top 10% of class:** 13
**Graduated top 25% of class:** 34
**Graduated top 50% of class:** 73

## COLLEGE GRADUATION REQUIREMENTS

**Course waivers allowed:** No
**Course substitutions allowed:** No
**In what courses:** N/A

## ADDITIONAL INFORMATION

**Environment:** The College is located on 19 acres 7 miles north of Washington, DC.

**Student Body**
  **Undergrad enrollment:** 1,172
  **Women:** 60%
  **Men:** 40%
  **In-state students:** 48%
  **Out-of-state:** 52%

**Cost Information**
  **In-state tuition:** $10,950
  **Out-of-state:** $10,950
  **Room & board:** $3,990

**Housing Information**
  **University housing:** Yes
  **Fraternity:** No
  **Sorority:** No
  **Living on campus:** 47%

  **Athletics:** NAIA

# FROSTBURG STATE UNIVERSITY

**MD**

Frostburg, MD 21532 • **Admissions:** 301-687-4201 • **Fax:** 301-687-7074
**Email:** admissions@fsu.edu • **Web:** www.fsu.umd.edu
**Support:** CS • **Institution:** 4 yr. Public

## LEARNING DISABILITY ADMISSIONS AND SERVICES

Frostburg State provides comprehensive support services for students with learning disabilities to assist them in achieving their potential. To be eligible for the Frostburg State University support services, admitted students must provide records of evaluation not more than three years old. Services include: advising and counseling by a qualified counselor familiar with each students needs; assistance in course selection; guaranteed schedules; liaison with faculty; representation at Academic Standards Committee meetings; tutoring and study skills workshops. The goal of the programs is to provide appropriate support services to enhance learning, and to strive for student self-advocacy, understanding of and independence in learning style.

## LEARNING DISABILITY ADMISSIONS INFORMATION

**Program Name:** Student Support Services/Disabled Student Services
**Program Director:** Suzzane Carroll Hall                 **Telephone:** 301-687-44481
**Contact Person:** Same as above

### ADMISSIONS

There is no special admission procedure for students with learning disabilities. All students must complete the mainstream program in high school and meet all requirements for the university and the State. There is a Student Support Services/Disability Support Services Information Form that must be completed by students to enroll in these programs. Admission to FSU is determined by the Admissions Office which assess an applicant's likelihood of success in a regular college program with Support Service assistance.

**College entrance exams required:** Yes          **Untimed accepted:** Yes
**Course entrance requirements:** Yes             **Interview required:** Y/N
**Diagnostic tests:** Yes
**Documentation:** Varies with disability: within 3 years

### ADDITIONAL INFORMATION

Basic Skills courses are available in time management, study techniques, organizational skills, and test taking strategies. Students who believe they may have a learning disability, but who have not been tested, may request testing and assessment for no fee. There is an orientation course to the university taught by an LD Specialist.

**Special education HS coursework accepted:** Yes, case-by-case                    **Essay required:** May be required
**Special application required:** No
**# of applications submitted each year:** N/A    **Submitted to:** N/A
**# of students receiving LD services:** 215+     **# of applications accepted each year:** N/A
**Acceptance into program means acceptance into college:** Students must be admitted and enrolled and then may request LD services.  There is an appeal procedure for students who are denied admission.

**Learning center:** Yes
**Kurzweil personal reader:** No
**LD specialists:** 3
**Allowed in exams:**
  **Calculator:** Yes
  **Dictionary:** Yes
  **Computer:** Yes
  **SpellCheck:** Yes

**Notetaker:** Yes
**Scribes:** Yes
**Proctors:** Yes
**Oral exams:** Yes
**Extended test time:** Yes
**Added cost:** None
**Distraction-free environ.:** Yes
**Tape recording in class:** Yes
**Books on tape:** Yes
**Taping of other books:** Yes

**Professional tutors:** Yes
**Peer tutors:** Yes
**Max. hrs/wk for services:** No limit
**Priority registration:** Yes
**Accomodations for students with ADD:** Yes
**How are professors notified of LD:** By the student and the Program Director

## GENERAL ADMISSIONS INFORMATION

**Director of Admissions:** Bernard Wynder

**Telephone:** 301-689-4201

### ENTRANCE REQUIREMENTS

Total high school units required/recommended: 14 total units are required; 4 English required, 3 math required, 2 science required, 2 foreign language required, 3 social studies required. Minimum combined SAT I score of 920 and minimum 2.7 GPA recommended. Special requirements: TOEFL is required of all international students.

**Application deadline:** Rolling
**Notification:** Rolling

**SAT or ACT preferred:** SAT
**Average GPA:** 2.6

## COLLEGE GRADUATION REQUIREMENTS

**Course waivers allowed:** Yes
**Course substitutions allowed:** Yes
**In what courses:** Math and science lab courses.

## ADDITIONAL INFORMATION

**Environment:** The university in located on 260 acres in the Appalachian Highlands in a small town 150 miles northwest of Baltimore.

**Student Body**
  **Undergrad enrollment:** 4,852
  **Women:** 49%
  **Men:** 51%
  **In-state students:** 86%
  **Out-of-state:** 14%

**Cost Information**
  **In-state tuition:** $3,280
  **Out-of-state:** $6,990
  **Room & board:** $4,770

**Housing Information**
  **University housing:** Yes
  **Fraternity:** No
  **Sorority:** No
  **Living on campus:** 45%

  **Athletics:** NCAA Div. III

# MD

# UNIVERSITY OF MARYLAND, COLLEGE PARK

College Park, MD 20742 • **Admissions:** 800-422-5867 • **Fax:** 301-314-9693
**Email:** um-admit@uga.umd.edu • **Web:** www.umcp.umd.edu
**Support:** CS • **Institution:** 4 yr. Public

## LEARNING DISABILITY ADMISSIONS AND SERVICES

The goal of Disability Support Services is to implement arrangements to meet the needs of students with learning disabilities. The student with a learning disability has the opportunity to develop skills through the services of the Learning Assistance Services as well as through accommodations as provided by Disability Support Services. Students are expected to make contact with instructors and negotiate any special accommodations. Students may request assistance from the Service Office in handling interactions with instructors. Commonly used services include testing assistance, notetakers, tutoring, counseling and reading. Besides the standard accommodations, students receive support through special study skills course workshops, mentoring and support groups.

## LEARNING DISABILITY ADMISSIONS INFORMATION

**Program Name:** Learning Assistance Services (LAS)
**Program Director:** William Scales          **Telephone:** 301-314-7682
**Contact Person:** Peggy Hayslip, LD Coordinator     **Telephone:** 301-314-9969

### ADMISSIONS

There is no special admissions or alternative admissions process for students with learning disabilities. Applicants with learning disabilities must meet general admission criteria. The admission decision is based on courses taken in high school, which include: 4 yrs. English, 3 yrs. social studies, 2 yrs. lab science, 3 yrs. math, and 2 yrs. foreign language; GPA; SAT/ACT; class rank; personal statement; recommendations; and the psycho-educational evaluation. The student may submit supporting documentation which will be considered during the decision making process. The Director of Learning Assistance Services may review the documentation and make a recommendation to the admission office. The final decision rests with the Office of Admissions.

**College entrance exams required:** Yes          **Untimed accepted:** Yes
**Course entrance requirements:** Yes          **Interview required:** Recommended
**Diagnostic tests:** Yes
**Documentation:** WAIS-R: W-J: Peabody: etc.: current

### ADDITIONAL INFORMATION

Notetakers are volunteers and could be students enrolled in the course. Tutoring is available for all students and is offered through LAS and other departments on campus. There is no centralized tutoring service. Priority registration is available. Services and accommodations are available to undergraduate and graduate students. There is a summer program for high school students which is not specifically for those with learning disabilities. However, these students could benefit from the Program.

**Special education HS coursework accepted:** Yes          **Essay required:** Recommended
**Special application required:** No          **Submitted to:** N/A
**# of applications submitted each year:** N/I          **# of applications accepted each year:** N/I
**# of students receiving LD services:** 350
**Acceptance into program means acceptance into college:** Students must be admitted to the university first and then may request services.

## LEARNING DISABILITY SERVICES

**Learning center:** No
**Kurzweil personal reader:** Yes
**LD specialists:** 1
**Allowed in exams:**
  **Calculator:** Yes
  **Dictionary:** Y/N
  **Computer:** Yes
  **SpellCheck:** Yes

**Notetaker:** Yes
**Scribes:** Yes
**Proctors:** Yes
**Oral exams:** Yes
**Extended test time:** Yes
**Added cost:** None
**Distraction-free environ.:** Yes
**Tape recording in class:** Yes
**Books on tape:** Yes
**Taping of other books:** Yes

**Professional tutors:** No
**Peer tutors:** Yes
**Max. hrs/wk for services:** Unlimited
**Priority registration:** Yes
**Accomodations for students with ADD:** Yes
**How are professors notified of LD:** By the student

## GENERAL ADMISSIONS INFORMATION

**Director of Admissions:** Linda Clement        **Telephone:** 301-314-8350

### ENTRANCE REQUIREMENTS

Total high school units required/recommended: 20 total units are recommended; 4 English recommended, 3 math recommended, 2 science recommended, 2 foreign language recommended, 3 social studies recommended. Special requirements: A portfolio is required for art program applicants. An audition is required for music program applicants. Portfolio required of architecture and design program applicants. TOEFL is required of international students whose SAT verbal score is below 480.

**Application deadline:** February 15
**Notification:** Rolling

**SAT or ACT preferred:** Either
**SAT Range:** 540–640V, 550–660M
**SAT II required:** Yes
**Average GPA:** 3.5

**Graduated top 10% of class:** 26
**Graduated top 25% of class:** 61
**Graduated top 50% of class:** 92

## COLLEGE GRADUATION REQUIREMENTS

**Course waivers allowed:** No
**Course substitutions allowed:** No
**In what courses:** There is an attempt to accommodate within the mathematics or foreign language classroom. Any requests for substitution must be reviewed by a committee.

## ADDITIONAL INFORMATION

**Environment:** Small town setting within proximity to Washington, D.C. and Baltimore.

**Student Body**
  **Undergrad enrollment:** 24,529
  **Women:** 48%
  **Men:** 52%
  **In-state students:** 76%
  **Out-of-state:** 24%

**Cost Information**
  **In-state tuition:** $4,460
  **Out-of-state:** $10,589
  **Room & board:** $5,807

**Housing Information**
  **University housing:** Yes
  **Fraternity:** Yes
  **Sorority:** Yes
  **Living on campus:** 36%

  **Athletics:** NCAA Div. I

# UNIVERSITY OF MARYLAND-EASTERN SHORE

**MD**

Princess Anne, MD 21853 • **Admissions:** 410-651-2200 • **Fax:** 410-651-7922
**Web:** www.umes.umd.edu
**Support:** S • **Institution:** 4 yr. Public

## LEARNING DISABILITY ADMISSIONS AND SERVICES

The Disabled Student Services assures the commitment of the university to provide access and equal opportunity to students with disabilities admitted to the university.

## LEARNING DISABILITY ADMISSIONS INFORMATION

**Program Name:** Disabled Student Services
**Program Director:** Dr. Diane Showell — **Telephone:** 410-651-6461
**Contact Person:** Georgiann H. Wing, Coordinator — **Telephone:** 410-651-6461

### ADMISSIONS

There is no special admission. All applicants must meet the same criteria.

**College entrance exams required:** Yes
**Course entrance requirements:** Yes
**Diagnostic tests:** Yes
**Documentation:** Varies depending on learning disability

**Untimed accepted:** Yes
**Interview required:** No

### ADDITIONAL INFORMATION

Tutoring is available in every subject for all students. There are skills courses offered in remedial math, reading and writing.

**Special education HS coursework accepted:** Yes
**Special application required:** No
**# of applications submitted each year:** 30
**# of students receiving LD services:** 25

**Essay required:** No
**Submitted to:** N/A
**# of applications accepted each year:** N/I

**Acceptance into program means acceptance into college:** No, must be admitted to the university first and then may request services.

## LEARNING DISABILITY SERVICES

**Learning center:** No
**Kurzweil personal reader:** Yes
**LD specialists:** 1
**Allowed in exams:**
  Calculator: N/I
  Dictionary: N/I
  Computer: N/I
  SpellCheck: N/I

**Notetaker:** Yes
**Scribes:** Yes
**Proctors:** Yes
**Oral exams:** Yes
**Extended test time:** Yes
**Added cost:** None
**Distraction-free environ.:** Yes
**Tape recording in class:** N/I
**Books on tape:** Yes
**Taping of other books:** N/I

**Professional tutors:** 4
**Peer tutors:** 8
**Max. hrs/wk for services:**
Unlimited
**Priority registration:** No
**Accomodations for students
with ADD:** No
**How are professors notified of
LD:** By the student and the
Program Director

## GENERAL ADMISSIONS INFORMATION

**Director of Admissions:** Dr. Rochelle Peoples      **Telephone:** 410-651-2200

### ENTRANCE REQUIREMENTS

Total high school units required/recommended: 20 total units are required; 4 English required, 3 math required, 2 foreign language required, 3 social studies required. Minimum combined SAT I score of 750 and minimum 2.5 GPA recommended. In-state applicants who have secondary school diploma and minimum C grade average may be admitted on basis of predictive index weighing SAT I scores and GPA. Special requirements: An audition is required for music program applicants. Specific requirements for engineering and music program applicants.

**Application deadline:** May 30
**Notification:** Rolling

**SAT or ACT preferred:** Either
**SAT Avg:** 430V, 410M
**Average GPA:** 2.54

## COLLEGE GRADUATION REQUIREMENTS

**Course waivers allowed:** Yes
**Course substitutions allowed:** Yes
**In what courses:** All pending core course requirements.

## ADDITIONAL INFORMATION

**Environment:** The university is located on a 600-acre campus in a rural area 15 miles south of Salisbury.

**Student Body**
  Undergrad enrollment: 2,862
  Women: 58%
  Men: 42%
  In-state students: 71%
  Out-of-state: 29%

**Cost Information**
  In-state tuition: $3,240
  Out-of-state: $7,776
  Room & board: $4,330

**Housing Information**
  University housing: Yes
  Fraternity: No
  Sorority: No
  Living on campus: 57%

  Athletics: NCAA Div. I

# MD

# TOWSON STATE UNIVERSITY

8000 York Road, Towson, MD 21252-0001 • **Admissions:** 410-830-3333 • **Fax:** 410-830-3030
**Email:** admissions@towson.edu • **Web:** www.towson.edu
**Support:** CS • **Institution:** 4 yr. Public

## LEARNING DISABILITY ADMISSIONS AND SERVICES

Towson State does not have a separate program for students with learning disabilities. Staff work individually with students to circumvent the handicap and to help students work with their own strongest compensating skills. The university policy is to ask students what their needs are rather than to present them with a 'plan' to which they must adapt. There is involvement in class selection. Professors are notified of students' disabilities which eliminates the need for students to 'explain 'or 'prove' their disability. Towson State also offers all students tutorial services, a Reading Center and a Writing Lab. All students requesting services and/or accommodations must have an interview with the Director of support services in order to establish what is necessary. Towson State University's program for students with learning disabilities is individualistic as the severity and compensating skills of the students are unique.

## LEARNING DISABILITY ADMISSIONS INFORMATION

**Program Name:** Office for Students with Disabilities (OSD)
**Program Director:** Ronnie Uhland                    **Telephone:** 410-830-2638
**Contact Person:** Same as above

### ADMISSIONS

There is no question on the application that inquires about a learning disability. Students with learning disabilities who want special consideration and/or services should provide documentation and information about their learning disability. Students will receive special admission consideration. Credentials are reviewed by a committee that has some flexibility in interpreting scores.

**College entrance exams required:** Yes          **Untimed accepted:** Yes
**Course entrance requirements:** Yes             **Interview required:** Recommended
**Diagnostic tests:** Yes
**Documentation:** WAIS-R; WRAT-R; W-J: within 3 years

### ADDITIONAL INFORMATION

Towson State University provides students with learning disabilities the necessary accommodations based on recent psycho-educational evaluations. These accommodations are based on recommendations from the evaluation. The Learning Center provides reading and study skills development services. The Writing Lab provides assistance for students who need improvement in writing skills. A quiet study area is available. Additionally, the The Office for Students with Disabilities provides: notetakers; a resource room to be used for quiets place to take a test; use of the services of a reader; extended testing time. Students must be registered with RFB to get taped textbooks. Those textbooks not available through RFB may be requested from OSD.

**Special education HS coursework accepted:** No     **Essay required:** Yes
**Special application required:** Yes               **Submitted to:** Program Director
**# of applications submitted each year:** N/I      **# of applications accepted each year:** N/I
**# of students receiving LD services:** 280
**Acceptance into program means acceptance into college:** Students must be admitted to the university first and then may request services.

## LEARNING DISABILITY SERVICES

**Learning center:** No
**Kurzweil personal reader:** Yes
**LD specialists:** 1
**Allowed in exams:**
  **Calculator:** Yes
  **Dictionary:** Yes
  **Computer:** Yes
  **SpellCheck:** Yes

**Notetaker:** Yes
**Scribes:** Yes
**Proctors:** Yes
**Oral exams:** Yes
**Extended test time:** Yes
**Added cost:** None
**Distraction-free environ.:** Yes
**Tape recording in class:** Yes
**Books on tape:** Yes
**Taping of other books:** Yes

**Professional tutors:** N/A
**Peer tutors:** Yes
**Max. hrs/wk for services:** Unlimited
**Priority registration:** No
**Accomodations for students with ADD:** Yes
**How are professors notified of LD:** By the student and the Program Director

## GENERAL ADMISSIONS INFORMATION

**Director of Admissions:** Angel Jackson          **Telephone:** 410-830-3333

### ENTRANCE REQUIREMENTS

Total high school units required/recommended: 20 total units are required; 4 English required, 3 math required, 2 science required, 2 foreign language required, 3 social studies required. Minimum combined SAT I score of 1100 and minimum 3.0 GPA required. Special requirements: An audition is required for music program applicants. TOEFL is required of all international students. Audition required of dance program applicants.

**Application deadline:** May 1
**Notification:** Rolling

**SAT or ACT preferred:** Either
**SAT Range:** 490–570V, 490–570M
**Average GPA:** 3.1

**Graduated top 10% of class:** 21
**Graduated top 25% of class:** 47
**Graduated top 50% of class:** 88

## COLLEGE GRADUATION REQUIREMENTS

**Course waivers allowed:** Yes
**Course substitutions allowed:** No
**In what courses:** Must appeal to Academic Standards Committee.

## ADDITIONAL INFORMATION

**Environment:** The school is located on 306 landscaped and wooded acres minutes from downtown Baltimore.

**Student Body**
  **Undergrad enrollment:** 13,063
  **Women:** 59%
  **Men:** 41%
  **In-state students:** 83%
  **Out-of-state:** 17%

**Cost Information**
  **In-state tuition:** $3,080
  **Out-of-state:** $8,158
  **Room & board:** $5,044

**Housing Information**
  **University housing:** Yes
  **Fraternity:** No
  **Sorority:** No
  **Living on campus:** 33%

  **Athletics:** NCAA Div. I

# WESTERN MARYLAND COLLEGE

2 College Hill, Westminster, MD 21157 • **Admissions:** 410-857-2230 • **Fax:** 410-857-2757
**Email:** admission@wmdc.edu • **Web:** www.wmdc.edu
**Support:** CS • **Institution:** 4 yr. Private

## LEARNING DISABILITY ADMISSIONS AND SERVICES

The goal of the college is to assist students with learning disabilities to be in college. More time is given to freshmen and transfer students to help with the transition into WMC. The Academic Skills Center provides 3 levels of services: Level I (no fee) students receive appropriate accommodations, tutoring, monthly support groups, and 2 hours a semester advising with ASC Coordinator; Level II ($750 fee) provides Level I services and pre-scheduling of courses, consulting with ASC coordinator, Study Lab, 5 hours per week of study skills tutoring, and assignment to an ASC mentor; Level III ($1,200 fee) provides services from Level I and Level II and diagnostic testing, planning, developmental implementation and evaluation of a yearly individualized academic program.

## LEARNING DISABILITY ADMISSIONS INFORMATION

**Program Name:** Academic Skills Center (ASC)
**Program Director:** Dr. Henry Reiff
**Contact Person:** Denise Bowen

**Telephone:** 410-857-2516
**Telephone:** 410-857-2504

### ADMISSIONS

Students with learning disabilities are encouraged to self-identify during the admissions process. Students who self-disclose will be assigned to an admission counselor with experience in this area. Applicants are referred to ASC and the ASC Coordinator gathers pertinent information and makes a recommendation to the Admissions Office. The high school may be contacted in order to gain a broader understanding of the student's ability. Applicants are encouraged to provide any information that will assist the Admissions Office with knowing more about the student.

**College entrance exams required:** Yes
**Course entrance requirements:** Yes
**Diagnostic tests:** Yes
**Documentation:** W-J psycho-educational battery; WAIS-R: within 2 years

**Untimed accepted:** Yes
**Interview required:** Recommended

### ADDITIONAL INFORMATION

Students must attend one Guidance Day during the summer prior to freshman year. Students with learning disabilities should attend an orientation meeting before college begins and schedule individual appointments with the Coordinator. Most freshmen register for 12-13 credits and this credit load each semester will ensure the amount of time to graduate. All students must pass one Math course. There is a basic math class and two math review courses for students needing more math foundation prior to taking the required course. One skill's class is offered and students have access to unlimited tutoring.

**Special education HS coursework accepted:** N/I
**Special application required:** No
**# of applications submitted each year:** 100
**# of students receiving LD services:** 100
**Acceptance into program means acceptance into college:** Students must be admitted to the College first and then may request services.

**Essay required:** Yes
**Submitted to:** N/A
**# of applications accepted each year:** 55

**Learning center:** Yes
**Kurzweil personal reader:** No
**LD specialists:** 3
**Allowed in exams:**
  **Calculator:** Yes
  **Dictionary:** Yes
  **Computer:** Yes
  **SpellCheck:** Yes

**Notetaker:** Yes
**Scribes:** Yes
**Proctors:** Yes
**Oral exams:** Yes
**Extended test time:** Yes
**Added cost:** Depends on Level of help: $750-$1,200.
**Distraction-free environ.:** Yes
**Tape recording in class:** Yes
**Books on tape:** Yes
**Taping of other books:** Yes

**Professional tutors:** Yes
**Peer tutors:** Yes
**Max. hrs/wk for services:** Peer tutors free; Professional tutors fee; Hours vary
**Priority registration:** Yes
**Accomodations for students with ADD:** Yes
**How are professors notified of LD:** By the student and the Program Director

## GENERAL ADMISSIONS INFORMATION

**Director of Admissions:** Martha O'Connell

**Telephone:** 410-857-2230

### ENTRANCE REQUIREMENTS

Total high school units required/recommended: 16 total units are required; 4 English required, 3 math required, 2 science required, 2 foreign language required, 3 social studies required. Minimum combined SAT I score of 1000 and minimum 2.5 GPA required. Special requirements: TOEFL is required of all international students.

**Application deadline:** March 15
**Notification:** April 1

**SAT or ACT preferred:** Either
**SAT Avg:** 557V, 556M
**Average ACT:** 24
**Average GPA:** 3.2

**Graduated top 10% of class:** 36
**Graduated top 25% of class:** 55
**Graduated top 50% of class:** 84

## COLLEGE GRADUATION REQUIREMENTS

**Course waivers allowed:** Yes
**Course substitutions allowed:** Yes
**In what courses:** Foreign language

## ADDITIONAL INFORMATION

**Environment:** The College is located on 160 acres in a small town 30 miles northwest of Baltimore.

**Student Body**
  **Undergrad enrollment:** 1,382
  **Women:** 54%
  **Men:** 46%
  **In-state students:** 65%
  **Out-of-state:** 35%

**Cost Information**
  **In-state tuition:** $16,125
  **Out-of-state:** $16,125
  **Room & board:** $5,365

**Housing Information**
  **University housing:** Yes
  **Fraternity:** Yes
  **Sorority:** Yes
  **Living on campus:** 90%

  **Athletics:** NCAA Div. III

# AMERICAN INTERNATIONAL COLLEGE

1000 State Street, Springfield, MA 01109 • **Admissions:** 413-747-7000 • **Fax:** 413-737-2803
**Email:** inquiry@aic.edu • **Web:** www.aic.edu
**Support:** SP • **Institution:** 4 yr. Private

## LEARNING DISABILITY ADMISSIONS AND SERVICES

The belief on which this program was founded is that individuals who are learning disabled can compensate for their difficulties and meet with success in the college environment. It is AIC's philosophy that the college is responsible for helping students with LD to become active participants in the learning process. AIC feels that the Supportive Learning Services Program has all the components necessary to allow for a successful college career for a student with learning disabilities. One test of a college's commitment to such a program is the amount of space allowed for the program's operation. The Curtis Blake Center at AIC that houses the program is dedicated entirely to providing services to students with LD. Metacognitive strategies are taught in order to help students use their intellect more efficiently. The learning environment of the student is modified to promote learning. Students must have the intellectual ability necessary to meet the demands of a college curriculum, as well as motivation and commitment. Students are mainstreamed and may receive a minimum of 2 hours of tutoring/studying strategies weekly. Students create an Individual Educational Plan with their tutor freshman year and may take as few as 4 courses each semester. Students generally stay in the program for four years.

## LEARNING DISABILITY ADMISSIONS INFORMATION

**Program Name:** Supportive Learning Services Program (SLSP)
**Program Director:** Professor Mary M. Saltus          **Telephone:** 413-747-6426
**Contact Person:** Susan Lempke

### ADMISSIONS

In addition to submitting an application to admissions, students interested in applying for the support program must also contact the Coordinator of SLSP. Applicants must schedule an on-campus interview with admissions and SLSP. Applicants must submit the results of the WAIS-R and accompanying report, relevant diagnostic material and information about supportive assistance in the past. The college requires a high school transcript and ACT/SAT scores. There should be a strong indication of achievement and motivation in the fields of knowledge studied. The majority of applicants have a GPA between 2.0-3.0. Courses required include 16 academic units from English, math, science and social studies. Foreign language is not required. The admission decision is made simultaneously between admissions and SLSP.

| | |
|---|---|
| **College entrance exams required:** Yes | **Untimed accepted:** Yes |
| **Course entrance requirements:** Yes | **Interview required:** Yes |
| **Diagnostic tests:** Yes | |
| **Documentation:** WAIS-R and report: W-J-R: within 3 years | |

### ADDITIONAL INFORMATION

At the heart of the services provided is a minimum of two hours of regularly scheduled direct, one-to-one assistance provided by a learning specialist. The specialist develops an individually tailored support program based on student's needs. Priority is given to practical assistance to help students negotiate demands of the curriculum. Provisions can be made for more basic remediation of the student's learning difficulties. Specialists assist in course selection, organizing work and study schedules, and as a resource. Students have access to skills seminars in many areas. Classes in reading, spelling, math, study strategies, time management, written language, and handwriting are offered. The Supportive Learning Services Center is only open to students who are participating in the program. Services and accommodations are available to undergraduate and graduate students.

**Special education HS coursework accepted:** Done on an individual basis
**Essay required:** No
**Special application required:** No
**# of applications submitted each year:** 280          **Submitted to:** N/A
**# of students receiving LD services:** 100          **# of applications accepted each year:** 35
**Acceptance into program means acceptance into college:** Simultaneous admission decision made by the program and admissions.

# LEARNING DISABILITY SERVICES

**Learning center:** Yes
**Kurzweil personal reader:** No
**LD specialists:** 10
**Allowed in exams:**
  **Calculator:** Y/N
  **Dictionary:** Y/N
  **Computer:** Yes
  **SpellCheck:** Y/N

**Notetaker:** No
**Scribes:** Yes
**Proctors:** Yes
**Oral exams:** Yes
**Extended test time:** Yes
**Added cost:** $1,650 for 2 hours per semester
**Distraction-free environ.:** Yes
**Tape recording in class:** Yes
**Books on tape:** Yes
**Taping of other books:** Yes

**Professional tutors:** 9
**Peer tutors:** No
**Max. hrs/wk for services:** Unlimited
**Priority registration:** No
**Accomodations for students with ADD:** Yes
**How are professors notified of LD:** By the Program Director and sometimes the student

# GENERAL ADMISSIONS INFORMATION

**Director of Admissions:** Peter J. Miller          **Telephone:** 413-737-6201

## ENTRANCE REQUIREMENTS

Total high school units required/recommended: 15 total units are required; 4 English required, 2 math required, 2 science required, 1 social studies required, 1 history required. Special requirements: TOEFL is required of all international students. 1 unit of chemistry required of nursing program applicants.

**Application deadline:** Rolling
**Notification:** Rolling

**SAT or ACT preferred:** SAT
**SAT Avg:** 456V, 487M
**SAT II required:** Yes
**Average GPA:** 2.7

**Graduated top 10% of class:** 9
**Graduated top 25% of class:** 22
**Graduated top 50% of class:** 67

# COLLEGE GRADUATION REQUIREMENTS

**Course waivers allowed:** No
**Course substitutions allowed:** No
**In what courses:** Foreign language not required for graduation. May use Pass/Fail option.

# ADDITIONAL INFORMATION

**Environment:** The school is located on 58 acres in Springfield 75 miles west of Boston and 30 miles north of Hartford.

**Student Body**
  **Undergrad enrollment:** 1,426
  **Women:** 52%
  **Men:** 48%
  **In-state students:** 56%
  **Out-of-state:** 44%

**Cost Information**
  **In-state tuition:** $9,750
  **Out-of-state:** $9,750
  **Room & board:** $5,310

**Housing Information**
  **University housing:** Yes
  **Fraternity:** No
  **Sorority:** No
  **Living on campus:** 58%

  **Athletics:** NCAA Div. II

# BRADFORD COLLEGE

320 South Main Street, Haverhill, MA 01835-7393 • **Admissions:** 508-372-7161 ext. 5271
**Fax:** 508-372-5240
**Email:** bradcoll@aol.com • **Web:** www.bradford.edu
**Support:** SP • **Institution:** 4 yr. Private

## LEARNING DISABILITY ADMISSIONS AND SERVICES

The College Learning Program at Bradford College offers a highly specialized service for students with diagnosed mild or moderate learning disabilities. The goal of the program is to help students become successful learners, capable of earning a college degree. The program focuses on reading, writing, and study skills, and provides a climate for optimum learning. The students work with the program's team of learning specialists. Bradford's caring approach fosters self-confidence, motivation, and achievement. Students attend weekly tutorials for each of their academic courses. At these individual and small group sessions, students are guided toward developing independent study techniques and strategies for their course assignments. Close communication is maintained between the Learning Center specialist and the faculty. During their second year at Bradford, students can opt to stay in the program full-time, receiving a weekly tutorial for each of their 4 academic courses or they can opt for half-time status, giving them 2 tutorials for their 4 academic courses. Junior and Senior years students can participate as a contract student. This provides them with one hourly tutorial per week, in a one-on-one setting with the learning specialist of their choice, to work on anything the student needs help with, except course content.

## LEARNING DISABILITY ADMISSIONS INFORMATION

**Program Name:** College Learning Program (CLP)
**Program Director:** Helen Page
**Contact Person:** Pat Davison

**Telephone:** 508-372-7161 ext.5312
**Telephone:** 508-372-7161 ext.5319

### ADMISSIONS

To be considered for CLP, students must have a diagnosed LD, average or above-average conceptual ability, good verbal skills, at least ninth-grade reading ability, and a strong commitment to a college education. Applicants should submit a high school transcript and the results of a WAIS-R evaluation done within the past 3 years, including subtest scores. An on-campus interview is required. Applicants must also submit the regular Bradford application form; 3 recommendations, including one from a learning specialist with whom the student has worked closely; 2 original essays—one is the required application essay and the other a graded essay submitted as course work, including the teacher's comments; and standardized diagnostic reading results documenting the reading grade level and comprehension level. ACT/SAT scores are not required for students with learning disabilities. General admissions require a 2.0 GPA; 4 yrs. English, 4 yrs. math, 1 yr. lab science, and 1 yr. social studies.

**College entrance exams required:** Yes (Not LD)
**Course entrance requirements:** Yes
**Diagnostic tests:** Yes
**Documentation:** WAIS-R; any reading comprehension test: within 3 years

**Untimed accepted:** Yes
**Interview required:** Yes

### ADDITIONAL INFORMATION

Students have access to one-on-one instruction. They spend one hour each week with a learning specialist for each of their courses. During these sessions, three or four students and a learning specialist discuss course materials, develop study strategies, determine key ideas and vocabulary, and prepare for exams. Exams can be taken in a testing accommodation's center which is distraction-free and coordinated by an accommodation's assistant. Students are given whatever extended-time or other modifications students negotiate with their professors. Further assistance is available with papers or class assignments. The program provides an unpressured learning environment. No grades or academic credit are given for participating in the program. During their second year at Bradford, students can begin to 'phase out' their involvement in the program. Juniors and seniors may use services on a limited basis. Students become self-advocates and independent learners.

**Special education HS coursework accepted:** No
**Special application required:** Yes
**# of applications submitted each year:** 130
**# of students receiving LD services:** 35

**Essay required:** Yes
**Submitted to:** Admissions Office
**# of applications accepted each year:** 50

**Acceptance into program means acceptance into college:** CLP and Admissions offer a joint decision.

## LEARNING DISABILITY SERVICES

**Learning center:** Yes
**Kurzweil personal reader:** No
**LD specialists:** 6
**Allowed in exams:**
  **Calculator:** Yes
  **Dictionary:** Yes
  **Computer:** Yes
  **SpellCheck:** Yes

**Notetaker:** Yes
**Scribes:** Yes
**Proctors:** Yes
**Oral exams:** No
**Extended test time:** Yes
**Added cost:** $4,000 per/year for Program; $750 Jr. & Sr. year
**Distraction-free environ.:** Yes
**Tape recording in class:** Yes
**Books on tape:** RFB
**Taping of other books:** Yes

**Professional tutors:** 6
**Peer tutors:** 0
**Max. hrs/wk for services:** 4 hours per/week
**Priority registration:** Yes
**Accomodations for students with ADD:** Yes
**How are professors notified of LD:** By the student and the Program Director

## GENERAL ADMISSIONS INFORMATION

**Director of Admissions:** William Dunfrey

**Telephone:** 508-372-7161

### ENTRANCE REQUIREMENTS

Total high school units required/recommended: 18 total units are required; 4 English required, 3 math required, 2 science required, 2 foreign language required, 2 social studies required, 2 history required. Minimum 2.0 GPA required. Special requirements: A portfolio is required for art program applicants.

**Application deadline:** Rolling
**Notification:** Rolling

**SAT or ACT preferred:** Either
**Average GPA:** 2.9

**Graduated top 10% of class:** 10
**Graduated top 25% of class:** 30
**Graduated top 50% of class:** 70

## COLLEGE GRADUATION REQUIREMENTS

**Course waivers allowed:** No
**Course substitutions allowed:** No
**In what courses:** There is no foreign language requirement; there is a minimal math requirement.

## ADDITIONAL INFORMATION

**Environment:** The college is located on 70 acres 35 miles north of Boston.

**Student Body**
  **Undergrad enrollment:** 588
  **Women:** 62%
  **Men:** 38%
  **In-state students:** 52%
  **Out-of-state:** 48%

**Cost Information**
  **In-state tuition:** $15,380
  **Out-of-state:** $15,380
  **Room & board:** $6,590

**Housing Information**
  **University housing:** Yes
  **Fraternity:** No
  **Sorority:** No
  **Living on campus:** 70%

  **Athletics:** NR

# CLARK UNIVERSITY

950 Main Street, Worcester, MA 01610 • **Admissions:** 508-793-7431 • **Fax:** 508-793-8821
**Email:** admissions@admissions.clarku.edu • **Web:** www.clarku.edu
**Support:** S • **Institution:** 4 yr. Private

## LEARNING DISABILITY ADMISSIONS AND SERVICES

The learning disabilities services at Clark University, based within the Academic Advising Center, was developed to advocate and support the needs of the student with learning disabilities in a college environment. Strategies are developed to help the student with learning disabilities cope with the increased demands of the college curriculum. Resources are available to students who experience difficulties, and who may require some support or wish to learn more about their own learning styles. Support services in the AAC are coordinated with services offered by the university's Writing Center, Math Clinic, and Dean of Students. The most successful students are the ones who accept their disability, develop good self-advocacy skills and are capable of good time management. The ultimate goal of Special Services is to help students improve their self-awareness and self-advocacy skills, and to assist them in being successful and independent in college.

## LEARNING DISABILITY ADMISSIONS INFORMATION

**Program Name:** Special Services
**Program Director:** Alan Bieri                     **Telephone:** 508-793-7468
**Contact Person:** Jen O'Loughlin, Admissions        **Telephone:** 508-793-7431

### ADMISSIONS

Special Services and the Office of Undergraduate Admissions work together in considering students for admission. Admission is based on ability, rather than disability. Applicants must meet standard admissions requirements. An interview with Clark's Special Services Office is highly recommended. If a student requires any classroom accommodations or support services, a diagnostic assessment completed within the last two years must be submitted, documenting the learning disability. This documentation is needed to evaluate the applicant's needs and determine what services the university can provide. The university looks at a student's upward trend in high school, as well as the challenge of the curriculum and the number of mainstream courses. Some special education courses in freshman year may be allowed if they have been followed by a college prep curriculum during the rest of high school. The Director of Special Services makes a recommendation to Admissions about the applicant, but the final decision rests with the Office of Admission.

| | |
|---|---|
| **College entrance exams required:** Yes | **Untimed accepted:** Yes |
| **Course entrance requirements:** Yes | **Interview required:** Recommended |
| **Diagnostic tests:** Yes | |
| **Documentation:** WAIS-R;W-J; Psycho-educational battery-R: within 2 years | |

### ADDITIONAL INFORMATION

An early orientation program 2 days prior to general orientation is designed to meet the needs of entering students with LD. This program is highly recommended as it provides intensive exposure to academic services on campus. Students take a reading comprehension and writing exam, and results are used to match students to the most appropriate academic program. Graduate students work with students on time management and organizational skills. Although notetakers are available, Special Services supplements with taping of lectures, and highly recommends that students use a cassette recorder with a count. It is also recommended that freshmen students take only three courses for the first semester. All students must complete one Math course in basic algebra prior to graduating. The overall GPA of Freshmen receiving services from Special Services is a 2.7. Services and accommodations are available to undergraduates and graduates.

| | |
|---|---|
| **Special education HS coursework accepted:** N/I | **Essay required:** Yes |
| **Special application required:** Yes | **Submitted to:** Director of Program |
| **# of applications submitted each year:** 150 | **# of applications accepted each year:** 70 |
| **# of students receiving LD services:** 150 | |

**Acceptance into program means acceptance into college:** Students must be accepted to the university first and then may request services.

# LEARNING DISABILITY SERVICES

**Learning center:** No
**Kurzweil personal reader:** No
**LD specialists:** No
**Allowed in exams:**
  **Calculator:** Yes
  **Dictionary:** Yes
  **Computer:** Yes
  **SpellCheck:** Yes

**Notetaker:** Yes
**Scribes:** Yes
**Proctors:** Yes
**Oral exams:** Yes
**Extended test time:** Yes
**Added cost:** None
**Distraction-free environ.:** Yes
**Tape recording in class:** Yes
**Books on tape:** Yes
**Taping of other books:** Yes

**Professional tutors:** No
**Peer tutors:** Yes
**Max. hrs/wk for services:** As needed
**Priority registration:** Yes
**Accomodations for students with ADD:** Yes
**How are professors notified of LD:** By the student and the Program Director

# GENERAL ADMISSIONS INFORMATION

**Director of Admissions:** Harold Wingood        **Telephone:** 508-793-7431

## ENTRANCE REQUIREMENTS

Total high school units required/recommended: 16 total units are recommended; 4 English recommended, 3 math recommended, 3 science recommended, 2 foreign language recommended, 2 social studies recommended. Special requirements: TOEFL is required of all international students.

**Application deadline:** February 1
**Notification:** April 1

**SAT or ACT preferred:** Either
**SAT Avg:** 565V, 559M
**Average ACT:** 25
**Average GPA:** 3.1

**Graduated top 10% of class:** 27
**Graduated top 25% of class:** 61
**Graduated top 50% of class:** 84

# COLLEGE GRADUATION REQUIREMENTS

**Course waivers allowed:** No
**Course substitutions allowed:** Yes
**In what courses:** Foreign language with appropriate documentation.

# ADDITIONAL INFORMATION

**Environment:** The university is located on 45 acres in a small city 38 miles west of Boston.

**Student Body**
  **Undergrad enrollment:** 1,840
  **Women:** 58%
  **Men:** 42%
  **In-state students:** 37%
  **Out-of-state:** 63%

**Cost Information**
  **In-state tuition:** $20,500
  **Out-of-state:** $20,500
  **Room & board:** $4,250

**Housing Information**
  **University housing:** Yes
  **Fraternity:** No
  **Sorority:** No
  **Living on campus:** 67%

  **Athletics:** NCAA Div. III

# CURRY COLLEGE

1071 Blue Hill Avenue, Milton, MA 02186 • **Admissions:** 617-333-2210 • **Fax:** 617-333-6860
**Email:** curryadm@curry.edu • **Web:** www.curry.edu:8080
**Support:** SP • **Institution:** 4 yr. Private

## LEARNING DISABILITY ADMISSIONS AND SERVICES

The Program for Advancement in Learning (PAL) at Curry College is a supportive program for students who are language/learning disabled. Students in the PAL Program participate fully in Curry College coursework and extra-curricular activities. The goal of PAL is to facilitate students' understanding of their individual learning styles and to achieve independence as learners. Students' empowerment is developed via intensive study of their own strengths, needs, and learning styles. PAL summer orientation session is recommended and an additional fee is required for this summer experience.

## LEARNING DISABILITY ADMISSIONS INFORMATION

**Program Name:** Program for Advancement in Learning (PAL)
**Program Director:** Dr. Lisa Ijiri                                    **Telephone:** 617-333-0500 ext. 2270
**Contact Person:** Same as above

### ADMISSIONS

Applicants must submit the regular application, fee, official transcript, SAT or ACT (recommended), a counselor or teacher recommendation, and the results of a WAIS-R test. Admissions to PAL is made jointly by Admissions and PAL. Acceptance into PAL is based on evidence of better-than-average compensational ability, strong reasoning ability and evidence of commitment to the learning process.

**College entrance exams required:** Recommended          **Untimed accepted:** Yes
**Course entrance requirements:** Yes                    **Interview required:** Recommended
**Diagnostic tests:** Yes
**Documentation:** WAIS-R; WJ-R: within 1 year

### ADDITIONAL INFORMATION

Students admitted to the PAL Program must commit to the program for at least 1 year, and have the option to continue with full or partial support beyond the first year. A 3-week 3-credit summer PAL orientation session is strongly recommended. Subject content tutoring is used to help develop strategies. The Center for Lifelong Learning (CLL) is the vehicle used for providing non-matriculated and marginal candidates the opportunity to prove their competence. Skills classes, for credit, are offered through the Essential Skills Center in developmental reading, writing and math.

**Special education HS coursework accepted:** N/I          **Essay required:** Yes
**Special application required:** Yes                     **Submitted to:** Director of Program
**# of applications submitted each year:** 600           **# of applications accepted each year:** 300
**# of students receiving LD services:** 400
**Acceptance into program means acceptance into college:** The admission decision is made jointly by PAL and the Office of Admission.

## LEARNING DISABILITY SERVICES

**Learning center:** Yes
**Kurzweil personal reader:** No
**LD specialists:** 28
**Allowed in exams:**
  **Calculator:** Y/N
  **Dictionary:** Y/N
  **Computer:** Y/N
  **SpellCheck:** Y/N

**Notetaker:** No
**Scribes:** No
**Proctors:** Yes
**Oral exams:** Y/N
**Extended test time:** Yes
**Added cost:** $1,625 per/yr. part/time; $3,250 per/yr. full time
**Distraction-free environ.:** Yes
**Tape recording in class:** Yes
**Books on tape:** Yes
**Taping of other books:** Yes

**Professional tutors:** Yes
**Peer tutors:** Yes
**Max. hrs/wk for services:** PAL Program hours on an individualized basis/ Essential Skills Ctr. is drop-in
**Priority registration:** No
**Accomodations for students with ADD:** Yes
**How are professors notified of LD:** By the student

## GENERAL ADMISSIONS INFORMATION

**Director of Admissions:** Janet C. Kelly          **Telephone:** 617-333-2211

### ENTRANCE REQUIREMENTS

Total high school units required/recommended: 16 total units are required; 4 English required, 3 math required, 2 science required, 2 foreign language required, 2 social studies required, 2 history required. Minimum SAT I scores of 400 in both verbal and math, rank in top half of secondary school class, and minimum 2.0 GPA recommended. Special requirements: TOEFL is required of all international students. Biology and chemistry, both with labs, required of nursing program applicants.

**Application deadline:** April 1
**Notification:** Rolling

**SAT or ACT preferred:** Either
**SAT Avg:** 450V, 440M
**Average GPA:** 2.5

**Graduated top 10% of class:** 10
**Graduated top 25% of class:** 40
**Graduated top 50% of class:** 90

## COLLEGE GRADUATION REQUIREMENTS

**Course waivers allowed:** No
**Course substitutions allowed:** Yes
**In what courses:** Varies

## ADDITIONAL INFORMATION

**Environment:** Curry's 120 acre campus in Milton, Massachusetts is minutes from metropolitan Boston.

**Student Body**
  **Undergrad enrollment:** 1,442
  **Women:** 51%
  **Men:** 49%
  **In-state students:** 63%
  **Out-of-state:** 37%

**Cost Information**
  **In-state tuition:** $15,250
  **Out-of-state:** $15,250
  **Room & board:** $5,815

**Housing Information**
  **University housing:** Yes
  **Fraternity:** No
  **Sorority:** No
  **Living on campus:** 60%

  **Athletics:** NCAA Div. III

# DEAN COLLEGE

99 Main St., Franklin, MA 02038 • **Admissions:** 508-541-1508 • **Fax:** 508-541-8726
**Support:** CS • **Institution:** 2 yr. Private

## LEARNING DISABILITY ADMISSIONS AND SERVICES

Dean College faculty and staff are committed to maintaining a caring and nurturing environment. While much of this support comes in the form of informal, face-to-face interactions, students will find that a number of programs have been developed specifically to provide students with structured guidance in both academics and student life. The Learning Center offers students academic support and assistance through the Berenson Writing Center, the Math Tutoring Program, Disability Support Services, and course-specific tutoring. Personalized Learning Services offers a comprehensive system of support for students with documented learning disabilities. The Center's staff include a writing specialist, three learning specialists, two math tutors, and a host of peer tutors providing assistance across the curriculum. The goal of PLS is to assist students in becoming confident, successful, independent learners. The FACTS Advising Center (Financial, Academic, Career, Transfer, and Student life) provides comprehensive assistance and information to students. Students are assigned a personal advising team to guide them as they move through the academic year.

## LEARNING DISABILITY ADMISSIONS INFORMATION

**Program Name:** Personalized Learning Services (PLS)
**Program Director:** N/A
**Contact Person:** Kevin Kelly, Director of Admissions

**Telephone:** N/A
**Telephone:** 508-541-1508

### ADMISSIONS

There is no special admission process for students with learning disabilities. All students submit the same general application. Every application is carefully reviewed by Admissions and students are selected based on their academic performance in high school, recommendations and personal accomplishments. Students who self disclose and submit documentation may have their materials reviewed by the LD specialist who will make a recommendation to Admissions. There is no simple formula applied to an application. Dean strives to make the best match between what they offer as an institution and each student's skills, interests and abilities. Students should have college prep including 4 yrs. English and 3 yrs. math. Interviews are not required but students must submit a counselor recommendation. SAT/ACT are optional but students may choose to submit the scores for evaluation.

**College entrance exams required:** No
**Course entrance requirements:** No
**Diagnostic tests:** Yes
**Documentation:** WAIS-R; within 2 years

**Untimed accepted:** Yes
**Interview required:** No

### ADDITIONAL INFORMATION

Accommodations may include, but are not limited to: taped texts; access to computers; scribes and notetakers; alternative testing modes; and extended time for testing. The Learning Center provides free academic assistance and support services for all students through tutoring, workshops, and study groups. Professional and peer tutors are available throughout the day to assist students in developing writing, math, and study skills, and to provide course specific tutoring. Personalized Learning Services offers tutorial support to students with documented LD, unique learning styles or other diagnosed learning needs. Students meet weekly with LD Specialist one-to-one or small groups. Learning and study strategies taught by specialist include: test taking; test preparation; notetaking skills; time management; academic organization; reading comprehension; research and writing skills; and self-awareness and advocacy. The fee is $500 per semester.

**Special education HS coursework accepted:** Yes
**Special application required:** No
**# of applications submitted each year:** N/A
**# of students receiving LD services:** N/I

**Essay required:** Yes
**Submitted to:** N/A
**# of applications accepted each year:** N/A

**Acceptance into program means acceptance into college:** Students must be admitted first and then may request LD services.

## LEARNING DISABILITY SERVICES

**Learning center:** Yes
**Kurzweil personal reader:** N/I
**LD specialists:** 3
**Allowed in exams:**
  **Calculator:** N/I
  **Dictionary:** N/I
  **Computer:** N/I
  **SpellCheck:** N/I

**Notetaker:** N/I
**Scribes:** N/I
**Proctors:** N/I
**Oral exams:** N/I
**Extended test time:** Yes
**Added cost:** $500 per semester
**Distraction-free environ.:** Yes
**Tape recording in class:** N/I
**Books on tape:** N/I
**Taping of other books:** N/I

**Professional tutors:** No
**Peer tutors:** No
**Max. hrs/wk for services:** N/I
**Priority registration:** N/I
**Accomodations for students with ADD:** N/I
**How are professors notified of LD:** N/I

## GENERAL ADMISSIONS INFORMATION

**Director of Admissions:** Walter Caffey          **Telephone:** 508-541-1547

**ENTRANCE REQUIREMENTS**
NR

**Application deadline:** NR          **SAT or ACT preferred:** NR
**Notification:** NR

## COLLEGE GRADUATION REQUIREMENTS

**Course waivers allowed:** No
**Course substitutions allowed:** No
**In what courses:** N/A

## ADDITIONAL INFORMATION

**Environment:** NR

**Student Body**
  **Undergrad enrollment:** NR
  **Women:** NR
  **Men:** NR
  **In-state students:** NR
  **Out-of-state:** NR

**Cost Information**
  **In-state tuition:** NR
  **Out-of-state:** NR

**Housing Information**
  **University housing:** Yes
  **Fraternity:** NR
  **Sorority:** NR
  **Living on campus:** NR

  **Athletics:** NR

# LESLEY COLLEGE

29 Everett Street, Cambridge, MA 02138 • **Admissions:** 617-349-8800 • **Fax:** 617-349-8150
**Email:** ugadm@mail.lesley.edu • **Web:** www.lesley.edu
**Support:** SP • **Institution:** 4 yr. Private

## LEARNING DISABILITY ADMISSIONS AND SERVICES

Threshold is a comprehensive college-based non-degree program, located on the campus of Lesley College. Students are highly motivated, lower-functioning individuals with LD and a strong desire to learn to live independently. Students spend 2 years on campus and ultimately receive 6 college credits and a certificate of completion. Most students continue with Treshold's Transition Year, which provides additional support as students enter the work world and embark upon independent living. The pre-certificate two-year program accommodates 48 students; the community-based, 12-month Transition Year typically serves 75% of the graduates. The Bridge Year is for students who need more structure following the initial 2 years: optimally it serves students by allowing them to move a "half-step" forward after graduation. It is a campus-based program providing the ideal setting to strengthen independent and vocational skills. Bridge students live with other first and second year students and follow the same academic calendar. The goal is to guide the "whole person" forward; to foster growth toward independence through a comprehensive curriculum that emphasizes vocational training, as well as courses that focus on independent living, psychological growth, effective use of leisure time, and creativity.

## LEARNING DISABILITY ADMISSIONS INFORMATION

**Program Name:** Threshold Program
**Program Director:** David Leslie
**Contact Person:** Jim Wilbur (Admissions)

**Telephone:** 617-349-8181

### ADMISSIONS

Threshold accepts up to 24 new students each year from a large number of applicants. Students apply by March 1 to be considered for September admission. During the prior winter, a required family interview enables an applicant to express his/her interests and also gives family members an opportunity to discuss the applicant's background. Reading and writing skills generally range upward from the 5th grade level. Vocational courses are strongly suggested but not required; no ACT/SAT; WAIS-R, PIAT or Woodcock Johnson, TAT or Rorschach all within the last year. While final acceptance decisions are made in April, at the conclusion of the interview administrators share with families their perceptions about how well the applicant might fit into Threshold. Most of the applicants have received years of special services in either public school resource rooms or in private settings for students with special needs. All have evidence of specific learning disabilities, a keen interest in working with people, and a strong desire to become independent adults.

**College entrance exams required:** No
**Course entrance requirements:** N/A
**Diagnostic tests:** Yes
**Documentation:** WAIS-R; W-J or PIAT; TAT or Rorschach; within 1 year

**Untimed accepted:** N/A
**Interview required:** Yes

### ADDITIONAL INFORMATION

Students initially experience 3 vocational options: early childhood, human services, and clerical services. In year two, students major in one of these areas. Faculty have expertise in educating students with special needs. Comprehensive support is provided and includes a weekly on-campus seminar, vocational supervision, and independent living advising. The Work World Advisors help students contend professionally with work-related issues, visit students on the job, maintain ongoing contact through regularly scheduled meetings, and help students improve on techniques learned in the vocational training component. Students work on increased development of conscientious work habits, such as punctuality, following directions, completing assigned tasks, and showing initiatives. Focus is also on general adjustment, dealing effectively with colleagues and superiors, and demonstrating responsibility, positive attitude, and reliable overall organization. The primary goal is to help students implement the skills needed to keep and succeed at jobs.

**Special education HS coursework accepted:** Yes
**Special application required:** Yes
**# of applications submitted each year:** 80
**# of students receiving LD services:** 70

**Essay required:** No
**Submitted to:** Jim Wilbur
**# of applications accepted each year:** 24

**Acceptance into program means acceptance into college:** Threshold students are housed on Lesley campus, but are not enrolled in the college.

## LEARNING DISABILITY SERVICES

**Learning center:** N/A
**Kurzweil personal reader:** N/A
**LD specialists:** N/A
**Allowed in exams:**
  **Calculator:** N/A
  **Dictionary:** N/A
  **Computer:** N/A
  **SpellCheck:** N/A

**Notetaker:** N/A
**Scribes:** N/A
**Proctors:** N/A
**Oral exams:** N/A
**Extended test time:** N/A
**Added cost:** None
**Distraction-free environ.:** N/A
**Tape recording in class:** N/A
**Books on tape:** N/A
**Taping of other books:** N/A

**Professional tutors:** N/A
**Peer tutors:** N/A
**Max. hrs/wk for services:** N/A
**Priority registration:** N/A
**Accomodations for students with ADD:** N/A
**How are professors notified of LD:** N/A

## GENERAL ADMISSIONS INFORMATION

**Director of Admissions:** Jim Wilbur

**Telephone:** 617-349-8181

### ENTRANCE REQUIREMENTS

Total high school units required/recommended: 13 total units are required; 17 total units are recommended; 4 English required, 2 math required, 3 math recommended, 1 science required, 3 science recommended, 2 foreign language required, 1 history required. Special requirements: TOEFL is required of all international students.

**Application deadline:** March 15
**Notification:** Rolling

**SAT or ACT preferred:** Either
**SAT Avg:** 500V, 480M
**SAT II required:** Yes
**Average GPA:** 2.8

**Graduated top 10% of class:** 6
**Graduated top 25% of class:** 36
**Graduated top 50% of class:** 90

## COLLEGE GRADUATION REQUIREMENTS

**Course waivers allowed:** N/A
**Course substitutions allowed:** N/A
**In what courses:** The program is a non-degree program and has no math or foreign language requirements.

## ADDITIONAL INFORMATION

**Environment:** The college is located in Cambridge with easy access to Harvard Square and Lesley College.

**Student Body**
  **Undergrad enrollment:** 508
  **Women:** 100%
  **Men:** 0%
  **In-state students:** 60%
  **Out-of-state:** 40%

**Cost Information**
  **In-state tuition:** $13,700
  **Out-of-state:** $13,700
  **Room & board:** $6,440

**Housing Information**
  **University housing:** Yes
  **Fraternity:** No
  **Sorority:** No
  **Living on campus:** 67%

  **Athletics:** NR

# MA UNIVERSITY OF MASSACHUSETTS-AMHERST

Admissions Center, Amherst, MA 01003 • **Admissions:** 413-545-0222
**Web:** www.umass.edu
**Support:** CS • **Institution:** 4 yr. Public

## LEARNING DISABILITY ADMISSIONS AND SERVICES

LDSS is a support service for all students with documented LD. Students are eligible for services if they can document their LD with the appropriate diagnostic evidence. To be eligible, all students must provide one or more of the following types of documentation: an individualized equational plan indicating LD from elementary or secondary school; a report from a state certified assessment center indicating LD; psycho-educational test results to be interpreted in the LDSS. Not all students with learning problems have learning disabilities. Only students with disabilities may be served by LDSS. Students whose predominate disability is a form of ADHD are served by the Program for Students with Psychological Disabilities and not LDSS. Each student enrolled in LDSS is assigned a Case Manager who is a graduate student in Education, Counseling or a related field. Case Managers have prior relevant professional experience and are supervised by professional staff. Students work with the same Case Manager for the entire academic year on 3 objectives: understanding and obtaining accommodations needed; identifying and utilizing resources; and identifying and implementing learning strategies to compensate for the disability. The goal of LDSS is for students to become independent self-advocated by the time they graduate.

## LEARNING DISABILITY ADMISSIONS INFORMATION

**Program Name:** Learning Disabilities Support Services (LDSS)
**Program Director:** Dr. Patricia Silver          **Telephone:** 413-545-4602
**Contact Person:** Amanda Zygmont

### ADMISSIONS

There is no special admissions criteria for students with learning disabilities. All admissions and support documents go through the Admissions Office. All applications on which the learning disabilities box is checked are reviewed individually by learning disabilities specialists. If any information is missing, the applicant will be notified. There is no quota on the number of students with LD who can be admitted to the university. Students who are otherwise qualified and have taken college preparatory courses in high school should submit a recent Individual Educational Plan and documentation.

**College entrance exams required:** Not in-state       **Untimed accepted:** Yes
**Course entrance requirements:** Yes                 **Interview required:** No
**Diagnostic tests:** Yes
**Documentation:** Depends on the learning disability: within 3 years

### ADDITIONAL INFORMATION

Students and Case Managers prepare Learning Style Sheets for professors requesting various accommodations such as: untimed exams, extended time on assignments, alternate form of tests, and notetaking. At mid-semester each professor who received a Learning Style Sheet receives a request from LDSS asking for the student's grades, attendance, and performance. There is individual tutoring for most introductory level courses and math skills, study skills, language arts, written expression, time management, learning strategies and organizational skills.Tutors are graduate students trained to work with LD. Students meet with tutors each week. Peer Mentor Network is an organization designed to support the needs of students with disabilities. Faculty Friends is a group of instructors nominated by Peer Mentor Network as outstanding in teaching and meeting the needs of students with disabilities. The university offers a special summer program for pre-college freshmen with learning disabilities.

**Special education HS coursework accepted:** No      **Essay required:** Yes
**Special application required:** No                   **Submitted to:** N/A
**# of applications submitted each year:** N/A         **# of applications accepted each year:** N/A
**# of students receiving LD services:** 550
**Acceptance into program means acceptance into college:** Students are admitted to the university and then reviewed for LD services.

# LEARNING DISABILITY SERVICES

**Learning center:** Yes
**Kurzweil personal reader:** Yes
**LD specialists:** Yes
**Allowed in exams:**
  **Calculator:** Yes
  **Dictionary:** Yes
  **Computer:** Yes
  **SpellCheck:** Yes

**Notetaker:** Yes
**Scribes:** Yes
**Proctors:** Yes
**Oral exams:** Yes
**Extended test time:** Yes
**Added cost:** None
**Distraction-free environ.:** Yes
**Tape recording in class:** Yes
**Books on tape:** Yes
**Taping of other books:** Yes

**Professional tutors:** 10
**Peer tutors:** No
**Max. hrs/wk for services:** Unlimited
**Priority registration:** Yes
**Accomodations for students with ADD:** Yes
**How are professors notified of LD:** By the student and the Program Director

# GENERAL ADMISSIONS INFORMATION

**Director of Admissions:** Arlene Cash

**Telephone:** 413-545-0222

## ENTRANCE REQUIREMENTS

Total high school units required/recommended: 17 total units are required; 4 English required, 3 math required, 3 science required, 2 foreign language required, 2 social studies required. Special requirements: A portfolio is required for art program applicants. An audition is required for music program applicants. TOEFL is required of all international students. 4 units of math required of business, computer science, engineering, and math program applicants. 1/2 unit of trigonometry recommended of physical sciences and math program applicants. 1 unit of chemistry required of nursing program applicants. Chemistry and physics required of engineering program applicants.

**Application deadline:** February 1
**Notification:** Rolling

**SAT or ACT preferred:** SAT
**SAT Avg:** 556V, 560M
**SAT II required:** Yes
**Average GPA:** 2.9

**Graduated top 10% of class:** 12
**Graduated top 25% of class:** 38
**Graduated top 50% of class:** 78

# COLLEGE GRADUATION REQUIREMENTS

**Course waivers allowed:** No
**Course substitutions allowed:** Yes
**In what courses:** College of Arts and Sciences students with a LD that prevents them from learning a foreign language may petition the Foreign Language Board for a modification of the requirement. If granted, courses which fulfill cultural intent and/or language awareness.

# ADDITIONAL INFORMATION

**Environment:** The university is located on 1,405 acres in a small town 90 miles west of Boston.

**Student Body**
  **Undergrad enrollment:** 19,467
  **Women:** 48%
  **Men:** 52%
  **In-state students:** 73%
  **Out-of-state:** 27%

**Cost Information**
  **In-state tuition:** $2,004
  **Out-of-state:** $8,952
  **Room & board:** $4,520

**Housing Information**
  **University housing:** Yes
  **Fraternity:** Yes
  **Sorority:** Yes
  **Living on campus:** 57%

  **Athletics:** NCAA Div. I

# MA
# MOUNT IDA COLLEGE

777 Dedham Street, Newton, MA 02159 • **Admissions:** 617-928-4535 • **Fax:** 617-928-4507
**Email:** micADMSN@Tiac.net • **Web:** www.mountida.edu
**Support:** SP • **Institution:** 2 yr. & 4 yr. Private

## LEARNING DISABILITY ADMISSIONS AND SERVICES

LOP provides additional academic support for students with LD. The program focuses on developing and strengthening individual learning styles which create successful, independent learning. Students are mainstreamed in a regular degree curriculum. Mount Ida goes the extra mile for all its students and the LOP is a natural extension of this philosophy. Students discover a supportive environment where a positive, successful experience is the goal. An important component of the LOP is the mentoring relationship with individual learning specialists. Mount Ida also has the Horizon Program to serve the needs of students not accepted into the LOP but who still demonstrate some academic promise and the ability to contribute to the college community. Horizon is a non-degree, transitional program; students take a reduced number of academic classes bolstered by non-academic support classes and tutorials; students achieving a minimum 2.0 GPA are eligible to transfer into LOP after their first year. Academic performance is not the only measure of success. A goal of the Horizon Program is to improve the quality of the college experience by providing a support network for better understanding of oneself, exchanging feelings and personal learning histories, and discovering a commonality that they are not alone in dealing with LD.

## LEARNING DISABILITY ADMISSIONS INFORMATION

**Program Name:** Learning Opportunities Program (LOP)
**Program Director:** Jill Mehler
**Contact Person:** Harold Duvall

**Telephone:** 617-928-4648
**Telephone:** 617-928-4553

### ADMISSIONS

There is no special admissions process for students with learning disabilities. Open admissions is available. ACT/SAT are not required for admission. An interview is strongly recommended. Students with disabilities should submit the WAIS-R; a test indicating appropriate reading grade level; and evaluative documentation of the learning disability. Some students may be admitted into a pilot program called Horizon which is a special admit program. It is a transition program prior to entering the LOP Program. Horizon reduces the academic challenge and increases support.

**College entrance exams required:** No
**Course entrance requirements:** No
**Diagnostic tests:** Yes
**Documentation:** Wechsler: within 3 years

**Untimed accepted:** N/A
**Interview required:** Yes

### ADDITIONAL INFORMATION

In the Learning Skills Laboratory students have an opportunity to work with Mount Ida faculty and students to improve study skills. Tutoring provided by professional tutors who are learning specialists is available two times per week. Each tutoring session is private and strategy based. These meetings focus on developing self-advocacy skills and independent learning skills. Other services include reduced course load, enrollment in Basic English, if needed, extended time testing, notetaking, diagnostic testing, course substitutions, and counseling. Study skills courses in Math and English are available. Additional support and content tutoring are offered in the Academic Success Center. The college also runs a Freshman Experience course specifically for students who may be underprepared for college that focuses on building the skills necessary to facilitate student success. Students work to identify and strengthen their individual learning styles.

**Special education HS coursework accepted:** Yes
**Special application required:** Yes
**# of applications submitted each year:** 349
**# of students receiving LD services:** 120

**Essay required:** No
**Submitted to:** Admissions
**# of applications accepted each year:** 274

**Acceptance into program means acceptance into college:** Students are admitted jointly into LOP and Mount Ida.

# LEARNING DISABILITY SERVICES

Learning center: No
Kurzweil personal reader: No
LD specialists: 10
Allowed in exams:
  Calculator: Yes
  Dictionary: Yes
  Computer: No
  SpellCheck: Yes

Notetaker: No
Scribes: No
Proctors: No
Oral exams: Yes
Extended test time: Yes
Added cost: $2,500 per year
Distraction-free environ.: Yes
Tape recording in class: Yes
Books on tape: No
Taping of other books: Yes

Professional tutors: 10
Peer tutors: 20
Max. hrs/wk for services: 4
Priority registration: Yes
Accomodations for students
with ADD: Yes
How are professors notified of
LD: By the student and the
Program Director

# GENERAL ADMISSIONS INFORMATION

Director of Admissions: Harold DuVall          Telephone: 617-928-4648

## ENTRANCE REQUIREMENTS
Total high school units required/recommended: 4 English recommended, 4 math recommended, 4 social studies recommended, 4 science recommended.

Application deadline: Rolling
Notification: Rolling

SAT or ACT preferred: Both are
recommended

# COLLEGE GRADUATION REQUIREMENTS

Course waivers allowed: Yes
Course substitutions allowed: Yes
In what courses: Limited, select courses affected the learning disability.

# ADDITIONAL INFORMATION

Environment: Mount Ida's 85-acre campus is in a suburban neighborhood 8 miles west of Boston.

Student Body
  Undergrad enrollment: 2,009
  Women: 60%
  Men: 40%
  In-state students: 75%
  Out-of-state: 25%

Cost Information
  In-state tuition: $12,230
  Out-of-state: $12,230
  Room & board: $8,460

Housing Information
  University housing: Yes
  Fraternity: No
  Sorority: No
  Living on campus: 45%

  Athletics: Intercollegiate sports

# NORTHEASTERN UNIVERSITY

360 Huntington Avenue, Boston, MA  02115 • **Admissions:** 617-437-2200 • **Fax:** 617-373-5106
**Email:** admissions@neu.edu • **Web:** www.neu.edu
**Support:** SP • **Institution:** 4 yr. Private

## LEARNING DISABILITY ADMISSIONS AND SERVICES

Persons with LD who need more intensive support may be interested in an independent highly structured LD program called The Learning Disability Program. Students meet with a psychologist and a learning disabilities specialist who acts as primary advisers to explore learning strengths and weaknesses, and develop specific goals for each quarter. On the basis of individual need, each student receives 3-5 hours of one-on-one tutoring each week. Program tutors maintain regular contact with instructors to monitor the student's progress. This privately sponsored program, only for students with learning disabilities, has an additional cost of $1,400 per/quarter and accepts a small number of students. The Disability Resource Center offers on-going support and counseling services, academic advising, student advocacy, and help with course and exam modifications for students with learning disabilities needing minimal assistance. Students who apply must have a learning disability documented through a recent evaluation and the willingness to use the resources and services of the program. The DRC serves students who have a wide range of learning problems, including specific reading or spelling disabilities, math disabilities, problems with organization, or difficulty maintaining attention. There is no charge for basic support services.

## LEARNING DISABILITY ADMISSIONS INFORMATION

**Program Name:** Disability Resource Program (DRC)
**Program Director:** Dean Ruth Bork                  **Telephone:** 617-373-2675
**Contact Person:** Debbi Hines, Coordinator          **Telephone:** 617-373-2675

### ADMISSIONS

There are two separate application processes involved in admission to Northeastern. Admission requirements to the university are the same for all students and any student may be eligible for help in the Disability Resource Center. Depending on the Program, courses and diagnosis of the student's learning disability, courses may be substituted for admission. There is a separate application and interview needed for The Learning Disability Program which is the independent program. Students must take a full 6-10 hour battery of tests for this program, and must also submit previous diagnostic tests. These students must have an interview and notification of acceptance is sent from the university Office of Admission.

**College entrance exams required:** Yes                **Untimed accepted:** Yes
**Course entrance requirements:** Yes                   **Interview required:** No
**Diagnostic tests:** Yes
**Documentation:** WAIS-R or WISC-R; psycho-educational evaluations: within 3 years

### ADDITIONAL INFORMATION

DRC services include: notetaking services; readers and scribes; academic advice related to the disability; liaison and advocacy services; counseling and referral services; support groups; "Basic Skills" courses taught by LD specialists are available in time management, learning strategies, study strategies, social skills, and perceptual skills. The LD Program provides more intensive services including on-on-one tutoring 3-5 hours per week and close monitoring of the student's progress. Services and accommodations are available for undergraduate and graduate students.

**Special education HS coursework accepted:** Decided by
Admissions                                              **Essay required:** No
**Special application required:** Yes                   **Submitted to:** Director of Program
**# of applications submitted each year:** N/I          **# of applications accepted each year:** N/I
**# of students receiving LD services:** 200+
**Acceptance into program means acceptance into college:** Students must be accepted by the university first and then may request LD services from DRC or admission to the LD Program.

## LEARNING DISABILITY SERVICES

**Learning center:** Yes
**Kurzweil personal reader:** Yes
**LD specialists:** 3
**Allowed in exams:**
  **Calculator:** Y/N
  **Dictionary:** Y/N
  **Computer:** Y/N
  **SpellCheck:** Y/N

**Notetaker:** Yes
**Scribes:** Yes
**Proctors:** Yes
**Oral exams:** Yes
**Extended test time:** Yes
**Added cost:** $1,400 per/quarter for the LD Program
**Distraction-free environ.:** Yes
**Tape recording in class:** Yes
**Books on tape:** Yes
**Taping of other books:** No

**Professional tutors:** Yes
**Peer tutors:** Yes
**Max. hrs/wk for services:** Unlimited
**Priority registration:** No
**Accomodations for students with ADD:** Yes
**How are professors notified of LD:** By the student or the Program Director

## GENERAL ADMISSIONS INFORMATION

**Director of Admissions:** Gary Bracker

**Telephone:** 617-373-2200

### ENTRANCE REQUIREMENTS

Total high school units required/recommended: 17 total units are recommended; 4 English recommended, 3 math recommended, 3 science recommended, 2 foreign language recommended, 3 social studies recommended, 2 history recommended. Special requirements: TOEFL is required of all international students.

**Application deadline:** March 1
**Notification:** Rolling

**SAT or ACT preferred:** SAT
**SAT Avg:** 547V, 548M
**Average ACT:** 23

**Graduated top 10% of class:** 16
**Graduated top 25% of class:** 44
**Graduated top 50% of class:** 79

## COLLEGE GRADUATION REQUIREMENTS

**Course waivers allowed:** No
**Course substitutions allowed:** Yes
**In what courses:** Substitute courses for foreign language and math.

## ADDITIONAL INFORMATION

**Environment:** The school is located on 55 acres in the city of Boston.

**Student Body**
  **Undergrad enrollment:** 11,387
  **Women:** 47%
  **Men:** 53%
  **In-state students:** 61%
  **Out-of-state:** 39%

**Cost Information**
  **In-state tuition:** $16,320
  **Out-of-state:** $16,320
  **Room & board:** $8,265

**Housing Information**
  **University housing:** Yes
  **Fraternity:** Yes
  **Sorority:** Yes
  **Living on campus:** 65%

  **Athletics:** NCAA Div. I

# PINE MANOR COLLEGE

400 Heath Street, Chestnut Hill, MA 02167 • **Admissions:** 617-731-7104 • **Fax:** 617-731-7199
**Email:** worshlis@pmc.edu • **Web:** www.pmc.edu
**Support:** CS • **Institution:** 2 yr. & 4 yr. Private

## LEARNING DISABILITY ADMISSIONS AND SERVICES

The Learning Resource Center is an expression of the college's strong commitment to the individual learning experience. The LRC supports and challenges students to realize their maximum academic potential in the way that best suits their individual learning styles. There are five professional tutors: Writing tutors, math tutors, Learning Specialists, and the Director who provide tutoring that is individually tailored to the learning style and needs of the student. The tutoring is not content-oriented, but rather strategy-based and process-oriented. The LRC hopes that students with learning disabilities enter college with some compensatory techniques and study skills. The Learning Specialists furnish guidance and academic skills assistance to students whose LD create a gap between their true capacity and daily performance. The LRC serves the whole college population free of charge, whether or not a student has a documented learning disability.

## LEARNING DISABILITY ADMISSIONS INFORMATION

**Program Name:** Learning Resource Center (LRC)
**Program Director:** Mary Walsh                **Telephone:** 800-PMC-1357
**Contact Person:** Same as above              **Telephone:** 617-731-7181

### ADMISSIONS

All applicants submit the same general application. Although not required, an interview is highly recommended. Admissions is done by the Office of Admissions. However, the Director of the LRC assists in interpreting testing and documentation and makes a recommendation to the office of Admissions. There is a special Optional Response Form that is used by the Learning Resource Center after the student is accepted.

**College entrance exams required:** Yes          **Untimed accepted:** Yes
**Course entrance requirements:** Yes            **Interview required:** Recommended
**Diagnostic tests:** No
**Documentation:** N/I

### ADDITIONAL INFORMATION

LRC staff works with the students on a regular, once or twice a week basis or on a drop-in basis. Students also work closely with their academic advisors. LRC tutors offer diagnosis and remediation for students in academic difficulty; enrichment for successful students; and assistance to faculty and staff. The Center can also obtain recorded textbooks and arrange for tutors and diagnostic testing. In addition, the following accommodations have proved useful: reduced course load each semester; additional time to complete exams, quizzes, or written assignments; and a separate room for examinations. Basic skills classes are offered in reading, math, learning strategies, written language, study strategies, and time management.

**Special education HS coursework accepted:** No      **Essay required:** Yes
**Special application required:** No                  **Submitted to:** N/A
**# of applications submitted each year:** N/A        **# of applications accepted each year:** N/A
**# of students receiving LD services:** 40
**Acceptance into program means acceptance into college:** Students must be admitted to the college prior to requesting services from the LRC.

## LEARNING DISABILITY SERVICES

**Learning center:** Yes
**Kurzweil personal reader:** No
**LD specialists:** 3
**Allowed in exams:**
  **Calculator:** Yes
  **Dictionary:** Yes
  **Computer:** Yes
  **SpellCheck:** Yes

**Notetaker:** Yes
**Scribes:** No
**Proctors:** No
**Oral exams:** Yes
**Extended test time:** Yes
**Added cost:** None
**Distraction-free environ.:** Yes
**Tape recording in class:** Yes
**Books on tape:** Yes
**Taping of other books:** Yes

**Professional tutors:** 5
**Peer tutors:** No
**Max. hrs/wk for services:** As many as needed
**Priority registration:** Yes
**Accomodations for students with ADD:** Yes
**How are professors notified of LD:** By the student or the Program Director

## GENERAL ADMISSIONS INFORMATION

**Director of Admissions:** Leslie Miles

**Telephone:** 617-731-7104

### ENTRANCE REQUIREMENTS

Total high school units required/recommended: 18 total units are recommended; 4 English recommended, 3 math recommended, 2 science recommended, 2 foreign language recommended, 2 social studies recommended.

**Application deadline:** Rolling
**Notification:** Rolling

**SAT or ACT preferred:** Either
**SAT Avg:** 361V, 386M
**Average ACT:** 19

**Graduated top 25% of class:** 10
**Graduated top 50% of class:** 30

## COLLEGE GRADUATION REQUIREMENTS

**Course waivers allowed:** Yes
**Course substitutions allowed:** Yes
**In what courses:** Students must petition for waivers of General Education requirements.

## ADDITIONAL INFORMATION

**Environment:** Pine Manor is located on a 79-acre campus in Chestnut Hill 5 miles west of Boston.

**Student Body**
  **Undergrad enrollment:** 370
  **Women:** 100%
  **Men:** 0%
  **In-state students:** 33%
  **Out-of-state:** 67%

**Cost Information**
  **In-state tuition:** $16,000
  **Out-of-state:** $16,000
  **Room & board:** $6,900

**Housing Information**
  **University housing:** Yes
  **Fraternity:** No
  **Sorority:** No
  **Living on campus:** 85%

  **Athletics:** NCAA Div. III

# SMITH COLLEGE

Elm Street, Northampton, MA 01063 • **Admissions:** 413-585-2500 • **Fax:** 413-585-2527
**Email:** admission@smith.edu • **Web:** www.smith.edu
**Support:** S • **Institution:** 4 yr. Private

## LEARNING DISABILITY ADMISSIONS AND SERVICES

Smith College does not have a formal LD program. However, the college is both philosophically committed and legally required to enable students with documented disabilities to participate in college programs by providing reasonable accommodations for them. The Office of Disabilities Services facilitates the provision of services and offers services aimed to eliminate barriers through modification of the program where necessary. A student may voluntarily register with ODS by completing a disability identification form and providing documentation of the disability, after which proper accommodations will be determined. Students with disabilities who need academic services are asked to make their needs known and to file timely request forms each semester with ODS for accommodations in course work. The college cannot make retroactive accommodations. Students are encouraged to tell professors about the accommodations needed. The college is responsible for providing that, within certain limits, students are not denied the opportunity to participate in college Programs on the basis of a disability. The college will provide support services to students for with appropriate evaluations and documentation. Students should contact the ODS for consultation and advice.

## LEARNING DISABILITY ADMISSIONS INFORMATION

**Program Name:** Office of Disability Services (ODS)
**Program Director:** Kris Kozuch, Coordinator          **Telephone:** 413-585-2071
**Contact Person:** Same as above

### ADMISSIONS

There is no special admissions procedure for students with learning disabilities. Tests that evaluate cognitive ability, achievement and information processing should be included with the regular application. It is also helpful to have a letter from a diagnostician documenting services which will be needed in college. SAT I and 3 SAT II Subject Tests are required or the ACT without SAT II Subject Tests. Leniency may be granted in regards to a high school's waiving of foreign language requirements due to a learning disability. High school courses recommended are 4 yrs. English composition and literature, 3 yrs. foreign language (or 2 years in each of 2 languages), 3 yrs. math, 2 yrs. science, and 2 yrs. history.

**College entrance exams required:** Yes          **Untimed accepted:** Yes
**Course entrance requirements:** No          **Interview required:** Yes
**Diagnostic tests:** Yes
**Documentation:** WAIS; WRAT; other psycho-educational testing: most recent

### ADDITIONAL INFORMATION

Because college and departmental requirements are implemented for sound academic reasons, Smith College does not provide waivers for required courses for students with LD. The support services assist students to meet their requirements through modifications to programs when necessary. Courses are available in quantitative skills, study skills, and time management skills. The Special Needs Action Group for Support is a cross-disability, student-led group which meets regularly to provide support and peer mentoring and to plan activities. Support services include: readers, note takers, scribes, assistive listening devices, typists, computing software and hardware, books on tape, writing counseling (more and/or longer appointments), peer tutoring, and time management/study skills training. If peer tutors are not available, other tutorial services may be sought. The college will not provide services that create an undue burden for the college.

**Special education HS coursework accepted:** No          **Essay required:** Yes
**Special application required:** No          **Submitted to:** N/A
**# of applications submitted each year:** N/A          **# of applications accepted each year:** N/A
**# of students receiving LD services:** 30
**Acceptance into program means acceptance into college:** Students must be accepted to the college first and then request services.

## LEARNING DISABILITY SERVICES

**Learning center:** No
**Kurzweil personal reader:** Yes
**LD specialists:** No
**Allowed in exams:**
  **Calculator:** Yes
  **Dictionary:** Yes
  **Computer:** Yes
  **SpellCheck:** Yes

**Notetaker:** Yes
**Scribes:** Yes
**Proctors:** No
**Oral exams:** Yes
**Extended test time:** Yes
**Added cost:** None
**Distraction-free environ.:** Yes
**Tape recording in class:** Yes
**Books on tape:** RFB
**Taping of other books:** Yes

**Professional tutors:** 2
**Peer tutors:** varies
**Max. hrs/wk for services:** Unlimited
**Priority registration:** Yes
**Accomodations for students with ADD:** Yes
**How are professors notified of LD:** By the student and the Service Director

## GENERAL ADMISSIONS INFORMATION

**Director of Admissions:** Nanci Tessier

**Telephone:** 413-585-2500

### ENTRANCE REQUIREMENTS
Total high school units required/recommended: 16 total units are recommended; 4 English recommended, 3 math recommended, 2 science recommended, 3 foreign language recommended, 2 social studies recommended, 2 history recommended.

**Application deadline:** January 15
**Notification:** April 1

**SAT or ACT preferred:** Either
**SAT Range:** 620–720V, 590–670M
**ACT Range:** 26–30
**Average GPA:** 3.7

**Graduated top 10% of class:** 53
**Graduated top 25% of class:** 85
**Graduated top 50% of class:** 97

## COLLEGE GRADUATION REQUIREMENTS

**Course waivers allowed:** No
**Course substitutions allowed:** No
**In what courses:** Smith College has no required courses to graduate.

## ADDITIONAL INFORMATION

**Environment:** The 204-acre campus is located in a small city 85 miles west of Boston and 15 minutes from Amherst.

**Student Body**
  **Undergrad enrollment:** 2,593
  **Women:** 100%
  **Men:** 0%
  **In-state students:** 20%
  **Out-of-state:** 80%

**Cost Information**
  **In-state tuition:** $21,360
  **Out-of-state:** $21,360
  **Room & board:** $7,250

**Housing Information**
  **University housing:** Yes
  **Fraternity:** No
  **Sorority:** No
  **Living on campus:** 90%

  **Athletics:** NCAA Div. III

# SPRINGFIELD COLLEGE

263 Alden Street, Springfield, MA 01109 • **Admissions:** 413-748-3136 • **Fax:** 413-748-3694
**Email:** admissions@spfldcol.edu • **Web:** www.spfldcol.edu
**Support:** CS • **Institution:** 4 yr. Private

## LEARNING DISABILITY ADMISSIONS AND SERVICES

Springfield College is committed to providing an equal educational opportunity and full participation in college activities for persons with disabilities. The Office of Student Support Services provides services which ensure that students with disabilities are given an equal educational opportunity and the opportunity for full participation in all college programs and activities. In addition to supporting students with disabilities, Student Support Services works with students who are having academic difficulty. Students can receive services by meeting with the Director of Student Support Services to verify eligibility for services, identify student needs, and determine appropriate services and accommodations. To receive services students must provide documentation of their learning disability which is current and comprehensive with specific evidence and identification of a learning disability. Documentation should be no older than three years.

## LEARNING DISABILITY ADMISSIONS INFORMATION

**Program Name:** Student Support Services
**Program Director:** Deb Dickens
**Contact Person:** Same as above

**Telephone:** 413-748-3100

### ADMISSIONS

There is no special admissions process for students with learning disabilities. All applicants must submit the same general application and meet the same admission criteria. There is not a minimum GPA required although the average GPA is a 3.0. Courses required include 4 yrs. English, 3 yrs. math, 2 yrs. history, and 2-3 yrs. science. The Admission decision is made by the Office of Admissions.

**College entrance exams required:** Yes
**Course entrance requirements:** Yes
**Diagnostic tests:** Yes
**Documentation:** Any psycho-educational testing: within 3 years

**Untimed accepted:** Yes
**Interview required:** Yes

### ADDITIONAL INFORMATION

Services provided through the Office of Student Support Services includes: taped textbooks; taped lectures; readers; alternative testing; notetakers; tutors; computers with spell-check; Reading Edge; reduced course loads; study skills and time management; course accommodations; course selection.

**Special education HS coursework accepted:** No
**Special application required:** No
**# of applications submitted each year:** N/A
**# of students receiving LD services:** 90-100

**Essay required:** Yes
**Submitted to:** N/A
**# of applications accepted each year:** N/A

**Acceptance into program means acceptance into college:** Students must be admitted to the college and then reviewed for services.

**Learning center:** No
**Kurzweil personal reader:** No
**LD specialists:** 1
**Allowed in exams:**
  **Calculator:** Yes
  **Dictionary:** Yes
  **Computer:** N/I
  **SpellCheck:** Yes

**Notetaker:** Yes
**Scribes:** Yes
**Proctors:** Yes
**Oral exams:** Yes
**Extended test time:** Yes
**Added cost:** None
**Distraction-free environ.:** Yes
**Tape recording in class:** Yes
**Books on tape:** N/I
**Taping of other books:** RFB

**Professional tutors:** No
**Peer tutors:** N/I
**Max. hrs/wk for services:** Unlimited
**Priority registration:** No
**Accomodations for students with ADD:** Yes
**How are professors notified of LD:** By the student and the Program Director

## GENERAL ADMISSIONS INFORMATION

**Director of Admissions:** Fred Bartlett

**Telephone:** 413-748-3136

### ENTRANCE REQUIREMENTS

Total high school units required/recommended: 16 total units are required; 4 English recommended, 2 math recommended, 2 science recommended, 2 social studies recommended. Special requirements: A portfolio is required for art program applicants. TOEFL is required of all international students.

**Application deadline:** April 1
**Notification:** Rolling

**SAT or ACT preferred:** SAT
**SAT Avg:** 495V, 505M

**Graduated top 10% of class:** 13
**Graduated top 25% of class:** 39
**Graduated top 50% of class:** 73

## COLLEGE GRADUATION REQUIREMENTS

**Course waivers allowed:** Yes
**Course substitutions allowed:** Yes
**In what courses:** N/I

## ADDITIONAL INFORMATION

**Environment:** NR

**Student Body**
  **Undergrad enrollment:** 2,046
  **Women:** 51%
  **Men:** 49%
  **In-state students:** 34%
  **Out-of-state:** 66%

**Cost Information**
  **In-state tuition:** $12,830
  **Out-of-state:** $12,830
  **Room & board:** $5,800

**Housing Information**
  **University housing:** Yes
  **Fraternity:** No
  **Sorority:** No
  **Living on campus:** 85%

  **Athletics:** NCAA Div. III

# ADRIAN COLLEGE

110 South Madison Street, Adrian, MI 49221 • **Admissions:** 800-877-2246 • **Fax:** 517-264-3331
**Email:** admission@adrian.edu • **Web:** www.adrian.edu
**Support:** CS • **Institution:** 4 yr. Private

## LEARNING DISABILITY ADMISSIONS AND SERVICES

There is extensive academic support services for all handicapped students. The more the students are mainstreamed in the high school, the greater their chances of success at Adrian in their mainstream program. There is no special or separate curriculum for students with learning disabilities. Project EXCEL is the umbrella program for all services at Adrian.

## LEARNING DISABILITY ADMISSIONS INFORMATION

**Program Name:** EXCEL
**Program Director:** Jane McCloskey          **Telephone:** 517-265-5161
**Contact Person:** Same as above

### ADMISSIONS

Students with learning disabilities must meet regular admission criteria. Students should demonstrate the ability to do college level work through an acceptable GPA in college preparatory classes, ACT (17+) or SAT, and a psychological report. Furthermore, by their senior year in high school, students should, for the most part, be mainstreamed. There is a special admissions program designed for students who demonstrate academic potential. This Special Admissions Status Program (SASP) requires students to sign a contract, maintain a certain GPA by the 1st semester, communicate with professors and meet with an advisor two times per week.

**College entrance exams required:** Yes          **Untimed accepted:** Yes
**Course entrance requirements:** Yes          **Interview required:** Recommended
**Diagnostic tests:** Yes
**Documentation:** Within 3 years

### ADDITIONAL INFORMATION

Course adaptations help to make courses more understandable. Skills classes are available in reading, math, and composition, and students are granted credit toward their GPA.

**Special education HS coursework accepted:** No          **Essay required:** No
**Special application required:** No          **Submitted to:** N/A
**# of applications submitted each year:** 10          **# of applications accepted each year:** N/I
**# of students receiving LD services:** 40
**Acceptance into program means acceptance into college:** Students must be accepted to the college first and then may request services.

## LEARNING DISABILITY SERVICES

**Learning center:** No
**Kurzweil personal reader:** Yes
**LD specialists:** 1
**Allowed in exams:**
  **Calculator:** Y/N
  **Dictionary:** Y/N
  **Computer:** Yes
  **SpellCheck:** Yes

**Notetaker:** Yes
**Scribes:** Yes
**Proctors:** Yes
**Oral exams:** Yes
**Extended test time:** Yes
**Added cost:** None
**Distraction-free environ.:** Yes
**Tape recording in class:** Yes
**Books on tape:** Yes
**Taping of other books:** Yes

**Professional tutors:** No
**Peer tutors:** Yes
**Max. hrs/wk for services:** Unlimited
**Priority registration:** No
**Accomodations for students with ADD:** Yes
**How are professors notified of LD:** By the student and the Program Director

## GENERAL ADMISSIONS INFORMATION

**Director of Admissions:** George Wolf

**Telephone:** 517-265-5161 ext. 4326

### ENTRANCE REQUIREMENTS
Total high school units required/recommended: 15 total units are recommended; 4 English recommended, 2 math recommended, 2 science recommended, 2 foreign language recommended, 2 social studies recommended, 2 history recommended. Minimum composite ACT score of 20, rank in top half of secondary school class, and minimum 2.5 GPA recommended.

**Application deadline:** August 15
**Notification:** Rolling

**SAT or ACT preferred:** Either
**SAT Avg:** 590V, 500M
**SAT II required:** Yes
**Average ACT:** 22
**Average GPA:** 3.1

**Graduated top 10% of class:** 24
**Graduated top 25% of class:** 42
**Graduated top 50% of class:** 84

## COLLEGE GRADUATION REQUIREMENTS

**Course waivers allowed:** Y/N
**Course substitutions allowed:** Y/N
**In what courses:** Depends on the situation

## ADDITIONAL INFORMATION

**Environment:** The school is located on 100 acres in a residential section of Michigan 35 miles northeast of Ann Arbor.

**Student Body**
  **Undergrad enrollment:** 1,049
  **Women:** 49%
  **Men:** 51%
  **In-state students:** 79%
  **Out-of-state:** 21%

**Cost Information**
  **In-state tuition:** $12,730
  **Out-of-state:** $12,730
  **Room & board:** $4,120

**Housing Information**
  **University housing:** Yes
  **Fraternity:** Yes
  **Sorority:** Yes
  **Living on campus:** 81%

  **Athletics:** NCAA Div. III

# MI AQUINAS COLLEGE

1607 Robinson Road SE, Grand Rapids, MI 49506-1799 • **Admissions:** 616-732-4460
**Fax:** 616-732-4431
**Email:** admissions@aquinas.edu • **Web:** www.aquinas.edu
**Support:** CS • **Institution:** 4 yr. Private

## LEARNING DISABILITY ADMISSIONS AND SERVICES

The mission of the the college is to provide a liberal arts education with a career orientation in a Catholic Christian context to all students capable of profiting from such an education regardless of gender, age, religion, racial background or disability. Aquinas College is committed to providing appropriate services and accommodations to students who demonstrate specific learning disabilities. The services are provided at no additional cost by the Academic Achievement Special Services on an individual need basis, so as to fulfill the Aquinas goal of enabling all students to reach their full academic potential. A counselor will help with academic advising, goal-setting, and career counseling with the students to improve those skills. Services are not mandatory. Students are encouraged to discuss their needs with a specialist to determine those services that will be most beneficial. DisABLED students succeed at Aquinas because they are self-motivated, capable, and wisely use the services as needed.

## LEARNING DISABILITY ADMISSIONS INFORMATION

**Program Name:** Academic Achievement Center
**Program Director:** Gary Kieff                    **Telephone:** 616-459-8281
**Contact Person:** Karen Broekstra

### ADMISSIONS

Students with a diagnosed learning disability are encouraged to take the ACT/SAT untimed if appropriate and to self-identify on the application. The admissions staff considers students on a number of factors, and if students include documentation with all other information it will be taken into consideration. The Academic Achievement Center will review documentation and provide a recommendation to the Admission Office. The final decision is made jointly by Admissions and the Academic Achievement Center for those students who self-disclose and provide documentation. Students must submit a minimum of 15 acceptable academic units from high school with a GPA of 2.5 or better. Once admitted, students are eligible to receive reasonable and appropriate services and accommodations. Alternative admission is available through Early Admissions, Transfer Students, Guest Status, Continuing Education, and Probationary Admit.

| | |
|---|---|
| **College entrance exams required:** No | **Untimed accepted:** N/A |
| **Course entrance requirements:** Yes | **Interview required:** Yes |
| **Diagnostic tests:** Yes | |
| **Documentation:** WAIS-R; WISC-R; WJ; SATA;TASK or TOWL-2: within 3 yrs. | |

### ADDITIONAL INFORMATION

Counselors help with academic advising, goal-setting, and career assessment. A specialist will assess the study skills of the student and work to improve these skills. Areas typically covered are textbook reading, notetaking, test preparation, test-taking strategies, and time management.  Special paper is available for notetaking, and taped texts and magazines are available.  Professional, one-to-one, basic skills tutoring is provided in writing, math, and computers. A specialist will work with students to set up a tutoring program when needed. Peer tutoring is available. Students are matched with other students with learning disabilities who serve as mentors. Memos are sent to professors which will introduce the student and provide a description of the disABILITY. Communication concerning the student's strengths, weaknesses, and learning style as well as coping mechanisms used previously are strongly encouraged. Specialists work with instructors to accommodate the student's individual test-taking needs.

| | |
|---|---|
| **Special education HS coursework accepted:** No | **Essay required:** No |
| **Special application required:** No | **Submitted to:** N/A |
| **# of applications submitted each year:** N/A | **# of applications accepted each year:** N/A |
| **# of students receiving LD services:** Approximately 40 | |

**Acceptance into program means acceptance into college:** Students must be accepted to the college first and then may be reviewed to receive services.

**Learning center:** Yes
**Kurzweil personal reader:** No
**LD specialists:** 1
**Allowed in exams:**
  **Calculator:** Yes
  **Dictionary:** Yes
  **Computer:** Yes
  **SpellCheck:** Yes

**Notetaker:** Yes
**Scribes:** Yes
**Proctors:** Yes
**Oral exams:** Yes
**Extended test time:** Yes
**Added cost:** None
**Distraction-free environ.:** Yes
**Tape recording in class:** Yes
**Books on tape:** Yes
**Taping of other books:** Yes

**Professional tutors:** 5
**Peer tutors:** 50
**Max. hrs/wk for services:** Unlimited
**Priority registration:** Yes
**Accomodations for students with ADD:** Yes
**How are professors notified of LD:** By the student and the Program Director

## GENERAL ADMISSIONS INFORMATION

**Director of Admissions:** Paula Romero          **Telephone:** 616-459-8281

### ENTRANCE REQUIREMENTS

Total high school units required/recommended: 15 total units are required; 4 English required, 3 math required, 3 science required, 4 social studies required. Rank in top 1/2 of secondary school class, and minimum 2.5 GPA required. Special requirements: TOEFL is required of all international students.

**Application deadline:** Rolling
**Notification:** Rolling

**SAT or ACT preferred:** ACT
**Average ACT:** 22
**Average GPA:** 3.2

**Graduated top 10% of class:** 20
**Graduated top 25% of class:** 46
**Graduated top 50% of class:** 76

## COLLEGE GRADUATION REQUIREMENTS

**Course waivers allowed:** Yes
**Course substitutions allowed:** Yes
**In what courses:** Depends on the individual case.

## ADDITIONAL INFORMATION

**Environment:** The college is located on 107 acres 6 miles east of Grand Rapids.

**Student Body**
  **Undergrad enrollment:** 1,825
  **Women:** 64%
  **Men:** 36%
  **In-state students:** 94%
  **Out-of-state:** 6%

**Cost Information**
  **In-state tuition:** $12,910
  **Out-of-state:** $12,910
  **Room & board:** $4,324

**Housing Information**
  **University housing:** Yes
  **Fraternity:** No
  **Sorority:** No
  **Living on campus:** 44%

  **Athletics:** NAIA

# MI CALVIN COLLEGE

3201 Burton Street, Southeast, Grand Rapids, MI 49546 • **Admissions:** 616-957-6106
**Fax:** 616-957-8551
**Email:** admissions@calvin.edu • **Web:** www.calvin.edu
**Support:** CS • **Institution:** 4 yr. Private

## LEARNING DISABILITY ADMISSIONS AND SERVICES

The mission of the Student Academic Services is to ensure that otherwise qualified students are able to benefit from a distinctly Christian education based on liberal arts. The Calvin community responds appropriately in a way that avoids handicapping the student with a disability.

## LEARNING DISABILITY ADMISSIONS INFORMATION

**Program Name:** Student Academic Services
**Program Director:** Dr. James Mackenzie
**Contact Person:** Sharon Juell/Margaret Vriend

**Telephone:** 616-957-6113

### ADMISSIONS

There are no special admissions for students with learning disabilities. Applicants are expected to have an ACT of 20 (19 English and 20 Math) or SAT of 810 (390 Verbal and 420 Math). Courses required include 3 yrs. English, 1 yr. algebra, 1 yr. geometry, and minimum of 2 yrs. in any two of the following fields: social science, language, or natural science; one of fields from math, foreign language, social science and natural science must include at least 3 yrs. of study. The Access Program is a conditional admission program for students who do not meet admission requirements, but show promise of developing into successful college students.

**College entrance exams required:** Yes
**Course entrance requirements:** Yes
**Diagnostic tests:** Yes
**Documentation:** Psycho-educational evaluations: within 3 years

**Untimed accepted:** Yes
**Interview required:** No

### ADDITIONAL INFORMATION

The Office of Student Academic Services is a learning center that is open to all students on campus. Skill classes are available in English, math and study skills. These classes may be taken for college credit. Services and accommodations are offered to undergraduate and graduate students. Students who self disclose and are admitted to the college are than reviewed for services.

**Special education HS coursework accepted:** Decided on an individual basis
**Essay required:** Yes
**Special application required:** No
**# of applications submitted each year:** 25
**# of students receiving LD services:** 75
**Acceptance into program means acceptance into college:** Students must be admitted to the college first and then may request services.

**Submitted to:** N/A
**# of applications accepted each year:** N/I

# LEARNING DISABILITY SERVICES

**Learning center:** Yes
**Kurzweil personal reader:** No
**LD specialists:** 1
**Allowed in exams:**
  **Calculator:** Y/N
  **Dictionary:** Y/N
  **Computer:** Y/N
  **SpellCheck:** Y/N

**Notetaker:** Yes
**Scribes:** Yes
**Proctors:** Yes
**Oral exams:** Y/N
**Extended test time:** Yes
**Added cost:** None
**Distraction-free environ.:** Y/N
**Tape recording in class:** Yes
**Books on tape:** Yes
**Taping of other books:** Yes

**Professional tutors:** 1
**Peer tutors:** 55
**Max. hrs/wk for services:**
Unlimited for LD
**Priority registration:** Yes
**Accomodations for students with ADD:** Yes
**How are professors notified of LD:** By the Director

# GENERAL ADMISSIONS INFORMATION

**Director of Admissions:** Dale D. Kuiper
**Telephone:** 616-957-6106

## ENTRANCE REQUIREMENTS

Total high school units required/recommended: 16 total units are required; 3 English required, 4 English recommended, 2 math required, 3 math recommended, 2 science required, 3 science recommended, 2 foreign language recommended, 3 social studies required. Required social studies units should include history. Required math units must include algebra and geometry. Minimum composite ACT score of 20 (combined SAT I score of 940) and minimum 2.5 GPA required. Special requirements: TOEFL is required of all international students.

**Application deadline:** Rolling
**Notification:** Rolling

**SAT or ACT preferred:** ACT
**SAT Avg:** 590V, 595M
**Average ACT:** 25
**Average GPA:** 3.5

**Graduated top 10% of class:** 30
**Graduated top 25% of class:** 56
**Graduated top 50% of class:** 85

# COLLEGE GRADUATION REQUIREMENTS

**Course waivers allowed:** No
**Course substitutions allowed:** Yes
**In what courses:** Foreign language with proper documentation.

# ADDITIONAL INFORMATION

**Environment:** The college is located on a 370-acre campus in a suburban area 7 miles southeast of Grand Rapids.

**Student Body**
  **Undergrad enrollment:** 3,993
  **Women:** 55%
  **Men:** 45%
  **In-state students:** 56%
  **Out-of-state:** 44%

**Cost Information**
  **In-state tuition:** $12,225
  **Out-of-state:** $12,225
  **Room & board:** $4,340

**Housing Information**
  **University housing:** Yes
  **Fraternity:** No
  **Sorority:** No
  **Living on campus:** 57%

  **Athletics:** NCAA Div. III

# FERRIS STATE UNIVERSITY

**MI**

901 State Street, Big Rapids, MI 49307 • **Admissions:** 616-592-2100 • **Fax:** 616-592-3944
**Email:** admissions@acto.ferris.edu • **Web:** about.ferris.edu
**Support:** CS • **Institution:** 2 yr. & 4 yr. Public

## LEARNING DISABILITY ADMISSIONS AND SERVICES

Ferris State is committed to a policy of equal opportunity for qualified students. The university believes to the fullest extent possible every student deserves the chance to have a positive college experience. Ferris State does not have a program for students with learning disabilities, but does provide a variety of support services and accommodations for students with documented learning disabilities which interfere with the learning process. Ferris State does not, however, attempt to rehabilitate learning disabilities. To obtain support services, an enrolled student needs to schedule an appointment with the Ferris special needs counselor, located in the Student Development Services Department. During this meeting, the student will complete a request for services application and a release form allowing the university to obtain a copy of the documentation of the disability. The disability documentation should be no more than five years old at the time of the application for services.

## LEARNING DISABILITY ADMISSIONS INFORMATION

**Program Name:** Special Needs Support Services
**Program Director:** Linda Travis, Dean University College
**Telephone:** 616-592-2216
**Contact Person:** Marcia C. Brayton or Joan Totten
**Telephone:** 616-592-3772

### ADMISSIONS

Students with learning disabilities submit the general application form, and should meet the same entrance criteria as all students. ACT scores are used for placement only. Students must be accepted and enrolled in order to receive support services. Sometimes a pre-admission interview is required if the GPA is questionable. In general students should have a 2.0 GPA, but some programs require a higher GPA and specific courses. The Special Needs Counselor is involved in the admissions decision when there is a question about academic preparedness.

**College entrance exams required:** Yes
**Course entrance requirements:** Yes
**Diagnostic tests:** Yes
**Documentation:** Psycho-educational Evaluation: within 5 years

**Untimed accepted:** Yes
**Interview required:** Recommended

### ADDITIONAL INFORMATION

Student Development Services offers tutoring for most courses. Flex tutoring is designed for in-depth clarification and review of subject material, and Workshop tutoring is designed for short-term, walk-in, assistance. The Collegiate Skills Program is designed to help academically under prepared students succeed in college by offering assistance in reading, writing, and study skills. Students also have an opportunity to develop skills in goal-setting, decision-making, and time management. The Academic Skills Center offers special instruction to assist students in improving their academic performance. Additionally the following are offered: admission assistance; early registration; counseling/career awareness; academic assistance; campus advocacy; case conferences with referring agencies; and referrals to appropriate university and community agencies.

**Special education HS coursework accepted:** Yes,
depending on GPA
**Special application required:** No
**# of applications submitted each year:** 50
**# of students receiving LD services:** 137

**Essay required:** No
**Submitted to:** N/A
**# of applications accepted each year:** Varies

**Acceptance into program means acceptance into college:** Students must be admitted to the university first and then may request services.

## LEARNING DISABILITY SERVICES

**Learning center:** No
**Kurzweil personal reader:** Yes
**LD specialists:** 1
**Allowed in exams:**
  **Calculator:** Y/N
  **Dictionary:** Yes
  **Computer:** Y/N
  **SpellCheck:** Yes

**Notetaker:** Yes
**Scribes:** Yes
**Proctors:** Yes
**Oral exams:** N/I
**Extended test time:** Yes
**Added cost:** None
**Distraction-free environ.:** Yes
**Tape recording in class:** Yes
**Books on tape:**
**Taping of other books:** Yes

**Professional tutors:** 10
**Peer tutors:** 140
**Max. hrs/wk for services:** Varies
**Priority registration:** Yes
**Accomodations for students with ADD:** Yes
**How are professors notified of LD:** By the student

## GENERAL ADMISSIONS INFORMATION

**Director of Admissions:** Don Mullens

**Telephone:** 616-592-2100

### ENTRANCE REQUIREMENTS

Total high school units required/recommended: 19 total units are recommended; 4 English recommended, 4 math recommended, 3 science recommended, 2 social studies recommended, 2 history recommended. Minimum 2.0 GPA required. Special requirements: TOEFL is required of all international students.

**Application deadline:** August 14
**Notification:** Rolling

**SAT or ACT preferred:** ACT
**ACT Required:** Yes
**Average ACT:** 19
**Average GPA:** 2.7

## COLLEGE GRADUATION REQUIREMENTS

**Course waivers allowed:** No
**Course substitutions allowed:** Varies
**In what courses:** N/I

## ADDITIONAL INFORMATION

**Environment:** The university is located on 600 acres 50 miles north of Grand Rapids.

**Student Body**
  **Undergrad enrollment:** 9,192
  **Women:** 44%
  **Men:** 56%
  **In-state students:** 95%
  **Out-of-state:** 5%

**Cost Information**
  **In-state tuition:** $3,812
  **Out-of-state:** $7,732
  **Room & board:** $4,792

**Housing Information**
  **University housing:** Yes
  **Fraternity:** Yes
  **Sorority:** Yes
  **Living on campus:** 45%

  **Athletics:** NCAA Div. II

# MICHIGAN STATE UNIVERSITY

East Lansing, MI 48824 • **Admissions:** 517-355-1855 • **Fax:** 517-353-7647
**Email:** ADM00@msu.edu • **Web:** www.msu.edu
**Support:** CS • **Institution:** 4 yr. Public

## LEARNING DISABILITY ADMISSIONS AND SERVICES

MSU is serious in their commitment to helping students no matter what the handicap. The OPHS mission is to be an advocate for the inclusion of handicapped students into the total university experience. The OPHS purpose is to respond to the needs of students by providing resources that equalize their chances for success, and support their full participation in all university programs, and to act as a resource for the university community and the community at large. OPHS has been responding to the needs of alternative learners for several years. Alternative learners are those individuals who exhibit a significant discrepancy between ability level and achievement in the school setting, which is not attributable to visual, hearing, or other factors. Alternative learners must provide recent documentation and history in the form of a school report, psychologist's assessment or certification by other recognized authority and must contain a clearly stated diagnosis. OPHS works to foster independence in the student's learning process. Staff specialists focus on freshmen and transfer students during their transition and adjustment to the university environment. As students learn to utilize appropriate accommodations and strategies, a greater sense of independence is achieved, although classroom accommodations may still be necessary. Eligibility for services requires documentation of the students' characteristics and history.

## LEARNING DISABILITY ADMISSIONS INFORMATION

**Program Name:** Office of Programs for Handicapper Students (OPHS)
**Program Director:** Marge Chmielewski          **Telephone:** 517-353-9642
**Contact Person:** Valerie Nilson

### ADMISSIONS

Admission for students with learning disabilities to the university is based on the same criteria as all other students. Students with learning disabilities are enrolled in the same programs and courses. MSU does not use a cut-off for test scores or GPA for admission. They look at the entire transcript, including the academic strength of the high school, the type of courses students have taken in high school, the trend of the grades, and the GPA of the academic, college preparatory courses. A letter of recommendation for students who may have borderline credentials could be included with the application. College Achievement Admissions Program (CAAP) is an alternative admissions procedure for students who have academic potential but who would be unable to realize that potential without special support services due to their economical, cultural, or educational background. Students with learning disabilities should not send any documentation to the Office of Admissions. All documentation should be sent to OPHS.

**College entrance exams required:** Yes          **Untimed accepted:** Yes
**Course entrance requirements:** Yes             **Interview required:** No
**Diagnostic tests:** Yes
**Documentation:** Refer to policy: within 3 years

### ADDITIONAL INFORMATION

The Alternative Learner Specialist is available by appointment to provide information to students. Accommodations include: taped texts; reading strategy tutoring and outlining technique tutoring; voice output computers; notetaking strategies and taping of lectures; extended time on tests, reader scribe, quiet room for tests, and test taking strategies; word processing and scribes; writing strategies tutoring, use of word processor; time management and study strategy tutoring; advocacy assistance from OPHS specialist and letters to professors; support groups through OPHS; and consultation with service providers.Various other resources on campus respond to the needs of alternative learners such as: Learning Resource Center; Office of Supportive Services; MSU Counseling Center; and Undergraduate University Division of Academic Advising.The Learning Resource Center works with students with learning characteristics on an individual basis to help the student learn to utilize appropriate learning strategies and to mediate their learning environment.

**Special education HS coursework accepted:** No          **Essay required:** No
**Special application required:** No                         **Submitted to:** N/A
**# of applications submitted each year:** N/A
**# of students receiving LD services:** 127              **# of applications accepted each year:** N/A

**Acceptance into program means acceptance into college:** Students must be admitted to the university first and then may request services.

**Learning center:** Yes
**Kurzweil personal reader:** Yes
**LD specialists:** 2
**Allowed in exams:**
  **Calculator:** Y/N
  **Dictionary:** Y/N
  **Computer:** Y/N
  **SpellCheck:** Y/N

**Notetaker:** Yes
**Scribes:** Yes
**Proctors:** Yes
**Oral exams:** Yes
**Extended test time:** Yes
**Added cost:** None
**Distraction-free environ.:** Yes
**Tape recording in class:** Yes
**Books on tape:** Yes
**Taping of other books:** Yes

**Professional tutors:** 1
**Peer tutors:** 8-10
**Max. hrs/wk for services:**
Unlimited
**Priority registration:** Yes
**Accomodations for students
with ADD:** Yes
**How are professors notified of
LD:** By the Student

## GENERAL ADMISSIONS INFORMATION

**Director of Admissions:** William Turner     **Telephone:** 517-355-8332

### ENTRANCE REQUIREMENTS

Total high school units required/recommended: 4 English recommended, 3 math recommended, 2 science recommended, 2 foreign language recommended, 3 social studies recommended, 1 history recommended. Minimum composite ACT score of 21. Special requirements: An audition is required for music program applicants.

**Application deadline:** Rolling
**Notification:** Rolling

**SAT or ACT preferred:** Either
**SAT Avg:** 540V, 550M
**SAT II required:** Yes
**Average ACT:** 23
**Average GPA:** 3.4

**Graduated top 10% of class:** 21
**Graduated top 25% of class:** 54
**Graduated top 50% of class:** 90

## COLLEGE GRADUATION REQUIREMENTS

**Course waivers allowed:** Y/N
**Course substitutions allowed:** Y/N
**In what courses:** Decided on a case-by-case basis.

## ADDITIONAL INFORMATION

**Environment:** Michigan State is located 1 hour from Ann Arbor and 1 1/2 hours from Detroit.

**Student Body**
  **Undergrad enrollment:** 32,318
  **Women:** 52%
  **Men:** 48%
  **In-state students:** 91%
  **Out-of-state:** 9%

**Cost Information**
  **In-state tuition:** $4,102
  **Out-of-state:** $11,167
  **Room & board:** $3,942

**Housing Information**
  **University housing:** Yes
  **Fraternity:** Yes
  **Sorority:** Yes
  **Living on campus:** 46%

  **Athletics:** NCAA Div. I

# UNIVERSITY OF MICHIGAN

1220 Student Activities Building, Ann Arbor, MI 48109-1316 • **Admissions:** 313-764-7433
**Fax:** 313-936-0740 • **Email:** ugadmiss@umich.edu • **Web:** www.umich.edu
**Support:** CS • **Institution:** 4 yr. Public

## LEARNING DISABILITY ADMISSIONS AND SERVICES

The philosophy of Services for Students with Disabilities is based on the legal actions described in Section 504 of the Rehabilitation Act of 1973. They are also dependent on self-advocacy of the students. They are "non-intrusive," giving the students the responsibility to seek out assistance. SSD offers selected student services which are not provided by other University of Michigan offices or outside organizations. SDS assists students in negotiating disability-related barriers to the pursuit of their education; strives to improve access to university programs, activities, and facilities; promotes increased awareness of disability issues on campus. SDS encourages inquiries for information. They will confidentially discuss concerns relating to a potential or recognized disability and, if requested, provide appropriate referrals for further assistance.

## LEARNING DISABILITY ADMISSIONS INFORMATION

**Program Name:** Services for Students with Disabilities (SSD)
**Program Director:** Stuart Segal                    **Telephone:** 313-763-3000
**Contact Person:** Same as above

### ADMISSIONS

Student with learning disabilities are expected to meet the same admission requirements as their peers. Courses required include: 4 yrs. English, 2 yrs. foreign language (4 yrs. recommended), 3 yrs. math (4 yrs. recommended including algebra, trig, and geometry, 2 yrs. biological and physical sciences (3 yrs. recommended), 3 yrs. history and the social sciences (2 yrs. history are recommended, including one year of U.S. history), 1 yr. hands-on computer study is strongly recommended, as is one year in the fine or performing arts, or equivalent preparation. Score range for the ACT is 25-29 and SAT 1170-1340. There is no set minimum for GPA as it is contingent on other factors. For students with learning disabilities, the admissions office will accept untimed test scores and letters of recommendation from LD specialists. When applying for admission to the University of Michigan, students with learning disabilities are encouraged to self-identify on the application form or by writing a cover letter.

| | |
|---|---|
| **College entrance exams required:** Yes | **Untimed accepted:** Yes |
| **Course entrance requirements:** Yes | **Interview required:** No |
| **Diagnostic tests:** For services | |
| **Documentation:** Psycho-educational testing: within 3 years | |

### ADDITIONAL INFORMATION

All accommodations are based on documented needs by the student. Services for students with learning disabilities include: volunteer readers; volunteer tutors; referral for psycho-educational assessments; selected course book loans for taping; Franklin Spellers; free cassette tapes; APH 4-track recorders; advocacy and referral; advocacy letters to professors; limited scholarships; newsletters; volunteer notetakers; carbonized notepaper; free photocopying of class notes; free course notes service for some classes; many students eligible for assisted earlier registration; adaptive technology; and library reading rooms. SSD also provides appropriate services for students with "other health related disabilities" such as ADHD. There is a special summer program at the university for high school students with learning disabilities. Services and accommodations are available for undergraduates and graduates.

| | |
|---|---|
| **Special education HS coursework accepted:** Yes | **Essay required:** Yes |
| **Special application required:** No | **Submitted to:** N/A |
| **# of applications submitted each year:** N/A | **# of applications accepted each year:** N/A |
| **# of students receiving LD services:** 250 | |

**Acceptance into program means acceptance into college:** Students must be admitted to the university and then reviewed for LD services.

# LEARNING DISABILITY SERVICES

**Learning center:** Yes
**Kurzweil personal reader:** Yes
**LD specialists:** 1
**Allowed in exams:**
  **Calculator:** Yes
  **Dictionary:** Yes
  **Computer:** Yes
  **SpellCheck:** Yes

**Notetaker:** Yes
**Scribes:** Yes
**Proctors:** No
**Oral exams:** No
**Extended test time:** Yes
**Added cost:** None
**Distraction-free environ.:** Yes
**Tape recording in class:** Yes
**Books on tape:** Yes
**Taping of other books:** Yes

**Professional tutors:** No
**Peer tutors:** No
**Max. hrs/wk for services:**
Depends on need
**Priority registration:** Yes
**Accomodations for students
with ADD:** Yes
**How are professors notified of
LD:** By the student

# GENERAL ADMISSIONS INFORMATION

**Director of Admissions:** Ted Spencer

**Telephone:** 313-647-0102

## ENTRANCE REQUIREMENTS

High school units required/recommended: 20 total units are recommended; 4 English recommended, 4 math recommended, 3 science recommended, 4 foreign language recommended, 3 social studies recommended, 1 history recommended.

**Application deadline:** 2/1
**Notification:** Rolling

**SAT or ACT preferred:** Both

# COLLEGE GRADUATION REQUIREMENTS

**Course waivers allowed:** No
**Course substitutions allowed:** Yes
**In what courses:** Foreign language substitution.

# ADDITIONAL INFORMATION

**Environment:** NR

**Student Body**
  **Undergrad enrollment:** 23,515
  **Women:** 49%
  **Men:** 51%
  **In-state students:** 72%
  **Out-of-state:** 28%

**Cost Information**
  **In-state tuition:** $5,850
  **Out-of-state:** $18,010

**Housing Information**
  **University housing:** Yes
  **Fraternity:** NR
  **Sorority:** NR
  **Living on campus:** 30%

  **Athletics:** NR

# NORTHERN MICHIGAN UNIVERSITY

MI

1401 Presque Isle Avenue, Marquette, MI 49855 • **Admissions:** 906-227-2650 • **Fax:** 906-227-1747
**Email:** admiss@nmu.edu • **Web:** www.nmu.edu
**Support:** CS • **Institution:** 4 yr. Public

## LEARNING DISABILITY ADMISSIONS AND SERVICES

Disability Services provides services and accommodations to all students with disabilities. The goals of Disability Services are to meet the individual needs of students. The Student Support Services is a multifaceted educational support project designed to assist students in completing their academic programs at Northern Michigan University. The Student Support Services professional staff, peer tutors, mentors and peer advisors, provide program participants with the individualized attention needed to successfully complete a college degree. This program is funded through the U.S. Department of Education. Federal Regulations require that all participants meet at least one of the following eligibility criteria: come from a low-income background; be a first generation college student; or have a physical or a learning disability.

## LEARNING DISABILITY ADMISSIONS INFORMATION

**Program Name:** Disability Services
**Program Director:** Lynn Walden, Coordinator          **Telephone:** 906-227-1550
**Contact Person:** Same as above

### ADMISSIONS

There is no special admissions for students with learning disabilities. All students submit the same general application, and are expected to have an ACT of 19 or higher and a high school GPA of at least 2.25 or above. There are no specific high school courses required for admissions although the university recommends 4 yrs. English, 4 yrs. math, 3 yrs. history/social studies, 3 yrs. science, 3 yrs. foreign language, 2 yrs. fine or performing arts, and 1 yr. computer instruction.

| | |
|---|---|
| **College entrance exams required:** Yes | **Untimed accepted:** Yes |
| **Course entrance requirements:** Yes | **Interview required:** No |
| **Diagnostic tests:** Yes | |
| **Documentation:** WAIS-R: tests of achievement; within 3 years | |

### ADDITIONAL INFORMATION

The Director of Disability Services works on a one-to-one basis with students as needed, and will also meet with students who do not have specific documentation if the they request assistance. Skill classes are offered in reading, writing, math, study skills, socio-cultural development, and interpersonal growth. No course waivers are granted for graduation requirements from NMU because the university views waivers as an institutional failure to educate its students with disabilities. Substitutions, however, are granted when appropriate. Services and accommodations are available for undergraduate and graduate students. Student Support Services provides each student with an individual program of educational support services including academic advising, basic skill building in reading, math and writing, counseling, career advisement, developmental skill build, mentoring, support groups and study groups, tutoring from paraprofessionals, specialized tutors, group tutoring or supplemental instruction, and workshops on personal development and study skills improvement. The e-mail address for Lynn Walden is lwalden@nmu.edu.

| | |
|---|---|
| **Special education HS coursework accepted:** Yes | **Essay required:** No |
| **Special application required:** Yes | **Submitted to:** Program Director |
| **# of applications submitted each year:** 80 | **# of applications accepted each year:** 80 |
| **# of students receiving LD services:** 80-170 | |

**Acceptance into program means acceptance into college:** Students must be admitted to the university first and then may request services.

**Learning center:** Yes
**Kurzweil personal reader:** Yes
**LD specialists:** 1
**Allowed in exams:**
  **Calculator:** Yes
  **Dictionary:** Yes
  **Computer:** Yes
  **SpellCheck:** Yes

**Notetaker:** Yes
**Scribes:** Yes
**Proctors:** Yes
**Oral exams:** Yes
**Extended test time:** Yes
**Added cost:** No
**Distraction-free environ.:** Yes
**Tape recording in class:** Yes
**Books on tape:** Yes
**Taping of other books:** Yes

**Professional tutors:** No
**Peer tutors:** 22
**Max. hrs/wk for services:** 2-4 hours per subject per/week. If additional is needed, outside agencies
**Priority registration:** Yes
**Accomodations for students with ADD:** Yes
**How are professors notified of LD:** By the Program Director

## GENERAL ADMISSIONS INFORMATION

**Director of Admissions:** Nancy Rehling

**Telephone:** 906-227-2650

### ENTRANCE REQUIREMENTS

Total high school units required/recommended: 4 English recommended, 4 math recommended, 3 history recommended, 3 science recommended, 3 foreign language recommended, 2 fine or performing arts recommended, 1 computer instruction recommended.

**Application deadline:** August 1
**Notification:** NR

**SAT or ACT preferred:** NR
**Average ACT:** 21
**Average GPA:** 2.85

## COLLEGE GRADUATION REQUIREMENTS

**Course waivers allowed:** No
**Course substitutions allowed:** Yes
**In what courses:** Substitutions permitted to fulfill graduation requirements with appropriate documentation.

## ADDITIONAL INFORMATION

**Environment:** The campus is located in an urban area about 300 miles north of Milwaukee, Wisconsin.

**Student Body**
  **Undergrad enrollment:** 7,144
  **Women:** 52%
  **Men:** 48%
  **In-state students:** 90%
  **Out-of-state:** 10%

**Cost Information**
  **In-state tuition:** $1,492
  **Out-of-state:** $5,264
  **Room & board:** $4,141

**Housing Information**
  **University housing:** Yes
  **Fraternity:** Yes
  **Sorority:** No
  **Living on campus:** 26%

  **Athletics:** NCAA Div. II

# SUOMI COLLEGE
Hancock, MI 49930

**Support:** SP • **Institution:** 2 yr. Private

## LEARNING DISABILITY ADMISSIONS AND SERVICES

Suomi's LD Program could change a student's life. Through the Program students will receive individual counseling, tutoring, academic advising, career counseling, and lots of support and encouragement. The LD Program is designed for students needing personalized attention and additional education before entering a liberal arts or career program. Careful academic planning is performed by the LD Director to ensure students carry a reasonable credit load that is sequential and well-balanced with attention to reading, written assignments and other course requirements. The faculty is supportive and written and verbal communication between the LD Director and faculty is frequent. Student performance is monitored and there are weekly scheduled meetings. The Director is the advisor and support person overseeing and coordinating each individual's program. Self-advocacy and compensatory skills are goals, rather then remediation. There is a 7-day orientation prior to freshman year. Advisors work with students during the orientation to plan the best course of study, provide advice and assurance that the student will get what is needed in the program, provide encouragement, and may even be able to match the student with professors whose style of teaching best complements the student's style of learning.

## LEARNING DISABILITY ADMISSIONS INFORMATION

**Program Name:** Learning Disabilities Program
**Program Director:** Carol Bates
**Contact Person:** Same as above

**Telephone:** 906-487-7258

### ADMISSIONS

General admission requirements must be met by all applicants. In addition, students with learning disabilities should submit an evaluation, within the last three years, documenting the learning disability; an IEP; and a handwritten essay by the student describing the learning disability. Sometimes a telephone interview or visitation is requested to help determine eligibility for the Program. An applicant must have the academic ability and background for work on a college level. Each applicant is evaluated individually by the Director of the Program and the admissions staff. Depending on the high school information provided, some students will be given the dual designation of LD/Pro-College if the Director of the Program feels the student may be "at risk."

**College entrance exams required:** No
**Course entrance requirements:** Yes
**Diagnostic tests:** Yes
**Documentation:** WAIS-R; WISC-R; W-J: within 3 years

**Untimed accepted:** N/A
**Interview required:** Recommended

### ADDITIONAL INFORMATION

The Program Director provides professors with a disability data sheet to request accommodations and also meets individually with faculty regarding student needs. Special services offered include: alternative testing; individual counseling; career counseling; auxiliary aids and services; academic advising; computer-based instruction; group and individualized courses; support from the Teaching/Learning Center; and support from Student Support Services. The Director of the Program is certified to teach students with learning disabilities, and will help them set up a plan for growth and strength in that areas that are challenging. Students will meet with their advisors once a week or for as much or as little time as is needed. Students may take skills classes, for non-college credit, in Reading and Study Strategies. There is a one week required summer orientation program for incoming freshmen.

**Special education HS coursework accepted:** No
**Special application required:** No
**# of applications submitted each year:** 15-25
**# of students receiving LD services:** 28

**Essay required:** No
**Submitted to:** N/A
**# of applications accepted each year:** 15-20

**Acceptance into program means acceptance into college:** The students are reviewed jointly by the LD Program and the Office of Admission to reach an admission decision.

## LEARNING DISABILITY SERVICES

Learning center: No
Kurzweil personal reader: Yes
LD specialists: 1
Allowed in exams:
  Calculator: Yes
  Dictionary: Y/N
  Computer: Yes
  SpellCheck: Yes

Notetaker: Yes
Scribes: Yes
Proctors: Yes
Oral exams: Yes
Extended test time: Yes
Added cost: No
Distraction-free environ.: Yes
Tape recording in class: Yes
Books on tape: Yes
Taping of other books: No

Professional tutors: 9
Peer tutors: 14
Max. hrs/wk for services:
Unlimited
Priority registration: No
Accomodations for students
with ADD: Yes
How are professors notified of
LD: By the student and the
Program Director

## GENERAL ADMISSIONS INFORMATION

Director of Admissions: Greg Timberlake

Telephone: 906-487-7310

### ENTRANCE REQUIREMENTS

An applicant must have the academic ability and background for work on a college level.

Application deadline: Rolling
Notification: NR

SAT or ACT preferred: Not
required

## COLLEGE GRADUATION REQUIREMENTS

Course waivers allowed: No
Course substitutions allowed: No
In what courses: N/A

## ADDITIONAL INFORMATION

Environment: The school is located in a beautiful and rugged area of the Upper Peninsula of Michigan.

Student Body
  Undergrad enrollment: 450
  Women: 69%
  Men: 31%
  In-state students: 76%
  Out-of-state: 24%

Cost Information
  In-state tuition: $9,500
  Out-of-state: $9,500

Housing Information
  University housing: Yes
  Fraternity: No
  Sorority: No
  Living on campus: 45%

  Athletics: Intramural sports

# AUGSBURG COLLEGE

MN

2211 Riverside Avenue South, Minneapolis, MN 55454 • **Admissions:** 612-330-1001
**Fax:** 612-330-1590
**Email:** daniels@augsburg.edu • **Web:** www.augsburg.edu
**Support:** SP • **Institution:** 4 yr. Private

## LEARNING DISABILITY ADMISSIONS AND SERVICES

The aim of the CLASS Program is to assist students in developing self-confidence, independence and self-advocacy skills in an academic setting. Augsburg has a commitment to recruit, retain and graduate students with learning disabilities who demonstrate the willingness and ability to participate in college-level learning. CLASS Program goals include: maximizing academic performance; assisting students in improving cognitive, affective, and psychomotor domains in order to become independent and confident learners; assist students in developing positive attitudes and confidence in their ability to learn; maintain standards of academic excellence among the students being served; and to advocate responsibility so that faculty, staff, and students gain a greater knowledge of and appreciation for the strengths and needs of the students served.

## LEARNING DISABILITY ADMISSIONS INFORMATION

**Program Name:** Center for Learning and Adaptive Student Services (CLASS)
**Program Director:** Sue Carlson                    **Telephone:** 612-330-1648
**Contact Person:** Same as above

### ADMISSIONS

Applicants with LD must first complete the Augsburg application form. Students with a 2.5 GPA, top 50% of class or a 20 ACT are automatically admissible. The CLASS Program can recommend admission for students who do not meet all criteria, but have the potential and desire to succeed with accommodations. Students complete a brief application form and submit LD documentation directly to CLASS. The written diagnostic report must contain a definite statement that a LD is present. Specific recommendations about accommodations and academic strengths and weaknesses are valuable. A formal interview will be scheduled to allow the student to provide information and receive more details about accommodations at Augsburg. Students admitted on probation or as high risk students must take a study skills class and earn 2.0 for the first year.

| | |
|---|---|
| **College entrance exams required:** Yes | **Untimed accepted:** Yes |
| **Course entrance requirements:** Yes | **Interview required:** Yes |
| **Diagnostic tests:** Yes | |

**Documentation:** WAIS-R; W-J- R (I.Q. and achievement): within 3 years

### ADDITIONAL INFORMATION

Students admitted into the Program are given individual assistance from application through graduation by learning specialists. Academic support includes: assistance with registration and advising; guidance with course work; assistance with writing; instruction in learning strategies and compensatory techniques; help with improving basic skills; advocacy; and support/resource group. Accommodations include: testing arrangements; access to computers and training; taped texts; the use of an Open Book Unbound Scanner; assistance in securing notetakers; assistance in obtaining tutors; and foreign language alternatives. There are also many community resources available. Services and accommodations are available for undergraduate and graduate students.

| | |
|---|---|
| **Special education HS coursework accepted:** Yes | **Essay required:** Yes |
| **Special application required:** Yes | **Submitted to:** CLASS Program |
| **# of applications submitted each year:** 90 | **# of applications accepted each year:** 46 |
| **# of students receiving LD services:** 115 | |

**Acceptance into program means acceptance into college:** Students must be accepted to the college first and then may request services.

## LEARNING DISABILITY SERVICES

**Learning center:** Yes
**Kurzweil personal reader:** Y/N
**LD specialists:** 3
**Allowed in exams:**
  **Calculator:** Yes
  **Dictionary:** Y/N
  **Computer:** Yes
  **SpellCheck:** Yes

**Notetaker:** Yes
**Scribes:** Yes
**Proctors:** Yes
**Oral exams:** Yes
**Extended test time:** Yes
**Added cost:** None
**Distraction-free environ.:** Yes
**Tape recording in class:** Yes
**Books on tape:** Yes
**Taping of other books:** Yes

**Professional tutors:** No
**Peer tutors:** 80
**Max. hrs/wk for services:** As needed
**Priority registration:** No
**Accomodations for students with ADD:** Yes
**How are professors notified of LD:** By the student

## GENERAL ADMISSIONS INFORMATION

**Director of Admissions:** Sally Daniels          **Telephone:** 612-330-1001

### ENTRANCE REQUIREMENTS

Total high school units required/recommended: 18 total units are recommended; 4 English recommended, 3 math recommended, 3 science recommended, 2 social studies recommended, 2 history recommended. Minimum composite ACT score of 20, rank in top half of secondary school class, and minimum 2.5 GPA recommended.

**Application deadline:** August 1
**Notification:** Rolling

**SAT or ACT preferred:** ACT
**SAT Avg:** 533V, 547M
**Average ACT:** 22
**Average GPA:** 3.18

**Graduated top 10% of class:** 21
**Graduated top 25% of class:** 44
**Graduated top 50% of class:** 73

## COLLEGE GRADUATION REQUIREMENTS

**Course waivers allowed:** Yes
**Course substitutions allowed:** Yes
**In what courses:** Foreign language and math.

## ADDITIONAL INFORMATION

**Environment:** The college is located on 25 acres near downtown Minneapolis.

**Student Body**
  **Undergrad enrollment:** 1,501
  **Women:** 54%
  **Men:** 46%
  **In-state students:** 83%
  **Out-of-state:** 17%

**Cost Information**
  **In-state tuition:** $13,850
  **Out-of-state:** $13,850
  **Room & board:** $4,986

**Housing Information**
  **University housing:** Yes
  **Fraternity:** No
  **Sorority:** No
  **Living on campus:** 45%

  **Athletics:** NCAA Div. III

# UNIVERSITY OF MINNESOTA-DULUTH

**MN**

10 University Drive, Duluth, MN 55812 • **Admissions:** 218-726-7171 • **Fax:** 218-726-6394
**Email:** umdadmis@d.umn.edu • **Web:** www.d.umn.edu
**Support:** CS • **Institution:** 4 yr. Public

## LEARNING DISABILITY ADMISSIONS AND SERVICES

The Learning Disabilities Program strives to help students understand their disability and be able to clearly explain how it affects them academically, and to be able to request the accommodations needed. The Learning Disability Program also provides guidance, advocacy and assistance to students with documented learning disabilities, so that they can achieve to their fullest potential. Services and accommodations are provided on an individual and flexible basis. Once admitted, students needing special services have the responsibility of contacting the Access Center. Services include skills enhancement courses, assistance in arranging alternative testing and evaluation methods, priority registration, support groups, proofreading of written projects, advocacy with faculty, and support groups to meet expressed needs of students.

## LEARNING DISABILITY ADMISSIONS INFORMATION

**Program Name:** Learning Disabilities Program
**Program Director:** Penny Cragun                          **Telephone:** 218-726-8727
**Contact Person:** Judy Bromen, LD Coordinator            **Telephone:** 218-726-7965

### ADMISSIONS

All students must meet the regular university admission requirements. Admission criteria includes an ACT of 19+ and rank in the top 1/3 of the high school class. Applicants who rank in the 40-65% of their class (or below) are reviewed individually. Students with an identified learning disability may have their applications evaluated by a committee of admissions and disability services personnel. These students must provide documentation of a learning disability from high school, independent psychological testing clinic or from a learning evaluation center. The admission decision is made jointly by the Program Director and the Director of Admission. Students who do not qualify for admission may take evening classes through Continuing Education. If they maintain a GPA of 2.0 or better they may be admitted to the regular college program.

**College entrance exams required:** Yes              **Untimed accepted:** Yes
**Course entrance requirements:** Yes                **Interview required:** No
**Diagnostic tests:** Yes
**Documentation:** Many standardized test results are acceptable: within 3 years

### ADDITIONAL INFORMATION

Any student admitted to the university with a verified learning disability is eligible for support services from the Access Center. There are skills enhancement courses in writing, math, and study strategies offered through the Achievement Center. At the beginning of each quarter students needing special services must contact the Access Center and also notify instructors of special needs. A Reading Edge machine is available for all students in the library. Services and accommodations are available for undergraduate and graduate students.

**Special education HS coursework accepted:** No       **Essay required:** No
**Special application required:** No                   **Submitted to:** N/A
**# of applications submitted each year:** N/A         **# of applications accepted each year:** No limit
**# of students receiving LD services:** 100
**Acceptance into program means acceptance into college:** Students must be admitted to the university first and then may request services.

**Learning center:** No
**Kurzweil personal reader:** No
**LD specialists:** 2
**Allowed in exams:**
  **Calculator:** Y/N
  **Dictionary:** Y/N
  **Computer:** Y/N
  **SpellCheck:** Y/N

**Notetaker:** Yes
**Scribes:** Yes
**Proctors:** Yes
**Oral exams:** Yes
**Extended test time:** Yes
**Added cost:** None
**Distraction-free environ.:** Yes
**Tape recording in class:** Yes
**Books on tape:** Yes
**Taping of other books:** Yes

**Professional tutors:** N/I
**Peer tutors:** 30
**Max. hrs/wk for services:** 5 hours of tutoring
**Priority registration:** Yes
**Accomodations for students with ADD:** Yes
**How are professors notified of LD:** By the student

## GENERAL ADMISSIONS INFORMATION

**Director of Admissions:** Gerald Allen          **Telephone:** 218-726-8801

### ENTRANCE REQUIREMENTS

Total high school units required/recommended: 14 total units are required; 4 English required, 3 math required, 3 science required, 2 foreign language required, 2 social studies required. Automatic admission for applicants ranking in top 35% of secondary school class. Selective admission to applicants in 40th to 64th percentile of secondary school class with minimum composite ACT score of 19.

**Application deadline:** August 1
**Notification:** Rolling

**SAT or ACT preferred:** ACT
**ACT Required:** Yes
**Average ACT:** 22
**Average GPA:** 70

**Graduated top 10% of class:** 16
**Graduated top 25% of class:** 46
**Graduated top 50% of class:** 84

## COLLEGE GRADUATION REQUIREMENTS

**Course waivers allowed:** By petition
**Course substitutions allowed:** By petition
**In what courses:** This is a case-by-case basis. math and foreign language courses have been waived after the student has made an honest attempt at mastery.

## ADDITIONAL INFORMATION

**Environment:** The university is located on a 250-acre campus in Duluth.

**Student Body**
  **Undergrad enrollment:** 7,100
  **Women:** 47%
  **Men:** 53%
  **In-state students:** 88%
  **Out-of-state:** 12%

**Cost Information**
  **In-state tuition:** $3,850
  **Out-of-state:** $11,004
  **Room & board:** $3,912

**Housing Information**
  **University housing:** Yes
  **Fraternity:** No
  **Sorority:** No
  **Living on campus:** 37%

  **Athletics:** NAIA

# MOORHEAD STATE UNIVERSITY

**MN**

1104 Seventh Avenue South, Moorhead, MN 56563 • **Admissions:** 218-236-2161 • **Fax:** 218-236-2168
Web: www.moorhead.msus.edu
**Support:** S • **Institution:** 4 yr. Public

## LEARNING DISABILITY ADMISSIONS AND SERVICES

The university is committed to ensuring that all students have equal access to programs and services. The office of Services to Students with Disabilities addresses the needs of students who have disabilities. Any student with a documented learning disability and who is a student at Moorhead State is eligible for services.

## LEARNING DISABILITY ADMISSIONS INFORMATION

**Program Name:** Disability Services
**Program Director:** Paula Ahles                     **Telephone:** 218-299-5859
**Contact Person:** Same as above

### ADMISSIONS

There is no special admissions for students with learning disabilities. All students must meet the same criteria including: a class rank in the top 50% or achieve the following scores on any of the standardized college admission tests; ACT 21+, PSAT 90+, or SAT 900+. They must also have 4 yrs. English, 3 yrs. math (2 algebra & 1 geometry), 3 yrs. science (1 biological, 1 physical science and at least one must include significant laboratory experiences), 3 yrs. social studies (including American history and at least 1 course that includes significant emphasis on geography), 3 electives chosen from at least 2 of the following; world language, world culture, visual and performing arts. The New Center offers an alternative way to begin university studies to students who reside within the MSU service region.

**College entrance exams required:** Yes          **Untimed accepted:** Yes
**Course entrance requirements:** Yes             **Interview required:** No
**Diagnostic tests:** Yes
**Documentation:** Flexible; Prefer within 3 years

### ADDITIONAL INFORMATION

Skills courses are offered in study skills and test anxiety, and students may earn credits for these courses. Services and accommodations are available for undergraduate and graduate students.

**Special education HS coursework accepted:** Y/N          **Essay required:** Yes, for special admission
**Special application required:** No                       **Submitted to:** N/A
**# of applications submitted each year:** N/I            **# of applications accepted each year:** N/A
**# of students receiving LD services:** 30-50
**Acceptance into program means acceptance into college:** Students must be accepted to the university first and then may request services.

## LEARNING DISABILITY SERVICES

**Learning center:** No
**Kurzweil personal reader:** No
**LD specialists:** No
**Allowed in exams:**
  **Calculator:** Yes
  **Dictionary:** Yes
  **Computer:** Yes
  **SpellCheck:** Yes

**Notetaker:** Yes
**Scribes:** Yes
**Proctors:** Yes
**Oral exams:** Yes
**Extended test time:** Yes
**Added cost:** None
**Distraction-free environ.:** Yes
**Tape recording in class:** Yes
**Books on tape:** Yes
**Taping of other books:** NR

**Professional tutors:** No
**Peer tutors:** Yes
**Max. hrs/wk for services:** Varies
**Priority registration:** Y/N
**Accomodations for students with ADD:** Yes
**How are professors notified of LD:** By the student and the Director

## GENERAL ADMISSIONS INFORMATION

**Director of Admissions:** Jean Lange          **Telephone:** 218-236-2161

### ENTRANCE REQUIREMENTS

Total high school units required/recommended: 13 total units are required; 4 English required, 3 math required, 3 science required, 3 social studies required. Elective units may be chosen from world languages, world culture, and the arts; applicants must take at least three units in at least two of these areas. Minimum composite ACT score of 21 (combined PSAT score of 90 or combined SAT I score of 900) and rank in top half of secondary school class required. Special requirements: An RN is required for nursing program applicants. TOEFL is required of all international students.

**Application deadline:** August 7
**Notification:** Rolling

**SAT or ACT preferred:** ACT
**SAT II required:** Yes
**Average ACT:** 22

**Graduated top 10% of class:** 11
**Graduated top 25% of class:** 11
**Graduated top 50% of class:** 11

## COLLEGE GRADUATION REQUIREMENTS

**Course waivers allowed:** Yes
**Course substitutions allowed:** Yes
**In what courses:** None specified. The student would appeal and their appeal would be considered.

## ADDITIONAL INFORMATION

**Environment:** A suburban campus located 240 miles northwest of Minneapolis.

**Student Body**
  **Undergrad enrollment:** 5,917
  **Women:** 61%
  **Men:** 39%
  **In-state students:** 60%
  **Out-of-state:** 40%

**Cost Information**
  **In-state tuition:** $2,355
  **Out-of-state:** $5,307
  **Room & board:** $2,958

**Housing Information**
  **University housing:** Yes
  **Fraternity:** Yes
  **Sorority:** Yes
  **Living on campus:** 26%

  **Athletics:** NAIA

# THE COLLEGE OF SAINT CATHERINE

**MN**

2004 Randolph Avenue, Saint Paul, MN 55105 • **Admissions:** 612-690-6505 • **Fax:** 612-690-8880
**Email:** stkate@stkate.edu
**Support:** CS • **Institution:** 4 yr. Private

## LEARNING DISABILITY ADMISSIONS AND SERVICES

The O'Neill Learning Center houses the special learning programs for students with learning disabilities. Accommodations are made on an individual basis. The centers' staff work with students and departments to provide reasonable and appropriate accommodations for access to and fair treatment in college programs and activities. The Learning Center and Counseling Center offer staff in-services to help them accommodate students with learning disabilities. A reduced course load is strongly suggested for first semester. Services include information sessions to access services, faculty consultations, and early registration. While the college does not have all the resources that students with learning disabilities may need, it is committed to responding flexibly to individual needs.

## LEARNING DISABILITY ADMISSIONS INFORMATION

**Program Name:** Services for Students with Disabilities
**Program Director:** Elaine McDonough
**Contact Person:** Barbara Mandel

**Telephone:** 612-690-6706

### ADMISSIONS

There is no special admission procedure for students with learning disabilities, although they tend to give special consideration if students self-disclose this information. The Director of Services for Students with Disabilities serves on the Admission Committee. The College of St. Catherine does not discriminate on the basis of disability in admission.

**College entrance exams required:** Yes
**Course entrance requirements:** Yes
**Diagnostic tests:** Yes
**Documentation:** Psycho-educational evaluation: within 3 years

**Untimed accepted:** Yes
**Interview required:** No

### ADDITIONAL INFORMATION

Drop-in help is available on a one-to-one basis from student assistants in writing, study skills, and time management. Students with learning disabilities also have access to support groups and practice in self-advocacy.

**Special education HS coursework accepted:** Yes
**Special application required:** No
**# of applications submitted each year:** N/I
**# of students receiving LD services:** 45
**Acceptance into program means acceptance into college:** Students must be admitted to the college first and then may request services.

**Essay required:** No
**Submitted to:** N/A
**# of applications accepted each year:** N/A

# LEARNING DISABILITY SERVICES

**Learning center:** Yes
**Kurzweil personal reader:** Yes
**LD specialists:** 2
**Allowed in exams:**
  **Calculator:** Yes
  **Dictionary:** Yes
  **Computer:** Yes
  **SpellCheck:** Yes

**Notetaker:** Yes
**Scribes:** Yes
**Proctors:** Yes
**Oral exams:** Yes
**Extended test time:** Yes
**Added cost:** None
**Distraction-free environ.:** Yes
**Tape recording in class:** Yes
**Books on tape:** RFB
**Taping of other books:** No

**Professional tutors:** N/I
**Peer tutors:** 13
**Max. hrs/wk for services:** No limit
**Priority registration:** Yes
**Accomodations for students with ADD:** Yes
**How are professors notified of LD:** By the student and the Program Director

# GENERAL ADMISSIONS INFORMATION

**Director of Admissions:** Mary Dockhn

**Telephone:** 612-690-6505

## ENTRANCE REQUIREMENTS

Total high school units required/recommended: 19 total units are recommended; 4 English recommended, 3 math recommended, 3 science recommended, 2 foreign language recommended, 3 social studies recommended, 1 history recommended.

**Application deadline:** August 15
**Notification:** Rolling

**SAT or ACT preferred:** Either
**SAT Avg:** 580V, 549M
**SAT II required:** Yes
**Average ACT:** 23
**Average GPA:** 3.4

**Graduated top 10% of class:** 21
**Graduated top 25% of class:** 41
**Graduated top 50% of class:** 80

# COLLEGE GRADUATION REQUIREMENTS

**Course waivers allowed:** No
**Course substitutions allowed:** Yes
**In what courses:** Foreign language

# ADDITIONAL INFORMATION

**Environment:** The college is located on 110 acres in an urban area in central St. Paul.

**Student Body**
  **Undergrad enrollment:** 2,198
  **Women:** 100%
  **Men:** 0%
  **In-state students:** 86%
  **Out-of-state:** 14%

**Cost Information**
  **In-state tuition:** $12,960
  **Out-of-state:** $12,960
  **Room & board:** $4,282

**Housing Information**
  **University housing:** Yes
  **Fraternity:** No
  **Sorority:** No
  **Living on campus:** 39%

  **Athletics:** NCAA Div. III

# UNIVERSITY OF SOUTHERN MISSISSIPPI

**MS**

Box 5166 Southern Station, Hattiesburg, MS 39406 • **Admissions:** 601-266-5000
**Fax:** 601-266-5148 • **Email:** admissions@usm.edu • **Web:** www.usm.edu
**Support:** CS • **Institution:** 4 yr. Public

## LEARNING DISABILITY ADMISSIONS AND SERVICES

The philosophy of USM is to provide services to students with learning disabilities to give them the maximum opportunity to complete a college education. The staff works closely with the Department of Special Education to assess the students' needs, provide funding for tutors and notetakers, and consulting with the academic faculty and staff to increase awareness of the students' needs and program objectives. The goal is to assist students in maintaining the required 2.0 GPA to remain in college.

## LEARNING DISABILITY ADMISSIONS INFORMATION

**Program Name:** Office of Services for Students with Disabilities (OSSD)
**Program Director:** Sheryl Glausier, Ph.D            **Telephone:** 601-266-5024
**Contact Person:** Same as above

### ADMISSIONS

There is no special application for students with learning disabilities. The admission decision for students with Learning Disabilities is made by the Director of OSSD. An interview is not required, but preferred. The university offers a pre-admission summer program.

**College entrance exams required:** Yes            **Untimed accepted:** Yes
**Course entrance requirements:** Yes               **Interview required:** Yes
**Diagnostic tests:** No
**Documentation:** Testing is done on campus

### ADDITIONAL INFORMATION

In order to receive reasonable accommodations for a disability, students must file an application with OSSD and provide current documentation of a disability. After an application is filed, students schedule an appointment with the OSSD Coordinator, complete an Intake Form, and establish a plan for reasonable accommodations and services. The OSSD helps students locate tutors, notetakers and other ancillary aids for their classwork. The office works with Vocational Rehabilitation in order to pay for these services. The office staff works with students on a one-to-one basis in order to determine how they learn best. There are remedial programs in math, writing and reading.

**Special education HS coursework accepted:** No            **Essay required:** No
**Special application required:** No                          **Submitted to:** N/A
**# of applications submitted each year:** N/A              **# of applications accepted each year:** N/A
**# of students receiving LD services:** N/A
**Acceptance into program means acceptance into college:** Students must be admitted and enrolled in the university and the may request services.

## LEARNING DISABILITY SERVICES

**Learning center:** Yes
**Kurzweil personal reader:** No
**LD specialists:** Yes
**Allowed in exams:**
  **Calculator:** Y/N
  **Dictionary:** No
  **Computer:** Yes
  **SpellCheck:** No

**Notetaker:** Yes
**Scribes:** Yes
**Proctors:** Yes
**Oral exams:** Yes
**Extended test time:** Yes
**Added cost:** $5 per/hour
**Distraction-free environ.:** Yes
**Tape recording in class:** Yes
**Books on tape:** Yes
**Taping of other books:** No

**Professional tutors:** Yes
**Peer tutors:** Yes
**Max. hrs/wk for services:** Varies
**Priority registration:** Yes
**Accomodations for students
with ADD:** Yes
**How are professors notified of
LD:** By the student

## GENERAL ADMISSIONS INFORMATION

**Director of Admissions:** Wayne Pife

**Telephone:** 601-266-5006

### ENTRANCE REQUIREMENTS

Total high school units required/recommended: 16 total units are required; 4 English required, 3 math required, 3 science required, 3 social studies required. One of the following is required: completion of the College Preparatory Curriculum (CPC) with a minimum 3.2 GPA; completion of the CPC with a minimum 2.5 GPA or rank in top half of class, and minimum composite ACT score of 16 (combined SAT I score of 770); completion of the CPC with a minimum 2.0 GPA and minimum composite ACT score of 18 (combined SAT I score of 850). Special requirements: An audition is required for music program applicants. TOEFL is required of all international students. Separate applications required of nursing school and honors college applicants.

**Application deadline:** August 10
**Notification:** Rolling

**SAT or ACT preferred:** ACT
**Average ACT:** 22

**Graduated top 10% of class:** 20
**Graduated top 25% of class:** 51
**Graduated top 50% of class:** 87

## COLLEGE GRADUATION REQUIREMENTS

**Course waivers allowed:** No
**Course substitutions allowed:** Yes
**In what courses:** Varies among majors.

## ADDITIONAL INFORMATION

**Environment:** The university is located on 840 acres in a small city 90 miles southeast of Jackson.

**Student Body**
  **Undergrad enrollment:** 10,647
  **Women:** 57%
  **Men:** 43%
  **In-state students:** 80%
  **Out-of-state:** 20%

**Cost Information**
  **In-state tuition:** $2,590
  **Out-of-state:** $5,410
  **Room & board:** $2,490

**Housing Information**
  **University housing:** Yes
  **Fraternity:** Yes
  **Sorority:** Yes
  **Living on campus:** 35%

  **Athletics:** NCAA Div. I

# MO EVANGEL COLLEGE

1111 North Glenstone, Springfield, MO 65802 • **Admissions:** 417-865-2811 • **Fax:** 417-865-9599
**Email:** admissions@mail9.evangel.edu • **Web:** www.evangel.edu
**Support:** CS • **Institution:** 4 yr. Private

## LEARNING DISABILITY ADMISSIONS AND SERVICES

The Center for Effective Learning is a place where caring people provide resources to enhance learning abilities. The philosophy of the Center for Effective Learning is to provide opportunities for all students to learn. "Learning is leaving one's self open for growth expanding one's life to include new thoughts, ideas, and dreams." "Learning is an ever-widening circle reaching farther and farther, touching more and more." "Learning is a foundation for an enriched life...which—even at its close—will not look back, but continually forward." (Syler, Director of the Center for Effective Learning). If students know how to learn, then they can learn the material for all their classes. The department focuses on learning/study skills, tutoring and individual counseling. The center offers study skills classes that will give students the necessary skills to function better academically, at the college level and in their life after college. The requirements for the skills classes are 3 hours of time weekly, creative homework, and most work done in the class. Current research at the college indicates that students who actively participate in these skill classes will improve their grade point average.

## LEARNING DISABILITY ADMISSIONS INFORMATION

**Program Name:** Center for Effective Learning
**Program Director:** Eleanor G. Syler, Ed.D.          **Telephone:** 417-865-2815 ext.7232
**Contact Person:** Same as above

### ADMISSIONS

There is no special application for students with learning disabilities. All students must meet the same admission criteria. Evangel College looks at the completed application, the ACT score, pastor's recommendation, and high school recommendation. Special admission is offered to students with ACT scores lower than 17. These students will be enrolled in Study Skills as well as other proficiency classes.

**College entrance exams required:** Yes          **Untimed accepted:** Yes
**Course entrance requirements:** Yes          **Interview required:** No
**Diagnostic tests:** No
**Documentation:** N/A

### ADDITIONAL INFORMATION

Some study skills classes are required for students who are admitted conditionally. The Center for Effective Learning is a special learning center which provides services for students with learning disabilities. There is a minimum of 13 credits required each semester. The center offers resources in such topics as: personal growth; goal setting; self-concept enrichment; stress management; memory and concentration; test taking; underlining; notetaking; outlining; reading a textbook; research; writing term papers; time scheduling; reading efficiency; and vocabulary. Additional resources include: the design and implementation of individualized programs with an instructor; personal professional counseling at no charge; career counseling with the Director of Career Development Services; reading labs for increased reading speed; and tutoring in other classes at no charge.

**Special education HS coursework accepted:** Yes, if meets the current criteria
**Essay required:** Yes
**Special application required:** No          **Submitted to:** N/A
**# of applications submitted each year:** N/A          **# of applications accepted each year:** N/A
**# of students receiving LD services:** 60-70 yearly
**Acceptance into program means acceptance into college:** Students must be admitted to the college first and then may request LD services.

**Learning center:** Yes
**Kurzweil personal reader:** No
**LD specialists:** 3
**Allowed in exams:**
  **Calculator:** Yes
  **Dictionary:** Yes
  **Computer:** Yes
  **SpellCheck:** Yes

**Notetaker:** No
**Scribes:** Yes
**Proctors:** Yes
**Oral exams:** Yes
**Extended test time:** Yes
**Added cost:** None
**Distraction-free environ.:** Yes
**Tape recording in class:** Yes
**Books on tape:** RFB
**Taping of other books:** Yes

**Professional tutors:** 2
**Peer tutors:** 6
**Max. hrs/wk for services:** Unlimited
**Priority registration:** No
**Accomodations for students with ADD:** Yes
**How are professors notified of LD:** By the student and the Program Director

## GENERAL ADMISSIONS INFORMATION

**Director of Admissions:** David Schoolfield

**Telephone:** 417-865-2815

### ENTRANCE REQUIREMENTS

Total high school units required/recommended: 15 total units are required; 3 English recommended, 2 math recommended, 1 science recommended, 2 social studies recommended. Rank in top half of secondary school class and minimum 2.0 GPA required.

**Application deadline:** August 1
**Notification:** Rolling

**SAT or ACT preferred:** ACT
**SAT II required:** Yes
**Average ACT:** 22

## COLLEGE GRADUATION REQUIREMENTS

**Course waivers allowed:** No
**Course substitutions allowed:** No
**In what courses:** N/A

## ADDITIONAL INFORMATION

**Environment:** The college is located on 80 acres in an urban area 225 miles west of St. Louis.

**Student Body**
  **Undergrad enrollment:** 1,574
  **Women:** 56%,
  **Men:** 44%
  **In-state students:** 42%
  **Out-of-state:** 58%

**Cost Information**
  **In-state tuition:** $7,700
  **Out-of-state:** $7,700
  **Room & board:** $3,440

**Housing Information**
  **University housing:** Yes
  **Fraternity:** No
  **Sorority:** No
  **Living on campus:** 90%

  **Athletics:** NAIA

# KANSAS CITY ART INSTITUTE

**MO**

4415 Warwick Boulevard, Kansas City, MO 64111 • **Admissions:** 816-931-5224 • **Fax:** 816-531-6296
**Email:** admiss@kcai.edu
**Support:** CS • **Institution:** 4 yr. Private

## LEARNING DISABILITY ADMISSIONS AND SERVICES

The Academic Resource Center is committed to the educational development of students at Kansas City Art Institute. A recognition of individual cognitive and creative styles of students of art and design is reflected in the comprehensive support service offered. The goal is to foster independent thinking and problem solving, resourcefulness and personal responsibility.

## LEARNING DISABILITY ADMISSIONS INFORMATION

**Program Name:** Academic Resource Center (ARC)
**Program Director:** Mary Magers
**Contact Person:** Same as above

**Telephone:** 816-561-4852 ex.310

### ADMISSIONS

All students have access to academic support services. Students with learning disabilities must demonstrate art ability through a portfolio review and meet a combination of academic criteria, like all applicants, but with a more specialized evaluation. Admitted students should have a minimum ACT of 20 or 950 SAT and a 2.5 GPA. There are no specific high school courses required for admission. If the criteria is not met, applicants are considered in depth via an admissions committee. An interview is recommended.

**College entrance exams required:** Yes
**Course entrance requirements:** Yes
**Diagnostic tests:** Yes
**Documentation:** Any psycho-educational battery: within 3 years

**Untimed accepted:** Yes
**Interview required:** Recommended

### ADDITIONAL INFORMATION

ARC is staffed with LD specialists and students are given assistance on an individual basis. ARC provides: specialized counseling to establish goals, communicate effectively, organize time, manage stress and balance academic and studio demands; critical thinking development to strengthen reading, writing, speaking skills, and refine creative problem-solving; writing assistance to learn techniques for the development, organization and editing of papers, resumes and artist statement; learning skills and strategies in notetaking, test preparation, study practices and management of course expectations; disability services for students with learning challenges, academic guidance and accommodations; testing for academic planning in individual learning and response styles; psycho-educational assessment to identify learning differences; workshops, study and support groups to facilitate learning and academic adjustment. Priority registration is not an issue because of specialized curriculum arrangements given to each student.

**Special education HS coursework accepted:** Y/N
**Special application required:** No
**# of applications submitted each year:** N/A
**# of students receiving LD services:** 15

**Essay required:** Yes
**Submitted to:** N/A
**# of applications accepted each year:** N/A

**Acceptance into program means acceptance into college:** Students must be admitted to the institute first and then may request LD services.

## LEARNING DISABILITY SERVICES

**Learning center:** Yes
**Kurzweil personal reader:** No
**LD specialists:** 1
**Allowed in exams:**
  **Calculator:** N/A
  **Dictionary:** No
  **Computer:** N/A
  **SpellCheck:** Yes

**Notetaker:** Y/N
**Scribes:** Y/N
**Proctors:** Yes
**Oral exams:** Y/N
**Extended test time:** Yes
**Added cost:** Student pays for notetaker
**Distraction-free environ.:** Yes
**Tape recording in class:** Yes
**Books on tape:** Yes
**Taping of other books:** Yes

**Professional tutors:** 2
**Peer tutors:** No
**Max. hrs/wk for services:** Unlimited
**Priority registration:** No
**Accomodations for students with ADD:** Yes
**How are professors notified of LD:** By the student and the Program Director

## GENERAL ADMISSIONS INFORMATION

**Director of Admissions:** Larry Stone

**Telephone:** 816-561-4852

### ENTRANCE REQUIREMENTS
Minimum GPA of 2.5

**Application deadline:** Rolling
**Notification:** NR

**SAT or ACT preferred:** Either
**SAT Avg:** 548V, 518M
**Average ACT:** 23

## COLLEGE GRADUATION REQUIREMENTS

**Course waivers allowed:** No
**Course substitutions allowed:** No
**In what courses:** N/A

## ADDITIONAL INFORMATION

**Environment:** The campus is located in an urban area in Kansas City.

**Student Body**
  **Undergrad enrollment:** 598
  **Women:** 44%
  **Men:** 56%
  **In-state students:** 20%
  **Out-of-state:** 80%

**Cost Information**
  **In-state tuition:** $16,320
  **Out-of-state:** $16,320
  **Room & board:** $4,694

**Housing Information**
  **University housing:** Yes
  **Fraternity:** No
  **Sorority:** No
  **Living on campus:** 20%

  **Athletics:** None

# SOUTHWEST MISSOURI STATE UNIVERSITY

**MO**

901 South National, Springfield, MO 65804 • **Admissions:** 417-836-5517 • **Fax:** 417-836-6334
**Email:** smsuinfo@uma • **Web:** www.smsu.edu
**Support:** CS • **Institution:** 4 yr. Public

## LEARNING DISABILITY ADMISSIONS AND SERVICES

The Learning Diagnostic Clinic is an academic support facility to assist students with LD. The staff includes psychologists and learning specialists. LDC provides two levels of academic support to 'qualified' individuals: One level of services are those services which comprise basic accommodations guaranteed to the 'qualified' students with disabilities under the law; these services are offered at no cost. The next level is called 'Project Success', an academic support program for college students with learning disabilities who desire more comprehensive services. This program provides academic and emotional support that will help to ease the transition to higher learning and the opportunity to function independently. Students applying to the Project Success Program are required to have a psycho-educational evaluation by the LDC staff to ensure the program is suitable for their needs and to provide appropriate accommodations. The fee for testing is $500. If background and documentation does not support a diagnosis of LD, alternatives and suggestions are discussed with the student. If the student wishes to appeal a decision not to provide services, he/she is referred to the ADA/504 Compliance Officer.

## LEARNING DISABILITY ADMISSIONS INFORMATION

**Program Name:** Learning Diagnostic Clinic (LDC)
**Program Director:** Sylvia T. Buse, Ph.D.
**Contact Person:** Terri Schrenk, M.S.

**Telephone:** 417-836-4787

### ADMISSIONS

Students must be admitted to the university to be eligible for the services, and students with learning disabilities must meet the same requirements for admission to the university as all other applicants. There is a special application to be completed as well as a required evaluation fee for students requesting special services. Eligibility for admissions is based on a sliding scale determined by ACT scores and class rank. Application procedures to Progress Success are: be accepted by the university; self-identifying and request application at LDC; submit application and requested information; date is reviewed and student is offered date for personal interview and testing or referred to other services; once interview and testing is completed the test data and information is evaluated by staff, student is accepted or offered alternative suggestions.

**College entrance exams required:** Yes
**Course entrance requirements:** Yes
**Diagnostic tests:** Yes
**Documentation:** Intelligence and Achievement Tests: within 2 years

**Untimed accepted:** Yes
**Interview required:** Yes

### ADDITIONAL INFORMATION

Students must self-identify as having a learning disability in order to request accommodations from LDC. Early referral permits the LDC more time to gather information and evaluate documentation. Appropriate accommodations are determined by the director and the student. The student is assigned to a graduate assistant who maintains contact, monitors progress, and assess the effectiveness of accommodations. Project Success staff provides intensive remediation, focusing upon written language and mathematics strategies; caseworkers provide assistance/advocacy skills; tutors, trained by the LDC, are available to students enrolled in the Project Success program; the fee for this level of accommodations is $1,000 per semester. Basic services from LDC may include assistance in obtaining recorded textbooks, testing accommodations, counseling, advisement, and notetaking assistance and there is no fee for basic services.

**Special education HS coursework accepted:** Yes
**Special application required:** No
**# of applications submitted each year:** N/A
**# of students receiving LD services:** 50-60

**Essay required:** No
**Submitted to:** N/A
**# of applications accepted each year:** N/A

**Acceptance into program means acceptance into college:** Students must be admitted to the university first and then may request an application to LDC or Project Success.

## LEARNING DISABILITY SERVICES

**Learning center:** Yes
**Kurzweil personal reader:** Yes
**LD specialists:** 3
**Allowed in exams:**
  **Calculator:** Y/N
  **Dictionary:** Y/N
  **Computer:** Y/N
  **SpellCheck:** Y/N

**Notetaker:** Yes
**Scribes:** Yes
**Proctors:** Yes
**Oral exams:** Yes
**Extended test time:** Yes
**Added cost:** $1,000 tutoring fee per/semester plus $500 for evaluation
**Distraction-free environ.:** Yes
**Tape recording in class:** Yes
**Books on tape:** RFB
**Taping of other books:** Yes

**Professional tutors:** 2
**Peer tutors:** Varies
**Max. hrs/wk for services:** Varies
**Priority registration:** Y/N
**Accomodations for students with ADD:** Yes
**How are professors notified of LD:** By the student and the Program Director

## GENERAL ADMISSIONS INFORMATION

**Director of Admissions:** Richard Davis

**Telephone:** 417-836-5517

### ENTRANCE REQUIREMENTS

Total high school units required/recommended: 16 total units are required; 4 English required, 3 math required, 2 science required, 3 social studies required. Applicants must meet one of the following requirements for admission: rank in top 53rd class rank percentile with minimum composite ACT score of 18 (combined SAT I score of 870); rank in 44th to 52nd class rank percentile with minimum composite ACT score of 19 (combined SAT I score of 910); or rank in 34th to 43rd class rank percentile with minimum composite ACT score of 20 (combined SAT I score of 959). Special requirements: An RN is required for nursing program applicants. TOEFL is required of all international students.

**Application deadline:** August 1
**Notification:** Rolling

**SAT or ACT preferred:** ACT

**Graduated top 10% of class:** 15
**Graduated top 25% of class:** 37
**Graduated top 50% of class:** 70

## COLLEGE GRADUATION REQUIREMENTS

**Course waivers allowed:** No
**Course substitutions allowed:** Y/N
**In what courses:** Special considerations are presented to department deans.

## ADDITIONAL INFORMATION

**Environment:** 200 acre rural campus located 170 miles from Kansas City and 120 miles from St. Louis.

**Student Body**
  **Undergrad enrollment:** 18,811
  **Women:** 54%
  **Men:** 46%
  **In-state students:** 94%
  **Out-of-state:** 6%

**Cost Information**
  **In-state tuition:** $2,670
  **Out-of-state:** $5,340
  **Room & board:** $3,340

**Housing Information**
  **University housing:** Yes
  **Fraternity:** Yes
  **Sorority:** Yes
  **Living on campus:** 22%

  **Athletics:** NCAA Div. I

# MO

# WASHINGTON UNIVERSITY IN SAINT LOUIS

Campus Box 1089, One Brookings Drive, Saint Louis, MO 63130-4899 • **Admissions:** 800-638-0700
**Fax:** 314-935-4290 • **Email:** admissions@wustl.edu • **Web:** www.wustl.edu
**Support:** CS • **Institution:** 4 yr. Private

## LEARNING DISABILITY ADMISSIONS AND SERVICES

Disabled Student Services recognizes that there are many types of disabilities which hinder a student in showing their true academic ability. It is the goal of DSS to treat students with disabilities as individuals with specific needs and to provide services responsive to those needs. DSS provides a wide range of services and accommodations to help remove barriers posed by the students' disabilities. Students are encouraged to be their own advocates and have the major responsibility for securing services and accommodations. Reasonable accommodations will be made to assist students in meeting their individual needs. It is the goal of DSS to incorporate students with disabilities into the mainstream of the university community.

## LEARNING DISABILITY ADMISSIONS INFORMATION

**Program Name:** Disabled Student Services (DSS)
**Program Director:** Daniel Herbst
**Contact Person:** Same as above

**Telephone:** 314-935-5040

### ADMISSIONS

Washington University gives full consideration to all applicants for admission. There is no special admissions process for students with learning disabilities. The student may choose to voluntarily identify themselves as learning disabled in the admissions process. If they chose to self-identify, details of the history and treatment of the disability, how the individual has met different academic requirements in light of the disability, and the relationship between the disability and academic record, help the university to understand more fully the applicant profile. This information can be helpful in the application process to explain, for example, lower grades in certain subjects. Washington University is a competitive school and they look for students with rigorous academic preparation including 4 yrs. English, 3-4 yrs. math, 3-4 yrs. science, 3-4 yrs. social studies, and 2 yrs. foreign language preferred but not required.

**College entrance exams required:** Yes
**Course entrance requirements:** Yes
**Diagnostic tests:** Yes
**Documentation:** Psycho-educational evaluation: within 4 years

**Untimed accepted:** Yes
**Interview required:** Yes

### ADDITIONAL INFORMATION

In order to receive services students with learning disabilities must submit documentation which identifies a specific learning disability. Students should also provide information regarding recommendations for necessary accommodations. The Learning Center services focus on reading, writing, vocabulary, time management and study techniques. Skills classes are offered in time management, rapid reading, and self-advocacy, but are not for credit. Services and accommodations are available for undergraduate and graduate students.

**Special education HS coursework accepted:** No
**Special application required:** No
**# of applications submitted each year:** N/A
**# of students receiving LD services:** 73

**Essay required:** Yes
**Submitted to:** N/A
**# of applications accepted each year:** N/A

**Acceptance into program means acceptance into college:** Students must be admitted to the university first and then may request LD services.

## LEARNING DISABILITY SERVICES

**Learning center:** Yes
**Kurzweil personal reader:** N/I
**LD specialists:** 1
**Allowed in exams:**
  **Calculator:** Yes
  **Dictionary:** Yes
  **Computer:** Yes
  **SpellCheck:** Yes

**Notetaker:** Yes
**Scribes:** Yes
**Proctors:** Yes
**Oral exams:** Yes
**Extended test time:** Yes
**Added cost:** None
**Distraction-free environ.:** Yes
**Tape recording in class:** Yes
**Books on tape:** Yes
**Taping of other books:** Yes

**Professional tutors:** No
**Peer tutors:** Yes
**Max. hrs/wk for services:**
Unlimited
**Priority registration:** No
**Accomodations for students
with ADD:** Yes
**How are professors notified of
LD:** By the student and the
Program Director

## GENERAL ADMISSIONS INFORMATION

**Director of Admissions:** Nanette Clift

**Telephone:** 314-935-6000

### ENTRANCE REQUIREMENTS

Total high school units required/recommended: 18 total units are recommended; 4 English recommended, 4 math recommended, 3 science recommended, 2 foreign language recommended, 3 social studies recommended. Rigorous secondary school academic program recommended. Special requirements: TOEFL is required of all international students. A portfolio is recommended for students applying to the Schools of Architecture and of Art, and it is required by these schools from those applying or academic scholarships.

**Application deadline:** January 15
**Notification:** April 1

**SAT or ACT preferred:** Either
**SAT Range:** 580–690V, 620–710M
**ACT Range:** 27–31

**Graduated top 10% of class:** 66
**Graduated top 25% of class:** 92
**Graduated top 50% of class:** 99

## COLLEGE GRADUATION REQUIREMENTS

**Course waivers allowed:** No
**Course substitutions allowed:** No
**In what courses:** N/A

## ADDITIONAL INFORMATION

**Environment:** The Washington University campus is located 7 miles west of St. Louis on 169 acres.

**Student Body**
  **Undergrad enrollment:** 5,033
  **Women:** 49%
  **Men:** 51%
  **In-state students:** 14%
  **Out-of-state:** 86%

**Cost Information**
  **In-state tuition:** $21,000
  **Out-of-state:** $21,000
  **Room & board:** $6,593

**Housing Information**
  **University housing:** Yes
  **Fraternity:** Yes
  **Sorority:** Yes
  **Living on campus:** 60%

  **Athletics:** NCAA Div. III

# WESTMINSTER COLLEGE

501 Westminster Avenue, Fulton, MO 65251 • **Admissions:** 800-475-3361 • **Fax:** 573-592-1255
**Email:** admissions@micro.wcmo.edu • **Web:** www.wcmo.edu
**Support:** SP • **Institution:** 4 yr. Private

## LEARNING DISABILITY ADMISSIONS AND SERVICES

The goal of the Learning Disabilities Program is to give students with learning disabilities the special attention they need to succeed in basically the same academic program as that pursued by regularly admitted students. Westminster offers the students a supportive environment, small classes, and professors who are readily accessible. The LD staff offers intensive instruction in reading, writing, and study skills. Much of the instruction is conducted on a one-to-one basis, and is directed to the student's specific problem. Close supervision of the curriculum is essential in the freshman year, and the students' progress is monitored for any difficulties that may arise. The staff is LD certified and faculty members have the specific role of providing LD support.

## LEARNING DISABILITY ADMISSIONS INFORMATION

**Program Name:** Learning Disabilities Program
**Program Director:** Hank F. Ottinger          **Telephone:** 314-592-1304
**Contact Person:** Same as above

### ADMISSIONS

There is a special application and admissions procedure for students with learning disabilities. Students submit: a completed Westminster College application form and a separate application form for the LD Program; results of an eye and hearing exam; WAIS-R; W-J; achievement tests; SAT score of 900+ or ACT score of 19+ (untimed); 2 copies of the high school transcript; recent reports from school counselors, learning specialists, psychologists or physicians who have diagnosed the applicant's disability; 4 recommendations from counselors or teachers familiar with the student's performance; and an evaluation from an educational specialist. An on-campus interview is required. The admission decision is made by the Learning Disabilities Program. Students are either admitted directly into the college and then reviewed for LD services or admitted into the LD Program which results in an admission to the college.

**College entrance exams required:** Yes          **Untimed accepted:** Yes
**Course entrance requirements:** Yes          **Interview required:** Yes
**Diagnostic tests:** Yes
**Documentation:** WRAT; WAIS-R; W-J: within 2 years

### ADDITIONAL INFORMATION

Students are mainstreamed and need a solid college prep background in high school. Learning resources include audio tapes of textbooks, self-instructional materials, special classes in study skills, reading and listening skills, test taking strategies, time management, English composition, and word processors to assist in writing instruction. The Student Development Center is a learning center that is open to all students.

**Special education HS coursework accepted:** Yes          **Essay required:** N/I
**Special application required:** Yes          **Submitted to:** Office of Admissions
**# of applications submitted each year:** 50-60          **# of applications accepted each year:** 10-13
**# of students receiving LD services:** 33
**Acceptance into program means acceptance into college:** Students are admitted jointly to the LD Program and the college.

## LEARNING DISABILITY SERVICES

**Learning center:** Yes
**Kurzweil personal reader:** No
**LD specialists:** 2
**Allowed in exams:**
  **Calculator:** Yes
  **Dictionary:** Y/N
  **Computer:** Yes
  **SpellCheck:** Yes

**Notetaker:** Yes
**Scribes:** Yes
**Proctors:** Yes
**Oral exams:** Yes
**Extended test time:** Yes
**Added cost:** $1,500 per/semester
Fresh. year: $750 upper class
per/semester
**Distraction-free environ.:** Yes
**Tape recording in class:** Yes
**Books on tape:** Yes
**Taping of other books:** Yes

**Professional tutors:** 2.5
**Peer tutors:** Varies
**Max. hrs/wk for services:** 2-5
**Priority registration:** No
**Accomodations for students
with ADD:** Yes
**How are professors notified of
LD:** By the Program Staff

## GENERAL ADMISSIONS INFORMATION

**Director of Admissions:** E. Norman Jones

**Telephone:** 314-642-3361 ext. 251

### ENTRANCE REQUIREMENTS

Total high school units required/recommended: 13 total units are required; 4 English required, 3 math required, 2 science required, 2 social studies required.

**Application deadline:** Rolling
**Notification:** Rolling

**SAT or ACT preferred:** ACT
**SAT Avg:** 561V, 540M
**SAT II required:** Yes
**Average ACT:** 25
**Average GPA:** 3.3

**Graduated top 10% of class:** 30
**Graduated top 25% of class:** 51
**Graduated top 50% of class:** 76

## COLLEGE GRADUATION REQUIREMENTS

**Course waivers allowed:** No
**Course substitutions allowed:** Y/N
**In what courses:** Students can petition the faculty.

## ADDITIONAL INFORMATION

**Environment:** The 250-acre college campus is located in a small town 20 miles east of Columbia, Missouri.

**Student Body**
  **Undergrad enrollment:** 662
  **Women:** 40%
  **Men:** 60%
  **In-state students:** 63%
  **Out-of-state:** 37%

**Cost Information**
  **In-state tuition:** $11,700
  **Out-of-state:** $11,700
  **Room & board:** $4,330

**Housing Information**
  **University housing:** Yes
  **Fraternity:** Yes
  **Sorority:** No
  **Living on campus:** 87%

  **Athletics:** NAIA

# MT MONTANA STATE UNIVERSITY-BILLINGS

1500 North 30th Street, Billings, MT 59101 • **Admissions:** 406-657-2158 • **Fax:** 406-657-2302
**Email:** adm_tempo@vicuna.emcmt.edu • **Web:** www.msubillings.edu
**Support:** S • **Institution:** 4 yr. Public

## LEARNING DISABILITY ADMISSIONS AND SERVICES

Montana State University-Billings has a policy of providing reasonable accommodations to qualified students with a documented disability. Students whose disabilities may require accommodations, such as exam accessibility or reader services, are encouraged to contact Disability Support Services at least four weeks before services are required. The guidelines utilized for providing services to students with learning disabilities are: 1) The student must meet the definition of learning disabled set forth by the National Joint Committee on Learning Disabilities; 2) The student must have a learning disability diagnosed by a professional qualified to diagnose, and a statement of the disability and a summary of academic strengths and weaknesses must be included; 3) Quantitative data acceptable for documentation must include standardized and informal measures including case histories, interviews and previous records that confirm the learning problem; 4) DSS reserves the right to determine whether a student qualifies for services.

## LEARNING DISABILITY ADMISSIONS INFORMATION

**Program Name:** Disability Support Services (DSS)
**Program Director:** Sharon Yazak
**Contact Person:** Same as above

**Telephone:** 406-657-2283

### ADMISSIONS

There is no special admission process for students with learning disabilities. All students must meet the same admission criteria. Freshmen applicants must meet one of the following conditions: 1) ACT of 22 or SAT 920; 2) 2.5 GPA; 3) Rank in the top 50% of the class. Students must have 4 yrs. English, 3 yrs. math (students are encouraged to take math in senior year), 3 yrs. social studies, 2 yrs. laboratory science (one year must be earth science, biology, chemistry, or physics), 2 yrs. chosen from foreign language, computer science, visual and performing arts, vocational education that meet the Office of Public Instruction guidelines. Students not meeting the college preparatory requirements have four options: 1) apply for an exemption by writing a letter and addressing special needs, talents or other reasons; 2) enroll part-time in a summer session 3) enroll as a part-time student with 7 or fewer credits or less the first semester; 4) attend a community college or other college and attempt at least 12 credits or make up any deficiency.

**College entrance exams required:** Yes
**Course entrance requirements:** Yes
**Diagnostic tests:** Yes
**Documentation:** Must clearly state a learning disability or ADHD.

**Untimed accepted:** Yes
**Interview required:** No

### ADDITIONAL INFORMATION

Students must request services, provide documentation specifying a learning disability or ADD, make an appointment for an intake with DSS, meet with professors at the beginning of each semester, and work closely with DSS. The DSS must keep documentation and intake on file, make a determination of accommodations, issue identification cards to qualified students, and serve as a resource and a support. Services available include: assistance in arranging course and testing accommodations; alternative testing; priority scheduling; technical assistance; liaison and referral services; taped textbooks; and career, academic, and counseling referrals. The use of computer, calculator, dictionary, or spell checker is at the discretion of the individual professor, and based on the documented needs of the student. Services and accommodations are available for undergraduate and graduate students.

**Special education HS coursework accepted:** Yes
**Special application required:** Yes
**# of applications submitted each year:** N/A
**# of students receiving LD services:** 60

**Essay required:** N/I
**Submitted to:** DSS
**# of applications accepted each year:** N/A

**Acceptance into program means acceptance into college:** Students must be admitted to the college and then may request LD services.

## LEARNING DISABILITY SERVICES

**Learning center:** No
**Kurzweil personal reader:** Yes
**LD specialists:** No
**Allowed in exams:**
  **Calculator:** Yes
  **Dictionary:** Yes
  **Computer:** Yes
  **SpellCheck:** Yes

**Notetaker:** Yes
**Scribes:** Yes
**Proctors:** Yes
**Oral exams:** Yes
**Extended test time:** Yes
**Added cost:** None
**Distraction-free environ.:** Yes
**Tape recording in class:** Yes
**Books on tape:** Yes
**Taping of other books:** Yes

**Professional tutors:** N/I
**Peer tutors:** N/I
**Max. hrs/wk for services:** Varies
**Priority registration:** Yes
**Accomodations for students with ADD:** Yes
**How are professors notified of LD:** By the student

## GENERAL ADMISSIONS INFORMATION

**Director of Admissions:** Karen Everett

**Telephone:** 406-657-2158

### ENTRANCE REQUIREMENTS

Total high school units required/recommended: 14 total units are required; 4 English required, 3 math required, 2 science required, 3 social studies required. Minimum composite ACT score of 22, rank in top half of secondary school class, or minimum 2.5 GPA required.

**Application deadline:** July 1
**Notification:** Rolling

**SAT or ACT preferred:** ACT
**SAT Avg:** 431V, 488M
**Average ACT:** 20
**Average GPA:** 3

**Graduated top 10% of class:** 7
**Graduated top 25% of class:** 27
**Graduated top 50% of class:** 62

## COLLEGE GRADUATION REQUIREMENTS

**Course waivers allowed:** Yes
**Course substitutions allowed:** Yes
**In what courses:** In foreign language and math under strict guidelines.

## ADDITIONAL INFORMATION

**Environment:** NR

**Student Body**
  **Undergrad enrollment:** 4,006
  **Women:** 63%
  **Men:** 37%
  **In-state students:** 94%
  **Out-of-state:** 6%

**Cost Information**
  **In-state tuition:** $2,388
  **Out-of-state:** $6,559
  **Room & board:** $4,050

**Housing Information**
  **University housing:** Yes
  **Fraternity:** No
  **Sorority:** No
  **Living on campus:** 11%

  **Athletics:** NR

# UNIVERSITY OF MONTANA

**MT**

101 Lodge, Missoula, MT 59812 • **Admissions:** 406-243-6266 • **Fax:** 406-243-5711
**Email:** admiss@selway.umt.edu • **Web:** www.umt.edu
**Support:** CS • **Institution:** 4 yr. Public

## LEARNING DISABILITY ADMISSIONS AND SERVICES

Disability Services for Students ensures equal access to the university by students with disabilities. DSS is a stand alone student affairs office at the university. It is staffed by more than ten full-time professionals. Students with learning disabilities have the same set of rights and responsibilities and the same set of services and accommodations offered other students with disabilities. Written documentation from a qualified diagnostician containing the diagnosis and functional limitation of the LD must be provided to DSS. It should be noted that DSS does not operate the same way many special education programs in secondary schools do. At the university, students have a right to access education; not a right to education. This means that DSS treats students as adults who succeed or fail on their own merits. Students should determine their needs, initiate requests for accommodations and follow up with the delivery of those rights. DSS refrains from seeking out individuals for interventionist actions. Once a student makes the disability and needs known to DSS, they will provide the accommodations which will grant the student the right of equal access. Transitioning from high school to college is enhanced when students grasp and apply the principles of self-advocacy.

## LEARNING DISABILITY ADMISSIONS INFORMATION

**Program Name:** Disability Services for Students (DSS)
**Program Director:** James Marks                    **Telephone:** 406-243-2373
**Contact Person:** Kristie Madsen                    **Telephone:** 406-243-5306

### ADMISSIONS

Admissions criteria is the same for all applicants. However, consideration will be given to students who do not meet the general admissions criteria. General admission criteria include: 22 ACT/ 1030 SAT; rank in the upper 50% of the class; 2.5 GPA. DSS will act as an advocate to students with learning disabilities during the admission process. Applicants not meeting admission criteria may request and receive a review of their eligibility by an admissions committee. Students should send documentation verifying the disability directly to the DSS office.

**College entrance exams required:** Yes            **Untimed accepted:** Yes
**Course entrance requirements:** Yes              **Interview required:** No
**Diagnostic tests:** Yes
**Documentation:** WAIS-R;one achievement battery unless ADD is considered: within 3 yrs.

### ADDITIONAL INFORMATION

Students with LD can expect reasonable accommodations to suit their individual needs. Accommodations may include a direct service or academic adjustment, but will not reduce the academic standards of the institution. Academic assistants at the university provide auxiliary aides such as: reading textbooks and other instructional materials; scribing assignments or tests; assisting in library research; and proofreading materials. Services may include: academic adjustments; admissions assistance; assistive technology; auxiliary aids; consultation with faculty; counseling; course waiver assistance; letter of verification; notetaking; orientation; priority registration; scribes; study skills course; test accommodations services; tutoring services. Academic adjustments may include: extended testing time; substitute course requirements; or lecture notes from instructors.

**Special education HS coursework accepted:** N/A        **Essay required:** No
**Special application required:** No                      **Submitted to:** N/A
**# of applications submitted each year:** N/A           **# of applications accepted each year:** N/A
**# of students receiving LD services:** 225
**Acceptance into program means acceptance into college:** Students must be admitted to the university and then reviewed for LD services.

# LEARNING DISABILITY SERVICES

**Learning center:** No
**Kurzweil personal reader:** Yes
**LD specialists:** 1
**Allowed in exams:**
  **Calculator:** Yes
  **Dictionary:** Y/N
  **Computer:** Yes
  **SpellCheck:** Yes

**Notetaker:** Yes
**Scribes:** Yes
**Proctors:** Yes
**Oral exams:** Yes
**Extended test time:** Yes
**Added cost:** 2 programs: 1/2 of total amt. or free
**Distraction-free environ.:** Yes
**Tape recording in class:** Yes
**Books on tape:** Yes
**Taping of other books:** RFB

**Professional tutors:** No
**Peer tutors:** N/A
**Max. hrs/wk for services:** 3-5 hours per class per week
**Priority registration:** Yes
**Accomodations for students with ADD:** Yes
**How are professors notified of LD:** By the student

# GENERAL ADMISSIONS INFORMATION

**Director of Admissions:** Frank Matoole

**Telephone:** 406-243-6266

## ENTRANCE REQUIREMENTS

Total high school units required/recommended: 14 total units are required; 4 English required, 3 math required, 2 science required, 2 foreign language recommended, 1 social studies required, 2 history required. Minimum composite ACT score of 22 (combined SAT I score of 930), rank in top half of secondary school class, and minimum 2.5 GPA required.

**Application deadline:** July 1
**Notification:** Rolling

**SAT or ACT preferred:** ACT
**SAT Avg:** 540V, 530M
**SAT II required:** Yes
**Average ACT:** 23
**Average GPA:** 3.1

**Graduated top 10% of class:** 16
**Graduated top 25% of class:** 49
**Graduated top 50% of class:** 100

# COLLEGE GRADUATION REQUIREMENTS

**Course waivers allowed:** Yes
**Course substitutions allowed:** Yes
**In what courses:** Any course that is not a core class depending upon the student's disability accommodations.

# ADDITIONAL INFORMATION

**Environment:** NR

**Student Body**
  **Undergrad enrollment:** 9,854
  **Women:** 51%
  **Men:** 49%
  **In-state students:** 70%
  **Out-of-state:** 30%

**Cost Information**
  **In-state tuition:** $2,766
  **Out-of-state:** $7,468
  **Room & board:** $4,162

**Housing Information**
  **University housing:** Yes
  **Fraternity:** Yes
  **Sorority:** Yes
  **Living on campus:** 28%

  **Athletics:** NCAA Div. I

# NORTHERN MONTANA COLLEGE

P.O. Box 7751, Havre, MT 59501 • **Admissions:** 406-265-3704 • **Fax:** 406-265-3777

**Support:** S • **Institution:** 4 yr. Public

## LEARNING DISABILITY ADMISSIONS AND SERVICES

Northern Montana College is a small college known for the individual care and attention given to students. Accommodations for learning disabilities are determined on a case-by-case basis. There is no specific program for students with learning disabilities. However, because of the small size of the student body, faculty are able to work closely with students and provide the necessary assistance they need to be successful. Student Support Services is a federally funded Trio program that is available to students who are either economically disadvantaged, the first in their family to attend college, or have a physical or learning disability. This environment on campus is less competitive and students work together. Students in need of a structured program must be willing to ask for services, and need to be aware that these are "reasonable accommodations" only. There is currently no process in place for students to request the substitution of a foreign language. Humanities is the only program that requires foreign language to graduate from the college. To be eligible for services or accommodations students are requested to provide current documentation that identifies a specific learning disability. The goal of the college is to see students become independent learners and their own self-advocates.

## LEARNING DISABILITY ADMISSIONS INFORMATION

**Program Name:** Student Support Services (SSS)
**Program Director:** John Donaldson
**Contact Person:** Linda Hoines

**Telephone:** 406-265-3783
**Telephone:** 406-265-3783 ex 3211

### ADMISSIONS

There is no special admission procedure. General admission requirements include: 1) GPA of 2.5; 2) rank in the top 50% of the class; 3) an ACT of 20 or SAT of 800. Students over the age of 22 do not need to submit ACT/SAT. In-state students must meet one of the 3 requirements and out-of-state students must meet 2 of the 3 requirements. Course requirements are 4 yrs. of English, 2 yrs. of lab science, 3 yrs. of math, 3 yrs. of History/Social science and 2 yrs. of approved electives. Some waivers or substitutions are allowed in some circumstances. Students not meeting the general admission criteria may still be admitted if they have a high school diploma or the GED. Typically these students are limited to twelve credits the first semester. Students may also be admitted as part-time students. There is also a special exemption for some students with special circumstances.

**College entrance exams required:** Yes
**Course entrance requirements:** Yes
**Diagnostic tests:** Yes
**Documentation:** Any given by a qualified professional; within 3 years preferred.

**Untimed accepted:** Yes
**Interview required:** No

### ADDITIONAL INFORMATION

Services are provided by Student Support Services. These services include testing accommodations; books on tape; oral exams; proctors; scribes; readers; and support groups. Very often when students need a reader for their exam the SSS will pre-tape the exam so that the students can be self-sufficient and listen to the exam on their own. There are skills courses offered for any student at the college. Professional tutors are available, but are not specifically for students with learning disabilities. All services and accommodations are available for undergraduate and graduate students.

**Special education HS coursework accepted:** Yes
**Special application required:** No
**# of applications submitted each year:** N/A
**# of students receiving LD services:** 30
**Acceptance into program means acceptance into college:** Students must be admitted to the college first and then may request services.

**Essay required:** No
**Submitted to:** N/A
**# of applications accepted each year:** N/A

# LEARNING DISABILITY SERVICES

**Learning center:** No
**Kurzweil personal reader:** No
**LD specialists:** No
**Allowed in exams:**
  **Calculator:** Yes
  **Dictionary:** Yes
  **Computer:** Yes
  **SpellCheck:** Yes

**Notetaker:** Yes
**Scribes:** Yes
**Proctors:** Yes
**Oral exams:** Yes
**Extended test time:** Yes
**Added cost:** None
**Distraction-free environ.:** Yes
**Tape recording in class:** Yes
**Books on tape:** Yes
**Taping of other books:** Yes

**Professional tutors:** 60
**Peer tutors:** 55
**Max. hrs/wk for services:**
Decided on a case-by-case basis
**Priority registration:** No
**Accomodations for students with ADD:** Yes
**How are professors notified of LD:** By the student

# GENERAL ADMISSIONS INFORMATION

**Director of Admissions:** Rose Spinker

**Telephone:** 406-265-3700 ex 3704

## ENTRANCE REQUIREMENTS

Total high school units required/recommended: 4 English recommended, 2 science recommended, 3 math recommended, 3 social studies recommended.

**Application deadline:** Rolling
**Notification:** NR

**SAT or ACT preferred:** Either

# COLLEGE GRADUATION REQUIREMENTS

**Course waivers allowed:** No
**Course substitutions allowed:** No
**In what courses:** There is currently no policy or procedure in place for course substitution. However, most of the majors do not require foreign language to graduate.

# ADDITIONAL INFORMATION

**Environment:** The college is located on 105 acres in a small town 115 miles north of Great Falls, MT.

**Student Body**
  **Undergrad enrollment:** 1,572
  **Women:** 54%
  **Men:** 46%
  **In-state students:** 97%
  **Out-of-state:** 3%

**Cost Information**
  **In-state tuition:** $2,330
  **Out-of-state:** $3,800

**Housing Information**
  **University housing:** Yes
  **Fraternity:** No
  **Sorority:** No
  **Living on campus:** 60%

  **Athletics:** Intramural, NAIA

# ROCKY MOUNTAIN COLLEGE

MT

1511 Poly Drive, Billings, MT 59102 • **Admissions:** 406-657-1026 • **Fax:** 406-259-9751
Web: www.rocky.edu
**Support:** CS • **Institution:** 4 yr. Private

## LEARNING DISABILITY ADMISSIONS AND SERVICES

Rocky Mountain College is committed to providing courses, programs, and services for students with disabilities. SAS provides a comprehensive support program for students with LD. To be eligible participants must meet one of the primary criteria: low-income family; first generation college student; or physical or learning disability. Participants must also be U.S. citizens and have an academic need for the program. Students are responsible for identifying themselves, providing appropriate documentation, and requesting reasonable accommodations. The program tailors services to meet the needs of the individuals. SAS welcomes applications from students who are committed to learning and who are excited about meeting the challenges of college with the support provided by the SAS staff. Research studies have shown that students who participate in student support services programs are more than twice as likely to remain in college and graduate as those students from similar backgrounds who do not participate in such programs. The SAS program is supported by a grant from the U.S. Department of Education and funds from Rocky Mountain College. The small size of the college, together with the caring attitude of the faculty and an excellent support program, make Rocky a "Learning Disability-friendly" college.

## LEARNING DISABILITY ADMISSIONS INFORMATION

**Program Name:** Services for Academic Success (SAS)
**Program Director:** Dr. Jane Van Dyk
**Contact Person:** Same as above

**Telephone:** 406-657-1128

### ADMISSIONS

There is no special admissions application for students with learning disabilities, and all applicants must meet the same criteria. However, to identify and provide necessary support services as soon as possible, students with disabilities are encouraged to complete a Services for Academic Success application form at the same time they apply for admission to Rocky. Recommended courses for admissions include: 4 yrs. English, 3 yrs. math, 3 yrs. social science, 2 yrs. lab science, and 2 yrs. foreign language. Students who do not meet the normal admission requirements may be admitted conditionally.

**College entrance exams required:** Yes          **Untimed accepted:** Yes
**Course entrance requirements:** Yes           **Interview required:** No
**Diagnostic tests:** Yes
**Documentation:** I.Q., reading, math, spelling, written lang.;cognitive process.: within 3 years.

### ADDITIONAL INFORMATION

SAS provides a variety of services tailored to meet a student's individual needs. Services are free to participants and include: developmental course work in reading, writing and mathematics; study skills classes; tutoring in all subjects; academic, career and personal counseling; graduate school counseling; accommodations for students with learning disabilities; alternative testing arrangements; taping of lectures or textbooks; cultural and academic enrichment opportunities; and advocacy. SAS staff meets with each student to talk about the supportive services the student needs, and then develops a semester plan. Skills classes for college credit are offered in math, English, and study skills.

**Special education HS coursework accepted:** N/I          **Essay required:** Yes
**Special application required:** No                       **Submitted to:** N/A
**# of applications submitted each year:** N/A            **# of applications accepted each year:** N/A
**# of students receiving LD services:** 30-40
**Acceptance into program means acceptance into college:** Students are admitted to the college first and them reviewed for services.

## LEARNING DISABILITY SERVICES

**Learning center:** Yes
**Kurzweil personal reader:** N/I
**LD specialists:** 1
**Allowed in exams:**
  **Calculator:** Yes
  **Dictionary:** Yes
  **Computer:** Yes
  **SpellCheck:** Yes

**Notetaker:** Yes
**Scribes:** Yes
**Proctors:** Yes
**Oral exams:** Yes
**Extended test time:** Yes
**Added cost:** None
**Distraction-free environ.:** Yes
**Tape recording in class:** Yes
**Books on tape:** Yes
**Taping of other books:** Yes

**Professional tutors:** 1
**Peer tutors:** 30-40
**Max. hrs/wk for services:** Unlimited
**Priority registration:** Yes
**Accomodations for students with ADD:** Yes
**How are professors notified of LD:** By the student and the Program Director

## GENERAL ADMISSIONS INFORMATION

**Director of Admissions:** Craig Gould

**Telephone:** 406-657-1025

### ENTRANCE REQUIREMENTS

Total high school units required/recommended: 4 English recommended, 3 math recommended, 2 science recommended.

**Application deadline:** Rolling
**Notification:** Rolling

**SAT or ACT preferred:** Either
**SAT Avg:** 424V, 458M
**Average ACT:** 22

**Graduated top 10% of class:** 7
**Graduated top 25% of class:** 27
**Graduated top 50% of class:** 51

## COLLEGE GRADUATION REQUIREMENTS

**Course waivers allowed:** Y/N
**Course substitutions allowed:** Y/N
**In what courses:** Substitutions and waivers are provided sometimes.

## ADDITIONAL INFORMATION

**Environment:** NR

**Student Body**
  **Undergrad enrollment:** 937
  **Women:** 53%
  **Men:** 47%
  **In-state students:** 68%
  **Out-of-state:** 32%

**Cost Information**
  **In-state tuition:** $9,994
  **Out-of-state:** $9,994
  **Room & board:** $4,992

**Housing Information**
  **University housing:** Yes
  **Fraternity:** No
  **Sorority:** No
  **Living on campus:** 35%

  **Athletics:** NAIA

# MT WESTERN MONTANA COLLEGE

710 South Atlantic, Dillon, MT 59725 • **Admissions:** 406-683-7331 • **Fax:** 406-683-7493
**Email:** k_leum@wmc.edu • **Web:** www.wmc.edu
**Support:** S • **Institution:** 4 yr. Public

## LEARNING DISABILITY ADMISSIONS AND SERVICES

Western Montana College strives to accommodate all students with special needs. These needs may be physical, social, and/or academic. Almost all services are free to the student. The Director of the Learning Center is in charge of making special accommodations available to the student with learning disabilities. If the student has a documented learning disability and requests special accommodations for a class, the student must contact the Director of the Learning Center so that arrangements can be made. The professor of the class, the Director of the Learning Center, and the student will meet to set up an individualized educational plan for that class and documentation will be kept on file in the Learning Center. Almost all services are free to the student.

## LEARNING DISABILITY ADMISSIONS INFORMATION

**Program Name:** Disability Services
**Program Director:** Clarence Kostelecky          **Telephone:** 406-683-7330
**Contact Person:** Same as above

### ADMISSIONS

The college has no special requirements other than those outlined by the state Board of Regents: a valid high school diploma or GED. Admission criteria for general admission include: 4 yrs. of English, 3 yrs. of math, and 3 yrs. of science, 3 yrs. social studies, and 2 yrs. from foreign language, computer science, visual or performing arts or vocational education; 2.5 GPA (minimum 2.0 for students with learning disabilities); 20 ACT or 960 SAT I; top 50% of the class. Students with documented learning disabilities may request waivers or substitutions in courses affected by the disability. Because Western Montana is a small college, each individual can set up an admissions plan. Some students can be admitted provisionally if they provide satisfactory evidence that they are prepared to pursue successfully the special courses required.

**College entrance exams required:** Yes          **Untimed accepted:** Yes
**Course entrance requirements:** Yes          **Interview required:** No
**Diagnostic tests:** Yes
**Documentation:** N/I

### ADDITIONAL INFORMATION

The Learning Center offers skill building classes in reading, writing and math. These classes don't count for GPA, but do for athletic eligibility. Students whose ACT or entrance tests show that they would profit from such instruction will be placed in courses which will best meet their needs and ensure a successful college career. Free tutoring is available in most areas on a drop-in basis and/or at prescribed times. Services and accommodations are available for undergraduate and graduate students.

**Special education HS coursework accepted:** Yes          **Essay required:** No
**Special application required:** N/A          **Submitted to:** N/A
**# of applications submitted each year:** N/A          **# of applications accepted each year:** N/A
**# of students receiving LD services:** 10
**Acceptance into program means acceptance into college:** Students must be admitted to the college first and then may request services.

## LEARNING DISABILITY SERVICES

**Learning center:** Yes
**Kurzweil personal reader:** No
**LD specialists:** No
**Allowed in exams:**
  **Calculator:** Yes
  **Dictionary:** Yes
  **Computer:** Yes
  **SpellCheck:** Yes

**Notetaker:** Yes
**Scribes:** Yes
**Proctors:** Yes
**Oral exams:** Yes
**Extended test time:** Yes
**Added cost:** None
**Distraction-free environ.:** Yes
**Tape recording in class:** Yes
**Books on tape:** Yes
**Taping of other books:** Yes

**Professional tutors:** 2
**Peer tutors:** 10
**Max. hrs/wk for services:**
Unlimited
**Priority registration:** Yes
**Accomodations for students
with ADD:** Yes
**How are professors notified of
LD:** By both the student and the
Director of services

## GENERAL ADMISSIONS INFORMATION

**Director of Admissions:** Kay Leum

**Telephone:** 406-683-7331

### ENTRANCE REQUIREMENTS

Total high school units required/recommended: 14 total units are required; 4 English required, 3 math required, 2 science required, 3 social studies required. Minimum composite ACT score of 20 (combined SAT I score of 960), rank in top half of secondary school class, and minimum 2.5 GPA required. Special requirements: TOEFL is required of all international students.

**Application deadline:** July 1
**Notification:** Rolling

**SAT or ACT preferred:** SAT
**Average ACT:** 20

## COLLEGE GRADUATION REQUIREMENTS

**Course waivers allowed:** Yes
**Course substitutions allowed:** Yes
**In what courses:** General education courses.

## ADDITIONAL INFORMATION

**Environment:** The college is located on 20 acres in a small town about 60 miles south of Butte.

**Student Body**
  **Undergrad enrollment:** 1,115
  **Women:** 44%
  **Men:** 56%
  **In-state students:** 90%
  **Out-of-state:** 10%

**Cost Information**
  **In-state tuition:** $2,400
  **Out-of-state:** $6,600
  **Room & board:** $3,800

**Housing Information**
  **University housing:** Yes
  **Fraternity:** No
  **Sorority:** No
  **Living on campus:** 40%

  **Athletics:** NAIA

# NE UNION COLLEGE

3800 South 48th Street, Lincoln, NE 68506 • **Admissions:** 402-486-2504 • **Fax:** 402-546-1217
**Email:** enroll@unionky.edu • **Web:** www.unionky.edu
**Support:** CS • **Institution:** 4 yr. Private

## LEARNING DISABILITY ADMISSIONS AND SERVICES

The Teaching Learning Center is a specialized program serving the Union College student with learning disabilities/dyslexia. Specific learning disabilities may affect, mildly or severely, one or more areas of academic performance while leaving other areas relatively unaffected. Courses that require large amounts of reading and language processing become extremely difficult. Students who find it necessary to expend large amounts of time and energy only to receive low grades become discouraged and often leave college if appropriate assistance is not available. The Teaching Learning Center offers assistance to the serious, capable student with learning disabilities at Union College who seeks to earn an undergraduate degree in a Christian environment. In order to qualify for accommodations a student must: have an IQ commensurate with college achievement; have a diagnosis based on current data which will be reviewed by the Teaching Leaning Center staff; complete admission procedures to Union College; take an untimed ACT; apply to the Teaching Learning Center and provide needed information; arrange for a 2 day visit to campus to complete diagnostic/prescriptive testing to determine needed accommodations and remediation.

## LEARNING DISABILITY ADMISSIONS INFORMATION

**Program Name:** Teaching Learning Center (TLC)
**Program Director:** Jennifer Forbes          **Telephone:** 402-486-2506
**Contact Person:** Anne Ballord

### ADMISSIONS

There is no special admission process for students with learning disabilities. All applicants are expected to meet the same admission criteria including: 2.0 GPA for for freshman development probation or 2.5 with no probationary admission; ACT/SAT; 3 yrs. English, 2 yrs. natural science, 2 yrs. history, 2 yrs. algebra, 3 yrs. selected from English, math, natural science, social studies, religion, modern foreign language, or vocational courses. Students with course deficiencies can be admitted and make up the deficiencies in college. Current documentation of the learning disability is required for the program. The staff from the Teaching Learning Center May review documentation from some applicants and provide a recommendation to the Office of Admissions regarding an admission decision. The final decision for admission into the Program is made by TLC.

| | |
|---|---|
| **College entrance exams required:** Yes | **Untimed accepted:** Yes |
| **Course entrance requirements:** Yes | **Interview required:** Yes |
| **Diagnostic tests:** Yes | |
| **Documentation:** WISC-R or WAIS;W-J or similar; within 3 years. | |

### ADDITIONAL INFORMATION

Reasonable accommodation is an individualized matter determined in consultation between the student, parents, project staff, and appropriate faculty members. Such accommodations may include but are not limited to: texts on tape; oral testing; individual testing; extended time/alternate assignments; notetakers; remediation; academic tutoring; counseling; instruction in word processing; assistance with term papers. Skills classes for college credit are offered in reading, spelling, math, and writing. Students with learning disabilities participating in the Teaching Learning Center program enroll in regular college classes although a light load is initially recommended.

| | |
|---|---|
| **Special education HS coursework accepted:** Yes | **Essay required:** No |
| **Special application required:** Yes | **Submitted to:** Program Director |
| **# of applications submitted each year:** N/A | **# of applications accepted each year:** N/A |
| **# of students receiving LD services:** 45 | |

**Acceptance into program means acceptance into college:** Students are admitted to the TLC program and the college jointly.

## LEARNING DISABILITY SERVICES

**Learning center:** Yes
**Kurzweil personal reader:** Yes
**LD specialists:** 4
**Allowed in exams:**
  **Calculator:** Y/N
  **Dictionary:** Yes
  **Computer:** Yes
  **SpellCheck:** Yes

**Notetaker:** Yes
**Scribes:** Yes
**Proctors:** Yes
**Oral exams:** Yes
**Extended test time:** Yes
**Added cost:** $400
**Distraction-free environ.:** Yes
**Tape recording in class:** Yes
**Books on tape:** Yes
**Taping of other books:** No

**Professional tutors:** 4
**Peer tutors:** Yes
**Max. hrs/wk for services:** 3-5
**Priority registration:** No
**Accomodations for students with ADD:** Yes
**How are professors notified of LD:** By both the student and the Program Director

## GENERAL ADMISSIONS INFORMATION

**Director of Admissions:** Tim Simon

**Telephone:** 402-486-2504

### ENTRANCE REQUIREMENTS
Special requirements: TOEFL is required of all international students.

**Application deadline:** August 1
**Notification:** NR

**SAT or ACT preferred:** NR

## COLLEGE GRADUATION REQUIREMENTS

**Course waivers allowed:** No
**Course substitutions allowed:** No
**In what courses:** So far a request for a course waiver or substitution has never been made to the college.

## ADDITIONAL INFORMATION

**Environment:** NR

**Student Body**
  **Undergrad enrollment:** NR
  **Women:** NR
  **Men:** NR
  **In-state students:** 25%
  **Out-of-state:** 75%

**Cost Information**
  **In-state tuition:** $9,550
  **Out-of-state:** $9,550
  **Room & board:** $3,120

**Housing Information**
  **University housing:** Yes
  **Fraternity:** No
  **Sorority:** No
  **Living on campus:** 66%

  **Athletics:** NR

# UNIVERSITY OF NEVADA-LAS VEGAS

NV

4505 South Maryland Parkway, Las Vegas, NV 89154 • **Admissions:** 702-895-3443
**Email:** witter@ccmail.nevada.edu • **Web:** www.nscee.edu/unlv/UNLV_Home_Page/OpenFolder.html
**Support:** S • **Institution:** 4 yr. Public

## LEARNING DISABILITY ADMISSIONS AND SERVICES

The Disability Resource Center (DRC) provides academic accommodations for students with documented disabilities who are otherwise qualified for university programs. Compliance with Section 504 requires that reasonable academic accommodations be made for students with disabilities. These accommodations might include: notetaking, testing accommodations, books on tape, readers, tutoring, priority registration, transition training, assistance with course registration and class monitoring, counseling, and information of the laws pertaining to disabilities. The center also serves as a resource area for all disability issues affecting students, faculty and staff. To establish services, students will need to provide the DRC with appropriate documentation of their disability. Each semester the student wishes to receive assistance, a review of current documentation and assessment of the course needs will be made to determine the appropriate academic accommodations. On some occasions there are decisions based on input from the students, faculty, and the designated DRC staff.

## LEARNING DISABILITY ADMISSIONS INFORMATION

**Program Name:** Disability Resource Center (DRC)
**Program Director:** Anita Stockbauer
**Contact Person:** Same as above

**Telephone:** 702-895-0866

### ADMISSIONS

All applicants are expected to meet the same admission criteria which includes a 2.5 GPA and 13 1/2 college prep courses or a 3.0 GPA and no specific high school courses. ACT/SAT are not required for admission, but are used for placement. Students are encouraged to self-disclose their learning disability and request information about services. DRC will assess the students documentation and write a recommendation to the Office of Admission based on the Director's opinion of the student's chance for success. Students denied admission may request assistance for an appeal through the Director of The Disability Resource Center. This requires a special application with an explanation of the circumstances of previous academic performance. Students and not the parents should call DRC to inquire about initiating an appeal of the denial. Some of these students may be offered Admission By Alternative Criteria. If admitted on probation the students must maintain a 2.0 GPA for the first semester. Others can enter on Special Status as a part-time student, take 15 credits and then transfer into the university.

**College entrance exams required:** Yes
**Course entrance requirements:** Yes
**Diagnostic tests:** Yes
**Documentation:** Psycho-educational evaluation; IEP: within 3 years.

**Untimed accepted:** Yes
**Interview required:** Recommended

### ADDITIONAL INFORMATION

The Disabilities Resource Center offers help to all students on campus who have a diagnosed disability. Following the evaluation students meet with DRC Director and staff to develop a plan for services. Students are encouraged to only enroll in 12 credit hours the first semester, including courses in abilities or skill development. Psychological services are available through the Counseling Office. There are also workshops offered in time management, organization, test taking strategies, and note taking skills. DRC offers workshops to teach classroom success techniques and self-advocacy skills. Assistance is provided year round to active students. Students remain active by signing a new contract for service before each semester. DRC hires enrolled students to be note takers, readers, scribes, and proctors. Services are available to undergraduate and graduate students.

**Special education HS coursework accepted:** Y/N
**Special application required:** Yes
**# of applications submitted each year:** N/A
**# of students receiving LD services:** 454

**Essay required:** No, unless appealing a denial
**Submitted to:** Office of Admission
**# of applications accepted each year:** N/A

**Acceptance into program means acceptance into college:** Students must be admitted to the university first (appeal process is available) and then may request services.

## LEARNING DISABILITY SERVICES

**Learning center:** Yes
**Kurzweil personal reader:** Yes
**LD specialists:** No
**Allowed in exams:**
  **Calculator:** Yes
  **Dictionary:** Yes
  **Computer:** Yes
  **SpellCheck:** Yes

**Notetaker:** Yes
**Scribes:** Yes
**Proctors:** Yes
**Oral exams:** Yes
**Extended test time:** Yes
**Added cost:** $20 per term—free for students with demonstrated financial need
**Distraction-free environ.:** Yes
**Tape recording in class:** Yes
**Books on tape:** Yes
**Taping of other books:** Yes

**Professional tutors:** Yes
**Peer tutors:** Yes
**Max. hrs/wk for services:** 2
**Priority registration:** Yes
**Accomodations for students with ADD:** Yes
**How are professors notified of LD:** By the student and the Program Director

## GENERAL ADMISSIONS INFORMATION

**Director of Admissions:** Susan Bozarth

**Telephone:** 702-895-3011

### ENTRANCE REQUIREMENTS

Total high school units required/recommended: 13 total units are required; 4 English required, 3 math required, 3 science required, 3 social studies required. Minimum 2.3 GPA required. Special requirements: TOEFL is required of all international students.

**Application deadline:** August 15
**Notification:** Rolling

**SAT or ACT preferred:** ACT
**SAT Avg:** 491V, 500M
**Average ACT:** 21
**Average GPA:** 3.52

**Graduated top 10% of class:** 17
**Graduated top 25% of class:** 50
**Graduated top 50% of class:** 85

## COLLEGE GRADUATION REQUIREMENTS

**Course waivers allowed:** No
**Course substitutions allowed:** Yes
**In what courses:** Foreign Language is only required for English majors and substitutions are available; math is required to graduate. All requests go to Academic Standard's Committee after initial approval from the College Advisor, Chair of the Department, Dean of the Deparment, and Director of DRC.

## ADDITIONAL INFORMATION

**Environment:** The university is located on 355 acres in an urban area minutes from downtown Las Vegas.

**Student Body**
  **Undergrad enrollment:** 15,663
  **Women:** 53%
  **Men:** 47%
  **In-state students:** 81%
  **Out-of-state:** 19%

**Cost Information**
  **In-state tuition:** $1,995
  **Out-of-state:** $7,430
  **Room & board:** $5,300

**Housing Information**
  **University housing:** Yes
  **Fraternity:** Yes
  **Sorority:** No
  **Living on campus:** 5%

  **Athletics:** NCAA Div. I

# COLBY-SAWYER COLLEGE

**NH**

100 Main Street, New London, NH 03257 • **Admissions:** 603-526-3700 • **Fax:** 603-526-3452
**Email:** csadmiss@colbysawyer.edu • **Web:** www.colby-sawyer.edu
**Support:** CS • **Institution:** 4 yr. Private

## LEARNING DISABILITY ADMISSIONS AND SERVICES

The goal of the Academic Development Center is to offer students with learning disabilities the same opportunities that the college extends to other students. This includes providing individualized, free of charge academic support services designed to enable Colby-Sawyer College students to realize their full academic potential. By way of implementation, the Academic staff are trained to meet the academic needs of the entire student body by providing supplemental assistance to those who need remedial help in specific courses and/or development of basic study skills, seek academic achievement beyond their already strong level, and/or have learning styles with diagnosed differences.

## LEARNING DISABILITY ADMISSIONS INFORMATION

**Program Name:** Academic Development Center
**Program Director:** N/I
**Contact Person:** Tom Mooney                    **Telephone:** 603-526-3713

### ADMISSIONS

There is no special admissions process for students with learning disabilities. Students must submit one recommendation from their counselor and one from a teacher. An essay is also required. It is recommended that students have at least 15 units of college preparatory courses. Students with documented learning disabilities may substitute courses for math or foreign language if those are the areas of deficit. GPA is evaluated in terms of factors that may have affected GPA, as well as a subjective assessment of students' chances of succeeding in college.

**College entrance exams required:** Yes          **Untimed accepted:** Yes
**Course entrance requirements:** Yes            **Interview required:** Yes
**Diagnostic tests:** Yes
**Documentation:** WAIS-R: within 3 years.

### ADDITIONAL INFORMATION

Essential to the success of the Academic Development Center is the informal, individualized, non-judgemental nature of the learning that occurs during tutoring sessions. Tutors must qualify for their jobs by presenting a GPA of 3.3 with no less than an A- in every course they designate as part of their area of expertise. Other services provided include: 1) Classroom modifications; students meet with a learning specialist to develop a "profile" which includes the student's learning style, learning strengths and weaknesses and recommendations to professors for accommodations; 2) Special help; Learning Specialists assist students in improving study skills, strengthening mathematic fundamentals and /or developing writing skills, 3) Academic advising; each student has a faculty advisor, interested in student progress, who confers with students at regular intervals to set and achieve goals and select courses.

**Special education HS coursework accepted:** Yes     **Essay required:** Yes
**Special application required:** No                  **Submitted to:** N/A
**# of applications submitted each year:** N/A        **# of applications accepted each year:** N/A
**# of students receiving LD services:** 65
**Acceptance into program means acceptance into college:** Students must be admitted to the college first and then may request services.

## LEARNING DISABILITY SERVICES

Learning center: Yes
Kurzweil personal reader: N/I
LD specialists: Yes
Allowed in exams:
  Calculator: Y/N
  Dictionary: Y/N
  Computer: Y/N
  SpellCheck: Yes

Notetaker: Y/N
Scribes: Y/N
Proctors: Y/N
Oral exams: Y/N
Extended test time: Y/N
Added cost: None
Distraction-free environ.: Y/N
Tape recording in class: Yes
Books on tape:
Taping of other books: Y/N

Professional tutors: 2
Peer tutors: 23
Max. hrs/wk for services:
Unlimited
Priority registration: Yes
Accomodations for students
with ADD: Yes
How are professors notified of
LD: By the student or the
Program Director

## GENERAL ADMISSIONS INFORMATION

Director of Admissions: Steve Cloniger

Telephone: 603-526-3702

### ENTRANCE REQUIREMENTS

Total high school units required/recommended: 15 total units are recommended; 4 English recommended, 3 math recommended, 2 science recommended, 2 foreign language recommended, 2 social studies recommended, 2 history recommended.

Application deadline: Rolling
Notification: Rolling

SAT or ACT preferred: Either
SAT Avg: 416V, 446M
Average ACT: 20

## COLLEGE GRADUATION REQUIREMENTS

Course waivers allowed: Yes
Course substitutions allowed: Yes
In what courses: Math, if it is not essential to the particular course of study.

## ADDITIONAL INFORMATION

Environment: 80-acre small town campus.

Student Body
  Undergrad enrollment: 675
  Women: 62%
  Men: 38%
  In-state students: 30%
  Out-of-state: 70%

Cost Information
  In-state tuition: $15,530
  Out-of-state: $15,530
  Room & board: $5,950

Housing Information
  University housing: Yes
  Fraternity: No
  Sorority: No
  Living on campus: 85%

  Athletics: NCAA Div. III

# NEW ENGLAND COLLEGE

26 Bridge Street, Henniker, NH 03242 • **Admissions:** 603-428-2223 • **Fax:** 603-428-7230
**Email:** admis@nec1.nec.edu • **Web:** www.nec.edu
**Support:** CS • **Institution:** 4 yr. Private

## LEARNING DISABILITY ADMISSIONS AND SERVICES

The Skills Center is a place to learn how to learn. Students have a variety of needs; writing term papers; reading speed; mathematics; confusion and anxiety about ability to perform as a college student; or a specific learning disability. The College Skills Center provides individual or small group tutoring, academic counseling and referral services. Although tutoring is available in most subject areas, the Center focuses primarily on helping first and second year students become independent and successful learners. The Skills Center provides the assistance required and the academic support services necessary for students with learning disabilities to be successful. This includes content area tutoring, time management skills and writing development to all students which will allow them to become independent learners. The college does not have a segregated program. The support services meet the needs of students who do not require a formal, structured program, but who can find success when offered support and advocacy by a trained and experienced staff in conjunction with small classes and personal attention by faculty. Typically these students have done well in "mainstream" programs in high school, when given assistance. Students with learning disabilities are encouraged to visit NEC and the Skills Center to determine whether the support services will adequately meet their academic needs.

## LEARNING DISABILITY ADMISSIONS INFORMATION

**Program Name:** College Skills Center
**Program Director:** Joanne MacEachron, Ph.D.          **Telephone:** 603-428-2218
**Contact Person:** Same as above

### ADMISSIONS

Students with learning disabilities submit the general New England College application. Students should have a 2.0 GPA. SAT/ACT are optional. Course requirements include: 4 yrs. English, 2 yrs. math, 2 yrs. science, and 2 yrs. social studies. Documentation of the learning disability should be submitted along with counselor and teacher recommendations. An interview is recommended. Successful applicants have typically done well in 'mainstream' programs in high school when given tutorial and study skills assistance. Summer Seminar Program is a 4 week Program open to all accepted students. Occasionally, NEC allows a handful of students to begin conditionally in the summer and tie admissions to performance in the summer program.

**College entrance exams required:** Yes          **Untimed accepted:** Yes
**Course entrance requirements:** Yes          **Interview required:** Recommended
**Diagnostic tests:** Yes
**Documentation:** WAIS-R; achievement tests in Reading, Math, etc: within 3 years.

### ADDITIONAL INFORMATION

Students may elect to use Skills Center services with regular appointments or only occasionally in response to particular or difficult assignments. The Center provides: tutoring in content areas; computer facilities; study skills instruction; time management strategies; writing support in planning, editing and proofreading; mathematics support; and referrals to other college services. The Center provides one-on-one writing support for all first year students taking WR 101-102. Students are encouraged to use the word processors to generate writing assignments, and to use the tutors to help plan and revise papers. The writing faculty works closely with the Center to provide coordinated and supportive learning for all students. The Skills Center has its own building and contains two classrooms, offices for faculty, and private tutoring areas. The Director is a learning disabilities specialist. Professional tutors work with students individually and in small groups. These services are provided in a secure and accepting atmosphere.

**Special education HS coursework accepted:** Yes, on a case-by-case basis          **Essay required:** Yes
**Special application required:** No          **Submitted to:** N/A
**# of applications submitted each year:** N/A          **# of applications accepted each year:** N/A
**# of students receiving LD services:** 125-130
**Acceptance into program means acceptance into college:** Students must be admitted to the college first and then may request services.

**Learning center:** Yes
**Kurzweil personal reader:** Yes
**LD specialists:** Yes
**Allowed in exams:**
  **Calculator:** Yes
  **Dictionary:** Yes
  **Computer:** Yes
  **SpellCheck:** Yes

**Notetaker:** No
**Scribes:** Y/N
**Proctors:** Yes
**Oral exams:** Y/N
**Extended test time:** Yes
**Added cost:** None
**Distraction-free environ.:** Yes
**Tape recording in class:** Y/N
**Books on tape:**
**Taping of other books:** N/I

**Professional tutors:** 12
**Peer tutors:** No
**Max. hrs/wk for services:** 3-4
**Priority registration:** No
**Accomodations for students with ADD:** Yes
**How are professors notified of LD:** By the student

## GENERAL ADMISSIONS INFORMATION

**Director of Admissions:** Donald Parker          **Telephone:** 603-428-2223

### ENTRANCE REQUIREMENTS

Total high school units required/recommended: 13 total units are required; 4 English required, 2 math required, 3 math recommended, 2 science required, 3 science recommended, 3 social studies required, 1 history required. Minimum 2.0 GPA recommended.

**Application deadline:** Rolling
**Notification:** Rolling

**SAT or ACT preferred:** NR
**Average GPA:** 2.72

**Graduated top 10% of class:** 10
**Graduated top 25% of class:** 33
**Graduated top 50% of class:** 73

## COLLEGE GRADUATION REQUIREMENTS

**Course waivers allowed:** Yes
**Course substitutions allowed:** Yes
**In what courses:** Math/statistics

## ADDITIONAL INFORMATION

**Environment:** The college is located in the town of Henniker on 212 acres 17 miles west of Concord.

**Student Body**
  **Undergrad enrollment:** 978
  **Women:** 43%
  **Men:** 57%
  **In-state students:** 20%
  **Out-of-state:** 80%

**Cost Information**
  **In-state tuition:** $15,784
  **Out-of-state:** $15,784
  **Room & board:** $5,920

**Housing Information**
  **University housing:** Yes
  **Fraternity:** Yes
  **Sorority:** Yes
  **Living on campus:** 60%

  **Athletics:** NCAA Div. III

# NEW HAMPSHIRE COLLEGE

**NH**

2500 North River Road, Manchester, NH 03106 • **Admissions:** 603-645-9611 • **Fax:** 603-645-9693
**Email:** admission@nhc.edu • **Web:** www.nhc.edu
**Support:** CS • **Institution:** 4 yr. Private

## LEARNING DISABILITY ADMISSIONS AND SERVICES

New Hampshire College does not have a formal learning disabilities program. The college does have a Learning Center which offers a wide range of academic support services. For the most part, successful students with learning disabilities will be those who are aware of their strengths and weaknesses and who actively seek help. The services of the Learning Center are not mandatory and students must request assistance. The college does not offer an alternative curriculum. The Learning Center is a support system, not an alternate road.

## LEARNING DISABILITY ADMISSIONS INFORMATION

**Program Name:** The Learning Center
**Program Director:** Richard Colfer
**Contact Person:** Same as above

**Telephone:** 603-645-9606

### ADMISSIONS

The college does not have a specific admission's process for students with learning disabilities. No pre-admission inquiry is made about applicants' disabilities, but self-disclosure can often be helpful in the admissions process. Through self-disclosure, an informed and fair decision can be made by the student and the college, regarding the suitability of New Hampshire College in the pursuit of a collegiate education. Students are encouraged to provide the following information: educational history including assessment measures and treatment of disability; accommodations needed; accommodations received in high school; coping skills that have been developed; and the relationship between the disability and the academic record.

**College entrance exams required:** Yes
**Course entrance requirements:** Yes
**Diagnostic tests:** Recommended
**Documentation:** Assessments and evaluations.

**Untimed accepted:** Yes
**Interview required:** Recommended

### ADDITIONAL INFORMATION

Tutoring is available on a one-to-one basis. Basic skills courses are offered in math, reading, and written language. College credit can be earned for reading and writing. The Learning Center is open to all students. Services and accommodations are available for undergraduate and graduate students. There is a very strong advising system in the freshman year.

**Special education HS coursework accepted:** No
**Special application required:** No
**# of applications submitted each year:** N/A
**# of students receiving LD services:** N/I

**Essay required:** Yes
**Submitted to:** N/A
**# of applications accepted each year:** N/A

**Acceptance into program means acceptance into college:** Students must be admitted to the college first and then may request services.

## LEARNING DISABILITY SERVICES

**Learning center:** Yes
**Kurzweil personal reader:** No
**LD specialists:** 1
**Allowed in exams:**
  **Calculator:** Yes
  **Dictionary:** Yes
  **Computer:** Yes
  **SpellCheck:** Yes

**Notetaker:** No
**Scribes:** No
**Proctors:** Yes
**Oral exams:** Yes
**Extended test time:** Yes
**Added cost:** None
**Distraction-free environ.:** Yes
**Tape recording in class:** Yes
**Books on tape:** No
**Taping of other books:** No

**Professional tutors:** 9-staff
**Peer tutors:** 40
**Max. hrs/wk for services:** As needed
**Priority registration:** Yes
**Accomodations for students with ADD:** Yes
**How are professors notified of LD:** By the student

## GENERAL ADMISSIONS INFORMATION

**Director of Admissions:** Brad Poznanski       **Telephone:** 800-NHC-4YOU

### ENTRANCE REQUIREMENTS
Total high school units required/recommended: 16 total units are required; 16 total units are recommended; 4 English required, 2 math required, 4 math recommended, 2 science recommended, 2 social studies recommended. Minimum 2.0 GPA and rank in top half of secondary school class recommended.

**Application deadline:** Rolling
**Notification:** Rolling

**SAT or ACT preferred:** SAT
**SAT Avg:** 475V, 473M
**Average GPA:** 2.6

**Graduated top 10% of class:** 3
**Graduated top 25% of class:** 10
**Graduated top 50% of class:** 40

## COLLEGE GRADUATION REQUIREMENTS

**Course waivers allowed:** No
**Course substitutions allowed:** No
**In what courses:** N/A

## ADDITIONAL INFORMATION

**Environment:** The college is located on 200 acres in a suburban area 55 miles north of Boston.

**Student Body**
  **Undergrad enrollment:** 3,975
  **Women:** 45%
  **Men:** 55%
  **In-state students:** 30%
  **Out-of-state:** 70%

**Cost Information**
  **In-state tuition:** $12,400
  **Out-of-state:** $12,400
  **Room & board:** $5,756

**Housing Information**
  **University housing:** Yes
  **Fraternity:** Yes
  **Sorority:** Yes
  **Living on campus:** 80%

  **Athletics:** NCAA Div. II

# UNIVERSITY OF NEW HAMPSHIRE

4 Garrison Avenue, Durham, NH 03824 • **Admissions:** 603-862-1360 • **Fax:** 603-862-0077
**Email:** admissions@unh.edu • **Web:** www.unh.edu/admissions/index.html
**Support:** S • **Institution:** 4 yr. Public

## LEARNING DISABILITY ADMISSIONS AND SERVICES

UNH encourages students to self-disclose within the admissions procedure. There is no LD program; rather services/ accommodations are based on student self-disclosure and obtaining the proper guidelines for documentation of LD. Testing must be comprehensive and minimally include: WAIS-R with subtest scores; Woodcock-Johnson; current levels of functioning in reading, mathematics and written language; information processing; current; have clear and specific evidence and identification of LD; include test scores/data; be completed by qualified professional; have suitable assessment instruments; and reports should include recommendations for accommodations. Eligibility for accommodations will be determined upon the student meeting with the Director of "ACCESS" (Disability Student Services Office). Students need to be aware that "being tested for a learning disability", "having old documentation" ( more than 3 years old), or, being "previously coded in secondary education" in and of itself, does not necessarily mean that the student will be currently qualified with a disability under federal laws in college. Services and accommodations at UNH can be defined as those generic activities offered to ensure educational opportunity for any student with a documented disability.

## LEARNING DISABILITY ADMISSIONS INFORMATION

**Program Name:** ACCESS
**Program Director:** N/I
**Contact Person:** Donna Marie Sorrentino    **Telephone:** 603-862-2607

### ADMISSIONS

Admissions criteria are the same for all applicants. Typically, students who are admitted to the university are in the top 30% of their class, have a "B" average in college preparatory courses, and have taken 4 years of college prep math, 3-4 years of a lab science, and 3-4 years of a foreign language; SAT I average range is 1050-1225 but there are no cut offs (or equivalent ACT). There are no alternative options for admissions.

**College entrance exams required:** Yes        **Untimed accepted:** Yes
**Course entrance requirements:** Yes          **Interview required:** No
**Diagnostic tests:** No
**Documentation:** Not at the time of admissions.

### ADDITIONAL INFORMATION

Academic accommodations provided based on documentation: individual scheduled meetings with ACCESS coordinator for guidance, advising and referrals; mediation and advocacy; notetakers; scribes; proctors; readers; taped texts; extended exam time; distraction free rooms for exams; alternative methods for exam administration; pre-registration priority scheduling; reduced course load; and faculty support letters. UNH does not provide a university-wide service or program for subject area tutoring; it is the student's responsibility to secure subject area tutoring. However, the Center for Academic Resources provides all students with: drop-in tutoring in selected courses; referrals to free academic assistance opportunities and to private pay tutors; individualized study skills assistance; and peer support for academic and personal concerns. There is a federally funded grant that allows some students to receive free peer tutoring and reading/writing assistance with a specialist.

**Special education HS coursework accepted:** Yes       **Essay required:** Yes
**Special application required:** N/A                     **Submitted to:** N/A
**# of applications submitted each year:** N/A           **# of applications accepted each year:** N/A
**# of students receiving LD services:** 225+
**Acceptance into program means acceptance into college:** Students must be admitted to the university and then reviewed for LD services.

# LEARNING DISABILITY SERVICES

**Learning center:** No
**Kurzweil personal reader:** No
**LD specialists:** No
**Allowed in exams:**
  **Calculator:** Yes
  **Dictionary:** Yes
  **Computer:** Yes
  **SpellCheck:** Yes

**Notetaker:** Yes
**Scribes:** Yes
**Proctors:** Yes
**Oral exams:** Yes
**Extended test time:** Yes
**Added cost:** None
**Distraction-free environ.:** Yes
**Tape recording in class:** Yes
**Books on tape:** Yes
**Taping of other books:** Yes

**Professional tutors:** N/I
**Peer tutors:** N/I
**Max. hrs/wk for services:** N/A
**Priority registration:** Yes
**Accomodations for students with ADD:** Yes
**How are professors notified of LD:** By the student and the Contact Person

# GENERAL ADMISSIONS INFORMATION

**Director of Admissions:** James Washington, Jr.           **Telephone:** 603-862-1360

## ENTRANCE REQUIREMENTS

Total high school units required/recommended: 18 total units are recommended; 4 English recommended, 4 math recommended, 4 science recommended, 3 social studies recommended. Minimum rank in top three-tenths of secondary school class. Special requirements: A portfolio is required for art program applicants. An audition is required for music program applicants. TOEFL is required of all international students.

**Application deadline:** February 1
**Notification:** April 15

**SAT or ACT preferred:** SAT
**SAT Avg:** 551V, 554M
**SAT II required:** Yes
**Average GPA:** 3.0

**Graduated top 10% of class:** 22
**Graduated top 25% of class:** 59
**Graduated top 50% of class:** 96

# COLLEGE GRADUATION REQUIREMENTS

**Course waivers allowed:** N/I
**Course substitutions allowed:** N/I
**In what courses:** New policy being developed/revised; for example, regarding foreign language requirements.

# ADDITIONAL INFORMATION

**Environment:** NR

**Student Body**
  **Undergrad enrollment:** 10,649
  **Women:** 56%
  **Men:** 44%
  **In-state students:** 60%
  **Out-of-state:** 40%

**Cost Information**
  **In-state tuition:** $4,020
  **Out-of-state:** $12,990
  **Room & board:** $4,354

**Housing Information**
  **University housing:** Yes
  **Fraternity:** Yes
  **Sorority:** Yes
  **Living on campus:** 55%

  **Athletics:** NCAA Div. I

# NOTRE DAME COLLEGE

2321 Elm Street, Manchester, NH 03104 • **Admissions:** 603-669-4298 • **Fax:** 603-644-8316
**Email:** admissions@nd.edu • **Web:** www.nd.edu
**Support:** S • **Institution:** 4 yr. Private

## LEARNING DISABILITY ADMISSIONS AND SERVICES

The Learning Disabilities support program at Notre Dame College is an accommodation, not a remediation program. All students are enrolled in regular classes. The Learning Enrichment Center is designed for the high school student who has the potential to earn a college degree, but needs support to compensate for a learning disability. Incoming students who wish to receive support should take the following steps: make an appointment with the Learning Enrichment Center Director to discuss concerns and necessary accommodations (the student should bring documentation of the learning disability to this meeting); take part in preparing a student profile with the Learning Enrichment Center Director; give copies of the completed student profile to each of the student's instructors; attend a weekly, pre-arranged meeting with the Learning Enrichment Center Director to monitor progress; seek tutoring as necessary or as recommended by the Learning Enrichment Center Director; and make a strong commitment to academics.

## LEARNING DISABILITY ADMISSIONS INFORMATION

**Program Name:** Learning Enrichment Center (LEC)

**Program Director:** Jane O'Neil                    **Telephone:** 603-669-42948
**Contact Person:** Same as above

### ADMISSIONS

Students with learning disabilities must submit a regular application for admission and be accepted under regular admission. The general admission requirements include: 4 yrs. English, 2 yrs. foreign language, 2 yrs. history, 2 yrs. math, 2 yrs. science, 2 yrs. social studies; 880 SAT I; 2.0 GPA. Applicants desiring admission to the Learning Enrichment Center are encouraged to self-disclose and submit documentation to admissions of a diagnosed learning disability by a certified professional. There is some flexibility in SAT range. Self-disclosed LD documentation should include: identification and description of the specific type of learning disability; description of the effects of the learning disability including strengths and weaknesses; learning style; and a recent Individualized Educational Plan. The admissions decision is made by both the Program Director and Admissions Director.

**College entrance exams required:** Yes          **Untimed accepted:** Yes
**Course entrance requirements:** Yes            **Interview required:** No
**Diagnostic tests:** Yes
**Documentation:** Psycho-educational-evaluation; IEP: within 2-3 years.

### ADDITIONAL INFORMATION

The Learning Enrichment Center provides a quiet atmosphere to offer academic support and appropriate accommodations to all students including students with documented learning disabilities. Services provided include: assistance in writing college-level papers; help in studying for major test and exams; guidance in study skills; tutoring in all subjects; workshops to review and relearn; individualized support services and appropriate accommodations for students with learning disabilities. Study skills classes for credit are offered in reading proficiency and basic English skills in writing.

**Special education HS coursework accepted:** Yes      **Essay required:** No
**Special application required:** No                    **Submitted to:** N/A
**# of applications submitted each year:** N/A         **# of applications accepted each year:** N/A
**# of students receiving LD services:** 28
**Acceptance into program means acceptance into college:** Students must be admitted to the college and then request services.

## LEARNING DISABILITY SERVICES

**Learning center:** Yes
**Kurzweil personal reader:** No
**LD specialists:** No
**Allowed in exams:**
  **Calculator:** Yes
  **Dictionary:** No
  **Computer:** Yes
  **SpellCheck:** No

**Notetaker:** Yes
**Scribes:** Yes
**Proctors:** Yes
**Oral exams:** Yes
**Extended test time:** Yes
**Added cost:** None
**Distraction-free environ.:** Yes
**Tape recording in class:** Yes
**Books on tape:**
**Taping of other books:** Y/N

**Professional tutors:** 2
**Peer tutors:** 20+
**Max. hrs/wk for services:**
Unlimited
**Priority registration:** No
**Accomodations for students
with ADD:** Yes
**How are professors notified of
LD:** By the student with a Profile
compiled by the Director of LEC

## GENERAL ADMISSIONS INFORMATION

**Director of Admissions:** Joseph P. Wagner           **Telephone:** 603-669-4298

### ENTRANCE REQUIREMENTS
Special requirements: TOEFL is required of all international students.

**Application deadline:** Rolling
**Notification:** NR

**SAT or ACT preferred:** NR

**Graduated top 10% of class:** 15
**Graduated top 25% of class:** 37
**Graduated top 50% of class:** 74

## COLLEGE GRADUATION REQUIREMENTS

**Course waivers allowed:**  Yes
**Course substitutions allowed:**  Yes
**In what courses:** On a case-by-case basis.

## ADDITIONAL INFORMATION

**Environment:** Notre Dame College is located on 7 acres in a suburban area north of Manchester.

**Student Body**
  **Undergrad enrollment:** 804
  **Women:** 68%
  **Men:** 32%
  **In-state students:** 77%
  **Out-of-state:** 23%

**Cost Information**
  **In-state tuition:** $11,440
  **Out-of-state:** $11,440
  **Room & board:** $5,295

**Housing Information**
  **University housing:** Yes
  **Fraternity:** No
  **Sorority:** No
  **Living on campus:** 34%

  **Athletics:** NAIA

# RIVIER COLLEGE

420 Main Street, Nashua, NH 03060 • **Admissions:** 603-888-1311 • **Fax:** 603-891-1799
**Email:** rivadmit@rivier.edu • **Web:** www.rivier.edu
**Support:** S • **Institution:** 4 yr. Private

## LEARNING DISABILITY ADMISSIONS AND SERVICES

Rivier College recognizes that learning styles differ from person to person. Physical, perceptual, or emotional challenges experienced by students may require additional supports and accommodations to equalize their opportunities for success. The college is committed to providing supports that allow all otherwise qualified individuals with disabilities an equal educational opportunity. Special Needs Services provides the opportunity for all individuals who meet academic requirements to be provided auxiliary services, facilitating their earning of a college education. To be eligible for support services students are required to provide appropriate documentation of their disabilities to the Coordinator of Special Needs Services. This documentation shall be provided from a professional in the field of psycho-educational testing or a physician and shall be current, within 3-5 years. This information will be confidential and is kept in the Coordinator's office for the purpose of planning appropriate support services. To access services students must contact the Coordinator of Special Needs Services before the start of each semester to schedule an appointment; provide documentation; and together the Coordinator and the student will discuss and arrange for support services specifically related to the disability.

## LEARNING DISABILITY ADMISSIONS INFORMATION

**Program Name:** Special Needs Services
**Program Director:** Lisa Baroody          **Telephone:** 603-888-1311 ext. 8497
**Contact Person:** Same as above

### ADMISSIONS

There is no special admissions process for students with learning disabilities. All applicants must meet the same criteria. Students should have a combined SAT of 700; GPA in the top 80%; and take college prep courses in high school. Applicants not meeting the general admission requirements may inquire about alternative admissions. The college has a probational admit that requires a student to maintain a minimum 2.0 GPA their first semester.

**College entrance exams required:** Yes          **Untimed accepted:** Yes
**Course entrance requirements:** Yes          **Interview required:** No
**Diagnostic tests:** Yes
**Documentation:** Standard IEP battery: within 2 years.

### ADDITIONAL INFORMATION

Services available include: academic, career, and personal counseling; preferential registration; classroom accommodations including tape recording of lectures, extended time for test completion, testing free from distractions, and notetakers; student advocacy; Writing & Learning Center for individualized instruction in writing and selected subject areas; individualized accommodations as developed by the Coordinator of Special Needs Services with the student. Skills classes are offered in English and math and students may take these classes for college credit. Services and accommodations are available for undergraduate and graduate students.

**Special education HS coursework accepted:** Yes          **Essay required:** Yes
**Special application required:** No          **Submitted to:** N/A
**# of applications submitted each year:** N/A          **# of applications accepted each year:** N/A
**# of students receiving LD services:** 12
**Acceptance into program means acceptance into college:** Students must be accepted to the college first and then may request services.

# LEARNING DISABILITY SERVICES

**Learning center:** No
**Kurzweil personal reader:** No
**LD specialists:** No
**Allowed in exams:**
  **Calculator:** Yes
  **Dictionary:** Yes
  **Computer:** Yes
  **SpellCheck:** Yes

**Notetaker:** Yes
**Scribes:** Yes
**Proctors:** Yes
**Oral exams:** Yes
**Extended test time:** Yes
**Added cost:** None
**Distraction-free environ.:** Yes
**Tape recording in class:** Yes
**Books on tape:** Yes
**Taping of other books:** No

**Professional tutors:** 4
**Peer tutors:** Yes
**Max. hrs/wk for services:** Unlimited
**Priority registration:** Yes
**Accomodations for students with ADD:** No
**How are professors notified of LD:** By both the student and the Director

# GENERAL ADMISSIONS INFORMATION

**Director of Admissions:** Jim Slattery

**Telephone:** 603-888-1311 ext. 8507

## ENTRANCE REQUIREMENTS

Total high school units required/recommended: 16 total units are required; 4 English required, 2 math required, 1 science required, 2 foreign language required, 2 social studies required, 1 history recommended. Special requirements: A portfolio is required for art program applicants. An RN is required for nursing program applicants. Algebra and chemistry required of nursing program applicants.

**Application deadline:** Rolling
**Notification:** Rolling

**SAT or ACT preferred:** SAT
**SAT Avg:** 480V, 460M
**Average GPA:** 2.6

**Graduated top 10% of class:** 5
**Graduated top 25% of class:** 23
**Graduated top 50% of class:** 63

# COLLEGE GRADUATION REQUIREMENTS

**Course waivers allowed:** Yes
**Course substitutions allowed:** Yes
**In what courses:** Each course substitution is looked at individually.

# ADDITIONAL INFORMATION

**Environment:** The college is located on 60 acres in a suburban area 40 miles north of Boston.

**Student Body**
  **Undergrad enrollment:** 1,728
  **Women:** 84%
  **Men:** 16%
  **In-state students:** 77%
  **Out-of-state:** 23%

**Cost Information**
  **In-state tuition:** $12,300
  **Out-of-state:** $12,300
  **Room & board:** $5,380

**Housing Information**
  **University housing:** Yes
  **Fraternity:** No
  **Sorority:** No
  **Living on campus:** 35%

  **Athletics:** NCAA Div. III

# FAIRLEIGH DICKINSON UNIVERSITY

West Passaic and Montross Avenue, Rutherford, NJ 07070 • **Admissions:** 201-460-5267
**Email:** admissions@fdu.edu • **Web:** www.fdu.edu
**Support:** SP • **Institution:** 2 yr. & 4 yr. Private

## LEARNING DISABILITY ADMISSIONS AND SERVICES

The Regional Center for College Students with LD offers a structured plan of intensive advisement, academic support and counseling services that is tailored to unique needs of students with LD. The goal is to provide a framework within which college students with LD will develop the confidence to succeed in their studies and the independence to do their best. Planning, learning strategies, professional tutors, counseling, and accommodations are the cornerstones of the Regional Center. Staffed by professionals with services at both the Teaneck and the Madison campus, the LD Program and special services are free of charge. Assistance to students is intensive and the Program is fully integrated into the coursework. Students are in touch with faculty on a regular basis. The Program encourages involvement in the community, particularly service-type activities relevant to the students with LD. Performance data is routinely reviewed to identify students in need of more intensive help. Upon admission students are invited to attend a Sumner orientation session. During this time, students meet with Center staff to develop an Individual Academic Plan in order to develop a class schedule with the right balance.

## LEARNING DISABILITY ADMISSIONS INFORMATION

**Program Name:** Regional Center for College Students with LD
**Program Director:** Dr. Mary Farrell          **Telephone:** 201-692-2087
**Contact Person:** Same as above

### ADMISSIONS

Admissions decisions are made jointly by Admissions and LD Program Director. Criteria include: documentation of LD made by licensed professionals dated within 24 months of the application; IQ in average to above average range; evidence of adequate performance in mainstream college prep high school courses; evidence of motivation as reflected in recommendations. Students enrolled in all special education high school classes are usually not admissible. Lower level mainstream classes are acceptable from high schools offering different levels in the same subjects. ACT/SAT are required but do not carry much weight. Grades are viewed as the best predictors for success. Students with a 2.5 GPA and 850 SAT can be accepted. General admissions require top 2/5 of class or B average and 850 SAT. If applicants are below a 2.5 GPA and 850 SAT they may be referred to Edward Williams College, a 2 year college located on the Teaneck campus which requires an 18 ACT or 600 SAT. Admission decisions are made after careful review.

| | |
|---|---|
| **College entrance exams required:** Yes | **Untimed accepted:** Yes |
| **Course entrance requirements:** Yes | **Interview required:** No |
| **Diagnostic tests:** Yes | |
| **Documentation:** WAIS-R, WJ; PEB or equivalent: within 2 years. | |

### ADDITIONAL INFORMATION

Edward Williams College, a 2 year liberal arts college on the campus, offers services and accommodations to students with learning disabilities who are not admissible to Farleigh Dickinson. FDU students already enrolled in the university may request LD assessments on campus for no charge. Skills class for no college credit are offered in math and writing. Tutorial sessions incorporate a variety of teaching techniques. There is a 13 to 1 ratio between student and LD specialists. Support sessions are small individualized and flexible. In sophomore year students can request tutoring for 3 courses. Students have priority registration. Most students are seen by 3-4 different LD specialists who regularly exchange views on academic and counseling issues. Services include: recorded textbooks; extended testing time and other class support; technological support; and supervised study to meet with specialists in study rooms.

| | |
|---|---|
| **Special education HS coursework accepted:** No | **Essay required:** No |
| **Special application required:** Yes | **Submitted to:** Director of Program |
| **# of applications submitted each year:** 225 | **# of applications accepted each year:** 40 |
| **# of students receiving LD services:** 120 | |

**Acceptance into program means acceptance into college:** Students are accepted jointly by the Regional Center for College Students with Learning Disabilities and the Office of Admissions.

# LEARNING DISABILITY SERVICES

**Learning center:** Yes
**Kurzweil personal reader:** No
**LD specialists:** 10
**Allowed in exams:**
  **Calculator:** Yes
  **Dictionary:** No
  **Computer:** Yes
  **SpellCheck:** Yes

**Notetaker:** No
**Scribes:** No
**Proctors:** Yes
**Oral exams:** Yes
**Extended test time:** Yes
**Added cost:** None
**Distraction-free environ.:** Yes
**Tape recording in class:** Yes
**Books on tape:** Yes
**Taping of other books:** No

**Professional tutors:** 10
**Peer tutors:** No
**Max. hrs/wk for services:** Fr/8 hrs; Soph/3 hrs; Jr/2 hrs; Sen/1 hr.; per week
**Priority registration:** Yes
**Accomodations for students with ADD:** Yes
**How are professors notified of LD:** By the Director fresh/soph year and the student junior/seniors year

# GENERAL ADMISSIONS INFORMATION

**Director of Admissions:** Dale Herold

**Telephone:** 201-692-7304

## ENTRANCE REQUIREMENTS

Total high school units required/recommended: 17 total units are required; 4 English required, 3 math required, 2 science required, 3 science recommended, 2 foreign language required, 2 history required. Minimum combined SAT I score of 930, or minimum combined SAT I score of 850 with either rank in top two-fifths of secondary school class or a minimum B. Special requirements: 3 units of college prep math (including trigonometry), chemistry, and physics required of biochemistry, chemistry, engineering, and management science program applicants. 3 units of college prep math (including trigonometry) required of computer science/science program applicants. 3 units of college prep mathematics (including algebra and plane geometry) required of engineering technology program applicants. biology and chemistry required of medical technology and nursing program applicants. biology, chemistry, and physics required of allied health program applicants.

**Application deadline:** Rolling
**Notification:** Rolling

**SAT or ACT preferred:** SAT

**Graduated top 10% of class:** 9
**Graduated top 25% of class:** 27
**Graduated top 50% of class:** 59

# COLLEGE GRADUATION REQUIREMENTS

**Course waivers allowed:** No
**Course substitutions allowed:** Yes
**In what courses:** Math and foreign language substitutions may be granted if candidate qualifies as per university policy.

# ADDITIONAL INFORMATION

**Environment:** The Teaneck campus is located on the banks of the Hackensack River. It is within walking distance of Edward Williams Junior College.

**Student Body**
  **Undergrad enrollment:** 7,010
  **Women:** 52%
  **Men:** 48%
  **In-state students:** 87%
  **Out-of-state:** 13%

**Cost Information**
  **In-state tuition:** $12,600
  **Out-of-state:** $12,600
  **Room & board:** $5,864

**Housing Information**
  **University housing:** Yes
  **Fraternity:** No
  **Sorority:** No
  **Living on campus:** 44%

  **Athletics:** NCAA Div. I

# GEORGIAN COURT COLLEGE

900 Lakewood Avenue, Lakewood, NJ 08701 • **Admissions:** 908-364-2200 • **Fax:** 908-367-3920
**Email:** admissions-ugrad@georgian.edu • **Web:** www.georgian.edu
**Support:** CS • **Institution:** 4 yr. Private

## LEARNING DISABILITY ADMISSIONS AND SERVICES

The Learning Center (TLC) Program is an assistance program designed to provide an environment for students with mild to moderate learning disabilities who desire a college education. The program is not one of remediation, but an individualized support program to assist candidates in becoming successful college students. Emphasis is placed on developing self-help strategies and study techniques. To be eligible for the TLC program all applicants must submit the following: documentation for learning disability by a certified professional within a school system or state certified agency; the documentation must be current within 3 years and must include identification and description of the learning disability including the student's level of academic performance and effect upon learning; a recent Individualized Education Plan; other evaluations or recommendations from professionals who have recently provided services to the student; and additional documentation upon request. All applicants must have a personal interview.

## LEARNING DISABILITY ADMISSIONS INFORMATION

**Program Name:** The Learning Center (TLC)
**Program Director:** Genevieve Van Pelt          **Telephone:** 908-364-2200 ext. 659
**Contact Person:** Same as above

### ADMISSIONS

Applicants must meet the following: 16 academics units that include 4 yrs. English; 2 yrs. foreign language; 2 yrs. math; 1 yr. lab science; 1 yr. history; electives. The class rank and transcript should give evidence of the ability to succeed in college. Students must submit the SAT. Conditional admission may be offered to some applicants. The Associate Director of Admissions is the liaison person between the admissions staff and the TLC.

**College entrance exams required:** Yes          **Untimed accepted:** Yes
**Course entrance requirements:** Yes          **Interview required:** Yes
**Diagnostic tests:** Yes
**Documentation:** Psycho-educational evaluation: within 3 years

### ADDITIONAL INFORMATION

College graduation requirements are not waived for TLC students. Reduced course load is recommended for students with learning disabilities, and program completion may take longer than 4 years. There is a social worker and counselor on staff of the TLC to help students as well. TLC offers the following: an individualized support program; scheduled tutorial sessions with a learning disabilities specialist; faculty liaison; academic counseling; priority registration; organizational skills including time management, test taking, notetaking, and outlining; study techniques; memory and concentration techniques; techniques for planning and writing research papers; and content-tutoring if needed.

**Special education HS coursework accepted:** No          **Essay required:** No
**Special application required:** No          **Submitted to:** N/A
**# of applications submitted each year:** 120          **# of applications accepted each year:** 12
**# of students receiving LD services:** 23
**Acceptance into program means acceptance into college:** Students are admitted jointly into the The Learning Center and Georgian Court College.

## LEARNING DISABILITY SERVICES

**Learning center:** No
**Kurzweil personal reader:** No
**LD specialists:** Yes
**Allowed in exams:**
  **Calculator:** Yes
  **Dictionary:** Yes
  **Computer:** Y/N
  **SpellCheck:** Y/N

**Notetaker:** Yes
**Scribes:** Yes
**Proctors:** Yes
**Oral exams:** Yes
**Extended test time:** Yes
**Added cost:** $2,000/year
**Distraction-free environ.:** Yes
**Tape recording in class:** Yes
**Books on tape:** No
**Taping of other books:** No

**Professional tutors:** Yes
**Peer tutors:** Yes
**Max. hrs/wk for services:** Varies
**Priority registration:** Yes
**Accomodations for students with ADD:** Y/N
**How are professors notified of LD:** By the student and the Program Director

## GENERAL ADMISSIONS INFORMATION

**Director of Admissions:** Sandra Zerby

**Telephone:** 908-364-2200

### ENTRANCE REQUIREMENTS
Total high school units required/recommended: 16 total units are required; 4 English required, 2 math required, 1 science required, 2 foreign language required, 1 history required. Minimum combined SAT I score of 860 (composite ACT score of 19) and rank in top half of secondary school class required. Special requirements: An audition is required for music program applicants.

**Application deadline:** August 1
**Notification:** Rolling

**SAT or ACT preferred:** SAT
**SAT Avg:** 478V, 466M
**SAT II required:** Yes

**Graduated top 10% of class:** 6
**Graduated top 25% of class:** 28
**Graduated top 50% of class:** 70

## COLLEGE GRADUATION REQUIREMENTS

**Course waivers allowed:** No
**Course substitutions allowed:** No
**In what courses:** N/A

## ADDITIONAL INFORMATION

**Environment:** Georgian Court College is a small private institution centrally located in New Jersey.

**Student Body**
  **Undergrad enrollment:** 1,667
  **Women:** 95%
  **Men:** 5%
  **In-state students:** 99%
  **Out-of-state:** 1%

**Cost Information**
  **In-state tuition:** $10,332
  **Out-of-state:** $10,332
  **Room & board:** $4,500

**Housing Information**
  **University housing:** Yes
  **Fraternity:** No
  **Sorority:** No
  **Living on campus:** 26%

  **Athletics:** NAIA

# JERSEY CITY STATE COLLEGE

2039 Kennedy Boulevard, Jersey City, NJ 07305 • **Admissions:** 201-200-3234 • **Fax:** 201-200-2044
**Email:** admissions@jcsi.jcstate.edu
**Support:** CS • **Institution:** 4 yr. Public

## LEARNING DISABILITY ADMISSIONS AND SERVICES

Project Mentor is a support program that "opens the door" to higher education for students with learning disabilities by providing them with a faculty mentor—a teacher, advisor and facilitator—for their entire college career. The goal of Project Mentor is to offer services and support to students so that they may be academically successful and independent in college. A four week pre-college Summer Orientation Program prepares students for success in an academic setting. This Orientation Program provides an intensive academic and personal challenge as well as an orientation to college life. A central theme unifies instruction in the learning strategies necessary for success in college, which notetaking, test taking and organizational skills are integrated with content and applied in a simulated college course. Students must present certification of a specific neurologically based learning disability/difference that causes a problem in one or more of the basic psychological processes involved in understanding or using language, spoken or written. Difficulty in listening, reading, writing, spelling or doing mathematical calculations are among the ways that the problem is demonstrated.

## LEARNING DISABILITY ADMISSIONS INFORMATION

**Program Name:** Project Mentor
**Program Director:** Dr. Myra Ehrlich             **Telephone:** 201-200-2091
**Contact Person:** Same as above

### ADMISSIONS

Students with LD must complete a regular application and should address their application to the attention of Project Mentor. There is a place on the application that the student may check a box indicating a learning disability. All applicants to Project Mentor are requested to: schedule an interview; submit recommendations or telephone calls from a high school counselor and/or teacher; a recent child study team evaluation. The admissions process involves a review of the psycho-educational report. They are looking for students with the intellectual potential to achieve in a 4 year college setting who were mostly in mainstream college prep classes in high school. Although SAT scores are required, they are not used for admission purposes. All applications from students with learning disabilities are referred to Project Mentor. Project faculty review applications and make recommendations to the admissions for acceptance, rejection or trial status for a Pre-college Summer Orientation Program. The staff considers each candidate individually. All entering freshmen in Project Mentor must attend the Summer Orientation Program.

**College entrance exams required:** Yes          **Untimed accepted:** Yes
**Course entrance requirements:** Yes          **Interview required:** Yes
**Diagnostic tests:** Yes
**Documentation:** WAIS; LD evaluation; social assessment: within 3 years.

### ADDITIONAL INFORMATION

Students meet once a week with mentors. Sessions might include instruction, counseling and/or referral to services available to all students at the college. Exclusive tutorials for Project Mentor students are staffed by highly trained professionals. Mentors help the students to negotiate accommodations with their professors. Extending the limits on examinations, providing tutorial assistance and permitting tape recording of lectures are among the types of accommodations provided. Professors try to provide for the special needs of students with learning differences/disabilities while maintaining appropriate academic standards.

**Special education HS coursework accepted:** No          **Essay required:** Yes
**Special application required:** No          **Submitted to:** N/A
**# of applications submitted each year:** 100 (approx.)          **# of applications accepted each year:** 20-25
**# of students receiving LD services:** 70
**Acceptance into program means acceptance into college:** Admission is given to the college and the Program at the same time.

## LEARNING DISABILITY SERVICES

**Learning center:** No
**Kurzweil personal reader:** No
**LD specialists:** 3
**Allowed in exams:**
  **Calculator:** Yes
  **Dictionary:** Yes
  **Computer:** Yes
  **SpellCheck:** Yes

**Notetaker:** Yes
**Scribes:** Yes
**Proctors:** Yes
**Oral exams:** Yes
**Extended test time:** Yes
**Added cost:** There is a fee for summer program; there are no other fees
**Distraction-free environ.:** Yes
**Tape recording in class:** Yes
**Books on tape:** Yes
**Taping of other books:** Yes

**Professional tutors:** 4-5
**Peer tutors:** No
**Max. hrs/wk for services:** As needed
**Priority registration:** Yes
**Accomodations for students with ADD:** Yes
**How are professors notified of LD:** By the student and the Program Director

## GENERAL ADMISSIONS INFORMATION

**Director of Admissions:** Samuel McGhee

**Telephone:** 201-200-3234

### ENTRANCE REQUIREMENTS

Total high school units required/recommended: 16 total units are required; 4 English required, 3 math required, 2 science required, 2 social studies required. Minimum combined SAT I score of 800, rank in top half of secondary school class, and minimum 2.5 GPA required. Special requirements: An audition is required for music program applicants. An RN is required for nursing program applicants. TOEFL is required of all international students.

**Application deadline:** June 1
**Notification:** Rolling

**SAT or ACT preferred:** SAT
**SAT Avg:** 496V, 478M
**Average GPA:** 2.5

**Graduated top 10% of class:** 11
**Graduated top 25% of class:** 32
**Graduated top 50% of class:** 70

## COLLEGE GRADUATION REQUIREMENTS

**Course waivers allowed:** No
**Course substitutions allowed:** No
**In what courses:** N/A

## ADDITIONAL INFORMATION

**Environment:** The college is located on 150 acres in a suburban area 20 miles west of New York City.

**Student Body**
  **Undergrad enrollment:** 6,213
  **Women:** 56%
  **Men:** 44%
  **In-state students:** 90%
  **Out-of-state:** 10%

**Cost Information**
  **In-state tuition:** $3,528
  **Out-of-state:** $4,998
  **Room & board:** $5,000

**Housing Information**
  **University housing:** Yes
  **Fraternity:** No
  **Sorority:** No
  **Living on campus:** 5%

  **Athletics:** NCAA Div. III

# KEAN COLLEGE OF NEW JERSEY

Morris Avenue, Union, NJ 07083 • **Admissions:** 908-527-2195 • **Fax:** 908-351-5187
**Email:** admitme@turbo.kean.edu • **Web:** www.kean.edu
**Support:** CS • **Institution:** 4 yr. Public

## LEARNING DISABILITY ADMISSIONS AND SERVICES

In the past, learning disabilities have often prevented students from pursuing higher education. Kean College believes, however, that qualified students who have difficulties processing oral and written material have the potential to earn a college degree if they are provided with certain individualized support services. These services are designed to help students compensate for their disabilities and to enable them to reach their educational and career potential. Students with learning disabilities attend the same classes and meet the same academic requirements as their peers. They also participate fully in Kean's social, athletic, and extracurricular activities. The goals of Project Excel are to help students develop skills they need in order to be successful as independent, involved, responsible learners, and to help students with learning disabilities use their own assets to become successful learners.

## LEARNING DISABILITY ADMISSIONS INFORMATION

**Program Name:** Project Excel
**Program Director:** Marie Segal, Ed.D.
**Contact Person:** Same as above

**Telephone:** 908-527-2380

### ADMISSIONS

There is no special admissions process for students with learning disabilities. All applicants must meet the same admission criteria which include: 4 yrs. English, 3 yrs. math, 2 yrs. social studies, 2 yrs. science, and 5 years of electives. SAT/ACT are required. The student must be highly motivated, able to do college work, be of at least average intelligence, have a documented learning disability, have areas of academic strength, and make a commitment to work responsibly and attend classes, tutoring, workshops, and counseling sessions. Students are encouraged to apply early, by March. Once accepted, students who choose to register with Project Excel may do so by providing complete documentation of a diagnosed disability.

**College entrance exams required:** Yes
**Course entrance requirements:** Yes
**Diagnostic tests:** Yes
**Documentation:** Educational evaluation: within 3 years

**Untimed accepted:** Yes
**Interview required:** Yes

### ADDITIONAL INFORMATION

There are a number of services available through project Excel: diagnostic assessments; academic; career; personal advisement/counseling; development of a College Education Plan (CEP) for the individual student; student advocacy with faculty; referral to other college services as appropriate; and tutoring in basic skills and course materials. All information about the student's learning disability is held in strict confidence. Information shared on or off campus is only done with the student's signed consent. LD assessments are available for a fee of $225 for a professional assessment and $140 for an assessment from a student intern. The fees are reduced for Kean students. All students in Project Excel select from the same schedule of classes and attend with all other students in the college.

**Special education HS coursework accepted:** Yes
**Special application required:** Yes
**# of applications submitted each year:** N/I
**# of students receiving LD services:** N/A
**Acceptance into program means acceptance into college:** Students are admitted to the college and then may request services through Project Excel.

**Essay required:** Yes
**Submitted to:** Program Director
**# of applications accepted each year:** N/I

## LEARNING DISABILITY SERVICES

**Learning center:** Yes

**Kurzweil personal reader:** No

**LD specialists:** Yes

**Allowed in exams:**

  **Calculator:** Yes

  **Dictionary:** Yes

  **Computer:** Yes

  **SpellCheck:** Yes

**Notetaker:** Yes

**Scribes:** Yes

**Proctors:** Yes

**Oral exams:** Yes

**Extended test time:** Yes

**Added cost:** None

**Distraction-free environ.:** Yes

**Tape recording in class:** Yes

**Books on tape:** Yes

**Taping of other books:** No

**Professional tutors:** N/A

**Peer tutors:** N/A

**Max. hrs/wk for services:** N/I

**Priority registration:** Yes

**Accomodations for students with ADD:** Yes

**How are professors notified of LD:** By the student

## GENERAL ADMISSIONS INFORMATION

**Director of Admissions:** Audley Bridges

**Telephone:** 908-527-2195

### ENTRANCE REQUIREMENTS

Total high school units required/recommended: 16 total units are required; 4 English required, 3 math required, 2 science required, 2 social studies required, and five courses in academic electives. Special requirements: An RN is required for nursing program applicants.

**Application deadline:** June 30

**Notification:** Rolling

**SAT or ACT preferred:** SAT

**SAT Avg:** 492V, 495M

**Graduated top 10% of class:** 6

**Graduated top 25% of class:** 43

**Graduated top 50% of class:** 76

## COLLEGE GRADUATION REQUIREMENTS

**Course waivers allowed:** No

**Course substitutions allowed:** No

**In what courses:** N/A

## ADDITIONAL INFORMATION

**Environment:** The College is located on 151 acres in a suburban area 20 miles west of New York City.

**Student Body**

  **Undergrad enrollment:** 9,879

  **Women:** 63%

  **Men:** 37%

  **In-state students:** 96%

  **Out-of-state:** 4%

**Cost Information**

  **In-state tuition:** $3,367

  **Out-of-state:** $4,684

  **Room & board:** $4,970

**Housing Information**

  **University housing:** Yes

  **Fraternity:** No

  **Sorority:** No

  **Living on campus:** 12%

  **Athletics:** NCAA Div. III

# MONMOUTH UNIVERSITY

Norwood and Cedar Avenues, W. Long Branch, NJ 07764-1898 • **Admissions:** 800-543-9671
**Fax:** 732-263-5166 • **Email:** cbenol@mondec.monmouth.edu • **Web:** www.monmouth.edu
**Support:** CS • **Institution:** 4 yr. Private

## LEARNING DISABILITY ADMISSIONS AND SERVICES

Monmouth College recognizes the special needs of students with learning disabilities who are capable, with appropriate assistance, of excelling in a demanding college environment. Comprehensive support services and a nurturing environment contribute to their success. Monmouth's commitment is to provide a learning process and atmosphere which allows students to pursue their educational goals, realize their full potential, contribute actively to their community and society, and to determine the direction of their lives. Students are enrolled in regular courses and are not isolated from the rest of the student body in any manner. Much of their success has to do with individual recognition of their specific learning needs combined with supportive faculty.

## LEARNING DISABILITY ADMISSIONS INFORMATION

**Program Name:** Support Services for Students with LD
**Program Director:** Ann Grad
**Contact Person:** Christine Barsony

**Telephone:** 908-571-3460
**Telephone:** 908-571-3456

### ADMISSIONS

Students who self-identify on their application and do not meet regular admission criteria are considered for admission through an alternate admission procedure. Applicants must submit their IEP or private professional evaluation including the WAIS-R and Woodcock-Johnson. Applicants should also submit letters of recommendations, reports of co-curricular involvement, and statement of high school support services. The admission decision is made jointly by the coordinator of Students with Disabilities, Director and Associate Director of Admissions, and Coordinator of Academic Support Services. Applicants may be asked to interview with the committee.

**College entrance exams required:** Yes
**Course entrance requirements:** Yes
**Diagnostic tests:** Yes
**Documentation:** WAIS-R; W-J psychoeducational battery; achievement with scores: within 3 yrs.

**Untimed accepted:** Yes
**Interview required:** Recommended

### ADDITIONAL INFORMATION

Services available to all identified students with a learning disability include: notetakers, testing accommodations, advocacy, and liaison between the student and the professor. Some services are optional and available to students for a comprehensive fee per/semester including: professional and peer tutoring, instruction in academic survival skills, counseling, and advising specific to the learning style.

**Special education HS coursework accepted:** Yes
**Special application required:** No
**# of applications submitted each year:** 120-150
**# of students receiving LD services:** 110

**Essay required:** No
**Submitted to:** N/A
**# of applications accepted each year:** 75

**Acceptance into program means acceptance into college:** Students are accepted jointly into the college and the LD Program.

# LEARNING DISABILITY SERVICES

**Learning center:** No
**Kurzweil personal reader:** Yes
**LD specialists:** 2
**Allowed in exams:**
  **Calculator:** Yes
  **Dictionary:** Yes
  **Computer:** Y/N
  **SpellCheck:** Y/N

**Notetaker:** Yes
**Scribes:** Yes
**Proctors:** Yes
**Oral exams:** Yes
**Extended test time:** Yes
**Added cost:** $1,250 per/year
**Distraction-free environ.:** Yes
**Tape recording in class:** Yes
**Books on tape:** Yes
**Taping of other books:** Yes

**Professional tutors:** Yes
**Peer tutors:** Yes
**Max. hrs/wk for services:** As needed
**Priority registration:** Yes
**Accomodations for students with ADD:** Yes
**How are professors notified of LD:** A letter delivered by the student

# GENERAL ADMISSIONS INFORMATION

**Director of Admissions:** David Waggoner

**Telephone:** 908-571-3456

## ENTRANCE REQUIREMENTS

Total high school units required/recommended: 16 total units are required; 4 English required, 3 math required, 2 science required, 2 history required. Minimum combined SAT I score of 830 and minimum 2.0 GPA required. Special requirements: An RN is required for nursing program applicants.

**Application deadline:** April 1
**Notification:** Rolling

**SAT or ACT preferred:** SAT
**SAT Avg:** 509V, 503M
**Average GPA:** 2.61

**Graduated top 10% of class:** 7
**Graduated top 25% of class:** 24
**Graduated top 50% of class:** 62

# COLLEGE GRADUATION REQUIREMENTS

**Course waivers allowed:** Yes
**Course substitutions allowed:** Yes
**In what courses:** Individual needs

# ADDITIONAL INFORMATION

**Environment:** The college is located on 125 acres in a suburb 60 miles south of New York City.

**Student Body**
  **Undergrad enrollment:** 3,875
  **Women:** 5,7%
  **Men:** 43%
  **In-state students:** 92%
  **Out-of-state:** 8%

**Cost Information**
  **In-state tuition:** $13,270
  **Out-of-state:** $13,270
  **Room & board:** $6,623

**Housing Information**
  **University housing:** Yes
  **Fraternity:** No
  **Sorority:** No
  **Living on campus:** 45%

  **Athletics:** NCAA Div. I

# RIDER UNIVERSITY

2083 Lawrenceville Road, Lawrenceville, NJ 08648 • **Admissions:** 609-896-5042 • **Fax:** 609-895-6645
**Email:** TOLA@rider1.rider.edu • **Web:** www.rider.edu
**Support:** CS • **Institution:** 4 yr. Private

## LEARNING DISABILITY ADMISSIONS AND SERVICES

The Education Enhancement Program offers a range of services to help students with documented learning disabilities obtain appropriate accommodations. These services include screening and referral, supplementary assessment, and instructional services. The goal of the Program is to assist students in becoming more independent and efficient learners. A Learning Disability Specialist meets individually with students who have learning disabilities and/or attention deficit disorder. Students must initiate the request for this meeting and must supply documentation of the disability. These learning disability specialists conduct an "intake interview" and, based on the information resulting from this interview, refer students to appropriate support services. They also determine the appropriate academic adjustments.

## LEARNING DISABILITY ADMISSIONS INFORMATION

**Program Name:** Education Enhancement Program
**Program Director:** Dr. Jacqueline Simon
**Contact Person:** Dr. Barbara Blandford

**Telephone:** 609-896-5241
**Telephone:** 609-896-5000 ext.7365

### ADMISSIONS

There is no special admissions process for students with learning disabilities. All students must submit the general University application. Admissions criteria is based on the following: high school academic record and GPA of 2.0 or better; SAT or ACT test results; and a college writing sample (essay). Courses required include 16 acceptable units from a college prep curriculum: 4 yrs. English, 2 yrs. math, sciences, foreign language, social science, and humanities. For students with a learning disability proper documentation recognizing the differing abilities of the student is requested. The Rider Achievement Program is for academically admissible students who are just below the admissions criteria for the regularly admitted student. The Educational Opportunity Fund Program is the state-funded program for academically disadvantaged or economically disadvantaged students.

**College entrance exams required:** Yes
**Course entrance requirements:** Yes
**Diagnostic tests:** Yes
**Documentation:** Educational and psychological tests; within 3 years

**Untimed accepted:** Yes
**Interview required:** If requested

### ADDITIONAL INFORMATION

The Rider Learning Center provides individual and small group tutoring in writing, reading comprehension, and study strategies. The staff offers study strategy workshops and students have access to computers. The Mathematics Skill Lab provides a math course for students who do not meet the placement criteria for college level math. The course is taught via individual tutoring, structured workshops, and computer-assisted instruction. The MSL staff offers weekly tutorial sessions for Finite Math, helps students prepare for the Algebra & Trig Qualifying Exam, and provides tutoring for other courses. Tutoring Services provide a peer tutoring program for students needing extra help. The Education Enhancement Program offers a course in College Reading and the English Department offers tutoring to improve composition skills.

**Special education HS coursework accepted:** Perhaps; each course is evaluated individually
**Essay required:** Yes
**Special application required:** No
**# of applications submitted each year:** N/A
**# of students receiving LD services:** Approximately 50 per semester
**Acceptance into program means acceptance into college:** Students must be admitted to the college first and then may request LD services.

**Submitted to:** N/A
**# of applications accepted each year:** N/A

# LEARNING DISABILITY SERVICES

**Learning center:** No
**Kurzweil personal reader:** No
**LD specialists:** 2
**Allowed in exams:**
  **Calculator:** Yes
  **Dictionary:** Y/N
  **Computer:** Y/N
  **SpellCheck:** Y/N

**Notetaker:** No
**Scribes:** Yes
**Proctors:** Yes
**Oral exams:** Yes
**Extended test time:** Yes
**Added cost:** None
**Distraction-free environ.:** Yes
**Tape recording in class:** Yes
**Books on tape:** Yes
**Taping of other books:** No

**Professional tutors:** 4
**Peer tutors:** 30
**Max. hrs/wk for services:** Usually not more than 3
**Priority registration:** Yes
**Accomodations for students with ADD:** Yes
**How are professors notified of LD:** By the student and the Program Director

# GENERAL ADMISSIONS INFORMATION

**Director of Admissions:** Susan Christian          **Telephone:** 609-896-5042

## ENTRANCE REQUIREMENTS

Total high school units required/recommended: 16 total units are required; 4 English required, 3 math recommended, 3 science recommended, 3 social studies recommended. Minimum combined SAT I score of 800 and rank in top half of secondary school class. Special requirements: Algebra I and II and geometry required of business, math, and science program applicants.

**Application deadline:** Rolling
**Notification:** Rolling

**SAT or ACT preferred:** SAT
**SAT Avg:** 505V, 509M
**SAT II required:** Yes

**Graduated top 10% of class:** 13
**Graduated top 25% of class:** 39
**Graduated top 50% of class:** 61

# COLLEGE GRADUATION REQUIREMENTS

**Course waivers allowed:** No
**Course substitutions allowed:** Yes
**In what courses:** There are no waivers of any courses. Substitutions are considered on a case-by-case basis through the Associate Deans. The courses would vary depending on students' individual disabilities and needs.

# ADDITIONAL INFORMATION

**Environment:** The college is located on a 353-acre campus between Princeton and Trenton, New Jersey.

**Student Body**
  **Undergrad enrollment:** 3,633
  **Women:** 60%
  **Men:** 40%
  **In-state students:** 73%
  **Out-of-state:** 27%

**Cost Information**
  **In-state tuition:** $14,400
  **Out-of-state:** $14,400
  **Room & board:** $6,030

**Housing Information**
  **University housing:** Yes
  **Fraternity:** Yes
  **Sorority:** Yes
  **Living on campus:** 70%

  **Athletics:** NCAA Div. I

# SETON HALL UNIVERSITY

400 South Orange Avenue, South Orange, NJ 07079 • **Admissions:** 973-761-9332
**Fax:** 973-761-93329452 • **Email:** thehall@shu.edu • **Web:** www.shu.edu
**Support:** S • **Institution:** 4 yr. Private

## LEARNING DISABILITY ADMISSIONS AND SERVICES

Student Support Services is an academic program that addresses the needs of all eligible undergraduates. The program provides individual and group tutoring in many disciplines. Academic, career, and other counseling services are also available. The program provides individual and group tutoring in many disciplines. Special emphasis is placed on mathematics, laboratory sciences, and business. Student Support Services is especially attentive to the needs of students who can provide professional documentation of specific disabilities. Every effort is made to accommodate the special academic needs of these students by recommending extended test-time and a distraction-free testing environment.

## LEARNING DISABILITY ADMISSIONS INFORMATION

**Program Name:** Student Support Services
**Program Director:** Raynette Gardner
**Contact Person:** Reverend Ray Frazier

**Telephone:** 201-761-9166
**Telephone:** 201-761-9168

### ADMISSIONS

There is no special admissions for students with learning disabilities, and all applicants must meet the same admission criteria. Courses required include: 4 yrs. English, 3 yrs. math, 1 yr. lab science, 2 yrs. foreign language, 2 yrs. social studies, and 4 electives. The minimum SAT is 900. Students need to rank in the top 2/5 of their class and a minimum 2.5 GPA is recommended.

**College entrance exams required:** Yes
**Course entrance requirements:** Yes
**Diagnostic tests:** Yes
**Documentation:** Depends on the student's needs

**Untimed accepted:** Yes
**Interview required:** No

### ADDITIONAL INFORMATION

In coordinating its activities with other departments of the university, (such as Residence Life and Academic Services), Student Support Services works to assure that the university remains in compliance with all federal laws and regulations. The Program also assists students in arranging for notetakers and obtaining adaptive equipment and textbooks or cassette tapes.

**Special education HS coursework accepted:** No
**Special application required:** N/A
**# of applications submitted each year:** N/A
**# of students receiving LD services:** 30
**Acceptance into program means acceptance into college:** Students must be admitted to the university first and then may request LD services.

**Essay required:** No
**Submitted to:** N/A
**# of applications accepted each year:** N/A

# LEARNING DISABILITY SERVICES

**Learning center:** No
**Kurzweil personal reader:** Yes
**LD specialists:** No
**Allowed in exams:**
  **Calculator:** N/A
  **Dictionary:** N/A
  **Computer:** N/A
  **SpellCheck:** N/A

**Notetaker:** Yes
**Scribes:** No
**Proctors:** Yes
**Oral exams:** Yes
**Extended test time:** Yes
**Added cost:** None
**Distraction-free environ.:** Yes
**Tape recording in class:** Yes
**Books on tape:** Yes
**Taping of other books:** No

**Professional tutors:** Yes
**Peer tutors:** Yes
**Max. hrs/wk for services:**
Depends on needs and availability
**Priority registration:** No
**Accomodations for students with ADD:** Yes
**How are professors notified of LD:** By the student and the Program Director

# GENERAL ADMISSIONS INFORMATION

**Director of Admissions:** Ed Blankmeyer          **Telephone:** 201-761-9332

## ENTRANCE REQUIREMENTS

Total high school units required/recommended: 16 total units are required; 4 English required, 3 math required, 1 science required, 2 foreign language required, 2 social studies required. Minimum combined SAT I score of 900, rank in top two-fifths of secondary school class, and minimum 2.5 GPA recommended. Special requirements: 2 units of lab science required of nursing program applicants.

**Application deadline:** March 1
**Notification:** Rolling after January 1

**SAT or ACT preferred:** Either
**SAT Avg:** 519V, 518M
**ACT Range:** 21–22
**Average GPA:** 3.0

**Graduated top 10% of class:** 13
**Graduated top 25% of class:** 32
**Graduated top 50% of class:** 67

# COLLEGE GRADUATION REQUIREMENTS

**Course waivers allowed:** No
**Course substitutions allowed:** No
**In what courses:** N/A

# ADDITIONAL INFORMATION

**Environment:** The university is located on 58 acres in a suburban area 14 miles west of New York City.

**Student Body**
  **Undergrad enrollment:** 4,096
  **Women:** 52%
  **Men:** 48%
  **In-state students:** 84%
  **Out-of-state:** 16%

**Cost Information**
  **In-state tuition:** $12,300
  **Out-of-state:** $12,300
  **Room & board:** $6,796

**Housing Information**
  **University housing:** Yes
  **Fraternity:** No
  **Sorority:** No
  **Living on campus:** 50%

  **Athletics:** NCAA Div. I

# NEW MEXICO STATE UNIVERSITY

**NM**

Box 30001, Department 3004, Las Cruces, NM 88003 • **Admissions:** 505-646-3121 • **Fax:** 505-646-6330
**Email:** admissions@nmsu.edu • **Web:** www.nmsu.edu
**Support:** S • **Institution:** 4 yr. Public

## LEARNING DISABILITY ADMISSIONS AND SERVICES

Services for Students with disAbilities is a component of the Office of Student Development. The staff are committed to providing information and services which assist students with disabilities in personal and academic adjustment to the university community. Services for Students with disAbilities provide assistance with procuring auxiliary aids, coordinating services and resources, and discussing special needs and accommodations, and serving as consultants regarding questions about various accommodations. They work with students to ensure that they have access to all programs and services that will effect their full participation in the campus community. Students are encouraged to contact Services for Students with disAbilities to discuss needs and to register for the program. Students should complete the Petition for Services for Students with disAbilities and return it with the appropriate documentation for evaluation and review. A review committee will determine eligibility, the specific services and accommodations to be provided, and the student will be notified by the Coordinator. This process takes time and students are encouraged to start the process as soon as possible.

## LEARNING DISABILITY ADMISSIONS INFORMATION

**Program Name:** Services for Students with DisAbilities
**Program Director:** Mary Thumann, Coordinator          **Telephone:** 505-646-1921
**Contact Person:** Same as above

### ADMISSIONS

Admission criteria is the same for all students. Admissions can be on a regular status or provisional status. Regular admission: high school GPA 2.0 and 20 ACT or high school GPA 2.5 or 21 ACT or 970 SAT. Course requirements include 4 yrs. English, 2 yrs. science, 3 yrs. math, and 1 yr. foreign language. Provisional status is possible for students who have a high school grade average of 2.1 and 18 ACT. Students admitted provisionally must take at least 6 but not more than 12 credits in a regular semester and at least 3, but not more than 6, in a summer session.

**College entrance exams required:** Yes          **Untimed accepted:** Yes
**Course entrance requirements:** Yes          **Interview required:** No
**Diagnostic tests:** Yes
**Documentation:** Accepted from diagnostician or psychologist; within 3 years

### ADDITIONAL INFORMATION

The Center for Learning Assistance offers students the skills they need to excel in college. Students work with learning facilitators to develop or maximize the skills needed for college success. Assistance is offered in time management, concentration, memory, test preparation, test-taking, listening/notetaking, textbook reading techniques, math/science study skills, reasoning skills, writing, spelling, and grammar. Student Support Services is a program of academic and personal support with the goal of improving the retention and graduation of undergraduate students with disabilities. A mentor is provided for all participants to help motivate them and tutors help with study skills in specific subjects. Students may have tutors in two subjects and can meet weekly. Other services available are: early registration; notetaking services; readers; and test accommodations including extended time, a quiet location, scribes, readers, or other assistance with exams. All services are free.

**Special education HS coursework accepted:** Yes          **Essay required:** No
**Special application required:** Yes          **Submitted to:** Coordinator, Disabled Student Programs
**# of applications submitted each year:** N/A          **# of applications accepted each year:** N/A
**# of students receiving LD services:** 89
**Acceptance into program means acceptance into college:** Students must be admitted to the university first and then may request LD services.

## LEARNING DISABILITY SERVICES

**Learning center:** No
**Kurzweil personal reader:** Yes
**LD specialists:** No
**Allowed in exams:**
 Calculator: Y/N
 Dictionary: Y/N
 Computer: Y/N
 SpellCheck: Y/N

**Notetaker:** Yes
**Scribes:** Yes
**Proctors:** Yes
**Oral exams:** Yes
**Extended test time:** Yes
**Added cost:** None
**Distraction-free environ.:** Yes
**Tape recording in class:** Yes
**Books on tape:** Yes
**Taping of other books:** Yes

**Professional tutors:** No
**Peer tutors:** Yes
**Max. hrs/wk for services:**
Unlimited
**Priority registration:** Yes
**Accomodations for students
with ADD:** Yes
**How are professors notified of
LD:** By the student and the
Director of Services

## GENERAL ADMISSIONS INFORMATION

**Director of Admissions:** Angela Moss

**Telephone:** 505-646-3121

### ENTRANCE REQUIREMENTS

Total high school units required/recommended: 12 total units are required; 4 English required, 3 math required, 2 science required, 1 foreign language required. Minimum composite ACT score of 20 (combined SAT I score of 770) and minimum 2.25 GPA required.

**Application deadline:** Rolling
**Notification:** Rolling

**SAT or ACT preferred:** ACT
**Average ACT:** 22
**Average GPA:** 3.3

## COLLEGE GRADUATION REQUIREMENTS

**Course waivers allowed:** Yes
**Course substitutions allowed:** Yes
**In what courses:** Students need to negotiate with the college in which he/she is majoring.

## ADDITIONAL INFORMATION

**Environment:** The university is located on 5,800 acres in a suburban area 40 miles north of El Paso, Texas.

**Student Body**
 **Undergrad enrollment:** 11,872
 **Women:** 52%
 **Men:** 48%
 **In-state students:** 89%
 **Out-of-state:** 11%

**Cost Information**
 **In-state tuition:** $2,196
 **Out-of-state:** $7,152
 **Room & board:** $3,180

**Housing Information**
 **University housing:** Yes
 **Fraternity:** Yes
 **Sorority:** Yes
 **Living on campus:** 25%

 **Athletics:** NCAA Div. I

# NM

# COLLEGE OF SANTA FE

1600 St. Michael's Drive, Santa Fe, NM 87505 • **Admissions:** 505-473-6131 • **Fax:** 505-473-6127
**Email:** admission@fogelson.csf.edu • **Web:** www.state.nm.us/csf
**Support:** CS • **Institution:** 4 yr. Private

## LEARNING DISABILITY ADMISSIONS AND SERVICES

The Center for Academic Excellence is a federally funded Title IV Support Services Program designed to assist eligible students to graduate from CSF. There is no formal program at the college, but the students do have access to many services and accommodations. Students with learning disabilities may receive services in basic skills instruction of reading, study strategies, writing, math, humanities, and science. Students work with the professional staff to set up a support program that meets their specific needs. The initial meeting is during registration. The classes at the college of Santa Fe are small and students have access to meeting with their professors. There is a great deal of in-servicing that takes place on campus, and the instructors are very sensitive to the needs of students with learning disabilities. In order to be eligible for services students with learning disabilities must provide a current psychoeducational evaluation which identifies the learning disability. Once this documentation is on file with the Center for Academic Excellence, students may meet with staff to identify the necessary accommodations needed to be successful in college.

## LEARNING DISABILITY ADMISSIONS INFORMATION

**Program Name:** Center for Academic Excellence
**Program Director:** Marilyn P. Pressley, Ph.D.
**Contact Person:** Carol Conoboy

**Telephone:** 505-473-6447
**Telephone:** 505-473-6112

### ADMISSIONS

The students' learning disability must be documented by copies of diagnostic examinations not more than 3 years old. These tests are sent to the Admissions Office along with the CSF application. Students with learning disabilities are required to meet the general admission criteria. However, each applicant is evaluated individually. Academic Probation Support Program is available for students who are new or returning to CSF. These students may have performed inconsistently in high school or have a GPA lower then 2.0. If admitted, students must meet with a CAD support advisor and contract for weekly support for the semester.

**College entrance exams required:** Yes
**Course entrance requirements:** Yes
**Diagnostic tests:** Yes
**Documentation:** Psychoeducational evaluation: within 3 years

**Untimed accepted:** Yes
**Interview required:** Recommended

### ADDITIONAL INFORMATION

The following services are available: reading and study skills instructors to assist students in areas of comprehension and organization; mastery in time management, notetaking, textbook reading, and test taking. Assistance is also available in dealing with math anxiety and in integrating reading, writing, and study skills for specific courses. Staff is available to spend extra time with individual students who need additional assistance with various skills such as time management, organization, and studying techniques. There is a Reading and Study Skills Specialist who works one-on-one with students. Students are also assisted in developing self-advocacy skills.

**Special education HS coursework accepted:** N/I
**Special application required:** No
**# of applications submitted each year:** N/A
**# of students receiving LD services:** 150

**Essay required:** No
**Submitted to:** N/A
**# of applications accepted each year:** N/A

**Acceptance into program means acceptance into college:** Students are admitted to the college and to the Center for Academic Excellence at the same time.

## LEARNING DISABILITY SERVICES

**Learning center:** Yes
**Kurzweil personal reader:** No
**LD specialists:** Yes
**Allowed in exams:**
  **Calculator:** Yes
  **Dictionary:** Yes
  **Computer:** Yes
  **SpellCheck:** Yes

**Notetaker:** Yes
**Scribes:** Yes
**Proctors:** Yes
**Oral exams:** Yes
**Extended test time:** Yes
**Added cost:** None
**Distraction-free environ.:** Yes
**Tape recording in class:** Yes
**Books on tape:** Yes
**Taping of other books:** No

**Professional tutors:** 4
**Peer tutors:** 13
**Max. hrs/wk for services:** depends on needs and availability
**Priority registration:** No
**Accomodations for students with ADD:** Yes
**How are professors notified of LD:** By the student and the Program Director

## GENERAL ADMISSIONS INFORMATION

**Director of Admissions:** Monica Martinez          **Telephone:** 505-473-6133

### ENTRANCE REQUIREMENTS

Total high school units required/recommended: 16 total units are required; 3 English required, 4 English recommended, 2 math required, 4 math recommended, 2 science required, 4 science recommended, 2 social studies required, 1 history recommended. Minimum composite ACT score of 19 (combined SAT I score of 900) and minimum 2.5 GPA required. Special requirements: An audition is required for music program applicants. TOEFL is required of all international students. Audition required of performing arts program applicants.

**Application deadline:** March 15
**Notification:** Rolling

**SAT or ACT preferred:** Either
**SAT Avg:** 556V, 523M
**Average ACT:** 24
**Average GPA:** 3.1

**Graduated top 10% of class:** 17
**Graduated top 25% of class:** 44
**Graduated top 50% of class:** 75

## COLLEGE GRADUATION REQUIREMENTS

**Course waivers allowed:** N/A
**Course substitutions allowed:** N/A
**In what courses:** Foreign Language is not required to graduate from the college. All students must take the equivalent of Math 100 (Pre-Algebra). Students may waive out of this requirement by having a 20 on the Math portion of the ACT or a 400 on the Math section of the SAT I.

## ADDITIONAL INFORMATION

**Environment:** The college is located on 118 acres in a suburban area of Santa Fe.

**Student Body**
  **Undergrad enrollment:** 1,556
  **Women:** 57%
  **Men:** 43%
  **In-state students:** 40%
  **Out-of-state:** 60%

**Cost Information**
  **In-state tuition:** $11,796
  **Out-of-state:** $11,796
  **Room & board:** $4,400

**Housing Information**
  **University housing:** Yes
  **Fraternity:** No
  **Sorority:** No
  **Living on campus:** 52%

  **Athletics:** NR

# ADELPHI UNIVERSITY

Garden City, NY 11530 • **Admissions:** 516-877-3050 • **Fax:** 516-877-3039
**Email:** steiner/@adlibu.adelphi.edu • **Web:** www.adelphi.edu
**Support:** SP • **Institution:** 4 yr. Private

## LEARNING DISABILITY ADMISSIONS AND SERVICES

The approach of the Program provides an atmosphere where students with learning disabilities can realize their potential. The Program is specially designed for students who are unable to process oral and written materials in conventional ways, but who excel in other ways. Adelphi's program for students with learning disabilities provides each student with the support of an inter-disciplinary team of experienced professionals in tutoring and counseling. All instruction, counseling, and assessment is provided by more than fifteen professionals with advanced degrees in special education and social work. Students meet individually with an educator and a counselor who work as a team. There is a mandatory 5 week Summer Program prior to freshman year.  Students must attend tutoring sessions 2 times a week, participate in all the program's services, and sign an agreement acknowledging their academic commitment. Parents are involved in the entire process. Students attend classes in their chosen major, meet standard academic requirements, and participate in Adelphi's Core Curriculum, a rigorous and integrated series of courses designed to engage the student's mind and cultivate intellect in the tradition of liberal learning. The goal is independence in the academic and the real world.

## LEARNING DISABILITY ADMISSIONS INFORMATION

**Program Name:** Program for College Students with Learning Disabilities
**Contact Person:** Sandra Holzinger or Susan O'Sullivan          **Telephone:** 516-877-4710

### ADMISSIONS

The Admissions Committee reviews all submitted materials for a total picture of strengths and disabilities. Applicants with LD who show an ability to succeed academically are invited to interview. They must submit a high school transcript,  documentation of LD,  ACT/SAT scores, and a handwritten essay answering the question "What special considerations should the Admissions Committee take into account when evaluating your application?" The Director of the Program is actively involved in the admissions decision. Motivation, college prep courses, average or higher IQ (WAIS-R), interview, documentation, and a recommendation from an LD specialist are other factors which are used in making an admission decision. Prior to applying applicants should attend a group information session conducted by the Program for College Students with LD. The university is seeking highly motivated and socially mature individuals with average or above average intelligence who are capable of handling full academic schedules.

| | |
|---|---|
| **College entrance exams required:** Yes | **Untimed accepted:** Yes |
| **Course entrance requirements:** Yes | **Interview required:** Yes |
| **Diagnostic tests:** Yes | |
| **Documentation:** WAIS-R: within 1 year | |

### ADDITIONAL INFORMATION

Students receive intensive academic tutoring and individual counseling which is begun in the summer program. Course content and requirements are never compromised for students with learning disabilities, but program procedures do help to ease the way in the classroom—for example: in individual tutorials professional special educators teach how to get the most of studies; instructors are privately notified in writing and by phone if Program students are in their classes; students may tape record class lectures if notetaking is difficult; learning-specialists work closely with the Center to coordinate extended-time testing; individual counseling enables students to understand their behavior, reduce anxiety, and grow emotionally. There is an 80% retention rate and 10% of these students make the Dean's list. Services and accommodations are available for undergraduate and graduate students.

| | |
|---|---|
| **Special education HS coursework accepted:** Yes | **Essay required:** Yes |
| **Special application required:** No | **Submitted to:** N/A |
| **# of applications submitted each year:** 150 | **# of applications accepted each year:** 75 |
| **# of students receiving LD services:** 100 | |

**Acceptance into program means acceptance into college:** Students must be admitted to the university and then request consideration for the Program.

## LEARNING DISABILITY SERVICES

**Learning center:** Yes
**Kurzweil personal reader:** Yes
**LD specialists:** 7
**Allowed in exams:**
  **Calculator:** Y/N
  **Dictionary:** Y/N
  **Computer:** Yes
  **SpellCheck:** Y/N

**Notetaker:** Yes
**Scribes:** Yes
**Proctors:** Yes
**Oral exams:** Yes
**Extended test time:** Yes
**Added cost:** $1,900 per/semester
**Distraction-free environ.:** Yes
**Tape recording in class:** Yes
**Books on tape:** Yes
**Taping of other books:** Yes

**Professional tutors:** 7
**Peer tutors:** No
**Max. hrs/wk for services:** 3
**Priority registration:** Yes
**Accomodations for students with ADD:** Yes
**How are professors notified of LD:** By the student and the Program Director

## GENERAL ADMISSIONS INFORMATION

**Director of Admissions:** Esther Goodcuff          **Telephone:** 516-877-3050

### ENTRANCE REQUIREMENTS

Total high school units required/recommended: 16 total units are recommended; 4 English recommended, 3 math recommended, 3 science recommended, 4 social studies recommended. Minimum combined SAT I score of 950 and minimum 2.5 GPA recommended. Special requirements: A portfolio is required for art program applicants. An audition is required for music program applicants. TOEFL is required of all international students. Audition required of performing arts program applicants. Portfolio required of technical theater program applicants.

**Application deadline:** Rolling          **SAT or ACT preferred:** Either
**Notification:** Rolling

## COLLEGE GRADUATION REQUIREMENTS

**Course waivers allowed:** No
**Course substitutions allowed:** Yes
**In what courses:** Composition

## ADDITIONAL INFORMATION

**Environment:** The university is located on a 75-acre campus 20 miles from New York City.

**Student Body**
  **Undergrad enrollment:** NR
  **Women:** 66%
  **Men:** 34%
  **In-state students:** 91%
  **Out-of-state:** 9%

**Cost Information**
  **In-state tuition:** $12,800
  **Out-of-state:** $12,800
  **Room & board:** $6,450

**Housing Information**
  **University housing:** Yes
  **Fraternity:** No
  **Sorority:** No
  **Living on campus:** 12%

  **Athletics:** NCAA Div. II

# COLGATE UNIVERSITY

13 Oak Drive, Hamilton, NY 13346 • **Admissions:** 315-824-7401 • **Fax:** 315-824-7544
**Email:** admission@center.colgate.edu • **Web:** www.colgate.edu
**Support:** CS • **Institution:** 4 yr. Private

## LEARNING DISABILITY ADMISSIONS AND SERVICES

Colgate provides for a small student body a liberal arts education that will expand individual potential and ability to participate effectively in society's affairs. There are many resources available for all students. Their goal is to offer resources and services within the campus-wide support system that are responsive to the various talents, needs, and preferences of students with disabilities. In order for the university to understand and prepare for the accommodations that may be requested, students are asked to complete a confidential self-assessment questionnaire and provide appropriate documentation about their disability. The Coordinator of Academic Support works with students and faculty to assure that the needs of students with disabilities are met; serves as clearinghouse for information about disabilities; provides training and individual consultation for all members of the Colgate community; provides academic counseling and individualized instruction; and advises the students with disabilities resource group. Students must contact the Director of the Academic Support in order to make the university aware of the existence of their learning disability. Seeking help early and learning to be a self-advocate are essential to college success.

## LEARNING DISABILITY ADMISSIONS INFORMATION

**Program Name:** Academic Program Services
**Program Director:** Lynn Waldman
**Contact Person:** Same as above

**Telephone:** 315-824-7225

### ADMISSIONS

There is no special admission process for students with learning disabilities. The Office of Admissions reviews the applications of all candidates for admission. The admission staff looks for evidence of substantial achievement in a rigorous secondary school curriculum and one counselor recommendation; standardized testing; personalized essay; and extracurricular involvement. Also valued are qualities such as curiosity, originality, thoughtfulness, and persistence. Admission is very competitive and criteria includes: 4 yrs. English, 3–4 yrs. math, 3–4 yrs. science, 3–4 yrs. social studies, 2–3 yrs. foreign language; ACT range 27–30 or SAT I 1250–1410 and 3 SAT II including Writing and 2 others of student choice.

**College entrance exams required:** Yes
**Course entrance requirements:** Yes
**Diagnostic tests:** Yes
**Documentation:** Psycho-educational testing: within 3 years

**Untimed accepted:** Yes
**Interview required:** No

### ADDITIONAL INFORMATION

Students are encouraged to seek help early; meet with professors at the beginning of each semester to discuss approaches and accommodations that will meet their needs; and seek assistance from the Coordinator of Academic Support, administrative adviser, and faculty adviser. Modifications in the curriculum are made on an individual basis. Colgate provides services in support of academic work on as-needed basis such as: assistance with notetakers; tape-recorded lectures; tutors, readers; and assistive technology. Skills courses are offer in writing (for credit), reading, and study skills. Services and accommodations are available for undergraduate and graduate students.

**Special education HS coursework accepted:** No
**Special application required:** No
**# of applications submitted each year:** N/A
**# of students receiving LD services:** 50

**Essay required:** Yes
**Submitted to:** N/A
**# of applications accepted each year:** N/A

**Acceptance into program means acceptance into college:** Students must be admitted to the university and then reviewed for LD services.

# LEARNING DISABILITY SERVICES

**Learning center:** Yes
**Kurzweil personal reader:** No
**LD specialists:** 1
**Allowed in exams:**
  **Calculator:** Yes
  **Dictionary:** Yes
  **Computer:** Yes
  **SpellCheck:** Yes

**Notetaker:** Yes
**Scribes:** Yes
**Proctors:** Yes
**Oral exams:** Yes
**Extended test time:** Yes
**Added cost:** None
**Distraction-free environ.:** Yes
**Tape recording in class:** Yes
**Books on tape:** RFB
**Taping of other books:** Yes

**Professional tutors:** Yes
**Peer tutors:** Yes
**Max. hrs/wk for services:**
Unlimited
**Priority registration:** Yes
**Accomodations for students**
**with ADD:** Yes
**How are professors notified of**
**LD:** By the student

# GENERAL ADMISSIONS INFORMATION

**Director of Admissions:** Mary F. Hill

**Telephone:** 315-824-7401

## ENTRANCE REQUIREMENTS
Total high school units required/recommended: 16 total units are recommended; 4 English recommended, 4 math recommended, 3 science recommended, 2 social studies recommended. Special requirements: TOEFL is required of all international students.

**Application deadline:** January 15
**Notification:** April 1

**SAT or ACT preferred:** Either
**SAT Avg:** 637V, 644M
**SAT II required:** Yes
**Average ACT:** 28
**Average GPA:** 3.45

**Graduated top 10% of class:** 54
**Graduated top 25% of class:** 88
**Graduated top 50% of class:** 100

# COLLEGE GRADUATION REQUIREMENTS

**Course waivers allowed:** Y/N
**Course substitutions allowed:** Y/N
**In what courses:** All requests are considered case-by-case; Foreign Language is required for graduation from the university.

# ADDITIONAL INFORMATION

**Environment:** NR

**Student Body**
  **Undergrad enrollment:** 2,849
  **Women:** 52%
  **Men:** 48%
  **In-state students:** 34%
  **Out-of-state:** 66%

**Cost Information**
  **In-state tuition:** $22,610
  **Out-of-state:** $22,610
  **Room & board:** $6,110

**Housing Information**
  **University housing:** Yes
  **Fraternity:** Yes
  **Sorority:** Yes
  **Living on campus:** 75%

  **Athletics:** NCAA Div. I

# NY CONCORDIA COLLEGE (NY)

171 White Plains Road, Bronxville, NY 10708 • **Admissions:** 914-337-9300 • **Fax:** 914-395-4500
Email: admission@concordia-ny.edu • **Web:** www.concordia-ny.edu
**Support:** SP • **Institution:** 4 yr. Private

## LEARNING DISABILITY ADMISSIONS AND SERVICES

Concordia Connection is a program for students with learning disabilities who have demonstrated the potential to earn a college degree. Their commitment is to provide an intimate, supportive, and caring environment where students with special learning needs can experience college as a successful and rewarding endeavor. This is a mainstream program. Students are fully integrated into the college. During the fall and spring semesters students are registered for 4 to 5 classes. Additionally, students are registered for a one-credit independent study incorporating: weekly, one-hour group session with the Director and staff that focus on the development of individualized learning strategies; and a minimum of two additional study sessions per week with Concordia Connection staff to address specific course requirements. Progress is monitored and assessment of learning potential and academic levels is provided. The Program's assistant director serves as the freshman advisor and coordinates support services. Enrollment is limited to 15 students. A 3-day summer orientation and academic seminar is required for all new Concordia Connection students.

## LEARNING DISABILITY ADMISSIONS INFORMATION

**Program Name:** The Concordia Connection
**Program Director:** George Groth, Psy.D.                     **Telephone:** 914-337-9300 ext. 2361
**Contact Person:** David Doring                               **Telephone:** 914-337-9300 ext. 2184

### ADMISSIONS

Students wishing to apply should submit the following documents to the Admissions Office: a Concordia Application; current transcript; SAT/ACT; documentation of LD which must minimally include a WAIS-R profile with subtest scores within the past year and the most recent IEP; recommendations from LD specialist and guidance counselor; essay describing the nature of the LD and the effect on learning patterns and reason for pursuing college. Visits are encouraged. Student must be a high school graduate, have a diagnosed LD, have college prep courses, be emotionally stable and committed to being successful. General admissions criteria include: "B" average; ACT/SAT are used to assess strengths and weaknesses rather than for acceptance or denial; college preparatory courses in high school (foreign language is recommended but not required). Students with learning disabilities who self-disclose and provide documentation will be reviewed by the Office of Admission and the Director of Concordia Connection.

**College entrance exams required:** Yes                 **Untimed accepted:** Yes
**Course entrance requirements:** Yes                    **Interview required:** Yes
**Diagnostic tests:** Yes
**Documentation:** WAIS-R, W-J-R: within 18 months

### ADDITIONAL INFORMATION

The Concordia Connection provides services to all students which include test taking modifications, taped text books, computer access, and tutoring. Although there are no charges for students requesting peer tutoring, there is a $1,500 per semester charge for program services. Skills courses for credit are offered in time management, organizational skills and study skills. The 3-day summer orientation helps students: get acquainted with support services; get exposure to academic expectations; review components and requirements of the freshman year; develop group cohesion; and explore individual-ized needs and strategies for seeking assistance.

**Special education HS coursework accepted:** Depends on content    **Essay required:** Yes
**Special application required:** No                                **Submitted to:** N/A
**# of applications submitted each year:** 40                       **# of applications accepted each year:** Approximately 12–15

**# of students receiving LD services:** 23
**Acceptance into program means acceptance into college:** Students must be admitted to the college and then request services. Some are reviewed by the LD program which provides a recommendation to admission.

# LEARNING DISABILITY SERVICES

**Learning center:** Yes
**Kurzweil personal reader:** No
**LD specialists:** 2
**Allowed in exams:**
 **Calculator:** Yes
 **Dictionary:** Yes
 **Computer:** Yes
 **SpellCheck:** Yes

**Notetaker:** Yes
**Scribes:** Yes
**Proctors:** Yes
**Oral exams:** Y/N
**Extended test time:** Yes
**Added cost:** $1,500 per/semester; peer tutors are no charge
**Distraction-free environ.:** Yes
**Tape recording in class:** Yes
**Books on tape:** Yes
**Taping of other books:** Yes

**Professional tutors:** 1
**Peer tutors:** 10
**Max. hrs/wk for services:** Based on need and resources
**Priority registration:** Yes
**Accomodations for students with ADD:** Yes
**How are professors notified of LD:** By the student and the Program Director

# GENERAL ADMISSIONS INFORMATION

**Director of Admissions:** Thomas Weede          **Telephone:** 914-337-9300 ext. 2150

## ENTRANCE REQUIREMENTS

Total high school units required/recommended: 16 total units are required; 4 English required, 2 math required, 3 science required, 2 social studies required. Minimum rank in top half of secondary school class and minimum 3.0 GPA required. Special requirements: An audition is required for music program applicants. TOEFL is required of all international students.

**Application deadline:** Rolling
**Notification:** Rolling

**SAT or ACT preferred:** Either
**SAT Range:**460–570V, 450–550M
**Average GPA:** 3.0

# COLLEGE GRADUATION REQUIREMENTS

**Course waivers allowed:** Yes
**Course substitutions allowed:** Yes
**In what courses:** Substitution of American Sign Language for foreign language.

# ADDITIONAL INFORMATION

**Environment:** NR

**Student Body**
 **Undergrad enrollment:** 496
 **Women:** 56%
 **Men:** 44%
 **In-state students:** 68%
 **Out-of-state:** 32%

**Cost Information**
 **In-state tuition:** $11,400
 **Out-of-state:** $11,400
 **Room & board:** $5,310

**Housing Information**
 **University housing:** Yes
 **Fraternity:** No
 **Sorority:** No
 **Living on campus:** 65%

 **Athletics:** NR

# CORNELL UNIVERSITY

**NY**

410 Thurston Avenue, Ithaca, NY 14850 • **Admissions:** 607-255-5241 • **Fax:** 607-255-5242
**Email:** admissions@cornell.edu • **Web:** www.cornell.edu
**Support:** S • **Institution:** 4 yr. Private & Public

## LEARNING DISABILITY ADMISSIONS AND SERVICES

Cornell University is committed to ensuring that all qualified persons with disabilities have the opportunity to participate in its educational programs and services on an equal basis. The university's aim is to provide that opportunity in an integrated setting that encourages the sharing of experiences among all students and faculty and staff members. Students with LD must provide OEO with verification of specific LD. Students need to provide this documentation well in advance of actual enrollment to enable OEO to identify and assist in implementing appropriate reasonable accommodations. A learning profile based on a psychoeducational evaluation by a learning specialist is most helpful in describing needed support services and classroom accommodations. Students are requested to meet with each professor at the beginning of the semester to discuss accommodation needs. Letters will be sent to faculty members describing classroom accommodations when required. The goal is to empower students to achieve maximum independence through the use of adaptive technology and compensatory strategies. Students are provided with the accommodations they require to perform at their maximum potential while being encouraged to become good self advocates. Each student is the best judge of which services work best for him or her.

## LEARNING DISABILITY ADMISSIONS INFORMATION

**Program Name:** Disability Services, Office of Equal Opportunity
**Program Director:** Joan B. Fisher
**Contact Person:** Same as above

**Telephone:** 607-255-3976

### ADMISSIONS

Cornell does not have a special admission process for students with learning disabilities. All students applying to Cornell are expected to meet the same admissions criteria. General admission requirements include 16 units of English, math, science, social studies, and foreign language. All of the 7 colleges have their own specific requirements. Admissions is very competitive and most of the admitted students rank, at least, in the top 20% of the class. Students with learning disabilities who wish to self-disclose are encouraged to write a personal statement that will provide insight into the nature of the disability and how the student has compensated for the areas of deficit. All documentation should be sent directly to OEO.

**College entrance exams required:** Yes                    **Untimed accepted:** Yes
**Course entrance requirements:** Yes                       **Interview required:** Y/N
**Diagnostic tests:** Yes
**Documentation:** A basic psycho-educational battery; within 3 years

### ADDITIONAL INFORMATION

Students are encouraged to complete a Disability Self-Identification Form that is enclosed with the acceptance materials. OEO welcomes a condensed version of the psychoeducational evaluation that could provide specific information regarding the disability and services/accommodations recommended. Once OEO has received a Learning Profile, the OEO will help students find tutors, notetakers, readers, recorded books, and work with professors to arrange for oral examinations and/or extended time on tests. Diagnostic testing, remedial courses, and tutors specifically trained to work with students with learning disabilities are not available at Cornell. The Learning Skills Center does provide general supportive services which include classes and workshops in specific areas such as organizational skills, notetaking, and a peer support group that meets on a regular basis. There is a Learning Skills Center which is open to all students. Skills classes are offered in reading comprehension, study skills, and notetaking. All services and accommodations are available for undergraduate and graduate students.

**Special education HS coursework accepted:** No          **Essay required:** Yes
**Special application required:** No                         **Submitted to:** N/A
**# of applications submitted each year:** N/A             **# of applications accepted each year:** N/A
**# of students receiving LD services:** 196
**Acceptance into program means acceptance into college:** Students must be admitted to the university first and then may request services.

**Learning center:** No
**Kurzweil personal reader:** Yes
**LD specialists:** No
**Allowed in exams:**
  **Calculator:** Yes
  **Dictionary:** Yes
  **Computer:** Yes
  **SpellCheck:** Yes

**Notetaker:** Yes
**Scribes:** Yes
**Proctors:** Yes
**Oral exams:** Yes
**Extended test time:** Yes
**Added cost:** None
**Distraction-free environ.:** Yes
**Tape recording in class:** Yes
**Books on tape:** Yes
**Taping of other books:** Yes

**Professional tutors:** No
**Peer tutors:** Yes
**Max. hrs/wk for services:** Unlimited
**Priority registration:** Yes
**Accomodations for students with ADD:** Yes
**How are professors notified of LD:** By the student and the Program Director

# GENERAL ADMISSIONS INFORMATION

**Director of Admissions:** Nancy Hargrave Meislahn        **Telephone:** 607-255-5241

## ENTRANCE REQUIREMENTS

Total high school units required/recommended: 16 total units are required; 4 English required, 3 math required, 2 science recommended, 2 social studies recommended. Other requirements vary significantly depending upon program. Applicants must have satisfactory knowledge of subjects required by individual colleges for admission to those colleges. Special requirements: TOEFL is required of all international students. Interview and portfolio required of applicants to College of Architecture, Art, and Planning. Interview required of applicants to School of Hotel Administration and School of Industrial and Labor Relations.

**Application deadline:** January 1
**Notification:** Early April

**SAT or ACT preferred:** Either
**SAT Range:** 600–700V, 640–730M

**Graduated top 10% of class:** 81
**Graduated top 25% of class:** 94
**Graduated top 50% of class:** 100

# COLLEGE GRADUATION REQUIREMENTS

**Course waivers allowed:** Yes
**Course substitutions allowed:** Yes
**In what courses:** Foreign language in the College of Arts and Science

# ADDITIONAL INFORMATION

**Environment:** Cornell is located 45 minutes from Syracuse on the southern end of Lake Cayuga in the Finger Lakes Region.

**Student Body**
  **Undergrad enrollment:** 13,512
  **Women:** 47%
  **Men:** 53%
  **In-state students:** 49%
  **Out-of-state:** 51%

**Cost Information**
  **In-state tuition:** $21,914
  **Out-of-state:** $21,914
  **Room & board:** $7,110

**Housing Information**
  **University housing:** Yes
  **Fraternity:** Yes
  **Sorority:** Yes
  **Living on campus:** 47%

  **Athletics:** NCAA Div. I

# HOFSTRA UNIVERSITY

**NY**

100 Hofstra University, Hempstead, NY 11549 • **Admissions:** 516-463-6700 • **Fax:** 516-560-7660
**Email:** hofstra@hofstra.edu • **Web:** www.hofstra.edu
**Support:** SP • **Institution:** 4 yr. Private

## LEARNING DISABILITY ADMISSIONS AND SERVICES

The PALS P rogram seeks candidates who have been diagnosed as learning disabled and show above-average intellectual ability and emotional stability. The program concentrates on identifying qualified applicants for entrance to the university, and on enhancing the skills that will help students achieve academic success. This program is part of the Division of Special Studies. Normally, candidates will be accepted into PALS for a period of one academic year. In the first semester students enroll in courses offered through DSS, and in the second semester they enroll in regular Hofstra classes.

## LEARNING DISABILITY ADMISSIONS INFORMATION

**Program Name:** Program for Academic Learning Skills  (PALS)
**Program Director:** I. H. Gotz, Ph.D.                    **Telephone:** 516-463-5840
**Contact Person:** Same as above

### ADMISSIONS

The Division of Special Studies, which administers PALS, has always conducted a highly individualized admissions process. Students with learning disabilities, who may be in the bottom 30% of their high school class and have an 800–850 SAT, may be eligible for the PALS Program. The interview is very important and students may be asked to write an essay at this time. Only 18 of the 100 students accepted into the Division of Special Studies are learning disabled. PALS is looking for students who have the academic ability and potential to be successful in college; self-knowledge and understanding of strengths and weaknesses; and a willingness to work hard. There are no specific high school course requirements for PALS. In cooperation with the Admissions Office, candidates are encouraged to apply for admission for the fall semester. Admission decisions are made jointly by PALS and the Office of Admissions.  Only in exceptional cases will applicants be admitted in midyear.

**College entrance exams required:** No                    **Untimed accepted:** Yes
**Course entrance requirements:** No                       **Interview required:** Yes
**Diagnostic tests:** Yes
**Documentation:** WAIS-R; IEP: within 1 year

### ADDITIONAL INFORMATION

There are waivers available, however, the university prefers to substitute courses where possible. Once admitted the students meet with a specialist 2 times a week, and information regarding progress is shared with the family. Basic skills courses are offered in spelling, learning strategies, study strategies, time management, written language, and social skills.

**Special education HS coursework accepted:** Yes          **Essay required:** No, but preferred
**Special application required:** Yes                      **Submitted to:** Director of Admissions
**# of applications submitted each year:** 350             **# of applications accepted each year:** 50
**# of students receiving LD services:** 150–180
**Acceptance into program means acceptance into college:** Students who are admitted to PALS are automatically admitted to the university.

## LEARNING DISABILITY SERVICES

**Learning center:** Yes
**Kurzweil personal reader:** Yes
**LD specialists:** 5
**Allowed in exams:**
  **Calculator:** Yes
  **Dictionary:** Yes
  **Computer:** Yes
  **SpellCheck:** Yes

**Notetaker:** Yes
**Scribes:** Yes
**Proctors:** Yes
**Oral exams:** Yes
**Extended test time:** Yes
**Added cost:** $4,625 for freshman year only
**Distraction-free environ.:** Yes
**Tape recording in class:** Yes
**Books on tape:** Yes
**Taping of other books:** Yes

**Professional tutors:** 5
**Peer tutors:** Yes
**Max. hrs/wk for services:** Unlimited
**Priority registration:** No
**Accomodations for students with ADD:** Yes
**How are professors notified of LD:** By the student and the Program Director

## GENERAL ADMISSIONS INFORMATION

**Director of Admissions:** Margaret Shields          **Telephone:** 516-463-6700

### ENTRANCE REQUIREMENTS

Total high school units required/recommended: 17 total units are required; 4 English required, 2 math required, 3 math recommended, 2 science required, 3 science recommended, 2 foreign language required, 3 social studies required. Minimum combined SAT I score of 1000 and rank in top third of secondary school class recommended. Special requirements: A portfolio is required for art program applicants. An audition is required for music program applicants. TOEFL is required of all international students.

**Application deadline:** Rolling
**Notification:** Rolling

**SAT or ACT preferred:** Either
**SAT Avg:** 535V, 535M
**SAT II required:** Yes
**Average ACT:** 22
**Average GPA:** 3

**Graduated top 10% of class:** 20
**Graduated top 25% of class:** 52
**Graduated top 50% of class:** 88

## COLLEGE GRADUATION REQUIREMENTS

**Course waivers allowed:** No
**Course substitutions allowed:** Yes
**In what courses:** Foreign language

## ADDITIONAL INFORMATION

**Environment:** Hempstead is a residential community in Long Island just outside New York City.

**Student Body**
  **Undergrad enrollment:** 8,431
  **Women:** 53%
  **Men:** 47%
  **In-state students:** 88%
  **Out-of-state:** 12%

**Cost Information**
  **In-state tuition:** $12,240
  **Out-of-state:** $12,240
  **Room & board:** $6,450

**Housing Information**
  **University housing:** Yes
  **Fraternity:** No
  **Sorority:** No
  **Living on campus:** 50%

  **Athletics:** NCAA Div. I

# IONA COLLEGE

**NY**

715 North Avenue, New Rochelle, NY 10801 • **Admissions:** 914-633-2502 • **Fax:** 914-633-2182
**Email:** tdelahunt@iona.edu • **Web:** www.iona.edu
**Support:** CS • **Institution:** 4 yr. Private

## LEARNING DISABILITY ADMISSIONS AND SERVICES

The College Assistance Program (CAP) of Iona College offers comprehensive support and services for students with LD. CAP is designed to encourage success by providing instruction tailored to individual strengths and needs. With success comes self-confidence and a greater ability to plan and achieve academic, personal, and career goals. Students take the standard full-time course requirements to ensure the level of quality education expected of all degree candidates. Tutors teach individually appropriate strategies which cross the disciplines. These skills are designed to facilitate the completion of assignments and to generate eventual academic independence. CAP staff encourage students to become active, involved members of the college community. All CAP freshmen must participate in a three week summer orientation; the aim is to provide students with a solid foundation from which the college experience can begin with confidence; the staff instruct and guide students in intensive writing instruction, study skills, organizational, and time management skills; students are oriented to the college and services; individual learning styles are explored, and opportunities are provided to practice self-advocacy; and several workshops are offered in areas that meet the student's specific needs; students create an individual schedule.

## LEARNING DISABILITY ADMISSIONS INFORMATION

**Program Name:** College Assistance Program (CAP)
**Program Director:** Madeline Packerman          **Telephone:** 914-633-2582
**Contact Person:** Same as above

### ADMISSIONS

All applicants must meet the same admission criteria which include: 4 yrs. English, 1 yr American history, 1 yr. social studies, 2 yrs. foreign language (waivers granted), 1 yr. natural science, and 3 yrs. math. Students must be admitted to the college prior to applying to CAP. Only after acceptance to the college should the applicant send the following to the CAP office: a complete psychological evaluation conducted within the past two years including the WAIS or WAIS-R subtest scores; a copy of the most recent Individualized Educational Plan; and 2 letters of recommendation (one from the learning disability instructor). A personal interview is required. Admission decisions are made jointly by Admissions and CAP. CAP is designed for students with learning disabilities who have been mainstreamed in their academic courses in high school. Students should be average or above average in intellectual ability, socially mature, emotionally stable, and motivated to work hard.

**College entrance exams required:** Yes          **Untimed accepted:** Yes
**Course entrance requirements:** Yes          **Interview required:** Yes
**Diagnostic tests:** Yes
**Documentation:** WAIS-R; IEP: within 2 years

### ADDITIONAL INFORMATION

CAP services include: summer college transition program; academic advising and program planning; priority registration; selection based on each student's learning style; 2 hours per week of scheduled individual tutoring with a professional learning specialist; additional tutoring sessions on as-need basis; small group tutoring and workshops; testing accommodations; alternative testing procedures; special equipment; self-advocacy training; referrals to additional services on campus; counseling services. Skills courses are available in reading, writing, and spelling. The CAP director works closely with the faculty to help them understand the problems faced by students with learning disabilities, and to explore creative ways to support the learning process. Services are available for undergraduate and graduate students. The Samuel Rudin Academic Resource Center offers free services to all students who wish to improve their learning skills or who want academic support. ARC provides free reasonable services to all students with documented LD.

**Special education HS coursework accepted:** No          **Essay required:** No
**Special application required:** No          **Submitted to:** N/A
**# of applications submitted each year:** 200+          **# of applications accepted each year:** 15–20
**# of students receiving LD services:** 65
**Acceptance into program means acceptance into college:** Students must be accepted to the college first and then may request admission to CAP.

## LEARNING DISABILITY SERVICES

**Learning center:** Yes
**Kurzweil personal reader:** No
**LD specialists:** 12
**Allowed in exams:**
  **Calculator:** Yes
  **Dictionary:** Yes
  **Computer:** Yes
  **SpellCheck:** Yes

**Notetaker:** Yes
**Scribes:** Yes
**Proctors:** Yes
**Oral exams:** Yes
**Extended test time:** Yes
**Added cost:** $1,000 per/semester
**Distraction-free environ.:** Yes
**Tape recording in class:** Yes
**Books on tape:** Yes
**Taping of other books:** Yes

**Professional tutors:** 10
**Peer tutors:** No
**Max. hrs/wk for services:** 2 hrs. scheduled, more hours are possible
**Priority registration:** Yes
**Accomodations for students with ADD:** Yes
**How are professors notified of LD:** By the student and the Program Director

## GENERAL ADMISSIONS INFORMATION

**Director of Admissions:** Brother Kevin Devlin    **Telephone:** 914-623-2017

### ENTRANCE REQUIREMENTS
Total high school units required/recommended: 16 total units are recommended; 4 English recommended, 3 math recommended, 1 social studies recommended, 1 history recommended. Rank in top half of secondary school class and minimum 2.5 GPA recommended. Special requirements: 2 units of lab science required of science program applicants.

**Application deadline:** Rolling
**Notification:** Rolling

**SAT or ACT preferred:** SAT
**SAT Avg:** 510V, 501M
**Average ACT:** 20
**Average GPA:** 82

**Graduated top 10% of class:** 11
**Graduated top 25% of class:** 33
**Graduated top 50% of class:** 49

## COLLEGE GRADUATION REQUIREMENTS

**Course waivers allowed:** No
**Course substitutions allowed:** Yes
**In what courses:** Foreign language and math

## ADDITIONAL INFORMATION

**Environment:** The college is located on 56 acres 20 miles northeast of New York City.

**Student Body**
  **Undergrad enrollment:** 2,500
  **Women:** 51%
  **Men:** 49%
  **In-state students:** 92%
  **Out-of-state:** 8%

**Cost Information**
  **In-state tuition:** $13,100
  **Out-of-state:** $13,100
  **Room & board:** $7,200

**Housing Information**
  **University housing:** Yes
  **Fraternity:** No
  **Sorority:** No
  **Living on campus:** 19%

  **Athletics:** NCAA Div. I

# LONG ISLAND UNIVERSITY-C.W. POST

720 Northern Boulevard, Brookville, NY 11548 • **Admissions:** 516-299-2413 • **Fax:** 516-299-2137
**Email:** admissions@collegehall.liunet.edu • **Web:** www.liunet.edu
**Support:** SP • **Institution:** 4 yr. Private

## LEARNING DISABILITY ADMISSIONS AND SERVICES

The ARC Program is a comprehensive support program designed for students with learning disabilities to help them achieve their academic potential in a university setting. The objective is to encourage students to become independent learners and self-advocates. Students participate in mainstream college courses and assume full responsibility for attendance in class and at the ARC. ARC staff communicates with professors, and students are tutored by graduate assistants. Students learn time management, reading, study and test-taking strategies, organizational skills, and notetaking techniques. The Center provides an environment which helps students demonstrate positive attitudes toward themselves and learning. ARC motto is "A serious Program for serious students". Center staff will work with serious students who are committed to earning a college degree. Students must apply for admission to the university to applying to ARC. Students admitted to the university and who identify themselves as LD are sent information and an application to apply to the ARC. Applications must include a Diagnostic Evaluation describing the specific LD; WAIS-R; and a handwritten essay indicating why the student is requesting admittance into the ARC. Once all of the information is on file the student will be invited to interview.

## LEARNING DISABILITY ADMISSIONS INFORMATION

**Program Name:** Academic Resource Center (ARC)
**Program Director:** Carol Rundlett                    **Telephone:** 516-299-2937
**Contact Person:** Same as above

### ADMISSIONS

The student must be admitted to the university first and then apply to the ARC. Acceptance into the university is separate and distinct from acceptance into the Center. Students should self disclose their learning disability. If the GPA or tests are low, students may be admitted through the Directed Studies Program. During an interview students must convince the Admissions Counselor that they have changed and are now willing to focus on studies. Motivation is very important. Students with an SAT below 800 or a Verbal below 450 are required to have either a B– average or 450 Verbal or 400 Math SAT. If students have a deficiency, the people responsible for testing must write letters stating what specifically in the test data indicates the students should be granted a waiver.

**College entrance exams required:** Yes          **Untimed accepted:** Yes
**Course entrance requirements:** Yes             **Interview required:** No, encouraged
**Diagnostic tests:** Yes
**Documentation:** WAIS-R; psychoeducational or neurological-psychological: within 1 year

### ADDITIONAL INFORMATION

Students work with Graduate Assistants on a one-to-one basis. Graduate Assistants are students enrolled in the School of Education who are pursuing master's degree. The Graduate Assistants help students make the transition from high school to college. They assist students in time management, organizational skills, note-taking techniques, study skills, and other learning strategies. Students are responsible for attendance and participation in meetings with the Graduate Assistants. Other services include: individualized learning strategies on a one-to-one basis 2 times a week; extended time and readers for exams; academic advisement and faculty liaison; and assistance in formulating an overall plan and structure when approaching an assignment. The Program is a four year program, but the majority of students opt to handle their own classwork at the end of sophomore year. Freshmen are limited to 12 credits for their first semester, and all must enroll in a Freshman Seminar. There are no special or remedial classes.

**Special education HS coursework accepted:** Yes       **Essay required:** Yes, 150 words in student's handwriting, describing disability

**Special application required:** Yes                    **Submitted to:** Director of Program
**# of applications submitted each year:** 200+         **# of applications accepted each year:** 40–50
**# of students receiving LD services:** 95
**Acceptance into program means acceptance into college:** Students must be accepted to the university first and then may request services through ARC (may appeal a denial).

# LEARNING DISABILITY SERVICES

**Learning center:** Yes
**Kurzweil personal reader:** No
**LD specialists:** 2
**Allowed in exams:**
  **Calculator:** Yes
  **Dictionary:** Yes
  **Computer:** Yes
  **SpellCheck:** Yes

**Notetaker:** Yes
**Scribes:** Yes
**Proctors:** Yes
**Oral exams:** Y/N
**Extended test time:** Yes
**Added cost:** $1,300 per/semester
**Distraction-free environ.:** Yes
**Tape recording in class:** Yes
**Books on tape:** Yes
**Taping of other books:** No

**Professional tutors:** 16
**Peer tutors:** Yes
**Max. hrs/wk for services:** Unlimited
**Priority registration:** No
**Accomodations for students with ADD:** Yes
**How are professors notified of LD:** By the student and the Program Director

# GENERAL ADMISSIONS INFORMATION

**Director of Admissions:** Christine Natali          **Telephone:** 516-299-2413

## ENTRANCE REQUIREMENTS

Total high school units required/recommended: 21 total units are required; 4 English required, 2 math required, 4 math recommended, 2 science required, 4 science recommended, 2 foreign language required, 3 social studies required, 4 social studies recommended, 3 history required. Minimum combined SAT I score of 900 and minimum grade average of 75 required. Special requirements: A portfolio is required for art program applicants. An audition is required for music program applicants. An RN is required for nursing program applicants. TOEFL is required of all international students.

**Application deadline:** Rolling
**Notification:** Rolling

**SAT or ACT preferred:** SAT
**SAT Avg:** 526V, 527M
**SAT II required:** Yes

**Graduated top 10% of class:** 24
**Graduated top 25% of class:** 49
**Graduated top 50% of class:** 79

# COLLEGE GRADUATION REQUIREMENTS

**Course waivers allowed:** Yes
**Course substitutions allowed:** No
**In what courses:** Foreign Language and Math

# ADDITIONAL INFORMATION

**Environment:** The college is located in Long Island about 30 minutes from New York City.

**Student Body**
  **Undergrad enrollment:** 4,670
  **Women:** 55%
  **Men:** 45%
  **In-state students:** 94%
  **Out-of-state:** 6%

**Cost Information**
  **In-state tuition:** $13,120
  **Out-of-state:** $13,120
  **Room & board:** $5,880

**Housing Information**
  **University housing:** Yes
  **Fraternity:** No
  **Sorority:** No
  **Living on campus:** 30%

  **Athletics:** NCAA Div. II

# MANHATTAN COLLEGE

**NY**

Manhattan College Parkway, Riverdale, NY 10471 • **Admissions:** 718-862-8000 • **Fax:** 718-862-8019
**Email:** admit@manhattan.edu • **Web:** www.manhattan.edu
**Support:** CS • **Institution:** 4 yr. Private

## LEARNING DISABILITY ADMISSIONS AND SERVICES

The philosophy and goal of the Learning Disability Program is to meet the specific needs of college students with learning disabilities to foster growth and independence, and achieve a college education, a career direction, and employment. This is a highly individualized student oriented program featuring "access-on-demand" and a totally integrated system with no segregated components. This is a fee-based program designed to enhance the academic progress of students with learning disabilities. Students enrolling in the LD program receive a multitude of enhanced small group workshops, and a specially designed three tier fee structure. The Specialized Resource Center serves all students with special needs. The mission of the Specialized Resource Center is to ensure educational opportunity for all students with special needs by providing access to full participation in campus life. This is accomplished by assisting students in arranging individualized support services.

## LEARNING DISABILITY ADMISSIONS INFORMATION

**Program Name:** Learning Disabilities Program
**Program Director:** Ross Pollack, Ed.D.                     **Telephone:** 718-862-7101
**Contact Person:** Anne Vaccaro, Coordinator           **Telephone:** 718-920-0409

### ADMISSIONS

All applicants are expected to meet the same admission criteria. These requirements include: 4 yrs. English, 2 yrs. foreign language, 2 yrs. science, 3 yrs. math, 3 yrs. social studies, 2 yrs. electives; scores on ACT/SAT are not definitive but give idea of potential; and a personal statement. Students with learning disabilities are encouraged to include the WAIS-R; educational testing; a handwritten essay; and a statement from their guidance counselor or special education teacher. The admission decision for students with learning disabilities who self-disclose is made jointly by the Office of Admissions and the Director of the Learning Disabilities Program. Applicants with learning disabilities may not be admitted into the enhanced LD Program prior to or concurrently with admission into the college. The college's general admissions committee shall make all admission decisions. Students who have been admitted to the college may then apply to the Enhanced LD Program. Students are accepted into college with appropriate documentation. There are no cut offs and no rejections for students who meet the admission criteria.

**College entrance exams required:** Yes                **Untimed accepted:** Yes
**Course entrance requirements:** Yes, core courses     **Interview required:** Recommended
**Diagnostic tests:** Yes
**Documentation:** WAIS-R; Psychoeducational (reading, math, written language)

### ADDITIONAL INFORMATION

The specialized Resource Center is staffed by a Director, a Coordinator, as well as a Learning Disabilities Specialist, and is a resource for students, faculty and the college at large. Use of the services is voluntary, strictly confidential, and without fee. A sampling of auxiliary aids and/or academic adjustments offered by the SRC for students providing appropriate documentation based on their individual needs include: priority registration; priority seating; alternative testing environments; readers; notetakers; scribes; access to adaptive technology; books on tape; and liaison with faculty and other college departments. Workshops are offered in math and study skills.

**Special education HS coursework accepted:** Yes       **Essay required:** Yes
**Special application required:** No                    **Submitted to:** Program Director
**# of applications submitted each year:** 100          **# of applications accepted each year:** No ceiling
**# of students receiving LD services:** 50
**Acceptance into program means acceptance into college:** Acceptance into the college means acceptance into program with proper documentation.

**Learning center:** Yes
**Kurzweil personal reader:** No
**LD specialists:** 2.5
**Allowed in exams:**
  **Calculator:** Yes
  **Dictionary:** Yes
  **Computer:** Yes
  **SpellCheck:** Yes

**Notetaker:** Yes
**Scribes:** Yes
**Proctors:** Yes
**Oral exams:** Yes
**Extended test time:** Yes
**Added cost:** None
**Distraction-free environ.:** Yes
**Tape recording in class:** Yes
**Books on tape:** Yes
**Taping of other books:** Yes

**Professional tutors:** No
**Peer tutors:** Varies
**Max. hrs/wk for services:** Unlimited
**Priority registration:** Yes
**Accomodations for students with ADD:** Yes
**How are professors notified of LD:** By the student with specialized forms

## GENERAL ADMISSIONS INFORMATION

**Director of Admissions:** Dean John Brennan      **Telephone:** 718-920-0907

### ENTRANCE REQUIREMENTS

Total high school units required/recommended: 16 total units are required; 4 English required, 3 math required, 4 math recommended, 2 science required, 3 science recommended, 2 foreign language required, 3 social studies required. Rank in top half of secondary school class and minimum grade average of 80 recommended.

**Application deadline:** March 1
**Notification:** Rolling

**SAT or ACT preferred:** SAT
**SAT Avg:** 514V, 516M
**SAT II required:** Yes
**Average GPA:** 3

**Graduated top 10% of class:** 23
**Graduated top 25% of class:** 67
**Graduated top 50% of class:** 77

## COLLEGE GRADUATION REQUIREMENTS

**Course waivers allowed:** Yes
**Course substitutions allowed:** Yes
**In what courses:** Each case viewed on individualized basis

## ADDITIONAL INFORMATION

**Environment:** The college is located on 47 acres in a the suburb of Riverdale, 12 miles north of midtown Manhattan.

**Student Body**
  **Undergrad enrollment:** 2,602
  **Women:** 50%
  **Men:** 50%
  **In-state students:** 83%
  **Out-of-state:** 17%

**Cost Information**
  **In-state tuition:** $13,800
  **Out-of-state:** $13,800
  **Room & board:** $7,150

**Housing Information**
  **University housing:** Yes
  **Fraternity:** No
  **Sorority:** No
  **Living on campus:** 50%

  **Athletics:** NCAA Div. I

# MANHATTANVILLE COLLEGE

2900 Purchase Street, Admissions Office, Purchase, NY 10577 • **Admissions:** 914-323-5464
**Fax:** 914-694-1732 • **Email:** jfbres@mville.edu • **Web:** www.manhattanville.edu
**Support:** CS • **Institution:** 4 yr. Private

## LEARNING DISABILITY ADMISSIONS AND SERVICES

The Higher Education Learning Program is designed to help the motivated and committed students with learning disabilities successfully meet the academic challenge of the college experience. The HELP program offers a range of support services for students with learning disabilities throughout their years of college. HELP remains focused on instruction and applications of compensatory strategies to college content courses. The first year program begins with a pre-freshman Summer experience and includes individualized tutoring, learning strategies course, and a reduced full time course load. Students review the characteristic behaviors of young adults with LD and analyze their own strengths and weaknesses. In addition, they contrast the demands of high school and college, discuss legally-mandated accommodations, and role-play the effective seeking of accommodations. The workshops enable students to establish a supportive relationship with others in the program and introduces students to the campus. Services are individualized and documented on an Individualized College Plan (ICP) to accommodate specific needs.

## LEARNING DISABILITY ADMISSIONS INFORMATION

**Program Name:** Higher Education Learning Program (HELP)
**Program Director:** Dr. Rebecca Rich           **Telephone:** 914-323-5143
**Contact Person:** Same as above

### ADMISSIONS

Applicants must meet the requirements for general admission. The admission decision is made jointly by the Office of Admissions and the Director of HELP. Applicants must submit diagnostic testing identifying the learning disability, 2 teacher recommendations (one must be English), a reference form completed by an LD teacher or tutor, and a signed student contract. Candidates must interview with admissions and the HELP Program after submitting an application.

**College entrance exams required:** Yes          **Untimed accepted:** Yes
**Course entrance requirements:** Yes          **Interview required:** Yes
**Diagnostic tests:** Yes
**Documentation:** WAIS-R; Reading tests, and writing samples: within 1 year

### ADDITIONAL INFORMATION

Freshman year HELP students take a four course load and must attend tutoring sessions 3 times a week. Students are encouraged to tape lectures, and tutor coordinators act as advocates to assist students in arranging for accommodations. Applications of Learning Theory is an inter-disciplinary course which provides modeling structure. Practice through instructional class sessions and individual sessions serve to monitor the application of the skills. Sophomore year through senior year students are provided with support services. The nature and extent of this support is determined by individual need. All instruction in the Program is provided by professionals with advanced degrees in special education who are experienced in working with students with learning disabilities.

**Special education HS coursework accepted:** determined on an individual basis
**Essay required:** Yes
**Special application required:** No          **Submitted to:** N/A
**# of applications submitted each year:** Varies          **# of applications accepted each year:** N/A
**# of students receiving LD services:** N/A
**Acceptance into program means acceptance into college:** Acceptance to HELP and the college are simultaneous.

## LEARNING DISABILITY SERVICES

**Learning center:** Yes
**Kurzweil personal reader:** No
**LD specialists:** 3
**Allowed in exams:**
  **Calculator:** Yes
  **Dictionary:** Yes
  **Computer:** Y/N
  **SpellCheck:** Y/N

**Notetaker:** Yes
**Scribes:** Yes
**Proctors:** Yes
**Oral exams:** Yes
**Extended test time:** Yes
**Added cost:** $3,000, freshman year only; $2,000, subsequent years
**Distraction-free environ.:** Yes
**Tape recording in class:** Yes
**Books on tape:** Yes
**Taping of other books:** Yes

**Professional tutors:** 1+
**Peer tutors:** Yes
**Max. hrs/wk for services:** 3 times a week required for the first year
**Priority registration:** N/I
**Accomodations for students with ADD:** Yes
**How are professors notified of LD:** By the student and the Program Director

## GENERAL ADMISSIONS INFORMATION

**Director of Admissions:** NR

**Telephone:** 914-694-2200 ext. 349

### ENTRANCE REQUIREMENTS

Total high school units required/recommended: 4 English required, 2 math required, 2 science required, 2 foreign language required, 2 social studies required, 2 history required. Minimum 3.0 GPA recommended. Special requirements: A portfolio is required for art program applicants. An audition is required for music program applicants.

**Application deadline:** Rolling
**Notification:** Rolling

**SAT or ACT preferred:** SAT
**SAT Avg:** 515V, 500M
**SAT II required:** Yes
**Average ACT:** 24
**Average GPA:** 3.0

**Graduated top 10% of class:** 30
**Graduated top 25% of class:** 45
**Graduated top 50% of class:** 90

## COLLEGE GRADUATION REQUIREMENTS

**Course waivers allowed:** No
**Course substitutions allowed:** No
**In what courses:** N/A

## ADDITIONAL INFORMATION

**Environment:** The college is located on a 100-acre campus in a suburban area 25 miles north of New York City.

**Student Body**
  **Undergrad enrollment:** 906
  **Women:** 65%
  **Men:** 35%
  **In-state students:** 72%
  **Out-of-state:** 28%

**Cost Information**
  **In-state tuition:** $16,120
  **Out-of-state:** $16,120
  **Room & board:** $7,680

**Housing Information**
  **University housing:** Yes
  **Fraternity:** No
  **Sorority:** No
  **Living on campus:** 75%

  **Athletics:** NCAA Div. III

# NY

# MARIST COLLEGE

North Road, Poughkeepsie, NY 12601 • **Admissions:** 914-575-3000 • **Fax:** 800-436-5483
**Email:** HWW@ musica.marista.edu • **Web:** www.marist.edu
**Support:** CS • **Institution:** 4 yr. Private

## LEARNING DISABILITY ADMISSIONS AND SERVICES

Marist College believes that bright, motivated students with specific learning disabilities are more similar than different to other college students and can achieve a higher education. Marist offers a program of support for students with learning disabilities through the Learning Disabilities Program. Students receive a complement of academic services designed to meet individual needs. The program focuses on the development and use of strategies to promote independence and personal success. The philosophy of the Program does not emphasize remediation, but rather the development of compensatory strategies. Each student is enrolled in credit-bearing courses and completes the same degree requirements as all students. Program staff work closely with faculty and administration and students are encouraged to discuss their learning disability with faculty. The goal is for each student to achieve the maximum level of independence possible and to become an effective self-advocate. Participation in the Program is available on a continual basis for as long as the Specialist and the student agree that is necessary.

## LEARNING DISABILITY ADMISSIONS INFORMATION

**Program Name:** Office of Special Services/LD Program
**Program Director:** Linda Cooper
**Contact Person:** Same as above

**Telephone:** 914-575-3274

### ADMISSIONS

Students with LD must submit an application for admission and all required materials to the Office of Admissions. A Supplementary Application for the LD Support Program must also be completed and sent directly to the OSS. Additionally, students must submit to the OSS the results of the WAIS-R, including subtest scores; calculated IQ and narrative; achievement testing with current levels of functioning in reading, mathematics and written language; an unedited essay describing the impact of the LD on academic achievement; and a $10 fee. SAT/ACT scores are not required of students with LD. After applications have been reviewed, those most qualified and suited to the Program will be invited to interview. Students accepted into the Program should have an acceptance and understanding of their LD; know their academic strengths and weaknesses; have college prep courses; provide recommendations which communicate strengths, motivation to succeed, and willingness to accept and access supports; and have sound study skills and work habits. Admission to the Program is competitive and students are encouraged to apply early. There is no Early Decision option.

**College entrance exams required:** No
**Course entrance requirements:** Yes
**Diagnostic tests:** Yes
**Documentation:** WAIS-R; within 3 years

**Untimed accepted:** Yes
**Interview required:** Yes

### ADDITIONAL INFORMATION

Upon enrollment students complete a comprehensive survey of abilities and attitudes toward academics. This survey is combined with diagnostic evaluations and the comprehensive record of students' performance to develop an Individual Support Service Plan. Students meet an LD specialist 2 times a week and typically concentrate on writing skills, notetaking, organizational skills, study skills, and testing strategies. Accommodations may include: adaptive testing procedures; notetakers/tape recorders; scribes; taped textbooks/personal readers; use of adaptive equipment. A Program fee is charged only for the services of the Learning Specialist. Students in the Program also have access to content tutors and a counselor who can address academic, career, and personal issues. Services and accommodations are available for undergraduate and graduate students.

**Special education HS coursework accepted:** No
**Special application required:** Yes
**# of applications submitted each year:** 250–300
**# of students receiving LD services:** 125

**Essay required:** Yes
**Submitted to:** Special Services
**# of applications accepted each year:** 25–30

**Acceptance into program means acceptance into college:** Students are admitted jointly into the college and the LD Program.

## LEARNING DISABILITY SERVICES

**Learning center:** N/I
**Kurzweil personal reader:** Yes
**LD specialists:** Yes
**Allowed in exams:**
  **Calculator:** Yes
  **Dictionary:** Yes
  **Computer:** Yes
  **SpellCheck:** Yes

**Notetaker:** Yes
**Scribes:** Yes
**Proctors:** Yes
**Oral exams:** Yes
**Extended test time:** Yes
**Added cost:** $1,100 per/semester
**Distraction-free environ.:** Yes
**Tape recording in class:** Yes
**Books on tape:** Yes
**Taping of other books:** Yes

**Professional tutors:** 4
**Peer tutors:** 60
**Max. hrs/wk for services:** Unlimited
**Priority registration:** Yes
**Accomodations for students with ADD:** Yes
**How are professors notified of LD:** By the student and the Program Director

## GENERAL ADMISSIONS INFORMATION

**Director of Admissions:** Sean Kaylor

**Telephone:** 914-575-3226

### ENTRANCE REQUIREMENTS

Total high school units required/recommended: 16 total units are required; 4 English recommended, 3 math recommended, 2 science recommended, 3 social studies recommended, 2 history recommended. Minimum combined SAT I score of 900, rank in top two-fifths of secondary school class, and minimum grade average of 80 required. Special requirements: 4 units of math recommended for computer science and science program applicants.

**Application deadline:** March 1
**Notification:** Rolling

**SAT or ACT preferred:** Either
**SAT Avg:** 541V, 533M
**SAT II required:** Yes
**Average ACT:** 25

## COLLEGE GRADUATION REQUIREMENTS

**Course waivers allowed:** Yes
**Course substitutions allowed:** Yes
**In what courses:** Varies, mostly in math

## ADDITIONAL INFORMATION

**Environment:** The college is located on 120 acres in upstate New York 75 miles from New York City.

**Student Body**
  **Undergrad enrollment:** 3,935
  **Women:** 57%
  **Men:** 43%
  **In-state students:** 60%
  **Out-of-state:** 40%

**Cost Information**
  **In-state tuition:** $11,400
  **Out-of-state:** $11,400
  **Room & board:** $6,300

**Housing Information**
  **University housing:** Yes
  **Fraternity:** No
  **Sorority:** No
  **Living on campus:** 70%

  **Athletics:** NCAA Div. I

# NEW YORK INSTITUTE OF TECHNOLOGY

P.O. Box 8000, Old Westbury, NY 11568 • **Admissions:** 516-686-7520 • **Fax:** 516-626-0419
**Email:** ADMISSIONS@ACL.NYIT.EDU • **Web:** www.nyit.edu
**Support:** CS • **Institution:** 4 yr. Private

## LEARNING DISABILITY ADMISSIONS AND SERVICES

The goal of the Greater Opportunities for the Learning Disabled (GOLD) Program is to graduate each student with a college degree making a positive transition from high school to college to career.

## LEARNING DISABILITY ADMISSIONS INFORMATION

**Program Name:** GOLD Program
**Program Director:** Dr. Sheila Meindl
**Contact Person:** Margaret Morrow

**Telephone:** 516-686-7655
**Telephone:** 516-686-7655

### ADMISSIONS

In addition to the regular application the following are required: Students with learning disabilities should have an average to above average intelligence as measured by the WAIS-R; a high school diploma, not an IEP; and educational testing in reading, math and written language. A 2.5 GPA is expected and New York students must have the New York State General or Regents Diploma.

**College entrance exams required:** No
**Course entrance requirements:** New York Regents
**Diagnostic tests:** Yes
**Documentation:** Psychoeducational evaluation: within 2 years

**Untimed accepted:** N/A
**Interview required:** Yes

### ADDITIONAL INFORMATION

Skills classes are offered in reading, math, written language and some of these classes are for college credit. Many of the in-class accommodations require professor permission. Services and accommodations are available for undergraduate and graduate students. The university offers a summer program for students with learning disabilities, as well as, a special summer program for pre-college freshmen with learning disabilities.

**Special education HS coursework accepted:** No
**Special application required:** Yes
**# of applications submitted each year:** 50
**# of students receiving LD services:** 53

**Essay required:** Yes
**Submitted to:** Program Director
**# of applications accepted each year:** N/A

**Acceptance into program means acceptance into college:** Students must be admitted to the university first and then may request services.

## LEARNING DISABILITY SERVICES

**Learning center:** Yes
**Kurzweil personal reader:** No
**LD specialists:** Yes
**Allowed in exams:**
  **Calculator:** Y/N
  **Dictionary:** Y/N
  **Computer:** Y/N
  **SpellCheck:** Y/N

**Notetaker:** Yes
**Scribes:** Yes
**Proctors:** Yes
**Oral exams:** Yes
**Extended test time:** Yes
**Added cost:** $4,540.00 per/year
**Distraction-free environ.:** Yes
**Tape recording in class:** Y/N
**Books on tape:** Yes
**Taping of other books:** No

**Professional tutors:** 18
**Peer tutors:** No
**Max. hrs/wk for services:** 3.5
**Priority registration:** Yes
**Accomodations for students with ADD:** Yes
**How are professors notified of LD:** By the student and the Program Director

## GENERAL ADMISSIONS INFORMATION

**Director of Admissions:** Beverly Tota

**Telephone:** 516-686-7655

### ENTRANCE REQUIREMENTS

Total high school units required/recommended: 4 English required, 2 math required, 2 science required, 3 social studies required. Minimum SAT I scores of 400 verbal and 450 math recommended. Minimum SAT I scores of 400 verbal and 500 required of engineering program applicants. Minimum combined SAT I score of 830 required of architecture program applicants. Minimum combined SAT I score of 1100, grade average of 90, and rank in top tenth of secondary school class required of B.S./D.Osteopathy program applicants. Special requirements: A portfolio is required for art program applicants. TOEFL is required of all international students.

**Application deadline:** Rolling
**Notification:** Rolling

**SAT or ACT preferred:** SAT

## COLLEGE GRADUATION REQUIREMENTS

**Course waivers allowed:** Y/N
**Course substitutions allowed:** Y/N
**In what courses:** It depends on the course

## ADDITIONAL INFORMATION

**Environment:** The Institute is located on 750 acres in a suburban area 25 miles east of New York City.

**Student Body**
  **Undergrad enrollment:** 6,737
  **Women:** 30%
  **Men:** 70%
  **In-state students:** 94%
  **Out-of-state:** 6%

**Cost Information**
  **In-state tuition:** $9,300
  **Out-of-state:** $9,300
  **Room & board:** $6,220

**Housing Information**
  **University housing:** Yes
  **Fraternity:** Yes
  **Sorority:** Yes
  **Living on campus:** 10%

  **Athletics:** NCAA Div. II

# NEW YORK UNIVERSITY

22 Washington Square North, New York, NY 10011 • **Admissions:** 212-998-4500 • **Fax:** 212-995-4902
**Email:** nyuadmit@uccvm.edu • **Web:** www.nyu.edu
**Support:** CS • **Institution:** 4 yr. Private

## LEARNING DISABILITY ADMISSIONS AND SERVICES

Success in college depends on such things as motivation, intelligence, talent, problem-solving abilities, and hard work. For students with learning disabilities these traits must be complimented by an understanding of their learning style and their ways of compensating for their disability. Access to Learning strives to help students capitalize on their strengths and minimize the impact of their learning disability. The goal of the Access To Learning program is to assist students with learning disabilities to achieve the highest level of academic independence and progress possible. Access to Learning provides support services and accommodations to all NYU students with learning disabilities. There is no fee. The Program can assist students in coping with their learning disability while working towards independence, competence, and a college degree.

## LEARNING DISABILITY ADMISSIONS INFORMATION

**Program Name:** Access to Learning
**Program Director:** Georgeann duChossois          **Telephone:** 212-998-4980
**Contact Person:** Jean Colaio

### ADMISSIONS

NYU is a competitive university which provides a challenging academic environment. Any student who applies, including students with learning disabilities, must demonstrate the potential to do well. As part of the admission decision, a learning disability specialist may be consulted for recommendations for students who self-disclose their learning disability. Students with learning disabilities typically have to work hard and manage their time well, but also find that they learn and accomplish a great deal at NYU. General admission criteria includes: 4 yrs. English, 3 yrs. math, science, 2 yrs. foreign language, and 3 yrs. social studies; SAT/ACT and SAT II for the B.A./M.D. Program.

**College entrance exams required:** Yes          **Untimed accepted:** Yes
**Course entrance requirements:** Yes          **Interview required:** No
**Diagnostic tests:** Yes
**Documentation:** Full psychoeducational evaluation: within 3 years

### ADDITIONAL INFORMATION

Services provided include: Learning Strategies Sessions with a specialist to develop compensatory skills in testing strategies, reading efficiency, effective writing, and time management; organization, proofreading, notetaking, and study skills; weekly support meetings with peers; test accommodations which could include extended time, private test rooms, use of a computer or calculator, reader, scribe, and alternative formats for tests; assistance in arranging for taping of lecture and ordering books on tape; priority seating; and technology such as Franklin Spellers, computers, and readers. Not all students need all of these services. An accommodation plan is made with each student based on individual needs, keeping in mind the goal of encouraging independence.

**Special education HS coursework accepted:** Yes          **Essay required:** Yes
**Special application required:** No          **Submitted to:** N/A
**# of applications submitted each year:** N/A          **# of applications accepted each year:** N/A
**# of students receiving LD services:** 300
**Acceptance into program means acceptance into college:** Students must be admitted to university first and then request services.

# LEARNING DISABILITY SERVICES

**Learning center:** Yes
**Kurzweil personal reader:** Yes
**LD specialists:** Yes
**Allowed in exams:**
  **Calculator:** Y/N
  **Dictionary:** Y/N
  **Computer:** Y/N
  **SpellCheck:** Y/N

**Notetaker:** Yes
**Scribes:** Yes
**Proctors:** Yes
**Oral exams:** Y/N
**Extended test time:** Yes
**Added cost:** No
**Distraction-free environ.:** Yes
**Tape recording in class:** Yes
**Books on tape:** RFB
**Taping of other books:** Yes

**Professional tutors:** Yes
**Peer tutors:** No
**Max. hrs/wk for services:** 1–2
**Priority registration:** Y/N
**Accomodations for students with ADD:** Yes
**How are professors notified of LD:** By the student

# GENERAL ADMISSIONS INFORMATION

**Director of Admissions:** Richard Avitabile

**Telephone:** 212-998-4500

## ENTRANCE REQUIREMENTS

Total high school units required/recommended: 16 total units are required; 4 English required, 3 math required, 2 science required, 2 foreign language required, 3 social studies required. Specific requirements vary by program. Three SAT II exams required of applicants to B.A./M.D. program. Special requirements: Submission of creative material or audition required of art, music, and performing arts program applicants and applicants to non-performance areas in the School of the Arts.

**Application deadline:** January 15
**Notification:** April 1

**SAT or ACT preferred:** Either
**SAT Range:** 600–690V, 590–690M
**SAT II required:** Yes
**ACT Range:** 27–29

**Graduated top 10% of class:** 60
**Graduated top 25% of class:** 94
**Graduated top 50% of class:** 99

# COLLEGE GRADUATION REQUIREMENTS

**Course waivers allowed:** Y/N
**Course substitutions allowed:** Y/N
**In what courses:** Determined by an Academic Standards Committee on a case-by-case basis

# ADDITIONAL INFORMATION

**Environment:** NR

**Student Body**
  **Undergrad enrollment:** 14,177
  **Women:** 58%
  **Men:** 42%
  **In-state students:** 60%
  **Out-of-state:** 40%

**Cost Information**
  **In-state tuition:** $21,730
  **Out-of-state:** $21,730
  **Room & board:** $8,170

**Housing Information**
  **University housing:** Yes
  **Fraternity:** Yes
  **Sorority:** No
  **Living on campus:** 41%

  **Athletics:** NCAA Div. III

# ROCHESTER INSTITUTE OF TECHNOLOGY

One Lomb Memorial Drive, Rochester, NY 14623 • **Admissions:** 716-475-6631 • **Fax:** 716-475-7424
**Email:** admissions@rit.edu • **Web:** www.rit.edu
**Support:** SP • **Institution:** 4 yr. Private

## LEARNING DISABILITY ADMISSIONS AND SERVICES

RIT offers "Insight Program" a transition year for students with LD. Students live on campus and in addition to skill-building experience, are enrolled in credit-bearing classes. The Alternative Learning Department provides insight and support on students' natural learning style, strengths, and how best to access them to reach their highest potential. Founded in current neurophysiological research, ALD is committed to assisting individuals in recognizing and accessing their learning abilities rather than disabilities. A full complement of programs and services is provided to assist students in strengthening areas of academic concern and/or weakness; to assist in understanding and refining the learning process; and to assist in using academic resources more effectively. It is mandatory for students with LD to participate in a six week series of workshops designed to enhance performance at RIT. Students may self-select the intervention level they feel most appropriately meets their specific needs. Students' progress is reviewed on a quarterly basis and level adjustment recommendations are reviewed on an individual basis. Their goal is to facilitate a smooth transition into college and foster self-sufficiency.

## LEARNING DISABILITY ADMISSIONS INFORMATION

**Program Name:** Alternative Learning Department
**Program Director:** Jacqueline Lynch Czamanske (Chair)      **Telephone:** 716-475-2215
**Contact Person:** Same as above

### ADMISSIONS

There is no special admissions process for students with learning disabilities. However, students with learning disabilities should include diagnostic information with their application. Although an interview is not required, it is recommended. The required scores on the SAT or ACT will depend on the college the student is applying to within RIT. It is also helpful to identify compensatory strategies used in high school and what will be needed for success in college. The admission decision is made jointly by the Program Chairperson and Director of Admission.

**College entrance exams required:** Yes                  **Untimed accepted:** Yes
**Course entrance requirements:** Yes                     **Interview required:** Recommended
**Diagnostic tests:** Yes
**Documentation:** WAIS-R; Achievement tests: as current as possible

### ADDITIONAL INFORMATION

"Insight Program" provides: instruction in whole-brain study techniques; self-advocacy training; career exploration; assistive technology and compensatory skill training; critical thinking skill development; multi-sensory phonetic reading/writing remediation; diagnostic/prescriptive sensory motor integration; 4 credits per period. ALD has 3 levels for students with LD. Level I: self-sufficient students who require minimal support interventions. Level II: initial support and progress monitoring on a weekly basis with LD specialist; organizational skills; notetaking strategies; study strategies; academic and social-emotional issues; peer support network. Level III: intensified structured monitoring; daily, small group appointments assist with daily plan; cost from $265 to $740 per quarter. All levels have access to student "Orton Affiliate Group"; Math and Writing Labs; study skills workshops; notetaking coordination; advocacy services; Learning 101 (mandatory); Individualized faculty-level math.

**Special education HS coursework accepted:** N/I        **Essay required:** Recommended
**Special application required:** No                       **Submitted to:** N/A
**# of applications submitted each year:** 200+          **# of applications accepted each year:** 50
**# of students receiving LD services:** 280
**Acceptance into program means acceptance into college:** Students are admitted to the Institute and ALD simultaneously.

**Learning center:** Yes
**Kurzweil personal reader:** Yes
**LD specialists:** 11
**Allowed in exams:**
  **Calculator:** Yes
  **Dictionary:** Yes
  **Computer:** Yes
  **SpellCheck:** Yes

**Notetaker:** Yes
**Scribes:** Yes
**Proctors:** Yes
**Oral exams:** Yes
**Extended test time:** Yes
**Added cost:** After 2 hours, $5 per/hr. for peer tutoring; $250–$750 Program
**Distraction-free environ.:** Yes
**Tape recording in class:** Yes
**Books on tape:** Yes
**Taping of other books:** Yes

**Professional tutors:** Yes
**Peer tutors:** Yes
**Max. hrs/wk for services:** 2
**Priority registration:** Yes
**Accomodations for students with ADD:** Yes
**How are professors notified of LD:** By the student

## GENERAL ADMISSIONS INFORMATION

**Director of Admissions:** Dan Shelly

**Telephone:** 716-475-6631

### ENTRANCE REQUIREMENTS

Total high school units required/recommended: 16 total units are recommended; 4 English recommended, 3 math recommended, 3 science recommended, 4 social studies recommended. Special requirements: A portfolio is required for art program applicants. Early application and supplementary information required of applicants to physician assistant program.

**Application deadline:** March 15
**Notification:** Rolling

**SAT or ACT preferred:** Either
**SAT Range:** 520–630V, 530–650 M
**ACT Range:** 22–28
**Average GPA:** 88

**Graduated top 10% of class:** 27
**Graduated top 25% of class:** 61
**Graduated top 50% of class:** 87

## COLLEGE GRADUATION REQUIREMENTS

**Course waivers allowed:** Yes
**Course substitutions allowed:** Yes
**In what courses:** Varies

## ADDITIONAL INFORMATION

**Environment:** R.I.T. is located on a 1,300 acre campus 5 miles south of the city of Rochester, the third largest city in New York State.

**Student Body**
  **Undergrad enrollment:** 8125
  **Women:** 34%
  **Men:** 66%
  **In-state students:** 59%
  **Out-of-state:** 41%

**Cost Information**
  **In-state tuition:** $16,083
  **Out-of-state:** $16,083
  **Room & board:** $6,417

**Housing Information**
  **University housing:** Yes
  **Fraternity:** Yes
  **Sorority:** Yes
  **Living on campus:** 79%

  **Athletics:** NCAA Div. III

# SAINT BONAVENTURE UNIVERSITY

P.O. Box D, St. Bonaventure, NY 14778 • **Admissions:** 716-375-2400 • **Fax:** 716-375-2005
**Email:** anaz@sbu.edu • **Web:** www.sbu.edu
**Support:** CS • **Institution:** 4 yr. Private

## LEARNING DISABILITY ADMISSIONS AND SERVICES

St. Bonaventure does not operate a specialized LD program but does provide services to students with identified disabilities. In the spirit of the Federal mandates, reasonable accommodations are made for otherwise qualified students with disabilities. St. Bonaventure's Teaching and Learning Center is an intrinsic element of the university's goal of academic excellence. The credo is 'to assist, not do.' The students need to accept responsibility for their own academic excellence and assistance will be provided.

## LEARNING DISABILITY ADMISSIONS INFORMATION

**Program Name:** Services for Students with Disabilities
**Program Director:** Debra A. Bookmiller, Coordinator          **Telephone:** 716-375-2066
**Contact Person:** Same as above

### ADMISSIONS

Students with learning disabilities must meet regular admission standards. Students, after acceptance, are encouraged to self-disclose their learning disability and provide appropriate documentation to the Office of Services For Students with Disabilities. Documentation is reviewed and appropriate accommodations are made. ACT average score is 23–24; SAT average score is 1070–1110; high school average score is 86. Course requirements include: 4 yrs. English, 4 yrs. social studies, 3 yrs. math, 3 yrs. science, 2 yrs. foreign language (recommended).

**College entrance exams required:** Yes          **Untimed accepted:** Yes
**Course entrance requirements:** Yes          **Interview required:** Recommended
**Diagnostic tests:** Yes
**Documentation:** WAIS-R; IEP: some memory and/or perceptual test: within 3 years

### ADDITIONAL INFORMATION

Students with LD may obtain assistance with assessing learning strengths and weaknesses, and consult one-on-one or in groups to acquire a greater command of a subject, get help with a specific assignment, or discuss academic challenges. SBU's one semester course 'SBU Success' (for credit) help's new students acclimate to college by covering topics such as notetaking skills, test taking strategies, and memory techniques. All entering freshmen with learning disabilities are strongly encouraged to take this course. Academic Restoration Program (2nd semester students) is mandated for some students to start at SBU. Peer support group is available upon student request. Students give presentations in classes to demonstrate what it is like to have a learning disability. Services and accommodations are available to undergraduate and graduate students.

**Special education HS coursework accepted:** Yes, if college equivalent
**Essay required:** Recommended
**Special application required:** No
**# of applications submitted each year:** N/A          **Submitted to:** N/A
**# of students receiving LD services:** 67          **# of applications accepted each year:** N/A
**Acceptance into program means acceptance into college:** Students must be admitted to the university first and then may request services.

# LEARNING DISABILITY SERVICES

**Learning center:** Yes
**Kurzweil personal reader:** No
**LD specialists:** 1
**Allowed in exams:**
  **Calculator:** Yes
  **Dictionary:** Y/N
  **Computer:** Yes
  **SpellCheck:** Yes

**Notetaker:** Yes
**Scribes:** Yes
**Proctors:** Yes
**Oral exams:** Yes
**Extended test time:** Yes
**Added cost:** None
**Distraction-free environ.:** Yes
**Tape recording in class:** Yes
**Books on tape:** Yes
**Taping of other books:** Yes

**Professional tutors:** 1
**Peer tutors:** 43
**Max. hrs/wk for services:** As needed and as available
**Priority registration:** No
**Accomodations for students with ADD:** Yes
**How are professors notified of LD:** By the student and the Program Director

# GENERAL ADMISSIONS INFORMATION

**Director of Admissions:** Alex Nazemet

**Telephone:** 716-375-2400

## ENTRANCE REQUIREMENTS

Total high school units required/recommended: 16 total units are required; 4 English required, 3 math required, 3 science required, 2 foreign language required, 4 social studies required. Minimum combined SAT I score of 1050, rank in top two-fifths of secondary school class, and minimum 3.0 GPA recommended.

**Application deadline:** April 15
**Notification:** Rolling

**SAT or ACT preferred:** Either
**SAT Avg:** 532V, 532M
**Average ACT:** 23

**Graduated top 10% of class:** 19
**Graduated top 25% of class:** 44
**Graduated top 50% of class:** 73

# COLLEGE GRADUATION REQUIREMENTS

**Course waivers allowed:** No
**Course substitutions allowed:** Yes
**In what courses:** Foreign Language

# ADDITIONAL INFORMATION

**Environment:** The university is located on 600 acres in a rural area 70 miles southeast of Buffalo.

**Student Body**
  **Undergrad enrollment:** 1,839
  **Women:** 52%
  **Men:** 48%
  **In-state students:** 78%
  **Out-of-state:** 22%

**Cost Information**
  **In-state tuition:** $11,919
  **Out-of-state:** $11,919
  **Room & board:** $5,326

**Housing Information**
  **University housing:** Yes
  **Fraternity:** No
  **Sorority:** No
  **Living on campus:** 76%

  **Athletics:** NCAA Div. I

# SAINT LAWRENCE UNIVERSITY

Canton, NY 13617 • **Admissions:** 315-379-5261
**Web:** www.stlawu.edu
**Support:** S • **Institution:** 4 yr. Private

## LEARNING DISABILITY ADMISSIONS AND SERVICES

The Office of Special Needs provides services to members of the university who either have identified themselves or believe they may have some type of learning disability. The Office has several purposes: to serve students who are learning-challenged by documented disabilities; to help students get the academic help that they need; to put students in touch with other people on campus who can help; to advise and counsel students; to educate everyone on campus about special needs. The office works with students in developing Individual Education Accommodations Plans for the purpose of receiving reasonable accommodations in their educational and residential life concerns. The service will also make referrals and advocate at several on-campus services, and if necessary, connect with state or regional support agencies. There is a Writing Center for help with writing assignments; Peer Tutors, for general assistance with academic work; and a Counseling Center and Health Center.

## LEARNING DISABILITY ADMISSIONS INFORMATION

**Program Name:** Office of Special Needs
**Program Director:** John Meagher, Director
**Contact Person:** Same as above

**Telephone:** 315-379-5104

### ADMISSIONS

There is no special admissions process for students with learning disabilities. All applicants must meet the same admission criteria which include: Courses recommended of 4 yrs. English, 3 yrs. math, 3 yrs. science, 3 yrs. foreign language, 3 yrs. social studies; SAT/ACT with the average SAT being 1130; an interview is recommended and can be done off campus with an alumni representative.

**College entrance exams required:** Yes
**Course entrance requirements:** Yes
**Diagnostic tests:** Yes
**Documentation:** Given by any qualified psychologist

**Untimed accepted:** Yes
**Interview required:** No

### ADDITIONAL INFORMATION

Students need to be self-starters (to seek out the service early and follow through). They need to share as soon as possible the official documents that describe the learning disability so that the office can help develop the Individual Educational Accommodation Plan (IEAP). As soon as possible, students need to notify the professors and people in various offices about the learning disability. The Director of Services sends a memo to each professor which describes the student's IEAP, discloses that the student is a documented and endorsed learning challenged student on file with the Office of Special Needs, and lists the accommodations necessary for the student to be successful in the course. Services and accommodations are available for undergraduate and graduate students.

**Special education HS coursework accepted:** Yes
**Special application required:** No
**# of applications submitted each year:** N/A
**# of students receiving LD services:** 119
**Essay required:** N/I
**Submitted to:** N/A
**# of applications accepted each year:** N/A

**Acceptance into program means acceptance into college:** Students must be accepted to the university first and then may request services.

## LEARNING DISABILITY SERVICES

**Learning center:** No
**Kurzweil personal reader:** Yes
**LD specialists:** No
**Allowed in exams:**
  **Calculator:** Yes
  **Dictionary:** Yes
  **Computer:** Yes
  **SpellCheck:** Yes

**Notetaker:** Yes
**Scribes:** Yes
**Proctors:** Yes
**Oral exams:** Yes
**Extended test time:** Yes
**Added cost:** None
**Distraction-free environ.:** Yes
**Tape recording in class:** Yes
**Books on tape:** Yes
**Taping of other books:** No

**Professional tutors:** No
**Peer tutors:** Yes
**Max. hrs/wk for services:**
Unlimited
**Priority registration:** Yes
**Accomodations for students
with ADD:** Yes
**How are professors notified of
LD:** By the student and the
Program Director

## GENERAL ADMISSIONS INFORMATION

**Director of Admissions:** Kathryn Mullaney         **Telephone:** 315-379-5261

### ENTRANCE REQUIREMENTS
Total high school units required/recommended: 16 total units are required; 4 English recommended, 3 math recommended, 3 science recommended, 3 social studies recommended.

**Application deadline:** February 15         **SAT or ACT preferred:** Either
**Notification:** Rolling after March 15         **SAT Avg:** 510V, 575M

## COLLEGE GRADUATION REQUIREMENTS

**Course waivers allowed:** No
**Course substitutions allowed:** No
**In what courses:** N/A

## ADDITIONAL INFORMATION

**Environment:** The university is located on 1,000 acres in a rural area 80 miles south of Ottawa, Canada.

**Student Body**
  **Undergrad enrollment:** 1,965
  **Women:** 50%
  **Men:** 50%
  **In-state students:** 48%
  **Out-of-state:** 52%

**Cost Information**
  **In-state tuition:** $20,410
  **Out-of-state:** $20,410
  **Room & board:** $6,110

**Housing Information**
  **University housing:** Yes
  **Fraternity:** Yes
  **Sorority:** Yes
  **Living on campus:** 96%

  **Athletics:** NCAA Div. III

# SAINT THOMAS AQUINAS COLLEGE

**NY**

125 Route 340, Sparkill, NY 10976 • **Admissions:** 914-398-4100 • **Fax:** 914-398-4224
**Email:** joestacenroll@rockland.net • **Web:** www.stac.edu
**Support:** SP • **Institution:** 4 yr. Private

## LEARNING DISABILITY ADMISSIONS AND SERVICES

The services provided in 'The STAC Exchange' Program are extremely comprehensive, and based on research and actual experiences with undergraduates who have learning process dysfunctions. STAC's program focuses on the development of critical thinking, abstract reasoning, and independent learning skills. The aim is to break the pattern of dependency often created for students with these dysfunctions, to foster a spirit of independence in learning, and to inspire confidence in the students's own abilities. As the students progress each year, the program is designed to gradually reduce the need for some services. The approach of the Program is learning strategies. At the heart of the Program are the Seminars conducted by eleven Program Mentors. These instructional units are small group sessions, each covering a specific learning strategy. The objective is to enable each student to reach his or her optimum level of learning independence. They do not tutor students through college; they teach them the tools to use so that they can learn independently. The students are required to participate in a unique summer program prior to freshman year; the students learn to use their learning strengths, to develop improved thinking skills, to enhance time management and organizational skills, and to develop a sense of confidence about themselves; the program integrates academic work, learning strategies, and social skills.

## LEARNING DISABILITY ADMISSIONS INFORMATION

**Program Name:** 'The STAC Exchange'
**Program Director:** Dr. MariJanet Doonan                    **Telephone:** 914-398-4230
**Contact Person:** Same as above

### ADMISSIONS

Students may apply to STAC with documentation of a diagnosis of LD by certified professionals. Students should be high school seniors/graduates; have college prep courses in high school; and be motivated to continue learning. Documentation needed: high school diploma; documentation of LD including identification and description of specific LD as the primary handicapping condition, effects of LD on academic performance including learning strengths and weaknesses, complete psychological exam including an analysis of abstract reasoning skills using subtest scores from WAIS, and latest IEP showing diagnosis, placement, long and short term goals, type of assistance received; ACT/SAT; STAC application; 3 recommendations from LD specialist, counselor,teacher; and handwritten statement stating why she/he wishes to attend college and how STAC could be beneficial; and agree to participate in the research nature of the Program. The admission decision is made jointly by Admissions and STAC; space is limited; early application is encouraged; acceptance into STAC is extremely competitive. Admitted students must attend a summer program.

| | |
|---|---|
| **College entrance exams required:** Yes | **Untimed accepted:** Yes |
| **Course entrance requirements:** Yes | **Interview required:** Yes |
| **Diagnostic tests:** Yes | |
| **Documentation:** WAIS-R; IEP; W-J:  within 1 year | |

### ADDITIONAL INFORMATION

Program Mentors conduct seminars in small groups and students must attend. Each Seminar design begins with basic learning strategies and guides students to mastery of specific approaches upon which further learning can be built. Students remain in a Seminar until they master the requisite strategy. Students meet twice weekly with a Mentor for help transferring competencies learned in the Seminars into course content areas. These sessions are different from traditional tutoring as it is expected that students come to these sessions to increase understanding of their materials, having completed the preliminary work for the assignment. Basic seminars include: organization, time management, pre-reading, listening techniques, notetaking, test taking, oral communication, interpersonal communication, memory techniques, critical thinking skills, problem solving, and self-advocacy.  Other services include: taped text, alternate exam strategies, counseling, media usage, editorial assistance, tape recorders, computer assistance, and career seminars.

| | |
|---|---|
| **Special education HS coursework accepted:** Y/N | **Essay required:** Yes |
| **Special application required:** Yes | **Submitted to:** Program Director |
| **# of applications submitted each year:** 180–200 | **# of applications accepted each year:** 35 |
| **# of students receiving LD services:** 85 | |

**Acceptance into program means acceptance into college:** Students are admitted to the college and then to STAC.

# LEARNING DISABILITY SERVICES

**Learning center:** Yes
**Kurzweil personal reader:** Yes
**LD specialists:** Yes
**Allowed in exams:**
  **Calculator:** Yes
  **Dictionary:** Yes
  **Computer:** Yes
  **SpellCheck:** Yes

**Notetaker:** No
**Scribes:** Yes
**Proctors:** Yes
**Oral exams:** Yes
**Extended test time:** Yes
**Added cost:** $3,000 per/year
**Distraction-free environ.:** Yes
**Tape recording in class:** Yes
**Books on tape:** Yes
**Taping of other books:** Yes

**Professional tutors:** Mentors
**Peer tutors:** No
**Max. hrs/wk for services:**
Generally 4–6 hrs. per/week but
as often as needed
**Priority registration:** Yes
**Accomodations for students
with ADD:** Yes
**How are professors notified of
LD:** By the student and the
Program Director

# GENERAL ADMISSIONS INFORMATION

**Director of Admissions:** Joe Chillo

**Telephone:** 914-398-4000

## ENTRANCE REQUIREMENTS

Total high school units required/recommended: 17 total units are required; 4 English required, 2 math required, 2 science required, 1 foreign language required, 1 history required. Minimum SAT I scores of 400 in both Verbal and Math, rank in top half of secondary school class.

**Application deadline:** Rolling
**Notification:** Rolling

**SAT or ACT preferred:** SAT
**SAT Avg:** 510V, 490M
**SAT II required:** Yes
**Average GPA:** 2.8

**Graduated top 10% of class:** 15
**Graduated top 25% of class:** 48
**Graduated top 50% of class:** 88

# COLLEGE GRADUATION REQUIREMENTS

**Course waivers allowed:** No
**Course substitutions allowed:** No
**In what courses:** Rarely; has not been an issue

# ADDITIONAL INFORMATION

**Environment:** The school is located on 43 acres in a suburban area 15 miles from New York City.

**Student Body**
  **Undergrad enrollment:** 2,101
  **Women:** 61%
  **Men:** 39%
  **In-state students:** 60%
  **Out-of-state:** 40%

**Cost Information**
  **In-state tuition:** $10,500
  **Out-of-state:** $10,500
  **Room & board:** $6,700

**Housing Information**
  **University housing:** Yes
  **Fraternity:** No
  **Sorority:** No
  **Living on campus:** 30%

  **Athletics:** NAIA

# STATE UNIVERSITY OF NEW YORK AT ALBANY

**NY**

1400 Washington Avenue, Albany, NY 12222 • **Admissions:** 518-442-5435 • **Fax:** 518-442-5418
**Email:** ugadmit@safnet.albany.edu • **Web:** www.albany.edu
**Support:** S • **Institution:** 4 yr. Public

## LEARNING DISABILITY ADMISSIONS AND SERVICES

The mission at the university is to provide a quality educational program to students with dyslexia /learning disabilities. The Disabled Student Services Program offers a full complement of support services to ensure students with disabilities equal access to the University at Albany. The Learning Disabilities Resource Program is a Division of Student Affairs that seeks to empower students with LD to become successful decision makers and problem solvers. Additionally, the LDRP promotes increased sensitivity to and appreciation for the uniqueness of students with learning disabilities. The goal of the LDRP is to provide general support for students as they attempt to gain access to services and accommodations necessary to their success. The Program provides a Writing Center staffed by faculty, advocacy, assistance with recommended courses, tutoring assistance, and a willingness to explore innovative ways of providing the most efficient assistance possible.

## LEARNING DISABILITY ADMISSIONS INFORMATION

**Program Name:** Learning Disabilities Resource Program (LDRP)
**Program Director:** Nancy Belowich-Negron          **Telephone:** 518-442-5491
**Contact Person:** Same as above

### ADMISSIONS

There is no special application for applicants with learning disabilities. Applicants who self-disclose may have their application files reviewed by the Director of the LDRP and the Office of Admissions. Letters of recommendation, auxiliary testing, and a personal interview are helpful. Students must present 18 units from high school acceptable to the university, SAT 950, high school average 85%, class rank in the top 1/3.

**College entrance exams required:** Yes          **Untimed accepted:** Yes
**Course entrance requirements:** Yes          **Interview required:** Recommended
**Diagnostic tests:** Yes
**Documentation:** IEP; WAIS-R; flexible: within 3 years

### ADDITIONAL INFORMATION

Services include: pre-admission review of the applicant's file in conjunction with admissions and individual counseling and advisement to applicants and their families; counseling and support; auxiliary aids and services such as testing accommodations, assistance in locating notetakers and tutors, reading services, and loan of tape recorders; information and referral to campus resources; and consultation and advocacy. Students diagnosed with ADD who have documented learning disabilities may receive support from the LDRP, or in some cases, from the Office of Disabled Student Services.

**Special education HS coursework accepted:** Y/N          **Essay required:** No
**Special application required:** No          **Submitted to:** N/A
**# of applications submitted each year:** N/A          **# of applications accepted each year:** N/A
**# of students receiving LD services:** 125
**Acceptance into program means acceptance into college:** Students must be accepted to the university first and then may request services.

# LEARNING DISABILITY SERVICES

**Learning center:** No
**Kurzweil personal reader:** No
**LD specialists:** No
**Allowed in exams:**
  **Calculator:** Yes
  **Dictionary:** No
  **Computer:** Yes
  **SpellCheck:** Yes

**Notetaker:** Yes
**Scribes:** Yes
**Proctors:** Yes
**Oral exams:** Yes
**Extended test time:** Yes
**Added cost:** $6.00 per/hour
**Distraction-free environ.:** Yes
**Tape recording in class:** Yes
**Books on tape:** Yes
**Taping of other books:** Yes

**Professional tutors:** N/I
**Peer tutors:** Yes
**Max. hrs/wk for services:** As needed
**Priority registration:** Yes
**Accomodations for students with ADD:** Yes
**How are professors notified of LD:** By the student and the Program Director

# GENERAL ADMISSIONS INFORMATION

**Director of Admissions:** Dr. Micheleen Treadwell          **Telephone:** 518-442-5435

## ENTRANCE REQUIREMENTS

Total high school units required/recommended: 18 total units are required; 4 English required, 2 math required, 2 science required, 3 social studies required. Minimum combined SAT I score of 1100, rank in top quarter of secondary school class, and minimum 86 grade average recommended. Special requirements: A portfolio is required for art program applicants. An audition is required for music program applicants.

**Application deadline:** February 15
**Notification:** Rolling

**SAT or ACT preferred:** SAT
**SAT Avg:** 569V, 581M
**Average GPA:** 87.3

**Graduated top 10% of class:** 14
**Graduated top 25% of class:** 52
**Graduated top 50% of class:** 91

# COLLEGE GRADUATION REQUIREMENTS

**Course waivers allowed:** No
**Course substitutions allowed:** Yes
**In what courses:** Determined on a case-by-case basis

# ADDITIONAL INFORMATION

**Environment:** Urban campus on 515 acres located on the fringe of the state capitol.

**Student Body**
  **Undergrad enrollment:** 9,622
  **Women:** 48%
  **Men:** 52%
  **In-state students:** 97%
  **Out-of-state:** 3%

**Cost Information**
  **In-state tuition:** $3,400
  **Out-of-state:** $8,300
  **Room & board:** $5,241

**Housing Information**
  **University housing:** Yes
  **Fraternity:** Yes
  **Sorority:** Yes
  **Living on campus:** 54%

  **Athletics:** NCAA Div. III

# BINGHAMTON UNIVERSITY

**NY**

P.O. Box 6000, Binghamton, NY 13902 • **Admissions:** 607-777-2171 • **Fax:** 607-777-4445
**Email:** admit@binghamton.edu • **Web:** www.binghamton.edu
**Support:** S • **Institution:** 4 yr. Public

## LEARNING DISABILITY ADMISSIONS AND SERVICES

The Services for Students with Disabilities Office provides assistance to students with physical or learning disabilities. They operate on the philosophy that the individuals they serve are students first and that their disabilities are secondary. Support services assist students in taking advantage of the opportunities at Binghamton and in making their own contributions to the university community.

## LEARNING DISABILITY ADMISSIONS INFORMATION

**Program Name:** Services for Students with Disabilities
**Program Director:** B. Jean Fairbairn                    **Telephone:** 607-777-2686
**Contact Person:** Same as above

### ADMISSIONS

Suny Binghamton welcomes applications from all qualified individuals. While there are no special admissions procedures or academic programs expressly for students with disabilities, the Services for Students with Disabilities Office provides a wide range of support services to enrolled students. Diagnostic tests are not required for admissions, but students are encouraged to meet with the Director of Services for Students with Disabilities and to provide documentation in order to determine appropriate accommodations. Through non-matriculated enrollment, students can take courses but are not enrolled in a degree program. If they do well, they may then apply for matriculation, using credits earned toward their degree.

**College entrance exams required:** Yes               **Untimed accepted:** Yes
**Course entrance requirements:** Yes                  **Interview required:** Encouraged
**Diagnostic tests:** Yes
**Documentation:** Psychoeducational Evaluation; completed no earlier than 11th or 12th grade

### ADDITIONAL INFORMATION

Tutorial services are provided at no charge for four hours per week. However, SSD can arrange for more than four hours per week at the student's expense. The university's Center for Academic Excellence provides peer tutoring to any student at no cost. The university has offered courses in College Study and Coping Skills and Applying Study Skills to Career Research. Availability of these courses each year is dependent on staffing. Students are given memos of reasonable accommodation written by the Director of Services for Students with Disabilities to be given to their professors. Services and accommodations are available for undergraduate and graduate students.

**Special education HS coursework accepted:** No         **Essay required:** Yes
**Special application required:** No                     **Submitted to:** N/A
**# of applications submitted each year:** N/A           **# of applications accepted each year:** N/A
**# of students receiving LD services:** 40
**Acceptance into program means acceptance into college:** Students must be admitted to the university and then request services.

**Learning center:** No
**Kurzweil personal reader:** Yes
**LD specialists:** No
**Allowed in exams:**
  **Calculator:** Yes
  **Dictionary:** Yes
  **Computer:** Yes
  **SpellCheck:** Yes

**Notetaker:** Yes
**Scribes:** Yes
**Proctors:** Yes
**Oral exams:** Yes
**Extended test time:** Yes
**Added cost:** None
**Distraction-free environ.:** Yes
**Tape recording in class:** Yes
**Books on tape:** Yes
**Taping of other books:** Yes

**Professional tutors:** No
**Peer tutors:** as needed
**Max. hrs/wk for services:** 4 hours per week; more hours at the student's expense
**Priority registration:** Y/N
**Accomodations for students with ADD:** Yes
**How are professors notified of LD:** By the student

## GENERAL ADMISSIONS INFORMATION

**Director of Admissions:** Geoffrey Gould     **Telephone:** 607-777-2171

### ENTRANCE REQUIREMENTS

Total high school units required/recommended: 21 total units are recommended; 4 English required, 3 math required, 4 math recommended, 4 science recommended, 2 social studies recommended, 2 history recommended. Special requirements: TOEFL is required of all international students. 3 units of one foreign language or 2 units of two languages required of Harpur College applicants. 1 unit of chemistry and 1 unit of biology recommended of nursing program applicants.

**Application deadline:** February 15
**Notification:** Rolling

**SAT or ACT preferred:** Either
**SAT Avg:** 595V, 619M
**Average GPA:** 3.5

**Graduated top 10% of class:** 52
**Graduated top 25% of class:** 94
**Graduated top 50% of class:** 100

## COLLEGE GRADUATION REQUIREMENTS

**Course waivers allowed:** No
**Course substitutions allowed:** Yes
**In what courses:** Foreign language substitutions are available when justified to the Academic Standards Committee of Harpur College, the only college at the university with a foreign language requirement.

## ADDITIONAL INFORMATION

**Environment:** NR

**Student Body**
  **Undergrad enrollment:** 9,349
  **Women:** 53%
  **Men:** 47%
  **In-state students:** 96%
  **Out-of-state:** 4%

**Cost Information**
  **In-state tuition:** $3,400
  **Out-of-state:** $8,300
  **Room & board:** $4,814

**Housing Information**
  **University housing:** Yes
  **Fraternity:** No
  **Sorority:** No
  **Living on campus:** 53%

  **Athletics:** NCAA Div. III

# NY

# STATE UNIVERSITY OF NEW YORK AT CANTON

Canton, NY 13617-1098 • Admissions: 315-386-7123

**Support:** S • **Institution:** 2 yr. Public

## LEARNING DISABILITY ADMISSIONS AND SERVICES

At the State University of New York-Caton, College of Technology the Accommodative Services Program is equipped to help students with learning disabilities make a smooth transition to college, and receive the necessary accommodations to ensure their academic success. Prospective students are welcome to contact the Accommodative Service office with any questions. Although students with learning disabilities may register at the office at any time during their stay at SUNY-Canton, they are encouraged to do so as early as possible. Students must register at the office in order to obtain the special resources and services. It is the students responsibility to self-disclose, provide appropriate documentation, and request accommodations.

## LEARNING DISABILITY ADMISSIONS INFORMATION

**Program Name:** Accommodative Services (AS)
**Program Director:** Debora L. Camp
**Contact Person:** Same as above

**Telephone:** 315-386-7121

### ADMISSIONS

All students follow the same admissions procedure and are evaluated similarly for specific course placement. There are no specific course requirements as the requirements vary per curriculum. All students must have a high school diploma or the GED equivalent.

**College entrance exams required:** No
**Course entrance requirements:** Yes
**Diagnostic tests:** Yes
**Documentation:** WAIS-R: within 2–3 years

**Untimed accepted:** Yes
**Interview required:** Preferred

### ADDITIONAL INFORMATION

There are a number of support services offered on campus: Academic Advisement; Academic Computing Center; Canton Special Services Program; Counseling Center; Educational Opportunity Program; Learning Center; Math Lab; Writing Center; Tutoring; Science Learning Center; and Accounting Lab. Acceptance into the university ensures the student will receive the services they request.

**Special education HS coursework accepted:** No
**Special application required:** No
**# of applications submitted each year:** N/A
**# of students receiving LD services:** 90
**Acceptance into program means acceptance into college:** Students must be admitted to the university first and then may request services.

**Essay required:** No
**Submitted to:** N/A
**# of applications accepted each year:** N/A

# LEARNING DISABILITY SERVICES

**Learning center:** Yes
**Kurzweil personal reader:** Yes
**LD specialists:** No
**Allowed in exams:**
  **Calculator:** Yes
  **Dictionary:** Yes
  **Computer:** Yes
  **SpellCheck:** Yes

**Notetaker:** Yes
**Scribes:** Yes
**Proctors:** Yes
**Oral exams:** Yes
**Extended test time:** Yes
**Added cost:** None
**Distraction-free environ.:** Yes
**Tape recording in class:** Yes
**Books on tape:** Yes
**Taping of other books:** Yes

**Professional tutors:** Yes
**Peer tutors:** Yes
**Max. hrs/wk for services:** On an as-need basis
**Priority registration:** Yes
**Accomodations for students with ADD:** Yes
**How are professors notified of LD:** By the student and the Program Director

# GENERAL ADMISSIONS INFORMATION

**Director of Admissions:** Michael Brophy

**Telephone:** 315-386-7123

## ENTRANCE REQUIREMENTS
Minimum of high school diploma or GED equivalent.

**Application deadline:** NR
**Notification:** NR

**SAT or ACT preferred:** NR

# COLLEGE GRADUATION REQUIREMENTS

**Course waivers allowed:** No
**Course substitutions allowed:** Yes
**In what courses:** Upon approval by Dean's office; must satisfy graduation requirements.

# ADDITIONAL INFORMATION

**Environment:** The 550-acre campus is 135 miles northeast of Syracuse.

**Student Body**
  **Undergrad enrollment:** 1,831
  **Women:** 45%
  **Men:** 55%
  **In-state students:** 99%
  **Out-of-state:** 1%

**Cost Information**
  **In-state tuition:** $3,200
  **Out-of-state:** $8, 300

**Housing Information**
  **University housing:** Yes
  **Fraternity:** Yes
  **Sorority:** Yes
  **Living on campus:** 46%

  **Athletics:** NJCAA

# NY STATE UNIVERSITY OF NEW YORK AT DEHLI

Delhi, NY 13753 • **Admissions:** 607-746-4000

**Support:** CS • **Institution:** 2 yr. Public

## LEARNING DISABILITY ADMISSIONS AND SERVICES

SUNY Delhi provides students with learning disabilities with academic support services and equipment which includes professional tutors; exams in a distraction-free environment; submission of exams on tape or dictating exams to an attendant; remedial courses in Reading, math, English, Study Skills; enlarged video display computer terminals. The Coordinator of Services often confers with students regarding their unique learning, study, and time management needs.

## LEARNING DISABILITY ADMISSIONS INFORMATION

**Program Name:** Academic Success
**Program Director:** Leslie Mokay          **Telephone:** 607-746-4585
**Contact Person:** Jody Fiorini          **Telephone:** 607-746-4590

### ADMISSIONS

The admission requirements are the same for all students. It is always helpful if students with learning disabilities present themselves as confident, independent, goal-oriented, and self-directed learners. To be eligible for services students must disclose information about their learning disability with the regular application form. ASSET scores are used for placement within courses.

**College entrance exams required:** Yes          **Untimed accepted:** Yes
**Course entrance requirements:** No          **Interview required:** Recommended
**Diagnostic tests:** Yes
**Documentation:** WAIS-R; Achievement tests: within 3 years

### ADDITIONAL INFORMATION

Students may dictate exams or submit exams on tape. The coordinator of services for students with learning disabilities is available to answer any questions regarding academic and non-academic matters. The coordinator also serves as a campus referral service.

**Special education HS coursework accepted:** Yes          **Essay required:** No
**Special application required:** Yes          **Submitted to:** Contact Person
**# of applications submitted each year:** N/I          **# of applications accepted each year:** N/I
**# of students receiving LD services:** 172
**Acceptance into program means acceptance into college:** Students must be admitted to the college and then request services.

## LEARNING DISABILITY SERVICES

**Learning center:** No
**Kurzweil personal reader:** Yes
**LD specialists:** Yes
**Allowed in exams:**
  **Calculator:** Yes
  **Dictionary:** Yes
  **Computer:** Yes
  **SpellCheck:** Yes

**Notetaker:** Yes
**Scribes:** Yes
**Proctors:** Yes
**Oral exams:** Yes
**Extended test time:** Yes
**Added cost:** None
**Distraction-free environ.:** Yes
**Tape recording in class:** Yes
**Books on tape:** Yes
**Taping of other books:** No

**Professional tutors:** 3
**Peer tutors:** Yes
**Max. hrs/wk for services:** 2 hours per/course
**Priority registration:** No
**Accomodations for students with ADD:** Yes
**How are professors notified of LD:** By the student and the Program Director

## GENERAL ADMISSIONS INFORMATION

**Director of Admissions:** Gary S. Cole

**Telephone:** 607-746-4550

### ENTRANCE REQUIREMENTS
3 yrs. math recommended.

**Application deadline:** Rolling
**Notification:** NR

**SAT or ACT preferred:** NR

## COLLEGE GRADUATION REQUIREMENTS

**Course waivers allowed:** Yes
**Course substitutions allowed:** Yes
**In what courses:** Math in special situations

## ADDITIONAL INFORMATION

**Environment:** Small town setting on 1,100 acres in upstate New York.

**Student Body**
  **Undergrad enrollment:** 2,332
  **Women:** 42%
  **Men:** 58%
  **In-state students:** 99%
  **Out-of-state:** 1%

**Cost Information**
  **In-state tuition:** $2,415
  **Out-of-state:** $5,500

**Housing Information**
  **University housing:** Yes
  **Fraternity:** Yes
  **Sorority:** N/I
  **Living on campus:** 50%

  **Athletics:** NJCAA

# STATE UNIVERSITY OF NEW YORK AT FARMINGDALE

Farmingdale, NY 11735 • **Admissions:** 516-420-2200
**Support:** CS • **Institution:** 2 yr. & 4 yr. Public

## LEARNING DISABILITY ADMISSIONS AND SERVICES

There is no LD program at the college, but the Office for Students with Disabilities is dedicated to the principle that equal opportunity to realize one's full potential should be available to all students. In keeping with this philosophy, the staff offers individualized services to students with disabilities in accordance with their needs. Students may meet individually with a learning disability specialist for one hour per week or in group meetings. Services include: academic remediation with emphasis on compensatory strategies; study skills strategies training; test accommodations; time management instruction; tutoring; and self-understanding of disability. The services offered strive to install independence, self-confidence, and self advocacy skills.

## LEARNING DISABILITY ADMISSIONS INFORMATION

**Program Name:** Support Services for Students with Disabilities
**Program Director:** Malka Edelman                **Telephone:** 516-420-2411
**Contact Person:** Same as above

### ADMISSIONS

There is no special admissions procedure for applicants with learning disabilities. Students should self-identify on the application. Admission decisions are made by the Office of Admission. Students should submit psychoeducational reports, letters of recommendation, and request a personal interview. Students are not required to take the SAT/ACT or to have the New York State Regent's Diploma. The university is on "rolling admissions." Almost all of the programs accept students throughout the year.

**College entrance exams required:** Recommended        **Untimed accepted:** Yes
**Course entrance requirements:** Yes                   **Interview required:** No
**Diagnostic tests:** Yes
**Documentation:** WAIS-R; WJPE: within 3 years

### ADDITIONAL INFORMATION

The college would like the high school Individualized Educational Plan (IEP) and the WAIS-R to help identify the services necessary to help the student to be successful. Pre-college Pathways Program has more flexible entrance requirements. Elementary Algebra is the minimum requirement in math.

**Special education HS coursework accepted:** Yes      **Essay required:** No
**Special application required:** No                   **Submitted to:** N/A
**# of applications submitted each year:** N/A          **# of applications accepted each year:** All admitted students can receive services

**# of students receiving LD services:** 175
**Acceptance into program means acceptance into college:** Students must be admitted to the university first (can appeal a denial) and then may request services.

## LEARNING DISABILITY SERVICES

**Learning center:** No
**Kurzweil personal reader:** No
**LD specialists:** 20
**Allowed in exams:**
  **Calculator:** Yes
  **Dictionary:** Yes
  **Computer:** Yes
  **SpellCheck:** Yes

**Notetaker:** Yes
**Scribes:** Yes
**Proctors:** Yes
**Oral exams:** Yes
**Extended test time:** Yes
**Added cost:** None
**Distraction-free environ.:** Yes
**Tape recording in class:** Yes
**Books on tape:** RFB
**Taping of other books:** Yes

**Professional tutors:** Yes
**Peer tutors:** Yes
**Max. hrs/wk for services:**
Unlimited
**Priority registration:** No
**Accomodations for students with ADD:** Yes
**How are professors notified of LD:** By the student

## GENERAL ADMISSIONS INFORMATION

**Director of Admissions:** Jeff Stein

**Telephone:** 516-420-2200

### ENTRANCE REQUIREMENTS

High school diploma. Course requirements vary by curriculum.

**Application deadline:** Rolling
**Notification:** NR

**SAT or ACT preferred:** NR

## COLLEGE GRADUATION REQUIREMENTS

**Course waivers allowed:** Yes
**Course substitutions allowed:** Yes
**In what courses:** Provided for foreign language and math

## ADDITIONAL INFORMATION

**Environment:** Farmingdale is a small town located within easy access to New York City.

**Student Body**
  **Undergrad enrollment:** 5,800
  **Women:** 47%
  **Men:** 53%
  **In-state students:** 98%
  **Out-of-state:** 2%

**Cost Information**
  **In-state tuition:** $2,980
  **Out-of-state:** $6,550

**Housing Information**
  **University housing:** Yes
  **Fraternity:** 1%
  **Sorority:** 1%
  **Living on campus:** 10%

  **Athletics:** NJCAA

# STATE UNIVERSITY OF NEW YORK AT STONY BROOK

Stony Brook, NY 11794 • **Admissions:** 516-632-6868 • **Fax:** 516-632-9898
**Email:** admissions@sunysb.edu • **Web:** www.sunysb.edu • **Support:** S • **Institution:** 4 yr. Public

## LEARNING DISABILITY ADMISSIONS AND SERVICES

The Stony Brook campus only provides support services; there is no program for students with learning disabilities.

## LEARNING DISABILITY ADMISSIONS INFORMATION

**Program Name:** Disabilities Services
**Program Director:** Carol Dworkin                    **Telephone:** 516-632-6748
**Contact Person:** Same as above

### ADMISSIONS
There is no special admissions process for students with learning disabilities. There is limited flexibility in terms of the required GPA considered, but students with learning disabilities may be reviewed with a GPA between 80–85% rather than 85% or above. Very little emphasis is placed on SAT scores. The Director of Disability Services will review documentation from students with learning disabilities and provide a recommendation to the Office of Admission.

**College entrance exams required:** N/A          **Untimed accepted:** Yes
**Course entrance requirements:** Yes              **Interview required:** No
**Diagnostic tests:** Yes
**Documentation:** Psychoeducational battery: within 3 years

### ADDITIONAL INFORMATION
Students are given assistance in locating tutors and a fee is charged per hour for tutoring. Services and accommodations are available to undergraduate and graduate students. No skills classes are offered.

**Special education HS coursework accepted:** No     **Essay required:** No
**Special application required:** No                 **Submitted to:** No
**# of applications submitted each year:** N/A       **# of applications accepted each year:** N/I
**# of students receiving LD services:** 95
**Acceptance into program means acceptance into college:** Students must be admitted to the university first and then may request services.

## LEARNING DISABILITY SERVICES

**Learning center:** No
**Kurzweil personal reader:** Yes
**LD specialists:** 1
**Allowed in exams:**
  **Calculator:** Y/N
  **Dictionary:** Y/N
  **Computer:** Y/N
  **SpellCheck:** Y/N

**Notetaker:** Yes
**Scribes:** Yes
**Proctors:** Yes
**Oral exams:** Y/N
**Extended test time:** Yes
**Added cost:** None, except fee for tutoring
**Distraction-free environ.:** Yes
**Tape recording in class:** Y/N
**Books on tape:** RFB
**Taping of other books:** No

**Professional tutors:** No
**Peer tutors:** N/I
**Max. hrs/wk for services:** Unlimited
**Priority registration:** Yes
**Accomodations for students with ADD:** Yes
**How are professors notified of LD:** Both the student and the Program Director

## GENERAL ADMISSIONS INFORMATION

**Director of Admissions:** Gigi Lamens

**Telephone:** 516-632-6868

### ENTRANCE REQUIREMENTS

Total high school units required/recommended: 4 English recommended, 3 math recommended, 3 science recommended, 3 foreign language recommended, 3 social studies recommended. Special requirements: Chemistry, physics, and 4 units of math recommended of engineering program applicants. Applicants planning to major in computer science must successfully complete one semester at Stony Brook. Additional requirements for upper-division nursing and engineering program applicants.

**Application deadline:** July 10
**Notification:** Rolling

**SAT or ACT preferred:** Either
**SAT Avg:** 520V, 560M
**SAT II required:** Yes
**Average GPA:** 3.0

**Graduated top 10% of class:** 23
**Graduated top 25% of class:** 63
**Graduated top 50% of class:** 95

## COLLEGE GRADUATION REQUIREMENTS

**Course waivers allowed:** N/I
**Course substitutions allowed:** No
**In what courses:** Substitution of 2 culture courses in place of foreign language. Specific math disability supported by documentation can be accommodated in relation to the university. Math requirements only—not requirements in a major.

## ADDITIONAL INFORMATION

**Environment:** The University is located on 1100 acres in a suburban area on Long Island, 60 miles from New York City.

**Student Body**
  **Undergrad enrollment:** 11,267
  **Women:** 51%
  **Men:** 49%
  **In-state students:** 98%
  **Out-of-state:** 2%

**Cost Information**
  **In-state tuition:** $3,400
  **Out-of-state:** $8,300
  **Room & board:** $5,594

**Housing Information**
  **University housing:** Yes
  **Fraternity:** No
  **Sorority:** No
  **Living on campus:** 50%

  **Athletics:** NCAA Div. III

# STATE UNIVERSITY OF NEW YORK
# COLLEGE OF TECHNOLOGY AT ALFRED

Alfred, NY 14802 • **Admissions:** 800-4-ALFRED
**Support:** CS • **Institution:** 2 yr. Public

## LEARNING DISABILITY ADMISSIONS AND SERVICES

Project 5 is a program for students with temporary or permanent disabilities. The "5" represents the major categories of the disabling conditions: physical, medical, learning, hearing, and visual. After students with disabilities are identified, appropriate services are provided depending on individual needs. The Student Development Center houses a team of dedicated professionals committed to fostering the personal and academic growth of all Alfred State College students. The centralized nature of the Center allows for an important and efficient link among those college supportive services that are dedicated to maximizing student growth and student success. The Alfred State Opportunity Program (ASOP) is an extended program designed to improve the student's opportunity to be academically successful. It allows for reduced course loads and college preparatory developmental courses which assist students in meeting curricular prerequisites. The Probation Intervention Program (PIP) assists freshmen on academic probation to attain "good standing" status through study skills instruction and one-to-one contact with a counselor. Students with disabilities should contact Learning Assistance and must provide adequate documentation before accommodations/services will be provided. The SSD Counselor determines the extent of services provided.

## LEARNING DISABILITY ADMISSIONS INFORMATION

**Program Name:** Services for Students with Disabilities
**Program Director:** Cora Dzubak                    **Telephone:** 607-587-4122
**Contact Person:** Same as above

### ADMISSIONS

There is no special admission process for students with learning disabilities. All applicants must meet the same admission criteria. The minimum core courses that are preferred include: 4 yrs. English, 3 yrs. math, 3 yrs. science, 3 yrs. social science, 2 yrs. foreign language, and 1 yr. Art. The minimum GPA is 2.0. The Alfred State Opportunity Program allows students to take three years to complete a two year program.

**College entrance exams required:** No          **Untimed accepted:** N/A
**Course entrance requirements:** Preferred      **Interview required:** No
**Diagnostic tests:** Yes
**Documentation:** WISC-R; WAIS; Kaufman; within 3 years

### ADDITIONAL INFORMATION

Services available through Project 5 include: individual academic skills development; notetakers and scribes; readers; peer tutors; taped texts; testing accommodations; extended curricular programs; referral to other offices and agencies; specialized equipment loan; advocacy; and registration. The ASOP program provides counseling, extensive advising, and tutoring. Peer and professional tutors are available by appointment and provide course-specific assistance such as answers to questions, clarification of information, and drill and/or review for exams. EOP tutoring program provides mandated assistance to students in the EOP. First year students meet weekly for supplemental instruction in math and science curses. Academic Skills Assistance for reading improvement, student success, and study skills can be provided through individual appointments, small group seminars, classroom instruction, or computer tutorials.

**Special education HS coursework accepted:** Yes       **Essay required:** No
**Special application required:** No                    **Submitted to:** N/A
**# of applications submitted each year:** N/A          **# of applications accepted each year:** N/A
**# of students receiving LD services:** 175
**Acceptance into program means acceptance into college:** Students must be admitted to the college and then may request LD services.

## LEARNING DISABILITY SERVICES

**Learning center:** Yes
**Kurzweil personal reader:** Yes
**LD specialists:** 1
**Allowed in exams:**
  **Calculator:** Yes
  **Dictionary:** Yes
  **Computer:** Yes
  **SpellCheck:** Yes

**Notetaker:** Yes
**Scribes:** Yes
**Proctors:** Yes
**Oral exams:** Yes
**Extended test time:** Yes
**Added cost:** None
**Distraction-free environ.:** Yes
**Tape recording in class:** Yes
**Books on tape:** Yes
**Taping of other books:** Yes

**Professional tutors:** 2
**Peer tutors:** 30
**Max. hrs/wk for services:**
Unlimited
**Priority registration:** Yes
**Accomodations for students
with ADD:** Yes
**How are professors notified of
LD:** By the student and the
Director of Services

## GENERAL ADMISSIONS INFORMATION

**Director of Admissions:** Deb Goodrich

**Telephone:** 800-4-ALFRED

### ENTRANCE REQUIREMENTS
NR

**Application deadline:** NR
**Notification:** NR

**SAT or ACT preferred:** NR

## COLLEGE GRADUATION REQUIREMENTS

**Course waivers allowed:** No
**Course substitutions allowed:** Yes
**In what courses:** Mathematics

## ADDITIONAL INFORMATION

**Environment:** NR

**Student Body**
  **Undergrad enrollment:** NR
  **Women:** NR
  **Men:** NR
  **In-state students:** NR
  **Out-of-state:** NR

**Cost Information**
  **In-state tuition:** NR
  **Out-of-state:** NR

**Housing Information**
  **University housing:** Yes
  **Fraternity:** NR
  **Sorority:** NR
  **Living on campus:** NR

  **Athletics:** NR

# SYRACUSE UNIVERSITY

**NY**

201 Tolley, Administration Building, Syracuse, NY 13244 • **Admissions:** 315-443-3611
**Email:** orange@suadmin.syr.edu • **Web:** www.syr.edu
**Support:** CS • **Institution:** 4 yr. Private

## LEARNING DISABILITY ADMISSIONS AND SERVICES

The Center for Academic Achievement provides an integrated network of academic support, counseling, and advising services to meet the individual needs of students with diagnosed learning disabilities. Every student with learning disabilities who is accepted to the university is eligible for services, and must provide diagnostic information from which appropriate academic accommodations are determined. The staff is very supportive and sensitive to the needs of the students. Services are provided by a professional staff who sincerely care about the needs of every student. The program enables students to develop a sense of independence as they learn to advocate for themselves and become involved in their college education.

## LEARNING DISABILITY ADMISSIONS INFORMATION

**Program Name:** Learning Disability Services (LDSS)
**Program Director:** James Duah-Agyeman          **Telephone:** 315-443-2622
**Contact Person:** Bethany Heaton Crawford        **Telephone:** 315-443-4498

### ADMISSIONS

All students must meet regular admission standards and submit the general application form. General admission criteria includes: 4 yrs. English, 3–4 yrs. math, 3–4 yrs. science, 3–4 yrs. social studies, 2 yrs. foreign language; 25 ACT or 1100+ SAT I; B average or 80% or 3.0 GPA. However, consideration will be given to standardized testing scores in light of the disability, and less weight is put on ACT and SAT. Students with learning disabilities may request substitutions for high school math or foreign language if documentation can substantiate a disability in any one of these areas. Students should include current testing and documentation. Student should write an accompanying letter describing the learning disability and their goals and the services needed. Students' grades should show an upward trend. In the event an applicant is denied admission to a specific course of study, an alternative offer may be suggested.

**College entrance exams required:** Yes          **Untimed accepted:** Yes
**Course entrance requirements:** Yes             **Interview required:** Recommended
**Diagnostic tests:** Yes
**Documentation:** I.Q., Achievement, and other relevant results: within 3 years

### ADDITIONAL INFORMATION

Students with identified LD are provided with an integrated network of academic and counseling services to meet their individual needs. Services include: notetakers, proofreaders, readers for exams and textbooks, tutors, counseling, and advising. Accommodations include: time extensions for exams, papers, or projects; alternative testing methods; and spelling waivers. The Center provides each student with an Accommodation letter to be used when the students meet with instructors to verify their LD status. To take advantage of these support services, diagnosed students must submit recent documentation of their learning disability. The Summer Institute Program is a 6 week program designed to enrich academic experience and ensure a smooth transition from high school to college with academic advising, orientation, tutoring, and career planning and counseling. There is also a summer program for high school students with learning disabilities. Services are offered to undergraduate and graduate students.

**Special education HS coursework accepted:** No        **Essay required:** Yes
**Special application required:** No                    **Submitted to:** N/A
**# of applications submitted each year:** N/A          **# of applications accepted each year:** N/A
**# of students receiving LD services:** 450
**Acceptance into program means acceptance into college:** Students must be admitted to the university first and then may request services.

## LEARNING DISABILITY SERVICES

**Learning center:** Yes
**Kurzweil personal reader:** Yes
**LD specialists:** 2
**Allowed in exams:**
  **Calculator:** Yes
  **Dictionary:** Y/N
  **Computer:** Yes
  **SpellCheck:** Yes

**Notetaker:** Yes
**Scribes:** Yes
**Proctors:** Yes
**Oral exams:** Yes
**Extended test time:** Yes
**Added cost:** 15–20 hour per/sem. are free; then $7.65 per/hr.
**Distraction-free environ.:** Yes
**Tape recording in class:** Yes
**Books on tape:** Yes
**Taping of other books:** N/I

**Professional tutors:** Yes
**Peer tutors:** Yes
**Max. hrs for services:** 20 hrs.: Fr/Sop; 18 hrs.: Jr/Sr; 15 hrs.: graduates; per semester
**Priority registration:** Yes
**Accomodations for students with ADD:** Yes
**How are professors notified of LD:** By the student

## GENERAL ADMISSIONS INFORMATION

**Director of Admissions:** Dean David Smith
**Telephone:** 315-443-2300

### ENTRANCE REQUIREMENTS

Total high school units required/recommended: 20 total units are required; 4 English required, 3 math required, 3 science required, 2 foreign language required, 3 social studies required. Special requirements: A portfolio is required for art program applicants. TOEFL is required of all international students. Portfolio required of architecture program applicants. An audition is required for music and drama applicants.

**Application deadline:** February 1
**Notification:** March 15

**SAT or ACT preferred:** SAT
**SAT Range:** 530–630V, 540–640M
**SAT II required:** Yes
**Average GPA:** 3.3

**Graduated top 10% of class:** 33
**Graduated top 25% of class:** 77
**Graduated top 50% of class:** 95

## COLLEGE GRADUATION REQUIREMENTS

**Course waivers allowed:** No
**Course substitutions allowed:** Yes
**In what courses:** Students can petition for substitutions for math or foreign language in most colleges. The substitutions must be approved by each colleges' academic committee. Documentation which specifically recommends this as an accommodation must be on file in the LD

## ADDITIONAL INFORMATION

**Environment:** The school is located on 200 acres set on a hill overlooking the city of Syracuse.

**Student Body**
  **Undergrad enrollment:** 10,180
  **Women:** 52%
  **Men:** 48%
  **In-state students:** 44%
  **Out-of-state:** 56%

**Cost Information**
  **In-state tuition:** $17,550
  **Out-of-state:** $17,550
  **Room & board:** $7,760

**Housing Information**
  **University housing:** Yes
  **Fraternity:** Yes
  **Sorority:** Yes
  **Living on campus:** 70%

  **Athletics:** NCAA Div. I

# APPALACHIAN STATE UNIVERSITY

**NC**

Boone, NC 28608 • **Admissions:** 704-262-2120 • **Fax:** 704-262-3296
**Email:** admissions@conrad.appstate.edu • **Web:** www.acs.appstate.edu
**Support:** CS • **Institution:** 4 yr. Public

## LEARNING DISABILITY ADMISSIONS AND SERVICES

The university LD Program is part of a larger academic support service called the Learning Assistance Program. The LD Program is designed to provide academic services for students who self-identify on a voluntary basis and attend regular classes. Students with learning disabilities are totally integrated throughout the university community. Students are expected to communicate with their instructors regarding their specific needs. The Coordinator of Services works with students and faculty to implement needed services and accommodations. The needs of each student are considered and treated individually in consultation with the student and are based on current documentation of the learning disability.

## LEARNING DISABILITY ADMISSIONS INFORMATION

**Program Name:** Learning Disability Program
**Program Director:** Arlene J. Lundquist                    **Telephone:** 704-262-2291
**Contact Person:** Same as above

### ADMISSIONS

Students with learning disabilities are admitted to the university through the regular admission procedure. The minimum admissions requirements include: 4 yrs. English, 3 yrs. math, 3 yrs. science (1 in biology and 1 in a physical science), 2 yrs. social science, and recommend 2 yrs. foreign language, including 1 course in math and foreign language in senior year. Applicants may self-disclose on their applications. This information would support their application for admission. Personal statement, letters of recommendations, and school activities provide additional useful information. Once students have been accepted by the university, a form is provided in which the students can identify their disability. This identification process is necessary for the students to have access to the services of the LD Program. Students not regularly admissible may request a review of their application with additional or updated information.

| | |
|---|---|
| **College entrance exams required:** Yes | **Untimed accepted:** Yes |
| **Course entrance requirements:** Yes | **Interview required:** No |
| **Diagnostic tests:** Yes | |
| **Documentation:** WAIS-R: W-J: within 3 years | |

### ADDITIONAL INFORMATION

Tutoring is provided on a one-to-one basis for assistance with course content, as well as guidance in developing or improving learning skills. Tutors are trained in working with each student. Basic skills courses are available in written language, math, time management, and study strategies. Skills courses for no credit are offered in English and math. Services and accommodations are available for undergraduates and graduates.

| | |
|---|---|
| **Special education HS coursework accepted:** No | **Essay required:** No |
| **Special application required:** No | **Submitted to:** N/A |
| **# of applications submitted each year:** N/A | **# of applications accepted each year:** N/A |
| **# of students receiving LD services:** 200 | |

**Acceptance into program means acceptance into college:** Students must be accepted into university first and then must identify and provide documentation to be eligible for assistance.

# LEARNING DISABILITY SERVICES

**Learning center:** No
**Kurzweil personal reader:** Yes
**LD specialists:** Yes
**Allowed in exams:**
  **Calculator:** Y/N
  **Dictionary:** Y/N
  **Computer:** Y/N
  **SpellCheck:** Y/N

**Notetaker:** Yes
**Scribes:** Yes
**Proctors:** Yes
**Oral exams:** Yes
**Extended test time:** Yes
**Added cost:** None
**Distraction-free environ.:** Yes
**Tape recording in class:** Yes
**Books on tape:** RFB
**Taping of other books:** RFB

**Professional tutors:** N/I
**Peer tutors:** N/I
**Max. hrs/wk for services:** Unlimited
**Priority registration:** Yes
**Accomodations for students with ADD:** Yes
**How are professors notified of LD:** By the student and the Program Director

# GENERAL ADMISSIONS INFORMATION

**Director of Admissions:** Joe Watts

**Telephone:** 704-262-2120

## ENTRANCE REQUIREMENTS

Total high school units required/recommended: 20 total units are required; 4 English required, 3 math required, 3 science required, 2 social studies required, 2 foreign language recommended. English units must emphasize grammar, composition, and literature; math units must include algebra I and II and geometry or higher-level course for which algebra II is a prerequisite; science units must include at least 1 unit of life or biological science and 1 unit of physical science; social studies units must include 1 unit of U.S. history. 1 unit each of foreign language and math taken in 12th year recommended. Minimum combined SAT I score of 960 (composite ACT score of 21), rank in top fifth of secondary school class, and minimum 3.1 GPA recommended. Special requirements: A portfolio is required for art program applicants. An audition is required for music program applicants.

**Application deadline:** March 31
**Notification:** February 28

**SAT or ACT preferred:** SAT
**SAT Avg:** 540V, 540M
**Average ACT:** 24
**Average GPA:** 3.4

**Graduated top 10% of class:** 41
**Graduated top 25% of class:** 89
**Graduated top 50% of class:** 99

# COLLEGE GRADUATION REQUIREMENTS

**Course waivers allowed:** No
**Course substitutions allowed:** Yes
**In what courses:** There are no waivers and substitutions are not automatic. Done on case-by-case basis via a hearing procedure.

# ADDITIONAL INFORMATION

**Environment:** A 255-acre campus in a small town 90 miles northwest of Winston-Salem.

**Student Body**
  **Undergrad enrollment:** 10,878
  **Women:** 52%
  **Men:** 48%
  **In-state students:** 90%
  **Out-of-state:** 10%

**Cost Information**
  **In-state tuition:** $1,793
  **Out-of-state:** $8,947
  **Room & board:** $2,840

**Housing Information**
  **University housing:** Yes
  **Fraternity:** Yes
  **Sorority:** Yes
  **Living on campus:** 40%

  **Athletics:** NCAA Div. I

# BELMONT ABBEY COLLEGE

100 Belmont-Mount Holly Road, Belmont, NC  28012 • **Admissions:** 704-825-6665 • **Fax:** 704-825-6670
**Email:** admissions@bac.edu • **Web:** www.bac.edu
**Support:** S • **Institution:** 4 yr. Private

## LEARNING DISABILITY ADMISSIONS AND SERVICES

Support Services which foster independence and promote academic success are available for students identified as Learning Disabled and having Attention Deficit Hyperactivity Disorder (ADHD). Services include development of an Individualized Educational Support Plan; non-directive support consultation providing assistance with study skills, compensating strategies, time management, organization, etc. Reasonable accommodations are developed with the student. Consultation with faculty is offered per the student's request. A student must complete the LD Support Services Application and sign a Participation Consent Form to be eligible for these specific support services which are above those required by Section 504 and the ADA. Referral to this program can also be made by students, parents, or faculty for students who appear "at risk" for learning difficulties/differences or who are under academic distress. Questions or concerns regarding learning disabilities or the support services available will be responded to in a confidential manner.

## LEARNING DISABILITY ADMISSIONS INFORMATION

**Program Name:** Learning Disability Support Services
**Program Director:** Janet K. Baxter                    **Telephone:** 704-825-6820
**Contact Person:** Same as above

### ADMISSIONS

Students with learning disabilities must meet the minimum admissions criteria, notify the  Director of the Learning Disability Program after admission, complete an application to the Support Service, supply current (within 3 years) assessment information, and visit the campus for a personal interview with the Director. Information provided is requested on a volunteer and confidential basis in an effort to encourage greater participation of applicants. An interview is recommended. Regular admission criteria include an ACT of 19+ and SAT I of 900, GPA of 2.3, and 4 yrs. English, 2 yrs. social studies, 2 yrs. science, 2 yrs. foreign language (may be waived), 3 yrs. math, and 3 yrs. electives. Applicants who do not meet the minimum admission standards may be reviewed by the Admissions Committee and may be offered an Admission Committee admit.

**College entrance exams required:** Yes          **Untimed accepted:** Yes
**Course entrance requirements:** Yes            **Interview required:** Recommended
**Diagnostic tests:** Yes
**Documentation:** WISC-R; WAIS-R: W-J: within 3 years

### ADDITIONAL INFORMATION

A 'First Year Program' is offered.  First year students will be assigned specially trained academic advisors who will also serve as mentors and seminar instructors throughout the first year. These advisors will remain with each student until the student formally declares a major. This program is designed to assist with key transitions issues, involves whole class and team meetings scheduled throughout the Fall and Spring semesters of the first year. These meetings are designed to facilitate a student's relationship with the advisor, develop a class identity, enhance skills in life management, and provide key information for students to effectively manage the transition from high school to college.

**Special education HS coursework accepted:** No      **Essay required:** No
**Special application required:** Yes                **Submitted to:** Director of Support Services
**# of applications submitted each year:** 30–40      **# of applications accepted each year:** N/I
**# of students receiving LD services:** 15
**Acceptance into program means acceptance into college:** Students must be admitted to the college first and then may request services.

# LEARNING DISABILITY SERVICES

**Learning center:** No
**Kurzweil personal reader:** No
**LD specialists:** No
**Allowed in exams:**
  **Calculator:** No
  **Dictionary:** No
  **Computer:** No
  **SpellCheck:** No

**Notetaker:** No
**Scribes:** No
**Proctors:** No
**Oral exams:** No
**Extended test time:** Yes
**Added cost:** None
**Distraction-free environ.:** Yes
**Tape recording in class:** Y/N
**Books on tape:** No
**Taping of other books:** No

**Professional tutors:** No
**Peer tutors:** No
**Max. hrs/wk for services:**
Tutoring is offered in existing college resources for all students.
**Priority registration:** Yes
**Accomodations for students with ADD:** Yes
**How are professors notified of LD:** By the student

# GENERAL ADMISSIONS INFORMATION

**Director of Admissions:** Denis Stokes      **Telephone:** 704-825-6665

## ENTRANCE REQUIREMENTS

Total high school units required/recommended: 16 total units are required; 4 English required, 3 math required, 2 science required, 2 foreign language required, 1 social studies required, 1 history required. Minimum combined SAT I score of 850, rank in top quarter of secondary school class, and minimum 2.3 GPA recommended.

**Application deadline:** August 1
**Notification:** Rolling

**SAT or ACT preferred:** SAT
**SAT Avg:** 490V, 471M
**Average GPA:** 2.9

**Graduated top 10% of class:** 13
**Graduated top 25% of class:** 53
**Graduated top 50% of class:** 70

# COLLEGE GRADUATION REQUIREMENTS

**Course waivers allowed:** Yes
**Course substitutions allowed:** Yes
**In what courses:** Determined on a case-by-case basis

# ADDITIONAL INFORMATION

**Environment:** Located in a small town 12 miles southwest of Charlotte, North Carolina.

**Student Body**
  **Undergrad enrollment:** 831
  **Women:** 56%
  **Men:** 44%
  **In-state students:** 61%
  **Out-of-state:** 39%

**Cost Information**
  **In-state tuition:** $9,920
  **Out-of-state:** $9,920
  **Room & board:** $5,346

**Housing Information**
  **University housing:** Yes
  **Fraternity:** No
  **Sorority:** No
  **Living on campus:** 45%

  **Athletics:** NAIA

# NC
## DAVIDSON COLLEGE

P.O. Box 1719, Davidson, NC 28036 • **Admissions:** 704-892-2230 • **Fax:** 704-892-2016
**Email:** admissions@davidson.edu • **Web:** www.davidson.edu
**Support:** CS • **Institution:** 4 yr. Private

## LEARNING DISABILITY ADMISSIONS AND SERVICES

As a small liberal arts college, Davidson has a concern for each student's individual intellectual, spiritual, and social develop-ment. In keeping with this concern, services for students with learning disabilities are individualized according to their strengths and weaknesses.There is not a specific program which provides services or accommodations. Rather, students with identified learning disabilities receive support through the Dean of Students. The first step for Davidson students experiencing learning difficulties is to undergo an evaluation by a learning specialist designated by the college. The college requires that all students, even those previously tested, work with these professionals since they are most familiar with Davidson College curricular requirements. It may be possible for previously tested students to expedite this process by making the results of those tests available to the college psychologist. This testing is usually done at the student's expense, although alternative arrangements can be made in the case of financial need. With the student's permission, the psycholo-gist makes available to the college a diagnosis, recommendations for compensatory learning strategies to be used by the student, and recommendations for services and accommodations to be provided by the college.

## LEARNING DISABILITY ADMISSIONS INFORMATION

**Program Name:** Support services for students with LD
**Program Director:** N/A                                          **Telephone:** N/A
**Contact Person:** Leslie Marsicano, Assoc. Dean of Students **Telephone:** 704-892-2225

### ADMISSIONS

There is no special application for students with learning disabilities. All applicants are expected to meet the same admission criteria (excluding consideration for exceptional circumstances). Students must have 4 yrs. English, 2 yrs. intermediate math, 1 yr. geometry, 2 yrs. foreign language, 1 yr. history, 2–4 yrs. science. Substitutions may be allowed for any of these required courses with adequate documentation as required by the law. Further questions regarding services for students with learning disabilities may be directed to the Davidson College Admission Office or the Office of the Dean of Students. Prospective students visiting the campus should arrange an appointment with the Associate Dean of Students as well as an Admission officer. Deferred admission requires successful year at another institution before enrollment at Davidson.

| | |
|---|---|
| **College entrance exams required:** Yes | **Untimed accepted:** Yes |
| **Course entrance requirements:** Yes | **Interview required:** No |
| **Diagnostic tests:** Yes | |
| **Documentation:** By college-approved specialist after admission | |

### ADDITIONAL INFORMATION

The psychologist at Davidson College might recommend that the student be allowed to use a small cassette recorder to record lectures and augment notetaking. Using these recommendations as a guide, a learning plan is designed for the individual student that enhances his/her learning strengths and compensates for learning difficulties. When possible, accommodations in teaching methods and course requirements are included in this plan. If the psychologist recommends the waiver of a particular course requirement, such a request is forwarded to the Curriculum Requirements Committee. This Committee may approve the waiver of a particular requirement or substitute another, more appropriate requirement. Workshops for no credit are available in notetaking, study skills, writing and test-taking strategies.

| | |
|---|---|
| **Special education HS coursework accepted:** N/I | **Essay required:** Yes |
| **Special application required:** No | **Submitted to:** N/A |
| **# of applications submitted each year:** N/A | **# of applications accepted each year:** N/A |
| **# of students receiving LD services:** 42 | |

**Acceptance into program means acceptance into college:** Student must be admitted to the college first, and then be tested by a psychologist recommended by the college, prior to obtaining services.

# LEARNING DISABILITY SERVICES

**Learning center:** No
**Kurzweil personal reader:** No
**LD specialists:** 1
**Allowed in exams:**
  **Calculator:** Yes
  **Dictionary:** Yes
  **Computer:** Yes
  **SpellCheck:** Yes

**Notetaker:** Yes
**Scribes:** Yes
**Proctors:** N/A
**Oral exams:** Y/N
**Extended test time:** Yes
**Added cost:** $7.00 per/hr. for peer tutoring
**Distraction-free environ.:** Yes
**Tape recording in class:** Yes
**Books on tape:** Yes
**Taping of other books:** Yes

**Professional tutors:** 1
**Peer tutors:** 100
**Max. hrs/wk for services:** Unlimited
**Priority registration:** No
**Accomodations for students with ADD:** Yes
**How are professors notified of LD:** By both the student and the Associate Dean of Students

# GENERAL ADMISSIONS INFORMATION

**Director of Admissions:** Dean Nancy Cable          **Telephone:** 704-892-2235

## ENTRANCE REQUIREMENTS
Total high school units required/recommended: 17 total units are required; 4 English required, 3 math required, 4 math recommended, 3 science required, 4 science recommended, 2 foreign language required, 1 history required, 2 history recommended. Special requirements: TOEFL is required of all international students.

**Application deadline:** January 15
**Notification:** Before April 1

**SAT or ACT preferred:** Either
**SAT Avg:** 657V, 664M
**Average ACT:** 28

**Graduated top 10% of class:** 77
**Graduated top 25% of class:** 94
**Graduated top 50% of class:** 100

# COLLEGE GRADUATION REQUIREMENTS

**Course waivers allowed:** Yes
**Course substitutions allowed:** Yes
**In what courses:** Foreign language and math when recommended by the psychologist and approved by the Curriculum Requirements Committee. This committee may approve the waiver or substitute another more appropriate requirement.

# ADDITIONAL INFORMATION

**Environment:** NR

**Student Body**
  **Undergrad enrollment:** 1,613
  **Women:** 49%
  **Men:** 51%
  **In-state students:** 24%
  **Out-of-state:** 76%

**Cost Information**
  **In-state tuition:** $20,595
  **Out-of-state:** $20,595
  **Room & board:** $5,918

**Housing Information**
  **University housing:** Yes
  **Fraternity:** No
  **Sorority:** No
  **Living on campus:** 92%

  **Athletics:** NCAA Div. I

# NC

# DUKE UNIVERSITY

2138 Campus Drive, Box 90586, Durham, NC 27708 • **Admissions:** 919-684-3214 • **Fax:** 919-681-8941
**Email:** askduke@admiss.duke.edu • **Web:** www.duke.edu
**Support:** CS • **Institution:** 4 yr. Private

## LEARNING DISABILITY ADMISSIONS AND SERVICES

Duke University does not provide a formal, highly structured program for students with learning disabilities. The university does provide, however, significant academic support services for students through the Academic Skills Center (ASC). Students who submit appropriate documentation of their learning disability to the ASC Clinical Director are eligible for assistance in obtaining reasonable academic adjustments and auxiliary aids. In addition, the ASC Clinical Director and Instructors can provide individualized instruction in academic skills and learning strategies, academic support counseling, and referrals for other services. Students with learning disabilities voluntarily access and use the services of the ASC, just as they might access and use other campus resources. Student interactions with the ASC staff are confidential. The goals of the support services for students with learning disabilities are in keeping with the goals of all services provided through the ASC: to help students achieve their academic potential within the context of a competitive university setting; to promote a disciplined approach to study; and to foster active, independent learners.

## LEARNING DISABILITY ADMISSIONS INFORMATION

**Program Name:** Academic Skills Center (ASC)
**Program Director:** Russell Colver/ Mary F. Peete      **Telephone:** 919-684-5917
**Contact Person:** Mary F. Peete

### ADMISSIONS

There is no special admission process for students with learning disabilities. All applicants must meet the general Duke admissions criteria. Admission to Duke is highly competitive and most applicants are in the top 10% of their class. Most applicants have completed a demanding curriculum in high school including many Advanced Placement and Honors courses. Services and accommodations may be requested after enrollment in Duke.

**College entrance exams required:** Yes          **Untimed accepted:** Yes
**Course entrance requirements:** Yes            **Interview required:** Recommended
**Diagnostic tests:** Yes
**Documentation:** Current testing: within 3 years

### ADDITIONAL INFORMATION

Assistance is available as needed from the students' Academic Dean and the Clinical Director of ASC. Students are encouraged to consult with their faculty advisor and the ASC, well in advance of registration, to determine the appropriate measures for particular courses. There is one staff member with special learning disability training, and 3 staff members who are writing/learning strategy instructors. Documentation and diagnostic tests are required for accommodations, not admissions. Students may also receive peer tutoring in introductory-level courses in several disciplines through the ASC Peer Tutoring Program. Up to 12 hours of tutoring in each course is offered at no additional charge. Students need to understand their learning disability, be able to self-advocate, and know what accommodations are necessary to assist them in being successful in college. Students are expected to work out reasonable accommodations with each of their professors. Outside testing referrals are made at the student's expense.

**Special education HS coursework accepted:** No          **Essay required:** Yes
**Special application required:** No                       **Submitted to:** N/A
**# of applications submitted each year:** N/A            **# of applications accepted each year:** N/A
**# of students receiving LD services:** N/I
**Acceptance into program means acceptance into college:** Students must be admitted to the university first and then may request services.

**Learning center:** Yes
**Kurzweil personal reader:** No
**LD specialists:** 1
**Allowed in exams:**
  **Calculator:** Yes
  **Dictionary:** Yes
  **Computer:** Yes
  **SpellCheck:** Yes

**Notetaker:** Yes
**Scribes:** No
**Proctors:** No
**Oral exams:** No
**Extended test time:** Yes
**Added cost:** None
**Distraction-free environ.:** Yes
**Tape recording in class:** Yes
**Books on tape:** Yes
**Taping of other books:** N/I

**Professional tutors:** 3
**Peer tutors:** 8
**Max. hrs/wk for services:** 1
**Priority registration:** No
**Accomodations for students with ADD:** Yes
**How are professors notified of LD:** By the student's Academic Dean

# GENERAL ADMISSIONS INFORMATION

**Director of Admissions:** Christoph Guttentag        **Telephone:** 919-684-3214

## ENTRANCE REQUIREMENTS
Total high school units required/recommended: 15 total units are recommended; 4 English required, 3 math recommended, 3 science recommended, 3 foreign langauage recommended, 2 social studies recommended. Special requirements: TOEFL is required of all international students. 4 units of math and 1 unit of physics or chemistry required of engineering program applicants.

**Application deadline:** January 2
**Notification:** April 5

**SAT or ACT preferred:** Either
**SAT Range:** 640–730V, 650–750M
**Average ACT:** 30

**Graduated top 25% of class:** 95
**Graduated top 50% of class:** 100

# COLLEGE GRADUATION REQUIREMENTS

**Course waivers allowed:** No
**Course substitutions allowed:** No
**In what courses:** No waivers or substitutions. However, students are only required to complete specific courses in 5 out of 6 subject areas including foreign language, arts and literature, civilization, qualitative reasoning, social sciences, or natural sciences.

# ADDITIONAL INFORMATION

**Environment:** The university is on 8500 acres in a suburban area 285 miles southwest of Washington, DC.

**Student Body**
  **Undergrad enrollment:** 6,272
  **Women:** 49%
  **Men:** 51%
  **In-state students:** 14%
  **Out-of-state:** 86%

**Cost Information**
  **In-state tuition:** $20,520
  **Out-of-state:** $20,520
  **Room & board:** $6,605

**Housing Information**
  **University housing:** Yes
  **Fraternity:** Yes
  **Sorority:** No
  **Living on campus:** 82%

  **Athletics:** NCAA Div. I

# EAST CAROLINA UNIVERSITY

Fifth Street, Greenville, NC 27858 • **Admissions:** 919-328-6640 • **Fax:** 919-328-6945
**Email:** admis@ecuvm.cis.ecu.edu • **Web:** www.ecu.edu
**Support:** S • **Institution:** 4 yr. Public

## LEARNING DISABILITY ADMISSIONS AND SERVICES

Through the Department for Disability Support Services, the university seeks to meet individual needs by coordinating and implementing internal policy regarding programs, services, and activities for individuals with disabilities. The Department functions as a source of information and advice and as a communication link among individuals with disabilities, faculty and staff members, state rehab agencies, and the community at large. The overall purpose of the university's program for students with learning disabilities is to provide auxiliary support services, so they may derive equal benefits from all that East Carolina University has to offer. Individuals with learning disabilities and attention deficit disorders are required to provide the department with proper documentation of their disability. An acceptable psych educational evaluation administered within the past three years must be submitted to qualify for services. Students should schedule a meting with the Department well in advance of the beginning of their first semester to prevent delays in the planning of services. Students with LD or ADD will receive a letter describing the services required to give to their instructors. With the exception of tutorial services for personal use, academic support services are provided at no cost.

## LEARNING DISABILITY ADMISSIONS INFORMATION

**Program Name:** Department for Disability Support Services
**Program Director:** C. C. Rowe
**Contact Person:** Same as above

**Telephone:** 919-328-6799

### ADMISSIONS

A student with a disability applies for admission and is considered for admission in the same manner as any other applicant. Neither the nature nor the severity of one's disability is used as a criterion for admission. Students with learning disabilities are admitted solely on academic qualifications. Out-of-state students must present slightly higher GPAs and test scores, but the minimum is 2.0 depending on the SAT. Test scores vary but the minimum out-of-state ACT 19 and in-state 17. The minimum SAT out-of-state is 1000 an in-state 900. Students must have taken 3 yrs. English, 2 yrs. social science, 3 yrs.science (1 yr. biology, 1 yr. physical science), and 3 yrs. math.

**College entrance exams required:** Yes
**Course entrance requirements:** Yes
**Diagnostic tests:** Yes
**Documentation:** WAIS-R; WJA+B; Bender-Gestalt: MMPI: within 3 years

**Untimed accepted:** Yes
**Interview required:** Recommended

### ADDITIONAL INFORMATION

Once admitted to the university, students must self-identify and register with the Department for Disability Support Services. Students must show official verification of their disability. Students will be assigned to academic advisors from the Department. Once students enter their major fields of study, the Department will still be available to provide advising assistance but never to the exclusion of the individual's assigned academic advisor. Alternative testing accommodations may include: extended time, oral testing, private testing, a noise-free environment, reader-assisted test taking, and other arrangements that satisfy the needs of the student. A maximum of double time can be allowed for student to complete a test or an exam. There are several laboratories available including: The Writing Center, Reading Center, Mathematics Center, the Academic Support Center, and Computer Lab. Students pay for private tutoring.

**Special education HS coursework accepted:** Yes, as
long as it is an equivalent course
**Special application required:** No
**# of applications submitted each year:** N/A
**# of students receiving LD services:** 200

**Essay required:** Yes
**Submitted to:** N/A
**# of applications accepted each year:** N/A

**Acceptance into program means acceptance into college:** Students must be admitted to the university first and then may request services.

**Learning center:** Yes
**Kurzweil personal reader:** Yes
**LD specialists:** No
**Allowed in exams:**
  **Calculator:** Yes
  **Dictionary:** No
  **Computer:** Yes
  **SpellCheck:** No

**Notetaker:** Yes
**Scribes:** Yes
**Proctors:** Yes
**Oral exams:** Yes
**Extended test time:** Yes
**Added cost:** Students pay for private tutors
**Distraction-free environ.:** Yes
**Tape recording in class:** Yes
**Books on tape:** Yes
**Taping of other books:** Yes

**Professional tutors:** N/I
**Peer tutors:** 10–15
**Max. hrs/wk for services:** Depends on need of student
**Priority registration:** Yes
**Accomodations for students with ADD:** Yes
**How are professors notified of LD:** By the student

## GENERAL ADMISSIONS INFORMATION

**Director of Admissions:** Dr. Thomas E. Powell, Jr.       **Telephone:** 919-757-6640

### ENTRANCE REQUIREMENTS
Total high school units required/recommended: 4 English required, 3 math required, 3 science required, 2 foreign language required, 2 social studies required, 1 history required. Minimum 2.0 GPA required and rank in top half of secondary school class recommended. Minimum combined SAT I score of 800 required of in-state applicants; minimum combined SAT I score of 900 required of out-of-state applicants. Special requirements: An audition is required for music program applicants.

**Application deadline:** March 15
**Notification:** Rolling

**SAT or ACT preferred:** Either
**SAT Avg:** 509V, 506M
**Average ACT:** 20
**Average GPA:** 3.11

**Graduated top 10% of class:** 15
**Graduated top 25% of class:** 42
**Graduated top 50% of class:** 84

## COLLEGE GRADUATION REQUIREMENTS

**Course waivers allowed:** No
**Course substitutions allowed:** Yes
**In what courses:** Foreign language under special circumstances

## ADDITIONAL INFORMATION

**Environment:** The school is located on over 370 acres within the city of Greenville and 85 miles from Raleigh.

**Student Body**
  **Undergrad enrollment:** 14,409
  **Women:** 58%
  **Men:** 42%
  **In-state students:** 86%
  **Out-of-state:** 14%

**Cost Information**
  **In-state tuition:** $874
  **Out-of-state:** $8,028
  **Room & board:** $3,480

**Housing Information**
  **University housing:** Yes
  **Fraternity:** No
  **Sorority:** Yes
  **Living on campus:** 32%

  **Athletics:** NCAA Div. I

# LENOIR-RHYNE COLLEGE

Hickory, NC 28603 • **Admissions:** 704-328-7300 • **Fax:** 704-328-7378
**Email:** admissions@lrc.edu • **Web:** www.lrc.edu
**Support:** CS • **Institution:** 4 yr. Private

## LEARNING DISABILITY ADMISSIONS AND SERVICES

The Student Academic Support Service Center provides services free of charge to all enrolled students, with the exception of one-to-one tutoring. The college offers a program of limited support services for students with learning disabilities. Group tutoring for certain courses is available free of charge to students who request it from the course instructor. Instruction is provided by selected peer tutors. Near the beginning of each semester a list of courses in which tutoring sessions will be provided is published in the *Lenoir-Rhynean* and a copy of these courses is available in the Center. There is also a computer-based program designed to help students who want to improve their skills in reading, writing, and mathematics is available in the SASSC. This program includes diagnostic tests, instructional programs, and practice tests to help students improve their basic skills. "Learning Plus" instruction helps students identify where they may need assistance offers self-paced practice and instructional assistance and provides extensive feedback.

## LEARNING DISABILITY ADMISSIONS INFORMATION

**Program Name:** Student Academic Support Service Center (SASSC)
**Program Director:** Dr. Thomas Fauquet          **Telephone:** 704-328-7275
**Contact Person:** Mrs. Sonnie Cooke             **Telephone:** 704-328-7343

### ADMISSIONS

There is no special admissions process for students with Learning Disabilities. All students are reviewed on an individual case-by-case basis. Basic admissions criteria include: 2.5 GPA, top 50% class rank, 850 SAT or 17 ACT, 4 yrs. English, 3 yrs. math, 1 yr. History, 2 yrs. foreign language (substitution allowed).

**College entrance exams required:** Yes          **Untimed accepted:** Yes
**Course entrance requirements:** Yes            **Interview required:** No
**Diagnostic tests:** Yes
**Documentation:** No

### ADDITIONAL INFORMATION

"Learning Plus" is also used as a tool to test general knowledge strengths and weaknesses for prospective teachers. Students take a Skills Profile test to assess their general knowledge. From this assessment "Learning Plus" will recommend areas of instruction based on the student's areas of weakness. This instruction is self-paced and provides immediate feedback on answers given, along with reason for the answers. The Early Warning System advises students when improvement will be needed to meet graduation requirements. Letters of Concern are sent to students at mid-term. Letters of Warning are sent at the end of each semester. At the end of each semester the progress of all students will be reviewed by the Academic Standing Committee. Some students will be placed on probation or suspended. Students on probation are monitored, and students suspended must apply for readmission. SASSC offers a Computer Lab, Math Assistance for students with special needs, and a Writing Center for free, confidential assistance with writing.

**Special education HS coursework accepted:** Yes          **Essay required:** No
**Special application required:** N/A                     **Submitted to:** N/A
**# of applications submitted each year:** N/A           **# of applications accepted each year:** N/A
**# of students receiving LD services:** 27
**Acceptance into program means acceptance into college:** Students not admitted are reviewed by the LD program which provides a recommendation to admissions. Once admitted they may request services.

**Learning center:** Yes
**Kurzweil personal reader:** N/I
**LD specialists:** 1
**Allowed in exams:**
  **Calculator:** Yes
  **Dictionary:** Y/N
  **Computer:** Y/N
  **SpellCheck:** Y/N

**Notetaker:** Yes
**Scribes:** Yes
**Proctors:** Yes
**Oral exams:** Yes
**Extended test time:** Yes
**Added cost:** None
**Distraction-free environ.:** Yes
**Tape recording in class:** Yes
**Books on tape:** RFB
**Taping of other books:** No

**Professional tutors:** N/I
**Peer tutors:** N/I
**Max. hrs/wk for services:**
Unlimited
**Priority registration:** Yes
**Accomodations for students
with ADD:** Yes
**How are professors notified of
LD:** By the student and the
Program Director

## GENERAL ADMISSIONS INFORMATION

**Director of Admissions:** Timothy L. Jackson

**Telephone:** 704-328-7300

### ENTRANCE REQUIREMENTS

Total high school units required/recommended: 16 total units are required; 4 English required, 3 math required, 1 science required, 2 foreign language required, 1 history required. Rank in top half of secondary school class and minimum 2.5 GPA required. Special requirements: An audition is required for music program applicants.

**Application deadline:** Rolling
**Notification:** Rolling

**SAT or ACT preferred:** SAT
**SAT Range:** 440–530V, 440–550M
**Average ACT:** 21
**Average GPA:** 3.2

**Graduated top 10% of class:** 15
**Graduated top 25% of class:** 42
**Graduated top 50% of class:** 76

## COLLEGE GRADUATION REQUIREMENTS

**Course waivers allowed:** Yes
**Course substitutions allowed:** Yes
**In what courses:** Not indicated

## ADDITIONAL INFORMATION

**Environment:** NR

**Student Body**
  **Undergrad enrollment:** 1,474
  **Women:** 63%
  **Men:** 37%
  **In-state students:** 67%
  **Out-of-state:** 33%

**Cost Information**
  **In-state tuition:** $12,036
  **Out-of-state:** $12,036
  **Room & board:** $4,400

**Housing Information**
  **University housing:** Yes
  **Fraternity:** Yes
  **Sorority:** Yes
  **Living on campus:** 56%

  **Athletics:** NCAA Div. II

# NC NORTH CAROLINA STATE UNIVERSITY

Box 7001, Raleigh, NC 27695 • **Admissions:** 919-515-2434 • **Fax:** 919-515-5039
**Email:** undergrad_admissions@ncsu.edu • **Web:** www.ncsu.edu
**Support:** CS • **Institution:** 4 yr. Public

## LEARNING DISABILITY ADMISSIONS AND SERVICES

Services for students with learning disabilities are handled by the LD Coordinator through Disability Services for Students. The functions of the Coordinator include identifying students with learning disabilities, helping to accommodate and interpret the needs of these students to the faculty, and providing services to students according to their individual needs. Support groups meet periodically to provide workshops, mutual support, and awareness of handicapped issues to the university community. The purpose of the services is to ensure that students with documented learning disabilities receive appropriate accommodations in order to equalize their opportunities while studying at NCSU.

## LEARNING DISABILITY ADMISSIONS INFORMATION

**Program Name:** Disability Services for Students (DSS)
**Program Director:** Patricia Smith          **Telephone:** 919-515-7653
**Contact Person:** Lelia S. Brettmann, Coordinator     **Telephone:** 919-515-8829

### ADMISSIONS

Admission to the university for students with learning disabilities is determined on the basis of academic qualifications, and they are considered in the same manner as any other applicant. There is no pre-admission question regarding a learning disability. A cover letter from applicants, stating that a learning disability exists, alerts the admission staff to consider that there may be unusual circumstances. Self-disclosure of the learning disability could explain the high school record, such as late diagnosis and onset of LD accommodations or difficulty in particular subjects.

**College entrance exams required:** Yes          **Untimed accepted:** Yes
**Course entrance requirements:** Yes           **Interview required:** No
**Diagnostic tests:** Yes
**Documentation:** WAIS-R: WJPEB-R, part II: within 3 years

### ADDITIONAL INFORMATION

All enrolled students may receive services and accommodations through the Coordinator of learning disabilities of the DSS if they present appropriate documentation. The documentation should include a written report with a statement specifying areas of learning disabilities. If new needs are identified, services are modified or developed to accommodate them.

**Special education HS coursework accepted:** Yes        **Essay required:** No
**Special application required:** No                **Submitted to:** N/A
**# of applications submitted each year:** N/A          **# of applications accepted each year:** N/A
**# of students receiving LD services:** 250
**Acceptance into program means acceptance into college:** Students must be admitted to the university first and then may request services.

**Learning center:** No
**Kurzweil personal reader:** No
**LD specialists:** 1
**Allowed in exams:**
  Calculator: Y/N
  Dictionary: Y/N
  Computer: Yes
  SpellCheck: Yes

**Notetaker:** Yes
**Scribes:** Yes
**Proctors:** Yes
**Oral exams:** Y/N
**Extended test time:** Yes
**Added cost:** None
**Distraction-free environ.:** Yes
**Tape recording in class:** Yes
**Books on tape:** Yes
**Taping of other books:** Y/N

**Professional tutors:** Yes
**Peer tutors:** Yes
**Max. hrs/wk for services:** 3+ hours per course
**Priority registration:** Yes
**Accomodations for students with ADD:** Yes
**How are professors notified of LD:** By the student and the Program Director

# GENERAL ADMISSIONS INFORMATION

**Director of Admissions:** George R. Dixon

**Telephone:** 919-515-2011

## ENTRANCE REQUIREMENTS

Total high school units required/recommended: 20 total units are required; 4 English required, 3 math required, 4 math recommended, 3 science required, 2 foreign language required, 2 social studies required, 1 history required. Special requirements: A portfolio is required for art program applicants. TOEFL is required of all international students.

**Application deadline:** February 1
**Notification:** Rolling

**SAT or ACT preferred:** Either
**SAT Avg:** 565V, 584M
**Average ACT:** 23
**Average GPA:** 3.65

**Graduated top 10% of class:** 30
**Graduated top 25% of class:** 71
**Graduated top 50% of class:** 98

# COLLEGE GRADUATION REQUIREMENTS

**Course waivers allowed:** No
**Course substitutions allowed:** No
**In what courses:** Only in very rare cases

# ADDITIONAL INFORMATION

**Environment:** The university sits on 623 acres in the central part of the state, and has an adjacent 900-acre research campus.

**Student Body**
  Undergrad enrollment: 19,026
  Women: 40%
  Men: 60%
  In-state students: 89%
  Out-of-state: 11%

**Cost Information**
  In-state tuition: $2,200
  Out-of-state: $10,732
  Room & board: $4,350

**Housing Information**
  University housing: Yes
  Fraternity: Yes
  Sorority: Yes
  Living on campus: 35%

  Athletics: NCAA Div. I

# UNIVERSITY OF NORTH CAROLINA-CHAPEL HILL

Jackson Hall UADM CB2200, Chapel Hill, NC 27599 • **Admissions:** 919-966-3621 • **Fax:** 919-962-3045
**Email:** uadm@email.unc.edu • **Web:** www.unc.edu
**Support:** CS • **Institution:** 4 yr. Public

## LEARNING DISABILITY ADMISSIONS AND SERVICES

Learning Disabilities Services (LDS) is one of seven units of Academic Support Services in the College of Arts and Sciences. The mission of LDS is to assist students in achieving their academic potential within the regular, academically competitive university curriculum. LDS works with students who are eligible for services. LDS is responsible for determining the reasonable accommodations that will reduce barriers caused by a student's disability without lowering the academic standards of the student's coursework. LDS is the service provider to students with documented LD/ADD. A student's documented disability becomes the foundation for accommodations, the student's desire to learn new ways to learn becomes the foundation for direct services. Accommodations are changes made by the university in how the students take in or express information. This is why the accommodations are determined case-by-case, based on each student's specific documented disability. Direct services focus on changes that students can make in how they learn. Services are offered in addition to the accommodations required by law. Students can meet as often as weekly in one-to-one sessions to learn more about their disability, develop self-advocacy skills, obtain referrals, and practice learning strategies.

## LEARNING DISABILITY ADMISSIONS INFORMATION

**Program Name:** Learning Disabilities Services
**Program Director:** Jane Byron          **Telephone:** 919-962-7227
**Contact Person:** Same as above

### ADMISSIONS

If the student discloses a disability during admissions, his or her application is reviewed by Subcommittee "D" of the Admissions Committee. This Subcommittee is made up of a number of campus professionals with expertise in disabilities, including the Director of the Learning Disabilities Services. If a student who is reviewed by this Subcommittee is admitted, the student is then automatically eligible to use LDS. Students with disabilities who apply for admissions have the right to refrain from disclosing. If, after being admitted, a student wishes to use LDS, that student would then submit documentation to be reviewed by the LD team.

**College entrance exams required:** Yes          **Untimed accepted:** Yes
**Course entrance requirements:** Yes          **Interview required:** No
**Diagnostic tests:** Yes
**Documentation:** WAIS-R or WISC-R and WJ-R or SAT: within 3 years

### ADDITIONAL INFORMATION

Accommodations provided include: notetakers; taped textbooks; tutors in math or foreign language; extended time on tests; a distraction-free test environment; a reader during exams; a scribe to write dictated test answers; and a computer for writing test answers. Using the student's current coursework, LDS can teach a range of strategies including: how to plan, draft, and edit papers; how to take lecture notes and reading notes; how to read critically and efficiently; how to manage time; and how to prepare for and take exams. Group experiences are available to students each semester, based on their expressed interests. These can include support groups that promote understanding, acceptance and pride; academic workshops that allow students to help each other learn specific skills; seminars that provide topical information from campus experts as well as other students; and panel discussions between students and university personnel. Each summer the university also provides a number of "orientation activities" to incoming students.

**Special education HS coursework accepted:** N/I          **Essay required:** Yes
**Special application required:** No          **Submitted to:** N/A
**# of applications submitted each year:** 86          **# of applications accepted each year:** 67
**# of students receiving LD services:** 240
**Acceptance into program means acceptance into college:** Students who self-disclose will be reviewed by Subcommittee D consisting of the LDS Director and Admissions.

# LEARNING DISABILITY SERVICES

**Learning center:** Yes
**Kurzweil personal reader:** No
**LD specialists:** 4
**Allowed in exams:**
  **Calculator:** Y/N
  **Dictionary:** Y/N
  **Computer:** Y/N
  **SpellCheck:** Y/N

**Notetaker:** Yes
**Scribes:** Yes
**Proctors:** Yes
**Oral exams:** Yes
**Extended test time:** Yes
**Added cost:** None
**Distraction-free environ.:** Yes
**Tape recording in class:** Yes
**Books on tape:** Yes
**Taping of other books:** Yes

**Professional tutors:** Yes
**Peer tutors:** Yes
**Max. hrs/wk for services:** 2
**Priority registration:** Yes
**Accomodations for students with ADD:** Yes
**How are professors notified of LD:** By the student and the Program Director

# GENERAL ADMISSIONS INFORMATION

**Director of Admissions:** James C. Walters

**Telephone:** 919-996-3621

## ENTRANCE REQUIREMENTS

Total high school units required/recommended: 16 total units are required; 4 English required, 3 math required, 3 science required, 2 foreign language required, 2 social studies required. Rigorous college-preparatory program recommended. Special requirements: An audition is required for music program applicants. TOEFL is required of all international students.

**Application deadline:** January 15
**Notification:** March

**SAT or ACT preferred:** SAT
**SAT Avg:** 610V, 611M
**Average GPA:** 4.0

**Graduated top 10% of class:** 72
**Graduated top 25% of class:** 92
**Graduated top 50% of class:** 99

# COLLEGE GRADUATION REQUIREMENTS

**Course waivers allowed:** No
**Course substitutions allowed:** Yes
**In what courses:** Each case is taken on an individual basis. Substitutions are possible in foreign language and math.

# ADDITIONAL INFORMATION

**Environment:** NR

**Student Body**
  **Undergrad enrollment:** 15,363
  **Women:** 59%
  **Men:** 41%
  **In-state students:** 76%
  **Out-of-state:** 24%

**Cost Information**
  **In-state tuition:** $2,161
  **Out-of-state:** $10,693
  **Room & board:** $4,500

**Housing Information**
  **University housing:** Yes
  **Fraternity:** Yes
  **Sorority:** Yes
  **Living on campus:** 44%

  **Athletics:** NCAA Div. I

# UNIVERSITY OF NORTH CAROLINA-CHARLOTTE

9201 University City Boulevard, Charlotte, NC 28223-0001 • **Admissions:** 704-547-2213 • **Fax:** 704-510-6483
**Email:** UNCCADM@email.uncc.edu • **Web:** www.uncc.edu
**Support:** S • **Institution:** 4 yr. Public

## LEARNING DISABILITY ADMISSIONS AND SERVICES

The professional staff in Disability Services assists students with learning disabilities to meet their individual needs. In all possible cases, UNC Charlotte will use existing resources for educational auxiliary aids. Services could include registration assistance, orientation to available services, individualized educational plan, special testing arrangements, counseling, and peer support services.

## LEARNING DISABILITY ADMISSIONS INFORMATION

**Program Name:** Disability Services
**Program Director:** Jane Rochester
**Contact Person:** Same as above

**Telephone:** 704-547-4354

### ADMISSIONS

All applicants must meet the general admissions requirements and any special requirements for acceptance into a particular program of study. Students go through the regular application process. Applicants with learning disabilities are encouraged to provide information about their learning disability at the time of application for admission. The university reserves the right to withhold the admission of any applicant who fails to meet any of the requirements for admission. Students who are not otherwise qualified, and who provide documentation of a learning disability, may be reviewed by the Disability Services who will give a recommendation to the Office of Admissions. Once students have been admitted and enrolled they may request the necessary services.

**College entrance exams required:** Yes
**Course entrance requirements:** Yes
**Diagnostic tests:** Yes
**Documentation:** Psychoeducational evaluation: within 3 years

**Untimed accepted:** Yes
**Interview required:** Recommended

### ADDITIONAL INFORMATION

Tutoring is available on a one-to-one basis. Students with learning disabilities can access services through the Learning Assistance Center and Writing Center. Workshops are offered in Math, Learning Strategies, Time Management, Study Strategies, and Written Language.

**Special education HS coursework accepted:** Yes
**Special application required:** No
**# of applications submitted each year:** N/A
**# of students receiving LD services:** 132
**Acceptance into program means acceptance into college:** Students must be admitted to the university first and then may request services.

**Essay required:** No
**Submitted to:** N/A
**# of applications accepted each year:** N/A

# LEARNING DISABILITY SERVICES

**Learning center:** Yes
**Kurzweil personal reader:** Yes
**LD specialists:** No
**Allowed in exams:**
  **Calculator:** NR
  **Dictionary:** Yes
  **Computer:** Yes
  **SpellCheck:** Yes

**Notetaker:** Yes
**Scribes:** Yes
**Proctors:** Yes
**Oral exams:** Yes
**Extended test time:** Yes
**Added cost:** None
**Distraction-free environ.:** Yes
**Tape recording in class:** Yes
**Books on tape:** Yes
**Taping of other books:** Yes

**Professional tutors:** No
**Peer tutors:** Yes
**Max. hrs/wk for services:** 4
**Priority registration:** Yes
**Accomodations for students with ADD:** Yes
**How are professors notified of LD:** By the student and the Program Director

# GENERAL ADMISSIONS INFORMATION

**Director of Admissions:** Craig Fulton          **Telephone:** 704-547-2213

## ENTRANCE REQUIREMENTS

Total high school units required/recommended: 16 total units are required; 4 English required, 3 math required, 2 science required, 2 foreign language required, 2 social studies required. Additional units of foreign language, math, world history, health education, and/or a minimum of 3 academic courses in the 12th year recommended. Minimum combined SAT I score of 850, rank in top half of secondary school class, and minimum 2.0 GPA required. Special Requirements: An audition is required for music program applicants. Minimum SAT I, score of 400 in math and ACT score of 20 in math required of business administration and architecture program applicants. Portfolio and interview required of architecture program applicants. Solid geometry and trigonometry required of architecture and engineering program applicants. Minimum SAT I score of 450 in math required of applicants to the Coll of Engineering; minimum SAT I score of 500 in math required of applicants to a specific department within the Coll of Engineering.

**Application deadline:** July 1
**Notification:** Rolling

**SAT or ACT preferred:** SAT
**SAT Avg:** 512V, 511M
**Average ACT:** 21
**Average GPA:** 3.25

**Graduated top 10% of class:** 16
**Graduated top 25% of class:** 51
**Graduated top 50% of class:** 96

# COLLEGE GRADUATION REQUIREMENTS

**Course waivers allowed:** No
**Course substitutions allowed:** Yes
**In what courses:** Foreign language if supported by documentation and only done on a case-by-case basis

# ADDITIONAL INFORMATION

**Environment:** The university is located on 1,000 acres 8 miles northeast of Charlotte.

**Student Body**
  **Undergrad enrollment:** 12,220
  **Women:** 52%
  **Men:** 48%
  **In-state students:** 90%
  **Out-of-state:** 10%

**Cost Information**
  **In-state tuition:** $1,716
  **Out-of-state:** $8,870
  **Room & board:** $3,386

**Housing Information**
  **University housing:** Yes
  **Fraternity:** Yes
  **Sorority:** No
  **Living on campus:** 26%

  **Athletics:** NCAA Div. I

# UNIVERSITY OF NORTH CAROLINA-GREENSBORO

1000 Spring Garden Street, Greensboro, NC 27412 • **Admissions:** 910-334-5243 • **Fax:** 910-334-3009
**Email:** undergrad_admissions@uncg.edu • **Web:** www.uncg.edu
**Support:** CS • **Institution:** 4 yr. Public

## LEARNING DISABILITY ADMISSIONS AND SERVICES

The University of North Carolina-Greensboro is committed to equality of educational opportunities for qualified students with disabilities. The goal of Disabled Student Services is to provide a full range of academic accommodations. Students who need tests offered in a non-traditional format may request this service. Modifications may include extended time, private room, reader, scribe, or use of word processor for essay examinations. Documentation must verify the use of special accommodations. The DSS Office provides a handbook for students to use as a helpful guide in making their experiences at UNCG a positive one.

## LEARNING DISABILITY ADMISSIONS INFORMATION

**Program Name:** Disabled Student Services
**Program Director:** Patricia Bailey          **Telephone:** 910-334-5440
**Contact Person:** Liz Shilliday

### ADMISSIONS

There is no special admissions process for students with learning disabilities. Admissions is competitive and based on academic qualifications. Students with learning disabilities must submit the regular application and are considered for admission in the same manner as any other applicant. No pre-admission inquiry regarding the learning disability is made. However, it is helpful for the student to write a cover letter stating that a specific disability exists if support services will be necessary. This alerts the Admissions staff to take this into consideration. It is highly recommended that the SAT or ACT be taken on an untimed basis if this gives a better estimate of the student's ability.

**College entrance exams required:** Yes          **Untimed accepted:** Yes
**Course entrance requirements:** Yes          **Interview required:** No
**Diagnostic tests:** Yes
**Documentation:** WISC;WAIS; W-J Part B; within 3 years

### ADDITIONAL INFORMATION

DSS has several computers with word processors for registered students. Trained staff members are available for counseling to assist students with academic and/or personal problems. Voluntary notetakers are solicited through DSS, and photocopying is available. Students will meet with their faculty advisor to discuss courses that need to be taken, and DSS will 'stamp' the students' registration cards to verify that they are registered with DSS and warrant priority registration. Assistance in securing taped textbooks through Recording for the Blind is provided, and a file of available readers is available for instances when materials are not available through RFB. Students are provided with information regarding campus tutorials and labs. Individual tutors are provided when it seems necessary. Students can receive help with study skills and time management techniques.

**Special education HS coursework accepted:** N/I          **Essay required:** No
**Special application required:** No          **Submitted to:** N/A
**# of applications submitted each year:** N/I          **# of applications accepted each year:** N/I
**# of students receiving LD services:** 180
**Acceptance into program means acceptance into college:** Students must be admitted to the university first and then may request services.

# LEARNING DISABILITY SERVICES

**Learning center:** No
**Kurzweil personal reader:** Yes
**LD specialists:** Yes
**Allowed in exams:**
  **Calculator:** No
  **Dictionary:** No
  **Computer:** Yes
  **SpellCheck:** Yes

**Notetaker:** Yes
**Scribes:** Yes
**Proctors:** Yes
**Oral exams:** Yes
**Extended test time:** Yes
**Added cost:** Yes
**Distraction-free environ.:** Yes
**Tape recording in class:** Yes
**Books on tape:** Yes
**Taping of other books:** Yes

**Professional tutors:** N/I
**Peer tutors:** Yes
**Max. hrs/wk for services:**
Depends on need of student
**Priority registration:** Yes
**Accomodations for students
with ADD:** Yes
**How are professors notified of
LD:** By the student

# GENERAL ADMISSIONS INFORMATION

**Director of Admissions:** Charles Rickard          **Telephone:** 914-334-5243

## ENTRANCE REQUIREMENTS

Total high school units required/recommended: 15 total units are required; 4 English required, 3 math required, 3 science required, 2 foreign language required, 2 social studies required. Science units must include 1 unit of life or biological science and 1 unit of physical science. Social studies units must include 1 unit of U.S. history and 1 unit of history, economics, sociology, or civics. Special requirements: A portfolio is required for art program applicants. An audition is required for music program applicants.

**Application deadline:** August 1
**Notification:** Rolling

**SAT or ACT preferred:** SAT
**SAT Avg:** 530V, 514M
**Average ACT:** 20
**Average GPA:** 3.32

**Graduated top 10% of class:** 13
**Graduated top 25% of class:** 41
**Graduated top 50% of class:** 83

# COLLEGE GRADUATION REQUIREMENTS

**Course waivers allowed:** No
**Course substitutions allowed:** Yes
**In what courses:** Decided on a case-by-case basis in Foreign Language (exception rather than the rule).

# ADDITIONAL INFORMATION

**Environment:** The university is located on 178 acres in an urban area in Greensboro.

**Student Body**
  **Undergrad enrollment:** 9,694
  **Women:** 66%
  **Men:** 34%
  **In-state students:** 90%
  **Out-of-state:** 10%

**Cost Information**
  **In-state tuition:** $1,016
  **Out-of-state:** $9,584
  **Room & board:** $3,940

**Housing Information**
  **University housing:** Yes
  **Fraternity:** Yes
  **Sorority:** Yes
  **Living on campus:** 33%

  **Athletics:** NCAA Div. I

# NC

# UNIVERSITY OF NORTH CAROLINA-WILMINGTON

601 South College Road, Wilmington, NC 28403 • **Admissions:** 910-962-3243 • **Fax:** 910-962-3038
**Email:** admissions@uncwil.edu • **Web:** www.uncwil.edu
**Support:** CS • **Institution:** 4 yr. Public

## LEARNING DISABILITY ADMISSIONS AND SERVICES

The university's goal is to provide access to all of its academic programs, support services, and extracurricular activities, and to enrich academic and vocational experience while in college. The coordinator of the Disabled Student Services meets with the student in order to apprise special needs, make referrals, and arrange for special accommodations. The university has devoted much time and energy to meeting the requirements of Section 504 and ADA. This effort is exemplified by the accommodating services offered through DSS for students with learning disabilities and by special cooperation of the faculty. As the number of students with learning disabilities attending UNCW increases, so does their commitment to make facilities and programs more accessible.

## LEARNING DISABILITY ADMISSIONS INFORMATION

**Program Name:** Disabled Student Services
**Program Director:** Dr. Phillip Sharp          **Telephone:** 910-395-3746
**Contact Person:** Ginny Lundeen

### ADMISSIONS

Students with learning disabilities must meet the same entrance requirements as all other applicants. The average SAT for entering freshmen is 960 and the average GPA is 3.0+.

**College entrance exams required:** Yes          **Untimed accepted:** Yes
**Course entrance requirements:** Yes          **Interview required:** No
**Diagnostic tests:** Yes
**Documentation:** WAIS-R; test of achievement, neuropsychiatric screening: within 3 yrs.

### ADDITIONAL INFORMATION

Services are provided based on individual need as assessed through recent diagnostic information and personal interview. As new needs are identified, services may be modified or developed to accommodate them. Newly accepted students interested in services should complete and sign the disclosure form which is included with the letter of acceptance. This information should then be forwarded to the Student Development Center. Current documentation must be sent to the Coordinator of DSS after acceptance to the university. Diagnostic testing must be conducted by a licensed professional, and an adequate report must include specific educational recommendations and a DSM IV code. Priority registration is available to all returning students registered with DSS. Services and accommodations are offered to undergraduate and graduate students.

**Special education HS coursework accepted:** No          **Essay required:** Yes
**Special application required:** Yes          **Submitted to:** DSS
**# of applications submitted each year:** N/A          **# of applications accepted each year:** N/A
**# of students receiving LD services:** 70
**Acceptance into program means acceptance into college:** Students must be admitted to the university first and then may request services.

## LEARNING DISABILITY SERVICES

**Learning center:** Yes
**Kurzweil personal reader:** Yes
**LD specialists:** 1
**Allowed in exams:**
  **Calculator:** Y/N
  **Dictionary:** Y/N
  **Computer:** Y/N
  **SpellCheck:** Y/N

**Notetaker:** Yes
**Scribes:** Yes
**Proctors:** Yes
**Oral exams:** Yes
**Extended test time:** Yes
**Added cost:** None
**Distraction-free environ.:** Yes
**Tape recording in class:** Yes
**Books on tape:** Yes
**Taping of other books:** Yes

**Professional tutors:** No
**Peer tutors:** 15
**Max. hrs/wk for services:**
Depends on need
**Priority registration:** Yes
**Accomodations for students
with ADD:** Yes
**How are professors notified of
LD:** By the student

## GENERAL ADMISSIONS INFORMATION

**Director of Admissions:** Doug Johnson        **Telephone:** 910-395-3243

### ENTRANCE REQUIREMENTS

Total high school units required/recommended: 20 total units are required; 4 English required, 3 math required, 3 science required, 2 foreign language required, 2 social studies required, 1 history required. Applicants may be admitted with deficiency in foreign language units but must complete requirement before graduation. Minimum combined SAT I score of 800 and minimum 2.0 GPA required.

**Application deadline:** February 15
**Notification:** Rolling

**SAT or ACT preferred:** SAT
**SAT Avg:** 454V, 512M
**Average ACT:** 22

**Graduated top 10% of class:** 19
**Graduated top 25% of class:** 62
**Graduated top 50% of class:** 93

## COLLEGE GRADUATION REQUIREMENTS

**Course waivers allowed:** Yes
**Course substitutions allowed:** Yes
**In what courses:** Foreign language

## ADDITIONAL INFORMATION

**Environment:** The university is located on 650-acre urban campus.

**Student Body**
  **Undergrad enrollment:** 7,980
  **Women:** 59%
  **Men:** 41%
  **In-state students:** 87%
  **Out-of-state:** 13%

**Cost Information**
  **In-state tuition:** $874
  **Out-of-state:** $8,028
  **Room & board:** $3,910

**Housing Information**
  **University housing:** Yes
  **Fraternity:** No
  **Sorority:** No
  **Living on campus:** 23%

  **Athletics:** NCAA Div. I

# SAINT ANDREWS PRESBYTERIAN COLLEGE

**NC**

1700 Dogwood Mile, Laurinburg, NC 28352 • **Admissions:** 910-277-5555 • **Fax:** 910-277-5087
**Email:** admissions@sapc.edu • **Web:** www.sapc.edu
**Support:** CS • **Institution:** 4 yr. Private

## LEARNING DISABILITY ADMISSIONS AND SERVICES

St. Andrews Presbyterian College acknowledges its responsibility, both legally and educationally for students with learning disabilities by providing reasonable accommodations. These services do not guarantee success, but endeavor to assist the student in pursuing a quality post-secondary education. The Academic Services Coordinator provides intensive one-to-one assistance in order to aid participants in their regular course work. Faculty and peer tutors work with students and the program faculty to provide additional help in a variety of disciplines and to provide accommodations when appropriate.

## LEARNING DISABILITY ADMISSIONS INFORMATION

**Program Name:** Special Academic Services
**Program Director:** Beth McSwain                    **Telephone:** 910-277-5331
**Contact Person:** Anne Todd                         **Telephone:** 910-277-5558

### ADMISSIONS

Each application is reviewed on an individual basis. Factors considered are: SAT minimum 700 or ACT minimum of 17; high school profile and courses attempted, as well as GPA with a minimum of 2.0; essay; counselor and/or teacher recommendation; motivation, career goals, and study skills (assessed through interview). Alternative admission can be offered through the Assist Program, which serves students whose academic record or test scores are below for ordinary admission. Application to the Assist Program is by referral only. Recommendations must come from the high school counselor.

**College entrance exams required:** Yes          **Untimed accepted:** Yes
**Course entrance requirements:** Yes              **Interview required:** Yes
**Diagnostic tests:** Yes
**Documentation:** WAIS-R or WAIS-III; Ach. Tests; Cognitive Process: within 3 years

### ADDITIONAL INFORMATION

The Assist Program, a one year program, is designed for students who show academic promise but who have not developed their talents in measurable ways. The Program provides 30 students a carefully supervised, highly-structured program of study to assist them in reaching their potential for academic success. Each student is assigned 2 advisors; participates in a special seminar involving note taking, methods for remembering lectures and films, group discussions and readings. Individual counseling to encourage students facing a wide range of assessment situations, including a special session on reducing "test anxiety."

**Special education HS coursework accepted:** No      **Essay required:** Yes
**Special application required:** No                  **Submitted to:** N/A
**# of applications submitted each year:** 50         **# of applications accepted each year:** N/I
**# of students receiving LD services:** 22
**Acceptance into program means acceptance into college:** Students must be admitted to the college first and then may request services.

## LEARNING DISABILITY SERVICES

**Learning center:** Yes
**Kurzweil personal reader:** No
**LD specialists:** 1
**Allowed in exams:**
  **Calculator:** Yes
  **Dictionary:** Yes
  **Computer:** Yes
  **SpellCheck:** Yes

**Notetaker:** Yes
**Scribes:** Yes
**Proctors:** Yes
**Oral exams:** Yes
**Extended test time:** Yes
**Added cost:** None
**Distraction-free environ.:** Yes
**Tape recording in class:** Yes
**Books on tape:** Yes
**Taping of other books:** No

**Professional tutors:** 1
**Peer tutors:** varies
**Max. hrs/wk for services:**
Unlimited
**Priority registration:** No
**Accomodations for students
with ADD:** Yes
**How are professors notified of
LD:** By the student and the
Program Director

## GENERAL ADMISSIONS INFORMATION

**Director of Admissions:** Anne Todd       **Telephone:** 800-763-0198

### ENTRANCE REQUIREMENTS

Total high school units required/recommended: 20 total units are recommended; 4 English recommended, 3 math recommended, 3 science recommended, 1 social studies recommended, 1 history recommended, 2 foreign language recommended. Minimum SAT I scores of 450 in both verbal and math and minimum 2.0 GPA recommended.

**Application deadline:** NR
**Notification:** Rolling

**SAT or ACT preferred:** Either
**SAT Avg:** 520V, 495M
**Average GPA:** 2.85

## COLLEGE GRADUATION REQUIREMENTS

**Course waivers allowed:** Yes
**Course substitutions allowed:** Yes
**In what courses:** Decision made on a case-by-case basis

## ADDITIONAL INFORMATION

**Environment:** The college is located on 600 acres in a small town 40 miles southwest of Fayetteville.

**Student Body**
  **Undergrad enrollment:** 662
  **Women:** 54%
  **Men:** 46%
  **In-state students:** 34%
  **Out-of-state:** 66%

**Cost Information**
  **In-state tuition:** $12,015
  **Out-of-state:** $12,015
  **Room & board:** $5,300

**Housing Information**
  **University housing:** Yes
  **Fraternity:** No
  **Sorority:** No
  **Living on campus:** 90%

  **Athletics:** NCAA Div. II

# NC

# WAKE FOREST UNIVERSITY

Box 7305 Reynolda Station, Winston-Salem, NC  27109 • **Admissions:** 910-758-5201 • **Fax:** 910-758-6074
**Email:** admissions@wfu.edu • **Web:** www.wfu.edu
**Support:** CS • **Institution:** 4 yr. Private

## LEARNING DISABILITY ADMISSIONS AND SERVICES

The LAP offers support for academic success. All students are eligible for group tutoring sessions in basic academic subjects. Those students enrolled in the LAP Academic Skills Program are also eligible for individual tutoring services. LAP tutors are specially trained to focus on academic skill building within course content areas. The students with learning disabilities have a series of conferences with staff members who specialize in academic skills, and who help design an overall study plan to improve scholastic performance in those areas needing assistance. If special course accommodations are needed, the Director will serve as an advocate for the students with members of the faculty.

## LEARNING DISABILITY ADMISSIONS INFORMATION

**Program Name:** Learning Assistance Program (LAP)
**Program Director:** Sandra C. Chadwick                **Telephone:** 910-759-5929
**Contact Person:** same as above

### ADMISSIONS

No special admissions. Students with learning disabilities submit the general Wake Forest University application and are expected to meet the same admission criteria as all applicants. Services are available to all enrolled students with documentation on file. Students are encouraged to provide a recent psychoeducational evaluation.

**College entrance exams required:** Yes        **Untimed accepted:** Yes
**Course entrance requirements:** Yes          **Interview required:** No
**Diagnostic tests:** Yes
**Documentation:** Psychoeducational evaluation: within 1 year

### ADDITIONAL INFORMATION

Applications are accepted for course substitutions. The Learning Assistance Program staff will assist students with learning disabilities with learning new approaches to studying and what will impact on reading and comprehension, notetaking, time management, study organization, memory, motivation, and self-modification.

**Special education HS coursework accepted:** No    **Essay required:** Yes
**Special application required:** No               **Submitted to:** N/A
**# of applications submitted each year:** N/A     **# of applications accepted each year:** N/A
**# of students receiving LD services:** N/I
**Acceptance into program means acceptance into college:** Students must be accepted to the university first and then may request services.

# LEARNING DISABILITY SERVICES

**Learning center:** No
**Kurzweil personal reader:** No
**LD specialists:** 2
**Allowed in exams:**
  **Calculator:** Yes
  **Dictionary:** Yes
  **Computer:** Yes
  **SpellCheck:** Yes

**Notetaker:** Yes
**Scribes:** N/I
**Proctors:** N/I
**Oral exams:** Yes
**Extended test time:** Yes
**Added cost:** None
**Distraction-free environ.:** Yes
**Tape recording in class:** Yes
**Books on tape:** Yes
**Taping of other books:** No

**Professional tutors:** Yes
**Peer tutors:** Yes
**Max. hrs/wk for services:** 3
**Priority registration:** N/I
**Accomodations for students with ADD:** N/I
**How are professors notified of LD:** By the student and the Program Director

# GENERAL ADMISSIONS INFORMATION

**Director of Admissions:** William G. Starling       **Telephone:** 910-759-5201

## ENTRANCE REQUIREMENTS

Total high school units required/recommended: 16 total units are required; 4 English required, 3 math required, 1 science required, 2 foreign language required, 2 social studies required, 2 history required. Special Requirements: TOEFL is required of all international students.

**Application deadline:** January 15
**Notification:** April 1

**SAT or ACT preferred:** NR
**SAT Range:** 620–700V, 600–690M

**Graduated top 10% of class:** 69
**Graduated top 25% of class:** 94
**Graduated top 50% of class:** 99

# COLLEGE GRADUATION REQUIREMENTS

**Course waivers allowed:** No
**Course substitutions allowed:** No
**In what courses:** N/A

# ADDITIONAL INFORMATION

**Environment:** The 550-acre campus is located in the Piedmont region of North Carolina.

**Student Body**
  **Undergrad enrollment:** 3,771
  **Women:** 50%
  **Men:** 50%
  **In-state students:** 30%
  **Out-of-state:** 70%

**Cost Information**
  **In-state tuition:** $18,500
  **Out-of-state:** $18,500
  **Room & board:** $5,100

**Housing Information**
  **University housing:** Yes
  **Fraternity:** Yes
  **Sorority:** Yes
  **Living on campus:** 80%

  **Athletics:** NCAA Div. I

# WESTERN CAROLINA UNIVERSITY

**NC**

Cullowhee, NC  28723 • **Admissions:** 704-227-7317 • **Fax:** 704-227-7319
**Email:** cauley@wcu.edu • **Web:** www.wcu.edu
**Support:** CS • **Institution:** 4 yr. Public

## LEARNING DISABILITY ADMISSIONS AND SERVICES

The Disabled Student Services Program attempts to respond to the needs of students with learning disabilities by making services and equipment available as needed, and by making judicious use of reading and tutoring services. Each student in the program is assigned a counselor/advisor. The students must meet with this counselor at least twice a month to discuss topics such as academic progress, study skills, adjustment to college life, career decision-making, or personal concerns. In addition, students may take specially designed classes in English, reading, and study skills.

## LEARNING DISABILITY ADMISSIONS INFORMATION

**Program Name:** Disability Student Services/Student Support Services
**Program Director:** Dr. Bonita Jacobs                    **Telephone:** 704-227-7234
**Contact Person:** Same as above

### ADMISSIONS

Students with learning disabilities are admitted under the same admission standards as students who have no learning disability. Non-standardized ACT/SAT are acceptable. Students who are admitted are encouraged to take the Summer Term Enrichment Program (STEP) in order to 'jump-start' their introduction to college. Students not admissible through the regular admission process may be offered a probationary admission and must begin in the summer prior to freshman year. The admission decision is made by the Admission Office.

**College entrance exams required:** Yes          **Untimed accepted:** Yes
**Course entrance requirements:** Yes            **Interview required:** No
**Diagnostic tests:** Yes
**Documentation:** W-J; IQ tests: within 3 years

### ADDITIONAL INFORMATION

To qualify for services students must be enrolled at the university, be evaluated within the last 3 years, be willing to participate in additional evaluation to confirm the disability, and be willing to participate in planning support services. Admitted students should maintain good class attendance, strive for good grades, cooperate with counselors and advisors, set realistic career goals, and meet with LD team. Services and accommodations are available for undergraduate and graduate students.

**Special education HS coursework accepted:** No          **Essay required:** N/I
**Special application required:** Yes                      **Submitted to:** Program Director
**# of applications submitted each year:** 145            **# of applications accepted each year:** All who are
**# of students receiving LD services:** 145
**Acceptance into program means acceptance into college:** Students must be admitted to the university first and then may request services.

**Learning center:** Yes
**Kurzweil personal reader:** Yes
**LD specialists:** 2
**Allowed in exams:**
  **Calculator:** Yes
  **Dictionary:** Yes
  **Computer:** Yes
  **SpellCheck:** Yes

**Notetaker:** Yes
**Scribes:** Yes
**Proctors:** Yes
**Oral exams:** Yes
**Extended test time:** Yes
**Added cost:** None
**Distraction-free environ.:** Yes
**Tape recording in class:** Yes
**Books on tape:** Yes
**Taping of other books:** Yes

**Professional tutors:** No
**Peer tutors:** No
**Max. hrs/wk for services:** varies
**Priority registration:** Yes
**Accomodations for students with ADD:** Yes
**How are professors notified of LD:** By the student

## GENERAL ADMISSIONS INFORMATION

**Director of Admissions:** Drumont I. Bowman, Jr.          **Telephone:** 704-227-7317

### ENTRANCE REQUIREMENTS

Total high school units required/recommended: 20 total units are required; 4 English required, 3 math required, 3 science required, 2 social studies required, 1 history required, 2 foreign language required. Minimum SAT I scores of 350 in both verbal and math, rank in top half of secondary school class, and minimum 2.0 GPA recommended. Special Requirements: An audition is required for music program applicants. TOEFL is required of all international students. Aptitude exam required of music program applicants.

**Application deadline:** June 1
**Notification:** Rolling

**SAT or ACT preferred:** SAT
**SAT Avg:** 495V, 488M
**SAT II required:** Yes
**YAverage ACT:** 18
**Average GPA:** 3.03

**Graduated top 10% of class:** 9
**Graduated top 25% of class:** 27
**Graduated top 50% of class:** 66

## COLLEGE GRADUATION REQUIREMENTS

**Course waivers allowed:** Varies
**Course substitutions allowed:** Yes
**In what courses:** Individually considered

## ADDITIONAL INFORMATION

**Environment:** The university is located on 400 acres in a rural area 50 miles southwest of Asheville.

**Student Body**
  **Undergrad enrollment:** 5,674
  **Women:** 51%
  **Men:** 49%
  **In-state students:** 93%
  **Out-of-state:** 7%

**Cost Information**
  **In-state tuition:** $874
  **Out-of-state:** $8,028
  **Room & board:** $2,674

**Housing Information**
  **University housing:** Yes
  **Fraternity:** Yes
  **Sorority:** Yes
  **Living on campus:** 55%

  **Athletics:** NCAA Div. I

# NC WINGATE UNIVERSITY

Wingate, NC 28174 • **Admissions:** 800-755-5550 • **Fax:** 704-233-8110
**Email:** admit@wingate.edu • **Web:** www.wingate.edu
**Support:** CS • **Institution:** 4 yr. Private

## LEARNING DISABILITY ADMISSIONS AND SERVICES

Wingate University provides a program designed to assist students with diagnosed specific learning disabilities/dyslexia. Wingate University is aware that the students with learning disabilities may be successful in the college environment, provided that their special needs are recognized and proper services are made available to them. The Program Director works closely with each student in an effort to maximize the opportunity for a successful college experience. While each student will have specific needs, there are some modes of assistance available to assist each student with the maximum support necessary. This assistance will include identifying strengths and weaknesses, balancing course selections, pre-registration, access to word processing, oral testing, extra testing time, taped texts, and tutoring. Success will be determined by the motivation and initiative of the individual student in seeking available assistance.

## LEARNING DISABILITY ADMISSIONS INFORMATION

**Program Name:** Specific Learning Disabilities
**Program Director:** Dr. Lucia R. Karnes          **Telephone:** 704-233-8269
**Contact Person:** Linda Stedje-Larson, Coordinator

### ADMISSIONS

In order to ensure that the individual needs of each student are met, enrollment in the program is limited. Applications are reviewed thoroughly by the admissions committee and the Program Director. Students should: complete high school with a C average; have been identified or diagnosed by a qualified professional; supply supportive testing information with the application; provide satisfactory SAT (900+) or ACT (20+); have an interview; provide assurance of motivation to attend Wingate University; and submit application for admission with all required documentation by March 15.

**College entrance exams required:** Yes          **Untimed accepted:** Yes
**Course entrance requirements:** Yes          **Interview required:** Yes
**Diagnostic tests:** Yes
**Documentation:** IQ performance, verbal, full-range: within 3 years

### ADDITIONAL INFORMATION

Services for enrolled students include: developing a plan for study, including choice of major, proper class load, and selection of professors; informing faculty; regular evaluation sessions; and additional guidance through the college's counseling program. The Academic Resources Center is used by individuals and groups at every point on the academic scale, from freshman trying to understand English Literature to seniors who are preparing for law boards.

**Special education HS coursework accepted:** Yes          **Essay required:** Yes
**Special application required:** No          **Submitted to:** N/A
**# of applications submitted each year:** N/A          **# of applications accepted each year:** N/A
**# of students receiving LD services:** 81
**Acceptance into program means acceptance into college:** Students must be accepted to the university first and then may request services.

## LEARNING DISABILITY SERVICES

**Learning center:** Yes
**Kurzweil personal reader:** No
**LD specialists:** 2
**Allowed in exams:**
  **Calculator:** Y/N
  **Dictionary:** Yes
  **Computer:** Yes
  **SpellCheck:** Yes

**Notetaker:** Y/N
**Scribes:** Y/N
**Proctors:** Y/N
**Oral exams:** Y/N
**Extended test time:** Y/N
**Added cost:** None
**Distraction-free environ.:** Y/N
**Tape recording in class:** Y/N
**Books on tape:** Yes
**Taping of other books:** No

**Professional tutors:** No
**Peer tutors:** Yes
**Max. hrs/wk for services:**
Unlimited
**Priority registration:** Yes
**Accomodations for students with ADD:** Yes
**How are professors notified of LD:** By the Coordinator of Support Services

## GENERAL ADMISSIONS INFORMATION

**Director of Admissions:** Walter P. Crutchfield, III          **Telephone:** 704-233-8200

### ENTRANCE REQUIREMENTS

Total high school units required/recommended: 4 English recommended, 3 math recommended, 2 science recommended, 1 social studies recommended, 2 history recommended, 2 foreign language recommended. Minimum 2.0 GPA required. Special Requirements: TOEFL is required of all international students.

**Application deadline:** Rolling
**Notification:** Rolling

**SAT or ACT preferred:** SAT
**SAT Avg:** 504V, 506M
**Average ACT:** 22
**Average GPA:** 3

**Graduated top 10% of class:** 16
**Graduated top 25% of class:** 35
**Graduated top 50% of class:** 70

## COLLEGE GRADUATION REQUIREMENTS

**Course waivers allowed:** No
**Course substitutions allowed:** No
**In what courses:** N/A

## ADDITIONAL INFORMATION

**Environment:** The university is located on 330 acres in a small town 25 miles east of Charlotte.

**Student Body**
  **Undergrad enrollment:** 1,200
  **Women:** 48%
  **Men:** 52%
  **In-state students:** 52%
  **Out-of-state:** 48%

**Cost Information**
  **In-state tuition:** $10,650
  **Out-of-state:** $10,650
  **Room & board:** $3,850

**Housing Information**
  **University housing:** Yes
  **Fraternity:** Yes
  **Sorority:** Yes
  **Living on campus:** 90%

  **Athletics:** NAIA

# NORTH DAKOTA STATE COLLEGE OF SCIENCE

**ND**

880 North 6th Street, Wahpeton, ND 58076-0002 • **Admissions:** 800-342-4325
**Fax:** 701-671-2145
**Support:** CS • **Institution:** 2 yr. Public

## LEARNING DISABILITY ADMISSIONS AND SERVICES

The philosophy of the Study Services for Students with Disabilities is to address the individual needs of students with learning disabilities, assure access to the academic, cultural and recreational offerings of the campus, assist students in moving toward independence and self-sufficiency and provide appropriate study services as requested by the individual student. This Program is a coordinated program of the Learning Skills Center (LSC) and the Career Guidance Coordinators. To receive services students must provide documentation; make their learning disability known to Study Services; identify the assistance needed to succeed in college; and self-advocate to get this assistance. The Learning Skills Center provides assistance to students needing to strengthen college-level academic skills. The Learning Skills Center houses an Open Center where students may take various individualized, self-paced courses designed to build listening, spelling, vocabulary, and computer skills. The Open Center is the heart of the LSC because from there students are directed to appropriate areas of study based on needs and interests. For more individualized instruction, alternative math courses are taught in the Math/Science Lab.

## LEARNING DISABILITY ADMISSIONS INFORMATION

**Program Name:** Study Services for Student with Disabilities
**Program Director:** Rene Moen                          **Telephone:** 701-671-2623
**Contact Person:** Doris Bruesch                         **Telephone:** 701-671-2623

### ADMISSIONS

Admission to the college is open to any student with a high school diploma or the GED. There are no specific course requirements, GPA, or tests scores. Students must submit the ACT/SAT but these scores are not used for admission purposes. Students with learning disabilities should submit the general application for admission. After the applicant has been accepted by NDSCS, contact should be made with Study Services for Students with Disabilities. At this time students should provide documentation of the disability in order to be eligible to receive services and accommodations.

**College entrance exams required:** Yes          **Untimed accepted:** Yes
**Course entrance requirements:** No              **Interview required:** No
**Diagnostic tests:** Yes
**Documentation:** Psychological reports

### ADDITIONAL INFORMATION

The Learning Center is available for all students on campus. Other important services offered in addition to the self-paced courses are: tutorials/software; tutoring; oral/untimed testing; class notes and textbook study guides; taped textbooks; and video tapes. Located in the Center are the following: Math/Science Lab; Reading Lab; Study Services; and Writing Lab. The College Prep Program is for students who are not ready to enter college without some additional preparation. College Prep serves as a transitional bridge. The mission of College Prep is to help students develop skills needed for success in college and beyond. Individual needs are assessed through personal interview and testing, and a program of study is then tailored for the student. When advisable, one or two college transfer courses can be taken along with the College Prep classes. Students with LD participate in classes that focus on skill development and uses accommodations provided through the LSC. This program is open to any student.

**Special education HS coursework accepted:** Yes          **Essay required:** No
**Special application required:** No                        **Submitted to:** N/A
**# of applications submitted each year:** N/A             **# of applications accepted each year:** N/A
**# of students receiving LD services:** 44

**Acceptance into program means acceptance into college:** Students must be admitted to the college first and then may request services.

**Learning center:** Yes
**Kurzweil personal reader:** No
**LD specialists:** 2
**Allowed in exams:**
  **Calculator:** Yes
  **Dictionary:** No
  **Computer:** N/I
  **SpellCheck:** N/I

**Notetaker:** Yes
**Scribes:** Yes
**Proctors:** Yes
**Oral exams:** Yes
**Extended test time:** Yes
**Added cost:** No
**Distraction-free environ.:** Yes
**Tape recording in class:** Yes
**Books on tape:** Yes
**Taping of other books:** Yes

**Professional tutors:** 8
**Peer tutors:** 19
**Max. hrs/wk for services:** Yes
**Priority registration:** No
**Accomodations for students with ADD:** Yes
**How are professors notified of LD:** By the student and the Program Director

## GENERAL ADMISSIONS INFORMATION

**Director of Admissions:** Keath Borchert

**Telephone:** 701-671-2189

### ENTRANCE REQUIREMENTS
High school diploma, ACT/SAT.

**Application deadline:** NR
**Notification:** NR

**SAT or ACT preferred:** NR

## COLLEGE GRADUATION REQUIREMENTS

**Course waivers allowed:** N/I
**Course substitutions allowed:** N/I
**In what courses:** N/I

## ADDITIONAL INFORMATION

**Environment:** NR

**Student Body**
  **Undergrad enrollment:** NR
  **Women:** NR
  **Men:** NR
  **In-state students:** NR
  **Out-of-state:** NR

**Cost Information**
  **In-state tuition:** NR
  **Out-of-state:** NR

**Housing Information**
  **University housing:** Yes
  **Fraternity:** NR
  **Sorority:** NR
  **Living on campus:** NR

  **Athletics:** NR

# NORTH DAKOTA STATE UNIVERSITY

University Station Box 5454, Fargo, ND 58105 • **Admissions:** 701-231-8643 • **Fax:** 701-231-8802
**Email:** nuadmiss@plains.nodak.edu • **Web:** www.ndsu.nodak.edu/index.nojs.shtml
**Support:** CS • **Institution:** 4 yr. Public

## LEARNING DISABILITY ADMISSIONS AND SERVICES

The mission of Students with Disabilities Service is to assist students with disabilities in obtaining optimal access to educational programs, facilities, and employment at NDSU. Toward this end, the staff collaborates with other Counseling Center staff, in providing consultation with students regarding accommodations that are therapeutic to their development as human beings and students. DS will provide equal access to academic programs; to promote self-awareness and advocacy; to educate the student body and faculty on disability-related issues; and to provide reasonable and appropriate accommodations. The staff educates faculty regarding the accommodation needs of students and works to ensure compliance with the Americans with Disabilities Act.

## LEARNING DISABILITY ADMISSIONS INFORMATION

**Program Name:** Disabilities Services
**Program Director:** Catherine Anderson
**Contact Person:** or Liz Sepe

**Telephone:** 701-231-7671
**Telephone:** 701-231-7714

### ADMISSIONS

Students with learning disabilities submit the general application form, and are expected to meet the same admission standards as all applicants. The ACT range is 20–22 and the minimum GPA is a 2.5. Applicants are expected to have high school courses in math including algebra and above, English, lab sciences, and social studies. Students with learning disabilities may include a self-disclosure or information explaining or documenting the disability. When necessary, an admission decision is made jointly by the Director of the Program and the Admissions Office. In this case the Disabilities Services would review the documentation and provide a recommendation to Admissions. Students can be admitted conditionally on probation and are required to take a study skills course.

**College entrance exams required:** Yes
**Course entrance requirements:** Yes
**Diagnostic tests:** Yes
**Documentation:** Combination of W-J-R, WAIS, Nelson-Denny, etc.: within 3 yrs.

**Untimed accepted:** Yes
**Interview required:** No

### ADDITIONAL INFORMATION

Skills courses are offered in study strategies, reading, computers, math, and science. A technology lab/resource room is available for student use. Assessment, counseling, and remedial support are coordinated through the Center for Student Counseling and Personal Growth. In addition, individual counseling, group support, career counseling, and personal/academic enrichment classes are offered. The NDSU Student Support Services Program provides tutoring and small group instruction. Students with appropriate documentation may request alternative testing accommodations. Skills classes are offered for credit for students with learning disabilities and ADHD. Additionally, Disability Services offers support groups for students with ADHD. Services and accommodations are available for undergraduate and graduate students.

**Special education HS coursework accepted:** Yes
**Special application required:** No
**# of applications submitted each year:** N/A
**# of students receiving LD services:** 80

**Essay required:** Not required but it can help
**Submitted to:** N/A
**# of applications accepted each year:** N/A

**Acceptance into program means acceptance into college:** Student must be admitted to the university first and then may request services.

## LEARNING DISABILITY SERVICES

**Learning center:** No
**Kurzweil personal reader:** Yes
**LD specialists:** 1
**Allowed in exams:**
  **Calculator:** Y/N
  **Dictionary:** Y/N
  **Computer:** Yes
  **SpellCheck:** Y/N

**Notetaker:** No
**Scribes:** Yes
**Proctors:** Yes
**Oral exams:** Y/N
**Extended test time:** Yes
**Added cost:** None
**Distraction-free environ.:** Yes
**Tape recording in class:** Yes
**Books on tape:** Yes
**Taping of other books:** Yes

**Professional tutors:** Yes
**Peer tutors:** No
**Max. hrs/wk for services:** 3 hours per week per class
**Priority registration:** Yes
**Accomodations for students with ADD:** Yes
**How are professors notified of LD:** By the student and the Program Director

## GENERAL ADMISSIONS INFORMATION

**Director of Admissions:** Kate Hangen

**Telephone:** 701-231-8643

### ENTRANCE REQUIREMENTS

Total high school units required/recommended: 13 total units are required; 4 English required, 3 math required, 3 science required, 3 social studies required. Minimum composite ACT score of 21 and minimum 2.5 GPA or minimum 2.5 GPA and rank in top half of secondary school class required of applicants deficient in any one of the required core units. Special Requirements: An audition is required for music program applicants. Minimum math ACT score of 23 or rank in top third of secondary school class with minimum math ACT score of 20 required of electrical/electronics engineering program applicants. Rank in top third of secondary school class required of mechanical engineering program applicants. Minimum composite ACT score of 22 recommended of architecture program applicants.

**Application deadline:** August 15
**Notification:** Rolling

**SAT or ACT preferred:** ACT
**Average ACT:** 23
**Average GPA:** 3.33

**Graduated top 10% of class:** 17
**Graduated top 25% of class:** 55
**Graduated top 50% of class:** 90

## COLLEGE GRADUATION REQUIREMENTS

**Course waivers allowed:** No
**Course substitutions allowed:** Yes
**In what courses:** Sometimes course substitutions are allowed, but never waivers

## ADDITIONAL INFORMATION

**Environment:** The university is located in a small city 250 miles from Minneapolis, Sioux Falls, and Winnipeg, Canada.

**Student Body**
  **Undergrad enrollment:** 8,664
  **Women:** 43%
  **Men:** 57%
  **In-state students:** 60%
  **Out-of-state:** 40%

**Cost Information**
  **In-state tuition:** $2,236
  **Out-of-state:** $5,970
  **Room & board:** $3,135

**Housing Information**
  **University housing:** Yes
  **Fraternity:** Yes
  **Sorority:** Yes
  **Living on campus:** 26%

  **Athletics:** NCAA Div. II

OH

# BOWLING GREEN STATE UNIVERSITY

Bowling Green, OH 43403 • **Admissions:** 419-372-2086 • **Fax:** 419-372-6955
Email: admissions@bgnet.bgsu.edu • **Web:** www.bgsu.edu
**Support:** S • **Institution:** 4 yr. Public

## LEARNING DISABILITY ADMISSIONS AND SERVICES

The philosophy of the university is to level the playing field for students with LD and/or ADHD through the provisions of appropriate accommodations and advocacy. The Office of Disability Resources is evidence of BGSU's commitment to provide a support system which assists in conquering obstacles that persons with disabilities may encounter as they pursue their educational goals and activities. Their hope is to recognize the diverse talents that persons with disabilities have to offer to the university and the community. The Office of Disability Services provides services on an as-need basis. Students who have a documented disability which precludes learning a Foreign Language may petition for an exemption from the language requirement. The Study Skills Lab is open to all BGSU students, and the extent of participation is determined by the student. No grades are given in at the Lab, participation is voluntary and the program is individualized. The Lab is not a tutorial service, but students will be shown efficient techniques for studying, reading textbooks, notetaking, time management, and strategies for effective test-taking and test-preparation. Students are scheduled according to need and personal goals. Student may attend a workshop and/or request a standing weekly appointment.

## LEARNING DISABILITY ADMISSIONS INFORMATION

**Program Name:** Office of Disability Resources (OODR)
**Program Director:** Rob Cunningham
**Contact Person:** Same as above

**Telephone:** 419-372-8495

### ADMISSIONS

There is no special application or special admissions process. Core courses preferred include: 4 yrs. English, 3 yrs. math, 3 yrs. science, 3 yrs. social studies, 2 yrs. foreign language, 1 yr. art. Students with LD may substitute Foreign Language with another core course. The minimum GPA is approximately 2.0. Students with LD submit the regular application and are encouraged to self-disclose their LD and arrange an interview with the OODR to allow staff to discuss any documentation they may require and any concerns of the students. Additional information such as school or medical history which describes specific strengths and weaknesses is helpful in determining services necessary, once admitted. Information documenting the LD should be sent to OODR. Students should submit the results of a psychoeducational evaluation or other testing and documentation which establishes the presence of a specific LD. Students should indicate accommodations that have worked successfully in high school. There is a Summer Freshman Program for freshmen applicants who do not meet the academic standards for fall admission.

**College entrance exams required:** Yes
**Course entrance requirements:** Yes
**Diagnostic tests:** Yes
**Documentation:** Flexible: within 3 years

**Untimed accepted:** Yes
**Interview required:** No

### ADDITIONAL INFORMATION

General services include:priority registration; advising by sharing information on instructor's teaching and testing styles; Writing Lab for effective strategies; Study Skills Center for effective study skills, test taking strategies, time management, and textbook reading skills; Math Lab is a walk-in-lab for understanding basic and advanced concepts; Computerized technology; notetakers, readers, and scribes; letters to professors explaining the disability and modifications needed; advocacy; and books on tape. To be eligible for test accommodations, students are required to provide documentation which provides a clear indication/recommendation for the need requested. Staff work with the student to reach consensus on the type of accommodation. Test accommodations may include: extended time; oral exams; take-home exams; open-book exams; reader; scribe; computer and spellcheck or grammar check; calculators; scratch paper with lines; speller's dictionaries on exams; question clarification; modification of test response format; quiet room.

**Special education HS coursework accepted:** Yes
**Special application required:** No
**# of applications submitted each year:** N/A
**# of students receiving LD services:** 175

**Essay required:** No
**Submitted to:** N/A
**# of applications accepted each year:** N/A

**Acceptance into program means acceptance into college:** Students must be accepted to the university first and then may request services.

**Learning center:** No
**Kurzweil personal reader:** No
**LD specialists:** No
**Allowed in exams:**
  **Calculator:** Yes
  **Dictionary:** Y/N
  **Computer:** Yes
  **SpellCheck:** Y/N

**Notetaker:** Yes
**Scribes:** No
**Proctors:** Yes
**Oral exams:** Yes
**Extended test time:** Yes
**Added cost:** None
**Distraction-free environ.:** Yes
**Tape recording in class:** Yes
**Books on tape:** No
**Taping of other books:** Yes

**Professional tutors:** Yes
**Peer tutors:** Yes
**Max. hrs/wk for services:** 6–8
**Priority registration:** Yes
**Accomodations for students with ADD:** Yes
**How are professors notified of LD:** By the student and the Program Director

## GENERAL ADMISSIONS INFORMATION

**Director of Admissions:** Michael D. Walsh          **Telephone:** 419-372-2086

### ENTRANCE REQUIREMENTS

Total high school units required/recommended: 16 total units are recommended; 4 English recommended, 3 math recommended, 3 science recommended, 3 social studies recommended, 2 foreign languages recommended. Minimum composite ACT score of 20 (combined SAT I score of 920) and minimum 2.0 GPA required. Special Requirements: An audition is required for music program applicants.

**Application deadline:** February 1
**Notification:** Rolling

**SAT or ACT preferred:** ACT
**SAT Avg:** 449V, 497M
**Average ACT:** 22
**Average GPA:** 3.12

**Graduated top 10% of class:** 14
**Graduated top 25% of class:** 45
**Graduated top 50% of class:** 85

## COLLEGE GRADUATION REQUIREMENTS

**Course waivers allowed:** Yes
**Course substitutions allowed:** Yes
**In what courses:** Foreign language

## ADDITIONAL INFORMATION

**Environment:** The 1,250-acre campus is in a small town 25 miles south of Toledo.

**Student Body**
  **Undergrad enrollment:** 14,912
  **Women:** 57%
  **Men:** 43%
  **In-state students:** 92%
  **Out-of-state:** 8%

**Cost Information**
  **In-state tuition:** $4,190
  **Out-of-state:** $8,930
  **Room & board:** $3,914

**Housing Information**
  **University housing:** Yes
  **Fraternity:** Yes
  **Sorority:** Yes
  **Living on campus:** 48%

  **Athletics:** NCAA Div. I

# CASE WESTERN RESERVE UNIVERSITY

University Circle, 10900 Euclid Avenue, Cleveland, OH 44106 • **Admissions:** 216-368-4450
**Fax:** 216-368-5111 • **Email:** xx329@po.cwru.edu • **Web:** www.cwru.edu
**Support:** S • **Institution:** 4 yr. Private

## LEARNING DISABILITY ADMISSIONS AND SERVICES

The goals of Educational Support Services are to provide reasonable accommodations and serve as an advocate for individuals with diagnosed learning disabilities. ESS ensures that students with disabilities have access to services and accommodations needed to make the college experience a positive and successful one. ESS provides academic support, special accommodations, and personal encouragement.

## LEARNING DISABILITY ADMISSIONS INFORMATION

**Program Name:** Educational Support Services (ESS)
**Program Director:** Mayo Bulloch                    **Telephone:** 216-368-5230
**Contact Person:** Same as above

### ADMISSIONS

Students with learning disabilities are encouraged to apply to CWRU. Admission is highly competitive, but all applicants are evaluated on an individual basis. Students who feel additional information would be helpful to the Admission Committee are encouraged to provide diagnostic information about their individual situation. General admission criteria include: 4 yrs. English, 3 yrs. Math, 3 yrs. Social Science, 1 yr. Science, and 2–4 yrs. Foreign Language. Students must also submit a writing sample and are encouraged to have an interview. Most admitted students rank in the top 20% of their class and have SAT I of 1180–1380 or ACT of 27–31.

**College entrance exams required:** Yes          **Untimed accepted:** Yes
**Course entrance requirements:** Yes             **Interview required:** Recommended
**Diagnostic tests:** No
**Documentation:** Students may provide diagnostic information if desired

### ADDITIONAL INFORMATION

Skills courses are offered in Study and Learning Strategies, Time Management, and Reading. It is helpful for students to provide information regarding the nature of their disability so that services may be accommodated to their needs. High performing students do well with the peer tutors available through the Educational Support Services. These tutors are students who have successfully completed the appropriate course work and have been approved by faculty. Special arrangements are made by ESS for students to have alternative testing such as additional time and proctored examinations in alternative settings. Students with LD are eligible for books on tape through RFB. The ESS center has reading improvement software, word processing, and all network applications. A reading strategies tutorial program for one credit taught by a graduate student is also available for students with LD.

**Special education HS coursework accepted:** No        **Essay required:** Yes
**Special application required:** No                     **Submitted to:** N/A
**# of applications submitted each year:** N/A          **# of applications accepted each year:** N/I
**# of students receiving LD services:** 25
**Acceptance into program means acceptance into college:** Students must be admitted to the university first and then may request services.

# LEARNING DISABILITY SERVICES

**Learning center:** Yes
**Kurzweil personal reader:** Yes
**LD specialists:** No
**Allowed in exams:**
  **Calculator:** Y/N
  **Dictionary:** Yes
  **Computer:** Y/N
  **SpellCheck:** Yes

**Notetaker:** Yes
**Scribes:** Yes
**Proctors:** Yes
**Oral exams:** Yes
**Extended test time:** Yes
**Added cost:** None
**Distraction-free environ.:** Yes
**Tape recording in class:** Yes
**Books on tape:**
**Taping of other books:** Y/N

**Professional tutors:** No
**Peer tutors:** Yes
**Max. hrs/wk for services:**
Unlimited peer tutoring
**Priority registration:** Yes
**Accomodations for students
with ADD:** Yes
**How are professors notified of
LD:** By the student and the
Program Director

# GENERAL ADMISSIONS INFORMATION

**Director of Admissions:** William Conley          **Telephone:** 216-368-4450

## ENTRANCE REQUIREMENTS

Total high school units required/recommended: 16 total units are required; 4 English required, 3 math required, 1 science required, 4 social studies recommended, 2–4 foreign language recommended. Special Requirements: A portfolio is required for art program applicants. An audition is required for music program applicants. TOEFL is required of all international students. 4 units of math and 2 units of lab science, including chemistry, recommended of math and science program applicants. 4 units of math, 1 unit of chemistry, and 1 unit of physics recommended of engineering program applicants. 2 units of lab science, including chemistry, recommended of premedical studies program applicants. Portfolio recommended of art education program applicants. Audition required of music education program applicants. SAT II (math I or II and chemistry and/or physics) recommended of engineering, math, and science program applicants.

**Application deadline:** February 1
**Notification:** April 1

**SAT or ACT preferred:** Either
**SAT Range:** 600–710 V,
640–740 M
**SAT II required:** Yes
**ACT Range:** 27–31

**Graduated top 10% of class:** 72
**Graduated top 25% of class:** 94
**Graduated top 50% of class:** 99

# COLLEGE GRADUATION REQUIREMENTS

**Course waivers allowed:** No
**Course substitutions allowed:** Yes
**In what courses:** English Composition

# ADDITIONAL INFORMATION

**Environment:** The university is located on 128 acres 4 miles east of downtown.

**Student Body**
  **Undergrad enrollment:** 3,679
  **Women:** 42%
  **Men:** 58%
  **In-state students:** 65%
  **Out-of-state:** 35%

**Cost Information**
  **In-state tuition:** $17,100
  **Out-of-state:** $17,100
  **Room & board:** $4,860

**Housing Information**
  **University housing:** Yes
  **Fraternity:** Yes
  **Sorority:** Yes
  **Living on campus:** 75%

  **Athletics:** NCAA Div. III

# CENTRAL OHIO TECHNICAL COLLEGE

**OH**

Newark, OH 43055 • Admissions: 614-366-9222

Support: CS • Institution: 2 yr. Public

## LEARNING DISABILITY ADMISSIONS AND SERVICES

The goals of the Disability Services are to foster self-advocacy and independence. The Disability Services provides diagnostic testing, counseling and accommodations for students with learning disabilities. This is the only college in Ohio which provided free complete testing with a neuropsychologist. Placement tests are given after admissions. Developmental Education and Disability Services (DE/DS) is the academic support unit in Student Support Services. DE/DS provides programs and services to any student desiring to strengthen academic skills. Students need to self-identify before scheduling classes. Early notice is needed for some services, such as alternate testing and recorded textbooks. The college advocates meeting the unique needs of students with disabilities, and accommodations provided allow for equal access to higher education.

## LEARNING DISABILITY ADMISSIONS INFORMATION

**Program Name:** Disability Services
**Program Director:** Phyllis E. Thompson, Ph.D        **Telephone:** 614-366-9246
**Contact Person:** same as above

### ADMISSIONS

Admission is open to all applicants with a high school diploma or the GED except in health programs. There are no specific course requirements. ACT/SAT tests are not required. To receive accommodations, diagnostic test results and diagnosis must be within the past three years.

**College entrance exams required:** No        **Untimed accepted:** N/A
**Course entrance requirements:** Yes        **Interview required:** No
**Diagnostic tests:** Yes
**Documentation:** WAIS-R; W-J: within 3 years

### ADDITIONAL INFORMATION

The Developmental Education Center is a learning center for students with learning disabilities. Students who received learning disability services, such as tutoring during the high school senior year are automatically eligible for services. The tutoring program includes peer tutoring in almost any course, scheduled at the student's convenience for two hours each week per course. The Academic Skills Lab has a Macintosh Computer Lab; resources to improve reading, math and language skills; word processing; and study aids for some courses and national tests. The Study Skills Workshop Series provide assistance in improving study skills and 50-minute workshops on time management, learning styles/memory, test preparing and taking, reading textbooks effectively, and notetaking. Students also have access to: proctors; individualized instruction designed to meet special needs; advocacy assistance; diagnosis counseling; and assistance with accommodations.

**Special education HS coursework accepted:** Yes        **Essay required:** No
**Special application required:** No        **Submitted to:** N/A
**# of applications submitted each year:** N/A        **# of applications accepted each year:** N/A
**# of students receiving LD services:** 70
**Acceptance into program means acceptance into college:** Students must be admitted to the college first and then may request services.

**Learning center:** Yes
**Kurzweil personal reader:** Yes
**LD specialists:** 1
**Allowed in exams:**
  **Calculator:** Yes
  **Dictionary:** Yes
  **Computer:** Yes
  **SpellCheck:** Yes

**Notetaker:** Yes
**Scribes:** Yes
**Proctors:** Yes
**Oral exams:** Yes
**Extended test time:** Yes
**Added cost:** None
**Distraction-free environ.:** Yes
**Tape recording in class:** Yes
**Books on tape:** Yes
**Taping of other books:** Yes

**Professional tutors:** No
**Peer tutors:** 60
**Max. hrs/wk for services:** Unlimited
**Priority registration:** No
**Accommodations for students with ADD:** Yes
**How are professors notified of LD:** By the student

## GENERAL ADMISSIONS INFORMATION

**Director of Admissions:** John Merrin          **Telephone:** 614-366-3151

### ENTRANCE REQUIREMENTS
Asset Placement Test accepted; test may be waived for minimum combined SAT score of 500, or ACT score of 20.

**Application deadline:** rolling          **SAT or ACT preferred:** See above
**Notification:** rolling

## COLLEGE GRADUATION REQUIREMENTS

**Course waivers allowed:** No
**Course substitutions allowed:** No
**In what courses:** N/A

## ADDITIONAL INFORMATION

**Environment:** The campus is located in a small town with easy access to Columbus.

**Student Body**
  **Undergrad enrollment:** 1,898
  **Women:** 70%
  **Men:** 30%
  **In-state students:** 99%
  **Out-of-state:** 1%

**Cost Information**
  **In-state tuition:** $2,124
  **Out-of-state:** $2,337

**Housing Information**
  **University housing:** Yes
  **Fraternity:** No
  **Sorority:** No
  **Living on campus:** 8%

  **Athletics:** Intercollegiate

# UNIVERSITY OF CINCINNATI

Institutional Planning, Mail Location 127, Cincinnati, OH 45221 • **Admissions:** 513-556-1100
**Fax:** 513-556-2046 • **Email:** admissions@uc.edu • **Web:** www.uc.edu
**Support:** S • **Institution:** 4 yr. Public

## LEARNING DISABILITY ADMISSIONS AND SERVICES

The University of Cincinnati does not have a specific structured learning disability program. However, students with learning disabilities who utilize the available services and resources of the university find they can be successful in achieving their academic objectives. The goal of Disability Services is to provide the necessary accommodations to students in order for them to become successful and independent learners. All students who register for classes during priority registration are guaranteed all of their classes. Some students with learning disabilities are encouraged to take a minimal load of 6 hours. Remedial developmental courses are available along with campus-wide tutoring. There is special consideration for testing, and a specialized mini computer lab.

## LEARNING DISABILITY ADMISSIONS INFORMATION

**Program Name:** Disability Services
**Program Director:** Stanley Henderson
**Contact Person:** Lawrence Goodall

**Telephone:** 513-556-3244
**Telephone:** 513-556-6816

### ADMISSIONS

There is no special admissions procedure for students with learning disabilities. The Admissions Office looks at each individual situation; there is no set rule for admissions and waivers. All students submit the general university application form. Course requirements and waivers depend upon the college within the university. General course requirements include: 4 yrs. English, 3 yrs. math (4 for engineering), 2 yrs. science, 2 yrs. social studies, and 2 yrs. foreign language (not required in Business) or can substitute American Sign Language. University College is a 2-year Associate Degree program which has an "open door" policy, no minimum GPA, no required tests, and no course requirements for entrance. Students may transfer to other majors after one year if they are doing well with a 3.0 GPA or may transfer automatically into one of the 4-year majors after receiving an Associate Degree. Students with learning disabilities are encouraged to request an interview, which their parents may attend.

**College entrance exams required:** Yes
**Course entrance requirements:** Yes
**Diagnostic tests:** Yes
**Documentation:** Psychological evaluation: within 3 years

**Untimed accepted:** Yes
**Interview required:** Yes

### ADDITIONAL INFORMATION

Disabilities Services provides services and accommodations that are mandated under federal law. Students with learning disabilities must provide documentation identifying a learning disability in order to receive services. Students with attention deficit disorder will need to provide medical documentation identifying ADD in order to receive accommodations. This documentation must be filed with Disability Services. Services available include readers, scribes, tests on computer, loan of equipment, and library disability services. All tutors are graduate students, and there is no fee for tutoring. University College offers developmental courses in Effective Reading, Psychology, English for Effective Communication, and Mathematics, as well as a Math Lab and a College Study course.

**Special education HS coursework accepted:** According to the college
**Essay required:** No
**Special application required:** No
**# of applications submitted each year:** N/A
**# of students receiving LD services:** 250

**Submitted to:** N/A
**# of applications accepted each year:** N/A

**Acceptance into program means acceptance into college:** Student must be admitted to the university first and then may request services.

## LEARNING DISABILITY SERVICES

**Learning center:** No
**Kurzweil personal reader:** Yes
**LD specialists:** No
**Allowed in exams:**
  **Calculator:** Yes
  **Dictionary:** Yes
  **Computer:** Yes
  **SpellCheck:** Yes

**Notetaker:** Yes
**Scribes:** Yes
**Proctors:** Yes
**Oral exams:** Yes
**Extended test time:** Yes
**Added cost:** None
**Distraction-free environ.:** Yes
**Tape recording in class:** Yes
**Books on tape:** Yes
**Taping of other books:** Yes

**Professional tutors:** Grads
**Peer tutors:** Yes
**Max. hrs/wk for services:**
Unlimited
**Priority registration:** Yes
**Accommodations for students with ADD:** Yes
**How are professors notified of LD:** By the student and the Director of Disability Services

## GENERAL ADMISSIONS INFORMATION

**Director of Admissions:** James D. Williams, Director of Enrollment Mgt.       **Telephone:** 513-556-6999

### ENTRANCE REQUIREMENTS

Total high school units required/recommended: 16 total units are required; 4 English required, 3 math required, 2 science required, 2 foreign language required, and 2 social studies required. Special Requirements: Two or more years of college required of pharmacy program applicants.

**Application deadline:** December 15
**Notification:** Rolling

**SAT or ACT preferred:** ACT
**SAT Avg:** 548V, 556M
**Average ACT:** 23

**Graduated top 10% of class:** 19
**Graduated top 25% of class:** 45
**Graduated top 50% of class:** 79

## COLLEGE GRADUATION REQUIREMENTS

**Course waivers allowed:** Yes
**Course substitutions allowed:** Yes
**In what courses:** Foreign language and math

## ADDITIONAL INFORMATION

**Environment:** The university is located on 392 acres in downtown Cincinnati.

**Student Body**
  **Undergrad enrollment:** 21,272
  **Women:** 48%
  **Men:** 52%
  **In-state students:** 93%
  **Out-of-state:** 7%

**Cost Information**
  **In-state tuition:** $3,918
  **Out-of-state:** $9,805
  **Room & board:** $4,881

**Housing Information**
  **University housing:** Yes
  **Fraternity:** Yes
  **Sorority:** Yes
  **Living on campus:** 16%

  **Athletics:** NCAA Div. I

# HOCKING COLLEGE

**OH**

3301 Hocking Parkway, Nelsonville, OH 45764 • **Admissions:** 614-753-3591
**Fax:** 614-753-1452
**Support:** CS • **Institution:** 2 yr. Public

## LEARNING DISABILITY ADMISSIONS AND SERVICES

The ACCESS CENTER is dedicated to serving the various needs of individuals with disabilities and to promote their full participation in college life. The Educational Coordinator for students with disabilities helps any student with a learning disability successfully adjust to college life by finding the right fit between the instructional offerings of Hocking College and his/her own individualized learning and personal needs. This is accomplished in part by working with assessment and counseling professionals to assist students in identifying individualized programs of study and means for success by more closely aligning interest and abilities with instructor and program effectiveness.

## LEARNING DISABILITY ADMISSIONS INFORMATION

**Program Name:** ACCESS CENTER
**Program Director:** Bonnie Prince, Ph.D.
**Contact Person:** Kim Powell

**Telephone:** 614-753-3591 ext. 2114
**Telephone:** 614-753-3591 ext. 2230

### ADMISSIONS

Open enrollment for any student with a high school diploma or equivalent. Students are not required to take any specific courses or have any specific test score on the ACT/SAT. Students requesting accommodations or services for learning disabilities must be admitted and enrolled, and then they may request services. Current documentation should be submitted.

**College entrance exams required:** No
**Course entrance requirements:** None
**Diagnostic tests:** Yes
**Documentation:** None

**Untimed accepted:** N/A
**Interview required:** No

### ADDITIONAL INFORMATION

Quest for Success is a program designed especially for new students to help them prepare to start technical classes in the fall. Additional services include professional tutors in some mathematics and communications courses, Compu-Lenz to enlarge type on a computer screen and reduce glare, academic advising, and an Educational Coordinator to act as a liaison with college instructors and community agencies.

**Special education HS coursework accepted:** Yes
**Special application required:** No
**# of applications submitted each year:** N/A
**# of students receiving LD services:** 150

**Essay required:** Yes
**Submitted to:** N/A
**# of applications accepted each year:** N/A

**Acceptance into program means acceptance into college:** Students must be admitted to the college first and then may request LD services.

## LEARNING DISABILITY SERVICES

**Learning center:** Yes
**Kurzweil personal reader:** No
**LD specialists:** Yes
**Allowed in exams:**
  **Calculator:** Y/N
  **Dictionary:** Y/N
  **Computer:** Y/N
  **SpellCheck:** Y/N

**Notetaker:** Yes
**Scribes:** Yes
**Proctors:** Yes
**Oral exams:** Yes
**Extended test time:** Yes
**Added cost:** None
**Distraction-free environ.:** Yes
**Tape recording in class:** Yes
**Books on tape:** Yes
**Taping of other books:** Yes

**Professional tutors:** Yes
**Peer tutors:** Yes
**Max. hrs/wk for services:** Unlimited
**Priority registration:** No
**Accommodations for students with ADD:** Yes
**How are professors notified of LD:** By the student and the Program Director

## GENERAL ADMISSIONS INFORMATION

**Director of Admissions:** Dr. Candy Vancko      **Telephone:** 614-753-3591

### ENTRANCE REQUIREMENTS
High school diploma or GED equivalent.

**Application deadline:** NR      **SAT or ACT preferred:** NR
**Notification:** NR

## COLLEGE GRADUATION REQUIREMENTS

**Course waivers allowed:** Y/N
**Course substitutions allowed:** Y/N
**In what courses:** Varies

## ADDITIONAL INFORMATION

**Environment:** The college is located on 150 acres in a rural area with easy access to Columbus.

**Student Body**
  **Undergrad enrollment:** NR
  **Women:** NR
  **Men:** NR
  **In-state students:** NR
  **Out-of-state:** NR

**Cost Information**
  **In-state tuition:** NR
  **Out-of-state:** NR

**Housing Information**
  **University housing:** NR
  **Fraternity:** NR
  **Sorority:** NR
  **Living on campus:** NR

  **Athletics:** NR

# OH

# KENT STATE UNIVERSITY

P.O. Box 5190, Kent, OH 44242 • **Admissions:** 800-988-KENT • **Fax:** 330-672-2499
**Email:** kentadm@admissions.kent.edu • **Web:** www.kent.edu
**Support:** CS • **Institution:** 4 yr. Public

## LEARNING DISABILITY ADMISSIONS AND SERVICES

The goals and philosophy of the Student Disability Services program are to promote student independence and self-advocacy at the college level. The university believes that the ability to do college work is highly correlated with grades in high school. Students with learning disabilities who receive accommodations in high school and who are academically successful are most likely to be successful at KSU. If an LD support system has been available, and the student has been diligent and still has a low GPA in high school, lack of skills or disabilities may be too severe for that student to be successful at KSU. Students should meet with an SDS staff member 6 months before enrollment to discuss needs and accommodations.

## LEARNING DISABILITY ADMISSIONS INFORMATION

**Program Name:** Student Disability Services
**Program Director:** N/A
**Contact Person:** Dr. Janet Filer

**Telephone:**
**Telephone:** 330-672-3391

### ADMISSIONS

Students with LD must meet the same admission criteria as all other applicants. There is no special admissions procedure for students with learning disabilities. However, the high school may adjust GPA if the student was not diagnosed until late in high school. Documentation of disability is required. In addition to having completed standard college preparatory courses, applicants should be able to type or use a computer and a calculator and have skills in performing addition, subtraction, multiplication and division using natural numbers, integers, fractions and decimals. Students should also have highly developed study skills based on their specific strengths. Students who have been in the upper 60% of their high school class, have an ACT score of 15+ or SAT of 620+ do very well at KSU.

**College entrance exams required:** Yes
**Course entrance requirements:** Yes
**Diagnostic tests:** Yes
**Documentation:** Multifactored educational assessment; IEP: within 3 years

**Untimed accepted:** Yes
**Interview required:** Yes

### ADDITIONAL INFORMATION

It is recommended that all documentation be submitted prior to enrolling, as services include academic assistance in selecting courses. There is a Summer Transition Program available for a limited number of probationary admitted students with learning disabilities. The program includes help with study and time management skills, academic assessment, group counseling, and an introduction to the university. All students with documentation of a learning disability may utilize the academic and counseling services, such as: academic advising; developmental education courses for freshmen students with deficits in reading, writing, math and English; individual and small group tutoring; support groups; and individual and group study-skills help through the Learning Development Program. Services and accommodations are available for under-graduate and graduate students.

**Special education HS coursework accepted:** No
**Special application required:** Yes
**# of applications submitted each year:** N/A
**# of students receiving LD services:** 198
**Acceptance into program means acceptance into college:** Students must be accepted to the university first and then may request services or appeal a denial.

**Essay required:** No
**Submitted to:** Director of Program
**# of applications accepted each year:** N/A

## LEARNING DISABILITY SERVICES

**Learning center:** Yes
**Kurzweil personal reader:** Yes
**LD specialists:** 1
**Allowed in exams:**
  **Calculator:** Yes
  **Dictionary:** No
  **Computer:** Yes
  **SpellCheck:** Yes

**Notetaker:** No
**Scribes:** Yes
**Proctors:** Yes
**Oral exams:** Yes
**Extended test time:** Yes
**Added cost:** None
**Distraction-free environ.:** Yes
**Tape recording in class:** Yes
**Books on tape:** Yes
**Taping of other books:** Yes

**Professional tutors:** 8
**Peer tutors:** 100
**Max. hrs/wk for services:** 2 hours, limited to math and composition
**Priority registration:** Yes
**Accommodations for students with ADD:** Yes
**How are professors notified of LD:** By the student and the Program Director

## GENERAL ADMISSIONS INFORMATION

**Director of Admissions:** Charles E. Richard          **Telephone:** 330-672-2444

### ENTRANCE REQUIREMENTS

Total high school units required/recommended: 16 total units are recommended; 4 English recommended, 3 math recommended, 3 science recommended, 3 social studies recommended. Minimum combined SAT I score of 870 (composite ACT score of 21), rank in top half of secondary school class, and minimum 2.1 GPA recommended. Special Requirements: An audition is required for music program applicants. Additional requirements for architecture, business, education, fashion design, fashion merchandising, flight, the honors college, interior design, nursing, and six-year M.D. program applicants.

**Application deadline:** March 15
**Notification:** Rolling

**SAT or ACT preferred:** Either
**SAT Avg:** 512V, 501M
**SAT II required:** Yes
**Average ACT:** 21
**Average GPA:** 2.8

**Graduated top 10% of class:** 10
**Graduated top 25% of class:** 29
**Graduated top 50% of class:** 62

## COLLEGE GRADUATION REQUIREMENTS

**Course waivers allowed:** No
**Course substitutions allowed:** Yes
**In what courses:** Decisions are made by individual colleges, and they depend on the student's major

## ADDITIONAL INFORMATION

**Environment:** The university is a residential campus located on 1,200 acres 45 miles southeast of Cleveland.

**Student Body**
  **Undergrad enrollment:** 15,982
  **Women:** 60%
  **Men:** 40%
  **In-state students:** 92%
  **Out-of-state:** 8%

**Cost Information**
  **In-state tuition:** $4,288
  **Out-of-state:** $7,768
  **Room & board:** $4,030

**Housing Information**
  **University housing:** Yes
  **Fraternity:** Yes
  **Sorority:** Yes
  **Living on campus:** 37%

  **Athletics:** NCAA Div. I

# OH

# MIAMI UNIVERSITY

Oxford, OH 45056 • **Admissions:** 513-529-2531 • **Fax:** 513-529-1550
**Email:** admission@muohio.edu • **Web:** www.muohio.edu
**Support:** CS • **Institution:** 4 yr. Public

## LEARNING DISABILITY ADMISSIONS AND SERVICES

The LD Program assists students in becoming independent and successful learners, preparing for meaningful careers, and achieving a positive college experience. The program staff coordinate university and community resources to meet the academic and personal needs of students with LD; assist faculty in understanding the characteristics and needs of these students; and provide services on an individual, confidential basis to students with appropriate documentation. All students with LD or ADHD are ultimately responsible for their own academic adjustment, including class attendance, assignments, and all other course requirements. It is the student's responsibility to ask for assistance. Appropriate services and accommodations are determined through a flexible, interactive process that involves the student and the Coordinator, and arranged through dialogue with faculty and staff responsible for implementing many of these services or accommodations. Decisions on services and accommodations for students with LD are made on the basis of the disability documentation and the functional limitations caused by the disability, as well as the current needs of the student. Students with ADHD must meet with the LD Coordinator to initiate services after discussing disability-related needs and providing verification of the disability.

## LEARNING DISABILITY ADMISSIONS INFORMATION

**Program Name:** Learning Disabilities Program
**Program Director:** Lois Philips
**Contact Person:** same as above

**Telephone:** 513-529-8741

### ADMISSIONS

Applicants with LD are encouraged to meet with the LD Coordinator during the college search process to discuss the LD support program, the nature and extent of their disability, the types of accommodations that may be needed, and the program and course requirements in their field of study. Students with LD are admitted to Miami through the regular admission process; therefore, it is important to ensure that the information in the application accurately reflects a student's academic ability and potential. Thus, students may choose to indicate in their application the presence of an LD or ADHD, either through a personal essay or the "extenuating circumstances" statement. Also, students may voluntarily choose to submit other information which may help the Office of Admission to understand their unique learning strengths and needs.

**College entrance exams required:** Yes
**Course entrance requirements:** Yes
**Diagnostic tests:** Yes
**Documentation:** WAIS-R, WIPEP, other achievement/processing measures: within 2-3 years

**Untimed accepted:** Yes
**Interview required:** No

### ADDITIONAL INFORMATION

Support services for students with learning disabilities include: transition information; admission counseling; priority registration; classroom accommodations such as test modifications, extended exam time, etc.; academic assistance such as tutoring and study skills assistance; mentoring in learning strategies, time management and coping strategies; liaison with faculty; campus advocacy; and counseling and career awareness. The Orton Student Association is a student organization which provides a support system—academically, socially, emotionally, and personally—to students with LD. The group encourages and promotes student and faculty awareness of these conditions through outreach efforts. The Terry A. Gould LD Fund is an endowed account providing funds for instructional materials, program expenses, and conference opportunities for students with LD. The Office of Learning Assistance works with students encountering academic difficulties. The Tutorial Assistance Program provides peer tutors.

**Special education HS coursework accepted:** Yes
**Special application required:** No
**# of applications submitted each year:** N/A
**# of students receiving LD services:** 300

**Essay required:** No
**Submitted to:** N/A
**# of applications accepted each year:** N/A

**Acceptance into program means acceptance into college:** Students must be admitted to the university first and then reviewed for services.

## LEARNING DISABILITY SERVICES

**Learning center:** Yes
**Kurzweil personal reader:** Yes
**LD specialists:** 1
**Allowed in exams:**
  **Calculator:** Yes
  **Dictionary:** N/I
  **Computer:** Yes
  **SpellCheck:** Yes

**Notetaker:** No
**Scribes:** No
**Proctors:** Yes
**Oral exams:** Yes
**Extended test time:** Yes
**Added cost:** None
**Distraction-free environ.:** Yes
**Tape recording in class:** Yes
**Books on tape:** Yes
**Taping of other books:** Yes

**Professional tutors:** No
**Peer tutors:** 270
**Max. hrs/wk for services:** Unlimited
**Priority registration:** Yes
**Accommodations for students with ADD:** Yes
**How are professors notified of LD:** By the student

## GENERAL ADMISSIONS INFORMATION

**Director of Admissions:** Dr. James McCoy          **Telephone:** 513-529-2531

### ENTRANCE REQUIREMENTS

Total high school units required/recommended: 16 total units are recommended; 4 English recommended, 3 math recommended, 3 science recommended, and 2 social studies recommended. Special Requirements: A portfolio is required for art program applicants. An audition is required for music program applicants. Interview required of architecture program applicants.

**Application deadline:** January 31
**Notification:** March 15

**SAT or ACT preferred:** Either
**SAT Range:** 560-640V, 560-650M
**ACT Range:** 24–28
**Average GPA:** 3.5

**Graduated top 10% of class:** 38
**Graduated top 25% of class:** 80
**Graduated top 50% of class:** 97

## COLLEGE GRADUATION REQUIREMENTS

**Course waivers allowed:** Yes
**Course substitutions allowed:** Yes
**In what courses:** In foreign language and math if not essential requirements for graduation in the student's major

## ADDITIONAL INFORMATION

**Environment:** NR

**Student Body**
  **Undergrad enrollment:** 13,640
  **Women:** 55%
  **Men:** 45%
  **In-state students:** 73%
  **Out-of-state:** 27%

**Cost Information**
  **In-state tuition:** $4,210
  **Out-of-state:** $9,966
  **Room & board:** $4,440

**Housing Information**
  **University housing:** Yes
  **Fraternity:** Yes
  **Sorority:** No
  **Living on campus:** 45%

  **Athletics:** NCAA Div. I

# COLLEGE OF MOUNT SAINT JOSEPH

5701 Delhi Road, Cincinnati, OH 45233 • **Admissions:** 513-244-4200 • **Fax:** 513-244-4629
**Email:** edward eckel@mail.msj.edu • **Web:** www.msj.edu
**Support:** SP • **Institution:** 4 yr. Private

## LEARNING DISABILITY ADMISSIONS AND SERVICES

Project Excel is a comprehensive, academic support program for students with learning disabilities enrolled in the college. The program's goals are to assist students in the transition from a secondary program to a college curriculum, and to promote the development of learning strategies and compensatory skills which will enable students to achieve success in a regular academic program. The structure of the program and supportive environment at the Mount give Project Excel its singular quality. Project Excel offers students individualized attention and a variety of support services to meet specific needs, including: supervised tutoring by certified LD teachers; monitoring of student progress; instruction in learning strategies, time management and coping skills; and academic advising with attention to the students' specific learning needs. Students admitted to the program must maintain a 2.25 overall GPA, and their progress is evaluated on an ongoing basis. Study time is crucial for a successful college experience, and the Study Sessions Policy governing student participation is in effect for freshmen.

## LEARNING DISABILITY ADMISSIONS INFORMATION

**Program Name:** Project Excel
**Program Director:** Jane Pohlman                    **Telephone:** 513-244-4623
**Contact Person:** Same as above

### ADMISSIONS

Admission to Project Excel is multi-stepped, including: an interview with the Program Director; complete general admission application; complete Project Excel forms (general information, applicant goal and self-assessment, and educational data completed by high school); psychoeducational evaluation; transcript; ACT minimum of 15 or SAT of 700-740; and a recommendation. The application is reviewed by Project Excel Director and Project Excel Admission Committee. The diagnostic evaluation must indicate the presence of specific LD and provide reasonable evidence that the student can successfully meet college academic requirements. Academic performance problems which exist concomitantly with a diagnosed ADD/ADHD will be considered in the review of the student's diagnostic profile. A psychoeducational evaluation to meet documentation requirements can be arranged through Project Excel if the applicant does not have assessment data to satisfy the admission requirement. Students can be admitted to the college through Project Excel. Students not meeting all Excel admission requirements may be admitted part-time or on a probationary basis. Apply early.

**College entrance exams required:** Yes          **Untimed accepted:** Yes
**Course entrance requirements:** Yes              **Interview required:** Yes
**Diagnostic tests:** Yes
**Documentation:** School records and forms verifying a learning disability: within 1 year

### ADDITIONAL INFORMATION

Students not meeting admission requirements can take up to 6 hours per semester to a maximum of 13 hours. At that point, if they have a 2.0+ GPA they are admitted to the college. Project Excel students are assisted with course and major selection. Students are offered individualized attention and a variety of support services to meet specific needs, including: supervised tutoring; monitoring of student progress; writing lab; notetakers; accommodated testing; instruction in learning strategies, time management, and coping skills; liaison with faculty; and academic advising with attention to specific learning needs. Students enroll in regular classes and must fulfill the same course requirements as all Mount students. The curriculum is closely supervised, and specialized instruction is offered in writing, reading, and study skills to fit the individual needs of the students. The program director serves as student advisor. There is a summer program for high school students with LD, as well as a program for pre-college freshmen.

**Special education HS coursework accepted:** No        **Essay required:** Yes
**Special application required:** Yes                    **Submitted to:** Director of Project Excel
**# of applications submitted each year:** 30-40         **# of applications accepted each year:** 15-20
**# of students receiving LD services:** 50-60
**Acceptance into program means acceptance into college:** Students are either admitted directly into Excel and the college; or Excel reviews applicant and recommends to Admissions; or they are admitted to the college.

## LEARNING DISABILITY SERVICES

**Learning center:** Yes
**Kurzweil personal reader:** No
**LD specialists:** 2
**Allowed in exams:**
 **Calculator:** N/I
 **Dictionary:** Yes
 **Computer:** Yes
 **SpellCheck:** Yes

**Notetaker:** Yes
**Scribes:** Yes
**Proctors:** Yes
**Oral exams:** Yes
**Extended test time:** Yes
**Added cost:** $3,000 Level I-fresh/soph.
$800-$2,400 Level II- jr/senior
**Distraction-free environ.:** Yes
**Tape recording in class:** Yes
**Books on tape:** N/I
**Taping of other books:** Yes

**Professional tutors:** 7
**Peer tutors:** No
**Max. hrs/wk for services:** Unlimited
**Priority registration:** No
**Accommodations for students with ADD:** Yes
**How are professors notified of LD:** By the Program Director

## GENERAL ADMISSIONS INFORMATION

**Director of Admissions:** Ed Eckel

**Telephone:** 513-244-4531

### ENTRANCE REQUIREMENTS

Total high school units required/recommended: 13 total units are required; 4 English required, 2 math required, 4 math recommended, 2 science required, 4 science recommended, 2 foreign language required, 41 social studies required, 3 social studies recommended, and 1 history required. Minimum composite ACT score of 19 (SAT I scores of 400 verbal and 440 math), rank in top three-fifths of secondary school class, and minimum 2.25 GPA required. Special Requirements: An audition is required for music program applicants. Chemistry required of science and nursing program applicants.

**Application deadline:** August 15
**Notification:** Rolling

**SAT or ACT preferred:** Either
**SAT Avg:** 520V, 540M
**SAT II required:** Yes
**Average ACT:** 22
**Average GPA:** 3.2

**Graduated top 10% of class:** 20
**Graduated top 25% of class:** 52
**Graduated top 50% of class:** 85

## COLLEGE GRADUATION REQUIREMENTS

**Course waivers allowed:** Yes
**Course substitutions allowed:** Yes
**In what courses:** Decision made on a case-by-case basis

## ADDITIONAL INFORMATION

**Environment:** The Mount is a Catholic, coeducational, liberal arts college located approximately 15 miles from downtown Cincinnati.

**Student Body**
 **Undergrad enrollment:** 1,383
 **Women:** 68%
 **Men:** 32%
 **In-state students:** 85%
 **Out-of-state:** 15%

**Cost Information**
 **In-state tuition:** $11,300
 **Out-of-state:** $11,300
 **Room & board:** $4,730

**Housing Information**
 **University housing:** Yes
 **Fraternity:** No
 **Sorority:** No
 **Living on campus:** 30%

 **Athletics:** NAIA

# MUSKINGUM COLLEGE

163 Stormont Street, New Concord, OH 43762 • **Admissions:** 614-826-8137 • **Fax:** 614-826-8404
**Email:** dkellar@muskingum.edu • **Web:** www.muskingum.edu
**Support:** SP • **Institution:** 4 yr. Private

## LEARNING DISABILITY ADMISSIONS AND SERVICES

The PLUS Program provides students who have disabilities with the opportunity to reach their academic potential while at Muskingum College. A learning-strategies instructional model administered by a professional staff is the basis for PLUS support. Students may revise full program participation to maintenance (reduced fee) or independence (no fee) based on academic achievement. A full range of accommodations in addition to a structured tutorial are provided through the Center for Advancement of Learning, the framework for academic support at Muskingum College. Program participants must maintains a minimum of one hour of individual tutoring time per week for each class. The program offers no remedial or developmental instruction, encourages individual responsibility for learning, and acknowledges successful individual efforts. The Program offers qualified students individual or small group content-based learning strategies, instruction and content tutorial support.

## LEARNING DISABILITY ADMISSIONS INFORMATION

**Program Name:** PLUS Program
**Program Director:** Jen Navicky, Dir. of Admissions
**Contact Person:** Michelle Butler

**Telephone:** 614-826-8280

### ADMISSIONS

Students may apply to the college and the PLUS program after completing the junior year of high school. Admission for students with learning disabilities is based on a careful evaluation of all the materials that are submitted with the application. Students must submit: a completed application for admission; ACT/SAT; current psychoeducational evaluation documenting disability and administered by a licensed psychologist or medical diagnosis of ADD; copy of current IEP and transition plan; and a detailed request for and description of auxiliary accommodations being requested. The student is evaluated for potential for academic success as a participant in the PLUS Program. Admission policies are flexible for students with LD, but a good distribution among college prep courses is helpful. Students should submit recommendations from teachers or guidance counselor. Applicants are reviewed, and selected candidates are invited to interview. Space in the program is limited, and early application is encouraged. The admission decision is made jointly by the Program Director and Admissions Director.

**College entrance exams required:** Yes
**Course entrance requirements:** Yes
**Diagnostic tests:** Yes
**Documentation:** WAIS-R III;  WJ-R: within 3 years

**Untimed accepted:** Yes
**Interview required:** Yes

### ADDITIONAL INFORMATION

PLUS guides students toward increasing learning independence; assigns students to  Academic Advisors and Program Advisors; and assists students in determining how to balance courses and create an appropriate load each semester. Professionals provide tutorial services and coordinate appropriate testing and instructional accommodations. Students are provided with a combination of individual and small group tutorial support. Students participating in the full program must maintain a minimum of one contact hour of tutoring per week for each course. PLUS maintenance is recommended for upperclassmen as they progress successfully in college. High school juniors and seniors with LD can participate in a comprehensive, two-week summer experience, "First Step", to help them make the transition to college. The primary emphasis is on the application of learning strategies within the context of a college-level expository course. The program focuses on social and emotional changes associated with the transition to college.

**Special education HS coursework accepted:** No
**Special application required:** Yes
**# of applications submitted each year:** 150
**# of students receiving LD services:** 130
**Acceptance into program means acceptance into college:** Admissions to the PLUS program is an automatic admission to the college.

**Essay required:** Yes
**Submitted to:** Admissions Director
**# of applications accepted each year:** 75

**Learning center:** Yes
**Kurzweil personal reader:** No
**LD specialists:** 3
**Allowed in exams:**
  **Calculator:** Y/N
  **Dictionary:** Y/N
  **Computer:** Yes
  **SpellCheck:** Yes

**Notetaker:** No
**Scribes:** Yes
**Proctors:** Yes
**Oral exams:** Yes
**Extended test time:** Yes
**Added cost:** $900 per semester for full program $1,800 full year
**Distraction-free environ.:** Yes
**Tape recording in class:** Yes
**Books on tape:** Yes
**Taping of other books:** Yes

**Professional tutors:** 13
**Peer tutors:** No
**Max. hrs/wk for services:** Unlimited
**Priority registration:** Yes
**Accommodations for students with ADD:** Yes
**How are professors notified of LD:** By the student and the Program Director

## GENERAL ADMISSIONS INFORMATION

**Director of Admissions:** Doug Kellar          **Telephone:** 614-826-8041

### ENTRANCE REQUIREMENTS

Total high school units required/recommended: 15 total units are required; 4 English recommended, 3 math recommended, 3 science recommended, 2 social studies recommended, and 2 history recommended. Minimum 2.3 GPA in college prep courses required.

**Application deadline:** August 1
**Notification:** Rolling

**SAT or ACT preferred:** Either

**Graduated top 10% of class:** 29
**Graduated top 25% of class:** 53
**Graduated top 50% of class:** 80

## COLLEGE GRADUATION REQUIREMENTS

**Course waivers allowed:** No
**Course substitutions allowed:** No
**In what courses:** Waivers are not necessary

## ADDITIONAL INFORMATION

**Environment:** The college is located on 215 acres in a rural area 70 miles east of Columbus.

**Student Body**
  **Undergrad enrollment:** 1,201
  **Women:** 49%
  **Men:** 51%
  **In-state students:** 85%
  **Out-of-state:** 15%

**Cost Information**
  **In-state tuition:** $9,850
  **Out-of-state:** $9,850
  **Room & board:** $4,280

**Housing Information**
  **University housing:** Yes
  **Fraternity:** Yes
  **Sorority:** Yes
  **Living on campus:** 90%

  **Athletics:** NCAA Div. III

# OH OBERLIN COLLEGE

Admissions Office, Carnegie Boulevard, Oberlin, OH 44074 • **Admissions:** 216-775-8121
**Fax:** 216-775-6905 • **Email:** ad.mail@ocvaxc.cc.oberlin.edu • **Web:** www.oberlin.edu
**Support:** CS • **Institution:** 4 yr. Private

## LEARNING DISABILITY ADMISSIONS AND SERVICES

The student with a Learning Disability is continually challenged to maximize his or her potential. Personnel from the Office of Services for Students with Disabilities understand that challenge and provide services, as well as coordinate accommodations, to meet the needs of students who have disabilities. The goal is to maximize all the student's educational potential while helping him/her develop and maintain independence. The program philosophy is one that encourages self-advocacy. Students who are diagnosed by personnel from the Office for Services for Students with Disabilities as having a learning disability, as well as those who can provide documentation of a current diagnosis of a learning disability, are eligible for services. To verify a previously diagnosed learning disability, a student must provide a psychological assessment, educational test results, and a recent copy of an Individualized Education Program that specifies placement in a learning disabilities program. These documents will be reviewed by personnel from OSSD to determine eligibility. Students requesting services are interviewed by a learning disability counselor before a service plan is developed or initiated.

## LEARNING DISABILITY ADMISSIONS INFORMATION

**Program Name:** Office of Services for Students with Disabilities
**Program Director:** Dean Kelly, Ph.D          **Telephone:** 216-775-8467
**Contact Person:** same as above

### ADMISSIONS

There is no special admissions procedure for students with learning disabilities. All applicants must meet the same admission requirements. Courses required include 4 yrs. English and math and at least 3 yrs. social science and science. GPA is typically a "B" average or better. ACT scores range between 25-30; SAT I scores range between 1100-1320 and SAT II scores range between 560-680 on each Reasoning Test. Students who self-disclose and provide documentation may have their files read by OSSD, who will provide a recommendation to the Office of Admissions. Students who can provide valid and recent documentation of a psychoeducational diagnosis of a learning disability may receive services.

**College entrance exams required:** Yes          **Untimed accepted:** Yes
**Course entrance requirements:** Yes          **Interview required:** N/I
**Diagnostic tests:** Yes
**Documentation:** WAIS; W-J; others: within 3 years

### ADDITIONAL INFORMATION

There is a Learning Resource Center and an Adaptive Technology Center, which are available for all students. Skills classes are offered, for college credit, in reading, study skills and writing. OSSD can arrange one or all of the following services for students with learning disabilities: quiet space for exams; extended examination time, usually time and one-half, but up to twice the time typically allotted, based on diagnosis; oral exams; scribes who write down wording verbatim during exams; individual academic, personal and vocational counseling; peer support groups for the development of academic strategies and psychosocial adjustments; computer resources for additional academic skill development and assistance; taped textbooks based on careful planning and lead time; priority academic scheduling; peer tutoring; diagnostic testing; new student orientation assistance; and faculty/staff consultation. In addition, OSSD can provide information about other support services sponsored by the college.

**Special education HS coursework accepted:** Yes          **Essay required:** Yes
**Special application required:** No          **Submitted to:** N/A
**# of applications submitted each year:** 25-30          **# of applications accepted each year:** 20-25
**# of students receiving LD services:** 112
**Acceptance into program means acceptance into college:** Students must be admitted to the college first and then may request services.

**Learning center:** Yes
**Kurzweil personal reader:** Yes
**LD specialists:** 2
**Allowed in exams:**
  **Calculator:** Yes
  **Dictionary:** Yes
  **Computer:** Yes
  **SpellCheck:** Yes

**Notetaker:** Yes
**Scribes:** Yes
**Proctors:** Yes
**Oral exams:** Yes
**Extended test time:** Yes
**Added cost:** None
**Distraction-free environ.:** Yes
**Tape recording in class:** Yes
**Books on tape:** Yes
**Taping of other books:** Yes

**Professional tutors:** 4
**Peer tutors:** 35+
**Max. hrs/wk for services:** Unlimited
**Priority registration:** Yes
**Accommodations for students with ADD:** Yes
**How are professors notified of LD:** By the student and the Program Director

## GENERAL ADMISSIONS INFORMATION

**Director of Admissions:** Debra Chermonte          **Telephone:** 216-775-8411

### ENTRANCE REQUIREMENTS

Total high school units required/recommended: 17 total units are recommended; 4 English recommended, 4 math recommended, 3 science recommended, and 3 social studies recommended. Special Requirements: An audition is required for music program applicants. TOEFL is required of all international students.

**Application deadline:** January 15
**Notification:** April 1

**SAT or ACT preferred:** Either
**SAT Avg:** 670V, 633M
**SAT II required:** Yes
**Average ACT:** 28
**Average GPA:** 3.4

**Graduated top 10% of class:** 46
**Graduated top 25% of class:** 80
**Graduated top 50% of class:** 99

## COLLEGE GRADUATION REQUIREMENTS

**Course waivers allowed:** No
**Course substitutions allowed:** Yes
**In what courses:** Foreign language

## ADDITIONAL INFORMATION

**Environment:** The college is located on 440 acres in a small town 35 miles southwest of Cleveland.

**Student Body**
  **Undergrad enrollment:** 2,842
  **Women:** 58%
  **Men:** 42%
  **In-state students:** 9%
  **Out-of-state:** 91%

**Cost Information**
  **In-state tuition:** $21,425
  **Out-of-state:** $21,425
  **Room & board:** $6,174

**Housing Information**
  **University housing:** Yes
  **Fraternity:** No
  **Sorority:** No
  **Living on campus:** 75%

  **Athletics:** NCAA Div. III

# OHIO STATE UNIVERSITY-COLUMBUS

**OH**

Third Floor Lincoln Tower, 1800 Cannon Drive, Columbus, OH 43210 • **Admissions:** 614-292-3980
**Fax:** 614-292-4818 • **Email:** admissions@ohio-state.edu • **Web:** www.acs.ohio-state.edu
**Support:** CS • **Institution:** 4 yr. Public

## LEARNING DISABILITY ADMISSIONS AND SERVICES

The mission of the Office for Disability Services is threefold: to seek to ensure that students can freely and actively partici-pate in all facets of university life; to provide and coordinate support services and programs to maximize educational potential; and to increase the level of awareness among all members of the University community so that students with disabilities are able to perform at a level only by their abilities—not their disabilities. The Office for Disability Services helps students in their efforts to attain an excellent college education by promoting self-advocacy skills, self-understanding, and independence. Staff members are specialists in learning disabilities. Students are assigned to a counselor who understands their disability. Counselors assist and advise students about how to make the most of college life and, more importantly, will advise students on how to succeed academically. Disability Services matches services with students' needs. The staff recommends specific services, but students select the services that are suitable for them based upon recommendations.

## LEARNING DISABILITY ADMISSIONS INFORMATION

**Program Name:** Office for Disability Services
**Program Director:** Ann Yurcison                    **Telephone:** 614-292-3307
**Contact Person:** Lois Burke

### ADMISSIONS

Students with LD are admitted under the same criteria as their peers. However, consideration can be given to students with LD with support from the Office for Disability Services in instances where the student's rank, GPA or lack of courses, such as Foreign Language, have affected their performance at school. Applicants interested in services should submit a general application for admission to the Admissions Office; complete the section on the application form that gives students the option to disclose their disability; and submit documentation of the disability to ODS, including the latest I.E.P. and the results of the last psychoeducational testing. ODS will review the application; look at coursework and deficiencies; review services received in high school and determine if the student's needs can be met at OSU if the student is not normally admissible; look at when diagnosis was made and at the IEP; and make a recommendation to Admissions. ODS will send a letter acknowledging receipt of the documentation. The letter will indicate whether services needed can be provided and if additional information is necessary.

**College entrance exams required:** Yes          **Untimed accepted:** Yes
**Course entrance requirements:** Yes             **Interview required:** No
**Diagnostic tests:** Yes
**Documentation:** Psychoeducational battery, general IQ plus achievement tests: within 3 years

### ADDITIONAL INFORMATION

ODS is staffed by many specialists, including learning disability specialists and 10 counselors. The LD specialists will meet with students once a week. ODS can arrange for services including: quiet studio space for exams; extended exam time; readers and/or scribes; computers for essay exams; access to class notes; taped textbooks through RFB; taping of text-books not available through RFB; peer support groups to help develop academic strategies and psychosocial adjustment; peer tutoring for assistance in learning specific class material; diagnostic testing for learning disabilities; orientation assis-tance, including scheduling and training to assist in accessing services; Computer Learning Center and assistance in computer usage; priority academic scheduling; faculty-staff consultation; and family consultation. Non-credit workshops are offered on academic effectiveness from the Counseling Center and the Reading/Study Skills Program.

**Special education HS coursework accepted:** N/I          **Essay required:** No
**Special application required:** No                        **Submitted to:** N/A
**# of applications submitted each year:** N/A            **# of applications accepted each year:** N/A
**# of students receiving LD services:** 450
**Acceptance into program means acceptance into college:** Students must be admitted to the university and then may request services.

# LEARNING DISABILITY SERVICES

**Learning center:** No
**Kurzweil personal reader:** Yes
**LD specialists:** Yes
**Allowed in exams:**
  **Calculator:** Y/N
  **Dictionary:** Y/N
  **Computer:** Y/N
  **SpellCheck:** Y/N

**Notetaker:** No
**Scribes:** Yes
**Proctors:** Yes
**Oral exams:** Y/N
**Extended test time:** Yes
**Added cost:** None
**Distraction-free environ.:** Yes
**Tape recording in class:** Yes
**Books on tape:** Yes
**Taping of other books:** Yes

**Professional tutors:** No
**Peer tutors:** Yes
**Max. hrs/wk for services:** Varies
**Priority registration:** Yes
**Accommodations for students with ADD:** Yes
**How are professors notified of LD:** By the student

# GENERAL ADMISSIONS INFORMATION

**Director of Admissions:** Scott F. Healy

**Telephone:** 614-292-3980

## ENTRANCE REQUIREMENTS

Total high school units required/recommended: 15 total units are required; 20 total units are recommended; 4 English required, 3 math required, 4 math recommended, 2 science required, 3 science recommended, 2 foreign language required, and 2 social studies required. Special Requirements: A portfolio is required for art program applicants. An audition is required for music program applicants. An audition is required for applicants to dance program.

**Application deadline:** February 15
**Notification:** Rolling

**SAT or ACT preferred:** Either
**SAT Range:** 500–620V, 500–630M
**ACT Range:** 21–27

**Graduated top 10% of class:** 24
**Graduated top 25% of class:** 50
**Graduated top 50% of class:** 81

# COLLEGE GRADUATION REQUIREMENTS

**Course waivers allowed:** No
**Course substitutions allowed:** Yes
**In what courses:** No waivers are allowed. Sometimes students can petition for a Foreign Language substitution after attempting Foreign Language in college

# ADDITIONAL INFORMATION

**Environment:** Urban area located 4 miles from downtown Columbus.

**Student Body**
  **Undergrad enrollment:** 35,486
  **Women:** 47%
  **Men:** 53%
  **In-state students:** 90%
  **Out-of-state:** 10%

**Cost Information**
  **In-state tuition:** $3,468
  **Out-of-state:** $10,335
  **Room & board:** $4,907

**Housing Information**
  **University housing:** Yes
  **Fraternity:** Yes
  **Sorority:** Yes
  **Living on campus:** 10%

  **Athletics:** NCAA Div. I

# OH OHIO UNIVERSITY

Athens, OH 45701 • **Admissions:** 614-593-1000 • **Fax:** 614-593-0191
**Email:** uadmiss1@ohiou.edu • **Web:** www.ohiou.edu
**Support:** CS • **Institution:** 4 yr. Public

## LEARNING DISABILITY ADMISSIONS AND SERVICES

The Office for Institutional Equity helps students with disabilities coordinate the services needed to enjoy full participation in academic programs and campus life. Students are heard, advised and assisted in achieving goals. Students are urged to have confidence in their abilities and to feel comfortable talking with their professors about their disability. Accommodations are a result of collaborative efforts between the student, faculty, and staff of the Office for Institutional Equity. The goal is to identify and strategize a plan to assist the student in achieving success in his/her educational pursuits. Students should provide the Office for Institutional Equity with a course schedule the first week of the quarter in order for professors to be notified of the student's status in the class. Students also need to communicate with professors in advance of requesting accommodations. Extra time to complete assignments and take tests can be arranged. Students should also take advantage of the tutoring sessions that can be arranged. It is very important that students understand that the accommodations requested may not be the ones considered reasonable by the university.

## LEARNING DISABILITY ADMISSIONS INFORMATION

**Program Name:** Office for Institutional Equity/Disability Services
**Program Director:** Katherine Fahey     **Telephone:** 614-593-2620
**Contact Person:** same as above

### ADMISSIONS

Applicants with learning disabilities are expected to meet the same admission criteria as all other applicants. General admission is Top 30% with 21 ACT or 990 SAT or top 50% with 23 ACT or 1060 SAT. Other colleges have different admission criteria. Core courses required are 4 English, 3 math, 3 science, 3 social studies, 2 foreign language, and 1 yr. fine arts. Students can be admitted with deficiencies. Applicants with learning disabilities who meet the criteria should send documentation to special services after admission. Those students not meeting the admission criteria are encouraged to self-disclose. This disclosure and accompanying documentation will be reviewed by Admissions. Students, in general, must demonstrate the ability to perform in a mainstream academic setting where support is available when needed. Counselor recommendation is very helpful for students who do not meet the traditional criteria.

**College entrance exams required:** Yes     **Untimed accepted:** Yes
**Course entrance requirements:** Yes     **Interview required:** No
**Diagnostic tests:** Yes
**Documentation:** N/I

### ADDITIONAL INFORMATION

General services provided include: advising; referral and liaison; academic adjustments and classroom accommodations; priority scheduling; free tutoring through the Academic Advancement Center (4 hours per course per week); and tutoring in writing and reading skills. Skills classes are offered in learning strategies, college reading skills, reading, speed and vocabulary. Services are available to undergraduate and graduate students.

**Special education HS coursework accepted:** Yes, with appropriate explanation
**Essay required:** Optional
**Special application required:** No     **Submitted to:** N/A
**# of applications submitted each year:** N/A     **# of applications accepted each year:** N/A
**# of students receiving LD services:** 278
**Acceptance into program means acceptance into college:** Students must be admitted to the university first and then may request services.

# LEARNING DISABILITY SERVICES

**Learning center:** Yes
**Kurzweil personal reader:** Yes
**LD specialists:** Yes
**Allowed in exams:**
  **Calculator:** Yes
  **Dictionary:** Yes
  **Computer:** Yes
  **SpellCheck:** Yes

**Notetaker:** Yes
**Scribes:** Yes
**Proctors:** Yes
**Oral exams:** Yes
**Extended test time:** Yes
**Added cost:** No
**Distraction-free environ.:** Yes
**Tape recording in class:** Yes
**Books on tape:** Yes
**Taping of other books:** Yes

**Professional tutors:** No
**Peer tutors:** Yes
**Max. hrs/wk for services:** 4 hrs. per course per week through the Academic Advancement Center
**Priority registration:** Yes
**Accommodations for students with ADD:** Yes
**How are professors notified of LD:** By the student and the Director of Services

# GENERAL ADMISSIONS INFORMATION

**Director of Admissions:** Kip Howard          **Telephone:** 614-593-2620

## ENTRANCE REQUIREMENTS

Total high school units required/recommended: 17 total units are recommended; 4 English recommended, 3 math recommended, 3 science recommended, 2 foreign languages, and 3 social studies recommended. Rank in top half of secondary school class recommended. Minimum 2.5 GPA recommended. Special Requirements: A portfolio is required for art program applicants. An audition is required for music program applicants. An RN is required for nursing program applicants.

**Application deadline:** February 1
**Notification:** Rolling

**SAT or ACT preferred:** ACT
**SAT Avg:** 555V, 551M
**SAT II required:** Yes
**Average ACT:** 24
**Average GPA:** 3.2

**Graduated top 10% of class:** 21
**Graduated top 25% of class:** 56
**Graduated top 50% of class:** 93

# COLLEGE GRADUATION REQUIREMENTS

**Course waivers allowed:** No
**Course substitutions allowed:** No
**In what courses:** Any substitution would be specific to each individual and his/her learning disability. This is not done as a general rule

# ADDITIONAL INFORMATION

**Environment:** NR

**Student Body**
  **Undergrad enrollment:** 16,075
  **Women:** 53%
  **Men:** 47%
  **In-state students:** 91%
  **Out-of-state:** 9%

**Cost Information**
  **In-state tuition:** $4,275
  **Out-of-state:** $8,994
  **Room & board:** $4,548

**Housing Information**
  **University housing:** Yes
  **Fraternity:** Yes
  **Sorority:** Yes
  **Living on campus:** 42%

  **Athletics:** NCAA Div. I

# UNIVERSITY OF TOLEDO

**OH**

2801 West Bancroft, Toledo, OH 43606 • **Admissions:** 419-530-2696 • **Fax:** 419-530-4504
Email: adm0017@uoft01.utoledo.edu • **Web:** www.utoledo.edu
**Support:** CS • **Institution:** 4 yr. Public

## LEARNING DISABILITY ADMISSIONS AND SERVICES

The University of Toledo see their students as people first. And they strive always to provide a nurturing environment that can help strengthen the student as a whole human being—mind, body, and spirit. The goal of the Office of Accessibility is to provide comprehensive academic support services to allow for equal opportunity in pursuing a post-secondary education. Students with learning disabilities should identify the nature of their disability and/or attention deficit disorder and provide this information to the Office of Accessibility along with current psychoeducational evaluation or medical diagnosis of ADHD. Students should provide information about the support services received in high school. The Office of Accessibility respects the right to privacy for each student and maintains confidentiality. The support service personnel, faculty directly involved with the student's classes, academic advisers, and administrative staff members exchange information with the Office of Accessibility pertaining to the nature of the student's disability, accommodations requested, and academic status. Students must sign a form indicating their understanding of the release of information for the Office of Accessibility and giving permission to release the information.

## LEARNING DISABILITY ADMISSIONS INFORMATION

**Program Name:** Office of Accessibility
**Program Director:** Pamela Emch                    **Telephone:** 419-530-4981
**Contact Person:** same as above

### ADMISSIONS

There is no separate admissions process for students with Learning Disabilities. All students must meet the same admission criteria. Admissions standards include: GPA of at least 2.0 or the equivalent of a "C" GPA; 18 ACT or higher for Ohio residents and 21 ACT or 1000 SAT score for non-Ohio residents; 4 yrs. English, 3 yrs. math, 3 yrs. science, 3 yrs. social studies, and 2 yrs. foreign language; and high school graduation requirements fulfilled or successful passing score on the GED. Ohio residents not meeting these requirements are reviewed on an individual basis for admission consideration. Some programs, including Engineering, Nursing, Physical Therapy, Pharmacy, Pre-Medical, Pre-Dentistry, and Pre-Veterinary have higher requirements.

**College entrance exams required:** Yes          **Untimed accepted:** Yes
**Course entrance requirements:** Yes             **Interview required:** No
**Diagnostic tests:** Yes
**Documentation:** Any psychoeducational testing: within 5 years

### ADDITIONAL INFORMATION

The Office of Accessibility requests a Program Information Form giving background information and disability-related information. There are no limitations on the number of students who can receive services and accommodations. Students are automatically accepted into the program once they are admitted to the university and provide appropriate documentation. The following support services are provided upon request: notetaking services; reader services, texts on tape and a one-on-one reader; extension of time for quizzes and tests, proctors to help with reading or/and writing; tutoring services, including one-on-one tutoring in all subjects and small group tutoring in specific subjects; counseling for academic advising, social/interpersonal counseling, and disability advising; instructor contact, personal memos and liaison between student and professor; registration assistance, advanced registration, priority registration; scholarship funds; Challenged Individuals Association for students; and adaptive computer room.

**Special education HS coursework accepted:** Yes       **Essay required:** No
**Special application required:** N/A                    **Submitted to:** N/A
**# of applications submitted each year:** N/A          **# of applications accepted each year:** N/A
**# of students receiving LD services:** 694
**Acceptance into program means acceptance into college:** Students are admitted to the university and then reviewed by LD services.

## LEARNING DISABILITY SERVICES

**Learning center:** No
**Kurzweil personal reader:** No
**LD specialists:** 4
**Allowed in exams:**
 **Calculator:** Yes
 **Dictionary:** Yes
 **Computer:** Yes
 **SpellCheck:** Yes

**Notetaker:** Yes
**Scribes:** Yes
**Proctors:** Yes
**Oral exams:** Yes
**Extended test time:** Yes
**Added cost:** None
**Distraction-free environ.:** Yes
**Tape recording in class:** Yes
**Books on tape:** Yes
**Taping of other books:** Yes

**Professional tutors:** Varies
**Peer tutors:** 75+
**Max. hrs/wk for services:** Unlimited
**Priority registration:** Yes
**Accommodations for students with ADD:** Yes
**How are professors notified of LD:** By the student and the Program Director

## GENERAL ADMISSIONS INFORMATION

**Director of Admissions:** Kent Hopkins

**Telephone:** 419-530-2696

### ENTRANCE REQUIREMENTS

Total high school units required/recommended: 4 English required, 3 math required, 3 science recommended, 2 foreign languages, 2 social studies recommended, 1 history recommended. 3 units of math must include 2 units of algebra and 1 unit of plane geometry. Minimum composite ACT score of 18 (combined SAT I score of 1000) recommended for in-state applicants; minimum composite ACT score of 21 (combined SAT I score of 1000) and minimum 2.0 GPA required of out-of-state applicants. Open admissions policy for in-state applicants. Special Requirements: An audition is required for music program applicants. 4 units of math and science required of engineering program applicants; 2 units of algebra and 1 unit of plane geometry required of applicants to other programs. Foreign language required of arts and sciences and secondary-education program applicants.

**Application deadline:** Rolling
**Notification:** Rolling

**SAT or ACT preferred:** ACT
**SAT Avg:** 447V, 504M
**SAT II required:** Yes
**Average ACT:** 20
**Average GPA:** 2.9

## COLLEGE GRADUATION REQUIREMENTS

**Course waivers allowed:** Yes
**Course substitutions allowed:** Yes
**In what courses:** Foreign language

## ADDITIONAL INFORMATION

**Environment:** The University of Toledo is located on a 305-acre campus in Toledo, Ohio.

**Student Body**
 **Undergrad enrollment:** 18,187
 **Women:** 52%
 **Men:** 48%
 **In-state students:** 88%
 **Out-of-state:** 12%

**Cost Information**
 **In-state tuition:** $3,778
 **Out-of-state:** $9,063
 **Room & board:** $4,092

**Housing Information**
 **University housing:** Yes
 **Fraternity:** Yes
 **Sorority:** Yes
 **Living on campus:** 12%

 **Athletics:** NCAA Div. I

# URSULINE COLLEGE

2550 Lander Road, Pepper Pike, OH 44124 • **Admissions:** 216-449-4203 • **Fax:** 216-449-3180
**Email:** dgiaco@en.com • **Web:** www.en.com/ursweb/index.htm
**Support:** CS • **Institution:** 4 yr. Private

## LEARNING DISABILITY ADMISSIONS AND SERVICES

Ursuline College is a small Catholic women's college committed to helping students with learning disabilities succeed in their courses and become independent learners. The Program for Students with Learning Disabilities is a voluntary, comprehensive fee-paid program. The goals of the Program for Students with Learning Disabilities include providing a smooth transition to college life, helping students learn to apply the most appropriate learning strategies in college courses, and teaching self-advocacy skills. To be eligible for the PSLD, a student must present documentation of an LD, which consists of a WAIS-R, the Woodcock-Johnson, and any other standardized measures of achievement. The psychoeducational evaluation must clearly indicate that the student has a specific learning disability and should have been conducted within the last three years. Students must have average to above-average intellectual ability and an appropriate academic foundation to succeed in a four-year liberal arts college.

## LEARNING DISABILITY ADMISSIONS INFORMATION

**Program Name:** Program for Students with LD (PSLD)
**Program Director:** Cynthia Russell
**Contact Person:** Beverly Broadsky (LD Specialist)

**Telephone:** 216-646-8123
**Telephone:** 216-449-2046

### ADMISSIONS

To participate in the PSLD, students must first meet with the LD specialist to discuss whether the program is suitable for them. Students must then meet the requirements for clear or conditional admission to the college by applying to the admission's office and completing all regular admission procedures. Students with Learning Disabilities must meet the same requirements for admission to the college as all other students: 2.5 GPA and an ACT score of 17 or 900 SAT for a "clear" admission. Courses recommended include: 4 yrs. English, 3 yrs. social studies, 3 yrs. math, 3 yrs. science, 2 yrs. foreign language. A student may receive a "conditional" admission if the GPA and ACT are lower, and if admitted would be limited to 12 credit hours per semester for the first year. The final admission decision is made by the Office of Admissions.

**College entrance exams required:** Yes
**Course entrance requirements:** Yes
**Diagnostic tests:** Yes
**Documentation:** WAIS-R, WJ-R, SAT II tests: within 3 years

**Untimed accepted:** Yes
**Interview required:** Yes for PSLD

### ADDITIONAL INFORMATION

The PSLD is a new program which features: a two-day orientation which provides a smooth transition to the college, acquaints students with mentors and other students in PSLD, and introduces students to high-tech equipment and computers in the LRC; individual bi-weekly one-hour sessions with LD specialist to work on developing time-management and organizational skills, design learning strategies for success in college, and learn notetaking and test-taking skills; individual weekly one-hour sessions with a writing specialist who provides assistance with writing assignments in specific courses, and helps with developing skills in writing effective sentences, paragraphs and essays; weekly academic-skills support groups with LD specialist to learn coping skills, develop self-advocacy skills, and receive support for dealing with classroom issues; and academic advising for guidance on choosing appropriate courses and scheduling appropriate number of credits each semester.

**Special education HS coursework accepted:** Yes
**Special application required:** No
**# of applications submitted each year:** N/A
**# of students receiving LD services:** 20

**Essay required:** Yes
**Submitted to:** N/A
**# of applications accepted each year:** N/A

**Acceptance into program means acceptance into college:** Students are admitted to the college first and then reviewed for PSLD.

## LEARNING DISABILITY SERVICES

**Learning center:** Yes
**Kurzweil personal reader:** Yes
**LD specialists:** 1
**Allowed in exams:**
  **Calculator:** Yes
  **Dictionary:** No
  **Computer:** Yes
  **SpellCheck:** Yes

**Notetaker:** Yes
**Scribes:** Yes
**Proctors:** Yes
**Oral exams:** Yes
**Extended test time:** Yes
**Added cost:** $1,000 per/yr. for PSLD
**Distraction-free environ.:** Yes
**Tape recording in class:** Yes
**Books on tape:** Yes
**Taping of other books:** Yes

**Professional tutors:** 1
**Peer tutors:** 15
**Max. hrs/wk for services:** 4 hours per week with peer tutors for a nominal fee
**Priority registration:** Y/N
**Accommodations for students with ADD:** Yes
**How are professors notified of LD:** By the student, who takes a letter to the faculty and gets a signature

## GENERAL ADMISSIONS INFORMATION

**Director of Admissions:** Dennis Giacomino

**Telephone:** 216-449-4203

**ENTRANCE REQUIREMENTS**
NR

**Application deadline:** Rolling
**Notification:** NR

**SAT or ACT preferred:** NR
**SAT Avg:** 404V, 434M
**Average ACT:** 21

**Graduated top 10% of class:** 12
**Graduated top 25% of class:** 41
**Graduated top 50% of class:** 77

## COLLEGE GRADUATION REQUIREMENTS

**Course waivers allowed:** No
**Course substitutions allowed:** Yes
**In what courses:** Substitutions are allowed if the student has a documented disability in math and has approval of department head of the major. There is no foreign language requirement.

## ADDITIONAL INFORMATION

**Environment:** NR

**Student Body**
  **Undergrad enrollment:** NR
  **Women:** NR
  **Men:** NR
  **In-state students:** 99%
  **Out-of-state:** 1%

**Cost Information**
  **In-state tuition:** $10,710
  **Out-of-state:** $10,710
  **Room & board:** $4,330

**Housing Information**
  **University housing:** Yes
  **Fraternity:** No
  **Sorority:** No
  **Living on campus:** 6%

  **Athletics:** NR

# WRIGHT STATE UNIVERSITY

**OH**

3640 Colonel Glenn Highway, Dayton, OH 45435 • **Admissions:** 937-775-3333 • **Fax:** 937-775-5795
**Email:** admissions@wright.edu • **Web:** www.wright.edu
**Support:** CS • **Institution:** 4 yr. Public

## LEARNING DISABILITY ADMISSIONS AND SERVICES

The university is dedicated to the elimination of barriers which prevent intellectually qualified individuals with disabilities from attending colleges and universities across the country. Students with disabilities are encouraged to participate in all facets of university life according to their abilities and interests and to develop independence and responsibility to the fullest extent possible. The philosophy of the university is intended to stimulate students to pursue the career of study regardless of their learning disability. Through the Office of Disability Services, the university provides a comprehensive array of services on a campus with a long history of commitment to students with physical, visual and/or learning disabilities. Students with learning disabilities may use a variety of services which will allow them to be equal and competitive in the classroom. A pre-service interview is required of all prospective students to discuss service needs. Eligibility for services is determined after documentation is received and the student has an individual interview.

## LEARNING DISABILITY ADMISSIONS INFORMATION

**Program Name:** Office of Disability Services
**Program Director:** Steve Simon
**Contact Person:** Judy Cantrell

**Telephone:** 937-775-5680

### ADMISSIONS

Open admission policy for in-state students. ACT/SAT are used for placement, not admission. Students with LD must meet the identical criteria as all applicants, and must be accepted prior to requesting. However, out-of-state students are encouraged to self-disclose their learning disability and submit documentation to the OSD prior to applying to the university if they would like to discuss eligibility for admission and services available on campus, and determine if Wright State is a good fit for them. The Director of Disability Services encourages students and their families to visit and interview. The Director does have the opportunity to provide some information to Admissions relating to students who may not have received any services in high school or who were identified late in high school or who were never identified as have learning disabilities. Students with a college prep curriculum in high school have been more successful at Wright State than those who took a general curriculum. The final decision rests with Admissions.

**College entrance exams required:** Yes
**Course entrance requirements:** Yes
**Diagnostic tests:** Yes
**Documentation:** WAIS-R; WRAT; W-J: within 3 years

**Untimed accepted:** Yes
**Interview required:** Yes

### ADDITIONAL INFORMATION

To determine eligibility for support services after admission, the following are required: results of psychological testing; a "Request for Support Services" form completed by the student; and a transcript of high school classes completed, as well as of any post-secondary courses taken. Students must write a 100-word handwritten, uncorrected statement about why they are requesting support services through the Learning Disabilities Program. Application for services for the LD Program is separate and not connected to the application to the university. Once enrolled, students may use a variety of services which will allow them to be equal and competitive in the classroom. Services available include: test proctoring, individual and group counseling, a Learning Disabilities Orientation, a club/support group, and a class entitled "Academic Coping Strategies for Students with Learning Disabilities." There are 30-40 tutors on staff. Interview and documentation are required.

**Special education HS coursework accepted:** N/I
**Special application required:** Yes
**# of applications submitted each year:** 150
**# of applications accepted each year:** All who are eligible
**# of students receiving LD services:** 285
**Acceptance into program means acceptance into college:** Students must be accepted to the university first and then request services.

**Essay required:** No
**Submitted to:** Program Director

# LEARNING DISABILITY SERVICES

**Learning center:** No
**Kurzweil personal reader:** Yes
**LD specialists:** Yes
**Allowed in exams:**
 **Calculator:** Yes
 **Dictionary:** Yes
 **Computer:** Yes
 **SpellCheck:** Yes

**Notetaker:** Yes
**Scribes:** Yes
**Proctors:** Yes
**Oral exams:** Yes
**Extended test time:** Yes
**Added cost:** As indicated above
**Distraction-free environ.:** Yes
**Tape recording in class:** Yes
**Books on tape:** Yes
**Taping of other books:** Yes

**Professional tutors:** No
**Peer tutors:** 100
**Max. hrs/wk for services:** 1 hr./ class/week no charge; $5.50 per hr. thereafter
**Priority registration:** No
**Accommodations for students with ADD:** Yes
**How are professors notified of LD:** By the student and the Program Director

# GENERAL ADMISSIONS INFORMATION

**Director of Admissions:** Ken Davenport

**Telephone:** 937-873-5700

## ENTRANCE REQUIREMENTS

Total high school units required/recommended: 16 total units are required; 4 English required, 3 math required, 3 science required, 2 foreign language required, and 3 social studies required. Minimum composite ACT score of 17 (combined SAT I score of 700), minimum 2.0 GPA, and college preparatory courses recommended of in-state applicants. Minimum composite ACT score of 20, minimum 2.5 GPA, and rank in top half of secondary school class recommended for out-of-state applicants. Special Requirements: TOEFL is required of all international students. Audition required of theater program applicants.

**Application deadline:** August 15
**Notification:** Rolling

**SAT or ACT preferred:** ACT
**SAT Avg:** 501V, 500M
**SAT II required:** Yes
**Average ACT:** 21
**Average GPA:** 2.9

**Graduated top 10% of class:** 11
**Graduated top 25% of class:** 30
**Graduated top 50% of class:** 62

# COLLEGE GRADUATION REQUIREMENTS

**Course waivers allowed:** No
**Course substitutions allowed:** Yes
**In what courses:** Substitutions are usually requested in Foreign Language or Math. Substitutions and not waivers are granted depending upon the nature and extent of the disability.

# ADDITIONAL INFORMATION

**Environment:** The university is located on 645 acres 8 miles northeast of Dayton.

**Student Body**
 **Undergrad enrollment:** 11,843
 **Women:** 53%
 **Men:** 47%
 **In-state students:** 97%
 **Out-of-state:** 3%

**Cost Information**
 **In-state tuition:** $3,600
 **Out-of-state:** $7,200
 **Room & board:** $4,180

**Housing Information**
 **University housing:** Yes
 **Fraternity:** No
 **Sorority:** No
 **Living on campus:** 15%

 **Athletics:** NCAA Div. I

# OKLAHOMA STATE UNIVERSITY

**OK**

104 Whitehurst Hall, Admissions Office, Stillwater, OK 74078 • **Admissions:** 405-744-6876
**Fax:** 405-744-5285 • **Email:** glr6458@okway.okstate.edu • **Web:** pio.okstate.edu
**Support:** S • **Institution:** 4 yr. Public

## LEARNING DISABILITY ADMISSIONS AND SERVICES

Oklahoma State University does not have a formal learning disabilities program, but uses a service-based model to assist the students in obtaining the necessary accommodations for specific learning disabilities. Students with learning disabilities may request priority enrollment and a campus orientation to assist in scheduling classes. Other services developed in coordination with the Special Education area work to minimize the students' difficulties in relation to coursework. These services could include test accommodations, course substitutions and independent study. The underlying philosophy of this program is to provide assistance to students to facilitate their academic progress. SDS also acts as a resource for faculty and staff.

## LEARNING DISABILITY ADMISSIONS INFORMATION

**Program Name:** Student Disability Services (SDS)
**Program Director:** Debra Swoboda
**Contact Person:** Same as above

**Telephone:** 405-744-7116

### ADMISSIONS

Although there is no special admissions policy for students with learning disabilities, a strong counselor recommendation could help a student who does not meet general admission requirements. In general, applicants with learning disabilities must meet the same specific requirements of the program in which they wish to enroll. Admitted students are encouraged to contact DSS to discuss special services or accommodations.

**College entrance exams required:** Yes          **Untimed accepted:** Yes
**Course entrance requirements:** Yes            **Interview required:** No
**Diagnostic tests:** Yes
**Documentation:** Certification of the learning disability

### ADDITIONAL INFORMATION

The purpose of alternative admissions is to provide a mechanism for students desiring to attend the university who may not qualify under the published criteria. These students must present their case as an exception and establish evidence of potential success. Five percent may be admitted on probation. The university also operates the Oklahoma City Technical Institute, which offers 2-year, career-oriented programs.

**Special education HS coursework accepted:** No      **Essay required:** No
**Special application required:** No                  **Submitted to:** N/A
**# of applications submitted each year:** N/A       **# of applications accepted each year:** N/A
**# of students receiving LD services:** 32
**Acceptance into program means acceptance into college:** Students must be admitted to the university first and then may request services.

# LEARNING DISABILITY SERVICES

**Learning center:** No
**Kurzweil personal reader:** Yes
**LD specialists:** No
**Allowed in exams:**
  **Calculator:** Yes
  **Dictionary:** Yes
  **Computer:** Yes
  **SpellCheck:** Yes

**Notetaker:** Yes
**Scribes:** Yes
**Proctors:** Yes
**Oral exams:** Yes
**Extended test time:** Yes
**Added cost:** None
**Distraction-free environ.:** Yes
**Tape recording in class:** Yes
**Books on tape:** Yes
**Taping of other books:** Yes

**Professional tutors:** No
**Peer tutors:** No
**Max. hrs/wk for services:** Unlimited
**Priority registration:** Yes
**Accommodations for students with ADD:** Yes
**How are professors notified of LD:** By the student and the Program Director

# GENERAL ADMISSIONS INFORMATION

**Director of Admissions:** Gordon Reese

**Telephone:** 405-744-6876

## ENTRANCE REQUIREMENTS

Total high school units required/recommended: 11 total units are required; 4 English required, 3 math required, 2 science required, 2 foreign languages, and 2 history required. Minimum composite ACT score of 21 (combined SAT I score of 990) or rank in top third of secondary school class and minimum 3.0 GPA required. Special Requirements: TOEFL is required of all international students.

**Application deadline:** August 18
**Notification:** Rolling

**SAT or ACT preferred:** ACT
**SAT Avg:** 560V, 568M
**Average ACT:** 24
**Average GPA:** 3.5

**Graduated top 10% of class:** 30
**Graduated top 25% of class:** 60
**Graduated top 50% of class:** 89

# COLLEGE GRADUATION REQUIREMENTS

**Course waivers allowed:** Yes
**Course substitutions allowed:** Yes
**In what courses:** In math and foreign language

# ADDITIONAL INFORMATION

**Environment:** This 415-acre campus is located in a small city 65 miles north of Oklahoma City.

**Student Body**
  **Undergrad enrollment:** 14,124
  **Women:** 46%
  **Men:** 54%
  **In-state students:** 93%
  **Out-of-state:** 7%

**Cost Information**
  **In-state tuition:** $2,148
  **Out-of-state:** $5,838
  **Room & board:** $3,988

**Housing Information**
  **University housing:** Yes
  **Fraternity:** Yes
  **Sorority:** Yes
  **Living on campus:** 23%

  **Athletics:** NCAA Div. I

# UNIVERSITY OF OKLAHOMA

**OK**

1000 Asp Avenue, Norman, OK 73019 • **Admissions:** 405-325-2251 • **Fax:** 405-325-7124
**Email:** admissions@ou.edu • **Web:** www.ou.edu
**Support:** S • **Institution:** 4 yr. Public

## LEARNING DISABILITY ADMISSIONS AND SERVICES

The Office of Disabled Student Services provides support services and is committed to the goal of achieving equal educational opportunity and full participation for students with disabilities. In many cases, these services are developed in response to expressed student needs. There are no special LD or remedial classes. Students are encouraged to be self-advocates in making requests for reasonable academic accommodations. Assistance is to be used to support the accomplishment of educational goals. The coordinator of services sponsors the OU Association for Disabled Students, a student organization that provides a recognized forum for support, regular meetings and social and recreational activities. Students must provide psychoeducational evaluations documenting learning disabilities in order to receive services. The evaluation should include full-scale, performance, and verbal IQ scores; scores from aptitude-achievement comparisons; and a summary and recommendations.

## LEARNING DISABILITY ADMISSIONS INFORMATION

**Program Name:** Disabled Student Services
**Program Director:** Suzette Dyer (Coordinator)
**Contact Person:** Same as above

**Telephone:** 405-325-3163

### ADMISSIONS

Admission requirements for students with learning disabilities are the same as for all other students. The university accepts ACT/SAT scores given under special conditions. Students should submit the general application form and letters of recommendation, and may request a personal interview. Course requirements include 4 yrs. English, 3 yrs. science, 3 yrs. math, and 2 yrs. social studies. ACT score required is 22+ and/or SAT scores required are 1030+. The expected GPA is a 3.0.

**College entrance exams required:** Yes
**Course entrance requirements:** Yes
**Diagnostic tests:** Yes
**Documentation:** WAIS-R; WJ-R: within 3 years preferred

**Untimed accepted:** Yes
**Interview required:** No

### ADDITIONAL INFORMATION

After receiving academic advisement from the college, the student should make an appointment with Disabled Student Services. The Office will also provide a personal campus orientation upon request. Services offered, based on individual needs, include: alternative testing, readers, scribes, notetakers (who are volunteers), tutors, tape-recorded texts and library assistance. Tutoring is provided on a one-to-one basis by peer tutors. Services are available for undergraduate and graduate students.

**Special education HS coursework accepted:** Yes
**Special application required:** No
**# of applications submitted each year:** N/A
**# of students receiving LD services:** 70
**Acceptance into program means acceptance into college:** Students must be admitted to the university first and then may request services.

**Essay required:** No
**Submitted to:** N/I
**# of applications accepted each year:** N/A

## LEARNING DISABILITY SERVICES

**Learning center:** No
**Kurzweil personal reader:** Yes
**LD specialists:** No
**Allowed in exams:**
  **Calculator:** Yes
  **Dictionary:** Yes
  **Computer:** Yes
  **SpellCheck:** Yes

**Notetaker:** Yes
**Scribes:** Yes
**Proctors:** Yes
**Oral exams:** Yes
**Extended test time:** Yes
**Added cost:** None
**Distraction-free environ.:** Yes
**Tape recording in class:** Yes
**Books on tape:** Yes
**Taping of other books:** Yes

**Professional tutors:** Yes
**Peer tutors:** No
**Max. hrs/wk for services:** As needed
**Priority registration:** Yes
**Accommodations for students with ADD:** Yes
**How are professors notified of LD:** By the student or the Program Director

## GENERAL ADMISSIONS INFORMATION

**Director of Admissions:** Marc Borish

**Telephone:** 405-325-2251

### ENTRANCE REQUIREMENTS

Total high school units required/recommended: 15 total units are required; 4 English required, 3 math required, 2 science required, 2 social studies required, and 2 history required. Minimum combined SAT I score of 1030 (composite ACT score of 22) or rank in top third of secondary school class and minimum 3.0 GPA required. Special Requirements: A portfolio is required for art program applicants. An audition is required for music program applicants. TOEFL is required of all international students.

**Application deadline:** July 15
**Notification:** Rolling

**SAT or ACT preferred:** Either
**SAT II required:** Yes
**Average ACT:** 24
**Average GPA:** 3.5

**Graduated top 10% of class:** 31
**Graduated top 25% of class:** 60
**Graduated top 50% of class:** 87

## COLLEGE GRADUATION REQUIREMENTS

**Course waivers allowed:** No
**Course substitutions allowed:** Yes
**In what courses:** Students may petition for a substitution in foreign language

## ADDITIONAL INFORMATION

**Environment:** The 3,107-acre campus is located in a suburb 17 miles south of Oklahoma City.

**Student Body**
  **Undergrad enrollment:** 13,250
  **Women:** 46%
  **Men:** 54%
  **In-state students:** 85%
  **Out-of-state:** 15%

**Cost Information**
  **In-state tuition:** $2,178
  **Out-of-state:** $5,868
  **Room & board:** $3,904

**Housing Information**
  **University housing:** Yes
  **Fraternity:** Yes
  **Sorority:** Yes
  **Living on campus:** 19%

  **Athletics:** NCAA Div. I

# UNIVERSITY OF TULSA

**OK**

600 South College Avenue, Tulsa, OK 74104 • **Admissions:** 918-631-2307
**Email:** admission@utulsa.edu • **Web:** www.utulsa.edu
**Support:** CS • **Institution:** 4 yr. Private

## LEARNING DISABILITY ADMISSIONS AND SERVICES

The policy of the University of Tulsa, in keeping with the Americans with Disabilities Act, is to provide reasonable accommodations for students with disabilities, including students with learning disabilities. Students who have specific disabilities which might impact their full access and participation in university programs are urged to provide the relevant documentation and make an appointment with the Coordinator of the Center for Student Academic Support. The Center for Student Academic Support is committed to helping students succeed academically and believes in providing each student with the most appropriate range of resources necessary for his/her progress. Ability and access services have been established to ensure that every reasonable effort is made to provide equal educational access to students with permanent or temporary disabilities.

## LEARNING DISABILITY ADMISSIONS INFORMATION

**Program Name:** Center for Student Academic Support
**Program Director:** Dr. Jane Owens
**Contact Person:** Same as above

**Telephone:** 918-631-2334

### ADMISSIONS

The student with learning disabilities needs to complete the application form and intake sheet. Also required is documentation presented from a doctor stating diagnostic material and diagnosis of the disorder. General admission requirements include: 4 yrs. English, 3 yrs. math, 4 yrs. science, and 2 yrs. foreign language. No course substitutions are allowed. The average ACT is above a 21 and for the SAT 1080-1140. Students applying to the Nursing or Athletic Training programs must submit a special application.

**College entrance exams required:** Yes
**Course entrance requirements:** Yes
**Diagnostic tests:** Yes
**Documentation:** Those appropriate for the disability: within the academic year

**Untimed accepted:** Yes
**Interview required:** Yes

### ADDITIONAL INFORMATION

Accommodations students might qualify for depending upon their documentation and needs include: extended time on tests; priority registration; testing in self-contained environment; use of spelling aids on written exams; texts on tape; notetakers; preferential seating; tests given orally; and enlarged print tests. Concerns regarding requests for a referral for evaluation of a learning disability should be directed to the Coordinator of the Center for Student Academic Support.

**Special education HS coursework accepted:** Yes
**Special application required:** Yes
**# of applications submitted each year:** N/I
**# of students receiving LD services:** 25
**Acceptance into program means acceptance into college:** Students must be admitted to the university and then may request services.

**Essay required:** Yes
**Submitted to:** Center for Student Academic Support
**# of applications accepted each year:** N/I

# LEARNING DISABILITY SERVICES

**Learning center:** Yes
**Kurzweil personal reader:** Yes
**LD specialists:** Varies
**Allowed in exams:**
  **Calculator:** Y/N
  **Dictionary:** Y/N
  **Computer:** No
  **SpellCheck:** No

**Notetaker:** Yes
**Scribes:** Yes
**Proctors:** Yes
**Oral exams:** Yes
**Extended test time:** Yes
**Added cost:** $3.00 per hr. fee for peer tutoring
**Distraction-free environ.:** Yes
**Tape recording in class:** Yes
**Books on tape:** Yes
**Taping of other books:** Yes

**Professional tutors:** N/I
**Peer tutors:** Yes
**Max. hrs/wk for services:** Unlimited
**Priority registration:** Yes
**Accommodations for students with ADD:** Yes
**How are professors notified of LD:** By both the student and the Program Director

# GENERAL ADMISSIONS INFORMATION

**Director of Admissions:** John Corso        **Telephone:** 918-631-2633

## ENTRANCE REQUIREMENTS

Total high school units required/recommended: 15 total units are recommended; 4 English recommended, 3 math recommended, 3 science recommended, 2 foreign languages, and 3 social studies recommended. Special requirements: 4 units of math required of engineering and physical sciences program applicants. Audition required of music and theatre scholarship applicants. Portfolio required of art scholarship applicants.

**Application deadline:** Rolling
**Notification:** Rolling

**SAT or ACT preferred:** Either
**SAT Avg:** 598V, 584M
**Average ACT:** 24
**Average GPA:** 3.6

**Graduated top 10% of class:** 34
**Graduated top 25% of class:** 64
**Graduated top 50% of class:** 91

# COLLEGE GRADUATION REQUIREMENTS

**Course waivers allowed:** No
**Course substitutions allowed:** Yes
**In what courses:** Foreign language and math, depending on documentation, strengths and weaknesses, and whether the course is a fundamental part of major. Final decision made by committee.

# ADDITIONAL INFORMATION

**Environment:** NR

**Student Body**
  **Undergrad enrollment:** 2,945
  **Women:** 54%
  **Men:** 46%
  **In-state students:** 55%
  **Out-of-state:** 45%

**Cost Information**
  **In-state tuition:** $12,850
  **Out-of-state:** $12,850
  **Room & board:** $4,252

**Housing Information**
  **University housing:** Yes
  **Fraternity:** Yes
  **Sorority:** Yes
  **Living on campus:** 60%

  **Athletics:** NCAA Div. I

# OR OREGON STATE UNIVERSITY

Corvallis, OR 97331 • **Admissions:** 503-737-4411
**Email:** osuadmit@ccmail.orst.edu • **Web:** www.orst.edu
**Support:** S • **Institution:** 4 yr. Public

## LEARNING DISABILITY ADMISSIONS AND SERVICES

OSU is committed to providing equal opportunity for higher education to academically qualified students without regard to a disability. Services for Students with Disabilities (SSD) strives to be sensitive to the individual needs of students by offering a variety of services. Services rendered are dependent on the type of learning disability. Services are provided to ensure an equal opportunity to succeed but do not guarantee success. Self-advocacy and independence are promoted. SSD is available for all students who need extra services. The Educational Opportunities Program (EOP) offers students who are learning-disabled, economically disadvantaged, or first-generation college-bound a variety of remedial courses for credit. EOP tries to provide tutoring for any undergraduate class if tutors are available. To be recognized as a person with a learning disability, students are required to submit documentation from a qualified educational evaluator. Preferred diagnostic testing would include at least one test in each of the following categories: cognitive, achievement, and processing. Other documentation specifying a learning disability without testing in the three categories mentioned must include an in-depth valid assessment of the disability by a qualified professional.

## LEARNING DISABILITY ADMISSIONS INFORMATION

**Program Name:** Services for Students with Disabilities (SSD)
**Program Director:** Tracy Bentley-Townlin      **Telephone:** 541-737-3661
**Contact Person:** Same as above

### ADMISSIONS

All students must submit the general application for admission. If a student does not meet admissions requirements, the student will be denied. Enclosed with the notification, the student will receive information regarding petitioning for special admission. Students who want to petition their admission into OSU on the basis of a learning disability must submit all information required in the petition. The Director of SSD helps to make admission decisions and may recommend EOP for the student with LD. Regular admission requires a 3.0 GPA and special admit a 2.5. Students requesting services should self identify; submit documentation of their LD, including educational history and diagnostic testing administered by professionals, and include information describing cognitive strengths and weaknesses, recommendations for accommodations or services, and any other additional information in the form of a family history. Students must also submit a handwritten 1-2 page statement outlining educational goals and explaining motivation to succeed at OSU.

**College entrance exams required:** Yes       **Untimed accepted:** Yes
**Course entrance requirements:** Yes          **Interview required:** No
**Diagnostic tests:** Yes
**Documentation:** IQ;  Achievement tests; Processing tests: within 3 years

### ADDITIONAL INFORMATION

Students with LD, whether admitted regularly or as special admits are encouraged to apply for additional assistance from the Educational Opportunities Program's Special Services Project, which can provide special counseling, tutoring, and intensive practice in study skills. Accommodations in instruction and related academic work may include alternative test methods such as extended testing time, use of resources such as calculators and dictionaries, and the waiver and/or substitution of appropriate core course requirements. Accommodations are negotiated with instructors, academic departments, and the college as appropriate. Personal counseling is available through the Counseling Center and SSD. EOP will review documentation and will provide extra help in selecting programs, including placement in study skills classes, and English and math classes with fewer students enrolled. There is also a course for students with LD to get assistance with notetaking. The Director acts as a liaison between student and faculty.

**Special education HS coursework accepted:** No      **Essay required:** Yes (should note learning disability)
**Special application required:** Yes                 **Submitted to:** Program Director
**# of applications submitted each year:** N/I         **# of applications accepted each year:** 15
**# of students receiving LD services:** 150
**Acceptance into program means acceptance into college:** Students must be admitted to the university first and then may request services.

# LEARNING DISABILITY SERVICES

**Learning center:** No
**Kurzweil personal reader:** Yes
**LD specialists:** No
**Allowed in exams:**
  **Calculator:** Y/N
  **Dictionary:** Y/N
  **Computer:** Y/N
  **SpellCheck:** Y/N

**Notetaker:** Yes
**Scribes:** Yes
**Proctors:** Yes
**Oral exams:** Y/N
**Extended test time:** Yes
**Added cost:** None
**Distraction-free environ.:** Yes
**Tape recording in class:** Yes
**Books on tape:** Yes
**Taping of other books:** No

**Professional tutors:** No
**Peer tutors:** Yes
**Max. hrs/wk for services:** Offered through EOP for all students, as available
**Priority registration:** Yes
**Accommodations for students with ADD:** Yes
**How are professors notified of LD:** By the student and the Program Director, depending on services

# GENERAL ADMISSIONS INFORMATION

**Director of Admissions:** Kay Conrad

**Telephone:** 541-737-0582

## ENTRANCE REQUIREMENTS

Total high school units required/recommended: 14 total units are required; 4 English required, 3 math required, 2 science required, 2 social studies required, and 1 history required. Minimum 3.0 GPA in all subjects or GPA and satisfactory ACT or SAT I scores required.

**Application deadline:** March 1
**Notification:** Rolling

**SAT or ACT preferred:** Either

# COLLEGE GRADUATION REQUIREMENTS

**Course waivers allowed:** Yes
**Course substitutions allowed:** Yes
**In what courses:** On a case-by-case basis and also dependent on the major selected

# ADDITIONAL INFORMATION

**Environment:** The university is located on 530 acres in a small town 85 miles south of Portland.

**Student Body**
  **Undergrad enrollment:** 11,430
  **Women:** 43%
  **Men:** 57%
  **In-state students:** 85%
  **Out-of-state:** 15%

**Cost Information**
  **In-state tuition:** $3,432
  **Out-of-state:** $10,420
  **Room & board:** $4,587

**Housing Information**
  **University housing:** Yes
  **Fraternity:** Yes
  **Sorority:** Yes
  **Living on campus:** 34%

  **Athletics:** NCAA Div. I

# UNIVERSITY OF OREGON

1217 University of Oregon, Eugene, OR 97403 • **Admissions:** 541-346-3201 • **Fax:** 541-346-2537
**Email:** fdyke@oregon.uoregon.edu • **Web:** www.uoregon.edu
**Support:** S • **Institution:** 4 yr. Public

## LEARNING DISABILITY ADMISSIONS AND SERVICES

The University of Oregon does not have a formalized program for students with learning disabilities, but there are several support offices offering services. Disability Services coordinates services and provides advocacy and support to students with documented learning disabilities. Eligibility for services must be supported by professional documentation of disability and need for services. Accommodations are determined on a case-by-case basis. Students who feel they are eligible for services should meet with the Counselor for Students with Disabilities. At this meeting students will be able to discuss the documentation process, services available, and their educational goals. Disability Services will work with students and faculty members to best accommodate needs. A general letter explaining the particular disability and suggested accommodations will be written, by request, to share with faculty at the students' discretion. This letter is reissued each academic term to designated instructors. Students with learning disabilities should be motivated, hard-working, and willing to take responsibility for meeting their educational goals.

## LEARNING DISABILITY ADMISSIONS INFORMATION

**Program Name:** Disability Services
**Program Director:** Hilary Gerdes, Ph.D.
**Contact Person:** Same as above

**Telephone:** 541-346-3211

### ADMISSIONS

Students with learning disabilities must meet the same admission criteria as all other applicants. Courses recommended for admission include: 4 yrs. English, 3 yrs. math, 2 yrs. science, 2 yrs. foreign language, 3 yrs. social studies, and 2 yrs. electives. The average SAT is 1140, and the average GPA is 3.3. Students not meeting the regular admission requirements who have extenuating circumstances due to a learning disability, may request additional consideration of their application by a special committee. A completed application form, a writing sample, two letters of recommendation, and documentation of the disability with information about how it has influenced the students' ability to meet minimum admission requirements are required for special admission consideration based on disability.

**College entrance exams required:** Yes
**Course entrance requirements:** Yes
**Diagnostic tests:** Yes
**Documentation:** WAIS-R; W-J: within 3 years

**Untimed accepted:** Yes
**Interview required:** No

### ADDITIONAL INFORMATION

Students are encouraged to take an active role in utilizing the services. Once admitted, students should meet with the counselor to discuss educational goals. Documentation will be put on file. Services available include: notetakers; books on tape; modification of testing procedures, including additional testing time, audiotaped answers, having someone write dictated answers, large print, or taking the exam in a quiet location; Adaptive Technology Lab; and faculty liaison to assist in communicating needs to instructors, and to help negotiate reasonable accommodations in courses and programs. The Office of Academic Advising provides counseling and assessment of progress toward graduation. There is a support group for "unique learners." The university requires 2 writing classes for graduation. In addition, the B.S degree requires 1 year of college math or 2 years of foreign language for a B.A degree. Writing and math labs are available.

**Special education HS coursework accepted:** Yes, but evaluated case-by-case
**Essay required:** No
**Special application required:** No
**# of applications submitted each year:** N/A
**# of students receiving LD services:** 300+

**Submitted to:** N/A
**# of applications accepted each year:** N/A

**Acceptance into program means acceptance into college:** Students must be admitted to the university first and then may request LD services.

**Learning center:** No
**Kurzweil personal reader:** Yes
**LD specialists:** No
**Allowed in exams:**
  **Calculator:** Yes
  **Dictionary:** Yes
  **Computer:** Yes
  **SpellCheck:** Yes

**Notetaker:** Yes
**Scribes:** Yes
**Proctors:** Yes
**Oral exams:** Yes
**Extended test time:** Yes
**Added cost:** $5-$8 per hour
**Distraction-free environ.:** Yes
**Tape recording in class:** Yes
**Books on tape:** Yes
**Taping of other books:** Yes

**Professional tutors:** Yes
**Peer tutors:** Yes
**Max. hrs/wk for services:** Varies
**Priority registration:** Yes
**Accommodations for students with ADD:** Yes
**How are professors notified of LD:** By the student and the Program Director

## GENERAL ADMISSIONS INFORMATION

**Director of Admissions:** Martha Pitts

**Telephone:** 541-346-3201

### ENTRANCE REQUIREMENTS

Total high school units required/recommended: 14 total units are required; 4 English required, 3 math required, 2 science required, 2 foreign language required, and 3 social studies required. Minimum 3.0 GPA required. Special requirements: A portfolio is required for art program applicants. An audition is required for music program applicants. Portfolio required of architecture program applicants.

**Application deadline:** March 1
**Notification:** Rolling

**SAT or ACT preferred:** Either
**SAT Avg:** 550V, 550M
**SAT II required:** Yes
**Average GPA:** 3.3

## COLLEGE GRADUATION REQUIREMENTS

**Course waivers allowed:** No
**Course substitutions allowed:** Yes
**In what courses:** In extreme cases only with appropriate documentation.

## ADDITIONAL INFORMATION

**Environment:** The university is located on 250 acres in an urban area of Eugene.

**Student Body**
  **Undergrad enrollment:** 13,874
  **Women:** 52%
  **Men:** 48%
  **In-state students:** 60%
  **Out-of-state:** 40%

**Cost Information**
  **In-state tuition:** $3,646
  **Out-of-state:** $12,014
  **Room & board:** $4,646

**Housing Information**
  **University housing:** Yes
  **Fraternity:** Yes
  **Sorority:** Yes
  **Living on campus:** 19%

  **Athletics:** NCAA Div. I

# WESTERN OREGON UNIVERSITY

**OR**

345 North Monmouth Avenue, Monmouth, OR 97361 • **Admissions**: 503-838-8211
**Fax**: 503-838-8289 • **Email**: wolfgram@fsa.wosc.osshe.edu • **Web**: www.wosc.osshe.edu
**Support**: S • **Institution**: 4 yr. Public

## LEARNING DISABILITY ADMISSIONS AND SERVICES

The mission of the Office of Disability Services is to remove barriers to learning for students with disabilities, and to help ensure that these students access the tools and processes they need to create a successful experience at Western and beyond. These goals are realized by providing support services and information to help students develop skills such as self-advocacy, independence, identification and use of resources, appropriate use of problem-solving techniques and accepting responsibility for one's actions. The ODS strives to meet the individual needs of students with disabilities. The College Enrichment Program (CEP) is designed to help students find success in college. The program's goals are to help CEP students: develop writing, math, learning and critical thinking skills; maintain the necessary GPA to achieve individual goals; develop interpersonal communication skills; and achieve autonomy and maintain a sense of self-worth. Students who could benefit from CEP are those who enter college without being completely prepared. CEP staff focus on working with individual needs. Eligibility is based on federal guidelines determined by 1) first-generation college-bound; 2) financial need; or 3) physical or learning disability; additionally, the student must have demonstrated academic need for the program.

## LEARNING DISABILITY ADMISSIONS INFORMATION

**Program Name:** Office of Disability Services
**Program Director:** Martha Smith
**Contact Person:** Same as above

**Telephone:** 503-838-8250

### ADMISSIONS

There are no special admissions criteria. General admission requires a 2.75 GPA and ACT/SAT scores which are used only as alternatives to the required GPA. Course requirements include 4 yrs. English, 3 yrs. math, 2 yrs. science, 3 yrs. social science, and 2 yrs. of the same foreign language. Alternatives to course requirements require either a score of 470 or above on 3 SAT II Subject Tests. A limited number of students who do not meet the regular admission requirements, alternatives, or exceptions may be admitted through special action of an admissions committee. These students must submit by January 1 for 1st session and May 1 for the 2nd session, a personal letter of petition stating why they don't meet the admission requirements and what they are doing to make up deficiencies, and three letters of recommendation from school and community members.

**College entrance exams required:** Yes
**Course entrance requirements:** Yes
**Diagnostic tests:** Yes
**Documentation:** More than one test showing specific disabilities; within 3 years.

**Untimed accepted:** Yes
No

### ADDITIONAL INFORMATION

Skills classes are offered in academic survival strategies (no credit) and critical thinking (college credit). Other services include: advocacy; computer stations; notetakers; readers and taping services; alternative testing; advisement; advocacy; and assistance with registration. CEP offers counseling; basic math courses; advising; individualized instruction in reading, study skills, writing and critical thinking; monitor programs; and workshops on study skills, research writing, math anxiety, rapid reading, notetaking, and time management. Services and accommodations are available for undergraduate and graduate students.

**Special education HS coursework accepted:** No
**Special application required:** Yes
**# of applications submitted each year:** N/A
**# of students receiving LD services:** 45

**Essay required:** No
**Submitted to:** Program Director
**# of applications accepted each year:** N/A

**Acceptance into program means acceptance into college:** Students must be admitted to the college first and then may request services.

# LEARNING DISABILITY SERVICES

**Learning center:** No
**Kurzweil personal reader:** No
**LD specialists:** No
**Allowed in exams:**
  **Calculator:** Yes
  **Dictionary:** Yes
  **Computer:** Yes
  **SpellCheck:** Yes

**Notetaker:** Yes
**Scribes:** Yes
**Proctors:** Yes
**Oral exams:** Yes
**Extended test time:** Yes
**Added cost:** None
**Distraction-free environ.:** Yes
**Tape recording in class:** Yes
**Books on tape:** Yes
**Taping of other books:** Yes

**Professional tutors:** No
**Peer tutors:** Yes
**Max. hrs/wk for services:** N/A
**Priority registration:** No
**Accommodations for students with ADD:** Yes
**How are professors notified of LD:** By the student and the Program Director

# GENERAL ADMISSIONS INFORMATION

**Director of Admissions:** Allison Marshall

**Telephone:** 503-838-8211

## ENTRANCE REQUIREMENTS
Total high school units required/recommended: 4 English required, 3 math required, 2 science required, 3 social studies, 2 of other college prep courses.

**Application deadline:** 4/15
**Notification:** NR

**SAT or ACT preferred:** NR

# COLLEGE GRADUATION REQUIREMENTS

**Course waivers allowed:** No
**Course substitutions allowed:** Yes
**In what courses:** The decision is made on a case-by-case basis; there are no standard substitute classes

# ADDITIONAL INFORMATION

**Environment:** Western Oregon State College is located on 134 acres in a rural area 15 miles west of Salem.

**Student Body**
  **Undergrad enrollment:** 3,908
  **Women:** 58%
  **Men:** 42%
  **In-state students:** 90%
  **Out-of-state:** 10%

**Cost Information**
  **In-state tuition:** $2,985
  **Out-of-state:** $8,475

**Housing Information**
  **University housing:** Yes
  **Fraternity:** No
  **Sorority:** No
  **Living on campus:** 30%

  **Athletics:** Intramural

# PA
# CLARION UNIVERSITY OF PENNSYLVANIA

Clarion, PA 16214 • **Admissions:** 814-226-2306 • **Fax:** 814-226-2039
**Web:** www.clarion.edu
**Support:** CS • **Institution:** 4 Yr. Public

## LEARNING DISABILITY ADMISSIONS AND SERVICES

Clarion does not have a "special admissions" policy for students with learning disabilities, nor does it offer a structured "LD Program." The Student Support Services Program works to ensure educational parity for students with learning disabilities within a mainstream setting. Academic accommodations and support focuses on minimizing the effects of the disability. The Special Services Program is the university's primary vehicle for providing a Tutoring Center and Academic Support Center, which are available to all students but are especially beneficial for students with learning disabilities. These services are free of charge and include extensive peer tutoring, study skills workshops and individual "learning to learn" activities.

## LEARNING DISABILITY ADMISSIONS INFORMATION

**Program Name:** Special Services Program
**Program Director:** Gregory K. Clary
**Contact Person:** Same as above

**Telephone:** 814-226-2347

### ADMISSIONS

Students with learning disabilities who wish to be admitted to the university must meet regular admission requirements. As part of the application process, students are encouraged to provide documentation of their learning disability in order to establish a clear need for individualized support services. Students should also include a copy of their Individualized Educational Plan from high school. Students not meeting the general admission criteria may be admitted by either the Academic Support Acceptance (these students are referred to Special Services) or Summer Start (probationary admittance).

**College entrance exams required:** Yes
**Course entrance requirements:** Yes
**Diagnostic tests:** Yes
**Documentation:** WAIS-R; W-J: within 3 years

**Untimed accepted:** Yes
**Interview required:** Recommended

### ADDITIONAL INFORMATION

The staff in Student Support Services serve as liaisons between students and faculty to provide special considerations when appropriate. The program also provides academic advising, diagnostic testing, tutoring, special topic seminars, and reading/study skills workshops. Services and accommodations are available to undergraduate and graduate students.

**Special education HS coursework accepted:** Yes
**Special application required:** No
**# of applications submitted each year:** N/A
**# of students receiving LD services:** 60

**Essay required:** Yes
**Submitted to:** N/A
**# of applications accepted each year:** N/A

**Acceptance into program means acceptance into college:** Students must be accepted to the university first and then may request services.

# LEARNING DISABILITY SERVICES

Learning center: No
Kurzweil personal reader: Yes
LD specialists: 1
Allowed in exams:
  Calculator: Y/N
  Dictionary: Y/N
  Computer: Y/N
  SpellCheck: Y/N

Notetaker: No
Scribes: Yes
Proctors: Yes
Oral exams: Yes
Extended test time: Yes
Added cost: None
Distraction-free environ.: Yes
Tape recording in class: Yes
Books on tape: Yes
Taping of other books: No

Professional tutors: No
Peer tutors: 20
Max. hrs/wk for services: 1 hour per week/per course
Priority registration: Yes
Accommodations for students with ADD: Yes
How are professors notified of LD: By the student and the Program Director

# GENERAL ADMISSIONS INFORMATION

Director of Admissions: John S. Shropshire        Telephone: 814-226-2306

## ENTRANCE REQUIREMENTS

Total high school units required/recommended: 16 total units are required; 4 English required, 2 math required, 4 math recommended, 2 science required, 4 science recommended, and 4 social studies required. Special requirements: A portfolio is required for art program applicants. An audition is required for music program applicants. 1 unit of chemistry and 1 unit of algebra or higher math, taken within five years of secondary school graduation, required of nursing program applicants. NLN pre-entrance test also required of nursing program applicants.

Application deadline: Rolling
Notification: Rolling

SAT or ACT preferred: Either
SAT Avg: 408V, 445M

Graduated top 10% of class: 8
Graduated top 25% of class: 34
Graduated top 50% of class: 71

# COLLEGE GRADUATION REQUIREMENTS

Course waivers allowed: Yes
Course substitutions allowed: Yes
In what courses: Determined case-by-case

# ADDITIONAL INFORMATION

Environment: The university is located on 100 acres in a small town 85 miles northeast of Pittsburgh.

Student Body
  Undergrad enrollment: 5,249
  Women: 60%
  Men: 40%
  In-state students: 92%
  Out-of-state: 8%

Cost Information
  In-state tuition: $3,362
  Out-of-state: $8,566
  Room & board: $3,160

Housing Information
  University housing: Yes
  Fraternity: No
  Sorority: No
  Living on campus: 35%

  Athletics: NCAA Div. II

PA

# COLLEGE MISERICORDIA

301 Lake Street, Dallas, PA 18612 • **Admissions:** 717-675-4449 • **Fax:** 717-675-2441
**Email:** admiss@miseri.edu • **Web:** www.miseri.edu
**Support:** SP • **Institution:** 4 yr. Private

## LEARNING DISABILITY ADMISSIONS AND SERVICES

All students who participate in the Alternate Learners Project (ALP) are enrolled in regular college classes. In most cases, they take a carefully selected, reduced credit load each semester. Students who participate in ALP are supported by an assortment of services delivered by a specially trained full-time staff. Services include "Learning Strategies," which are designed to make students more efficient, and accommodations designed to work around students' disabilities whenever possible. Upon entry each student develops an Individual Education Plan and signs a contract agreeing to weekly meetings with mentors. The ultimate goal of ALP is to help students with learning disabilities succeed in college.

## LEARNING DISABILITY ADMISSIONS INFORMATION

**Program Name:** Alternative Learners Project (ALP)
**Program Director:** Dr. Joseph Rogan          **Telephone:** 717-674-6347
**Contact Person:** Same as above

### ADMISSIONS

College Misericordia's experience with students with learning disabilities is that students who are highly motivated and socially mature have an excellent chance to be successful. Each applicant has to secure a standard admissions form, enclose a written cover letter summarizing the learning disability and indicate a desire to participate in the ALP. Additionally, a copy of the psychological report should be submitted along with the high school transcript and 3 letters of recommendation (one must be written by a special education professional). Class rank is usually above top 60%. ACT/SAT are required but not used in any way for LD admissions. Students and their parents will be invited to interviews. This interview is very important. The admission decision is made jointly by the Program Director and the Director of Admissions.

**College entrance exams required:** Yes          **Untimed accepted:** Yes
**Course entrance requirements:** Yes          **Interview required:** Yes
**Diagnostic tests:** Yes
**Documentation:** Recent psychological including WAIS-R: within 18 months

### ADDITIONAL INFORMATION

All students served by ALP are asked to attend a summer program ($1,600) to learn strategies, understand needed accommodations, and learn about the college. The college, not ALP, offers several skills courses (non-credited) in basic areas such as reading, writing and math. Services and accommodations are available for undergraduate and graduate students. College Misericordia offers a summer program for high school students with learning disabilities.

**Special education HS coursework accepted:** No          **Essay required:** Yes
**Special application required:** No          **Submitted to:** N/A
**# of applications submitted each year:** 150          **# of applications accepted each year:** 24
**# of students receiving LD services:** 51
**Acceptance into program means acceptance into college:** There is a joint acceptance between ALP and the Office of Admissions.

## LEARNING DISABILITY SERVICES

**Learning center:** Yes
**Kurzweil personal reader:** Yes
**LD specialists:** 5
**Allowed in exams:**
  **Calculator:** Yes
  **Dictionary:** Yes
  **Computer:** Yes
  **SpellCheck:** Yes

**Notetaker:** Yes
**Scribes:** Yes
**Proctors:** Yes
**Oral exams:** Yes
**Extended test time:** Yes
**Added cost:** None
**Distraction-free environ.:** Yes
**Tape recording in class:** Yes
**Books on tape:** Yes
**Taping of other books:** N/I

**Professional tutors:** 3
**Peer tutors:** Yes
**Max. hrs/wk for services:**
Unlimited
**Priority registration:** Yes
**Accommodations for students with ADD:** No
**How are professors notified of LD:** By the Program Director

## GENERAL ADMISSIONS INFORMATION

**Director of Admissions:** Jane Deesoye          **Telephone:** 717-674-6460

### ENTRANCE REQUIREMENTS

High school units required/recommended: 4 English recommended, 4 math recommended, 4 science recommended, 4 social studies recommended, and 4 history recommended. Special requirements: TOEFL is required of all international students. Chemistry or biology recommended of nursing program applicants. Chemistry recommended of occupational therapy program applicants. Biology and physics recommended of radiologic technology program applicants. Chemistry, biology, and trigonometry recommended of pre-medicine program applicants.

**Application deadline:** Rolling
**Notification:** Rolling

**SAT or ACT preferred:** SAT
**SAT Avg:** 510V, 500M
**SAT II required:** Yes
**Average ACT:** 23
**Average GPA:** 3

**Graduated top 10% of class:** 26
**Graduated top 25% of class:** 54
**Graduated top 50% of class:** 70

## COLLEGE GRADUATION REQUIREMENTS

**Course waivers allowed:** Yes
**Course substitutions allowed:** Yes
**In what courses:** Non-essential areas. If a course is "essential" it is not waived or substituted

## ADDITIONAL INFORMATION

**Environment:** The college is located on a 100-acre campus in a suburban small town 9 miles south of Wilkes-Barre.

**Student Body**
  **Undergrad enrollment:** 1,590
  **Women:** 75%
  **Men:** 25%
  **In-state students:** 80%
  **Out-of-state:** 20%

**Cost Information**
  **In-state tuition:** $13,120
  **Out-of-state:** $13,120
  **Room & board:** $6,150

**Housing Information**
  **University housing:** Yes
  **Fraternity:** Yes
  **Sorority:** Yes
  **Living on campus:** 53%

  **Athletics:** NAIA

# DREXEL UNIVERSITY

3141 Chestnut Street, Philadelphia, PA 19104 • **Admissions:** 215-895-2000 • **Fax:** 215-895-1508
**Email:** admunder@post.drexel.edu • **Web:** www.drexel.edu
**Support:** CS • **Institution:** 4 yr. Private

## LEARNING DISABILITY ADMISSIONS AND SERVICES

Drexel does not have a learning disability program, but services are provided through the Office of Disability Services. ODS helps students achieve their personal and educational goals through assistance from the staff. Programs are designed to develop academic and life skills, increase cultural awareness, contribute to career planning and development, and lend the support necessary to complete a college degree. The program offers two four-week residential summer programs, which are designed to prepare incoming freshmen to adjust to academic life. College Prep or English as a Second Language admit 60 students to strengthen academics and study skills. There is no cost for the summer programs. Documentation is required prior to the provision of accommodations. The verification of a disability should include a diagnosis, a description of the functional limitations that may affect performance, necessary accommodations, and the printed and signed name of a person qualified or certified to assess the disability. To obtain accommodations, students must register by submitting documentation to the ODS. Students are encouraged to submit documentation early in the process in order to receive accommodations in a timely manner.

## LEARNING DISABILITY ADMISSIONS INFORMATION

**Program Name:** Office of Disability Services (ODS)
**Program Director:** Patrice Miller
**Contact Person:** Marilyn Longo/Bill Welsh          **Telephone:** 215-895-2960

### ADMISSIONS

The regular admission requirements are the same for all students, and there is no special process for students with learning disabilities. Students are encouraged to self-disclose and provide current documentation of their learning disabilities. General admission criteria include: Recommended courses of 4 yrs. English, 3 yrs. math, 1 yr. science, 1 yr. social studies, 7 years electives (chosen from English, math, science, social studies, foreign language, history, or mechanical drawing); interview recommended; average SAT is 1010, average GPA is 3.1, and 89% of the admitted students are in the top 60% of their high school graduating class.

| | |
|---|---|
| **College entrance exams required:** Yes | **Untimed accepted:** Yes |
| **Course entrance requirements:** Yes | **Interview required:** Yes |
| **Diagnostic tests:** No | |
| **Documentation:** Documentation is needed to provide services | |

### ADDITIONAL INFORMATION

Services provided are: tutors; readers; notetakers; proofreaders; LD specialists; personal academic and career counseling; liaison between student, faculty and administration; priority scheduling; instructional modifications; augmented classes offered in math and English; and remedial services in study skills, writing, reading and math, time management, self-advocacy enhancement, and disability education for staff, faculty, and students. The Office of Disability Services also provides assistance with academic accommodations and learning strategies, and follows through on all Affirmative Action and ADA requirements.

| | |
|---|---|
| **Special education HS coursework accepted:** Yes | **Essay required:** Yes |
| **Special application required:** No | **Submitted to:** N/A |
| **# of applications submitted each year:** N/A | **# of applications accepted each year:** N/A |
| **# of students receiving LD services:** 75 | |
| **Acceptance into program means acceptance into college:** Students must be admitted to the university first and then may request LD services. | |

# LEARNING DISABILITY SERVICES

**Learning center:** Yes
**Kurzweil personal reader:** No
**LD specialists:** 1
**Allowed in exams:**
  **Calculator:** Yes
  **Dictionary:** Y/N
  **Computer:** No
  **SpellCheck:** No

**Notetaker:** Yes
**Scribes:** Yes
**Proctors:** Yes
**Oral exams:** Yes
**Extended test time:** Yes
**Added cost:** None
**Distraction-free environ.:** Yes
**Tape recording in class:** Yes
**Books on tape:** Yes
**Taping of other books:** Yes

**Professional tutors:** Yes
**Peer tutors:** Yes
**Max. hrs/wk for services:**
Unlimited
**Priority registration:** No
**Accommodations for students
with ADD:** Yes
**How are professors notified of
LD:** By the student and the
Program Coordinator

# GENERAL ADMISSIONS INFORMATION

**Director of Admissions:** Donald Dickason      **Telephone:** 215-895-2400

## ENTRANCE REQUIREMENTS

Total high school units required/recommended: 16 total units are recommended; 4 English recommended, 3 math recommended, 1 science recommended, and 1 social studies recommended. Elective units must be in English, history, math, science, social science, foreign language, or mechanical drawing. Special requirements: TOEFL is required of all international students. One additional unit in both math and science required of applicants to College of Engineering, College of Science, and to commerce/engineering program offered by College of Business and Administration.

**Application deadline:** Rolling
**Notification:** Rolling

**SAT or ACT preferred:** Either
**SAT Avg:** 554V, 584M

**Graduated top 10% of class:** 25
**Graduated top 25% of class:** 58
**Graduated top 50% of class:** 89

# COLLEGE GRADUATION REQUIREMENTS

**Course waivers allowed:** Yes
**Course substitutions allowed:** Yes
**In what courses:** Done on a case-by-case basis

# ADDITIONAL INFORMATION

**Environment:** The campus is located on 38 acres near the center of Philadelphia.

**Student Body**
  **Undergrad enrollment:** 6,805
  **Women:** 32%
  **Men:** 68%
  **In-state students:** 67%
  **Out-of-state:** 33%

**Cost Information**
  **In-state tuition:** $13,680
  **Out-of-state:** $13,680
  **Room & board:** $6,718

**Housing Information**
  **University housing:** Yes
  **Fraternity:** Yes
  **Sorority:** Yes
  **Living on campus:** 25%

  **Athletics:** NCAA Div. I

# EAST STROUDSBURG UNIV. OF PENNSYLVANIA

200 Prospect Street, East Stroudsburg, PA 18301 • **Admissions:** 717-424-3542 • **Fax:** 717-422-3933
**Web:** www.esu.edu
**Support:** CS • **Institution:** 4 yr. Public

## LEARNING DISABILITY ADMISSIONS AND SERVICES

There is no special program for students with learning disabilities at East Stroudsburg University. However, the university is committed to supporting otherwise qualified students with learning disabilities in their pursuit of an education. Disability Services offers learning-disabled students academic and social support and acts as their advocate on campus. Students are encouraged to meet with the coordinator, once accepted, to schedule classes and to develop compensatory skills. Tutors are trained to be sensitive to individual learning styles.

## LEARNING DISABILITY ADMISSIONS INFORMATION

**Program Name:** Disability Services
**Program Director:** Edith F. Miller
**Contact Person:** Same as above

**Telephone:** 717-422-3825

### ADMISSIONS

Students with learning disabilities file the general application form, and are encouraged to complete the section titled "Disabilities Information," and forward documentation of their disability to Disability Services. Notification of a learning disability is used as a part of the admissions process only if the student is denied admission. At this time the admissions office waits for a recommendation from the learning-disability specialist. The Office of Academic Support may request that the admissions office re-evaluate the student's application in light of information on the disability.

**College entrance exams required:** Yes
**Course entrance requirements:** Yes
**Diagnostic tests:** Yes
**Documentation:** Psychological evaluation; IEP: most current

**Untimed accepted:** Yes
**Interview required:** No

### ADDITIONAL INFORMATION

There is a pre-admission summer program for Pennsylvania residents only called the "Summer Intensive Study Program." All entering freshmen and their parents are invited to participate in a 2-day summer orientation. Drop-in labs are offered in math and writing, as are study skills workshops. Students with learning disabilities may work individually with the Disability Services Coordinator. All students enrolled in the university have the opportunity to take skills classes in reading, composition, and math. Other services include workshops in time management and test-taking strategies as well as support groups. Services and accommodations are available for undergraduate and graduate students.

**Special education HS coursework accepted:** Yes

**Special application required:** Yes
**# of applications submitted each year:** 143
**# of students receiving LD services:** 150

**Essay required:** Yes, for entrance into Freshman English
**Submitted to:** Program Director
**# of applications accepted each year:** 60

**Acceptance into program means acceptance into college:** Students must be admitted to the university first and then may request consideration for Disability Services.

## LEARNING DISABILITY SERVICES

**Learning center:** Yes
**Kurzweil personal reader:** Yes
**LD specialists:** 1
**Allowed in exams:**
  **Calculator:** Yes
  **Dictionary:** Yes
  **Computer:** Yes
  **SpellCheck:** Yes

**Notetaker:** Yes
**Scribes:** Yes
**Proctors:** Yes
**Oral exams:** Yes
**Extended test time:** Yes
**Added cost:** None
**Distraction-free environ.:** Yes
**Tape recording in class:** Yes
**Books on tape:** Yes
**Taping of other books:** No

**Professional tutors:** 50
**Peer tutors:** 50
**Max. hrs/wk for services:** 2 hours per course
**Priority registration:** Yes
**Accommodations for students with ADD:** Yes
**How are professors notified of LD:** By the student and the Program Director

## GENERAL ADMISSIONS INFORMATION

**Director of Admissions:** Alan T. Chesterton          **Telephone:** 717-424-3834

### ENTRANCE REQUIREMENTS

Special requirements: Minimum SAT I score of 500 in Math required of computer science program applicants.

**Application deadline:** March 1
**Notification:** March 1

**SAT or ACT preferred:** Either

**Graduated top 10% of class:** 7
**Graduated top 25% of class:** 25
**Graduated top 50% of class:** 67

## COLLEGE GRADUATION REQUIREMENTS

**Course waivers allowed:** No
**Course substitutions allowed:** Yes
**In what courses:** Substitutions for math and foreign language

## ADDITIONAL INFORMATION

**Environment:** The 813-acre campus is set in the foothills of the Pocono Mountains.

**Student Body**
  **Undergrad enrollment:** 4,564
  **Women:** 56%
  **Men:** 44%
  **In-state students:** 72%
  **Out-of-state:** 28%

**Cost Information**
  **In-state tuition:** $3,368
  **Out-of-state:** $8,566
  **Room & board:** $3,626

**Housing Information**
  **University housing:** Yes
  **Fraternity:** Yes
  **Sorority:** No
  **Living on campus:** 45%

  **Athletics:** NCAA Div. II

# EDINBORO UNIVERSITY OF PENNSYLVANIA

**PA**

Edinboro, PA 16444 • **Admissions:** 814-732-2761 • **Fax:** 814-732-2420
**Email:** CARLIN@edinboro.edu • **Web:** www.edinboro.edu
**Support:** CS • **Institution:** 4 yr. Public

## LEARNING DISABILITY ADMISSIONS AND SERVICES

Edinboro is actively involved in providing services for students with learning disabilities. OSD provides services that are individually directed by the program staff according to expressed needs. There are different levels of services offered depending on the student's needs. Level A offers supervised study sessions with trained mentors 2 hours per day, with additional hours based on academic progress; writing specialists 1-2 hours weekly; computer lab; study lab; required appointment every two weeks with professional staff to review progress; and all services in Level D. To be eligible for Level B students must maintain a 2.5 GPA and complete two or more semesters at Level A: supervised study sessions with peer mentor 1 hour per day and 2 more hours based on progress; writing specialists 1-2 hours weekly; computer lab; study lab; a required appointment every two weeks with professional staff; and all services listed in Level D. Level C requires 2.5 GPA and one semester at Level B: peer mentoring up to 6 hours weekly; writing specialists 1-2 hours weekly; computer lab; study lab; and all services in Level D. Level D provides: assistance in arranging academic accommodations, including alternate test arrangements; priority scheduling; consultation with staff; and tape-recorded textbooks.

## LEARNING DISABILITY ADMISSIONS INFORMATION

**Program Name:** Office for Students with Disabilities (OSD)
**Program Director:** N/A                                    **Telephone:** 814-732-2462
**Contact Person:** Kathleen Strosser

### ADMISSIONS

Students with learning disabilities submit the general application form. Upon receipt of the application from the Admissions Office, it is suggested that students identify any special services that may be required and contact OSD so that a personal interview may be scheduled. Occasionally, OSD staff are asked for remarks on certain files, but it is not part of the admission decision. Students must provide a multifactored educational assessment; grade-level scores in reading, vocabulary and comprehension, math, and spelling; an individual intelligence test administered by a psychologist, including a list of the tests given; and a list of recommended accommodations. Students with learning disabilities who self disclose are admitted to the college and then reviewed for services.

**College entrance exams required:** Yes            **Untimed accepted:** Yes
**Course entrance requirements:** No                **Interview required:** Recommended
**Diagnostic tests:** Yes
**Documentation:** WAIS-R or WISC-R and achievement testing: within 3 years

### ADDITIONAL INFORMATION

Students with learning disabilities are paired with peer tutors who help them with study skills, organizational skills, and time-management skills. Students are recommended for different levels of services based on their needs. Students cannot be required to choose a particular level, but OSD strongly recommends that students enroll for Level A if they have less than a 2.5 GPA. Specific academic scheduling needs may be complex, but students working through OSD are given priority in academic scheduling. The Life Skills Center is a training area designed to enable students with disabilities to maximize their personal independence while completing their academic programs. Educational modules are available in consumer affairs, financial management, functional skills, communication, time management, and career planning.

**Special education HS coursework accepted:** Yes          **Essay required:** No
**Special application required:** No                        **Submitted to:** N/A
**# of applications submitted each year:** N/A             **# of applications accepted each year:** N/A
**# of students receiving LD services:** 240
**Acceptance into program means acceptance into college:** Students must be admitted to the university first and then may request services. from OSD.

**Learning center:** No
**Kurzweil personal reader:** Yes
**LD specialists:** 2
**Allowed in exams:**
  **Calculator:** Yes
  **Dictionary:** Yes
  **Computer:** Yes
  **SpellCheck:** Yes

**Notetaker:** No
**Scribes:** Yes
**Proctors:** Yes
**Oral exams:** Yes
**Extended test time:** Yes
**Added cost:** Per semester: Level A/$660; Level B/$660; Level C/$198; Level D/free
**Distraction-free environ.:** Yes
**Tape recording in class:** Yes
**Books on tape:** Yes
**Taping of other books:** Yes

**Professional tutors:** Yes
**Peer tutors:** Mentors
**Max. hrs/wk for services:** 12
**Priority registration:** Yes
**Accommodations for students with ADD:** Yes
**How are professors notified of LD:** By the student

## GENERAL ADMISSIONS INFORMATION

**Director of Admissions:** Mr. Terrence Carlin       **Telephone:** 814-732-2761

### ENTRANCE REQUIREMENTS

Special requirements: An audition is required for music program applicants. TOEFL is required of all international students.

**Application deadline:** Rolling
**Notification:** Rolling

**SAT or ACT preferred:** SAT
**SAT II required:** Yes

## COLLEGE GRADUATION REQUIREMENTS

**Course waivers allowed:** No
**Course substitutions allowed:** Yes
**In what courses:** Case-by-case basis

## ADDITIONAL INFORMATION

**Environment:** Edinboro University is located on 600 acres in a small town 20 miles south of Erie.

**Student Body**
  **Undergrad enrollment:** 6,035
  **Women:** 60%
  **Men:** 40%
  **In-state students:** 94%
  **Out-of-state:** 6%

**Cost Information**
  **In-state tuition:** $3,368
  **Out-of-state:** $8,566
  **Room & board:** $3,616

**Housing Information**
  **University housing:** Yes
  **Fraternity:** No
  **Sorority:** No
  **Living on campus:** 31%

  **Athletics:** NCAA Div. II

# GANNON UNIVERSITY

University Square, Erie, PA 16541 • **Admissions:** 814-871-7240 • **Fax:** 814-871-5803
**Email:** admissions@cluster.gannon.edu • **Web:** www.gannon.edu
**Support:** SP • **Institution:** 4 yr. Private

## LEARNING DISABILITY ADMISSIONS AND SERVICES

Gannon's Program for Students with LD (PSLD) provides special support services for students who have been diagnosed with either LD or ADHD yet who are highly motivated for academic achievement and have average-to-gifted intellectual potential. PSLD faculty are committed to excellence and strive to offer each student individually designed instruction. Students in the program may select any academic major offered by the university. Freshman-year support includes weekly individual sessions with instructor-tutors and a writing specialist, and small group meetings with a reading specialist. Also provided are a study-skills course and an advocacy seminar, which includes participation in small group counseling. Students declare a major at the beginning of the sophomore year and attend all regularly scheduled classes. There is limited space in PSLD, and students should check the appropriate box on the admissions application if this service applies. Gannon University provides a student-centered environment that helps to prepare undergraduate students for leadership roles within the university in their chosen careers and in the communities which they serve. Gannon assists students in achieving their intellectual, social, emotional and spiritual potential.

## LEARNING DISABILITY ADMISSIONS INFORMATION

**Program Name:** Program for Students with Learning Disabilities
**Program Director:** Sister Joyce Lowery, SSJ, M.Ed.     **Telephone:** 814-871-5326
**Contact Person:** Jane Benson, M.Ed.     **Telephone:** 814-871-5360

### ADMISSIONS

Besides the regular application and interview there is a special admissions process for the student with learning disabilities. Applicants must submit a psychoeducational evaluation, a high school transcript, 3 letters of recommendation, a short written paragraph about why they want to go to Gannon University, and a paragraph about why there is a need for support services. Students must also have a personal interview which can be conducted by telephone. Students with learning disabilities who are admitted conditionally must enter as undeclared majors until they can achieve a 2.0 GPA. Special Education high school courses are accepted in certain situations.

**College entrance exams required:** Yes     **Untimed accepted:** Yes
**Course entrance requirements:** Yes     **Interview required:** Yes
**Diagnostic tests:** Yes
**Documentation:** WISC or WAIS and reading test

### ADDITIONAL INFORMATION

Specific features of the program include: twice-weekly tutoring sessions with the program instructors to review course material, learn study skills relevant to material from courses, learn test-taking skills relevant to particular courses, and focus on specific needs; weekly sessions with the writing specialists for reviewing, editing and brainstorming. A two-credit Advocacy Seminar course is part of the course load of first semester; this course covers self-advocacy, motivational techniques, college survival skills, the law and learning disabilities, and learning styles and strategies. Additional services available are: computer access and/or tutoring; taped textbooks; taping of classes; extended time on exams; scribes and/or dictated; oral exams; and exams by instructors. There is an additional fee of $600 for support services.

**Special education HS coursework accepted:** Yes     **Essay required:** Yes
**Special application required:** Yes     **Submitted to:** Admissions
**# of applications submitted each year:** 50     **# of applications accepted each year:** 10-16
**# of students receiving LD services:** 60
**Acceptance into program means acceptance into college:** The Director of PSLD accepts students into the program and the university.

## LEARNING DISABILITY SERVICES

**Learning center:** Yes
**Kurzweil personal reader:** Yes
**LD specialists:** 1
**Allowed in exams:**
  **Calculator:** Y/N
  **Dictionary:** Yes
  **Computer:** Yes
  **SpellCheck:** Yes

**Notetaker:** No
**Scribes:** Yes
**Proctors:** Yes
**Oral exams:** Yes
**Extended test time:** Yes
**Added cost:** $600 for the academic year
**Distraction-free environ.:** Yes
**Tape recording in class:** Yes
**Books on tape:** RFB
**Taping of other books:** Yes

**Professional tutors:** 6
**Peer tutors:** 0
**Max. hrs/wk for services:** 2 1/2 hours per week
**Priority registration:** Y/N
**Accommodations for students with ADD:** Yes
**How are professors notified of LD:** By the student and the Program Director

## GENERAL ADMISSIONS INFORMATION

**Director of Admissions:** Beth Nemenz

**Telephone:** 814-871-5336

### ENTRANCE REQUIREMENTS
Total high school units required/recommended: 16 total units are required; 4 English required, 2 math required, 4 math recommended, 2 science required, 4 science recommended, 2 foreign language required, 2 social studies required, and 4 social studies recommended. Rank in top 1/2 of secondary school class and minimum 2.5 GPA required; minimum required test scores vary by program. Minimum secondary school unit requirements vary by program.

**Application deadline:** Rolling
**Notification:** Rolling

**SAT or ACT preferred:** SAT
**SAT Avg:** 550V, 550M
**Average ACT:** 24
**Average GPA:** 3.3

**Graduated top 10% of class:** 24
**Graduated top 25% of class:** 58
**Graduated top 50% of class:** 89

## COLLEGE GRADUATION REQUIREMENTS

**Course waivers allowed:** N/A
**Course substitutions allowed:** N/A
**In what courses:** No decision has been made at this time

## ADDITIONAL INFORMATION

**Environment:** The university is located on 13 acres in Erie, PA, an urban area 135 miles north of Pittsburgh.

**Student Body**
  **Undergrad enrollment:** 2,826
  **Women:** 56%
  **Men:** 44%
  **In-state students:** 82%
  **Out-of-state:** 18%

**Cost Information**
  **In-state tuition:** $11,980
  **Out-of-state:** $11,980
  **Room & board:** $4,860

**Housing Information**
  **University housing:** Yes
  **Fraternity:** Yes
  **Sorority:** Yes
  **Living on campus:** 40%

  **Athletics:** NCAA Div. II

# KUTZTOWN UNIVERSITY OF PENNSYLVANIA

Kutztown, PA 19530 • **Admissions:** 610-683-4060 • **Fax:** 610-683-1375
**Email:** admissions@kutztown.edu • **Web:** www.kutztown.edu
**Support:** CS • **Institution:** 4 yr. Public

## LEARNING DISABILITY ADMISSIONS AND SERVICES

The philosophy of the university is to provide equal opportunity to all individuals. The Services for Students with Disabilities provides all necessary and reasonable services while fostering independence in the students. The services provided are in accordance with the needs of the students and the academic integrity of the institution. The Office acts as an information and referral resource, provides direct services, coordinates services provided by other departments/agencies, and serves as a liaison between students with disabilities and university personnel working with students. Since information regarding a student's disability is not obtained through the admission process, it is the student's responsibility upon acceptance to the university to identify him/herself to the Program. Students are encouraged to this as early as possible upon admission, or even when contemplating application. This will provide an opportunity to assess the university's capability of responding to special needs and provide the students with opportunity to assess the services available at the university. The DAD/504 Coordinator works together with all university offices to help provide specific services as warranted by a diagnosis or clear need as well as creative solutions to problems with which students with disabilities are confronted.

## LEARNING DISABILITY ADMISSIONS INFORMATION

**Program Name:** Services for Students with Disabilities
**Program Director:** Barbara N. Peters
**Contact Person:** Same as above

**Telephone:** 610-683-4108

### ADMISSIONS

There is no special admissions process for students with learning disabilities. All applicants are expected to meet the same admission criteria, which include college prep courses; SAT I of 900 with exceptions. Admission requirements are not so high that they impede access. An admissions exceptions committee considers applications that may warrant exceptions to the general admission standards. Students may enter through Extended Learning and upon earning 21 credits, a student may be considered for regular matriculation. In-state residents who do not predict a 2.0 GPA may be considered for a 5-week Summer Developmental Studies Session.

**College entrance exams required:** Yes
**Course entrance requirements:** Yes
**Diagnostic tests:** Yes
**Documentation:** Given by a qualified tester; within 3 years

**Untimed accepted:** Yes
**Interview required:** No

### ADDITIONAL INFORMATION

The Coordinator of Human Diversity Programming is the initial resource person and record keeper who validates the existence of a disability and the need for any specific accommodations, and contacts faculty and other individuals who have reason to receive information. Academic assistance is provided through the Department of Developmental Studies. Students with LD are eligible to receive: services and accommodations prescribed in the psychoeducational evaluation, extended time on exams, use of tape recorder, use of calculator, testing in a separate location, readers, spell and grammar check on written assignments, scribes, four-track cassette, tutorial assistance, early advisement and preregistration, computer assistive technology, and referrals. Individualized study skills assessments are made and tutorial assistance is provided. Skills classes are offered in study skills, stress management, and remedial math, English and reading, and ESL. Tutors are available to all students and arrangements are made at no cost to the student.

**Special education HS coursework accepted:** Yes
**Special application required:** No
**# of applications submitted each year:** N/A
**# of students receiving LD services:** 152
**Acceptance into program means acceptance into college:** Students must be accepted to the university first and then may request services.

**Essay required:** No
**Submitted to:** N/A
**# of applications accepted each year:** N/A

## LEARNING DISABILITY SERVICES

**Learning center:** Yes
**Kurzweil personal reader:** Yes
**LD specialists:** Yes
**Allowed in exams:**
  **Calculator:** N/I
  **Dictionary:** N/I
  **Computer:** Yes
  **SpellCheck:** Yes

**Notetaker:** Yes
**Scribes:** Yes
**Proctors:** Yes
**Oral exams:** Yes
**Extended test time:** Yes
**Added cost:** None
**Distraction-free environ.:** Yes
**Tape recording in class:** Yes
**Books on tape:** No
**Taping of other books:** Yes

**Professional tutors:** No
**Peer tutors:** Yes
**Max. hrs/wk for services:** As needed and as available
**Priority registration:** Yes
**Accommodations for students with ADD:** Yes
**How are professors notified of LD:** By the student and the Program Director

## GENERAL ADMISSIONS INFORMATION

**Director of Admissions:** George McKinley       **Telephone:** 610-683-4472

### ENTRANCE REQUIREMENTS

Total high school units required/recommended: 16 total units are recommended; 4 English recommended, 3 math recommended, 2 science recommended, 2 foreign language recommended, 2 social studies recommended, 2 history recommended. Rank in top half of secondary school class and minimum B average required. Additional requirements vary by program. Special requirements: A portfolio is required for art program applicants. An RN is required for nursing program applicants. TOEFL is required of all international students.

**Application deadline:** Rolling
**Notification:** Rolling

**SAT or ACT preferred:** Either
**SAT Avg:** 501V, 483M

**Graduated top 10% of class:** 5
**Graduated top 25% of class:** 20
**Graduated top 50% of class:** 82

## COLLEGE GRADUATION REQUIREMENTS

**Course waivers allowed:** Yes
**Course substitutions allowed:** Yes
**In what courses:** Only with strong diagnostic recommendation through the Academic Exceptions Committee—foreign language and math

## ADDITIONAL INFORMATION

**Environment:** The university is located on 325 acres in a rural area 90 miles north of Philadelphia.

**Student Body**
  **Undergrad enrollment:** 6,925
  **Women:** 58%
  **Men:** 42%
  **In-state students:** 92%
  **Out-of-state:** 8%

**Cost Information**
  **In-state tuition:** $3,368
  **Out-of-state:** $8,566
  **Room & board:** $3,500

**Housing Information**
  **University housing:** Yes
  **Fraternity:** No
  **Sorority:** No
  **Living on campus:** 41%

  **Athletics:** NCAA Div. II

# MERCYHURST COLLEGE

Glenwood Hills, Erie, PA 16546 • **Admissions:** 814-824-2202 • **Fax:** 814-824-2071
**Email:** mwhelan@paradise.mercy.edu
**Support:** SP • **Institution:** 4 yr. Private

## LEARNING DISABILITY ADMISSIONS AND SERVICES

The specialized program at Mercyhurst College is designed to assist students who have been identified as LD. The emphasis is on students' individual strengths, abilities and interests, as well as learning deficits. This program consists of a structured, individualized set of experiences designed to assist students with LD to get maximum value from their educational potential and earn a college degree. Students selecting the Structured Program for students with learning differences pay an additional fee for this service and must submit: a recent psychological evaluation that includes the WAIS or WISC-R scores within 2 years; 3 letters of recommendation, 1 each from a math, English, LD teacher or guidance counselor; SAT/ACT; and a written statement from a professional documenting the student's learning disability. Students choosing the Structured Program option must attend a summer session prior to entrance; classes may include Learning Strategies, Basic Writing, Communications, Career Planning, and Computer Competency. The program lasts 5 weeks and costs approximately $1600 (includes room, board, and tuition). Students with learning differences who feel that they do not require a structured program may opt to receive support services through the Academic Support Center at no additional charge.

## LEARNING DISABILITY ADMISSIONS INFORMATION

**Program Name:** Program for Students with Learning Differences
**Program Director:** Dr. Barbara Weigert      **Telephone:** 814-824-2450
**Contact Person:** Tina King      **Telephone:** 814-824-2450

### ADMISSIONS

To be eligible for any of the services at Mercyhurst, students with LD must adhere to the regular admission requirements and meet the regular admission criteria. General admission criteria include: 2.5 GPA; ACT 19+ or SAT 900+; 4 yrs. English, 2 yrs. social science, 3 yrs. math, 2 yrs. science, 2 yrs. foreign language (waivers and substitutions are determined on an individual basis). Students who do not meet the regular admissions standards are referred to Mercyhurst-McAuley and/or Mercyhurst-North East for consideration into the 2-year division. The college reserves the right to reject any student not meeting admission standards. The admission decisions are made jointly by the Director of Programs for Students with Learning Differences and the Office of Admission. Upon acceptance to the college, if the student wishes special services, she/he must identify herself/himself to the Admissions Office and, at that time, choose to receive services in 1 of 2 options available to students with documented learning differences. These programs are a structured program and a basic service program.

| | |
|---|---|
| **College entrance exams required:** Yes | **Untimed accepted:** Yes |
| **Course entrance requirements:** Yes | **Interview required:** No |
| **Diagnostic tests:** Yes | |
| **Documentation:** WISC or WAIS-R; complete psychological: within 2 years | |

### ADDITIONAL INFORMATION

The Structured Program for Students with Learning Differences provides special services including: Advisory Board; advocacy; alternative testing; books on tape though RFB; community skills; drop-in services; Kurzweil Personal Reader; mid-term progress reports; notetakers; peer tutoring; professional advising/priority registration; special 5-week Summer Orientation Program prior to freshman year; special section of Basic Writing; special section of Math Problem Solving; study hall (required of all freshman); and a support group. The Academic Support Department employs a student advocate, "Mr. Help," whose job is to listen to any question a student has and to help find the answer. Any student can receive free tutoring in any course through the Academic Success Center on a walk-in basis.

| | |
|---|---|
| **Special education HS coursework accepted:** Yes | **Essay required:** No |
| **Special application required:** No | **Submitted to:** N/A |
| **# of applications submitted each year:** N/A | **# of applications accepted each year:** N/A |
| **# of students receiving LD services:** 50 | |

**Acceptance into program means acceptance into college:** Students must be admitted to the college and then reviewed for LD services.

## LEARNING DISABILITY SERVICES

**Learning center:** Yes
**Kurzweil personal reader:** Yes
**LD specialists:** 2
**Allowed in exams:**
  **Calculator:** Yes
  **Dictionary:** No
  **Computer:** Yes
  **SpellCheck:** Yes

**Notetaker:** Yes
**Scribes:** No
**Proctors:** Yes
**Oral exams:** No
**Extended test time:** Yes
**Added cost:** Fees range from $500-$1000 for services
**Distraction-free environ.:** Yes
**Tape recording in class:** Yes
**Books on tape:** No
**Taping of other books:** No

**Professional tutors:** No
**Peer tutors:** 40
**Max. hrs/wk for services:** No limit/ free tutoring
**Priority registration:** Yes
**Accommodations for students with ADD:** Yes
**How are professors notified of LD:** By the student and the Program Director

## GENERAL ADMISSIONS INFORMATION

**Director of Admissions:** Matthew Whelan

**Telephone:** 814-824-2573

### ENTRANCE REQUIREMENTS

Total high school units required/recommended: 18 total units are recommended; 4 English recommended, 3 math recommended, 3 science recommended, 2 foreign language recommended, 3 social studies recommended, 2 history recommended. Minimum combined SAT I score of 800, rank in top 1/2 of secondary school class, or minimum 2.5 GPA recommended. Special requirements: A portfolio is required for art program and dance program applicants.

**Application deadline:** Rolling
**Notification:** Rolling

**SAT or ACT preferred:** Either
**SAT Avg:** 549V, 532M
**SAT II required:** Yes
**Average ACT:** 23
**Average GPA:** 3.4

**Graduated top 10% of class:** 16
**Graduated top 25% of class:** 42
**Graduated top 50% of class:** 85

## COLLEGE GRADUATION REQUIREMENTS

**Course waivers allowed:** No
**Course substitutions allowed:** No
**In what courses:** N/A

## ADDITIONAL INFORMATION

**Environment:** The 80-acre campus of Mercyhurst overlooks Lake Erie.

**Student Body**
  **Undergrad enrollment:** 2,635
  **Women:** 52%
  **Men:** 48%
  **In-state students:** 63%
  **Out-of-state:** 37%

**Cost Information**
  **In-state tuition:** $10,920
  **Out-of-state:** $10,920
  **Room & board:** $4,500

**Housing Information**
  **University housing:** Yes
  **Fraternity:** No
  **Sorority:** No
  **Living on campus:** 78%

  **Athletics:** NCAA Div. II

# PENNSYLVANIA STATE UNIV.-UNIVERSITY PARK

**PA**

University Park, PA 16802 • **Admissions:** 814-865-5471 • **Fax:** 814-863-7590
**Email:** admissions@psu.edu • **Web:** www.psu.edu
**Support:** CS • **Institution:** 4 yr. Public

## LEARNING DISABILITY ADMISSIONS AND SERVICES

The goal of Penn State's academic support services for students with learning disabilities is to ensure that they receive appropriate accommodations so that they can function independently and meet the academic demands of a competitive university. Students with learning disabilities should be able to complete college-level courses with the help of support services and classroom accommodations. In order to receive any of the support services, students must submit documentation of their learning disability to the Learning Disability Specialist in the Office for Disability Services. Documentation should be a psychoeducational report from a certified or licensed psychologist done within the past 3 years.

## LEARNING DISABILITY ADMISSIONS INFORMATION

**Program Name:** Learning Disabilities Support Services
**Program Director:** Marianne Karwacki          **Telephone:** 814-863-2291
**Contact Person:** Same as above

### ADMISSIONS

There is no special application process for students with learning disabilities, and these students are considered for admission on the same basis as other applicants. However, students with LD may self-identify on the application. If the high school grades and the test scores are low, students may submit a letter explaining why their ability to succeed in college is higher than indicated by their academic records. The Admissions Office will consider this information as it is voluntarily provided. The acceptable ACT or SAT score will depend upon the high school grades and class rank of the student. Two-thirds of the evaluation is based on high school grades, and 1/3 on test scores. Once admitted, students must submit documentation of their learning disability in order to receive support services. Students may seek admission as a provisional or non-degree student if they do not have criteria required for admission as a degree candidate. Any student may enroll as a non-degree student.

| | |
|---|---|
| **College entrance exams required:** Yes | **Untimed accepted:** Yes |
| **Course entrance requirements:** Yes | **Interview required:** No |
| **Diagnostic tests:** Yes | |

**Documentation:** WAIS-R: W-J; neuropsychological if appropriate: within 3 years

### ADDITIONAL INFORMATION

Students with LD are encouraged to participate in the Buddy Program; incoming students are matched with a 'senior buddy' who is a current student with a disability, and is available to share experiences with a junior buddy. Other services include: locating audiotaped textbooks; arranging course substitutions with academic departments (when essential requirements are not involved); test accommodations; and individual counseling. Assistance with note taking is offered through the Office for Disability Services. Services are offered in a mainstream setting. The Learning Assistance Center operates a Math Center, Tutoring Center, Writing Center, and Computer Learning Center. Students may receive academic help either individually or in small groups for a number of different courses. One-to-one academic assistance is available though the Office of Disability Services. Graduate clinicians provide individual assistance with study skills, time management and compensatory learning strategies.

| | |
|---|---|
| **Special education HS coursework accepted:** Y/N | **Essay required:** No |
| **Special application required:** No | **Submitted to:** N/A |
| **# of applications submitted each year:** N/A | **# of applications accepted each year:** N/A |
| **# of students receiving LD services:** 275 | |

**Acceptance into program means acceptance into college:** Students must be admitted to the university and then may request LD services.

## LEARNING DISABILITY SERVICES

**Learning center:** Yes
**Kurzweil personal reader:** Yes
**LD specialists:** 1
**Allowed in exams:**
  **Calculator:** Yes
  **Dictionary:** Y/N
  **Computer:** Yes
  **SpellCheck:** Yes

**Notetaker:** Yes
**Scribes:** Yes
**Proctors:** Yes
**Oral exams:** Yes
**Extended test time:** Yes
**Added cost:** None
**Distraction-free environ.:** Yes
**Tape recording in class:** Yes
**Books on tape:** Yes
**Taping of other books:** Yes

**Professional tutors:** No
**Peer tutors:** 20
**Max. hrs/wk for services:** 3
**Priority registration:** Yes
**Accommodations for students with ADD:** Yes
**How are professors notified of LD:** By the student

## GENERAL ADMISSIONS INFORMATION

**Director of Admissions:** Dr. Geoff Harford          **Telephone:** 814-865-5471

### ENTRANCE REQUIREMENTS

Total high school units required/recommended: 15 total units are required; 4 English required, 3 math required, 3 science required, 2 foreign language recommended.

**Application deadline:** Nov. 30
**Notification:** Rolling

**SAT or ACT preferred:** SAT
**SAT Avg:** 593V, 617M
**Average GPA:** 3.7

**Graduated top 10% of class:** 54
**Graduated top 25% of class:** 90
**Graduated top 50% of class:** 97

## COLLEGE GRADUATION REQUIREMENTS

**Course waivers allowed:** No
**Course substitutions allowed:** Yes
**In what courses:** Foreign language if a student's documentation supports the need for it.

## ADDITIONAL INFORMATION

**Environment:** The school is located on over 5,000 acres in a small city 90 miles west of Harrisburg.

**Student Body**
  **Undergrad enrollment:** 31,009
  **Women:** 45%
  **Men:** 55%
  **In-state students:** 81%
  **Out-of-state:** 19%

**Cost Information**
  **In-state tuition:** $5,250
  **Out-of-state:** $11,746
  **Room & board:** $4,176

**Housing Information**
  **University housing:** Yes
  **Fraternity:** Yes
  **Sorority:** Yes
  **Living on campus:** 36%

  **Athletics:** NCAA Div. I

# WIDENER UNIVERSITY

One University Place, Chester, PA 19013 • **Admissions:** 610-499-4126 • **Fax:** 610-499-4425
**Email:** admissions.office@widener.edu • **Web:** www.widener.edu/widener.html
**Support:** CS • **Institution:** 4 yr. Private

## LEARNING DISABILITY ADMISSIONS AND SERVICES

'ENABLE' is a personalized academic advising and counseling service. The ENABLE support service is designed to help students with learning disabilities who meet university entrance requirements, to cope with the rigors of academic life. Students are assigned counselors who help them understand and accept their disabilities; provide academic advice; individualize learning strategies; teach self-advocacy; and link the students with the Reading and Academic Skills Center, Math Lab, Writing Center, and tutoring services. This office assures that professors understand which accommodations are needed.

## LEARNING DISABILITY ADMISSIONS INFORMATION

**Program Name:** ENABLE
**Program Director:** LaVerne Ziegenfuss, Psy.D.        **Telephone:** 610-499-1270
**Contact Person:** Same as above

### ADMISSIONS

Students with learning disabilities submit the general application form. Admission decisions are made jointly by the Office of Admissions and the Director of ENABLE. Students should submit documentation, essay, and recommendations. ACT scores range between 17-27 and SAT scores range between 750-1300. There are no specific course requirements for admissions. High school GPA range is 2.0-4.0.

**College entrance exams required:** Yes          **Untimed accepted:** Yes
**Course entrance requirements:** Yes          **Interview required:** Recommended
**Diagnostic tests:** Yes
**Documentation:** WAIS; Achievement: within 3 years

### ADDITIONAL INFORMATION

The Writing Center provides assistance with writing assignments and is staffed by professors. The Math Center offers individualized and group tutoring and is staffed by professors and experienced tutors. The Reading Skills Center assists in improving reading comprehension and study skills. Skills classes are available in college reading, math, and English and only 3 credits are accepted for college credit. The Academic Skills Program assists students who receive less than a 2.0 GPA in the fall semester.

**Special education HS coursework accepted:** Yes          **Essay required:** Yes
**Special application required:** No          **Submitted to:** N/A
**# of applications submitted each year:** N/A          **# of applications accepted each year:** N/A
**# of students receiving LD services:** 90
**Acceptance into program means acceptance into college:** Students must be accepted to university first and then may request services.

## LEARNING DISABILITY SERVICES

**Learning center:** Yes
**Kurzweil personal reader:** Yes
**LD specialists:** 3
**Allowed in exams:**
  **Calculator:** Yes
  **Dictionary:** Yes
  **Computer:** Yes
  **SpellCheck:** Yes

**Notetaker:** Yes
**Scribes:** Yes
**Proctors:** Yes
**Oral exams:** Yes
**Extended test time:** Yes
**Added cost:** None
**Distraction-free environ.:** Yes
**Tape recording in class:** Yes
**Books on tape:** Yes
**Taping of other books:** No

**Professional tutors:** 8
**Peer tutors:** 20
**Max. hrs/wk for services:** Unlimited
**Priority registration:** Yes
**Accommodations for students with ADD:** Yes
**How are professors notified of LD:** By the student

## GENERAL ADMISSIONS INFORMATION

**Director of Admissions:** Dan Bowers

**Telephone:** 610-499-4126

### ENTRANCE REQUIREMENTS

Total high school units required/recommended: 18 total units are recommended; 4 English recommended, 3 math recommended, 3 science recommended, 2 foreign languages recommended, 2 social studies recommended, 2 history recommended. Minimum SAT I scores of 400 in both Verbal and Math, rank in top 1/2 of secondary school class, and minimum 2.5 GPA recommended. Special requirements: TOEFL is required of all international students. Audition required for music program scholarships.

**Application deadline:** Rolling
**Notification:** Rolling

**SAT or ACT preferred:** SAT
**SAT Avg:** 480V, 475M
**Average GPA:** 2.75

**Graduated top 10% of class:** 22
**Graduated top 25% of class:** 66
**Graduated top 50% of class:** 91

## COLLEGE GRADUATION REQUIREMENTS

**Course waivers allowed:** No
**Course substitutions allowed:** No
**In what courses:** N/A

## ADDITIONAL INFORMATION

**Environment:** The university's 105-acre campus is located 15 miles south of Philadelphia.

**Student Body**
  **Undergrad enrollment:** 3,968
  **Women:** 47%
  **Men:** 53%
  **In-state students:** 55%
  **Out-of-state:** 45%

**Cost Information**
  **In-state tuition:** $14,380
  **Out-of-state:** $14,380
  **Room & board:** $6,200

**Housing Information**
  **University housing:** Yes
  **Fraternity:** Yes
  **Sorority:** Yes
  **Living on campus:** 67%

  **Athletics:** NCAA Div. III

# BROWN UNIVERSITY

45 Prospect Street, Box 1876, Providence, RI 02912 • **Admissions:** 401-863-2378 • **Fax:** 401-863-9595
**Email:** admissions@brown.edu • **Web:** www.brown.edu
**Support:** CS • **Institution:** 4 yr. Private

## LEARNING DISABILITY ADMISSIONS AND SERVICES

Brown University strives to assist students with learning disabilities to provide them with the tools they need to succeed in their adult lives. The Students with Alternative Learning Styles is a mainstreaming program providing accommodations and services to enable students with learning disabilities to succeed at Brown. Counseling is available, as well as the Writing Center, Computer Center, and Student-to-Student (a peer counseling group). Testing accommodations are available. Students may petition to take a reduced load.

## LEARNING DISABILITY ADMISSIONS INFORMATION

**Program Name:** Students with Alternative Learning Styles
**Program Director:** Robert Shaw, Dean
**Contact Person:** Admissions Office

**Telephone:** 401-863-2378

### ADMISSIONS

Admission is very competitive and all students are required to submit the same application form and meet the same standards.

**College entrance exams required:** Yes
**Course entrance requirements:** Yes
**Diagnostic tests:** No
**Documentation:** All information is helpful

**Untimed accepted:** Yes
**Interview required:** No

### ADDITIONAL INFORMATION

Students determine what group of courses to take and there are no specific courses required for graduation. Students who have weaker writing skills may request assistance from a Writing Fellow trained to work with dyslexics. Services and accommodations are available for undergraduate and graduate students.

**Special education HS coursework accepted:** No
**Special application required:** No
**# of applications submitted each year:** N/A
**# of students receiving LD services:** 200
**Acceptance into program means acceptance into college:** Students must be accepted to the university first and then may request services.

**Essay required:** Yes
**Submitted to:** N/A
**# of applications accepted each year:** N/A

## LEARNING DISABILITY SERVICES

**Learning center:** No
**Kurzweil personal reader:** Yes
**LD specialists:** 1
**Allowed in exams:**
  **Calculator:** Yes
  **Dictionary:** Yes
  **Computer:** Yes
  **SpellCheck:** Yes

**Notetaker:** Yes
**Scribes:** No
**Proctors:** No
**Oral exams:** No
**Extended test time:** Yes
**Added cost:** None
**Distraction-free environ.:** Yes
**Tape recording in class:** Yes
**Books on tape:** No
**Taping of other books:** No

**Professional tutors:** N/I
**Peer tutors:** N/I
**Max. hrs/wk for services:** N/I
**Priority registration:** No
**Accommodations for students with ADD:** Yes
**How are professors notified of LD:** By the student and the Dean

## GENERAL ADMISSIONS INFORMATION

**Director of Admissions:** Michael Goldberger          **Telephone:** 401-863-2378

### ENTRANCE REQUIREMENTS

Total high school units required/recommended: 16 total units are required; 4 English required, 3 math required, 3 science required, 3 foreign language required, 2 history required. Electives should be from computer science, foreign language, history, math, or science. Different distributions of units required of S.B. program applicants and 8-year Liberal Arts/Medical Education Program applicants. Special requirements: TOEFL is required of all international students.

**Application deadline:** January 1
**Notification:** April 1

**SAT or ACT preferred:** SAT
**SAT Avg:** 620V, 680M
**Average ACT:** 28

**Graduated top 10% of class:** 87
**Graduated top 25% of class:** 95
**Graduated top 50% of class:** 99

## COLLEGE GRADUATION REQUIREMENTS

**Course waivers allowed:** No
**Course substitutions allowed:** Yes
**In what courses:** Varies

## ADDITIONAL INFORMATION

**Environment:** The university is located on 146 acres in an urban area 45 miles south of Boston.

**Student Body**
  **Undergrad enrollment:** 5,992
  **Women:** 52%
  **Men:** 48%
  **In-state students:** 4%
  **Out-of-state:** 96%

**Cost Information**
  **In-state tuition:** $21,592
  **Out-of-state:** $21,592
  **Room & board:** $6,538

**Housing Information**
  **University housing:** Yes
  **Fraternity:** Yes
  **Sorority:** Yes
  **Living on campus:** 80%

  **Athletics:** NCAA Div. I

# JOHNSON & WALES UNIVERSITY

8 Abbott Park Place, Providence, RI 02903 • **Admissions:** 1-800-343-2565
**Fax:** 401-598-2948
**Support:** CS • **Institution:** 2 yr. & 4 yr. Private

## LEARNING DISABILITY ADMISSIONS AND SERVICES

Johnson and Wales University is dedicated to providing reasonable accommodations to allow students with learning disabilities to succeed in their academic pursuits. While maintaining the highest academic integrity, the university strives to balance scholarship with support services, which will assist special needs students to function in the post-secondary learning process. Accommodations could include decelerated load, preferential scheduling, oral or untimed exams, notetakers, LD support group, individualized tutoring, and a special needs advisor. It is important that these students identify themselves and present the appropriate neurological, medical and/or psychoeducational documentation as soon as possible. Recommendations for specific accommodations will be based on the student's individual needs and learning style. The goal of the Student Success Department is to support students in their efforts to develop their talents, empower them to direct their own learning, and lead them on the pathways of success.

## LEARNING DISABILITY ADMISSIONS INFORMATION

**Program Name:** Student Success/Special Needs
**Program Director:** Meryl Bernstein
**Contact Person:** Same as above

**Telephone:** 401-598-4689

### ADMISSIONS

There is no special application process. After regular admissions has been completed and the student is accepted, the student should self-identify and verify the learning disability with the appropriate neurological, medical and/or psychoeducational documentation. This would include tests administered by the student's high school or private testing service within the past 3 years. Once admitted, the coordinator of the program will meet with the student, and recommendations for specific accommodations will be based on the student's individual needs and learning styles. Any student admitted conditionally will be closely monitored by an academic counselor and must maintain a GPA of 2.0. (2 terms below a 2.0 may result in dismissal).

**College entrance exams required:** No
**Course entrance requirements:** No
**Diagnostic tests:** Yes
**Documentation:** Flexible: within 3 years

**Untimed accepted:** N/A
**Interview required:** No

### ADDITIONAL INFORMATION

Academic counselors establish initial contact with probational, conditional, and special needs students. Counselors monitor and review grades and enforce academic policies. Students are allowed to take a reduced course load. Career counselors and personal counselors are also available. Program of Assisted Studies (PAS) provides a structured delivery of fundamental math, language and major skills courses with a strong emphasis on learning strategy instruction and professional advising and tutoring. The Learning Center offers group and/or one-to-one tutoring, writing skills, culinary skills, grammar fundamentals, study groups and supplemental instruction groups. Freshman requirements include a course in study and social adjustment skills, and a course to teach effective job-search techniques, including career planning, personal development, resume writing, and interview techniques. Services and accommodations are available for undergraduate and graduate students.

**Special education HS coursework accepted:** Yes
**Special application required:** No
**# of applications submitted each year:** N/A
**# of students receiving LD services:** 500+

**Essay required:** No
**Submitted to:** N/A
**# of applications accepted each year:** N/A

**Acceptance into program means acceptance into college:** Students must be accepted to the university first and then may request services.

## LEARNING DISABILITY SERVICES

**Learning center:** Yes
**Kurzweil personal reader:** No
**LD specialists:** 5
**Allowed in exams:**
  **Calculator:** Y/N
  **Dictionary:** Yes
  **Computer:** Yes
  **SpellCheck:** Yes

**Notetaker:** Yes
**Scribes:** Yes
**Proctors:** Yes
**Oral exams:** Yes
**Extended test time:** Yes
**Added cost:** None
**Distraction-free environ.:** Yes
**Tape recording in class:** Yes
**Books on tape:** Yes
**Taping of other books:** No

**Professional tutors:** 4
**Peer tutors:** 35
**Max. hrs/wk for services:** Unlimited
**Priority registration:** Yes
**Accommodations for students with ADD:** Yes
**How are professors notified of LD:** By the Program Director

## GENERAL ADMISSIONS INFORMATION

**Director of Admissions:** Ken DiSaia

**Telephone:** 401-598-1000

### ENTRANCE REQUIREMENTS
NR

**Application deadline:** NR
**Notification:** NR

**SAT or ACT preferred:** NR

## COLLEGE GRADUATION REQUIREMENTS

**Course waivers allowed:** No
**Course substitutions allowed:** Yes
**In what courses:** Foreign language

## ADDITIONAL INFORMATION

**Environment:** The university is located on 100 acres with easy access to Boston.

**Student Body**
  **Undergrad enrollment:** 8,884
  **Women:** 45%
  **Men:** 55%
  **In-state students:** 10%
  **Out-of-state:** 90%

**Cost Information**
  **In-state tuition:** $10,554
  **Out-of-state:** $10,554

**Housing Information**
  **University housing:** Yes
  **Fraternity:** Yes
  **Sorority:** Yes
  **Living on campus:** 51%

  **Athletics:** NR

# PROVIDENCE COLLEGE

River Avenue and Eaton Street, Providence, RI 02918 • **Admissions:** 401-865-2535
**Fax:** 401-865-2826 • **Email:** pcadmission@providence.edu • **Web:** www.providence.edu
**Support:** CS • **Institution:** 4 yr. Private

## LEARNING DISABILITY ADMISSIONS AND SERVICES

There is no formal program for students with learning disabilities. However, the Director of the Office of Academic Services and the faculty of the college are very supportive and are diligent about providing comprehensive services. The goal of the college is to be available to assist students whenever help is requested. After admission, the Director meets with the LD students during the summer, prior to entry, to help them select the appropriate courses for freshman year. Students are monitored for 4 years.

## LEARNING DISABILITY ADMISSIONS INFORMATION

**Program Name:** Office of Academic Services
**Program Director:** Rose A. Boyle
**Contact Person:** Ann Marie Coleman

**Telephone:** 401-865-2494

### ADMISSIONS

There is no special admissions process for students with learning disabilities. However, an interview is highly recommended, during which individualized coursework is examined. General course requirements include 4 yrs. English, 3 yrs. math, 3 yrs. foreign language, 2 yrs. lab science, 2 yrs. social studies, and 2 yrs. electives. Students with learning disabilities who have lower test scores, but a fairly good academic record, may be accepted. The admission committee has the flexibility to overlook poor test scores for students with learning disabilities. Those who have higher test scores and reasonable grades in college prep courses (C+/B) may also gain admission. Students should self-identify as learning disabled on their application.

**College entrance exams required:** Yes
**Course entrance requirements:** Yes
**Diagnostic tests:** Yes
**Documentation:** WAIS-R; Reading and Achievement Tests: within 3 years

**Untimed accepted:** Yes
**Interview required:** Recommended

### ADDITIONAL INFORMATION

All learning disability documentation should be sent to the Office of Academic Services. This information will help in determining the types of services the students will need. Skills seminars, for no credit, are offered in study techniques and test taking strategies. Services and accommodations are available for undergraduate and graduate students.

**Special education HS coursework accepted:** No
**Special application required:** No
**# of applications submitted each year:** N/A
**# of students receiving LD services:** 150

**Essay required:** Yes
**Submitted to:** N/A
**# of applications accepted each year:** N/A

**Acceptance into program means acceptance into college:** Students must be accepted to the college first and then may request services.

## LEARNING DISABILITY SERVICES

**Learning center:** No
**Kurzweil personal reader:** Yes
**LD specialists:** 2
**Allowed in exams:**
  **Calculator:** Y/N
  **Dictionary:** Yes
  **Computer:** Yes
  **SpellCheck:** Yes

**Notetaker:** Yes
**Scribes:** Yes
**Proctors:** Yes
**Oral exams:** Yes
**Extended test time:** Yes
**Added cost:** None
**Distraction-free environ.:** Yes
**Tape recording in class:** Yes
**Books on tape:** Yes
**Taping of other books:** Yes

**Professional tutors:** N/I
**Peer tutors:** 35
**Max. hrs/wk for services:** No limit for students with learning disabilities
**Priority registration:** Yes
**Accommodations for students with ADD:** Yes
**How are professors notified of LD:** By the Program Director

## GENERAL ADMISSIONS INFORMATION

**Director of Admissions:** William Di Brienza

**Telephone:** 401-865-2535

### ENTRANCE REQUIREMENTS

Total high school units required/recommended: 18 total units are required; 4 English required, 3 math required, 2 science required, 3 math recommended, 3 science recommended, 3 foreign language required, 4 foreign language recommended, 2 social studies required, 1 history required. Minimum SAT I scores of 510 Verbal and 550 Math (composite ACT score of 25), rank in top 1/3 of secondary school class, and minimum 3.0 GPA recommended. Special requirements: TOEFL is required of all international students. 4 units each of math and science recommended of Biology, Chemistry, and Pre-engineering Program applicants.

**Application deadline:** February 1
**Notification:** April 1

**SAT or ACT preferred:** Either
**SAT Avg:** 576V, 571M
**Average ACT:** 26

**Graduated top 10% of class:** 30
**Graduated top 25% of class:** 69
**Graduated top 50% of class:** 94

## COLLEGE GRADUATION REQUIREMENTS

**Course waivers allowed:** Yes
**Course substitutions allowed:** Yes
**In what courses:** Depends on student's disability

## ADDITIONAL INFORMATION

**Environment:** Providence College is on a 105-acre campus located in a small city 50 miles south of Boston.

**Student Body**
  **Undergrad enrollment:** 3,653
  **Women:** 58%
  **Men:** 42%
  **In-state students:** 11%
  **Out-of-state:** 89%

**Cost Information**
  **In-state tuition:** $16,350
  **Out-of-state:** $16,350
  **Room & board:** $6,919

**Housing Information**
  **University housing:** Yes
  **Fraternity:** No
  **Sorority:** No
  **Living on campus:** 72%

  **Athletics:** NCAA Div. I

# LIMESTONE COLLEGE

115 College Drive, Gaffney, SC 29340 • **Admissions:** 864-489-7151
**Email:** 74114.1034@compuseco •
**Support:** S • **Institution:** 4 yr. Private

## LEARNING DISABILITY ADMISSIONS AND SERVICES

Program for Alternative Learning Styles (PALS) was developed to service students with learning disabilities. Therefore, only students with documented learning disabilities are eligible to receive program services. For Program purposes, LD refers to students with average to above average intelligence (above 90), who have a discrepancy between measured intelligence and achievement. The PALS Program's biggest advantage is the tracking system that is in place for the PALS students. Each student is very carefully monitored as to their progress in each course they take. The students who are not successful are typically those students who do not take advantage of the system. With the tracking system the students in PALS are in no danger of "falling between the cracks." The tracking system is specifically designed to keep the professors, the director, and the students informed as to their progress toward a degree from Limestone College. A student may not be successful at Limestone College, but it will not be because of being lost in the crowd.

## LEARNING DISABILITY ADMISSIONS INFORMATION

**Program Name:** Program for Alternative Learning Styles
**Program Director:** Dr. Joe Pitts
**Contact Person:** Same as above

**Telephone:** 864-488-4534

### ADMISSIONS

Students must submit a high school transcript with a diploma or GED certificate, SAT or ACT scores, and the general college application. In addition, students wishing to receive services through PALS must submit a copy of their most recent psychological report (within 3 years), documenting the existence of a learning disability. Only evaluations by certified school psychologists will be accepted. In addition, only intelligence test scores from the Stanford Binet and/or Wechsler Scales will be acceptable. All available information is carefully reviewed prior to acceptance. It is strongly recommended that a student applying to PALS arrange an on-campus interview with the director of PALS. Students may be admitted provisionally provided they are enrolled in PALS.

**College entrance exams required:** Yes
**Course entrance requirements:** Yes
**Diagnostic tests:** Yes
**Documentation:** Wechsler Scales; Stanford Binet: within 3 years

**Untimed accepted:** Yes
**Interview required:** Recommended

### ADDITIONAL INFORMATION

During the regular academic year, students will receive special instruction in the area of study skills. The Director of PALS is in constant communication with students concerning grades, tutors, professors, accommodations, time management, and study habits. Tutorial services are provided on an individual basis so that all students can reach their maximum potential. Skills classes are offered in math and reading. Other services include counseling, time management skills, and screening for the best ways to make accommodations.

**Special education HS coursework accepted:** N/I
**Special application required:** Yes
**# of applications submitted each year:** 25
**# of students receiving LD services:** 17

**Essay required:** N/I
**Submitted to:** Director of Program
**# of applications accepted each year:** 12

**Acceptance into program means acceptance into college:** Students are admitted simultaneously into the college and to the PALS program.

# LEARNING DISABILITY SERVICES

**Learning center:** No
**Kurzweil personal reader:** No
**LD specialists:** No
**Allowed in exams:**
  **Calculator:** Y/N
  **Dictionary:** Y/N
  **Computer:** Y/N
  **SpellCheck:** Y/N

**Notetaker:** Yes
**Scribes:** Yes
**Proctors:** Yes
**Oral exams:** Yes
**Extended test time:** Yes
**Added cost:** $3,000 per year
**Distraction-free environ.:** Yes
**Tape recording in class:** Yes
**Books on tape:** Yes
**Taping of other books:** No

**Professional tutors:** Yes
**Peer tutors:** Yes
**Max. hrs/wk for services:**
Unlimited
**Priority registration:** No
**Accommodations for students
with ADD:** Y/N
**How are professors notified of
LD:** By the student and the
Director

# GENERAL ADMISSIONS INFORMATION

**Director of Admissions:** John Lancaster

**Telephone:** 864-488-4553

## ENTRANCE REQUIREMENTS

Special requirements: TOEFL is required of all international students.

**Application deadline:** Rolling
**Notification:** NR

**SAT or ACT preferred:** NR
**SAT Avg:** 440V, 480M
**Average ACT:** 22

**Graduated top 10% of class:** 5
**Graduated top 25% of class:** 40
**Graduated top 50% of class:** 80

# COLLEGE GRADUATION REQUIREMENTS

**Course waivers allowed:** Yes
**Course substitutions allowed:** No
**In what courses:** Foreign language

# ADDITIONAL INFORMATION

**Environment:** The campus is located in an urban area 45 miles south of Charlotte.

**Student Body**
  **Undergrad enrollment:** 310
  **Women:** 45%
  **Men:** 55%
  **In-state students:** 88%
  **Out-of-state:** 12%

**Cost Information**
  **In-state tuition:** $8,200
  **Out-of-state:** $8,200
  **Room & board:** $3,700

**Housing Information**
  **University housing:** Yes
  **Fraternity:** Yes
  **Sorority:** Yes
  **Living on campus:** 65%

  **Athletics:** Intramural

# UNIVERSITY OF SOUTH CAROLINA-COLUMBIA

Office of Admissions, Columbia, SC 29208 • **Admissions:** 803-777-7700 • **Fax:** 803-777-5415
**Email:** admissions-ugrad@sc.edu • **Web:** www.csd.scarolina.edu
**Support:** CS • **Institution:** 4 yr. Public

## LEARNING DISABILITY ADMISSIONS AND SERVICES

The university's Learning Disability Program (LPD) provides educational support and assistance to students with learning disabilities who have the potential for success in a competitive university setting. The Program is specifically designed to empower them with the confidence to become self-advocates and to take an active role in their education. The university works with each student on an individualized basis to match needs with appropriate services. The services are individually tailored to provide educational support and assistance to students based on their specific needs. The Program recommends and coordinates support services with faculty, administrators, advisors, and deans' offices. The nature and severity of a learning disability may vary considerably. For this reason, the individual needs of each student determine which support services and accommodations are recommended. All requests are based on documented diagnostic information regarding each student's specific learning disability. The first step in accessing services from the LDP is to self-disclose the learning disability and arrange an interview. During the interview, staff members will discuss the student's educational background and will determine which services best fit his/her needs.

## LEARNING DISABILITY ADMISSIONS INFORMATION

**Program Name:** Learning Disability Program (LPD)
**Program Director:** Deborah C. Haynes
**Contact Person:** Same as above

**Telephone:** 803-777-6142

### ADMISSIONS

There is no special application or admission process for students with LD. Required scores on the SAT and ACT vary with high school. Applicants must have a cumulative C+ average on defined college preparatory courses including: 4 yrs. English, 3 yrs. math, 2 yrs. science, 2 yrs. social studies, 2 yrs. foreign language,1 yr. elective and 1 yr. physical education; 1200 SAT or 27 ACT. Admissions is based on a combination of test score and the grades in high school core courses. If they are denied admission or feel they do not meet the required standards, students may petition the Admissions Committee for an exception to the regular admissions requirements. Once admitted, students should contact the Educational Support Services Center to arrange an interview to determine which services are necessary to accommodate their needs.

**College entrance exams required:** Yes
**Course entrance requirements:** Yes
**Diagnostic tests:** Yes
**Documentation:** N/I

**Untimed accepted:** Yes
**Interview required:** No

### ADDITIONAL INFORMATION

Services are individually tailored to provide educational support and assistance. All requests are based on documented diagnostic information. The program is designed to provide educational support and assistance including analysis of learning needs to determine appropriate interventions, consulting with the faculty about special academic needs, monitoring of progress by a staff member, study skills training, and tutorial referrals. Special program accommodations may include a reduced course load of 9 hours, auditing a course before taking it for credit, taking an incomplete course due to the need for additional time, withdrawal from a course at any time without grade penalty with approval, waivers /substitutions for problematic courses, and expanded pass/fail options. Special classroom accommodations may include tape recorders, notetakers, alternative test procedures, alternative assignments, oral presentation of written assignments, monitoring of progress, and access to calculators/ dictionaries in class or on tests.

**Special education HS coursework accepted:** No
**Special application required:** No
**# of applications submitted each year:** N/A
**# of students receiving LD services:** 95

**Essay required:** No
**Submitted to:** N/A
**# of applications accepted each year:** N/A

**Acceptance into program means acceptance into college:** Students must be admitted to the university first (may appeal a denial) and then may request LD services.

## LEARNING DISABILITY SERVICES

**Learning center:** No
**Kurzweil personal reader:** Yes
**LD specialists:** 1
**Allowed in exams:**
  **Calculator:** Yes
  **Dictionary:** Yes
  **Computer:** Y/N
  **SpellCheck:** Y/N

**Notetaker:** Yes
**Scribes:** Yes
**Proctors:** Yes
**Oral exams:** Yes
**Extended test time:** Yes
**Added cost:** No
**Distraction-free environ.:** Yes
**Tape recording in class:** Yes
**Books on tape:** No
**Taping of other books:** Yes

**Professional tutors:** N/I
**Peer tutors:** N/I
**Max. hrs/wk for services:** Unlimited
**Priority registration:** Yes
**Accommodations for students with ADD:** Yes
**How are professors notified of LD:** By the student and the Program Director

## GENERAL ADMISSIONS INFORMATION

**Director of Admissions:** Ms. Terry Davis

**Telephone:** 800-868-5872

### ENTRANCE REQUIREMENTS

Total high school units required/recommended: 16 total units are required; 4 English required, 3 math required, 2 science required, 2 foreign language required, 2 social studies required. Minimum 2.0 GPA or 15 academic secondary school units required. Special requirements: TOEFL is required of all international students.

**Application deadline:** Rolling
**Notification:** Rolling

**SAT or ACT preferred:** Either
**SAT Avg:** 537V, 530M
**ACT Range:** 20–26

**Graduated top 10% of class:** 31
**Graduated top 25% of class:** 75
**Graduated top 50% of class:** 94

## COLLEGE GRADUATION REQUIREMENTS

**Course waivers allowed:** Yes
**Course substitutions allowed:** Yes
**In what courses:** Students with learning disabilities may petition their college for substitution of the required foreign language if the requirement is not an integral part of the degree program.

## ADDITIONAL INFORMATION

**Environment:** The university is located on 242 acres in downtown Columbia.

**Student Body**
  **Undergrad enrollment:** 15,747
  **Women:** 54%
  **Men:** 46%
  **In-state students:** 81%
  **Out-of-state:** 19%

**Cost Information**
  **In-state tuition:** $3,380
  **Out-of-state:** $8,575
  **Room & board:** $3,690

**Housing Information**
  **University housing:** Yes
  **Fraternity:** Yes
  **Sorority:** Yes
  **Living on campus:** 40%

  **Athletics:** NCAA Div. I

# SC SOUTHERN WESLEYAN UNIVERSITY

P.O. Box 1020, Central, SC 29630 • **Admissions:** 803-639-2453
**Fax:** 864-639-0826
**Support:** CS • **Institution:** 4 yr. Private

## LEARNING DISABILITY ADMISSIONS AND SERVICES

Southern Wesleyan University provides the environment for success. In accepting students with learning disabilities, the university is committed to providing special services and assistance to these students. Services are provided after an assessment of the students' particular needs. The objectives of the SWU Program is to help students with learning disabilities make a smooth transition from high school to college, provide faculty with instructional methods, and to help students know that they can graduate and be successful. Southern Wesleyan has a very friendly student body and everyone works together like a family.

## LEARNING DISABILITY ADMISSIONS INFORMATION

**Program Name:** Learning Disabilities
**Program Director:** Randy Becker
**Contact Person:** Jim Wilerson

**Telephone:** N/I
**Telephone:** 864-639-2453

### ADMISSIONS

Applicants with learning disabilities are reviewed on the basis of high school transcript, SAT or ACT, personal interview, recommendations and psychoeducational evaluation. Students may be conditionally admitted with less than a 'C' average or SAT lower than 740 or ACT lower than 19, or rank in the bottom 50%. High school courses should include: 4 yrs. English; 2 yrs. math; 2 yrs. science; 2 yrs. social studies. Applicants not meeting these requirements may be admitted conditionally (on academic warning), on probation, or provisionally.

**College entrance exams required:** Yes
**Course entrance requirements:** Yes
**Diagnostic tests:** Yes
**Documentation:** Psychoeducational evaluations

**Untimed accepted:** Yes
**Interview required:** Recommended

### ADDITIONAL INFORMATION

There is a liaison person between faculty and students. Professors are available to students after class. Modifications can be made in test taking which could include extended time and a quiet place to take exams. Additionally, students may receive assistance with note taking. There are peer group study sessions for those students wishing this type of study experience.

**Special education HS coursework accepted:** Yes
**Special application required:** No
**# of applications submitted each year:** N/A
**# of students receiving LD services:** 8

**Essay required:** No
**Submitted to:** N/A
**# of applications accepted each year:** N/A

**Acceptance into program means acceptance into college:** Students are admitted directly into the university and to special services for exceptional students on campus with appropriate documentation.

## LEARNING DISABILITY SERVICES

**Learning center:** Yes
**Kurzweil personal reader:** N/I
**LD specialists:** Yes
**Allowed in exams:**
  **Calculator:** Yes
  **Dictionary:** Yes
  **Computer:** N/A
  **SpellCheck:** N/A

**Notetaker:** Yes
**Scribes:** Yes
**Proctors:** Yes
**Oral exams:** Yes
**Extended test time:** Yes
**Added cost:** $5 per/hour for some tutoring
**Distraction-free environ.:** Yes
**Tape recording in class:** Yes
**Books on tape:** Yes
**Taping of other books:** Yes

**Professional tutors:** Yes
**Peer tutors:** Yes
**Max. hrs/wk for services:** As needed
**Priority registration:** No
**Accommodations for students with ADD:** Yes
**How are professors notified of LD:** By the student and the Program Director

## GENERAL ADMISSIONS INFORMATION

**Director of Admissions:** Tim Wilkerson

**Telephone:** 864-639-2453

### ENTRANCE REQUIREMENTS
Special requirements: TOEFL is required of all international students.

**Application deadline:** Rolling
**Notification:** NR

**SAT or ACT preferred:** NR
**SAT Avg:** 388V, 434M

**Graduated top 10% of class:** 7
**Graduated top 25% of class:** 26
**Graduated top 50% of class:** 57

## COLLEGE GRADUATION REQUIREMENTS

**Course waivers allowed:** No
**Course substitutions allowed:** No
**In what courses:** N/A

## ADDITIONAL INFORMATION

**Environment:** The college is located midway between Charlotte, NC, and Atlanta, GA, within sight of the Blue Ridge Mountains.

**Student Body**
  **Undergrad enrollment:** 1,277
  **Women:** 59%
  **Men:** 41%
  **In-state students:** 85%
  **Out-of-state:** 15%

**Cost Information**
  **In-state tuition:** $9,416
  **Out-of-state:** $9,416
  **Room & board:** $3,380

**Housing Information**
  **University housing:** Yes
  **Fraternity:** No
  **Sorority:** No
  **Living on campus:** 14%

  **Athletics:** NAIA

# BLACK HILLS STATE UNIVERSITY

1200 University Avenue, Spearfish, SD 57799 • **Admissions:** 605-642-6343 • **Fax:** 605-642-6022
**Email:** Jbery@mystic.bhsu.edu • **Web:** www.bhsu.edu
**Support:** S • **Institution:** 2 yr. & 4 yr.  Public

## LEARNING DISABILITY ADMISSIONS AND SERVICES

Student Support Services ensures equal access and opportunities to educational programs for students with learning disabilities. Within the program, the Disabilities Coordinator provides a wide range of services, including consultation on disability issues and awareness to the campus. A campus counselor provides support and encouragement through a disabilities support group. The Special Education faculty are LD specialists and LD certified. Everyone works together to ensure success for students with disabilities.

## LEARNING DISABILITY ADMISSIONS INFORMATION

**Program Name:** Student Support Services
**Program Director:** Sharon Hemmingson
**Contact Person:** Ann Anderson, Coordinator

**Telephone:** 605-642-6643
**Telephone:** 605-642-6099

### ADMISSIONS

General admission requirements include a C average or an ACT of 20 or rank in upper 2/3 for residents or upper 1/2 for non-residents. In addition students must complete the following high school course work; 4 yrs. English, 2 yrs. lab science and 3 yrs. math or 2 yrs. math and 2 yrs. lab science, 3 yrs. social studies, 1/2 yr. of fine arts and 1/2 yr. of computer science. Students who do not meet the admission requirements for general admissions will be admitted to the Junior College at Black Hills State. Course deficiencies must be satisfied within 2 years of admittance. There is complete open enrollment for summer courses also. Transfer students who do not meet admission requirements will be admitted on probationary status.

**College entrance exams required:** Yes
**Course entrance requirements:** Yes
**Diagnostic tests:** Yes
**Documentation:** Any testing that is available

**Untimed accepted:** Yes
**Interview required:** No

### ADDITIONAL INFORMATION

Black Hills State University offers Special Education as a major in the School of Education and the professors are specialists certified in learning disabilities. The Academic Skills Center provides tutors, and the Student Support Services will hire tutors in areas the Academic Skills Center are unable to provide. Study skills, supplemental instruction in algebra and English are available for non-credit.

**Special education HS coursework accepted:** Not for college credit
**Essay required:** No
**Special application required:** Yes
**# of applications submitted each year:** 5
**# of students receiving LD services:** 26

**Submitted to:** Director of Program
**# of applications accepted each year:** All who apply

**Acceptance into program means acceptance into college:** Students must be accepted to the university first and then may request services.

## LEARNING DISABILITY SERVICES

**Learning center:** No
**Kurzweil personal reader:** No
**LD specialists:** No
**Allowed in exams:**
 **Calculator:** Yes
 **Dictionary:** Yes
 **Computer:** Yes
 **SpellCheck:** Yes

**Notetaker:** Yes
**Scribes:** Yes
**Proctors:** Yes
**Oral exams:** Yes
**Extended test time:** Yes
**Added cost:** None
**Distraction-free environ.:** Yes
**Tape recording in class:** Yes
**Books on tape:** Yes
**Taping of other books:** Yes

**Professional tutors:** 2
**Peer tutors:** 25
**Max. hrs/wk for services:** As needed/as available
**Priority registration:** No
**Accommodations for students with ADD:** Yes
**How are professors notified of LD:** By the student and the Program Director

## GENERAL ADMISSIONS INFORMATION

**Director of Admissions:** April Meeker          **Telephone:** 605-642-6567

### ENTRANCE REQUIREMENTS

Total high school units required/recommended: 14 total units are required; 4 English required, 3 math required, 3 science required, 3 social studies required. Minimum composite ACT score of 18, rank in top 3/5 of secondary school class, or minimum 2.6 GPA required. Special requirements: TOEFL is required of all international students.

**Application deadline:** Rolling
**Notification:** Rolling

**SAT or ACT preferred:** ACT
**SAT II required:** Yes
**Average ACT:** 19

## COLLEGE GRADUATION REQUIREMENTS

**Course waivers allowed:** Yes
**Course substitutions allowed:** Yes
**In what courses:** Evaluated on an individual basis. Waivers are not recommended.

## ADDITIONAL INFORMATION

**Environment:** The university is located on 123 acres in a small town 45 miles northwest of Rapid City.

**Student Body**
 **Undergrad enrollment:** 3,997
 **Women:** 58%
 **Men:** 42%
 **In-state students:** 74%
 **Out-of-state:** 26%

**Cost Information**
 **In-state tuition:** $1,646
 **Out-of-state:** $4,840
 **Room & board:** $2,537

**Housing Information**
 **University housing:** Yes
 **Fraternity:** No
 **Sorority:** No
 **Living on campus:** 22%

 **Athletics:** NAIA

# NORTHERN STATE UNIVERSITY

1200 South Jay Street, Aberdeen, SD 57401 • **Admissions:** 605-626-2544 • **Fax:** 605-626-2431
**Email:** admission1@wolf.northern.edu • **Web:** www.northern.edu
**Support:** CS • **Institution:** 4 yr. Public

## LEARNING DISABILITY ADMISSIONS AND SERVICES

The Learning Center at Northern State University is designed to provide services to benefit the student. Each case is determined on an individual basis and the plan of action is dependent solely on the unique needs of the student. The main goal of the Program in the future is to provide quality service and expand to provide additional services not currently offered at NSU.

## LEARNING DISABILITY ADMISSIONS INFORMATION

**Program Name:** Learning Center
**Program Director:** Paul Kraft
**Contact Person:** Same as above

**Telephone:** 605-626-2371

### ADMISSIONS

As a gateway university, the students are admitted via individual decision. Adaptations are made for taking the ACT and special admission is in order. Each student is considered individually. Special Admit is an open policy for any student with an ACT of 15 and ranking in the top 3/4 of their high school class. Students with learning disabilities may request to be evaluated on a Learning Disability status or to be admitted via a special unit. Courses required for general admissions include: 3 yrs. English, 3 yrs. math, 3 yrs. social studies.

**College entrance exams required:** Yes
**Course entrance requirements:** Yes
**Diagnostic tests:** No
**Documentation:** N/A

**Untimed accepted:** Yes
**Interview required:** No

### ADDITIONAL INFORMATION

All students who do not meet the entrance requirements can be admitted to Northern State University as a special admit, or on a probationary period for 1 semester. If the student maintains or achieves a 2.0 GPA, he/she is taken off the special admit. Skills classes are offered in reading, math, writing, and "College Success." Services and accommodations are available for undergraduate and graduate students.

**Special education HS coursework accepted:** No
**Special application required:** No
**# of applications submitted each year:** N/A
**# of students receiving LD services:** 96+

**Essay required:** No
**Submitted to:** N/A
**# of applications accepted each year:** N/A

**Acceptance into program means acceptance into college:** Students must be admitted and enrolled in the university and then may request to be reviewed for LD services.

## LEARNING DISABILITY SERVICES

**Learning center:** Yes
**Kurzweil personal reader:** No
**LD specialists:** 2
**Allowed in exams:**
  **Calculator:** Yes
  **Dictionary:** Yes
  **Computer:** Yes
  **SpellCheck:** Yes

**Notetaker:** Yes
**Scribes:** Yes
**Proctors:** Yes
**Oral exams:** Yes
**Extended test time:** Yes
**Added cost:** None
**Distraction-free environ.:** Yes
**Tape recording in class:** Yes
**Books on tape:** Yes
**Taping of other books:** Yes

**Professional tutors:** 3
**Peer tutors:** 15-25
**Max. hrs/wk for services:**
Unlimited
**Priority registration:** Yes
**Accommodations for students
with ADD:** Yes
**How are professors notified of
LD:** By the student and the
Program Director

## GENERAL ADMISSIONS INFORMATION

**Director of Admissions:** Steve Ochsner

**Telephone:** 605-626-2544

### ENTRANCE REQUIREMENTS

Total high school units required/recommended: 13 total units are required; 4 English required, 3 math required, 3 social studies required. Minimum composite ACT score of 18, rank in top 3/5 of secondary school class, or minimum 2.6 GPA required. Special requirements: TOEFL is required of all international students.

**Application deadline:** August 15
**Notification:** Rolling

**SAT or ACT preferred:** ACT

**Graduated top 25% of class:** 35
**Graduated top 50% of class:** 74

## COLLEGE GRADUATION REQUIREMENTS

**Course waivers allowed:** Yes
**Course substitutions allowed:** Yes
**In what courses:** Depends on the class and the disability.

## ADDITIONAL INFORMATION

**Environment:** NR

**Student Body**
  **Undergrad enrollment:** 2,871
  **Women:** 57%
  **Men:** 43%
  **In-state students:** 95%
  **Out-of-state:** 5%

**Cost Information**
  **In-state tuition:** $1,646
  **Out-of-state:** $4,840
  **Room & board:** $2,340

**Housing Information**
  **University housing:** Yes
  **Fraternity:** No
  **Sorority:** No
  **Living on campus:** 37%

  **Athletics:** NAIA

# SOUTH DAKOTA STATE UNIVERSITY

Box 2201, Brookings, SD 57007 • **Admissions:** 605-688-4121 • **Fax:** 605-688-6384
**Email:** sdsuadms@adm.state.edu •
**Support:** S • **Institution:** 4 yr. Public

## LEARNING DISABILITY ADMISSIONS AND SERVICES

South Dakota State University is committed to providing equal opportunities for higher education to academically qualified students with learning disabilities who have a reasonable expectation of college success. The university does not offer a specialized curriculum, but it does share responsibility with students for modifying programs to meet individual needs. Students needing specialized tutoring service in reading and writing may have to seek assistance from Vocational Rehabilitation or personally pay for such help. The key to success in college includes planning and preparing for college, and the ability and openness to realize strengths and limitations.

## LEARNING DISABILITY ADMISSIONS INFORMATION

**Program Name:** Disabled Student Services (DSS)
**Program Director:** N/I
**Contact Person:** James W. Carlson

**Telephone:** N/I
**Telephone:** 605-688-4496

### ADMISSIONS

Students with learning disabilities are required to submit the general application form. If they do not meet all of the course requirements, they may be admitted conditionally based on ACT scores or class rank. Courses required include 4 yrs. English, 2-3 yrs. math, 1/2 yr. computer science, 3 yrs. social studies, 2-3 yrs. science, and 1/2 yr. art or music. Students deficient in course requirements need an ACT of 22 (in-state or Minnesota) or 23 from out-of-state.

**College entrance exams required:** Yes
**Course entrance requirements:** Yes
**Diagnostic tests:** No
**Documentation:** WAIS-R; WISC-R; WRAT

**Untimed accepted:** Yes
**Interview required:** Recommended

### ADDITIONAL INFORMATION

A skills course is available in Mastering Lifelong Skills. Test proctoring for additional time, as well as reading or writing assistance with classroom exams can be arranged. DSS will also assist students who are learning disabled with finding readers or notetakers.

**Special education HS coursework accepted:** No
**Special application required:** Yes
**# of applications submitted each year:** 60
**# of students receiving LD services:** 44

**Essay required:** No
**Submitted to:** DSS
**# of applications accepted each year:** N/I

**Acceptance into program means acceptance into college:** Students must be admitted to the university first and then may request services.

# LEARNING DISABILITY SERVICES

**Learning center:** No
**Kurzweil personal reader:** Yes
**LD specialists:** No
**Allowed in exams:**
  **Calculator:** Yes
  **Dictionary:** Y/N
  **Computer:** Yes
  **SpellCheck:** N/I

**Notetaker:** No
**Scribes:** Yes
**Proctors:** Yes
**Oral exams:** Yes
**Extended test time:** Yes
**Added cost:** None
**Distraction-free environ.:** Yes
**Tape recording in class:** Yes
**Books on tape:** Yes
**Taping of other books:** No

**Professional tutors:** No
**Peer tutors:** Yes
**Max. hrs/wk for services:** N/I
**Priority registration:** Yes
**Accommodations for students with ADD:** Yes
**How are professors notified of LD:** By the student or the Program Director

# GENERAL ADMISSIONS INFORMATION

**Director of Admissions:** Dean Hofland

**Telephone:** 605-688-4121

## ENTRANCE REQUIREMENTS

Total high school units required/recommended: 14 total units are required; 4 English required, 3 math required, 3 science required, 3 social studies required, and 1/2 unit each of fine arts and computer science required. Minimum composite ACT score of 18, rank in top 3/5 of class, or minimum 2.6 GPA required. Special requirements: An audition is required for music program applicants.

**Application deadline:** Rolling
**Notification:** Rolling

**SAT or ACT preferred:** NR
**ACT Required:** Yes
**Average ACT:** 22

**Graduated top 10% of class:** 15
**Graduated top 25% of class:** 40
**Graduated top 50% of class:** 75

# COLLEGE GRADUATION REQUIREMENTS

**Course waivers allowed:** No
**Course substitutions allowed:** No
**In what courses:** N/A

# ADDITIONAL INFORMATION

**Environment:** The school is located on 220 acres in a rural area 50 miles north of Sioux Falls.

**Student Body**
  **Undergrad enrollment:** 7,356
  **Women:** 48%
  **Men:** 52%
  **In-state students:** 74%
  **Out-of-state:** 26%

**Cost Information**
  **In-state tuition:** $1,696
  **Out-of-state:** $5,376
  **Room & board:** $2,344

**Housing Information**
  **University housing:** Yes
  **Fraternity:** Yes
  **Sorority:** Yes
  **Living on campus:** 38%

  **Athletics:** NCAA Div. II

# LEE COLLEGE

P.O. Box 3450, Cleveland, TN 37311 • **Admissions:** 423-614-8500 • 800-533-9930

**Support:** CS • **Institution:** 4 yr. Private

## LEARNING DISABILITY ADMISSIONS AND SERVICES

Lee College provides a quality Academic Support Program for students. This service is free to students. It is the goal of the Lee College Academic Support Program to empower students to actualize all the academic potential that they can. Lee College offers a Peer Tutorial Program which hires the best students on campus to share their time, experience and insight in the course or courses that are most difficult for the students who need tutoring. In addition, the college provides direct assistance for any student to verify a learning disability or Attention Deficit Disorder. For these students, Lee College provides support teams, testing adjustments, classroom adjustments, tutoring, and personal monitoring. Students must initiate the request for special accommodations by applying at the Academic Support Program Office. Lee College is committed to the provision of reasonable accommodations for students with disabilities.

## LEARNING DISABILITY ADMISSIONS INFORMATION

**Program Name:** Academic Support Program
**Program Director:** Debrah Murray
**Contact Person:** Same as above

**Telephone:** 423-614-8175

### ADMISSIONS

Each applicant is reviewed on a case-by-case basis. Each student must be able to perform successfully with limited support. Students who do not meet the college policy for entrance are referred to a special committee for possible probational acceptance.

**College entrance exams required:** Yes
**Course entrance requirements:** No
**Diagnostic tests:** Yes
**Documentation:** I.Q and current achievement tests: within 3 years

**Untimed accepted:** Yes
**Interview required:** Yes

### ADDITIONAL INFORMATION

The Program is staffed by professional counselors, math and reading instructors and a tutoring coordinator. The Center has listening and study lab instructional materials, group study/discussion rooms, and tutoring services. The Program provides readers in place of books on tape. Benefits included in the program are: tutoring sessions with friendly and comfortable surroundings; 2 hours of tutoring per week per student; tutoring in any subject including biology, psychology, English, mathematics, religion, science, sociology, history, and foreign language.

**Special education HS coursework accepted:** Yes
**Special application required:** Yes
**# of applications submitted each year:** 25
**# of students receiving LD services:** 40

**Essay required:** No
**Submitted to:** Academic Support
**# of applications accepted each year:** 80%

**Acceptance into program means acceptance into college:** Students must be admitted to the college first and then may request services.

## LEARNING DISABILITY SERVICES

**Learning center:** No
**Kurzweil personal reader:** N/I
**LD specialists:** 2
**Allowed in exams:**
  **Calculator:** No
  **Dictionary:** No
  **Computer:** No
  **SpellCheck:** No

**Notetaker:** Yes
**Scribes:** Yes
**Proctors:** Yes
**Oral exams:** Yes
**Extended test time:** Yes
**Added cost:** No
**Distraction-free environ.:** Yes
**Tape recording in class:** Yes
**Books on tape:** No
**Taping of other books:** No

**Professional tutors:** No
**Peer tutors:** 43
**Max. hrs/wk for services:** 2 hours per student, per subject
**Priority registration:** Yes
**Accommodations for students with ADD:** Yes
**How are professors notified of LD:** By the student and the Program Director

## GENERAL ADMISSIONS INFORMATION

**Director of Admissions:** Gary Ray

**Telephone:** 423-614-8500

**ENTRANCE REQUIREMENTS**
NR

**Application deadline:** Rolling
**Notification:** Rolling

**SAT or ACT preferred:** NR

## COLLEGE GRADUATION REQUIREMENTS

**Course waivers allowed:** No
**Course substitutions allowed:** No
**In what courses:** N/A

## ADDITIONAL INFORMATION

**Environment:** The college is located in a small town on 40 acres 25 miles from Chattanooga.

**Student Body**
  **Undergrad enrollment:** 2,400
  **Women:** 56%
  **Men:** 44%
  **In-state students:** 17%
  **Out-of-state:** 83%

**Cost Information**
  **In-state tuition:** $4,734
  **Out-of-state:** $4,734

**Housing Information**
  **University housing:** Yes
  **Fraternity:** Yes
  **Sorority:** Yes
  **Living on campus:** 65%

  **Athletics:** NAIA

# TN THE UNIVERSITY OF MEMPHIS

Memphis, TN 38152 • **Admissions:** 901-678-2169 • **Fax:** 901-678-3053
**Web:** www.memphis.edu
**Support:** CS • **Institution:** 4 yr. Public

## LEARNING DISABILITY ADMISSIONS AND SERVICES

The LD Program is designed to enhance academic strengths, provide support for areas of weakness, and build skills to help students compete in the college environment. The program encourages development of life-long learning skills as well as personal responsibility for academic success. Training in college survival skills and regular meetings with the LD Coordinator are emphasized during the first year to aid in the transition to college. Specific services are tailored to individual needs, considering one's strengths, weaknesses, course requirements, and learning styles. Students with LD are integrated into regular classes and are held to the same academic standards as other students; however, academic accommodations are available to assist them in meeting requirements. The LD program places responsibility on students to initiate services and follow through with services once they are arranged. Most students who use the appropriate services are successful in their academic pursuits.

## LEARNING DISABILITY ADMISSIONS INFORMATION

**Program Name:** Learning Disability Program
**Program Director:** Dona Sparger                    **Telephone:** 901-678-2880
**Contact Person:** Susan TePaske                      **Telephone:** 901-678-2880

### ADMISSIONS

If applicants with learning disabilities or ADHD choose to disclose their disability and provide professional medical documentation, exceptions to the regular admissions criteria may be made on an individual basis. Applicants should have at least a 17 ACT Composite or 2.0 GPA, and no more than 3 high school curriculum deficiencies, only 1 of which can be math. Applicants who request admissions exceptions will be asked to provide 2 academic recommendations and a personal letter in addition to the documentation. Students requesting admissions exceptions based on learning disabilities or attention deficit disorders will have their documentation reviewed by the LD Coordinator to determine if the documentation is sufficient to meet qualifying criteria.

**College entrance exams required:** Yes            **Untimed accepted:** Yes
**Course entrance requirements:** Yes               **Interview required:** Yes, for Alternative Admission
**Diagnostic tests:** Yes
**Documentation:** WAIS-R; W-J: within the last year

### ADDITIONAL INFORMATION

Remedial and developmental courses are available in basic math, algebra and composition for credit. Non-credit instruction is available in notetaking, time management, and organization skills. The university also offers LD orientation, early registration, training in word processing, use of computers and adaptive software, preferential classroom seating, LD student organization, special section of "Introduction to the University" for LD students geared to their needs. Services and accommodations are available for undergraduate and graduate students.

**Special education HS coursework accepted:** Yes       **Essay required:** Yes
**Special application required:** No                    **Submitted to:** N/A
**# of applications submitted each year:** N/A          **# of applications accepted each year:** N/A
**# of students receiving LD services:** 225
**Acceptance into program means acceptance into college:** Students must be accepted to the university first and then may request services.

## LEARNING DISABILITY SERVICES

**Learning center:** Yes
**Kurzweil personal reader:** Yes
**LD specialists:** 1
**Allowed in exams:**
  **Calculator:** Yes
  **Dictionary:** Yes
  **Computer:** Yes
  **SpellCheck:** Yes

**Notetaker:** Yes
**Scribes:** Yes
**Proctors:** Yes
**Oral exams:** Yes
**Extended test time:** Yes
**Added cost:** None
**Distraction-free environ.:** Yes
**Tape recording in class:** Yes
**Books on tape:** Yes
**Taping of other books:** Yes

**Professional tutors:** Yes
**Peer tutors:** Yes
**Max. hrs/wk for services:**
Unlimited
**Priority registration:** Yes
**Accommodations for students
with ADD:** Yes
**How are professors notified of
LD:** By both the student and the
Director

## GENERAL ADMISSIONS INFORMATION

**Director of Admissions:** David Wallace

**Telephone:** 901-678-2678

### ENTRANCE REQUIREMENTS
Total high school units required/recommended: 14 total units are required; 16 total units are recommended; 3 math required, 4 math recommended, 2 science required, 3 science recommended, 2 foreign language required, 2 social studies recommended. Minimum composite ACT score of 20 and minimum 2.0 GPA required; minimum composite ACT score of 20 and minimum 3.0 GPA recommended. Special requirements: TOEFL is required of all international students.

**Application deadline:** August 1
**Notification:** Rolling

**SAT or ACT preferred:** ACT
**Average ACT:** 22

## COLLEGE GRADUATION REQUIREMENTS

**Course waivers allowed:** Yes
**Course substitutions allowed:** Yes
**In what courses:** Foreign language

## ADDITIONAL INFORMATION

**Environment:** The university is located on 1,159 acres in an urban area.

**Student Body**
  **Undergrad enrollment:** 15,485
  **Women:** 57%
  **Men:** 43%
  **In-state students:** 88%
  **Out-of-state:** 12%

**Cost Information**
  **In-state tuition:** $2,112
  **Out-of-state:** $6,448
  **Room & board:** $2,470

**Housing Information**
  **University housing:** Yes
  **Fraternity:** Yes
  **Sorority:** No
  **Living on campus:** 13%

  **Athletics:** NCAA Div. I

# RHODES COLLEGE

2000 North Parkway, Memphis, TN 38112 • **Admissions:** 901-843-3700 • **Fax:** 901-843-3719
**Email:** adminfo@rhodes.edu • **Web:** www.rhodes.edu
**Support:** S • **Institution:** 4 yr. Private

## LEARNING DISABILITY ADMISSIONS AND SERVICES

Students wishing to request services and accommodations for learning disabilities must contact the Disability Service Office. The Coordinator of Disability Services assists with academic accommodations or arranging for other specific services. The coordinator meets with students to obtain an informal educational history and assist in developing an individualized accommodation plan. Students with a documented disability do have equal access to courses, programs, services, jobs, and activities; may request individualized professional assessment of the documentation supporting the disability and its impact on functioning in an academic environment; reasonable and appropriate accommodations, academic adjustments, and/or auxiliary aids; appropriate confidentiality of all information pertaining to the disability with the choice of to whom to disclose the disability; and information reasonably available in accessible formats. Rhodes does not offer comprehensive diagnostic evaluation for determining disabilities; a special disability-related tutorial program; a reduced standard for academic performance; an exemption from graduation requirements; or credit for effort in place of demonstrated competence in the content of a course. The essential requirements of an academic course need not be modified to accommodate an individual with a disability. Rhodes complies with Section 504 and the ADA in providing reasonable accommodations to qualified students with disabilities.

## LEARNING DISABILITY ADMISSIONS INFORMATION

**Program Name:** Disability Services
**Program Director:** None
**Contact Person:** Peggy Harlow

**Telephone:** N/A
**Telephone:** 901-726-3994

### ADMISSIONS

Rhodes does not have a special application process for students with learning disabilities. All applicants must submit the general application and meet the same admission criteria. Students must have taken 4 yrs English, 2 yrs. foreign language, 2 yrs. laboratory science, 2 yrs. history/social science, and 3 yrs. math. There is no minimum GPA or cutoff scores for the ACT/SAT. Sometimes the foreign language may be waived if it is not offered at the high school. Students are encouraged to self-disclose the learning disability and to provide current diagnostic testing to Disability Services if they plan to attend Rhodes and request services and accommodations.

**College entrance exams required:** Yes
**Course entrance requirements:** Yes
**Diagnostic tests:** Yes
**Documentation:** Psychoeducational evaluation; within 3 years

**Untimed accepted:** Yes
**Interview required:** Recommended

### ADDITIONAL INFORMATION

The Coordinator will meet with the student to refine the specific accommodation requests and discuss how the plan can be carried out. In cases where there is a delay in obtaining the required documentation, provisional accommodations can be arranged. Students are given copies of their accommodation plan so they can present it to each professor. Examples of the types of accommodations that can be provided, if warranted by the disability and substantiated by documentation, include but are not limited to the following: preferential classroom seating, readers, notetakers, adaptive technology, extended time for tests, and permission to tape lectures. All students on campus have access to: supplemental instruction in certain courses; a Writing Center; math assistance; study skills workshops in time management, concentration, motivation, notetaking, test-taking and test preparation; peer assistants; academic advisors; career counseling; and short-term confidential counseling.

**Special education HS coursework accepted:** N/I
**Special application required:** No
**# of applications submitted each year:** N/A
**# of students receiving LD services:** N/I

**Essay required:** Yes
**Submitted to:** N/A
**# of applications accepted each year:** N/A

**Acceptance into program means acceptance into college:** Students must be admitted and enrolled in the college and then request services.

# LEARNING DISABILITY SERVICES

Learning center: No
Kurzweil personal reader: No
LD specialists: No
Allowed in exams:
  Calculator: Yes
  Dictionary: Yes
  Computer: Yes
  SpellCheck: Yes

Notetaker: Yes
Scribes: Yes
Proctors: No
Oral exams: Yes
Extended test time: Yes
Added cost: N/I
Distraction-free environ.: Yes
Tape recording in class: Yes
Books on tape: Yes
Taping of other books: Yes

Professional tutors: N/I
Peer tutors: 25+
Max. hrs/wk for services: N/I
Priority registration: N/I
Accommodations for students
with ADD: Yes
How are professors notified of
LD: By the student and the
Director

# GENERAL ADMISSIONS INFORMATION

Director of Admissions: Therese Buscher          Telephone: 901-726-3700

## ENTRANCE REQUIREMENTS

Total high school units required/recommended: 16 total units are required; 4 English required, 3 math required, 2 science required, 2 foreign language required, 2 social studies required. Minor program deviations may be accepted from applicants of superior ability. Special requirements: TOEFL is required of all international students.

Application deadline: February 1
Notification: April 1

SAT or ACT preferred: Either
SAT Range: 590–690V, 590–680M
ACT Range: 26–30
Average GPA: 3.62

Graduated top 10% of class: 61
Graduated top 25% of class: 83
Graduated top 50% of class: 99

# COLLEGE GRADUATION REQUIREMENTS

Course waivers allowed: No
Course substitutions allowed: No
In what courses: Substitutions are not normally given

# ADDITIONAL INFORMATION

Environment: NR

Student Body
  Undergrad enrollment: 1,419
  Women: 55%
  Men: 45%
  In-state students: 31%
  Out-of-state: 69%

Cost Information
  In-state tuition: $16,392
  Out-of-state: $16,392
  Room & board: $5,110

Housing Information
  University housing: Yes
  Fraternity: No
  Sorority: No
  Living on campus: 77%

  Athletics: NCAA Div. III

# UNIVERSITY OF TENNESSEE AT CHATTANOOGA

615 McCallie Avenue, Chattanooga, TN 37403 • **Admissions:** 423-755-4662 • **Fax:** 423-755-4157
**Email:** steve-king@utc.edu • **Web:** www.utc.edu
**Support:** CS • **Institution:** 4 yr. Public

## LEARNING DISABILITY ADMISSIONS AND SERVICES

The College Access Program (CAP) at the university provides academic, social, and emotional support for students with learning disabilities. CAP provides academic advisement, tutoring in all coursework, career planning, counseling, social skills development, survival skills, career advisement, word processing skills, untimed tests, freshmen orientation, and psychological testing. "Start Smart" is a summer seminar for CAP students to prepare them for university coursework and general adjustment to the university.

## LEARNING DISABILITY ADMISSIONS INFORMATION

**Program Name:** College Access Program (CAP)
**Program Director:** Dr. Patricia B. Kopetz          **Telephone:** 423-755-4006
**Contact Person:** Danny Williams                     **Telephone:** 423-755-4056

### ADMISSIONS

Students with LD submit a general application to the Admissions Office and a special application to CAP. Applicants to CAP should also submit a LD evaluation, a transcript and 2 letters of recommendation. Minimum admissions requirements are: 2.0 GPA, 16 ACT or 640 SAT and 4 yrs. English, 3 math, 2 lab science, 1 American history, 1 European history or world history or world geography, 2 yrs. foreign language, and 1 yr. fine arts. Students may be admitted conditionally if they fall below these guidelines. If the course deficiency is in the area of the LD, an appeals committee will sometimes allow a probationary admittance if CAP also accepts the student. Students admitted on condition must earn at least a 1.0 GPA 1st semester or suspension will result. The Dean of Admissions or admission committee may recommend conditions for acceptance.

**College entrance exams required:** Yes          **Untimed accepted:** Yes
**Course entrance requirements:** Yes             **Interview required:** Yes
**Diagnostic tests:** Yes
**Documentation:** W-J: WAIS-R; Achievement battery: within 3 years

### ADDITIONAL INFORMATION

CAP does not, as a matter of policy, seek on a student's behalf, a waiver of any coursework. Students admitted conditionally may be required to carry a reduced course-load, take specific courses, have a specific advisor, and take specific programs of developmental study. Upper-class and graduate student tutors, trained to work with students with learning disabilities, hold regularly scheduled, individualized tutoring sessions. The Coordinator matches tutors with CAP students according to learning styles. Social skills development activities may involve video and role-playing situations in group form as well as during informal gatherings. There is a monthly publication, *The CAPsule*, for CAP students and parents. UTC offers developmental math and English courses for institutional credit. Services and accommodations are available for undergraduate and graduate students.

**Special education HS coursework accepted:** Y/N          **Essay required:** Yes
**Special application required:** Yes                       **Submitted to:** CAP
**# of applications submitted each year:** 90              **# of applications accepted each year:** 45
**# of students receiving LD services:** 160
**Acceptance into program means acceptance into college:** Students must be admitted to the university first in order to participate in CAP.

**Learning center:** Yes
**Kurzweil personal reader:** Yes
**LD specialists:** 5
**Allowed in exams:**
  **Calculator:** Y/N
  **Dictionary:** Yes
  **Computer:** Yes
  **SpellCheck:** Yes

**Notetaker:** No
**Scribes:** Yes
**Proctors:** Yes
**Oral exams:** Yes
**Extended test time:** Yes
**Added cost:** $500 per semester; paid by TN Dept. Human Services if okay by Voc Rehab
**Distraction-free environ.:** Yes
**Tape recording in class:** Yes
**Books on tape:** Yes
**Taping of other books:** Yes

**Professional tutors:** 8
**Peer tutors:** 25-30
**Max. hrs/wk for services:** Unlimited
**Priority registration:** Yes
**Accommodations for students with ADD:** Yes
**How are professors notified of LD:** By the student

## GENERAL ADMISSIONS INFORMATION

**Director of Admissions:** Patsy Reynolds

**Telephone:** 423-755-4662

### ENTRANCE REQUIREMENTS

NR

**Application deadline:** August 1
**Notification:** NR

**SAT or ACT preferred:** NR
**Average ACT:** 22
**Average GPA:** 3.1

## COLLEGE GRADUATION REQUIREMENTS

**Course waivers allowed:** No
**Course substitutions allowed:** No
**In what courses:** N/A

## ADDITIONAL INFORMATION

**Environment:** The university is located on 60 acres in an urban area in Chattanooga.

**Student Body**
  **Undergrad enrollment:** 7,021
  **Women:** 56%
  **Men:** 44%
  **In-state students:** 90%
  **Out-of-state:** 10%

**Cost Information**
  **In-state tuition:** $2,064
  **Out-of-state:** $6,400
  **Room & board:** $4,547

**Housing Information**
  **University housing:** Yes
  **Fraternity:** Yes
  **Sorority:** No
  **Living on campus:** 16%

  **Athletics:** NCAA Div. I

# UNIVERSITY OF TENNESSEE AT MARTIN

Admin. Bldg. Rm.201, Martin, TN  38238 • **Admissions:** 800-829-UTM1 • **Fax:** 901-587-7029
**Email:** admitme@utm.edu • **Web:** www.utm.edu
**Support:** CS • **Institution:** 4 yr. Public

## LEARNING DISABILITY ADMISSIONS AND SERVICES

The university believes students with learning disabilities can achieve success in college without academic compromise and can become productive, self-sufficient members of society. Students who participate in Program Access for College Enhancement (P.A.C.E.) are given diagnostic testing and evaluations after applications are submitted. A preliminary interview will include a review of previous assessments of the disability and the collection of background information. If the results of the P.A.C.E. evaluation show that the academic and social needs of the student can be met by P.A.C.E. services, the student will work with a learning disabilities specialist to develop an individually designed program. university staff who work with P.A.C.E. students receive training in understanding learning disabilities and teaching strategies that meet the individual student's needs. Graduate supervisors coordinate support services.  P.A.C.E. is designed to complement and supplement existing university support services available for all students.

## LEARNING DISABILITY ADMISSIONS INFORMATION

**Program Name:** Program Access for College Enhancement
**Program Director:** Dr. Barbara Gregory                **Telephone:** 901-587-7195
**Contact Person:** Same as above

### ADMISSIONS

Basically applicants must meet regular admission criteria including: 16 ACT and 2.6 GPA or 19 ACT and 2.2 GPA. Some applicants are considered through Qualified Admission with a 14 ACT and 2.25 GPA. Each student is considered based on background, test scores, strengths/weaknesses, and motivation. Qualified students with LD should apply directly to both the P.A.C.E. Center and the Office of Admissions. Students must complete all steps in both admission processes before an admission decision can be made. To be certain consideration is given to the learning disability, university decisions on acceptance are determined by both the P.A.C.E. Center and the Admissions Office. Applicants are selected on the basis of intellectual potential (average to superior), motivation, academic preparation, and willingness to work hard.

**College entrance exams required:** Yes          **Untimed accepted:** Yes
**Course entrance requirements:** Yes            **Interview required:** Yes
**Diagnostic tests:** Yes
**Documentation:** WAIS, W-J; within 2 years

### ADDITIONAL INFORMATION

All freshmen students with LD selected to participate in P.A.C.E. and admitted for fall semester must attend the first summer session program. Students take 1 selected university class in the mornings. In the afternoons, P.A.C.E. second staff teach learning strategies that can be applied to all future courses so that the students will have hands-on experience using the skills. The summer program will also address improvements in reading, spelling, written language, or math skills. Equally important are small group sessions to help students improve social skills. Priority registration is provided to freshmen only. Students with ADHD must have comprehensive documentation in order to receive accommodations and services. Services and accommodations are provided to undergraduate and graduate students.

**Special education HS coursework accepted:** Limited     **Essay required:** Yes
**Special application required:** Yes                     **Submitted to:** Director
**# of applications submitted each year:** 30-40          **# of applications accepted each year:** N/I
**# of students receiving LD services:** 50
**Acceptance into program means acceptance into college:** Simultaneous admission to the university and P.A.C.E.

## LEARNING DISABILITY SERVICES

**Learning center:** Yes
**Kurzweil personal reader:** Yes
**LD specialists:** 1
**Allowed in exams:**
  **Calculator:** Y/N
  **Dictionary:** Y/N
  **Computer:** Yes
  **SpellCheck:** Yes

**Notetaker:** Yes
**Scribes:** Yes
**Proctors:** Yes
**Oral exams:** Yes
**Extended test time:** Yes
**Added cost:** $500 per/semester
**Distraction-free environ.:** Yes
**Tape recording in class:** Yes
**Books on tape:** Yes
**Taping of other books:** Yes

**Professional tutors:** 4
**Peer tutors:** 20
**Max. hrs/wk for services:** Unlimited
**Priority registration:** Y/N
**Accommodations for students with ADD:** Yes
**How are professors notified of LD:** By the student and the Program Director

## GENERAL ADMISSIONS INFORMATION

**Director of Admissions:** Judy Rayburn          **Telephone:** 901-587-7032

### ENTRANCE REQUIREMENTS
Special requirements: TOEFL is required of all international students.

**Application deadline:** August 1
**Notification:** NR

**SAT or ACT preferred:** NR
**Average ACT:** 22
**Average GPA:** 3.1

## COLLEGE GRADUATION REQUIREMENTS

**Course waivers allowed:** No
**Course substitutions allowed:** Yes
**In what courses:** Math, foreign language

## ADDITIONAL INFORMATION

**Environment:** The university is located on a 200-acre campus in a small town 100 miles north of Memphis.

**Student Body**
  **Undergrad enrollment:** 5,368
  **Women:** 57%
  **Men:** 43%
  **In-state students:** 96%
  **Out-of-state:** 4%

**Cost Information**
  **In-state tuition:** $1,924
  **Out-of-state:** $6,260
  **Room & board:** $3,444

**Housing Information**
  **University housing:** Yes
  **Fraternity:** Yes
  **Sorority:** Yes
  **Living on campus:** 55%

  **Athletics:** NR

# ABILENE CHRISTIAN UNIVERSITY

**TX**

Box 29000, Abilene, TX 79699 • **Admissions:** 915-674-2650 • **Fax:** 915-674-2130
**Email:** info@admissions.acu.edu • **Web:** www.acu.edu
**Support:** CS • **Institution:** 4 yr. Private

## LEARNING DISABILITY ADMISSIONS AND SERVICES

Alpha Academic Services is a student support service program funded under Title IV legislation governing TRIO programs. The university strives to assist students in programs that move them toward independence in learning and living. The staff are specially-trained instructors, peer tutors, counselors and administrators who focus on the problems encountered by college students. Staff members help qualifying students find and apply solutions to their problems. Students qualify for services if they are a first generation college student, economically disadvantaged, or a student with a disability. Alpha means one-on-one help and the instruction and tutoring is tailored to the students' unique needs. Students with learning disabilities may receive special accommodation services to assist them in achieving success in their university studies. Documentation of the disability is required in order to receive disability accommodations. Students must make an appointment to determine if they qualify to receive services.

## LEARNING DISABILITY ADMISSIONS INFORMATION

**Program Name:** Alpha Academic Services
**Program Director:** Gloria Bradshaw          **Telephone:** 915-674-2750
**Contact Person:** Same as above

### ADMISSIONS

All students must meet the same criteria for admission. There is no special admission process for students with learning disabilities. Regular admissions includes: 19+ ACT or 910+ SAT I; college preparatory courses; no specific GPA. Some students not meeting the admission criteria may be admitted conditionally. Students admitted conditionally must take specified courses in a summer term and demonstrate motivation and ability.

**College entrance exams required:** Yes          **Untimed accepted:** Yes
**Course entrance requirements:** Yes          **Interview required:** Yes
**Diagnostic tests:** Yes
**Documentation:** WAIS-R; WJPB; others as indicated: within 3 years preferred

### ADDITIONAL INFORMATION

Alpha Academic Services provides opportunities in: individual instruction in basic skills areas such as writing, math, or study skills; assessment of learning preferences, strengths and weaknesses; instruction and tutoring designed to fit the student's particular learning preferences and strengths, and academic needs; classroom help if needed such as readers, notetakers, alternative testing arrangements; personal, career and academic counseling; and workshops on topics such as time management skills, resume writing, career placement, and study skills.

**Special education HS coursework accepted:** Yes          **Essay required:** Yes
**Special application required:** Yes          **Submitted to:** Alpha Academic Services
**# of applications submitted each year:** 30-40          **# of applications accepted each year:** 25-35
**# of students receiving LD services:** 95
**Acceptance into program means acceptance into college:** Students must be admitted to the university and then may request admission to Alpha Academic Services.

## LEARNING DISABILITY SERVICES

**Learning center:** Yes
**Kurzweil personal reader:** Yes
**LD specialists:** 2
**Allowed in exams:**
  **Calculator:** Y/N
  **Dictionary:** Yes
  **Computer:** Y/N
  **SpellCheck:** Y/N

**Notetaker:** Yes
**Scribes:** Yes
**Proctors:** Yes
**Oral exams:** Yes
**Extended test time:** Yes
**Added cost:** None
**Distraction-free environ.:** Yes
**Tape recording in class:** Yes
**Books on tape:** Yes
**Taping of other books:** Y/N

**Professional tutors:** 3
**Peer tutors:** 15
**Max. hrs/wk for services:** 1 hour per week guaranteed; unlimited access
**Priority registration:** No
**Accomodations for students with ADD:** Yes
**How are professors notified of LD:** By the student

## GENERAL ADMISSIONS INFORMATION

**Director of Admissions:** Don King

**Telephone:** 915-674-2650

### ENTRANCE REQUIREMENTS

Total high school units required/recommended: 21 total units are required; 23 total units are recommended; 4 English required, 1 math required, 2 science required, 2 foreign language required, 1 social studies required, 1 history required. Rank in top half of secondary school class and minimum combined SAT I score of 910 (minimum ACT score of 19) required. Special requirements: TOEFL is required of all international students.

**Application deadline:** Rolling
**Notification:** Rolling

**SAT or ACT preferred:** Either
**SAT Avg:** 541V, 534M
**SAT II required:** Yes
**Average ACT:** 23
**Average GPA:** 3.4

**Graduated top 10% of class:** 23
**Graduated top 25% of class:** 50
**Graduated top 50% of class:** 79

## COLLEGE GRADUATION REQUIREMENTS

**Course waivers allowed:** Yes
**Course substitutions allowed:** Yes
**In what courses:** Depends on specific circumstances

## ADDITIONAL INFORMATION

**Environment:** NR

**Student Body**
  **Undergrad enrollment:** 3,754
  **Women:** 52%
  **Men:** 48%
  **In-state students:** 79%
  **Out-of-state:** 21%

**Cost Information**
  **In-state tuition:** $922
  **Out-of-state:** $922
  **Room & board:** $3,810

**Housing Information**
  **University housing:** Yes
  **Fraternity:** No
  **Sorority:** No
  **Living on campus:** 47%

  **Athletics:** NCAA Div. II

# UNIVERSITY OF HOUSTON

Office of Admissions, Houston, TX 77204-2161 • **Admissions:** 713-743-1010 • **Fax:** 713-743-9633
**Email:** admissions@uh.edu • **Web:** www.uh.edu/home.html
**Support:** CS • **Institution:** 4 yr. Public

## LEARNING DISABILITY ADMISSIONS AND SERVICES

The Center for Students with DisABILITIES provides a wide variety of academic support services to students with all types of disabilities. Their goal is to help ensure that these otherwise qualified students are able to successfully compete with non-disabled students by receiving equal educational opportunities in college as mandated by law. Through advocacy efforts and a deliberate, ongoing, public education program, the staff strives to heighten the awareness of needs, legal rights, and abilities of persons with handicapping conditions.

## LEARNING DISABILITY ADMISSIONS INFORMATION

**Program Name:** Center for Students with DisABILITIES
**Program Director:** Caroline Gergely                  **Telephone:** 713-743-5400
**Contact Person:** Same as above

### ADMISSIONS

If an applicant to one of those programs with different requirements does not meet the stated standards, but does meet the general admission requirements, then that applicant may be admitted to the university with an undeclared status. General admission requirements are: Top 10%, no minimum on SAT or ACT; 1st quarter 920 SAT I or 19 ACT; 2nd quarter 1010 SAT I or 21 ACT; 3rd quarter 1100 SAT I or 24 ACT; 4th quarter 1180 SAT I or 26 ACT. Courses required are 2 yrs. English, 3 yrs. math, 2 yrs. science, 3 yrs. social studies. Applicants who do not qualify for admission may request a further review through the Individual Admission Process. The review will be based on an overall assessment of each applicant's circumstances in respect to potential for academic success.

**College entrance exams required:** Yes                  **Untimed accepted:** Yes
**Course entrance requirements:** Yes                  **Interview required:** No
**Diagnostic tests:** Yes
**Documentation:** WAIS-R, WJ-R; or a neuropsych. evaluation; within 3 years

### ADDITIONAL INFORMATION

Students who come from an educationally and/or economically disadvantaged background may be eligible to participate in the UH 'Challenger Program' which is designed to provide intense support to students who face obstacles in their efforts to successfully complete college. Services to all students include: tutoring, counseling, financial aid advisement, and social enrichment. Remedial reading, writing, and study skills courses for 3 hours of non-college credit are offered. There are also remedial courses for credit in English and college algebra. Other services include assistance with petitions for course substitutions, peer support groups, free carbonized paper for notetaking, textbooks and class handouts put on tape by office staff or volunteer readers and advocacy for student's legal rights to "reasonable and necessary accommodations" in their course work. Extended tutoring is available at the Learning Support Services and Math Lab.

**Special education HS coursework accepted:** Yes, after a review
**Essay required:** No
**Special application required:** No                  **Submitted to:** N/A
**# of applications submitted each year:** N/A                  **# of applications accepted each year:** N/A
**# of students receiving LD services:** 185
**Acceptance into program means acceptance into college:** Students must be admitted to the university first and then may request services.

# LEARNING DISABILITY SERVICES

**Learning center:** No
**Kurzweil personal reader:** Yes
**LD specialists:** Yes
**Allowed in exams:**
  **Calculator:** Y/N
  **Dictionary:** Yes
  **Computer:** Yes
  **SpellCheck:** Yes

**Notetaker:** No
**Scribes:** Yes
**Proctors:** Yes
**Oral exams:** Yes
**Extended test time:** Yes
**Added cost:** No
**Distraction-free environ.:** Yes
**Tape recording in class:** Yes
**Books on tape:** Yes
**Taping of other books:** Yes

**Professional tutors:** No
**Peer tutors:** Yes
**Max. hrs/wk for services:** Unlimited
**Priority registration:** Yes
**Accomodations for students with ADD:** Yes
**How are professors notified of LD:** By the Director of Services and the student

# GENERAL ADMISSIONS INFORMATION

**Director of Admissions:** Susan Zweig

**Telephone:** 713-743-9570

## ENTRANCE REQUIREMENTS

Total high school units required/recommended: 12 total units are required; 4 English required, 3 math required, 2 science required, 3 social studies required. Foreign language is recommended. Class rank determines minimum SAT I or ACT score requirements; generally ranges from combined SAT I score of 800 (composite ACT score of 19) for applicants in top quarter of secondary school class to combined SAT I score of 1100 (composite ACT score of 27) for those in bottom quarter. Minimum SAT I Verbal score of 400 (ACT English score of 19) required of all applicants. Special requirements: An audition is required for music program applicants. SAT II (Chemistry) required of engineering program applicants in place of foreign language.

**Application deadline:** July 1
**Notification:** Rolling

**SAT or ACT preferred:** Either
**SAT Avg:** 525V, 541M
**Average ACT:** 22
**Average GPA:** 3.2

**Graduated top 10% of class:** 27
**Graduated top 25% of class:** 57
**Graduated top 50% of class:** 87

# COLLEGE GRADUATION REQUIREMENTS

**Course waivers allowed:** No-P.E. only
**Course substitutions allowed:** Yes
**In what courses:** Substitutions possible in math and foreign language if these are courses that impact the disability, and only after a demonstrated effort with tutoring and testing accommodations to take the courses.

# ADDITIONAL INFORMATION

**Environment:** The university is located on 540 acres in an urban area 3 miles from Houston.

**Student Body**
  **Undergrad enrollment:** 21,522
  **Women:** 52%
  **Men:** 48%
  **In-state students:** 93%
  **Out-of-state:** 7%

**Cost Information**
  **In-state tuition:** $816
  **Out-of-state:** $5,904
  **Room & board:** $4,405

**Housing Information**
  **University housing:** Yes
  **Fraternity:** Yes
  **Sorority:** Yes
  **Living on campus:** 9%

  **Athletics:** NCAA Div. I

# TX

# LAMAR UNIVERSITY

Lamar Station, Box 10001, Beaumont, TX 77710 • **Admissions:** 409-880-8353 • **Fax:** 409-880-8463
**Web:** www.lamar.edu
**Support:** S • **Institution:** 4 yr. Public

## LEARNING DISABILITY ADMISSIONS AND SERVICES

Services are designed to help students become successful on the Lamar campus. Students with learning disabilities could qualify for registration assistance, tutoring, and other personalized services. Students are encouraged to notify the Coordinator of Services that specific disabilities exist, the modification needed, and preferably a conference prior to registration will allow the appropriate accommodations to be made. Prior to registration, students are requested to notify the Coordinator of Handicapped Services for students with disabilities regarding assistance and/or accommodation they anticipate will be needed during the course of instruction for which they plan to register.

## LEARNING DISABILITY ADMISSIONS INFORMATION

**Program Name:** Services for Students with Disabilities (SFSWD)
**Program Director:** Callie Trahan, Coordinator          **Telephone:** 409-880-8026
**Contact Person:** Same as above

### ADMISSIONS

Applicants with learning disabilities must meet the general admission requirements. Services will be offered to enrolled students who notify the coordinator of Services for Students with Disabilities. Students must be in top 1/4 of their class and complete 14 "solid" credits to be admitted unconditionally including 4 yrs. English, 3 yrs. math, 2 yrs. science (physical science, biology, chemistry, physics, or geology), 2 1/2 yrs. social science, 2 1/2 yrs. electives (foreign language is recommended). A very limited number of applicants not meeting the pre-requisites may be admitted on "individual approval". Those not in top 1/4 must achieve a minimum composite score of 900 SAT/20 ACT and be in 2nd quarter of class; or 1000 SAT/21 ACT in the 3rd quarter; or 1100 SAT/24 ACT in the 4th quarter. Some students may be considered on an Individual Approval basis if they fail to meet Unconditional Admission. These students are subject to: mandatory advisement; 6 credit limit in summer and 14 in fall term; successfully complete 9 hours with 2.0 GPA; and must meet these provisions or leave for 1 year.

**College entrance exams required:** Yes
**Course entrance requirements:** Yes
**Diagnostic tests:** Yes
**Documentation:** Yes

**Untimed accepted:** Yes
**Interview required:** Recommended

### ADDITIONAL INFORMATION

SFSWD offers a variety of services designed to assist students in becoming full-participating members of the University. Services or accommodations could include: priority registration; alternative testing accommodations; copying of class notes; class room accommodations; counseling for academic, personal and vocational needs; notetakers; readers; textbooks on tape; and tutoring. Professional staff assist students with questions, problem solving, adjustment, decision making, goal planning, testing, and development of learning skills. Skills classes in study skills are offered, including developmental writing, reading, and math for credit. Students are referred to other offices and personnel in accord with the needs and intents of the individual. Services and accommodations are available for undergraduate and graduate students.

**Special education HS coursework accepted:** N/I
**Special application required:** No
**# of applications submitted each year:** N/A
**# of students receiving LD services:** 31

**Essay required:** No
**Submitted to:** N/A
**# of applications accepted each year:** N/A

**Acceptance into program means acceptance into college:** Students must be admitted to the university first and then may request services.

# LEARNING DISABILITY SERVICES

**Learning center:** No
**Kurzweil personal reader:** Yes
**LD specialists:** No
**Allowed in exams:**
  **Calculator:** Yes
  **Dictionary:** Yes
  **Computer:** Yes
  **SpellCheck:** Yes

**Notetaker:** Yes
**Scribes:** Yes
**Proctors:** Yes
**Oral exams:** Yes
**Extended test time:** Yes
**Added cost:** N/A
**Distraction-free environ.:** Yes
**Tape recording in class:** Yes
**Books on tape:** Yes
**Taping of other books:** No

**Professional tutors:** Yes
**Peer tutors:** 15
**Max. hrs/wk for services:** Varies
**Priority registration:** Yes
**Accomodations for students with ADD:** Yes
**How are professors notified of LD:** By the student and the Program Director

# GENERAL ADMISSIONS INFORMATION

**Director of Admissions:** Jim Rush

**Telephone:** 409-880-8354

## ENTRANCE REQUIREMENTS

Total high school units required/recommended: 16 total units are recommended; 4 English recommended, 3 math recommended, 2 science recommended, 2 social studies recommended. Rank in top 2/3 of secondary school class or minimum combined SAT I score of 700 required of graduates of non-accredited secondary schools. Special requirements: TOEFL is required of all international students. 2 units of algebra, 1/2 unit of trigonometry, 1 unit of chemistry, and 1 unit of physics required of engineering program applicants. Special application, health exam, and letters of recommendation required of nursing and allied health program applicants.

**Application deadline:** August 1
**Notification:** Rolling

**SAT or ACT preferred:** SAT
**SAT Avg:** 413V, 459M
**Average ACT:** 20

**Graduated top 10% of class:** 10
**Graduated top 25% of class:** 27
**Graduated top 50% of class:** 90

# COLLEGE GRADUATION REQUIREMENTS

**Course waivers allowed:** No
**Course substitutions allowed:** Yes
**In what courses:** Must be determined to not be an essential element of degree.

# ADDITIONAL INFORMATION

**Environment:** The university is located on 200 acres in an urban area 90 miles east of Houston.

**Student Body**
  **Undergrad enrollment:** 9,496
  **Women:** 53%
  **Men:** 47%
  **In-state students:** 99%
  **Out-of-state:** 1%

**Cost Information**
  **In-state tuition:** $864
  **Out-of-state:** $4,752
  **Room & board:** $3,040

**Housing Information**
  **University housing:** Yes
  **Fraternity:** Yes
  **Sorority:** Yes
  **Living on campus:** 11%

  **Athletics:** NCAA Div. I

# TX

# MIDWESTERN STATE UNIVERSITY

3410 Taft Boulevard, Wichita Falls, TX 76308 • **Admissions:** 940-689-4321 • **Fax:** 940-689-4042
**Email:** schoolrelations@nexus.mwsu.edu • **Web:** www.mwsu.edu
**Support:** S • **Institution:** 4 yr. Public

## LEARNING DISABILITY ADMISSIONS AND SERVICES

In accordance with Section 504 of the federal Rehabilitation Act of 1973 and the Americans with Disabilities Act of 1990, Midwestern State University endeavors to make reasonable adjustments in its policies, practices, services, and facilities to ensure equal opportunity for qualified persons with disabilities to participate in all educational programs and activities. Students requiring special accommodation or auxiliary aids must make application for such assistance through the Office of Disability Accommodations. The Office of Disability Accommodations focuses on helping students to negotiate all aspects of adapting to college life. These include academic, personal, career, and social concerns. To obtain services, students must be accepted for admissions at MSU, complete an application form from the Office of Disability Accommodation, and supply verification of the disability.

## LEARNING DISABILITY ADMISSIONS INFORMATION

**Program Name:** Office of Disability Accommodations
**Program Director:** Debra J. Higginbotham
**Contact Person:** Same as above

**Telephone:** 817-689-4618

### ADMISSIONS

Unconditional acceptance by the university is available to the student who graduates from an accredited high school with 4 yrs. of English, 3 yrs. math, 2 yrs. science, 60% high school rank, an ACT of 20 or more, or SAT of 840 or more. Admission by Review is an alternative admissions with the same high school units as mentioned previously, but a high school rank between 40% and 60%, an ACT between 14 and 19, or an SAT of 560-839.

**College entrance exams required:** Yes
**Course entrance requirements:** Yes
**Diagnostic tests:** Yes
**Documentation:** WAIS-R; W-J: within 3 years

**Untimed accepted:** Yes
**Interview required:** No

### ADDITIONAL INFORMATION

The Office of Disability Accommodation arranges accommodations for the student with special needs. Help includes: priority registration; testing arrangements; classroom accessibility; special equipment; and counseling for personal, academic, or vocational concerns. Skills courses for credit are offered in study skills and time management. Services and accommodations are available for undergraduate and graduate students.

**Special education HS coursework accepted:** Yes
**Special application required:** No
**# of applications submitted each year:** N/A
**# of students receiving LD services:** 23
**Acceptance into program means acceptance into college:** Students must be accepted to the university first and then may request services.

**Essay required:** No
**Submitted to:** N/A
**# of applications accepted each year:** N/A

# LEARNING DISABILITY SERVICES

**Learning center:** No
**Kurzweil personal reader:** No
**LD specialists:** No
**Allowed in exams:**
  **Calculator:** Yes
  **Dictionary:** Yes
  **Computer:** Yes
  **SpellCheck:** Yes

**Notetaker:** Yes
**Scribes:** Yes
**Proctors:** Yes
**Oral exams:** Yes
**Extended test time:** Yes
**Added cost:** None
**Distraction-free environ.:** Yes
**Tape recording in class:** Yes
**Books on tape:** No
**Taping of other books:** No

**Professional tutors:** Yes
**Peer tutors:** Varies
**Max. hrs/wk for services:** Based on need
**Priority registration:** Yes
**Accomodations for students with ADD:** Yes
**How are professors notified of LD:** By the Program Director

# GENERAL ADMISSIONS INFORMATION

**Director of Admissions:** Barbara Merkle
**Telephone:** 817-689-4334

## ENTRANCE REQUIREMENTS

Total high school units required/recommended: 4 English required, 3 math required, 2 science required. Minimum composite ACT score of 20 (combined SAT I score of 950R) or rank in top 2/5 of secondary school class required. Special requirements: TOEFL is required of all international students.

**Application deadline:** August 7
**Notification:** Rolling

**SAT or ACT preferred:** Either
**SAT Avg:** 471V, 479M
**SAT II required:** Yes
**Average ACT:** 20

**Graduated top 10% of class:** 5
**Graduated top 25% of class:** 27
**Graduated top 50% of class:** 56

# COLLEGE GRADUATION REQUIREMENTS

**Course waivers allowed:** Yes
**Course substitutions allowed:** Yes
**In what courses:** Waivers and substitutions require an individual review by the Office of Disability Accommodations, Chair of the Department, and Vice President of Academics.

# ADDITIONAL INFORMATION

**Environment:** The campus is located 135 miles northwest of Dallas.

**Student Body**
  **Undergrad enrollment:** 4,954
  **Women:** 55%
  **Men:** 45%
  **In-state students:** 93%
  **Out-of-state:** 7%

**Cost Information**
  **In-state tuition:** $768
  **Out-of-state:** $5,904
  **Room & board:** $3,470

**Housing Information**
  **University housing:** Yes
  **Fraternity:** Yes
  **Sorority:** No
  **Living on campus:** 12%

  **Athletics:** NAIA

# UNIVERSITY OF NORTH TEXAS

**TX**

P.O. Box 13797 NT Station, Denton, TX 76203 • **Admissions:** 817-565-2681 • **Fax:** 817-565-4930
**Web:** www.unt.edu
**Support:** CS • **Institution:** 4 yr. Public

## LEARNING DISABILITY ADMISSIONS AND SERVICES

The goal of the Office of Disability Accommodations is to ensure that qualified students with disabilities have access to reasonable and appropriate services and learning resources needed to facilitate matriculation and successful completion of academic programs at the university. Serving as a liaison to ensure that assistance and/or accommodation/adjustments are available for students with disabilities to enable them full access to the educational facilities and services at the university. The Office provides consultation and assistance to academic and general service offices in making adaptations and adjustments for students with disabilities. They also provide alternative testing sites and proctors when the academic department is unable to provide assistance.

## LEARNING DISABILITY ADMISSIONS INFORMATION

**Program Name:** Office of Disability Accommodations
**Program Director:** Steve Pickett, M.S., C.R.C.
**Contact Person:** Dee Wilson

**Telephone:** 817-565-4323

### ADMISSIONS

Students must apply directly to the Admissions Office and meet the current requirements. When a student makes a written request for waivers to admission requirements, the request is sent to an individual approval review committee for consideration. Students in the top 10% of their high school class must submit ACT/SAT, scores but no specific score is required; students in the remainder of top quarter need minimum 920 SAT I or 19 ACT; the 2nd quarter need a minimum 1010 SAT I or 21 ACT; the 3rd quarter need a minimum 1100 SAT I or 24 ACT; and the 4th quarter need a minimum 1180 SAT I or 27 ACT. If a student is not accepted, there is an appeal process on the basis of the learning disability. These students may need letters of support, a statement of commitment from the student, and an evaluation of the documentation by the Disability Office. Admission decisions are made by the Office of Admissions and the Office of Disability Accommodations.

**College entrance exams required:** Yes
**Course entrance requirements:** Yes
**Diagnostic tests:** Yes
**Documentation:** WAIS-R; WRAT-R; Nelson-Denny Reading Test; Bender-G.; within 3 yrs.

**Untimed accepted:** Yes
**Interview required:** No

### ADDITIONAL INFORMATION

The Center for Development Studies provides tutoring to build academic knowledge and skills in various subject areas; academic counseling to plan class schedules and to evaluate areas of strengths and weaknesses, personal counseling to develop greater self-understanding and to learn ways to cope with adjustments to college and the pressures of life, and study skills assessment for evaluating and improving academic performance. Skills courses for credit are offered in time management, career choice, and study skills. Students requesting a distraction-free environment for tests must provide the appropriate documentation. Calculators, dictionaries, computers, and spellcheckers are allowed with instructor's approval. Services and accommodations are available for undergraduate and graduate students.

**Special education HS coursework accepted:** No
**Special application required:** No
**# of applications submitted each year:** N/A
**# of students receiving LD services:** 225+

**Essay required:** Yes, for students appealing a denial
**Submitted to:** N/A
**# of applications accepted each year:** N/A

**Acceptance into program means acceptance into college:** Students must be admitted to the university first and then may request services. Students denied admission may appeal the decision.

# LEARNING DISABILITY SERVICES

**Learning center:** No
**Kurzweil personal reader:** Yes
**LD specialists:** 1
**Allowed in exams:**
 **Calculator:** Yes
 **Dictionary:** Y/N
 **Computer:** Y/N
 **SpellCheck:** Y/N

**Notetaker:** Yes
**Scribes:** Yes
**Proctors:** Yes
**Oral exams:** Yes
**Extended test time:** Yes
**Added cost:** None
**Distraction-free environ.:** Yes
**Tape recording in class:** Yes
**Books on tape:** Yes
**Taping of other books:** Yes

**Professional tutors:** No
**Peer tutors:** Yes
**Max. hrs/wk for services:** Unlimited
**Priority registration:** Yes
**Accomodations for students with ADD:** Yes
**How are professors notified of LD:** By the student and the Program Director

# GENERAL ADMISSIONS INFORMATION

**Director of Admissions:** Marcilla Collinsworth

**Telephone:** 817-565-2681

## ENTRANCE REQUIREMENTS

No minimum SAT I or ACT scores required of applicants in top 10% of secondary school class. Minimum combined SAT I score of 800 (composite ACT score of 19) required of those in remainder of top quarter. Minimum combined SAT I score of 900 (composite ACT score of 21) required of those in 2nd quarter. Minimum combined SAT I score of 1000 (composite ACT score of 24) required of those in 3rd quarter. Minimum combined SAT I score of 1100 (composite ACT score of 27) required of those in 4th quarter. Special requirements: An audition is required for music program applicants.

**Application deadline:** June 15
**Notification:** Rolling

**SAT or ACT preferred:** Either
**SAT Avg:** 467V, 526M
**Average ACT:** 23

**Graduated top 10% of class:** 23
**Graduated top 25% of class:** 51
**Graduated top 50% of class:** 86

# COLLEGE GRADUATION REQUIREMENTS

**Course waivers allowed:** Yes
**Course substitutions allowed:** Yes
**In what courses:** This is looked at on an approval basis by each department. Approval is dependent on the student's situation. It is not automatically approved.

# ADDITIONAL INFORMATION

**Environment:** The university is located on 425 acres in an urban area 35 miles north of Dallas/Ft. Worth.

**Student Body**
 **Undergrad enrollment:** 19,181
 **Women:** 51%
 **Men:** 49%
 **In-state students:** 95%
 **Out-of-state:** 5%

**Cost Information**
 **In-state tuition:** $768
 **Out-of-state:** $5,904
 **Room & board:** $3,766

**Housing Information**
 **University housing:** Yes
 **Fraternity:** Yes
 **Sorority:** Yes
 **Living on campus:** 18%

 **Athletics:** NCAA Div. I

# SCHREINER COLLEGE

**TX**

2100 Memorial Boulevard, Kerrville, TX 78028 • **Admissions:** 210-896-5411 • **Fax:** 210-896-3232

**Support:** SP • **Institution:** 4 yr. Private

## LEARNING DISABILITY ADMISSIONS AND SERVICES

Extensive learning support is given to each student and the ultimate goal is for students to be able to succeed without special help. The Learning Support Services Program (LSS) is staffed by LD specialists and many tutors. Students with learning disabilities are enrolled in regular college courses and receive individual tutorial assistance in each subject. The goal of the service is to help students succeed in a rigorous academic environment.

## LEARNING DISABILITY ADMISSIONS INFORMATION

**Program Name:** Learning Support Services
**Program Director:** Jude Gallik
**Contact Person:** Same as above

**Telephone:** 210-896-5411 ext. 271

### ADMISSIONS

Proof of high school diploma and all significant materials relevant to the specific learning disability must be submitted. Applicants should be enrolled in regular, mainstream English courses in high school. The Woodcock-Johnson Achievement Battery is preferred but other tests are accepted. An interview is required and is an important part of the admissions decision. Applicants are considered individually, and selected on the basis of their intellectual ability, motivation, academic preparation, and potential for success. LSS students are admitted contingent upon their participation in the program. Students admitted into the Learning Support Services Program are automatically admitted into the college.

**College entrance exams required:** Yes
**Course entrance requirements:** Yes
**Diagnostic tests:** Yes
**Documentation:** WAIS-R; W-J: within 1 year

**Untimed accepted:** Yes
**Interview required:** Yes

### ADDITIONAL INFORMATION

Schreiner College offers both an Associates Degree and a Bachelor's Degree. Skills courses are available in study strategies, test taking, notetaking, reading, math, and written language. There is a professional counselor on staff.

**Special education HS coursework accepted:** Yes
**Special application required:** Yes
**# of applications submitted each year:** 50
**# of students receiving LD services:** 90

**Essay required:** No
**Submitted to:** Admissions
**# of applications accepted each year:** 35

**Acceptance into program means acceptance into college:** Students admitted into the Learning Support Program are automatically admitted into the college.

## LEARNING DISABILITY SERVICES

**Learning center:** Yes
**Kurzweil personal reader:** No
**LD specialists:** 2
**Allowed in exams:**
  **Calculator:** Y/N
  **Dictionary:** Yes
  **Computer:** Yes
  **SpellCheck:** Yes

**Notetaker:** Yes
**Scribes:** Yes
**Proctors:** Yes
**Oral exams:** Yes
**Extended test time:** Yes
**Added cost:** $3,365
**Distraction-free environ.:** Yes
**Tape recording in class:** Yes
**Books on tape:** Yes
**Taping of other books:** Yes

**Professional tutors:** 25
**Peer tutors:** 2
**Max. hrs/wk for services:** Unlimited
**Priority registration:** No
**Accomodations for students with ADD:** N/I
**How are professors notified of LD:** By the student and the Program Director

## GENERAL ADMISSIONS INFORMATION

**Director of Admissions:** Michael Paris

**Telephone:** 800-343-4919

### ENTRANCE REQUIREMENTS
NR

**Application deadline:** August 1
**Notification:** NR

**SAT or ACT preferred:** NR
**SAT Avg:** 410V, 490M
**Average ACT:** 21

**Graduated top 10% of class:** 19
**Graduated top 25% of class:** 51
**Graduated top 50% of class:** 82

## COLLEGE GRADUATION REQUIREMENTS

**Course waivers allowed:** No
**Course substitutions allowed:** Yes
**In what courses:** Math and foreign language on limited basis

## ADDITIONAL INFORMATION

**Environment:** The college is located on 175 acres in a rural wooded area 60 miles northwest of San Antonio.

**Student Body**
  **Undergrad enrollment:** 620
  **Women:** 54%
  **Men:** 46%
  **In-state students:** 96%
  **Out-of-state:** 4%

**Cost Information**
  **In-state tuition:** $9,735
  **Out-of-state:** $9,735
  **Room & board:** $6,380

**Housing Information**
  **University housing:** Yes
  **Fraternity:** No
  **Sorority:** No
  **Living on campus:** 54%

  **Athletics:** NAIA

# SOUTHWEST TEXAS STATE UNIVERSITY

601 University Drive, San Marcos, TX 78666 • **Admissions:** 512-245-2364 • **Fax:** 512-245-8088
**Email:** admissions@swt.edu • **Web:** www.swt.edu
**Support:** CS • **Institution:** 4 yr. Public

## LEARNING DISABILITY ADMISSIONS AND SERVICES

The mission of the Office of Disability Services (ODS) is to assist students with disabilities to independently achieve their educational goals and enhance their leadership development by ensuring equal access to all programs, activities, and services. This is accomplished through a decentralizing approach in providing education and awareness so that programs, activities, and services are conducted "in the most integrated setting appropriate". Students with learning disabilities are encouraged to self-identify and to submit documentation once admitted. By identifying and assessing student needs, ODS provides direct services and refers students to appropriate resources on and off campus. ODS also promotes awareness of the special needs and abilities of students with disabilities through educational events and outreach activities. The following campus agencies provide students with special academic support services: ODS, Learning Resource Center, and Student Learning Assistance Center.

## LEARNING DISABILITY ADMISSIONS INFORMATION

**Program Name:** Office of Disability Services (ODS)
**Program Director:** Gina Schultz
**Contact Person:** Same as above

**Telephone:** 512-245-3451

### ADMISSIONS

The admission procedure is the same for all students regardless of their disability. General admission requirements include: 4 yrs. English, 3 yrs. math, 2 yrs. science, 3 yrs. social studies, 1/2 yr. economics, and 2 yrs. foreign language; 2.0 GPA or determined by class rank; 22 ACT is average and 850 SAT is mid 50%. Students who are not accepted are free to write letters of appeal to Admissions. All decisions are made by the Admissions Office. Probationary admission plans are available. Students not meeting the required rank in class may be admitted by review through Predicted Academic Success Option (PASO): students in top 3/4 may submit 7th semester transcript and a request that a PASO formula be attempted. (Students who rank in the 4th quarter are not eligible for the Predicted Academic Success Option). The formula used is an individual's high school rank in combination with ACT or SAT scores. If admitted, these students are placed on a 1-semester contract set by the Director of Admissions.

**College entrance exams required:** Yes
**Course entrance requirements:** Yes
**Diagnostic tests:** Yes
**Documentation:** WISC-R; Achievement measures & cognitive abilities: within 5 yrs.

**Untimed accepted:** Yes
**Interview required:** No

### ADDITIONAL INFORMATION

Student Support Services provides one-on-one tutoring in limited subject areas. Remedial courses and an effective learning course are offered. An academic support group course covering various topics is offered for credit. Services and accommodations are available for undergraduate and graduate students.

**Special education HS coursework accepted:** Yes
**Special application required:** No
**# of applications submitted each year:** N/A
**# of students receiving LD services:** 350
**Acceptance into program means acceptance into college:** Students must be admitted to the university first and then may request services.

**Essay required:** No
**Submitted to:** N/A
**# of applications accepted each year:** N/A

## LEARNING DISABILITY SERVICES

**Learning center:** No
**Kurzweil personal reader:** Yes
**LD specialists:** Yes
**Allowed in exams:**
  **Calculator:** Yes
  **Dictionary:** Yes
  **Computer:** Yes
  **SpellCheck:** Yes

**Notetaker:** No
**Scribes:** Yes
**Proctors:** Yes
**Oral exams:** Yes
**Extended test time:** Yes
**Added cost:** None
**Distraction-free environ.:** Yes
**Tape recording in class:** Yes
**Books on tape:** Yes
**Taping of other books:** Yes

**Professional tutors:** Yes
**Peer tutors:** Yes
**Max. hrs/wk for services:** Offered through Student Support Services
**Priority registration:** Yes
**Accomodations for students with ADD:** Yes
**How are professors notified of LD:** By the student

## GENERAL ADMISSIONS INFORMATION

**Director of Admissions:** Fernando Yarrito

**Telephone:** 512-245-2364

### ENTRANCE REQUIREMENTS

Total high school units required/recommended: 17 total units are required; 4 English required, 3 math required, 3 science required, 2 foreign language required, 3 social studies required, 4 social studies recommended. No minimum SAT I or ACT scores required of applicants ranking in top 10% of secondary school class; minimum combined SAT I score of 920 (composite ACT score of 20) required of applicants ranking in next 15%; minimum combined SAT I score of 1010 (composite ACT score of 22) required of applicants ranking in 2nd quarter; minimum combined SAT I score of 1180 (composite ACT score of 26) required of applicants ranking in 3rd quarter; minimum combined SAT I score of 1270 (composite ACT score of 29) required of applicants ranking in 4th quarter. Special requirements: An audition is required for music program applicants. TOEFL is required of all international students.

**Application deadline:** July 1
**Notification:** Rolling

**SAT or ACT preferred:** Either
**SAT Avg:** 533V, 515M
**Average ACT:** 21

**Graduated top 10% of class:** 15
**Graduated top 25% of class:** 50
**Graduated top 50% of class:** 94

## COLLEGE GRADUATION REQUIREMENTS

**Course waivers allowed:** No
**Course substitutions allowed:** Yes
**In what courses:** Foreign language

## ADDITIONAL INFORMATION

**Environment:** The 1,091-acre campus is located 30 miles south of Austin, and within easy access of San Antonio.

**Student Body**
  **Undergrad enrollment:** 17,677
  **Women:** 54%
  **Men:** 46%
  **In-state students:** 98%
  **Out-of-state:** 2%

**Cost Information**
  **In-state tuition:** $960
  **Out-of-state:** $7,380
  **Room & board:** $3,787

**Housing Information**
  **University housing:** Yes
  **Fraternity:** No
  **Sorority:** No
  **Living on campus:** 26%

  **Athletics:** NCAA Div. I

# TX

# TEXAS A&M UNIVERSITY

College Station, TX 77843 • **Admissions:** 409-845-3741

**Support:** S • **Institution:** 4 yr. Public

## LEARNING DISABILITY ADMISSIONS AND SERVICES

The Department of Student Life Services with Disabilities (SSWD) works to enable all students with disabilities to participate in the full range of college experiences. The philosophy is to empower students, with the skills needed, to act as their own advocates and succeed in the mainstream of the university environment. Individual programs are developed for each student's needs. Services include: tutoring from peer tutors or qualified tutors from the community, test accommodations, curriculum modification, and skills courses in study strategies and time management.

## LEARNING DISABILITY ADMISSIONS INFORMATION

**Program Name:** Students with Disabilities
**Program Director:** Dr. Jo Hudson                    **Telephone:** 409-845-1637
**Contact Person:** Same as above

### ADMISSIONS

Applicants with learning disabilities submit the general application form and are considered under the same guidelines as all applicants. Students may have their application reviewed by requesting special consideration based on their disability and by providing letters of recommendation from their high school counselor stating what accommodations are needed in college to be successful. Admissions will be affected by the student's record indicating success with provided accommodations along with any activities and leadership skills. Students not meeting academic criteria for automatic admission may be offered admission to a Summer Provisional Program. These students must take 9 credits and receive a grade of "C" in each of the courses.

| | |
|---|---|
| **College entrance exams required:** Yes | **Untimed accepted:** Yes |
| **Course entrance requirements:** Yes | **Interview required:** No |
| **Diagnostic tests:** Yes | |
| **Documentation:** WAIS-R or WRAT-R: within 2-3 years | |

### ADDITIONAL INFORMATION

Skill classes in math, reading and writing are offered to the entire student body though the Center for Academic Enhancement. Some of these classes may be taken for college credit. Services and accommodations are available for undergraduate and graduate students. Services include a new Learning Technology Laboratory equipped with state of the art technology for students with disabilities including text-to-speech scanning for personal computer use.

| | |
|---|---|
| **Special education HS coursework accepted:** No | **Essay required:** No |
| **Special application required:** No | **Submitted to:** N/A |
| **# of applications submitted each year:** N/A | **# of applications accepted each year:** N/A |
| **# of students receiving LD services:** N/I | |

**Acceptance into program means acceptance into college:** Students must be admitted to the university first and then may request services.

## LEARNING DISABILITY SERVICES

**Learning center:** Yes
**Kurzweil personal reader:** Yes
**LD specialists:** No
**Allowed in exams:**
  **Calculator:** Yes
  **Dictionary:** Yes
  **Computer:** Yes
  **SpellCheck:** Yes

**Notetaker:** Yes
**Scribes:** Yes
**Proctors:** Yes
**Oral exams:** Yes
**Extended test time:** Yes
**Added cost:** $6 - $10 per/hour
**Distraction-free environ.:** Yes
**Tape recording in class:** Yes
**Books on tape:** Yes
**Taping of other books:** Yes

**Professional tutors:** No
**Peer tutors:** Yes
**Max. hrs/wk for services:**
Unlimited/available for all
students
**Priority registration:** Yes
**Accomodations for students
with ADD:** Yes
**How are professors notified of
LD:** By the student and a
support letter from SSWD

## GENERAL ADMISSIONS INFORMATION

**Director of Admissions:** Dr. Gary Engelgau          **Telephone:** 409-845-1031

### ENTRANCE REQUIREMENTS
NR

**Application deadline:** NR          **SAT or ACT preferred:** NR
**Notification:** NR

## COLLEGE GRADUATION REQUIREMENTS

**Course waivers allowed:** No
**Course substitutions allowed:** Yes
**In what courses:** Course substitution is determined by the Dean of the college in which the student is enrolled
in consultation with SSWD. Courses essential to a major are not substituted.

## ADDITIONAL INFORMATION

**Environment:** The school is located on over 5,000 acres in a college town of 100,000 about 90 miles from
Houston.

**Student Body**
  **Undergrad enrollment:** 31,914
  **Women:** 46%
  **Men:** 54%
  **In-state students:** 95%
  **Out-of-state:** 5%

**Cost Information**
  **In-state tuition:** $1,020
  **Out-of-state:** $7,440

**Housing Information**
  **University housing:** Yes
  **Fraternity:** Yes
  **Sorority:** Yes
  **Living on campus:** 31%

  **Athletics:** NCAA Div. 1

# TEXAS A & M UNIVERSITY-KINGSVILLE

Campus Box 105, Kingsville, TX  78363 • **Admissions:** 512-593-2315 • **Fax:** 512-593-2195

**Support:** S • **Institution:** 4 yr. Public

## LEARNING DISABILITY ADMISSIONS AND SERVICES

The university is committed to making every effort to assure that the needs of disabled students are met. Services vary according to the nature of the disability and are provided by the Center for Life Services and Wellness. Counseling services offer educational, vocational and personal consultations, as well as tutoring, testing, and academic advising. Students with learning disabilities have access to notetakers, readers, writers, and other assistance that the university can provide.  All students entering college as freshmen (or transfers with less then 30 hours) have the university's commitment to improve student achievement, retention, depth, and quality of instruction and services.

## LEARNING DISABILITY ADMISSIONS INFORMATION

**Program Name:** Disabled Student Services
**Program Director:** Diane Brown-Pearson
**Contact Person:** Pat Berson

**Telephone:** 512-593-3302
**Telephone:** 512-593-3024

### ADMISSIONS

All applicants must meet the same general admission criteria.  Admissions is very similar to "open door" admissions and thus most applicants are admitted either conditionally or unconditionally, or on probation. ACT score range is 16+ or greater or SAT is 610+ or greater. There are no specific courses required for entrance; however, it is recommended that students take 4 yrs. English, 3 yrs. math, 3 yrs. science, 4 yrs. social studies, 3 yrs. foreign language, 1/2 yr. health, 1 1/2 yrs. physical education, 1 yr. computer, 1 yr.  art/speech, and 3 yrs. electives. Students with learning disabilities are encouraged to self-disclose during the application process. There are 2 types of admission plans, conditional and unconditional. Unconditional admission is met by achieving 970 or greater on the SAT. Conditional admission is achieved by scoring 810-960 on the SAT.

**College entrance exams required:** Yes
**Course entrance requirements:** No
**Diagnostic tests:** No
**Documentation:** N/I

**Untimed accepted:** Yes
**Interview required:** No

### ADDITIONAL INFORMATION

Each freshman receives academic endorsement, developmental educational classes in writing, math or reading (if necessary), tutoring or study groups, and academic rescue programs for students in academic jeopardy. Skills classes are offered for no credit in stress management and test anxiety. Services and accommodations are available to undergraduate and graduate students.

**Special education HS coursework accepted:** Yes
**Special application required:** No
**# of applications submitted each year:** N/A
**# of students receiving LD services:** 9

**Essay required:** No
**Submitted to:** N/A
**# of applications accepted each year:** N/A

**Acceptance into program means acceptance into college:** Students must be admitted to the university first and then may request services.

## LEARNING DISABILITY SERVICES

**Learning center:** Yes
**Kurzweil personal reader:** Yes
**LD specialists:** No
**Allowed in exams:**
  **Calculator:** Yes
  **Dictionary:** No
  **Computer:** Yes
  **SpellCheck:** Yes

**Notetaker:** Yes
**Scribes:** Yes
**Proctors:** Yes
**Oral exams:** Yes
**Extended test time:** Yes
**Added cost:** None
**Distraction-free environ.:** Yes
**Tape recording in class:** Yes
**Books on tape:** Yes
**Taping of other books:** No

**Professional tutors:** No
**Peer tutors:** 10
**Max. hrs/wk for services:** Case-by-case decision
**Priority registration:** No
**Accomodations for students with ADD:** Yes
**How are professors notified of LD:** By the student and the Program Director

## GENERAL ADMISSIONS INFORMATION

**Director of Admissions:** Joseph Estrada          **Telephone:** 512-595-2011

### ENTRANCE REQUIREMENTS

Total high school units required/recommended: 4 English recommended, 3 math recommended, 3 science recommended, 4 social studies recommended, 3 foreign language recommended, 1/2 health recommended, 1 1/2 physical education recommended, 1 computer course recommended, 1 fine art/speech recommended, 3 electives recommended.

**Application deadline:** Open          **SAT or ACT preferred:** NR
**Notification:** NR

## COLLEGE GRADUATION REQUIREMENTS

**Course waivers allowed:** Yes
**Course substitutions allowed:** Yes
**In what courses:** Case-by-case decision made by the Provost

## ADDITIONAL INFORMATION

**Environment:** The 246-acre university campus is located 40 miles southwest of Corpus Christi.

**Student Body**
  **Undergrad enrollment:** 31,914
  **Women:** 46%
  **Men:** 54%
  **In-state students:** 95%
  **Out-of-state:** 5%

**Cost Information**
  **In-state tuition:** $1,020
  **Out-of-state:** $7,440

**Housing Information**
  **University housing:** Yes
  **Fraternity:** Yes
  **Sorority:** Yes
  **Living on campus:** 35%

  **Athletics:** NCAA Div. 1

# TX TEXAS TECH UNIVERSITY

Box 45005, Lubbock, TX 79409 • **Admissions:** 806-742-1482 • **Fax:** 806-742-0980
**Email:** A5MJG@TTU.EDU • **Web:** www.ttu.edu
**Support:** S • **Institution:** 4 yr. Public

## LEARNING DISABILITY ADMISSIONS AND SERVICES

It is the philosophy of Texas Tech University to serve each student on a case-by-case basis. All services rendered are supported by adequate documentation. We firmly believe that all students should be and will become effective self-advocates. Students with disabilities attending Texas Tech will find numerous programs designed to provide services and to promote access to all phases of university activity. Such programming is coordinated through the Dean of Students office with the assistance of an advisory committee of both disabled and non-disabled students, faculty, and staff. Services to disabled students are offered through a decentralized network of university and non-university resources. This means that many excellent services are available but that it is up to the student to initiate them. Each student is encouraged to act as his or her own advocate and take the major responsibility for securing services and accommodations. The Disabled Student Services team, Dean of Students Office, faculty and staff are supportive in this effort.

## LEARNING DISABILITY ADMISSIONS INFORMATION

**Program Name:** Disabled Student Services
**Program Director:** Charley L.Tiggs, Ass't. Dean of Students   **Telephone:** 806-742-2192
**Contact Person:** Same as above

### ADMISSIONS

There is no special admissions process for students with learning disabilities, and all applicants must meet the same criteria. All students must have 4 yrs. English, 3 yrs. math, 2 1/2 yrs. social studies, 2 yrs. science, and 3 1/2 yrs. electives. Any applicant who scores a 1200 on the SAT or a 29 on the ACT is automatically admitted regardless of class rank. Some students are admissible who do not meet the stated requirements, but must have a 2.0 GPA for a provisional admission. After a student is admitted, Disabled Student Services requires documentation that provides a diagnosis, an indication of the severity of the disability, and offers recommendations for accommodations, in order for students to receive services.

| | |
|---|---|
| **College entrance exams required:** Yes | **Untimed accepted:** Yes |
| **Course entrance requirements:** Yes | **Interview required:** No |
| **Diagnostic tests:** Yes | |
| **Documentation:** Neuropsychological evaluation: within 3 years | |

### ADDITIONAL INFORMATION

Support services through the Disabled Student Services include Academic Support Services, which can help students develop habits that will enable them to get a good education. Students may receive academic support services in the PASS (Programs for Academic Support Services) Center which is open to all students on campus. Services offered free of charge include: tutor referral services (paid by student); study skills group; hour-long workshops that target a variety of subjects from "Overcoming Math Anxiety" to "Preparing for Final"; a self-help learning lab with videotapes; computerize-assisted instruction;  individual consultations assisting students with specific study problems; and setting study skills improvement goals. All students with learning disabilities are offered priority registration. Services and accommodations are available for undergraduate and graduate students.

| | |
|---|---|
| **Special education HS coursework accepted:** Yes | **Essay required:** No |
| **Special application required:** Yes | **Submitted to:** N/A |
| **# of applications submitted each year:** N/A | **# of applications accepted each year:** N/A |
| **# of students receiving LD services:** 450 | |

**Acceptance into program means acceptance into college:** Students must be admitted to the university first and then may request services.

## LEARNING DISABILITY SERVICES

**Learning center:** Yes
**Kurzweil personal reader:** Yes
**LD specialists:** No
**Allowed in exams:**
  **Calculator:** Yes
  **Dictionary:** Y/N
  **Computer:** Yes
  **SpellCheck:** Yes

**Notetaker:** Yes
**Scribes:** Yes
**Proctors:** Yes
**Oral exams:** Yes
**Extended test time:** Yes
**Added cost:** None
**Distraction-free environ.:** Yes
**Tape recording in class:** Yes
**Books on tape:** Yes
**Taping of other books:** No

**Professional tutors:** Yes
**Peer tutors:** Yes
**Max. hrs/wk for services:** Unlimited
**Priority registration:** Yes
**Accomodations for students with ADD:** Yes
**How are professors notified of LD:** By the student

## GENERAL ADMISSIONS INFORMATION

**Director of Admissions:** Dale Grusing          **Telephone:** 806-742-2192

### ENTRANCE REQUIREMENTS

Total high school units required/recommended: 17 total units are required; 4 English required, 3 math required, 2 science required, 2 social studies required. Applicants meeting 1 of the following requirements are guaranteed admission: rank in top 1/10 of secondary school class; rank in top 1/4 with minimum combined SAT I score of 1000 (composite ACT score of 22); rank in 2nd quarter with minimum combined SAT I score of 1180 (composite ACT score of 27); or rank in bottom half with minimum combined SAT I score of 1270 (composite ACT score of 29). Others may be admitted as space permits. Special requirements: TOEFL is required of all international students.

**Application deadline:** August 1
**Notification:** Rolling

**SAT or ACT preferred:** Either
**SAT Avg:** 522V, 530M
**SAT II required:** Yes
**Average ACT:** 22

**Graduated top 10% of class:** 22
**Graduated top 25% of class:** 51
**Graduated top 50% of class:** 86

## COLLEGE GRADUATION REQUIREMENTS

**Course waivers allowed:** No
**Course substitutions allowed:** Yes
**In what courses:** Possible in math or foreign language

## ADDITIONAL INFORMATION

**Environment:** The university is located on 1,839 acres in an urban area in Lubbock.

**Student Body**
  **Undergrad enrollment:** 20,420
  **Women:** 46%
  **Men:** 54%
  **In-state students:** 93%
  **Out-of-state:** 7%

**Cost Information**
  **In-state tuition:** $1,020
  **Out-of-state:** $7,440
  **Room & board:** $4,200

**Housing Information**
  **University housing:** Yes
  **Fraternity:** No
  **Sorority:** No
  **Living on campus:** 25%

  **Athletics:** NCAA Div. I

# UNIVERSITY OF TEXAS-PAN AMERICAN

1201 West University Drive, Edinburg, TX 78539 • **Admissions:** 512-381-2206

**Support:** S • **Institution:** 4 yr. Public

## LEARNING DISABILITY ADMISSIONS AND SERVICES

The Office of Services for Persons with Disabilities (OSPO) is a component of the Division of Student Affairs at the University of Texas-Pan American. It is designed and committed to providing support services to meet the educational, career, and personal needs of persons with disabilities attending or planning to attend the university. Students requesting accommodations must put their requests in writing, must provide documentation from a professional person who is qualified to diagnose and verify the particular disability; and the testing and documentation must be current within 3 years. The Office of Persons with Disabilities will use the documentation to properly prepare an assistance plan for the student to use while enrolled at the university. It typically takes at least 30 days to process requests for services or accommodations.

## LEARNING DISABILITY ADMISSIONS INFORMATION

**Program Name:** Office of Services for Persons with Disabilities
**Program Director:** Ruben Garza                **Telephone:** 210-316-7005
**Contact Person:** Same as above

### ADMISSIONS

Students with learning disabilities must meet the same admission requirements as all other applicants. The criteria for entering freshmen are: a high school diploma denoting graduation with "Honors" or "Advanced" or rank in the top 50% or 20+ ACT or 1200+ SAT; 4 yrs. English, 4 yrs. math, 3 yrs. science, 4 yrs. social studies, 3 yrs. foreign language, 1 yr. fine arts, 1 1/2 PE, 1/2 health, 0-1 yr. computers, and 2 1/2 electives. Students not meeting these criteria may enroll through the Provisional Enrollment Program (PEP). PEP students must: attend orientation, be advised by counseling center, select classes prescribed, participate in non-credit programs to develop study and academic skills. PEP students with a total of 9 or more hours may fulfill criteria for regular admission by meeting specific requirements in GPA and completion of attempted hours. PEP students who do not have a 2.0 GPA after 9 hours can take an additional semester if they have at least a 1.5 GPA and meet successful completion of attempted hours. Some students not eligible to continue may petition the Admissions Committee.

**College entrance exams required:** Yes              **Untimed accepted:** Yes
**Course entrance requirements:** Yes                **Interview required:** Recommended
**Diagnostic tests:** Yes
**Documentation:** Left to the discretion of professional completing assessment; within 5 years

### ADDITIONAL INFORMATION

The OSPD provides the following services: assessment for special needs; notetakers; readers and writers; advisement, counseling and guidance; assistance with admissions, orientation, registration; referral services to other university units; liaison between students, faculty, staff, and others; resolution to problems/concerns; computer hardware and software; reading machine. Skills classes for credit are offered in time management, test-taking strategies, notetaking skills, reading text, and stress management. The OSPD assists students prepare appeals and works with faculty/administrators to secure waivers. Services and accommodations are available for undergraduate and graduate students.

**Special education HS coursework accepted:** No        **Essay required:** No
**Special application required:** No                    **Submitted to:** N/A
**# of applications submitted each year:** N/A          **# of applications accepted each year:** N/A
**# of students receiving LD services:** 34
**Acceptance into program means acceptance into college:** Students must be admitted to the university first and then may request services.

## LEARNING DISABILITY SERVICES

**Learning center:** Yes
**Kurzweil personal reader:** Yes
**LD specialists:** No
**Allowed in exams:**
  **Calculator:** Yes
  **Dictionary:** Yes
  **Computer:** Yes
  **SpellCheck:** Yes

**Notetaker:** Yes
**Scribes:** Yes
**Proctors:** Yes
**Oral exams:** Yes
**Extended test time:** Yes
**Added cost:** None
**Distraction-free environ.:** Yes
**Tape recording in class:** Yes
**Books on tape:** Yes
**Taping of other books:** Yes

**Professional tutors:** 15
**Peer tutors:** 50
**Max. hrs/wk for services:** 40 hours
**Priority registration:** Yes
**Accomodations for students with ADD:** Yes
**How are professors notified of LD:** By the student and the Director of OSPD

## GENERAL ADMISSIONS INFORMATION

**Director of Admissions:** David Zuniga          **Telephone:** 210-381-2206

### ENTRANCE REQUIREMENTS

Special requirements: TOEFL is required of all international students.

**Application deadline:** August 1
**Notification:** NR

**SAT or ACT preferred:** NR
**Graduated top 25% of class:** 46
**Graduated top 50% of class:** 46

## COLLEGE GRADUATION REQUIREMENTS

**Course waivers allowed:** Yes
**Course substitutions allowed:** Yes
**In what courses:** It depends on the degree plan. Requests can be made through the Program Advisors, Department Chairs, and the VP for Academic Affairs.

## ADDITIONAL INFORMATION

**Environment:** NR

**Student Body**
  **Undergrad enrollment:** NR
  **Women:** NR
  **Men:** NR
  **In-state students:** NR
  **Out-of-state:** NR

**Cost Information**
  **In-state tuition:** $991
  **Out-of-state:** $3,486
  **Room & board:** $1,241

**Housing Information**
  **University housing:** Yes
  **Fraternity:** No
  **Sorority:** No
  **Living on campus:** 5%

  **Athletics:** NCAA Div. I

# BRIGHAM YOUNG UNIVERSITY

Provo, UT 84602 • **Admissions:** 801-378-4636 • **Fax:** 801-378-7860
**Email:** admissions@byu.edu • **Web:** www.byu.edu
**Support:** CS • **Institution:** 4 yr. Private

## LEARNING DISABILITY ADMISSIONS AND SERVICES

The Services to Students with Learning Disabilities (SSLD) program works to provide individualized programs to meet the specific needs of each student, assisting in developing strengths to meet the challenges, and making arrangements for accommodations and special services as required.

## LEARNING DISABILITY ADMISSIONS INFORMATION

**Program Name:** Services to Students with Learning Disabilities
**Program Director:** Paul Bryd                     **Telephone:** 801-378-2767
**Contact Person:** Same as above

### ADMISSIONS

There is no special admission process for students with learning disabilities. Suggested courses include: 4 yrs. English, 3-4 yrs. math, 2-3 yrs. science, 2 yrs. history or government, 2 yrs. foreign language, and 2 yrs. of literature or writing. Evaluations are made on an individualized basis with a system weighted for college prep courses and core classes.

**College entrance exams required:** Yes          **Untimed accepted:** Yes
**Course entrance requirements:** Yes             **Interview required:** No
**Diagnostic tests:** Yes
**Documentation:** N/I

### ADDITIONAL INFORMATION

Workshops are offered for non-credit. The following are some examples: Math anxiety, memory, overcoming procrastination, self-appreciation, stress management, test-taking, textbook comprehension, time management, and communication. Additional services include counseling support and advising. Services and accommodations are available for undergraduate and graduate students.

**Special education HS coursework accepted:** Yes       **Essay required:** Yes
**Special application required:** No                     **Submitted to:** N/A
**# of applications submitted each year:** N/A          **# of applications accepted each year:** N/A
**# of students receiving LD services:** 101
**Acceptance into program means acceptance into college:** Students must be admitted to the university first and then may request services.

## LEARNING DISABILITY SERVICES

**Learning center:** No
**Kurzweil personal reader:** No
**LD specialists:** Yes
**Allowed in exams:**
  **Calculator:** Yes
  **Dictionary:** Yes
  **Computer:** Yes
  **SpellCheck:** Yes

**Notetaker:** Yes
**Scribes:** No
**Proctors:** Yes
**Oral exams:** Yes
**Extended test time:** Yes
**Added cost:** None
**Distraction-free environ.:** Yes
**Tape recording in class:** Yes
**Books on tape:** Yes
**Taping of other books:** Yes

**Professional tutors:** No
**Peer tutors:** N/I
**Max. hrs/wk for services:** Unlimited
**Priority registration:** Yes
**Accomodations for students with ADD:** Yes
**How are professors notified of LD:** By both the student and the Program Director

## GENERAL ADMISSIONS INFORMATION

**Director of Admissions:** Tom M. Gourley          **Telephone:** 801-378-4594

### ENTRANCE REQUIREMENTS

Total high school units required/recommended: 18 total units are recommended; 4 English recommended, 3 math recommended, 2 science recommended, 2 foreign language recommended, 2 history recommended. Minimum ACT score in mid-20s and minimum 3.0 GPA recommended. Special requirements: TOEFL is required of all international students.

**Application deadline:** February 15
**Notification:** Rolling

**SAT or ACT preferred:** ACT
**SAT II required:** Yes
**ACT required:** Yes
**Average ACT:** 27
**Average GPA:** 3.7

**Graduated top 10% of class:** 48
**Graduated top 25% of class:** 79
**Graduated top 50% of class:** 96

## COLLEGE GRADUATION REQUIREMENTS

**Course waivers allowed:** Yes
**Course substitutions allowed:** Yes
**In what courses:** N/I

## ADDITIONAL INFORMATION

**Environment:** The university is located in a suburban area 45 miles south of Salt Lake City.

**Student Body**
  **Undergrad enrollment:** 26,553
  **Women:** 52%
  **Men:** 48%
  **In-state students:** 30%
  **Out-of-state:** 70%

**Cost Information**
  **In-state tuition:** $2,530
  **Out-of-state:** $2,530
  **Room & board:** $3,930

**Housing Information**
  **University housing:** Yes
  **Fraternity:** No
  **Sorority:** No
  **Living on campus:** 20%

  **Athletics:** NCAA Div. I

# SOUTHERN UTAH UNIVERSITY

351 West Center, Cedar City, UT 84720 • **Admissions:** 801-586-7740 • **Fax:** 801-865-8223
**Email:** adminfo@suu.edu • **Web:** www.suu.edu
**Support:** S • **Institution:** 4 yr. Public

## LEARNING DISABILITY ADMISSIONS AND SERVICES

The philosophy of the Student Support Services (SSS) is to promote self-sufficiency and achievement. Student Support Services assists college students with developmental classes, skills courses, academic and tutorial support, and advisement. In particular, disabled students are encouraged and supported in advocating for themselves. The university provides a full variety of services and accommodations for all disabled students. The academic support coordinator assists students with enrollment in SSS and helps them identify academic areas where they feel a need to strengthen skills to assure college success.

## LEARNING DISABILITY ADMISSIONS INFORMATION

**Program Name:** Student Support Services
**Program Director:** Lynne J. Brown                    **Telephone:** 801-586-7771
**Contact Person:** Pamela France                       **Telephone:** 801-586-7848

### ADMISSIONS

Students with learning disabilities submit the general application form. Students must have at least a 2.0 GPA and show competency in English, math, science and social studies. The university uses an admissions index derived from the combination of the high school GPA and results of either the ACT or SAT. If students are not admissible through the regular process, special consideration by a Committee Review can be gained through reference letters and a personal letter. The university is allowed to admit 5% in "flex" admission. These applications are reviewed by a committee consisting of the Director of Support Services and representatives from the Admissions Office. Students are encouraged to self-disclose their learning disability and submit documentation.

**College entrance exams required:** Yes                **Untimed accepted:** Yes
**Course entrance requirements:** Yes                   **Interview required:** No
**Diagnostic tests:** Yes
**Documentation:** Psychoeducational evaluations: within 3 years

### ADDITIONAL INFORMATION

Tutoring is available in small groups or one-to-one, free of charge. Basic skills classes, for credit, are offered in English, reading, math, math anxiety, language, and study skills.

**Special education HS coursework accepted:** No        **Essay required:** Yes
**Special application required:** Yes                   **Submitted to:** SSS/ Pamela France
**# of applications submitted each year:** 30           **# of applications accepted each year:** N/I
**# of students receiving LD services:** 30
**Acceptance into program means acceptance into college:** Students must be admitted to the university first and then may request services.

# LEARNING DISABILITY SERVICES

**Learning center:** Yes
**Kurzweil personal reader:** Yes
**LD specialists:** No
**Allowed in exams:**
  **Calculator:** Yes
  **Dictionary:** Yes
  **Computer:** Yes
  **SpellCheck:** Yes

**Notetaker:** Yes
**Scribes:** Yes
**Proctors:** Yes
**Oral exams:** Yes
**Extended test time:** Yes
**Added cost:** None
**Distraction-free environ.:** Yes
**Tape recording in class:** Yes
**Books on tape:** Yes
**Taping of other books:** Yes

**Professional tutors:** 4
**Peer tutors:** 12-20
**Max. hrs/wk for services:**
Unlimited
**Priority registration:** Yes
**Accomodations for students
with ADD:** Yes
**How are professors notified of
LD:** By the student and the
Program Director

# GENERAL ADMISSIONS INFORMATION

**Director of Admissions:** Dale Orton

**Telephone:** 801-586-7742

## ENTRANCE REQUIREMENTS

Total high school units required/recommended: 11 total units are recommended; 4 English recommended, 3 math recommended, 2 science recommended, 1 social studies recommended, 1 history recommended. Minimum ACT scores and GPA required based on admissions index. Special requirements: TOEFL is required of all international students. Nursing program applicants must apply through Weber State U.

**Application deadline:** July 1
**Notification:** Rolling

**SAT or ACT preferred:** ACT
**SAT Avg:** 498V, 487M
**Average ACT:** 22
**Average GPA:** 3.39

**Graduated top 10% of class:** 7
**Graduated top 25% of class:** 25
**Graduated top 50% of class:** 56

# COLLEGE GRADUATION REQUIREMENTS

**Course waivers allowed:** Yes
**Course substitutions allowed:** Yes
**In what courses:** Only on an individual basis after Southern Utah University policy process is completed.

# ADDITIONAL INFORMATION

**Environment:** The university is in a small town 150 miles north of Las Vegas.

**Student Body**
  **Undergrad enrollment:** 5,426
  **Women:** 56%
  **Men:** 44%
  **In-state students:** 90%
  **Out-of-state:** 10%

**Cost Information**
  **In-state tuition:** $1,386
  **Out-of-state:** $5,238
  **Room & board:** $2,070

**Housing Information**
  **University housing:** Yes
  **Fraternity:** Yes
  **Sorority:** Yes
  **Living on campus:** 10%

  **Athletics:** NCAA Div. I

# UTAH STATE UNIVERSITY

University Hill, Logan, UT 84322 • **Admissions:** 801-797-1079
**Email:** admit@admissions.usu.edu • **Web:** www.usu.edu
**Support:** S • **Institution:** 4 yr. Public

## LEARNING DISABILITY ADMISSIONS AND SERVICES

The mission of DRC is to provide support services to students with learning disabilities (and physical disabilities) in order to assist them in meeting their academic and personal goals. Staff members coordinate university support services, and help the students identify their needs, and overcome educational or attitudinal barriers that may prevent them from reaching their full educational potential. The DRC works to tailor services to students' individual needs. Many students use a combination of services to assist them academically, including: campus orientation, registration referral, and academic advising to help students feel comfortable and to promote academic services.

## LEARNING DISABILITY ADMISSIONS INFORMATION

**Program Name:** Disability Resource Center (DRC)
**Program Director:** Diane Craig Baum                     **Telephone:** 801-750-2444
**Contact Person:** Natalie Sterling                       **Telephone:** 801-750-3434

### ADMISSIONS

All students submit the regular application. However, there is a box on the application to be used to voluntarily disclose information about a learning disability. If the Admissions committee does not admit the student with a learning disability, the student may request the Disability Resource Program to become an advocate in an appeal process. Students who know they have a learning disability should contact the DRC to find out the details. Each student is assessed individually for admission. Consideration is given to waiving certain entrance requirements, such as flexibility on the GPA, course requirements, and SAT or ACT scores (lower than 17 on the ACT).

**College entrance exams required:** Yes                  **Untimed accepted:** Yes
**Course entrance requirements:** Yes                     **Interview required:** No
**Diagnostic tests:** Yes
**Documentation:** W-J; Any other psychoeducational testing: within 3 years

### ADDITIONAL INFORMATION

Peer tutoring is available on a one-to-one basis or in small groups. Basic skills courses are offered in time management, learning strategies, reading, math, and study strategies. The DRC has developed an assistive technology lab with computers and adaptive equipment to promote independence in conducting research and completing class assignments. Scholarships are available.

**Special education HS coursework accepted:** Yes, if college appropriate
**Essay required:** No
**Special application required:** Yes                      **Submitted to:** Disability Resource Center
**# of applications submitted each year:** Varies          **# of applications accepted each year:** Anyone who applies is admitted
**# of students receiving LD services:** 150 (approximately)
**Acceptance into program means acceptance into college:** Students must be admitted to university first and then may request services.

## LEARNING DISABILITY SERVICES

**Learning center:** No
**Kurzweil personal reader:** Yes
**LD specialists:** No
**Allowed in exams:**
  **Calculator:** Yes
  **Dictionary:** Yes
  **Computer:** Y/N
  **SpellCheck:** Y/N

**Notetaker:** Yes
**Scribes:** Yes
**Proctors:** Yes
**Oral exams:** Yes
**Extended test time:** Yes
**Added cost:** None
**Distraction-free environ.:** Yes
**Tape recording in class:** Yes
**Books on tape:** Yes
**Taping of other books:** Yes

**Professional tutors:** Yes
**Peer tutors:** 30
**Max. hrs/wk for services:** Varies
**Priority registration:** Yes
**Accomodations for students
with ADD:** Yes
**How are professors notified of
LD:** By the student

## GENERAL ADMISSIONS INFORMATION

**Director of Admissions:** Rod Clark

**Telephone:** 801-750-1096

### ENTRANCE REQUIREMENTS

Total high school units required/recommended: 18 total units are required; 4 English required, 3 math required, 3 science required, 2 foreign language recommended, 3 social studies required. Minimum composite ACT score of 20 and minimum 2.6 GPA required.

**Application deadline:** July 1
**Notification:** Rolling

**SAT or ACT preferred:** ACT
**SAT II required:** Yes
**Average ACT:** 22
**Average GPA:** 3.3

**Graduated top 10% of class:** 26
**Graduated top 25% of class:** 53
**Graduated top 50% of class:** 84

## COLLEGE GRADUATION REQUIREMENTS

**Course waivers allowed:** Yes
**Course substitutions allowed:** Yes
**In what courses:** Requests are handled on a case-by-case basis.

## ADDITIONAL INFORMATION

**Environment:** The university is located on 332 acres 96 miles north of Salt Lake City.

**Student Body**
  **Undergrad enrollment:** 16,703
  **Women:** 51%
  **Men:** 49%
  **In-state students:** 70%
  **Out-of-state:** 30%

**Cost Information**
  **In-state tuition:** $1,701
  **Out-of-state:** $5,979
  **Room & board:** $3,579

**Housing Information**
  **University housing:** Yes
  **Fraternity:** Yes
  **Sorority:** Yes
  **Living on campus:** 14%

  **Athletics:** NCAA Div. I

# CHAMPLAIN COLLEGE

P.O. Box 670, Burlington, VT 05402-0670 • **Admissions:** 802-860-2700 • **Fax:** 802-860-2775
**Support:** S • **Institution:** 2 & 4 yr. Private

## LEARNING DISABILITY ADMISSIONS AND SERVICES

Champlain College does not offer a special program for students with learning disabilities. Support services and academic accommodations are available when needed. Students with learning disabilities meet individually with a counselor at the start of the semester and are assisted in developing a plan of academic support. The counselor acts as liaison between the student and faculty. The Student Resource Center offers peer tutoring, writing assistance, accounting lab, math lab, and a study skill workshop series in notetaking, mastering a college text, writing, revising and editing papers and personal counseling. Students must provide documentation of the disability to Support Services for Students with Disabilities which should include: the most recent educational evaluation performed by a qualified individual—a letter from any educational support service provider who has recently worked with the student would be most helpful—the letter should include information about the nature of the disability and the support services and/or program modifications provided.

## LEARNING DISABILITY ADMISSIONS INFORMATION

**Program Name:** Support Services for Students with Disabilities
**Program Director:** N/I
**Contact Person:** Becky Peterson, Coordinator & Counselor   **Telephone:** 802-860-2700 ext. 2605

### ADMISSIONS

There is no special admissions procedure for students with learning disabilities. Admissions are fairly flexible, although some requirements for certain majors are more difficult. Upward grade trend is very helpful and a good senior year is looked upon favorably. Recommendations are crucial. The college is very sensitive to students with learning disabilities and is most interested in determining if the students can succeed. Students may take a reduced load of 12 credits and still be considered full-time.

**College entrance exams required:** No
**Course entrance requirements:** Yes
**Diagnostic tests:** Yes
**Documentation:** Whatever is most current

**Untimed accepted:** N/A
**Interview required:** Encouraged

### ADDITIONAL INFORMATION

Students with LD who self-disclose receive a special needs form from the Coordinator of Support Services for Students with Disabilities, after they have enrolled in college courses. The coordinator meets with each student during the first week of school. The first appointment includes a discussion about the student's disability and the academic accommodations that will be needed. Accommodations could include but are not limited to: tutoring, extended time for tests (in the Resource Center), readers for tests, use of computer, peer notetakers, tape recording lecture, and books on tape. With the student's permission, faculty members receive a letter describing the student's disability, and discussing appropriate accommodations. The coordinator will continue to act as a liaison between students and faculty, consult with tutors, monitor students' academic progress, and consult with faculty as needed. Freshman Focus, a course designed to assist students in making a smooth transition to college, is available for students in certain majors.

**Special education HS coursework accepted:** Y/N
**Special application required:** No
**# of applications submitted each year:** N/A
**# of students receiving LD services:** 80

**Essay required:** Yes
**Submitted to:** N/A
**# of applications accepted each year:** N/A

**Acceptance into program means acceptance into college:** Students must be admitted to the college first and then may request services.

# LEARNING DISABILITY SERVICES

**Learning center:** Yes
**Kurzweil personal reader:** N/I
**LD specialists:** No
**Allowed in exams:**
  **Calculator:** Yes
  **Dictionary:** Y/N
  **Computer:** Y/N
  **SpellCheck:** Y/N

**Notetaker:** Yes
**Scribes:** Yes
**Proctors:** Yes
**Oral exams:** Yes
**Extended test time:** Yes
**Added cost:** None
**Distraction-free environ.:** Yes
**Tape recording in class:** Yes
**Books on tape:** RFB
**Taping of other books:** Yes

**Professional tutors:** No
**Peer tutors:** 25
**Max. hrs/wk for services:** 2 hrs./ per course per week
**Priority registration:** No
**Accomodations for students with ADD:** Yes
**How are professors notified of LD:** By the student and the Coordinator

# GENERAL ADMISSIONS INFORMATION

**Director of Admissions:** Josephine Churchill

**Telephone:** 802-860-2727

## ENTRANCE REQUIREMENTS
High school transcript and letters of recommendation.

**Application deadline:** NR
**Notification:** NR

**SAT or ACT preferred:** NR

# COLLEGE GRADUATION REQUIREMENTS

**Course waivers allowed:** No
**Course substitutions allowed:** Y/N
**In what courses:** Decided on a case-by-case basis.

# ADDITIONAL INFORMATION

**Environment:** The college is located on 16 acres in a small city surrounded by rural area mountains and Lake Champlain.

**Student Body**
  **Undergrad enrollment:** 2,047
  **Women:** 58%
  **Men:** 42%
  **In-state students:** 75%
  **Out-of-state:** 25%

**Cost Information**
  **In-state tuition:** $8,670
  **Out-of-state:** $8,670

**Housing Information**
  **University housing:** Yes
  **Fraternity:** No
  **Sorority:** No
  **Living on campus:** 36%

  **Athletics:** NJCAA

# GREEN MOUNTAIN COLLEGE

**VT**

One College Circle, Poultney, VT 05764 • **Admissions:** 802-287-8208 • **Fax:** 802-287-8099
**Email:** admiss@greenmtn.edu • **Web:** www.greenmtn.edu
**Support:** CS • **Institution:** 4 yr. Private

## LEARNING DISABILITY ADMISSIONS AND SERVICES

Green Mountain College provides accommodation for students with documented learning differences. They believe that every student has the potential for academic success and they strive to support students while teaching them independence and self-advocacy. The Learning Center (LC) functions as the primary source of information regarding academic issues relating to disabilities. Students seeking academic accommodations must self-identify and submit valid documentation of their learning needs. The LC staff determines which students are eligible for academic accommodations and works with the student and staff to develop and implement an accommodation plan that will allow the student an opportunity to succeed at college. Progress is monitored to ensure access to the necessary supports and to assist in fostering self-advocacy. The LC has 6 main functions: to provide academic support, primarily through one-on-one, small group, general content area tutoring; to serve as the campus Writing Center; to support courses specifically designed for underprepared students; to provide support for foreign students; to be the campus center for academic issues relating to disabilities; and to provide workshops and seminars and events with the goal of improving learning skills.

## LEARNING DISABILITY ADMISSIONS INFORMATION

**Program Name:** The Learning Center
**Program Director:** Jack Clay                    **Telephone:** 801-287-8232
**Contact Person:** Same as above

### ADMISSIONS

There is no special admissions process for students with learning disabilities. Students face the same admission criteria, which include: ACT score of 19 or SAT score of 900; 2.0 GPA; 4 yrs. English, 2-3 yrs. history/social studies, 2 yrs. science (with lab), 3 yrs. math, and 2 yrs. foreign language. All applications are carefully considered with the best interest of both the student and the college in mind. Green Mountain College has a probationary admission which limits the course load of the new student while requiring the student to make use of support services.

**College entrance exams required:** Yes          **Untimed accepted:** Yes
**Course entrance requirements:** Yes             **Interview required:** No
**Diagnostic tests:** Yes
**Documentation:** Psychological/educational testing: within 3 years

### ADDITIONAL INFORMATION

The Learning Center provides support services to all students. The tutoring program uses a three tiered approach: a drop-in clinic for immediate but temporary academic assistance, individually scheduled tutoring, or a more extensive schedule of 1, 2, or 3 tutoring sessions per week for tutorial help throughout a course. The Writing Center is open during drop-in hours. All new students take placement tests to assess their achievement in reading and mathematics. Students whose work is unsatisfactory are requested to rewrite assignments with the help of the Learning Center staff. Students underprepared in math are advised to take Basic Math or Beginning Algebra, and tutoring is available.

**Special education HS coursework accepted:** Yes          **Essay required:** Yes
**Special application required:** No                        **Submitted to:** N/A
**# of applications submitted each year:** N/A             **# of applications accepted each year:** N/A
**# of students receiving LD services:** 25
**Acceptance into program means acceptance into college:** Students must be admitted to the college and then reviewed for LC services.

## LEARNING DISABILITY SERVICES

**Learning center:** Yes
**Kurzweil personal reader:** No
**LD specialists:** 1
**Allowed in exams:**
  **Calculator:** Yes
  **Dictionary:** Yes
  **Computer:** Yes
  **SpellCheck:** Yes

**Notetaker:** Yes
**Scribes:** Yes
**Proctors:** Yes
**Oral exams:** Yes
**Extended test time:** Yes
**Added cost:** None
**Distraction-free environ.:** Yes
**Tape recording in class:** Yes
**Books on tape:** Yes
**Taping of other books:** No

**Professional tutors:** 4
**Peer tutors:** 10
**Max. hrs/wk for services:** Unlimited
**Priority registration:** Yes
**Accomodations for students with ADD:** Yes
**How are professors notified of LD:** By the student and the Program Director

## GENERAL ADMISSIONS INFORMATION

**Director of Admissions:** Peter Freyberg

**Telephone:** 801-287-8208

### ENTRANCE REQUIREMENTS

Total high school units required/recommended: 16 total units are required; 4 English required, 2 math required, 2 science required, 1 social studies required, 1 history required. Minimum combined SAT I score of 800 (composite ACT score of 19) and minimum 2.5 GPA recommended.

**Application deadline:** Rolling
**Notification:** Rolling

**SAT or ACT preferred:** SAT
**SAT Avg:** 498V, 476M
**Average ACT:** 20
**Average GPA:** 2.66

**Graduated top 10% of class:** 8
**Graduated top 25% of class:** 22
**Graduated top 50% of class:** 53

## COLLEGE GRADUATION REQUIREMENTS

**Course waivers allowed:** No
**Course substitutions allowed:** No
**In what courses:** N/A

## ADDITIONAL INFORMATION

**Environment:** NR

**Student Body**
  **Undergrad enrollment:** 585
  **Women:** 51%
  **Men:** 49%
  **In-state students:** 8%
  **Out-of-state:** 92%

**Cost Information**
  **In-state tuition:** $14,360
  **Out-of-state:** $14,360
  **Room & board:** $3,190

**Housing Information**
  **University housing:** Yes
  **Fraternity:** No
  **Sorority:** No
  **Living on campus:** 93%

  **Athletics:** NAIA

# JOHNSON STATE COLLEGE

**VT**

RR2, Box 75, Johnson, VT 05656 • **Admissions:** 802-635-1219 • **Fax:** 802-635-1230
**Email:** jscapply@badgr.jfc.vsc.edu • **Web:** www.jsc.vsc.edu
**Support:** CS • **Institution:** 4 yr. Public

## LEARNING DISABILITY ADMISSIONS AND SERVICES

Johnson State College provides services to students with learning disabilities through the Special Services Counselor. The fundamental purpose is to provide students with the appropriate services necessary to allow full participation in all Johnson State College academic programs. Students with learning disabilities are integrated fully into the college community. This is a TRIO Program for 250 students meeting eligibility criteria, which include at least one of the following areas: be enrolled in 1 or more basic skills courses; SAT scores below 300 on either Verbal or Math sections; earned a G.E.D.; has below average high school grades; has not completed Algebra II or its equivalent in high school; or was conditionally accepted to the college. Students must also meet 1 of 3 criteria: (1) have a documented disability; (2) be a 1st generation college student; and (3) be economically disadvantaged. Eligible students receive intensive support services through the Academic Support Services Program. The Learning Resource Center provides a friendly and supportive environment for any student who is academically struggling or underprepared to meet their educational goals. Services include: group and peer tutoring, Math Lab, Writer's Workshop, and study skills booklets.

## LEARNING DISABILITY ADMISSIONS INFORMATION

**Program Name:** Academic Support Services
**Program Director:** Sara Henry
**Contact Person:** Same as above

**Telephone:** 802-635-2356 ext. 259

### ADMISSIONS

Upon consultation with the Academic Support Services office, all students with learning disabilities who demonstrate the academic ability to be successful are accepted. Modifications to entrance requirements are accommodated if a student is otherwise admissible. Course requirements include 4 yrs. English, 2 yrs. science, 2 yrs. social science and 3 yrs. math. High school GPA range can be between "B–/C+." The SAT score ranges between 700-940 for the middle 50%.

**College entrance exams required:** Yes
**Course entrance requirements:** Yes
**Diagnostic tests:** Yes
**Documentation:** Cognitive measurement—WAIS-R and achievement tests: within 3 years

**Untimed accepted:** Yes
**Interview required:** No

### ADDITIONAL INFORMATION

Academic Support Services provides: priority tutoring, academic advising, personal counseling, career exploration and development, College Survival Skills training workshops, and assistance with establishing appropriate and reasonable accommodations. Students should be self-advocates and are responsible for notifying instructors to arrange for accommodations. The Skill Program is designed to support high school graduates. This innovative learning experience will help make the transition from high school to college a more positive and rewarding experience for students needing strong academic and individual support. The Skill Program is 17 weeks and students earn 4 college credits through a student-centered program designed to teach self-advocacy, critical inquiry, study skills, and general college survival skills. Students develop individual educational plans consistent with their short- and long-term educational goals. This begins 2 weeks prior to freshman year and continues through 15 weeks of fall semester.

**Special education HS coursework accepted:** Yes
**Special application required:** No
**# of applications submitted each year:** N/A
**# of students receiving LD services:** 104

**Essay required:** Yes
**Submitted to:** N/A
**# of applications accepted each year:** N/A

**Acceptance into program means acceptance into college:** Students must be admitted to the university and then may request services.

## LEARNING DISABILITY SERVICES

**Learning center:** Yes
**Kurzweil personal reader:** N/I
**LD specialists:** 1
**Allowed in exams:**
  **Calculator:** Yes
  **Dictionary:** Yes
  **Computer:** Yes
  **SpellCheck:** Yes

**Notetaker:** Yes
**Scribes:** Yes
**Proctors:** Yes
**Oral exams:** Yes
**Extended test time:** Yes
**Added cost:** None
**Distraction-free environ.:** Yes
**Tape recording in class:** Yes
**Books on tape:** Yes
**Taping of other books:** Yes

**Professional tutors:** No
**Peer tutors:** Yes
**Max. hrs/wk for services:** Unlimited
**Priority registration:** N/I
**Accomodations for students with ADD:** Yes
**How are professors notified of LD:** By the student

## GENERAL ADMISSIONS INFORMATION

**Director of Admissions:** Jonathan H. Henry

**Telephone:** 802-635-2356

### ENTRANCE REQUIREMENTS

Total high school units required/recommended: 16 total units are required; 4 English required, 3 math required, 2 science required, 2 social studies required, 2 history required. Applicants who rank in top half of secondary school class with a minimum C+ accepted. Special requirements: TOEFL is required of all international students.

**Application deadline:** Rolling
**Notification:** Rolling

**SAT or ACT preferred:** SAT
**SAT Avg:** 500V, 480M

**Graduated top 10% of class:** 2
**Graduated top 25% of class:** 12
**Graduated top 50% of class:** 39

## COLLEGE GRADUATION REQUIREMENTS

**Course waivers allowed:** Yes
**Course substitutions allowed:** Yes
**In what courses:** Determined on a case-by-case basis as needed and requested by the student.

## ADDITIONAL INFORMATION

**Environment:** The college is located in a rural area 45 miles northeast of Burlington.

**Student Body**
  **Undergrad enrollment:** 1,569
  **Women:** 47%
  **Men:** 53%
  **In-state students:** 73%
  **Out-of-state:** 27%

**Cost Information**
  **In-state tuition:** $3,780
  **Out-of-state:** $8,760
  **Room & board:** $5,086

**Housing Information**
  **University housing:** Yes
  **Fraternity:** No
  **Sorority:** No
  **Living on campus:** 55%

  **Athletics:** NCAA Div. III

# LANDMARK COLLEGE

Putney, VT 05346 • **Admissions:** 802-387-4767

**Support:** SP • **Institution:** 2 yr. Private

## LEARNING DISABILITY ADMISSIONS AND SERVICES

Landmark College is designed exclusively for high-potential students with dyslexia, specific learning disabilities, and/or ADHD. It is the only accredited college in the nation for students with LD/ADHD. More than 100 members of the faculty and professional staff devote their entire attention to providing the finest possible program for these students. The goal is to prepare students to enter or return to college. At Landmark, students do not bypass difficulties by using notetakers, taped books, or taking exams orally. Students must do their own work and Landmark teaches them how. Landmark's approach is unique and includes an individually designed tutorial program, very small classes, structured assignments, and an emphasis on constantly improving language and study skills.

## LEARNING DISABILITY ADMISSIONS INFORMATION

**Program Name:** Landmark College
**Program Director:** Frances Sopper
**Contact Person:** Same as above

**Telephone:** 802-387-6718

### ADMISSIONS

Landmark College serves students whose academic skills have not been developed to a level equal to their intellectual capacity. Students must have average to superior intellectual potential, diagnosis of dyslexia, specific LD or ADHD, and high motivation. Applicants must have a willingness to undertake a rigorous academic program that does not provide bypass methods such as notetakers, books on tape, or oral exams. Focus instead is on individualized, intensive development and honing of academic skills. Qualified students must have a testing session and interview. An admission decision is made at this time. ACT/SAT are not required. There are no specific course requirements for admission, but students must take courses that lead to a high school diploma or the GED. Students may apply for admission for summer, fall, or spring semesters.

**College entrance exams required:** No
**Course entrance requirements:** N/A
**Diagnostic tests:** Yes
**Documentation:** WAIS-R; complete psychoeducational evaluation: within 2 years

**Untimed accepted:** Yes
**Interview required:** Yes

### ADDITIONAL INFORMATION

Skills Development Summer Sessions ($6,475) help students develop the language and study skills needed for success in college. This program is open to students from other colleges, or recent high school graduates, as well as those planning to attend Landmark. Students can get help with writing, reading, study skills, and understanding their own learning styles. Skills classes are offered to students on campus in study skills, math, written language, oral language and content courses.

**Special education HS coursework accepted:** Yes
**Special application required:** No
**# of applications submitted each year:** N/A
**# of students receiving LD services:** 240
**Acceptance into program means acceptance into college:** The Program and the college are one and the same.

**Essay required:** Yes
**Submitted to:** N/A
**# of applications accepted each year:** N/A

## LEARNING DISABILITY SERVICES

**Learning center:** Yes
**Kurzweil personal reader:** No
**LD specialists:** Yes
**Allowed in exams:**
  **Calculator:** Yes
  **Dictionary:** Yes
  **Computer:** Yes
  **SpellCheck:** Yes

**Notetaker:** No
**Scribes:** No
**Proctors:** No
**Oral exams:** No
**Extended test time:** Yes
**Added cost:** None
**Distraction-free environ.:** Yes
**Tape recording in class:** Yes
**Books on tape:** No
**Taping of other books:** No

**Professional tutors:** 105
**Peer tutors:** No
**Max. hrs/wk for services:** Unlimited
**Priority registration:** No
**Accomodations for students with ADD:** Yes
**How are professors notified of LD:** Not necessary as all students are learning disabled

## GENERAL ADMISSIONS INFORMATION

**Director of Admissions:** Frances Sopper

**Telephone:** 802-387-6718

**ENTRANCE REQUIREMENTS**
NR

**Application deadline:** Rolling
**Notification:** NR

**SAT or ACT preferred:** Not required

## COLLEGE GRADUATION REQUIREMENTS

**Course waivers allowed:** No
**Course substitutions allowed:** No
**In what courses:** N/A

## ADDITIONAL INFORMATION

**Environment:** The college is located on 125 acres overlooking the Connecticut River Valley and the hills of Vermont and New Hampshire.

**Student Body**
  **Undergrad enrollment:** 240
  **Women:** 28%
  **Men:** 72%
  **In-state students:** 5%
  **Out-of-state:** 95%

**Cost Information**
  **In-state tuition:** $24,500
  **Out-of-state:** $24,500

**Housing Information**
  **University housing:** Yes
  **Fraternity:** No
  **Sorority:** No
  **Living on campus:** 100%

  **Athletics:** Intercollegiate, intramural

# NORWICH UNIVERSITY

655 Main Street, Northfield, VT 05663 • **Admissions:** 802-485-2001 • **Fax:** 802-485-2032
**Email:** nuadm@norwichedu • **Web:** www.norwich.edu
**Support:** CS • **Institution:** 4 yr. Private

## LEARNING DISABILITY ADMISSIONS AND SERVICES

The Learning Support Center (LSC) offers comprehensive support services in all areas of academic life. While Norwich does not have a formal program for students with learning disabilities, the university does offer support services on a voluntary basis. Students are instructed by the center staff in Freshman Academic Survival Training (FAST), which covers a wide range of study and college survival skills. The Center's staff works closely with advisors and faculty members, and are strong advocates for students with learning disabilities. The university stresses autonomy by providing a level of support that assists students with becoming responsible, thinking adults, well-acquainted with their own needs and able to articulate them. Services are provided by a staff of professionals that includes LD reading specialists, study skills/writing specialists, and a basic math specialist. The professional staff is supplemented by a trained, well-supervised student tutorial staff.

## LEARNING DISABILITY ADMISSIONS INFORMATION

**Program Name:** Learning Support Center (LSC)
**Program Director:** Paula A. Gills                    **Telephone:** 802-485-2130
**Contact Person:** Same as above

### ADMISSIONS

Students with learning disabilities submit a general application. Admission criteria include: high school GPA of a C or better; SAT of 850 or equivalent ACT; participation in activities; and strong college recommendations from teachers, counselors or coaches. There are no course waivers for admission, but some limited course substitutions are allowed. The university is flexible on ACT/SAT test scores. Students with learning disabilities should provide detailed information about any existing handicap. A complete psychodiagnostic evaluation is required. A small number of students who do not meet the general admission requirements may be admitted if they show promise. An interview is highly recommended.

**College entrance exams required:** Yes          **Untimed accepted:** Yes
**Course entrance requirements:** Yes             **Interview required:** Recommended
**Diagnostic tests:** Yes
**Documentation:** WAIS-R; Auditory-visual; Educ. achievement: within 4 years

### ADDITIONAL INFORMATION

A telephone conversation or personal meeting with the LSC support personnel is encouraged prior to the start of college, so that work can begin immediately on preparing an individualized program. Students are responsible for meeting with each professor to discuss accommodations. Services begin with Freshman Placement Testing designed to assess each individual's level of readiness for college-level reading, writing and math. Other services include course advising in companion with an assigned academic advisor, and advocacy for academic petitions. Skills classes are offered in time management and general study techniques. Services and accommodations are available for undergraduate and graduate students.

**Special education HS coursework accepted:** Yes      **Essay required:** Highly recommended
**Special application required:** No                   **Submitted to:** N/A
**# of applications submitted each year:** N/A         **# of applications accepted each year:** N/A
**# of students receiving LD services:** 130
**Acceptance into program means acceptance into college:** Students must be admitted to the university first and then may request services.

## LEARNING DISABILITY SERVICES

**Learning center:** Yes
**Kurzweil personal reader:** No
**LD specialists:** 2
**Allowed in exams:**
  **Calculator:** Y/N
  **Dictionary:** Y/N
  **Computer:** Yes
  **SpellCheck:** Yes

**Notetaker:** Yes
**Scribes:** Yes
**Proctors:** Yes
**Oral exams:** Yes
**Extended test time:** Yes
**Added cost:** None
**Distraction-free environ.:** Yes
**Tape recording in class:** Yes
**Books on tape:** RFB
**Taping of other books:** Yes

**Professional tutors:** 8
**Peer tutors:** 15-20
**Max. hrs/wk for services:**
Depends on staff availability
**Priority registration:** Yes
**Accomodations for students
with ADD:** Yes
**How are professors notified of
LD:** By the student and the LSC
Director

## GENERAL ADMISSIONS INFORMATION

**Director of Admissions:** Frank Griffis

**Telephone:** 802-485-2001

### ENTRANCE REQUIREMENTS

Total high school units required/recommended: 4 English required, 3 math required, 2 science required, 2 social studies required. Special requirements: TOEFL is required of all international students.

**Application deadline:** Rolling
**Notification:** NR

**SAT or ACT preferred:** NR
**SAT II required:** Yes

**Graduated top 10% of class:** 8
**Graduated top 25% of class:** 29
**Graduated top 50% of class:** 58

## COLLEGE GRADUATION REQUIREMENTS

**Course waivers allowed:** No
**Course substitutions allowed:** Yes
**In what courses:** Foreign language

## ADDITIONAL INFORMATION

**Environment:** 2 campuses located in Northfield (traditional) and Montpelier (low residency) are located 50 miles southeast of Burlington.

**Student Body**
  **Undergrad enrollment:** NR
  **Women:** 40%
  **Men:** 60%
  **In-state students:** 34%
  **Out-of-state:** 66%

**Cost Information**
  **In-state tuition:** $14,634
  **Out-of-state:** $14,634
  **Room & board:** $5,536

**Housing Information**
  **University housing:** Yes
  **Fraternity:** No
  **Sorority:** No
  **Living on campus:** 77%

  **Athletics:** NCAA Div. III

# SOUTHERN VERMONT COLLEGE

Monument Avenue Extension, Bennington, VT 05201 • **Admissions:** 802-442-5427 • **Fax:** 802-442-5427
**Email:** admis@svc.edu • **Web:** www.svc.edu
**Support:** SP • **Institution:** 2 yr. & 4 yr. Private

## LEARNING DISABILITY ADMISSIONS AND SERVICES

The Learning Disability Program at Southern Vermont College offers a highly supportive environment for students with special educational needs. Students who participate in the program are offered a wide range of support services tailored to their individual needs, and regularly scheduled tutorial sessions for academic support, study skills, and compensatory strategies. Students accepted into the program must also commit to accessing support services during their 1st year. Support remains available throughout their college stay.

## LEARNING DISABILITY ADMISSIONS INFORMATION

**Program Name:** Learning Disability Program
**Program Director:** Linda Crowe
**Contact Person:** Same as above

**Telephone:** 802-442-5427

### ADMISSIONS

If a student with a documented learning disability does not meet regular admissions criteria, the LD Coordinator and review committee will further examine documentation and evaluation information. Each case is decided on an individual basis. Required documentation includes: WAIS-R (within 2 years) with individual subscores indicating at least average ability in abstract reasoning; recent individualized achievement tests indicating grade equivalents in reading skills/comprehension, math, and written language skills. General admissions criteria include: a minimum GPA of 2.0; 3 yrs. English, 2 yrs. Math, 2 yrs. Science (can substitute); No ACT/SAT is required. Occasionally, if a student does not meet regular admissions standards or meet all indicators of college success, a conditional acceptance may be offered to the summer ACTion Program. Admissions decisions are made by the Office of Admissions and the Director of the Learning Disabilities Program.

**College entrance exams required:** Optional
**Course entrance requirements:** Yes
**Diagnostic tests:** Yes
**Documentation:** Achievement testing: W-J; WAIS-R: within 2 years

**Untimed accepted:** Yes
**Interview required:** Yes

### ADDITIONAL INFORMATION

Skill workshops are offered for credit in study skills; notetaking; and memory strategies. The ACTion Program works with students during the school year to help them with academic and/or personal problems. There is walk-in tutoring with trained tutors. The LD staff works with students and instructors to find learning strategies to help them succeed in college. Students may be placed in one of three classes: English composition and college math to master skills; literature course to improve general reading skills; and basic math, which is a self-paced course to strengthen math skills. Summer ACTion program is available to all students accepted into Fall Freshman class. SVC's Summer ACTion Program was created for students who wish to benefit from its basic skills courses. This Program provides: courses in literature, English composition, college algebra, and intro to psychology; small class size and individual attention; study halls and tutorials; cultural events; dorm life; sports and recreation; field trips; and paid work experience.

**Special education HS coursework accepted:** Yes
**Special application required:** No
**# of applications submitted each year:** 80
**# of students receiving LD services:** 70

**Essay required:** Yes
**Submitted to:** N/A
**# of applications accepted each year:** 25

**Acceptance into program means acceptance into college:** Students are admitted directly into LD Program resulting in admission to the college; or LD Program provides a recommendation to Admissions.

## LEARNING DISABILITY SERVICES

**Learning center:** Yes
**Kurzweil personal reader:** No
**LD specialists:** 2
**Allowed in exams:**
  **Calculator:** Y/N
  **Dictionary:** No
  **Computer:** Yes
  **SpellCheck:** Yes

**Notetaker:** Yes
**Scribes:** Y/N
**Proctors:** Yes
**Oral exams:** Y/N
**Extended test time:** Yes
**Added cost:** None
**Distraction-free environ.:** Yes
**Tape recording in class:** Yes
**Books on tape:** RFB
**Taping of other books:** No

**Professional tutors:** 2
**Peer tutors:** 9
**Max. hrs/wk for services:** Unlimited
**Priority registration:** Yes
**Accomodations for students with ADD:** Yes
**How are professors notified of LD:** By the student

## GENERAL ADMISSIONS INFORMATION

**Director of Admissions:** Todd Crandall          **Telephone:** 802-378-2782

### ENTRANCE REQUIREMENTS

Total high school units required/recommended: 3 English recommended, 2 math recommended, 2 science recommended.
Special requirements: An RN is required for nursing program applicants.

**Application deadline:** Rolling
**Notification:** Rolling

**SAT or ACT preferred:** Either
**SAT Avg:** 440V, 450M

**Graduated top 10% of class:** 3
**Graduated top 25% of class:** 19
**Graduated top 50% of class:** 61

## COLLEGE GRADUATION REQUIREMENTS

**Course waivers allowed:** Yes
**Course substitutions allowed:** Yes
**In what courses:** Math course substitution considered only if, in spite of demonstrated efforts to master college Math course material, the student has met with limited success.

## ADDITIONAL INFORMATION

**Environment:** The college is located in a town of 17,000, forty miles northeast of Albany, New York.

**Student Body**
  **Undergrad enrollment:** 697
  **Women:** 58%
  **Men:** 42%
  **In-state students:** 42%
  **Out-of-state:** 58%

**Cost Information**
  **In-state tuition:** $8,370
  **Out-of-state:** $8,370
  **Room & board:** $4,304

**Housing Information**
  **University housing:** Yes
  **Fraternity:** No
  **Sorority:** No
  **Living on campus:** 30%

  **Athletics:** NCAA Div. III

# UNIVERSITY OF VERMONT

Office of Admissions, 194 South Prospect Street, Burlington, VT 05401 • **Admissions:** 802-656-3480
**Fax:** 802-656-8611 • **Email:** admissions@uvm.edu • **Web:** www.uvm.edu/indexjscript.html
**Support:** CS • **Institution:** 4 yr. Public

## LEARNING DISABILITY ADMISSIONS AND SERVICES

The university provides a multidisciplinary program for students with LD. The Office of Specialized Student Services (OSSS) works closely with students having learning problems to ensure that campus-wide resources are used effectively. Initially, a comprehensive assessment is undertaken to identify students' strengths and weaknesses in learning. This information is used to carefully design classroom and study accommodations to compensate for learning problems. Through this process, students and program staff have identified a number of techniques and strategies to enable success at class and study tasks. The academic advising process for student with LD involves 2 offices: The academic advisor assigned by the college, and the professional staff of the OOSS who review tentative semester schedules to balance course format, teaching style, and work load with a student's learning strengths. The Learning Cooperative offers individual tutoring and assistance with reading, writing, study skills, and time management. The Writing Center assists with proofing and feedback on writing assignments. There are no developmental courses, only tutoring. This is an individualized support service program designed to equalize educational opportunities for students with learning disabilities.

## LEARNING DISABILITY ADMISSIONS INFORMATION

**Program Name:** Office of Specialized Student Services
**Program Director:** Nancy Oliker, Ph.D.                    **Telephone:** 802-656-7753
**Contact Person:** Susan Krasnow/Nancy Oliker           **Telephone:** 802-656-8615

### ADMISSIONS

Students are encouraged to voluntarily provide documentation of their disability. A clear understanding of the students' strengths and weaknesses in learning, and the influence of the disability on the current and past educational process, will enable a broader assessment of ability to meet academic qualifications, requirements, and rigors of UVM. Students with LD should submit a current educational evaluation that includes a measure of cognitive functioning and documentation of the learning problem(s). Students with ADHD are encouraged to provide documentation and information on how the ADHD had an impact on the educational setting. Course requirements include 4 yrs. English, 3 yrs. social science, 3 yrs. math, 2 yrs. physical sciences, and 2 yrs. foreign language. (Math and foreign language can be waived with appropriate documentation). Special education courses are acceptable if the student's high school gives high school credit for the courses. There is no minimum SAT score (average SAT is 1000). Generally students rank in the top 1/3 of their high school class.

**College entrance exams required:** Yes                **Untimed accepted:** Yes
**Course entrance requirements:** Yes                   **Interview required:** No
**Diagnostic tests:** Yes
**Documentation:** WAIS-R; W-J 1 or 2; or other similar tests: within 3 years

### ADDITIONAL INFORMATION

UVM provides a multidisciplinary program for students with learning disabilities that emphasizes: development of academic accommodations; academic adjustments including notetaking, course requirement substitution, course load reduction, extended time on exams, alternate test formats and computer/speller availability; auxiliary services including taped tests, reader services, tutorial services, writing skill development, proofing services, reading skill development; academic advising and course selection; priority registration services; learning strategies and study skills training; LD support group and counseling; faculty consultation and in-service training; and diagnostic screening and evaluation. Students with ADHD with appropriate documentation may receive help with class schedules, study activities to fit individual learning styles, support services, or accommodations in test conditions, course loads, and/or program requirements because of the severity of the disability.

**Special education HS coursework accepted:** Yes      **Essay required:** Yes
**Special application required:** No                    **Submitted to:** N/A
**# of applications submitted each year:** N/A          **# of applications accepted each year:** N/A
**# of students receiving LD services:** 450
**Acceptance into program means acceptance into college:** Students must be admitted and then may request services. Some students are reviewed by the LD program which provides consultation to admissions.

# LEARNING DISABILITY SERVICES

**Learning center:** Yes
**Kurzweil personal reader:** No
**LD specialists:** 3
**Allowed in exams:**
  **Calculator:** Yes
  **Dictionary:** Y/N
  **Computer:** Yes
  **SpellCheck:** Yes

**Notetaker:** Yes
**Scribes:** Yes
**Proctors:** Yes
**Oral exams:** Yes
**Extended test time:** Yes
**Added cost:** $7 per hr. for tutoring unless qualified for TRIO grant
**Distraction-free environ.:** Yes
**Tape recording in class:** Yes
**Books on tape:** Yes
**Taping of other books:** Yes

**Professional tutors:** Varies
**Peer tutors:** Yes
**Max. hrs/wk for services:** Varies
**Priority registration:** Yes
**Accomodations for students with ADD:** Yes
**How are professors notified of LD:** By the student and the Program Director

# GENERAL ADMISSIONS INFORMATION

**Director of Admissions:** Barbara O'Reilly          **Telephone:** 802-656-3370

## ENTRANCE REQUIREMENTS

Total high school units required/recommended: 16 total units are required; 4 English required, 3 math required, 2 science required, 2 foreign language required, 3 social studies required. Additional electives strongly recommended; nonacademic electives may be counted. Qualified in-state applicants accepted first; out-of-state applicants then accepted on competitive basis. Special requirements: TOEFL is required of all international students. Trigonometry required of business, engineering, mathematics, physical therapy, and science program applicants; biology, chemistry, and physics required of physical therapy program applicants; chemistry and physics required of engineering program applicants; biology and chemistry required of professional nursing program applicants. Audition required of music performance program applicants.

**Application deadline:** February 1
**Notification:** March 15

**SAT or ACT preferred:** SAT
**SAT Avg:** 564V, 565M
**SAT II required:** Yes

**Graduated top 10% of class:** 15
**Graduated top 25% of class:** 49
**Graduated top 50% of class:** 90

# COLLEGE GRADUATION REQUIREMENTS

**Course waivers allowed:** Yes
**Course substitutions allowed:** Yes
**In what courses:** Depends on departmental/college approval

# ADDITIONAL INFORMATION

**Environment:** The university is located on 425 acres by Lake Champlain 90 miles south of Montreal.

**Student Body**
  **Undergrad enrollment:** 7,375
  **Women:** 54%
  **Men:** 46%
  **In-state students:** 41%
  **Out-of-state:** 59%

**Cost Information**
  **In-state tuition:** $6,732
  **Out-of-state:** $16,824
  **Room & board:** $4,706

**Housing Information**
  **University housing:** Yes
  **Fraternity:** Yes
  **Sorority:** Yes
  **Living on campus:** 47%

  **Athletics:** NCAA Div. I

# VERMONT TECHNICAL COLLEGE

Randolph Center, VT 05061 • **Admissions:** 802-728-1000

**Support:** CS • **Institution:** 2 yr. Public

## LEARNING DISABILITY ADMISSIONS AND SERVICES

The goal of the Services for Students with Disabilities Program is to ensure equal access to all VTC programs for all qualified students with disabilities; to help students develop the necessary skills to be effective at VTC and beyond; to further students' understanding of how their disabilities effects them in school, work, and social settings.

## LEARNING DISABILITY ADMISSIONS INFORMATION

**Program Name:** Services for Students with Disabilities
**Program Director:** Barbara Bendix      **Telephone:** 802-728-1278
**Contact Person:** Same as above

### ADMISSIONS

There is no special admissions process for students with learning disabilities.  In general, students have a GPA of 80% or higher. There is no cut-off score for the SAT. The Program Director can make recommendations to waive certain admission criteria if they discriminate against a student with a learning disability, and other evidence of a student's qualifications exist. General course requirements include: algebra I & II, geometry, and physics or chemistry for engineering programs. Many students meet with the Disability Coordinator during the application process to discuss their needs. There are 2 alternative admission plans. The 2nd plan is the Summer Bridge Program which is a 4-week math/physics and language arts program as preparation for marginal freshmen who do not require the 3-year Program option. This option is for engineering students who need longer than 2 years to complete the program.

**College entrance exams required:** Yes        **Untimed accepted:** Yes
**Course entrance requirements:** Yes         **Interview required:** Recommended
**Diagnostic tests:** Yes
**Documentation:** WAIS-R; or WISC-R: or W-J and achievement test: within 3 years

### ADDITIONAL INFORMATION

The Disabilities Coordinator provides a variety of services which include: assessment of students' academic needs, coordination of tutoring to provide assistance with course material, disabilities forum for students to share experiences and academic strategies that they have learned with other students. Individual tutoring is provided in writing and study skills, such as time management, effective text book reading, learning strategies, and stress management. Also available are academic and career counseling and coordination of accommodations. There is a Learning Center which is open to all students on campus.

**Special education HS coursework accepted:** Yes     **Essay required:** No
**Special application required:** No              **Submitted to:** N/A
**# of applications submitted each year:** N/A      **# of applications accepted each year:** N/A
**# of students receiving LD services:** 35
**Acceptance into program means acceptance into college:** Students must be admitted to the college first and then may request services.

## LEARNING DISABILITY SERVICES

**Learning center:** Yes
**Kurzweil personal reader:** Yes
**LD specialists:** Yes
**Allowed in exams:**
  **Calculator:** Y/N
  **Dictionary:** Y/N
  **Computer:** Y/N
  **SpellCheck:** Y/N

**Notetaker:** Yes
**Scribes:** No
**Proctors:** Yes
**Oral exams:** Yes
**Extended test time:** Yes
**Added cost:** None
**Distraction-free environ.:** Yes
**Tape recording in class:** Yes
**Books on tape:** RFB
**Taping of other books:** No

**Professional tutors:** 16
**Peer tutors:** 12
**Max. hrs/wk for services:** Unlimited
**Priority registration:** Yes
**Accomodations for students with ADD:** Yes
**How are professors notified of LD:** By the student

## GENERAL ADMISSIONS INFORMATION

**Director of Admissions:** Rosemary Distel      **Telephone:** 802-728-1243

### ENTRANCE REQUIREMENTS
Total high school units required/recommended: 3 math and 2 science required for the Engineering Program; 2 math and 2 science required for all others.

**Application deadline:** NR      **SAT or ACT preferred:** NR
**Notification:** NR

## COLLEGE GRADUATION REQUIREMENTS

**Course waivers allowed:** No
**Course substitutions allowed:** No
**In what courses:** N/A

## ADDITIONAL INFORMATION

**Environment:** The college is located on 544 acres in a rural area.

**Student Body**
  **Undergrad enrollment:** 872
  **Women:** 25%
  **Men:** 75%
  **In-state students:** 70%
  **Out-of-state:** 30%

**Cost Information**
  **In-state tuition:** $4,380
  **Out-of-state:** $4,936

**Housing Information**
  **University housing:** Yes
  **Fraternity:** No
  **Sorority:** No
  **Living on campus:** 79%

  **Athletics:** Intramurals, Intercollegiate

# FERRUM COLLEGE

P.O. Box 1000, Ferrum, VA 24088 • **Admissions:** 540-365-2121 • **Fax:** 540-365-4269
**Email:** admissions@ferrum.edu • **Web:** www.ferrum.edu
**Support:** CS • **Institution:** 4 yr. Private

## LEARNING DISABILITY ADMISSIONS AND SERVICES

Ferrum College does not have a program for students with learning disabilities, but does provide services to students with disabilities documentation. Ferrum also does not offer a comprehensive program or monitoring services. Students motivated to accept the assistance and academic accommodations offered frequently find Ferrum's services to be excellent.

## LEARNING DISABILITY ADMISSIONS INFORMATION

**Program Name:** Academic Resources Center
**Program Director:** Nancy S. Beach                    **Telephone:** 540-365-4290
**Contact Person:** Same as above

### ADMISSIONS

Ferrum is proactive in terms of the admissions process for students with documentation of a disability. All students first go through the admissions process. If students are not admitted through the general admissions process, the committee can be requested to reconsider with the presentation of the documentation and a recommendation from the disability service provider. Those applicants who do not meet general admission criteria are encouraged to have an interview with the Office of Admissions. General admission criteria include: 4 yrs. English, 1 yr. math (3 recommended), 1 yr. science (3 recommended), 2 yrs. foreign language, and 3 yrs. social studies are recommended; SAT/ACT required (average ACT is 18 and average SAT I is 1040); the average GPA is 2.6.

**College entrance exams required:** Yes                **Untimed accepted:** Yes
**Course entrance requirements:** Yes                  **Interview required:** Y/N
**Diagnostic tests:** Yes
**Documentation:** Psychoeducational evaluation: within 3 years

### ADDITIONAL INFORMATION

The Academic Resources Center is a learning center available for students with learning disabilities as well as all other students on campus. Some of the tutoring is provided by volunteer professors. Skills classes are offered for credit in study skills. Ferrum College offers a summer program for pre-college freshmen with learning disabilities.

**Special education HS coursework accepted:** N/I          **Essay required:** Optional
**Special application required:** No                      **Submitted to:** N/A
**# of applications submitted each year:** N/A            **# of applications accepted each year:** N/A
**# of students receiving LD services:** N/A
**Acceptance into program means acceptance into college:** Students must be admitted to the college first and then may request services. There is an appeal process for students denied admission.

## LEARNING DISABILITY SERVICES

**Learning center:** Yes
**Kurzweil personal reader:** Yes
**LD specialists:** 1
**Allowed in exams:**
  **Calculator:** Y/N
  **Dictionary:** Yes
  **Computer:** Yes
  **SpellCheck:** Yes

**Notetaker:** Yes
**Scribes:** Yes
**Proctors:** Yes
**Oral exams:** Yes
**Extended test time:** Yes
**Added cost:** None
**Distraction-free environ.:** Yes
**Tape recording in class:** Yes
**Books on tape:** Yes
**Taping of other books:** RFB

**Professional tutors:** Yes
**Peer tutors:** Yes
**Max. hrs/wk for services:** Unlimited
**Priority registration:** Yes
**Accomodations for students with ADD:** Yes
**How are professors notified of LD:** By the student and the Program Director

## GENERAL ADMISSIONS INFORMATION

**Director of Admissions:** Michael Novak

**Telephone:** 540-365-4290

### ENTRANCE REQUIREMENTS

Total high school units required/recommended: 21 total units are recommended; 4 English required, 1 math required, 3 math recommended, 1 science required, 3 science recommended, 2 foreign languages, 3 social studies recommended. Foreign language recommended.

**Application deadline:** August 1
**Notification:** Rolling

**SAT or ACT preferred:** SAT
**SAT Avg:** 451V, 445M
**SAT II required:** Yes
**Average GPA:** 2.6

**Graduated top 10% of class:** 7
**Graduated top 25% of class:** 23
**Graduated top 50% of class:** 44

## COLLEGE GRADUATION REQUIREMENTS

**Course waivers allowed:** Y/N
**Course substitutions allowed:** Y/N
**In what courses:** Discussed on a case-by-case basis.

## ADDITIONAL INFORMATION

**Environment:** NR

**Student Body**
  **Undergrad enrollment:** 1,075
  **Women:** 42%
  **Men:** 58%
  **In-state students:** 81%
  **Out-of-state:** 19%

**Cost Information**
  **In-state tuition:** $10,750
  **Out-of-state:** $10,750
  **Room & board:** $4,850

**Housing Information**
  **University housing:** Yes
  **Fraternity:** No
  **Sorority:** No
  **Living on campus:** 81%

  **Athletics:** NCAA Div. III

# GEORGE MASON UNIVERSITY

4400 University Drive, Fairfax, VA 22030 • **Admissions:** 703-993-2400 • **Fax:** 703-993-4622
**Email:** adm@gmu.edu • **Web:** www.gmu.edu
**Support:** S • **Institution:** 4 yr. Public

## LEARNING DISABILITY ADMISSIONS AND SERVICES

The university does not maintain a specific program for students with learning disabilities. However, George Mason is committed to providing appropriate services and accommodations to allow identified students with disabilities to access programs. The Disability Support Services (DSS) offered is responsible for assuring that students receive the services to which they are entitled. Students must provide documentation and complete a Faculty Contact Sheet to receive documentation. DSS must confirm the students' requests for services.

## LEARNING DISABILITY ADMISSIONS INFORMATION

**Program Name:** Disability Support Services
**Program Director:** Paul Bousel
**Contact Person:** Paul Bousel/ Cathie Axe

**Telephone:** 703-993-2474

### ADMISSIONS

Students with learning disabilities must submit the general George Mason University undergraduate application and meet the same requirements as all other applicants. Students are encouraged to self-disclose and provide documentation of their disability. Letters of recommendation are helpful for explaining weaknesses or problematic areas. Students who have deficiencies in required courses may request a waiver of the requirement. These requests are considered on an individual basis. General admission criteria include: 4 yrs. English, 3 yrs. math (4 recommended), 1 yr. science (3 recommended), 3 yrs. foreign language, 3 yrs. social studies (4 recommended), and 3-4 electives; ACT/SAT; an interview is required.

**College entrance exams required:** Yes
**Course entrance requirements:** Yes
**Diagnostic tests:** Yes
**Documentation:** Psychoeducational evaluation: within 3 years

**Untimed accepted:** Yes
**Interview required:** Yes

### ADDITIONAL INFORMATION

Students with learning disabilities may request: extended testing time or alternative formats for exams, extended time for in-class writing assignments or short-term projects, notetakers, or use of a word processor for essay exams if documentation supports these modifications. Learning Services is a resource center for all students on campus. The center offers self-help skills classes in time management, organizational skills, and test taking strategies. There is a Freshman Orientation class offered for credit and some sections of this class are geared toward academic skills.

**Special education HS coursework accepted:** Yes
**Special application required:** No
**# of applications submitted each year:** N/A
**# of students receiving LD services:** 350
**Acceptance into program means acceptance into college:** Students must be admitted to the university first and then may request services.

**Essay required:** Recommended
**Submitted to:** N/A
**# of applications accepted each year:** N/A

# LEARNING DISABILITY SERVICES

**Learning center:** No
**Kurzweil personal reader:** Yes
**LD specialists:** No
**Allowed in exams:**
  **Calculator:** Yes
  **Dictionary:** Yes
  **Computer:** Yes
  **SpellCheck:** Yes

**Notetaker:** Yes
**Scribes:** Yes
**Proctors:** Yes
**Oral exams:** Yes
**Extended test time:** Yes
**Added cost:** $7-9 per hour peer tutor
**Distraction-free environ.:** Yes
**Tape recording in class:** Yes
**Books on tape:** Yes
**Taping of other books:** Yes

**Professional tutors:** No
**Peer tutors:** Yes
**Max. hrs/wk for services:** As needed
**Priority registration:** Yes
**Accomodations for students with ADD:** Yes
**How are professors notified of LD:** By the student and the Program Director

# GENERAL ADMISSIONS INFORMATION

**Director of Admissions:** Patricia Riordan, Dean          **Telephone:** 703-993-2400

## ENTRANCE REQUIREMENTS

Total high school units required/recommended: 16 total units are required; 22 total units are recommended; 4 English required, 3 math required, 4 math recommended, 1 science required, 3 science recommended, 2 foreign language required, 3 foreign language recommended, 3 social studies required, 4 social studies recommended. Special requirements: A portfolio is required for art program applicants. An audition is required for music program applicants. TOEFL is required of all international students.

**Application deadline:** February 1
**Notification:** April 1

**SAT or ACT preferred:** Either
**Average GPA:** 3.1

**Graduated top 10% of class:** 17
**Graduated top 25% of class:** 46
**Graduated top 50% of class:** 96

# COLLEGE GRADUATION REQUIREMENTS

**Course waivers allowed:** No
**Course substitutions allowed:** Yes
**In what courses:** Foreign language and, in some instances, in analytical reasoning with specific documentation provided.

# ADDITIONAL INFORMATION

**Environment:** The university is located on 682 acres in a suburban area 18 miles southwest of Washington, D.C.

**Student Body**
  **Undergrad enrollment:** 13,331
  **Women:** 55%
  **Men:** 45%
  **In-state students:** 85%
  **Out-of-state:** 15%

**Cost Information**
  **In-state tuition:** $4,242
  **Out-of-state:** $11,952
  **Room & board:** $5,080

**Housing Information**
  **University housing:** Yes
  **Fraternity:** No
  **Sorority:** No
  **Living on campus:** 29%

  **Athletics:** NCAA Div. I

# HAMPTON UNIVERSITY

Hampton, VA 23668 • **Admissions:** 757-727-5328 • **Fax:** 757-727-5084
**Email:** admissions@cs.hampton.edu • **Web:** www.cs.hamptonu.edu
**Support:** S • **Institution:** 4 yr. Private

## LEARNING DISABILITY ADMISSIONS AND SERVICES

Hampton University does not have a program specifically for students with learning disabilities. However, some special services are provided as needed on an individual basis. It is the belief of the university that students, regardless of their backgrounds, can achieve academically if they take advantage of the educational support services available. Student Support Services is a program to assist students in achieving and maintaining the academic performance level required for satisfactory academic standing at the university; thereby, increasing their chances of graduating. Student Support Services also encourages students to continue their educational training beyond the undergraduate level. The goal of the Program is to develop and implement educational services and activities in an effort to motivate and aid students toward the achievement of their personal, social, academic, and career goals. Student Support Services is a federally funded program. In order to qualify for the Program, students must be enrolled at Hampton University, be a citizen or permanent resident of the United States, and must be either low-income, 1st generation college student or an individual with a disability.

## LEARNING DISABILITY ADMISSIONS INFORMATION

**Program Name:** Student Support Services
**Program Director:** Jean Williamson                    **Telephone:** 757-727-5493
**Contact Person:** Letizia Gambrell-Boone

### ADMISSIONS

There is no special admission process for students with learning disabilities. All students are expected to meet the same admission criteria which include: 4 yrs. English, 3 yrs. math, 2 yrs. science, 2 yrs. history, and 6 electives; ACT/SAT with a minimum SAT of 800; rank in the top 50% of the class; and have a minimum GPA of 2.0. Some students may be admitted through the summer 'Bridge' Program if SAT scores are below 800 or the students are deficient in course requirements. These students take Placement Exams to determine the need for English, writing, reading or science courses. 20% of the class is admitted through Bridge.

**College entrance exams required:** Yes            **Untimed accepted:** Yes
**Course entrance requirements:** Yes               **Interview required:** No
**Diagnostic tests:** Yes
**Documentation:** Psychoeducational evaluation: within 3 years

### ADDITIONAL INFORMATION

Program services include: Special orientation, counseling, career planning, special academic advising, reduced course load, tutoring, course modifications, alternate forms of testing, notetakers, tape recording permitted in courses, transcriber for tapes, trained tutors, and a special tutoring area for students with learning disabilities. Pre-college Program is open to all students. Freshmen on probation may take 2 non-repeating courses in Summer school and get "C" or better and return for sophomore year. The Office of Testing Services provides Section 504 accommodations.

**Special education HS coursework accepted:** Yes        **Essay required:** No
**Special application required:** No                      **Submitted to:** N/A
**# of applications submitted each year:** N/A           **# of applications accepted each year:** N/A
**# of students receiving LD services:** 15
**Acceptance into program means acceptance into college:** Students must be admitted to the university first and then may request services.

## LEARNING DISABILITY SERVICES

**Learning center:** No
**Kurzweil personal reader:** No
**LD specialists:** No
**Allowed in exams:**
  **Calculator:** Yes
  **Dictionary:** Yes
  **Computer:** Y/N
  **SpellCheck:** yes

**Notetaker:** Yes
**Scribes:** Y/N
**Proctors:** Y/N
**Oral exams:** Yes
**Extended test time:** Yes
**Added cost:** None
**Distraction-free environ.:** Yes
**Tape recording in class:** Yes
**Books on tape:** Yes
**Taping of other books:** Yes

**Professional tutors:** Yes
**Peer tutors:** 21
**Max. hrs/wk for services:** As needed
**Priority registration:** Yes
**Accomodations for students with ADD:** Yes
**How are professors notified of LD:** By the student and the Program Director

## GENERAL ADMISSIONS INFORMATION

**Director of Admissions:** Leonard Jones

**Telephone:** 757-727-5328

### ENTRANCE REQUIREMENTS

Total high school units required/recommended: 17 total units are required; 4 English required, 3 math required, 2 science required, 2 history required. Minimum combined SAT I score of 800, rank in top 1/2 of secondary school class, and minimum 2.0 GPA required.

**Application deadline:** March 15
**Notification:** Rolling

**SAT or ACT preferred:** Either
**SAT Avg:** 482V, 512M
**Average ACT:** 20
**Average GPA:** 2.9

**Graduated top 10% of class:** 25
**Graduated top 25% of class:** 63
**Graduated top 50% of class:** 94

## COLLEGE GRADUATION REQUIREMENTS

**Course waivers allowed:** No
**Course substitutions allowed:** Yes
**In what courses:** Foreign language

## ADDITIONAL INFORMATION

**Environment:** The university is located on 204 acres 15 miles west of Norfolk.

**Student Body**
  **Undergrad enrollment:** 5,155
  **Women:** 60%
  **Men:** 40%
  **In-state students:** 30%
  **Out-of-state:** 70%

**Cost Information**
  **In-state tuition:** $8,198
  **Out-of-state:** $8,198
  **Room & board:** $3,878

**Housing Information**
  **University housing:** Yes
  **Fraternity:** No
  **Sorority:** No
  **Living on campus:** 55%

  **Athletics:** NCAA Div. II

# JAMES MADISON UNIVERSITY

Undergraduate Admission, Harrisonburg, VA 22807 • **Admissions:** 540-568-6147 • **Fax:** 540-568-7846
**Email:** gotojmu@jmu.edu • **Web:** www.jmu.edu
**Support:** S • **Institution:** 4 yr. Public

## LEARNING DISABILITY ADMISSIONS AND SERVICES

The Office of Disability Service (ODS) does not have a formal LD Program, but students with learning disabilities are assisted individually and are eligible for appropriate accommodations. It is the goal of ODS to assist students in the developmental process of transition to higher education, independence, and effective self-advocacy. ODS recognizes that each student is an individual with unique needs so services are tailored to the varying needs of the student. The Coordinator functions as a liaison between students and the university community, and provides support in obtaining accommodations for equalizing academic success in the classroom. If the student is eligible for re-evaluation through the school system, it is strongly advised to take advantage of the service before leaving high school. Current documentation with recommendations for post-secondary accommodations are crucial for providing appropriate services in college. Course substitution requests are dealt with on an individual basis. They may be appropriate for students for whom a particular subject has been a continuously documented obstacle to academic progress. Students should notify ODS upon enrollment if they want to seek a substitution for a course requirement. Substitutions are not guaranteed.

## LEARNING DISABILITY ADMISSIONS INFORMATION

**Program Name:** Office of Disability Services
**Program Director:** Lou Hedrick                    **Telephone:** 540-568-6705
**Contact Person:** Same as above

### ADMISSIONS

The admissions team at JMU is highly sensitive and knowledgeable concerning students with learning disabilities and the admissions process. While there are no special criteria for students with learning disabilities and entrance requirements are the same for all students, the admissions committee is able to give thorough consideration to students who provide documentation of the learning disability (evaluation, I.E.P. and/or description of services received in high school). After admission to JMU, documentation will be forwarded to the ODS. Current recommendations for post-secondary accommodations are crucial for providing appropriate services in college. There are no specific courses required for admission into James Madison. The average SAT is 1140. The university uses class rank as one of the criteria reviewed, but does not use GPA.

**College entrance exams required:** Yes          **Untimed accepted:** Yes
**Course entrance requirements:** Yes             **Interview required:** No
**Diagnostic tests:** Yes
**Documentation:** WAIS-R; achievement, information processing: within 4 years

### ADDITIONAL INFORMATION

Some of the commonly used services are priority registration, Support Lab which houses equipment, academic advisors and academic services, and course scheduling information. Classroom accommodations include: extended time for tests and written assignments, testing in a distraction free environment, modification of exam format, volunteer notetakers, use of tape recorders in class, oral testing, scribes, use of computers for tests, and individual assistance as needed. Other university services include Reading and Writing Lab, Counseling and Student Development Center, and Academic Advising. Basic workshops for no credit are offered in study skills and self-advocacy. Services and accommodations are available for undergraduate and graduate students.

**Special education HS coursework accepted:** N/I      **Essay required:** Yes
**Special application required:** No                    **Submitted to:** N/A
**# of applications submitted each year:** N/A          **# of applications accepted each year:** N/A
**# of students receiving LD services:** 90
**Acceptance into program means acceptance into college:** Students must be admitted to the university first and then may request services.

# LEARNING DISABILITY SERVICES

**Learning center:** Yes
**Kurzweil personal reader:** Yes
**LD specialists:** No
**Allowed in exams:**
  **Calculator:** Yes
  **Dictionary:** Yes
  **Computer:** Yes
  **SpellCheck:** Yes

**Notetaker:** Yes
**Scribes:** Yes
**Proctors:** Yes
**Oral exams:** Yes
**Extended test time:** Yes
**Added cost:** Auxiliary costs for purchase of cassettes or NCR paper
**Distraction-free environ.:** Yes
**Tape recording in class:** Yes
**Books on tape:** Yes
**Taping of other books:** No

**Professional tutors:** No
**Peer tutors:** No
**Max. hrs/wk for services:** Maximum hours per week for services are unlimited
**Priority registration:** Yes
**Accomodations for students with ADD:** Yes
**How are professors notified of LD:** By the student and the Program Director

# GENERAL ADMISSIONS INFORMATION

**Director of Admissions:**                                   **Telephone:** 540-568-6147

## ENTRANCE REQUIREMENTS

Total high school units required/recommended: 22 total units are recommended; 4 English recommended, 4 math recommended, 4 science recommended, 4 foreign language recommended, 1 social studies recommended, 2 history recommended. Minimum combined SAT I score of 800 required of all applicants; rank in top 1/2 of secondary school class recommended of in-state applicants and rank in top 1/3 of secondary school class recommended of out-of-state applicants. Special requirements: A portfolio is required for art program applicants. An audition is required for music program applicants. TOEFL is required of all international students. Supplemental application and interview required of nursing program applicants.

**Application deadline:** January 15
**Notification:** April 1

**SAT or ACT preferred:** SAT
**SAT range:** 540–630V, 550–630M
**SAT II required:** Yes

# COLLEGE GRADUATION REQUIREMENTS

**Course waivers allowed:** No
**Course substitutions allowed:** Yes
**In what courses:** Foreign language and math; Only substitutions typically when documentation is very recent, and specifically points to the need.

# ADDITIONAL INFORMATION

**Environment:** The university is located in the Shenandoah Valley surrounded by the Blue Ridge Mountains and the Alleghenies, 120 miles from Washington, D.C.

**Student Body**
  **Undergrad enrollment:** 11,643
  **Women:** 55%
  **Men:** 45%
  **In-state students:** 70%
  **Out-of-state:** 30%

**Cost Information**
  **In-state tuition:** $4,104
  **Out-of-state:** $8,580
  **Room & board:** $4,884

**Housing Information**
  **University housing:** Yes
  **Fraternity:** Yes
  **Sorority:** Yes
  **Living on campus:** 50%

  **Athletics:** NCAA Div. I

# LIBERTY UNIVERSITY

**VA**

P.O. Box 20000, Lynchburg, VA 24506 • **Admissions:** 800-522-6225 • **Fax:** 804-582-2617
**Web:** www.liberty.edu
**Support:** CS • **Institution:** 4 yr. Private

## LEARNING DISABILITY ADMISSIONS AND SERVICES

The primary purpose of the Bruckner Learning Center is to offer reading and study skills assistance to all students. The Center provides individualized peer tutoring regularly or on a drop-in basis for English or math. There are 3 1-semester hour courses provided for students wishing to develop reading and study skills. These courses include; college Study Strategies, college Reading Improvement, and Individualized Laboratory in Reading and Study Strategies.

## LEARNING DISABILITY ADMISSIONS INFORMATION

**Program Name:** Bruckner Learning Center
**Program Director:** Barbara Sherman
**Contact Person:** Denton McHaney

**Telephone:** 804-582-2226

### ADMISSIONS

All applicants with a high school diploma or equivalent are admissible. No ACT/SAT are required for admission and no specific GPA is required. Any test scores submitted are used for placement only. It is requested that students submit, to Admissions, their latest IEP and/or psychological testing profile or other written information that describes their learning disability and any classroom accommodations suggested. Bruckner Learning Center will review documentation submitted and provide a recommendation to the Office of Admissions. The final admission decision is made by Admissions.

**College entrance exams required:** Not required
**Course entrance requirements:** No
**Diagnostic tests:** Yes
**Documentation:** IEP or latest psychoeducational evaluation

**Untimed accepted:** N/A
**Interview required:** No

### ADDITIONAL INFORMATION

If a student's entrance test scores indicate a deficiency in English or Math, then the student will enroll in a basic composition class, and a fundamentals of math class, as well. With students' permission, instructors are provided with a written communication providing information about the students' specific disability and suggestions of appropriate accommodations. Students with a specific learning disability can be assigned to a faculty advisor who has had training in LD. This person advises students concerning academic loads and acts as a liaison between instructors and students regarding classroom accommodations. The Bruckner Learning Center provided individualized peer tutoring in most subjects on a weekly or drop-in basis.

**Special education HS coursework accepted:** No
**Special application required:** No
**# of applications submitted each year:** N/A
**# of students receiving LD services:** 110
**Acceptance into program means acceptance into college:** Students must be admitted to the university first and then may request services.

**Essay required:** Yes
**Submitted to:** N/A
**# of applications accepted each year:** N/A

## LEARNING DISABILITY SERVICES

**Learning center:** Yes
**Kurzweil personal reader:** No
**LD specialists:** 2
**Allowed in exams:**
  **Calculator:** N/I
  **Dictionary:** Y/N
  **Computer:** Yes
  **SpellCheck:** Yes

**Notetaker:** No
**Scribes:** No
**Proctors:** Yes
**Oral exams:** Yes
**Extended test time:** Yes
**Added cost:** None
**Distraction-free environ.:** Yes
**Tape recording in class:** Yes
**Books on tape:** Yes
**Taping of other books:** No

**Professional tutors:** No
**Peer tutors:** 30
**Max. hrs/wk for services:** As needed
**Priority registration:** Yes
**Accomodations for students with ADD:** Yes
**How are professors notified of LD:** By the student and the Program Director

## GENERAL ADMISSIONS INFORMATION

**Director of Admissions:** Jay Spencer

**Telephone:** 800-522-6225

### ENTRANCE REQUIREMENTS

Total high school units required/recommended: 12 total units are recommended; 4 English recommended, 3 math recommended, 2 science recommended, 1 foreign language recommended, 1 social studies recommended, 1 history recommended. Special requirements: TOEFL is required of all international students.

**Application deadline:** August 1
**Notification:** Rolling

**SAT or ACT preferred:** SAT

## COLLEGE GRADUATION REQUIREMENTS

**Course waivers allowed:** No
**Course substitutions allowed:** No
**In what courses:** N/A

## ADDITIONAL INFORMATION

**Environment:** The 5,200-acre university is located in a suburban area 45 miles east of Roanoke.

**Student Body**
  **Undergrad enrollment:** 3,603
  **Women:** 49%
  **Men:** 51%
  **In-state students:** 26%
  **Out-of-state:** 74%

**Cost Information**
  **In-state tuition:** $7,680
  **Out-of-state:** $7,680
  **Room & board:** $4,800

**Housing Information**
  **University housing:** Yes
  **Fraternity:** No
  **Sorority:** No
  **Living on campus:** 76%

  **Athletics:** NCAA Div. I

# OLD DOMINION UNIVERSITY

5215 Hampton Boulevard, Norfolk, VA 23529 • **Admissions:** 757-683-3000 • **Fax:** 757-683-3255
**Web:** www.odu.edu
**Support:** CS • **Institution:** 4 yr. Public

## LEARNING DISABILITY ADMISSIONS AND SERVICES

Student Support Services is a TRIO Program funded by the U.S. Department of Education providing academic support. The Program is oriented to meet the needs of students according to their development level. Typically students are newly diagnosed or recently transitioning to campus. The Program assists students in achieving and maintaining the academic performance level required for satisfactory academic standing at the university, thereby increasing their chances of graduating. Services include: on-site orientation programs, taped materials, tutorial services by peers, oral testing, untimed testing, and individual counseling. The students are respected as the primary source for knowledge of their needs.

## LEARNING DISABILITY ADMISSIONS INFORMATION

**Program Name:** Disability Services
**Program Director:** Dr. Nancy Olthoff, Ph.D.          **Telephone:** 757-683-4655
**Contact Person:** Same as above

### ADMISSIONS

There is no special admissions process for students with learning disabilities. Students are encouraged to include a cover letter identifying their learning disabilities and explaining weaknesses that may have affected their academic records. If students self-identify during the admissions process, the information may be used to support the student's application, but may not be used to their detriment. Clear and specific evidence and identification of a LD must be stated and the report must be conducted and written by a qualified professional. Students not meeting regular admission standards may be admitted through the Academic Opportunity Program. This is for 300 students with low tests but high GPA. Others may be admitted through a Summer Transition Program or Individual Admission for non-traditional students. General admission criteria include: 4 yrs. English, 3 yrs. math, 3 yrs. science, 2 yrs. foreign language, 3 yrs. social studies, and 3 yrs. history; ACT/SAT (with a minimum SAT of 850 and at least a 400 in the Verbal and the Math); rank in the top 1/2 of the class; and have a minimum GPA of 2.0

**College entrance exams required:** Yes               **Untimed accepted:** Yes
**Course entrance requirements:** Recommended          **Interview required:** No
**Diagnostic tests:** Yes
**Documentation:** WAIS-R; WISC-R; W-J: within 3 years

### ADDITIONAL INFORMATION

Counseling and advising, study skills instruction, reading, writing, math instruction, and tutorial assistance are available. Program staff design support services that focus on students' learning styles and special needs. There is a special section of Spanish for students with learning disabilities to meet the foreign language requirements as well as developmental math, reading, spelling, and writing.

**Special education HS coursework accepted:** Yes, if equivalent to HS course work
**Essay required:** No
**Special application required:** Yes                   **Submitted to:** Director of Program
**# of applications submitted each year:** N/A          **# of applications accepted each year:** All who
provide adequate documentation
**# of students receiving LD services:** 175
**Acceptance into program means acceptance into college:** Students must be admitted to the university first and then may request services.

## LEARNING DISABILITY SERVICES

**Learning center:** No
**Kurzweil personal reader:** Yes
**LD specialists:** 1
**Allowed in exams:**
   **Calculator:** Yes
   **Dictionary:** Yes
   **Computer:** Yes
   **SpellCheck:** Yes

**Notetaker:** Yes
**Scribes:** Yes
**Proctors:** Yes
**Oral exams:** Yes
**Extended test time:** Yes
**Added cost:** None
**Distraction-free environ.:** Yes
**Tape recording in class:** Yes
**Books on tape:** Yes
**Taping of other books:** Yes

**Professional tutors:** Yes
**Peer tutors:** Yes
**Max. hrs/wk for services:** Varies
**Priority registration:** Yes
**Accomodations for students with ADD:** Yes
**How are professors notified of LD:** By the student and the Program Director

## GENERAL ADMISSIONS INFORMATION

**Director of Admissions:** Patricia Cavendar          **Telephone:** 757-683-3637

### ENTRANCE REQUIREMENTS

Total high school units required/recommended: 18 total units are required; 4 English required, 3 math required, 3 science required, 2 foreign language required, 3 social studies required, 3 history required. Minimum combined SAT I score of 850 (minimum scores of 400 in both Verbal and Math), rank in top 1/2 of secondary school class, and minimum 2.0 GPA recommended. Special requirements: A portfolio is required for art program applicants. An audition is required for music program applicants. TOEFL is required of all international students. Minimum SAT I Math score of 500 required of engineering program applicants.

**Application deadline:** June 1
**Notification:** Rolling

**SAT or ACT preferred:** SAT
**SAT Avg:** 452V, 515M
**Average GPA:** 2.8

**Graduated top 10% of class:** 16
**Graduated top 25% of class:** 46
**Graduated top 50% of class:** 80

## COLLEGE GRADUATION REQUIREMENTS

**Course waivers allowed:** No
**Course substitutions allowed:** Yes
**In what courses:** Waivers are not available. Substitutions may be applied for in special cases.

## ADDITIONAL INFORMATION

**Environment:** The university is located on 46 acres in a suburban area of Norfolk.

**Student Body**
   **Undergrad enrollment:** 8,346
   **Women:** 53%
   **Men:** 47%
   **In-state students:** 87%
   **Out-of-state:** 13%

**Cost Information**
   **In-state tuition:** $3,990
   **Out-of-state:** $10,350
   **Room & board:** $4,540

**Housing Information**
   **University housing:** Yes
   **Fraternity:** Yes
   **Sorority:** Yes
   **Living on campus:** 20%

   **Athletics:** NCAA Div. I

# VA VIRGINIA INTERMONT COLLEGE

1013 Moore Street, Bristol, VA 24201 • **Admissions:** 540-669-6101 • **Fax:** 540-669-5763
**Email:** viadmit@vic.edu • **Web:** www.vic.edu
**Support:** CS • **Institution:** 4 yr. Private

## LEARNING DISABILITY ADMISSIONS AND SERVICES

Student Support Services is a federally funded program providing free supportive services to students who participate in the program. There are extensive services offered to those with LD. The objective of the services is to help students stay in school and graduate. The department consists of a Director/Counselor, School Psychologist/LD Specialist, Tutor Coordinator, and an Administrative Assistant. Students work voluntarily with the staff as individuals or as a team to develop individual plans of support. Staff members act as advocates for students with faculty and administration and provide general faculty awareness and understanding of overall student needs without disclosure of confidentiality. It is their experience that students with LD who are willing to work hard can successfully complete a degree program at Virginia Intermont. They have a commitment to the significance of the individual and to the value of personalizing education. The college provides quality education with extensive support services and accommodations, rather than altering admissions criteria or course requirements. Once admitted, students are encouraged to submit documentation of any special needs. This is usually in the form of psychoeducational test data and IEP from high school. All accommodations are provided solely on a voluntary basis.

## LEARNING DISABILITY ADMISSIONS INFORMATION

**Program Name:** Student Support Services
**Program Director:** Talmage Dobbins          **Telephone:** 703-669-6101 ext. 215
**Contact Person:** Barbara Holbrook          **Telephone:** 703-669-6101 ext. 216

### ADMISSIONS

There is no special admissions procedure for the student with a learning disability. However, the general application should include documentation related to the learning disability. This information should be submitted to the Office of Admissions. Testing done by a high school psychologist is acceptable. General admission criteria include: an ACT of 18 or SAT of 780; 2.0 GPA; and a minimum of 15 units including 4 yrs. English, 2 yrs. math, 1 yr. lab science, 2 yrs. social science, and 6 yrs. electives. Virginia Intermont is more concerned with the student's quality of preparation than with the precise numerical distribution of requirements. Students not having the proper high school preparation or not meeting the normal admissions criteria will be required to take developmental courses as needed in math, english and reading. These courses would not count toward graduation, and the student would be limited to 14 hours in the 1st semester.

**College entrance exams required:** Yes          **Untimed accepted:** Yes
**Course entrance requirements:** Yes          **Interview required:** Recommended
**Diagnostic tests:** Yes
**Documentation:** WISC-R or WAIS-R; W-J: within 4 years

### ADDITIONAL INFORMATION

Students with LD will be offered appropriate accommodations recommended by the Learning Specialist based on the nature of the handicapping condition. Accommodations and/or services available to eligible students include: Individual personal and academic counseling, Freshman Placement Test accommodations, testing accommodations, computer tests, taped tests, peer and staff tutoring emphasizing unique techniques as needed, support groups, academic advising, diagnostic testing, liaison with faculty, tape recording of classes, assistance with course selection and registration, and optional reduced course load. A few accommodations require appointments, though generally there is an open door policy. Education 100 (1 credit) taught by Student Support Services staff, is designed for students interested in improving academic skills. Topics covered in this course are: individual learning styles, time-study management, notetaking, textbook reading, memory strategies, test taking strategies, and test anxiety reduction.

**Special education HS coursework accepted:** No          **Essay required:** No, unless requested
**Special application required:** No          **Submitted to:** N/A
**# of applications submitted each year:** N/A          **# of applications accepted each year:** N/A
**# of students receiving LD services:** 26
**Acceptance into program means acceptance into college:** Students must be accepted to the college first and then may request LD services.

## LEARNING DISABILITY SERVICES

**Learning center:** Yes
**Kurzweil personal reader:** No
**LD specialists:** 1
**Allowed in exams:**
  **Calculator:** Yes
  **Dictionary:** Yes
  **Computer:** Yes
  **SpellCheck:** Yes

**Notetaker:** Yes
**Scribes:** Yes
**Proctors:** Yes
**Oral exams:** Yes
**Extended test time:** Yes
**Added cost:** None
**Distraction-free environ.:** Yes
**Tape recording in class:** Yes
**Books on tape:** Yes
**Taping of other books:** Yes

**Professional tutors:** 1
**Peer tutors:** 35
**Max. hrs/wk for services:** Generally 3 hrs. per week for tutoring; unlimited for other services
**Priority registration:** No
**Accomodations for students with ADD:** Yes
**How are professors notified of LD:** By student and the Program Director

## GENERAL ADMISSIONS INFORMATION

**Director of Admissions:** Robin Cozart

**Telephone:** 703-669-6101

### ENTRANCE REQUIREMENTS

Total high school units required/recommended: 16 total units are required; 4 English required, 2 math required, 1 science required, 2 social studies required. Minimum "C" average. Special requirements: Specific programs require additional admission forms.

**Application deadline:** Rolling
**Notification:** Rolling

**SAT or ACT preferred:** Either
**SAT Avg:** 470V, 447M
**SAT II required:** Yes
**Average ACT:** 19
**Average GPA:** 2.9

**Graduated top 10% of class:** 11
**Graduated top 25% of class:** 26
**Graduated top 50% of class:** 66

## COLLEGE GRADUATION REQUIREMENTS

**Course waivers allowed:** No
**Course substitutions allowed:** No
**In what courses:** N/A

## ADDITIONAL INFORMATION

**Environment:** The college is located on a 16-acre campus in the Blue Ridge Mountains.

**Student Body**
  **Undergrad enrollment:** 451
  **Women:** 68%
  **Men:** 32%
  **In-state students:** 63%
  **Out-of-state:** 37%

**Cost Information**
  **In-state tuition:** $10,450
  **Out-of-state:** $10,450
  **Room & board:** $4,700

**Housing Information**
  **University housing:** Yes
  **Fraternity:** No
  **Sorority:** No
  **Living on campus:** 47%

  **Athletics:** NAIA

# UNIVERSITY OF VIRGINIA

Office of Admission, P.O. Box 9017, Charlottesville, VA 22906 • **Admissions:** 804-982-3200
**Fax:** 804-982-2858 • **Email:** undergrad-admission@virginia.edu • **Web:** www.virginia.edu
**Support:** CS • **Institution:** 4 yr. Public

## LEARNING DISABILITY ADMISSIONS AND SERVICES

The University of Virginia believes in making academic progress accessible to students with learning disabilities. The Learning Needs and Evaluation Center (LNEC) is the coordinating agency for services to all students with disabilities. The LNEC provides academic support services to meet specialized needs of students with learning and other disabilities. The center provides educational/cognitive assessments or referrals to any matriculated student for the purpose of identifying and documenting learning disabilities. Each student entering, who self-discloses a learning disability, is given a card to be completed and housed in the center. This information is to be shared, with the student's permission, with university personnel who have an educational need to know. Once a learning disability is documented, the center assigns appropriate and reasonable accommodations and serves as a liaison with faculty and administrators. The center's primary purpose is to support the academic well-being of students with disabilities.

## LEARNING DISABILITY ADMISSIONS INFORMATION

**Program Name:** Learning Needs and Evaluation Center
**Program Director:** N/I
**Contact Person:** Hilary L. Morgan

**Telephone:** 804-982-3200

### ADMISSIONS

The students with learning disabilities go through the same admissions procedure as all incoming applicants. After admission to the university, students must contact the LNEC in order to receive services. Students with learning disabilities admitted to the university have qualified for admission because of their ability. No criteria for admission is waived because of a disability. However, no students with learning disabilities who are qualified are denied because of their disability. Should a candidate self-disclose a learning disability, any information which is missing, because of the disability, may be allowed or differentially weighted. All applicants to UVA have outstanding grades, high rank in their high school class, excellent performance in Advanced Placement and Honor courses, superior performance on ACT/SAT I and SAT II, extracurricular success, special talents, and interests and goals. Letters of recommendation are required.

**College entrance exams required:** Yes
**Course entrance requirements:** Yes
**Diagnostic tests:** Yes
**Documentation:** Any valid documentation

**Untimed accepted:** Yes
**Interview required:** No

### ADDITIONAL INFORMATION

The Learning Needs and Evaluation Center addresses such things as personal social skills, alternative speaking, reading, writing methods, and referral for tutors. Staff also consult with students about academic difficulties. Skills classes are offered for credit in study skills and time management. Services and accommodations are available for undergraduate and graduate students.

**Special education HS coursework accepted:** Yes
**Special application required:** No
**# of applications submitted each year:** N/A
**# of students receiving LD services:** 230
**Acceptance into program means acceptance into college:** Students must be admitted to the university first and then may request services.

**Essay required:** Yes
**Submitted to:** N/A
**# of applications accepted each year:** N/A

## LEARNING DISABILITY SERVICES

**Learning center:** Yes
**Kurzweil personal reader:** Yes
**LD specialists:** 3
**Allowed in exams:**
 **Calculator:** Yes
 **Dictionary:** Yes
 **Computer:** Yes
 **SpellCheck:** Yes

**Notetaker:** Yes
**Scribes:** Yes
**Proctors:** Yes
**Oral exams:** Yes
**Extended test time:** Yes
**Added cost:** None
**Distraction-free environ.:** Yes
**Tape recording in class:** Yes
**Books on tape:** Yes
**Taping of other books:** Yes

**Professional tutors:** Yes
**Peer tutors:** Yes
**Max. hrs/wk for services:**
Individualized
**Priority registration:** Yes
**Accomodations for students
with ADD:** Yes
**How are professors notified of
LD:** By the student with a letter
from the Center

## GENERAL ADMISSIONS INFORMATION

**Director of Admissions:** John Blackburn          **Telephone:** 804-982-3200

### ENTRANCE REQUIREMENTS

Total high school units required/recommended: 16 total units are required; 4 English required, 4 math required, 2 science required, 2 foreign language required, 1 social studies required. More competitive requirements for out-of-state applicants. Special Requirements: TOEFL is required of all international students. Chemistry and physics required of engineering program applicants.

**Application deadline:** January 2
**Notification:** April 1

**SAT or ACT preferred:** SAT
**SAT Avg:** 643V, 653M

**Graduated top 10% of class:** 79
**Graduated top 25% of class:** 96
**Graduated top 50% of class:** 99

## COLLEGE GRADUATION REQUIREMENTS

**Course waivers allowed:** Yes
**Course substitutions allowed:** Y/N
**In what courses:** Waivers allowed in the area of foreign language or by policy for others.

## ADDITIONAL INFORMATION

**Environment:** The 2,440-acre campus is located in a small city 70 miles northwest of Richmond.

**Student Body**
 **Undergrad enrollment:** 12,211
 **Women:** 52%
 **Men:** 48%
 **In-state students:** 66%
 **Out-of-state:** 34%

**Cost Information**
 **In-state tuition:** $4,786
 **Out-of-state:** $15,030
 **Room & board:** $4,279

**Housing Information**
 **University housing:** Yes
 **Fraternity:** Yes
 **Sorority:** Yes
 **Living on campus:** 48%

 **Athletics:** NCAA Div. I

# WA EASTERN WASHINGTON UNIVERSITY

MS 148, Cheney, WA 99004 • **Admissions:** 509-359-2397 • **Fax:** 509-359-4330
**Email:** admissions@ewu.edu • **Web:** www.ewu.edu
**Support:** S • **Institution:** 4 yr. Public

## LEARNING DISABILITY ADMISSIONS AND SERVICES

Academically qualified students with disabilities are an integral part of the student population at EWU, and providing equal opportunities is a campus-wide responsibility and commitment. Although the university does not offer a specialized curricula, personnel work with students to modify programs to meet individual needs. Disability Suppory Services (DSS) is dedicated to the coordination of appropriate and reasonable accommodations for students with disabilities. These accommodations are based on individual needs so that each student may receive an equal opportunity to learn to participate in campus life; to grow emotionally and socially; and to successfully complete a program of study that will enable them to be self-supporting while remaining as independent as possible. This is facilitated through support services, information sharing, advisement, and referral when requested. Students who wish services and support need to contact the DSS Office so that the disability can be verified, needs determined, and timely accommodations made. In most cases, documentation by a professional service provider will be necessary. Information is kept strictly confidential. However, it is important to share information that will enable DSS staff to provide appropriate, reasonable, and timely services tailored to individual needs.

## LEARNING DISABILITY ADMISSIONS INFORMATION

**Program Name:** Disability Support Services
**Program Director:** Karen Raver
**Contact Person:** Same as above

**Telephone:** 509-359-2293

### ADMISSIONS

Individuals with disabilities are admitted via the standard admissions criteria that apply to all students. Untimed ACT and SAT scores are accepted. General admissibility is based on an index using GPA and test scores. Required courses include: 4 yrs. English, 3 yrs. math, 3 yrs. social science, 2 yrs. science (1 yr. lab), 2 yrs. foreign language (American Sign Language accepted), and 1 yr. arts or academic elective. Special education courses are acceptable if they are courses that are regularly taught in the high school. However, all applicants must complete the required core courses. Students who do not meet grade and test score admission scale may provide additional information to the Admission Office and request consideration through the Admission Committee.

**College entrance exams required:** Yes
**Course entrance requirements:** Yes
**Diagnostic tests:** Yes
**Documentation:** WAIS-R; WJ; WRAT; IEP; within 3 years

**Untimed accepted:** Yes
**Interview required:** No

### ADDITIONAL INFORMATION

Examples of services for students with specific learning disabilities include: taped texts; equipment loan; alternative testing arrangements such as oral, extended time, relocation of testing site; notetakers; tutorial assistance (available to all students); referral to Learning Skills Center, Writers' Center, Mathematics Lab; accessible computer stations; and Kurzweil reading machine. Examples of services for students with ADHD are: consultation regarding reasonable and effective accommodations with classroom professors; alternative testing; books on tape; notetakers; taped lectures; equipment loans; referrals to Learning Skills Center, Math Lab, Writers' Center, and Counseling and Psychological services; information on ADHD; and informal counseling. Skills classes for credit are offered in math, reading, time management, study skills, and writing skills. There is a Learning Skills Center and a Writing Center which are open to all students. Services and accommodations are offered to undergraduate and graduate students.

**Special education HS coursework accepted:** Yes
**Special application required:** No
**# of applications submitted each year:** N/A
**# of students receiving LD services:** 46

**Essay required:** No
**Submitted to:** N/A
**# of applications accepted each year:** N/A

**Acceptance into program means acceptance into college:** Students must be admitted to the university first and then may request services.

## LEARNING DISABILITY SERVICES

Learning center: Yes
Kurzweil personal reader: Yes
LD specialists: No
Allowed in exams:
  Calculator: Yes
  Dictionary: Yes
  Computer: Yes
  SpellCheck: Yes

Notetaker: Yes
Scribes: Yes
Proctors: Yes
Oral exams: Yes
Extended test time: Yes
Added cost: None
Distraction-free environ.: Yes
Tape recording in class: Yes
Books on tape: Yes
Taping of other books: Yes

Professional tutors: 7
Peer tutors: 10
Max. hrs/wk for services: 19
Priority registration: Yes
Accomodations for students
with ADD: Yes
How are professors notified of
LD: By the Program Director
initially

## GENERAL ADMISSIONS INFORMATION

Director of Admissions: Keith Raver

Telephone: 509-359-2397

### ENTRANCE REQUIREMENTS

Total high school units required/recommended: 15 total units are required; 4 English required, 3 math required, 4 math recommended, 2 science required, 2 foreign language required, 3 social studies required, 4 social studies recommended. Special Requirements: TOEFL is required of all international students. Audition required of B.F.A. music program applicants.

Application deadline: July 1
Notification: Rolling

SAT or ACT preferred: Either
SAT Avg: 500V, 498M
Average ACT: 21
Average GPA: 3.29

## COLLEGE GRADUATION REQUIREMENTS

Course waivers allowed: Yes
Course substitutions allowed: Yes
In what courses: Foreign language

## ADDITIONAL INFORMATION

Environment: The university is located on 35 acres in a small town 18 miles southwest of Spokane.

Student Body
  Undergrad enrollment: 6,326
  Women: 58%
  Men: 42%
  In-state students: 91%
  Out-of-state: 9%

Cost Information
  In-state tuition: $2,430
  Out-of-state: $8,616
  Room & board: $4,293

Housing Information
  University housing: Yes
  Fraternity: Yes
  Sorority: No
  Living on campus: 11%

  Athletics: NCAA Div. II

# WA WASHINGTON STATE UNIVERSITY

342 French Administration Building, Pullman, WA 99164 • **Admissions:** 509-335-5586
**Fax:** 509-335-4902 • **Email:** admissions@wsu.edu • **Web:** www.wsu.edu
**Support:** CS • **Institution:** 4 yr. Public

## LEARNING DISABILITY ADMISSIONS AND SERVICES

The Disability Resource Center assists students who have a disability by providing academic and personal support services. The program may also refer students to other service programs that may assist them in achieving their academic goals. DRC will help students overcome potential obstacles so that they may be successful in their area of study. All academic adjustments are authorized on an individual basis. DRC coordinates services for students with LD. The program offers academic support through advising, and individualized and group instruction in many different areas. To be eligible for assistance, students must be currently enrolled at Washington State University. They also must submit documentation of their disability. For a learning disability, the student must submit a written report that includes test scores and evaluation. The student with a disability is the best source of information regarding necessary accommodations. It is the student's responsibility to request accommodations if desired. It is important to remember that even though two individuals may have the same disability, they may not necessarily need the same academic adjustments. DRC works with students and instructors to determine and implement appropriate academic adjustments. Many adjustments are simple creative alternatives for traditional ways of learning.

## LEARNING DISABILITY ADMISSIONS INFORMATION

**Program Name:** Disability Resource Center
**Program Director:** Marshall Mitchell
**Contact Person:** Same as above

**Telephone:** 509-335-1566

### ADMISSIONS

All students must meet the general admission requirements. The university looks at the combination of the score on the ACT/SAT and the high school GPA. The standard admission criteria is based on an index score determined by 75% GPA and 25% SAT/ACT. If an applicant does not meet standard admission criteria and has a documented learning disability, a special admission may be offered. Only 15% of new admissions may be offered under 'special admission.' Documentation of the learning disability and diagnostic tests given less than 3 years before application should be included with the application. The admission decision is made jointly by the Office of Admission and the Director of the Disability Resource Center.

**College entrance exams required:** Yes
**Course entrance requirements:** Yes
**Diagnostic tests:** Yes
**Documentation:** WAIS-R or WISC-R; W-J: within 3-5 years

**Untimed accepted:** Yes
**Interview required:** Recommended

### ADDITIONAL INFORMATION

General assistance to students with learning disabilities includes: pre-admission counseling; information about disabilities; referral to appropriate community resources; academic, personal, and career counseling; information about accommodations; information about the laws pertaining to individuals with disabilities; and self-advocacy. Typical academic adjustments for students with learning disabilities may include notetakers and/or audiotape class sessions; extra exam time or alternative testing arrangements; visual, aural, and tactile demonstrations incorporated into instruction; textbook taping or one-to-one readers; extended time for exams; essay exams taken on computer; computers with voice output and spellcheckers. Services and accommodations are available for undergraduate and graduate students.

**Special education HS coursework accepted:** Yes
**Special application required:** No
**# of applications submitted each year:** N/A
**# of students receiving LD services:** 240
**Acceptance into program means acceptance into college:** Students must be accepted to the university first (can appeal a denial) and then may request services.

**Essay required:** Yes, for special admissions
**Submitted to:** N/A
**# of applications accepted each year:** N/A

**Learning center:** Yes
**Kurzweil personal reader:** No
**LD specialists:** 1
**Allowed in exams:**
  **Calculator:** Y/N
  **Dictionary:** Y/N
  **Computer:** Yes
  **SpellCheck:** Yes

**Notetaker:** Yes
**Scribes:** Yes
**Proctors:** Yes
**Oral exams:** Yes
**Extended test time:** Yes
**Added cost:** None
**Distraction-free environ.:** Yes
**Tape recording in class:** Yes
**Books on tape:** Yes
**Taping of other books:** N/I

**Professional tutors:** No
**Peer tutors:** 50
**Max. hrs/wk for services:** Unlimited
**Priority registration:** Yes
**Accomodations for students with ADD:** Yes
**How are professors notified of LD:** By the student

# GENERAL ADMISSIONS INFORMATION

**Director of Admissions:** Ms. Terry Flynn          **Telephone:** 509-335-5586

## ENTRANCE REQUIREMENTS

Total high school units required/recommended: 15 total units are required; 4 English required, 3 math required, 2 science required, 2 foreign language required, 3 social studies required, 3 units of social science/history also required. Special requirements: A portfolio is required for art program applicants. An audition is required for music program applicants.

**Application deadline:** May 1
**Notification:** Rolling

**SAT or ACT preferred:** Either
**Average GPA:** 3.4

**Graduated top 10% of class:** 40
**Graduated top 25% of class:** 74
**Graduated top 50% of class:** 98

# COLLEGE GRADUATION REQUIREMENTS

**Course waivers allowed:** Yes
**Course substitutions allowed:** Yes
**In what courses:** Foreign language

# ADDITIONAL INFORMATION

**Environment:** The university is located on 600 acres in a small town 80 miles south of Spokane.

**Student Body**
  **Undergrad enrollment:** 16,686
  **Women:** 50%
  **Men:** 50%
  **In-state students:** 88%
  **Out-of-state:** 12%

**Cost Information**
  **In-state tuition:** $3,142
  **Out-of-state:** $9,758
  **Room & board:** $4,150

**Housing Information**
  **University housing:** Yes
  **Fraternity:** Yes
  **Sorority:** Yes
  **Living on campus:** 43%

  **Athletics:** NCAA Div. I

# WV DAVIS & ELKINS COLLEGE

100 Campus Drive, Elkins, WV 26241 • **Admissions:** 304-637-1900 • **Fax:** 304-637-1419
**Email:** admiss@dne.wvnet.edu • **Web:** www.dne.wvnet.edu
**Support:** SP • **Institution:** 4 yr. Private

## LEARNING DISABILITY ADMISSIONS AND SERVICES

Davis & Elkins is one of only 3 colleges in West Virginia to offer a program for students with learning disabilities. Since 1987 this program has been earning a reputation for results. What's more, the college has a lasting commitment to working personally with students with learning disabilities to help them achieve their very best. The goal of the LD Program is to provide the specialized services needed for success in college. The Program at Davis & Elkins College is based on the needs of the individual student, and personnel are trained by the Special Services Director to meet specialized needs. An individualized, diagnostic, prescriptive approach is used, stressing learning strategies that provide students with the learning tools to function independently. To be eligible to participate in the LD Program, a student must meet 3 criteria: (1) must have a diagnosed learning disability, (2) must be accepted for admission to Davis & Elkins, (3) must receive the recommendation of a high school counselor, LD specialist, or psychologist, stating that enrollment n the program will be beneficial. Students intending to enter the college in the fall and be part of the Learning Disabilities Program may find it beneficial to attend the summer "Head Start for College" Program.

## LEARNING DISABILITY ADMISSIONS INFORMATION

**Program Name:** Learning Disability Special Services
**Program Director:** Dr. Margaret N. Turner          **Telephone:** 304-637-1354
**Contact Person:** Same as above

### ADMISSIONS

All applications are screened by the Special Services Director and the Director of Admissions. Students must be admitted to Davis & Elkins College prior to being considered for Special Services. The admissions counselors have been trained to recognize potentially successful students with learning disabilities. Students requesting services must send a high school transcript; psychological tests within the last 3 years; recommendation for participation in the program by an LD teacher, LD specialist, counselor or psychologist; copy of recent IEP; and a handwritten essay requesting services and indicating why services are being requested. A limited number of students participate in the William James Center for students who have potential for success but need greater development of personal skills and study habits. This is not a program designed for LD, although students with LD are eligible to participate.

**College entrance exams required:** No                 **Untimed accepted:** Yes
**Course entrance requirements:** Yes                    **Interview required:** Recommended
**Diagnostic tests:** Yes
**Documentation:** Complete psychological and academic battery; within 3 years

### ADDITIONAL INFORMATION

Services include: individual sessions with certified LD specialists; individualized programs focusing on improved writing skills; test taking techniques; notetaking and textbook usage; and time management strategies. Specialists help students develop a personalized program focusing on improving written work, identifying class expectations and preparing work to that level of expectation, test-taking skills, using textbooks and taking notes, and managing time effectively. Students also receive advising and registration assistance based on assessment information. Some students are referred to "Student Alert" Program for assistance in personal or academic counseling. Personnel in the LD Program also assist the students with course selection and registration; orientation to college life; monitoring of classes throughout the year and help interpreting feedback from professors; coordination of tutoring, additional counseling, and career planning; and instructional program modification as needed.

**Special education HS coursework accepted:** No          **Essay required:** Yes
**Special application required:** Yes                     **Submitted to:** Director of Program
**# of applications submitted each year:** Fluctuates     **# of applications accepted each year:** 90%
**# of students receiving LD services:** 95
**Acceptance into program means acceptance into college:** Students must be admitted to the university first and then may request services.

# LEARNING DISABILITY SERVICES

**Learning center:** Yes
**Kurzweil personal reader:** No
**LD specialists:** 6
**Allowed in exams:**
  **Calculator:** Yes
  **Dictionary:** Yes
  **Computer:** Yes
  **SpellCheck:** Yes

**Notetaker:** Yes
**Scribes:** N/I
**Proctors:** Yes
**Oral exams:** Yes
**Extended test time:** Yes
**Added cost:** $2,390/year
**Distraction-free environ.:** Yes
**Tape recording in class:** Yes
**Books on tape:** Yes
**Taping of other books:** No

**Professional tutors:** Yes
**Peer tutors:** Yes
**Max. hrs/wk for services:** As needed
**Priority registration:** Yes
**Accomodations for students with ADD:** Y/N
**How are professors notified of LD:** By student and the Special Services Director

# GENERAL ADMISSIONS INFORMATION

**Director of Admissions:** Kevin Chenowath

**Telephone:** 304-636-1900 ext.1301

## ENTRANCE REQUIREMENTS
NR

**Application deadline:** Rolling
**Notification:** Rolling

**SAT or ACT preferred:** NR
**SAT Avg:** 482V, 457M
**Average ACT:** 20
**Average GPA:** 3.0

**Graduated top 10% of class:** 12
**Graduated top 25% of class:** 31
**Graduated top 50% of class:** 63

# COLLEGE GRADUATION REQUIREMENTS

**Course waivers allowed:** No
**Course substitutions allowed:** No
**In what courses:** N/A

# ADDITIONAL INFORMATION

**Environment:** The college is located in a community of 10,000 in the foothills of the Allegheny Mountains.

**Student Body**
  **Undergrad enrollment:** 732
  **Women:** 60%
  **Men:** 40%
  **In-state students:** 60%
  **Out-of-state:** 40%

**Cost Information**
  **In-state tuition:** $10,580
  **Out-of-state:** $10,580
  **Room & board:** $4,890

**Housing Information**
  **University housing:** Yes
  **Fraternity:** Yes
  **Sorority:** Yes
  **Living on campus:** 50%

  **Athletics:** NCAA Div. II

# MARSHALL UNIVERSITY

**WV**

400 Hal Greer Boulevard, Huntington, WV 25755 • **Admissions:** 304-696-3160 • **Fax:** 304-696-3135
**Email:** admissions@marshall.edu • **Web:** www.marshall.edu
**Support:** SP • **Institution:** 4 yr. Public

## LEARNING DISABILITY ADMISSIONS AND SERVICES

Higher Education for Learning Problems (H.E.L.P.) encourages a feeling of camaraderie between the students enrolled in the Program. H.E.L.P. provides an individual tutoring program in course work, exceptions in testing, and a remedial program. Students work with LD specialists one-to-one, to improve reading, writing and language skills. Counseling is provided on-site, and the large professional staff offers a variety of additional services. This program boasts a 95% success rate with students.

## LEARNING DISABILITY ADMISSIONS INFORMATION

**Program Name:** Higher Education for Learning Problems (H.E.L.P.)
**Program Director:** Dr. Barbara P. Guyer          **Telephone:** 304-696-6317
**Contact Person:** Lynne Weston          **Telephone:** 304-696-6316

### ADMISSIONS

There is a special admissions procedure to follow for students with learning disabilities. These students must submit: an application; updated psychological and educational evaluation; 1-page, handwritten, statement by the student (no assistance) regarding why college is desirable; and 2 recommendations stating why the recommenders feel the students should attend college. Interviews are required; minimum GPA of 2.0, ACT 17+, or SAT 810+ (tests are unimportant for LD admit), plus 4 yrs. English, 3 yrs. social studies, and 2 yrs. math. Students should schedule interview before January, and submit application to H.E.L.P. no less than 1 year in advance of the proposed entry date to college. All applications must be received by December 31. Marshall University has a probationary admission if the reason for low GPA or test scores is convincing. There is a required 5-week summer H.E.L.P. Program for these in-coming freshmen.

**College entrance exams required:** Yes          **Untimed accepted:** Yes
**Course entrance requirements:** Yes          **Interview required:** Yes
**Diagnostic tests:** Yes
**Documentation:** WAIS-R: within 3 yrs./ achievement tests: within 1 year

### ADDITIONAL INFORMATION

The Summer Learning Disabilities Program is offered through H.E.L.P. to incoming freshmen with learning disabilities. The Program includes teachers with master's degrees in learning disabilities; a graduate assistant for each teacher who assists with tutoring course work (tutors are matched to students who have a learning style compatible to the teaching style of the tutor); no more than 5 students per group; notetaking skills and study skills; test-taking strategies; organization of time; improvement of basic skills in reading, spelling, written language, and mathematics; improvement of self-esteem and self-confidence. The cost is $1000 for West Virginia residents, $1300 for Metro area residents, and $2000 for non-West Virginia residents. This does not include registration classes students may take through the university. Students sign a release allowing H.E.L.P. to talk to professors and parents. There is also a summer program for elementary and secondary students with learning disabilities.

**Special education HS coursework accepted:** Yes          **Essay required:** Yes
**Special application required:** Yes          **Submitted to:** H.E.L.P. Program
**# of applications submitted each year:** 300+          **# of applications accepted each year:** 40-45
**# of students receiving LD services:** N/I
**Acceptance into program means acceptance into college:** Students must be accepted to the university first and then may request admission to H.E.L.P.

## LEARNING DISABILITY SERVICES

**Learning center:** Yes
**Kurzweil personal reader:** Yes
**LD specialists:** Yes
**Allowed in exams:**
  **Calculator:** Y/N
  **Dictionary:** Y/N
  **Computer:** No
  **SpellCheck:** Y/N

**Notetaker:** No
**Scribes:** Yes
**Proctors:** Yes
**Oral exams:** Yes
**Extended test time:** Yes
**Added cost:** 1 hr. per wk $450; 2 hrs. $900; 3 hrs. $1350; 4 hrs. $1800; 5 hrs. $2250; 6 hrs. $2700; 7 hrs. $3150
**Distraction-free environ.:** Yes
**Tape recording in class:** Yes
**Books on tape:** Yes
**Taping of other books:** Yes

**Professional tutors:** 10
**Peer tutors:** Yes
**Max. hrs/wk for services:** Unlimited
**Priority registration:** Yes
**Accomodations for students with ADD:** Yes
**How are professors notified of LD:** By the student

## GENERAL ADMISSIONS INFORMATION

**Director of Admissions:** James Harless          **Telephone:** 800-642-3463

### ENTRANCE REQUIREMENTS

Total high school units required/recommended: 11 total units are required; 4 English required, 2 math required, 2 science required, 2 foreign language recommended, 3 social studies required. Minimum composite ACT score of 17 or minimum 2.0 GPA required. Special Requirements: An audition is required for music program applicants. TOEFL is required of all international students. Minimum composite ACT score of 18 and separate application required of nursing program applicants.

**Application deadline:** August 15
**Notification:** Rolling

**SAT or ACT preferred:** ACT
**Average ACT:** 22
**Average GPA:** 3.2

## COLLEGE GRADUATION REQUIREMENTS

**Course waivers allowed:** Yes
**Course substitutions allowed:** Yes
**In what courses:** Foreign language

## ADDITIONAL INFORMATION

**Environment:** Marshall University is a 55-acre urban campus located 140 miles east of Lexington, KY.

**Student Body**
  **Undergrad enrollment:** 8,778
  **Women:** 55%
  **Men:** 45%
  **In-state students:** 86%
  **Out-of-state:** 14%

**Cost Information**
  **In-state tuition:** $2,116
  **Out-of-state:** $5,878
  **Room & board:** $4,240

**Housing Information**
  **University housing:** Yes
  **Fraternity:** Yes
  **Sorority:** Yes
  **Living on campus:** NR

  **Athletics:** NCAA Div. I

# WEST VIRGINIA WESLEYAN COLLEGE

**WV**

59 College Avenue, Buckhannon, WV  26201 • **Admissions:** 304-473-8510 • **Fax:** 304-473-8187
**Email:** admission@admin.wvwc.edu • **Web:** www.wvwc.edu
**Support:** SP • **Institution:** 4 yr. Private

## LEARNING DISABILITY ADMISSIONS AND SERVICES

The Special Support Services Program (SSSP) is designed to help students with diagnosed perceptual learning disabilities to succeed in college and to prepare for a productive career. Students are mainstreamed into regular classes and assisted by a variety of people and services coordinated by Wesleyan's Learning Center. Most SSSP students at Wesleyan complete their degree requirements in 4 to 5 years, which is less time than the national average. In the first year, students with learning disabilities take: College Study Strategies, Critical Issues in Personal Development, and a practicum of their choice. Other learning services include all those guaranteed under the ADA Act plus personal counseling, assigned professional support person, specialized individualization, specialized computer lab with instructional support, reading programs, notetakers, special individual assistance and help in developing self-monitoring skills, Learning Center lab staffed by professionals Sunday through Thursday evenings, special daytime hours available on Saturdays, and evaluation of progress with annual recommendations. The goals of the Program are to meet the interests and needs of students, and provide them with the tools to become independent learners.

## LEARNING DISABILITY ADMISSIONS INFORMATION

**Program Name:** Special Support Services Program
**Program Director:** Phyllis Coston
**Contact Person:** Wilma Whitlock

**Telephone:** 304-473-8380

### ADMISSIONS

All students must submit the regular application, high school transcript, SAT/ACT, 3 letters of recommendation, and have an interview on campus. The completed application must be submitted by December 15. The interview is an important component of the process and student motivation is the key. The GPA usually ranges from 2.0-3.5 and the ACT score range is 18-27 or SAT 800-1400, although applicants with LD may be accepted with lower scores. Courses generally include 4 yrs. English, 3 yrs. math, 2 yrs. science, 2 yrs. social studies, 1 yr. history, and 3 yrs. electives. Foreign language is not a requirement. Each applicant is reviewed individually. Students should self-identify in the application process, and request an interview with the Learning Center prior to December 1. The Academic Dean has the authority to offer special admission to some students not admitted through the regular application process. Application decisions are made jointly by the Director of Admission and the Director of SSSP.  Everything should be sent to the Office of Admission prior to December 1.  March 1 is the preferred application deadline.

**College entrance exams required:** Yes

**Untimed accepted:** Yes

**Course entrance requirements:** Yes

**Interview required:** Yes

**Diagnostic tests:** Yes

**Documentation:** WAIS-R or WISC-R; W-J; and all educational assessments: within 2 years

### ADDITIONAL INFORMATION

SSSP includes academic advising by an advisor sensitive to the needs of students with LD and preferential preregistration during freshman year; diagnostic testing to help determine learning activities and individual practicums; special test taking accommodations such as extended time, use of computer, use of a tape recorder, or a reader; recorded textbooks which could improve speed and comprehension in reading; tutoring services in group and individual sessions; proofreading; Learning Center Courses during the 1st year in College Study Strategies, Critical Issues in Personal Development, or a practicum; individual practicums; professional support person; personal counseling; computer lab with support; reading programs; notetakers; individual assistance and help in developing self-monitoring skills; evaluation of progress with annual recommendations; and a professional staff. West Virginia Wesleyan offers a summer program for high school students with learning disabilities.

**Special education HS coursework accepted:** Yes, should be mainstreamed by Junior year
**Essay required:** Yes
**Special application required:** No

**Submitted to:** N/A

**# of applications submitted each year:** N/A

**# of applications accepted each year:** N/A

**# of students receiving LD services:** 220

**Acceptance into program means acceptance into college:** Students are admitted jointly into the college and SSSP.

## LEARNING DISABILITY SERVICES

**Learning center:** Yes
**Kurzweil personal reader:** Yes
**LD specialists:** 3
**Allowed in exams:**
 **Calculator:** Y/N
 **Dictionary:** Y/N
 **Computer:** Yes
 **SpellCheck:** Yes

**Notetaker:** Yes
**Scribes:** Yes
**Proctors:** Yes
**Oral exams:** No
**Extended test time:** Yes
**Added cost:** Level I/$3700; Level II/$2000; Level III/$1000; Level IV/$500
**Distraction-free environ.:** Yes
**Tape recording in class:** Yes
**Books on tape:** Yes
**Taping of other books:** Yes

**Professional tutors:** Yes
**Peer tutors:** Varies
**Max. hrs/wk for services:** No limit
**Priority registration:** Yes
**Accomodations for students with ADD:** Yes
**How are professors notified of LD:** By the Program Director and student

## GENERAL ADMISSIONS INFORMATION

**Director of Admissions:** Robert Skinner

**Telephone:** 304- 473-8510

### ENTRANCE REQUIREMENTS

Total high school units required/recommended: 17 total units are required; 21 total units are recommended; 4 English required, 3 math required, 2 science required, 2 foreign language required, 2 social studies required, 3 social studies recommended, 1 history required, 2 history recommended. Minimum combined SAT I score of 900 (composite ACT score of 21), rank in top half of secondary school class, and minimum 2.85 GPA recommended. Special Requirements: A portfolio is required for art program applicants. An audition is required for music program applicants.

**Application deadline:** August 15
**Notification:** Rolling

**SAT or ACT preferred:** Either
**SAT Avg:** 527V, 521M
**SAT II required:** Yes
**Average ACT:** 23
**Average GPA:** 3.2

**Graduated top 10% of class:** 24
**Graduated top 25% of class:** 50
**Graduated top 50% of class:** 80

## COLLEGE GRADUATION REQUIREMENTS

**Course waivers allowed:** No
**Course substitutions allowed:** Yes
**In what courses:** In any course where the request is appropriate.

## ADDITIONAL INFORMATION

**Environment:** The college is located on 80 acres 135 miles from Pittsburgh in the Appalachian foothills.

**Student Body**
 **Undergrad enrollment:** 1,531
 **Women:** 55%
 **Men:** 45%
 **In-state students:** 49%
 **Out-of-state:** 51%

**Cost Information**
 **In-state tuition:** $14,975
 **Out-of-state:** $14,975
 **Room & board:** $3,915

**Housing Information**
 **University housing:** Yes
 **Fraternity:** Yes
 **Sorority:** No
 **Living on campus:** 82%

 **Athletics:** NAIA

# WI ALVERNO COLLEGE

3401 South 39th Street, P.O. Box 343922, Milwaukee, WI 53234 • **Admissions:** 414-382-6000
**Fax:** 414-382-6354 • **Email:** alvadmsh@execpc.com • **Web:** www.alverno.edu
**Support:** S • **Institution:** 4 yr. Private

## LEARNING DISABILITY ADMISSIONS AND SERVICES

Alverno College is a small liberal arts college for women with approximately 2,500 students. There is an Instructional Services Center (ISC) that provides academic support to Alverno students, and to assist Alverno applicants to meet admissions requirements. The ISC offers courses in reading, writing and critical thinking, math, and algebra in order to develop academic skills as required on the basis of new student assessment results; students may take ISC courses for academic enrichment. ISC also offers course-based study groups and workshops to provide an opportunity for small groups of students to study together under the direction of a peer tutor or an ISC teacher. There is also a Coordinator of Support Services for Students with Learning Disabilities. The goal of Support Services is to assist the student to meet her academic potential through understanding her learning needs, development of strategies and accommodations to maximize her strengths, and development of self-advocacy with faculty.

## LEARNING DISABILITY ADMISSIONS INFORMATION

**Program Name:** Instructional Services Center
**Program Director:** Nancy Bornstein
**Contact Person:** Colleen Barnett, Coordinator

**Telephone:** 414-382-6353
**Telephone:** 414-382-6026

### ADMISSIONS

Admission criteria is the same for all students coming directly from high school. General admission requirements include: 19+ ACT; 17 academic credits in college prep courses with recommendations including 4 yrs. English, 2 yrs. foreign language, 3 yrs. math, 3 yrs. science, 3 yrs. social studies; and rank in the top 1/2 of graduating class. There is a pre-college program for students who do not meet the admissions criteria but have academic potential.

**College entrance exams required:** Yes
**Course entrance requirements:** Yes
**Diagnostic tests:** Yes
**Documentation:** WAIS-R; WJ-R; WRAT-R: within 5-8 years

**Untimed accepted:** Yes
**Interview required:** No

### ADDITIONAL INFORMATION

Classes are offered at a beginning level in reading, writing, math, and algebra. There is also one class offered in interpreting language practices that assists students who need to be taught to read and write. Students may not substitute courses for Math courses required to graduate, but intensive assistance is provided. Tutoring is provided through Instructional Services, and there is an Academic Support Group for students with learning disabilities that meets every 2-3 weeks to discuss topics such as; self-advocacy, problem solving, writing letters, and communicating with professors. The college has a Math Resource Center and a Writing Resource Center available for all students.

**Special education HS coursework accepted:** N/A
**Special application required:** No
**# of applications submitted each year:** N/A
**# of students receiving LD services:** 58

**Essay required:** Yes
**Submitted to:** N/A
**# of applications accepted each year:** N/A

**Acceptance into program means acceptance into college:** Students must be admitted to the college first and then may request services.

# LEARNING DISABILITY SERVICES

**Learning center:** No
**Kurzweil personal reader:** No
**LD specialists:** No
**Allowed in exams:**
  **Calculator:** Yes
  **Dictionary:** Yes
  **Computer:** Yes
  **SpellCheck:** Yes

**Notetaker:** Yes
**Scribes:** Yes
**Proctors:** Yes
**Oral exams:** Yes
**Extended test time:** Yes
**Added cost:** None
**Distraction-free environ.:** Yes
**Tape recording in class:** Yes
**Books on tape:** No
**Taping of other books:** No

**Professional tutors:** 10
**Peer tutors:** Yes
**Max. hrs/wk for services:** Unlimited
**Priority registration:** No
**Accomodations for students with ADD:** Yes
**How are professors notified of LD:** By the student and the Program Director

# GENERAL ADMISSIONS INFORMATION

**Director of Admissions:** Colleen Hayes         **Telephone:** 414-382-6100

## ENTRANCE REQUIREMENTS

Total high school units required/recommended: 17 total units are required; 4 English recommended, 3 math recommended, 3 science recommended, 2 foreign language recommended, 4 social studies recommended, 3 history recommended. Minimum composite ACT score of 19, rank in top half of secondary school class, and minimum 2.5 GPA recommended. Special requirements: biology and chemistry required of music therapy program applicants. Biology, chemistry, and algebra required of nursing program applicants. Biology, chemistry, algebra, and geometry recommended of nuclear medicine technology program applicants. Audition (or tape) and music theory exam required of music program applicants.

**Application deadline:** August 1
**Notification:** Rolling

**SAT or ACT preferred:** ACT
**SAT II required:** Yes
**Average ACT:** 20
**Average GPA:** 3.0

**Graduated top 10% of class:** 7
**Graduated top 25% of class:** 36
**Graduated top 50% of class:** 68

# COLLEGE GRADUATION REQUIREMENTS

**Course waivers allowed:** No
**Course substitutions allowed:** No
**In what courses:** Foreign language not required to graduate. Students must take a College Algebra class to graduate.

# ADDITIONAL INFORMATION

**Environment:** The campus is located in a suburban area on the southwest side of Milwaukee.

**Student Body**
  **Undergrad enrollment:** 2,191
  **Women:** 100%
  **Men:** 0%
  **In-state students:** 97%
  **Out-of-state:** 3%

**Cost Information**
  **In-state tuition:** $9,672
  **Out-of-state:** $9,672
  **Room & board:** $4,040

**Housing Information**
  **University housing:** Yes
  **Fraternity:** No
  **Sorority:** No
  **Living on campus:** 11%

  **Athletics:** NR

# WI

# BELOIT COLLEGE

700 College Avenue, Beloit, WI 53511 • **Admissions:** 608-363-2500 • **Fax:** 608-363-2717
**Email:** admiss@beloit.edu • **Web:** www.beloit.edu
**Support:** CS • **Institution:** 4 yr. Private

## LEARNING DISABILITY ADMISSIONS AND SERVICES

The goal of the Educational Development Program (EDP) is to provide support services and accommodations individually tailored to the needs of each student to enable the successful completion of the baccalaureate degree. EDP is a campus resource that provides opportunities for students to succeed. Beloit College students can qualify for EDP services based on any one of the following: 1) parents' educational attainment, 2) family income, 3) need for academic support, 4) need for special services. EDP is funded through Beloit College in cooperation with the US Department of Education. Participation is on a first-come, first-served basis for those who qualify and by the discretion of project staff.

## LEARNING DISABILITY ADMISSIONS INFORMATION

**Program Name:** Educational Development Program
**Program Director:** Gail Pizarro
**Contact Person:** Same as above
**Telephone:** 608-363-2031

### ADMISSIONS

There is no special admissions procedure for students with learning disabilities. Each student is reviewed individually and the final decision is made by the Office of Admission. The college is competitive in admissions, but there are no cut-offs for GPA or test scores.

**College entrance exams required:** Yes
**Course entrance requirements:** Yes
**Diagnostic tests:** No
**Documentation:** N/A

**Untimed accepted:** Yes
**Interview required:** No

### ADDITIONAL INFORMATION

The Beloit Learning Resource Center offers additional services to the students in the areas of tutoring, study skills and time management, math and science tutoring and study groups, improvement of writing skills, advising, mentoring, reading speed and comprehension and computer usage. Counseling services are offered in personal group counseling, career guidance, and crisis intervention. Faculty contribute examples of past tests from a variety of courses that are housed in a Test file. Individual and self-help programs and small group workshops are available. Assessment tools are offered to help students determine individual strengths and weakness in reading rate, comprehension, and vocabulary, and there are a variety of handouts covering a wide range of academic skill areas such as studying, math, footnoting, and test taking.

**Special education HS coursework accepted:** Yes
**Special application required:** Yes
**# of applications submitted each year:** N/A
**# of students receiving LD services:** 10-12

**Essay required:** Yes
**Submitted to:** Program Director
**# of applications accepted each year:** N/A

**Acceptance into program means acceptance into college:** Students must be admitted to the college first and then may request services.

# LEARNING DISABILITY SERVICES

Learning center: Yes
Kurzweil personal reader: No
LD specialists: Yes
Allowed in exams:
  Calculator: Yes
  Dictionary: Y/N
  Computer: Y/N
  SpellCheck: Y/N

Notetaker: Yes
Scribes: Yes
Proctors: Yes
Oral exams: Yes
Extended test time: Yes
Added cost: None
Distraction-free environ.: Yes
Tape recording in class: Yes
Books on tape: No
Taping of other books: Yes

Professional tutors: Yes
Peer tutors: Yes
Max. hrs/wk for services:
Unlimited
Priority registration: Y/N
Accomodations for students
with ADD: Yes
How are professors notified of
LD: By the student and Program
Director

# GENERAL ADMISSIONS INFORMATION

Director of Admissions: Alan McIvor

Telephone: 608-363-2380

## ENTRANCE REQUIREMENTS

Total high school units required/recommended: 16 total units are required; 4 English recommended, 3 math recommended, 3 science recommended, 2 foreign language recommended, 3 social studies recommended. Rank in top 1/2 of secondary school class recommended.

Application deadline: Rolling
Notification: Rolling

SAT or ACT preferred: Either
SAT Avg: 610V, 590M
Average ACT: 26
Average GPA: 3.5

Graduated top 10% of class: 31
Graduated top 25% of class: 80
Graduated top 50% of class: 93

# COLLEGE GRADUATION REQUIREMENTS

Course waivers allowed: No
Course substitutions allowed: No
In what courses: N/A

# ADDITIONAL INFORMATION

Environment: The college is located 50 miles south of Madison, 90 miles northwest of Chicago.

Student Body
  Undergrad enrollment: 1,270
  Women: 57%
  Men: 43%
  In-state students: 23%
  Out-of-state: 77%

Cost Information
  In-state tuition: $18,850
  Out-of-state: $18,850
  Room & board: $4,140

Housing Information
  University housing: Yes
  Fraternity: Yes
  Sorority: Yes
  Living on campus: 95%

  Athletics: NCAA Div. III

# EDGEWOOD COLLEGE

**WI**

855 Woodrow Street, Madison, WI 53711 • **Admissions:** 608-257-4861 • **Fax:** 608-257-1455

**Support:** CS • **Institution:** 4 yr. Private

## LEARNING DISABILITY ADMISSIONS AND SERVICES

The Assistance to Students with Learning Disabilities (ASLD) Program is available for incoming freshmen who have demonstrated a learning disability. This Program is designed to support students in their regular coursework throughout their Edgewood College career. Each student accepted into the Program will participate in the ASLD Summer Program and will be eligible to receive support services. Skills courses are available in math, reading, and writing. Weekly or biweekly meetings are held with the Learning Skills Coordinator to monitor students' progress and special services.

## LEARNING DISABILITY ADMISSIONS INFORMATION

**Program Name:** Assistance to Students with Learning Disabilities
**Program Director:** Kathie Moran, Coordinator
**Contact Person:** Same as above

**Telephone:** 608-257-4861
**Telephone:** 1-800-444-4861

### ADMISSIONS

General admissions criteria require students to meet 2 out of 3 categories: 18 ACT, 2.5 GPA or upper 50% of class. In addition to the regular admission application and requirements, applicants with learning disabilities should submit: the ASLD Program application, letters of recommendation from 2 high school teachers/counselors, documentation of the learning disability, and have an on-campus interview with the Program Director. If a student with a learning disabily is denied admission, that student may request reconsideration from the Admissions Committee and send additional documentation. The Admission decision is made jointly by the Director of Admission and the Director of ASLD.

**College entrance exams required:** Yes
**Course entrance requirements:** Yes
**Diagnostic tests:** Yes
**Documentation:** W-J; WAIS-R or WISC-R request all subtests scores: within 2 years

**Untimed accepted:** Yes
**Interview required:** Yes

### ADDITIONAL INFORMATION

During the Summer Program, admitted students meet with college personnel to plan for needed support services. The plan is based on Edgewood College placement test scores, diagnostic tests, and information about the individual's learning disability. Students also participate in study skills workshops.

**Special education HS coursework accepted:** No
**Special application required:** Yes
**# of applications submitted each year:** 10-15
**# of students receiving LD services:** 30

**Essay required:** Yes
**Submitted to:** ASLD Program
**# of applications accepted each year:** 5

**Acceptance into program means acceptance into college:** Students must be admitted to the college and then request consideration for the ASLD Program or other services.

# LEARNING DISABILITY SERVICES

**Learning center:** No
**Kurzweil personal reader:** No
**LD specialists:** 1
**Allowed in exams:**
 **Calculator:** Y/N
 **Dictionary:** Y/N
 **Computer:** Y/N
 **SpellCheck:** Y/N

**Notetaker:** Yes
**Scribes:** Yes
**Proctors:** Yes
**Oral exams:** Yes
**Extended test time:** Yes
**Added cost:** None
**Distraction-free environ.:** Yes
**Tape recording in class:** Yes
**Books on tape:** Yes
**Taping of other books:** No

**Professional tutors:** 1
**Peer tutors:** 10
**Max. hrs/wk for services:** Unlimited
**Priority registration:** No
**Accomodations for students with ADD:** Yes
**How are professors notified of LD:** As directed by student

# GENERAL ADMISSIONS INFORMATION

**Director of Admissions:** Kevin Kucera

**Telephone:** 608-257-4861

## ENTRANCE REQUIREMENTS

NR

**Application deadline:** August 1
**Notification:** NR

**SAT or ACT preferred:** NR
**ACT Range:** 17–25

**Graduated top 10% of class:** 24
**Graduated top 25% of class:** 63
**Graduated top 50% of class:** 94

# COLLEGE GRADUATION REQUIREMENTS

**Course waivers allowed:** No
**Course substitutions allowed:** Yes
**In what courses:** Math and foreign language, depending on major, severity of the learning disability, and a history of attempting the course with supported services.

# ADDITIONAL INFORMATION

**Environment:** The college is located in Madison, a university-oriented city.

**Student Body**
 **Undergrad enrollment:** NR
 **Women:** NR%
 **Men:** NR%
 **In-state students:** 90%
 **Out-of-state:** 10%

**Cost Information**
 **In-state tuition:** $9,000
 **Out-of-state:** $9,000
 **Room & board:** $3,800

**Housing Information**
 **University housing:** Yes
 **Fraternity:** No
 **Sorority:** No
 **Living on campus:** 33%

 **Athletics:** NAIA

*EDGEWOOD COLLEGE*

# MARIAN COLLEGE OF FOND DU LAC

45 South National Avenue, Fond du Lac, WI 54935 • **Admissions:** 414-923-7650 • **Fax:** 414-923-7154
**Email:** admit@mariancoll.edu
**Support:** CS • **Institution:** 4 yr. Private

## LEARNING DISABILITY ADMISSIONS AND SERVICES

Academic Support Services is not a program, but does offer services for students with learning disabilities. The ultimate goal of these services is to provide the academic, social, and emotional support to students in order that they may maintain at least a 2.0 GPA and persevere to earn a college degree. Academic Support Services strives to provide a 'neutral' area within which students can be accepted for who they are, and can begin moving towards meeting their own personal and academic goals.

## LEARNING DISABILITY ADMISSIONS INFORMATION

**Program Name:** Academic Support Services
**Program Director:** Connie Rodriquez Leyner
**Contact Person:** Same as above

**Telephone:** 414-923-8117

### ADMISSIONS

There is no special application or admissions procedure for students with learning disabilities. Admission criteria includes a 2.0 GPA, top 50% of class, and ACT of 18. All students, not just those with learning disabilities, are asked to meet 2/3 of these criteria. Students who do not meet 2/3 may be asked to submit 3 letters of recommendation supporting their ability to succeed in college-level coursework. Students also may be asked to schedule a visit to Marian for a pre-admission interview during which their skills, attitudes, motivation, and self-understanding will be informally assessed. Students admitted provisionally may be admitted with limited credit status and may be required to take a freshman seminar course. Special education course work is accepted, but students are encouraged to be fully mainstreamed by senior year with minimal monitoring.

**College entrance exams required:** Yes
**Course entrance requirements:** Yes
**Diagnostic tests:** Yes
**Documentation:** WAIS-R; WISC-R; W-J and achievement tests: within 3 years

**Untimed accepted:** Yes
**Interview required:** Yes, for borderline candidates

### ADDITIONAL INFORMATION

The Peer Tutoring Program helps students gain the confidence and skill necessary to successfully complete coursework. To receive assistance students must disclose their disability. Skill classes are offered in English, math and study skills, as well as computer assisted instruction in math and basic skill areas. Other services include information on community, state and national resources; assistance in writing and proofreading papers and assignments; tutors (individual and group); liaison service; assistance in working with instructors, and course scheduling. Calculators are allowed in exams for students with a documented disability in math, and dictionaries are allowed in exams for students with a documented disability in written language. Assistance is determined for each individual based on assessment. Services are available for undergraduate and graduate students.

**Special education HS coursework accepted:** Yes
**Special application required:** No
**# of applications submitted each year:** 15-20
**# of students receiving LD services:** 74

**Essay required:** No
**Submitted to:** N/A
**# of applications accepted each year:** N/I

**Acceptance into program means acceptance into college:** No, must be admitted to the college first and then may request services.

## LEARNING DISABILITY SERVICES

Learning center: Yes
Kurzweil personal reader: No
LD specialists: 2
Allowed in exams:
 Calculator: Y/N
 Dictionary: Y/N
 Computer: Yes
 SpellCheck: Yes

Notetaker: Yes
Scribes: Yes
Proctors: Yes
Oral exams: Yes
Extended test time: Yes
Added cost: None
Distraction-free environ.: Yes
Tape recording in class: Yes
Books on tape: Yes
Taping of other books: No

Professional tutors: 3
Peer tutors: 25-50
Max. hrs/wk for services: Unlimited
Priority registration: No
Accomodations for students with ADD: Yes
How are professors notified of LD: By the student and Program Director

## GENERAL ADMISSIONS INFORMATION

**Director of Admissions:** Carol Reichenberger

**Telephone:** 414-923-7650

### ENTRANCE REQUIREMENTS
Total high school units required/recommended: 16 total units are required; 3 English required, 4 English recommended, 2 math required, 2 science recommended, 2 foreign language recommended, 2 social studies recommended. Minimum composite ACT score of 18, rank in top half of secondary school class, and minimum 2.0 GPA required. Special Requirements: 1 unit of chemistry and 1 unit of biology required of nursing program applicants.

**Application deadline:** July 1
**Notification:** Rolling

**SAT or ACT preferred:** ACT
**Average ACT:** 20

**Graduated top 10% of class:** 15
**Graduated top 25% of class:** 41
**Graduated top 50% of class:** 70

## COLLEGE GRADUATION REQUIREMENTS

**Course waivers allowed:** No
**Course substitutions allowed:** No
**In what courses:** Not requested or needed; students have taken directed study-type classes to fulfill their math requirement; work one-to-one with tutor and weekly with instructor; 1 year to complete semester course; must attempt required course in traditional manner.

## ADDITIONAL INFORMATION

**Environment:** Marian College is located on 50 acres in a suburb of Fond-du-Lac 60 miles north of Milwaukee.

**Student Body**
 Undergrad enrollment: 1,856
 Women: 67%
 Men: 33%
 In-state students: 80%
 Out-of-state: 20%

**Cost Information**
 In-state tuition: $10,560
 Out-of-state: $10,560
 Room & board: $3,800

**Housing Information**
 University housing: Yes
 Fraternity: Yes
 Sorority: Yes
 Living on campus: 55%

 Athletics: NAIA

# WI | RIPON COLLEGE

P.O. Box 248, Ripon, WI 54971 • **Admissions:** 920-748-8102 • **Fax:** 920-748-7243
**Email:** adminfo@mac.ripon.edu • **Web:** www.ripon.edu
**Support:** S • **Institution:** 4 yr. Private

## LEARNING DISABILITY ADMISSIONS AND SERVICES

The Educational Development Program (EDP) provides a wide variety of services on the campus including academic and personal counseling, study skills information and tutoring. Although the focus of the program is on 1st generation students, students of higher need, and students who are learning disabled, other students who feel they might qualify are encouraged to contact the EDP office. EDP is a voluntary program that has been in existence at Ripon College since 1974. For the many students who have used its services, EDP has provided a network of support for academic, financial, and personal concerns. A group of peer contacts serves EDP by meeting regularly with students to facilitate communication between EDP participants and the office staff. For students who qualify, EDP offers free tutoring in specific subject areas. (All campus tutoring is also available). The tutors are upperclass students who have been recommended by their professors and trained by the EDP staff. These tutors serve as a supplement to faculty assistance. The aim of the tutoring program is to help students develop independent learning skills and improve their course grades. Although federal guidelines require a restriction on who "qualifies" the door to EDP remains open to all eligible students.

## LEARNING DISABILITY ADMISSIONS INFORMATION

**Program Name:** Student Support Services
**Program Director:** Dan Kehin
**Contact Person:** Same as above

**Telephone:** 414-748-8107

### ADMISSIONS

Students with learning disabilities are screened by admissions and must meet the same admission criteria as all other applicants. There is no set GPA required; courses required include 4 yrs. English, algebra and geometry, 2 yrs. natural science, 2 yrs. social studies, and 7 additional units. Students with learning disabilities who self-disclose are referred to Student Support Services when making prospective visits to the campus in order to ascertain specific needs and abilities of the student.

**College entrance exams required:** Yes
**Course entrance requirements:** Yes
**Diagnostic tests:** Yes
**Documentation:** W-J;I.Q.: within 3 years

**Untimed accepted:** Yes
**Interview required:** Yes

### ADDITIONAL INFORMATION

The Educational Development Program provides tutoring in subject areas; skills classes for no credit in time management, notetaking, test taking strategies, reading college texts, writing papers, studying for and taking exams, and setting goals; and counseling/guidance. Student Support Services provides intensive study groups, LD support groups, and internships. EDP provides students with peer contacts who provide students with one-on-one support and is useful in helping students adjust to college life, to provide a contact for the student to go to with problems or issues, organize group tutoring, and to help students open their minds and see hope in their future.

**Special education HS coursework accepted:** Yes
**Special application required:** No
**# of applications submitted each year:** N /A
**# of students receiving LD services:** 10

**Essay required:** Yes
**Submitted to:** N/A
**# of applications accepted each year:** N/A

**Acceptance into program means acceptance into college:** Students must be admitted to the college and then may request services.

**Learning center:** No
**Kurzweil personal reader:** No
**LD specialists:** No
**Allowed in exams:**
  **Calculaor::** Yes
  **Dictionary:** No
  **Computer:** No
  **SpellCheck:** No

**Notetaker:** Yes
**Scribes:** Yes
**Proctors:** Yes
**Oral exams:** Yes
**Extended test time:** Yes
**Added cost:** None
**Distraction-free environ.:** Yes
**Tape recording in class:** Yes
**Books on tape:** Yes
**Taping of other books:** No

**Professional tutors:** 40
**Peer tutors:** 14
**Max. hrs/wk for services:** 3 hrs. per week per course
**Priority registration:** No
**Accomodations for students with ADD:** Yes
**How are professors notified of LD:** By the student and the Director of services

## GENERAL ADMISSIONS INFORMATION

**Director of Admissions:** Paul Weeks

**Telephone:** 414-748-8107

### ENTRANCE REQUIREMENTS

Total high school units required/recommended: 17 total units are required; 4 English required, 2 math required, 4 math recommended, 2 science required, 4 science recommended, 2 foreign language recommended, 2 social studies required, 4 social studies recommended, 2 history recommended. Rank in top 1/4 of secondary school class recommended. Special requirements: TOEFL is required of all international students.

**Application deadline:** March 15
**Notification:** Rolling

**SAT or ACT preferred:** Either
**SAT Avg:** 576V, 541M
**SAT II required:** Yes
**Average ACT:** 24
**Average GPA:** 3.3

**Graduated top 10% of class:** 27
**Graduated top 25% of class:** 49
**Graduated top 50% of class:** 94

## COLLEGE GRADUATION REQUIREMENTS

**Course waivers allowed:** Yes
**Course substitutions allowed:** Yes
**In what courses:** Foreign language

## ADDITIONAL INFORMATION

**Environment:** NR

**Student Body**
  **Undergrad enrollment:** 734
  **Women:** 57%
  **Men:** 43%
  **In-state students:** 61%
  **Out-of-state:** 39%

**Cost Information**
  **In-state tuition:** $16,780
  **Out-of-state:** $16,780
  **Room & board:** $4,400

**Housing Information**
  **University housing:** Yes
  **Fraternity:** Yes
  **Sorority:** Yes
  **Living on campus:** 97%

  **Athletics:** NCAA Div. III

# WI
# UNIVERSITY OF WISCONSIN-EAU CLAIRE

105 Garfield Avenue, Eau Claire, WI 54701 • **Admissions:** 715-836-5415 • **Fax:** 715-836-2380
**Email:** ask-uwec@uwec.edu • **Web:** www.uwec.edu
**Support:** CS • **Institution:** 4 yr. Public

## LEARNING DISABILITY ADMISSIONS AND SERVICES

The university does not have a separate program for students with learning disabilities. However, many services provided would be beneficial. Documentation of a learning disability is required to receive services. Students should meet with someone in the Special Services Office 2 months before enrolling to ensure that needed services are in place. Academic adjustments or accommodations will be provided to meet the students' needs. The purpose of academic accommodations is not to give the students an unfair advantage, but to keep the students from having an unfair disadvantage. In no way will the standards of the university be compromised.

## LEARNING DISABILITY ADMISSIONS INFORMATION

**Program Name:** Services for Students with Disabilities (SSD)
**Program Director:** Joseph C. Hisrich                    **Telephone:** 715-836-4542
**Contact Person:** Beth Hicks

### ADMISSIONS

Individuals with learning disabilities complete the standard university application form and must meet the regular university admission criteria. Applicants should rank in the top 50% of their class. Courses required include 4 yrs. English, 3 yrs. math, 3 yrs. natural science, 3 yrs. social science, 2 yrs. foreign language, and 2 courses in any academic course or art, music, speech, and computer science. Students not admitted in the fall, may find a January admission somewhat less competitive. Students must submit an ACT score and take placement tests in English, math, and other appropriate areas. Conditional student status is given during the summer and second semester of the academic year.

**College entrance exams required:** Yes                   **Untimed accepted:** Yes
**Course entrance requirements:** Yes                      **Interview required:** No
**Diagnostic tests:** Yes
**Documentation:** LD assessment: within 3 years

### ADDITIONAL INFORMATION

Students must provide documentation prior to receiving appropriate accommodations. Collegiate Bridge Program (5-week summer program), is offered mainly to minority students, 1st generation and disadvantaged students. Students with learning disabilities are eligible candidates. Conditionally admitted students automatically receive an application. The Academic Skills Center offers individualized tutoring in math preparation and background, composition, reading and study skills. Many departments on campus provide tutors to help students with course content. Students complete a form for professors identifying appropriate accommodation requests. Students who are denied accommodations can appeal any denial by filing a complaint with the Affirmative Action Review Board. Services and accommodations are available to undergraduate and graduate students.

**Special education HS coursework accepted:** Y/N          **Essay required:** No
**Special application required:** No                        **Submitted to:** N/A
**# of applications submitted each year:** N/A             **# of applications accepted each year:** N/A
**# of students receiving LD services:** 80
**Acceptance into program means acceptance into college:** Students must be admitted to the university first and then may request services.

## LEARNING DISABILITY SERVICES

**Learning center:** No
**Kurzweil personal reader:** No
**LD specialists:** 1
**Allowed in exams:**
  Calculator: Y/N
  Dictionary: Y/N
  Computer: Y/N
  SpellCheck: Y/N

**Notetaker:** Yes
**Scribes:** Yes
**Proctors:** Yes
**Oral exams:** Yes
**Extended test time:** Yes
**Added cost:** None
**Distraction-free environ.:** Yes
**Tape recording in class:** Yes
**Books on tape:** Yes
**Taping of other books:** Yes

**Professional tutors:** No
**Peer tutors:** 30-40
**Max. hrs/wk for services:** Unlimited
**Priority registration:** Yes
**Accomodations for students with ADD:** Yes
**How are professors notified of LD:** By the student or the Program Director (if requested)

## GENERAL ADMISSIONS INFORMATION

**Director of Admissions:** Roger W. Groenewold          **Telephone:** 715-836-5415

### ENTRANCE REQUIREMENTS
Total high school units required/recommended: 17 total units are required; 4 English required, 3 math required, 3 science required, 2 foreign language required, 3 social studies required. Minimum composite ACT score of 22 and rank in top 1/2 of secondary school class required. Special requirements: An audition is required for music program applicants.

**Application deadline:** Rolling
**Notification:** Rolling

**SAT or ACT preferred:** ACT
**SAT Avg:** 543V, 557M
**Average ACT:** 23

**Graduated top 10% of class:** 19
**Graduated top 25% of class:** 49
**Graduated top 50% of class:** 87

## COLLEGE GRADUATION REQUIREMENTS

**Course waivers allowed:** No
**Course substitutions allowed:** Yes
**In what courses:** Substitutions are assessed on an individual basis. The college dean reviews and gives approval. Courses can be substituted if not required by major, minor or program, such as foreign language and math

## ADDITIONAL INFORMATION

**Environment:** The 333-acre campus is an urban setting 95 miles east of Minneapolis.

**Student Body**
  Undergrad enrollment: 10,023
  Women: 60%
  Men: 40%
  In-state students: 82%
  Out-of-state: 18%

**Cost Information**
  In-state tuition: $2,574
  Out-of-state: $8,038
  Room & board: $2,904

**Housing Information**
  University housing: Yes
  Fraternity: Yes
  Sorority: Yes
  Living on campus: 35%

  Athletics: NAIA

# UNIVERSITY OF WISCONSIN-LACROSSE

**WI**

1725 State Street, LaCrosse, WI 54601 • **Admissions:** 608-785-8067 • **Fax:** 608-785-6695
**Web:** www.uwlax.edu
**Support:** CS • **Institution:** 4 yr. Public

## LEARNING DISABILITY ADMISSIONS AND SERVICES

The goal of the Services for Students with Special Needs is to provide academic accommodations for students with learning disabilities in order for them to participate fully at the university. A number of academic and personal support services are available. Students must provide documentation (completed within the last 3 years) to verify the disability. The mission is to identify, reduce, or eliminate barriers in education for students with disabilities within the most integrated setting possible. The Adult Learning Disabilities Section is a service of Gundersen Clinic. It provides an interdisciplinary approach to identifying, evaluating and treating the learning problems of adults.

## LEARNING DISABILITY ADMISSIONS INFORMATION

**Program Name:** Services for Students with Disabilities
**Program Director:** June Reinert, Coordinator          **Telephone:** 608-785-6900
**Contact Person:** Same as above

### ADMISSIONS

Admission criteria includes an ACT of 23 and a class rank in the top 35%. There is limited admission for students with learning disabilities if they are close to the regular admission requirements. Students with learning disabilities are encouraged to self-disclose their disability. These applications are automatically referred to the Program Director who will then request a recent psychological report, 3 letters of recommendation, and a personal interview. The admissions office is sensitive to the Director's opinions and will admit students recommended, who can succeed, even if these students do not meet standard admissions requirements.

**College entrance exams required:** Yes          **Untimed accepted:** Yes
**Course entrance requirements:** Yes          **Interview required:** No
**Diagnostic tests:** Yes
**Documentation:** WAIS; W-J: within 3 years

### ADDITIONAL INFORMATION

The Program Director writes a letter to all the student's professors explaining the student's learning disability and describing necessary modifications. The Program Director meets with freshmen once a week. There is also a support group which meets twice a month. Services include taped texts, testing accommodations, notetakers, and remedial courses. Students are encouraged to get tutoring through the academic departments. Tutorial assistance is offered through each department within the university. Skills classes are offered in reading, remedial English, and mathematics. Services and accommodations are available for undergraduate and graduate students.

**Special education HS coursework accepted:** No          **Essay required:** No
**Special application required:** Yes          **Submitted to:** Director of Program
**# of applications submitted each year:** 40          **# of applications accepted each year:** N/I
**# of students receiving LD services:** 140
**Acceptance into program means acceptance into college:** Students must be admitted to the university first and then may request LD services.

## LEARNING DISABILITY SERVICES

**Learning center:** No
**Kurzweil personal reader:** Yes
**LD specialists:** Yes
**Allowed in exams:**
  **Calculator:** Y/N
  **Dictionary:** Y/N
  **Computer:** Y/N
  **SpellCheck:** Yes

**Notetaker:** Yes
**Scribes:** Yes
**Proctors:** Yes
**Oral exams:** N/I
**Extended test time:** Yes
**Added cost:** None
**Distraction-free environ.:** Yes
**Tape recording in class:** Yes
**Books on tape:** Yes
**Taping of other books:** Yes

**Professional tutors:** No
**Peer tutors:** Yes
**Max. hrs/wk for services:**
Unlimited
**Priority registration:** Yes
**Accomodations for students
with ADD:** Yes
**How are professors notified of
LD:** By the student

## GENERAL ADMISSIONS INFORMATION

**Director of Admissions:** Timothy R. Lewis

**Telephone:** 608-785-8067

### ENTRANCE REQUIREMENTS

Total high school units required/recommended: 17 total units are required; 4 English required, 3 math required, 4 math recommended, 3 science required, 4 science recommended, 3 social studies required. Minimum composite ACT score of 23 and rank in top 3/5 of secondary school class or minimum composite ACT score of 21 and rank in top 35% of secondary school class required. Special requirements: Interview required of physical therapy and physician assistant program applicants.

**Application deadline:** Rolling
**Notification:** Rolling

**SAT or ACT preferred:** ACT
**SAT II required:** Yes
**ACT required:** Yes
**Average ACT:** 23

**Graduated top 10% of class:** 21
**Graduated top 25% of class:** 57
**Graduated top 50% of class:** 94

## COLLEGE GRADUATION REQUIREMENTS

**Course waivers allowed:** Yes
**Course substitutions allowed:** Yes
**In what courses:** Decision is made on an individual basis.

## ADDITIONAL INFORMATION

**Environment:** The university is located on 119 acres, in a small city 140 miles west of Madison.

**Student Body**
  **Undergrad enrollment:** 8,435
  **Women:** 56%
  **Men:** 44%
  **In-state students:** 85%
  **Out-of-state:** 15%

**Cost Information**
  **In-state tuition:** $2,570
  **Out-of-state:** $7,740
  **Room & board:** $2,800

**Housing Information**
  **University housing:** Yes
  **Fraternity:** Yes
  **Sorority:** Yes
  **Living on campus:** 33%

  **Athletics:** NCAA Div. III

# UNIVERSITY OF WISCONSIN-MADISON

140 Petenson Office Building, 750 University Avenue, Madison, WI 53706 • **Admissions:** 608-262-3961
**Fax:** 608-262-1429 • **Email:** ON.WISCONSIN@mail.admin.wisc.edu • **Web:** www.wisc.edu
**Support:** CS • **Institution:** 4 yr. Public

## LEARNING DISABILITY ADMISSIONS AND SERVICES

UW-Madison believes that students with disabilities add valuable diversity to the campus, and those who have the potential to succeed academically should have their exceptional circumstances taken into account. The university cannot inquire about a disability and no one is obligated to provide this information. However, some students may strengthen their applications by disclosing the disability. This information will only be considered in cases where the student would not otherwise be admissible. When an applicant discloses a disability during the application process, the Admissions Office notifies the McBurney Center. The center sends information to the applicant, including detailed instructions on the application procedure. Making good decisions about college requires carefully considering the match between interests and abilities and the expectations and support available on the campus. Students should consider: the competitiveness of their high school and how this compares to Madison in terms of academic challenge, size and level of disability related services; the current use of disability-related services, and if these are similar to the support services offered at the university; self-advocacy skills; if the academic abilities match interests and if these are realistic.

## LEARNING DISABILITY ADMISSIONS INFORMATION

**Program Name:** McBurney Disability Resource Center
**Program Director:** Cathy Trueba                    **Telephone:** 602-263-2741
**Contact Person:** Same as above

### ADMISSIONS

The admission process is the same  for all applicants. Applicants not meeting these criteria who self-disclose a disability can have their documentation reviewed by an Admissions Office liaison, and then sent to McBurney Center. The disability could become a factor in admission by providing documentation clearly establishing the presence of a disability, showing an impact of the disability on education, and having a record of academic achievement that meets guidelines and suggests potential success. Factors in alternative admissions review process include disability information, grades, rank, tests, course requirements completed, and potential for success. Examples include date of diagnosis or onset of disability, a disability that occurs in high school causing lower grades will be reviewed with the disability and recovery being considered, the interactions between the disability and curricular requirements. If course requirements are directly impacted by the disability resulting in low grades or the absence of courses, the GPA will be reviewed with and without those courses.

**College entrance exams required:** Yes                    **Untimed accepted:** Yes
**Course entrance requirements:** Yes                    **Interview required:** No
**Diagnostic tests:** Yes
**Documentation:** Normed to age; intelligence, achievement, cognitive processing; within 3 yrs.

### ADDITIONAL INFORMATION

The documentation must be completed by a professional qualified to diagnose a LD; must include results of a clinical interview and descriptions of the testing procedures, instruments used, test and sub-test results reported in standard scores as well as percentile rank and grade scores where useful, interpretation and recommendations based on data gathered; be comprehensive and include test results where applicable in intelligence, reading, math, spelling, written language, language processing and cognitive processing skills. Testing should carefully examine areas of concern/weakness as well as areas of strengths; include a clear diagnostic statement based on the tests results and personal history. Students may be eligible for advocacy/liaison with faculty and staff, alternative testing accommodations, curriculum modifications, disability management advising, learning skills training, liaison with Voc Rehab, McBurney Learning Resource Room card, notetaker, peer support groups, priority registration, taped texts, and course materials.

**Special education HS coursework accepted:** Possibly, depends on the description of course
**Essay required:** No
**Special application required:** No                    **Submitted to:** N/A
**# of applications submitted each year:** N/A          **# of applications accepted each year:** N/A
**# of students receiving LD services:** Approximately 300
**Acceptance into program means acceptance into college:** Reviewed by McBurney only if not regularly admissible. The final decision is made by the Admission Office. Once admitted, students must request services.

# LEARNING DISABILITY SERVICES

**Learning center:** Yes
**Kurzweil personal reader:** N/I
**LD specialists:** 2
**Allowed in exams:**
  **Calculator:** Y/N
  **Dictionary:** Y/N
  **Computer:** Y/N
  **SpellCheck:** Y/N

**Notetaker:** Yes
**Scribes:** Yes
**Proctors:** Yes
**Oral exams:** Yes
**Extended test time:** Yes
**Added cost:** No
**Distraction-free environ.:** Yes
**Tape recording in class:** Yes
**Books on tape:** Yes
**Taping of other books:** Yes

**Professional tutors:** N/I
**Peer tutors:** N/I
**Max. hrs/wk for services:** 1 hour every two weeks on an average
**Priority registration:** Yes
**Accomodations for students with ADD:** Yes
**How are professors notified of LD:** By the student

# GENERAL ADMISSIONS INFORMATION

**Director of Admissions:** Keith White, Acting Director     **Telephone:** 608-262-3961

## ENTRANCE REQUIREMENTS

Total high school units required/recommended: 17 total units are required; 22 total units are recommended; 4 English required, 3 math required, 4 math recommended, 3 science required, 4 science recommended, 2 foreign language required, 4 foreign language recommended, 3 social studies required, 4 social studies recommended. Special requirements: An audition is required for music program applicants. TOEFL is required of all international students. Portfolio recommended of art program applicants.

**Application deadline:** February 1
**Notification:** Rolling

**SAT or ACT preferred:** Either
**SAT Avg:** 610V, 620M
**Average ACT:** 26
**Average GPA:** 3.7

**Graduated top 10% of class:** 43
**Graduated top 25% of class:** 85
**Graduated top 50% of class:** 99

# COLLEGE GRADUATION REQUIREMENTS

**Course waivers allowed:** No
**Course substitutions allowed:** Yes
**In what courses:** Foreign language

# ADDITIONAL INFORMATION

**Environment:** NR

**Student Body**
  **Undergrad enrollment:** 26,910
  **Women:** 51%
  **Men:** 49%
  **In-state students:** 70%
  **Out-of-state:** 30%

**Cost Information**
  **In-state tuition:** $2,881
  **Out-of-state:** $9,636
  **Room & board:** $3,829

**Housing Information**
  **University housing:** Yes
  **Fraternity:** Yes
  **Sorority:** Yes
  **Living on campus:** 7%

  **Athletics:** NCAA Div. I

# UNIVERSITY OF WISCONSIN-MILWAUKEE

P.O. Box 413, Milwaukee, WI 53201 • **Admissions:** 414-229-3800 • **Fax:** 414-229-6977
**Email:** admissions@uwm.edu • **Web:** www.uwm.edu
**Support:** CS • **Institution:** 4 yr. Public

## LEARNING DISABILITY ADMISSIONS AND SERVICES

The Learning Disabilities Program offers a wide range of support services. The goal of the program is to provide an environment that encourages the development of the unique talents of each student. This program is well suited for those who can function independently with some academic support. There is an emphasis on mainstreaming, and participation to the fullest extent in the total life of the university community. Services provided include taped textbooks, tutorial services, special arrangements for test taking, notetakers, communication with professors, monitoring, and priority registration.

## LEARNING DISABILITY ADMISSIONS INFORMATION

**Program Name:** Learning Disabilities Program
**Program Director:** Laurie Gramatzki                    **Telephone:** 414-229-6239
**Contact Person:** Same as above

### ADMISSIONS

Admission into UMW is necessary for participation in the LD Program. Students apply directly to the Admissions office. The LD Program does not make admission decisions. Students should send documentation to the LD Program, and once admitted to the university, the students will be contacted by the LD Program. The Director of the LD Program can assist students with the admission process, and can make informal recommendations to the admission office on an individual basis. Students not regularly admissible, who are serious about continuing their education, and show potential for university study, may apply through the Academic Opportunity Center (AOC) . Students should submit a UWM application; send transcripts; take AOC placement tests; submit ACT/SAT; and schedule an interview. Approximately 60-75 students submit applications yearly through AOC. There is no limit on the number of students who can be admitted through the AOC each year.

**College entrance exams required:** Yes                    **Untimed accepted:** Yes
**Course entrance requirements:** Yes                    **Interview required:** Recommended
**Diagnostic tests:** Yes
**Documentation:** WAIS-R; Woodcock Johnson; tests of achievement: within 3 years

### ADDITIONAL INFORMATION

Students who may not be regularly admissible based on low GPA, ACT, SAT or rank in class or who lack academic units, or those who would benefit from intensive advising, may want to apply directly to AOC on their UWM application. Students will need to take the AOC test series, including math, English, and the Nelson Denny Reading Test to identify which accommodations can be requested. Students must also have an interview with an advisor in the AOC. The AOC will evaluate the student's potential in making an admission decision. AOC offers intensive advising, basic skills courses, and additional academic support.

**Special education HS coursework accepted:** Yes          **Essay required:** No
**Special application required:** No                       **Submitted to:** N/A
**# of applications submitted each year:** N/A            **# of applications accepted each year:** N/A
**# of students receiving LD services:** 230
**Acceptance into program means acceptance into college:** Students are admitted to the university first and then may request services. Some students may apply directly through AOC.

**Learning center:** No
**Kurzweil personal reader:** Yes
**LD specialists:** 1
**Allowed in exams:**
  **Calculator:** Yes
  **Dictionary:** Yes
  **Computer:** Yes
  **SpellCheck:** Y/N

**Notetaker:** Yes
**Scribes:** Yes
**Proctors:** Yes
**Oral exams:** Y/N
**Extended test time:** Yes
**Added cost:** None
**Distraction-free environ.:** Yes
**Tape recording in class:** Yes
**Books on tape:** Yes
**Taping of other books:** Yes

**Professional tutors:** No
**Peer tutors:** Yes
**Max. hrs/wk for services:** 2-3 hours per/week
**Priority registration:** Yes
**Accomodations for students with ADD:** Yes
**How are professors notified of LD:** By the student and the Program Director

## GENERAL ADMISSIONS INFORMATION

**Director of Admissions:** Beth Weckmueller          **Telephone:** 414-229-6164

### ENTRANCE REQUIREMENTS

Total high school units required/recommended: 17 total units are required; 4 English required, 3 math required, 4 math recommended, 3 science required, 4 science recommended, 2 social studies required. Minimum ACT score of 21 and rank in top half of secondary school class required of in-state applicants; minimum ACT score of 21 (combined SAT I score of 920) and rank in top half of secondary school class required of out-of-state applicants. Special Requirements: An audition is required for music program applicants. TOEFL is required of all international students. 4 units each of math and English and 1 unit each of chemistry and physics recommended of applicants to College of Engineering and Applied Science.

**Application deadline:** June 30
**Notification:** Rolling

**SAT or ACT preferred:** ACT
**SAT II required:** Yes
**Average ACT:** 22

**Graduated top 10% of class:** 8
**Graduated top 25% of class:** 28
**Graduated top 50% of class:** 67

## COLLEGE GRADUATION REQUIREMENTS

**Course waivers allowed:** Yes
**Course substitutions allowed:** Yes
**In what courses:** Determined on an individual basis

## ADDITIONAL INFORMATION

**Environment:** The university is located on 90 acres in a residential area 90 miles north of Chicago.

**Student Body**
  **Undergrad enrollment:** 17,032
  **Women:** 52%
  **Men:** 48%
  **In-state students:** 97%
  **Out-of-state:** 3%

**Cost Information**
  **In-state tuition:** $3,102
  **Out-of-state:** $9,965
  **Room & board:** $4,040

**Housing Information**
  **University housing:** Yes
  **Fraternity:** Yes
  **Sorority:** No
  **Living on campus:** 11%

  **Athletics:** NCAA Div. I

# UNIVERSITY OF WISCONSIN-OSHKOSH

**WI**

Dempsey Hall 135, 800 Algoma Boulevard, Oshkosh, WI 54901 • **Admissions:** 920-424-0202
**Fax:** 920-424-1098 • **Email:** oshadmuw@uwosh.edu • **Web:** www.uwosh.edu
**Support:** SP • **Institution:** 4 yr. Public

## LEARNING DISABILITY ADMISSIONS AND SERVICES

Project Success (PS) is a language remediation project that is based on mastering the entire sound structure of the English language. These students are academically able and determined to succeed, in spite of a pronounced problem in a number of areas. Help is offered in the following ways: by direct remediation of deficiencies through the Orton-Gillingham Technique; one-to-one tutoring assistance; math and writing labs; guidance and counseling with scheduling course work and interpersonal relations; untimed exams; and by providing an atmosphere that is supportive. The goal is for students to become language independent in and across all of these major educational areas: math, spelling, reading, writing, comprehension and study skills. As full-time university students they will acquire language independence by mastering the entire phonemic structure of the American English language.

## LEARNING DISABILITY ADMISSIONS INFORMATION

**Program Name:** Project Success
**Program Director:** Dr. Robert T. Nash
**Contact Person:** Same as above
**Telephone:** 414-424-1033

### ADMISSIONS

Students should apply to Project Success in their sophomore year of high school. Applicants apply by writing a letter, in their own handwriting, indicating interest in the Program and why they are interested. Applications are processed on a first-come, first-served basis. Those interested should apply at least 2-3 years prior to desired entrance. Students and parents will be invited to interview. The interview is used to assess family dynamics in terms of support for the student, and reasons for wanting to attend college. The Director is looking for motivation, stability and the ability of the students to describe the disability. Acceptance into Project Success does not grant acceptance into the university. Admission to the university and acceptance into Project Success is a joint decision but a separate process is required for each. General admissions procedures must be followed before acceptance into the special program can be offered. ACT/SAT or GPA are not critical. Accepted students for Project Success are required to register for a summer term prior to freshman year.

**College entrance exams required:** Yes
**Course entrance requirements:** Yes
**Diagnostic tests:** Yes
**Documentation:** Testing done by Program Director at Project Success

**Untimed accepted:** Yes
**Interview required:** Yes

### ADDITIONAL INFORMATION

Incoming freshmen to Project Success must participate in an 8-week summer school program consisting of simultaneous multi-sensory instructional procedures (SMSIP). This procedure is used to teach study skills, reading, spelling, writing, and mathematical operations. Students are eligible for tutoring services and untimed testing opportunities. Services and accommodations are available for undergraduate and graduate students.

**Special education HS coursework accepted:** Yes
**Essay required:** No, just a letter expressing interest in program
**Special application required:** Yes
**# of applications submitted each year:** 60-75
**# of students receiving LD services:** 200-225
**Submitted to:** Director of Program
**# of applications accepted each year:** 54-60
**Acceptance into program means acceptance into college:** Students are accepted jointly to Project Success and the university; however, they must submit separate applications for the program and the university.

## LEARNING DISABILITY SERVICES

Learning center: Yes
Kurzweil personal reader: No
LD specialists: 3
Allowed in exams:
  Calculator: Yes
  Dictionary: Yes
  Computer: Yes
  SpellCheck: No

Notetaker: No
Scribes: No
Proctors: Yes
Oral exams: No
Extended test time: Yes
Added cost: None
Distraction-free environ.: Yes
Tape recording in class: Yes
Books on tape: No
Taping of other books: No

Professional tutors: 3
Peer tutors: 36
Max. hrs/wk for services: 5 hrs. for individual; unlimited group
Priority registration: No
Accomodations for students with ADD: Yes
How are professors notified of LD: By the student and the Director

## GENERAL ADMISSIONS INFORMATION

Director of Admissions: August Helgerson          Telephone: 414-424-0202

### ENTRANCE REQUIREMENTS

Total high school units required/recommended: 17 total units are required; 4 English required, 3 math required, 3 science required, 3 social studies required. Minimum composite ACT score of 23 required or rank in top 1/2 of secondary school class required. Special requirements: An audition is required for music program applicants.

Application deadline: August 1
Notification: Rolling

SAT or ACT preferred: ACT
SAT II required: Yes
ACT required: Yes
Average ACT: 22

Graduated top 10% of class: 11
Graduated top 25% of class: 34
Graduated top 50% of class: 85

## COLLEGE GRADUATION REQUIREMENTS

Course waivers allowed: Yes
Course substitutions allowed: Yes
In what courses: As it relates to the foreign language requirement, UW-Oshkosh has special accommodations in place.

## ADDITIONAL INFORMATION

Environment: The campus is located 3 hours north of Chicago and 2 hours northeast of Madison.

Student Body
  Undergrad enrollment: 8,751
  Women: 57%
  Men: 43%
  In-state students: 96%
  Out-of-state: 4%

Cost Information
  In-state tuition: $2,550
  Out-of-state: $8,320
  Room & board: $2,658

Housing Information
  University housing: Yes
  Fraternity: Yes
  Sorority: Yes
  Living on campus: 35%

  Athletics: NCAA Div. III

# UNIVERSITY OF WISCONSIN-STEVENS POINT

WI

Main Street, Stevens Point, WI 54481 • **Admissions:** 715-346-2441 • **Fax:** 715-346-2558
**Email:** admiss@uwsp.edu • **Web:** www.uwsp.edu
**Support:** CS • **Institution:** 4 yr. Public

## LEARNING DISABILITY ADMISSIONS AND SERVICES

The university does not have a formal program or a specialized curriculum for students with LD; rather provides all of the services appropriate to ensure equal access to all programs. Their philosophy is to provide what is mandated in order to enhance the student's academic success, and also, to convey their concern for the student's total well-being. The Director is a strong advocate for students. Students are encouraged to meet with the Director prior to admissions for information about the services. A full range of accommodations are provided. The services provide a multisensory approach developing compensatory skills, not remediation; and utilize a developmental model for advising as well as psychosocial adjustment. Student success is contingent on many factors; some responsibilities belong to the student, others belong the university, and others are shared by both. Students should make an appointment at the beginning of each semester; should not miss appointments; register with RFB for taped texts; make their needs known; be a self-advocate. The Office of Disability Services (ODS) provides students with accommodations that are appropriate for the disability. Together, ODS and the student can work toward effective accommodations and utilization of support services and establish a working relationship based on trust and communication.

## LEARNING DISABILITY ADMISSIONS INFORMATION

**Program Name:** Office of Disability Services
**Program Director:** John Timcak
**Contact Person:** Same as above

**Telephone:** 715-346-3365

### ADMISSIONS

There is no separate admission procedure for students with learning disabilities. However, students are encouraged to make a pre-admission inquiry and talk to the Director of Disability Services. Students with learning disabilities who do not meet the combined class rank and ACT test score criteria of 64 should send a letter of recommendation from the high school LD specialist or counselor. Students should also meet with the Director of Disabled Student Services at Stevens Point if support is needed in the application process. The Director of Admission does have the flexibility to admit students with learning disabilities on a case-by-case basis.

**College entrance exams required:** Yes
**Course entrance requirements:** Yes
**Diagnostic tests:** Yes
**Documentation:** WAIS-R; W-J; Bender, etc.: as appropriate

**Untimed accepted:** Yes
**Interview required:** Recommended

### ADDITIONAL INFORMATION

ODS provides: accommodations that are appropriate to the disability, orientation assistance, taped textbooks, notetakers, proctors and scribes, adaptive testing, priority registration, assistance with life skills and advising, referral to tutoring and writing assistance, time management and study strategies training, notification to faculty/staff regarding necessary accommodations, assessment and referral services for those not yet diagnosed, and a commitment to keeping scheduled appointments and a corresponding commitment to being timely. The Tutoring-Learning Center schedules 30-minute tutoring sessions and small-group tutoring; tutoring is free for students wanting help with reading or writing assignments. Tutoring in subject areas is done in groups and there is a $10 enrollment fee; however, for most students, the fee is covered by various support programs.

**Special education HS coursework accepted:** No
**Special application required:** No
**# of applications submitted each year:** N/A
**# of students receiving LD services:** 150

**Essay required:** No
**Submitted to:** N/A
**# of applications accepted each year:** N/A

**Acceptance into program means acceptance into college:** Students must be admitted to the university first and then may request services.

## LEARNING DISABILITY SERVICES

**Learning center:** Yes
**Kurzweil personal reader:** No
**LD specialists:** Yes
**Allowed in exams:**
  **Calculator:** Yes
  **Dictionary:** Yes
  **Computer:** Yes
  **SpellCheck:** Yes

**Notetaker:** Yes
**Scribes:** Yes
**Proctors:** Yes
**Oral exams:** Yes
**Extended test time:** Yes
**Added cost:** None
**Distraction-free environ.:** Yes
**Tape recording in class:** Yes
**Books on tape:** Yes
**Taping of other books:** Yes

**Professional tutors:** Yes
**Peer tutors:** Yes
**Max. hrs/wk for services:** 2
hours per/class
**Priority registration:** Yes
**Accomodations for students
with ADD:** Yes
**How are professors notified of
LD:** By the student and the
Program Director

## GENERAL ADMISSIONS INFORMATION

**Director of Admissions:** John Larsen **Telephone:** 715-346-2441

### ENTRANCE REQUIREMENTS

Total high school units required/recommended: 17 total units are required; 4 English required, 3 math required, 3 science required, 3 social studies required. Minimum composite ACT score of 24 or secondary school rank in the 65th percentile required. Special requirements: TOEFL is required of all international students. Minimum 2.5 GPA required of applicants to professional studies programs in School of Education and of applicants to Divisions of Business and Economics, Biology, and Medical Technology. Minimum 2.75 GPA required of paper science and communicative disorders program applicants.

**Application deadline:** Rolling
**Notification:** Rolling

**SAT or ACT preferred:** NR
**SAT II required:** Yes
**ACT required:** Yes
**Average ACT:** 22

**Graduated top 10% of class:** 12
**Graduated top 25% of class:** 43
**Graduated top 50% of class:** 87

## COLLEGE GRADUATION REQUIREMENTS

**Course waivers allowed:** Yes
**Course substitutions allowed:** Yes
**In what courses:** On a case-by-case basis if not essential for the major.

## ADDITIONAL INFORMATION

**Environment:** The University of Wisconsin at Stevens Point is located on 335 acres 110 miles north of Madison.

**Student Body**
  **Undergrad enrollment:** 8,024
  **Women:** 53%
  **Men:** 47%
  **In-state students:** 92%
  **Out-of-state:** 8%

**Cost Information**
  **In-state tuition:** $2,650
  **Out-of-state:** $8,400
  **Room & board:** $3,260

**Housing Information**
  **University housing:** Yes
  **Fraternity:** Yes
  **Sorority:** Yes
  **Living on campus:** 39%

  **Athletics:** NCAA Div. III

# UNIVERSITY OF WISCONSIN-WHITEWATER

WI

800 West Main Street, Whitewater, WI 53190 • **Admissions:** 414-472-1234 • **Fax:** 414-472-1515
**Email:** uwwadmit@uwwvax.uww.edu • **Web:** www.uww.edu
**Support:** CS • **Institution:** 4 yr. Public

## LEARNING DISABILITY ADMISSIONS AND SERVICES

The University of Wisconsin-Whitewater offers support services for students with learning disabilities including tutoring, teaching strategies for long term success, test-taking accommodations, and notetakers.

## LEARNING DISABILITY ADMISSIONS INFORMATION

**Program Name:** Project ASSIST
**Program Director:** Deb Hall
**Contact Person:** Same as above

**Telephone:** 414-472-5239
**Telephone:** 414-472-4788

### ADMISSIONS

All applicants must meet the same criteria for admission. General criteria include: ACT 18 or a lower ACT if the student is in the top 50% of the class. Students apply to the University Admissions first, after a decision is made to admit or deny, the Director of Project ASSIST reviews the file to decided whether to make an exception for admission or whether the student may use services. If the Director needs to make an exception for admissions, then the Summer Transition program is required and students receive 2 years of support. Summer Transition Program is only offered to students with learning disabilities.

**College entrance exams required:** Yes
**Course entrance requirements:** Yes
**Diagnostic tests:** Yes
**Documentation:** WAIS-R; W-J: within 3 years

**Untimed accepted:** Yes
**Interview required:** Yes

### ADDITIONAL INFORMATION

Students may have LD assessments on campus for $250. Skills courses are offered for no credit in reading comprehension and writing.

**Special education HS coursework accepted:** N/I
**Special application required:** Yes
**# of applications submitted each year:** N/I
**# of students receiving LD services:** 150

**Essay required:** No
**Submitted to:** Project ASSIST
**# of applications accepted each year:** 150

**Acceptance into program means acceptance into college:** Students must be admitted to the university and then request services. Project ASSIST reviews some applications and makes recommendations to admissions.

# LEARNING DISABILITY SERVICES

**Learning center:** Yes
**Kurzweil personal reader:** No
**LD specialists:** Yes
**Allowed in exams:**
  **Calculator:** Y/N
  **Dictionary:** Yes
  **Computer:** Yes
  **SpellCheck:** Yes

**Notetaker:** Yes
**Scribes:** Yes
**Proctors:** Yes
**Oral exams:** Y/N
**Extended test time:** Yes
**Added cost:** Depends on one-to-one support
**Distraction-free environ.:** Yes
**Tape recording in class:** Yes
**Books on tape:** RFB
**Taping of other books:** Yes

**Professional tutors:** 2
**Peer tutors:** 40
**Max. hrs/wk for services:** Unlimited
**Priority registration:** No
**Accomodations for students with ADD:** Yes
**How are professors notified of LD:** By the student

# GENERAL ADMISSIONS INFORMATION

**Director of Admissions:** Ion Sherman

**Telephone:** 414-472-1440

## ENTRANCE REQUIREMENTS

Total high school units required/recommended: 16 total units are required; 4 English required, 3 math required, 3 science required, 3 social studies required. Secondary school rank in top 1/2 required; minimum composite ACT score of 20 recommended. Special requirements: An audition is required for music program applicants. TOEFL is required of all international students.

**Application deadline:** Rolling
**Notification:** Rolling

**SAT or ACT preferred:** ACT
**SAT II required:** Yes
**Average ACT:** 22

**Graduated top 10% of class:** 11
**Graduated top 25% of class:** 35
**Graduated top 50% of class:** 83

# COLLEGE GRADUATION REQUIREMENTS

**Course waivers allowed:** No
**Course substitutions allowed:** No
**In what courses:** N/A

# ADDITIONAL INFORMATION

**Environment:** NR

**Student Body**
  **Undergrad enrollment:** 9,157
  **Women:** 54%
  **Men:** 46%
  **In-state students:** 93%
  **Out-of-state:** 7%

**Cost Information**
  **In-state tuition:** $2,560
  **Out-of-state:** $7,920
  **Room & board:** $2,700

**Housing Information**
  **University housing:** Yes
  **Fraternity:** Yes
  **Sorority:** Yes
  **Living on campus:** 45%

  **Athletics:** NCAA Div. III

# WY
## SHERIDAN COLLEGE

Sheridan, WY 82801
307-674-6446
**Support:** S • **Institution:** 2 yr. Public

## LEARNING DISABILITY ADMISSIONS AND SERVICES

Sheridan College has limited services available for students with learning disabilities. Students who have been enrolled in Special Education classes in high school may find that the college does not have the extensive services necessary for them to be successful. Students need to be self sufficient, because only a small percentage of the time of the 2 advisor/counselors is available to work with students with disabilities. Students requesting accommodations must provide psychoeducational evaluations and have these sent to the Counseling/Testing Offices. The college reserves the right to evaluate whether it can serve the needs of students.

## LEARNING DISABILITY ADMISSIONS INFORMATION

**Program Name:** Learning Center
**Program Director:** Norma Campbell
**Contact Person:** Marilyn Davidson

**Telephone:** 307-674-6446

### ADMISSIONS

There are no special admission procedures or criteria for students with learning disabilities. The college has open admissions and any student with a high school diploma or the GED is eligible to attend. All students are treated the same and must submit the general college application for admission. Any information on learning disabilities provided is voluntarily given by the student. Students with learning disabilities must submit psychoeducational evaluations, and Sheridan has an educational Diagnostician to test a limited number of referrals. The admission decision is made by the Director of the Program.

**College entrance exams required:** No
**Course entrance requirements:** N/I
**Diagnostic tests:** Yes
**Documentation:** Psycho-educational evaluation: within 3 years

**Untimed accepted:** N/A
**Interview required:** No

### ADDITIONAL INFORMATION

The college also offers tutoring, quiet places to take tests, readers, extended testing time, recorder, notetakers, and the availability of a few Franklin Spellers. Remediation courses are offered in arithmetic skills, spelling, vocabulary, reading, writing, and algebra. Other aids for students with learning disabilities include test taking strategies, books on tape, tutoring one-on-one or small groups in the Learning Center, and GED preparation and testing. Support services include career testing and evaluation, peer counseling, personal and career development.

**Special education HS coursework accepted:** N/I
**Special application required:** No
**# of applications submitted each year:** No
**# of students receiving LD services:** N/A
**Acceptance into program means acceptance into college:** Students must be admitted to the college and then reviewed for LD services.

**Essay required:** No
**Submitted to:** N/A
**# of applications accepted each year:** N/A

**Learning center:** No
**Kurzweil personal reader:** No
**LD specialists:** No
**Allowed in exams:**
  **Calculator:** Yes
  **Dictionary:** Yes
  **Computer:** Yes
  **SpellCheck:** Yes

**Notetaker:** No
**Scribes:** No
**Proctors:** Yes
**Oral exams:** Yes
**Extended test time:** Yes
**Added cost:** None
**Distraction-free environ.:** Yes
**Tape recording in class:** Yes
**Books on tape:** Yes
**Taping of other books:** Yes

**Professional tutors:** Yes
**Peer tutors:** Yes
**Max. hrs/wk for services:** N/I
**Priority registration:** Yes
**Accomodations for students with ADD:** Yes
**How are professors notified of LD:** By the student and the Program Director

## GENERAL ADMISSIONS INFORMATION

**Director of Admissions:** Ken Carlson

**Telephone:** 307-674-6446

**ENTRANCE REQUIREMENTS**

NR

**Application deadline:** NR
**Notification:** NR

**SAT or ACT preferred:** NR

## COLLEGE GRADUATION REQUIREMENTS

**Course waivers allowed:** No
**Course substitutions allowed:** No
**In what courses:** N/A

## ADDITIONAL INFORMATION

**Environment:** The college is located on 64 acres.

**Student Body**
  **Undergrad enrollment:** 2,998
  **Women:** 59%
  **Men:** 41%
  **In-state students:** 94%
  **Out-of-state:** 6%

**Cost Information**
  **In-state tuition:** $690
  **Out-of-state:** $1,872

**Housing Information**
  **University housing:** Yes
  **Fraternity:** No
  **Sorority:** No
  **Living on campus:** 5%

  **Athletics:** NJCAA

# UNIVERSITY OF WYOMING

**WY**

Admissions Office, Box 3435, Laramie, WY 82071 • **Admissions:** 307-766-5160 • **Fax:** 307-766-2606
**Email:** undergraduate.admission@uwyo.edu • **Web:** www.uwyo.edu
**Support:** S • **Institution:** 4 yr. Public

## LEARNING DISABILITY ADMISSIONS AND SERVICES

The University Disability Support Services (UDSS) offers academic support services to students with LD and physically handicapped students. The goals are to promote the independence and self-sufficiency of students, and to encourage the provision of equal opportunities in education for students with disabilities. Any student enrolled at UW who has a documented disability is eligible for assistance. UDSS provides disability-related accommodations and services, technical assistance, consultations, and resource information. Recommended documentation includes: a clear statement of the LD (documentation should be current, preferably within the last 3 years); a summary of assessment procedures and evaluation instruments used to make the diagnosis and a summary of the results, including standardized or percentile score which support the diagnosis (LD testing must be comprehensive, including a measure of both aptitude and achievement in the areas of reading, mathematics and written language); a statement of strengths and needs that will impact the student's ability to meet the demands of college; and suggestions of reasonable accommodations which might be appropriate. Accommodations are collaboratively determined by the student and the assigned Disability Support Service Coordinator.

## LEARNING DISABILITY ADMISSIONS INFORMATION

**Program Name:** University Disability Support Services
**Program Director:** Chris Primus          **Telephone:** 307-766-6189
**Contact Person:** Same as above

### ADMISSIONS

Students with learning disabilities must meet general admission requirements. If the students are borderline and have a documented learning disability, they are encouraged to self-identify to the Director. Students who were diagnosed late in high school or began utilizing services late may be able to explain how this had an impact on academics. Students with learning disabilities who meet the general admission criteria request LD services after being admitted. Conditional admission is granted with GPA of 2.5 or GPA 2.25 and 20 ACT or SAT of 960. Students with learning disabilities not meeting admission criteria and not qualifying for assured or conditional admission may have their applications reviewed by the LD Program director. The LD Director will make a recommendation to the Office of Admission.

**College entrance exams required:** Yes     **Untimed accepted:** Yes
**Course entrance requirements:** Yes       **Interview required:** No
**Diagnostic tests:** Yes
**Documentation:** A record of a learning disability administered by qualified specialist

### ADDITIONAL INFORMATION

Services include priority registration, readers, assistance with study skills, notetaking, test preparation, word processing orientation; equipment loan assistance, tutor referral, and advocacy for students via University Committee on Campus Access for the Disabled. Auditory systems are also used to provide access to print mediums for persons with LD. Synthesized speech reinforces visual cues; grammar checking software is available to proof documents and to improve writing skills; writing skills may be improved through the use of word prediction software; Dragon Dictate, a voice recognition program, may benefit those students who have learning disabilities that affect written expression. All students must take 1 course in math or quantitative reasoning to graduate.

**Special education HS coursework accepted:** Yes     **Essay required:** No
**Special application required:** Yes                 **Submitted to:** Program Director
**# of applications submitted each year:** N/I         **# of applications accepted each year:** No limit
**# of students receiving LD services:** 90
**Acceptance into program means acceptance into college:** Students must be admitted to the university first and then may apply for services.

**Learning center:** Yes
**Kurzweil personal reader:** Yes
**LD specialists:** No
**Allowed in exams:**
  **Calculator:** Yes
  **Dictionary:** Yes
  **Computer:** Yes
  **SpellCheck:** Yes

**Notetaker:** Yes
**Scribes:** Yes
**Proctors:** Yes
**Oral exams:** Yes
**Extended test time:** Yes
**Added cost:** No
**Distraction-free environ.:** Yes
**Tape recording in class:** Yes
**Books on tape:** Yes
**Taping of other books:** Yes

**Professional tutors:** Yes
**Peer tutors:** Yes
**Max. hrs/wk for services:** As available
**Priority registration:** Yes
**Accomodations for students with ADD:** Yes
**How are professors notified of LD:** By the student and the Program Director

## GENERAL ADMISSIONS INFORMATION

**Director of Admissions:** James Mansfield

**Telephone:** 307-766-5160

### ENTRANCE REQUIREMENTS

Total high school units required/recommended: 18 total units are recommended; 4 English recommended, 3 math recommended, 3 science recommended, 3 social studies recommended, 1 art or music recommended, 1 speech recommended, 1 computer science recommended, 2 foreign language recommended. Minimum composite ACT score of 19 and minimum 2.5 GPA recommended.

**Application deadline:** August 10
**Notification:** Rolling

**SAT or ACT preferred:** ACT
**Average ACT:** 24
**Average GPA:** 3.4

**Graduated top 10% of class:** 27
**Graduated top 25% of class:** 53
**Graduated top 50% of class:** 82

## COLLEGE GRADUATION REQUIREMENTS

**Course waivers allowed:** No
**Course substitutions allowed:** Yes
**In what courses:** Substitutions are possible for foreign language and some math course requirements.

## ADDITIONAL INFORMATION

**Environment:** The University is located on 785 acres in a small town 128 miles north of Denver.

**Student Body**
  **Undergrad enrollment:** 8,820
  **Women:** 52%
  **Men:** 48%
  **In-state students:** 73%
  **Out-of-state:** 27%

**Cost Information**
  **In-state tuition:** $2,326
  **Out-of-state:** $7,414
  **Room & board:** $4,245

**Housing Information**
  **University housing:** Yes
  **Fraternity:** Yes
  **Sorority:** Yes
  **Living on campus:** 33%

  **Athletics:** NCAA Div. I

# QUICK CONTACT REFERENCE LIST

## ALABAMA

| Institution | City/State/Zip | Contact | Service | Phone |
|---|---|---|---|---|
| Auburn U. | Auburn U., AL 36849 | Kelly Haynes | Prog. for Auburn Stud. with Disabilities | 205-884-2096 |
| Auburn U. | Montgomery, AL 36117 | Nancy McDaniel | Special Services | 334-244-3468 |
| Gadsden State CC | Gadsden, AL 35999 | Joan Williamson | Student Services | 205-549-8271 |
| Jacksonville State U. | Jacksonville, AL 36265 | Daniel Miller | Disabled Student Services | 205-782-5093 |
| Samford U. | Birmingham, AL 35229 | Dr. Richard Franklin | #504 Compliance | 205-870-2901 |
| U. of Alabama | Birmingham, AL 35294 | Larie Ross-Hunter | Handicapped Student Services | 205-934-4205 |
| U. of Alabama | Huntsville, AL 35899 | Delois Smith | Student Development Services | 205-890-6203 |
| U. of Alabama | Tuscaloosa, AL 35487-0304 | Pat Friend-Nesmith | Disability Services | 205-348-4285 |
| U. of S. Alabama | Mobile, AL 36688 | Bernita Pulmas | Special Student Services | 334-460-7212 |
| U. of Montevallo | Montevallo, AL 35115 | Deborah McCune | Serv. for Students with Disabilities | 205-665-6250 |

## ALASKA

| Institution | City/State/Zip | Contact | Service | Phone |
|---|---|---|---|---|
| SheldonJackson C. | Sitka, AK 99835 | Alice Zellhuber | Learning Assistance Program | 907-747-5235 |
| U. of Alaska | Anchorage, AK 99508 | Lyn Stoller | Disability Support Services | 907-786-4530 |
| U. of Alaska | Fairbanks, AK 99775 | Diane Preston | Services for Students with Disabilities | 907-474-5655 |

## ARIZONA

| Institution | City/State/Zip | Contact | Service | Phone |
|---|---|---|---|---|
| Arizona State U. | Tempe, AZ 85287-3202 | Deb Taska | Disability Resources for Students | 602-965-6484 |
| Coconino CC | Flagstaff, AZ 86004 | Larisa McClung | Disability Resource | 520-527-1222 |
| Gateway CC | Phoenix, AZ 85034 | Esther Schon | Special Services | 602-392-5049 |
| Mesa C. C. | Mesa, AZ 85202 | Judith Taussig | Student Special Services | 602-461-7449 |
| N. Arizona U. | Flagstaff, AZ 86011-6045 | Karen Wise | Disability Support Services | 520-523-7252 |
| Pima C. C | Tucson, AZ 85702 | Dr. Patricia Richard | Disabled Student Resources | 520-884-6986 |
| Phoenix C. | Phoenix, AZ 85013 | Ginny Bugh | Special Services | 602-285-7477 |
| U. of Arizona | Tucson, AZ 85721 | Diane Perreira | SALT | 520-621-1427 |

## ARKANSAS

| Institution | City/State/Zip | Contact | Service | Phone |
|---|---|---|---|---|
| Arkansas State U. | State Univ., AR 72467 | Jennifer Rice-Mason | Disability Services | 501-972-3964 |
| Harding U. | Searcy, AR 72149-0001 | Dr. Linda Thompson | Student Support Services | 501-279-4416 |
| Henderson St. U. | Arkadelphia, AR 71999 | Vickie Faust | Project Connect | 501-230-5251 |
| NW Arkansas CC. | Bentonville, AR 72712 | Betty Hopper | Disability Service | 501-636-7202 |
| S. Arkansas U. | Magnolia, AR 71753 | Paula Washinton-Woods | Student Disability Special Services | 501-235-4145 |
| U. of Arkansas | Fayetteville, AR 72701 | Dr. Riqua Serebreni | Office for Campus Access | 501-575-3104 |
| U. of Arkansas | Little Rock, AR 72204 | Susan Queller | Support Services | 501-569-3143 |
| U. of Arkansas | Pine Bluff, AR 71511 | Steve Smith | Disability Services | 501-543-8512 |
| U. of Central Arkansas | Conway, AR 72035 | Daryl McGee | Support Services | 501-450-3135 |
| U. of the Ozarks | Clarksville, AR 72830 | Julia Frost | Jones Learning Center Program | 501-979-1401 |

# CALIFORNIA

| College | Location | Contact | Service | Phone |
|---|---|---|---|---|
| Bakersfield C. | Bakersfield, CA 93311 | Joyce Kirst | Support Services Program | 805-395-4520 |
| Biola U. | LaMirada, CA 90639 | DeAnn Decker | Services to the Disabled | 310-903-4874 |
| Butte Community C. | Oroville, CA 95965 | Richard Dunn | Services for Students with Disabilities | 916-895-2455 |
| Cabrillo C. | Aptos, CA 95003 | Deborah Shulman | Learning Skills Program | 408-479-6220 |
| Cabrillo College | Santa Cruz, CA 95060 | Richard Griffiths | Disabled Student Services | 408-479-6220 |
| Calif. Poly. State U. | San Luis Obispo, CA 93407 | William Bailey | Disabled Student Services | 805-756-1395 |
| Calif. State.Poly U. | Pomona, CA 91768 | Jane Mathis-Lowe | Disabled Student Services | 909-869-3270 |
| California State U. | Bakersfield, CA 93311 | Tim Bohan | Services for Students with Disabilities | 805-664-3360 |
| California State U. | Chico, CA 95929 | Ed Daniels | Disabled Student Services | 916-898-5959 |
| California State U. | Fullerton, CA 92634 | Debra Fletcher | Counseling & LD Services | 714-773-3117 |
| California State U. | Hayward, CA 94563 | Beth Darrow | Disabled Student Services | 510-254-6854 |
| California State U. | Long Beach, CA 90840 | David Sanfilippo | Disabled Student Services | 310-985-5401 |
| California State U. | Northridge, CA 91330 | Drs.L.Axelrod/J.Zui | Office of Disability Student Services | 818-885-2684 |
| California State U. | Sacramento, CA 95819 | Patricia Sonntag | Services to Students with Disabilities | 916-278-7821 |
| California State U. | San Bernardino, CA 92407 | Barbara Sovereign | Learning Disabilities Program | 909-880-5239 |
| California State U. | San Marcos, CA 92096 | Cynthia Moore | Disabled Student Services | 310-750-4800 |
| California State U. | Turlock, CA 95382 | Lee Bettencourt | Disabled Student Services | 209-667-3159 |
| Cerritos Comm. C. | Norwalk, CA 90650 | Bob Hughlett | DSPS | 310-860-2451 |
| Chapman U. | Orange, CA 92666 | Violet Champa | Academic Support Services | 714-744-7055 |
| Citrus Community C. | Glendora, CA 91741 | Judy Wong-Henmi | Disabled Student Program | 818-914-8677 |
| City C. San Francisco | Orinda, CA 94563 | K. Kerr-Schochet | Disabled Studdent Services | 415-452-5565 |
| College of Redwoods | Crescent Cty, CA 95531 | Sandra Nightingale | Disabled Student Spec. | 707-464-7457 |
| Columbia Comm. C. | Sonora, CA 95370 | Suzanne Patterson | Disabled Student Programs & Services | 209-588-5133 |
| Cuesta College | San Luis Obispo, CA 93403 | Dr. Lynn Frady | Learning Skills/Disab. Student Services | 805-546-3148 |
| De Anza C. | Sunnyvale, CA 94087 | Marilyn Rosenthal | Educational Diagnostic Center | 408-864-8472 |
| E. Los Angeles C. | Monterey Pk, CA 90025 | Therese Demir | DSPNS | 213-265-8745 |
| El Camino C. | Torrance, CA 90506 | Lucinda Aborn | Special Resource Center | 310-660-3296 |
| Foothill C. | Los Altos, CA 94022 | Charlene Maltzman | STEP | 415-949-7619 |
| Grossmont C. | Ramona, CA 92065 | Mary Paschke | LD Services | 619-789-9706 |
| Humboldt State U. | Arcata, CA 95521 | Theresa Jordan | Disabled Student Services | 707-826-4678 |
| John F. Kennedy U. | Orinda, CA 94563 | Lois Jones-Rasberry | Student Services | 510-253-4317 |
| Kings River Comm. C. | Reedley, CA 93654 | Lynn Mancini | Disabled Student Services | 209-638-0332 |
| Lake Tahoe CC | S. Lake Tahoe, CA 96150 | Kathleen Conway | Disabled Student Programs & Serv. | 916-541-4660 |
| Laney C. | El Sobrante, CA 94803 | Carol Dalissio | Disabled Student Programs & Serv. | 510-464-3432 |
| Long Beach City C. | Long Beach, CA 90808 | Mark Matsui | Disabled Student Program & Services | 310-938-4548 |
| Los Angeles City C. | Los Angeles, CA 90039 | Susan Matranga | LD Services | 213-662-1299 |
| Loyola Marymount U. | Los Angeles, CA 90045 | Joanna Boval | Disabled Student Services | 310-338-4535 |
| Master's College | Newhall, CA 91322 | Donna Hall | National Institute of Learning Disabilities | 805-259-3082 |

| Institution | City/State | Contact | Office/Program | Phone |
|---|---|---|---|---|
| Menlo C. | Atherton, CA 94027 | Kathryn Lanson | Academic Success | 415-688-3854 |
| Occidental College | Los Angeles, CA 90041 | Rae McCormick | Center for Teaching | 213-259-2545 |
| Oxnard College | Oxnard, CA 93033 | Ellen Young | Disabled Student Program & Services | 805-986-5830 |
| Pasadena City C. | Pasadena, CA 91106 | Bianca Richards | Disabled Students Programs & Serv. | 818-585-7127 |
| Saddleback C. | Carlsbad, CA 92008 | Randy Anderson | Special Services | 714-582-4750 |
| San Diego City C. | San Diego, CA 92101 | Helen Elias | Disabled Student Program & Serv. | 619-230-2513 |
| San Diego State U. | San Diego, CA 92182 | Dr. Frank Siehien | Disabled Student Services | 619-514-6473 |
| San Francisco State U. | San Francisco, CA 94132 | Deidre Defreese | Disability Resource Center | 415-338-6356 |
| San Jose State | San Jose, CA 95192 | Martin Schulter | Disability Resource Center | 408-924-6000 |
| Santa Barbara City C. | Santa Barbara, CA 93109 | Janet Shapiro | Disabled Student Services | 805-965-0581 |
| Santa Clara U. | Santa Clara, CA 95053 | Ramon Chacon | Disabled Student Resources | 408-554-4109 |
| Santa Monica C. | Santa Monica, CA 90405 | Ann Maddox | Learning Specialist Program | 213-452-9265 |
| Santa Rosa Jr. C. | Santa Rosa, CA 95401 | Pattie Wegman | Disability Resource Department | 707-527-4906 |
| Sierra C. | Rocklin, CA 95677 | Denise Stone | Learning Opportunities Ctr. | 916-789-2697 |
| Sonoma State U. | Rohnert Park, CA 94928 | Anthony Tusler | Disability Resource Center | 707-664-2166 |
| Stanford U. | Palo Alto, CA 94305 | Joan Bisajano | Disability Resource Center | 415-723-1066 |
| Taft College | Taft, CA 93268 | Jeff Ross | Disabled Student Services | 805-763-4282 |
| U. of California | Berkeley, CA 94720 | Connie Chiba | Disabled Students Program | 510-642-0518 |
| U. of California | Davis, CA 95616 | Christine O'Dell | Disability Resource Center | 916-752-2971 |
| U. of California | Irvine, CA 92697 | Dr. Ron Blosser | Disability Services | 714-824-7494 |
| U. of California | Los Angeles, CA 90024 | Arline Halpaer | UCLA LD Program | 310-825-1501 |
| U. of California | Riverside, CA 92521 | Marcia Schiffer | Disabled Student Services | 714-787-4538 |
| U. of California | La Jolla, CA 92093 | Roberta Gimblett | Disabled Student Services | 619-534-3160 |
| U. of California | Riverside, CA 92521 | Marcia Schiffer | Disabled Student Services | 909-787-4538 |
| U. of California | Santa Barbara, CA 93106 | Diane Glenn | Disabled Student Services | 805-893-2182 |
| U. of California | Santa Cruz, CA 95064 | Margaret Keith | Disabled Student Services | 408-459-2089 |
| U. of the Pacific | Stockton, CA 95211 | Howard Houck | Learning Disability Support Service | 209-946-3219 |
| U. of Redlands | Redlands, CA 92373 | Judy Bowman | Academic Support Service | 909-335-4079 |
| U. of San Diego | San Diego, CA 92110 | Kken Chep | Counseling Center | 619-260-4674 |
| U. of San Francisco | San Francisco, CA 94117 | Cally Salzman | Services For Students with LD | 415-666-6876 |
| U. of Southern Calif. | Los Angeles, CA 90089 | Janet Ewart Eddy | Learning Disabilities Support Services | 213-740-0776 |
| Whittier College | Whittier, CA 90608 | Gail Harris | Learning Support Services | 310-907-4840 |

## COLORADO

| Institution | City/State | Contact | Office/Program | Phone |
|---|---|---|---|---|
| Colorado Mt. C. | Glenwood Spr., CO 81601 | Shirley Bowen | Developmental Education | 303-945-8691 |
| Colo. Sch.of Mines | Golden, CO 80401 | Ron Brummett | Student Development & Career Center | 303-273-3357 |
| Colorado State U. | Fort Collins, CO 80523 | Rosemary Kreston | Office of Disabled Student Services | 970-491-6385 |
| Fort Lewis C. | Durango, CO 81301 | Robert Lundquist | Learning Assistance Center | 970-247-7383 |
| Mesa State C. | Grand Junction, CO 81501 | Sandra Wymore | TLC/PLD | 303-243-7830 |

| Institution | City/State | Contact | Program | Phone |
|---|---|---|---|---|
| Northeastern Jr.C. | Sterling, CO 80751 | Nancy Mann | Study Skills Services | 303-522-6600 |
| Regis C. | Denver, CO 80221 | Victoria McCabe | Freshman Commitment Program | 303-458-3572 |
| U. of Colorado | Boulder, CO 80309-0107 | Terri Bodhaine | Learning Disability Program | 303-492-8671 |
| U. of Colorado | Colo. Springs, CO 80920 | JoAnne Hill | Supplemental Services | 719-593-3265 |
| U. of Denver | Denver, CO 80208 | Ted May | Learning Effectiveness Program | 303-871-4293 |
| U. of N. Colorado | Greeley, CO 80639 | Nancy Kauffman | Disability Access Center | 970-351-2289 |
| U. Southern Colorado | Pueblo, CO 81001 | Rose M.E. Duran | Disability Services Office | 719-549-2292 |
| Western State C. | Gunnison, CO 81231 | Jan Edwards | Disability Services | 303-943-2130 |

### CONNECTICUT

| Institution | City/State | Contact | Program | Phone |
|---|---|---|---|---|
| Briarwood C. | Southington, CT 06489 | Barbara Mackay | Services for Students with LD | 860-628-4751 |
| Central Ct. State U. | New Britain, CT 06050 | George Tenney | Special Student Services | 860-827-7651 |
| Connecticut C. | New London, CT 06320 | Betsy Burris | Writing Center | 203-439-2122 |
| E. Connecticut State | Willimantic, CT 06226 | Deb Cohen | Special Services for Students with Disab. | 860-465-4302 |
| Fairfield U. | Fairfield, CT 06430 | Rev. W.L. O.Neil | Student Support Services | 203-254-4000 |
| Housatonic C. | Bridgeport, CT 06608 | Peter Anderheggen | Disability Support Services | 203-579-6427 |
| Mitchell C. | New London, CT 06320 | Joseph Madaus | Learning Resource Center | 860-701-5142 |
| Quinnipiac C. | Hamden, CT 06518 | John Jarvis | Learning Services | 203-287-5390 |
| Southern Conn. St. U. | New Haven, CT 06515 | Suzanne Tucker | Disability Resource Office | 203-392-6828 |
| U. of Connecticut | W.Hartford, CT 06117 | J. Thierfeld-Brown | Disability Support Services | 860-570-9188 |
| U. of Connecticut | Storrs, CT 06269 | Dr. Joan McGuire | Univ. Prog. for LD Students | 860-486-0178 |
| U. of Hartford | W. Hartford, CT 06117 | Sharon Truex | Learning Plus | 860-768-4522 |
| U. of New Haven | West Haven, CT 06516 | Linda Copney-Okeke | Disabilty Accomm. Services | 203-932-7331 |
| Wesleyan U. | Middletown, CT 06457 | Marie Heathcock | Learning Disabilities Services | 860-344-7900 |
| W. Connecticut State | Danbury, CT 06810 | Helen Kreuger | Student with Disabilities Services | 203-837-9252 |
| Yale University | New Haven, CT 06520 | F.Fay Hanson | Resident Office on Disabilities | 203-432-2324 |

### DELAWARE

| Institution | City/State | Contact | Program | Phone |
|---|---|---|---|---|
| Deleware Tech CC | Georgetown, DE 19947 | Bonnie Hall | Student Support Services | 302-856-5400 |
| U. of Delaware | Newark, DE 19716 | Ruth Smith | Academic services Center | 302-831-1639 |

### DISTRICT OF COLUMBIA

| Institution | City/State | Contact | Program | Phone |
|---|---|---|---|---|
| American U. | Washington, DC 20016 | Helen Steinberg | Learning Services Program | 202-885-3360 |
| Catholic U. of America | Washington, DC 20064 | Lorraine Krusa | Multicultural & Special Services | 202-319-5618 |
| Gallaudet U. | Washington, DC 20002 | John Raymer | Prog. for Stud. with other Disabilities | 202-651-5256 |
| George Washington U. | Washington, DC 20052 | Christy Willis | Disabled Student Services | 202-994-8250 |
| Georgetown U. | Washington, DC 20057 | Dr. Norma Jo Eitington | Learning Services | 202-687-4082 |
| Mt. Vernon C. | Washington, DC 20007 | Mary Ann Hollinger | Dept. of Academic Programs | 202-625-4569 |
| Trinity C. | Washington, DC 20017 | Lois Haid | Academic Support | 202-884-9647 |

## FLORIDA

| Institution | Location | Contact | Service | Phone |
|---|---|---|---|---|
| Barry U. | Miami Shores, FL 33161 | Eileen McDonough | Academic Instructional Services | 305-899-3480 |
| Beacon C. | Leesburg, FL 34748 | Deborah Townley | Beacon Coll. for Learning Disabled | 352-787-7660 |
| Broward CC | F.Lauderdale, FL 33301 | Jaffrie Grossman | Disability Services | 305-761-7555 |
| Edison CC | Fort Myers, FL 33906 | Nanci Karczewski | Disablty Services | 941-489-9427 |
| Embry-Riddle Aero. U. | Daytona Beach, FL 32114 | Maureen Bridger | Disability Student Services | 904-226-7917 |
| Florida A & M | Tallahassee, FL 32307 | Dr. Sharon M. Wooten | Learning Devel. & Evaluation Ctr. | 904-599-8474 |
| Florida Atlantic | Boca Raton, FL 33431 | Beverly Warde | Off. for Students with Disabilities | 407-367-3880 |
| Florida International U. | Miami, FL 33199 | Brenda Russel | Disabled Student Services | 305-348-3532 |
| Florida State U. | Tallahassee, FL 32306 | Robin Leach | Student Disability Resource Ctr. | 904-644-9569 |
| Gulf Coast CC | Panama City, FL 32401 | Linda Van Dalen | Disability Student Services | 904-872-3834 |
| Hillsborough CC | Tampa, FL 33631-3127 | Dr. Leonard Bryant,Jr. | Disabled Services | 813-253-7021 |
| Indian River CC | Fort Pierce, FL 34981 | Mary Sylvester | Disability Services | 216-987-5106 |
| Jacksonville U. | Jacksonville, FL 32211 | Janet Johnson | Student Support Services | 904-744-3950 |
| Lynn University | Boca Raton, FL 33431 | Dr. Marsha Glines | The Advancement Program | 407-994-0770 |
| Pensacola Jr.C. | Pensacola, FL 32504 | Linda Sheppard | Disabled Student Services | 904-484-1637 |
| St. Thomas U. | Miami, FL 33054 | Susan Angulo | Academic Enhancement | 305-625-6000 |
| Santa Fe CC. | Gainsville, FL 32606 | Doug Fols | Student Support Services | 352-295-5948 |
| Seminole CC | Sanford, FL 32773 | Dorothy Paishon | Disabled Students Services | 407-328-2109 |
| St. Petersburg Jr.C | St.Petersburg, FL 33733 | Susan Blanchard | LD Support Program | 813-791-3721 |
| U. of Central Florida | Orlando, FL 32816 | Louise Friderici | Student Disability Services | 407-823-2371 |
| U. of Florida | Gainesville, FL 32611 | James Costello | Students with Disabilities | 352-392-1261 |
| Univ. of Miami | Coral Gables, FL 33124-4616 | Nicola Cumiskey | Off. for Students with Disabilities | 305-284-6434 |
| U. of S. Florida | Tampa, FL 33620 | Melba Sanchez | LD Support Services | 914-359-4331 |
| U. of Tampa | Tampa, FL 33606 | Helene Silverman | Academic Enrichment Center | 813-253-3333 |

## GEORGIA

| Institution | Location | Contact | Service | Phone |
|---|---|---|---|---|
| Andrew C. | Cuthbert , GA 31740 | Carol Trieble | Academic Support Services | 912-732-6813 |
| Armstrong State C | Savannah, GA 31419 | Jan Jones | Disability Services | 912-927-5271 |
| Brenau Women's C. | Gainesville, GA 30501 | Dr. Vincent Yamilkoski | Learning Center | 770-534-6134 |
| Clark Atlanta U. | Atlanta, GA 30314 | Geneva Miller | Disability Services | 404-880-8043 |
| Columbus State U. | Columbus, GA 31907 | Roderick Jungbauer | Special Needs | 708-568-2330 |
| Darton College | Albany, GA 31707 | Louis Emond | Disabled Student Services | 912-430-6729 |
| Dekalb College | Clarkston, GA 30021 | Lisa Fowler | Ctr. for Disability Services | 404-299-4118 |
| Emory U. | Atlanta, GA 30322 | Deborah Hyde | Disabled Student Services | 404-727-1070 |
| Gainesville C. | Gainesville, GA 30503 | Diane Carpenter | Disability Services | 770-718-3855 |
| Georgia Southern C. | Statesboro, GA 30460 | Wayne Akins | Disability Services | 912-871-1566 |
| Georgia Inst. of Tech. | Atlanta, GA 30332 | Katy Landers | Disabled Student Services | 404-894-2564 |
| Georgia State U. | Atlanta, GA 30303 | Carol Pearson | Office of Student Development | 404-651-1487 |

| College | Location | Contact | Office | Phone |
|---|---|---|---|---|
| Life C. | Marietta, GA 30060 | Ann Drake | Academic Assistance Center | 770-426-2725 |
| Oglethorpe U. | Atlanta, GA 30319 | Mary Kay Jennings | LD Services | 404-364-8869 |
| Reinhardt C. | Walenska, GA 30183 | Sylvia Robertson | Academic Support Office | 770-720-5567 |
| South Poltech. St. U. | Marietta, GA 30060 | Charlotte Janis | Disability Services | 770-528-7226 |
| Spellman C. | Atlanta, GA 30314 | Coletta Hassell | Disability Servies | 404-223-7590 |
| U. of Georgia | Athens, GA 30602 | Dr. N. Greg/R. Jackson | Learning Disabilities Center | 706-542-4589 |
| Valdosta State C. | Valdosta, GA 31698 | Maggie Viverette | Special Services Program | 912-245-2498 |

## HAWAII

| College | Location | Contact | Office | Phone |
|---|---|---|---|---|
| Chaminade U. | Honolulu, HI 96816 | Mary Wilkinson | Student Support Services | 808-735-4881 |
| Hawaii CC. | Hilo, HI 96720 | Karen Kane | Ha'awi Kokua Program | 808-933-3741 |
| U. of Hawaii | Hilo, HI 96720 | Barbara Lee | Students with Disabilities | 808-974-7616 |
| U. of Hawaii | Honolulu, HI 96822 | Ann Ito | KOKUA Program | 808-956-7511 |

## IDAHO

| College | Location | Contact | Office | Phone |
|---|---|---|---|---|
| Boise State U. | Boise, ID 83725 | Blaine Eckles | Special Services | 208-385-1583 |
| Idaho State U. | Pocatello, ID 83209 | Robert Campbell | Ctr. of Serv. for Students with Disab. | 208-236-3599 |
| Lewis Clark St. C. | Lewiston, ID 83501 | Loren Hajduk | Advising & Disability Services | 208-799-2211 |
| U. of Idaho | Moscow, ID 83843 | Meredith Goodwin | Student Support Services | 208-885-6746 |

## ILLINOIS

| College | Location | Contact | Office | Phone |
|---|---|---|---|---|
| Aurora U. | Aurora, IL 60506 | Maureen Connolly | Learning Center | 630-644-5521 |
| Barat C. | Lake Forest, IL 60045 | Dr. Pamela Adelman | Learning Opportunities Program | 847-234-3000 |
| Chicago St. U. | Chicago, IL 60628 | Sandra Saunders | Disabled Student Services | 773-995-4401 |
| College of Lake County | Grayslake, IL 60030 | Bill Freitag | Special Needs | 847-223-6601 |
| College of DuPage | Glen Ellyn, IL 60137 | Jackqueline Reuland | Special Student Services | 630-942-2306 |
| DePaul U. | Chicago, IL 60614 | Karen Wold | Productive Learning Strategies | 312-325-7000 |
| Eastern Illinois U. | Charleston, IL 61920 | Martha Jacques | Office of Disability Services | 217-581-6583 |
| Elgin CC. | Elgin, IL 60123 | Annabelle Rhoades | Disability Services | 847-697-1000 |
| Harper C. | Palatine, IL 60067 | Tom Thompson | Center for Students with Disabilities | 708-925-6266 |
| Illinois Benedictine C. | Lisle, IL 60532 | Jane Smith | Student Support Services | 708-960-1500 |
| Illinois Inst. of Tech. | Chicago, IL 60616 | Charles Merbitz | Disability Resources | 312-567-8862 |
| Illinois State U. | Normal, IL 61790 | Dr. Judy Smithson | Disability Concerns | 309-438-5853 |
| John Wood CC | Quincy, IL 62301 | Rose-Marie Akers | Support Learning Services | 217-224-6500 |
| Joliet Junior C. | Joliet, IL 60436 | Jewell Dennis | Special Needs Program | 815-729-9020 |
| Kankakee CC | Kankakee, IL 60901 | Kevin Kennedy | Special Population | 815-933-0332 |
| Lake Forest C. | Lake Forest, IL 60045 | Elizabeth Fischer | Support Services | 847-735-5200 |
| Lakeland C. | Mattoon, IL 61938 | Cindy Campbell | Special Needs Resources | 217-234-5259 |
| Lincoln C. | Lincoln, IL 62656 | Paula Knopp | Supportive Educational Services | 800-569-0556 |
| Loyola U. | Chicago, IL 60626 | Pennie Marcus | Services for Students with Disability | 773-508-3197 |

| Institution | Location | Contact | Service | Phone |
|---|---|---|---|---|
| McHenry CC | Crystal Lake, IL 60012 | Howard Foreman | Special Needs | 815-455-8710 |
| Morraine Valley CC | Palos Hills, IL 60465 | Mary Schafer | Student Support Services | 708-974-5330 |
| Morton C. | Cicero, IL 60650 | Susan Pierce | Special Needs | 708-656-8000 |
| National-Louis U. | Evanston, IL 60201 | Anna Hannond | Center for Academic Development | 847-475-1100 |
| North Central C. | Naperville, IL 60566 | Deanne Wiedeman | Ld/ADD Services | 630-637-5266 |
| Northeastern Il. U. | Chicago, IL 60625 | Rita Brusca-Vega | Special Services | 312-583-4050 |
| Northern Illinois U. | DeKalb, IL 60115 | Nancy Kasinski | Ctr. for Access Ability Resources | 815-753-1303 |
| Oakton Community C. | Des Plaines, IL 60016 | Linda McCann | ASSIST | 847-635-1759 |
| Parkland C. | Champaign, IL 61821 | Norman Lambert | Disability Services | 217-351-7632 |
| Roosevelt U. | Chicago, IL 60605 | Nancy Litke | Learning Support Services Program | 312-341-3810 |
| Rosary C. | River Forest, IL 60305 | Louis Tenzis | Student Support Services | 312-366-2490 |
| St. Xavier C. | Chicago, IL 60655 | Loretta Kardatzke | Learning Assistance Center | 773-298-3330 |
| School of Art Instit. | Chicago, IL 60603 | Susan Whitlow | Learning Center | 312-345-3595 |
| Southern Illinois U. | Carbondale, IL 62901 | Barbara Cordoni | Achieve Program | 618-453-6120 |
| Southern Illinois U. | Edwardsville, IL 62020 | Jane Floyd-Hendey | Disability Support Services | 618-692-3782 |
| U. of Chicago | Chicago, IL 60637 | Margaret Fallers | Office of Admission | 773-702-8650 |
| U. of Illinois | Champaign, IL 61801 | Brad Hedrick | Rehabilitation Education Services | 217-333-4602 |
| U. of Illinois-Chicago | Chicago, IL 60607 | Jean Gorman | Disability Services | 312-996-8332 |
| Waubonsee Comm. C. | Sugar Grove, IL 60554 | Iris Jorstad | Access Center for Students with Disab. | 708-466-4811 |
| Western Illinois U. | Macomb, IL 61455 | Joam Green | Disabled Student Services | 309-298-2512 |
| Will. Rainey Harper CC | Palatine, IL 60067 | Tom Thompson | Center for Students with Disabilities | 847-925-6266 |

## INDIANA

| Institution | Location | Contact | Service | Phone |
|---|---|---|---|---|
| Anderson U. | Anderson, IN 46012 | Rinda Vogelgesang | Program for Learning Disabled | 317-641-4226 |
| Ball State U. | Muncie, IN 47306 | Richard Harris | Office of Disabled Students | 317-285-5293 |
| Butler U. | Indianapolis, IN 46208 | Mary Paugh | Special Student Services | 800-368-6852 |
| DePauw U. | Greencastle, IN 46135 | Madeline Eagon | Office of Admission | 800-447-2495 |
| Earlham C. | Richmond, IN 47374 | David Gerth | Student Support Services | 317-983-1341 |
| Goshen C. | Goshen, IN 46526 | Martha Hooley | Learning Resource Center | 219-535-7535 |
| Indiana State U. | Terre Haute, IN 47809 | Rita Worrell | Stu. Support Services | 812-237-2301 |
| Indiana U. | Bloomington, IN 47405 | Steve Morris | Disabled Student Services | 812-855-7578 |
| Indiana U.-East | Richmond, IN 47374 | Sabrina Pennington | Student Support Services | 317-973-8302 |
| Indiana U.-Purdue U. | Indianapolis, IN 46202 | Pamela King | Adaptive Educ. Services | 317-278-2050 |
| Indiana U.-South Bend | South Bend, IN 46634 | Mark Dosch | Disabled Student Services | 219-237-4479 |
| Indiana U.- S.E. | New Albany, IN 47150 | Jodi Taylor | Students with Disabilities | 812-941-2243 |
| IUPU-Ft. Wayne | Ft. Wayne, IN 46805 | Randy Borst | Disabled Student Services | 219-481-6658 |
| Indiana Wesleyan U. | Marion, IN 46953 | Dr. Neil McFarlane | Student Support Services | 317-677-2257 |
| IVY Tech. | Fort Wayne, IN 46805 | Debra Clarke | Disabity Servcies | 219-480-4207 |
| IVY Tech. St. C. | Evansville, IN 47710 | Peg Ehlen | Special Needs | 812-429-1386 |

| College | Location | Contact | Service | Phone |
|---|---|---|---|---|
| Manchester C. | N. Manchester, IN 46962 | Denise Howe | Services for Stud. with Disabilities | 219-982-5076 |
| Marion C. | Indianapolis, IN 46222 | Kimberly Tyson | Learning Center | 317-929-0317 |
| Purdue U.- Calumet | Hammond, IN 46323 | Berry Fitzner | Serv. for students with Disabilities | 219-989-2455 |
| Purdue U. | W. Lafayette, IN 47907 | Paula Micka | Adaptive Programs | 317-494-1245 |
| St. Francis C. | Fort Wayne, IN 46808 | Sandra Pass | Academic Support Services | 219-434-3288 |
| St. Joseph's C. | Rensselaer, IN 47978 | Tom Dukes | Counseling Services | 219-866-6116 |
| Taylor U. | Upland, IN 46989 | Edwin Welch | Academic Support | 317-998-5523 |
| Tri-State U. | Angola, IN 46703 | Patrick Manning | Special students | 219-665-4171 |
| U. of Evansville | Evansville, IN 47722 | Dr. Howard Rosenblatt | Student Life Center | 812-479-2500 |
| U. of Indianapolis | Indianapolis, IN 46227 | Drs. P.Cook/N.O'Dell | B.U.I.L.D. | 317-788-3369 |
| U. of Notre Dame | Notre Dame, IN 46556 | Scott Howland | Office of Students with Disabilities | 219-631-7141 |
| U. of S. Indiana | Evansville, IN 47712 | Leslie Swanson | Counseling Center | 812-464-1867 |
| Valparaiso U. | Valparaiso, IN 46383 | Katharine Antommaria | Academic Support Services | 219-464-5318 |
| Vincennes U. | Vincennes, IN 47591 | J.Kavanaugh/S. Laue | S.T.E.P. | 812-888-4485 |
| Wabash C. | Crawfordsville, IN 4793 | Lucy Brooks | Academic Support Services | 765-361-6352 |

## IOWA

| College | Location | Contact | Service | Phone |
|---|---|---|---|---|
| Coe C. | Cedar Rapids, IA 52402 | Lois Kabela-Coates | Educational Support Program | 319-399-8500 |
| Cornell C. | Mt. Vernon, IA 52314 | Ricci Henderson | Counseling & Student Support Services | 319-895-4292 |
| Des Moines Area CC | Ankney, IA 50021 | Carol Grimm | Academic Achievement | 515-964-6268 |
| Drake U. | Des Moines, IA 50311 | Amy Desenberg-Wihes | Disability Resource Center | 515-271-3100 |
| Graceland C. | Laomoni, IA 50140 | Carl McGuire | Student Support Services | 515-784-5449 |
| Grand View C. | Des Moines, IA 50316 | Jane Molden | Learning Disability Program | 515-263-2884 |
| Grinnell C. | Grinnell, IA 50112 | Jo Calhoun | Academic Advising Office | 515-269-3702 |
| Hawkeye CC | Waterloo, IA 50704 | Dianne Shoultz | Special Needs/JTPA | 319-296-4014 |
| Indiana Hills C. C. | Ottumwa, IA 52501 | Judith K. Brickey | Transition Program | 515-683-5125 |
| Iowa Central C.C. | Ft. Dodge, IA 50501 | Barbara McClannahan | Special Needs | 515-576-7201 |
| Iowa State U. | Ames, IA 50011 | Joyce Packwood | Services for Students with Disabilities | 515-294-1020 |
| Iowa Wesleyan U. | Mt. Pleasant, IA 52641 | Linda Widmer | Learning Center | 319-385-6332 |
| Iowa Western C. C. | Council Bluffs, IA 51502 | Bonny Gioiello | Student Support Services/Career Ctr. | 712-325-3282 |
| Loras C. | Dubuque, IA 52004 | Dianne Gibson | Learning Disabilities Program | 319-588-7134 |
| Luther C. | Decorah, IA 52101 | Perry-O Sliwa | Learning Skills Center | 319-387-1270 |
| Mt. St. Clare C. | Clinton, IA 52732 | Art Belair | Student Support Services | 319-242-4153 |
| St. Ambrose U. | Davenport, IA 52803 | Andy Kaiser | Services for Students with Disabilities | 319-333-6275 |
| Scott CC-E.Iowa CC | Bettendorf, IA 52722 | Jerri Crabtree | Student Support Services | 319-359-7531 |
| Southeastern CC | W. Burlington, IA 52655 | Curt Bloom | Special Populations | 319-752-2731 |
| U. of Dubuque | Dubuque, IA 52001 | Lavinia Pattee | Learning Center | 319-589-3218 |
| U. of Iowa | Iowa City, IA 52242 | Mary Richard | Student Disability Services | 319-335-1462 |
| U. of Northern Iowa | Cedar Falls, IA 50614 | Dr. Edward Morris | Disability Services | 319-273-2676 |

| College | Contact | Address | Program/Service | Phone |
|---|---|---|---|---|
| Waldorf College | Rebecca S. Hill | Forest City, IA 50436 | LD Program | 515-582-8207 |
| Wartburg C. | Alexander Smith | Waverly, IA 50677 | Dean of Students Office | 319-352-8260 |

## KANSAS

| College | Contact | Address | Program/Service | Phone |
|---|---|---|---|---|
| Bethel C. | Sandee Zerger | N. Newton, KS 67117 | Center for Academic Development | 316-283-5359 |
| Butler City CC | Liane Fowler | Eldorado, KS 67042 | Special Needs & Services | 316-322-3166 |
| Colby CC | Deb Kohn | Colby, KS 67701 | Student Support Services | 913-462-3984 |
| Emporia State U. | Trudi Benjamin | Emporia, KS 66901 | Project Challenge | 316-341-5097 |
| Hutchinson CC | Linda Dermyer | Hutchison, KS 67502 | Student Support Services | 316-665-3554 |
| Kansas City Art Inst. | Patricia Jachowicz | Kansas City, KS 64111 | Academic Resource Center | 816-931-5224 |
| Johnson City CC | Holly Dressler | Overland Park, KS 66210 | Disability Support Services | 913-469-3830 |
| Kansas City CC | Valerie Webb | Kansas City, KS 66112 | Disability Resource Center | 913-596-9670 |
| Kansas State U. | Gretchen Holden | Manhattan, KS 66505 | Disabled Student Services | 913-532-6441 |
| Pratt CC | Jaynce English | Pratt, KS 67124 | Disability Servcies | 316-672-5641 |
| U. of Kansas | Michael Shuttic | Lawrence, KS 66006 | Student Assistance Center | 913-864-4064 |
| Wichita State U. | Grady Landrum | Wichita, KS 67260-0132 | Resource Center for Independence | 316-689-3309 |

## KENTUCKY

| College | Contact | Address | Program/Service | Phone |
|---|---|---|---|---|
| Bellarmine C. | Ruth Gavy | Louisville, KY 40205 | Student Affairs | 502-452-8153 |
| Brescia C. | Tersea Riley | Owensboro, KY 42301 | Student Support Services | 502-686-4259 |
| E. Kentucky U. | Harry Moberly | Richmond, KY 40475 | Project SUCCESS | 606-622-1500 |
| Lexington CC | Marlene Huff | Lexington, KY 40506 | Disability Support Services | 606-257-6068 |
| Moorhead St. | Debra Reed | Moorhead, KY 40351 | Disability Servcies | 606-783-2005 |
| Murray State U. | Annzette Fields | Murray, KY 42071 | Student Support Services | 502-762-4327 |
| N. Kentucky U. | A. Dale Adams | Highland Hts., KY 41009 | Disability Services | 606-572-9518 |
| Thomas More C. | Barbara Davis | Crestview Hills, KY 41017 | Student Support Services | 606-344-3521 |
| Southeast CC | Richard Richmond | Cumberland, KY 40823 | Student Support Services | 606-589-2145 |
| U. of Kentucky | Jacob Karnes | Lexington, KY 40506 | Disability Resource Center | 606-257-2754 |
| U. of Louisville | Cathy Patus | Louisville, KY 40292 | Disabled Student Services | 502-552-6938 |
| W. Kentucky U. | Huda Melky | Bowling Green, KY 42101 | Office for Disability Services | 502-745-5004 |

## LOUISIANA

| College | Contact | Address | Program/Service | Phone |
|---|---|---|---|---|
| Louisiana C. | Vickie Kelly | Pineville, LA 71359 | PASS | 318-487-7629 |
| Louisiana State U. | Traci Bryant | Baton Rouge, LA 70803 | Disabled Services Office | 504-388-5919 |
| Loyola U. | Sara Smith | New Orleans, LA 70118 | Academic Enrichment & Disability Serv. | 504-865-2990 |
| Nichols State U. | Randall Moore | Thibodaux, LA 70310 | Dyslexia Center | 504-448-4214 |
| S. Eastern Louisiana U. | Deborrah Hebert | Hammond, LA 70402 | Student Life | 504-549-5040 |
| S. U. at New Orleans | Zelma Frnak | New Orleans, LA 70126 | Student Support Services | 504-286-5106 |
| Tulane U. | Cathy Swanson | New Orleans, LA 70118 | Counseling/ERC | 504-865-5113 |
| U. of New Orleans | Janice Lyn | New Orleans, LA 70148 | Disabled Student Services | 504-286-6222 |

| College | City/State | Service | Contact | Phone |
|---|---|---|---|---|
| U. SW Louisiana | Lafayette, LA 70504 | Disabled Student Services | Page Salley | 318-482-5252 |

## MAINE

| College | City/State | Service | Contact | Phone |
|---|---|---|---|---|
| Bates C. | Lewiston, ME 04240 | Student Services | Celeste Branham | 207-786-6202 |
| Bowdoin C. | Brunswick, ME 04011 | Student Affairs | Margaret Hazlett | 207-725-3879 |
| Colby College | Waterville, ME 04901 | Student Support Services | Mark Serdjenian | 207-872-3106 |
| Eastern Tech. C. | Bangor, ME 04401 | Disability Services | Lois Marchand | 207-941-4655 |
| Kennebec Valley tech. | Fairfield, ME 04937 | Student with Disabilities | Karen Normandin | 207-453-5020 |
| N. Maine Tech. C. | Presque Isle, ME 04769 | Special Services | Laura Flagg | 207-769-2461 |
| S. Maine Tech C. | South Portland, ME 04106 | Learning Assistance Center | Gail Rowe | 207-767-9536 |
| Unity C. | Unity, ME 04988 | Learning Resource Center | James Horan | 207-948-3131 |
| U. of Maine | Augusta, ME 04330 | Cornerstone Program | Calene Spencer | 207-621-3464 |
| U. of Maine | Farmington, ME 04938 | Learning Assistance Center | Claire Nelson | 207-778-7295 |
| U. of Maine | Orono, ME 04469 | Onward Program Services | Ann Smith | 207-581-2319 |
| U. of Maine | Presque Isle, ME 04769 | Student Support Services Program | Myrna McGaffin | 207-768-9400 |
| U. of New England | Biddeford, ME 04005 | Individual Learning Program | Pamela Leone | 207-283-0171 |
| U. of Southern Maine | Portland, ME 04103 | Academic Support Services | Joyce Branaman | 207-780-4706 |

## MARYLAND

| College | City/State | Service | Contact | Phone |
|---|---|---|---|---|
| Allegheny C. | Cumberland, MD 21502 | Instructional Assistance Ctr. | Valerie Hager | 301-724-7700 |
| Anne Arundel CC | Arnold, MD 21012 | Student Services | Deborah Conway | 410-541-2307 |
| Baltimore City CC. | Baltimore, MD 21215 | Disabled Student Services | A. Quismat Gorham | 410-462-7977 |
| Carroll CC. | Westminster, MD 21157 | Student Support Services | Sherry Glass | 410-876-9600 |
| Catonsville CC | Catonsville, MD 21228 | Special Student Population | Jill Brooks-Hodge | 410-455-4718 |
| Cecil C. | North East, MD 20901 | Academic Advising | Debbie Farris | 410-287-6060 |
| Charles Co. CC | La Plata, MD 20646 | Academic Support | Jay Marciano | 301-934-2251 |
| Columbia Union C. | Takoma Park, MD 20912 | Summer Start | Dr. Betty Howard | 301-891-4106 |
| Essex CC | Baltimore, MD 21237 | Disability Services | Marion Herb | 410-780-6741 |
| Frostburg State U. | Frostburg, MD 21532 | Disabled Student Services | Suzzane Hall | 301-687-4481 |
| Goucher C. | Baltimore, MD 21204 | Special Student Services | Frona Brown | 410-337-6178 |
| Hartford CC. | Bel Air, MD 21015 | Special Services | Patricia Burton | 410-836-4452 |
| Hood C. | Frederick, MD 21701 | Disability Services | Lynn Schlossberh | 301-696-3421 |
| Howard CC. | Columbia, MD 21044 | Learning Assistance Center | Janice Marks | 410-992-4800 |
| John Hopkins U. | Baltimore, MD 21218 | Academic Advising | Yvonne Theodore | 410-516-8075 |
| Loyola C. | Baltimore, MD 21210 | Support Services | Andrea Buonincontro | 410-617-3522 |
| Montgomery C. | Rockville, MD 20850 | Disability Support Services | Janet Merrick | 301-294-9672 |
| Morgan State U. | Baltimore, MD 21251 | Counselin Center | N. Dobson-Hopkins | 410-319-3131 |
| Towson State U. | Towson, MD 21204 | Off. for Students with Disabilities | Ronnie Upland | 410-830-2638 |
| U. of Baltimore | Baltimore, MD 21201 | Disabled Student Services | Jacquelyn Truelove | 410-837-4775 |

| Institution | Location | Contact | Service | Phone |
|---|---|---|---|---|
| U. of Maryland | College Park, MD 20742 | William Scales | Disability Support Services | 301-314-7682 |
| U. Maryland-E.Shore | Princes Anne, MD 21853 | Georgann Wing | Disabled Student Services | 410-651-6461 |
| Western Maryland C. | Westminster, MD 21157 | Dr. Henry Reiff | Academic Skills Center | 410-857-2516 |

## MASSACHUSETTS

| Institution | Location | Contact | Service | Phone |
|---|---|---|---|---|
| Anna Marie C. | Paxton, MA 01612 | Oliva Tarleton | Learning Center | 508-849-3356 |
| American International | Springfield, MA 01109 | Prof. Mary Saltus | Supportive Learning Services Program | 413-747-6426 |
| Amherst U. | Amherst, MA 01002 | Frances Tuleja | Serv. for Stud. with Disabilities | 413-527-8132 |
| Aquinas C. | Newton, MA 02158 | Louise Silva | Academic Success Center | 617-969-4400 |
| Assumption C. | Worchester, MA 01615 | Allen Bruehl | Academic Support Center | 508-767-7311 |
| Babson C. | Babson Pk, MA 02157 | Allison Chase | Disability Services | 617-239-4433 |
| Bentley C. | Waltham, MA 02154 | Dr. Brenda Hawks | Counseling and Student Development | 617-891-2274 |
| Berklee C. of Music | Boston, MA 02215 | Bob Mulvey | Special Services | 617-266-1400 |
| Berkshire CC | Pittsfield, MA 01201 | Pamela Farron | Students with Disabilities | 413-499-4660 |
| Boston C. | Chestnut Hill, MA 02167 | John Hennessey | Disabled Student Services | 617-552-3310 |
| Boston U. | Boston, MA 02215 | Dr. Lorriane Wolf | Office of Disability Services | 617-353-6880 |
| Bradford C. | Bradford, MA 01835 | Helen Page | College Learning Program | 508-372-7161 |
| Brandeis U. | Waltham, MA 02254 | Walter Anthony Jr. | Academic Affairs | 617-736-3460 |
| Bridgewater St. C. | Bridgewater, MA 02325 | Martha Jones | Office for Students with Disabilities | 508-697-1278 |
| Clark U. | Worcester, MA 01610 | Alan Bieri | Special Services | 508-793-7468 |
| C. of Holy Cross | Worcester, MA 01610 | Matthew Toth | Counseling Ctr. | 508-793-3363 |
| Curry C. | Milton, MA 02186 | Dr. Lisa Ijiri | PAL Program | 617-335-0500 |
| Dean College | Franklin, MA 02038 | Kevin Kelly | Personalized Learning Services | 508-541-1508 |
| Emerson C. | Boston, MA 02116 | Anthony Bashir | Learning Assistance Center | 617-824-8500 |
| Endicott C. | Beverly, MA 01915 | Jane Lang | Student Support Program | 508-927-0585 |
| Fitchburg State C. | Fitchburg, MA 01420 | Debra Horton | Disability Services | 508-345-2151 |
| Framingham St. | Framingham, MA 01701 | Dennis Polselli | Disabled Student Services | 508-626 4627 |
| Gordon C. | Wenham, MA 01984 | Ann Seavy | Academic Support | 508-927-2300 |
| Hampshire C. | Amherst, MA 01002 | Andy Korenewsky | Student Services | 413-582-5412 |
| Harvard U. | Cambridge, MA 02138 | Louise Russell | Student Disability Resource Ctr. | 617-496-8707 |
| Holyoke C.C. | Holyoke, MA 01040 | Maureen Conroy | Office for Students with Disabilities | 413-538-7000 |
| Johnson & Wales | Providence, MA 02903 | Meryl Berstein | Special Needs | 401-456-5982 |
| Lesley C. | Cambridge, MA 02138 | David Leslie | Threshold | 617-349-8181 |
| Mass. Bay CC | Wellesley Hls, MA 02181 | Cynthia Zafft | Disability Services | 617-239-2287 |
| Massasoit CC | Brockton, MA 02402 | Stanley Oliver | Disability Servcies | 508-588-9100 |
| Mt. Ida C. | Newton Ctr, MA 02159 | Jill Mehler | Learning Opportunities | 617-928-4648 |
| Mt. Wachusett CC. | Gardner, MA 01440 | Nancy Kennedy | ACCESS | 508-632-6600 |
| N. Adams State C. | N. Adams, MA 01247 | Linda Neville | Learning Center | 413-664-6673 |
| N. Shore CC. | Danvers, MA 01923 | Jane Coviello | Student Support Center | 508-762-4000 |

| College | Location | Contact | Program | Phone |
|---|---|---|---|---|
| Northeastern U. | Boston, MA 02115 | Dr. Ruth K. Bork | Disability Resource Center | 617-373-2675 |
| Pine Manor C. | Chestnut Hill, MA 02167 | Mary Walsh | Learning Resource Center | 617-731-7181 |
| Quinsigamond CC. | Worcester, MA 01606 | JoAnne Sharac | Supported Education Program | 508-854-4295 |
| Salem State CC | Salem, MA 01970 | Margo Druschel | Students with Disabilities | 508-741-6217 |
| Simmons C. | Boston, MA 02115 | Carolyn Holland | Supportive Instructional Services | 617-738-2471 |
| Smith C. | Northampton, MA 01063 | Kris Kozuch | Office of Disability Services | 413-585-2071 |
| Springfield C. | Springfield, MA 01109 | Deb Dickens | Student Support Services | 413-748-3100 |
| Springfield Tech. CC | Springfield, MA 01105 | Mary Moriarty | Disabled Student Services | 413-781-7822 |
| St. Coll. at N. Adams | N. Adams, MA 01247 | Terry Miller | Ctr. for Academic Advancement | 413-662-5272 |
| Stonehill C. | N.Easton, MA 02357 | Richard Grant | Academic Services | 508-230-1306 |
| Suffolk U. | Boston, MA 02108 | David Pfeiffer | Support Servcies | 617-573-8316 |
| Tufts U. | Medford, MA 02155 | Libby Sweetnam | Academic Resource Center | 617-627-3159 |
| U. of Massachusetts | Amherst, MA 01003 | Linda Vincent | Learning Disabled Student Services | 413-545-0333 |
| U. of Massachusetts | Boston, MA 02125 | Bill Pollard | Project Reach | 617-287-7390 |
| U. Massachusetts | N. Dartmouth, MA 02747 | Carole Johnson | Disabled Students | 508-999-8711 |
| Wheaton C. | Norton, MA 02766 | Carol Suisman | Office of Advising | 508-285-8215 |
| Wellesley C. | Wellesley, MA 02181 | Barbara Boger | Learning & Teaching Center | 617-283-2092 |
| W. New England C. | Springfield, MA 01119 | Carol Morecki-Oberg | LD Services | 413-782-4111 |
| Wheelock C. | Boston, MA 02215 | Mary McCormac | Academic Advising | 617-734-5200 |
| Williams C. | Williamstown, MA 01267 | Amy Fahnestock | Disability Services | 413-597-4037 |
| Worcester State C. | Worcester, MA 01602 | Dennis Lindblom | Disability Services | 508-793-8000 |
| Worcester Poly. Inst. | Worcester, MA 01609 | Ann Garvin | Office of Academic Advising | 508-831-5381 |

## MICHIGAN

| College | Location | Contact | Program | Phone |
|---|---|---|---|---|
| Adrian C. | Adrian, MI 49221 | Jane McCloskey | EXCEL Program | 517-265-5161 |
| Alma C. | Alma, MI 48801 | Kalindi Trieatley | Center for Student Development | 517-463-7225 |
| Aquinas C. | Grand Rapids, MI 49506 | Gary Kieff | Academic Achievement Center | 616-459-8281 |
| Calvin C. | Grand Rapids, MI 49546 | James MacKenzie | Student Academic Services | 619-957-6113 |
| Central Michigan U. | Mt.Pleasant, MI 48859 | Carol Wojcik | Academic Assistance | 517-774-3018 |
| Delta C. | Univ. Ctr., MI 48710 | Dave Murley | Learning Disabilities Services | 517-686-9573 |
| Ferris State U. | Big Rapids, MI 49307 | M.Campbell-Brayton | Special Needs Support Services | 616-592-3661 |
| Grand Rapids CC. | Grand Rapids, MI 49503 | Anne Sherman | Handicapped Student Services | 616-771-4140 |
| Grand Valley State | Allendale, MI 49410 | John Pedraza | Student Support Services | 616-895-2490 |
| Hope C. | Holland, MI 49422 | Jacqueline Heisler | Academic Support Center | 616-395-7830 |
| Kellogg CC. | Battle Creek, MI 49017 | Janice McNearney | Support Services | 616-965-3931 |
| Lansing CC. | Lansing, MI 48901 | Pamela Davis | Center for Student Support | 517-483-1188 |
| Madonna U. | Livonia, MI 48150 | Michael Meldrum | Educational Support Services | 313-432-5641 |
| Marygrove C. | Detroit, MI 48221 | Blanche Glimps | LD Support Services | 313-862-8000 |
| Michigan State U. | East Lansing, MI 48824 | Margaret Chmielewski | Program for Handicapped Services | 517-353-9642 |

| Institution | Location | Contact | Service | Phone |
|---|---|---|---|---|
| Michigan Tech. U. | Houghton, MI 49931 | Dr. Gloria Melton | Handicapper Services | 906-487-2212 |
| North Central Mich. C. | Petoskey, MI 49770 | Daniel Linnenberg | Special Populations | 616-348-6687 |
| Northern Michigan U. | Marquette, MI 49855 | Lynn Walden | Disability Services | 906-227-1550 |
| Oakland CC. | Auburn Hills, MI 48326 | June Czopek | Special Needs | 810-471-7588 |
| Oakland U. | Rochester, MI 48309 | Lisa McGill | Disability Support Servcies | 810-370-3266 |
| Saginaw Valley St. U. | University Ctr, MI 48710 | Cynthia Woiderski | Disability Services | 517-790-4168 |
| Schoolcraft Cc. | Livonia, MI 48152 | Sirkka Gudan | LAC | 313-462-4436 |
| SW Michigan C. | Dowagiac, MI 49047 | Susan Searight | Special Needs | 616-782-1312 |
| Suomi C. | Hancock, MI 49930 | Carol Bates | Learning Disabilities Program | 906-487-7258 |
| U. of Michigan | Ann Arbor, MI 48109 | Stuart Segal | Services for Students with Disabilities | 313-763-3000 |
| U. of Michigan | Flint, MI 48502 | Shawn Potter | Student Development Center | 810-238-0015 |
| Wayne State U. | Detroit, MI 48202 | Deborah Daiek | Handicapper Educational Services | 313-577-3165 |
| Western Michigan U. | Kalamazoo, MI 49008 | Beth Den Hartigh | Special Services Program | 616-387-2116 |

## MINNESOTA

| Institution | Location | Contact | Service | Phone |
|---|---|---|---|---|
| Augsburg C. | Minneapolis, MN 55454 | Kate Storey | Ctr. for Learning & Adaptive Stu. Serv. | 612-330-1218 |
| Behel C. | St. Paul, MN 55112 | Gretchen Wrobel | Disability Services | 612-638-6403 |
| Bimidji State U. | Bimidji, MN 55601 | Kathi Hagen | Educational Development Ctr. | 218-755-3883 |
| Carleton College | Northfield, MN 55057 | Hudlin Wagner | Support Services | 507-646-4190 |
| Century C. | White Bear Lk., MN 55110 | Mary Bataglia | Disability Access | 612-779-3354 |
| C. of St. Benedict | St. Joseph, MN 56374 | Michelle Sauer | Student Support Services | 320-363-5687 |
| C. of St. Catherine | St. Paul, MN 55105 | Elaine McDonough | Learning Programs | 612-690-6706 |
| C. of St. Scholastic | Duluth, MN 55811 | Jay Newcomb | Academic Support Services | 218-723-6552 |
| Concordia C. | Moorhead, MN 56562 | Monica Kersting | Center for Educ. Couns./Per. Growth | 218-299-3514 |
| Fond du lac CC. | Cloquet, MN 55720 | Anita Hanson | Office of Student with Disabilities | 218-879-0800 |
| Gustavus Adolophus C. | St. Peter, MN 56082 | Julie Johnson | Academic Advising | 507-933-6124 |
| Hamline U. | St. Paul, MN 55104 | Barbara Simmons | Study Resource Center | 612-641-2417 |
| Hibbing Comm. Coll. | Hibbing, MN 55746 | Barbara Anderson | Disability Services | 218-262-6775 |
| Inverhills CC. | Invergr. Hts., MN 55076 | Virginia Spurr | Disabled Student Services | 612-450-8628 |
| Itaska CC | Grand Rapids, MN 55744 | Beth Claussen | Student Services | 218-327-4166 |
| Lake Superior C. | Duluth, MN 55811 | Molly Johnson | Disability Services | 218-722-2801 |
| Lakewood CC. | White Bear Lk., MN 55110 | Karen Kodzik | Disability Access Center | 612-779-3354 |
| Macalester C. | St. Paul, MN 55105 | Lisa Broek | Learning Skills Center | 612-696-6220 |
| Mankato State U. | Mankato, MN 56002 | Audrey Metro | Student with LD | 507-389-2825 |
| Mesabi CC | Virginia, MN 55792 | Jane Sakrison-Chilcote | Disability Services | 218-749-7791 |
| Minneapolis CC. | Minneapolis, MN 55403 | Judy Schuck | Office for Students with Disabilities | 612-341-7549 |
| Moorhead State U. | Moorhead, MN 56563 | Paula Ahles | Disability Services | 218-299-5859 |
| Normandale CC. | Bloomington, MN 55431 | Mary Jibben | DEEDS | 612-832-6422 |
| N. Hennepin CC | Brooklyn Pk., MN 55445 | Sheryl Olson | Disability Services | 612-493-0556 |

| College | City | Contact | Service | Phone |
|---|---|---|---|---|
| Northwestern C. | St. Paul, MN 55113 | Jackie Gleny | Student Support Services | 612-631-5257 |
| Riverland CC | Austin, MN 55912 | Mindyi Askelson | Students Success Center | 507-433-0558 |
| Rochester CC. | Rochester, MN 55904 | Janell Holter | SSSP | 507-285-7568 |
| St. Cloud State U. | St. Cloud, MN 56301 | Sharon Oliver | Handicapped Student Services | 320-654-5089 |
| St. John's U. | Collegeville, MN 56321 | Fr. Tony Hellenberg | Academic Advising | 612-363-2248 |
| St. Mary's U. | Winona, MN 55987 | Jane Ochrymowyzc | Academic Skills Center | 507-457-1421 |
| St. Olaf C. | Northfield, MN 55057 | Kathy Quade | LD Support Services | 507-646-3288 |
| Southwest State U. | Marshall, MN 56258 | Eve Nichols | Learning Resource Center | 507-537-7285 |
| U. of Minnesota | Crookston, MN 56716 | Laurie Wilson | Office for Students with Disabilities | 218-281-8587 |
| U. of Minnesota | Duluth, MN 55812 | Penny Cragun | Learning Disability Program | 218-726-8727 |
| U. of Minnesota | Minneapolis, MN 55455 | Carol Hill | Students with Disabilities | 612-624-2893 |
| U. of Minnesota | Morris, MN 56267 | Nancy South | Disability Services | 320-589-6178 |
| U. of Minnesota | Twin Cities, MN 55455 | Sue Kroeger | Students with Disabilities | 612-624-4120 |
| U. of St. Thomas | St. Paul, MN 55105 | Jeannine Harff | Special Services | 612-962-6055 |
| Winona State U. | Winona, MN 55987 | Nancy Dumke | Learning Center | 507-457-5543 |

## MISSISSIPPI

| College | City | Contact | Service | Phone |
|---|---|---|---|---|
| Mississippi St. U. | Mississippi, MS 39762 | Leslie Betha | PAACS | 601-325-7919 |
| U. of Mississippi | University, MS 38677 | Ardessa Minor | Serv. for Students with Disabilities | 601-266-5007 |
| U. of S. Mississippi | Hattiesburg, MS 39406 | Sheryl Glausier | Office of Support Services | 601-266-5024 |
| William Carey C. | Hattiesburg, MS 39401 | Brenda Waldrip | Student Support Services | 601-582-6208 |

## MISSOURI

| College | City | Contact | Service | Phone |
|---|---|---|---|---|
| Columbia College | Coloumbia, MO 65216 | Kim McHale | Center for Academic Enrichment | 800-231-2391 |
| Evangel C. | Springfield, MO 65802 | Eleanor Syler | Ctr. for Effective Learning | 417-865-2815 |
| Fontbonne C. | St. Louis, MO 63105 | Jane Snyder | Academic Resources | 314-889-4571 |
| Kansas City Art Inst. | Kansas City, MO 64111 | Mary Majers | Academic Resource Center | 816-561-4852 |
| Lindenwood C. | St.Charles, MO 63301 | Tonie Isenhour | Disability Services | 314-949-4949 |
| Maple Woods CC | Kansas City, MO 64156 | Barbara Schaefer | Special Needs | 816-437-3192 |
| Metropolitan CC | Kansas City, MO 64111 | Joan Friend | Support Services | 816-759-1164 |
| Mineral Area C. | Park Hills, MO 63601` | Margaret Scobee | Special Services | 314-431-4593 |
| Missouri S. St. Coll. | Joplin, MO 64801 | Ellen Dodsey | Learning Center | 417-625-9670 |
| Missouri Valley C. | Marshall, MO 65340 | Marilyn Ehlert | Support Services | 816-831-4157 |
| Missouri West. St. C. | St.Joseph, MO 64507 | Ellen Smither | Non-traditional Student Center | 816-271-4280 |
| NE Missouri State | Kirksville, MO 63501 | T.W. Sorrell | Services for Indiv. with Disabilities | 816-785-4478 |
| Northwest Mo. St. U. | Maryville, MO 64468 | Phil Kenkel | Student Support Services | 816-562-1861 |
| Penn Valley CC. | Kansas Ciry, MO 64110 | Connie Spies | Special Needs | 816-759-4152 |
| St. Charles City CC. | Saint Peters, MO 63376 | Pam Bova | Disabled Student Services | 314-922-8247 |
| St. Louis CC.-Meramec | St. Louis, MO 63122 | Linda Nissenbaum | Disabled Student Services | 314-984-7654 |

| Institution | Location | Contact | Service | Phone |
| --- | --- | --- | --- | --- |
| St. Louis C.-Floriss.V. | St. Louis, MO 63135 | Suelaine Matthews | Project Ability | 314-595-4549 |
| St. Louis CC. | St. Louis, MO 63110 | Claudia Felsen | Support Services | 314-644-9260 |
| St. Louis U. | St. Louis, MO 63103 | M. Kay Balthazor | Student Eduaction & Services Ctr. | 314-977-2930 |
| Southwest Mo. St. U. | Springfield, MO 65804 | Sylvia Buse | Learning Diagnostic Clinic | 417-836-4787 |
| Three River CC. | Poplar Bluff, MO 63901 | Mack Warren | Student Support Services | 573-840-9650 |
| Truman State U. | Kirksville, MO 63501 | T.W. Sorrell | Services for Individuals with Dis. | 816-785-4478 |
| U. of Missouri | Columbia, MO 65211 | Carma Messerli | Access Office | 314-882-4696 |
| U. of Missouri | Kansas City, MO 64110 | DeAnne G. Steinle | Services for Students with Disabilities | 816-235-5696 |
| U. of Missouri | Rolla, MO 65401 | Dr. Wendell Ogrosky | Counseling & Testing | 573-341-4954 |
| U. of Missouri | St. Louis, MO 63120 | Marilyn Ditto | Special Student Program | 314-516-5211 |
| Washington U. | St. Louis, MO 63130 | Daniel Herbst | Disabled Student  Services | 314-935-4062 |
| Westminster C. | Fulton, MO 65251 | Henry F. Ottinger | Learning Disabilities Program | 314-592-1304 |
| William Jewell C. | Liberty, MO 64068 | David Maltby | LD Support Services | 816-781-7700 |

## MONTANA

| Institution | Location | Contact | Service | Phone |
| --- | --- | --- | --- | --- |
| Montana State U. | Billings, MT 59101-0298 | Sharon Yasik | Disability Support Services | 406-657-2283 |
| Montana State U. | Bozeman, MT 59717 | Sandy Mandell | Learning Skills Advance By Choice | 406-994-2824 |
| Montana St. U. North. | Havre, MT 59501 | Linda Hoines | Student Support Services | 406-265-3783 |
| Rocky Mountain C. | Billings, MT 5912 | Dr. Jane Van Dyk | Services for Academic Success | 406-657-1070 |
| U.of Montana | Missoula, MT 59812 | James Marks | Disability Services for Students | 406-243-2373 |
| Western Montana C. | Dillon, MT 59725 | Clarence Kostelecky | Disability Services | 406-683-7330 |

## NEBRASKA

| Institution | Location | Contact | Service | Phone |
| --- | --- | --- | --- | --- |
| Concordia C. | Seward, NE 68434 | Grace Dolak | Academic Support Services | 402-643-7250 |
| Creighton U. | Omaha, NE 68178 | Denise LeClaire | Educational Opportunity Programs | 402-280-2749 |
| Dana College | Blair, NE 68008 | Lori Nielsen | Academic Support Services | 402-426-7334 |
| Doane College | Crete, NE 68333 | Sherri Hanigan | Student Support Services | 402-826-8586 |
| Metropolitan CC. | Omaha, NE 68103 | Mark Carta | Special Needs Program | 402-449-8505 |
| Southeast CC. | Lincoln, NE 68520 | Darlene Williams | Disability Services | 402-437-2625 |
| Union C. | Lincoln, NE 68506 | Jennifer Forbes | Teaching Learning Center | 402-486-2506 |
| U. of Nebraska | Lincoln, NE 68588 | Christy Horn | Services for Stud. With Disabilities | 402-472-3417 |
| U. of Nebraska | Omaha, NE 68182 | Janice Leuenbergere | Learning Center | 402-554-2992 |
| Wayne State C. | Wayne, NE 68787 | Mary O'Boyle | Student Support Services | 402-375-7204 |
| W. Nebraska CC. | Scottsbluff, NE 69361-1899 | Vanessa Harrison | Counseling Center | 308-635-6120 |

## NEVADA

| Institution | Location | Contact | Service | Phone |
| --- | --- | --- | --- | --- |
| U. of Nevada | Las Vegas, NV 89154 | Anita Stockbower | Learning Abilities Center | 702-895-0866 |
| U. of Nevada | Reno, NV 89507 | Mary Zabel | Disabled Student Services | 702-784-6000 |
| W. Nevada CC | Carson City, NV 89703 | Kim Ashley | Student Support Services | 702-887-3156 |

## NEW HAMPSHIRE

| College | Location | Contact | Program | Phone |
|---|---|---|---|---|
| Colby-Sawyer C. | New London, NH 03257 | Tom Mooney | Academic Development | 603-526-3713 |
| Dartmouth C. | Hanover, NH 03755 | Nancy Pompian | Student Disabilities | 603-646-2014 |
| Franklin Pierce C. | Rindge, NH 03461 | Dr. Carol Sitterly | Academic Services | 603-899-4044 |
| Keene State C. | Keene, NH 03435 | Maria Dinting | Aspire Project | 603-358-2390 |
| New England C. | Henniker, NH 03242 | Dr. Joanne MacEachran | College Skills Center | 603-428-2218 |
| New Hampshire C. | Manchester, NH 03106 | Richard Colfer | The Learning Center | 603-645-9606 |
| New Hampshire Tech. | Manchester, NH 03102 | Cate Weir | Support Services | 603-668-6706 |
| Notre Dame C. | Manchester, NH 03275 | Jane O'Neil | Learning Enrichment Center | 603-664-8316 |
| Rivier College | Nashua, NH 03104 | Lisa Baroody | Special Need Services | 603-888-1311 |
| U. of New Hampshire | Ctr. Barnstead, NH 03225 | Donna Sorrentino | Affirmative Action | 603-862-2607 |

## NEW JERSEY

| College | Location | Contact | Program | Phone |
|---|---|---|---|---|
| Bergen CC | Paramus, NJ 07652 | Lynne Crawford | Student Support Services | 201-447-9211 |
| Brookdale CC. | Lincroft, NJ 07738 | Elizabeth Twoby | Adaptive Services | 908-224-2730 |
| Camden County College | Blackwood, NJ 08012 | Anne-Marie Hoyle | PACS Program | 609-227-7200 |
| Centenary C. | Hackettstown, NJ 07840 | Jeffery Zimdahl | Learning Disabilities Services | 908-852-4696 |
| County C. of Morris | Randolph, NJ 07869 | Audrey Melillo | Horizons Program | 201-328-5284 |
| Drew U. | Madison, NJ 07940 | Patricia Naylor | Pgm. - Stud. w/Learning Disabilities | 201-408-3103 |
| Farleigh-Dickinson | Teaneck, NJ 07666 | Dr. Mary Farrell | Regional Ctr. College Students with LD | 201-692-2087 |
| Georgian Court C. | Lakewood, NJ 08701 | Genevieve Van Pelt | The Learning Center | 908-367-2200 |
| Jersey City State C. | Jersey City, NJ 07305 | Dr. Myrna Ehrlich | Project Mentor | 201-200-3120 |
| Kean College | Union, NJ 07083 | Dr. Marie Segal | Project Excel | 908-527-2380 |
| Middlesex City C. | Edison, NJ 08818 | Joan Ikle | Project Connections | 908-906-2507 |
| Monmouth C. | W. Long Branch, NJ 07764 | Ann Grad | Support Serv. for Students with Disab. | 908-571-3460 |
| Monmouth U. | W. Long Branch, NJ 07764 | Carol Giroud | Students with Disabilities | 908-571-3671 |
| Ocean County C. | Toms River, NJ 08754 | Maureen Reustle | Project Academic Skills Support | 908-255-0456 |
| Princeton U. | Princeton, NJ 08544 | Sandra Silverman | Disability Services | 609-258-3054 |
| Ramapo C. | Mahwah, NJ 07430 | Jean Balutanski | Office of Special Services | 201-529-7513 |
| Raritan Valley CC. | Somerville, NJ 08876 | Linda Baum | LD Services | 908-526-1200 |
| Rider University | Lawrenceville, NJ 08648 | Jacqueline Simon | Education Enhancement Program | 609-896-5244 |
| Rutgers U. | New Brunswick, NJ 08903 | Patricia Grove | Learning Resource Center | 908-932-1660 |
| Salem CC | Carneys Point , NJ 08069 | Richard Duffy | Special Population | 609-299-2606 |
| Seton Hall U. | Rutherford, NJ 07070 | Ray Frazier | Student Support Services | 201-761-9168 |
| Sussex CC. | Newton, NJ 07860 | Jean Coen | LD Program | 201-300-2153 |
| Trenton State C. | Trenton, NJ 08650-4700 | Ann Degennaro | Office For Stud. with Differing Abilities | 609-771-2571 |
| Union County C. | Cranford, NJ 07016 | Linda Miraglia-Smith | Services for Students with Disabilities | 908-709-7083 |

## NEW MEXICO

| Institution | Contact | Location | Service | Phone |
|---|---|---|---|---|
| College of Santa Fe | Carol Conoboy | Santa Fe, NM 87505-7634 | Ctr. for Academic Excellence | 505-473-6112 |
| E. New Mexico U. | Linda Green | Roswell, NM 88202 | Special Services | 505-624-7289 |
| N. Mexico Jr. C. | Marilyn Jackson | Hobbs, NM 88240 | Special Needs Services | 505-392-5411 |
| New Mexico State | M. Reynolds-Jackson | Las Cruces, NM 88003 | Services for Students with disAbilities | 505-646-6840 |
| Santa Fe CC. | Jill Douglas | Santa Fe, NM 87502 | Special Services | 505-471-8200 |
| U. of New Mexico | Juan Candelaria | Albuquerque, NM 87131 | Special Services Program | 505-277-3506 |

## NEW YORK

| Institution | Contact | Location | Service | Phone |
|---|---|---|---|---|
| Adelphi U. | Sandra Holzinger | Garden City, NY 11530 | Program for College Students with LD | 516-877-4710 |
| Alfred State-SUNY | Cora Dzubak | Alfred, NY 14802 | Project 5 | 607-587-4122 |
| Barnard C. | Susan Quinby | New York, NY 10027 | Office for Disabled Services | 212-854-4634 |
| Bronx CC. | Joanettia Grier | Bronx, NY 10453 | Disabled Students | 212-220-6444 |
| Brooklyn C. | Roberta Adelman | Brooklyn, NY 11210 | Students with Disabilities | 718-951-5363 |
| Broome CC. | Bruce Pomeroy | Binghamton, NY 134902 | Student Support Services | 607-778-5234 |
| Buffalo State C. | Karen Johnson | Buffalo, NY 14222 | Academic Skills Center | 716-878-4041 |
| Canisius C. | Dan Ryan | Buffalo, NY 14208 | Disabled Student Services | 716-888-3748 |
| Cayuga CC. | David Charland | Auburn, NY 13021 | Services for Students with Special Needs | 315-255-1743 |
| Colgate U. | Lynn Waldman | Hamilton, NY 13346 | Academic Support Program | 315-824-7225 |
| C. of New Rochelle | Joan Bristol | New Rochelle, NY 10805 | Student Services | 914-654-5364 |
| C. of Staten Island | Margaret Venditti | Staten Island, NY 10304 | Disability Services | 718-982-2513 |
| College of St. Rose | Mary Van Der Zee | Albany, NY 12203 | Disabled Student Services | 518-454-5299 |
| Columbia-Greene CC. | Anne Siddall | Hudson, NY 12534 | Students with Disabilities | 518-828-4181 |
| Columbia U. | Lynne Bejoian | New York, NY 10027 | Office of Student Affairs | 212-854-2388 |
| Concordia C. | George Groth | Bronxville, NY 10708 | Concordia Connection | 914-337-9300 |
| Cornell U. | Joan Fisher | Ithaca, NY 14853 | Office of Equal Opportunity | 607-255-3976 |
| Corning CC. | Judy Northrop | Corning, NY 14830 | Counseling for Students with Disab. | 607-962-9459 |
| Culinary Inst. of Amer. | Frederick Gainer | Hyde Park, NY 12538 | Student Development | 914-452-9600 |
| D'Youville C. | Carolyn Boone | Buffalo, NY 14201 | Disability Services | 716-881-7728 |
| Finger Lakes Comm.C. | Patricia Malinowski | Canandaigua, NY 14424 | Services for a Student with a LD | 716-394-3500 |
| Fordham U. | Elliott Palais | Bronx, NY 10458 | TRIO | 718-817-4821 |
| Hamilton C. | Louise Peckingham | Clinton, NY 13323 | Student Support Services | 315-859-4106 |
| Hofstra U. | Dr. Ignacio Gotz | Hempstead, NY 11550 | Prog. for Academic Learning Skills | 516-463-5291 |
| Houghton C. | Susan Hice | Houghton, NY 14744 | Academic Support Center | 716-567-9239 |
| Hudson Valley CC. | Pablo Negron | Troy, NY 12180 | Disabled Student Services | 518-270-7154 |
| Hunter C. CUNY | Sandra LaPorta | New York, NY 10021 | Office for Students with Disabilities | 212-772-4857 |
| Iona College | Madeline Pacherman | New Rochelle, NY 10801 | College Assistance Program | 914-633-2582 |
| Jamestown CC. | Nancy Callahan | Jamestown, NY 14702 | Services for Students with Disabilities | 716-665-5220 |
| Jefferson CC. | Anita Canizares | Watertown, NY 13601 | Learning Skills Center | 315-786-2377 |

| College | Location | Contact | Service | Phone |
| --- | --- | --- | --- | --- |
| Kingsborough CC. | Brooklyn, NY 11235 | Anthony Colarossi | Special Services | 718-368-5175 |
| LaGuardia CC | Long Island City, NY 11101 | Matthew Joffe | Off. for Students with Disabilities | 718-482-5278 |
| LeMoyne C. | Syracuse, NY 13214 | Anne Herron | Academic Support Center | 315-445-4118 |
| Lehman C/CUNY | Bronx, NY 10468 | Marcos Gonzalez | Disability Issues | 718-960-1589 |
| Long Island C.W. Post | Brookville, NY 11548 | C. Rundlett | Academic Resource Center | 516-299-2937 |
| Manhattan College | Riverdale, NY 10471 | Dr. Ross Pollack | Specialized Resource Center | 718-862-8000 |
| Manhattanville C. | Purchase, NY 10577 | Rebecca Rich | Higher Education Learning Program | 914-323-5143 |
| Marist C. | Poughkeepsie, NY 12601 | Linda Cooper | Learning Disabilities Program | 914-575-3274 |
| Marymount Manhattan | New York, NY 10021 | Adele Schwartz | LD College Students | 212-517-0501 |
| Marymount C. | Tarrytown, NY 10591 | Jason Berner | Learning Services | 914-332-8310 |
| Mercy C. | Dobbs Ferry, NY 10522 | Terry Rich | Support Services | 914-693-4500 |
| Mohawk Valley CC. | Utica, NY 13501 | Lynn Igoe | Serv. to Stud. with Disabilities | 315-792-5413 |
| Molloy C. | Rockville Ctr, NY 11570 | Sr.Therese Forker | Students with Special Needs | 516-678-5000 |
| Nassau CC. | Garden Cty., NY 11530 | Victor Margolis | Disabled Student Services | 516-572-7178 |
| New York Inst.of Tech | Old Westbury, NY 11568 | Kate Beckman | GOLD | 516-686-7976 |
| New York U. | New York City, NY 10011 | Georgeanne du Chossios | Access to Learning | 212-998-4980 |
| NYU Para Educator Ctr. | New York, NY 10003 | Dr. Jane Herzog | Para Educator Ctr. for Young Adults | 212-998-5800 |
| Niagara U. | Niagara U., NY 14109 | Diane Stoelting | Individualized Instruction | 716-286-8076 |
| Onondaga CC. | Syracuse, NY 13215 | Roger Purdy | Off. of Serv. Students with Spec. Needs | 315-469-2245 |
| Paul Smith's C. | Paul Smith's, NY 12970 | Carol McKillip | Special Services | 518-327-6425 |
| Purchase C. | Purchase, NY 10577 | Ronnie Mait | Special students | 914-251-6035 |
| Rensselaer Poly. Inst. | Troy, NY 12180 | Debra Hamilton | Disabled Student Services | 518-276-2746 |
| Roberts Wesleyan C. | Rochester, NY 14624 | Carol Ernsthausen | Learning Center | 716-594-6270 |
| Rochester Inst. Tech | Rochester, NY 14623 | Jacqueline Czamanske | Alternative Learning Department | 716-475-2215 |
| Rockland CC. | Suffern, NY 10901 | Ellen Spergel | Office of Disability Services | 914-574-4312 |
| St. Bonaventure | S. Bonaventure, NY 14778 | Debra Bookmiller | Services for Students with Disabilities | 716-375-2066 |
| St, John's U. | Jamaica, NY 11439 | Jackie Lochrie | Student Life | 718-990-6568 |
| St. Lawrence U. | Canton, NY 13617 | John Meagher | Office of Special Needs | 315-379-5104 |
| St. Thomas Aquinas | Sparkill, NY 10976 | Dr. Marijanet Doonan | The "STAC" Exchange | 914-398-4230 |
| Schenectady CC. | Schenectady, NY 12305 | Martha Asselin | Disabled Student Services | 518-381-1200 |
| SUNY at Albany | Albany, NY 12222 | N. Belowich-Negron | LD Resource Program | 518-442-5491 |
| SUNY at Binghamton | Binghamton, NY 13902 | Jean Fairbairn | Services for Students with Disab. | 607-777-2686 |
| SUNY at Brockport | Brockport, NY 14420 | Mildred Portela | Office for Students with Disabilities | 716-395-5409 |
| SUNY at Buffalo | Buffalo, NY 14260 | Sarah Bihr | Office of Disability Services | 716-645-2000 |
| SUNYC at Buffalo | Buffalo, NY 14222 | Marianne Savino | Special Services | 716-878-4041 |
| SUNY-Cortland | Cortland, NY 13045 | Sharon Scheibel | Disability Services | 607-753-2937 |
| SUNY at Farmingdale | Farmingdale, NY 11735 | Malka Edelman | Support Services | 516-420-2411 |
| SUNY-Fredonia | Fredonia, NY 14063 | Liza Smith | Disabled Student Services | 716-673-3270 |
| SUNY at Geneseo | Geneseo, NY 14454 | Kelly Clark | Special Programs | 716-245-5620 |

| Institution | Location | Contact | Service | Phone |
| --- | --- | --- | --- | --- |
| SUNY New Paltz | New Paltz, NY 12561 | KKristen Proctor | Disabled Student Services | 914-257-3020 |
| SUNY at Oneonta | Oneonta, NY 13820 | Sandra Denicore | Learning Support Services | 607-436-2137 |
| SUNY at Oswego | Oswego, NY 13126 | Harry Shock | Learning Enhancement Office | 315-341-2240 |
| SUNY at Plattsburgh | Plattsburgh, NY 12901 | Cordelia Drake | Student Support Services | 518-564-2810 |
| SUNY at Potsdam | Potsdam, NY 13676 | Tamara Durant | Disabled Student Services | 315-267-3267 |
| SUNY at Stony Brook | Stony Brook, NY 11794 | Carol Dworkin | Support Services for Students with LD | 516-632-6748 |
| SUNYC of Technology | Alfred, NY 14802 | Kathryn Fosegan | Project 5 | 607-587-4122 |
| SUNYC of Technology | Canton, NY 13617 | Debora Camp | Accommodative Services Program | 315-386-7121 |
| SUNYC of Technology | Cobelskill, NY 12043 | Anne Campbell | Counseling Center | 518-234-5211 |
| SUNYC of Technology | Delhi, NY 13753 | Leslie Mokay | Academic Success | 607-746-4585 |
| SUNYC of Technology | Farmingdale, NY 11735 | Malka Edelman | Support Services | 516-420-2411 |
| Syracuse U. | Syracuse, NY 13244 | James Duah-Agyeman | Learning Disability Services | 315-443-2622 |
| Tompkins Cortland CC. | Dryden, NY 13035 | Kathryn Wunerlich | Learning Assistance Services | 607-844-8211 |
| U. of Albany | Albany, NY 12222 | Nancy Belowich-Negron | Acad. Assist. for Students with LD | 518-442-5490 |
| Union C. | Schenectady, NY 12308 | Kate Schurick | Support Services | 518-388-6061 |
| U. of Rochester | Rochester, NY 14627 | Vicki Roth | Learning Assistance | 716-275-9049 |
| Utica C. | Utica, NY 13502 | Stephen Pattarini | Academic Support Services | 315-792-3032 |
| Vassar C. | Poughkeepsie, NY 12601 | Ellen Zahariadis | Academic Resource Center | 914-437-7584 |
| Wagner College | Staten Island, NY 10301 | Ruth Anna Perri | Academic Advisement Center | 718-390-3340 |
| Westchester CC. | Valhalla, NY 10595 | Marcia Kalkut | Disabled Students | 914-785-6552 |

## NORTH CAROLINA

| Institution | Location | Contact | Service | Phone |
| --- | --- | --- | --- | --- |
| Appalachian State U. | Boone, NC 28608 | Arlene Lundquist | Learning Disability Program | 704-262-2291 |
| Ashville-Buncombe C. | Ashville, NC 28801 | Deborah Harmon | Special Needs | 704-254-1921 |
| Belmont Abbey C. | Belmont, NC 28012 | Janet Baxter | Learning Disability Support Program | 704-825-6820 |
| Central Piedmont CC. | Charlotte, NC 28235 | Gus Boukouvalas | Services for Students with Disabilities | 704-342-6556 |
| Davidson C. | Davidson, NC 28036 | Leslie Marsicana | Student Support Services | 704-892-2225 |
| Duke U. | Durham, NC 27708 | R. Colver/M. Peete | Academic Skills Center | 919-684-5917 |
| East Carolina U. | Greenville, NC 27858 | C.C. Rowe | Office of Disability Support Services | 919-328-6799 |
| Elon C. | Elon College, NC 27244 | Priscilla Haworth | Student Support Services | 910-584-2212 |
| Guilford C. | Greensboro, NC 27410 | Sue Williams Keith | Academic Skills Center | 919-316-2000 |
| Guilford Tech. CC. | Jamestown, NC 27282 | Angela Leak | Academic Support Services | 919-334-4822 |
| Lenoir-Rhyne C. | Hickory, NC 28603 | Thomas Fauquet | Student Academic Support Service | 704-328-7275 |
| Mars Hill C. | Mars Hill, NC 28754 | Barbara McKinney | Student Support Services | 704-689-1464 |
| Nash CC. | Rocky Mount, NC 27804 | John Browning | Student Support Services | 919-443-4011 |
| North Carolina St. U. | Raleigh, NC 27695 | Patricia Smith | Disability Student Services | 919-737-7653 |
| Richmond CC. | Hamlet, NC 28345 | Gilbert Montgomery | Instructional Services | 910-582-7000 |
| Rockingham CC. | Wentworth, NC 27375 | LaVonne James | Disability Services | 910-342-4261 |
| Southwestern CC. | Sylva, NC 28779 | Steve Conlin | Student Support Services | 704-586-4091 |

| College | Location | Contact | Service | Phone |
|---|---|---|---|---|
| U. of N. Carolina | Chapel Hill, NC 27599 | Jane Byron | Learning Disabilities Services | 919-962-7227 |
| U. of N. Carolina | Charlotte, NC 28223 | Jane Rochester | Disability Services | 704-547-4357 |
| U. of N. Carolina | Wilmington, NC 28403 | Phillip Sharp | Disabled Student Services | 919-395-3746 |
| Wake Forest U. | Winston-Salem, NC 27109 | Diane Mitchell | Learning Assistance Program | 910-759-5201 |
| Western Carolina U. | Cullowhee, NC 28723 | Dr. Bonita Jacobs | Disability Student Services | 704-227-7234 |
| West Piedmont CC. | Morgantown, NC 28655 | Susan Andrea | Disabled Student Services | 704-438-6050 |
| Wake Tech. CC. | Raleigh, NC 27603 | Sheila Hite | Services for Handicap. Students | 919-772-0750 |
| W. Carolina U. | Cullowhee, NC 28723 | Carol Mellen | Student Support Services | 704-227-7127 |
| Wingate University | Wingate, NC 28174 | Dr.L Karnes | Specific Learning Disabilities | 704-233-8269 |
| Winston-Salem St. U. | Winston-Salem, NC 27006 | Myra Waddell | Academic Resource Center | 919-750-5000 |

## NORTH DAKOTA

| College | Location | Contact | Service | Phone |
|---|---|---|---|---|
| Bismarck State C. | Bismarck, ND 58506 | Gerie Hase | Learning Skills Center | 701-224-5426 |
| Dickinsson State U. | Dickinson, ND 58601 | Philip Covington | Student Developement | 701-227-2686 |
| Minot State U. | Minot, ND 58702 | Dawn Rorvig | Counseling Services | 701-857-3371 |
| North Dakota St. C. | Wahpeton, ND 58075 | Rene Moen | Study Serv. for Students with Disab. | 701-671-2335 |
| North Dakota St. U. | Fargo, ND 58105 | Catherine Anderson | Students with Disability Services | 701-231-7671 |
| United Tribes Tech.C. | Bismarck, ND 58504 | Jane Hilsendager | Special Services | 701-255-3285 |
| U. of N. Dakota | Grand Forks, ND 58202 | Deborah Glennen | Disability Support Services | 701-777-3425 |
| U. of N. Dakota | Williston, ND 58801 | Stephanie Turcotte | Disability Support Services | 701-774-4220 |

## OHIO

| College | Location | Contact | Service | Phone |
|---|---|---|---|---|
| Antioch C. | Yellow Springs, OH 45387 | Judy Kinatner | Support Services | 513-767-6473 |
| Ashland U. | Ashland, OH 44805 | Suzanne Salvo | Classroom Support Services | 419-289-5904 |
| Baldwin- Wallace C. | Berea, OH 44017 | Jane Boomer | Learning Center | 216-826-2147 |
| Bowling Green State U. | Bowling Green, OH 43403 | Rob Cunningham | Office of Disability Services | 419-372-8495 |
| Capital U. | Columbus, OH 43209 | I. Phillips-Carmichael | Disability Services | 800-289-6289 |
| Case W. Reserve U. | Cleveland, OH 44106 | Mayo Bulloch | Educational Support Services | 216-368-3059 |
| Central Ohio Tech. C. | Newark, OH 43055 | Dr. Phyllis Thompson | Disability Services | 614-366-9246 |
| Clark St. CC. | Springfield, OH 45505 | Jean Chepp | Office of Student Development | 513-328-6081 |
| Cleveland State U. | Cleveland, OH 44115 | Michael Zuccaro | Disability Services | 216-687-2015 |
| C. of Wooster | Wooster, OH 44691 | Pam Rose | Learning Center | 330-263-2595 |
| C. of Mt. St. Joseph | Cincinnati, OH 45233 | Jane Pohlman | Project Excel | 513-244-4623 |
| Columbus St. CC. | Columbus, OH 43216 | Wayne Cocchi | Disability Services | 614-227-2629 |
| Cuyahoga CC.-Western | Parma, OH 44130 | Deena Strome | Access Office for Accommodation | 216-987-2052 |
| Denison U. | Granville, OH 43023 | Ms.Stuart Oremus | Educational Services | 614-587-6489 |
| Franklin U. | Columbus, OH 43215 | Rick McIntosh | Disability Services | 614-341-6415 |
| Hiram C. | Hiram, OH 44234 | Lynn Taylor | Counseling | 330-569-5233 |
| Hocking Technical C. | Nelsonville, OH 45764 | Kim Powell | Access Center | 614-753-3591 |

| Institution | Location | Contact | Service | Phone |
|---|---|---|---|---|
| Kent State U. | Kent, OH 44242 | Janet Filer | Student Disability Services | 330-672-3391 |
| Kenyon C. | Gambier, OH 43022 | Jane Martindell | Academic Advising | 614-427-5145 |
| Lakeland CC. | Kirtland, OH 44094 | Alan Kirsh | Special Student Services | 216-953-7245 |
| Lorain City CC. | Elyria, OH 44035 | Ruth Porter | Office for Special Needs Services | 216-366-4058 |
| Lourdes C. | Sylvania, OH 43560 | Kim Naumann | Learning Resource Center | 419-885-3211 |
| Marietta C. | Marietta, OH 45750 | Dr. Marilyn Pasquarelli | Counseling Center | 614-374-4784 |
| Miami U.-Hamilton | Hamilton, OH 45011 | Mary Vogel | Special Services | 513-785-3211 |
| Miami U. | Oxford, OH 45056 | Lois Phillips | Learning Disabilities Program | 513-529-6841 |
| Muskingum C. | New Concord, OH 43762 | Jen Navicki | PLUS Program | 614-826-8280 |
| N. Centrl.Tech. C.Ftd | Mansfield, OH 44901 | Leslie Harris | Disability Services | 419-755-4753 |
| Oberlin C. | Oberlin, OH 44074 | Dr. Dean Kelly | Off. of Services for Students with Disab. | 216-775-8467 |
| Ohio Dominican C. | Columbus, OH 43219 | Rose Ann Kalister | Academic Development | 614-251-4511 |
| Ohio Northern U. | Ada, OH 45810 | Karen Condeni | Office of Admissions | 419-772-2260 |
| Ohio State U. | Columbus, OH 43210 | Ann Yurcisin | Office for Disabilities Services | 614-292-3307 |
| Ohio State U. | Marion, OH 43302 | Margaret Hazelett | Learning Disabilities Services | 614-389-2361 |
| Ohio State U. | Newark, OH 43055 | Phillip Thompson | Disability Services | 614-366-9246 |
| Ohio U. | Athens, OH 45701 | Catherine Fahey | Off. for Institutional Equity/Disab. Serv. | 614-593-2620 |
| Ohio Wesleyan U. | Delaware, OH 43015 | R. Blake Michael | Academic Advising | 614-368-3275 |
| Otterbein College | Westerville, OH 43081 | Ellen Kasulis | Learning Assistance Center | 614-898-1362 |
| Owens CC | Toledo, OH 43699 | Debra Sanchez | Disability Resource Services | 419-661-7504 |
| Raymond Walters C. | Cincinnati, OH 45236 | Julie Gibson | Disability Services | 513-745-5670 |
| Shawnee State U. | Portsmouth, OH 45662 | Eustace Matthews | Special Needs | 614-355-2276 |
| Sinclair CC. | Dayton, OH 45402 | Lisa Badia | Disability Services | 937-449-5113 |
| Terra State CC. | Fremont, OH 43420 | Richard Newman | Disability Services | 419-334-8400 |
| U. of Akron | Akron, OH 44325 | Grace Olmstead | Serv. for Stud. with Disabilities | 216-972-7928 |
| U. of Cincinnati | Cincinnati, OH 45221 | Stanley Henderson | Disability Services | 513-556-3244 |
| U. of Dayton | Dayton, OH 45469 | Bea Bedard | Disabled Student Services | 513-229-2229 |
| U. of Findlay | Findlay, OH 45840 | Donna Smith | Supporting Skills System | 419-422-8313 |
| U. of Toledo | Toledo, OH 43606 | Pamela Emch | Physically or Mentally Challenged | 419-530-4981 |
| Ursuline C. | Pepper Pike, OH 44124 | Cynthia Russell | PSLD | 216-646-8123 |
| Washinton St. CC. | Marietta, OH 45750 | Deborah Thomas | Student Development | 614-374-8716 |
| Wright State U. | Dayton, OH 45435 | Stephen Simon | Learning Disabilities Program | 513-775-5680 |
| Xavier U. | Cincinnati, OH 45207 | Sarah Kelly | Learning Assistance Program | 513-745-3280 |

## OKLAHOMA

| Institution | Location | Contact | Service | Phone |
|---|---|---|---|---|
| Cameron U. | Lawton, OK 73505 | Suzanne Aplin | Student Support Services | 405-581-2352 |
| Oklahoma City CC. | Oklahoma City, OK 73159 | Keith Leafdale | Services to Students with Disabilities | 405-682-1611 |
| Oklahoma State U. | Stillwater, OK 74078 | Debra Swoboda | Disabled Student Services | 405-744-7116 |
| Phillips U. | Enid, OK 73701 | Kibby Rose | Support Services | 405-548-2208 |

| College | City | Contact | Service | Phone |
|---|---|---|---|---|
| Southeastern OK St.U. | Durant, OK 74701 | Jan Anderson | Student Support Services Prog. | 405-924-0121 |
| Tulsa Junior C. | Tulsa, OK 74119 | Yolanda Williams | Disabled Student Resource Center | 918-631-7115 |
| U. of Oklahoma | Norman, OK 73026 | Suzette Dyer | Disabled Student Services | 405-325-3163 |
| U. of Tulsa | Tulsa, OK 74104 | Jane Owens | Student Academic Support | 918-631-2334 |

## OREGON

| College | City | Contact | Service | Phone |
|---|---|---|---|---|
| Blue Mt. CC. | Pendleton, OR 97801 | Cynthia Hilden | Special Services Office | 541-278-5796 |
| Chemeketa CC. | Salem, OR 97309 | Tiffany Borden | Off. for Persons with Disabilities | 503-399-5192 |
| Lane CC. | Eugene, OR 97405 | Leigh Alice Petty | Disabled Student Services | 541-747-4501 |
| Linn-Benton CC. | Albany, OR 97321 | Paula Grigsby | Disabled Student Services | 503-917-4683 |
| Mt. Hood CC. | Gresham, OR 97030 | Debbie Derr | Disability Services | 503-667-7650 |
| Oregon Instit. Tech | Klamath, OR 97601 | Ron McCutcheon | Campus Access and Equality | 541-885-1031 |
| Oregon State U. | Corvallis, OR 97331 | Tracy Bentley | Services for Students with Disabilities | 541-737-3661 |
| Portland State U. | Portland, OR 97207 | Lisa Cavendor | Info. & Academic Support Ctr. | 503-725-4005 |
| Rogue CC. | Grants Pass, OR 97527 | Bonnie Reeg | Support Services | 541-471-3527 |
| S. Oregon State C. | Ashland, OR 97520 | Patricia Sloan | Disabled Student Services | 503-552-6213 |
| Umpqua CC. | Roseburg, OR 97470 | Barbara Stoner | Disability Services | 503-440-4600 |
| U. of Oregon | Eugene, OR 97403 | Dr. Hilary Gerdes | Disability Services | 541-346-3211 |
| W. Baptist C. | Salem, OR 97301 | Faythe Moore | Disability Services | 503-375-7015 |
| W. Oregon State U. | Monmouth, OR 97361 | Martha Smith | Office of Disability Services | 503-838-8250 |
| Willamette U. | Salem, OR 97301 | Robin Smithtro | Off. of Serv. for Students with Disab. | 503-370-6471 |

## PENNSYLVANIA

| College | City | Contact | Service | Phone |
|---|---|---|---|---|
| Albright C. | Reading, PA 19612 | R. Jane Williams | Counseling Center | 215-921-2381 |
| Allentown C. | Ctr. Valley, PA 18034 | Rosiland Smith-Edman | Learning Center | 610-282-1100 |
| Bryn Mauw C. | Bryn Maur, PA 19010 | Jeanne Simon Angell | Accessibility | 610-526-7322 |
| Bucknell U. | Lewisburg, PA 17837 | Maureen Murphy | Support Services | 717-524-1301 |
| Bucks County CC. | Newton, PA 18940 | M. Stevens-Cooper | Prog. for Students with Disabilities | 215-968-8463 |
| Cabrini C. | Radnor, PA 19087 | Stephanie Bell | LD Services | 610-902-8572 |
| California U. of Penn. | California, PA 15419 | Albertha Graham | CARE Program | 412-938-4012 |
| Carlow C. | Pittsburgh, PA 15213 | Andrea Beranek | Learning Center | 412-578-6136 |
| Carnegie Mellon U. | Pittsburgh, PA 15213 | Linda Hooper | Learning Services | 412-268-6878 |
| Chatham C. | Pittsburg, PA 15232 | Janet James | Support SDervices | 412-354-1611 |
| Clarion U. of Penn. | Clarion, PA 16214 | Gregory Clary | Special Services Program | 814-226-2347 |
| CC of Allegheny Cty. | Pittsburgh, PA 15212 | Mary Beth Doyle | Handicapped Services | 412-237-4614 |
| CC. of Philadelphia | Philadelphia, PA 19130 | Joan Monroe | Educational Support Services | 215-751-8474 |
| CCAC C. North | Pittsburgh, PA 15237 | Kathleen White | Special Services | 412-369-3686 |
| College Misericordia | Dallas, PA 18612 | Dr. Joseph Rogan | Alternative Learners Project | 717-675-1281 |
| Delaware Valley C. | Doylestown, PA 18901 | Cynthia King | Learning Support | 215-489-2490 |

| Institution | Location | Contact | Service | Phone |
|---|---|---|---|---|
| Dickinson C. | Carlisle, PA 17013 | Kate Brooks | Disabled Student Services | 717-245-1740 |
| Drexel U. | Philadelphia, PA 19104 | Patrice Miller | Office of Student Supportive Services | 215-895-2960 |
| East Stroudsburg U. | E. Stroudsburg, PA 18301 | Edith Miller | Disability Services | 717-422-3825 |
| Edinboro U. of Penn. | Edinboro, PA 16444 | Kathleen Strosser | Office for Students with Disabilities | 814-732-2462 |
| Franklin & Marshall | Lancaster, PA 17604 | Kenneth John | Counseling Services | 717-291-4083 |
| Gannon U. | Erie, PA 16541 | Sister J. Lowery | Program for Students with LD | 814-871-5326 |
| Gettysburg C. | Gettysburg, PA 17325 | Gailann Rickert | Academic Advising | 717-337-6587 |
| Harcum Jr. C. | Bryn Mawr, PA 19010 | Penny Caldwell | Talent Development | 215-526-6034 |
| Indiana U. of Penn. | Indiana, PA 15705 | Catherine Dugan | Disabled Student Services | 412-357-4067 |
| King's C. | Wilkes-Barre, PA 18711 | Jacintha Burke | Academic Skills Center | 717-826-5800 |
| Kutztown U. | Kutztown, PA 19530 | Barbara Peters | Services for Students with Disabilities | 610-683-4108 |
| Lehigh University | Bethlehem, PA 18015 | Cheryl Ashcroft | Academic Support Services | 215-758-4152 |
| Lock Haven U. of Penn. | Lock Haven, PA 17745 | Nate Hosley | Student Support Services | 717-893-2324 |
| Luzerne Cty CC. | Naanticoke, PA 18634 | Anna Mary McHugh | Learning Support Services | 717-829-7399 |
| Lycoming C. | Williamsport, PA 17701 | Diane Bonner | Academic Resource Center | 717-321-4052 |
| Mercyhurst C. | Erie, PA 16546 | Dr. Barbara Weigert | Prog. for Stud. with Learning Differences | 814-824-2450 |
| Messiah C. | Grantham a, PA 17027 | Keith Drahn | Disability Services | 717-766-2511 |
| Millersville U. of PA | Millersville, PA 17551 | Gerald Burkhardt | Academic Advisement | 717-872-3257 |
| Montgomery Col. CC. | Blue Bell, PA 19422 | Saul Finkle | Services for Students with Disab. | 215-641-6574 |
| Muhlenberg C. | Allentown, PA 18104 | Wendy Cole | Academic Support Services | 610-821-3200 |
| Northampton Comm C. | Bethlehem, PA 18017 | Laranie Demshock | Services for Learning Disabled | 215-861-5342 |
| Penn. C. of Tech. | Williamsport, PA 17701 | Mary Lou Morollo | Serv. for Students with Disabilities | 717-326-3761 |
| Penn State-Delaware | Media, PA 19063 | Sharon Manco | Support Services | 610-892-1461 |
| Penn State-Mt. Alto | Mount Alto, PA 17237 | Nanette Hatzes | Learning Center | 717-749-6045 |
| Pennsylvania State U. | Univ. Park, PA 16802 | Marianne Karwacki | Learning Disabilities Support Services | 814-863-2291 |
| Peirce C. | Philadelphia, PA 19102 | Patricia Rucker | Disability Services | 215-545-6400 |
| Robert Morris College | Corapolis, PA 15108 | Marian Alverson | Disabled Student Services | 412-262-8349 |
| Shippensburg U. | Shippensburg, PA 17257 | Lois Waters | Social Equity | 717-532-1161 |
| Slippery Rock U. | Slippery Rock, PA 16057 | Linda Mattice Smith | Disability Services | 412-738-2016 |
| St. Joseph's U. | Philadelphia, PA 19131 | Jim Scott | Students with Disabilities | 610-660-1774 |
| Temple U. | Philadelphia, PA 19122 | Dorothy Cebula | Disability Resources & Services | 215-204-1280 |
| U. of Pennsylvania | Philadelphia, PA 19104 | Alice Nagle | Program for People with Disabilities | 215-898-6993 |
| U. of Pittsburgh | Johnstown, PA 15904 | Dianna Van Blerkom | Learning Resource Center | 814-269-7107 |
| U. of Pittsburgh | Pittsburgh, PA 15260 | Marcie Roberts | Disability Resources & Services | 412-648-7890 |
| U. of Scranton | Scranton, PA 18510 | Mary McAndrew | Learning Resource Center | 717-941-4038 |
| U. of the Arts | Philadelphia, PA 19102 | Stephanie Bell | Student Services | 215-875-2254 |
| Washington & Jefferson | Washington, PA 15301 | Mary Jane Jones | Academic Support Program | 412-228-9331 |
| West Chester U. | Westchester, PA 19383 | Martin Patwell | Disability Services | 610-436-3217 |
| Westmoreland Cty.C. | Youngwood, PA 15697 | Mary Ellen Barres | Student Support Services | 412-925-4189 |

| Institution | City/State/Zip | Contact | Program | Phone |
|---|---|---|---|---|
| Widener U. | Chester, PA 19013 | LaVerne Ziegenfuss | ENABLE | 610-499-1270 |
| Wilkins U. | Wilkes-Barre, PA 18766 | Judith Fremont | Learning Center | 717-831-4150 |

## RHODE ISLAND

| Institution | City/State/Zip | Contact | Program | Phone |
|---|---|---|---|---|
| Brown U. | Providence, RI 02912 | Robert Shaw | Stu.With Alternative Learning Styles | 401-863-2378 |
| Bryant College | Smithfield, RI 02917 | Dr. Martha Ucci | Counseling Center | 401-232-6045 |
| CC. of Rhode Island | Warwick, RI 02856 | Julie White | Access to Opportunity | 401-825-2305 |
| Johnson & Whales C. | Providence, RI 02903 | Meryl Berstein | Special Needs/ Student Success | 800-343-2565 |
| New England Inst. Tech. | Warwick, RI 02886 | Doreen Lasiew | Academic Skills Center | 401-739-5000 |
| Providence C. | Providence, RI 02918 | Rose Boyle | Academic Services | 401-865-2494 |
| U. of Rhode Island | Kingston, RI 02881 | Pamela Rohland | Disability Services | 401-874-1000 |

## SOUTH CAROLINA

| Institution | City/State/Zip | Contact | Program | Phone |
|---|---|---|---|---|
| Clemson U. | Clemson, SC 29634 | Shirley Davis | Planning & Research | 864-656-3181 |
| College of Charleston | Charleston, SC 29424 | Bobbie Lindstrom | SNAP Services | 803-953-5981 |
| Francis Marion U. | Florence, SC 29501 | David Kahn | Guidance & Placement | 803-661-1290 |
| Johnson & Wales | Charleston, SC 29403 | Dale Crowell | special Needs | 803-727-3028 |
| Limestone C. | Gaffney, SC 29340 | Joe Pitts | PALS | 864-488-4534 |
| S. Carolina State | Orangeburg, SC 29117 | Belinda Smalls | Handicapped Prog. | 803-536-7024 |
| Southern Wesleyan U. | Central, SC 29630 | Randy Becker | Learning Disabilities | 864-639-2453 |
| The Citadel | Charleston, SC 29409 | Dr. Barbara Zaremba | Support Services for LD Students | 803-953-5000 |
| Trident Tech. C. | Charleston, SC 29423 | Pam Middleton | Serv. for Students with Disabilities | 803-572-6222 |
| U. of S. Carolina | Aiken, SC 29801 | Linda Matthews | Office of Special Services | 803-641-3317 |
| USC-Coastal Carolina | Conway, SC 29526 | J. Mazurkiewicz | Counseling Services | 803-347-3161 |
| U. of South Carolina | Columbia, SC 29208 | Karen Pettus | Learning Disability Program | 803-777-6142 |
| U. of S. Carolina | Lancaster, SC 29721 | Deborah Cureton | Academic Success Center | 803-285-7471 |
| U. of S. Carolina | Spartburg, SC 29303 | Stephanie Boyd | Disability Services | 864-503-5123 |
| York Tech.C. | Clover, SC 29730 | Nita Forrest | Student Support Services | 803-324-3130 |

## SOUTH DAKOTA

| Institution | City/State/Zip | Contact | Program | Phone |
|---|---|---|---|---|
| Augustana C. | Sioux Falls, SD 57107 | Katie Poole | Student Services | 605—336-4496 |
| Black Hills St. U. | Spearfish, SD 57783 | Ann Anderson | Student Support Services | 605-642-6099 |
| Dakota State U. | Madison, SD 57042 | Naancy Moose | Support Services | 605-252-5269 |
| National C. | Rapid City, SD 57709 | Susan Watton | Learning Center | 605-394-4821 |
| Northrn State U. | Aberdeen, SD 57401 | Paul Kraft | Learning Center | 605-626-2371 |
| South Dakota State U. | Brookings, SD 57007 | James W. Carlson | Disabled Student Services | 605-688-4496 |
| U. of S. Dakota | Vermillion, SD 57069 | Elaine Pearson | Disability Services | 605-677-6389 |

## TENNESSEE

| Institution | City/State/Zip | Contact | Program | Phone |
|---|---|---|---|---|
| Chattanooga St. CC. | Chattanooga, TN 37406 | Betty Soward | Disability Services | 423-697-4421 |

| College | Location | Contact | Service | Phone |
| --- | --- | --- | --- | --- |
| Cleveland St. CC. | Cleveland, TN 37320 | Mark Wilson | Student Development | 423-478-6217 |
| E. Tennessee St. | Johnson Cty., TN 37614 | Heidi Bimrose | Disabled Student Services | 423-439-4841 |
| Lee C. | Cleveland, TN 37311 | Ginger Sands | Academic Support Program | 423-478-7434 |
| Middle TN St. U. | Murfreesboro, TN 37132 | John Harris | Handicapped Student Services | 615-898-2783 |
| Pellissippi St. Tech. C. | Knoxville, TN 37933 | Judy Fischer Mathis | Services for Students with Disabilities | 423-694-6751 |
| Roane State CC. | Harriman, TN 37748 | Barbara Neal | Disability Services | 423-882-4570 |
| Rhodes C. | Memphis, TN 38112 | Peggy Harlow | Services for Students with Disabilities | 901-726-3994 |
| Tennessee Tech U. | Cookeville, TN 38505 | Sammie Young | Disabled Services | 615-372-6318 |
| U. of Memphis | Memphis, TN 38152 | Dona Sparger | Learning Disability Program | 901-678-2880 |
| U. of Tennessee | Chattanooga, TN 37403 | Dr. Patricia Kopetz | College Access Program | 423-755-4006 |
| U. of Tennessee | Knoxville, TN 37996 | J. ScottBey Howard | Disabled Student Services | 423-974-6087 |
| U. of Tennessee | Martin, TN 38238 | Dr. Barbara Gregory | P.A.C.E. | 901-587-7125 |
| U. of Tennesse | Memphis, TN 38163 | Cynthia Jordan | Student Academic Support Serv. | 901-448-5056 |
| Vanderbilt U. | Nashville, TN 37235 | Michael Miller | Opportunity Development Center | 615-322-4705 |

## TEXAS

| College | Location | Contact | Service | Phone |
| --- | --- | --- | --- | --- |
| Abilene Christian U. | Abilene, TX 79699 | Gloria Bradshaw | Alpha Academic Services | 915-674-2750 |
| Amarillo C. | Amarillo, TX 79178 | Lloyd Meroney | Accessibility | 806-371-5436 |
| Ambassador C. | Big Sandy, TX 75755 | John Good | Disability Support Services | 903-636-2062 |
| Austin CC. | Cedar Park, TX 78613 | Meredith Ross-Chong | Special Services | 512-223-2012 |
| Blinn C. | Brenham, TX 77868 | Patricia Moran | Disability Resources | 409-830-4157 |
| Central Texas C. | Killeen, TX 76540 | Jose Aponte | Disability Support Services | 817-526-1339 |
| Eastfield C. | Mesquite, TX 75150 | Reva Rattan | Services for Special Populations | 972-860-7032 |
| El Paso CC. | El Paso, TX 79998 | Ann Westbrook | Center for Students with Disabilities | 915-594-2675 |
| Lamar U. Tech. Inst. | Beaumont, TX 77705 | Callie Trahan | Services for Students with Disabilities | 409-880-8026 |
| Lamar U.-Orange | Orange, TX 77630 | Ann Taylor | Disability Services | 409-882-3379 |
| Lamar U. Port Arthur | Port Arthur, TX 77641 | Pamela Hunter | Special Poplulations | 409-983-4921 |
| Laredo CC. | Laredo, TX 78040 | Sylvia Trevino | Special Population | 210-721-5137 |
| Lee C. | Baytown, TX 77522 | Rosemary Coffman | Disabilities Services | 713-425-6384 |
| Midwestern St. U. | Wichita Falls, TX 76308 | Debra Higginbotham | Office of Disability Accommodations | 817-689-4618 |
| N. Lake C. | Irving, TX 75038 | Mary Ciminelli | Special Services | 214-273-3165 |
| Palo Alto C. | San Antonio, TX 78224 | Sharon Dresser | Special Populations | 210-921-5287 |
| Schreiner C. | Kerrville, TX 78028 | Jude Gallik | Learning Support Services Program | 512-896-5411 |
| St. Philip's College | San Antonio, TX 78203 | Rhonda Rapp | Learning Disability Program | 210-531-3474 |
| St. Edward's U.. | Austin, TX 78704 | Bunny Smith | Learning Assistance Center | 512-448-8561 |
| Southern Methodist | Dallas, TX 75275 | Sandra Mufkopf | Services for Students with Disabilities | 214-268-2065 |
| South Plains C. | Lubbock, TX 79401 | Maggie Seymour | Special Services | 806-747-0576 |
| S.W. Texas St. U. | San Marcos, TX 78666 | Gina Schuetz | Office of Disability Services | 512-245-3451 |
| Stephen F. Austin St. U. | Nacogdoches, TX 75962 | Lucy Stringer | Disability Services | 409-468-3004 |

| College | Location | Service | Contact | Phone |
|---|---|---|---|---|
| Texas A & M | Kingsville, TX 78363 | Services for Students with Disabilities | D. Brown-Pearson | 512-5953-3991 |
| Texas A & M. U. | College Station, TX 77843 | Services for Students with Disabilities | Jo Hudson | 409-845-1637 |
| Texas Christian U. | Ft. Worth, TX 76129 | Acad. Serv. for Students with Disab. | Jennifer Lowrance | 817-921-7486 |
| Texas Women's U. | Denton, TX 76204 | Disabled Student Services | Juliette Rizzo | 817-898-3835 |
| Texas Tech. U. | Lubbock, TX 79409 | Disabled Student Services | Charley Tiggs | 806-742-2192 |
| Tyler Jr. C. | Tyler, TX 75711 | Support Services | Vickie Geisel | 903-510-2395 |
| U. of Houston | Houston, TX 77058 | Disability Services | Margie Skyles | 713-283-2627 |
| U. of Houston | Houston, TX 77204 | Center for Students with Disabilities | Caroline Gergely | 713-743-5400 |
| U. of Houston-Dwntwn | Houston, TX 77002 | Disabled Student Services | Duraese Hall | 713-221-8430 |
| U. of North Texas | Denton, TX 76203 | Office of Disability Accommodations | Steve Pickett | 817-565-4323 |
| U. of Texas | Arlington, TX 76019 | Office of Counseling & Career Development | Cheryl Cardell | 817-273-2011 |
| U. of Texas-Austin | Austin, TX 78713 | Serv. for students with Disabilities | Sondra Marks | 512-471-6259 |
| U. of Texas-Brnsville | Brownsville, TX 78520 | Disability Services | Stephen Wilder | 210—544-8292 |
| U. of Texas-Dallas | Richardson, TX 75083 | Special Services | Tracy Cole | 972-883-2098 |
| U. of Texas-Edinburg | Edinburg, TX 78539 | Disability Services | Garza Ruben | 210-381-2585 |
| U. of Texas- El Paso | El Paso, TX 79968 | Disabled Student Services | Susan Lopez | 915-747-7481 |
| U. of Texas-S.Antonio | San Antonio, TX 78249 | Disabled Student Services | Lorraine Donham | 210-458-4157 |
| U. of Texas-Pan Amer. | Edinburg, TX 78539 | Office or Serv. for Persons with Disab. | Ruben Garza | 210-316-7005 |
| West State Texas U. | Canyon, TX 79016 | Special Populations Counseling Center | Kay Kropff | 806-656-2392 |

## UTAH

| College | Location | Service | Contact | Phone |
|---|---|---|---|---|
| Brigham Young U. | Provo, UT 84602 | Counseling & Development Center | Paul Byrd | 801-378-2767 |
| College of E. Utah | Price, UT 84501 | Student Support Services | Colleen Quigley | 801-637-0489 |
| Salt Lake CC. | Salt Lake Cty, UT 84130 | Disability Resource Center | Kay Fulton | 801-957-4659 |
| Snow C. | Ephraim, UT 84627 | Student Support Services | Cyndi Crabb | 801-283-4021 |
| Southern Utah U. | Cedar City, UT 84720 | Student Support Services | Pamela France | 801-586-7848 |
| U. of Utah | Salt Lake City, UT 84112 | Serv. for Stud. with Learning Disabilities | Olga Nadeau | 801-581-5020 |
| Utah State U. | Logan, UT 84322 | Disability Resource Center | Diane Baum | 801-797-2444 |
| Utah Valley CC. | Orem, UT 84058 | Students with Disabilities | Curtis Pendelton | 801-222-8000 |
| Weber State C. | Ogden, UT 84408 | Physically Challenged Students | LaMar Kap | 801-626-6413 |

## VERMONT

| College | Location | Service | Contact | Phone |
|---|---|---|---|---|
| Burlington College | Burlington, VT 05401 | Educational Resource Center | Donna Levin | 8-2-862-9616 |
| Castleton St. C. | Castleton, VT 05735 | Student Support Services | Joan Mulligan | 802-468-5611 |
| Champlain C. | Burlington, VT 05402 | Student Resource Center | Rebecca Peterson | 802-658-0800 |
| Green Mountain C. | Poultney, VT 05764 | The Learning Center | Jack Clay | 802-287-8208 |
| Johnson State C. | Johnson, VT 05656 | Academic and Support Services | Sara Henry | 802-635-2356 |
| Landmark C. | Putney, VT 05346 | Landmark College/Pre-College | Francis Sopper | 802-387-6718 |
| Lyndon State C. | Lyndonville, VT 05851 | Project EXCELL | Dan Daley | 802-626-6210 |

| School | Location | Contact | Service | Phone |
|---|---|---|---|---|
| Marlboro C. | Marlboro, VT 05344 | Hilly Van Loon | Advising | 802-257-4333 |
| Middlebury C. | Middlebury, VT 05753 | Elizabeth Charistensen | Support Services | 802-443-5851 |
| Norwich U. | Northfield, VT 05663 | Paula Gills | Learning Support Center | 802-485-2130 |
| St. Michael's C. | Colchester, VT 05439 | Dr. David Landers | Student Resource Center | 802-654-2000 |
| Southern Vermont C. | Bennington, VT 05201 | Linda Crowe | Learning Disability Program | 802-442-5427 |
| Trinity C. | Burlington, VT 05401 | Linda Gustafson | Learning Resource Center | 802-658-0337 |
| U. of Vermont | Burlington, VT 05405 | Nancy Oliker | Office of Specialized Student Services | 802-656-7753 |
| Vermont Technical C. | Randolph, VT 05061 | Barbara Bendix | Services for Students with Disabilities | 802-728-1278 |

## VIRGINIA

| School | Location | Contact | Service | Phone |
|---|---|---|---|---|
| Blue Ridge CC. | Weyers Cave, VA 24486 | John Downey | Disability Services | 540-234-9261 |
| Christopher Newport C. | Newport News, VA 23606 | Melissa Whitt | Services to Students with Disabilities | 757-594-7047 |
| Clinch Valley C. | Wise, VA 24293 | Julia Heise | Student Support Services | 703-328-0176 |
| C. of William & Mary | Williamsburg, VA 23185 | Lisa Bickley | Disabilities Services | 804-221-2510 |
| E. Mennonite U. | Harrisonburg, VA 22801 | J. Coryell Hedrick | Learning Center | 540-432-4233 |
| Ferrum C. | Ferrum, VA 24088 | Nancy Beach | Disability Services | 540-365-4262 |
| George Mason U. | Fairfax, VA 22030 | Paul Bousel | Disability Support Services | 703-993-2474 |
| Hampton U. | Hampton, VA 23668 | L. Gambell-Boone | Student Support Services | 757-729-5493 |
| Hollins C. | Roanoke, VA 24020 | Rita Foster | Student Support Services | 540-362-6404 |
| James Madison | Harrisonburg, VA 22807 | Lou Hedrick | Office of Disability Services | 540-568-6705 |
| Liberty U. | Lynchburg, VA 24506 | Barbara Sherman | Bruckner Learning Center | 804-582-2226 |
| Longwood C. | Farmville, VA 23901 | Scott Lissner | Academic Support Services | 804-395-2591 |
| Lynchburg C. | Lynchburg, VA 24501 | Ann Smith | Disabled StudentServices | 804-541-8300 |
| Mary Washington C. | Fredericksburg, VA 22401 | Tricia Tracy | Office of Academic Services | 540-654-4694 |
| Marymount U. | Arlington, VA 22207 | Sr. Irene Cody | Disabled Student Services | 703-284-1605 |
| New River CC. | Dublin, VA 24060 | Jeannanne Dixon | Leap Center | 540-674-3600 |
| Old Dominican U. | Norfolk, VA 23529 | Dr. Nancy Olthoff | Disability Services | 757-683-4655 |
| Patrick Henry CC. | Martinsville, VA 24115 | Scott Guebert | Student Support Services | 540-656-0257 |
| Radford U. | Radford, VA 24142 | Linda Conrads | Disabled Student Services | 540831-5226 |
| Randolph- Macon C. | Ashland, VA 23005 | Sherry Schlenke | Learning Disabilities Support Services | 804-752-7343 |
| Richard Bland C. | Petersburg, VA 23805 | Gracie Balley | ADA Services | 804-862-6244 |
| Roanoke C. | Salem, VA 24153 | Dr. Camille Miller | Student Support Services | 703-375-2219 |
| St. Paul's C. | Lawrenceville, VA 23868 | Dorothy Goodson | Disability Services | 804-848-3111 |
| Sweet Briar C. | Sweet Briar, VA 24595 | Laura Symons | Academic Resource Center | 804-381-6278 |
| Thomas Nelson CC. | Hampton, VA 23670 | Thomas Kellen | Disabled Student Services | 757-825-2827 |
| Tidewater CC. | Portsmouth, VA 23703 | Sue Rice | LD Services | 804-683-2874 |
| U. of Richmond | Richmond, VA 23173 | Hope Walton | Academic Skills Center | 804-289-8626 |
| U. of Virginia | Charlottesville, VA 22903 | Eleanor Cartwright | Learning Needs & Evaluation Center | 804-243-5180 |
| Virginia Intermont C. | Bristol, VA 24201 | Talmadge Dobbins | Student Support Services | 703-669-6101 |

| College | Location | Contact | Service | Phone |
|---|---|---|---|---|
| Virginia Poly. Inst. | Blacksbury, VA 24061 | Virginia Reilly | Disabled Student Services | 703-231-3787 |
| VA Commonwealth U. | Richmond, VA 23284 | Rosemary Kelso | ADA Services | 804-828-1347 |
| Virginia State U. | Petersburg, VA 23806 | Mae Fitchett | Student Enrichment Center | 804-524-5000 |
| VA Tech. | Blacksburg, VA 24061 | Virginia Reilly | Special Services | 540-231-3787 |
| Virginia Wesleyan C. | Norfolk, VA 23502 | Fayne Pearson | Disability Services | 757-455-3246 |
| Virginia Western CC. | Roanoke, VA 24038 | Michael Henderson | Student Support Services | 540-857-7289 |
| U. of Virginia | Charlottesville, VA 22903 | Jim Clack | Learning Needs & Evaluation Ctr. | 804-243-5180 |

## WASHINGTON

| College | Location | Contact | Service | Phone |
|---|---|---|---|---|
| Bates Tech. C. | Tacoma, WA 98405 | Daniel Eberle | Special Needs | 206-596-1698 |
| Central Washington U. | Ellensburg, WA 98926 | Robert Harden | Disabled Student Services | 509-963-2171 |
| Clark College | Vancouver, WA 98663 | Duane Henry | Disabled Services | 360-992-2835 |
| E. Washington U. | Cheney, WA 99004 | Karen Raver | Disability Support Services | 509-359-2293 |
| Everett CC. | Everette, WA 98201 | Roxanna Hansen | Disabled Student Services | 206-388-9272 |
| Evergreen State U. | Olympia, WA 98505 | Linda Pickering | Access & Service Office | 360-866-6000 |
| Gonzaga U. | Spokaane, WA 99258 | Amy Lopes Wasson | Disability Support Services | 509-328-4220 |
| Grays Harbor C. | Aberdeen, WA 98520 | George Caldwell | Disabled Student Services | 360-538-4068 |
| N. Seattle CC. | Seattle, WA 98103 | Bateman Harris | Disabled Student Services | 206-527-7307 |
| Pacific Lutheran U. | Tacoma, WA 98447 | Alene Klein | Counseling & Testing | 206-535-7206 |
| Pacific Union C. | Tacoma, WA 98447 | Wanda Wentworth | Academic Assistance | 206-535-7520 |
| Pierce C. | Tacoma, WA 98446 | Deborah Wynn | Special Needs | 206-964-6527 |
| Saint Martin C. | Lacey, WA 98503 | Deborah DeBow | Disability Support Services | 360-438-4580 |
| Seattle Central CC. | Seattle, WA 98122 | Alfred Souma | Disabled Student Services | 206-587-4169 |
| Seattle Pacific U. | Seattle, WA 98119 | Judy Mackenzie | Disabled Student Services | 206-281-2018 |
| Seattle U. | Seattle, WA 98122 | Carol Schneider | The Learning Center | 206-296-5740 |
| Skagit Valley College | Mt.Vernon, WA 98273 | Eric Anderson | Disabled Student Services | 360-416-7818 |
| Spokane Falls CC. | Spokane, WA 99204 | Ben Webinger | Disability and Support Services | 509-533-3437 |
| Tacoma CC. | Tacoma, WA 98465 | Marie Markham | Disability Services | 206-566-5339 |
| U. of Puget Sound | Tacoma, WA 98416 | John Hickey | Support Servcies | 206-756-3203 |
| U. of Washington | Seattle, WA 98195 | Dyane Haynes | Disabled Student Services | 206-543-8924 |
| Washington State U. | Pullman, WA 99164 | Marshall Mitchell | Disability Resource Center/SALC | 509-335-4357 |
| Western Washington U. | Bellingham, WA 98225 | David Brunnemer | Disabled Student Services | 306-650-3083 |
| Whatcom CC. | Bellingham, WA 98226 | Lynn Blackwell | Disabled Student Services | 360-676-2170 |
| Yakima Valley CC. | Yakima, WA 98907 | Mark Cornett | Disability Services | 509-575-2350 |

## WEST VIRGINIA

| College | Location | Contact | Service | Phone |
|---|---|---|---|---|
| Davis & Elkins C. | Elkins, WV 26241 | Dr. Margaret Turner | LD Special Services | 304-637-1384 |
| Marshall U. | Huntington, WV 25755 | Dr. Barbara Guyer | H.E.L.P. Program for Learning Problems | 304-696-6317 |
| W. Virginia State U. | Institute, WV 25112 | Jacqueline Burns | Collegiate Support Services | 304-766-3000 |

| Institution | Location | Contact | Service | Phone |
|---|---|---|---|---|
| W. Virginia Tech. | Montgomery, WV 25136 | Dale Fox | Student Support Services | 304-442-3188 |
| W. Virginia U. | Morgantown, WV 26506 | Gordon Kent | Office of Disability Services | 304-293-6700 |
| W. Vir. Wesleyan C. | Buckhannon, WV 26201 | Phyllis Coston | Special Support Services Program | 304-473-8380 |

## WISCONSIN

| Institution | Location | Contact | Service | Phone |
|---|---|---|---|---|
| Alverno C. | Milwaukee, WI 53234 | Nancy Bornstein | Instructional Services | 414-382-6353 |
| Beloit C. | Beloit, WI 53511 | Gail Pizarro | Educational Development Prog. | 608-363-2031 |
| Cardinal Stritch C. | Milwaukee, WI 53217 | Marcia Laskey | Acadeic Support | 414-352-5400 |
| Carroll C. | Waukesha, WI 53186 | Dr. Ellen Barclay | Learning Center | 414-524-7100 |
| Carthage C. | Kenosha, WI 53140 | Laura Busch | Pace Center | 800-551-4768 |
| Concordia U. | Mequon, WI 53097 | Jean Timpel | Tutoring Center | 414-243-4216 |
| Edgewood C. | Madison, WI 53711 | Kathie Moran | Assistance to Students with LD | 608-257-4861 |
| Gateway Tech. C. | Kenosha, WI 53144 | Jo Bailey | Support Services | 414-656-6960 |
| Lawrence U. | Appleton, WI 54912 | M. Hemwall, Assoc.Dean | Disability Services | 414-832-6530 |
| Marian C. | Fond du Lac, WI 54935 | C. Rodrigues Leyrer | Academic Support Services | 414-923-8117 |
| Marquette U. | Milwaukee, WI 53233 | Patricia Almon | Disability Services | 414-224-1645 |
| Midstate Tech. C. | Wisc. Rapids, WI 54494 | John Bellanti | Special Needs Services | 715-422-5452 |
| Milwaukee Inst. of Art | Milwaukee, WI 53202 | Jennifer Crandall | Academic Support | 414-276-7889 |
| Milwaukee Sch. of Eng. | Milwaukee, WI 53201 | Carol Thompson | Student Support Services | 414-277-7281 |
| Northland College | Ashland, WI 54806 | Melinda Merrill | Academic Skills | 715-682-1803 |
| Ripon C. | Ripon, WI 54971 | Dan Khrin | Student Support Services | 414-748-8107 |
| St. Norbert C. | de Pere, WI 54115 | Carole Basak | Academic Mastery Program | 414-337-1321 |
| U. of Wisconsin | Eau Claire, WI 54702 | Joseph Hisrich | Serv. for Students with Disabilities | 715-836-4542 |
| U. of Wisconsin | Green Bay, WI 54311 | Elizabeth MacNeille | Educational Support | 414-465-2343 |
| U. of Wisconsin | La Crosse, WI 54601 | June Reinert | Services for Students with Disabilities | 608-785-6900 |
| U. of Wisconsin | Madison, WI 53715 | Cathleen Trueba | McBurney Resource Center | 608-263-2741 |
| U. of Wisconsin | Milwaukee, WI 53201 | Laurie Gramatzki | Learning Disabilities Program | 414-229-6239 |
| U. of Wisconsin | Oshkosh, WI 54901 | Dr. Robert Nash | Project Success | 414-424-1033 |
| U. of Wisconsin | Parkside, WI 53141 | Renee Sartin Kirby | Learning Disabilities Support Services | 414-595-2610 |
| U. of Wisconsin | Platteville, WI 53818 | Bernie Bernhardt | Special Services | 608-342-1817 |
| U. of Wisconsin | River Falls, WI 54022 | Dr. John Haman | Challenge Program | 715-425-3884 |
| U. of Wisconsin | Stevens Point, WI 54481 | John Timcak | Disabled Student Services | 715-346-3361 |
| U. of Wisconson-Stout | Menomonie, WI 54751 | Scott Bay | Student Support Services | 715-232-2995 |
| U. of Wisconsin | Superior, WI 54880 | Eloise Lozar | Special Services | 715-394-8185 |
| U. of Wisconsin | Whitewater, WI 53190 | Deb Hall | Project Assist | 414-472-5239 |
| Viterbo C. | La Crosse, WI 54601 | Wayne Wojciechowski | Learning Center | 608-796-3085 |
| W. Wisconsin Tech. C. | La Crosse, WI 54602 | Kristina Puent | Services for Students with Special Needs | 608-789-9873 |
| Wisc. Indianhead Tech. | Shell Lake, WI 54871 | Desmond Connley | Disability Services | 715-468-2815 |

## WYOMING

| School | Location | Contact | Service | Phone |
|---|---|---|---|---|
| Laramie County CC. | Cheyenne, WY 82007 | Patty Pratz | Student Success Center | 307-778-5222 |
| Sheridan College | Sheridan, WY 82801 | Norma Campbell | Learning Center | 307-674-6446 |
| U. of Wyoming | Laramie, WY 82071 | Chris Primus | Disability Support Services | 307-766-6189 |

## CANADA/ALBERTA

| School | Location | Contact | Service | Phone |
|---|---|---|---|---|
| Grant MacEwan CC. | Edmonton AB T51 2P2, Canada | A. Parrish-Craig | Counseling & Special Services | 403-483-5811 |
| Lethbridge CC | Lethbridge AB T1K 1L6, Canada | Julie Deimert | Support Services | 403-320-3244 |
| N. Alberta Inst. Tech. | Edmonton AB T5G 2R1, Canada | Shirley Kabachia | Services to Disabled Students | 403-471-7551 |
| S.Alberta Inst. Tech. | Calgary AB T2M OL4, Canada | Judy Murphy | Students with Disabilities | 403-284-7013 |
| U. of Alberta | Edmonton AB T6G 2E8, Canada | Marion Vosahlo | Disabled Student Services | 403-492-3381 |

## CANADA/BRITISH COLUMBIA

| School | Location | Contact | Service | Phone |
|---|---|---|---|---|
| Camosun C. | Victoria V8P 4X8, Canada | Susan McArthur | Adult Special Education | 604-370-3325 |
| Capilano C. | N. Vancouver V71 3H5, Canada | Jolene Bordewick | Disability Support Services | 604-983-7527 |
| C. of New Caledonia | Pr.George V2N 1P8, Canada | Fran Miller | ASE Division | 604-562-2131 |
| Kwantlen College | Surrey V3T 5H8, Canada | Susanne Dadson | Services for Stud. with Disabilities | 604-599-2003 |
| Langara C. | Vancouver V5Y 2Z6, Canada | Wendy Keenlyside | Disabled Students | 604-323-5635 |
| Okanagan C. | Kelowna V1Y 4X8, Canada | Valerie Best | Disability Services | 250-762-5445 |
| Simon Fraser U. | Burnaaby V5A 1S6, Canada | Jeff Sugarman | Learning & Study | 604-291-3877 |
| U. of N. British Colum. | Prince Grge V2L 5P2, Canada | Jim Leonard | Student Services | 250-960-6362 |
| U. of British Columbia | Vancouver V6T 1Z1, Canada | Ruth Warick | Disabilities Resource Center | 604-822-4677 |
| U. of Victoria | Victoria V8W 3P2, Canada | David Clode | Student & Ancillary Services | 250-721-8024 |

## CANADA/MANITOBA

| School | Location | Contact | Service | Phone |
|---|---|---|---|---|
| U. Of Manitoba | Winnipeg R3T 2N2, Canada | Susan Ness | Disabilities Services | 204-474-6213 |
| U. of Winnipeg | Winnipeg R3B 2E9, Canada | Carlene Besner | Services for Stud. with Special Needs | 204-786-9771 |

## CANADA/NEW BRUNSWICK

| School | Location | Contact | Service | Phone |
|---|---|---|---|---|
| Mt. Allison U. | Sackville E0A 3C0, Canada | Jane Drover | Center for Learning Assistance | 506-364-2527 |
| U. of New Brunswick | Fredericton E3B 6E3, Canada | Sandra Latchford | Learning Center | 506-453-3515 |

## CANDA/NEWFOUNDLAND

| School | Location | Contact | Service | Phone |
|---|---|---|---|---|
| Mem. U. Newfoundland | St. John's A1G 5S7, Canada | Donna Hardy | Student Development | 709-737-7593 |

## CANADA/NOVA SCOTIA

| School | Location | Contact | Service | Phone |
|---|---|---|---|---|
| Dalhousie U. | Halifax B3H 4J2, Canada | Lynn Shokry | Services for Students w/Disabilities | 902-494-7077 |
| St. Mary's U. | Halifax NS B3H 3C3, Canada | David Leitch | Support for Disabled Students | 902-420-5449 |

## CANADA/ONTARIO

| School | Location | Contact | Service | Phone |
|---|---|---|---|---|
| Algoma U. C. | S. Ste.Marie P6A 2G4, Canada | Judy Syrette | Special Needs | 705-949-2301 |

| Institution | Address | Contact | Service | Phone |
|---|---|---|---|---|
| Cambrian C. | Sudbury P3A 3V8, Canada | S. Alcorn MacKay | Special Needs Center | 705-566-8101 |
| Canadore C. | N. Bay P1B 8K9, Canada | Dawson Pratt | Special Needs Services | 705-474-7600 |
| Carleton U. | Ottawa K1S 5B6, Canada | Larry McCloskey | Services for the Disabled | 613-520-6608 |
| Centennial C. | Scarborough M1K 5E9, Canada | Irene Volinets | Special Needs | 416-694-3241 |
| Durham C. | Oshawa L1H 7L7, Canada | Patricia Revell | Special Needs | 416-576-0210 |
| Fanshawe C. | London N5V 1W2, Canada | Bill Aarts | Counseling & Student Life | 519-452-4282 |
| George Brown C. | Toronto M5T 2T9, Canada | Margueritge Wales | Special Needs | 416-867-2620 |
| Humber College | Rexdale M9W 5L7, Canada | Craig Barrett | Special Needs Office | 416-675-6622 |
| Lakehead U. | Thunder By P7B 5E1, Canada | Donna Grau | Learning Assistance | 807-343-8086 |
| Loyalist College | Belleville K8N 5B9, Canada | Catherine O'Rourke | Special Needs | 613-962-0633 |
| Mohawk College | Hamilton L8N 3T2, Canada | Rachel Mathews | Special Needs Office | 416-575-2331 |
| Nippissig U. College | N. Bay P1B 8L7, Canada | Bonnie Houston | Special Needs Services | 705-474-6431 |
| Ontarion C. of Art | Toronto M5T 1W1, Canada | Cynthia Richardson | Special Needs | 416-977-6000 |
| Queen's U. | Kingston K7L 3N6, Canada | Allyson Harrison | Special Needs | 613-545-6279 |
| Seneca College | N. York M2J 2X5, Canada | Arthur Burke | Special Needs | 416-491-5050 |
| St. Clair C. | Windsor N9A 6S4, Canada | June Egan | Special Needs | 519-966-1656 |
| St. Lawrence C. | Brockville K6V 5X3, Canada | Gall Easton | Special Needs | 613-345-0660 |
| Sheridan C. | Oakville L6H 2L1, Canada | Linda DeJong | Special Needs | 905-845-9430 |
| Trent U. | Peterborough K9J 7B8, Canada | Eunice Lund-Lucas | Special Needs | 705-748-1281 |
| U. of W. Ontario | London N6A 3K7, Canada | Susan Weaver | Disabled Student Services | 519-661-2147 |
| U. of Waterloo | Waterloo N2L 3G1, Canada | Rose Padacz | Services for Disabled Persons | 519-885-1211 |
| U. of Windsor | Windsor N9B 3P4, Canada | Michael Hoouston | Office of Student Affairs | 519-253-4232 |
| York U. | N.York M3J 1P3, Canada | Marc Wilchesky | LD Programs | 416-736-5297 |

## CANADA/PRINCE EDWARD ISLAND

| Institution | Address | Contact | Service | Phone |
|---|---|---|---|---|
| Holland C. | Charlottetn PE C1A 4Z1, Canada | Brian McMillan | Support Services | 902-566-9561 |

## CANADA/QUEBEC

| Institution | Address | Contact | Service | Phone |
|---|---|---|---|---|
| Concordia U. | Montreal PQ H4B 1R6, Canada | Leo Bissonnette | Services for Disabled Students | 514-848-3518 |
| Dawson C. | Montreal H3Z 1A4, Canada | Alice Havel | Services for Students with Disabilities | 514-931-8731 |
| John Abbott C. | St.An.Belvue.H9X 3L9, Canada | Gail Booth | Special Needs Learning Center | 514-457-6610 |
| McGill U. | Montreal H3A 1X1, Canada | Joan Wolforth | Special Services | 514-398-6009 |

## SASKATCHEWAN

| Institution | Address | Contact | Service | Phone |
|---|---|---|---|---|
| SIAST-Kelsey | Saskatoon S7K 6B1, Canada | Jim Kessler | Dept. of Disabilities Services | 306-933-6445 |
| U. of Saskatchewan | Saskatoon S7N 0W0, Canada | Jacklin Andrews | Disabled Student Services | 306-966-5773 |

## CANADA/YUKON

| Institution | Address | Contact | Service | Phone |
|---|---|---|---|---|
| Yukon C. | Yukon Y1A 5K4, Canada | Catalina Colaci | Special Education | 403-668-8785 |

# DEFINITIONS OF TESTING INSTRUMENTS AND ASSESSMENTS

## Intelligence Tests

**STANFORD BINET** Stanford Binet Intelligence Scale, Fourth Edition
This scale is administered to individuals aged 2 through adulthood. Verbal responses are emphasized more than nonverbal responses. Thus, children tested at age 2 might score quite differently when tested on another IQ test several years later.

**WISC-III** Wechsler Intelligence Scale for Children III
The WISC-III is a revision of the Wechsler Intelligence Scale for Children-Revised (WISC-R). The WISC-III is given to children ages 6 through 16, and it measures general intelligence. This scale provides three IQ scores: verbal, performance, and full-scale, yielding information about strengths and weaknesses in language and performance areas.

| WAIS-R | Wechsler Adult Intelligence Scale—Revised |
|---|---|
| | This scale tests verbal and non-verbal intelligence of adults aged 16 and over. Adolescents between the ages of 16 and 18 who are in high school must have this test conducted. This test is used to identify areas of learning strengths, learning weaknesses, or disabilities. |

## Achievement Tests

| PIAT-R | The PIAT-R is an updated, revised, and re-standardized battery of the old PIAT, and includes a new Written Expression subtest. This test is used to measure general academic achievement in reading mechanics and comprehension, spelling, math, and general knowledge. The PIAT-R is normed from kindergarten through 12th grade and ages 5 through 18 years. |
|---|---|
| SDAT | Stanford Diagnostic Achievement Tests |
| | The SDAT is a test that measures performance in academic subjects such as spelling, grammar, arithmetic, and reading. This test also provides instructional objectives and suggestions for teaching. |
| TOWL | Test of Written Language |
| | The TOWL is a test used to identify strengths and weaknesses in various writing abilities. It can be used to compare students to their peers, and determine who perform poorer or better in written expression. |
| WRAT-R | Wide Range Achievement Test—Revised |
| | The WRAT-R evaluates oral reading, spelling, and arithmetic computation. This test is used from kindergarten through college, and scores are by grade level for each skill. |
| WJ-R | Woodcock Johnson Psychoeducational Battery—Revised |
| | The WJ-R is a battery of tests used from pre-school through adult level to measure achievement in reading, math, written language, and general knowledge. These tests also assess the level of academic versus non-academic accomplishments. |

# Index

# ABOUT THE AUTHORS

Marybeth Kravets is the College Consultant at Deerfield High School, a public high school in Deerfield, Illinois. She has been part of the Counseling Department for 18 years. She received her A.B. in Education from the University of Michigan, Ann Arbor, Michigan, and her M.A. in Counseling from Wayne State University, Detroit, Michigan. Kravets is the President of the Illinois Association for College Admission Counseling; a member of many professional organizations; has appeared as a guest on the "NBC Today Show" as well as other television and radio shows; has published many articles in journals and magazines; and has presented at major national conferences on the understanding of learning disabilities and the transition process for students with learning disabilities from high school to college. She is married to Alan Kravets and they have four children and three grandchildren.

Imy Falik Wax is a certified licensed psycho-therapist, educational consultant, and currently in private family practice. She has worked with the adolescent population and their families in social service settings as well as in high schools. She received her B.S. from Mills College of Education, New York City, New York, and her M.S. from Hunter College, New York City, New York. She is a member of a number of professional and parent organizations. She has presented at both professional and parent conferences on the topic of "The Emotional Expectations of Parenting a Child with Learning Disabilities" and has published articles in several professional and parent journals. Imy also conducts workshops for parents on raising children with learning disabilities and/or attention deficit disorder. She has appeared as a guest on the "NBC Today Show" as well as other television and radio shows. She is married to Howard Wax and has four children, two learning disabled and one who is also attention deficit disordered. Her daughter, Deborah, was the inspiration for this book.

# NOTES

# NOTES

# NOTES

# NOTES

# NOTES

# FIND US...

## International

**Hong Kong**
4/F Sun Hung Kai Centre
30 Harbour Road, Wan Chai,
Hong Kong
Tel: (011)85-2-517-3016

**Japan**
Fuji Building 40, 15-14
Sakuragaokacho, Shibuya Ku,
Tokyo 150, Japan
Tel: (011)81-3-3463-1343

**Korea**
Tae Young Bldg, 944-24,
Daechi- Dong, Kangnam-Ku
The Princeton Review- ANC
Seoul, Korea 135-280,
South Korea
Tel: (011)82-2-554-7763

**Mexico City**
PR Mex S De RL De Cv
Guanajuato 228 Col. Roma
06700 Mexico D.F., Mexico
Tel: 525-564-9468

**Montreal**
666 Sherbrooke St.
West, Suite 202
Montreal, QC H3A 1E7 Canada
Tel: (514) 499-0870

**Pakistan**
1 Bawa Park - 90 Upper Mall
Lahore, Pakistan
Tel: (011)92-42-571-2315

**Spain**
Pza. Castilla, 3 - 5º A, 28046
Madrid, Spain
Tel: (011)341-323-4212

**Taiwan**
155 Chung Hsiao East Road
Section 4 - 4th Floor,
Taipei R.O.C., Taiwan
Tel: (011)886-2-751-1243

**Thailand**
Building One, 99 Wireless Road
Bangkok, Thailand 10330
Tel: (662) 256-7080

**Toronto**
1240 Bay Street, Suite 300
Toronto M5R 2A7 Canada
Tel: (800) 495-7737
Tel: (716) 839-4391

**Vancouver**
4212 University Way NE,
Suite 204
Seattle, WA 98105
Tel: (206) 548-1100

## National (U.S.)

We have over 60 offices around the U.S. and
run courses in over 400 sites. For courses and
locations within the U.S. call **1 (800) 2/Review**
and you will be routed to the nearest office.

# MORE EXPERT ADVICE

*from*

## THE PRINCETON REVIEW

We help hundreds of thousands of students improve their test scores and get into college each year. If you want to give yourself the best chances for getting into the college of your choice, we can help you get the highest test scores, the best financial aid package, and make the most informed choices with our comprehensive line of books for the college bound student. Here's to your success and good luck!

**CRACKING THE SAT & PSAT**
**1998 EDITION**
0-679-78405-5 $18.00

**CRACKING THE SAT & PSAT WITH SAMPLE TESTS ON DISK 1998 EDITION**
0-679-7404-7 • $29.95
WIN/MAC compatible

**CRACKING THE SAT & PSAT WITH SAMPLE TESTS ON CD-ROM 1998 EDITION**
0-679-78403-9 • $29.95
WIN/MAC compatible

**SAT MATH WORKOUT**
0-679-75363-X • $15.00

**SAT VERBAL WORKOUT**
0-679-75362-1 • $16.00

**INSIDE THE SAT BOOK/CD-ROM**
1-884536-56-5 • $34.95
WIN/MAC compatible

**CRACKING THE ACT 1997-98 EDITION**
0-679-77856-X • $18.00

**CRACKING THE ACT WITH SAMPLE TESTS ON CD-ROM 1997-98 EDITION**
0-679-77857-8 • $29.95
WIN/MAC compatible

**COLLEGE COMPANION**
Real Students, True Stories, Good Advice
0-679-76905-6 • $15.00

**STUDENT ADVANTAGE GUIDE TO COLLEGE ADMISSIONS**
Unique Strategies for Getting into the College of Your Choice
0-679-74590-4 • $12.00

**PAYING FOR COLLEGE WITHOUT GOING BROKE**
**1998 EDITION**
Insider Strategies to Maximize Financial Aid and Minimize College Costs
0-679-77363-0 • $18.00

**THE BEST 311 COLLEGES**
**1998 EDITION**
The Buyer's Guide to College
0-679-78397-0 • $18.00

**THE COMPLETE BOOK OF COLLEGES**
**1998 EDITION**
0-679-78398-9 • $26.00

**COLLEGE ADVISOR**
1-884536-43-3 • $21.50
WIN/MAC compatible

# WE ALSO HAVE BOOKS TO HELP YOU SCORE HIGH ON

## THE SAT II, AP, AND CLEP EXAMS:

**CRACKING THE AP BIOLOGY 1997-98 EDITION**
0-679-76927-7 $16.00

**CRACKING THE AP CALCULUS AB & BC 1997-98 EDITION**
0-679-76926-9 $16.00

**CRACKING THE AP CHEMISTRY 1997-98 EDITION**
0-679-76928-5 $16.00

**CRACKING THE AP ENGLISH LITERATURE 1997-98 EDITION**
0-679-76924-2 $16.00

**CRACKING THE AP U.S. HISTORY 1997-98 EDITION**
0-679-76925-0 $16.00

**CRACKING THE CLEP 1998 EDITION**
0-679-77867-5 $20.00

**CRACKING THE SAT II: BIOLOGY 1997-98 EDITION**
0-679-77863-2 $17.00

**CRACKING THE SAT II: CHEMISTRY 1997-98 EDITION**
0-679-77860-8 $17.00

**CRACKING THE SAT II: ENGLISH 1997-98 EDITION**
0-679-77858-6 $17.00

**CRACKING THE SAT II: FRENCH 1997-98 EDITION**
0-679-77865-9 $17.00

**CRACKING THE SAT II: HISTORY 1997-98 EDITION**
0-679-77861-6 $17.00

**CRACKING THE SAT II: MATH 1997-98 EDITION**
0-679-77864-0 $17.00

**CRACKING THE SAT II: PHYSICS 1997-98 EDITION**
0-679-77859-4 $17.00

**CRACKING THE SAT II: SPANISH 1997-98 EDITION**
0-679-77862-4 $17.00

www.review.com

# Expert Advice

Counselor-O-Matic

Pop Surveys

Paying for It

www.review.com

www.review.com

**THE PRINCETON REVIEW**

Getting In

Word du Jour

www.review.com

www.review.com

College Talk

Find-O-Rama College Search

www.review.com

Includes FREE Offer — MSN The Microsoft Network

SAT Survival

Best Schools

www.review.com